T0181900

# Lecture Notes in Computer Science     12698

More information about this subseries at http://www.springer.com/series/7410

Anne Canteaut · François-Xavier Standaert (Eds.)

# Advances in Cryptology – EUROCRYPT 2021

40th Annual International Conference on the Theory
and Applications of Cryptographic Techniques
Zagreb, Croatia, October 17–21, 2021
Proceedings, Part III

 Springer

*Editors*
Anne Canteaut (iD)
Inria
Paris, France

François-Xavier Standaert (iD)
UCLouvain
Louvain-la-Neuve, Belgium

ISSN 0302-9743          ISSN 1611-3349  (electronic)
Lecture Notes in Computer Science
ISBN 978-3-030-77882-8          ISBN 978-3-030-77883-5  (eBook)
https://doi.org/10.1007/978-3-030-77883-5

LNCS Sublibrary: SL4 – Security and Cryptology

This Springer imprint is published by the registered company Springer Nature Switzerland AG
The registered company address is: Gewerbestrasse 11, 6330 Cham, Switzerland

# Preface

Eurocrypt 2021, the 40th Annual International Conference on the Theory and Applications of Cryptographic Techniques, was held in Zagreb, Croatia, during October 17–21, 2021.[1] The conference was sponsored by the International Association for Cryptologic Research (IACR). Lejla Batina (Radboud University, The Netherlands) and Stjepan Picek (Delft University of Technology, The Netherlands) were responsible for the local organization.

We received a total of 400 submissions. Each submission was anonymized for the reviewing process and was assigned to at least three of the 59 Program Committee (PC) members. PC members were allowed to submit at most two papers. The reviewing process included a rebuttal round for all submissions. After extensive deliberations the PC accepted 78 papers. The revised versions of these papers are included in this three-volume proceedings.

The PC decided to give Best Paper Awards to the papers *"Non-Interactive Zero Knowledge from Sub-exponential DDH"* by Abhishek Jain and Zhengzhong Jin, *"On the (in)security of ROS"* by Fabrice Benhamouda, Tancrède Lepoint, Julian Loss, Michele Orrù, and Mariana Raykova and *"New Representations of the AES Key Schedule"* by Gaëtan Leurent and Clara Pernot. The authors of these three papers received an invitation to submit an extended version of their work to the *Journal of Cryptology*. The program also included invited talks by Craig Gentry (Algorand Foundation) and Sarah Meiklejohn (University College London).

We would like to thank all the authors who submitted papers. We know that the PC's decisions can be very disappointing, especially rejections of good papers which did not find a slot in the sparse number of accepted papers. We sincerely hope that these works will eventually get the attention they deserve.

We are indebted to the PC and the external reviewers for their voluntary work. Selecting papers from 400 submissions covering the many areas of cryptologic research is a huge workload. It has been an honor to work with everyone. We owe a big thank you to Kevin McCurley for his continuous support in solving all the minor issues we had with the HotCRP review system, to Gaëtan Leurent for sharing his MILP programs which made the papers assignments much easier, and to Simona Samardjiska who acted as Eurocrypt 2021 webmaster.

Finally, we thank all the other people (speakers, sessions chairs, rump session chairs…) for their contribution to the program of Eurocrypt 2021. We would also like to thank the many sponsors for their generous support, including the Cryptography Research Fund that supported student speakers.

April 2021

Anne Canteaut
François-Xavier Standaert

---

[1] This preface was written before the conference took place, under the assumption that it will take place as planned in spite of travel restrictions due to COVID-19.

# Eurocrypt 2021

**The 40th Annual International Conference on the Theory
and Applications of Cryptographic Techniques**

Sponsored by the *International Association for Cryptologic Research*
Zagreb, Croatia
October 17–21, 2021

## General Co-chairs

Lejla Batina — Radboud University, The Netherlands
Stjepan Picek — Delft University of Technology, The Netherlands

## Program Committee Chairs

Anne Canteaut — Inria, France
François-Xavier Standaert — UCLouvain, Belgium

## Program Committee

Shweta Agrawal — IIT Madras, India
Joël Alwen — Wickr, USA
Foteini Baldimtsi — George Mason University, USA
Marshall Ball — Columbia University, USA
Begül Bilgin — Rambus - Cryptography Research, The Netherlands
Nir Bitansky — Tel Aviv University, Israel
Joppe W. Bos — NXP Semiconductors, Belgium
Christina Boura — University of Versailles, France
Wouter Castryck — KU Leuven, Belgium
Kai-Min Chung — Academia Sinica, Taiwan
Jean-Sébastien Coron — University of Luxembourg, Luxembourg
Véronique Cortier — LORIA, CNRS, France
Geoffroy Couteau — CNRS, IRIF, Université de Paris, France
Luca De Feo — IBM Research Europe, Switzerland
Léo Ducas (Area Chair: Public-Key Crypto) — CWI, Amsterdam, The Netherlands
Orr Dunkelman — University of Haifa, Israel
Stefan Dziembowski (Area Chair: Theory) — University of Warsaw, Poland
Thomas Eisenbarth — University of Lübeck, Germany
Dario Fiore — IMDEA Software Institute, Spain
Marc Fischlin — TU Darmstadt, Germany

# Additional Reviewers

Mark Abspoel
Hamza Abusalah
Alexandre Adomnicai
Archita Agarwal
Divesh Aggarwal
Shashank Agrawal
Gorjan Alagic
Martin R. Albrecht
Ghada Almashaqbeh
Bar Alon
Miguel Ambrona
Ghous Amjad
Prabhanjan Ananth
Toshinori Araki
Victor Arribas
Gilad Asharov
Roberto Avanzi
Melissa Azouaoui
Christian Badertscher
Saikrishna
  Badrinarayanan
Karim Baghery
Victor Balcer
Laasya Bangalore
Magali Bardet
James Bartusek
Balthazar Bauer
Carsten Baum
Christof Beierle
James Bell
Fabrice Benhamouda
Iddo Bentov
Olivier Bernard
Sebastian Berndt
Pauline Bert
Ward Beullens
Benjamin Beurdouche
Ritam Bhaumik
Erica Blum
Alexandra Boldyreva
Jonathan Bootle
Nicolas Bordes
Katharina Boudgoust

Florian Bourse
Xavier Boyen
Elette Boyle
Zvika Brakerski
Lennart Braun
Gianluca Brian
Marek Broll
Olivier Bronchain
Chris Brzuska
Benedikt Bünz
Chloe Cachet
Matteo Campanelli
Federico Canale
Ignacio Cascudo
Gaëtan Cassiers
Avik Chakraborti
Benjamin Chan
Eshan Chattopadhyay
Panagiotis Chatzigiannis
Shan Chen
Yanlin Chen
Yilei Chen
Yu Chen
Alessandro Chiesa
Ilaria Chillotti
Seung Geol Choi
Arka Rai Choudhuri
Michele Ciampi
Daniel Coggia
Benoît Cogliati
Ran Cohen
Andrea Coladangelo
Sandro Coretti-Drayton
Craig Costello
Daniele Cozzo
Ting Ting Cui
Debajyoti Das
Poulami Das
Bernardo David
Alex Davidson
Gareth Davies
Lauren De Meyer
Thomas Debris-Alazard

Leo de Castro
Thomas Decru
Jean Paul Degabriele
Akshay Degwekar
Amit Deo
Patrick Derbez
Itai Dinur
Christoph Dobraunig
Yevgeniy Dodis
Jack Doerner
Jelle Don
Benjamin Dowling
Eduoard Dufour Sans
Yfke Dulek
Frédéric Dupuis
Sylvain Duquesne
Avijit Dutta
Ehsan Ebrahimi
Kasra Edalat Nejdat
Naomi Ephraim
Thomas Espitau
Andre Esser
Grzegorz Fabiański
Xiong Fan
Antonio Faonio
Sebastian Faust
Serge Fehr
Patrick Felke
Rune Fiedler
Ben Fisch
Matthias Fitzi
Antonio Flórez-Gutiérrez
Cody Freitag
Georg Fuchsbauer
Ariel Gabizon
Nicolas Gama
Chaya Ganesh
Rachit Garg
Pierrick Gaudry
Romain Gay
Peter Gaži
Nicholas Genise
Craig Gentry

Marilyn George
Adela Georgescu
David Gerault
Essam Ghadafi
Satrajit Ghosh
Irene Giacomelli
Aarushi Goel
Junqing Gong
Alonso González
S. Dov Gordon
Louis Goubin
Marc Gourjon
Rishab Goyal
Lorenzo Grassi
Elijah Grubb
Cyprien de Saint Guilhem
Aurore Guillevic
Aldo Gunsing
Chun Guo
Qian Guo
Felix Günther
Iftach Haitner
Mohammad Hajiabadi
Mathias Hall-Andersen
Ariel Hamlin
Lucjan Hanzlik
Patrick Harasser
Dominik Hartmann
Eduard Hauck
Phil Hebborn
Javier Herranz
Amir Herzberg
Julia Hesse
Shoichi Hirose
Martin Hirt
Akinori Hosoyamada
Kathrin Hövelmanns
Andreas Hülsing
Ilia Iliashenko
Charlie Jacomme
Christian Janson
Stanislaw Jarecki
Ashwin Jha
Dingding Jia

Daniel Jost
Kimmo Järvinen
Guillaume Kaim
Chethan Kamath
Pritish Kamath
Fredrik Kamphuis
Ioanna Karantaidou
Shuichi Katsumata
Jonathan Katz
Tomasz Kazana
Marcel Keller
Mustafa Khairallah
Louiza Khati
Hamidreza Khoshakhlagh
Dakshita Khurana
Ryo Kikuchi
Eike Kiltz
Elena Kirshanova
Agnes Kiss
Karen Klein
Michael Klooß
Alexander Koch
Lisa Kohl
Vladimir Kolesnikov
Dimitris Kolonelos
Ilan Komargodski
Yashvanth Kondi
Venkata Koppula
Adrien Koutsos
Hugo Krawczyk
Stephan Krenn
Ashutosh Kumar
Ranjit Kumaresan
Po-Chun Kuo
Rolando L. La Placa
Thijs Laarhoven
Jianchang Lai
Virginie Lallemand
Baptiste Lambin
Eran Lambooij
Philippe Lamontagne
Rio Lavigne
Jooyoung Lee
Alexander Lemmens

Nikos Leonardos
Matthieu Lequesne
Antonin Leroux
Gaëtan Leurent
Jyun-Jie Liao
Damien Ligier
Huijia Lin
Benjamin Lipp
Maciej Liskiewicz
Qipeng Liu
Shengli Liu
Tianren Liu
Yanyi Liu
Chen-Da Liu-Zhang
Alex Lombardi
Patrick Longa
Vadim Lyubashevsky
Fermi Ma
Mimi Ma
Urmila Mahadev
Nikolaos Makriyannis
Giulio Malavolta
Damien Marion
Yoann Marquer
Giorgia Marson
Chloe Martindale
Ange Martinelli
Michael Meyer
Pierre Meyer
Andrew Miller
Brice Minaud
Ilya Mironov
Tal Moran
Saleet Mossel
Tamer Mour
Pratyay Mukherjee
Marta Mularczyk
Pierrick Méaux
Yusuke Naito
Joe Neeman
Patrick Neumann
Khoa Nguyen
Ngoc Khanh Nguyen
Phong Nguyen

Tuong-Huy Nguyen
Jesper Buus Nielsen
Ryo Nishimaki
Abderrahmane Nitaj
Anca Nitulescu
Lamine Noureddine
Adam O'Neill
Maciej Obremski
Cristina Onete
Michele Orru
Emmanuela Orsini
Carles Padro
Mahak Pancholi
Omer Paneth
Dimitris Papachristoudis
Sunoo Park
Anat Paskin-Cherniavsky
Alice Pellet-Mary
Olivier Pereira
Léo Perrin
Thomas Peters
Duy-Phuc Pham
Krzyszof Pietrzak
Jérôme Plût
Bertram Poettering
Yuriy Polyakov
Antigoni Polychroniadou
Alexander Poremba
Thomas Prest
Cassius Puodzius
Willy Quach
Anaïs Querol
Rahul Rachuri
Hugues Randriam
Adrian Ranea
Shahram Rasoolzadeh
Deevashwer Rathee
Mayank Rathee
Divya Ravi
Christian Rechberger
Michael Reichle
Jean-René Reinhard
Joost Renes
Nicolas Resch

João Ribeiro
Silas Richelson
Tania Richmond
Doreen Riepel
Peter Rindal
Miruna Rosca
Michael Rosenberg
Mélissa Rossi
Yann Rotella
Alex Russell
Théo Ryffel
Carla Ràfols
Paul Rösler
Rajeev Anand Sahu
Olga Sanina
Pratik Sarkar
Alessandra Scafuro
Christian Schaffner
Peter Scholl
Tobias Schmalz
Phillipp Schoppmann
André Schrottenloher
Jörg Schwenk
Adam Sealfon
Okan Seker
Jae Hong Seo
Karn Seth
Barak Shani
Abhi Shelat
Omri Shmueli
Victor Shoup
Hippolyte Signargout
Tjerand Silde
Mark Simkin
Luisa Siniscalchi
Daniel Slamanig
Benjamin Smith
Fang Song
Jana Sotáková
Pierre-Jean Spaenlehauer
Nicholas Spooner
Akshayaram Srinivasan
Damien Stehlé
Marc Stevens

Siwei Sun
Mehrdad Tahmasbi
Quan Quan Tan
Stefano Tessaro
Florian Thaeter
Aishwarya
  Thiruvengadam
Mehdi Tibouchi
Radu Titiu
Oleksandr Tkachenko
Yosuke Todo
Junichi Tomida
Ni Trieu
Eran Tromer
Daniel Tschudi
Giorgos Tsimos
Ida Tucker
Michael Tunstall
Akin Ünal
Dominique Unruh
Bogdan Ursu
Christine van Vredendaal
Wessel van Woerden
Marc Vauclair
Serge Vaudenay
Muthu
  Venkitasubramaniam
Damien Vergnaud
Gilles Villard
Fernando Virdia
Satyanarayana Vusirikala
Riad Wahby
Hendrik Waldner
Alexandre Wallet
Haoyang Wang
Hoeteck Wee
Weiqiang Wen
Benjamin Wesolowski
Jan Wichelmann
Luca Wilke
Mary Wootters
David Wu
Jiayu Xu
Sophia Yakoubov

Shota Yamada
Takashi Yamakawa
Sravya Yandamuri
Kang Yang
Lisa Yang

Kevin Yeo
Eylon Yogev
Greg Zaverucha
Mark Zhandry
Jiayu Zhang

Ruizhe Zhang
Yupeng Zhang
Vassilis Zikas
Paul Zimmermann
Dionysis Zindros

# Contents – Part III

**Garbled Circuits**

LogStack: Stacked Garbling with $O(b \log b)$ Computation . . . . . . . . . . . . . 3
  *David Heath and Vladimir Kolesnikov*

Large Scale, Actively Secure Computation from LPN and Free-XOR
Garbled Circuits . . . . . . . . . . . . . . . . . . . . . . . . . . . . . . . . . . . . 33
  *Aner Ben-Efraim, Kelong Cong, Eran Omri, Emmanuela Orsini,*
  *Nigel P. Smart, and Eduardo Soria-Vazquez*

Threshold Garbled Circuits and Ad Hoc Secure Computation . . . . . . . . . . . . 64
  *Michele Ciampi, Vipul Goyal, and Rafail Ostrovsky*

**Indistinguishability Obfuscation**

Indistinguishability Obfuscation from Simple-to-State Hard Problems:
New Assumptions, New Techniques, and Simplification . . . . . . . . . . . . . . 97
  *Romain Gay, Aayush Jain, Huijia Lin, and Amit Sahai*

Candidate Obfuscation via Oblivious LWE Sampling . . . . . . . . . . . . . . . . 127
  *Hoeteck Wee and Daniel Wichs*

**Non-Malleable Commitments**

Black-Box Non-interactive Non-malleable Commitments . . . . . . . . . . . . . . 159
  *Rachit Garg, Dakshita Khurana, George Lu, and Brent Waters*

Non-interactive Distributional Indistinguishability (NIDI)
and Non-malleable Commitments . . . . . . . . . . . . . . . . . . . . . . . . . . . 186
  *Dakshita Khurana*

**Zero-Knowledge Proofs**

Public-Coin Statistical Zero-Knowledge Batch Verification Against
Malicious Verifiers . . . . . . . . . . . . . . . . . . . . . . . . . . . . . . . . . . . 219
  *Inbar Kaslasi, Ron D. Rothblum, and Prashant Nalini Vasudevanr*

Efficient Range Proofs with Transparent Setup from Bounded
Integer Commitments. . . . . . . . . . . . . . . . . . . . . . . . . . . . . . . . . . . 247
  *Geoffroy Couteau, Michael Klooß, Huang Lin, and Michael Reichle*

Towards Accountability in CRS Generation . . . . . . . . . . . . . . . . . . . . . . .      278
    *Prabhanjan Ananth, Gilad Asharov, Hila Dahari, and Vipul Goyal*

**Property-Preserving Hash Functions and ORAM**

Robust Property-Preserving Hash Functions for Hamming Distance
and More. . . . . . . . . . . . . . . . . . . . . . . . . . . . . . . . . . . . . . . . . . . .      311
    *Nils Fleischhacker and Mark Simkin*

Alibi: A Flaw in Cuckoo-Hashing Based Hierarchical ORAM Schemes
and a Solution . . . . . . . . . . . . . . . . . . . . . . . . . . . . . . . . . . . . . . . . .      338
    *Brett Hemenway Falk, Daniel Noble, and Rafail Ostrovsky*

Structured Encryption and Dynamic Leakage Suppression . . . . . . . . . . . . .      370
    *Marilyn George, Seny Kamara, and Tarik Moataz*

**Blockchain**

Dynamic Ad Hoc Clock Synchronization . . . . . . . . . . . . . . . . . . . . . . . .      399
    *Christian Badertscher, Peter Gaži, Aggelos Kiayias, Alexander Russell,
    and Vassilis Zikas*

TARDIS: A Foundation of Time-Lock Puzzles in UC . . . . . . . . . . . . . . . .      429
    *Carsten Baum, Bernardo David, Rafael Dowsley, Jesper Buus Nielsen,
    and Sabine Oechsner*

**Privacy and Law Enforcement**

On the Power of Multiple Anonymous Messages: Frequency Estimation
and Selection in the Shuffle Model of Differential Privacy . . . . . . . . . . . . . .      463
    *Badih Ghazi, Noah Golowich, Ravi Kumar, Rasmus Pagh,
    and Ameya Velingker*

Non-Interactive Anonymous Router. . . . . . . . . . . . . . . . . . . . . . . . . . . .      489
    *Elaine Shi and Ke Wu*

Bifurcated Signatures: Folding the Accountability vs. Anonymity Dilemma
into a Single Private Signing Scheme . . . . . . . . . . . . . . . . . . . . . . . . . . .      521
    *Benoît Libert, Khoa Nguyen, Thomas Peters, and Moti Yung*

Abuse Resistant Law Enforcement Access Systems . . . . . . . . . . . . . . . . . .      553
    *Matthew Green, Gabriel Kaptchuk, and Gijs Van Laer*

**Author Index** . . . . . . . . . . . . . . . . . . . . . . . . . . . . . . . . . . . . . . . . .      585

# Garbled Circuits

# LogStack: Stacked Garbling
# with $O(b \log b)$ Computation

David Heath$^{(\boxtimes)}$ and Vladimir Kolesnikov

Georgia Institute of Technology, Atlanta, GA, USA
{heath.davidanthony,kolesnikov}@gatech.edu

**Abstract.** Secure two party computation (2PC) of arbitrary programs can be efficiently achieved using garbled circuits (GC). Until recently, it was widely believed that a GC proportional to the entire program, including parts of the program that are entirely discarded due to conditional branching, must be transmitted over a network. Recent work shows that this belief is *false*, and that communication proportional only to the longest program execution path suffices (Heath and Kolesnikov, CRYPTO 20, [HK20a]). Although this recent work reduces needed communication, it *increases* computation. For a conditional with $b$ branches, the players use $O(b^2)$ computation (traditional GC uses only $O(b)$).

Our scheme LogStack reduces stacked garbling computation from $O(b^2)$ to $O(b \log b)$ with *no* increase in communication over [HK20a]. The cause of [HK20a]'s increased computation is the oblivious collection of *garbage labels* that emerge during the evaluation of inactive branches. Garbage is collected by a *multiplexer* that is costly to generate. At a high level, we redesign stacking and garbage collection to avoid quadratic scaling.

Our construction is also more *space efficient*: [HK20a] algorithms require $O(b)$ space, while ours use only $O(\log b)$ space. This space efficiency allows even modest setups to handle large numbers of branches.

[HK20a] assumes a random oracle (RO). We track the source of this need, formalize a simple and natural added assumption on the base garbling scheme, and remove reliance on RO: LogStack is secure in the standard model. Nevertheless, LogStack can be instantiated with typical GC tricks based on non-standard assumptions, such as free XOR and half-gates, and hence can be implemented with high efficiency.

We implemented LogStack (in the RO model, based on half-gates garbling) and report performance. In terms of wall-clock time and for fewer than 16 branches, our performance is comparable to [HK20a]'s; for larger branching factors, our approach clearly outperforms [HK20a]. For example, given 1024 branches, our approach is 31× faster.

**Keywords:** 2PC · Garbled circuits · Conditional branching · Stacked garbling

## 1 Introduction

Secure two party computation (2PC) of programs representable as Boolean circuits can be efficiently achieved using garbled circuits (GC). However,

© International Association for Cryptologic Research 2021
A. Canteaut and F.-X. Standaert (Eds.): EUROCRYPT 2021, LNCS 12698, pp. 3–32, 2021.
https://doi.org/10.1007/978-3-030-77883-5_1

circuit-based MPC in general is problematic because conditional control flow does not have an efficient circuit representation: in the cleartext program, only the taken execution is computed whereas in the circuit *all* branches must be computed.

Until recently, it was assumed that the players must not only compute all branches, but also transmit a string of *material* (i.e., the garbled circuit itself) proportional to the entire circuit. Since communication is the GC bottleneck, transmitting this large string was problematic for programs with conditionals.

Stacked Garbling [HK20a], which we interchangeably call Stacked Garbled Circuit (SGC), shows that expensive branching-based communication is unnecessary: the players need only send enough material for the single longest branch. This single piece of *stacked* material can be re-used across all conditional branches, substantially reducing communication. Unfortunately, this improvement comes with one important downside: SGC requires the players to compute more than they would have without stacking. In particular, for a conditional with $b$ branches, the [HK20a] GC generator must evaluate under encryption each branch $b - 1$ times and hence must pay $O(b^2)$ total computation. In contrast, standard garbling uses computation linear in the number of branches.

In this work, we present a new SGC construction that incurs only $O(b \log b)$ computation for both players while retaining the important communication improvement of [HK20a]. The construction also features improved space complexity: while [HK20a] requires the generator to store $O(b)$ intermediate garblings, both Eval and Gen in our construction use only $O(\log b)$ space. Finally, the construction features low constants and hence opens the door to using SGC even in the presence of high branching factors without prohibitive computation.

## 1.1  A Case for High Branching Factor

Branching is ubiquitous in programming, and our work significantly improves the secure evaluation of programs with branching. Moreover, the efficient support of *high branching factor* is more important than it may first appear.

Efficient branching enables optimized handling of *arbitrary control flow*, including repeated and/or nested loops. Specifically, we can repeatedly refactor the source program until the program is a single loop whose body conditionally dispatches over straightline fragments of the original program.[1] However, these types of refactorings often lead to conditionals with high branching factor.

As an example, consider a program $P$ consisting of a loop $L_1$ followed by a loop $L_2$. Assume the total number of loop iterations $T$ of $P$ is known, as is usual in MPC. For security, we must protect the number of iterations $T_1$ of $L_1$ and $T_2$ of $L_2$. Implementing such a program with standard Yao GC requires us to execute loop $L_1$ $T$ times and then to execute $L_2$ $T$ times. SGC can simply execute $\mathsf{Stack}(L_1, L_2)$ $T$ times, a circuit with a significantly smaller garbling. This observation corresponds to the following refactoring:

$$\texttt{while(e}_0\texttt{)\{s}_0\texttt{\}; while(e}_1\texttt{)\{s}_1\texttt{\}} \longrightarrow \texttt{while(e}_0 \vee \texttt{e}_1\texttt{)\{ if(e}_0\texttt{)\{s}_0\texttt{\} else \{s}_1\texttt{\} \}}$$

---

[1] As a brief argument that this is possible, consider that a CPU has this structure: in this case the 'straightline fragments' are the instruction types handled by the CPU.

where $s_i$ are nested programs and $e_i$ are predicates on program variables.[2] The right hand side is friendlier to SGC, since it substitutes a loop by a conditional. Now, consider that $s_0$ and $s_1$ might themselves have conditionals that can be flattened into a single conditional with all branches. By repeatedly applying such refactorings, even modest programs can have conditionals with high branching factors. High-performance branching, enabled by our approach, allows the efficient and secure evaluation of such programs.

In this work, we do not further explore program refactorings as an optimization. However, we firmly believe that SGC is an essential tool that will enable research into this direction, including CPU emulation-based MPC. As argued above, performance in the presence of high branching factor is essential.

## 1.2   [HK20a] and Its $O(b^2)$ Computation

Our approach is similar to that of [HK20a]: we also stack material to decrease communication. The key difference is our reduced computation. It is thus instructive to review [HK20a], focusing on the source of its quadratic scaling.

The key idea of SGC is that the circuit generator Gen garbles, starting from seeds, each branch $C_i$. He then *stacks* these $b$ garbled circuits, yielding only a single piece of material proportional to the longest branch: $M = \bigoplus_i \hat{C}_i$.[3] Because garblings are expanded from short seeds, the seeds are compact representations of the garblings. Although it would be insecure for the evaluator Eval to receive *all* seeds from Gen, [HK20a] show that it *is secure* for her to receive seeds corresponding to the inactive branches. Let $\alpha$ be the id of the active branch. Eval can reconstruct from seeds the garbling of each inactive branch, use XOR to unstack the material $\hat{C}_\alpha$, and evaluate $C_\alpha$ normally. Of course, what is described so far is not secure: the above procedure implies that Eval knows $\alpha$, which she does not in general know and which she should not learn.

Thus, [HK20a] supplies to Eval a 'bad' seed for the active branch: i.e., she receives a seed that is different yet indistinguishable from the seed used by Gen. From here, Eval simply *guesses which branch is taken* (she in fact tries all $b$ branches) and evaluates this guessed branch with the appropriately reconstructed material. For security, each guess is unverifiable by Eval. Still, when she guesses right, she indeed evaluates the taken branch and computes valid GC output labels. When she guesses wrong, she evaluates the branch with so-called garbage material (material that is a random-looking string, not an encryption of circuit truth tables), and computes *garbage output labels* (i.e., labels that are not the encryption of 0 or 1, but are random-looking strings). To proceed past the exit of the conditional and continue evaluation, it is necessary to 'collect' these garbage labels by obliviously discarding them in favor of the valid labels.[4]

---

[2] To be pedantic, this specific refactoring is not always valid: $s_1$ might mutate variables used in $e_0$. Still, similar, yet more notationally complex, refactorings are always legal.

[3] Note, [HK20a], as do we in this work, pad each GC material $\hat{C}_i$ with uniform bits before stacking. This ensures all $\hat{C}_i$ are of the same length.

[4] Of course, the final output labels of the conditional are fresh, such that they cannot be cross-referenced with those obtained in branch evaluation.

[HK20a] collect garbage without interaction using a garbled gadget called a *multiplexer*. The multiplexer can be non-interactively constructed by Gen, but only if he *knows all possible garbage labels*. Once this is satisfied, it is easy for Gen to produce a gadget (e.g., appropriate garbled translation tables) that eliminates garbage and propagates the active branch's output labels.

**Gen's Uncertainty.** It is possible for Gen to acquire all garbage labels. [HK20a] achieve this by having Gen emulate the actions of Eval on all inactive branches. To see how this can be done, consider Gen's knowledge and uncertainty about the garbled evaluation. There are three sources of Gen's uncertainty:

- The input values to each inactive branch. This is the largest source of uncertainty (the number of possibilities are exponential in the number of input wires), but the easiest to handle. [HK20a] introduce a simple trick: they add an additional garbled gadget, the *demultiplexer*, that 'zeros out' the wires into the inactive branches. This fully resolves this source of uncertainty.
- The index of the active branch, which we denote by truth.
- Eval's guess of the value of truth, which we denote by guess.

In total, there are $b^2$ (truth, guess) combinations. Crucially, each of these combinations leads to Eval evaluating a *unique combination of a circuit and material*. Hence, there are $b^2$ possible sets of labels ($b(b - 1)$ garbage sets of labels and $b$ valid sets of labels) that the evaluator can compute.

To acquire all possible garbage labels such that he can build the garbage collecting multiplexer, the [HK20a] generator assumes an all-zero inputs for each inactive branch and emulates "in his head" Eval's evaluation of all possible (truth, guess) combinations. This requires that Gen evaluate $b(b - 1)$ times on garbage material. This is the source of the $O(b^2)$ computation.

## 1.3   Top-Level Intuition for $O(b \log b)$ Stacked Garbling

Our main contribution is the reduction of SGC computation from $O(b^2)$ to $O(b \log b)$. To this end, we redesign stacking/unstacking to *reduce Gen's uncertainty*. By doing so, we reduce the computation needed to implement garbage collection. In this section we provide our highest-level intuition for the construction. Section 2.1 continues in greater detail.

Recall from Sect. 1.2 the sources of Gen's uncertainty, which result in $b^2$ evaluations inside Gen's emulation of Eval: there are $b$ possible values for both variables truth and guess (truth $\in \{0, b - 1\}$, guess $\in \{0, b - 1\}$). For each fixed pair (truth, guess), Gen has a fully deterministic view of Eval's garbled evaluation, and hence a deterministic view of the garbage she computes. Gen uses the garbage labels to construct the garbage collecting multiplexer.

Our main idea is to consolidate the processing of many such (truth, guess) pairs by ensuring that Eval's execution is the same across these (truth, guess) pairs. This would further reduce Gen's uncertainty and save computation.

Here is how we approach this. Wlog, let $b = 2^k$ for some $k \in \mathbb{N}$ and consider a balanced binary tree with the $b$ branches at the leaves. For each leaf $\ell$, define the *sibling subtree at level $i$* (or *$i$-th sibling subtree*) to be the subtree rooted in a sibling of the $i$-th node on the path to $\ell$ from the tree root. Thus, each branch has $\log b$ sibling subtrees. We call the root of a sibling subtree of a leaf $\ell$ a *sibling root of $\ell$*. Note, the $\log b$ sibling subtrees of a leaf $\ell$ cover all leaves except for $\ell$. For example, consider Fig. 1. There, node $C_3$ has sibling roots $\mathcal{N}_2, \mathcal{N}_{0,1}, \mathcal{N}_{4,7}$.

We reduce the number of possible (truth, guess) combinations by changing the semantics of truth. truth will not denote the active branch. Instead truth will now be defined *with respect to a given guess* guess. In particular, truth will denote the sibling subtree of guess that contains the active branch (truth = 0 denotes a correct guess). For a fixed guess, there are $\log b + 1$ choices for this truth. If Gen and Eval can efficiently process each of these $b \log b$ (truth, guess) combinations (they can!), we achieve the improved $O(b \log b)$ computation.

## 1.4   Our Contributions

[HK20a] shows that GC players need not send a GC proportional to the entire circuit. Instead, communication proportional to only the longest program execution path suffices. However, their improved communication comes at a cost: for a conditional with $b$ branches, the players use $O(b^2)$ computation.

This is a usually a worthwhile trade-off: GC generation is usually much faster than network transmission (cf. our discussion in Sect. 1.5). However, as the branching factor grows, computation can quickly become the bottleneck due to quadratic scaling. Thus, as we argue in Sect. 1.1, a more computationally efficient technique opens exciting possibilities for rich classes of problems.

This work presents LogStack, an improvement to SGC that features improved computation without compromising communication. Our contributions include:

- Improved time complexity. For $b$ branches, LogStack reduces time complexity from $O(b^2)$ to $O(b \log b)$.
- Improved space complexity. For $b$ branches, our algorithms require $O(\log b)$ space, an improvement from [HK20a]'s $O(b)$ requirement.
- High concrete performance. In total, the players together garble or evaluate the $b$ branches a total of $\frac{7}{2} b \log b + 2b$ times. These concrete results translate to implementation performance: for fewer than 16 branches, our wall-clock runtime is similar to that of [HK20a]. At higher branching factors, we clearly outperform prior work (see Sect. 7).
- A formalization in the [BHR12] framework (as modified by [HK20a]) proved secure under standard assumptions. [HK20a] proved SGC secure by assuming a random oracle. We prove security assuming only a pseudorandom function.

## 1.5   When to Use LogStack: A High-Level Costs Consideration

We now informally discuss a broad question of practical importance:

"If my program has complex control flow, how can I most efficiently implement it for 2PC?"

To make the question more precise, we assume that 'most efficiently' means 'optimized for shortest total wall-clock time'. Since (1) GC is often the most practical approach to 2PC, (2) the GC bottleneck is communication, (3) 'complex control flow' implies conditional behavior, and (4) SGC improves communication for programs with conditional behavior, SGC plays an important role in answering this question. Of course, the cryptographic technique is not the only variable in the optimization space. Program transformations, such as described in Sect. 1.1, also play a crucial role. These variables are related: some program transformations may lead to a blowup in the number of branches. While SGC alleviates the communication overhead of this blowup, the players still incur $b \log b$ computational overhead. So choosing which program transformations to apply depends also on the performance characteristics of the cryptographic scheme.

Despite the fact that the optimization space for total wall-clock time is complex, we firmly believe the following claim: using LogStack over standard GC will *almost always improve performance*. The rest of this section argues this claim.

*Computation vs communication.* To discuss how to best apply LogStack, we establish approximate relative costs of GC computation and communication.

Based on our experiments, a commodity laptop running a single core can generate GC material at about 3× the network bandwidth of a 1 Gbps channel. However, while 1 Gbps is a typical speed in the LAN setting, WAN speeds are much lower, e.g. 100 Mbps. Other network speeds (bluetooth, cellular) are lower still. Even on a LAN and even in a data center, typically we should not assume that our MPC application is allowed to consume the entire channel bandwidth. Rather, we should aim to use as small a fraction of the bandwidth as possible. Based on this discussion, and erring on the conservative side, we choose 100 Mbps as "typical" available bandwidth.

Computation is a much more available resource. Today, commodity laptops have four physical cores. Higher-end computing devices, such as desktop CPUs and GPUs have higher numbers of cores and/or per-core processing power, resulting in yet higher GC computation-to-transmission ratio. Precomputation, if available, can also be seen as a way to increase the available compute resource. SGC, even when using our more sophisticated algorithms, is highly parallelizable. It is easy to engage *many* cores to achieve proportional performance improvement. Based on this discussion, and erring on the conservative side, we choose 2 physical cores as a lower end of "typical" available computational power.

Given a typical setting with 2 cores and a 100 Mbps channel, we arrive at an approximation that GC computation is ≈ 60× faster than GC transmission.

*Assumption: fixed target circuit.* To gain a foothold on answering our broad question, we start by ruling out program transformations and consider only cryptographic protocols. Thus, we consider a fixed *baseline circuit* against which we measure SGC and LogStack performance. That is, our baseline is a circuit $\mathcal{C}$ with conditionals, to which we apply garbling scheme directly, and to which we do not apply any program transformations. We may compare 2PC based on LogStack with Yao GC, both instantiated with half-gates [ZRE15].

*Rule of thumb: always apply* **LogStack**. Assuming our approximated speed ratio of GC generation/transmission, and with a few caveats described next, using **LogStack** for branching will *always* improve over standard GC.

This is easy to see. **Gen** and **Eval** together run a more computationally demanding process, garbling and evaluating branches exactly $\frac{7}{2}b \log b + 2b$ total times ($\frac{5}{2}b \log b + b$ garblings and $b \log b + b$ evaluations). Consider a conditional with $b$ branches. Classic GC will transmit $b$ branches. During this time, **Gen** and **Eval** could have instead performed $60b$ branch garbling/evaluations. **LogStack** garbles/evaluates $\frac{7}{2}b \log b$ branches. Thus, the point where computation crosses over to become the bottleneck is obtained by solving $\frac{7}{2}b \log b > 60b$, the solution to which is $b \gtrsim 2^{17} = 131072$ branches. Of course, this is a "rule-of-thumb" estimate and is based on the conservative assumptions discussed above.

If instead a full 1 Gbps channel is available (i.e. 10× of our network resource assumption), to arrive at the same cross over point, we would need ten times more cores than our computational resource assumption. That equates to 20 cores; such power is available on mainstream servers.

We conclude that applying **LogStack** improves wall clock time for nearly all reasonable baseline circuits and settings.

*Limits on circuit transformations imposed by computational costs.* Above, we established that **LogStack** is almost always better than standard GC for circuits with branching. It is harder to provide heuristics or even rough suggestions regarding which circuit transformations (cf. in Sect. 1.1) to apply, and how aggressively they should be applied in conjunction with **LogStack** secure evaluation. We emphasize that our computational improvement opens a *much* wider optimization space than what was possible with the prior scheme [HK20a]. We leave detailed investigation into this direction as exciting future work.

## 2 Technical Overview of Our Approach

We now informally present our construction with sufficient detail to introduce the most interesting technical challenges and solutions.

### 2.1 $O(b \log b)$ Stacked Garbling

Our main contribution is the reduction of SGC computation from $O(b^2)$ to $O(b \log b)$. Our constants are also low: altogether **Gen** issues $\frac{3}{2}b \log b + b$ calls to Gb and $b \, logb$ calls to Ev. **Eval** issues $b \log b$ calls to Gb and $b$ calls to Ev.

We continue the discussion from Sect. 1.3 in more detail. Our main task is the garbage collection of output labels of *incorrectly guessed* (**truth**, **guess**) combinations where **guess** is **Eval**'s guess of the active branch, and **truth** defines the active branch w.r.t. **guess**. Wlog, let $b$ be a power of 2 to simplify notation. Consider a binary tree where the leaves are the $b$ branches $\mathcal{C}_0, ..., \mathcal{C}_{b-1}$. The tree provides an infrastructure to group branches and to unify processing.

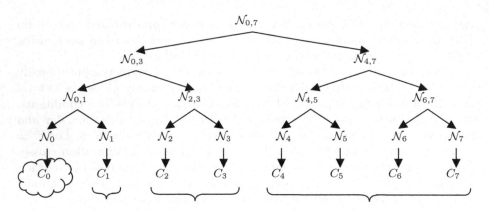

**Fig. 1.** Suppose there are eight branches $C_0$ through $C_7$, and suppose Eval guesses that $C_0$ is the taken branch. If the taken branch is in the subtree $C_4$ through $C_7$, Eval will generate the same garbage material for the entire subtree, regardless of which branch is actually taken. By extension, $C_0$ can only be evaluated against $\log 8 = 3$ garbage material strings: one for each sibling subtree (sibling subtrees are bracketed). Hence $C_0$ has only three possible sets of garbage output labels.

Fix one of $b$ choices for guess. In contrast with [HK20a], which then considers $b$ choices for truth independently from guess, we define truth *in relation* to guess, and consider fewer truth options. Namely, we let truth denote the sibling subtree of guess that contains the active branch (cf. notation Sect. 1.3). Given a fixed incorrect guess, there are only $\log b$ choices for truth.[5] While we have redefined truth, the active branch ID $\alpha$ continues to point to the single active branch. Our garbled gadgets compute functions of $\alpha$.

For concreteness, consider the illustrative example of an 8-leaf tree in Fig. 1 where guess $= 0$. The discussion and arguments pertaining to this special case generalize to arbitrary $b$ and guess.

Consider the four scenarios where one of the branches $C_4 - C_7$ is active. These four scenarios each correspond to truth $= 1$: $C_4 - C_7$ all belong to the level-1 sibling subtree of $C_0$. We ensure that Eval's unstacking and evaluation in each of these four cases is *identical*, and hence she evaluates the same garbage output labels in these four cases. More generally, we achieve identical processing for all leaves of each sibling subtree. Let $\alpha$ denote the index of the active branch. That is, $\alpha$ is a $\log b$-bit integer that points to the active branch.

**Actions and gadgets of Gen.** In the context of the example in Fig. 1, Gen garbles branches $C_0, ..., C_7$ as follows. Recall, the active branch ID $\alpha$ is available to Gen in the form of garbled labels. Gen chooses a random seed for the root of the tree (denoted $s_{0,7}$ for the 8-leaf tree in Fig. 1), and uses it to pseudorandomly derive seeds for each node of the tree. This is done in the standard manner, e.g.,

---

[5] We focus on garbage collection and consider only incorrect guesses; managing output labels of the correctly guessed branches is straightforward and cheap.

- INPUTS: the active branch id $\alpha$ and the number of branches $b$.
- OUTPUTS: a sequence of evaluator seeds that form a binary tree:

$$\mathsf{es}_{0,b-1}, \mathsf{es}_{0,\frac{b-1}{2}}, \mathsf{es}_{\frac{b-1}{2}+1,b-1}, \ldots, \mathsf{es}_0, \mathsf{es}_1, \ldots \mathsf{es}_{b-1}$$

such that for each node $\mathcal{N}$:

$$\mathsf{es}_{\mathcal{N}} = \begin{cases} s_{\mathcal{N}}, & \text{if } \mathcal{N} \text{ is a sibling root of } \alpha \\ s'_{\mathcal{N}}, & \text{otherwise} \end{cases}$$

where $s'_{\mathcal{N}}$ is a uniform string indistinguishable from $s_{\mathcal{N}}$.

**Fig. 2.** The `SortingHat` functionality. `SortingHat` is responsible for conveying only the sibling root seeds of $\alpha$ to `Eval`. For every other node, `Eval` obtains a different, but indistinguishable, seed that, when garbled, generates garbage material. `SortingHat` is easily implemented as a garbled circuit gadget (i.e., built from garbled rows).

the immediate children of a seed $s$ are the PRF evaluations on inputs 0 and 1 with the key $s$. `Gen` uses each leaf seed $s_i$ to garble the corresponding branch $\mathcal{C}_i$ and stacks all garbled branches $M = \bigoplus_i \hat{\mathcal{C}}_i$. This material $M$ is the large string that `Gen` ultimately sends across the network to `Eval`. We note two facts about $M$ and about the active branch $\alpha$.

1. **Correctness:** if `Eval` obtains the $\log b$ seeds of the sibling roots of $\alpha$, then she can regarble all circuits $\hat{\mathcal{C}}_{i \neq \alpha}$, unstack by XORing with $M$, and obtain $\hat{\mathcal{C}}_\alpha$, allowing her to correctly evaluate $\mathcal{C}_\alpha$.
2. **Security:** `Eval` must not obtain any correct seed corresponding to any ancestor of $\alpha$. If she did, she would learn (by garbling) the encoding of wire labels which would allow her to decrypt all intermediate wire values in $\mathcal{C}_\alpha$. Instead, `Eval` will obtain 'garbage' seeds indistinguishable yet distinct from the correct seeds generated by `Gen`.

To facilitate garbled evaluation of the conditional and meet the requirements of these two facts, in addition to $M$, `Gen` generates and sends to `Eval` a small (linear in the number of branches with small constants) garbled gadget that we call `SortingHat`.[6] `SortingHat` aids `Eval` in her reconstruction of branch material. `SortingHat` takes as input labels corresponding to $\alpha$ and produces candidate seeds for each node in the tree. For each node $\mathcal{N}$, `SortingHat` constructs a correct seed $s_{\mathcal{N}}$ if and only if $\mathcal{N}$ is a sibling root of the leaf $\alpha$ (see Fig. 2). `SortingHat` can be implemented as a collection of garbled rows. Importantly, since this is a fixed gadget, when evaluated on a node $\mathcal{N}$ that is not a sibling root of $\alpha$, `Eval` will obtain a *fixed* seed that is predictable to `Gen`.

---

[6] In J.K. Rowling's Harry Potter universe, the 'sorting hat' is a magical object that assigns new students to different school houses based on personality. Our `SortingHat` 'sorts' nodes of trees into two categories based on $\alpha$: those that are 'good' (i.e., sibling roots of $\alpha$) and those that are 'bad'.

For example in Fig. 1, if the active branch is $\alpha = 4$, then applying `SortingHat` to nodes $\mathcal{N}_{0,3}, \mathcal{N}_{6,7}, \mathcal{N}_5$ reconstructs the correct seeds $s_{0,3}, s_{6,7}, s_5$. Applying `SortingHat` to other nodes constructs fixed garbage seeds. If instead $\alpha = 3$, then `SortingHat` reconstructs the correct seeds $s_{4,7}, s_{0,1}, s_2$. Critically, the garbage seeds reconstructed in both cases, e.g. for node $\mathcal{N}_{4,5}$, are the same.

**Actions of `Eval`.** It is now intuitive how `Eval` proceed with unstacking. She applies `SortingHat` and obtains a tree of random-looking seeds; of $2b$ seeds, only $\log b$ seeds just off the path to $\alpha$ (corresponding to $\alpha$'s sibling roots) are correct. `Eval` guesses `guess`; assuming `guess`, she uses only the sibling seeds of `guess` to derive all $b - 1$ leaf seeds not equal to `guess`. She then garbles the $b - 1$ branches $\mathcal{C}_i$ and unstacks the corresponding GCs $\hat{\mathcal{C}}_i$.

If `guess` $= \alpha$, `Eval` derives the intended leaf seeds $s_{i \neq \alpha}$, unstacks the intended garbled circuits $\hat{\mathcal{C}}_{i \neq \alpha}$, and obtains the correct GC $\hat{\mathcal{C}}_\alpha$. Consider the case where `Eval` guesses wrong. `Eval` simply unstacks wrong branches garbled with the wrong seeds. Since `Eval` never receives any additional valid seeds, there is no security loss. We next see that the number of different garbage labels we must collect is small, and further that they can be collected efficiently.

**$O(b \log b)$ computational cost accounting.** Let Gb and Ev be procedures that respectively garble/evaluate a GC. Consider how many such calls are made by `Eval`. Consider branch $\mathcal{C}_i$. It is garbled $\log b$ times, once with a seed (ultimately) derived from each seed on the path to the root. Thus, the total number of calls by `Eval` to Gb is $b \log b$ and to Ev is exactly $b$.

To construct the garbage collecting multiplexer, `Gen` must obtain all possible garbage labels. We demonstrate that the total cost to the generator is $O(b \log b)$ calls to both Gb and Ev. First, consider only Gb and consider the number of ways `Eval` can garble a specific circuit $\mathcal{C}_i$. Clearly, this is exactly $\log b + 1$.

Now, consider `Gen`'s number of calls to Ev. Recall that our goal was to ensure that `Eval` constructs the same garbage output labels for a branch $\mathcal{C}_i$ in each scenario where $\alpha$ is in some fixed sibling subtree of $\mathcal{C}_i$. The logic of `SortingHat` ensures that `Eval` obtains the same sibling root seeds in each of these scenarios, and therefore she constructs the same garblings. Hence, since there are $\log b$ sibling subtrees of $\mathcal{C}_i$, $\mathcal{C}_i$ has only $\log b$ possible garbage output labels. Thus, in order to emulate `Eval` in all settings and obtain all possible garbage output labels, `Gen` must garble and evaluate each branch $\log b$ times.

## 2.2 Technical Difference Between Our and [HK20a] Binary Braching

A careful reader familiar with [HK20a] may notice that they present two versions of stacked garbling. The first handles high branching factors by recursively *nesting* conditionals. Nested conditionals can be viewed as a binary tree. This first approach is then discarded in favor of a second, more efficient vector approach. Our work advocates binary branching and yet substantially improves over [HK20a]'s vectorized approach. Why is our binary branching better?

The problem with [HK20a]'s recursive construction is that Eval recursively garbles the garbage-collecting multiplexer for nested sub-conditionals. Doing so leads to a recursive emulation whereby Eval emulates herself (and hence Gen emulates himself as well). This recursion leads to quadratic cost for both players. The way out is to treat the multiplexer separately, and to opt not to stack it. If multiplexers are not stacked, then Eval need not garble them, and hence Eval need never emulate herself. On top of this, we reduce the number of ways that individual branches can be garbled via our SortingHat.

**A note on nested branches.** Nested branches with complex sequencing of instructions emerge naturally in many programs. Our approach operates directly over vectors of circuits and treats them as binary trees. This may at first seem like a disadvantage, since at the time the first nested branching decision is made, it may not yet be possible to make *all* branching decisions. There are two natural ways LogStack can be used in such contexts:

1. Although we advocate for vectorized branching, LogStack does support nested evaluation. Although nesting is secure and correct, we do not necessarily recommend it. Using LogStack in this recursive manner yields quadratic computation overhead.
2. Refactorings can be applied to ensure branches are vectorized. For example, consider the following refactoring:

$$\text{if } (e_0) \{ s_0; \text{if } (e_1) \{ s_1 \} \text{ else } \{ s_2 \} \} \text{ else } \{ s_3; s_4 \} \longrightarrow$$

$$\text{if } (e_0) \{ s_0 \} \text{ else } \{ s_3 \}; \text{switch}(e_0 + e_0 e_1) \{ s_4 \} \mid \{ s_2 \} \mid \{ s_1 \}$$

   Where $s_i$ are programs, $e_i$ are predicates on program variables, and where $s_0, s_3$ do not modify variables in $e_0$. This refactoring has replaced a nested conditional by a sequence of two 'vectorized' conditionals, and hence made the approach amenable to our efficient algorithms.

## 2.3   Memory Efficiency of LogStack

The [HK20a] approach forces Gen to store many intermediate garblings: for conditionals with $b$ branches he requires $O(b)$ space. In contrast, LogStack has low space requirements: its algorithms run in $O(\log b)$ space. We briefly discuss why [HK20a] requires linear space and how our approach improves this.

In the [HK20a] approach, Eval obtains $b-1$ good seeds for all but the active branch and a bad seed for the active branch. When Eval then makes a particular guess, she attempts to uncover the material for guess by XORing the stacked material (sent by Gen) with $b-1$ reconstructed materials; she 'unstacks' her $b-1$ materials corresponding to all branches that are not equal to guess. Recall that Gen emulates Eval for all combinations of (truth, guess) where truth $\neq$ guess to compute garbage outputs. The most intuitive way to proceed, and the strategy [HK20a] uses, is for Gen to once and for all garble all circuits using the 'good' seeds and garble all circuits using the 'bad' seeds, and to store all materials in two large vectors. Let $M_i$ be the good material for a branch $C_i$ and let $M_i'$ be the bad material. Now let $j = \texttt{truth}$ and $k = \texttt{guess}$. To emulate all possible bad evaluations, Gen evaluates $C_k$ using the material $M_k \oplus M_j \oplus M_j'$: i.e., he emulates Eval when correctly unstacking all material except $M_k$ (which she will not attempt to unstack because she wishes to evaluate $C_k$) and $M_j$ (which she attempts to unstack, but fails and instead adds $M_j'$). Because Gen considers all $j, k$ combinations, it is not clear how Gen can compute all values $M_k \oplus M_j \oplus M_j'$ without either (1) storing intermediate garblings in $O(b)$ space or (2) repeatedly garbling each branch at great cost. [HK20a] opts for the former.

In contrast, because of LogStack's binary tree structure, we can eagerly stack material together as it is constructed to save space. E.g., consider again the example in Fig. 4 where Eval guesses that $C_0$ is active. Recall, she garbles the entire right subtree starting from the seed for node $\mathcal{N}_{4,7}$, and Gen emulates this same behavior with the bad seed. For both players, the material corresponding to individual circuits, say $M_4$ corresponding to $C_4$, is *not interesting or useful*. Only the stacked material $M_4 \oplus .. \oplus M_7$ is useful for guessing $C_0$ (and more generally for guessing all circuits in the subtree $\mathcal{N}_{0,3}$). Thus, instead of storing all material separately, the players both XOR material for subtrees together as soon as it is available. This trick is the basis for our low space requirement.

There is one caveat to this trick: the 'good' garbling of each branch $C_i$ *is* useful throughout Gen's emulation of Eval. Hence, the straightforward procedure would be for Gen to once and for all compute the good garblings of each branch and store them in a vector, consuming $O(b)$ space. This is viable, and indeed has lower runtime constants than presented elsewhere in this work: Gen would invoke Gb only $b \log b + b$ times. We instead trade in some concrete time complexity in favor of dramatically improved space complexity. Gen garbles the branches using good seeds an extra $\frac{1}{2} b \log b$ times, and hence calls Gb a total of $\frac{3}{2} b \log b + b$ times. These extra calls to Gb allow Gen to avoid storing a large vector of materials, and our algorithms run in $O(\log b)$ space.

## 2.4   Stacked Garbling with and Without Random Oracles

[HK20a] (and we) focus only on branching and leave the handling of low level gates to another *underlying* garbling scheme, Base. [HK20a] assumes nothing about Base except that it satisfies the standard [BHR12] properties, as well as their *stackability* property. However, they do not preclude Base's labels from being related to each other, which presents a security problem: Base's labels are used to garble rows, but if the labels are related they cannot be securely used as PRF keys. [HK20a] handles the possible use of related keys by using a RO.

We introduce a stronger requirement on Base, which we call *strong stackability*. Informally, we additionally require that *all* output labels of Base are uniformly random. This is sufficient to prove security in the standard model.

Of course, RO-based security theorems and proofs also work, and our gadgets could be slightly optimized in a natural manner under this assumption.

# 3   Related Work

GC is the most popular and often the fastest approach to secure two-party computation. Until recently, it was believed that it is necessary to transmit the entire GC during 2PC, even for inactive conditional branches. Recent breakthrough work [HK20a] showed that this folklore belief is false, and that it suffices to only transmit GC material proportional to the longest execution path.

We focus our comparison with prior work on [HK20a], and then review other related work, such as universal circuits and earlier stacked garbling work.

*Comparison with* [HK20a]. As discussed in Sect. 1.1, programs with conditionals with high branching factor may be a result of program transformations aimed at optimizing GC/SGC performance. While the protocol of [HK20a] is concretely efficient, its quadratic computational cost presents a limitation even in settings with relatively modest branching factor $b$. This significantly limits the scope of program transformations which will be effective for SGC.

Our work archives total computational cost proportional to $3.5b \log b$, and effectively removes the computational overhead of the SGC technique as a constraining consideration[7], as discussed in Sect. 1.5.

Memory management is a significant performance factor in GC in general, and in particular in [HK20a] garbling. Retrieving an already-garbled material from RAM may take similar or longer time than regarbling from scratch while operating in cache. In addition to significantly improving computation (i.e. number of calls to Gb and Ev), our approach offers improved memory utilization (see Sects. 1.4 and 2.3). [HK20a] requires that a linear number of garbled circuits be kept in RAM. For larger circuits this can become a problem. For example, the garbling of a 1M AND-gate circuit occupies 32 MB in RAM. If a machine can dedicate 2 GB to garbling, a maximum of 64 branches of this size can be handled. This ignores additional constant space costs, which are not necessarily low. In contrast, we use only $O(\log b)$ space, and hence can fit the garblings of large numbers of branches into memory. In our experiments, we ran our implementation on a circuit with 8192 SHA-256 branches, a circuit that altogether holds > 385M AND-gates. Our peak memory usage was at around 100 MB ([HK20a] would require more than 12 GB of space to run this experiment).

In sum, as discussed at length in Sects. 1.5 and 2.3 and Sect. 7, we essentially eliminate the concern of increased computation due to Stacked Garbling for typical settings and open the door to the possibility of applying a large class of efficiency-improving program transformations on the evaluated program.

*Universal circuits.* An alternate technique for handling conditional branching is to implement a *universal circuit* [Val76], which can represent any conditional branch. We discuss universal circuits [LMS16, KS16, GKS17, ZYZL19, AGKS20,

---

[7] We stress that branches must still be garbled, and extreme program transformations, such as stacking *all* possible program control flows, may be impractical computationally due to the exponential number of branches.

KKW17] in more detail in the full version of this paper. In short, SGC is a more practical approach to conditional branching in most scenarios.

*Other related work.* Kolesnikov [Kol18] was the first to separate the GC *material* from circuit topology. This separation was used to improve GC branching given that the GC generator Gen knows the active branch. Subsequently, [HK20b] considered a complementary setting where the GC evaluator Eval knows the active branch, and used it to construct efficient ZK proofs for circuits with branching. Our work follows the line of work initiated by [Kol18, HK20b]; it is for general 2PC and is constant-round.

As discussed in [HK20a], interaction, such as via the output selection protocol of [Kol18], can be used to collect garbage efficiently (computation linear in $b$). However, a communication round is added for each conditional branch. In many scenarios, non-interactive 2PC (such as what we achieve) is preferred.

Designing efficient garbling schemes under standard assumptions (i.e. using only PRFs) is a valuable research direction. [GLNP15] impressively implement garbled table generation and evaluation with speed similar to that of fixed-key AES. [GLNP15] cannot use the Free XOR technique [KS08], which requires circularity assumptions [CKKZ12], but nevertheless implement XOR Gates with only one garbled row and AND gates with two rows.

## 4   Notation and Assumptions

*Notation.* Our notation is mostly consistent with the notation of [HK20a].

- Our garbling scheme is called LogStack. We sometimes refer to it by the abbreviation LS, especially when referring to its algorithms.
- 'Gen' is the circuit generator. We refer to Gen as he, him, his, etc.
- 'Eval' is the circuit evaluator. We refer to Eval as she, her, hers, etc.
- '$\mathcal{C}$' is a circuit. $\text{inpSize}(\mathcal{C})$ and $\text{outSize}(\mathcal{C})$ respectively compute the number of input/output wires to $\mathcal{C}$.
- $x \mid y$ denotes the concatenation of strings $x$ and $y$.
- Following SGC terminology introduced by [Kol18], $M$ refers to GC *material*. Informally, material is just a collection of garbled tables, i.e. the garbling data which, in conjunction with circuit topology and input labels, is used to compute output labels.
- We use $m$ to denote the size of material, i.e. $m = |M|$.
- Variables that represent vectors are denoted in bold, e.g. $\boldsymbol{x}$. We index vectors using bracket notation: $\boldsymbol{x}[0]$ accesses the 0th index of $\boldsymbol{x}$.
- We extensively use binary trees. Suppose $t$ is such a tree. We use subscript notation $t_i$ to denote the $i$th leaf of $t$. We use pairs of indexes to denote internal nodes of the tree. I.e., $t_{i,j}$ is the root of the subtree containing the leaves $t_i..t_j$. $t_{i,i}$ (i.e. the node containing only $i$) and $t_i$ both refer to the leaf: $t_{i,i} = t_i$. It is sometimes convenient to refer to a (sub)tree index abstractly. For this, we write $\mathcal{N}_{i,j}$ or, when clear from context, simply write $\mathcal{N}$.

- We write $a \leftarrow_\$ S$ to denote that $a$ is drawn uniformly from the set $S$.
- $\overset{c}{=}$ denotes computational indistinguishability.
- $\kappa$ denotes the computational security parameter and can be understood as the length of PRF keys (e.g. 128).

We evaluate GCs with input labels that are generated independently of the GC material and do not match the GC. We call such labels *garbage labels*. During GC evaluation, garbage labels propagate to the output wires and must eventually be obliviously dropped in favor of valid labels. We call the process of canceling out output garbage labels *garbage collection*.

*Assumptions.* LogStack is secure in the standard model. However, higher efficiency of both the underlying scheme Base and of our garbled gadgets can be achieved under the RO assumption. Our implementation uses half-gates as Base, and relies on a random oracle (RO).

# 5   The LogStack Garbling Scheme

In this section, we formalize our construction, LogStack. Throughout this section, consider a conditional circuit with $b$ branches. For simplicity, we ignore the number input and output wires.

We adopt the above simplification because branching factor is the most interesting aspect of LogStack. We emphasize that ignoring inputs/outputs does not hide high costs. While we scale with the product of the number of inputs and $b$ (and respectively the product of number of outputs and $b$), the constants are low (see Sect. 7 for evidence). Thus, inputs/outputs are of secondary concern to the circuit size, which is often far larger than the number of inputs/outputs.

Consider garbled circuits $\hat{\mathcal{C}}_i$ corresponding to each branch $\mathcal{C}_i$. Let $m$ be the size of the largest such garbling: $m = \max_i |\hat{\mathcal{C}}_i|$. Given branching factor $b$, LogStack features:

- $O(m)$ communication complexity.
- $O(mb \log b)$ time complexity.
- $O(m \log b)$ space complexity.

LogStack is formalized as a *garbling scheme* [BHR12]. Garbling schemes abstract the details of GC such that protocols can be written generically. That is, LogStack is a modular collection of algorithms, not a protocol. Our formalization specifically uses the modified garbling scheme framework of [HK20a], which separates the *topology* of circuits (i.e., the concrete circuit description) from circuit material (i.e., the collections of encryptions needed to securely evaluate the circuit), an important modification for SGC.

A garbling scheme is a tuple of five algorithms:

$$(\mathsf{ev}, \mathsf{Ev}, \mathsf{Gb}, \mathsf{En}, \mathsf{De})$$

- ev specifies circuit semantics. For typical approaches that consider only low-level gates, ev is often left implicit since its implementation is generally understood. We explicate ev to formalize conventions of conditional evaluation.
- Ev specifies how Eval securely evaluates the GC.
- Gb specifies how Gen garbles the GC.
- En and De specify the translation of cleartext values to/from GC labels. That is, En specifies how player inputs translate to input labels and De specifies how outputs labels translate to cleartext outputs.

Correct garbling schemes ensure that the garbled functions Gb, En, Ev, and De achieve the semantics specified by ev.

Before we present our garbling scheme LogStack, we introduce the formal syntax of the circuits it manipulates. Because our focus is conditional branching, we assume an *underlying garbling scheme* Base. Base is responsible for handling the collections of low level gates (typically AND and XOR gates) that we refer to as *netlists*. In our implementation, we instantiate Base with the efficient half-gates scheme of [ZRE15]. We do not specify the syntax of netlists, and entirely leave their handling to Base. Our circuit syntax is defined inductively: Let $\mathcal{C}_0, \mathcal{C}_1$ be two arbitrary circuits and $\mathcal{C}$ be a vector of arbitrary circuits. The space of circuits is defined as follows:

$$\mathcal{C} ::= \mathsf{Netlist}(\cdot) \mid \mathsf{Cond}(\mathcal{C}) \mid \mathsf{Seq}(\mathcal{C}_0, \mathcal{C}_1)$$

That is, a circuit is either (1) a netlist, (2) a conditional dispatch over a vector of circuits (our focus), or (3) a sequence of two circuits. Sequences of circuits are necessary to allow arbitrary control flow.

With our syntax established, we are ready to present our algorithms.

**Construction 1 (LogStack).** *LogStack is the tuple of algorithms:*

$$(LS.ev, LS.Ev, LS.Gb, LS.En, LS.De)$$

*Definitions for each algorithm are listed in Fig. 3.*

We discuss correctness and security of Construction 1 in Sect. 6. Due to lack of space, proofs of these properties are in the full version of this paper.

In terms of efficiency, LogStack satisfies the following property:

**Theorem 1.** *Let Base be a garbling scheme satisfying the following property:*

- *Let $C$ be an arbitrary netlist and let $s$ be the size of material generated by invoking Base.Gb on $C$. Let both Base.Ev and Base.Gb, invoked on $C$, run in $O(s)$ time and $O(s)$ space.*

*Then Construction 1 instantiated with Base satisfies the following property.*

- *Let $\mathcal{C}$ be a vector of $b$ arbitrary netlists. Let $m$ be the maximum size of the garblings constructed by calling Base.Gb on each of these $b$ netlists. Then both LS.Ev and LS.Gb, invoked on $\mathsf{Cond}(\mathcal{C})$, run in $O(mb \log b)$ time and $O(m \log b)$ space.*

LS.ev($\mathcal{C}, \boldsymbol{x}$) :
  ▷ What are the circuit semantics?
  switch $\mathcal{C}$ :
    case Netlist($\cdot$) : return Base.ev($\mathcal{C}, \boldsymbol{x}$)
    case Seq($\mathcal{C}_0, \mathcal{C}_1$) : return LS.ev($\mathcal{C}_1$, LS.ev($\mathcal{C}_0, \boldsymbol{x}$))
    case Cond($\boldsymbol{\mathcal{C}}$) :
      ▷ split branch index from input
      $\alpha \mid \boldsymbol{x}' \leftarrow \boldsymbol{x}$
      ▷ Run the active branch.
      return LS.ev($\boldsymbol{\mathcal{C}}[\alpha], \boldsymbol{x}'$)

LS.Ev($\mathcal{C}, M, \boldsymbol{X}$) :
  ▷ How does Eval evaluate the GC?
  switch($\mathcal{C}$) :
    case Netlist($\cdot$) : return Base.Ev($\mathcal{C}, M, \boldsymbol{X}$)
    case Seq($\mathcal{C}_0, \mathcal{C}_1$) :
      $M_0 \mid M_{tr} \mid M_1 \leftarrow M$
      return LS.Ev($\mathcal{C}_1, M_1, trans$.Ev(LS.Ev($\mathcal{C}_0, M_0, \boldsymbol{X}$), $M_{tr}$))
    case Cond($\boldsymbol{\mathcal{C}}$) : return EvCond($\boldsymbol{\mathcal{C}}, M, \boldsymbol{X}$)

LS.En($e, \boldsymbol{x}$) :
  ▷ How do inputs map to labels?
  ▷ This works for all projective schemes:
  $\boldsymbol{X} \leftarrow \lambda$
  for $i \in 0..\text{inpSize}(\mathcal{C})-1$ :
    $(X^0, X^1) \leftarrow e[i]$
    if $\boldsymbol{x}[i] = 0$ : $\{ \boldsymbol{X}[i] \leftarrow X^0 \}$ else : $\{ \boldsymbol{X}[i] \leftarrow X^1 \}$
  return $\boldsymbol{X}$

LS.Gb($1^\kappa, \mathcal{C}, S$) :
  ▷ How does Gen garble the GC?
  ▷ $S$ is an explicit seed.
  switch $\mathcal{C}$ :
    case Netlist($\cdot$) :
      return Base.Gb($1^\kappa, \mathcal{C}, S$)
    case Seq($\mathcal{C}_0, \mathcal{C}_1$) :
      ▷ Derive seeds for two circuits.
      $S_0 \leftarrow F_S(0)$
      $S_1 \leftarrow F_S(1)$
      $(M_0, e_0, d_0) \leftarrow$ LS.Gb($1^\kappa, \mathcal{C}_0, S_0$)
      $(M_1, e_1, d_1) \leftarrow$ LS.Gb($1^\kappa, \mathcal{C}_1, S_1$)
      ▷ Labels out of $\mathcal{C}_0$ must be *translated*
      ▷ to labels into $\mathcal{C}_1$.
      $M_{tr} \leftarrow trans$.Gb($d_0, e_1$)
      $M \leftarrow M_0 \mid M_{tr} \mid M_1$
      return $(M, e_0, d_1)$
    case Cond($\boldsymbol{\mathcal{C}}$) : return GbCond($\boldsymbol{\mathcal{C}}, S$)

LS.De($d, \boldsymbol{Y}$) :
  ▷ How do labels map to outputs?
  ▷ This works for all projective schemes:
  $\boldsymbol{y} \leftarrow \lambda$
  for $i \in 0..\text{outSize}(\mathcal{C})-1$ :
    $(Y^0, Y^1) \leftarrow d[i]$
    if $\boldsymbol{Y}[i] = Y^0$ : $\boldsymbol{y}[i] \leftarrow 0$
    else if $\boldsymbol{Y}[i] = Y^1$ : $\boldsymbol{y}[i] \leftarrow 1$
    else : ABORT
  return $\boldsymbol{y}$

**Fig. 3.** Our garbling scheme LogStack. The included algorithms are typical except for the handling of conditionals. Ev and Gb delegate the core of our approach: EvCond (Fig. 5) and GbCond (Fig. 6).

Standard garbling schemes, e.g. the half-gates scheme [ZRE15], achieve the efficiency required by Theorem 1, since they simply handle each gate individually.

Lemmas that support Theorem 1 are formally stated and proved in the full version of this paper.

Proofs of these lemmas follow from inspecting our recursive algorithms and (1) counting the number of calls to the underlying scheme's algorithms and (2) counting the number of garblings kept in scope.

We now draw attention to two key details of algorithms in Fig. 3: (1) LS.Ev delegates to a subprocedure EvCond and (2) LS.Gb delegates to a subprocedure GbCond. All details of conditionals are handled by these two subprocedures. Aside from these delegations, the algorithms in Fig. 3 are relatively unsurprising: the algorithms closely match [HK20a]'s construction and essentially provide infrastructure needed to host our contribution. We briefly discuss the most relevant details of these algorithms before returning to an extended discussion of EvCond and GbCond (c.f. Sect. 5.1):

- **Projectivity.** LogStack is a *projective garbling scheme* [BHR12]. Projectivity requires that the input *encoding string e* and output *decoding string d* have a specific format: they must both be a vector of pairs of labels such that the left element of each pair is a label encoding logical 0 and the right element of each pair is a label encoding 1. Thus, LS.En and LS.De are straightforward mappings between cleartext values and encoding/decoding strings.
- **Sequences and Translation.** In a sequence of two circuits, all output wires of the first circuit are passed as the inputs to the second. Because these two circuits are garbled starting from different seeds, the output labels from $C_0$ will not match the required input encoding of $C_1$. We thus implement a *translation* component (*trans*.Ev and *trans*.Gb) that implements via garbled rows a straightforward translation from one encoding to another. Our scheme securely implements the translator, and all other gadgets, using a PRF ([HK20a] used an RO). This simplification is possible because of the stronger property, strong stackability, that we require of the underlying garbling scheme (see Sect. 6).

## 5.1   Algorithms for Handling of Conditionals

With the remaining formalization out of the way, we focus on conditional branching. Our goal is to formalize EvCond and GbCond, the key sub-procedures invoked by LS.Ev and LS.Gb respectively. Our presentation is a formalization of discussion in Sect. 2; the following explores the technical aspects of our construction, but the reader should refer to Sect. 2 for unifying high level intuition.

**Demultiplexer and Multiplexer.** Before we discuss handling the body of conditionals, we briefly discuss entering and leaving a conditional. That is, we describe the *demultiplexer* (entry) and *multiplexer* (exit) components.

   The demultiplexer is responsible for (1) forwarding the conditional's inputs to the active branch $C_\alpha$ and (2) forwarding specially prepared garbage inputs to each branch $C_{i \neq \alpha}$. The demultiplexer computes the following function for each wire input $x$ to each branch $C_i$ with respect to the active index $\alpha$:

$$demux(x, i, \alpha) = \begin{cases} x, & \text{if } i = \alpha \\ \bot, & \text{otherwise} \end{cases}$$

where $\bot$ is a specially designated constant value. In the GC, the label corresponding to $\bot$ is independent yet indistinguishable from the corresponding 0 and 1 labels: independence is crucial for security. The demultiplexer is easily implemented by garbled rows. The number of required rows is proportional to the number of branches and the conditional's number of inputs. EvCond and

GbCond make use of *demux*.Ev and *demux*.Gb, procedures which implement the above function via GC. Although we do not, for simplicity, formally describe these, we emphasize that they are a straightforward implementation of garbled rows.

The multiplexer is central to our approach. It non-interactively eliminates garbage outputs from inactive branches. Despite its central role, if Gen knows the garbage outputs from each branch, the multiplexer's implementation is simple. Specifically, suppose each branch $C_i$ has an output $x_i$ that should propagate if that branch is active. The multiplexer computes the following function:

$$mux(x_0, ..., x_{b-1}, \alpha) = x_\alpha$$

Given that (1) each value $x_{i \neq \alpha}$ is a fixed constant $\perp$, at least with respect to a given $\alpha$ (a property that we carefully arrange via the demultiplexer), and (2) Gen knows the value of each of these fixed constants (the central point of our work), then the above *mux* function is easily implemented as a collection of garbled rows. The number of required rows is proportional to the number of branches and the number of the conditional's outputs. EvCond and GbCond make use of *mux*.Ev and *mux*.Gb, procedures which implement the above function via GC. As with the demultiplexer, we do not formalize these procedures in detail, but their implementation is a straightforward handling of garbled rows.

**Garbling Subtrees.** Recall, we organize the $b$ branches into a binary tree. For *each* internal node of the tree, both EvCond and GbCond perform a common task: they garble all branches in the entire subtree rooted at that node and stack together all material. These subtrees are garbled according to seeds given by the SortingHat, formally defined in Fig. 2. Like the demultiplexer and multiplexer, the GC implementation of SortingHat is a straightforward handling of garbled rows: we assume procedures SortingHat.Ev and SortingHat.Gb which implement this handling.

We next define a procedure, GbSubtreeFromSeed (Fig. 4), which performs the basic task of garbling and stacking an entire subtree. GbSubtreeFromSeed recursively descends through the subtree starting from its root, uses a PRF to derive child seeds from the parent seed, and at the leaves garbles the branches. As the recursion propagates back up the tree, the procedure stacks the branch materials together (and concatenates input/output encodings). The recursion tracks two integers $i$ and $j$, denoting the range of branches $C_i..C_j$ that are to be stacked together. EvCond and GbCond use a similar strategy, and all three algorithms maintain an invariant that $i, j$ refers to a valid node $\mathcal{N}_{i,j}$ in the binary tree over the $b$ branches. EvCond and GbCond invoke GbSubtreeFromSeed at *every* node. This entails that both procedures garble each branch $C_i$ more than once, but with different seeds. As discussed in Sect. 2, this repeated garbling is key to reducing the total number of garbage outputs that Eval can compute.

```
GbSubtreeFromSeed(C, i, j, seed) :
    if i = j :     ▷ Base case of 1 branch.
      return Gb(C[i], seed)
    else :
        ▷ Expand child seeds using PRF.
        seed_L ← F_seed(0)
        seed_R ← F_seed(1)
        ▷ Recursively garble both child trees and stack material.
        k ← halfway(i, j)
        M_L, e_L, d_L ← GbSubtreeFromSeed(C, i, k, seed_L)
        M_R, e_R, d_R ← GbSubtreeFromSeed(C, k + 1, j, seed_R)
        return (M_L ⊕ M_R, e_L | e_R, d_L | d_R)


halfway(i, j) :
    ▷ Simple helper for splitting range of branches (approximately) in half.
    return i + ⌊ (j − i)/2 ⌋
```

**Fig. 4.** The helper algorithm `GbSubtreeFromSeed` starts from a single seed at the root of a subtree $\mathcal{N}_{i,j}$, derives all seeds in the subtree, garbles all branches in the subtree, and stacks (using XOR) all resultant material. The procedure also returns the input/output encodings for all branches.

**Evaluating Conditionals.** We now formalize the procedure `EvCond` by which `Eval` handles a vector of conditionals (Fig. 5). The core of `EvCond` is delegated to a recursive subprocedure `EvCond'`. `EvCond'` carefully manages material and uses the garblings of sibling subtrees to evaluate each branch while limiting the possible number of garbage outputs. `EvCond'` is a formalization of the high level procedure described in Sect. 2: `Eval` recursively descends through the tree, constructing and unstacking garblings of subtrees in the general case. When she finally reaches the leaf nodes, she simply evaluates. In the base case $i = \alpha$, she will have correctly unstacked all material except $M_\alpha$ (because she has good seeds for the sibling roots of $\alpha$), and hence evaluates correctly. All other cases $i \neq \alpha$ will lead to garbage outputs that `Gen` must also compute. Other than the delegation to `EvCond'`, `EvCond` simply invokes `SortingHat.Ev` to obtain her seeds, invokes $demux.\text{Ev}$ to propagate valid inputs to $\mathcal{C}_\alpha$, and, after evaluating all branches, invokes $mux.\text{Ev}$ to collect garbage outputs from all $\mathcal{C}_{i \neq \alpha}$.

**Garbling Conditionals.** Finally, we formalize `Gen`'s procedure for handling vectors of conditional branches, `GbCond` (Fig. 6).

1. `GbCond` recursively derives a binary tree of good seeds via `DeriveSeedTree`. This call uses a PRF to recursively derive seeds in the standard manner.

$\text{EvCond}(\boldsymbol{C}, M, X):$

  $b \leftarrow |\boldsymbol{C}|$

  ▷ Parse the active branch index from the rest of the input.

  $\alpha \mid X' \leftarrow X$

  ▷ Parse material for gadgets and body of conditional.

  $M_{\texttt{SortingHat}} \mid M_{dem} \mid M_{cond} \mid M_{mux} \leftarrow M$

  ▷ Run $\texttt{SortingHat}$ to compute all of $\texttt{Eval}$'s seeds.

  $\text{es} \leftarrow \texttt{SortingHat.Ev}(\alpha, M_{\texttt{SortingHat}})$

  ▷ Run the demultiplexer to compute input for each branch $\mathcal{C}_i$.

  $\boldsymbol{X}_{cond} \leftarrow demux.\text{Ev}(\alpha, X, M_{dem})$

  ▷ We define a recursive subprocedure that evaluates $\mathcal{C}_i - \mathcal{C}_j$ using material $M$.

  $\text{EvCond}'(i, j, M_{i,j}):$

    if $i = j$:

      ▷ Base case: compute output by evaluating the branch normally.

      ▷ This base case corresponds to $\texttt{guess} = i$.

      ▷ Accumulate output labels into the vector $\boldsymbol{Y}_{cond}$ (for later garbage collection).

      $\boldsymbol{Y}_{cond}[i] \leftarrow \text{Ev}(\mathcal{C}_i, M, \boldsymbol{X}_{cond}[i])$

    else:

      $k \leftarrow \texttt{halfway}(i, j)$

      ▷ Garble the right subtree using the available seed,

      ▷ unstack, and recursively evaluate the left subtree.

      $M_{k+1,j}, \cdot, \cdot \leftarrow \texttt{GbSubtreeFromSeed}(\boldsymbol{C}, k+1, j, \text{es}_{k+1,j})$

      $\text{EvCond}'(i, k, M_{i,j} \oplus M_{k+1,j})$

      ▷ Symmetrically evaluate the right subtree.

      $M_{i,k}, \cdot, \cdot \leftarrow \texttt{GbSubtreeFromSeed}(\boldsymbol{C}, i, k, \text{es}_{i,k})$

      $\text{EvCond}'(k+1, j, M_{i,j} \oplus M_{i,k})$

  ▷ Start recursive process from the top of the tree.

  $\text{EvCond}'(0, b-1, M_{cond})$

  ▷ Eliminate garbage and propagate $\boldsymbol{Y}_\alpha$ via the multiplexer.

  return $mux.\text{Ev}(\alpha, \boldsymbol{Y}_{cond}, M_{mux})$

**Fig. 5.** $\texttt{Eval}$'s procedure, $\texttt{EvCond}$, for evaluating a conditional with $b$ branches. $\texttt{EvCond}$ evaluates each branch; $b-1$ evaluations result in garbage outputs and one (the evaluation of $\mathcal{C}_\alpha$) results in valid outputs. The multiplexer collects garbage and propagates output from $\mathcal{C}_\alpha$. $\texttt{EvCond}$ involves $b \log b$ calls to $\texttt{Gb}$ (via $\texttt{GbSubtreeFromSeed}$), and each branch evaluation is done with respect to the garbling of that branch's sibling subtrees.

---

$\mathsf{GbCond}(\mathcal{C}, S)$ :

  $b \leftarrow |\mathcal{C}|$

  ▷ Recursively derive all 'good' seeds for the entire tree.

  $s \leftarrow \mathsf{DeriveSeedTree}(S, b)$

  ▷ Sample input/output encodings for the conditional.

  $e \leftarrow \mathsf{GenProjection}(S, \mathsf{inpSize}(\mathsf{Cond}(\mathcal{C})))$

  $d \leftarrow \mathsf{GenProjection}(S, \mathsf{outSize}(\mathsf{Cond}(\mathcal{C})))$

  ▷ Parse encoding into encoding of $\alpha$ and encoding of rest of input.

  $e_\alpha \mid e' \leftarrow e$

  ▷ Garble $\mathsf{SortingHat}$ based on the encoding of $\alpha$.

  ▷ This outputs material as well as the tree of all 'bad' seeds $s'$.

  $M_{\mathsf{SortingHat}}, s' \leftarrow \mathsf{SortingHat.Gb}(e_\alpha, s)$

  ▷ Construct the stacked material and input encodings for each branch.

  $M_{cond}, e_{cond}, d_{cond} \leftarrow \mathsf{GbSubtreeFromSeed}(\mathcal{C}, 0, b-1, s_{0,b-1})$

  ▷ The demux conditionally translates the input encoding $e'$

  ▷ to one of the branch encodings in $e_{cond}$ based on $e_\alpha$.

  $M_{dem}, \Lambda_{in} \leftarrow demux.\mathsf{Gb}(e_\alpha, e', e_{cond})$

  ▷ Compute all possible garbage outputs.

  $\Lambda_{out} \leftarrow \mathsf{ComputeGarbage}(\mathcal{C}, M_{cond}, \Lambda_{in}, s, s')$

  ▷ The demultiplexer collects garbage outputs.

  $M_{mux} \leftarrow mux.\mathsf{Gb}(e_\alpha, d, d_{cond}, \Lambda_{out})$

  $\mathbf{return}\ (M_{\mathsf{SortingHat}} \mid M_{dem} \mid M_{cond} \mid M_{mux}, e, d)$

---

**Fig. 6.** The algorithm for garbling a conditional vector. Given $b$ branches, $\mathsf{GbCond}$ returns (1) the stacked material, (2) the input encoding string, (3) all $b$ output decoding strings, and (4) all $b \log b$ possible garbage output label vectors.

2. $\mathsf{GbCond}$ invokes $\mathsf{GenProjection}$ to select uniform input/output encodings $e$ and $d$: $e$ and $d$ are vectors of pairs of labels that are the valid input/output labels for the overall conditional. Our use of $\mathsf{GenProjection}$ is straightforward and similar to that of [HK20a].
3. $\mathsf{GbCond}$ uses $\mathsf{SortingHat.Gb}$ to garble the $\mathsf{SortingHat}$ functionality of Fig. 2. As input, $\mathsf{GbCond}$ provides the tree of good seeds $s$ and the encoding of the active branch id $e_\alpha$. As output, $\mathsf{Gen}$ receives the tree of all bad seeds. $\mathsf{GbCond}$ needs these bad seeds, in addition to the good seeds he already knows, to emulate $\mathsf{Eval}$ making a bad guess.
4. $\mathsf{GbCond}$ uses $\mathsf{GbSubtreeFromSeed}$ to derive stacked material $M_{cond}$ from the root seed. $M_{cond}$ is the material that $\mathsf{Gen}$ ultimately sends to $\mathsf{Eval}$.
5. $\mathsf{GbCond}$ calls $demux.\mathsf{Gb}$ to compute the demultiplexer garbled rows. This call also returns $\Lambda_{in}$, the collection of garbage input labels for each branch: essential information that allows $\mathsf{Gen}$ to emulate $\mathsf{Eval}$.

ComputeGarbage($\mathcal{C}, M, \Lambda_{in}, s, s'$) :

  ▷ We first define a recursive subprocedure.

  ComputeGarbage$'(i, j, M_{i,j}, \boldsymbol{M}')$ :

    ▷ Compute all possible garbage outputs from branches $\mathcal{C}_i - \mathcal{C}_j$.

    ▷ $\boldsymbol{M}'$ is a vector of the bad garblings of all sibling roots of the current node.

    if $i = j$ :

      ▷ Base case: loop over all possible garbage material

      ▷ and accumulate garbage outputs into $\Lambda_{out}$.

      $acc \leftarrow M_{i,i}$

      for $k \in 0..|\boldsymbol{M}'| - 1$ :

        ▷ Emulate all possible bad evaluations of $\mathcal{C}_i$.

        $acc \leftarrow acc \oplus \boldsymbol{M}'[k]$

        $\Lambda_{out}[i][k] \leftarrow \mathsf{Ev}(\mathcal{C}[i], acc, \Lambda_{in}[k])$

    else :

      $k \leftarrow \mathtt{halfway}(i, j)$

      ▷ Compute the good material for both subtrees.

      $M_{i,k}, \cdot, \cdot \leftarrow \mathtt{GbSubtreeFromSeed}(\mathcal{C}, i, k, s_{i,k})$

      $M_{k+1,j} \leftarrow M_{i,j} \oplus M_{i,k}$

      ▷ Compute the bad material for both subtrees.

      $M'_{i,k}, \cdot, \cdot \leftarrow \mathtt{GbSubtreeFromSeed}(\mathcal{C}, i, k, s'_{i,k})$

      $M'_{k+1,j}, \cdot, \cdot \leftarrow \mathtt{GbSubtreeFromSeed}(\mathcal{C}, k + 1, j, s'_{k+1,j})$

      ▷ Recursively compute all garbage outputs.

      ComputeGarbage$'(i, k, (M_{k+1,j} \oplus M'_{k+1,j}) \mid \boldsymbol{M}')$

      ComputeGarbage$'(k + 1, j, (M_{i,k} \oplus M'_{i,k}) \mid \boldsymbol{M}')$

 

  $b \leftarrow |\mathcal{C}|$

  ▷ Start the recursive process using the top level material $M$

  ▷ and using the empty vector of bad sibling material.

  ComputeGarbage$'(0, b - 1, M, [\,])$

  return $\Lambda_{out}$

**Fig. 7.** ComputeGarbage allows Gen to compute the possible garbage output labels from evaluation of inactive branches. Specifically, the algorithm takes as arguments (1) the vector of conditional branches $\mathcal{C}$, (2) the 'good' material for the conditional $M$, (3) the garbage input labels $\Lambda_{in}$, (4) the tree of 'good' seeds (i.e. the seeds used by Gen to generate $M$) $s$, and (5) the tree of 'bad' seeds $s'$. The algorithm outputs $\Lambda_{out}$, the vector (length $b$) of vectors (each length $\log b$) of output labels from each branch.

With this accomplished, GbCond's remaining task is to encrypt the garbage-collecting multiplexer. However, it is not clear how this can be achieved unless Gen *knows all garbage outputs* that Eval might compute. Thus, GbCond first invokes ComputeGarbage (Fig. 7), a procedure which emulates all of Eval's bad guesses.

ComputeGarbage delegates to the recursive subprocedure ComputeGarbage'. This recursive procedure walks down the tree, maintaining two key variables: (1) $M_{i,j}$ holds the correct material for the current subtree $\mathcal{N}_{i,j}$ and (2) $M'$ holds a vector of bad materials of the incorrectly garbled sibling roots of $\mathcal{N}_{i,j}$. In the general case, these variables are simply appropriately updated via calls to GbSubtreeFromSeed. Thus, in the base case, the garbage materials for all sibling roots of the considered leaf are available. Additionally, all garbage inputs into each branch are available in the vector $\Lambda_{in}$. So, at the leaves we can compute all garbage outputs for each branch by calling Ev on the proper combinations of garbage material and labels. We store all garbage outputs into the global vector $\Lambda_{out}$, which is returned by the overall procedure, and then ultimately used by GbCond to call $mux$.Gb.

## 6   LogStack Correctness/Security

We discuss LogStack's correctness and security properties. We formalize our theorems in the [BHR12] framework (as modified by [HK20a]), which requires a candidate garbling scheme to be **correct**, **oblivious**, **private**, and **authentic**.

In addition, [HK20a] introduced a new property, **stackability**, which formalizes the class of garbling schemes whose garblings can be securely stacked; hence stackable schemes are candidate underlying schemes. In this work, we strengthen the definition of stackability. This strengthening, which we call **strong stackability**, allows us to prove security under standard assumptions (an improvement over [HK20a], which required a random oracle assumption). Strong stackability is strictly stronger than stackability: all strongly stackable schemes are stackable, and all lemmas that hold for stackable schemes hold also for strongly stackable schemes. A key application of this second fact is that all stackable schemes are trivially **oblivious**, so all strongly stackable schemes are oblivious. We prove security given a strongly stackable, correct, authentic, private underlying scheme.

[HK20a] showed that several standard garbling schemes are stackable, including the state-of-the-art half-gates technique [ZRE15]. We later argue that such schemes either are strongly stackable without modification or can be easily adjusted. Hence, our implementation can assume an RO and use half-gates as its underlying scheme to achieve high performance.

LogStack is itself strongly stackable, giving flexibility in usage: while by design LogStack handles vectors of conditional branches, we also support arbitrarily nested conditional control flow without modifying the source program. We note that this nested usage *does not* give $O(b \log b)$ computation, and so vectorized branches should favored where possible.

Due to a lack of space, we postpone most proofs to the full version of this paper.

## 6.1   Correctness

**Definition 1 (Correctness).** *A garbling scheme is* **correct** *if for all circuits* $C$, *all input strings* $x$ *of length* $\texttt{inpSize}(C)$, *and all pseudorandom seeds* $S$:

$$De(d, Ev(C, M, En(e, x))) = ev(C, x)$$

*where* $(M, e, d) = Gb(1^\kappa, C, S)$

A correct scheme implements the semantics specified by ev. Proof of the following is formalized in the full version of this paper.

**Theorem 2.** *If* Base *is correct, then* LogStack *is correct.*

## 6.2   Security

The following definition is derived from the corresponding definition of [HK20a]; we discuss its motivation (support for PRF-based garbling gadgets) and technical differences with [HK20a] immediately after we present it formally below.

**Definition 2 (Strong Stackability).** *A scheme is* **strongly stackable** *if:*

1. *For all circuits* $C$ *and all inputs* $x$,

$$(C, M, En(e, x)) \stackrel{c}{=} (C, M', X')$$

   *where* $S$ *is uniformly drawn,* $(M, e, \cdot) = Gb(1^\kappa, C, S)$, $X' \leftarrow_\$ \{0,1\}^{|X|}$, *and* $M' \leftarrow_\$ \{0,1\}^{|M|}$.
2. *The scheme is* **projective** *[BHR12].*
3. *There exists an efficient deterministic procedure* colorPart *that maps strings to* $\{0,1\}$ *such that for all* $C$ *and all projective label pairs* $A^0, A^1 \in d$:

$$colorPart(A^0) \neq colorPart(A^1)$$

   *where* $S$ *is uniformly drawn and* $(\cdot, \cdot, d) \leftarrow Gb(1^\kappa, C\ S)$.
4. *There exists an efficient deterministic procedure* keyPart *that maps strings to* $\{0,1\}^\kappa$ *such that for all* $C$ *and all projective label pairs* $A^0, A^1 \in d$:

$$keyPart(A^0) \mid keyPart(A^1) \stackrel{c}{=} \{0,1\}^{2\kappa}$$

   *where* $S$ *is uniformly drawn and* $(\cdot, \cdot, d) \leftarrow Gb(1^\kappa, C\ S)$.

The above definition is given by [HK20a], with the exception of point 4. Informally, stackability ensures (a) that circuit garblings 'look random' and (b) that our scheme can manipulate labels generated by the underlying scheme. Since strong stackability simply adds point 4, the following lemma is immediate:

**Lemma 1.** *Every strongly stackable scheme is stackable.*

We briefly explain the role of colorPart and keyPart. As with [HK20a], we use the output labels of the underlying scheme as keys in subsequent garbled gadgets. The keyPart procedure allows us to extract a *suitable PRF key* from each label. At the same time, we make use of the classic point-and-permute trick to reduce the number of PRF calls needed to evaluate garbled gadgets: we use the colorPart as the bit that instructs which garbled row to decrypt. Note that because we essentially 'split' each output label into a key and a color, we 'lose' bits of the underlying scheme's labels when we invoke keyPart. We stress that this is not an issue: the required key length for the next PRF application can be restored as we require keyPart output to be $\kappa$ bits long. All point-and-permute schemes have a similar approach.

The added requirement (point 4) allows us to relax our security assumptions in comparison to [HK20a]. For each projective output pair $A^0, A^1$, we require that keyPart($A^0$) and keyPart($A^1$) are unrelated. This is achieved by requiring that the concatenation of these two strings is indistinguishable from a random string of the same length. This allows us to circumvent a problem: the [HK20a] definition allowed labels in the underlying scheme to be arbitrarily related. More precisely, while point 1 requires that any particular set of labels seen by Eval look random, it does not require that *all labels together* look random. This was problematic, because the output labels of the underlying scheme were used to implement garbled tables, so the two possibly related labels were both used as PRF keys. Using related keys is outside the scope of the standard PRF security definition. Thus, [HK20a] were forced to assume the existence of a random oracle to ensure possible relationships in the output decoding string did not compromise security. By adding point 4, we ensure that the *entire* decoding string 'looks random', so all labels must be independent. This added requirement on the underlying scheme allows us to push our proofs through in the standard model.

Many standard schemes are compatible with strong stackability: if the scheme is stackable and has randomly chosen output labels, it trivially satisfies our definition. Free XOR based schemes [KS08] use pairs of labels separated by a fixed constant $\Delta$, and so are not *a priori* strongly stackable. However, it is easy to adjust such schemes such that the final output gates return independent labels. As a final note, while our scheme is secure in the standard model, we of course adopt any additional security assumptions from the chosen underlying scheme: e.g., instantiating LogStack with the efficient Half Gates scheme [ZRE15] requires us to assume the existence of a circular correlation robust hash function.

We prove the following in the full version of this paper. The proof utilizes properties of Base and of a PRF to show that LogStack's garblings 'looks random'.

**Theorem 3.** *If Base is strongly stackable, then LogStack is strongly stackable.*

**Definition 3 (Obliviousness).** *A garbling scheme is **oblivious** if there exists a simulator $\mathcal{S}_{obv}$ such that for any circuit $\mathcal{C}$ and all inputs $x$ of length* inpSize($\mathcal{C}$), *the following are indistinguishable:*

$$(\mathcal{C}, M, \boldsymbol{X}) \overset{c}{=} \mathcal{S}_{obv}(1^\kappa, \mathcal{C})$$

where $S$ is uniform, $(M, e, \cdot) = Gb(1^\kappa, \mathcal{C}, S)$ and $\boldsymbol{X} = En(e, \boldsymbol{x})$.

Obliviousness ensures that the garbled circuit with input labels can be simulated, and hence reveals no extra information to Eval. [HK20a] proved that every stackable scheme is trivially oblivious: drawing a random string of the correct length is a suitable simulator. This fact, combined with Lemma 1 and Theorem 3 implies two immediate facts:

**Lemma 2.** *Every strongly stackable scheme is oblivious.*

**Theorem 4.** *If Base is strongly stackable, then LogStack is oblivious.*

**Definition 4 (Authenticity).** *A garbling scheme is **authentic** if for all circuits $\mathcal{C}$, all inputs $\boldsymbol{x}$ of length* inpSize$(\mathcal{C})$*, and all poly-time adversaries $\mathcal{A}$ the following probability is negligible in $\kappa$:*

$$Pr\left(\boldsymbol{Y}' \neq Ev(\mathcal{C}, M, \boldsymbol{X}) \wedge De(d, \boldsymbol{Y}') \neq \bot\right)$$

where $S$ is uniform, $(M, e, d) = Gb(1^\kappa, \mathcal{C}, S)$, $\boldsymbol{X} = En(e, \boldsymbol{x})$, and $\boldsymbol{Y}' = \mathcal{A}(\mathcal{C}, M, \boldsymbol{X})$.

Authenticity ensures that an adversary cannot compute GC output labels except by running the scheme as intended.

We prove the following in the full version of this paper. The proof utilizes properties of Base and of a PRF to show that an adversary cannot compute GC output labels except by running LogStack.

**Theorem 5.** *If Base is authentic, then LogStack is authentic.*

**Definition 5 (Privacy).** *A garbling scheme is **private** if there exists a simulator $\mathcal{S}_{prv}$ such that for any circuit $\mathcal{C}$ and all inputs $\boldsymbol{x}$ of length* inpSize$(\mathcal{C})$*, the following are computationally indistinguishable:*

$$(M, \boldsymbol{X}, d) \overset{c}{=} \mathcal{S}_{prv}(1^\kappa, \mathcal{C}, \boldsymbol{y}),$$

where $S$ is uniform, $(M, e, d) = Gb(1^\kappa, \mathcal{C}, S)$, $\boldsymbol{X} = En(e, \boldsymbol{x})$, and $\boldsymbol{y} = ev(\mathcal{C}, \boldsymbol{x})$.

Privacy ensures that Eval, who is given access to $(M, \boldsymbol{X}, d)$, learns nothing except what can be learned from the output $\boldsymbol{y}$. I.e., Gen's input is protected.

We prove the following in the full version of this paper. The proof utilizes properties of Base and of a PRF to show that Eval's view can be simulated.

**Theorem 6.** *If Base is private, authentic, and strongly stackable, then LogStack is private.*

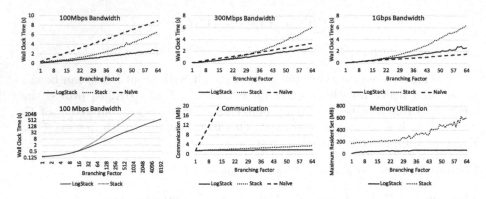

**Fig. 8.** Experimental evaluation of LogStack as compared to [HK20a]'s Stack and to basic half-gates [ZRE15] ('naïve' branching). We compare in terms of wall-clock time on different simulated network bandwidths (top). We performed an extended wall-clock time comparison to Stack (bottom left). Both LogStack and Stack greatly outperform basic half-gates in terms of total bandwidth consumption (bottom center), and LogStack greatly outperforms Stack in terms of memory consumption (bottom right).

## 7    Instantiation and Experimental Evaluation

We implemented LS in ∼ 1500 lines of C++ and used it to instantiate a semi-honest 2PC protocol. We instantiated Base using the half-gates [ZRE15], allowing high concrete performance. Our implementation thus relies on non-standard assumptions. We use computational security parameter $\kappa = 127$; the 128th bit is reserved for point and permute. Our implementation spawns additional threads to make use of inherent parallelism available in GbCond and EvCond.

Our experiments were each performed on a MacBook Pro laptop with an Intel Dual-Core i5 3.1 GHz processor and 8 GB of RAM.

We compared our implementation to basic half-gates [ZRE15] and to the Stack SGC of [HK20a]. Figure 8 plots the results of our experiments.

We consider end-to-end wall-clock time, bandwidth consumption, and memory utilization. All branches implement the SHA-256 netlist, which has 47726 AND gates, 179584 XOR gates, and 70666 NOT gates. A GC for each branch has size 1.45 MB. It is, of course, unrealistic that a conditional would have the same circuit in each branch. However, we choose this benchmark because SHA-256 has become somewhat of a community standard and because our goal is only to analyze performance. We ensure our implementation does not cheat: it cannot recognize that branches are the same and hence cannot shortcut the evaluation.

**Bandwidth consumption** is the easiest metric to analyze. The communication chart in Fig. 8 plots communication as a function of branching factor. As expected, Stack's and LogStack's communication remains almost constant, while half-gates' grows linearly and immediately dominates. LogStack is slightly leaner than Stack because of low-level improvements to LogStack's demultiplexer. This small improvement should not be counted as a significant advantage over Stack.

**Memory utilization** was measured as a function of branching factor. We compare our scheme to Stack (half-gates memory utilization is constant, since garblings can be streamed across the network and immediately discarded). Our chart shows Stack's linear and LogStack's logarithmic space consumption. In settings with many branches, improved space consumption is essential. For example, we ran LogStack on a circuit with 8192 SHA-256 branches, a circuit that has > 385M AND gates. Our peak memory usage was ∼ 100 MB, while [HK20a] would require more than 12 GB of space to run this experiment.

**Wall-clock time** to complete an end-to-end 2PC protocol is our most comprehensive metric. We plot three charts for 1 to 64 branches (on networks with 100, 300, and 1000 Mbps bandwidth) comparing each of the three approaches. We also explored more extreme branching factors, running conditionals with branching factors at every power of 2 from $2^0$ to $2^{13}$ in the 100 Mbps setting.

In the 1 Gbps network setting, as expected, naïve half-gates leads. As discussed in Sect. 1.5, two cores (our laptop) indeed cannot keep up with the available network capacity. However, doubling the number of cores would already put us ahead of naïve, and any further computation boost would correspondingly improve our advantage. We are about 3× faster than Stack.

In the 300 Mbps network setting, we outperform naïve. Because we range over the same number of branches, we are the same factor ≈ 3× faster than Stack.

The more typical 100 Mbps setting shows the advantage of SGC. Both Stack and LogStack handily beat naïve.

Finally, we experimented with large branching factors. LogStack scales well; we ran up to 8192 branches as it was sufficient to show a trend. Due to its logarithmic memory utilization, LogStack would run on a practically arbitrary number of branches. In contrast, Stack exhibited limited scaling. We ran up to 1024 branches with Stack, enough to show a trend, and after which our experiments started to take too long. LogStack ran 2PC for a 1024-branch conditional in ∼ 67s, while Stack took ∼ 2050s, ∼ 31× slower than LogStack.

**Acknowledgements.** This work was supported in part by NSF award #1909769, by a Facebook research award, and by Georgia Tech's IISP cybersecurity seed funding (CSF) award.

# References

[AGKS20] Alhassan, M.Y., Günther, D., Kiss, Á., Schneider, T.: Efficient and scalable universal circuits. J. Cryptol. **33**(3), 1216–1271 (2020)

[BHR12] Bellare, M., Hoang, V.T., Rogaway, P.: Foundations of garbled circuits. In: Yu, T., Danezis, G., Gligor, V.D. (eds.) ACM CCS 2012, pp. 784–796. ACM Press, October 2012

[CKKZ12] Choi, S.G., Katz, J., Kumaresan, R., Zhou, H.-S.: On the security of the "Free-XOR" technique. In: Cramer, R. (ed.) TCC 2012. LNCS, vol. 7194, pp. 39–53. Springer, Heidelberg (2012). https://doi.org/10.1007/978-3-642-28914-9_3

[GKS17]  Günther, D., Kiss, Á., Schneider, T.: More efficient universal circuit constructions. In: Takagi, T., Peyrin, T. (eds.) ASIACRYPT 2017, Part II. LNCS, vol. 10625, pp. 443–470. Springer, Cham (2017). https://doi.org/10.1007/978-3-319-70697-9_16

[GLNP15]  Gueron, S., Lindell, Y., Nof, A., Pinkas, B.: Fast garbling of circuits under standard assumptions. In: Ray, I., Li, N., Kruegel, C. (eds.) ACM CCS 2015, pp. 567–578. ACM Press, October 2015

[HK20a]  Heath, D., Kolesnikov, V.: Stacked garbling. In: Micciancio, D., Ristenpart, T. (eds.) CRYPTO 2020, Part II. LNCS, vol. 12171, pp. 763–792. Springer, Cham (2020). https://doi.org/10.1007/978-3-030-56880-1_27

[HK20b]  Heath, D., Kolesnikov, V.: Stacked garbling for disjunctive zero-knowledge proofs. In: Canteaut, A., Ishai, Y. (eds.) EUROCRYPT 2020, Part III. LNCS, vol. 12107, pp. 569–598. Springer, Cham (2020). https://doi.org/10.1007/978-3-030-45727-3_19

[KKW17]  Kennedy, W.S., Kolesnikov, V., Wilfong, G.: Overlaying conditional circuit clauses for secure computation. In: Takagi, T., Peyrin, T. (eds.) ASIACRYPT 2017, Part II. LNCS, vol. 10625, pp. 499–528. Springer, Cham (2017). https://doi.org/10.1007/978-3-319-70697-9_18

[Kol18]  Kolesnikov, V.: Free IF: how to omit inactive branches and implement S-universal garbled circuit (almost) for free. In: Peyrin, T., Galbraith, S. (eds.) ASIACRYPT 2018, Part III. LNCS, vol. 11274, pp. 34–58. Springer, Cham (2018). https://doi.org/10.1007/978-3-030-03332-3_2

[KS08]  Kolesnikov, V., Schneider, T.: Improved garbled circuit: free XOR gates and applications. In: Aceto, L., Damgård, I., Goldberg, L.A., Halldórsson, M.M., Ingólfsdóttir, A., Walukiewicz, I. (eds.) ICALP 2008, Part II. LNCS, vol. 5126, pp. 486–498. Springer, Heidelberg (2008). https://doi.org/10.1007/978-3-540-70583-3_40

[KS16]  Kiss, Á., Schneider, T.: Valiant's universal circuit is practical. In: Fischlin, M., Coron, J.-S. (eds.) EUROCRYPT 2016, Part I. LNCS, vol. 9665, pp. 699–728. Springer, Heidelberg (2016). https://doi.org/10.1007/978-3-662-49890-3_27

[LMS16]  Lipmaa, H., Mohassel, P., Sadeghian, S.: Valiant's universal circuit: improvements, implementation, and applications. Cryptology ePrint Archive, Report 2016/017 (2016). http://eprint.iacr.org/2016/017

[Val76]  Valiant, L.G.: Universal circuits (preliminary report). In: STOC, pp. 196–203. ACM Press, New York (1976)

[ZRE15]  Zahur, S., Rosulek, M., Evans, D.: Two halves make a whole. In: Oswald, E., Fischlin, M. (eds.) EUROCRYPT 2015, Part II. LNCS, vol. 9057, pp. 220–250. Springer, Heidelberg (2015). https://doi.org/10.1007/978-3-662-46803-6_8

[ZYZL19]  Zhao, S., Yu, Yu., Zhang, J., Liu, H.: Valiant's universal circuits revisited: an overall improvement and a lower bound. In: Galbraith, S.D., Moriai, S. (eds.) ASIACRYPT 2019, Part I. LNCS, vol. 11921, pp. 401–425. Springer, Cham (2019). https://doi.org/10.1007/978-3-030-34578-5_15

# Large Scale, Actively Secure Computation from LPN and Free-XOR Garbled Circuits

Aner Ben-Efraim[2]([✉]), Kelong Cong[1] ⓘ, Eran Omri[2] ⓘ, Emmanuela Orsini[1] ⓘ,
Nigel P. Smart[1,3] ⓘ, and Eduardo Soria-Vazquez[4] ⓘ

[1] imec-COSIC, KU Leuven, Leuven, Belgium
kelong.cong@esat.kuleuven.be, {emmanuela.orsini,nigel.smart}@kuleuven.be
[2] Department of Computer Science, Ariel Univeristy, Ariel, Israel
anermosh@post.bgu.ac.il
[3] Department of Computer Science, University of Bristol, Bristol, UK
[4] Department of Computer Science, Aarhus University, Aarhus, Denmark
eduardo@cs.au.dk

**Abstract.** We (MPC) protocol based on garbled circuits which is both actively secure and supports the free-XOR technique, and which has communication complexity $O(n)$ per party. This improves on a protocol of Ben-Efraim, Lindell and Omri which only achieved passive security, without support for free-XOR. Our construction is based on a new variant of LPN-based encryption, but has the drawback of requiring a rather expensive garbling phase. To address this issue we present a second protocol that assumes at least $n/c$ of the parties are honest (for an arbitrary fixed value $c$). This second protocol allows for a significantly lighter preprocessing, at the cost of a small sacrifice in online efficiency. We demonstrate the practicality of our evaluation phase with an implementation.

## 1 Introduction

The last decade has seen an enormous amount of progress in the practicality of actively secure multiparty computation (MPC), spanning many new designs and implementations of protocols based on both garbled circuits and secret sharing. Much of the developments have been in the dishonest majority case, where more than half of the parties can arbitrarily deviate from the protocol, trying to compromise privacy and correctness of computation. Despite this, there is still some gap between the complexities one can achieve in theory, and those which can be met by practical protocols in the real world.

Almost all of the most efficient protocols in the dishonest majority setting are designed in the so-called *preprocessing* model, in which parties first produce some input-independent correlated randomness which can be later used to evaluate the function. In secret-sharing-based protocols, the main goal of the preprocessing (or *offline*) phase is to generate secret-shared random multiplication triples,

© International Association for Cryptologic Research 2021
A. Canteaut and F.-X. Standaert (Eds.): EUROCRYPT 2021, LNCS 12698, pp. 33–63, 2021.
https://doi.org/10.1007/978-3-030-77883-5_2

which are consumed during the online computation to evaluate multiplication gates. In garbled-circuit-based protocols, the preprocessing generates a one-time garbled circuit which will be later evaluated on private inputs.

Recent protocols in both of the above paradigms have incredibly fast execution times in their online phases when the number of parties $n$ is relatively small (say less than 10), see for example SPDZ-like protocols [15,25,26,28] and SPDZ$_{2^k}$ [13,36], for the case of linear secret-sharing based MPC, and BMR-based protocols [22,39,40]. However, when we increase the number of parties this practicality drops off.

Secret-sharing based protocols [7,14,15,19,37], which work for both binary and arithmetic circuits, require a small amount of communication between (essentially) all parties for each layer of multiplication gates in the circuit, and hence their round complexity is linear in the depth of the circuit. This means that these protocols require very low bandwidth, and can be very efficient in a LAN (Local-Area-Networks) setting, but the large amount of rounds of communication and high latency make them less suited for the WAN (Wide-Area-Networks) setting, where the parties are usually geographically far apart from each other. If we consider the complexity of the online evaluation, secret-sharing based protocols have $O(n)$ complexity per gate per party[1].

Garbled circuit protocols, introduced by Yao [41] in the two-party setting and later generalized to the multiparty case by Beaver, Micali and Rogaway (BMR) [3], mainly work over binary circuits. In these protocols an "encrypted" version of the circuit is constructed in such a way that its evaluation does not require any communication beyond parties providing their "garbled" inputs. These protocols run in a constant number of rounds and are often slower than secret-sharing based protocols in a LAN setting due to their higher bandwidth requirements. Nevertheless, they are usually much faster in the WAN setting. For practical multiparty garbled-circuit protocols each evaluating party has to perform $O(n^2)$ operations. Thus the scalability of the online phase of secure multiparty computation protocols in a WAN setting, as the number of parties increases, is still an issue.

Theoretically, this is not a problem for multi-party garbled circuits. To achieve a protocol which has complexity $O(n)$ per party, one can take the standard two-party protocol by Yao [41] and then compute the garbling function via an $n$-party actively secure MPC system. The resulting garbled circuit will not depend on the number of parties, but the garbling itself will be highly inefficient as the underlying pseudo-random functions (PRFs) used in Yao's construction will need to be evaluated within MPC. Thus, while theoretically interesting, such an approach is unlikely to ever be practical.

The $O(n^2)$ complexity problem for practical BMR-based protocols led Ben-Efraim, Lindell and Omri [6] to present a *passively secure* BMR-based protocol

---

The complexity can be reduced to $O(1)$ for all but one of the parties in SPDZ-like protocols by 'opening' being performed in a king-followers fashion: Followers send their shares to the king, who then replies to all followers with the reconstructed value (hence $O(n)$ complexity for the king). For more details, see e.g. [15].

whose evaluation is independent of the number of parties and such that the garbling phase avoids to evaluate PRFs using generic MPC. This was done by utilizing a specific key-homomorphic PRF, for which two instantiations were given in the paper, one based on DDH in prime order groups and one based on Learning-with-Errors. The work of Ben-Efraim et al. provides a large-scale MPC protocol which is *almost practical*: their evaluation phase is concretely faster than previous works for large $n$, but more research is needed into the offline phase in order to make it practical. The efficiency of online evaluation is demonstrated through an implementation which shows that, roughly, their protocol is more efficient than its $O(n^2)$ counterpart [5] as soon as 100 parties take part in the MPC. However, this large-scale protocol suffers from two major drawbacks: firstly, it only deals with the case of passive adversaries, and secondly their techniques are not compatible with the important free-XOR optimization introduced by Kolesnikov and Schneider [27].

Another relevant large-scale, garbled-circuit based protocol is that proposed by Hazay, Orsini, Scholl and Soria-Vazquez [21]. Their result, which only deals with passive adversaries, shortens symmetric keys (as the ones for PRFs in the garbled circuit) in order to speed up computation and reduce communication. Security is then retained by relying on the length of the *concatenation* of all honest parties' keys, rather than on each of them individually. Such a protocol allows to evaluate each garble gate with $O(n^2\ell/\kappa)$ operations, compared to $O(n^2)$ of standard approaches, where $\kappa > \ell$ is the security parameter and $\ell$ is the key length. In subsequent work [20], the same authors extended their technique to the active setting, but only for secret-sharing based protocols, leaving actively secure garbled circuits with short keys as an open problem.

## 1.1   Our Contribution

In this paper we introduce a new $n$-party garbling technique and present two almost-practical, large-scale BMR-style protocols. Both the size and evaluation complexity of the resulting garbled circuits is $O(1)$, hence resulting in an online phase which has a complexity of $O(n)$ per party[2]. Our protocols are actively secure and employ the free-XOR optimization by Kolesnikov and Schneider [27].

*Obtaining Free-XOR.* Our construction takes inspiration from the work of Ben-Efraim et al. [6], but instead of basing the construction on key-homomorphic PRFs, we use an encryption scheme which is both key-homomorphic and message-homomorphic. In order to enable the free-XOR technique, we further need to restrict ourselves to message and key spaces of characteristic two. This rules out standard Ring-Learning-with-Errors (RLWE) based encryption schemes, for which the secret key and message spaces are modulo distinct primes. Instead, we introduce a new homomorphic encryption scheme based on the Learning-Parity-with-Noise (LPN) problem. We note that LPN-based encryption was also used by Appelbaum [1] in order to replace the random oracle with

---

[2] This increase in complexity is due to parties still needing to reconstruct the circuit and send their masked inputs around.

standard cryptographic assumptions in two-party, free-XOR garbled circuits. We would like to stress that the motivation (and also the resulting LPN construction) for our work is different, as we aim to build practical protocols for a large number of parties rather than a purely theoretical result related to cryptographic assumptions. A further overview of our new LPN garbling scheme can be found in the next subsection, and all its details appear in Sect. 3.

*Obtaining Active Security.* Our first protocol achieves active security by employing an actively-secure garbling phase which guarantees that the resulting secret-shared garbled circuit is correct. While in standard BMR all of the garbling, except the PRFs evaluations, is computed within an MPC protocol, we instead *entirely* generate the garbled gates in a distributed manner using an actively secure full-threshold MPC system. We will refer to this first protocol as *"authenticated garbling"*. This terminology resembles the authenticated-garbling technique by Wang, Ranellucci and Katz [38,39] (referred as WRK in the rest of the paper) and more recently by Yang, Wang and Zhang [40]. However, while their preprocessing phase is explicitly based on TinyOT-like protocols [17,33], which rely on Message Authentication Codes (MACs), our preprocessing works with any actively secure protocols.

In our construction each garbled AND gate consists of 4 rather than $4n$ ciphertexts as in previous BMR-style protocols. In the online phase, parties only need to broadcast shares of their inputs and perform a cheap, local computation that requires a single decryption per AND gate. However, this very efficient online evaluation comes at the price of a rather expensive preprocessing. Thus, whilst forming a potential bridge from what is theoretically possible to what is practically realisable, this protocol is only 'almost'-practical.

*Bridging the Gap.* To further bridge the gap between theory and practice, we also present a second construction with a more efficient preprocessing phase. We achieve this by relaxing some of the requirements in our garbling functionality, which becomes more similar to that described by Hazay, Scholl and Soria-Vazquez (HSS) [22]. In particular, we allow the shares of the garbled circuit to be *unauthenticated*: rather than producing LPN ciphertexts within an actively secure MPC engine, each party will locally produce *additive shares* of these ciphertexts. This effectively allows the adversary to introduce arbitrarily additive errors to corrupted parties' shares. To maintain active security, we need to introduce an extra check in the online evaluation, as we explain in Technical Overview (Sect. 1.2).

In order to achieve a better performance, this new construction assumes that there are at least $n/c$ honest parties, for an arbitrarily chosen constant $1 < c \leq n$. Since our goal is constructing efficient protocols for a large number of parties (typically more than one hundred), it is very reasonable to assume, in this setting, more than a single honest party.

*Experimental Validation.* We validate the claim that our protocol is almost-practical by demonstrating that the evaluation phase is indeed more efficient than other truly practical approaches when the number of parties is large. Thus, to turn our almost-practical protocol into a fully practical one, future works only need to concentrate on the garbling phase.

The concrete efficiency of our schemes crucially depends on the LPN parameters and the error correcting codes used to instantiate the two-key LPN based encryption scheme. We set the security of the scheme according to the work of Esser et al. [16] and instantiate the cryptosystem with concatenated codes (see the full version). We stress that our implementation should be taken more as a proof of feasibility than an optimized implementation of the proposed constructions. Moreover, we believe that using more efficient codes, like LDPC or QC-LDPC, the concrete efficiency of our protocols would improve significantly.

More concretely, in the full-threshold authenticated garbling case, experiments show that our evaluation phase will be more efficient than state of the art protocols such as HSS or WRK when the number of parties exceeds about 100. Notice HSS, WRK and the recent protocol of Yang et al. [40] have similar online efficiency, therefore, to concretely validate our claim, we compare the results of our experiments in the full-threshold case with the running times reported in [39]. Setting the statistical security parameter to 40, as in [39], we report a running time for AES-128 of 1.72 s (c.f. Table 2 in Sect. 6), compared to 1.87 s in a LAN setting and 2.3 s in a WAN setting reported in WRK [39] for 128 parties. These numbers from WRK will grow quadratically as the number of parties increases, whereas ours will remain constant.

In the scalable protocol by Ben-Efraim et al. [6] –only passively secure and without free-XOR– the authors also estimate that the cross over point from the $O(n^2)$ to the $O(n)$ protocols comes when $n$ is about 100. Thus we obtain roughly the same cross over point in the case of active security with free-XOR as Ben-Efraim et al. do for passive security with no free-XOR. When comparing our protocol to [6] we see that, assuming a circuit consisting solely of AND gates, our protocol is roughly six times slower than that of [6]. Whilst this penalty for obtaining active security can be considered too much, one needs to consider the effect over typical circuits, as our protocols evaluate XOR gates for free. Thus, in practice, our performance penalty to achieve active security compared to Ben-Efraim et al. is closer to just a 15% of slow down. The details of our implementation can be found in Sect. 6. In the full version we also provide an estimation of the overall complexity of our protocols.

## 1.2 Technical Overview

We now proceed to discuss our results and techniques in greater detail. They mainly revolve around two key ideas: how to use LPN encryption to allow $n$-party garbling with free-XOR, and how to achieve active security. We give an overview of these techniques below, more details can be found in the rest of the paper.

Since our constructions assume a circuit-based representation, we fix some conventions and notation we adopt across the paper. We consider binary circuits $C_f$ consisting of $|C_\wedge|$ AND gates, $|C_\oplus|$ XOR gates, each of which has two input wires, $u$ and $v$, and one output wire $w$. We use $g$ to indicate the gate index. Let $W$ be the set of all wires, $W_{in}$ and $W_{out}$ be the set of input and output wires, respectively, we assume $|W_{in}| = n_{in}$ and $|W_{out}| = n_{out}$. We denote by $W_{in_i}$ the set of input wires associated to party $P_i$, and likewise for output wires $W_{out_i}$.

*Background on BMR.* Most of the work in multi-party garbled circuits is based on the BMR protocol by Beaver, Micali and Rogaway [3], which has been recently improved by a sequence of works [5,22,29,30,39] both in the case of passive and active security. In this paper we follow the approach described in [5,22].

These protocols consist of two phases: an input-independent preprocessing phase where the garbled circuit is generated, and an online phase where parties locally evaluate the circuit obtaining the output of the computation. While in Yao's two-party protocol only one party, the garbler, creates the garbled circuit, in BMR all parties generate it in a distributed way. This means that, instead of having a single key associated to each wire of the circuit, in multiparty garbling we have $n$ keys for each wire, one for each party.

At the beginning of the preprocessing step, each party $P_i$ chooses a global correlation $\Delta^i \in \mathbb{F}_2^k$ to support free-XOR, and, for each wire $w$ that is not the output wire of a XOR gate, samples a random key $\mathbf{k}_{w,0}^i$, associated to the value 0, and sets $\mathbf{k}_{w,1}^i = \mathbf{k}_{w,0}^i \oplus \Delta^i$ for the value 1. Moreover, each $P_i$ samples a random wire mask $\lambda_w^i \in \mathbb{F}_2$, for all the input wires $w \in W_{in_i}$ and output wires of AND gates. Therefore the actual wire mask for such wires is given by $\lambda_w = \oplus_{i \in [n]} \lambda_w^i$.

In this way, XOR gates do not need any additional preprocessed material, as parties simply set $\mathbf{k}_{w,0}^i = \mathbf{k}_{u,0}^i \oplus \mathbf{k}_{v,0}^i$, $\mathbf{k}_{w,1}^i = \mathbf{k}_{w,0}^i \oplus \Delta^i$ and $\lambda_w = \lambda_u \oplus \lambda_v$ (where $u$ and $v$ are the input wires and $w$ is the output wire).

Let $g$ be denote an AND gate with input wires $u, v$ and output wire $w$. Given wire masks $\lambda_u, \lambda_v, \lambda_w$ and wire keys $\{\mathbf{k}_{u,\alpha}^i, \mathbf{k}_{v,\beta}^i, \mathbf{k}_{w,0}^i\}_{(\alpha,\beta) \in \{0,1\}^2, i \in [n]}$, parties generate a garbled gate corresponding to the AND truth table. It consists of four rows, indexed by the values $(\alpha, \beta) \in \{0,1\}^2$ on the input wires. Every row contains $n$ ciphertexts, each of which is encrypted under $2n$ keys as follows:

$$\tilde{g}_{\alpha,\beta}^j = \left( \bigoplus_{i=1}^n F_{\mathbf{k}_{u,\alpha}^i, \mathbf{k}_{v,\beta}^i}(g\|j) \right) \oplus \mathbf{k}_{w,0}^j \oplus \Delta^j \cdot ((\lambda_u \oplus \alpha) \cdot (\lambda_v \oplus \beta) \oplus \lambda_w), \quad (1)$$

where $j \in [n]$ represents the $j$-th ciphertext on the $(\alpha, \beta)$-row and $F$ is a double-key PRF. Note that, as free-XOR asks for every pair of keys $(\mathbf{k}_{w,0}^j, \mathbf{k}_{w,1}^j)$ to be correlated according to $\Delta^j$, we further need $F$ to be a circular 2-correlation robust PRF [22].

In the online phase, these encrypted truth tables, along with the input and output wire masks, are revealed to all parties so to allow local evaluation of the circuit. More precisely, in the input phase each party $P_i$ broadcasts values $\epsilon_w = \rho_w \oplus \lambda_w$, for each $w \in W_{in_i}$, where $\rho_w$ is the actual input and $\lambda_w$ the corresponding wire mask provided to $P_i$ with other preprocessed material. In response, every party $P_j$ broadcasts their key $\mathbf{k}_{w,\epsilon_w}^i$. Upon collecting all the keys and masked inputs, parties can start evaluating the circuit. At this point, this does not require any interaction. Given complete sets of input keys $(\mathbf{k}_{u,\epsilon_u}^1, \ldots, \mathbf{k}_{u,\epsilon_u}^n)$ and $(\mathbf{k}_{v,\epsilon_v}^1, \ldots, \mathbf{k}_{v,\epsilon_v}^n)$, it is possible to decrypt a single row of AND garbled gates obtaining $(\mathbf{k}_{w,\epsilon_w}^1, \ldots, \mathbf{k}_{w,\epsilon_w}^n)$. Note that during evaluation each party decrypts the entire row, requiring $n^2$ PRF evaluations. Once these output keys are obtained, every party $P_i$ can check that the $i$-th key corresponds to one of its keys $\mathbf{k}_{w,0}^i, \mathbf{k}_{w,1}^i$ generated in the garbling phase. This check allows: 1) To determine the masked output value, i.e. if $\mathbf{k}_{w,\epsilon_w}^i = \mathbf{k}_{w,0}^i$, $P_i$ sets $\epsilon_w = 0$, and $\epsilon_w = 1$ otherwise; 2) To ensure active security for the online evaluation.

Notice that, while [29] uses the actively secure SPDZ protocol [15] to create an *authenticated* secret-sharing of Eq. (1), Hazay et al. [22] show that, in order to obtain an actively secure BMR-style protocol, it is enough to generate an *unauthenticated* additive sharing of the garbled circuit, provided that the values $\Delta^j \cdot ((\lambda_u \oplus \alpha) \cdot (\lambda_v \oplus \beta) \oplus \lambda_w)$ in Eq. (1) are correctly generated.

*BMR Garbling with LPN Encryption.* We replace the circular 2-correlation robust PRF needed to allow the free-XOR technique in garbled circuit based protocols with a two-key symmetric encryption scheme based on LPN. By applying the key and message homomorphism, each garbled gate contains only a single ciphertext per row instead of $n$. However to achieve efficiency we need to modify the LPN encryption used in [1], as we have $n$ rather than two parties, and prove that our system still satisfies the Linear Related-Key and Key-Dependent-Message (LIN-RK-KDM) security needed to support the free-XOR optimization.

On the other hand, we cannnot naively modify the standard single-key LPN-based encryption scheme because of the free-XOR technique. Due to the key-homomorphism of LPN, there would be only two different keys –either $\mathbf{k}_{u,0} + \mathbf{k}_{v,0}$ or $\mathbf{k}_{u,0} + \mathbf{k}_{v,0} + \Delta$– encrypting each four-ciphertext gate entries in every garbled table (more details are in Sect. 3), essentially allowing the adversary to always decrypt half of them. We define a new scheme that still takes as input two keys but applies a permutation $\sigma$ to the second one. We prove that the newly defined scheme satisfies a related notion of LIN-RK-KDM security, which we denote by LIN-RK-KDM$^\sigma$, while supporting the use of free-XOR in our garbled circuits.

Using our new scheme, we can replace the $4 \cdot n$ ciphertexts given in Eq. (1) with 4 ciphertexts of the form

$$\tilde{g}_{\alpha,\beta} = \mathsf{Enc}\left((\mathbf{k}_{w,\epsilon_{w,\alpha,\beta}}, \epsilon_{w,\alpha,\beta}), (g\|\alpha\|\beta), (\mathbf{k}_{u,\alpha}, \mathbf{k}_{v,\beta})\right), \ (\alpha,\beta) \in \{0,1\}^2, \quad (2)$$

where the values $\epsilon_{w,\alpha,\beta} = (\lambda_u \oplus \alpha) \cdot (\lambda_v \oplus \beta) \oplus \lambda_w$, $\mathbf{k}_{w,\epsilon_{w,\alpha,\beta}} = \mathbf{k}_{w,0} \oplus \Delta \cdot \epsilon_{w,\alpha,\beta}$ correpond to the output public-value and output key, respectively.

*Obtaining Active Security.* We use the garbling technique just described to design our actively secure BMR protocols with linear online complexity in the number of parties. At a very high level the approach we follow to obtain active security is the same approach used in HSS, but with some significant differences.

The first one is clearly in the evaluation phase. In HSS, upon receiving all the input-wire keys and reconstructing the garbled circuit, parties evaluate the circuit locally by computing, for every AND gate, $n^2$ PRF evaluations. By subtracting those PRF outputs (see Eq. 1), they obtain the $n$ keys $(\mathbf{k}_{w,\epsilon_w}^1, \ldots, \mathbf{k}_{w,\epsilon_w}^n)$

corresponding to the AND gate's output, which can be used to evaluate subsequent gates. Since, during this operation, each party $P_i$ should recover one of its two possible output keys, $(\mathbf{k}_{w,0}^i, \mathbf{k}_{w,1}^i)$, checking whether this condition verifies is enough to guarantee active security for the online evaluation. In our case this is no longer true, because upon decryption any party obtains a single unknown output key, $\mathbf{k}_{w,\epsilon_w}$. For security reasons, such a key needs to remain unknown to all parties up to this step, therefore, if we just plug-in our new garbling into HSS, it is no longer possible to check that the keys obtained by evaluating AND gates are correct. We describe two different ways to overcome this issue.

The first method, described in Sect. 4 and corresponding to the fully authenticated LPN-based garbling, proposes to fully authenticate the entire garbled circuit, and not just the wire mask. This is achieved using any MPC protocol with active security and dishonest majority. In this way the garbled values opened during the circuit evaluation are guaranteed to be correct, leading to a very efficient online phase. However, this comes at the price of a rather expensive preprocessing.

In our second protocol, described in Sect. 5, we improve the practicality of the preprocessing phase while maintaining almost the same online efficiency. In order to do so, we increase the number of honest parties to $n/c$, with $c \in \mathbb{R}$ and $1 < c \le n$. The proposed protocol works for any $1 < c \le n$: when $c \ge 2$ we are in the dishonest majority setting and when $c = n$ we go back to the full threshold case.

By setting the LPN parameters in the right way, we can design a protocol where each party locally generates "weak" (in term of security) ciphertexts. Since an adversary will be able to see only the sum of these ciphertexts, we show that this is enough to obtain a secure protocol. The balance then has to be drawn to ensure that enough 'noise' is added by each party in creating their own LPN-based ciphertexts in order to ensure privacy, but not too much to still guarantee correctness. The garbling we use in this case is unauthenticated, like in HSS, with only few actively secure MPC operations. Since, as explained before, we cannot rely on the online check used in HSS, we need to introduce a new additional test. In a little more detail, for each output gate $g$, with input wire $u$ and output wire $w$, we construct a new garbled gate as

$$\tilde{g}_\alpha = \mathsf{Enc}\left((\xi_{w,\alpha}^1 \| \cdots \| \xi_{w,\alpha}^n), (g\|\alpha\|0), (\mathbf{k}_{u,\alpha}, \mathbf{0})\right), \ \alpha \in \{0,1\},$$

where each value $\xi_{w,\alpha}^i$ is generated by party $P_i$ and then secret-shared among all parties. In the online phase each $P_i$ decrypts $\tilde{g}_{\epsilon_u}$, where $\epsilon_u$ is the public value of $g$'s input wire, and checks if the $i$-entry in the obtained vector correspond to one of the two values $\xi_{w,0}^i, \xi_{w,1}^i$. This extra check per output gate is sufficient to guarantee active security of our second protocol.

## 2   Preliminaries

We denote by $\mathsf{sec}$ the security parameter. We say that a function $\mu : \mathbb{N} \to \mathbb{N}$ is *negligible* if, for every positive polynomial $p(\cdot)$ and all sufficiently large $\mathsf{sec}$, it holds that $\mu(\mathsf{sec}) < \frac{1}{p(\mathsf{sec})}$. We assume that all involved algorithms are probabilistic polynomial time Turing machines. We let $x \leftarrow X$ denote the uniformly random assignment to the variable $x$ from the set $X$, assuming a uniform distribution over $X$. We also write $x \leftarrow y$ as shorthand for $x \leftarrow \{y\}$. If $\mathcal{D}$ is a probability distribution over a set $X$, then we let $x \leftarrow \mathcal{D}$ denote sampling from $X$ with respect to the distribution $\mathcal{D}$. If $A$ is a (probabilistic) algorithm then we denote by $a \leftarrow A$ the assignment of the output of $A$ where the probability distribution is over the random tape of $A$. With $\mathsf{Ber}_\tau$ we denote the Bernoulli distribution of parameter $\tau$, i.e. $\Pr[x = 1 : x \leftarrow \mathsf{Ber}_\tau] = \tau$.

**Security Model.** The protocols presented in this work are proved secure in the Universal Composability framework of Canetti [12]. We consider security against a static, malicious adversary who corrupts a subset $I \subset \mathcal{P} = \{P_1, \ldots, P_n\}$ of parties at the beginning of the protocol.

We assume all parties are connected via authenticated channels as well as secure point-to-point channels and a broadcast channel. The default method of communication is through authenticated channels, unless otherwise specified.

**Randomized Functions:** To describe our garbling technique we follow the same approach used in [1] and use the terminology of randomized encodings for garbled circuits [23, 24].

A *randomized function* $f : X \times R \longrightarrow Y$ is a two argument function such that, for every input $x \in X$, we can think of $f(x)$ as a random variable which samples $r \in R$ and then applies $f(x; r)$. When an algorithm $A$ gets oracle access to a randomized function $f$ we assume $A$ only has control on the inputs $x$. We denote the resulting randomized function by $A^f$. We say that two randomized functions are *equivalent*, written $f \equiv g$, if for every input, their output is identically distributed.

A set of randomized functions $\{f_\mathbf{s}\}_{\mathbf{s} \in \{0,1\}^*}$, indexed by a key $\mathbf{s}$, is called a *collection of randomized functions* if $f_\mathbf{s}$ is a randomized function for every $\mathbf{s}$. In the following we drop the dependency on $\mathbf{s}$.

We say that two collections $\{f_\mathbf{s}\}$ and $\{g_\mathbf{s}\}$ of randomized functions are computationally indistinguishable, written $\{f_\mathbf{s}\} \overset{c}{\equiv} \{g_\mathbf{s}\}$, if the probability that an efficient adversary can distinguish between them, given oracle access to a function in $\{f_\mathbf{s}\}$ and a function in $\{g_\mathbf{s}\}$, is negligible.

Let $\{f_\mathbf{s}\}, \{g_\mathbf{s}\}, \{h_\mathbf{s}\}$ be collections of randomized functions, we have the following standard facts [32]:

- if $\{f_\mathbf{s}\} \overset{c}{\equiv} \{g_\mathbf{s}\}$ and $A$ is an efficient function then $\{A^{f_\mathbf{s}}\} \overset{c}{\equiv} \{A^{g_\mathbf{s}}\}$;
- if $\{f_\mathbf{s}\} \overset{c}{\equiv} \{g_\mathbf{s}\}$ and $\{g_\mathbf{s}\} \overset{c}{\equiv} \{h_\mathbf{s}\}$ then $\{f_\mathbf{s}\} \overset{c}{\equiv} \{h_\mathbf{s}\}$.

## 2.1 LIN-RK-KDM Security

We briefly recall the notion of (Linear) Related-Key and Key-Dependent-Message security [1, 2, 4, 9, 11] that we need in our constructions: Given a symmetric encryption scheme $\mathcal{E} = (\mathsf{Enc}, \mathsf{Dec})$ over the plaintext space $\mathcal{M} = \mathbb{F}_2^*$ and key space $\mathcal{K} = \mathbb{F}_2^{\text{sec}}$, we define two families of key-derivation and key-dependent message functions:

$$\Phi_{\text{RKA}} = \{\phi : \mathcal{K} \to \mathcal{K}\} \quad \text{and} \quad \Psi_{\text{KDM}} = \{\psi : \mathcal{K} \to \mathcal{M}\},$$

such that Related-Key and Key-Dependent-Message (RK-KDM) security can be defined through two oracles $\text{Real}_s$ and $\text{Fake}_s$, indexed by a key $\mathbf{s} \in \mathcal{K}$, as follows: for each query $(\phi, \psi) \in \Phi_{\text{RKA}} \times \Psi_{\text{KDM}}$, $\text{Real}_s$ returns a sample from the distribution $\text{Enc}(\psi(\mathbf{s}); \phi(\mathbf{s}))$ and $\text{Fake}_s$ a sample from the distribution $\text{Enc}(0^{|\psi(\mathbf{s})|}; \phi(\mathbf{s}))$.

**Definition 1 (RK-KDM secure encryption, [1]).** *We say that a symmetric encryption scheme* $\mathcal{E} = (\text{Enc}, \text{Dec})$ *is semantically-secure under* RK-KDM *attacks with respect to* $\Phi_{\text{RKA}}$ *and* $\Psi_{\text{KDM}}$ *if* $\text{Real}_s \stackrel{c}{\equiv} \text{Fake}_s$, *where* $\mathbf{s} \leftarrow \mathcal{K}$.

If both $\phi$ and $\psi$ are linear functions over $\mathbb{F}_2$, we refer to this notion as Linear Key-Related and Key-Dependent-Message (LIN-RK-KDM) security. In this case we can rewrite the oracles in a compact way:

$$\text{Real}_s : (\delta, \mathbf{m}, b) \longmapsto \text{Enc}(\mathbf{m} \oplus b \cdot \mathbf{s}, \ \delta \oplus \mathbf{s})$$
$$\text{Fake}_s : (\delta, \mathbf{m}, b) \longmapsto \text{Enc}(0^{|\mathbf{m}|}, \ \delta \oplus \mathbf{s}),$$

where $\mathbf{m} \in \mathcal{M}$ is a message, $\mathbf{s} \in \mathcal{K}$ a key, $b \in \mathbb{F}_2$ a bit and $\delta \in \mathbb{F}_2^{\text{sec}}$ a key-shift. Notice in computing $\mathbf{m} \oplus b \cdot \mathbf{s}$ we multiply $\mathbf{s}$ by $b$ bitwise, and then pad the result with $|\mathbf{m}| - k$ zeros to left before xor-ing with $\mathbf{m}$.

## 2.2  Error Correcting Codes

An $[\ell, \mathtt{m}, d]$ binary linear code $L$ is a subspace of dimension $\mathtt{m}$ of $\mathbb{F}_2^\ell$, where $\ell$ is the length of the code, $\mathtt{m}$ its dimension and $d$ its distance, i.e. the minimum (Hamming) distance between any distinct codewords in $L$. We denote by $G$ a *generator matrix* of $L$, that is any matrix in $\mathbb{F}_2^{\mathtt{m} \times \ell}$ whose rows form a basis for $L$. If $G$ has the form $[I_\mathtt{m}|P]$, where $I_\mathtt{m}$ is the $\mathtt{m} \times \mathtt{m}$ identity matrix, $G$ is said to be in *standard form*. A *parity-check matrix* for $L$ is a matrix in $\mathbb{F}_2^{(\ell - \mathtt{m}) \times \ell}$ such that $GH^T = 0$. A linear code can be uniquely specified either by its generator matrix or its parity-check matrix.

Given an $[\ell, \mathtt{m}, d]$ binary linear code $L$, we can define a pair of algorithms $(\text{Encode}, \text{Decode})$, where $\text{Encode}: \mathbb{F}_2^\mathtt{m} \to \mathbb{F}_2^\ell$ (resp. $\text{Decode}: \mathbb{F}_2^\ell \to \mathbb{F}_2^\mathtt{m}$) is an encoding (resp. decoding) algorithm, such that:

1. **Linearity:** For every pair of messages $\mathbf{x}_1, \mathbf{x}_2 \in \mathbb{F}_2^\mathtt{m}$ we have $\text{Encode}(\mathbf{x}_1) \oplus \text{Encode}(\mathbf{x}_2) = \text{Encode}(\mathbf{x}_1 \oplus \mathbf{x}_2)$.
2. $\lfloor (d-1)/2 \rfloor$**-Correction:** The decoding algorithm can correct any error of Hamming weight up to $\lfloor (d-1)/2 \rfloor$, i.e., for every message $\mathbf{x} \in \mathbb{F}_2^\mathtt{m}$ and every error vector $\mathbf{e} \in \mathbb{F}_2^\ell$ with at most $\lfloor (d-1)/2 \rfloor$ non-zero elements, it always holds that $\text{Decode}(\text{Encode}(\mathbf{x}) \oplus \mathbf{e}) = \text{Decode}(\text{Encode}(\mathbf{x})) = \mathbf{x}$.

We will also need the following more general property.

**Definition 2 (($\ell, \tau$)-Correction:).** *Let* $\mathsf{Ber}_\tau$ *be the Bernoulli distribution with parameter* $\tau$. *Given an* $[\ell, \mathfrak{m}, d]$ *binary linear code* $L$ *and a pair of efficient encoding and decoding algorithms,* (Encode, Decode), *we say that* $L$ *is* ($\ell, \tau$)-correcting *if, for any message* $\mathbf{x} \in \mathbb{F}_2^{\mathfrak{m}}$, *the decoding algorithm* Decode *will, with overwhelming probability, satisfy* $\mathsf{Decode}(\mathsf{Encode}(\mathbf{x}) \oplus \mathbf{e}) = \mathsf{Decode}(\mathsf{Encode}(\mathbf{x})) = \mathbf{x}$, *where* $\mathbf{e} \leftarrow \mathsf{Ber}_\tau^\ell$ *is a noise vector, and* $\mathsf{Ber}_\tau^\ell$ *is the distribution over* $\mathbb{F}_2^\ell$ *obtained by drawing each entry of the vector* $\mathbf{e}$ *independently according to* $\mathsf{Ber}_\tau$.

## 2.3   LPN-Based Encryption

The Learning Parity with Noise (LPN) problem [10,18] is a well-studied problem in learning and coding theory, and has recently found many applications in cryptography. In this section we introduce the decisional version of the LPN problem together with some variants of the standard LPN-based encryption scheme that we need in our garbling construction.

**Definition 3 (Decisional LPN).** *Let* $\ell, k \in \mathbb{N}$ *and* $\tau \in (0, 1/2)$, *the* $\mathsf{DLPN}_{\ell,k,\tau}$ *problem is to distinguish between the distributions given by*

$$\left\{ (C, \mathbf{c}) : C \leftarrow \mathbb{F}_2^{\ell \times k}, \; \mathbf{s} \leftarrow \mathbb{F}_2^k, \; \mathbf{e} \leftarrow \mathsf{Ber}_\tau^\ell, \; \mathbf{c} \leftarrow C \cdot \mathbf{s} \oplus \mathbf{e} \right\}$$

*and*

$$\left\{ (C, \mathbf{c}) : C \leftarrow \mathbb{F}_2^{\ell \times k}, \; \mathbf{c} \leftarrow \mathbb{F}_2^\ell \right\}.$$

The decisional and search variants of the LPN problem are polynomially equivalent, they have been extensively studied and are widely believed to be hard for any $\tau$. The DLPN assumption has been used to build various cryptographic primitives and, in particular, symmetric encryption schemes.

**Definition 4 (Standard LPN Encryption).** *Let* $\mathfrak{m}, k, \ell = \mathsf{poly}(\mathsf{sec})$ *be three integers. Let* $\mathcal{K} = \mathbb{F}_2^k$ *be the key space,* $\mathcal{C} = \mathbb{F}_2^{\ell \times k} \times \mathbb{F}_2^\ell$ *the ciphertext space and* $\mathcal{M} = \mathbb{F}_2^{\mathfrak{m}}$ *the message space. Let* $\tau \in (0, 1/2)$ *be a parameter defining the Bernoulli distribution* $\mathsf{Ber}_\tau^\ell$. *Finally, let* $G \in \mathbb{F}_2^{\ell \times \mathfrak{m}}$ *be a generator matrix for an* $[\ell, \mathfrak{m}, d]$ *binary linear code* $L$ *which is* ($\ell, \tau$)-correcting. *The (standard) LPN symmetric encryption scheme consists of the three following algorithms:*

- $\mathsf{KeyGen}_\tau^1(1^{\mathsf{sec}})$: *Given as input the security parameter* sec, *sample uniformly at random a secret key,* $\mathbf{s} \leftarrow \mathcal{K}$.
- $\mathsf{Enc}_\tau^1(\mathbf{m}, \mathbf{s})$: *Given a message* $\mathbf{m} \in \mathcal{M}$ *and the secret key* $\mathbf{s} \in \mathcal{K}$, *sample a matrix* $C \leftarrow \mathbb{F}_2^{\ell \times k}$, *noise* $\mathbf{e} \leftarrow \mathsf{Ber}_\tau^\ell$ *and output*

$$\mathbf{c} \leftarrow C \cdot \mathbf{s} \oplus \mathbf{e} \oplus G \cdot \mathbf{m}.$$

- $\mathsf{Dec}_\tau^1((C, \mathbf{c}), \mathbf{s})$: *Given a ciphertext* $(C, \mathbf{c})$ *and the secret key* $\mathbf{s}$, *compute* $\mathbf{c} \oplus C \cdot \mathbf{s}$ *and apply a decoding algorithm to recover* $\mathbf{m}$.

In [1], Appelbaum proved that (an extension of) the above encryption scheme is LIN-RK-KDM secure.

**Theorem 1.** *Assuming* $\mathsf{DLPN}_{\ell,k,\tau}$ *is hard, the encryption scheme* $(\mathsf{KeyGen}_\tau^1,$ $\mathsf{Enc}_\tau^1, \mathsf{Dec}_\tau^1)$ *is LIN-RK-KDM secure according to the above definition of LIN-RK-KDM security.*

Assuming the DLPN-problem is hard, it is easy to show that also the following nonce-based symmetric encryption scheme is IND-CPA, where it is required that a specific nonce is used only once for each key $\mathbf{s}$.

*An eXtendable Output Function (XOF).* A XOF is a way to model a random oracle that can produce outputs of any length. Implementations of such functions can be created from SHA-3 in a standardized manner [8,34].

**Definition 5 (XOF-Based LPN Encryption).** *Let* $\mathrm{m}, k, \ell = \mathsf{poly}(\mathsf{sec})$ *be three integers and* $\mathcal{K}, \mathcal{C}, \mathcal{M}$ *as in Definition 4. Let* $\tau \in (0, 1/2)$ *and* $G \in \mathbb{F}_2^{\ell \times \mathrm{m}}$ *be chosen in the same way as there too. Let a XOF* $H : \{0,1\}^* \longrightarrow \mathbb{F}_2^{\ell \times k}$ *be modelled as a random oracle. The XOF-Based LPN symmetric encryption scheme consists of the three following algorithms:*

- $\mathsf{KeyGen}_\tau^{\mathsf{XOF}}(1^{\mathsf{sec}})$*: Sample uniformly at random a secret key,* $\mathbf{s} \leftarrow \mathcal{K}$.
- $\mathsf{Enc}_\tau^{\mathsf{XOF}}((\mathbf{m}, \mathsf{nonce}), \mathbf{s})$*: Given a message* $\mathbf{m} \in \mathcal{M}$*, a key* $\mathbf{s} \in \mathcal{K}$ *and a string* $\mathsf{nonce}$*, sample noise* $\mathbf{e} \leftarrow \mathsf{Ber}_\tau^\ell$ *and compute*

$$C \leftarrow H(\mathsf{nonce}) \text{ and } \mathbf{c} \leftarrow C \cdot \mathbf{s} \oplus \mathbf{e} \oplus G \cdot \mathbf{m}.$$

- $\mathsf{Dec}_\tau^{\mathsf{XOF}}((C, \mathbf{c}), \mathbf{s})$*: Given a ciphertext* $(C, \mathbf{c})$*, compute* $\mathbf{c} \oplus C \cdot \mathbf{s}$ *and then apply error correction to recover* $\mathbf{m}$

The above LPN encryption scheme is trivially additively homomorphic in the message space, and is also key homomorphic if two encryptions with the same nonce value are added together. To reduce bandwidth and storage requirements, it is possible to define the ciphertext to be $(\mathsf{nonce}, \mathbf{c})$ instead of $(C, \mathbf{c})$.

Looking ahead, we will choose the parameters for our LPN-based encryption scheme based on recent analysis on the security of the LPN assumption by Esser et al. [16], which implies that the parameter $k$ in the scheme should be selected to be

$$k \geq \frac{\mathsf{sec}}{\log_2\left(\frac{1}{1-\tau}\right)}, \tag{3}$$

where $\mathsf{sec}$ is the (symmetric-key equivalent) security parameter and $\tau$ defines the noise rate. In what follows one should think of $\mathsf{sec}$ as being equal to 128 or 256.

### 2.4  Functionalities for Secret-Shared MPC

Our protocols make use of the functionality $\mathcal{F}_{\mathsf{MPC}}$ for MPC over binary circuits described in Fig. 1. The functionality is independent of how the values are stored and represented. In particular, we will need two different implementations of $\mathcal{F}_{\mathsf{MPC}}$, one achieving only passive security and the second achieving active security. Note that any generic MPC protocol can be used to practically instantiate

---

**Functionality** $\mathcal{F}_{\mathsf{MPC}}^{\mathsf{flag}}$

The functionality runs with parties $P_1, \ldots, P_n$ and an adversary $\mathcal{A}$.
It is parametrized by flag $\in \{\mathsf{Auth}, \mathsf{UnAuth}\}$. Given a set $ID$ of valid identifiers, all values are stored in the form $(varid, x)$, where $varid \in ID$.

**Initialize:** On input $(Init)$ from all parties. The adversary is assumed to have corrupted a subset $I$ of the parties.

**Input:** On input $(\mathsf{Input}, P_i, varid, x)$ from $P_i$, with $x \in \mathbb{F}_2$, and $(\mathsf{Input}, P_i, varid, ?)$ from all other parties, with $varid$ a fresh identifier.

**Add:** On command $(\mathsf{Add}, varid_1, varid_2, varid_3)$ from all parties:
  1. The functionality retrieves $(varid_1, x)$, $(varid_2, y)$ and stores $(varid_3, x \oplus y)$.

**Multiply:** On input $(\mathsf{Multiply}, varid_1, varid_2, varid_3)$ from all parties:
  1. The functionality retrieves $(varid_1, x)$, $(varid_2, y)$ and stores $(varid_3, x \cdot y)$.

**Output/Open:** On input $(\mathsf{Output/Open}, varid, i)$ from all honest parties the functionality retrieves $(varid, y)$, sends $y$ to the adversary, and waits for a reply. If $\mathcal{A}$ answers with $\mathsf{Deliver}$, then do one of the following:
  - If flag $= \mathsf{Auth}$: output $y$ to either all parties (if $i = 0$) or $P_i$ (if $i \neq 0$).
  - If flag $= \mathsf{UnAuth}$: $\mathcal{A}$ further specifies an additive error $e \in \mathbb{F}_2$. The functionality outputs $y + e$ to either all parties (if $i = 0$) or $P_i$ (if $i \neq 0$).
  
  In both cases, if $\mathcal{A}$ does not answer with $\mathsf{Deliver}$, output abort.

---

**Fig. 1.** The ideal functionality for MPC over $\mathbb{F}_2$

$\mathcal{F}_{\mathsf{MPC}}$ in our constructions. However, since TinyOT-like protocols, that rely on message authentication codes (MACs) to achieve active security, are currently the most efficient protocols on binary circuits and are used in previous works like HSS and WRK, we abuse notation and use $\mathcal{F}_{\mathsf{MPC}}^{\mathsf{Auth}}$ and $\mathcal{F}_{\mathsf{MPC}}^{\mathsf{UnAuth}}$ to distinguish between an active and a passive implementation of $\mathcal{F}_{\mathsf{MPC}}$. Also notice that each value in $\mathcal{F}_{\mathsf{MPC}}$ is uniquely identified by an identifier $varid \in ID$, where $ID$ is a set of identifiers.

After an **Initialize** step, the functionality allows the parties to provide their inputs, which can be added and multiplied using **Add** and **Multiply**, respectively. The functionality also provides an **Output/Open** command that allows values to be revealed either publicly or privately to a single party. Note we maintain the double notation **Output/Open** only to distinguish between output values and intermediate values that are opened during the execution of the protocol.

*Unauthenticated Values:* We denote $\langle x \rangle$ an additive sharing of $x$ over $\mathbb{F}_2$ generated by $\mathcal{F}_{\mathsf{MPC}}^{\mathsf{UnAuth}}$, where $x = \oplus_{i \in [n]} x^i$ with party $P_i$ holding the share $x^i \in \mathbb{F}_2$.

Looking ahead, using such a sharing we can perform arbitrary linear operations, however, upon opening values, an adversary is able to introduce an arbitrary additive error and reveal incorrect values. For this reason when we use unauthenticated values to instantiate our LPN-based protocol, we need to add an new mechanism to prevent these additive errors introducing a security weakness in the protocol.

*Authenticated Values:* We denote $[x]$ an actively secure additive sharing of $x$, for example using a fixed MAC scheme. Addition and multiplication of such elements will be represented by $[x] + [y]$ and $[x] \cdot [y]$.

To simplify notation we will use the following shorthands for inputing and outputting values to/from a party/all parties:

$$[x] \leftarrow \mathsf{Input}(P_i), \qquad x \leftarrow \mathsf{Output}([x], P_i), \qquad x \leftarrow \mathsf{Open}([x]),$$

$$\langle x \rangle \leftarrow \mathsf{Input}(P_i), \qquad x \leftarrow \mathsf{Output}(\langle x \rangle, P_i), \qquad x \leftarrow \mathsf{Open}(\langle x \rangle),$$

respectively in $\mathcal{F}_{\mathsf{MPC}}^{\mathsf{Auth}}$ and $\mathcal{F}_{\mathsf{MPC}}^{\mathsf{UnAuth}}$. If the type (authenticated/unauthenticated) of operation is not obvious from the context we will write $\mathsf{Input}^P$, $\mathsf{Output}^P$, $\mathsf{Open}^P$ for the unauthenticated variant, with no superscript added for the authenticated variant.

Trivially, from a $[x]$ sharing we can obtain (immediately and with no computation or communication) a $\langle x \rangle$ sharing of the same value. We denote this operation by $\langle x \rangle \leftarrow \mathsf{Convert}([x])$. Extension of this notation to act on elements $\mathbf{x} \in \mathbb{F}_2^k$, for various values of $k$, will be by using $[\mathbf{x}]$ and $\langle \mathbf{x} \rangle$ in the obvious way.

We can extend the $\mathcal{F}_{\mathsf{MPC}}$ functionality by a command, which we denote by $[x] \leftarrow \mathsf{GenBit}()$ which produces a shared random bit within the MPC engine. This command can be derived from the base commands by performing:

1. All parties call $[x^i] \leftarrow \mathsf{Input}(P_i)$, $x^i \in \mathbb{F}_2$.
2. Parties compute $[x] \leftarrow \oplus_i [x^i]$.

## 3   Free-XOR Garbling Using LPN

We now discuss how to garble a single AND gate using LPN-based encryption while maintaining the free-XOR invariant. Later on, in Sects. 4 and 5, we will show how this technique can be used in order to build our actively secure garbled-circuit based MPC protocols.

Our garbling method is similar to the one given in Eq. (1), with two main differences. Firstly and most importantly, we have a single ciphertext per row, rather than $n$ of them; secondly, we replace the circular 2-correlation robust PRF $F$ with a nonce-based, two-key symmetric encryption scheme based on LPN. Thus we obtain the garbling method given in Eq. (2).

To achieve this modification one could naively think of just adapting standard LPN encryption (c.f. Definition 4) to use two keys, where $\Delta = \bigoplus_{i=1}^{n} \Delta^i$, and, for $t \in \{u, v, w\}$, $\mathbf{k}_{t,0} = \bigoplus_{i=1}^{n} \mathbf{k}_{t,0}^i$ and $\mathbf{k}_{t,1} = \mathbf{k}_{t,0} \oplus \Delta$. Each garbled row $(\epsilon_u, \epsilon_v) \in \{0,1\}^2$ could then be set as:

$$\tilde{g}_{\epsilon_u, \epsilon_v} = (C, c), \quad C \leftarrow \mathbb{F}_2^{\ell \times k}, \quad c \leftarrow C \cdot (\mathbf{k}_{u,\epsilon_u} \oplus \mathbf{k}_{v,\epsilon_v}) \oplus \mathbf{e} \oplus G \cdot \mathbf{k}_{w,\epsilon_w} \qquad (4)$$

This naive solution does not result in a secure garbling method. To see this denote $\mathbf{s}_{\epsilon_u, \epsilon_v} = \mathbf{k}_{u,\epsilon_u} \oplus \mathbf{k}_{v,\epsilon_v}$, then due to free-XOR we would have that $\mathbf{s}_{\epsilon_u, \epsilon_v} = \mathbf{k}_{u,0} \oplus \mathbf{k}_{v,0} \oplus (\epsilon_u \oplus \epsilon_v) \cdot \Delta$, and hence $s_{0,0} = s_{1,1}$ as well as $s_{1,0} = s_{0,1}$. This would trivially allow corrupted parties to always decrypt half of the entries of every garbled gate, breaking completely the security of the scheme. A possible fix to this problem would be to sample two different matrices $C_u, C_v \leftarrow \mathbb{F}_2^{\ell \times k}$ and compute $c \leftarrow C_u \cdot \mathbf{k}_{u,\epsilon_u} \oplus C_v \cdot \mathbf{k}_{v,\epsilon_v} \oplus \mathbf{e} \oplus G \cdot \mathbf{k}_{w,\epsilon_w}$, but this would incur in increased computational costs due to the sampling of the matrices and the cost of calculating the matrix-vector products.

In order to avoid these issues in our garbling, while still maintaining security, we introduce a modification to the previously provided nonce-based version of LPN encryption. In particular, our scheme will take as input two keys in $\mathbb{F}_2^k$, but this time a permutation $\sigma \in S_k$ (where $S_k$ is the set of permutations on $k$ elements) will be applied to the second one.

**Definition 6 (XOF-Based Two-Key LPN Encryption).** *Let* $\mathfrak{m}, k, \ell =$ poly(sec) *be three integers. Let* $\mathcal{K} = \mathbb{F}_2^k \times \mathbb{F}_2^k$ *be the key space,* $\mathcal{C} = \mathbb{F}_2^{\ell \times k} \times \mathbb{F}_2^\ell$ *the ciphertext space and* $\mathcal{M} = \mathbb{F}_2^{\mathfrak{m}}$ *the message space. Let* $\tau \in (0, 1/2)$ *be a parameter defining a Bernoulli distribution and* $\sigma$ *a permutation in* $S_k$. *Finally, let* $G \in \mathbb{F}_2^{\ell \times \mathfrak{m}}$ *be a generator matrix for an* $[\ell, \mathfrak{m}, d]$ *binary linear code* $L$ *which is* $(\ell, \tau)$-*correcting (c.f. Definition 2). Let* $H : \{0,1\}^* \longrightarrow \mathbb{F}_2^{\ell \times k}$ *be a XOF. A XOF-based, two-key symmetric LPN encryption scheme* $\mathcal{E}_\tau^{\mathsf{XOF}}$ *is defined by the following algorithms:*

- KeyGen($1^{\mathsf{sec}}$): *Samples* $(\mathbf{k}_u, \mathbf{k}_v) \leftarrow \mathbb{F}_2^{2 \times k}$ *at random.*
- Enc$_\tau$(($\mathbf{m}$, nonce), ($\mathbf{k}_u, \mathbf{k}_v$)): *On input of a message* $\mathbf{m} \in \mathcal{M}$, *a pair of keys* ($\mathbf{k}_u, \mathbf{k}_v$) *and a string* nonce, *compute*

$$C \leftarrow H(\mathsf{nonce}),$$

$$\mathbf{c} \leftarrow C \cdot (\mathbf{k}_u \oplus \sigma(\mathbf{k}_v)) \oplus \mathbf{e} \oplus G \cdot \mathbf{m}, \quad \mathbf{e} \leftarrow \mathsf{Ber}_\tau^\ell.$$

- Dec(($C, \mathbf{c}$), ($\mathbf{k}_u, \mathbf{k}_v$)): *Compute* $\mathbf{c} \oplus C \cdot (\mathbf{k}_u \oplus \sigma(\mathbf{k}_v))$ *and then apply error correction to recover* $\mathbf{m}$.

Note that this scheme is message homomorphic, and it only requires to store nonce rather than $C$. In addition, when the same nonce is used, it is also key homomorphic.

Returning to our garbling proposal from the beginning of this section, now the key used to garble entry ($\epsilon_u, \epsilon_v$) of a given gate $g$ is $\mathbf{s}_{\epsilon_u, \epsilon_v} = \mathbf{k}_{u,\epsilon_u} \oplus \sigma(\mathbf{k}_{v,\epsilon_v})$. By substituting the free-XOR correlation, we see that security now relies on the secrecy of

$$\mathbf{s}_{\epsilon_u, \epsilon_v} = \mathbf{k}_{u,0} \oplus \sigma(\mathbf{k}_{v,0}) \oplus \epsilon_u \cdot \Delta \oplus \epsilon_v \cdot \sigma(\Delta), \tag{5}$$

and hence on four possible (distinct) values of $\mathbf{s}_{\epsilon_u, \epsilon_v}$. Nevertheless, the security analysis requires additional care. As it is always the case when using the free-XOR optimization, we have the problem that we are encrypting key-dependent messages (where the dependence is the free-XOR correlation $\Delta$), as well as we are using related keys when encrypting the inactive rows of a garbled gate. Explicitly, given the active row $\mathbf{s}_{\epsilon_u, \epsilon_v}$, for $(\alpha, \beta) \in \{0,1\}^2$ these inactive rows are:

$$\mathbf{s}_{\epsilon_u \oplus \alpha, \epsilon_v \oplus \beta} = \mathbf{s}_{\epsilon_u, \epsilon_v} \oplus \alpha \cdot \Delta \oplus \beta \cdot \sigma(\Delta).$$

Hence, once the parties learn any $\mathbf{s}_{\epsilon_u,\epsilon_v}$ by evaluating the garbled circuit, security for each of the three remaining rows is relying, respectively, on the secret values $\Delta, \sigma(\Delta)$ and $\Delta \oplus \sigma(\Delta)$. To define an appropriate way of dealing with this RK-KDM problem, we will first define the following variant of LPN.

**Definition 7 (DLPN$^\sigma$ Problem).** *Let $\sigma \in S_k$ be the set of permutations of $k$ elements and $\ell, k, \tau \in \mathbb{N}$. The DLPN$^\sigma_{\ell,k,\tau}$ problem is to distinguish between the two distributions given by*

$$\left\{ (C, \mathbf{c}, \sigma) : C \leftarrow \mathbb{F}_2^{\ell \times k}, \ \mathbf{s} \leftarrow \mathbb{F}_2^k, \ \mathbf{e} \leftarrow \mathsf{Ber}^\ell_\tau, \ \mathbf{c} \leftarrow C \cdot (\mathbf{s} \oplus \sigma(\mathbf{s})) \oplus \mathbf{e} \right\}$$

*and*

$$\left\{ (C, \mathbf{c}, \sigma) : C \leftarrow \mathbb{F}_2^{\ell \times k}, \ \mathbf{c} \leftarrow \mathbb{F}_2^\ell \right\},$$

*where $\mathsf{Ber}^\ell_\tau$ is the Bernoulli distribution with parameter $\tau$.*

Recalling that any permutationon of a finite set can be uniquely expressed as the product of disjoint cycles, we now show how the DLPN and DLPN$^\sigma$ problems are related to each other by the following Lemma, the proof of which is given in the full version.

**Lemma 1.** *Let $\sigma \in S_k$ be a permutation consisting of exactly $\tilde{k}$ disjoint cycles, the DLPN$_{\ell,k-\tilde{k},\tau}$ problem reduces to DLPN$^\sigma_{\ell,k,\tau}$ problem.*

In our construction, the permutation $\sigma$ will be chosen to map $(\delta_0, \ldots, \delta_{k-1}) \in \mathbb{F}_2^k$ to $(\delta'_0, \ldots, \delta'_{k-1})$, where $\delta'_j = \delta_{j-1 \pmod{k}}$. Note that this $\sigma$ consists of a single cycle of length $k$ and, hence, the security of DLPN$^\sigma$ is the same as that of DLPN with keys which are one bit shorter.

We are now just one step away from defining the right RK-KDM notion for our scheme. A detail that was overlooked in Eq. (4) is that the key space $\mathcal{K} = \mathbb{F}_2^k$ and the message space $\mathcal{M} = \mathbb{F}_2^\mathsf{m}$ are different, so we cannot write $G \cdot \mathbf{k}_{w,\epsilon_w}$. Furthermore, as in our protocols nobody will know neither $\mathbf{k}_{w,0}$ nor $\mathbf{k}_{w,1}$ (a problem which does not come up in previous works, because each $P_i$ has its own pair of keys $\mathbf{k}^i_{w,0}, \mathbf{k}^i_{w,1}$), we need the garbled gate to also encrypt explicitly the external value $\epsilon_w$.

We thus define an injection of the space $\mathcal{K} \times \mathbb{F}_2$ into the message space $\mathcal{M}$, which requires that $\mathsf{m} \geq k + 1$, via the following linear map:

$$\Psi : \begin{cases} \mathcal{K} \times \mathbb{F}_2 \longrightarrow \mathcal{M} \\ (\mathbf{k}, b) \longmapsto A \cdot (\mathbf{k}, b)^\mathsf{T} \end{cases}$$

for some matrix $A \in \mathbb{F}_2^{\mathsf{m} \times (k+1)}$. In order to make the image of $\Psi$ easily recognizable, so that we can efficiently recover its preimage when decrypting a garbled row, we pick the matrix $A$ in the map $\Psi$ such that we obtain:

$$\Psi : (\mathbf{k}, b) \longmapsto (0^{\mathsf{m}-k-1} \| \mathbf{k} \| b) = \begin{pmatrix} \mathbf{0}_{(\mathsf{m}-k-1) \times (k+1)} \\ I_k \| \mathbf{0}_{k \times 1} \\ \mathbf{0}_{1 \times k} \| 1 \end{pmatrix} \cdot \begin{pmatrix} \mathbf{k}^\mathsf{T} \\ b \end{pmatrix}.$$

This choice of matrix $A$ also simplifies somewhat the proof of Theorem 2 below.

We can now finally define the relevant notion of RK-KDM security for our scheme defined in Definition 6 (LIN-RK-KDM$^\sigma$ security), and show how we will use it to garble gates in our protocols. For security reasons, which will become apparent in the proofs, we need to make the assumption that the free-XOR correlation $\Delta \in \mathbb{F}_2^k$ is of the form $(1, \Delta', 0)$.

Let $\Delta = (1, \Delta', 0)$ with $\Delta' \leftarrow \mathbb{F}_2^{k-2}$ be a secret value. Let $H$ the XOF associated with the scheme (KeyGen$^{\mathsf{XOF}}$, Enc$_\tau^{\mathsf{XOF}}$, Dec$^{\mathsf{XOF}}$) of Definition 5. In the following we think of the encryption scheme as being defined with respect to three possible keys $\Delta$, $\sigma(\Delta)$, and $\Delta \oplus \sigma(\Delta)$ chosen by $(\alpha, \beta)$. The variable $\mathbf{k}$ is defining a linearly homomorphic relation with respect to one of the keys and $b$ is defining the linearly homomorphic key-dependent offset $\Psi(b \cdot \Delta, b)$. With this understanding we define the following oracles:

$$\mathsf{Real}_\Delta^\sigma : (\mathbf{k}, \alpha, \beta, \mathbf{m}, b, \mathsf{nonce}) \longmapsto$$

$$\mathsf{Enc}_\tau^{\mathsf{XOF}}(\ (\mathbf{m} \oplus \Psi(b \cdot \Delta, b), \ \mathsf{nonce}), \ \mathbf{k} \oplus \alpha \cdot \Delta \oplus \beta \cdot \sigma(\Delta)\ )$$

$$\mathsf{Fake}_\Delta^\sigma : (\mathbf{k}, \alpha, \beta, \mathbf{m}, b, \mathsf{nonce}) \longmapsto (H(\mathsf{nonce}), \ \mathbf{c}), \qquad \mathbf{c} \leftarrow \mathcal{C},$$

where $\mathcal{C}$ is the ciphertext space, and forbid the following kind of queries: Let $\{(\mathbf{k}_i, \alpha_i, \beta_i, \mathbf{m}_i, b_i, \mathsf{nonce})\}_{i=1}^q$ be a sequence of queries under the same nonce. Such a sequence is not allowed if and only if there exist coefficients $c_1, \ldots, c_q \in \mathbb{F}_2$, not all zero, such that $\sum_{i=1}^q c_i \cdot (\alpha_i, \beta_i) = (0, 0)$. We can now define our notion of LIN-RK-KDM$^\sigma$ security:

**Definition 8 (LIN-RK-KDM$^\sigma$ secure encryption).** *The encryption scheme* (KeyGen$^{\mathsf{XOF}}$, Enc$_\tau^{\mathsf{XOF}}$, Dec$^{\mathsf{XOF}}$) *is said to be LIN-RK-KDM$^\sigma$ secure if the two oracles* $\mathsf{Real}_\Delta^\sigma$ *and* $\mathsf{Fake}_\Delta^\sigma$ *are computationally indistinguishable, when we forbid the above queries.*

The reason for the forbidden queries is in order to stop the distinguisher $\mathcal{D}$ from mounting a trivial attack. Take for example the simplest forbidden query, where $\mathcal{D}$ simply asks once for $(\mathbf{k}, 0, 0, \mathbf{m}, b, \mathsf{nonce})$. As none of the three possible secret keys depending on $\Delta$ has been applied, then $\mathcal{D}$ can just decrypt using $\mathbf{k}$ and see whether the oracle was implementing Real or Fake. For longer sequences, the idea is essentially the same, as the key-homomorphism of LPN would otherwise allow $\mathcal{D}$ to mount the same kind of attack simply by computing the linear combination defined by the $c_i$ values.

**Theorem 2.** *Let* $\Delta = (1, \Delta', 0)$ *with* $\Delta' \leftarrow \mathbb{F}_2^{k-2}$ *be a secret value, then, assuming that DLPN is hard, the XOF-Based Two-Key LPN Encryption scheme (c.f. Definition 6) is LIN-RK-KDM$^\sigma$ secure, i.e.* $\mathsf{Real}_\Delta^\sigma \stackrel{c}{\equiv} \mathsf{Fake}_\Delta^\sigma$.

*Proof.* For the proof of this result, see the full version. $\qquad\square$

---

**The security game GarbleANDSec**

This is a game between a challenger and an adversary. The challenger has access to the oracles $\mathsf{Fake}_\Delta^\sigma$ or $\mathsf{Real}_\Delta^\sigma$, which we denote by $\mathcal{O}$,

1. The challenger picks three bits $\epsilon_u, \epsilon_v, \epsilon_w \in \{0,1\}$, three keys $\mathbf{k}_{u,\epsilon_u}, \mathbf{k}_{v,\epsilon_v}, \mathbf{k}_{w,\epsilon_w} \in \mathbb{F}_2^k$, a nonce $g$ and $b_u, b_v \in \{0,1\}$.
2. The challenger sets $b_w \leftarrow b_u \cdot b_v$ and $\lambda_t \leftarrow b_t \oplus \epsilon_t, t \in \{u,v,w\}$.
3. The challenger sets $\mathbf{k} \leftarrow \mathbf{k}_{u,\epsilon_u} \oplus \sigma(\mathbf{k}_{v,\epsilon_v})$.
4. The challenger computes the ciphertext

$$\mathsf{ct}_{\epsilon_u,\epsilon_v} \leftarrow \mathsf{Enc}_\tau (\ (\Psi(\mathbf{k}_{w,\epsilon_w}, \epsilon_w), (g\|\epsilon_u\|\epsilon_v)), (\mathbf{k}_{u,\epsilon_u}, \mathbf{k}_{v,\epsilon_v})\ )$$

5. For $\alpha, \beta \in \{0,1\}, (\alpha, \beta) \neq (\epsilon_u, \epsilon_v)$ set

$$\ell_{\alpha,\beta} = (\lambda_u \oplus \alpha) \cdot (\lambda_v \oplus \beta) \oplus b_w.$$

6. The challenger computes, for $(\alpha, \beta) \neq (\epsilon_u, \epsilon_v)$ the three remaining ciphertexts:

$$\mathsf{ct}_{\alpha,\beta} \leftarrow \mathcal{O}(\ \mathbf{k}, \ \epsilon_u \oplus \alpha, \ \epsilon_v \oplus \beta, \ \Psi(\mathbf{k}_{w,\epsilon_w}, \ \epsilon_w), \ \ell_{\alpha,\beta}, \ (g\|\alpha\|\beta)\ )$$

7. The ciphertexts $(\mathsf{ct}_{0,0}, \mathsf{ct}_{1,0}, \mathsf{ct}_{0,1}, \mathsf{ct}_{1,1})$ along with the keys values, $(\mathbf{k}_{u,\epsilon_u}, \epsilon_u)$ and $(\mathbf{k}_{v,\epsilon_v}, \epsilon_v)$, are returned to the adversary.
8. The adversary goal is to determine which oracle the challenger is using.

---

**Fig. 2.** The security game GarbleANDSec

We end this section by showing, *intuitively*, why the garbling method using our (XOF-Based) Two-Key LPN Encryption is secure. Consider the garbling game in Fig. 2, which models an adversary that is trying to learn something about a garbled AND gate, given only the pair of keys and external values for the active path. From our previous discussion, if the LIN-RK-KDM$^\sigma$ problem is hard then the adversary is clearly unable to win this game. We remark that this game just provides the intuition around the security of our garbling protocols, which will not explicitly use it in their respective proofs.

## 4   MPC from Fully Authenticated LPN-Garbling

We use the garbling technique introduced in the previous section to describe our first protocol. As we said before, we evaluate the entire garbled circuit using a generic, actively secure MPC protocol.

In particular, given a secret shared key $[\mathbf{k}]$, message $[\mathbf{m}]$, and noise vector $[\mathbf{e}]$ (obtained by calling GenBit() and Mult in $\mathcal{F}_{\mathsf{MPC}}^{\mathsf{Auth}}$), the parties can compute a secret shared ciphertext $(C, [\mathbf{c}])$, where $C$ is in the clear, using a double-key encryption scheme $\mathcal{E}_\tau^{\mathsf{XOF}}$ as described in Definition 6. Since both the generation and opening of the garbled circuit are done using an active secure MPC system, the reconstructed garbled circuit is guaranteed to be correct and thus there is no need for any consistency checks during the evaluation phase. The downside of

---

**Protocol $\Pi_{\mathsf{Garble}}$**

Let $\mathcal{E}_\tau^{\mathsf{XOF}} = \{\mathsf{KeyGen}_\tau, \mathsf{Enc}_\tau, \mathsf{Dec}_\tau\}$ be a XOF-based two-key LPN encryption scheme, where $\tau$ is a parameter of the scheme. Let $\mathcal{K} = \mathbb{F}_2^k$.

**Garbling:**

1. Each $P_i$ samples $\Delta^i \leftarrow \mathbb{F}_2^{k-2}$ and calls $\mathcal{F}_{\mathsf{MPC}}^{\mathsf{Auth}}$ to compute $[\Delta^i] \leftarrow \mathsf{Input}(P_i)$.
2. Set $[\Delta] \leftarrow (1, \mathbf{0}) \oplus \bigoplus_{i \in [n]} (0, [\Delta^i], 0)$.
3. For every input wire $w \in W_{\mathsf{in}}$ and output wire of an AND gate, parties do:
   - Call $\mathcal{F}_{\mathsf{MPC}}^{\mathsf{Auth}}$ obtaining a shared random bit $[\lambda_w] \leftarrow \mathsf{GenBit}()$.
   - Each $P_i$ samples $\mathbf{k}_{w,0}^i \leftarrow \mathcal{K}$ and call $\mathcal{F}_{\mathsf{MPC}}^{\mathsf{Auth}}$ on $[\mathbf{k}_{w,0}^i] \leftarrow \mathsf{Input}(P_i)$.
   - Set $[\mathbf{k}_{w,0}] \leftarrow \bigoplus_{i \in [n]} [\mathbf{k}_{w,0}^i]$ and $[\mathbf{k}_{w,1}] \leftarrow [\mathbf{k}_{w,0}] \oplus [\Delta]$.
4. For every wire $w$ in the circuit which is the output of a XOR gate:
   - Parties compute the mask on the output wire $[\lambda_w] \leftarrow [\lambda_u] \oplus [\lambda_v]$.
   - Parties compute $[\mathbf{k}_{w,0}] \leftarrow [\mathbf{k}_{v,0}] \oplus [\mathbf{k}_{v,0}]$ and set $[\mathbf{k}_{w,1}] \leftarrow [\mathbf{k}_{w,0}] \oplus [\Delta]$
5. For every wire $w$ in the circuit which is the output of an AND gate and for $\alpha, \beta \in \{0, 1\}$, parties call $\mathcal{F}_{\mathsf{MPC}}^{\mathsf{Auth}}$ to compute
   - (a) $[\epsilon_{w,\alpha,\beta}] \leftarrow ([\lambda_u] \oplus \alpha) \cdot ([\lambda_v] \oplus \beta) \oplus [\lambda_w]$.
   - (b) $[\mathbf{k}_{w,\alpha,\beta}] \leftarrow [\mathbf{k}_{w,0}] \oplus ([\Delta] \cdot [\epsilon_{w,\alpha,\beta}])$.
   - (c) The encryption $(C^{w,\alpha,\beta}, [\mathbf{c}^{w,\alpha,\beta}])$, given by

$$\mathsf{Enc}_\tau \ ( \ \Psi([\mathbf{k}_{w,\alpha,\beta}], [\epsilon_{w,\alpha,\beta}]), \ (g\|\alpha\|\beta) \ ), \ ([\mathbf{k}_{u,\alpha}], [\mathbf{k}_{v,\beta}]) \ ,$$

     where $g$ is a unique gate identifier.
   - (d) Parties call $\mathcal{F}_{\mathsf{MPC}}^{\mathsf{Auth}}$ to open the values $\lambda_w \leftarrow \mathsf{Output}([\lambda_w], P_i)$ corresponding to party $P_i$'s output values.

**Open Garbling:**

1. Parties call $\mathcal{F}_{\mathsf{MPC}}^{\mathsf{Auth}}$ to open $\mathbf{c}^{w,\alpha,\beta} \leftarrow \mathsf{Open}([\mathbf{c}^{w,\alpha,\beta}]), \alpha, \beta \in \{0, 1\}$.
2. Set the garbled gates to be $\tilde{g}_{w,\alpha,\beta} = (C^{w,\alpha,\beta}, \mathbf{c}^{w,\alpha,\beta})$ for $\alpha, \beta \in \{0, 1\}$.

---

**Fig. 3.** The protocol for authenticated garbling $\Pi_{\mathsf{Garble}}$

this simple approach is that the amount of multiplications required to produce noise vectors $[\mathbf{e}]$ with the right distribution could be prohibitively high in some scenarios.

## 4.1 Garbling

Our garble protocol $\Pi_{\mathsf{Garble}}$, is described in Fig. 3. First, the parties produce, in an actively-secure way, shares of the global key $[\Delta]$, the wire labels $[\mathbf{k}_{0,w}^i], [\mathbf{k}_{1,w}^i]$ and the wire masks $[\lambda_w]$ for the garbled circuit using $\mathcal{F}_{\mathsf{MPC}}^{\mathsf{Auth}}$. Then, for each AND gate $g$ with input wires $u, v$ and output wire $w$, and for each $\alpha, \beta \in \{0, 1\}$, the parties compute authenticated additive sharing of the values

$$[\epsilon_{w,\alpha,\beta}] \leftarrow ([\lambda_u] \oplus \alpha) \cdot ([\lambda_v] \oplus \beta) \oplus [\lambda_w].$$

Thus the garbled gate for each AND gate is obtained by calling $\mathcal{F}_{\mathsf{MPC}}^{\mathsf{Auth}}$ to evaluate the following encryptions

$$(C^{w,\alpha,\beta}, [\mathbf{c}^{w,\alpha,\beta}]) = \mathsf{Enc}_\tau^{\mathsf{XOF}}\Big( \; ( \Psi([\mathbf{k}_{w,\alpha,\beta}], [\epsilon_{w,\alpha,\beta}]), \; (g\|\alpha\|\beta) \;), \; ([\mathbf{k}_{u,\alpha}], [\mathbf{k}_{v,\beta}]) \; \Big)$$

where $\alpha, \beta \in \{0,1\}$, $g$ is a unique gate identifier and $\mathbf{k}_{w,\alpha,\beta} = k_{w,0} \oplus \epsilon_{w,\alpha,\beta} \cdot \Delta$. Finally, parties open the masks for all the output wires of the circuit, so that they will be able to recover the output at the end of the evaluation phase.

When the garbled circuit is opened, using $\mathcal{F}_{\mathsf{MPC}}^{\mathsf{Auth}}$, the parties reconstruct the four values $(C^{w,\alpha,\beta}, \mathbf{c}^{w,\alpha,\beta})$, $\alpha, \beta \in \{0,1\}$, and set these to be the garbled gates $\tilde{g}_{\alpha,\beta}$. Note that the first component $C^{w,\alpha,\beta}$ of the ciphertexts in the garbled gates does not need to be stored, as it can be generated on the fly by applying the XOF to the relevant nonce $= (g\|\alpha\|\beta)$.

In order to see how the garbling is correct, note that the output of the AND gate is exactly the value $(\lambda_u \oplus \alpha) \cdot (\lambda_v \oplus \beta)$. Hence, assuming $\lambda_w = 0$, we have two cases: if $(\lambda_u \oplus \alpha) \cdot (\lambda_v \oplus \beta) = 0$, then $\epsilon_{w,\alpha,\beta} = 0$ and $k_{w,\alpha,\beta} = k_{w,0}$; otherwise $\epsilon_{w,\alpha,\beta} = 1$ and $k_{w,\alpha,\beta} = k_{w,0} \oplus \Delta$. The result is reversed if $\lambda_w = 1$. In more formality, we state the following theorem. It has a relatively standard proof, which follows the pattern of previous works on $n$-party garbling, and can be found in the full version.

**Theorem 3.** *Let $\mathcal{E}_\tau^{\mathsf{XOF}}$ be a XOF-based two-key LPN encryption scheme with parameter $\tau$. The protocol $\Pi_{\mathsf{Garble}}$, given in Fig. 3, UC-securely computes the functionality $\mathcal{F}_{\mathsf{Preprocessing}}$ (see the full version) in the presence of a static, active adversary corrupting up to $n - 1$ parties in the $\mathcal{F}_{\mathsf{MPC}}^{\mathsf{Auth}}$-hybrid model.*

### 4.2   Evaluation

The protocol $\Pi_{\mathsf{Evaluate}}$, given in the full version, describes how parties evaluate the garbled circuit. This protocol is very similar to that of HSS, where everyone evaluates the garbled circuit obtained in the preprocessing phase by broadcasting their inputs XORed with the corresponding wire mask. The main difference with HSS is that, as there is a single output key $\mathbf{k}_{w,\epsilon_w}$ for every wire, rather than one such key per party, parties need to explicitly obtain the masked wire value $\epsilon_w$ when decrypting $\tilde{g}_{\epsilon_u,\epsilon_v}$. Once the whole circuit has been evaluated, making use of the output wire masks they obtained at the preprocessing stage, parties can unmask their corresponding outputs and learn their intended result.

It is important to note that, unlike in HSS and due to the active security of the base MPC system, all among the garbled circuit, input keys $\mathbf{k}_{w,\epsilon_w}$ and masked inputs $\epsilon_w$ are guaranteed to be correct. Since the rest of this phase is purely local computation, this essentially ensures the output is correct. The security of the protocol, provided by the following theorem, follows from adapting the proof of our more complex unauthenticated garbling protocol in Sect. 5. In other words, the proof of Theorem 4 is just a specialised version of the proof of Theorem 6.

**Theorem 4.** *Let $f$ be an n-party functionality and $\mathcal{E}_\tau^{\mathsf{XOF}}$ a XOF-based two-key LPN encryption scheme with parameter $\tau$. The protocol $\Pi_{\mathsf{Evaluate}}$ UC-securely* *computes f in the presence of a static, active adversary corrupting up to $n-1$ parties in the $\{\mathcal{F}_{\mathsf{MPC}}, \mathcal{F}_{\mathsf{Preprocessing}}\}$-hybrid model.*

# 5 MPC from Unauthenticated LPN-Garbling

Whilst the protocol described in the previous section is intuitive and achieves our goals for the evaluation phase, the usage of an authenticated garbling functionality incurs a larger number of oblivious operations in the preprocessing phase. In this section, we turn to use an unauthenticated preprocessing functionality, in the style of HSS, in order to improve the efficiency of this phase. Our unauthenticated garbling protocol makes clever use of the homomorphic properties of the LPN encryption scheme. This turns out to be especially efficient when a large proportion of parties are assumed to be honest. Our protocols and functionalities in this section are parametrised by a value $c \in \mathbb{R}$ that represents the proportion $1/c$ of parties that are assumed honest. In other words, our protocols will have $n/c$ honest parties, with $1 < c \leq n$. Note that when $2 \leq c$, we obtain a protocol which is secure against a dishonest majority, and by setting $c = n$ we would go back to the case of a full-threshold adversary. As expected, the value of $c$ greatly affects the performances of our construction. We remark that allowing the possibility of having more than a single honest party is a highly reasonable assumption in a large scale setting.

## 5.1 Garbling

In this section we describe how to implement the $\mathcal{F}_{\mathsf{Preprocessing}}^{n/c}$ functionality given in the full version. As this is a weaker functionality which allows the adversary to introduce additive errors in the garbled circuit, our implementing protocol will not need to produce the LPN ciphertexts and keys using a fully active implementation of $\mathcal{F}_{\mathsf{MPC}}$ as we did in Sect. 4.

The main idea of our unauthenticated garbling protocol is to use the homomorphic property of the LPN encryption scheme, i.e., abusing notation,

$$\Sigma_{i=1}^{n}\mathsf{Enc}_{\tau}^{\mathsf{XOF}}((\mathbf{m}^i, \mathsf{nonce}), \mathbf{s}^i) = \mathsf{Enc}_{\tau'}^{\mathsf{XOF}}((\Sigma_{i=1}^{n}\mathbf{m}^i, \mathsf{nonce}), \Sigma_{i=1}^{n}\mathbf{s}^i). \qquad (6)$$

However, note that the Bernoulli distribution resulting from the sum has parameter $\tau' > \tau$. Additionally, even given only the sum of the encryptions, the adversary can use the above homomorphic property to "remove" his own encryptions and remain with only the sum of the honest parties' encryptions. Thus, the sum of the honest parties' encryptions must still be secure.

We thus proceed as follows: we let each party locally generate a 'weak' LPN encryption for the garbled gates. The garbled gates are computed by summing these 'weak' encryptions. The 'weak' ciphertexts are never seen by the adversary, as the parties compute their sum using additive secret-sharing. Intuitively, if the adversary cannot learn any information on the keys and messages from the sum, then this gives the adversary the possibility of (only) an additive attack. Hence,

---

### Protocol $\Pi_{\mathsf{Garble}}^{n/c}$

Let $\mathcal{E}_\tau^{\mathsf{XOF}} = \{\mathsf{KeyGen}_\tau, \mathsf{Enc}_\tau, \mathsf{Dec}_\tau\}$ be a XOF-based two-key LPN encryption scheme, where $\tau$ is a parameter of the scheme. Let $\mathcal{K} = \mathbb{F}_2^k$. Let $[x]$ and $\langle x \rangle$ denote respectively an authenticated and unauthenticated additive sharing of $x$.

**Garbling:**
1. Each $P_i$ generates a random value $\Delta^i \in \mathbb{F}_2^{k-2}$ and call $\langle \Delta^i \rangle \leftarrow \mathsf{Input}^P(P_i)$ of $\mathcal{F}_{\mathsf{MPC}}$.
2. Set $\langle \Delta \rangle \leftarrow (1, \mathbf{0}) \oplus_i (0, \langle \Delta^i \rangle, 0)$. [a]
3. For every wire $w$ in the circuit which is either an input wire or the output of an AND gate, parties do as follows:
   - Create a secret random bit $[\lambda_w] \leftarrow \mathsf{GenBit}()$.
   - Each $P_i$ generates a random $\mathbf{k}_{w,0}^i \in \mathcal{K}$ and calls $\langle \mathbf{k}_{w,0}^i \rangle \leftarrow \mathsf{Input}^P(P_i)$.
   - Set $\langle \mathbf{k}_{w,0} \rangle \leftarrow \oplus_i \langle \mathbf{k}_{w,0}^i \rangle$ and $\langle \mathbf{k}_{w,1} \rangle \leftarrow \langle \mathbf{k}_{w,0} \rangle \oplus \langle \Delta \rangle$.
4. For every wire $w$ in the circuit which is the output of a XOR gate (with input wires $u$ and $v$) parties locally set:
   - $[\lambda_w] \leftarrow [\lambda_u] \oplus [\lambda_v]$.
   - $\langle \mathbf{k}_{w,0} \rangle \leftarrow \langle \mathbf{k}_{u,0} \rangle \oplus \langle \mathbf{k}_{v,0} \rangle$ and $\langle \mathbf{k}_{w,1} \rangle \leftarrow \langle \mathbf{k}_{w,0} \rangle \oplus \langle \Delta \rangle$.
5. For every wire $w$ in the circuit which is the output of an AND gate $g$ (with input wires $u$ and $v$), for $\alpha, \beta \in \{0,1\}$,
   (a) Parties call $\mathcal{F}_{\mathsf{MPC}}$ to compute $[\epsilon_{w,\alpha,\beta}] \leftarrow ([\lambda_u] \oplus \alpha) \cdot ([\lambda_v] \oplus \beta) \oplus [\lambda_w]$.
   (b) Parties call the command $\langle \epsilon_{w,\alpha,\beta} \cdot \Delta \rangle \leftarrow \mathsf{Bit} \times \mathsf{String}_{\langle \Delta \rangle}([\epsilon_{w,\alpha,\beta}])$. [a]
   (c) Parties locally compute $\langle \mathbf{k}_{w,\alpha,\beta} \rangle \leftarrow \langle \mathbf{k}_{w,0} \rangle \oplus \langle \epsilon_{w,\alpha,\beta} \cdot \Delta \rangle$.
   (d) Each party $P_i$ computes the encryptions $(C^{w,\alpha,\beta}, \mathbf{c}^{i,w,\alpha,\beta})$ given by

   $$\mathsf{Enc}_{\tau_e} \ (\ \Psi(\mathbf{k}_{w,\alpha,\beta}^i, \epsilon_{w,\alpha,\beta}^i), \ (g\|\alpha\|\beta)\ ), \ (\mathbf{k}_{u,\alpha}^i, \mathbf{k}_{v,\beta}^i)$$

   where $g$ is a unique gate identifier.
   (e) For every output gate $g$ associated to a set of parties $\hat{\mathcal{P}} \subseteq \mathcal{P}$, with input wire $u$ and output wire $w$, perform the following steps
   - Set $[\lambda_w] \leftarrow [\lambda_u]$.
   - For $\alpha \in \{0,1\}$, each $P_i \in \hat{\mathcal{P}}$ generates two random values $\xi_{w,\alpha}^i \in \{0,1\}^s$ and shares them as $\langle \xi_{w,\alpha}^i \rangle \leftarrow \mathsf{Input}^P(P_i)$.
   - For $\alpha \in \{0,1\}$ use the trick from step 5d above to construct the garbled row $\tilde{g}_\alpha = (C^{w,\alpha}, \mathbf{c}^{w,\alpha})$ corresponding to the encryption

   $$\mathsf{Enc}_{\tau_d} \ (\ (\xi_{w,\alpha}^{i_1}\|\ldots\|\xi_{w,\alpha}^{i_{|\hat{\mathcal{P}}|}}), \ (g\|\alpha\|0)\ ), \ (\mathbf{k}_{u,\alpha}, \mathbf{0})$$

6. Reveal to each $P_i$ their input and output wire masks: $\lambda_w \leftarrow \mathsf{Output}([\lambda_w], P_i), w \in W_{\mathsf{in}_i} \cup W_{\mathsf{out}_i}$.

**Open Garbling:**
1. Each $P_i$ calls $\langle \mathbf{c}^{i,w,\alpha,\beta} \rangle \leftarrow \mathsf{Input}^P(P_i)$. All parties then computes $\langle \mathbf{c}^{w,\alpha,\beta} \rangle = \oplus_{i \in [n]} \langle \mathbf{c}^{i,w,\alpha,\beta} \rangle$ and reveal the result (using $\ell$ calls to $\mathsf{Open}^P$) so that each party obtains the ciphertext $(C^{w,\alpha,\beta}, \mathbf{c}^{w,\alpha,\beta})$
2. The garbled gate is $\tilde{g}_{w,\alpha,\beta} = (C^{w,\alpha,\beta}, \mathbf{c}^{w,\alpha,\beta})$ for $\alpha, \beta \in \{0,1\}$.
3. Similarly, in output gates, for $\alpha \in \{0,1\}$ use the trick from step 1 in **Open Garbling** to reconstruct $\tilde{g}_{w,\alpha} = (C^{w,\alpha}, \mathbf{c}^{w,\alpha})$

---

[a] See Remark 1

---

**Fig. 4.** The protocol for unauthenticated garbling, with $n/c$ honest parties

this scheme works as long as the sum of $n$ 'weak' encryptions is decryptable and the sum of $n/c$ 'weak' encryptions is secure.

We now look at how to achieve these requirements. We introduce $\tau_s$ to denote the parameter of the Bernoulli distribution that we want the sum of any $n/c$ ciphertexts to achieve. For the local, weak encryptions, honest parties will use a parameter $\tau_e$. Lastly, the sum of all $n$ ciphertexts will have a Bernouilli distribution with a parameter that we will denote $\tau_d$. Below we analyse the relationship between the three $\tau$ parameters and give an example of how to select them in practice. Our analysis makes use of the following lemma [31].

**Lemma 2 (Piling Up Lemma).** *Let $X$ be binary random variable which is equal to one with probability $p = 1/2 - \epsilon$, where $\epsilon$ is the bias approximation, then we have*

$$\Pr[x_1 + \cdots + x_n = 1 : x_i \leftarrow X] = \frac{1}{2} - 2^{n-1} \cdot \epsilon^n.$$

Recall we have $n$ parties of which $n/c$ are honest, and in our garbling protocol each honest party will generate an LPN ciphertext with $\tau$ equal to $\tau_e$, with the adversary producing a ciphertext in any way it chooses. These ciphertexts are then secret shared, and the sum of all the $n$ ciphertexts is then released.

As explained, the adversary can determine the sum of the $n/c$ ciphertexts produced by the honest parties. These sum to a ciphertext whose underlying $\tau$ value, $\tau_s$, can be evaluated by the Piling Up Lemma. Thus, we have

$$\tau_s = \frac{1}{2} - 2^{n/c-1} \cdot \left(\frac{1}{2} - \tau_e\right)^{n/c} = \frac{1}{2} \cdot \left(1 - (1 - 2 \cdot \tau_e)^{n/c}\right).$$

We also require that, if the adversarial parties follow the protocol, the resulting ciphertext sum can be decrypted correctly. In other words we need to set $\tau_d$ such that

$$\tau_d = \frac{1}{2} - 2^{n-1} \cdot \left(\frac{1}{2} - \tau_e\right)^{n} = \frac{1}{2} \cdot (1 - (1 - 2 \cdot \tau_e)^{n}),$$

or

$$\tau_e = \frac{1}{2} \cdot \left(1 - (1 - 2 \cdot \tau_d)^{1/n}\right).$$

Note that this gives us

$$\tau_s = \frac{1}{2} \cdot \left(1 - \left(1 - 2 \cdot \left(\frac{1}{2} \cdot \left(1 - (1 - 2 \cdot \tau_d)^{1/n}\right)\right)\right)^{n/c}\right)$$

$$= \frac{1}{2} \cdot \left(1 - \left((1 - 2 \cdot \tau_d)^{1/n}\right)^{n/c}\right) = \frac{1}{2} \cdot \left(1 - (1 - 2 \cdot \tau_d)^{1/c}\right).$$

Therefore, we have proved the following fact.

**Lemma 3.** *Let $\tau_s, \tau_e, \tau_d$ be LPN parameters, as described above. For fixed $\tau_d$ the value of $\tau_s$ does not depend on the number of parties, but only on the proportion $c$ which is honest.*

Starting with a $\tau_d$, a desired security parameter sec and a proportion $c$, we can derive the LPN parameters $k$, $\tau_s$ and $\tau_e$. First, using $\tau_d$ and $c$, it is possible to derive $\tau_s$. Then, given sec and $\tau_s$, we can compute $k$ using Eq. (3). Finally, $\tau_e$, that parties use for encryption, is derived from $\tau_s$ and the number of parties $n$. For example, if we take $\tau_d = 1/8$ and a proportion of 20% honest parties, i.e. $c = 5$, then we find that $\tau_s = 0.02796$. For sec $= 128$ this implies we need to select $k = 3129$. For $n = 100$ parties we then have that the honest parties need to encrypt with parameter $\tau_e = 0.001436$. For more example for sec $= \{128, 256\}$ see the full version.

Using the above observations we define, in Fig. 4, the garbling protocol when $n/c$ parties are honest. Our protocol makes use of an operation, which allows us to compute an unauthenticated sharing of $\langle x \cdot \Delta \rangle$ given an authenticated sharing of a bit $[x]$, where $\Delta \in \{0,1\}^k$ is a global shared value. We denote this operation by

$$\langle x \cdot \Delta \rangle \leftarrow \mathsf{Bit} \times \mathsf{String}_{\langle \Delta \rangle}([x]).$$

We could naïvely implement this operation using Tiny-OT, but this would be highly inefficient since $\Delta \in \mathbb{F}_2^k$ and $k$ is very large as it is the dimension of the secret key space $\mathcal{K}$ of the underlying LPN encryption scheme. For this reason, in the full version, we show a more efficient bit-string multiplication protocol, that is still based on Tiny-OT. The new protocol requires that $n/c \geq s$, where $s$ is the statistical security parameter. Since $c$ is a constant, this requirement holds for sufficiently large $n$.[3]

*Remark 1.* Note that the way that the Bit $\times$ String operation is described in the full version, the shares of $\Delta$ are chosen inside the Bit $\times$ String protocol. However, this would make the unauthenticated garbling protocol description in Fig. 4 cumbersome. To simplify the presentation, we let the parties choose their shares of $\Delta$ at the beginning of the unauthenticated garbling protocol; this is possible since the $\Delta$ shares are used only locally before the Bit $\times$ String operation.

Compared with the evaluation phase of [22], we cannot rely on individual pairs of keys, $\mathbf{k}_{w,0}^i, \mathbf{k}_{w,1}^i$, in order to let a party $P_i$ decide whether to abort or not in the presence of errors in the garbled circuit. This is because only the sums of individual keys, $\mathbf{k}_{w,0}, \mathbf{k}_{w,1}$ are revealed, and these need to be hidden from all parties. Instead, we perform a check in the output gates as follows: given a set of parties $\hat{\mathcal{P}} \subseteq \mathcal{P}$ who receive an output of $C_f$ on wire $w$, a garbled output gate $g$, with input wire $u$ and output wire $w$, consists of the two following entries (one for each $\alpha \in \{0,1\}$):

$$g_\alpha \leftarrow \mathsf{Enc}_\tau^{\mathsf{XOF}} \Big( \big( (\xi_{w,\alpha}^{i_1} \| \cdots \| \xi_{w,\alpha}^{i_{|\hat{\mathcal{P}}|}}), (g\|\alpha\|0) \big), (\mathbf{k}_{u,\alpha}, \mathbf{0}) \Big)$$

where $\xi_{w,\alpha}^i \in \{0,1\}^s$ is a secret random value chosen by party $P_i$.[4]

---

[3] If the requirement does not hold, then this operation needs to be done using Tiny-OT directly as in [22]. Hence, this optimization is mainly for large-scale MPC.

[4] For simplicity, we assume the message space is at least $|\hat{\mathcal{P}}| \cdot s$ bits long. If the message space was only of $|\hat{\mathcal{P}}| \cdot s/r$ bits, one would compute $r$ ciphertext, each of them with the $\xi^i$ values of $|\hat{\mathcal{P}}|/r$ parties.

The security of our garbling protocol is then given by the following theorem, the proof of which is given in the full version.

**Theorem 5.** *Let $\mathcal{E}_\tau^{\mathsf{XOF}}$ be a XOF-based two-key LPN encryption scheme with parameter $\tau$. Let $\mathcal{F}_{\mathsf{BS}}$ be implemented by the* Bit × String *operation. The protocol $\Pi_{\mathsf{Garble}}^{n/c}$ described in Fig. 4 UC-securely computes $\mathcal{F}_{\mathsf{Preprocessing}}^{n/c}$ in the presence of a static, active adversary corrupting up to $(c-1)\cdot n/c$ parties in the $\{\mathcal{F}_{\mathsf{MPC}}, \mathcal{F}_{\mathsf{BS}}\}$-hybrid model, provided $n/c > s$ (where $s$ is the statistical security parameter).*

*Remark 2.* By implementing the Bit × String operation in the naïve way, using TinyOT as in [22], we could prove Theorem 5 in the $\{\mathcal{F}_{\mathsf{MPC}}, \mathcal{F}_{\mathsf{TinyOT}}\}$-hybrid model, without the $n/c > s$ requirement.

## 5.2   Evaluation

The evaluation procedure is given in the full version. This involves no operations with respect to the MPC functionality, but it requires two rounds of broadcast. The security of our evaluation protocol is given by the following theorem, the proof of which is given in the full version.

**Theorem 6.** *Let $f$ be an n-party functionality and $\mathcal{E}_\tau^{\mathsf{XOF}}$ a XOF-based two-key LPN encryption scheme with parameter $\tau$. The protocol $\Pi_{\mathsf{Evaluate}}^{n/c}$ UC-securely computes $f$ in the presence of a static, active adversary corrupting up to $(c - 1) \cdot n/c$ parties in the $\{\mathcal{F}_{\mathsf{MPC}}, \mathcal{F}_{\mathsf{Preprocessing}}^{n/c}\}$-hybrid model.*

Our proof follows the blueprint of the online proof of Hazay et al. [22]. More concretely, after the description of the simulator, we show that the adversary can succeed in introducing errors in the garbled circuit only with negligible probability, so ruling out this possibility we show that the ideal and real executions are indistinguishable trough a reduction to the LIN-RK-KDM$^\sigma$ security of the LPN-based encryption scheme $\mathcal{E}^{\mathsf{XOF}}$. Although the general idea of the proof is similar to [22], in our proof we need to take care of our new method of garbling AND gates, and prove that if the adversary introduces some errors such that the some value is not correct during the evaluation, then the final checks will fail with overwhelming probability.

# 6   Implementation and Experimental Results

To demonstrate the practicality of our design, we implemented the circuit evaluation step for both of our protocols, and tested them on a number of 'standard' test circuits, given in Table 1. For the preprocessing phase, we give an estimation of the communication complexity in the full version and compare it with the recent work of Yang et al. [40].

**Table 1.** Standard Test Circuits

| Circuit | No. ANDs | No. XORs | No. Invs |
|---|---|---|---|
| AES-128$(k, m)$ | 6400 | 28176 | 2087 |
| AES-192$(k, m)$ | 7168 | 32080 | 2317 |
| AES-256$(k, m)$ | 8832 | 39008 | 2826 |
| Keccak-f$(m)$ | 38400 | 115200 | 38486 |
| SHA-256-f$(H, f)$ | 22573 | 110644 | 1856 |
| SHA-512-f$(H, f)$ | 57947 | 286724 | 4946 |

The test circuits consisted of a combination of AND, XOR and INV gates. The SHA-256 and SHA-512 circuits implemented the compression function $f$ only for a single block message $m$. Further, we compare our results with existing work at the end of this section.

The hash function $H$ used to define our nonce-based LPN encryption function (Definition 6) is implemented using three variants. The first variant is based on the AES-KDF from NIST [35]. This is very fast but it is not indifferentiable from a random oracle, and thus not strictly a true XOF. The second variant is based on the SHA-3 based XOF derived from KMAC128 and KMAC256 given in [34]. The third variant is based on the Kangaroo-12 XOF from [8], which is also based on SHA-3 which provides 128-bits of security. For our two SHA-3 variants we used the library provided by the Keccak team https://keccak.team/. For the AES based KDF variant we used code using the Intel AES-NI instructions.

**Code Instantiation.** We use concatenated codes as our error correcting code. While they are not the fastest or offer the highest rate, we can easily calculate the exact failure probability, unlike the alternatives such as LDPC codes. This makes selecting a code according to the LPN parameters convenient. The concatenated codes we use has a Reed-Solomon outer code and a general linear inner code. The details of concatenated codes and their concrete instantiation is presented in the full version. We set the decoding failure probability to $2^{-s}$, and run experiments with $s = 40$ and 80. While finding the best error correcting code is not the goal of this work, we expect the performance to improve significantly when using a more efficient family of codes such as LDPC or quasi-cyclic LDPC.

**Online Implementation Results.** The expensive parts of the algorithms are the parts related to the evaluation of the garbled circuit; thus these were the parts of the algorithm we timed. Experiments were run on a Intel i7-7700K CPU 4.20 GHz machine with 32 GB of RAM.

For the authenticated garbling (resp. unauthenticated garbling) variant of our algorithm, we obtained the run-times presented in Table 2 (resp. Table 3) with decryption failure $s = 40$. For equivalent runtimes when $s = 80$ see the full version of the paper. In these tables the security level refers to the security of the

**Table 2.** Evaluation (in sec) of various circuits in the authenticated garbling case. Setting sec = 128 and $s = 40$, the LPN parameters are $(k, \mathsf{m}, \ell, \tau) = (664, 672, 7140, 1/8)$ and we use the error correcting given by $(L_o = [255, 84, 172], L_i = [28, 8, 15])$. For 256 bit security, the LPN parameters are $(k, \mathsf{m}, \ell, \tau) = (1328, 1332, 14819, 1/8)$ and the error correcting code is given by $(L_o = [511, 148, 364], L_i = [29, 9, 11])$. Details of these codes are given in the full version.

| Circuit | Execution Time (sec) | | | |
|---|---|---|---|---|
| | 128-bit Security | | | 256-bit Security |
| | AES-KDF | KMAC128 | Kangaroo | KMAC256 |
| AES-128$(k, m)$ | 1.72 | 6.64 | 4.04 | 35.4 |
| AES-192$(k, m)$ | 1.92 | 7.41 | 4.51 | 39.9 |
| AES-256$(k, m)$ | 2.35 | 9.13 | 5.58 | 48.9 |
| Keccak-f$(m)$ | 10.2 | 39.7 | 24.3 | 214 |
| SHA-256-f$(H, f)$ | 6.02 | 23.3 | 14.3 | 128 |
| SHA-512-f$(H, f)$ | 15.6 | 60.0 | 36.8 | 327 |

**Table 3.** Evaluation of various circuits in the unauthenticated garbling variant, using the AES-KDF, and $s = 40$. For the parameters for the LPN scheme, and the associated error correcting code we used those given in the full version.

| Circuit | Execution Time (s) | | | | | |
|---|---|---|---|---|---|---|
| | 128-bit Security | | | 256-bit Security | | |
| | $c = 2$ | $c = 5$ | $c = 10$ | $c = 2$ | $c = 5$ | $c = 10$ |
| AES-128$(k, m)$ | 10.5 | 50.4 | 77.5 | 16.9 | 80.2 | 538 |
| AES-192$(k, m)$ | 11.7 | 56.3 | 86.7 | 18.9 | 89.3 | 602 |
| AES-256$(k, m)$ | 14.4 | 69.1 | 106 | 23.4 | 110 | 742 |
| Keccak-f$(m)$ | 64.4 | 309 | 474 | 104 | 490 | 3333 |
| SHA-256-f$(H, f)$ | 36.7 | 176 | 271 | 59.5 | 284 | 1899 |
| SHA-512-f$(H, f)$ | 94.0 | 451 | 692 | 152 | 725 | 4848 |

underlying LPN function. Observe that the choice of the underlying method to generate the LPN matrix has a key effect on the performance of the system, with an AES based KDF being the most efficient. For the unauthenticated garbling variant, we only present runtimes using the efficient AES based KDF function. Concretely, when using AES-KDF, a majority (81%) of the CPU time is spent in decoding. When using KMAC128, the majority (84%) of the time is spent on KMAC128. Thus, the performance bottleneck varies with the choice of $H$.

We compare our scheme with some related work. In the authenticated garbling case, and the fastest implementation using an AES-KDF based for the function $H$, we obtain a throughput of roughly $266 \mu s$ per AND gate for $s = 40$. The experiments from [6], i.e. in the passive case, with no free-XOR, has a throughput of roughly 45 microseconds per *gate* (also with $s = 40$). Ignoring the fact we can perform free-XOR, this gives a cost of a factor of six for using our actively secure variant. However, this cost decreases when we look at typical circuits. For example the AES-128 circuit has $34,675$ AND and XOR gates, thus the protocol in [6] would take around 1.5 seconds, compared to our runtime of 1.72 seconds. Thus, the ability to cope with free-XOR means we only pay an extra 15% in performance for active security.

As a means of comparison with 'traditional' $n$-party garbled circuits via actively secure BMR with free-XOR, we extrapolated known run times of evaluating AES-128 using the HSS protocol. It would appear that our algorithm will provide a faster *evaluation* stage when the number of parties exceeds about 100 in the authenticated garbling case. This is confirmed by a comparison with [39] that reports an online running time of 2.3 s for AES with 128 parties in the WAN setting.

**Acknowledgements.** This work has been supported in part by ERC Advanced Grant ERC-2015-AdG-IMPaCT, by the Defense Advanced Research Projects Agency (DARPA) and Space and Naval Warfare Systems Center, Pacific (SSC Pacific) under contract No. N66001-15-C-4070, FA8750-19-C-0502 and HR001120C0085, by the Office of the Director of National Intelligence (ODNI), Intelligence Advanced Research Projects Activity (IARPA) via Contract No. 2019-1902070006, by the FWO under an Odysseus project GOH9718N, and by CyberSecurity Research Flanders with reference number VR20192203. Eduardo Soria-Vazquez was supported by the Carlsberg Foundation under the Semper Ardens Research Project CF18-112 (BCM). Aner Ben-Efraim and Eran Omri were supported by ISF grant 152/17, and by the Ariel Cyber Innovation Center in conjunction with the Israel National Cyber directorate in the Prime Minister's Office.

Any opinions, findings and conclusions or recommendations expressed in this material are those of the author(s) and do not necessarily reflect the views of any of the funders. The U.S. Government is authorized to reproduce and distribute reprints for governmental purposes notwithstanding any copyright annotation therein.

# References

1. Applebaum, B.: Garbling XOR gates "For Free" in the standard model. In: Sahai, A. (ed.) TCC 2013. LNCS, vol. 7785, pp. 162–181. Springer, Heidelberg (2013). https://doi.org/10.1007/978-3-642-36594-2_10
2. Applebaum, B., Harnik, D., Ishai, Y.: Semantic security under related-key attacks and applications. In: Chazelle, B. (ed.) ICS 2011, pp. 45–60. Tsinghua University Press, January 2011
3. Beaver, D., Micali, S., Rogaway, P.: The round complexity of secure protocols (extended abstract). In: 22nd ACM STOC, pp. 503–513. ACM Press, May 1990
4. Bellare, M., Kohno, T.: A theoretical treatment of related-key attacks: RKA-PRPs, RKA-PRFs, and applications. In: Biham, E. (ed.) EUROCRYPT 2003. LNCS, vol. 2656, pp. 491–506. Springer, Heidelberg (2003). https://doi.org/10.1007/3-540-39200-9_31
5. Ben-Efraim, A., Lindell, Y., Omri, E.: Optimizing semi-honest secure multiparty computation for the internet. In: Weippl, E.R., Katzenbeisser, S., Kruegel, C., Myers, A.C., Halevi, S. (eds.) ACM CCS 2016, pp. 578–590. ACM Press, October 2016

6. Ben-Efraim, A., Lindell, Y., Omri, E.: Efficient scalable constant-round MPC via garbled circuits. In: Takagi, T., Peyrin, T. (eds.) ASIACRYPT 2017, Part II. LNCS, vol. 10625, pp. 471–498. Springer, Cham (2017). https://doi.org/10.1007/978-3-319-70697-9_17

7. Ben-Or, M., Goldwasser, S., Wigderson, A.: Completeness theorems for non-cryptographic fault-tolerant distributed computation (extended abstract). In: 20th ACM STOC, pp. 1–10. ACM Press, May 1988

8. Bertoni, G., Daemen, J., Peeters, M., Van Assche, G., Van Keer, R., Viguier, B.: KANGAROOTWELVE: fast hashing based on KECCAK-p. In: Preneel, B., Vercauteren, F. (eds.) ACNS 2018. LNCS, vol. 10892, pp. 400–418. Springer, Cham (2018). https://doi.org/10.1007/978-3-319-93387-0_21

9. Black, J., Rogaway, P., Shrimpton, T.: Encryption-scheme security in the presence of key-dependent messages. In: Nyberg, K., Heys, H. (eds.) SAC 2002. LNCS, vol. 2595, pp. 62–75. Springer, Heidelberg (2003). https://doi.org/10.1007/3-540-36492-7_6

10. Blum, A., Furst, M., Kearns, M., Lipton, R.J.: Cryptographic primitives based on hard learning problems. In: Stinson, D.R. (ed.) CRYPTO 1993. LNCS, vol. 773, pp. 278–291. Springer, Heidelberg (1994). https://doi.org/10.1007/3-540-48329-2_24

11. Camenisch, J., Lysyanskaya, A.: An efficient system for non-transferable anonymous credentials with optional anonymity revocation. In: Pfitzmann, B. (ed.) EUROCRYPT 2001. LNCS, vol. 2045, pp. 93–118. Springer, Heidelberg (2001). https://doi.org/10.1007/3-540-44987-6_7

12. Canetti, R.: Universally composable security: a new paradigm for cryptographic protocols. In: 42nd FOCS, pp. 136–145. IEEE Computer Society Press, October 2001

13. Cramer, R., Damgård, I., Escudero, D., Scholl, P., Xing, C.: SPDZ$_{2^k}$: efficient MPC mod $2^k$ for dishonest majority. In: Shacham, H., Boldyreva, A. (eds.) CRYPTO 2018, Part II. LNCS, vol. 10992, pp. 769–798. Springer, Cham (2018). https://doi.org/10.1007/978-3-319-96881-0_26

14. Damgård, I., Nielsen, J.B.: Scalable and unconditionally secure multiparty computation. In: Menezes, A. (ed.) CRYPTO 2007. LNCS, vol. 4622, pp. 572–590. Springer, Heidelberg (2007). https://doi.org/10.1007/978-3-540-74143-5_32

15. Damgård, I., Pastro, V., Smart, N., Zakarias, S.: Multiparty computation from somewhat homomorphic encryption. In: Safavi-Naini, R., Canetti, R. (eds.) CRYPTO 2012. LNCS, vol. 7417, pp. 643–662. Springer, Heidelberg (2012). https://doi.org/10.1007/978-3-642-32009-5_38

16. Esser, A., Kübler, R., May, A.: LPN decoded. In: Katz, J., Shacham, H. (eds.) CRYPTO 2017, Part II. LNCS, vol. 10402, pp. 486–514. Springer, Cham (2017). https://doi.org/10.1007/978-3-319-63715-0_17

17. Frederiksen, T.K., Keller, M., Orsini, E., Scholl, P.: A unified approach to MPC with preprocessing using OT. In: Iwata, T., Cheon, J.H. (eds.) ASIACRYPT 2015, Part I. LNCS, vol. 9452, pp. 711–735. Springer, Heidelberg (2015). https://doi.org/10.1007/978-3-662-48797-6_29

18. Goldreich, O., Krawczyk, H., Luby, M.: On the existence of pseudorandom generators. In: Goldwasser, S. (ed.) CRYPTO 1988. LNCS, vol. 403, pp. 146–162. Springer, New York (1990). https://doi.org/10.1007/0-387-34799-2_12

19. Goldreich, O., Micali, S., Wigderson, A.: How to play any mental game or A completeness theorem for protocols with honest majority. In: Aho, A. (ed.) 19th ACM STOC, pp. 218–229. ACM Press, May 1987

20. Hazay, C., Orsini, E., Scholl, P., Soria-Vazquez, E.: Concretely efficient large-scale MPC with active security (or, TinyKeys for TinyOT). In: Peyrin, T., Galbraith, S. (eds.) ASIACRYPT 2018, Part III. LNCS, vol. 11274, pp. 86–117. Springer, Cham (2018). https://doi.org/10.1007/978-3-030-03332-3_4

21. Hazay, C., Orsini, E., Scholl, P., Soria-Vazquez, E.: TinyKeys: a new approach to efficient multi-party computation. In: Shacham, H., Boldyreva, A. (eds.) CRYPTO 2018, Part III. LNCS, vol. 10993, pp. 3–33. Springer, Cham (2018). https://doi.org/10.1007/978-3-319-96878-0_1

22. Hazay, C., Scholl, P., Soria-Vazquez, E.: Low cost constant round MPC combining BMR and oblivious transfer. In: Takagi, T., Peyrin, T. (eds.) ASIACRYPT 2017, Part I. LNCS, vol. 10624, pp. 598–628. Springer, Cham (2017). https://doi.org/10.1007/978-3-319-70694-8_21

23. Ishai, Y., Kushilevitz, E.: Randomizing polynomials: a new representation with applications to round-efficient secure computation. In: 41st FOCS, pp. 294–304. IEEE Computer Society Press, November 2000

24. Ishai, Y., Kushilevitz, E.: Perfect constant-round secure computation via perfect randomizing polynomials. In: Widmayer, P., Eidenbenz, S., Triguero, F., Morales, R., Conejo, R., Hennessy, M. (eds.) ICALP 2002. LNCS, vol. 2380, pp. 244–256. Springer, Heidelberg (2002). https://doi.org/10.1007/3-540-45465-9_22

25. Keller, M., Orsini, E., Scholl, P.: MASCOT: faster malicious arithmetic secure computation with oblivious transfer. In: Weippl, E.R., Katzenbeisser, S., Kruegel, C., Myers, A.C., Halevi, S. (eds.) ACM CCS 2016, pp. 830–842. ACM Press, October 2016

26. Keller, M., Pastro, V., Rotaru, D.: Overdrive: making SPDZ great again. In: Nielsen, J.B., Rijmen, V. (eds.) EUROCRYPT 2018, Part III. LNCS, vol. 10822, pp. 158–189. Springer, Cham (2018). https://doi.org/10.1007/978-3-319-78372-7_6

27. Kolesnikov, V., Schneider, T.: Improved garbled circuit: free XOR gates and applications. In: Aceto, L., Damgård, I., Goldberg, L.A., Halldórsson, M.M., Ingólfsdóttir, A., Walukiewicz, I. (eds.) ICALP 2008, Part II. LNCS, vol. 5126, pp. 486–498. Springer, Heidelberg (2008). https://doi.org/10.1007/978-3-540-70583-3_40

28. Larraia, E., Orsini, E., Smart, N.P.: Dishonest majority multi-party computation for binary circuits. In: Garay, J.A., Gennaro, R. (eds.) CRYPTO 2014, Part II. LNCS, vol. 8617, pp. 495–512. Springer, Heidelberg (2014). https://doi.org/10.1007/978-3-662-44381-1_28

29. Lindell, Y., Pinkas, B., Smart, N.P., Yanai, A.: Efficient constant round multiparty computation combining BMR and SPDZ. In: Gennaro, R., Robshaw, M. (eds.) CRYPTO 2015, Part II. LNCS, vol. 9216, pp. 319–338. Springer, Heidelberg (2015). https://doi.org/10.1007/978-3-662-48000-7_16

30. Lindell, Y., Smart, N.P., Soria-Vazquez, E.: More efficient constant-round multiparty computation from BMR and SHE. In: Hirt, M., Smith, A. (eds.) TCC 2016, Part I. LNCS, vol. 9985, pp. 554–581. Springer, Heidelberg (2016). https://doi.org/10.1007/978-3-662-53641-4_21

31. Matsui, M.: Linear cryptanalysis method for DES cipher. In: Helleseth, T. (ed.) EUROCRYPT 1993. LNCS, vol. 765, pp. 386–397. Springer, Heidelberg (1994). https://doi.org/10.1007/3-540-48285-7_33

32. Maurer, U.: Indistinguishability of random systems. In: Knudsen, L.R. (ed.) EUROCRYPT 2002. LNCS, vol. 2332, pp. 110–132. Springer, Heidelberg (2002). https://doi.org/10.1007/3-540-46035-7_8

33. Nielsen, J.B., Nordholt, P.S., Orlandi, C., Burra, S.S.: A new approach to practical active-secure two-party computation. In: Safavi-Naini, R., Canetti, R. (eds.) CRYPTO 2012. LNCS, vol. 7417, pp. 681–700. Springer, Heidelberg (2012). https://doi.org/10.1007/978-3-642-32009-5_40

34. NIST National Institute for Standards and Technology: SHA-3 derived functions: cSHAKE, KMAC, TupleHash and ParallelHash (2016). http://nvlpubs.nist.gov/nistpubs/SpecialPublications/NIST.SP.800-185.pdf

35. NIST National Institute for Standards and Technology: Recommendation for key derivation through extraction- then-expansion rev.1 (2018). https://nvlpubs.nist.gov/nistpubs/Legacy/SP/nistspecialpublication800-56c.pdf

36. Orsini, E., Smart, N.P., Vercauteren, F.: Overdrive2k: efficient secure MPC over $\mathbb{Z}_{2^k}$ from somewhat homomorphic encryption. In: Jarecki, S. (ed.) CT-RSA 2020. LNCS, vol. 12006, pp. 254–283. Springer, Cham (2020). https://doi.org/10.1007/978-3-030-40186-3_12

37. Rabin, T., Ben-Or, M.: Verifiable secret sharing and multiparty protocols with honest majority (extended abstract). In: 21st ACM STOC, pp. 73–85. ACM Press, May 1989

38. Wang, X., Ranellucci, S., Katz, J.: Authenticated garbling and efficient maliciously secure two-party computation. In: Thuraisingham, B.M., Evans, D., Malkin, T., Xu, D. (eds.) ACM CCS 2017, pp. 21–37. ACM Press, October/November 2017

39. Wang, X., Ranellucci, S., Katz, J.: Global-scale secure multiparty computation. In: Thuraisingham, B.M., Evans, D., Malkin, T., Xu, D. (eds.) ACM CCS 2017, pp. 39–56. ACM Press, October/November 2017

40. Yang, K., Wang, X., Zhang, J.: More efficient MPC from improved triple generation and authenticated garbling. Cryptology ePrint Archive, Report 2019/1104 (2019). https://eprint.iacr.org/2019/1104

41. Yao, A.C.C.: How to generate and exchange secrets (extended abstract). In: 27th FOCS, pp. 162–167. IEEE Computer Society Press, October 1986

# Threshold Garbled Circuits and Ad Hoc Secure Computation

Michele Ciampi[1]([✉]), Vipul Goyal[2], and Rafail Ostrovsky[3]

[1] The University of Edinburgh, Edinburgh, UK
michele.ciampi@ed.ac.uk
[2] NTT Research and CMU, Pittsburgh, PA, USA
goyal@cs.cmu.edu
[3] UCLA Department of Computer Science and Department of Mathematics,
Los Angeles, CA, USA
rafail@cs.ucla.edu

**Abstract.** Garbled Circuits (GCs) represent fundamental and powerful tools in cryptography, and many variants of GCs have been considered since their introduction. An important property of the garbled circuits is that they can be evaluated securely if and only if exactly 1 key for each input wire is obtained: no less and no more. In this work we study the case when: 1) some of the wire-keys are missing, but we are still interested in computing the output of the garbled circuit and 2) the evaluator of the GC might have both keys for a constant number of wires. We start to study this question in terms of non-interactive multi-party computation (NIMPC) which is strongly connected with GCs. In this notion there is a fixed number of parties ($n$) that can get correlated information from a trusted setup. Then these parties can send an encoding of their input to an evaluator, which can compute the output of the function. Similarly to the notion of *ad hoc secure computation* proposed by Beimel et al. [ITCS 2016], we consider the case when less than $n$ parties participate in the online phase, and in addition we let these parties colluding with the evaluator. We refer to this notion as *Threshold NIMPC*.

In addition, we show that when the number of parties participating in the online phase is a fixed threshold $l \leq n$ then it is possible to securely evaluate any $l$-input function. We build our result on top of a new secret-sharing scheme (which can be of independent interest) and on the results proposed by Benhamouda, Krawczyk and Rabin [Crypto 2017]. Our protocol can be used to compute any function in $NC^1$ in the information-theoretic setting and any function in $P$ assuming one-way functions.

As a second (and main) contribution, we consider a slightly different notion of security in which the number of parties that can participate in the online phase is not specified, and can be any number $c$ above the threshold $l$ (in this case the evaluator cannot collude with the other parties). We solve an open question left open by Beimel, Ishai and Kushilevitz [Eurocrypt 2017] showing how to build a secure protocol for the case when $c$ is constant, under the Learning with Errors assumption.

A. Canteaut and F.-X. Standaert (Eds.): EUROCRYPT 2021, LNCS 12698, pp. 64–93, 2021.
https://doi.org/10.1007/978-3-030-77883-5_3

# 1   Introduction

Garbled Circuits (GCs) have played a central role in cryptography. The basic version of GCs has been shown to be useful for secure computation as well as various other areas in cryptography because of its non-interactive nature [4,13, 19,25–27]. Various GC variants with additional properties have also played an important role: e.g. GC with free-XOR [24], adaptive GC [18,20,21], information-theoretic GCs [23], covert-garbled circuit [11], and arithmetic GC [2]. Moreover, in general, a garbled circuit can be viewed as a randomized encoding which in turn has played an important role even beyond cryptography in complexity theory [1]. A key property of a garbled circuit is its "decomposability", i.e., different input wire keys can be computed independently based on the value on that wire (also referred to as decomposable randomized encodings). This for example allows to use a separate 1-out-of-2 Oblivious Transfer (OT) for each input wire. In various applications, this property has played an important role, like in building functional encryption from attribute based encryption [14], and in building Non-Interactive Multi-Party Computation (NIMPC) [6] where different parties hold input values corresponding to different input wires. An important property of the garbled circuits is that they can be evaluated securely if and only if exactly 1 key for each input wire is obtained: no less and no more. Moreover, if the evaluator of the garbled circuit has more than one keys (even for a single wire) the security of the garbled circuit is (in general) compromised.

In this work, we ask the following natural question: *what if 1) the keys corresponding to some of the input wires are missing and 2) more than one key for a subset of wires is leaked to the adversary?*

In particular, suppose that a function is well defined even if only a subset of the inputs are present (e.g., the function simply computes the majority, some aggregate statistics like the median or the sorting on the inputs). Furthermore, suppose we only have the wire keys exactly for say $l$ wires (less than the total number of wires $n$) and that more than one key for a constant number of wires can be leaked to the adversary. *Can we obtain a garbled circuit construction that still allows one to securely compute the function output in this case?*

Here $l$ can be seen as a parameter for the GC construction. This notion, besides being intriguing and interesting in its own right, can also be seen as having natural applications to NIMPC. In NIMPC we can distinguish three main phases: *setup, online* and *evaluation*. In this, various parties with inputs and auxiliary information obtained during the setup phase, can encode their inputs and send this encoding to an *evaluator* during an online phase. The evaluator can then compute the output of the function without further interaction with the other parties. Basic constructions of NIMPC readily follows from GC. That is, the setup generates a garbled circuit with $n$ input wires for the function that needs to be computed. Each party $p_i$ receives two wire keys (one for the input 0 and one for the input 1) for the $i$-th wire. During the online phase each party sends the wire key which corresponds to its input to the evaluator. The evaluator, which now has $n$ wire keys, can evaluate the garbled circuit and obtain the output. Frequently cited example applications of NIMPC are voting and auctions [6,9]. However, in the case of voting, it is conceivable that several voters might never show up. Can we obtain a system where if a threshold number of voter votes, the result can be obtained? One could also even consider "attribute-based voting" where your attributes determine whether or not you are eligible to vote. For example, in deciding a tenure case, only voters having the attributes of "full professor" and "computer science department" might be eligible. The number and identity of such voters may not necessarily be known at the time of the NIMPC setup (and only an upper-bound on the number of voters is known). Let $n$ be total number of parties, the question we study in this paper is the following:

*"Is it possible to obtain a construction of garbled circuits for a function having $n$ input wires s.t. if the wire keys corresponding of $l \leq n$ wires are available, then the output can be securely computed even if both the keys for a constant number of wires are leaked to the adversary?"*

A partial answer to the above question has been given in [7], where the authors show how to obtain such a NIMPC protocol under the assumption that the evaluator does not collude with any of the other parties. Another partial answer has been given in [9], where the authors show how to obtain a NIMPC protocol that tolerates a constant number of corruption only for the case where $l = n$, where $n$ is the total number of parties involved in the protocol. However, to the best of our knowledge, we are the first to study the combination of the two problems. In [7] the authors consider another interesting notion called $(l, k)$-*secure ad hoc private simultaneous messages (PSM)*. This notion is similar to the notion of NIMPC, with the difference that 1) the parties cannot collude with the evaluator and 2) any number $k$ of parties might participate in the online phase of the protocol, with $k \geq l$. Beimel et al. [7] proved that such a notion (for generic values of $l$ and $k$) would imply obfuscation[1], and left open the following question:

*"Is it possible to obtain $(l, l + c)$-secure ad hoc PSM protocol for a constant $c$?".*

## 1.1    Our Contributions

Our contribution lies in studying of the above questions, providing a formal definition, and obtaining various constructions. Our most basic result is the following:

**Theorem 1** (informal). *If there exists an $l$-party NIMPC protocol for the $l$-input function $f$ which tolerates up to $t$ corruptions, then there exists an $n$-party Threshold NIMPC protocol that tolerates up to $t$ corruptions that can securely evaluate $f$ when only $l$ of the $n$ parties participate in the online phase.*

This can also naturally be seen as a threshold garbled circuit where the message received by the evaluator during the setup phase corresponds to the garbled circuit, whereas the two messages corresponding to two different possibilities of

---

[1] The authors of [7] propose inefficient constructions for general functions.

the input (i.e., either 0 or 1) for party $p_i$ can be seen as the two possible wire-keys for the $i$-th input wire. Our construction also relies on a conceptual tool which we call *positional secret sharing (PoSS)*, which we instantiate information theoretically. Please see the technical overview for more details. We note that our construction, additionally, has the feature that it can handle up to a constant number of corruptions (assuming the input of each player is a single bit). We build upon the construction of Benhamouda et al. [9] with tolerates up to a constant number of corruptions. Informally, this means that the evaluator may be able to compute multiple outputs of the function by flipping the input of the corrupted parties (since the corrupted parties can generate an encoding of both the inputs 0 and 1). However, the evaluator learns no more than having access to an ideal functionality which allows for computing such multiple outputs. As noted in [9], a construction tolerating an arbitrary number of corruptions in this setting implies indistinguishability obfuscation (iO) [3]. Our second (and main) technical construction is a protocol that retains its security even if more than $l$ input wire keys are given to an evaluator. Going back to the example of voting, while one may have an estimate on how the voter turnout will be (e.g., based on historical data), it might be hard to know the exact number of voters in advance. If the actual number of voters turns out to be even $l + 1$ (as opposed to $l$), all security guarantees cease to exist and our previous construction may become entirely insecure. Towards that end, we ask the following question:

*"Is it possible to design construction of garbled circuits where if anywhere between $l$ and $l + c$ inputs wire keys are obtained, the function output can be securely computed?*

In other words: can we have an $(l, l + c)$-secure ad hoc PSM protocol? Note that in this setting, the evaluator can compute multiple outputs by selecting any $l$-sized subset of the received inputs. While ideally, we would like to have $l + c = n$ (for a generic $c$), such a construction necessarily implies iO and indeed, using iO, a construction where $l + c = n$ can be readily obtained (we recall that $n$ is the total number of parties). However, since our focus is on using standard falsifiable assumptions, we restrict our attention to the case where $c$ is a constant. In addition, our construction allows the input of each party to be a string of arbitrary size. Our main theorem is the following:

**Theorem 2** (informal). *If the LWEs assumption holds, then there exists an n-party $(l, l + c)$-secure ad hoc PSM protocol that can securely evaluate an l-input function f when N parties participate in the online phase with $N \leq l + c \leq n$ for a constant c.*

We stress that $N$ does not need to be known in the setup phase. The last notion that we consider in this paper is *adaptive-ad-hoc PSM*. This notion, in addition to the notion of ad hoc PSM, gives to the evaluator the possibility to evaluate an $N$-input function $f_N$, where $N$ is the number of parties that participate in the online phase, with $N \leq l + c \leq n$. This notion gives the same security guarantees as to the notion of $(l, l+c)$-secure ad hoc PSM, but it allows an honest evaluator to evaluate a function even if more than $l$ parties participate in the online phase. It should be easy to see that such a notion can be easily realized using multiple instantiations of an ad hoc PSM scheme. Even in this case, the input of each party can be a string of arbitrary (bounded) length.

## 2 Technical Overview

We start illustrating a new secret sharing scheme which is instrumental for our constructions. Then we show how to use such a secret sharing scheme to construct a threshold NIMPC and an $(l, k)$-Ad Hoc PSM protocol.

### 2.1 Positional Secret Sharing (PoSS)

We consider the setting where there is a dealer, $n$ non-colluding parties $\{p_1, \ldots .p_n\}$ and an evaluator. A PoSS scheme allows a dealer to compute a secret sharing of $l$ secrets $x_1, \ldots, x_l$ with respect to a party index $j$ and distribute these shares among the $n$ parties. Let $S = (s_1, \ldots, s_n)$ be the output shares computed by the dealer. Any subset of parties of size $l$ can send their shares to an evaluator, and if the $j$-th party has the $\alpha$-th greatest index among these $l$ parties, then the evaluator can reconstruct the $\alpha$-th secret. If the party $p_j$ does not send its share then none of the secrets can be reconstructed (the $j$-th share goes always to the party $p_j$). To construct such a scheme we use a standard $t$-out-of-$m$ secret sharing scheme. In more detail, the dealer computes 3-out-of-3 secret sharing of $x_i$ obtaining $x_i^0$, $\tilde{x}_i$ and $x_i^1$. Then computes 1) an $(i-1)$-out-of-$(j-1)$ secret sharing of $x_i^1$ thus obtaining the shares $s_{i,1}, \ldots, s_{i,j-1}$, 2) an $(l-i)$-out-of-$(n-j)$ secret sharing of $x_i^0$ obtaining $s_{i,j+1}, \ldots, s_{i,n}$ and 3) defines $s_{i,i} := \tilde{x}_i$. The output of the sharing algorithm corresponds to $(s_1, \ldots, s_n)$ with $s_i := (s_{1,i}, \ldots, s_{l,i})$ for each $i \in [n]$. Intuitively, if the evaluator receives the shares $S' = (s_{i_1}, \ldots, s_{i_l})$ with $0 \le i_1 < \cdots < i_l \le n$ where $j = i_\alpha$ for some $\alpha$, then she can reconstruct $x_\alpha^0$ using the shares $s_{i_1}, \ldots, s_{i_{\alpha-1}}$, $x_\alpha^1$ using the shares $s_{i_{\alpha+1}}, \ldots, s_{i_l}$ and $\tilde{x}_\alpha$, which corresponds to the share $s_{i_\alpha}$. Note that all the other secrets $x_j$ are protected since there are not enough shares to either reconstruct $x_k^0$ or $x_k^1$ for each $k \in [l] - \{\alpha\}$. In the case where there is no $i_\alpha$ with $\alpha = j$, then none of the secrets can be reconstructed since one share of the 3-out-of-3 secret sharing will be missing for each of the secrets.

### 2.2 Threshold NIMPC

Let $f$ be an $l$-input function. To obtain a Threshold NIMPC for $f$ that tolerates $t$ corruptions we use a PoSS scheme in combination with a *standard* NIMPC protocol that supports $t$ corruptions and that can be used to evaluate $l$-input functions. Let $p_1, \ldots, p_n$ be the parties that could participate an execution of the protocol (we recall that a threshold NIMPC is parametrized by $l$, which represents the maximum number of parties that can participate in the online phase). The idea is to pre-compute an encoding of the input 0 (that we denote with $m_j^0$) and of the input 1 (that we denote with $m_j^1$) for each input slot

$j \in [l]$ of the NIMPC scheme. Then we run two instantiations of a PoSS for each party $p_i$. The first instantiation of the PoSS scheme is run on input the secrets $m_1^0, \ldots, m_l^0$ (and the index $i$ of the party) whereas the second is run using the secrets $m_1^1, \ldots, m_l^1$ (and the index $i$ of the party). Let $(s_{i,1}^0, \ldots, s_{i,n}^0)$ be the output shares of the first instantiation of the PoSS scheme, and $(s_{i,1}^1, \ldots, s_{i,n}^1)$ be the output of the second instantiation for the party $p_i$. All these shares are then distributed among the $n$ parties. During the online phase each party $p_i$ acts as follows. If the input of $p_i$ is $b_i = 0$ then $p_i$ sends all the shares but the one related to the second instantiation of the PoSS scheme for the index $i$ (i.e., $p_i$ does not send $s_{i,i}^1$), if $b_i = 1$ then $p_i$ sends all the shares but the one related to the first instantiation of the PoSS scheme for the index $i$ (i.e., $p_i$ does not send $s_{i,i}^0$). The security of the PoSS scheme guarantees that if a party $p_i$ does not send the share for one instantiation of PoSS that is run with respect to $i$, then nothing can be learned about the secrets encoded in that instantiation. In addition, for the case when $p_{i_\alpha}$ sends the share $s_{i_\alpha, i_\alpha}^b$ (with $b \in \{0, 1\}$), the PoSS security guarantees that only the secret in position $i_\alpha$ can be learned. Hence, the evaluator can compute $m_1^{b_{i_1}}, \ldots, m_l^{b_{i_l}}$ by running the reconstruction algorithms for the $l$ instantiations of the PoSS scheme for which at least $l$ shares have been provided.[2] These messages then can be used to run the evaluation algorithm of NIMPC protocol to obtain the output of $f$. In addition, if the NIMPC protocol used in the above construction supports up to $t$-corruption, so does our scheme. We allow only the corruption of the parties that are participating in the protocol. That is, if $l$ parties provide an input then the corrupted parties belong to this set of parties. We give no security guarantees in any other case (which would give to the colluding evaluator an additional share for the PoSS scheme reaching the total of $l + 1$ shares, compromising the security of the PoSS scheme, and in turn, the security of the underling NIMPC protocol). Given the implication of NIMPC with iO, for our construction we consider only the case when the input of each party is a bit, exactly as in [9] (our other constructions do not have this limitation).

## 2.3  $(l, k)$-Secure Ad Hoc PSM

The notion of $(l, k)$-secure ad hoc PSM is similar to the notion of threshold NIMPC with the following two differences: 1) provides the best possible security guarantees in the case when $N$ parties participate in the online phase for an unknown $N$ with $l \leq N \leq k$ and 2) the security holds only if the evaluator does not collude with the other parties. In this work we want to construct a $(l, l + c)$-secure ad hoc PSM for a constant $c$. Moreover, we want to construct a scheme that allows the input of each party being a bit-string (instead of one bit like in the previous construction). One might think that a threshold NIMPC protocol already satisfies this security notion. We start by describing what are the

---

[2] The shares of the PoSS scheme need to be opportunely permuted to not give a trivial advantage to the adversary. We refer the reader to the technical part of the paper for more detail.

problems in trying to prove that our threshold NIMPC is an ad hoc PSM, even considering the case when the input of each party is a bit, and then show how our construction works in an incremental fashion. In the threshold NIMPC showed above, if more than $l$ parties are participating to the online phase then more than one secret from each instantiation of the PoSS scheme would be leaked (by the definition of PoSS). Hence, it might be possible for a corrupt evaluator to learn an encoding of different messages for the same input-slots of the NIMPC protocol. Note that this problem could be mitigated if the underlying NIMPC protocol was secure against an arbitrary number of corruptions, but any such a scheme would imply iO. Luckily, we do not really need a NIMPC protocol that supports an arbitrary number of corruptions, but we need a protocol that remains secure in the case when an evaluator, given a set of input $X := (x_{i_1}, \ldots, x_{i_{l+c}})$, could run the NIMPC protocol on any subset of size $l$ of $X$. This property is clearly not enjoyed by a NIMPC protocol that supports a constant number of corruptions. Moreover, even if the problem of corruption and the problem that we are describing here seem related, it looks like a completely different technique is required. To see the problem from a different perspective, the issue of obtaining a secure NIMPC protocol in the case of corruption is related to the fact that an adversary could evaluate the function on strings that have hamming distance at most $t$ from each other. That is, an adversary can flip up to $t$-bits, obtaining up to $2^t$ different inputs. In our case, even for $c = 1$, an adversary obtains inputs that have hamming distance $l$ (where $l$ is a polynomial). This is because the adversary, for example, could remove one input in the first position and add a new input in the last position thus causing the shift of the inputs that have not been replaced. Therefore, if the strings are close in terms of editing distance, they could have more than $l$ hamming distance. For this reason, it is not clear how the techniques used to achieve security against corrupted parties (for example those used in [9]) would be helpful in our case.

**Quasi-secure Ad Hoc PSM.** We now describe how, at a very high level, our protocol works. We provide an incremental description, starting from a protocol that is not secure, and gradually modifying it until we reach our final result. Let us consider the simplified scenario where we have only four parties $p_1$, $p_2$, $p_3$ and $p_4$ and we want to construct a $(3, 4)$-Ad Hoc PSM protocol for the 3-input function $f$. As a main tool, we consider two simple two-party NIMPC protocols (that tolerate no corruption): $\Pi_1$ that realizes the function $g$, $\Pi_2$ that realizes the function $g_{\mathsf{OUT}}$. The function $g$, on input two values $(z_1, z_2)$ concatenates them and creates an encoding of $z_1 \| z_2$ for the first input slot of $\Pi_2$. The function $g_{\mathsf{OUT}}$ takes the two inputs $(z_1 \| z_2, z_3)$ and outputs $f(z_1, z_2, z_3)$.

Given $\Pi_1$ and $\Pi_2$, each party $p_i$ now prepares an encoding of its input $x_i$ for the first and the second input slot of $\Pi_1$ (let us call these encodings $\mathsf{Msg}_i^0$ and $\mathsf{Msg}_i^1$). In addition, each party $p_i$ computes an encoding of $x_i$ for the second input slot of $\Pi_2$ (let us call this $\mathsf{Msg}_i^2$). For each party $p_i$ then we run an instantiations of a PoSS scheme with input $(\mathsf{Msg}_i^1, \mathsf{Msg}_i^2, \mathsf{Msg}_i^3, i)$. The security of the PoSS schemes guarantees that if the parties that are participating in the online phase are, for example, $p_1$ $p_2$ and $p_4$, then the evaluator will be able to get $(\mathsf{Msg}_1^1, \mathsf{Msg}_2^2, \mathsf{Msg}_4^3)$ only. The evaluator, at this point can evaluate the function $g$ with the inputs of $p_1$ and $p_2$ by running the evaluation algorithm for $\Pi_1$ on input $\mathsf{Msg}_1^1$ and $\mathsf{Msg}_2^2$. The output of $\Pi_1$ can then be used in combination with $\mathsf{Msg}_4^3$ to run the evaluation algorithm of $\Pi_2$ to compute the final output. It should be easy to see that this scheme is a threshold-NIMPC protocol that tolerates no corruption. But we are now interested in the security of the protocol in the case when four parties participate in the online phase. In this case, the PoSS scheme allows the evaluator to get, for example, $(\mathsf{Msg}_1^1, \mathsf{Msg}_2^2, \mathsf{Msg}_4^3)$ and $(\mathsf{Msg}_2^1, \mathsf{Msg}_3^2, \mathsf{Msg}_4^3)$ at the same time. This means that the evaluator can run the evaluation algorithm of $\Pi_1$ using $(\mathsf{Msg}_1^1, \mathsf{Msg}_2^2)$ and $(\mathsf{Msg}_1^1, \mathsf{Msg}_3^2)$ thus obtaining two different encodings for different values for the first input slot of $\Pi_2$ (assuming that the $x_1 || x_2 \neq x_2 || x_3$). This corresponds to the case in which the evaluator can collude with a party to generate encodings of multiple inputs for the first input slot of $\Pi_2$. Since we do not want to assume that $\Pi_2$ is resilient against such an attack[3], we modify the protocol as follows:

- Instead of considering one protocol $\Pi_2$ that realizes the function $g_{\mathsf{OUT}}$, we consider $\lambda$ protocols[4]: $\Pi_2^1, \ldots, \Pi_2^\lambda$.
- Each input of $g$ now comes with two random values $v_1$ and $v_2$ that each party samples. Hence, the inputs of $g$ now can be seen as $(z_1 || v_1, z_2 || v_2)$.
- The function $g$, on input $z_1 || v_1$ and $z_2 || v_2$ computes $y = z_1 || z_2$ and the hash $\mathsf{H}(v_1 \oplus v_2)$ thus obtaining $\mathsf{sel} \in [\lambda]$. Then $g$ encodes $y$ accordingly to the protocol $\Pi_2^{\mathsf{sel}}$.
- The party $p_3$ and $p_4$ now compute an encoding of their input for the second input slot for all the protocols $\Pi_2^1, \ldots, \Pi_2^\lambda$.

This mechanism now partially solves the problem of the previous protocol. This is because a different combination of inputs for $\Pi_1$ yields to an encoding for a different protocol $\Pi_2^{\mathsf{sel}}$, with $\mathsf{sel} \in [\lambda]$. Indeed, if the $\Pi_1$ is run using the input contributed by $p_1$ and $p_2$ then the output of $\Pi_1$ corresponds to an encoding of the concatenation of $x_1 || x_2$ for the protocol $\Pi_2^{\mathsf{sel}}$ with $\mathsf{sel} = \mathsf{H}(v_1 \oplus v_2)$. If instead $\Pi_1$ is run using the input contributed by $p_1$ and $p_3$, then we have that $\mathsf{H}(v_1 \oplus v_2) \neq \mathsf{H}(v_1 \oplus v_3) = \mathsf{sel}'$ with some probability $1/p$ (that depends on the choice of $\lambda$ and on the random coins of the parties). Hence, the output of $\Pi_1$ corresponds to an encoding for the protocol $\Pi_2^{\mathsf{sel}'}$. Clearly, $\lambda$ needs to be polynomially related to the security parameter. This means that the probability of founding a collision for $\mathsf{H}$ is non-negligible (and if there is a collision then the security of this protocol collapses back to the security of the previous protocol). Later in this section we show how to solve this problem using the LWE assumption. Before discussing that, we note that this protocol has yet another issue. As we said, the evaluator can get the values $(\mathsf{Msg}_1^1, \mathsf{Msg}_2^2, \mathsf{Msg}_4^3)$ and $(\mathsf{Msg}_2^1, \mathsf{Msg}_3^2, \mathsf{Msg}_4^3)$ when all the parties participate in the online phase. Given that $\mathsf{Msg}_1^1$ and $\mathsf{Msg}_2^1$ represent the encoding of different values for the

---

[3] We recall that we do not know any NIMPC protocol that is secure in this setting when the inputs of $\Pi_2$ are bit strings unless from assuming iO.

[4] We discuss the size of $\lambda$ later in the paper.

first input slot of $\Pi_1$, then we have an issue similar to the one that we have just discussed. This time, we can solve this problem easily. We simply consider an instantiation of a NIMPC protocol that realizes the function $g$ which we denote with $\Pi_1^{i,j}$, which can be used only by the party $i, j$, with $i \in \{1, 2\}$ and $j \in \{2, 3, 4\}$. Then, for example, the party $p_1$ will compute an encoding for the first input slot of $\Pi_1^{1,2}$, $\Pi_1^{1,3}$ and $\Pi_1^{1,4}$, and use all of them as the input of the first instantiation of the PoSS scheme. For the protocol that we have just described, we can prove that for a suitable choice of $\lambda$ (given that $c$ is a constant value) the probability that there are no collisions in H is $1/p$ where $p$ is a polynomial. Hence, we can prove that the execution of our protocol is secure with probability $1/p$. We note that in this discussion we have assumed that the security of the PoSS scheme is not compromised even when more than $l$ parties provide their shares. In the technical part of the paper we show that our construction of PoSS enjoys a stronger notion, that is indeed sufficient to construct the protocol that we have just described. To extend the above construction to the case when the number of party is more than 4, and the threshold $l$ is an arbitrary value, we just need to consider a longer *chain* of 2-party NIMPC protocols. However, this generalization has to be done carefully to avoid an exponential blowup in the size of the messages. For more details on that, we refer the reader to Sect. 5.

**Fully Secure Ad Hoc PSM.** We denote the protocol that we have just described with $\Pi^{\mathsf{PSM}}$ and show how to use it to obtain an ad hoc PSM that is $(l, l + c)$-secure. To amplify the security of $\Pi^{\mathsf{PSM}}$ we make use of a homomorphic secret sharing (HSS) scheme for the function $f$ (we recall that $f$ is the $l$-input function that we want to evaluate). At a high level, a HSS allows each party $i$ to compute m shares of its input $x_i$ and distribute them among m servers using the algorithm $\mathsf{Share}^{\mathsf{HSS}}$ so that $x_i$ is hidden from any $\mathsf{m} - 1$ colluding servers. Each server $j$ can apply a local evaluation algorithm $\mathsf{Eval}^{\mathsf{HSS}}$ to its share of the $l$ inputs, and obtain an output share $y_j$. By combining all the output shares it is possible to obtain the output of the function, that is $y_1 \oplus \cdots \oplus y_{\mathsf{m}} = f(x_1, \ldots, x_l)$.[5] At a very high level, our protocol consists of m instantiations of $\Pi^{\mathsf{PSM}}$ where the $e$-th instantiation evaluates the function $G_e$ with $e \in [\mathsf{m}]$. The Function $G_e$ takes as input $l$ shares of the HSS scheme, and uses them as input of $\mathsf{Eval}^{\mathsf{HSS}}$ together with the *server index* $e$ (see the bottom of Fig. 6 for a formal specification of $G_e$). Each party $p_i$ that wants to participate in the protocol computes a secret sharing of its input thus obtaining m shares $(s_1, \ldots, s_{\mathsf{m}})$. Then $p_i$ uses the $e$-th share as input of the $e$-th instantiation of $\Pi^{\mathsf{PSM}}$. The evaluator runs the evaluation algorithm of the $e$-th instantiation of $\Pi^{\mathsf{PSM}}$ thus obtaining $y_e$ (which corresponds to the output of $\mathsf{Eval}^{\mathsf{HSS}}$ on input the $e$-th shares of all the parties) for each $e \in [\mathsf{m}]$. The output of the evaluation phase then corresponds to $y_1 \oplus \cdots \oplus y_{\mathsf{m}}$. We show that this protocol is secure as long as there is at least one execution of $\Pi^{\mathsf{PSM}}$ that is secure (i.e., simulatable). Moreover, by choosing m opportunely we can prove that at least one execution of $\Pi^{\mathsf{PSM}}$ is secure with overwhelming probability. Hence, at least one share of

---

[5] In our work we assume that the HSS is additive.

each of the inputs of the honest parties will be protected. Therefore, because of the security offered by the HSS, also the input of the parties will be protected.

**Adaptive-Ad-Hoc PSM.** It is straightforward to construct an adaptive-ad-hoc PSM having a $(l, l+c)$ ad hoc PSM $\Pi^{\mathsf{APSM}}$. Indeed, we just need to run $c$ instantiation of $\Pi^{\mathsf{APSM}}$, where each instantiation computes a function $f_\alpha$ with arity $\alpha$ for each $\alpha \in \{l, \dots, l+c\}$.

## 2.4 Related Work

The study of MPC protocols with restricted interaction was initiated by Halevi, Lindell, and Pinkas [16,17]. We have mentioned the work of Benhamouda et al. [9] which provides the first NIMPC protocol that tolerates up to a constant number of corruptions for all functions in $P$ under OWFs. In addition, the authors show how to obtain a more efficient NIMPC protocol for symmetric functions. The work [5] introduces the notion of ad hoc PSM and in [7] the authors propose many instantiations of such a primitive in the information-theoretic and computational setting. A result of [7] that is very related to our first contribution, is the construction of an ad hoc PSM protocol for a $k$-argument function $f : X^k \to Y$ from a NIMPC protocol for a *related* $n$-argument function $g : (X \cup \{\perp\})^n \to Y$. More precisely, the function $g$ outputs $\perp$ if there are more than $n - k$ inputs that are $\perp$, it outputs the output of $f$ if there are exactly $n - k$ inputs that are $\perp$, in any other cases the output of $g$ is undefined. The compiler that we propose is more generic and it preserves its security against colluding parties (if any). Always in [7] the authors propose an $(l, l+c)$-secure ad hoc PSM protocol for symmetric functions whose complexity is exponential in $l$, and prove that an $(l, k)$-ad hoc PSM protocols for simple functions with generic $(l, k)$ already implies obfuscation for interesting functions. In [8] the authors improve the efficiency of the protocols proposed in [7]. The work [16] try to make reusable the setup assuming more interactions between the parties, or assuming specific graphs of interaction patterns. In [15] the authors successfully remove the need of the parties to obtain correlated randomness from the setup phase via a PKI supplemented with a common random string under the iO assumption. In addition, the construction proposed in [15] tolerates arbitrary many corruptions.

## 3 Background

**Preliminaries.** We denote the security parameter by $\lambda$ and use "$||$" as concatenation operator (i.e., if $a$ and $b$ are two strings then by $a||b$ we denote the concatenation of $a$ and $b$). For a finite set $Q$, $x \xleftarrow{\$} Q$ denotes a sampling of $x$ from $Q$ with uniform distribution. We use "$=$" to check equality of two different elements (i.e. $a = b$ then...), "$\leftarrow$" as the assigning operator (e.g. to assign to $a$ the value of $b$ we write $a \leftarrow b$). and $:=$ to define two elements as equal. We use the abbreviation PPT that stands for probabilistic polynomial time. We use poly($\cdot$) to indicate a generic polynomial function. We assume familiarity with the notion of negligible function. We denote with $[n]$ the set $\{1, \ldots, n\}$, $\mathbb{N}_0$ the set of non-negative integers and with $\mathbb{N}$ the set of positive integer.

## 3.1  Secret Sharing

A secret sharing scheme allows a dealer to share a secret $m$ among $n$ parties $\mathcal{P} = \{p_1, \ldots, p_m\}$ such that any authorized subset (if any) of $\mathcal{P}$ can reconstruct the secret $m$, while the other parties learn nothing about $m$. We now give the definition of $l$-out-of-$n$ secret sharing.

**Definition 1 ($l$-out-of-$n$ secret sharing).** *A $l$-out-of-$n$ secret sharing scheme over a message space $\mathcal{M}$ is a pair of* PPT *algorithms (*Share, Reconstruct*) where:*

- Share *on input $x \in \mathcal{M}$ outputs $n$ shares $(s_1, \ldots, s_n)$;*
- Reconstruct *on input $l$ values (shares) outputs a message in $\mathcal{M}$;*

*satisfying the following requirements.*

- *Correctness.* $\forall x \in \mathcal{M}$, $\forall S = \{i_1, \ldots, i_l\} \subseteq \{1, \ldots, n\}$ *of size $l$,*
  $\text{Prob}\left[ x \leftarrow \text{Reconstruct}(s_{i_1}, \ldots, s_{i_l}) : (s_1, \ldots, s_n) \leftarrow \text{Share}(x) \right] = 1.$
- *Security.* $\forall x, x' \in \mathcal{M}$, $\forall S \subseteq \{1, \ldots, n\}$ *s.t. $|S| < l$, the following distributions are identical:* $\{(s_i)_{i \in S} : (s_1, \ldots, s_n) \leftarrow \text{Share}(x)\}$
  $\{(s'_i)_{i \in S} : (s'_1, \ldots, s'_n) \leftarrow \text{Share}(x')\}.$

## 3.2  Homomorphic Secret Sharing (HSS)

We consider HSS scheme that supports the evaluation of a function $f$ on shares of inputs $x_1, \ldots x_n$ that are originated from different clients. In this notion each client $i$ can compute $m$ shares of its input $x_i$ and distribute them between $m$ servers using the algorithm $\text{Share}^{\text{HSS}}$ so that $x_i$ is hidden from any $m-1$ colluding servers. Each server $j$ can apply a local evaluation algorithm $\text{Eval}^{\text{HSS}}$ to its share of the $n$ inputs, and obtains an output share $y_j$. The output $f(x_1, \ldots, x_n)$ is reconstructed by applying a decoding algorithm $\text{Dec}^{\text{HSS}}$ to the output shares $y_1, \ldots, y_m$.

**Definition 2 (HSS [10]).** *An $n$-client, $m$-server, $t$-secure homomorphic secret sharing scheme for a function $f : (\{0,1\}^\star)^{n+1} \rightarrow \{0,1\}^\star$, or $(n,m,t)$-HHS for short, is a triple of* PPT *algorithms ($\text{Share}^{\text{HSS}}$, $\text{Eval}^{\text{HSS}}$, $\text{Dec}^{\text{HSS}}$) where:*

- $\text{Share}^{\text{HSS}}(1^\lambda, i, x)$*: On input $1^\lambda$ (security parameter), $i \in [n]$ (client index) and $x \in \{0,1\}^\star$ (client input), the sharing algorithm $\text{Share}^{\text{HSS}}$ outputs $m$ input shares $(x^1, \ldots, x^m)$.*
- $\text{Eval}^{\text{HSS}}(j, x_0, (x_1^j, \ldots, x_n^j))$*: On input $j \in [m]$ (server index), $x_0 \in \{0,1\}^\star$ (common server input), and $x_1^j, \ldots, x_n^j$ ($j$-th share of each client input), the evaluation algorithm $\text{Eval}^{\text{HSS}}$ outputs $y^j \in \{0,1\}^\star$, corresponding to the server $j$'s share of $f(x_0; x_1, \ldots, x_n)$.*

– $\text{Dec}^{\text{HSS}}(y^1, \ldots, y^m)$: *On input* $(y^1, \ldots, y^m)$ *(list of output shares), the decoding algorithm* $\text{Dec}^{\text{HSS}}$ *computes a final output* $y \in \{0, 1\}^\star$.

The algorithm $(\text{Share}^{\text{HSS}}, \text{Eval}^{\text{HSS}}, \text{Dec}^{\text{HSS}})$ *should satisfy the following correctness and security requirements:*

– **Correctness:** *For any* $n + 1$ *inputs* $x_0, \ldots, x_n \in \{0, 1\}^\star$,

$$\text{Prob}[\forall i \in [n](x_i^1, \ldots x_i^m) \xleftarrow{\$} \text{Share}^{\text{HSS}}(1^\lambda, i, x_i), \forall j \in [m]\ y^j \xleftarrow{\$} \text{Eval}^{\text{HSS}}(j, x_0,$$
$$(x_1^j, \ldots, x_n^j)) : \text{Dec}^{\text{HSS}}(y^1, \ldots, y^m) = f(x_0; x_1, \ldots, x_n)] = 1 - \nu(\lambda).$$

– **Security:** *Consider the following semantic security challenge experiment for corrupted set of server* $T \subset [m]$:
   1. *The stateful adversary gives challenge index and inputs* $(i, x_0, x_1) \leftarrow \mathcal{A}(1^\lambda)$, *with* $i \in [n]$ *and* $|x_0| = |x_1|$.
   2. *The challenger samples* $b \xleftarrow{\$} \{0, 1\}$ *and* $(x^1, \ldots, x^m) \xleftarrow{\$} \text{Share}^{\text{HSS}}(1^\lambda, i, x_b)$.
   3. *The adversary outputs* $b' \leftarrow \mathcal{A}((x^j)_{j \in T})$ *given the shares for corrupted* $T$. *Denote by* $a := \text{Prob}[\,b = b'\,] - 1/2$ *the advantage of* $\mathcal{A}$ *in guessing* $b$ *in the above experiment, where probability is taken over the randomness of the challenger and of* $\mathcal{A}$. *For circuit size bound* $S = S(\lambda)$ *and advantage bound* $\alpha = \alpha(\lambda)$, *we say that an* $(n, m, t)$-HSS *scheme* $\Pi$ *is* $(S, \alpha)$-secure *if for all* $T \subset [m]$ *of size* $|T| \leq t$, *and all non-uniform adversaries* $\mathcal{A}$ *of size* $S(\lambda)$, *we have* $a \leq \alpha(\lambda)$. *We say that* $\Pi$ *is computationally secure if it is* $(S, 1/S)$-secure for all polynomials $S$.

In this work we consider only *additive* HSS schemes. An HHS scheme is additive if $\text{Dec}^{\text{HSS}}$ outputs the exclusive or of the $m$ output shares. For our construction we make use of an additive $(n, m, m-1)$-HSS scheme. Such a scheme can be constructed from the LWEs assumption [10,12].

## 4 Our Model

In this section we propose the formal definition of NIMPC. We give a more general definition that captures the case when up to $t$ parties can collude with the evaluator, and following [9,16,17], we refer to this notion as $t$-robust NIMPC. Then we give our new definition of threshold NIMPC which can be seen as a combination of the notion of NIMPC with the notion of ad hoc PSM proposed in [6]. Let $\mathcal{X}$ be a non-empty set and let $\mathcal{X}^n$ denote the Cartesian product $\mathcal{X}^n := \mathcal{X} \times \cdots \times \mathcal{X}$.

**Definition 3 (NIMPC Protocol. [9]).** *Let* $\mathcal{F} = (\mathcal{F}_n)_{n \in \mathbb{N}}$ *be an ensemble of sets* $\mathcal{F}_n$ *of functions* $f : \mathcal{X} \to \mathcal{Y}$, *where* $\mathcal{Y}$ *is a finite set. A non-interactive secure multiparty computation (NIMPC) protocol for* $\mathcal{F}$ *is a tuple of three algorithms* $\Pi := (\text{Setup}, \text{Msg}, \text{Eval})$, *where:*

– Setup *takes as input unary representations of* $n$ *and of the security parameter* $\lambda$, *and a representation of function* $f \in \mathcal{F}_n$ *and outputs a tuple* $(\rho_0, \rho_1, \ldots, \rho_n)$;

- Msg *takes as input a value* $\rho_i$, *and an input* $x_i \in \mathcal{X}$, *and deterministically outputs a message* $m_i$;
- Eval *takes as input a value* $\rho_0$ *and a tuple of n messages* $(m_1, \ldots, m_n)$ *and outputs an element in* $\mathcal{Y}$ *satisfying the following property:*
  Correctness. *For any* $n \in \mathbb{N}$, *security parameter* $\lambda \in \mathbb{N}_0$, $f \in \mathcal{F}_n$, $x :=$ $(x_1, \ldots, x_n) \in \mathcal{X}$, *and* $(\rho_0, \ldots, \rho_n) \stackrel{\$}{\leftarrow} \mathsf{Setup}(1^n, 1^\lambda, f)$,
  $\mathsf{Eval}(\rho_0, \mathsf{Msg}(\rho_1, x_1), \ldots, \mathsf{Msg}(\rho_n, x_n)) = f(x)$.

While the previous definition is abstract, in the sequel, we will often see NIMPC protocols as protocols with $n$ parties $p_1, \ldots, p_n$ with respective inputs $x_1, \ldots, x_n$ and an evaluator $p_0$. A polynomial-time NIMPC protocol for $\mathcal{F}$ is an NIMPC protocol (Setup, Msg, Eval) where Setup, Msg, and Eval run in polynomial time in $n$ and $\lambda$. In particular, functions $f \in \mathcal{F}$ should be representable by polynomial-size bit strings.

**Robustness.** For a subset $T = \{i_1, \ldots, i_t\} \subseteq [n]$ and $x = (x_1, \ldots, x_n)$, we denote by $\overline{x}_T$ the $t$-coordinate projection vector $(x_{i_1}, \ldots, x_{i_t})$. For a function $f : \mathcal{X}^n \rightarrow \mathcal{Y}$, we denote by $f|_{\overline{T}, x_{\overline{T}}}$ the function $f$ with the inputs corresponding to positions $\overline{T}$ fixed to the entries of the vector $x$. We now recall the notions of robustness for NIMPC protocols. Informally, $T$-robustness $T \subseteq \{1, \ldots, n\}$ for a set $T$ of colluding parties means that if $x_{\overline{T}}$ represents the inputs of the honest parties, then an evaluator colluding with the parties in set $T$ can compute the residual function $f|_{\overline{T}, x_{\overline{T}}}$ on any input $x_T$ but cannot learn anything else about the input of the honest parties. This describes the best privacy guarantee attainable in this adversarial setting. The formal definition is stated in terms of a simulator that can generate the view of the adversary (evaluator plus the colluding parties in set $T$) with sole oracle access to the residual function $f|_{\overline{T}, x_{\overline{T}}}$.

**Definition 4 (NIMPC Robustness [9]).** *Let* $n \in \mathbb{N}$ *and* $T \subseteq \{1, \ldots, n\}$. *A NIMPC protocol* $\Pi$ *is perfectly (resp., statistically, computationally) $T$-robust if there exists a* PPT *algorithm* Sim *(called simulator) such that for any* $f \in \mathcal{F}_n$ *and* $x_{\overline{T}} \in \mathcal{X}_{\overline{T}}$, *the following distributions are perfectly (resp., statistically, computationally) indistinguishable:* $\{\mathsf{Sim}^{f|_{\overline{T}, x_{\overline{T}}}}(1^n, 1^\lambda, T)\}, \{\mathsf{View}(1^n, 1^\lambda, f, T, x_{\overline{T}})\}$, *where* $\{\mathsf{View}(1^n, 1^\lambda, f, T, x_{\overline{T}})\}$ *is the view of the evaluator* $p_0$ *and of the colluding parties* $p_i$ *(for* $i \in T$*) from running* $\Pi := (\mathsf{Setup}, \mathsf{Msg}, \mathsf{Eval})$ *on input* $x_{\overline{T}}$ *for the honest parties: that is,* $((m_i)_{i \in \overline{T}}, \rho_0, (\rho_i)_{i \in T})$ *where* $(\rho_0, \ldots, \rho_n) \stackrel{\$}{\leftarrow}$ $\mathsf{Setup}(1^n, 1^\lambda, f)$ *and* $m_i \leftarrow \mathsf{Msg}(\rho_i, x_i)$ *for all* $i \in \overline{T}$ *where* $x_{\overline{T}} := (x_i)_{i \in \overline{T}}$. *Let* $t \in \mathbb{N}_0$ *be a function of $n$, then a NIMPC protocol* $\Pi$ *is perfectly (resp., statistically, computationally) $t$-robust if for any* $n \in \mathbb{N}$ *and any* $T \subseteq \{1, \ldots, n\}$ *of size at most* $t = t(n)$, $\Pi$ *is perfectly (resp., statistically, computationally) $T$-robust.*

Robustness does not necessarily imply that the simulator Sim is the same for any $n$ and $T$. In this and in the following notions we consider only PPT simulators since in this paper we focus only on efficiently simulatable protocols.

## 4.1   Threshold NIMPC

We introduce the new notion of *Threshold NIMPC*. A Threshold NIMPC is parametrized by $n$ and $l$ with $0 \leq l \leq n$, where $n$ denotes the number of parties and $l$ represents a threshold. Given a set of $n$ parties $\mathcal{P}$, any subset of $\mathcal{P}' \subseteq \mathcal{P}$ of size $l$ can evaluate the function $f : \mathcal{X}^l \to \mathcal{Y}$, where $\mathcal{Y}$ is a finite set and $\mathcal{X} = \{\{0,1\}^\lambda, \{1, \ldots n\}\}$. In more details, we assume that any party in $\mathcal{P}$ is univocally identified by an index $i \in [n]$. The setup algorithm and the algorithm used by the parties to generate an encoding of their inputs have the same interface as the algorithms of a NIMPC protocol. The difference is in the evaluation algorithm. In this notion we do not require all the $n$ parties to participate in the protocol in order to evaluate a function. That is, any subsets of $\mathcal{P}$ of size $l$ would allow the evaluator to compute the function $f$. Without loss of generality, we consider only functionalities whose output depends on the inputs of the parties, and on the indexes of the parties that contributed with these inputs. Formally, the class of function supported by our protocol is described in Fig. 1 (where $g$ can be any function).

---

**Input:** $\big((x_{i_1}, i_1), \ldots (x_{i_l}, i_l)\big)$ where $\{i_1, \ldots, i_l\} \subseteq [n]$, $x_{i_1}, \ldots, x_{i_l} \in \mathcal{X}$, $l \leq n$ and $n \in \mathbb{N}$.
**Output:** Let $(j_1, \ldots, j_l)$ be a permutation of the values $(i_1, \ldots, i_l)$ such that $1 \leq j_1 < j_2 < \cdots < j_{l-1} < j_l \leq n$ and output $\perp$ if such a permutation does not exist, else, output $g\big(x_{j_1}, \ldots, x_{j_l}\big)$

---

**Fig. 1.** Class of functionalities supported by our threshold NIMPC protocol.

**Definition 5 (Threshold NIMPC Protocol).** *Let $\mathcal{F} = (\mathcal{F}_l)_{l \in \mathbb{N}}$ be an ensemble of sets $\mathcal{F}_l$ of functions $f : \mathcal{X} \to \mathcal{Y}$, a Threshold NIMPC protocol for $\mathcal{F}$ is a tuple of three algorithms* $(\mathsf{Setup}^{\mathsf{th}}, \mathsf{Msg}^{\mathsf{th}}, \mathsf{Eval}^{\mathsf{th}})$, *where:*

- $\mathsf{Setup}^{\mathsf{th}}$ *takes as input unary representations of $n$, $l$ and of the security parameter $\lambda$ with $1 \leq l \leq n$, and a representation of function $f \in \mathcal{F}_l$ and outputs a tuple $(\rho_0, \rho_1, \ldots, \rho_n)$;*
- $\mathsf{Msg}^{\mathsf{th}}$ *takes as input a value $\rho_i$, and an input $x_i \in \mathcal{X}$, and deterministically outputs a message $m_i$;*
- $\mathsf{Eval}^{\mathsf{th}}$ *takes as input a value $\rho_0$ and a tuple of $n$ messages $(m_{j_1}, \ldots, m_{j_l})$ with $1 \leq j_1 < \cdots < j_l \leq n$ and outputs an element in $\mathcal{Y}$;*

*satisfying the following property:*

*Correctness. For any $n \in \mathbb{N}$, security parameter $\lambda \in \mathbb{N}_0$, $f \in \mathcal{F}_l$, $x :=$ $\big((x_{j_1}, j_1), \ldots, (x_{j_l}, j_l)\big) \in \mathcal{X}$, with $1 \leq j_1 < \cdots < j_l \leq n$ and $(\rho_0, \ldots, \rho_n) \xleftarrow{\$}$ $\mathsf{Setup}^{\mathsf{th}}(1^n, 1^l, 1^\lambda, f)$,*

$$\mathsf{Eval}^{\mathsf{th}}\big(\rho_0, \mathsf{Msg}^{\mathsf{th}}(\rho_{j_1}, x_{j_1}), \ldots, \mathsf{Msg}^{\mathsf{th}}(\rho_{j_l}, x_{j_l})\big) = f\big((x_{j_1}, j_1), \ldots, (x_{j_l}, j_l)\big).$$

**Definition 6 (Threshold NIMPC Security).** *Let* $n \in \mathbb{N}$, $K := \{j_1, \ldots, j_l\}$
*with* $1 \leq j_1 < \cdots < j_l \leq n$, $T \subseteq K$ *and* $\overline{T} := K - T$. *A Threshold NIMPC*
*protocol* $\Pi$ *is perfectly (resp., statistically, computationally) $T$-secure if there*
*exists a* PPT *algorithm* Sim *(called simulator) such that for any* $f \in \mathcal{F}_l$ *and* $x_{\overline{T}} \in$
$\mathcal{X}_{\overline{T}}$, *the following distributions are perfectly (resp., statistically, computationally)*
*indistinguishable:*

$$\{\mathsf{Sim}^{f|_{\overline{T}, x_{\overline{T}}}}(1^n, 1^l, 1^\lambda, T, K)\}, \{\mathsf{View}(1^n, 1^l, 1^\lambda, f, T, K, x_{\overline{T}})\}$$

*where* $\{\mathsf{View}(1^n, 1^l, 1^\lambda, f, T, K, x_{\overline{T}})\}$ *is the view of the evaluator* $p_0$ *and of the*
*colluding parties* $p_i$ *(for* $i \in T$*) from running* $\Pi$ *on input* $x_{\overline{T}}$ *for the honest*
*parties: that is,* $((m_i)_{i \in \overline{T}}, \rho_0, (\rho_i)_{i \in T})$ *where* $(\rho_0, \ldots, \rho_n) \xleftarrow{\$} \mathsf{Setup}(1^n, 1^l, 1^\lambda, f)$
*and* $m_i \leftarrow \mathsf{Msg}(\rho_i, x_i)$ *for all* $i \in \overline{T}$.[6] *Let* $t, l, n \in \mathbb{N}_0$ *be such that* $0 \leq t \leq l \leq n$,
*a Threshold NIMPC protocol* $\Pi$ *is perfectly (resp., statistically, computationally)*
$t$-*secure if for any* $K \subseteq [n]$ *with* $|K| \leq l$, *and any* $T \subseteq K$ *such that* $K = T \cup \overline{T}$
*with* $|T| \leq t$, $\Pi$ *is perfectly (resp., statistically, computationally) $T$-secure.*

### 4.2  Ad Hoc PSM

An $(l, t)$-secure ad hoc PSM protocol $\Pi$ is a 0-secure threshold NIMPC that
remains secure even if more than $l$ (and less than $t$) parties participate in the
online phase. In other words, the evaluator cannot collude with any of the other
parties, but the protocol remains secure for any number $N$ of parties participating in the protocol with $N \leq t$. Moreover, the evaluator can compute the output
if $N \geq l$. By secure here we mean that the adversary can evaluate the function
$f$ on any combination of size $l$ of the inputs provided by the honest parties and
learns nothing more than that. More formally, if $\overline{x} := ((x_{i_1}, i_1), \ldots, (x_{i_i}, i_N))$
represents the inputs of the $N$ parties participating in the online phase, then a
malicious party can compute $f$ on any input $\overline{x}_K$ where $K := \{j_1, \ldots, j_l\}$ with
$1 \leq j_1 < \cdots < j_l \leq n$, $K \subseteq \{i_1, \ldots, i_N\}$ but cannot learn anything else. This
describes the best privacy guarantee attainable in this setting. The formal definition is stated in terms of a simulator that can generate the view of the adversary
with sole oracle access to $\mathcal{O}_f$, where $\mathcal{O}_f$ takes as input a set $K := \{j_1, \ldots, j_l\}$ with
$1 \leq j_1 < \cdots < j_l \leq n$, $K \subseteq \{i_1, \ldots, i_N\}$ and returns $f((x_{j_1}, j_1), \ldots, (x_{j_l}, j_l))$.[7]
The definition that we provide is essentially the same as the one provided in [7],
we just use a different terminology to be consistent with our other definitions.

**Definition 7 (Ad Hoc PSM).** *Let* $n, l, t, \lambda \in \mathbb{N}_0$ *and* $K := \{j_1, \ldots, j_N\}$ *with*
$0 \leq j_1 < \cdots < j_N \leq n$ *such that* $0 \leq N \leq t$. *An ad hoc PSM protocol is perfectly*
*(resp., statistically, computationally) $K$-secure if there exists a* PPT *algorithm*
Sim *(called simulator) such that for any* $f \in \mathcal{F}_l$, $\overline{x} := (x_{j_1}, j_1), \ldots, (x_{j_N}, j_N)$, *the*

---

[6] $f|_{\overline{T}, x_{\overline{T}}}$ works as before, with the difference that it outputs $\bot$ in the case where less
    than $|K| < l$.
[7] The oracle outputs $\bot$ if $N < l$.

*following distributions are perfectly (resp., statistically, computationally) indistinguishable:*

$$\{\mathsf{Sim}^{\mathcal{O}_f}(1^n, 1^l, 1^\lambda, K)\}, \{\mathsf{View}(1^n, 1^l, 1^\lambda, f, K, \overline{x})\}$$

*where* $\{\mathsf{View}(1^n, 1^l, 1^\lambda, f, K, \overline{x})\}$ *is the view of the evaluator* $p_0$ *from running* $\Pi$ *on input* $\overline{x}$ *for the honest parties: that is,* $((m_i)_{i \in K}, \rho_0)$ *where* $m_i \leftarrow \mathsf{Msg}(\rho_i, x_i)$ *for all* $i \in K$ *and* $(\rho_0, \dots, \rho_n) \xleftarrow{\$} \mathsf{Setup}(1^n, 1^l, 1^\lambda, f)$. *We say that an ad hoc PSM protocol* $\Pi$ *is perfectly (resp., statistically, computationally)* $(l, t)$-*secure if for any* $N \leq t$, *any* $K := \{j_1, \dots, j_N\}$, $\Pi$ *is perfectly (resp., statistically, computationally)* $K$-*secure.*

## 4.3   Adaptive-Ad-Hoc PSM

An adaptive-ad-hoc PSM protocol is parametrized by the number of parties $n$, the threshold $l$, an integer $t$ with $0 \leq t \leq n$ and a set of functions $f_l, \dots, f_\beta$, and allows an honest evaluator to obtain the evaluation of a function $f_N$ if the number of parties that are participating in the protocol is $l \leq N \leq \beta$, for any $N \in \{l, \dots, \beta\}$. Informally, an adaptive-ad-hoc PSM protocol can be seen as a protocol that allows evaluating a function that accepts a variable number of inputs. We refer to the full version for the formal definition.

## 5   Positional Secret Sharing (PoSS)

In this section we propose new notions of secret sharing schemes, and provide an information theoretical instantiation of them. These new definitions represent one of the main building block of our NIMPC protocols. We now introduce the first notion that we call *Positional Secret Sharing (PoSS)*. Let $\mathcal{P} := \{p_1, \dots, p_n\}$ be a set of parties and $X := (x_1, \dots, x_l)$ be a sequence of secrets. A PoSS scheme is defined with respect to a party $p_j \in \mathcal{P}$. In a PoSS scheme a dealer can compute a secret sharing of $X$ thus obtaining $s_1, \dots, s_n$ and distribute $s_i$ to $p_i$ for all $i \in \{1, \dots, n\}$. Let $\mathcal{P}' := \{p_{j_1}, \dots, p_{j_l}\}$ be an arbitrary chosen set of $l$ parties with $0 \leq j_1 < j_2 < \cdots < j_{l-1} < j_l \leq n$. On input $(s_{j_1}, \dots, s_{j_l})$ with $j_\alpha = j$ for some $\alpha \in \{1, \dots, l\}$ an evaluator can compute $x_\alpha$ and nothing more. If there is no $j_\alpha = j$ or less than $l$ shares are available then all the secrets remain protected. We now propose a formal definition of PoSS.

**Definition 8 (Positional Secret Sharing).** *A PoSS scheme over a message space* $\mathcal{M}$ *is a pair of* PPT *algorithms (*$\mathsf{Share}^{\mathsf{PoSS}}$, $\mathsf{Reconstruct}^{\mathsf{PoSS}}$*) where:*

- $\mathsf{Share}^{\mathsf{PoSS}}$ *takes as input* $X := (x_1, \dots, x_l)$, *the number of parties* $n$ *and an index* $j \in [n]$, *and outputs* $n$ *shares* $(s_1, \dots, s_n)$;
- $\mathsf{Reconstruct}^{\mathsf{PoSS}}$ *takes as input* $l$ *values (shares), the index* $j$ *and outputs a message in* $\mathcal{M}$ *(where* $\mathcal{M}$ *denotes the message space);*

*satisfying the following requirements.*

**Correctness.** $\forall x_1, \ldots, x_l \in \mathcal{M}^l$, $\forall S = \{j_1, \ldots, j_l\} \subseteq \{1, \ldots, n\}$ with $j_1 < j_2 < \cdots < j_{l-1} < j_l$, if there exists $\alpha \in \{1, \ldots, l\}$ such that $j_\alpha = j$ then
$$\text{Prob}[x_\alpha \leftarrow \text{Reconstruct}^{\text{PoSS}}(s_{j_1}, \ldots, s_{j_l}, j) : (s_1, \ldots, s_n) \xleftarrow{\$} \text{Share}^{\text{PoSS}}((x_1,$$
$$\ldots, x_l), j)] = 1.$$

**Standard security.** $\forall (x_1, \ldots, x_l), (x_1', \ldots, x_l') \in \mathcal{M}^l$, $\forall S \subseteq \{1, \ldots, n\}$ s.t. $|S| < l$, the following distributions are identical:
$$\{(s_i)_{i \in S} : (s_1, \ldots, s_n) \xleftarrow{\$} \text{Share}^{\text{PoSS}}((x_1, \ldots, x_l), j)\}$$
$$\{(s_i')_{i \in S} : (s_1', \ldots, s_n') \xleftarrow{\$} \text{Share}^{\text{PoSS}}((x_1', \ldots, x_l'), j)\}$$

**Positional security.** $\forall (x_1, \ldots, x_l), (x_1', \ldots, x_l') \in \mathcal{M}^l$, $\forall S = \{j_1, \ldots, j_l\} \subseteq \{1, \ldots, n\}$ with $j_1 < j_2 < \cdots < j_{l-1} < j_l$:

1. if there exists $\alpha \in \{1, \ldots, l\}$ such that $j_\alpha = j$, the following distributions are identical:
$$\{(s_i)_{i \in S} : (s_1, \ldots, s_n) \xleftarrow{\$} \text{Share}^{\text{PoSS}}((x_1, \ldots, x_{\alpha-1}, x_\alpha, x_{\alpha+1} \ldots, x_l), j)\}$$
$$\{(s_i')_{i \in S} : (s_1', \ldots, s_n') \xleftarrow{\$} \text{Share}^{\text{PoSS}}((x_1', \ldots, x_{\alpha-1}', x_\alpha, x_{\alpha+1}', \ldots, x_l'), j)\}.$$

2. if $\nexists \alpha \in \{1, \ldots, l\}$ such that $j_\alpha = j$, the following distributions are identical:
$$\{(s_i)_{i \in S} : (s_1, \ldots, s_n) \xleftarrow{\$} \text{Share}^{\text{PoSS}}((x_1, \ldots, x_l), j)\}$$
$$\{(s_i')_{i \in S} : (s_1', \ldots, s_n') \xleftarrow{\$} \text{Share}^{\text{PoSS}}((x_1', \ldots, x_l'), j)\}$$

### 5.1   PoSS: Our Construction

We denote our scheme with $(\text{Share}^{\text{PoSS}^*}, \text{Reconstruct}^{\text{PoSS}^*})$. $\text{Share}^{\text{PoSS}^*}$ takes as input $X := (x_1, \ldots, x_l)$ and the index $j$ and executes the following steps.

– For $i = 1, \ldots, l$
  1. Pick $x_i^0, x_i^1 \xleftarrow{\$} \{0, 1\}^\lambda$ and compute $\tilde{x}_i \leftarrow x_i^0 \oplus x_i^1 \oplus x_i$.
  2. Construct an $(i-1)$-out-of-$(j-1)$ secret sharing for $x_i^0$ thus obtaining $s_{i,1}, \ldots, s_{i,j-1}$.
  3. Construct a $(l-i)$-out-of-$(n-j)$ secret sharing for $x_i^1$ thus obtaining $s_{i,j+1}, \ldots, s_{i,n}$.
  4. Define $s_{i,j} := \tilde{x}_i$.
– For $i = 1, \ldots, n$ set $s_i = (s_{1,i}, \ldots, s_{l,i})$.
– Output $(s_1, \ldots, s_n)$.

The algorithm $\text{Reconstruct}^{\text{PoSS}^*}$ takes as input $(s_{j_1}, \ldots, s_{j_l})$ and the index $j$, and executes the following steps.

1. If there does not exist $\alpha$ such that $j_\alpha = j$ then output $\perp$ else continue as follows.
2. For $i = 1, \ldots, l$ parses $s_{j_i}$ as $(s_{1,j_i}, \ldots, s_{l,j_i})$.
3. Use the shares $s_{\alpha,j_1}, \ldots, s_{\alpha,j_{\alpha-1}}$ to reconstruct $x_\alpha^0$.
4. Use the shares $s_{\alpha,j_{\alpha+1}}, \ldots, s_{\alpha,j_l}$ to reconstruct $x_\alpha^1$.
5. Output $x_\alpha \leftarrow x_\alpha^0 \oplus x_\alpha^1 \oplus s_{\alpha,j_\alpha}$.

We note passing that a PoSS scheme could be constructed from monotone span programs [22]. However, for some of our applications we need a PoSS scheme that is also secure under a stronger notion (*enhanced PoSS*). For this reason we have provided one ad-hoc scheme that relies on standard $k$-out-of-$m$ secret sharing and that can be proven secure under the notion of PoSS and its stronger variant.

**Theorem 1.** (Share$^{\mathsf{PoSS}^*}$, Reconstruct$^{\mathsf{PoSS}^*}$) *is a PoSS scheme.*

For this and the proofs of all the subsequent theorems, we refer the reader to the full version of the paper. We now present the notion of Enhanced Positional Secret Sharing (ePoSS). An ePoSS scheme is a PoSS scheme with an additional security property that guarantees the protection of some of the secret inputs even when an adversary obtains more than $l$ shares. In more detail, the notion of PoSS guarantees that when $l$ shares are available one of the $l$ secret can be reconstructed, and nothing about the other $l - 1$ secrets is leaked. The notion of ePoSS guarantees that even if an adversary has $l + c$ shares, then at least $l - c - 1$ secrets remain protected. In the same spirit as in the definition of PoSS, the notion of ePoSS specifies also which secrets remain protected depending on the indexes of the dealer (the second input of the sharing algorithm). We show that the construction provided in the previous section already satisfies this additional security property. The formal definition follows.

**Definition 9 (Enhanced Positional Secret Sharing).** *An* Enhanced Positional Secret Sharing *scheme over a message space* $\mathcal{M}$ *is a PoSS scheme described by the* PPT *algorithms* (Share$^{\mathsf{ePoSS}}$, Reconstruct$^{\mathsf{ePoSS}}$) *which satisfies the following additional property.*

**Enhanced Positional Security.** $\forall (x_1, \ldots, x_l), (x'_1, \ldots, x'_l) \in \mathcal{M}^l$, $\forall S = \{j_1, \ldots, j_{l+c}\} \subseteq \{1, \ldots, n\}$ *with* $j_1 < j_2 < \cdots < j_{l-1} < j_l < \cdots < j_{l+c}$:

1. *If there exists* $\alpha \in \{1, \ldots, l+c\}$ *such that* $j_\alpha = j$, *and* $c \leq l$ *then*

   1.1 *If* $\alpha \leq l$ *then the following distributions are identical (where* $\gamma = \min\{c, \alpha - 1\}$):

   $\{(s_i)_{i \in S} : (s_1, \ldots, s_n)$
   $\xleftarrow{\$}$ Share$^{\mathsf{ePoSS}}((x_1, \ldots, x_{\alpha-\gamma-1}, x_{\alpha-\gamma}, \ldots, x_{\alpha-1}, x_\alpha, \ldots, x_l), j)\}$
   $\{(s_i)_{i \in S} : (s_1, \ldots, s_n)$
   $\xleftarrow{\$}$ Share$^{\mathsf{ePoSS}}((x'_1, \ldots, x'_{\alpha-\gamma-1}, x_{\alpha-\gamma}, \ldots, x_\alpha, x'_{\alpha+1}, \ldots, x'_l), j)\}.$

   1.2 *If* $\alpha > l$ *the following distributions are identical:*

   $\{(s_i)_{i \in S} : (s_1, \ldots, s_n)$
   $\xleftarrow{\$}$ Share$^{\mathsf{ePoSS}}((x_1, \ldots, x_{\alpha-c-1}, x_{\alpha-c}, \ldots, x_{l-1}, x_l), j)\}$
   $\{(s_i)_{i \in S} : (s_1, \ldots, s_n)$
   $\xleftarrow{\$}$ Share$^{\mathsf{ePoSS}}((x'_1, \ldots, x'_{\alpha-c-1}, x_{\alpha-c}, \ldots, x_{l-1}, x_l), j)\}$

2. *if* $\nexists \alpha \in \{1, \ldots, l+c\}$ *such that* $j_\alpha = j$, *the following are identical:*

   $\{(s_i)_{i \in S} : (s_1, \ldots, s_n) \xleftarrow{\$}$ Share$^{\mathsf{ePoSS}}((x_1, \ldots, x_l), j)\}$
   $\{(s'_i)_{i \in S} : (s'_1, \ldots, s'_n) \xleftarrow{\$}$ Share$^{\mathsf{ePoSS}}((x'_1, \ldots, x'_l), j)\}$

It is easy to see that for $c = 0$ the properties of enhanced positional and positional security are equivalent and that for $c \geq l - 1$ none of the secrets is protected.

**Theorem 2.** $(\mathsf{Share}^{\mathsf{PoSS}^*}, \mathsf{Reconstruct}^{\mathsf{PoSS}^*})$ *is an Enhanced Positional Secret Sharing scheme*

## 6   Threshold NIMPC

In this section we show how to construct a $t$-secure NIMPC $\mathsf{NIMPC}^{\mathsf{th}} := (\mathsf{Setup}^{\mathsf{th}}, \mathsf{Msg}^{\mathsf{th}}, \mathsf{Eval}^{\mathsf{th}})$. That is, a threshold NIMPC protocol for $n$ parties, with threshold $l$ that supports up to $t$ corruptions. For our construction we make use of the following tools.

- A $t$-robust NIMPC protocol $\mathsf{NIMPC} := (\mathsf{Setup}, \mathsf{Msg}, \mathsf{Eval})$.
- A PoSS scheme $\mathsf{PSS} := (\mathsf{Share}^{\mathsf{PoSS}}, \mathsf{Reconstruct}^{\mathsf{PoSS}})$.

At a high level our protocol $\mathsf{NIMPC}^{\mathsf{th}}$ works as follows.

**Setup:** The algorithm $\mathsf{Setup}^{\mathsf{th}}$ runs the setup algorithm of the $t$-robust NIMPC protocol on input the unary representation of $l$ (the number of parties that will participate in the computation) thus obtaining $\tilde{\rho}_0, \ldots, \tilde{\rho}_l$. Then, for each $i \in \{1, \ldots, l\}$, $\mathsf{Setup}^{\mathsf{th}}$ computes an encoding of the input 0 and of the input 1 using NIMPC: $\tilde{m}_i^0 \leftarrow \mathsf{Msg}(\tilde{\rho}_i, 0)$, $\tilde{m}_i^1 \leftarrow \mathsf{Msg}(\tilde{\rho}_i, 1)$. As a final step, for all $i \in \{1, \ldots, l\}$, $\mathsf{Setup}^{\mathsf{th}}$ computes a positional secret sharing of the messages $(\tilde{m}_1^0, \ldots, \tilde{m}_k^0)$ using index $i$ thus obtaining $(s_{i,1}^0, \ldots, s_{i,n}^0)$, and a positional secret sharing of the messages $(\tilde{m}_1^1, \ldots, \tilde{m}_k^1)$, always for the index $i$, obtaining $(s_{i,1}^1, \ldots, s_{i,n}^1)$. The output of $\mathsf{Setup}^{\mathsf{th}}$ corresponds to $(\tilde{\rho}_0, \rho_1, \ldots, \rho_n)$ where $\rho_i := (s_{j,i}^0, s_{j,i}^1)_{j \in \{1, \ldots, n\}}$ for all $i \in \{1, \ldots, n\}$.

**Online Messages.** The party $p_i$ with input $\rho_i := (s_{j,i}^0, s_{j,i}^1)_{j \in \{1, \ldots, n\}}$ and the input $x_i \in \{0, 1\}$ sends $m_i := (s_{1,i}^0, s_{1,i}^1), \ldots, s_{i,i}^{x_i}, \ldots, (s_{n,i}^0, s_{n,i}^1)$

**Evaluation.** The evaluator $p_0$, on input $\tilde{\rho}_0, m_{j_1}, \ldots, m_{j_l}$ with $0 \leq j_1 < \cdots < j_l \leq n$, performs the following steps. For all $i \in \{1, \ldots, l\}$, let $b_i \in \{0, 1\}$ be such that $\tilde{m}_i \xleftarrow{\$} \mathsf{Reconstruct}^{\mathsf{PoSS}}(s_{j_i, j_1}^{b_i}, \ldots, s_{j_i, j_i}^{b_i}, \ldots, s_{j_i, j_l}^{b_i}, j_i)$ and $\tilde{m}_i \neq \perp$.[8] Then $p_0$ computes and outputs $\mathsf{Eval}(\tilde{\rho}_0, \tilde{m}_1, \ldots, \tilde{m}_l)$.

It is easy to see that in the above construction a malicious evaluator can learn the input of the honest party $p_i$ by only inspecting the bit $b_i$. To avoid this trivial attack we just need to permute the shares sent by the parties to the evaluator. We decided to not include this additional step into the informal description of the protocol to make it easier to read. We show how the complete scheme works in the formal description of the protocol proposed Fig. 2. Intuitively, the scheme is secure because of the following reasons:

---

[8] In this informal description of the protocol we assume that the algorithm $\mathsf{Reconstruct}^{\mathsf{PoSS}}$ outputs $\perp$ in the case that some of the input shares are ill formed (e.g., the input shares are the combination of different execution of the algorithm $\mathsf{Share}^{\mathsf{PoSS}}$).

---

**Setup**

1. Run $\mathsf{Setup}(1^l, 1^\lambda, f)$ obtaining $\tilde{\rho}_0, \ldots, \tilde{\rho}_l$.
2. For $i = 1, \ldots, l$ compute $\tilde{m}_i^0 \leftarrow \mathsf{Msg}(\tilde{\rho}_i, 0)$, $\tilde{m}_i^1 \leftarrow \mathsf{Msg}(\tilde{\rho}_i, 1)$
3. For $i = 1, \ldots, n$ pick the permutation bit $b_i \xleftarrow{\$} \{0, 1\}$, run
   3.1. $\mathsf{PSS}(\tilde{m}_1^0, \ldots, \tilde{m}_l^0, i)$ thus obtaining $(s_{i,1}^{b_i}, \ldots, s_{i,n}^{b_i})$ and run
   3.2. $\mathsf{PSS}(\tilde{m}_1^1, \ldots, \tilde{m}_l^1, i)$ obtaining $(s_{i,1}^{1-b_i}, \ldots, s_{i,n}^{1-b_i})$.
4. Output $(\rho_0, \rho_1, \ldots, \rho_n)$ where $\rho_0 := \tilde{\rho}_0$ and for $i = 1, \ldots, n$, $\rho_i := (b_i, (s_{j,i}^0, s_{j,i}^1)_{j \in \{1, \ldots, n\}})$.

**Online messages.** On input $x_i \in \{0, 1\}$ and $\rho_i$ the party $p_i$ does the following.

1. If $b_i = 0$ then set $s_{i,i} \leftarrow s_{i,i}^{x_i}$ and $d_i \leftarrow x_i$ else set $s_{i,i} \leftarrow s_{i,i}^{1-x_i}$ and $d_i \leftarrow 1 - x_i$.
2. Sends $m_i := ((s_{1,i}^0, s_{1,i}^1), \ldots, s_{i,i}, \ldots, (s_{n,i}^0, s_{n,i}^1), d_i)$.

**Evaluation**

1. On input $\rho_0, m_{j_1}, \ldots, m_{j_l}$ with $0 \le j_1 < \cdots < j_l \le n$, for $i = 1, \ldots, l$ compute $\tilde{m}_i \leftarrow \mathsf{Reconstruct}^{\mathsf{PoSS}}(s_{j_i, j_1}^{d_{j_i}}, \ldots, s_{j_i, j_i}, \ldots, s_{j_i, j_l}^{d_{j_i}}, j_i)$.
2. Compute and output $\mathsf{Eval}(\rho_0, \tilde{m}_1, \ldots, \tilde{m}_l)$.

---

**Fig. 2.** Our $t$-secure NIMPC

1. The *standard security* property of the PoSS scheme exposes only one between $\mathsf{Msg}(\tilde{\rho}_j, 0)$ and $\mathsf{Msg}(\tilde{\rho}_j, 1)$ for all $j \in [l]$ when $i_j \in [n]$ is the index of an honest party $p_{i_j}$. Indeed, an honest party $p_{i_j}$ will not send the share $s_{i_j, i_j}^{1-x_i}$ where $x_{i_j}$ denotes the input bit of $p_{i_j}$. Hence, there would not be enough shares to reconstruct $\mathsf{Msg}(\tilde{\rho}_i, 1 - x_{i_j})$.
2. The *positional security* guarantees that the adversary, with respect to a corrupted party $p_{i_k}$, can obtain only the two messages $\mathsf{Msg}(\tilde{\rho}_k, 0)$ and $\mathsf{Msg}(\tilde{\rho}_k, 1)$ (where $i_k \in [n]$ and $k \in [l]$).
3. The security of the $t$-robust NIMPC guarantees that even if for the corrupted parties $p_{c_1}, \ldots, p_{c_t}$ the adversary obtains $\mathsf{Msg}(\tilde{\rho}_i, 0)$ and $\mathsf{Msg}(\tilde{\rho}_i, 1)$ for each $i \in [t]$ this does not represent a problem.

**Theorem 3.** *If* NIMPC *is a $t$-robust NIMPC protocol, then* NIMPC$^{\mathsf{th}}$ *is a $t$-secure Threshold NIMPC protocol.*

## 7   Ad Hoc PSM

We start by showing how to construct an $(l, l + c)$-secure ad hoc PSM protocol, for an arbitrary non-negative integer $c$, for a very simple functionality that we call *message selector* and denote with $f^{\mathsf{msg\text{-}sel}}$. $f^{\mathsf{msg\text{-}sel}}$ takes $l$ inputs, and each input $i \in [l]$ consists of 1) a list of size $l$ of $\lambda$-bit strings and 2) and integer $i_o$ with $i_o \in [n]$ (this will represent the index of the party that is contributing to the input). The output of $f^{\mathsf{msg\text{-}sel}}$ corresponds to the concatenation of $l$ messages, where the message in position $j$ corresponds to the $j$-th message in the input list of the party with the $j$-th greatest index that is participating in the online phase. We propose a formal description of the function in Fig. 3. We denote our protocol with $\Pi^{\mathsf{msg\text{-}sel}} := (\mathsf{Setup}^{\mathsf{msg\text{-}sel}}, \mathsf{Msg}^{\mathsf{msg\text{-}sel}}, \mathsf{Eval}^{\mathsf{msg\text{-}sel}})$ and provide an informal description of it for the simplified case in which the input of each party is a list of bits (instead of list of $\lambda$-bit strings). In the formal description we consider the generic case where the input of each party is a list of $\lambda$-bit strings. At a very high level, the protocol $\Pi^{\mathsf{msg\text{-}sel}}$ works as follows.

---

**Input:** $\left((x_k^{i_1})_{k\in[l]}, i_1\right), \ldots \left((x_k^{i_l})_{k\in[l]}, i_l\right)$ where $\{i_1, \ldots, i_l\} \subseteq [n]$, $x_k^{i_1}, \ldots, x_k^{i_l} \in \{0,1\}^{\lambda}$, $l \leq n$ and $n, \lambda \in \mathbb{N}$.
**Output:** Let $(j_1, \ldots, j_l)$ be a permutation of the values $(i_1, \ldots, i_l)$ such that $0 \leq j_1 < j_2 < \cdots < j_{l-1} < j_l \leq n$, output $x_1^{j_1} || \ldots || x_l^{j_l}$

---

**Fig. 3.** $f^{\mathsf{msg\text{-}sel}}$

**Setup:** For each party indexed by $i \in \{1, \ldots, n\}$, $\mathsf{Setup}^{\mathsf{msg\text{-}sel}}$ generates $l$ random bits $b_1, \ldots, b_l$ that we call *permutation bits*. Then $\mathsf{Setup}^{\mathsf{msg\text{-}sel}}$ computes an enhanced PoSS of $(b_1, \ldots, b_l)$ for the index $i$, and an enhanced PoSS of $(1 - b_1, \ldots, 1 - b_l)$ for the index $i$ thus obtaining $(s_{i,1}^0, \ldots, s_{i,n}^0)$ and $(s_{i,1}^1, \ldots, s_{i,n}^1)$ respectively. Intuitively, the party $i$ will receive as a part of $\rho_i$ the permutation bits, and depending on his inputs he will send the corresponding permutation bits. For example, if the first input in the list of $p_i$ is 0 then $p_i$: 1) takes the permutation bit $b_1$ (if the input of $p_i$ is 1 then $p_1$ picks as the permutation bit $1 - b_i$) 2) and sends the permutation bit together with other pieces of information (more details will follow). The output of $\mathsf{Setup}^{\mathsf{msg\text{-}sel}}$ corresponds to $(\rho_0, \rho_1, \ldots, \rho_n)$ where $\rho_i := (s_{j,i}^0, s_{j,i}^1, b_j)_{j\in\{1,\ldots,n\}}$ for all $i \in \{1, \ldots, n\}$ and $\rho_0 := \bot$.

**Online Messages.** The party $p_i$ on input $\rho_i := (s_{j,i}^0, s_{j,i}^1, b_j)_{j\in\{1,\ldots,n\}}$ and the input bits $x_1, \ldots x_l$ computes $d_1 \leftarrow b_1$ if $x_1 = b_1$ and $d_1 \leftarrow 1 - b_1$ otherwise. Repeat the same for $x_2 \ldots x_l$ and sends $m_i := \left((s_{1,i}^0, s_{1,i}^1), \ldots, (s_{n,i}^0, s_{n,i}^1), (d_1, \ldots, d_l)\right)$.

**Evaluation.** The evaluator $p_0$, on input $\tilde{\rho}_0, m_{j_1}, \ldots, m_{j_l}$ with $0 \leq j_1 < \cdots < j_l \leq n$, does the following steps. For all $i \in \{1, \ldots, l\}$ compute $y_i^0 \leftarrow \mathsf{Reconstruct}^{\mathsf{PoSS}}(s_{j_i,j_1}^0, \ldots, s_{j_i,j_l}^0, j_i)$, $y_i^1 \leftarrow \mathsf{Reconstruct}^{\mathsf{PoSS}}(s_{j_i,j_1}^0, \ldots, s_{j_i,j_l}^0, j_i)$ and $\tilde{x}_i \leftarrow y_i^{d_{j_i}}$. The output of the evaluator then corresponds to $(\tilde{x}_1, \ldots, \tilde{x}_l)$. The security of our protocol relies on the security of the enhanced PoSS scheme. Informally, let $X := ((x_{i_1}, i_1), \ldots, (x_{i_N}, i_N))$ with $N \leq l + c$ be the inputs of the parties participating in the protocol (recall that each input represents a list of $l$ bits). The notion of ad hoc PSM guarantees that a malicious evaluator can learn only the output of $f^{\mathsf{msg\text{-}sel}}$ on input any possible set $S$ where $S := ((x_{j_1}, j_1), \ldots, (x_{j_l}, j_l)) \subseteq X$. Hence, the adversary can evaluate $f^{\mathsf{msg\text{-}sel}}$ on up to $\binom{l+c}{l}$ possible sets of inputs. Consider now the input of the party $p_{i_\alpha}$ be $x_{i_\alpha}$ and let $c < l$, then we have the two possible cases (when $c \geq l$ then the evaluator can obtain all the inputs).

- If $\alpha \leq l$ then $x_{i_\alpha}$ can be placed in the $\alpha$-th input slot of $f^{\mathsf{msg\text{-}sel}}$, or in any other position $i_{\alpha-1}, \ldots, i_{\alpha-\gamma}$ with $\gamma = \min\{c, \alpha - 1\}$.
- If $\alpha > l$ then $x_{i_\alpha}$ can be place in $l$-th input slot of $f^{\mathsf{msg\text{-}sel}}$, or in any other position $i_{l-1}, \ldots, i_{\alpha-c}$ given that $N = l + c$.

Any other value in the input list $x_{i_\alpha}$ of $p_{i_\alpha}$ has to be protected. We note that this is exactly the security that an ePoSS scheme can guarantee (Fig. 4).

---

**Common input:** Input length: $\lambda$, number of parties $n$, threshold $l$ and $c$.
**Setup:**

1. For $i = 1, \ldots, n$
   1.1. For each $k = 1, \ldots l$, For each $j = 1, \ldots, \lambda$ Pick $b_j^k \xleftarrow{\$} \{0, 1\}$.
   1.2. Run $\mathsf{PSS}(b_1^1 || \ldots || b_\lambda^1, b_1^2 || \ldots || b_\lambda^2, \ldots, b_1^l || \ldots || b_\lambda^l, i)$ thus obtaining $(s_{i,1}^0, \ldots, s_{i,n}^0)$.
   1.3. Run $\mathsf{PSS}(1 - b_1^1 || \ldots || 1 - b_\lambda^1, 1 - b_1^2 || \ldots || 1 - b_\lambda^2, \ldots, 1 - b_1^l || \ldots || 1 - b_\lambda^l, i)$ thus obtaining $(s_{i,1}^1, \ldots, s_{i,n}^1)$.
   1.4. Set $B_i = (b_1^k, \ldots, b_\lambda^k)_{k \in [l]}$.
2. Output $(\rho_0, \rho_1, \ldots, \rho_n)$ where $\rho_0 := \bot$ and for $i = 1, \ldots, n$, $\rho_i := (B_i, (s_{j,i}^0, s_{j,i}^1)_{j \in \{1, \ldots, n\}})$.

**Online messages**

1. On input $x_1^i, \ldots, x_l^i \in \{0, 1\}^\lambda$ and $\rho_i$ the party $p_i$ acts as follows.
   1.1. For each $k \in [l]$ parse $x_k^i$ as a $\lambda$ bit string $x_{k,1}, \ldots, x_{k,\lambda}$.
   1.2. For each $k \in [l], j \in [\lambda]$ if $x_{k,j} = b_j^k$ then set $d_j^k = b_j^k$ else set $d_j^k = 1 - b_j^k$.
   1.3. Set $D_i \leftarrow (d_1^k, \ldots, d_\lambda^k)_{k \in [l]}$.
   1.4. Send $m_i := (D_i, (s_{1,i}^0, s_{1,i}^1), \ldots, (s_{n,i}^0, s_{n,i}^1))$.

**Evaluation**

1. On input $\rho_0, m_{k_1}, \ldots, m_{k_l}$ with $0 \leq k_1 < \cdots < k_l \leq n$, for $i = 1, \ldots, l$ do the following
   1.1. Compute $y_{1,0} || \ldots || y_{\lambda,0} \leftarrow \mathsf{Reconstruct}^{\mathsf{PoSS}}(s_{k_i,k_1}^0, \ldots, s_{k_i,k_l}^0, k_i)$,
   1.2. Compute $y_{1,1} || \ldots || y_{\lambda,1} \leftarrow \mathsf{Reconstruct}^{\mathsf{PoSS}}(s_{k_i,k_1}^1, \ldots, s_{k_i,k_l}^1, k_i)$
   1.3. For $j = 1, \ldots, \lambda$ set $c \leftarrow d_j^i$, $x_{i,j} \leftarrow y_{j,c}$
2. Compute and output $x_{1,1} || \ldots || x_{1,\lambda}, \ldots, x_{l,1} || \ldots || x_{l,\lambda}$.

---

**Fig. 4.** Our $(l, l + c)$-secure ad hoc PSM for the message selector function $f^{\mathsf{msg\text{-}sel}}$.

**Theorem 4.** $\Pi^{\text{msg-sel}}$ *is a* $(l, l + c)$*-secure ad hoc PSM protocol.*

## 7.1   Ad Hoc PSM for All Functions

In this section we show how to construct a $(l, l + c)$-secure ad hoc PSM for any function $f$ and any constant $c$, which has a simulator that is successful with probability at least $p = e^{-1}$ (where $e$ is the Euler number). We denote this scheme with $\Pi^{\text{PSM}} := (\text{Setup}^{\text{PSM}}, \text{Msg}^{\text{PSM}}, \text{Eval}^{\text{PSM}})$ and to construct it we make use of the following tools.

- An $(l, l+c)$-secure ad hoc PSM $\Pi^{\text{msg-sel}} := (\text{Setup}^{\text{msg-sel}}, \text{Msg}^{\text{msg-sel}}, \text{Eval}^{\text{msg-sel}})$ for the message selector function described in the previous section.
- A hash function H with range size $\lambda' = \lambda^{2c+2}$.[9]
- A 2-party 0-robust NIMPC scheme $\Pi^{\text{2PC}} := (\text{Setup}, \text{Msg}, \text{Eval})$ for the function $g_k$ (which will be specified later) with the following additional properties:
  1. It accepts inputs of size $\delta = 2\lambda n + n\lambda\lambda'$, where $n$ represents the number of parties and $\lambda$ is the input size allowed by $\Pi^{\text{PSM}}$ (it also represents the security parameter);[10] and $\lambda'$ is the range size of H.
  2. The size of the output of Msg depends only on $\text{poly}(\lambda, \delta)$ and it is independent from the function that $\Pi^{\text{2PC}}$ is computing (whereas the output of Setup can grow with the size of the function being computed;
  3. The randomness required to run Setup is $\kappa := \text{poly}(\lambda)$.
- A PRG $\text{PRG} : \{0, 1\}^\lambda \to \{0, 1\}^\kappa$.

We start by giving a high level idea of how our construction works starting from a scheme that does not provide security but contains most of intuitions; then we gradually modify it until we get our final scheme.

**First attempt.** Let $\rho$ be the output of the setup phase of $\Pi^{\text{msg-sel}}$ and consider $(l - 1)$ instantiations of $\Pi^{\text{2PC}}$ which we denote with $\Pi_2^{\text{2PC}}, \ldots, \Pi_l^{\text{2PC}}$. We denote with $R_i, \rho_i^0, \rho_i^1$ the output of the setup phase of $\Pi_i^{\text{2PC}}$ for each $i \in \{2, \ldots, l\}$.

For each $i \in \{2, \ldots, l - 1\}$, an instantiation $\Pi_i^{\text{2PC}}$ will be used to evaluate the function $g_i$. The function $g_i$ takes two inputs $x^0 \in \{0, 1\}^\lambda, x^1 \in \{0, 1\}^\lambda$ and outputs $\text{Msg}(\rho_{i+1}^0, x^0 || x^1)$. That is, $g_i$ outputs an encoding of the message $x^0 || x^1$ for $\Pi_{i+1}^{\text{2PC}}$. The instantiation $\Pi_l^{\text{2PC}}$ is used to evaluate the function $g_l$, which takes as input $x_1 || x_2 || \ldots || x_{l-1}$ and $x_l$ and outputs $f(x_1, x_2, \ldots, x_{l-1}, x_l)$.

Each party $p_i$ on input $x \in \{0, 1\}^\lambda$, $\rho$, $\rho_2^1, \ldots \rho_l^1$ and $\rho_2^0$ does the following.

1. Encode the input $x$ for $\Pi_2^{\text{2PC}}$ by running $\text{Msg}(\rho_2^0, x)$ thus obtaining $m_1^0$.
2. For each $j \in \{2, \ldots, l\}$
   2.1 Encode the input $x$ for $\Pi_j^{\text{2PC}}$ by running $\text{Msg}(\rho_j^1, x)$ thus obtaining $m_j^1$
3. Run $\text{Msg}^{\text{msg-sel}}(\rho, m_2^0 || m_2^1 || m_3^1 || m_4^1 || \ldots || m_l^1)$ thus obtaining $\tilde{m}_i$ and output $m_i$.

---

[9] This function is defined as the hash function that on input $x$ outputs $x \mod \lambda'$.

[10] Our construction would work for inputs of size $\text{poly}(\lambda)$, but to not overburden the notation we consider only inputs of size $\lambda$ only.

The evaluation algorithm works as follows

1. Run $\mathsf{Eval}^{\mathsf{msg\text{-}sel}}$ on input $(\tilde{m}_{k_1}, \ldots, \tilde{m}_{k_l})$ thus obtaining $m_1^1, m_2^1, \ldots, m_l^1$ (we denote with $k_1, \ldots, k_l$ the indexes of the parties that are participating in the online phase).
2. Run $\mathsf{Eval}(R_2, m_1^0, m_2^1)$ thus obtaining $m_3^0$.
3. For each $j \in \{3, \ldots, l-1\}$ run $\mathsf{Eval}(R_j, m_j^0, m_j^1)$ thus obtaining $m_{j+1}^0$.
4. Output $\mathsf{Eval}(R_l, m_l^0, m_l^1)$

Despite being correct, the above protocol suffers of a security issue. If more than $l$ parties participate to the protocol, then a corrupted evaluator could be able to obtain the encoding of two different messages with respect to the same $\rho_j^1$ for some $j \in \{2, \ldots, l\}$, and this could harm the security of $\Pi_j^{2\mathsf{PC}}$.

**Second Attempt.** To solve this problem we give a different $\rho_j^1$ to each party. In this way, even if two different parties encode different messages we can still rely on the security of $\Pi^{2\mathsf{PC}}$. This approach requires a more sophisticated function $g_j$, since now the output of $g_j$ should contain an encoding of the previous inputs under $\Pi^{2\mathsf{PC}}$ which can be combined the with the next party's encoded message, whoever she is. Hence, we modify $g_j$ (for any $j$) to output multiple encodings, one for each party with index greater than $j$. Even if this approach never causes the same $\rho_j^1$ to be used twice on different inputs, now multiple encodings of different inputs under $\rho_j^0$ might be computed by a malicious evaluator. For example, an evaluator could construct the first input for $g_j$ using two different sequences on inputs (this is possible only if the evaluator has access to more than $l$ messages sent from the honest parties).

**Our Approach.** To mitigate (but not completely solve) the above problem, we modify the above protocol as follows.

1. From the setup phase each party $p_i$ receives $\rho_{j,i}^{\mathsf{sel},0}$ for each $\mathsf{sel} \in [\lambda']$ and each $j \in [l]$ (note that we need to run the setup of $\Pi^{2\mathsf{PC}}$ $\lambda'$ times more in this protocol).
2. Each party $p_i$ picks a random value $v_i$, and encodes this value together with its input by running $\mathsf{Msg}(\rho_{j,i}^{\mathsf{sel},0}, x_i \| v_i)$ for each $\mathsf{sel} \in \lambda'$ and $j \in \{2, \ldots, l\}$.
3. The function $g_j$ now takes as input $v^0 \| x^0$ and $v^1 \| x^1$, computes $\mathsf{sel}' \leftarrow \mathsf{H}(v^0 \oplus v^1)$ and outputs $\mathsf{Msg}(\rho_{j+1,i}^{\mathsf{sel}',0}, x^0 \| x^1 \| v^0 \oplus v^1)$ for each $i$ where $\mathsf{H}$ is an hash function with range size $\lambda'$.

This protocol remains secure as long the adversary is not able to find a combination of the messages that yields to a collision in the hash function. We can prove that with probability at least $e^{-1}$ the adversary does not find a collision. Intuitively, this holds because each hash function can be evaluated at most on $\binom{l+c}{l}$ different random values. Give that $c$ is a constant value we obtain that the number of possible inputs of $\mathsf{H}$ is at most $n^c$. Hence, for a suitable choice of $\lambda'$ we can show that our protocol is simulatable with probability $e^{-1}$. In the next section we show how to amplify the security to obtain a secure ad hoc PSM. For the formal description of $\Pi^{\mathsf{PSM}}$ and of $g_k$ we refer to Fig. 5.

**Common parameters:** Security parameter $\lambda$, H $\lambda' = \lambda^{2c+1}$, $n$, $l$, and $c$.

**Setup:**

- For each $i, j \in [n]$ with $i \neq j$ do the following.
    - Run $\mathsf{Setup}(1^2, g_2, 1^\lambda)$ thus obtaining $(R_{2,i}^j, \rho_{2,i}^{j,0}, \rho_{2,i}^{j,1})$.
- For each $k \in \{3, \ldots, l-1\}$, $i \in [n]$, sel $\in [\lambda']$ do the following.
    - Pick $r_{k,i}^{\mathsf{sel}} \xleftarrow{\$} \{0,1\}^\lambda$ and compute $\mathsf{PRG}(r_{k,i}^{\mathsf{sel}})$ thus obtaining $r$.
    - Run $\mathsf{Setup}(1^2, g_k, 1^\lambda; r)$ thus obtaining $(R_{k,i}^{\mathsf{sel}}, \rho_{k,i}^{\mathsf{sel},0}, \rho_{k,i}^{\mathsf{sel},1})$.
- For each sel $\in [\lambda']$ $i \in [n]$ run $\mathsf{Setup}(1^2, g_l, 1^\lambda)$ thus obtaining $(R_{l,i}^{\mathsf{sel}}, \rho_{l,i}^{\mathsf{sel},0}, \rho_{l,i}^{\mathsf{sel},1})$
- Run $\mathsf{Setup}^{\mathsf{msg\text{-}sel}}(1^n, 1^l, 1^\lambda, f^{\mathsf{msg\text{-}sel}})$ thus obtaining $(\rho_0^{\mathsf{th}}, \rho_1^{\mathsf{th}}, \ldots, \rho_n^{\mathsf{th}})$.
- For $i \leftarrow 1, \ldots, n$ pick $v_i \xleftarrow{\$} \{0,1\}^\lambda$ and set
$$\rho_i := (v_i, (r_{k,i}^{\mathsf{sel}})_{j > i})_{j \in [n] \mathsf{sel} \in [\lambda'], k \in \{3,\ldots,l\}}, (\rho_{k,i}^{\mathsf{sel},1})_{\mathsf{sel} \in [\lambda'], k \in \{3,\ldots,l\}},$$
$$(\rho_{2,j}^{i,0}, \rho_{2,i}^{j,1})_{j \in [n]-\{i\}}, \rho_i^{\mathsf{th}}) \text{ and } \rho_0 := \rho_0^{\mathsf{th}}, \{R_{k,i}^{\mathsf{sel}}\}_{\mathsf{sel} \in [\lambda'], i \in [n], k \in [l]}$$

**Online messages.** On input $x_i \in \{0,1\}^\lambda$ and $\rho_i$ the party $p_i$ does the following.

- For each $j \in [n] - \{i\}$ compute $m_{1,j}^{i,0} \leftarrow \mathsf{Msg}(\rho_{2,j}^{i,0}, (x_i, v_i))$.
- For each $j \in [n] - \{i\}$ compute $m_{2,i}^{j,1} \leftarrow \mathsf{Msg}(\rho_{2,i}^{j,1}, i||x_i||v_i||\{r_{3,c>i}^{\mathsf{sel},0}\}_{c \in [n]})$.
- For each $k \in \{3, \ldots, l-2\}$, sel $\in [\lambda']$ compute
$m_{k,i}^{\mathsf{sel},1} \leftarrow \mathsf{Msg}(\rho_{k,i}^{\mathsf{sel},1}, i||x_i||v_i||\{r_{k+1,j>i}^{\mathsf{sel},0}\}_{j \in [n], \mathsf{sel} \in [\lambda']})$
- For each sel $\in [\lambda']$ compute $m_{l,i}^{\mathsf{sel},1} \leftarrow \mathsf{Msg}(\rho_{l,i}^{\mathsf{sel},1}, x_i)$
- Compute and send
$m_i \leftarrow \mathsf{Msg}^{\mathsf{msg\text{-}sel}}(\rho_i^{\mathsf{th}}, (\{m_{1,j}^{i,0}\}_{j \in [n]-\{i\}}, \{m_{2,i}^{j,1}\}_{j \in [n]-\{i\}}, \ldots, \{m_{l,i}^{\mathsf{sel},1}\}_{\mathsf{sel} \in [\lambda']}, i))$

**Evaluation** On input $\rho_0, m_{k_1}, \ldots, m_{k_l}$ with $0 \leq k_1 < \cdots < k_l \leq n$:

- Run $\mathsf{Eval}(\rho_0^{\mathsf{th}}, m_{k_1}, \ldots, m_{k_l})$ thus obtaining
$\{m_{1,\mathsf{sel}}^{k_1,0}\}_{\mathsf{sel} \in [n]-\{k_1\}}, \{m_{2,k_2}^{\mathsf{sel},1}\}_{\mathsf{sel} \in [n]-\{k_2\}}, \ldots, \{m_{l-1,k_{l-1}}^{\mathsf{sel},1}\}_{\mathsf{sel} \in [\lambda']}, \{m_{l,k_l}^{\mathsf{sel},1}\}_{\mathsf{sel} \in [\lambda']}$.
- Run $\mathsf{Eval}(R_{2,k_2}^{k_1}, m_{1,k_2}^{k_1,0}, m_{2,k_2}^{k_1,1})$ thus obtaining $\{\mu_{3,i}^{\mathsf{sel},0}\}_{i \in [n]}$.
- For $j \leftarrow 3, \ldots, l-1$: Run $\mathsf{Eval}(R_{j,k_j}^{\mathsf{sel}'}, \mu_{j,k_j}^{\mathsf{sel}',0}, m_{j,k_j}^{\mathsf{sel}',1})$ thus obtaining $\{\mu_{j+1,i}^{\mathsf{sel}'',0}\}_{i \in [n]}$, set $\mathsf{sel}' \leftarrow \mathsf{sel}''$.
- Compute $y \leftarrow \mathsf{Eval}(R_{l,k_l}^{\mathsf{sel}'}, \mu_{l,k_l}^{\mathsf{sel}',0}, m_{l,k_l}^{\mathsf{sel}',1})$ and output $y$.

---

$g_k(x||v_1, j||y||v_2||\{r_{k+1,i>j}^{\mathsf{sel}}\}_{j \in [n], \mathsf{sel} \in [\lambda']})$ :
$v \leftarrow v_1 \oplus v_2$, $\mathsf{sel}' \leftarrow \mathsf{H}(v)$
For each $i \in \{j+1, \ldots, n\}$ compute
$r \leftarrow \mathsf{PRG}(r_{k+1,i}^{\mathsf{sel}'})$, $(R_{k+1,i}^{\mathsf{sel}'}, \rho_{k+1,i}^{\mathsf{sel}',0}, \rho_{k+1,i}^{\mathsf{sel}',1}) \leftarrow \mathsf{Setup}(1^n, 1^\lambda, g_{k+1}; r)$.
$\mu_{k+1,i}^{\mathsf{sel}',0} \leftarrow \mathsf{Msg}(\rho_{k+1,i}^{\mathsf{sel}',0}, x||y||v)$.
Return $\{\mu_{k+1,i}^{\mathsf{sel}',0}\}_{i \in \{j+1, \ldots, n\}}$
$g_l(x, y)$ : Parse $x$ as $l$ bit-strings of $\lambda$ bits $x_1, \ldots, x_{l-1}$ and compute and output $f(x_1, \ldots, x_{l-1}, y)$.

**Fig. 5.** Our ad hoc PSM for all functions that is secure with probability $e^{-1}$.

**Theorem 5.** *There exists a simulator that successfully satisfies the definition of $(l, l + c)$-secure ad hoc PSM with probability at least $e^{-1}$, for any constant $c$.*

*How to instantiate the 2-party 0-robust NIMPC scheme $\Pi^{2PC}$.* Our compiler requires non-standard requirement on the size of the messages of the protocol $\Pi^{2PC}$. As also noted in [9], 0-robust NIMPC protocol can be constructed from garbled circuits. And this construction would have all the properties that we need. At a high level the construction works as follows. Let $g$ be a two-input function where each input is of size $M$. In the setup phase a garbled circuit $\tilde{C}$ for the function $g$ and the corresponding wire keys $L_{0,1}, L_{1,1}, \ldots L_{0,M}, L_{1,M}, R_{0,1}, R_{1,1}, \ldots R_{0,M}, R_{1,M}$ are computed. Then $\rho = \tilde{C}$ is given to the evaluator, the keys $\rho_0 = L_{0,1}, L_{1,1}, \ldots L_{0,M}, L_{1,M}$ are given to to the party $p_0$ and the keys $\rho_1 = R_{0,1}, R_{1,1}, \ldots R_{0,M}, R_{1,M}$ are given to the party $p_1$. For the evaluation, the party $p_0$ on input $x \in \{0, 1\}^M$ parses it as a bit string $x_1, \ldots, x_M$ and sends to the evaluator $L_{x_1,1}, \ldots L_{x_M,M}$. The party $p_1$ does the same for its input $y$ but using the keys $\rho_1 = R_{0,1}, R_{1,1}, \ldots R_{0,M}, R_{1,M}$. The evaluator then uses the received keys and $\tilde{C}$ to compute $g(x, y)$. This construction is provided in [13], the only difference is that in their protocol the $\tilde{C}$ is sent by one of the parties instead in our case we assume that $\tilde{C}$ is already given to the evaluator from the setup phase. This construction has the property that we need since the size of the keys of the garbled circuit depends only on the security parameter and on the size of the inputs and *does not* depend on the size of the function $g$ [2]. Then can instantiate our protocol from one-way functions.

## 7.2  Fully Secure Ad Hoc PSM

We are now ready to provide a fully-secure ad hoc PSM $\Pi^{APSM}$ := $(\mathsf{Setup}^{APSM}, \mathsf{Msg}^{APSM}, \mathsf{Eval}^{APSM})$ that realizes any function $f$. We use the following tools.

- An $(l, l + c)$-secure ad hoc PSM protocol $\Pi^{PSM}$ := $(\mathsf{Setup}^{PSM}, \mathsf{Msg}^{PSM}, \mathsf{Eval}^{PSM})$ that supports up to a $n$ parties and that is simulatable with probability $\frac{1}{p}$ with $p \leq e$ (where $e$ is the Euler number).
- An additive $(l, \mathsf{m}, \mathsf{m} - 1)$-HSS Scheme for the function $f$ HSS := $(\mathsf{Share}^{HSS}, \mathsf{Eval}^{HSS}, \mathsf{Dec}^{HSS})$ where $\mathsf{m} := p\lambda$.

At a very high level our protocol consists of $\mathsf{m}$ instantiations of the $\Pi^{PSM}$ where the $j$-th instantiation evaluates the function $G_j$ with $j \in [\mathsf{m}]$. The Function $G_j$ takes as input $l$ shares of the HSS scheme, and uses them as input of $\mathsf{Eval}^{HSS}$ together with the *server index* $j$ (see bottom of Fig. 6 for a formal specification of $G_j$). Each party $p_i$ that wants to participate in the protocol computes a secret sharing of his input thus obtaining $\mathsf{m}$ shares. Then $p_i$ encodes each share by running $\mathsf{Msg}^{PSM}$ (one execution of $\mathsf{Msg}^{PSM}$ per share). The evaluator runs the evaluation algorithm of the $j$-th instantiation of $\Pi^{PSM}$ thus obtaining $y_j$ (which corresponds to the output of $\mathsf{Eval}^{HSS}$) for each $j \in [\mathsf{m}]$. The output of the evaluation phase then corresponds to $y_1 \oplus \cdots \oplus y_\mathsf{m}$. We show that this protocol is secure as long as there is at least one execution of $\Pi^{\mathsf{PSM}}$ that simulatable. Moreover, by choosing m opportunely we can prove that at least for one instantiation of $\Pi^{\mathsf{PSM}}$ the simulator is successful with overwhelming probability. Hence, at least one share of each of the inputs of the honest parties will be protected. Therefore, because of the security offered by the HSS, also the entire input of the parties will be protected. We refer to Fig. 6 for the formal description of $\Pi^{\mathsf{APSM}}$.

---

**Common parameters:** $\lambda$, $n$, $l$, $c$ where $l + c$ denotes the maximum number of active parties supported by the protocol and $\mathsf{m} = p\lambda$.

**Setup:**

1. For each $j \in \mathsf{m}$ run $\mathsf{Setup}^{\mathsf{PSM}}(1^n, 1^l, 1^\lambda, G_j)$ thus obtaining $\rho_0^j, \rho_1^j, \ldots, \rho_n^j$.
2. Output $\rho_0, \rho_1, \ldots, \rho_n$ with $\rho_0 := (\rho_0^j)_{j \in [\mathsf{m}]}, \rho_1 := (\rho_1^j)_{j \in [\mathsf{m}]}, \ldots \rho_n := (\rho_n^j)_{j \in [\mathsf{m}]}$

**Online messages.** On input $x_i \in \{0,1\}^\lambda$ and $\rho_i$ the party $p_i$ does the following.

1. For each $k \in [l]$ run $\mathsf{Share}^{\mathsf{HSS}}(1^\lambda, k, x)$ thus obtaining $x_i^{1,k}, \ldots x_i^{m,k}$.
2. For each $j \in \mathsf{m}$ run $\mathsf{Msg}^{\mathsf{PSM}}(\rho_i^j, ((x_i^{j,k})_{k \in [l]}, i))$ thus obtaining $m_i^j$.
3. Send $m_i := (m_i^j)_{j \in [\mathsf{m}]}$

**Evaluation**

1. On input $\rho_0, m_{k_1} := (m_{k_1}^j)_{j \in [\mathsf{m}]}, \ldots, m_{k_l} := (m_{k_l}^j)_{j \in [\mathsf{m}]}$ with $0 \le k_1 < \cdots < k_l \le n$ the evaluator does the following.
2. For each $j \in \mathsf{m}$ run $\mathsf{Eval}^{\mathsf{PSM}}(\rho_0^j, m_{k_1}^j, \ldots, m_{k_l}^j)$ thus obtaining $y^j$.
3. Output $y^1 \oplus \cdots \oplus y^{\mathsf{m}}$

---

The function $G_j$ with $j \in [\mathsf{m}]$ takes as input $((x_{i_1}^k)_{k \in [l]}, i_1), \ldots ((x_{i_l}^k)_{k \in [l]}, i_l)$ where $\{i_1, \ldots, i_l\} \subseteq [n]$, $x_{i_1}^k, \ldots, x_{i_l}^k \in \{0,1\}^\lambda$, $l \le n$ and $n, \lambda \in \mathbb{N}$, and outputs $\mathsf{Eval}^{\mathsf{HSS}}(j, x_{j_1}^1, \ldots, x_{j_l}^l)$ where $(j_1, \ldots, j_l)$ is a permutation of the values $(i_1, \ldots, i_l)$ such that $0 \le j_1 < j_2 < \cdots < j_{l-1} < j_l \le n$.

---

**Fig. 6.** Our fully secure ad hoc PSM for all functions

**Theorem 6.** $\Pi^{\mathsf{APSM}}$ *is a* $(l, l+c)$*-secure ad hoc PSM protocol for any constant* $c$.

Since $\Pi^{\mathsf{PSM}}$ can be constructed from OWFs and since the HSS scheme can be instantiated from the LWEs assumption [10,12] then our protocol can be instantiated assuming LWEs.

*Adaptive-ad-hoc PSM.* As we have anticipated in the introduction, it is straight-forward to construct a $(l, t)$-secure adaptive-ad-hoc PSM from a $(l, t)$-secure Ad Hoc PSM protocol. We refer to the full version for more detail.

**Acknowledgments.** Vipul Goyal is supported in part by the NSF award 1916939, DARPA SIEVE program, a gift from Ripple, a DoE NETL award, a JP Morgan Faculty Fellowship, a PNC center for financial services innovation award, and a Cylab seed funding award. Rafail Ostrovsky is supported in part by DARPA under Cooperative Agreement No: HR0011-20-2-0025, NSF Grant CNS-2001096, US-Israel BSF grant 2015782, Google Faculty Award, JP Morgan Faculty Award, IBM Faculty Research Award, Xerox Faculty Research Award, OKAWA Foundation Research Award, B. John Garrick Foundation Award, Teradata Research Award, and Lockheed-Martin Corporation Research Award. The views and conclusions contained herein are those of the authors and should not be interpreted as necessarily representing the official policies, either expressed or implied, of DARPA, the Department of Defense, or the U.S. Government. The U.S. Government is authorized to reproduce and distribute reprints for governmental purposes not withstanding any copyright annotation therein. Michele Ciampi is supported by H2020 project PRIVILEDGE #780477 and the work is done in part while consulting for Stealth Software Technologies, Inc.

# References

1. Applebaum, B.: Garbled circuits as randomized encodings of functions: a primer. In: Electronic Colloquium on Computational Complexity (ECCC), vol. 24, p. 67 (2017). https://eccc.weizmann.ac.il/report/2017/067
2. Applebaum, B., Ishai, Y., Kushilevitz, E.: How to garble arithmetic circuits. In: Ostrovsky, R. (ed.) 52nd Annual Symposium on Foundations of Computer Science, Palm Springs, CA, USA, 22–25 October 2011, pp. 120–129. IEEE Computer Society Press (2011). https://doi.org/10.1109/FOCS.2011.40
3. Barak, B., et al.: On the (im)possibility of obfuscating programs. In: Kilian, J. (ed.) CRYPTO 2001. LNCS, vol. 2139, pp. 1–18. Springer, Heidelberg (2001). https://doi.org/10.1007/3-540-44647-8_1
4. Beaver, D., Micali, S., Rogaway, P.: The round complexity of secure protocols (extended abstract). In: 22nd Annual ACM Symposium on Theory of Computing, Baltimore, MD, USA, 14–16 May 1990, pp. 503–513. ACM Press (1990). https://doi.org/10.1145/100216.100287
5. Beimel, A., Gabizon, A., Ishai, Y., Kushilevitz, E.: Distribution design. In: Sudan, M. (ed.) ITCS 2016: 7th Conference on Innovations in Theoretical Computer Science, Cambridge, MA, USA, 14–16 January 2016, pp. 81–92. Association for Computing Machinery (2016). https://doi.org/10.1145/2840728.2840759
6. Beimel, A., Gabizon, A., Ishai, Y., Kushilevitz, E., Meldgaard, S., Paskin-Cherniavsky, A.: Non-interactive secure multiparty computation. In: Garay, J.A., Gennaro, R. (eds.) CRYPTO 2014. LNCS, vol. 8617, pp. 387–404. Springer, Heidelberg (2014). https://doi.org/10.1007/978-3-662-44381-1_22
7. Beimel, A., Ishai, Y., Kushilevitz, E.: Ad hoc PSM protocols: secure computation without coordination. In: Coron, J.-S., Nielsen, J.B. (eds.) EUROCRYPT 2017, Part III. LNCS, vol. 10212, pp. 580–608. Springer, Cham (2017). https://doi.org/10.1007/978-3-319-56617-7_20

8.  Beimel, A., Kushilevitz, E., Nissim, P.: The complexity of multiparty PSM proto-
    cols and related models. In: Nielsen, J.B., Rijmen, V. (eds.) EUROCRYPT 2018,
    Part II. LNCS, vol. 10821, pp. 287–318. Springer, Cham (2018). https://doi.org/
    10.1007/978-3-319-78375-8_10
9.  Benhamouda, F., Krawczyk, H., Rabin, T.: Robust non-interactive multiparty com-
    putation against constant-size collusion. In: Katz, J., Shacham, H. (eds.) CRYPTO
    2017, Part I. LNCS, vol. 10401, pp. 391–419. Springer, Cham (2017). https://doi.
    org/10.1007/978-3-319-63688-7_13
10. Boyle, E., Gilboa, N., Ishai, Y., Lin, H., Tessaro, S.: Foundations of homomorphic
    secret sharing. In: Karlin, A.R. (ed.) ITCS 2018: 9th Innovations in Theoretical
    Computer Science Conference, Cambridge, MA, USA, 11–14 January 2018, vol.
    94, pp. 21:1–21:21. LIPIcs (2018). https://doi.org/10.4230/LIPIcs.ITCS.2018.21
11. Chandran, N., Goyal, V., Ostrovsky, R., Sahai, A.: Covert multi-party computa-
    tion. In: 48th Annual Symposium on Foundations of Computer Science, Provi-
    dence, RI, USA, 20–23 October 2007, pp. 238–248. IEEE Computer Society Press
    (2007). https://doi.org/10.1109/FOCS.2007.21
12. Dodis, Y., Halevi, S., Rothblum, R.D., Wichs, D.: Spooky Encryption and Its
    Applications. In: Robshaw, M., Katz, J. (eds.) CRYPTO 2016, Part III. LNCS,
    vol. 9816, pp. 93–122. Springer, Heidelberg (2016). https://doi.org/10.1007/978-
    3-662-53015-3_4
13. Feige, U., Kilian, J., Naor, M.: A minimal model for secure computation (extended
    abstract). In: 26th Annual ACM Symposium on Theory of Computing, Montréal,
    Québec, Canada, 23–25 May 1994, pp. 554–563. ACM Press (1994). https://doi.
    org/10.1145/195058.195408
14. Goldwasser, S., Kalai, Y.T., Popa, R.A., Vaikuntanathan, V., Zeldovich, N.:
    Reusable garbled circuits and succinct functional encryption. In: Boneh, D., Rough-
    garden, T., Feigenbaum, J. (eds.) 45th Annual ACM Symposium on Theory of
    Computing, Palo Alto, CA, USA, 1–4 June 2013, pp. 555–564. ACM Press (2013).
    https://doi.org/10.1145/2488608.2488678
15. Halevi, S., Ishai, Y., Jain, A., Komargodski, I., Sahai, A., Yogev, E.: Non-
    interactive multiparty computation without correlated randomness. In: Takagi,
    T., Peyrin, T. (eds.) ASIACRYPT 2017, Part III. LNCS, vol. 10626, pp. 181–211.
    Springer, Cham (2017). https://doi.org/10.1007/978-3-319-70700-6_7
16. Halevi, S., Ishai, Y., Jain, A., Kushilevitz, E., Rabin, T.: Secure multiparty com-
    putation with general interaction patterns. In: Sudan, M. (ed.) Proceedings of
    the 2016 ACM Conference on Innovations in Theoretical Computer Science, Cam-
    bridge, MA, USA, 14–16 January 2016, pp. 157–168. ACM (2016). https://doi.
    org/10.1145/2840728.2840760
17. Halevi, S., Lindell, Y., Pinkas, B.: Secure computation on the web: computing
    without simultaneous interaction. In: Rogaway, P. (ed.) CRYPTO 2011. LNCS,
    vol. 6841, pp. 132–150. Springer, Heidelberg (2011). https://doi.org/10.1007/978-
    3-642-22792-9_8
18. Hemenway, B., Jafargholi, Z., Ostrovsky, R., Scafuro, A., Wichs, D.: Adaptively
    Secure Garbled Circuits from One-Way Functions. In: Robshaw, M., Katz, J. (eds.)
    CRYPTO 2016, Part III. LNCS, vol. 9816, pp. 149–178. Springer, Heidelberg
    (2016). https://doi.org/10.1007/978-3-662-53015-3_6
19. Ishai, Y., Kushilevitz, E.: Randomizing polynomials: a new representation with
    applications to round-efficient secure computation. In: 41st Annual Symposium
    on Foundations of Computer Science, Redondo Beach, CA, USA, 12–14 November
    2000, pp. 294–304. IEEE Computer Society Press (2000). https://doi.org/10.1109/
    SFCS.2000.892118

20. Jafargholi, Z., Scafuro, A., Wichs, D.: Adaptively indistinguishable garbled circuits. In: Kalai, Y., Reyzin, L. (eds.) TCC 2017, Part II. LNCS, vol. 10678, pp. 40–71. Springer, Cham (2017). https://doi.org/10.1007/978-3-319-70503-3_2
21. Jafargholi, Z., Wichs, D.: Adaptive security of Yao's garbled circuits. In: Hirt, M., Smith, A. (eds.) TCC 2016, Part I. LNCS, vol. 9985, pp. 433–458. Springer, Heidelberg (2016). https://doi.org/10.1007/978-3-662-53641-4_17
22. Karchmer, M., Wigderson, A.: On span programs. In: Proceedings of Structures in Complexity Theory, pp. 102–111 (1993)
23. Kolesnikov, V.: Gate evaluation secret sharing and secure one-round two-party computation. In: Roy, B. (ed.) ASIACRYPT 2005. LNCS, vol. 3788, pp. 136–155. Springer, Heidelberg (2005). https://doi.org/10.1007/11593447_8
24. Kolesnikov, V., Schneider, T.: Improved garbled circuit: free XOR gates and applications. In: Aceto, L., Damgård, I., Goldberg, L.A., Halldórsson, M.M., Ingólfsdóttir, A., Walukiewicz, I. (eds.) ICALP 2008, Part II. LNCS, vol. 5126, pp. 486–498. Springer, Heidelberg (2008). https://doi.org/10.1007/978-3-540-70583-3_40
25. Lindell, Y., Pinkas, B.: A proof of security of Yao's protocol for two-party computation. J. Cryptol. 22(2), 161–188 (2008). https://doi.org/10.1007/s00145-008-9036-8
26. Naor, M., Pinkas, B., Sumner, R.: Privacy preserving auctions and mechanism design. In: Feldman, S.I., Wellman, M.P. (eds.) Proceedings of the First ACM Conference on Electronic Commerce (EC-99), Denver, CO, USA, 3–5 November 1999, pp. 129–139. ACM (1999). https://doi.org/10.1145/336992.337028
27. Yao, A.C.C.: How to generate and exchange secrets (extended abstract). In: 27th Annual Symposium on Foundations of Computer Science, Toronto, Ontario, Canada, 27–29, October 1986, pp. 162–167. IEEE Computer Society Press (1986). https://doi.org/10.1109/SFCS.1986.25

# Indistinguishability Obfuscation

# Indistinguishability Obfuscation from Simple-to-State Hard Problems: New Assumptions, New Techniques, and Simplification

Romain Gay[1]([⊠]), Aayush Jain[2], Huijia Lin[3], and Amit Sahai[2]

[1] IBM, Zurich, Switzerland
[2] UCLA, Los Angeles, CA 90095, USA
{aayushjain,sahai}@cs.ucla.edu
[3] University of Washington, Seattle, WA 98195, USA
rachel@cs.washington.edu

**Abstract.** In this work, we study the question of what set of simple-to-state assumptions suffice for constructing functional encryption and indistinguishability obfuscation ($i\mathcal{O}$), supporting all functions describable by polynomial-size circuits. Our work improves over the state-of-the-art work of Jain, Lin, Matt, and Sahai (Eurocrypt 2019) in multiple dimensions.

NEW ASSUMPTION: Previous to our work, all constructions of $i\mathcal{O}$ from simple assumptions required novel pseudorandomness generators involving LWE samples and constant-degree polynomials over the integers, evaluated on the error of the LWE samples. In contrast, Boolean pseudorandom generators (PRGs) computable by constant-degree polynomials have been extensively studied since the work of Goldreich (2000). (Goldreich and follow-up works study Boolean pseudorandom generators with constant-locality, which can be computed by constant-degree polynomials.) We show how to replace the novel pseudorandom objects over the integers used in previous works, with appropriate Boolean pseudorandom generators with sufficient stretch, when combined with LWE with binary error over suitable parameters. Both binary error LWE and constant degree Goldreich PRGs have been a subject of extensive cryptanalysis since much before our work and thus we back the plausibility of our assumption with security against algorithms studied in context of cryptanalysis of these objects.

NEW TECHNIQUES: we introduce a number of new techniques:

- We show how to build partially-hiding *public-key* functional encryption, supporting degree-2 functions in the secret part of the message, and arithmetic $\mathsf{NC}^1$ functions over the public part of the message, assuming only standard assumptions over asymmetric pairing groups.
- We construct single-ciphertext secret-key functional encryption for all circuits with *linear* key generation, assuming only the LWE assumption.

© International Association for Cryptologic Research 2021
A. Canteaut and F.-X. Standaert (Eds.): EUROCRYPT 2021, LNCS 12698, pp. 97–126, 2021.
https://doi.org/10.1007/978-3-030-77883-5_4

SIMPLIFICATION: Unlike prior works, our new techniques furthermore let us construct *public-key* functional encryption for polynomial-sized circuits directly (without invoking any bootstrapping theorem, nor transformation from secret-key to public key FE), and based only on the *polynomial hardness* of underlying assumptions. The functional encryption scheme satisfies a strong notion of efficiency where the size of the ciphertext grows only sublinearly in the output size of the circuit and not its size. Finally, assuming that the underlying assumptions are subexponentially hard, we can bootstrap this construction to achieve $i\mathcal{O}$.

# 1    Introduction

This paper studies the notion of indistinguishability obfuscation ($i\mathcal{O}$) for general programs computable in polynomial time [21,40,50], and develops several new techniques to strengthen the foundations of $i\mathcal{O}$. The key security property for $i\mathcal{O}$ requires that for any two equivalent programs $P_0$ and $P_1$ modeled as circuits of the same size, where "equivalent" means that $P_0(x) = P_1(x)$ for all inputs $x$, we have that $i\mathcal{O}(P_0)$ is computationally indistinguishable to $i\mathcal{O}(P_1)$. Furthermore, the obfuscator $i\mathcal{O}$ should run in probabilistically polynomial time.

This notion of obfuscation was coined by [21] in 2001. However, until 2013, there was not even a single candidate construction known. This changed with the breakthrough work of [40]. Soon after, the floodgates opened and a flurry of over 100 papers were published reporting applications of $i\mathcal{O}$ (e.g. [24,33,48,54,58,73] [38,42,53]). Not only did $i\mathcal{O}$ enable the first constructions of numerous important cryptographic primitives, $i\mathcal{O}$ also *expanded* the scope of cryptography, allowing us to mathematically approach problems that were previously considered the domain of software engineering. A simple example along these lines is the notion of *crippleware* [40]: Alice, a software developer, has developed a program P using powerful secrets, and wishes to sell her work. Before requiring payment, Alice is willing to share with Bob a weakened (or "crippled") version of her software. Now, Alice could spend weeks developing this crippled version $\widetilde{P}$ of her software, being careful not to use her secrets in doing so; or she could simply disable certain inputs to cripple it yielding an equivalent P', but this would run the risk of Bob hacking her software to re-enable those disabled features. $i\mathcal{O}$ brings this problem of software engineering into the realm of mathematical analysis. With $i\mathcal{O}$, Alice could avoid weeks of effort by simply giving to Bob $i\mathcal{O}(P')$, and because this is indistinguishable from $i\mathcal{O}(\widetilde{P})$, Alice is assured that Bob can learn no secrets.

Not only has $i\mathcal{O}$ been instrumental in realizing new cryptographic applications, it has helped us advance our understanding of long-standing theoretical questions. One such recent example is that of the first cryptographic evidence of the average-case hardness of the complexity class PPAD (which contains of the problem of finding Nash equilibrium). In particular, [24] constructed hard instances for the End Of the Line (EOL) problem assuming subexponentially secure $i\mathcal{O}$ and one-way functions.

*Our Contributions.* In this work, we show how to simplify, both technically and conceptually, the task of constructing secure $i\mathcal{O}$ schemes. Notably, the ideas we develop in this work helped pave the way for the recent first construction of $i\mathcal{O}$ from well-studied assumptions [56], resolving the central open question in the area of $i\mathcal{O}$. The follow-up work of [56] builds upon this paper.

We now discuss the contributions of our paper in detail.

*What Hardness Assumptions Suffice for Constructing $i\mathcal{O}$?* Given its importance, a crucial question is to identify what hardness assumptions, in particular, simple ones, suffice for constructing $i\mathcal{O}$. While it is hard to concretely measure simplicity in assumptions, important features include i) having succinct description, ii) being falsifiable and instance independent (e.g., independent of the circuit being obfuscated), and iii) consisting of only a constant number of assumptions, as opposed to families of an exponential number of assumptions. However, research on this question has followed a tortuous path over the past several years, and so far, despite of a lot of progress, before our work, no known $i\mathcal{O}$ constructions [3,5,9,10,13,18,20,22,29,31,37,40,41,45,46,55,60,61,63,64,70] were based on assumptions that have all above features.

*Our New Assumption.* In this work, building upon assumptions introduced in [10,55], we introduce a new simple-to-state assumption, that satisfies all the features enumerated above. We show how to provably achieve $i\mathcal{O}$ based only on our new assumption combined with standard assumptions, namely subexponentially secure Learning With Errors (LWE) problem [71], and subexponentially secure SXDH and bilateral DLIN assumptions over bilinear maps [27,57]. Let us now describe, informally, our new assumption. In this introductory description, we will omit discussion of parameter choices; however, they are crucial (even for standard assumptions), and we discuss them in detail in our technical sections. We start by describing the ingredients that will go into the assumption.

Constant-degree[1] Boolean PRGs generalize constant-locality Boolean PRGs, as for Boolean functions, locality upper bounds the degree. The latter is tightly connected to the fundamental topic of Constraint Satisfaction Problems (CSPs) in complexity theory, and were first proposed for cryptographic use by Goldreich [47] 20 years ago. The complexity theory and cryptography communities have jointly developed a rich body of literature on the cryptanalysis and theory of constant-locality Boolean PRGs [14–16,26,39,47,67,68]. Our new assumption first postulates that there exists a constant $d$-degree Boolean PRG, $G : \{0,1\}^n \rightarrow \{0,1\}^m$ with sufficient stretch $m \geq n^{\lceil \frac{d}{2} \rceil \cdot (0.5+\epsilon)+\rho}$ for some constants $\epsilon, \rho > 0$, whose output $r = G(x)$ should satisfy the standard notion of pseudorandomness. Furthermore, our assumption postulates that the pseudorandomness holds even when its Boolean input $x \in \{0,1\}^n$ is embedded in LWE samples as noises, and the samples are made public. The latter is known as *Learning With Binary Errors (LWBE)*, which has been studied over the

---

[1] Throughout this work, unless specified, by degree of boolean PRGs, we mean the degree of the polynomial computing the PRG over the reals.

last decade [17,35,36,66]. Our new assumption, combining Boolean PRGs and LWBE, is as follows:

*The* G-LWEleak-*security assumption (informal).*

$$\left(\{a_i, \langle a_i, s\rangle + e_i \bmod p\}_{i \in [n]}, G, G(e)\right) \; //e = (e_1, \ldots, e_n) \leftarrow \{0,1\}^n, \; a_i, s \leftarrow \mathbb{Z}_p^{n^{0.5+\epsilon}}$$

$$\approx \; \left(\{a_i, \langle a_i, s\rangle + e_i \bmod p\}_{i \in [n]}, G, r\right) \; //r \leftarrow \{0,1\}^m$$

As is evident here, this assumption is quite succinct, is falsifiable and instance-independent, does not involve an exponential family of assumptions, and does not use multilinear maps. Furthermore, the ingredients that make up the assumption – Constant-degree Boolean PRGs and LWBE – have a long history of study within cryptography and complexity theory. As we discuss in detail in the full version, this assumption avoids attacks by all known cryptanalytic techniques. We note that the parameter $n$ of LWBE samples is chosen to be sub-quadratic in the length $|s|$ of the secret. This is needed in order to avoid Arora-Ge attacks on LWBE [17], and also avoid all known algebraic attacks [35]. Indeed, the parameter choices we make are not possible using the previous work of [55], and the parameters used in [55] would render LWBE insecure.

*Comparison of Our Assumption with the Subsequent Follow-Up Work of* [56]. Our shift to considering Boolean PRGs in the context of the approach of [55] provided a conceptual starting point for the subsequent work of [56], which finally achieved $i\mathcal{O}$ from four well-founded assumptions: LPN over $\mathbb{F}_p$, LWE, Boolean PRGs in $NC^0$, and SXDH. Indeed, the work of [56] essentially succeeds in "separating" the two ingredients in our assumption above—that is, basing $i\mathcal{O}$ on LWBE and the security of Goldreich's PRG with appropriate parameters separately, through a novel leveraging of the LPN over $\mathbb{F}_p$ assumption. Indeed, their work goes further and actually eliminates the need for the LWBE assumption entirely, and also eliminates the parameter requirements that we needed for Goldreich's PRG.

*Complexity and Clarity in $i\mathcal{O}$ Constructions.* Another motivation for our work is to address the complexity of existing $i\mathcal{O}$ constructions. Current constructions of $i\mathcal{O}$ are rather complex in the sense they often rely on many intermediate steps, each of which incur a complexity blow up, both in the sense of computational complexity and in the sense of difficulty of understanding. Ideally, for the sake of simplicity, $i\mathcal{O}$ schemes would minimize the number of such transformations, and instead aim at a more direct construction. In our case, we solely rely on the generic transformation of [12,25], which shows that $i\mathcal{O}$ can be build from Functional Encryption [74], a primitive that was originally formulated by [28,69]. Roughly speaking, FE is a public-key or secret-key encryption scheme where users can generate restricted decryption keys, called functional keys, where each such key is associated with a particular function $f$. Such a key allows the decryptor to learn from an encryption of a plaintext $m$, the value $f(m)$, and nothing beyond that.

Previous constructions fell short in directly constructing a full-fledged FE needed for the implication of $i\mathcal{O}$ [12,25]. For example, the work of [55] first obtain a "weak" FE that: i) is *secret-key*, ii) only generates function keys associated with function computable *only by* $\mathsf{NC_0}$ *circuits*, iii) only ensures *weak security*, and iv) is based on subexponential hardness assumptions. Then, generic transformations are applied to "lift" the function class supported and the security level, which inevitably makes the final FE and $i\mathcal{O}$ schemes quite complex.

This state of affairs motivates simplifying $i\mathcal{O}$ constructions, for efficiency and simplicity itself, but also for making a technically deep topic more broadly accessible to the community. That is also one of the goals of this paper.

## 1.1 Our Results

Our main result is a simpler and more direct $i\mathcal{O}$ construction from the following assumptions.

**Theorem 1.** *There is a construction of $i\mathcal{O}$ for obfuscating all polynomial-sized circuits based on the following assumptions:*

- *There exists a constant-degree $d$ Boolean PRG $G : \{0,1\}^n \rightarrow \{0,1\}^m$ with sufficient stretch $m \geq n^{\lceil \frac{d}{2} \rceil \cdot (0.5+\epsilon)+\rho}$ for some constant $\epsilon, \rho > 0$, and satisfies subexponential G-LWEleak-security,*
- *the subexponential LWBE assumption, and*
- *the subexponential bilateral DLIN and SXDH assumption over asymmetric pairing groups.*

*Our Techniques and Additional Results.* Our construction of FE and $i\mathcal{O}$ are enabled by our new assumption and a number of new techniques designed to enable basing the security of $i\mathcal{O}$ on simple-to-state assumptions. We briefly summarize them here, but we elaborate on how they are used in the $i\mathcal{O}$ construction in the technical overview section immediately following this introduction.

*Single-Ciphertext Functional Encryption with Linear Key Generation.* We construct, assuming only LWE, a single-ciphertext secret-key functional encryption scheme able to give functional keys associated with any polynomial-sized circuit with depth bounded by $\lambda$, whose key generation and decryption algorithms have certain *simple structures*: i) The key generation algorithm computes a *linear* function on the master secret key and randomness, and ii) the decryption algorithm, given a ciphertext ct, a functional secret key $\mathsf{sk}_f$ associated with a function $f$ and the description of $f$ itself, first performs some deterministic computation on the ciphertext to get an intermediate ciphertext $\mathsf{ct}_f$, followed by simply subtracting the $\mathsf{sk}_f$ from it, and then rounds to obtain the outcome. This object is previously known as special homomorphic encryption in the literature [3, 6, 62]. However, prior constructions only handles functional keys associated with $\mathsf{NC_0}$ circuits (for those based on LWE) or $\mathsf{NC^1}$ circuits (for those based on ring LWE). In this work, we view it through the FE lens, and construct it from LWE for all functions computable by polynomial-size circuits with any depth bounded by the security parameter $\lambda$. Constructing such single-ciphertext (or single-key) FE (that do not have compact ciphertexts) from standard assumptions is a meaningful goal on its own. In the literature, there are constructions of single-ciphertext FE from the minimal assumption of public-key encryption [51,72], and several applications (e.g., [8]). However, they do not have the type of simple structures (e.g., linear key generation algorithm) our construction enjoys, and consequently cannot be used in our $i\mathcal{O}$ construction. These simple structural properties may also find uses in other applications.

*Partially-Hiding Functional Encryption for* $\mathsf{NC}^1$ *Public Computation and Degree-2 Private Computation.* Partially-hiding Functional Encryption (PHFE) schemes involve functional secret keys, each of which is associated with some 2-ary function $f$, and decryption of a ciphertext encrypting $(x, y)$ with such a key reveals $f(x, y)$, $x$, $f$, and nothing more about $y$. Since only the input $y$ is hidden, such an FE scheme is called partially-hiding FE. The notion was originally introduced by [51] where it was used to bootstrap FE schemes. A similar notion of partially-hiding predicate encryption was proposed and constructed by [52]. PHFE beyond the case of predicate encryption was first constructed by [11] for functions $f$ that compute degree-2 polynomials on the input $y$ and degree-1 polynomials in $x$, under the name of 3-restricted FE, in the secret-key setting. In this work, we construct a PHFE scheme from standard assumptions over bilinear pairing groups, that is *public-key* and supports functions $f$ that have degree 2 in the private input $y$, while performs an arithmetic $\mathsf{NC}^1$ computation on the public input $x$, More precisely, $f(x, y) = \langle g(x), q(y) \rangle$ where $g$ is computable by an arithmetic log-depth circuit and $q$ is a degree-2 polynomial. The previous best constructions of partially-hiding FE were secret-key, and could only handle $\mathsf{NC}_0$ computation on the public input [55].

This contribution is interesting in its own right, as a step forward towards broadening the class of functions supported by FE schemes from standard assumptions. In particular, it can be used to combine rich access-control and perform selective computation on the encrypted data. In that context, the public input $x$ represents some attributes, while the private input $y$ is the plaintext. Functional secret keys reveal the evaluation of a degree-2 polynomial on the private input if some policy access, represented by an $\mathsf{NC}^1$ arithmetic circuit evaluates to true on the attributes. This is the key-policy variant of a class of FE with rich access-control introduced in [2]. In the latter, the authors build an FE scheme where ciphertexts encrypt a Boolean formula (the public input) and a vector (the private input). Functional secret keys are associated with attributes and a vector of weights, and decryption yields the weighted sum of the plaintexts if the formula embedded in the ciphertext evaluates to true on the attributes embedded in the functional secret key. Their construction, as ours, rely on standard pairing assumptions, but only permits computation of *degree-1* polynomials on the private input. They also give a lattice-based construction, which is limited to identity-based access structures.

# 2    Technical Overview

Below, we will use several different encryption schemes, and adopt the following notation to refer to ciphertexts and keys of different schemes. For a scheme x (e.g., a homomorphic encryption scheme HE, or a functional encryption scheme FE), we denote by xct, xsk a ciphertext, or secret key of the scheme x. At times, we write xct($m$), xsk($f$) to make it explicit what is the encrypted message $m$ and the associated function $f$; and write xct($k, m$), xsk($k, f$) to make explicit what is the key $k$ they are generated from. We omit these details when they do not matter or are clear from the context.

## 2.1    Overview of Our FE Construction

*Basic Template of FE Construction in Prior Works.* We start with reviewing the basic template of FE construction in recent works [3,10,55]. FE allows one to generate so-called functional secret key fesk($f$) associated with a function $f$ that decrypts an encryption of a plaintext $\boldsymbol{x}$, fect($\boldsymbol{x}$) to $f(\boldsymbol{x})$. Security ensures that beyond the evaluation of the function $f$ on $\boldsymbol{x}$, nothing is revealed about $\boldsymbol{x}$. For constructing $i\mathcal{O}$, it suffices to have an FE scheme whose security is guaranteed against adversaries seeing only *a single functional secret key*, for a function with long output $f : \{0,1\}^n \rightarrow \{0,1\}^m$ and where the ciphertexts are *sublinearly-compact* in the sense that its size depends sublinearly in the output length $m$.

Towards this, the basic idea is encrypting the message using a Homomorphic Encryption scheme HE, which produces the ciphertext hect($\boldsymbol{s}, \boldsymbol{x}$), where $\boldsymbol{s}$ is the secret key of HE. It is possible to publicly evaluate homomorphically any function $f$ directly on the ciphertext to obtain an so-called output ciphertext hect($\boldsymbol{s}, f(\boldsymbol{x})$) $\leftarrow$ HEEval(hect, $f$), that encrypts the output $f(\boldsymbol{x})$. Then, we use another *much simpler* FE scheme to decrypt hect($\boldsymbol{s}, f(\boldsymbol{x})$) so as to reveal $f(\boldsymbol{x})$ and nothing more. Using this paradigm, the computation of the function $f$ is delegated to HE, while the FE only computes the decryption of HE. This is motivated by the fact that HE for arbitrary functions can be built from standard assumptions, while existing FE schemes is either not compact, in the sense that the ciphertext grows with the output size of the functions [49,72], or are limited to basic functions—namely, degree-2 polynomials at most, [19,43] for the public-key setting, [13,61] for the private-key setting[2] Furthermore, known HE schemes have very simple decryption—for most of them, it is simply computing an inner product, then rounding. That is, decryption computes $\langle \text{hect}_f, \boldsymbol{s} \rangle = p/2 \cdot f(\boldsymbol{x}) + e_f$ (mod $p$) for some modulus $p$, where $\boldsymbol{s}$ is the secret key of HE, and $e_f$ is a small, polynomially bounded error (for simplicity, in this overview, we assume w.l.o.g that $f(\boldsymbol{x}) \in \{0, 1\}$). While there are FE schemes that support computing inner products [1,4], sublinearly compact FE that also computes the rounding are

---

[2] As mentioned in the introduction, partially hiding functional encryption allows to further strengthen the function class supported, by essentially adding computation on a public input, however computation on the private input is still limited to degree 2.

currently our of reach. Omitting this rounding would reveal $f(x)$, but also $e_f$, which hurts the security of HE. Instead, we will essentially realize an approximate version of the rounding—thereby hiding the noise $e_f$.

A natural approach to hide the noises $e_f$ is to use larger, smudging noises. Since $e_f$ depends on the randomness used by HEEnc, and the function $f$, the smudging noises must be fresh for every ciphertext. Hard-wiring the smudging noise in the ciphertext, as done in [6], leads to non-succinct ciphertext, whose size grows linearly with the output size of the functions. Instead, we generate the smudging noises from a short seed, using a PRG. The latter must be simple enough to be captured by state of the art FE schemes.

Previous constructions use a weak pseudo-random generator, referred to as a noise generator NG, to generate many smudging noises $r = \mathsf{NG}(\mathsf{sd})$ for hiding $e_f$. To see how it works, suppose hypothetically that there is a noise generator computable by degree-2 polynomials. Then we can use 2FE, an FE scheme that support the generation of functional key for degree-2 polynomials, to compute $p/2 \cdot f(x) + e_f + \mathsf{NG}(\mathsf{sd})$, which reveals only $f(x)$ as desired. This gives a basic template of FE construction summarized below.

---

**Basic Template of FE Construction (Intuition only, does not work)**

$$\mathsf{fesk}(f) \text{ contains} : \qquad \mathsf{2fsk}(g)$$
$$\mathsf{fect}(x) \text{ contains} : \mathsf{hect}(s,x), \mathsf{2fct}(s\|\mathsf{sd})$$

---

*The basic idea is using HE with a one-time secret key $s$ to perform the computation and using a simple FE for degree-2 polynomials, 2FE, to decrypt the output ciphertext and add a smudging noise generated via a noise generator NG. That is, we would like $g(s\|\mathsf{sd}) = (p/2 \cdot f(x) + e_f + \mathsf{NG}(\mathsf{sd}))$. However, there are many challenges to making this basic idea work.*

---

Unfortunately, to make the above basic idea work, we need to overcome a series of challenges. Below, we give an overview of the challenges, how we solve them using new tools, new techniques, and new assumptions, and how our solutions compare with previous solutions. In later Subsects. 2.2, 2.3, and in the full version, we give more detail on our solutions.

*Challenge 1: No Candidate Degree-2 Noise Generator.* Several constraints are placed on the structure of the noise generators NG which renders their instantiation difficult.

- MINIMAL DEGREE. To use degree-2 FE to compute NG, the generator is restricted to have only degree 2 in the secret seed $\mathsf{sd}$.
- SMALL (POLY-SIZED) OUTPUTS. Existing degree-2 FE are implemented using pairing groups: They perform the degree-2 computation in the exponent of the groups, and obtain the output in the exponent of the target group. This means the output $p/2 \cdot f(x) + e_f + \mathsf{NG}(\mathsf{sd})$ resides in the exponent, and the

only way to extract $f(\boldsymbol{x}) \in \{0, 1\}$ is via brute force discrete logarithm to extract the whole $p/2 \cdot f(\boldsymbol{x}) + \boldsymbol{e}_f + \mathsf{NG}(\mathsf{sd})$. This in particular restricts $\mathsf{NG}$ to have polynomially bounded outputs.

Previous works [10,55] used new assumptions that combine LWE with constant-degree polynomials over the integers (see discussion in the introduction) to instantiate the noise generator. The resulting generator do not have exactly degree 2, but "close" to degree 2 in following sense:

**Degree "2.5" Noise Generator:** $\mathsf{NG}(\mathsf{pubsd}, \mathsf{privsd})$ is a polynomial in a public seed $\mathsf{pubsd}$ and a private seed $\mathsf{privsd}$ both of length $n'$, and has polynomial stretch. The seeds are jointly sampled $(\mathsf{pubsd}, \mathsf{privsd}) \leftarrow \mathcal{D}_{\mathsf{sd}}$ from some distribution and $\mathsf{pubsd}$ is made publc. Degree 2.5 means that $\mathsf{NG}$ has constant degree in $\mathsf{pubsd}$ and degree 2 in $\mathsf{privsd}$.

Previous degree-2.5 noise generators produce small integer outputs, and can only satisfy certain weak pseudo-randomness property (as opposed to standard pseudorandomness). To get a flavor, consider the fact that the outputs of previous candidates are exactly the outputs of some constant-degree polynomials computed over the integers. Individual output elements are not uniformly distributed in any range, and two output elements that depend on the same seed element are noticably correlated. Hence, they are not pseudorandom or even pseudo-independent. In this work, our new assumption combines Learning With Binary Errors (LWBE) and constant-degree *Boolean* PRGs, and gives new degree-2.5 noise generators with *Boolean outputs* as follows:

- $\mathsf{pubsd} = \{\boldsymbol{c}_i = (\boldsymbol{a}_i, \boldsymbol{a}_i \boldsymbol{s} + e_i)\}_{i \in [n]}$: LWBE samples where $\boldsymbol{s}, \boldsymbol{a}_i \leftarrow \mathbb{Z}_p^{n^{0.5+\epsilon}}$, $e_i \leftarrow \{0, 1\}$.
- $\mathsf{privsd} = \otimes(\boldsymbol{s} || -1)^{\lceil \frac{d}{2} \rceil}$: tensoring $(\boldsymbol{s} || -1)$ for $\lceil \frac{d}{2} \rceil$ times.
- $\mathsf{PRG}(\mathsf{pubsd}, \mathsf{privsd}) = G(\cdots || e_i = \langle \boldsymbol{c}_i, (\boldsymbol{s} || -1) \rangle || \cdots) = G(\boldsymbol{e})$, where $G$ is a constant degree Boolean PRG.

When the PRG $G$ has sufficient stretch $m \geq n^{\lceil \frac{d}{2} \rceil \cdot (0.5+\epsilon)+\rho}$ for some constant $\epsilon, \rho > 0$, our new generator has polynomial stretch $m = |\mathsf{pubsd}||\mathsf{privsd}|^{1+\epsilon'}$ for some $\epsilon'$ depending on $\epsilon, \rho$. Constant-degree Boolean PRGs are qualitatively different from constant-degree polynomials over the integers and have been extensively studied. Furthermore, our new assumption implies that the outputs of our generator are *pseudo-random* – in other words, we obtain a *degree-2.5 Boolean PRG*.

Not surprisingly, the stronger security property of degree-2.5 PRG lets us significantly simplify the construction and security proof.

*Challenge 2: How to Evaluate Degree 2.5 Polynomials?* To evaluate our degree-2.5 Boolean PRG, we need an FE scheme that is more powerful than 2FE. The notion of Partially-Hiding Functional Encryption PHFE, originally introduced by [52] in the form of Partially Hiding Predicate Encryption (PHPE), fits exactly this task. As mentioned in introduction, PHFE strengthens the functionality of FE by allowing the ciphertext $\mathsf{phfct}(x, y)$ to encode a public input $x$, in addition to the usual private input $y$. Decryption by a functional key $\mathsf{phfsk}(f)$ reveals $x$ and $f(x, y)$ and nothing else. The works of [10,55] constructed *private-key* PHFE for computing degree-2.5 polynomials (i.e., constant degree in $x$ and degree 2 in $y$) from pairing groups. (Like 2FE, the output is still computed in the exponent of the target group.) This suffices for evaluating degree-2.5 noise generator or PRG in the FE construction outlined above. The only drawback is that since PHFE is private-key, the resulting FE is also private-key.

In this work, we give a new construction of PHFE from pairing groups that is 1) public-key and 2) supports arithmetic $\mathsf{NC}^1$ computation on the public input— more specifically, $f(x, y) = \langle g(x), q(y) \rangle$ where $g$ is computable by an arithmetic log-depth circuit and $q$ is a degree-2 polynomial.

**Theorem 2 (Public-key $(\mathsf{NC}^1, \deg\text{-}2)$-PHFE, Informal).** *There is a construction of a public-key PHFE for arithmetic $\mathsf{NC}^1$ public computation and degree-2 private computation from standard assumptions over asymmetric pairing groups.*

This new construction allows us to obtain public key FE directly. Furthermore, our construction supports the most expressive class of functions among all known FE schemes from standard assumptions; we believe this is of independent interests.

*Challenge 3: How to Ensure Integrity?* Now that we have replaced 2FE with PHFE to compute degree-2.5 polynomials, the last question is how to ensure that PHFE decrypts only the right evaluated ciphertext $\mathsf{hect}_f$ (instead of any other ciphertext)? The function $g$ we would like to compute via PHFE is $g(s, \mathsf{pubsd}, \mathsf{privsd}) = \langle \mathsf{hect}_f, s \rangle + \mathsf{NG}(\mathsf{pubsd}, \mathsf{privsd})$. The difficulty is that $\mathsf{hect}_f$ is unknown at key-generation time or at encryption time (as it depends on both $f$ and $\mathsf{hect}(s, x)$), and is too complex for PHFE to compute (as the homomorphic evaluation has high polynomial depth). To overcome this, we replace homomorphic encryption with a *single-ciphertext* secret-key FE for polynomial size circuits with depth $\lambda$ with *linear key generation*, denoted as $\epsilon$-1LGFE, which has the following special structure.

---

**Single Ciphertext FE with Linear Key Generation**

| | |
|---|---|
| $\mathsf{PPGen}(1^\lambda)$ | : generate public parameters $\mathsf{pp}$ |
| $\mathsf{Setup}(1^\lambda, \mathsf{pp})$ | : generate master secret key $s \in \mathbb{Z}_p^\lambda$ |
| $\mathsf{Enc}(\mathsf{pp}, s)$ | : generates a ciphertext $\epsilon\text{-1LGFE.ct}$ |
| $\mathsf{KeyGen}(\mathsf{pp}, s, f)$ | : $\mathsf{pp}_f \leftarrow \mathsf{EvalPP}(\mathsf{pp}, f)$ , $r \leftarrow ([0, B-1] \cap \mathbb{Z})^m$, |
| | output $f$ and secret key, |
| | $\epsilon\text{-1LGFE.sk}(f) = \langle \mathsf{pp}_f, s \rangle - r$ |
| $\mathsf{Dec}(\epsilon\text{-1LGFE.ct}, (f, \epsilon\text{-1LGFE.sk}))$ | : $\epsilon\text{-1LGFE.ct}_f \leftarrow \mathsf{EvalCT}(\epsilon\text{-1LGFE.ct}, f)$ |
| | output $\frac{q}{2}y + e_f + r \leftarrow \epsilon\text{-1LGFE.ct} - \epsilon\text{-1LGFE.sk}$, |
| | $\|e_f\|_\infty \leq B'$ |

---

*The single-ciphertext FE has i) a key generation algorithm that is linear in the master secret key $s$ and randomness $r$, and ii) decryption first performs some computation on the ciphertext $\epsilon\text{-1LGFE.ct}$ to obtain an intermediate ciphertext $\epsilon\text{-1LGFE.ct}_f$, and then simply subtracts the secret key from $\epsilon\text{-1LGFE.ct}_f$, and obtains the output $y$ perturbed by a polynomially-bounded noise.*

---

We replace the ciphertext $\mathsf{hect}(s, x)$ now with a ciphertext $\epsilon\text{-1LGFE.ct}(s, x)$ of $\epsilon\text{-1LGFE}$. By the correctness and security of $\epsilon\text{-1LGFE}$, revealing $\epsilon\text{-1LGFE.sk}(f)$ only reveals the output $f(x)$. Hence, it suffices to use PHFE to compute the secret key. Thanks to the special structure of the key generation algorithm, this can be done in degree 2.5, using pseudoradnmonness $r$ expanded out via our degree-2.5 PRG. More concretely, PHFE computes the following degree-2.5 function $g$.

$$g(s\|\mathsf{pubsd}\|\mathsf{privsd}) = \langle \mathsf{pp}_f, s \rangle + r = \epsilon\text{-1LGFE.sk}(f), \qquad // \ g \text{ has degree 2.5}$$

$$\text{where } r_j = \sum_{k=0}^{\log B - 1} 2^k \mathsf{PRG}_{(j-1)\log B + k}(\mathsf{pubsd}, \mathsf{privsd}) \ .$$

One more technical caveat is that known pairing-based PHFE schemes actually compute the secret key $\epsilon\text{-1LGFE.sk}$ in the exponent of a target group element, which we denote by $[\epsilon\text{-1LGFE.sk}]_T$, where for any exponent $a \in \mathbb{Z}_p$, $[a]_T = g_T^a$ for a generator $g_T$. Thanks to the special structure of the decryption algorithm of $\epsilon\text{-1LGFE}$—namely, it is linear in $\epsilon\text{-1LGFE.sk}$—these group elements are sufficient for decryption. A decryptor can first compute $\epsilon\text{-1LGFE.ct}_f$ from $\epsilon\text{-1LGFE.ct}(s, x)$ and $f$ in the clear, then perform the decryption by subtracting $[\epsilon\text{-1LGFE.ct}_f - \epsilon\text{-1LGFE.sk}]_T$ in the exponent. This gives $[p/2 \cdot f(x) + e_f + r]_T$, whose exponent $p/2 \cdot f(x) + e_f + r$ can be extracted by enumrating all possible $e_f + r$, which are of polynomial size, and $f(x) \in \{0, 1\}$.

Our single-ciphertext FE with linear key generation is essentially the same notion as that of Special Homomorphic Encryption (SHE) used in [3,62]. SHE are homomorphic encryption with a special decryption equation $\mathsf{hect}_f - \langle \mathsf{pp}_f, s \rangle = p/2 \cdot f(x) + e_f$ where $\mathsf{pp}_f$ (as in $\epsilon\text{-1LGFE}$) can be computed efficiently from public parameters $\mathsf{pp}$ and $f$. We think it is more accurate to view this object as a functional encryption scheme, since what the special decryption equation gives is exactly a functional key $\langle \mathsf{pp}_f, s \rangle + r$ where $r$ are smudging noises for hiding $e_f$ to guarantee that only $p/2 \cdot f(x)$ is revealed.

Viewing this through the lens of FE brought us a significant benefit. Previous works constructed SHE by modifying the Brakerski-Vankuntanathan FHE scheme [32], but are limited to supporting $\mathsf{NC}^1$ computations based on RLWE [6], and $\mathsf{NC}_0$ based on LWE [6,62]. Instead, the FE lens led us to search for ideas in the predicate encryption literature. We show how to construct $\epsilon$-1LGFE for polynomial sized circuits with depth bounded by $\lambda$ from LWE by modifying the predicate encryption scheme of [52]. This new construction allowed us to construct FE for polynomial sized circuits with depth bounded by $\lambda$ directly without invoking any bootstrapping theorem from weaker function classes.

**Theorem 3 ($\epsilon$-1LGFE from LWE, informal).** *There is a construction of a single-ciphertext FE for polynomial size circuits of depth $\lambda$ with linear key generation as described above, from LWE.*

In summary, putting all the pieces together, our construction of FE for polynomial size circuits with depth $\lambda$ is depicted below. Comparing with previous constructions, it enjoys several features: 1) it is public key, 2) it can be based on the polynomial-hardness of underlying assumptions, 3) it has simpler proofs (e.g., no bootstrapping theorem).

---

**Our FE Construction**

    $\mathsf{fesk}(f)$ contains    :                       $\mathsf{phfsk}(g)$
    $\mathsf{fect}(x)$ contains    : $\epsilon$-$\mathsf{1LGFE.ct}(s, x)$ $\mathsf{phfct}(s\|\mathsf{pubsd}\|\mathsf{privsd})$

    $\mathsf{FEDec}(\mathsf{fect}, (f, \mathsf{fesk}))$ : $[\epsilon\text{-}\mathsf{1LGFE.sk}]_T \leftarrow \mathsf{PHFEDec}(\mathsf{phfct}, \mathsf{phfsk})$
                                       $\epsilon$-$\mathsf{1LGFE.ct}_f \leftarrow \mathsf{EvalCT}(\epsilon\text{-}\mathsf{1LGFE.ct}, f)$
                                       $[y + e_f + r]_T = \epsilon\text{-}\mathsf{1LGFE.ct}_f - [\epsilon\text{-}\mathsf{1LGFE.sk}]_T$
                                       extract $y + e_f + r$ and round to recover $y$

---

*The basic idea is using* $\mathsf{PHFE}$ *to compute a* $\epsilon$-1LGFE *secret key* $\epsilon$-$\mathsf{1LGFE.sk}(f)$ *in the exponent of the target group, and then decrypting the ciphertext* $\epsilon$-$\mathsf{1LGFE.ct}(s, x)$ *to reveal* $f(x)$ *only.*

---

The only aspect of our construction that we have not discussed explicitly is how to deal with the fact that the pseudorandom smudging error is of polynomial size, and therefore reveals a $1/poly$ amount of information. We thus need to amplify security, but because the source of our error is so simple, we are able to achieve this amplification in a simple and direct construction (found in the full version) that avoids any need to use hard-core measures or any other such sophisticated and/or delicate amplification technology.

## 2.2 Instantiating Our Assumption

To instantiate our assumption, we need to *choose a degree d PRG with a stretch more than* $n^{\lceil \frac{d}{2} \rceil \cdot (0.5+\delta)+\rho}$. The good news is that there is a rich body of literature on both ingredients of our assumption that existed way before our work to guide the choice. Binary LWE was first considered by [17] and then by [7,34,35,66]. Goldreich PRGs have been studied even before that. There are many prior works spanning areas in computer science devoted to cryptanalysis of these objects from lattice reduction algorithms and symmetric-key cryptanalysis, to algebraic algorithm tools such as the Gröbner basis algorithm and attacks arising from the Constraint Satisfaction Problem and Semi-Definite Programming literature. Guided by them, we list three candidates below. In the full-version [44], we survey many of these attack algorithms, and we compute approximate running times of the attacks arising out of these algorithms on our candidates. For the parameters we choose, all those attacks are subexponential time.

A Goldreich's PRG $G$ is defined by a predicate $P : \{0,1\}^{\ell'} \to \{0,1\}$, where $\ell'$ is the locality of the PRG, and a bipartiate input-output dependency graph $\Lambda$, which specifies for every output index $j \in [m]$, the subset $\Lambda(j) \subset [n]$ of input indexes of size $\ell'$ it depends on – the $j$'th output bit is simply set to $G(j) = P(\Lambda(j))$. Hence the degree of the PRG $G$ is identical to the degree of the predicate $P$. Usually, the input-output dependency graph $\Lambda$ is chosen at random, and the non-trivial part lies in choosing the predicate $P$.

*Instantiation 1.* The first instantiation is that of the predicate XORMAJ, which is a poplular PRG predicate [16,39].

$$\mathsf{XORMAJ}_{\ell,\ell}(x_1 \ldots, x_{2\ell}) = \oplus_{i \in [\ell]} x_i \oplus \mathsf{MAJ}(x_{\ell+1}, \ldots, x_{2\ell}).$$

The predicate above has a degree of $2 \cdot \ell$; thus, our construction require expansion $m > n^{\frac{\ell}{2}+\ell\delta+\rho}$. The predicate is $\ell+1$ wise independent and thus it provably resists subexponential time SoS refutation attacks when $m(n) \leq n^{\frac{\ell+1}{2}-c}$ for $c > 0$ [59]. All other known attacks that we consider and even the algebraic attacks when instantiated in our combined assumption require subexponential time. We refer the reader to the full-version [44] for a detailed discussion.

*Instantiation 2.* An slightly unsatisfactory aspect of the XORMAJ predicate is that the lower bound on the stretch of the PRG instantiated by XORMAJ for it to be useful in our FE construction is $> n^{\frac{\ell}{2}+\delta'}$, whereas the upper bound on the stretch to withstand existing attacks is very close $\leq n^{\frac{\ell+1}{2}-c}$, leaving only a tiny margin to work with. This motivates us to we consdier predicates with degree lower than the locality. One such predicate was analyzed in [65] for stretch upto $n^{1.25-c}$ for $c > 0$:

$$\mathsf{TSPA}(x_1, x_2, x_3, x_4, x_5) = x_1 \oplus x_2 \oplus x_3 \oplus ((x_2 \oplus x_4) \wedge (x_3 \oplus x_5)).$$

What is nice about this predicate is that, it has locality 5 but only degree 3; thus, our construction only require expansion $m > n^{\lceil \frac{3}{2} \rceil(0.5+\epsilon)+\rho} = n^{1+2\epsilon+\rho}$. In [65], it was proven that the PRG istantiated with TSPA resists subexponential time $\mathbb{F}_2$ linear and SoS attacks. We present analysis against other attacks in the full-version [44], all taking subexponential time.

*Instantiation 3.* We present a degree reduction transformation that takes as input a non-linear predicate $g : \{0,1\}^k \to \{0,1\}$ and constructs a predicate P.

$$\mathsf{P}_g(x_1 \dots, x_{2k+1}) = \oplus_{i \in [k+1]} x_i \oplus g(x_{k+2} \oplus x_2, \dots, x_{2k+1} \oplus x_{k+1}).$$

We show in the full version [44] that the predicate above has a locality of $2k+1$ but a degree equal to $k+1$; thus, our construction requires expansion $m > n^{\lceil \frac{k+1}{2} \rceil (0.5+\epsilon)+\rho}$. The predicate is also $k+1$ wise independent. We show that all known attacks run in subexponential time even when the stretch is bounded by $m \leq n^{\frac{k+1}{2}-\delta}$ for some $\delta > 0$. Thanks to the gap between the locality and degree, we now have a very large margin between the lower and upper bounds on the stretch. Hence, our work motivates the interesting question of studying such predicates.

## 2.3 Single Ciphertext Functional Encryption with Linear Key Generation

We describe our construction of a single-ciphertext (secret-key) FE scheme for all polynomial-sized circuits with depth bounded by $\lambda$, that have the simple structure outlined in Sect. 2, denoted as $\epsilon$-1LGFE, from LWE. In particular, the key generation and decryption algorithms have the following form, where $s$ is the master secret key and pp is the public parameters.

$$\mathsf{KeyGen}(\mathsf{pp}, s, f) \qquad : \mathsf{pp}_f \leftarrow \mathsf{EvalPP}(\mathsf{pp}, f) \ , \ r \leftarrow ([0, B-1] \cap \mathbb{Z})^m,$$
$$\text{output } f \text{ and secret key } \epsilon\text{-1LGFE.sk}(f) = \langle \mathsf{pp}_f, s \rangle - r$$
$$\mathsf{Dec}(\epsilon\text{-1LGFE.ct}, (f, \epsilon\text{-1LGFE.sk})) : \epsilon\text{-1LGFE.ct}_f \leftarrow \mathsf{EvalCT}(\epsilon\text{-1LGFE.ct}, f)$$
$$\text{output } \tfrac{q}{2} y + e_f + r \leftarrow \epsilon\text{-1LGFE.ct} - \epsilon\text{-1LGFE.sk}, \ |e_f|_\infty \leq B'$$

Importantly, decryption recovers a perturbed output where the error $e_f + r$ is polynomially bounded. As mentioned before, this object is essentially the same as the notion of Special Homomorphic Encryption (SHE) in the literature [6,62]. Previous SHE schemes are constructed by modifying existing homomorphic encryption schemes of [30,32]. These constructions are recursive and quite complex, and the overhead due to recursion prevents them from supporting computations beyond $\mathsf{NC}^1$. In this work, viewing through the FE lens, we search the literature of predicate encryption, and show how to modify the predicate encryption scheme of [52] (GVW) to obtain single-ciphertext FE with the desired structure. The GVW predicate encryption provide us with a single-ciphertext encryption scheme with the following properties:

- The public parameter generation algorithm PPGen samples a collection of random LWE matrices $A_i, B_j \leftarrow \mathbb{Z}_p^{n \times m}$, and sets the public parameters to $\mathsf{pp} = (\{A_i\}, \{B_j\})$.
- The setup algorithm Setup samples a master secret key constaining an LWE secret $s \leftarrow \chi^n$ drawn from the noise distribution $\chi$.

- The encryption algorithm to encrypt $x$, generates a ciphertext $\mathsf{hect}(x)$ containing two sets of LWE samples of form $c_i = s^T A_i + \widehat{x}_i G + e_i$ and $d_j = s^T B_j + \widehat{k}_j G + e'_j$, where $G \in \mathbb{Z}_p^{n \times m}$ is the gadget matrix, vk is a freshly sampled secret key of a homomorphic encryption scheme, and $e_i, e'_j \leftarrow \chi^m$ are LWE noises. Furthermore, $\widehat{x}_i$ is the $i$'th bit of a homomorphic encryption ciphertext of $x$ under key $k$.
- The predicate encryption scheme of [52] provides two homomorphic procedures: The $\mathsf{EvalCT}$ procedure homomorphically evaluate $f$ on $\{c_i, A_i\}$ and $\{d_j, B_j\}$ to obtain $c_f$, and the $\mathsf{EvalPP}$ seperately homormorphically evaluates on $\{A_i\}$ and $\{B_i\}$ to obtain $A_f$.
- The homomorphic evaluation outcomes $c_f, A_f$, has the property that the first coordinate $c_{f,1}$ of $c_f$ and the first column $A_{f,1}$ of $A_f$ satisfy the special decryption equation.

$$c_{f,1} - s^T A_{f,1} = f(x) \lfloor p/2 \rceil + e_f \quad \bmod p$$

The above described encryption scheme almost gives the FE scheme we want except for the issue that it has super-polynomially large decryption error $e_f$. Thus, we turn to reducing the norm of the decryption error, by applying the rounding (or modulus switch) technique in the HE literature [30]. Namely, to reduce the error norm by a factor of $p/q$ for a $q < p$, we multiply $c_{f,1}$ and $A_{f,1}$ with $q/p$ over the reals and then round to the nearest integer component wise. The rounding results satisfy the following equation

$$\lfloor \tfrac{q}{p} c_{f,1} \rceil - s^T \lfloor \tfrac{q}{p} A_{f,1} \rceil = f(x) \lfloor q/2 \rceil + \lfloor \tfrac{q}{p} e_f \rceil + \mathsf{error} \quad \bmod p$$

where the rounding error $\mathsf{error}$ is bounded by $|\mathsf{hesk}|_1 + O(1)$, which is polynomially bounded as the secret is sampled from the LWE noise distribution instead of uniformly.

We are now ready to instantiate the FE scheme we want. It uses the same public parameter generation, setup, and encryption algorithm. Now to generate a functional key for $f$, it first computes $A_f \leftarrow \mathsf{EvalPP}(\{A_i\}, \{B_j\})$ and sets $\mathsf{pp}_f = \lfloor \tfrac{q}{p} A_{f,1} \rceil$, and then outputs a functional key $\epsilon\text{-1LGFE.sk} = \langle \mathsf{pp}_f s \rangle - r$ where $r$ is a random vector of smudging noises of sufficiently large but still polynomially bounded magnitude. The decryption algorithm decrypts a ciphertext $\epsilon\text{-1LGFE.ct} = (\{c_i\}, \{d_j\})$ using a functional key $\epsilon\text{-1LGFE.sk}$ as follows: It first computes $c_f \leftarrow \mathsf{EvalPP}(\{A_i, c_i\}, \{B_j, d_j\})$, and sets $\epsilon\text{-1LGFE.ct}_f = \lfloor \tfrac{q}{p} c_{f,1} \rceil$, it then subtracts $\epsilon\text{-1LGFE.sk}$ from it, yielding $f(x) \lfloor q/2 \rceil + \lfloor \tfrac{q}{p} e_f \rceil + \mathsf{error} + r$ as desired.

# 3   Preliminaries

In this section, we describe preliminaries that are useful for rest of the paper. We denote the security parameter by $\lambda$. For any distribution $\mathcal{X}$, we denote by $x \leftarrow \mathcal{X}$ (or $x \leftarrow_R \mathcal{X}$) the process of sampling a value $x$ from the distribution $\mathcal{X}$.

Similarly, for a set $X$ we denote by $x \leftarrow X$ (or $x \leftarrow_R X$) the process of sampling $x$ from the uniform distribution over $X$. For an integer $n \in \mathbb{N}$ we denote by $[n]$ the set $\{1, .., n\}$. A function $\mathsf{negl} : \mathbb{N} \to \mathbb{R}$ is negligible if for every constant $c > 0$ there exists an integer $N_c$ such that $\mathsf{negl}(\lambda) < \lambda^{-c}$ for all $\lambda > N_c$.

By $\approx_c$ we denote the standard polynomial time computational indistinguishability. We say that two ensembles $\mathcal{X} = \{\mathcal{X}_\lambda\}_{\lambda \in \mathbb{N}}$ and $\mathcal{Y} = \{\mathcal{Y}_\lambda\}_{\lambda \in \mathbb{N}}$ are $(s(\lambda), \epsilon(\lambda))-$ indistinguishable if for every adversary $\mathcal{A}$ (modeled as a circuit) of size bounded by $s(\lambda)$ it holds that: $\left| \Pr_{x \leftarrow \mathcal{X}_\lambda}[\mathcal{A}(1^\lambda, x) = 1] - \Pr_{y \leftarrow \mathcal{Y}_\lambda}[\mathcal{A}(1^\lambda, y) = 1] \right| \leq \epsilon(\lambda)$ for every sufficiently large $\lambda \in \mathbb{N}$.

For a field element $a \in \mathbb{F}_{\mathsf{prmtr}}$ represented in $[-p/2, p/2]$, we say that $a \in [-B, B]$ for some positive integer $B$ if its representative in $[-p/2, p/2]$ lies in $[-B, B]$.

Throughout, when we refer to polynomials in security parameter, we mean constant degree polynomials that take positive value on non negative inputs. We denote by $\mathsf{poly}(\lambda)$ an arbitrary polynomial in security parameter satisfying the above requirements of non-negativity.

### 3.1 Pairing Groups

Throughout the paper, we use a sequence of asymmetric prime-order pairing groups:

$$\mathcal{G} = \{(p_\lambda, \mathbf{G}_{\lambda,1}, \mathbf{G}_{\lambda,2}, \mathbf{G}_{\lambda,T}, P_{\lambda,1}, P_{\lambda,2}, P_{\lambda,T}, e_\lambda)\}_{\lambda \in \mathbb{N}},$$

where for all $s \in \{1, 2, T\}$, $(\mathbf{G}_{\lambda,s}, +)$ is an cyclic group (for which we use additive notation) of order $p_\lambda = 2^{\lambda^{\Theta(1)}}$. $\mathbf{G}_{\lambda,1}$ and $\mathbf{G}_{\lambda,2}$ are generated by $P_{\lambda,1}$ and $P_{\lambda,2}$ respectively, and $e : \mathbf{G}_{\lambda,1} \times \mathbf{G}_{\lambda,2} \to \mathbf{G}_T$ is a non-degenerate bilinear map, that is, satisfying $e_\lambda(aP_{\lambda,1}, bP_{\lambda,2}) = abP_T$ for all integers $a, b \in \mathbb{Z}_p$, where $P_T = e(P_{\lambda,1}, P_{\lambda,2})$ is a generator of $\mathbf{G}_{\lambda,T}$. We require the group operations as well as the pairing operation to be efficiently computable. The rest of the paper will refer to this sequence of bilinear pairing groups, and the corresponding sequence of prime orders of the groups $\{p_\lambda\}_{\lambda \in \mathbb{N}}$. In the full version [44], we describe the assumptions bilateral DLIN and SXDH over such groups, which we use for our construction.

## 4 Functional Encryption Definitions

We denote by $\mathcal{F} = \cup_{n,d,\ell,\mathsf{size} \in \mathsf{poly}} \left( \{\mathcal{F}_{\lambda,n(\lambda),d(\lambda),\ell(\lambda),\mathsf{size}(\lambda)}\}_{\lambda \in \mathbb{N}} \right)$ an abstract function class, which is parameterized by $\lambda \in \mathbb{N}$ and four polynomials $n(\lambda), d(\lambda), \ell(\lambda), \mathsf{size}(\lambda)$. We call $\mathsf{prmtr}$ the tuple $(n, d, \ell, \mathsf{size})$. In this abstract class, every function $f \in \mathcal{F}_{\lambda,\mathsf{prmtr}}$ takes an input from $\mathcal{X}_{\lambda,\mathsf{prmtr}} \times \mathcal{Y}_{\lambda,\mathsf{prmtr}}$ and outputs in $\mathcal{Z}_{\lambda,\mathsf{prmtr}}$. We will specify what the exact denotes in the exact constructions. Two specific instantiations of those classes are described below:

- The function class $\mathcal{F}_{\lambda,\text{prmtr}}^{\text{CIRC}}$: Here $\mathcal{Y}_{\lambda,\text{prmtr}}$ consists of $\{0,1\}^n$, $\mathcal{X}_{\lambda,\text{prmtr}}$ is empty, $\mathcal{Z}_{\lambda,\text{prmtr}} = \{0,1\}^\ell$. This family consists of Boolean circuits of depth $d$ and size size.
- The function class $\mathcal{F}_{\lambda,\text{prmtr}}^{\text{PHFE}}$: Here $\mathcal{X}_{\lambda,\text{prmtr}} = \mathcal{Y}_{\lambda,\text{prmtr}} = \mathbb{Z}_{p_\lambda}^{O(n)}$ where $p_\lambda$ is the prime order for the group $\mathcal{G}_\lambda$. The class consists of certain kinds of arithmetic cicuits over $\mathbb{Z}_p$. We describe the exact class later when we need it.

Here we provide the relevant definition regarding functional encryption (FE) and partially-hiding FE (PHFE) along with several notions of efficiency and security properties. FE corresponds to the particular case where the public part of the message (referred to as $\mathcal{X}_{\lambda,\text{prmtr}}$ below) is empty.

**Definition 1.** *(Syntax of a PHFE Scheme.)  A partially-hiding functional encryption scheme,* PHFE, *for a functionality* $\{\mathcal{F}_{\lambda,\text{prmtr}} : \mathcal{X}_{\lambda,\text{prmtr}} \times \mathcal{Y}_{\lambda,\text{prmtr}} \rightarrow \mathcal{Z}_{\lambda,\text{prmtr}}\}_{\lambda,\text{prmtr}}$, *consists of the following PPT algorithms:*

- PPGen($1^\lambda$, prmtr) : *Given as input the security parameter* $1^\lambda$ *and additional parameters* prmtr $= (n, d, \ell, \text{size})$, *it outputs a string* pp. *We assume that* pp *is implicitly given as input to all the algorithms below.*
- Setup(pp): *Given as input* pp, *it outputs a public key* pk *and a master secret key* msk.
- Enc(pk, $(x, y)$): *Given as input the public key* pk *and a message* $(x, y)$ *with public part* $x \in \mathcal{X}_{\lambda,\text{prmtr}}$ *and private part* $y \in \mathcal{Y}_{\lambda,\text{prmtr}}$, *outputs the ciphertext* ct *along with the input* $x$.
- KeyGen(msk, $f$): *Given as input the master secret key* msk *and a function* $f \in \mathcal{F}_{\lambda,\text{prmtr}}$, *it outputs a functional decryption key* $\text{sk}_f$.
- Dec($\text{sk}_f$, $(x, \text{ct})$): *Given a functional decryption key* $\text{sk}_f$ *and a ciphertext* $(x, \text{ct})$, *it deterministically outputs a value* $z$ *in* $\mathcal{Z}_{\lambda,\text{prmtr}}$, *or* $\perp$ *if it fails.*

*Remark 1.* (On Secret Key Schemes.) An FE scheme is said to be secret-key is pk is empty, and the encryption algorithm takes as additional input the master secret key msk.

*Remark 2.* (On FE vs PHFE.) The syntax of FE is identical to PHFE described above except that for all $\lambda \in \mathbb{N}$, the set $\mathcal{X}_{\lambda,\text{prmtr}} = \emptyset$, that is, all the input remains private.

**Definition 2.** *(Correctness.)  A Partially hiding FE scheme* PHFE *for the functionality* $\mathcal{F} = \{\mathcal{F}_{\lambda,\text{prmtr}}\}_{\lambda,\text{prmtr}}$ *is correct if for security parameter* $\lambda \in \mathbb{N}$ *and every polynomials* $n, d, \ell, \text{size}$ *there exists a negligible function* $\text{negl}(\lambda)$ *such that for all messages* $(x, y) \in \mathcal{X}_{\lambda,\text{prmtr}} \times \mathcal{Y}_{\lambda,\text{prmtr}}$ *and all functions* $f \in \mathcal{F}$, *we have:*

$$\Pr \begin{bmatrix} \text{pp} \leftarrow \text{PPGen}(1^\lambda, \text{prmtr}) \\ (\text{pk}, \text{sk}) \leftarrow \text{Setup}(\text{pp}) \\ (x, \text{ct}) \leftarrow \text{Enc}(\text{pk}, (x, y)) \\ \text{sk}_f \leftarrow \text{KeyGen}(\text{sk}, f) \\ \text{Dec}(\text{sk}_f, x, \text{ct})) \neq f(x, y) \end{bmatrix} \leq \text{negl}(\lambda).$$

Now we give the security notions for PHFE and FE.

## 4.1  Security Definition

We discuss two security notions. First, for any constant $\epsilon \in (0,1]$, we present the notion of $\epsilon$-simulation security below:

**Definition 3 ($\epsilon$-simulation security).** *For all $\epsilon \in (0,1]$, we say a PHFE scheme for the functionality $\mathcal{F} = \{\mathcal{F}_{\lambda,\mathsf{prmtr}}\}_{\lambda,\mathsf{prmtr}}$ denoted by PHFE is $\epsilon$-simulation secure if there exists a (possibly stateful) PPT simulator $\mathcal{S} = (\widetilde{\mathsf{Setup}}, \widetilde{\mathsf{Enc}}, \widetilde{\mathsf{KeyGen}})$ such that for all stateful PPT adversaries $\mathcal{A} = (\mathcal{A}_1, \mathcal{A}_2)$, there exists a negligible function $\mathsf{negl}$ such that for all security parameters $\lambda \in \mathbb{N}$, all polynomials $\mathsf{prmtr} = (n, d, \ell, \mathsf{size})$, we have:*

$$\mathsf{adv}^{\mathsf{SIM}}_{\mathsf{PHFE},\mathcal{A}}(1^\lambda, \mathsf{prmtr}) := |\Pr[1 \leftarrow \mathsf{Real}^{\mathsf{PHFE}}_{\mathcal{A}}(1^\lambda, \mathsf{prmtr})] - \Pr[1 \leftarrow \mathsf{Ideal}^{\mathsf{PHFE}}_{\mathcal{A},\mathcal{S}}(1^\lambda, \mathsf{prmtr})]| < \mathsf{negl}(\lambda),$$

*where the experiments $\mathsf{Real}^{\mathsf{PHFE}}_{\mathcal{A}}(1^\lambda)$ and $\mathsf{Ideal}^{\mathsf{PHFE}}_{\mathcal{A},\mathcal{S}}(1^\lambda)$ are defined below. The differences between these two experiments are highlighted in red.*

---

$\mathsf{Real}^{\mathsf{PHFE}}_{\mathcal{A}}(1^\lambda, \mathsf{prmtr})$:

$(x^*, y^*) \in \mathcal{X}_{\lambda,\mathsf{prmtr}} \times \mathcal{Y}_{\lambda,\mathsf{prmtr}}, (f_j \in \mathcal{F}_{\lambda,\mathsf{prmtr}})_{j \in [Q_{\mathsf{sk}}]} \leftarrow \mathcal{A}_1(1^\lambda)$

$\mathsf{pp} \leftarrow \mathsf{PPGen}(1^\lambda, \mathsf{prmtr})$

$(\mathsf{pk}, \mathsf{msk}) \leftarrow \mathsf{Setup}(\mathsf{pp})$

$(x^*, \mathsf{ct}^*) \leftarrow \mathsf{Enc}(\mathsf{pk}, (x^*, y^*))$

$\forall j \in [Q_{\mathsf{sk}}]: \mathsf{sk}_{f_j} \leftarrow \mathsf{KeyGen}(\mathsf{msk}, f_j)$

$\alpha \leftarrow \mathcal{A}_2(\mathsf{pp}, \mathsf{pk}, (\mathsf{sk}_{f_j})_{j \in Q_{\mathsf{sk}}}, x^*, \mathsf{ct}^*)$

*Output $\alpha$.*

---

$\mathsf{Ideal}^{\mathsf{PHFE}}_{\mathcal{A},\mathcal{S}}(1^\lambda, \mathsf{prmtr})$:

$(x^*, y^*) \in \mathcal{X}_{\lambda,\mathsf{prmtr}} \times \mathcal{Y}_{\lambda,\mathsf{prmtr}}, (f_j \in \mathcal{F}_{\lambda,\mathsf{prmtr}})_{j \in [Q_{\mathsf{sk}}]} \leftarrow \mathcal{A}_1(1^\lambda)$

$\mathsf{pp} \leftarrow \mathsf{PPGen}(1^\lambda, \mathsf{prmtr})$

$(\widetilde{\mathsf{pk}}, \mathsf{td}) \leftarrow \widetilde{\mathsf{Setup}}(\mathsf{pp}), \omega \leftarrow \mathsf{Sample}(x^*, y^*, (f_j)_{j \in [Q_{\mathsf{sk}}]})$

$(x^*, \widetilde{\mathsf{ct}}^*) \leftarrow \widetilde{\mathsf{Enc}}(\mathsf{td}, \omega)$

$\forall j \in [Q_{\mathsf{sk}}] : \widetilde{\mathsf{sk}}_{f_j} \leftarrow \widetilde{\mathsf{KeyGen}}(\mathsf{td}, f_j, \omega)$

$\alpha \leftarrow \mathcal{A}_2\left(\mathsf{pp}, \widetilde{\mathsf{pk}}, (\widetilde{\mathsf{sk}}_{f_j})_{j \in Q_{\mathsf{sk}}}, x^*, \widetilde{\mathsf{ct}}^*\right)$

*Output $\alpha$.*

---

*The algorithm $\mathsf{Sample}$, given as input the tuple $\left(x^*, (f_j, f_j(x^*, y^*))_{j \in [Q_{\mathsf{sk}}]}\right)$, flips a biased coin. If the outcome is tails (which happens with probability $\epsilon$ over the coin flip), then it outputs $\omega = \left(x^*, (f_j, f_j(x^*, y^*))_{j \in [Q_{\mathsf{sk}}]}\right)$. If the outcome is heads (which happens with probability $1 - \epsilon$ over the coin flip), then it outputs $\omega = \left(x^*, y^*(f_j)_{j \in [Q_{\mathsf{sk}}]}\right)$.*

*Remark 3 (Standard simulation security).* If $\epsilon = 1$, the algorithm $\mathsf{Sample}$ always outputs $\omega = (x^*, (f_j, f_j(x^*, y^*))_{j \in [Q_{\mathsf{sk}}]})$, which corresponds to the standard simulation security definition.

*Remark 4 (Secret-Key schemes).* This definition can be easily adapted to a secret-key scheme simply by having the encryption algorithm get the additional input $\mathsf{msk}$.

*Remark 5 (Subexponential security).* If $\epsilon = 1$, and the negl above is $2^{-\lambda^{\Omega(1)}}$, then the scheme is said to satisfy subexponential security.

*Remark 6 (Number of functional decryption keys).* We say a a scheme is many-key secure if security holds for any polynomial $Q_{\mathsf{sk}}$, and one-key secure if $Q_{\mathsf{sk}} = 1$. When we do not specify it explicitly, we mean one-key security.

We also give an indistinguishability-based security definition.

**Definition 4 (IND security).** *We say an FE scheme* FE *for functionality* $\mathcal{F} = \{\mathcal{F}_{\lambda,\mathsf{prmtr}}\}_{\lambda \in \mathbb{N}}$ *is IND secure if for all stateful PPT adversaries* $\mathcal{A}$*, all polynomial parameters* $\mathsf{prmtr} = (n, d, \ell, \mathsf{size})$ *there exists a negligible function* negl *such that, we have:*

$$\mathsf{adv}^{\mathsf{IND}}_{\mathsf{FE},\mathcal{A}}(\lambda) := 2 \cdot |1/2 - \Pr[1 \leftarrow \mathsf{IND}^{\mathsf{FE}}_{\mathcal{A}}(1^\lambda, \mathsf{prmtr})]| < \mathsf{negl}(\lambda),$$

*where the experiment* $\mathsf{IND}^{\mathsf{FE}}_{\mathcal{A}}(1^\lambda, \mathsf{prmtr})$ *is defined below.*

---

$\mathsf{IND}^{\mathsf{FE}}_{\mathcal{A}}(1^\lambda, \mathsf{prmtr})$:

$\{x^i_0, x^i_1\}_{i \in [Q_{\mathsf{ct}}]}, \{f^j\}_{j \in [Q_{\mathsf{sk}}]} \leftarrow \mathcal{A}(1^\lambda)$

$\mathsf{pp} \leftarrow \mathsf{PPGen}(1^\lambda, \mathsf{prmtr})$

*Where* $\forall i \in [Q]$: $x^i_0, x^i_1 \in \mathcal{Y}_{\lambda,\mathsf{prmtr}}$, $\forall j \in [Q_{\mathsf{sk}}]$: $f^j \in \mathcal{F}_{\lambda,\mathsf{prmtr}}$

$(\mathsf{pk}, \mathsf{msk}) \leftarrow \mathsf{Setup}(\mathsf{pp})$, $b \leftarrow_R \{0,1\}$

$\forall i \in [Q_{\mathsf{ct}}] : \mathsf{ct}_i \leftarrow \mathsf{Enc}(\mathsf{pk}, x^i_b)$, $\forall j \in [Q_{\mathsf{sk}}] : \mathsf{sk}_j \leftarrow \mathsf{KeyGen}(\mathsf{msk}, f^j)$

$b' \leftarrow \mathcal{A}(\{\mathsf{ct}_i\}_{i \in [Q_{\mathsf{ct}}]}, \{\mathsf{sk}_j\}_{j \in [Q_{\mathsf{sk}}]}, \mathsf{pk})$

*Return* 1 *if* $b = b'$ *and* $\forall\, i \in [Q_{\mathsf{ct}}], j \in [Q_{\mathsf{sk}}], f^j(x^i_0) = f^j(x^i_1)$, 0 *otherwise.*

---

As for simulation security, we say that FE satisfies subexponential security if $\mathsf{negl}(\lambda) = 2^{-\lambda^{\Omega(1)}}$.

## 4.2   Efficiency Features

We now define various efficiency notions for PHFE (which are straightforward to adapt to FE).

**Definition 5 (Linear efficiency).**

*We say a PHFE for the functionality* $\mathcal{F} = \{\mathcal{F}_{\lambda,\mathsf{prmtr}}\}_{\lambda,\mathsf{prmtr}}$ *satisfies linear efficiency if there exists a polynomial* poly *such that for all security parameters* $\lambda \in \mathbb{N}$ *and all polynomial parameters* $\mathsf{prmtr} = (n, d, \ell, \mathsf{size})$*, all messages* $(x, y) \in \mathcal{X}_{\lambda,\mathsf{prmtr}} \times \mathcal{Y}_{\lambda,\mathsf{prmtr}}$*, all* pp *in the support of* $\mathsf{PPGen}(1^\lambda, \mathsf{prmtr})$*, all* $(\mathsf{pk}, \mathsf{msk})$ *in the support of* $\mathsf{Setup}(\mathsf{pp})$ *the size of the circuit computing* $\mathsf{Enc}(\mathsf{pk}, \cdot)$ *on the input* $(x, y)$ *is at most* $(|x| + |y|) \cdot \mathsf{poly}(\lambda)$*, for some fixed polynomial* poly *where* $|x|$ *and* $|y|$ *denote the size of* $x$ *and* $y$*, respectively.*

Now we define the notion of sublinearity for FE scheme for the functionality $\mathcal{F}$ (i.e. all polynomial circuits, defined in Sect. 3). It was shown in a series of works [12, 23, 25] that such FE schemes for P/poly imply obfuscation (assuming subexponential security).

**Definition 6 (Sublinearity).** *Let* FE *be an FE scheme for the functionality* $\mathcal{F} = \{\mathcal{F}_{\lambda,\mathsf{prmtr}}\}_{\lambda,\mathsf{prmtr}}$. *If there exists* $\epsilon \in (0,1)$ *and a polynomial* poly *such that for all tuple of polynomials* $\mathsf{prmtr} = (n, d, \ell, \mathsf{size})$, *all* $\lambda \in \mathbb{N}$, *all* pp *in the support of* $\mathsf{PPGen}(1^\lambda, \mathsf{prmtr})$, *all* (pk, msk) *in the support of* $\mathsf{Setup}(\mathsf{pp})$:

- *if the size of the circuit* $\mathsf{Enc}(\mathsf{pk}, \cdot)$ *is at most* $\mathsf{size}^{1-\epsilon} \cdot \mathsf{poly}(n, \lambda)$ *then* FE *is said to be sublinearly efficient. It is said to be compact if* $\epsilon = 1$.
- *if for all* $x \in \{0,1\}^n$, *all ciphertexts* ct *in the support of* $\mathsf{Enc}(\mathsf{pk}, x)$, *the size of* ct *is at most* $\mathsf{size}^{1-\epsilon} \cdot \mathsf{poly}(n, \lambda)$ *then* FE *is said to be sublinearly ciphertext-efficient.*
- *if for all* $x \in \{0,1\}^n$, *all ciphertexts* ct *in the support of* $\mathsf{Enc}(\mathsf{pk}, x)$, *the size of* ct *is at most* $\ell^{1-\epsilon} \cdot \mathsf{poly}(n, \lambda)$ *then* FE *is said to be sublinearly output-efficient.*

*Remark 7 (levelled linear efficiency, compactness, and sublinearity).* More generally, we say that the scheme satisfies levelled linear efficiency or levelled compactness, or levelled sublinearity if the multiplicative factor $\mathsf{poly}(n, \lambda)$ in Definition 5 or Definition 6 is replaced by $\mathsf{poly}(\lambda, n, d)$, i.e. the polynomial also depends on the depth bound $d$.

## 4.3 Structural Properties

Now we define some structural properties that are very specific to our construction. First we define the notion of special structure which captures the property of a function key can be generated just by applying a linear function of the master secret key over some field along with the fact that the decryption of a ciphertext is "almost linear" (specified below).

**Definition 7.** *(Special Structure\*.)   We say that a functional encryption scheme* FE *for* $\mathcal{F}^{\mathsf{CIRC}} = \{\mathcal{F}^{\mathsf{CIRC}}_{\lambda,\mathsf{prmtr}}\}_{\lambda,\mathsf{prmtr}}$ *satisfies special structure\* if there exist polynomials* $h_1, h_2, h_3, h_4$ *such that the following holds. Recall* $\mathcal{F}^{\mathsf{CIRC}}_{\lambda,\mathsf{prmtr}}$ *for* $\mathsf{prmtr} = (n, d, \ell, \mathsf{size})$ *consists of all Boolean circuits with* $n$ *bits of input,* $\ell$ *bits of output, depth* $d$ *and size* $\mathsf{size}$.

- *(PP Syntax.) The* pp *generated by the* $\mathsf{PPGen}(1^\lambda, \mathsf{prmtr})$ *algorithm contains a* $h_1(\lambda)$*-bit prime modulus* $p$.
- *(Linear secret key Structure.) The master secret key is a vector in* $\mathbf{s} \in \mathbb{Z}_p^{h_2(\lambda)}$. *For any function* $f \in \mathcal{F}_{\lambda,\mathsf{prmtr}}$, *let* $f = \{f_i\}_{i \in [\ell]}$ *denote the circuit computing* $i^{th}$ *bit of* $f$. *The functional secret key is of the form* $\mathsf{sk}_f = \{\mathsf{sk}_{f_i}\}_{i \in [\ell]}$ *where each* $\mathsf{sk}_{f_i} = \langle \mathsf{pp}_{f_i}, \mathbf{s} \rangle + e_i \bmod p$ *where* $e_i \leftarrow_R \{0, \dots, h_3(\lambda, n, \ell, d)\}$ *and* $\mathsf{pp}_{f_i}$ *is some deterministic polynomial time computable function of* pp *and* $f_i$.
- *(Linear + Round Decryption with polynomial decryption error.) There exists a deterministic poly-time algorithm such that given an encryption* ct *of* $m \in \{0,1\}^n$ *and a function* $f = (f_1, \dots, f_\ell) \in \mathcal{F}_{\lambda,\mathsf{prmtr}}$, *for every* $i \in [\ell]$, *computes* $\mathsf{ct}_{f_i}$ *such that* $|\mathsf{ct}_{f_i} - \langle \mathsf{pp}_{f_i}, \mathbf{s} \rangle - f_i(m) \lceil \frac{p}{2} \rceil| \le h_4(\lambda, d, \ell, \mathsf{size})$. *Given the secret-key for a function* $f = (f_1, \dots, f_\ell)$, *this can be used to recover* $f(m) = (f_1(m), \dots, f_\ell(m))$.

*Outline. In the rest of the paper, we just discuss one of the aspect, which is to construct an from a* PHFE *scheme, an* $\epsilon$-1LGFE *scheme and an* sPRG *an* $\epsilon$-secure Functional Encryption *scheme. We show how to construct each of these primitives in the full version [44]. We also show in the full version how to amplify its security resulting into a sublinearly efficient Functional Encryption scheme. Such a scheme can be used to build* $i\mathcal{O}$ *using known results [12, 25].*

# 5  Definition of Structured-Seed PRG

We recall the notion of a structured seed PRG sPRG [56].

**Definition 8 (Syntax of Structured-Seed Pseudo-Random Generators (sPRG)).** *Let* $\tau$ *be a positive constant. A structured-seed Boolean PRG,* sPRG, *with stretch* $\tau$ *that maps* $(n \cdot \mathsf{poly}(\lambda))$-*bit binary strings into* $(m = n^\tau)$-*bit strings, where* poly *is a fixed polynomial, is defined by the following PPT algorithms:*

- PPGen($1^\lambda, 1^n$) *takes as input the security parameter* $\lambda$, *and an input length* $1^n$, *which is a polynomial in* $\lambda$. *It outputs public parameters* pp, *which amongst other things contains an odd prime modulus* $p(\lambda)$ *which is* poly($\lambda$) *bit prime for some polynomial independent of* $n$.
- IdSamp(pp) *samples a function index* $I$.
- SdSamp($I$) *jointly samples two binary strings, a public seed and a private seed,* sd $=$ (P, S). *These are vectors over* $\mathbb{Z}_p$. *The combined dimension of these vectors is* $n \cdot$ poly($\lambda$).
- Eval($I$, sd) *computes a string in* $\{0,1\}^m$.

*Remark 8 (The modulus* $p(\lambda)$*).* The size of the modulus $p(\lambda)$ is some fixed polynomial in the security parameter $\lambda$ independent of $n$.

*Remark 9 (Polynomial Stretch.).* We say that an sPRG has polynomial stretch if $\tau > 1$ for some constant $\tau$.

*Remark 10 (Linear Efficiency.).* We say that an sPRG has linear-efficiency if the time to sample sd is $n \cdot$ poly($\lambda$).

*Remark 11 (On* poly($\lambda$) *multiplicative factor in the seed length.).* As opposed to a standard Boolean PRG definition where the length of the output is set to be $n^\tau$ where $n$ is the seed length, we allow the length of the seed to increase multiplicatively by a fixed polynomial poly in a parameter $\lambda$. Looking ahead, one should view $n$ as an arbitrary large polynomial in $\lambda$, and hence sPRG will be expanding in length.

**Definition 9 (Security of sPRG).** *A structured-seed Boolean PRG,* sPRG, *satisfies*

**Pseudorandomness:** *Let $\lambda \in \mathbb{N}$ be the security parameter, let $n(\lambda)$ be a polynomial in $\lambda$. Then, following distributions are indistinguishable.*

$$(\mathsf{pp}, I, \mathsf{P}, \ \mathsf{Eval}(I, \mathsf{sd}))$$
$$(\mathsf{pp}, \ I, \ \mathsf{P}, \ \boldsymbol{r} \ )$$

*where* $\mathsf{pp} \leftarrow \mathsf{PPGen}(1^\lambda, 1^n)$, $I \leftarrow \mathsf{IdSamp}(\mathsf{pp})$, $\mathsf{sd} \leftarrow \mathsf{SdSamp}(I)$, $\boldsymbol{r} \leftarrow \{0,1\}^m$.

**Definition 10 (Complexity and degree of sPRG).** *Let $D \in \mathbb{N}$, let $\lambda \in \mathbb{N}$ and $n = n(\lambda)$ be arbitrary positive polynomial in $\lambda$, and $p = p(\lambda)$ denote a prime modulus which is sampled during $\mathsf{PPGen}$. Let $\mathbb{C}$ be a complexity class. A sPRG has complexity $\mathbb{C}$ in the public seed and degree $D$ in private seed over $\mathbb{Z}_p$, denoted as, $\mathsf{sPRG} \in (\mathbb{C}, \deg D)$, if for every $I$ in the support of $\mathsf{IdSamp}(1^\lambda, 1^n)$, there exists an algorithm $\mathsf{Process}_I$ in $\mathbb{C}$ and an $m(n)$-tuple of polynomials $Q_I$ that can be efficiently generated from $I$, such that for all $\mathsf{sd}$ in the support of $\mathsf{SdSamp}(I)$, it holds that:*

$$\mathsf{Eval}(I, \mathsf{sd}) = Q_I(\mathsf{P}', \mathsf{S}) \ over \ \mathbb{Z}_p, \ \mathsf{P}' = \mathsf{Process}_I(\mathsf{P}),$$

*where $Q_I$ has degree 1 in $\mathsf{P}$ and degree $D$ in $\mathsf{S}$.*

We remark that the above definition generalizes the standard notion of families of PRGs in two aspects: 1) the seed consists of a public part and a private part, jointly sampled and arbitrarily correlated, and 2) the seed may not be uniform. In the full version, we show how to construct an sPRG from our new assumption $\mathsf{G\text{-}LWEleak}_{D,\epsilon,\rho}$.

# 6    Construction of $\epsilon$-Simulation Secure FE

In this section, we construct a $\epsilon$-simulation secure public-key functional encryption scheme $\mathsf{FE}$ for circuits $\mathcal{F}^{\mathsf{CIRC}} = \{\mathcal{F}^{\mathsf{CIRC}}_{\lambda,\mathsf{prmtr}}\}_{\lambda,\mathsf{prmtr}}$ for some $\epsilon \in (0,1)$. $\mathcal{F}^{\mathsf{CIRC}}_{\lambda,\mathsf{prmtr}}$ is the function class where for all $\lambda$ and all polynomials $\mathsf{prmtr} = (n, d, \ell, \mathsf{size})$ it denotes the set of Boolean circuits with input length $n(\lambda)$, depth at most $d(\lambda)$, output length $\ell(\lambda)$, and size at most $\mathsf{size}(\lambda)$. It uses the following ingredients:

- $\epsilon$-1LGFE: a secret-key FE scheme for the function class $\mathcal{F}^{\mathsf{CIRC}}$ defined above, satisfying the following properties:
    - (Security.) 1-key single ciphertext $\epsilon$-simulation security as in Definition 4 for some constant $\epsilon \in (0,1)$ specified later. Note that although the scheme is for a single key, it however allows circuits with multiple output bits.
    - (Efficiency.) *levelled* compactness as in Definition 5. In particular, ciphertext size as well as the size of encryption circuit is $\mathsf{poly}(\lambda, n, d)$, independent of the function size $\mathsf{size}$ and output length $\ell$.
    - (Structural property.) Special Structure* as per Definition 7. Recall, it says that:

    \* (PP Syntax.) The pp generated by the $\mathsf{PPGen}(1^\lambda, \mathsf{prmtr})$ algorithm contains a $h_1(\lambda)$-bit prime modulus which is the modulus of the bilinear map $\mathcal{G}_\lambda$, $p$.

    \* (Linear secret key Structure.) The master secret key is a vector in $\boldsymbol{s} \in \mathbb{Z}_p^{h_2(\lambda)}$. For any function $f \in \mathcal{F}_{\lambda,\mathsf{prmtr}}$, let $f = \{f_i\}_{i \in [\ell]}$ denote the circuit computing $i^{th}$ bit of $f$. The functional secret key is of the form $\mathsf{sk}_f = \{\mathsf{sk}_{f_i}\}_{i \in [\ell]}$ where each $\mathsf{sk}_{f_i} = \langle \mathsf{pp}_{f_i}, \boldsymbol{s} \rangle + e_i \mod p$ where $e_i \leftarrow_{\mathrm{R}} \{0, \dots, h_3(\lambda, n, \ell, d)\}$ and $\mathsf{pp}_{f_i}$ is some deterministic polynomial time computable function of $\mathsf{pp}$ and $f_i$. For our construction below we require that $h_3(\lambda, n, \ell, d) = 2^t - 1$ for some natural number $t = O(\log(n \cdot d \cdot \ell \cdot \mathsf{size}))$. We can always choose an a constant $\epsilon \in (0, 1)$ for the construction in the full version [44] such that there exists an $\epsilon$-1LGFE scheme with this property, satisfying $\epsilon$-simulation security. We use that value of $\epsilon$.

    \* (Linear + Round Decryption with polynomial decryption error.) There exists a deterministic poly-time algorithm such that given an encryption $\mathsf{ct}$ of $m \in \{0,1\}^n$ and a function $f = (f_1, \dots, f_\ell) \in \mathcal{F}_{\lambda,\mathsf{prmtr}}^{\mathsf{CIRC}}$, for every $i \in [\ell]$, computes $\mathsf{ct}_{f_i}$ such that $|\mathsf{ct}_{f_i} - \langle \mathsf{pp}_{f_i}, \boldsymbol{s} \rangle - f_i(m) \lceil \frac{p}{2} \rceil| \leq h_4(\lambda, d, \ell, \mathsf{size})$. Given the secret-key for a function $f = (f_1, \dots, f_\ell)$, this can be used to recover $f(m) = (f_1(m), \dots, f_\ell(m))$.

Such a scheme is constructed in the full version [44].

- PHFE: a public-key PHFE for the class of functions $\mathcal{F}^{\mathsf{PHFE}}$ defined with respect to bilinear groups of order $p$ (which is the same as the modulus of $\epsilon$-1LGFE) and is in fact the order of group $\mathcal{G}_\lambda$. $\mathcal{F}^{\mathsf{PHFE}} = \{\mathcal{F}_{\lambda,n'}^{\mathsf{PHFE}}\}_{\lambda,n'}$ for every polynomial $n'$ consists of all functions $f$ that takes an input of the form $(\boldsymbol{x}, \boldsymbol{y}) \in \mathbb{Z}_p^{n'} \times \mathbb{Z}_p^{n'}$, and computes $f(\boldsymbol{x}, \boldsymbol{y}) = [\sum_{j,k} f_{j,k}(\boldsymbol{x}) \cdot y_j \cdot y_k]_T \in \mathbf{G}_T$ where $f_{j,k}$ is a constant degree polynomial over $\boldsymbol{x}$ (i.e. an arithmetic circuit in $\mathsf{NC}^0$), and $\mathbf{G}_T$ denotes the target group (see def pairings). The scheme PHFE satisfies the following properties:
  - (Security.) 1-simulation security for unbounded key queries.
  - (Efficiency.) Linear run-time as per Definition 5.

  Such a scheme is constructed in the full version. We set $n'$ later.
- sPRG: a structured-seed PRG with stretch $\tau > 1$, linear efficiency as per Definition 8. This sPRG works with the modulus $p(\lambda)$ of the bilinear map $\mathcal{G}_\lambda$. The evaluation algorithm of sPRG computes an arithmetic $\mathsf{NC}^0$ circuit on the public part of the seed, and a degree-2 polynomial on the secret part of the seed, that is, $\mathsf{sPRG} \in (\mathsf{arith}\text{-}\mathsf{NC}^0, \deg 2)$. This sPRG is implementable by $\mathcal{F}^{\mathsf{PHFE}}$.

We now describe the construction.

*Parameters:* For sPRG, we set the length parameter to be $\ell^{\frac{1}{\tau}} \cdot \lambda$. Thus, $\ell_{\mathsf{sPRG}} = \ell^{\frac{1}{\tau}} \mathsf{poly}(\lambda)$ is the number of $\mathbb{Z}_p$ elements in the sPRG seed for some polynomial poly independent of the $\ell$. Define $n' = h_2(\lambda, d) + \ell_{\mathsf{sPRG}}$. Let $t = \log_2(h_3(\lambda, n, \ell, d) + 1)$.

*Construction:* Please refer to the construction in Fig. 1.

---

FE.PPGen($1^\lambda$, prmtr) :

Given $1^\lambda$ and the tuple of polynomials prmtr $= (n, \text{size}, d, \ell)$, it samples PHFE.pp $\leftarrow$ PHFE.PPGen($1^\lambda, 1^{n'}$), $\epsilon$-1LGFE.pp $\leftarrow$ $\epsilon$-1LGFE.PPGen($1^\lambda$, prmtr) and sPRG.pp $\leftarrow$ sPRG.PPGen($1^\lambda, 1^{\ell^{\frac{1}{\tau}} \cdot \lambda}$), $I \leftarrow$ sPRG.IdSamp(sPRG.pp). Let $p$ denote the prime modulus of $\mathcal{G}_\lambda$. Output pp $= $ (PHFE.pp, $\epsilon$-1LGFE.pp, sPRG.pp, $I, p$).

FE.Setup(pp) : Run PHFE.Setup(PHFE.pp) $\to$ (PHFE.pk, PHFE.msk). Set and output FE.pk $=$ PHFE.pk and FE.msk $=$ PHFE.msk.

FE.Enc(FE.pk, $m \in \{0, 1\}^n$) :

  – msk$'$ $\leftarrow$ $\epsilon$-1LGFE.Setup($\epsilon$-1LGFE.pp)
  – ct$_1$ $\leftarrow$ $\epsilon$-1LGFE.Enc(msk$'$, $m$).
  – $(P, S) \leftarrow$ SdSamp($I$).
  – ct$_2$ $\leftarrow$ PHFE.Enc(PHFE.pk, $(P, (S, \text{msk}'))$).

It returns ct $=$ (ct$_1$, ct$_2$).

FE.KeyGen(FE.msk, $C$) : Given as input a circuit $C \in \mathcal{F}_{\text{prmtr}}$, denote $C = (C_1, \ldots, C_\ell)$ where each $C_i$ is the circuit computing the $i^{th}$ output bit of $C$. For every $i \in [\ell]$, do the following:

  – let $\epsilon$-1LGFE.pp$_{C_i}$ be the vector computed deterministically from $\epsilon$-1LGFE.pp and $C_i$ such that sk$_{C_i}$ $\approx$ $\langle \text{msk}', \epsilon\text{-1LGFE.pp}_{C_i} \rangle$ (see the linear secret key structure in Definition 7).
  – Compute sk$_{C_i}$ $\leftarrow$ PHFE.KeyGen(PHFE.msk, $f_i$) where $f_i$ takes as input $(P, (S, \text{msk}'))$ and outputs $\langle \text{msk}', \epsilon\text{-1LGFE.pp}_{C_i} \rangle + \sum_{j \in [1, t]} 2^{j-1} \cdot r_{(i-1) \cdot t + j}$, where for all $\theta \in [m]$, $r_\theta$ denotes the $\theta$'th bit output by sPRG.Eval($I$, sd) $\in \{0, 1\}^m$.

It returns sk$_C$ $=$ (sk$_{C_1}, \ldots$ sk$_{C_\ell}$).

FE.Dec(sk$_C$, ct) : Parse sk$_C$ $=$ (sk$_{C_1}, \ldots, \text{sk}_{C_\ell}$) and ct $=$ (ct$_1$, ct$_2$). For every $i \in [\ell]$, do the following:

  – By the special structure* of $\epsilon$-1LGFE, compute ct$_{C,i}$ using the ciphertext ct$_1$.
  – Compute $[w_i]_T \leftarrow$ PHFE.Dec(sk$_{C_i}$, ct$_2$).
  – Compute $[z_i]_T = [\text{ct}_{C_i} - w_i]_T$.
  – Check if $|z_i| \leq h_3(\lambda, n, d, \ell) + h_4(\lambda, n, d, \ell)$ (by brute-force). If so set $y_i = 0$. Otherwise, set $y_i = 1$. Output $(y_1, \ldots, y_\ell)$.

---

**Fig. 1.** Construction of Functional Encryption Scheme FE.

Due to lack of space, we argue correctness, efficiency and security properties in the full version [44].

**Acknowledgements.** Aayush Jain was partially supported by grants listed under Amit Sahai, a Google PhD fellowship. Huijia Lin was supported by NSF grants CNS-1528178, CNS-1929901, CNS-1936825 (CAREER), the Defense Advanced Research Projects Agency (DARPA) and Army Research Office (ARO) under Contract No. W911NF-15-C-0236, and a subcontract No. 2017-002 through Galois.

Amit Sahai was supported in part from DARPA SAFEWARE and SIEVE awards, NTT Research, NSF Frontier Award 1413955, and NSF grant 1619348, BSF grant 2012378, a Xerox Faculty Research Award, a Google Faculty Research Award, an equipment grant from Intel, and an Okawa Foundation Research Grant. This material is based upon work supported by the Defense Advanced Research Projects Agency through Award HR00112020024 and the ARL under Contract W911NF-15-C- 0205.

The views expressed are those of the authors and do not reflect the official policy or position of the Department of Defense, DARPA, ARO, Simons, Intel, Okawa Foundation, ODNI, IARPA, DIMACS, BSF, Xerox, the National Science Foundation, NTT Research, Google, or the U.S. Government.

# References

1. Abdalla, M., Bourse, F., De Caro, A., Pointcheval, D.: Simple functional encryption schemes for inner products. In: Katz, J. (ed.) PKC 2015. LNCS, vol. 9020, pp. 733–751. Springer, Heidelberg (2015). https://doi.org/10.1007/978-3-662-46447-2_33

2. Abdalla, M., Catalano, D., Gay, R., Ursu, B.: Inner-product functional encryption with fine-grained access control. Cryptology ePrint Archive, Report 2020/577 (2020). https://eprint.iacr.org/2020/577

3. Agrawal, S.: Indistinguishability obfuscation without multilinear maps: new methods for bootstrapping and instantiation. In: Ishai, Y., Rijmen, V. (eds.) EUROCRYPT 2019, Part I. LNCS, vol. 11476, pp. 191–225. Springer, Cham (2019). https://doi.org/10.1007/978-3-030-17653-2_7

4. Agrawal, S., Libert, B., Stehlé, D.: Fully secure functional encryption for inner products, from standard assumptions. In: Robshaw, M., Katz, J. (eds.) CRYPTO 2016, Part III. LNCS, vol. 9816, pp. 333–362. Springer, Heidelberg (2016). https://doi.org/10.1007/978-3-662-53015-3_12

5. Agrawal, S., Pellet-Mary, A.: Indistinguishability obfuscation without maps: attacks and fixes for noisy linear FE. In: Canteaut, A., Ishai, Y. (eds.) EUROCRYPT 2020, Part I. LNCS, vol. 12105, pp. 110–140. Springer, Cham (2020). https://doi.org/10.1007/978-3-030-45721-1_5

6. Agrawal, S., Rosen, A.: Functional encryption for bounded collusions, revisited. In: Kalai, Y., Reyzin, L. (eds.) TCC 2017, Part I. LNCS, vol. 10677, pp. 173–205. Springer, Cham (2017). https://doi.org/10.1007/978-3-319-70500-2_7

7. Albrecht, M.R., Cid, C., Faugère, J.-C., Fitzpatrick, R., Perret, L.: Algebraic algorithms for LWE problems. ACM Commun. Comput. Algebra **49**(2), 62 (2015)

8. Ananth, P., Brakerski, Z., Segev, G., Vaikuntanathan, V.: From selective to adaptive security in functional encryption. In: Gennaro, R., Robshaw, M. (eds.) CRYPTO 2015, Part II. LNCS, vol. 9216, pp. 657–677. Springer, Heidelberg (2015). https://doi.org/10.1007/978-3-662-48000-7_32

9. Ananth, P., Gupta, D., Ishai, Y., Sahai, A.: Optimizing obfuscation: avoiding Barrington's theorem. In: ACM CCS, pp. 646–658 (2014)

10. Ananth, P., Jain, A., Lin, H., Matt, C., Sahai, A.: Indistinguishability obfuscation without multilinear maps: new paradigms via low degree weak pseudorandomness and security amplification. In: Boldyreva, A., Micciancio, D. (eds.) CRYPTO 2019, Part III. LNCS, vol. 11694, pp. 284–332. Springer, Cham (2019). https://doi.org/10.1007/978-3-030-26954-8_10

11. Ananth, P., Jain, A., Sahai, A.: Indistinguishability obfuscation without multilinear maps: IO from LWE, bilinear maps, and weak pseudorandomness. IACR Cryptology ePrint Archive 2018:615 (2018)

12. Ananth, P., Jain, A.: Indistinguishability obfuscation from compact functional encryption. In: Gennaro, R., Robshaw, M. (eds.) CRYPTO 2015, Part I. LNCS, vol. 9215, pp. 308–326. Springer, Heidelberg (2015). https://doi.org/10.1007/978-3-662-47989-6_15

13. Ananth, P., Sahai, A.: Projective arithmetic functional encryption and indistinguishability obfuscation from degree-5 multilinear maps. In: Coron, J.-S., Nielsen, J.B. (eds.) EUROCRYPT 2017, Part I. LNCS, vol. 10210, pp. 152–181. Springer, Cham (2017). https://doi.org/10.1007/978-3-319-56620-7_6

14. Applebaum, B.: Pseudorandom generators with long stretch and low locality from random local one-way functions. In: Karloff, H.J., Pitassi, T. (eds.) 44th ACM STOC, pp. 805–816. ACM Press, May 2012

15. Applebaum, B., Bogdanov, A., Rosen, A.: A dichotomy for local small-bias generators. In: Cramer, R. (ed.) TCC 2012. LNCS, vol. 7194, pp. 600–617. Springer, Heidelberg (2012). https://doi.org/10.1007/978-3-642-28914-9_34

16. Applebaum, B., Lovett, S.: Algebraic attacks against random local functions and their countermeasures. In: Wichs, D., Mansour, Y. (eds.) 48th ACM STOC, pp. 1087–1100. ACM Press, June 2016

17. Arora, S., Ge, R.: New algorithms for learning in presence of errors. In: Aceto, L., Henzinger, M., Sgall, J. (eds.) ICALP 2011, Part I. LNCS, vol. 6755, pp. 403–415. Springer, Heidelberg (2011). https://doi.org/10.1007/978-3-642-22006-7_34

18. Badrinarayanan, S., Miles, E., Sahai, A., Zhandry, M.: Post-zeroizing obfuscation: new mathematical tools, and the case of evasive circuits. In: Fischlin, M., Coron, J.-S. (eds.) EUROCRYPT 2016. LNCS, vol. 9666, pp. 764–791. Springer, Heidelberg (2016). https://doi.org/10.1007/978-3-662-49896-5_27

19. Baltico, C.E.Z., Catalano, D., Fiore, D., Gay, R.: Practical functional encryption for quadratic functions with applications to predicate encryption. In: Katz, J., Shacham, H. (eds.) CRYPTO 2017, Part I. LNCS, vol. 10401, pp. 67–98. Springer, Cham (2017). https://doi.org/10.1007/978-3-319-63688-7_3

20. Barak, B., Garg, S., Kalai, Y.T., Paneth, O., Sahai, A.: Protecting obfuscation against algebraic attacks. In: Nguyen, P.Q., Oswald, E. (eds.) EUROCRYPT 2014. LNCS, vol. 8441, pp. 221–238. Springer, Heidelberg (2014). https://doi.org/10.1007/978-3-642-55220-5_13

21. Barak, B., et al.: On the (im)possibility of obfuscating programs. In: Kilian, J. (ed.) CRYPTO 2001. LNCS, vol. 2139, pp. 1–18. Springer, Heidelberg (2001). https://doi.org/10.1007/3-540-44647-8_1

22. Bartusek, J., Ishai, Y., Jain, A., Ma, F., Sahai, A., Zhandry, M.: Affine determinant programs: a framework for obfuscation and witness encryption. In: Vidick, T. (ed.) 11th Innovations in Theoretical Computer Science Conference, ITCS 2020, Seattle, Washington, USA, 12–14 January 2020. LIPIcs, vol. 151, pp. 82:1–82:39. Schloss Dagstuhl - Leibniz-Zentrum für Informatik (2020)

23. Bitansky, N., Nishimaki, R., Passelègue, A., Wichs, D.: From cryptomania to obfustopia through secret-key functional encryption. In: Hirt, M., Smith, A. (eds.) TCC 2016, Part II. LNCS, vol. 9986, pp. 391–418. Springer, Heidelberg (2016). https://doi.org/10.1007/978-3-662-53644-5_15
24. Bitansky, N., Paneth, O., Rosen, A.: On the cryptographic hardness of finding a Nash equilibrium. In: Guruswami, V. (ed.) 56th FOCS, pp. 1480–1498. IEEE Computer Society Press, October 2015
25. Bitansky, N., Vaikuntanathan, V.: Indistinguishability obfuscation from functional encryption. In: Guruswami, V. (ed.) 56th FOCS, pp. 171–190. IEEE Computer Society Press, October 2015
26. Bogdanov, A., Qiao, Y.: On the security of Goldreich's one-way function. Comput. Complex. **21**(1), 83–127 (2012)
27. Boneh, D., Franklin, M.: Identity-based encryption from the Weil pairing. In: Kilian, J. (ed.) CRYPTO 2001. LNCS, vol. 2139, pp. 213–229. Springer, Heidelberg (2001). https://doi.org/10.1007/3-540-44647-8_13
28. Boneh, D., Sahai, A., Waters, B.: Functional encryption: definitions and challenges. In: Ishai, Y. (ed.) TCC 2011. LNCS, vol. 6597, pp. 253–273. Springer, Heidelberg (2011). https://doi.org/10.1007/978-3-642-19571-6_16
29. Brakerski, Z., Döttling, N., Garg, S., Malavolta, G.: Candidate iO from homomorphic encryption schemes. In: Canteaut, A., Ishai, Y. (eds.) EUROCRYPT 2020. LNCS, vol. 12105, pp. 79–109. Springer, Cham (2020). https://doi.org/10.1007/978-3-030-45721-1_4
30. Brakerski, Z., Gentry, C., Vaikuntanathan, V.: (Leveled) fully homomorphic encryption without bootstrapping. In: Innovations in Theoretical Computer Science 2012, Cambridge, MA, USA, 8–10 January 2012, pp. 309–325 (2012)
31. Brakerski, Z., Rothblum, G.N.: Virtual black-box obfuscation for all circuits via generic graded encoding. In: Lindell, Y. (ed.) TCC 2014. LNCS, vol. 8349, pp. 1–25. Springer, Heidelberg (2014). https://doi.org/10.1007/978-3-642-54242-8_1
32. Brakerski, Z., Vaikuntanathan, V.: Fully homomorphic encryption from ring-LWE and security for key dependent messages. In: Rogaway, P. (ed.) CRYPTO 2011. LNCS, vol. 6841, pp. 505–524. Springer, Heidelberg (2011). https://doi.org/10.1007/978-3-642-22792-9_29
33. Brzuska, C., Farshim, P., Mittelbach, A.: Indistinguishability obfuscation and UCEs: the case of computationally unpredictable sources. In: Garay, J.A., Gennaro, R. (eds.) CRYPTO 2014, Part I. LNCS, vol. 8616, pp. 188–205. Springer, Heidelberg (2014). https://doi.org/10.1007/978-3-662-44371-2_11
34. Buchmann, J., Göpfert, F., Player, R., Wunderer, T.: On the hardness of LWE with binary error: revisiting the hybrid lattice-reduction and meet-in-the-middle attack. In: Pointcheval, D., Nitaj, A., Rachidi, T. (eds.) AFRICACRYPT 2016. LNCS, vol. 9646, pp. 24–43. Springer, Cham (2016). https://doi.org/10.1007/978-3-319-31517-1_2
35. Caho, S., Tibouchi, M., Abe, M.: Sample-time trade-off for the Arora-Ge attack on binary LWE. In: Symposium on Cryptography and Information Theory (2019)
36. Sun, C., Tibouchi, M., Abe, M.: Revisiting the hardness of binary error LWE. Cryptology ePrint Archive, Report 2020/666 (2020). https://eprint.iacr.org/2020/666
37. Chen, Y., Vaikuntanathan, V., Wee, H.: GGH15 beyond permutation branching programs: proofs, attacks, and candidates. In: Shacham, H., Boldyreva, A. (eds.) CRYPTO 2018, Part II. LNCS, vol. 10992, pp. 577–607. Springer, Cham (2018). https://doi.org/10.1007/978-3-319-96881-0_20

38. Cohen, A., Holmgren, J., Nishimaki, R., Vaikuntanathan, V., Wichs, D.: Watermarking cryptographic capabilities. In: STOC (2016)
39. Couteau, G., Dupin, A., Méaux, P., Rossi, M., Rotella, Y.: On the concrete security of Goldreich's pseudorandom generator. In: Peyrin, T., Galbraith, S. (eds.) ASIACRYPT 2018, Part II. LNCS, vol. 11273, pp. 96–124. Springer, Cham (2018). https://doi.org/10.1007/978-3-030-03329-3_4
40. Garg, S., Gentry, C., Halevi, S., Raykova, M., Sahai, A., Waters, B.: Candidate indistinguishability obfuscation and functional encryption for all circuits. In: 54th FOCS, pp. 40–49. IEEE Computer Society Press, October 2013
41. Garg, S., Miles, E., Mukherjee, P., Sahai, A., Srinivasan, A., Zhandry, M.: Secure obfuscation in a weak multilinear map model. In: Hirt, M., Smith, A. (eds.) TCC 2016, Part II. LNCS, vol. 9986, pp. 241–268. Springer, Heidelberg (2016). https://doi.org/10.1007/978-3-662-53644-5_10
42. Garg, S., Pandey, O., Srinivasan, A.: Revisiting the cryptographic hardness of finding a Nash equilibrium. In: Robshaw, M., Katz, J. (eds.) CRYPTO 2016, Part II. LNCS, vol. 9815, pp. 579–604. Springer, Heidelberg (2016). https://doi.org/10.1007/978-3-662-53008-5_20
43. Gay, R.: A new paradigm for public-key functional encryption for degree-2 polynomials. In: Kiayias, A., Kohlweiss, M., Wallden, P., Zikas, V. (eds.) PKC 2020, Part I. LNCS, vol. 12110, pp. 95–120. Springer, Cham (2020). https://doi.org/10.1007/978-3-030-45374-9_4
44. Gay, R., Jain, A., Lin, H., Sahai, A.: Indistinguishability obfuscation from simple-to-state hard problems: new assumptions, new techniques, and simplification. IACR Cryptology ePrint Archive 2020:764 (2020)
45. Gentry, C., Jutla, C.S., Kane, D.: Obfuscation using tensor products. In: Electronic Colloquium on Computational Complexity (ECCC), vol. 25, p. 149 (2018)
46. Gentry, C., Lewko, A.B., Sahai, A., Waters, B.: Indistinguishability obfuscation from the multilinear subgroup elimination assumption. IACR Cryptology ePrint Archive 2014:309 (2014)
47. Goldreich, O.: Candidate one-way functions based on expander graphs. In: Electronic Colloquium on Computational Complexity (ECCC), vol. 7, no. 90 (2000)
48. Goldwasser, S., et al.: Multi-input functional encryption. In: Nguyen, P.Q., Oswald, E. (eds.) EUROCRYPT 2014. LNCS, vol. 8441, pp. 578–602. Springer, Heidelberg (2014). https://doi.org/10.1007/978-3-642-55220-5_32
49. Goldwasser, S., Kalai, Y.T., Popa, R.A., Vaikuntanathan, V., Zeldovich, N.: Reusable garbled circuits and succinct functional encryption. In: Boneh, D., Roughgarden, T., Feigenbaum, J. (eds.) 45th ACM STOC, pp. 555–564. ACM Press, June 2013
50. Goldwasser, S., Kalai, Y.T., Rothblum, G.N.: One-time programs. In: Wagner, D. (ed.) CRYPTO 2008. LNCS, vol. 5157, pp. 39–56. Springer, Heidelberg (2008). https://doi.org/10.1007/978-3-540-85174-5_3
51. Gorbunov, S., Vaikuntanathan, V., Wee, H.: Functional encryption with bounded collusions via multi-party computation. In: Safavi-Naini, R., Canetti, R. (eds.) CRYPTO 2012. LNCS, vol. 7417, pp. 162–179. Springer, Heidelberg (2012). https://doi.org/10.1007/978-3-642-32009-5_11
52. Gorbunov, S., Vaikuntanathan, V., Wee, H.: Predicate encryption for circuits from LWE. In: Gennaro, R., Robshaw, M. (eds.) CRYPTO 2015, Part II. LNCS, vol. 9216, pp. 503–523. Springer, Heidelberg (2015). https://doi.org/10.1007/978-3-662-48000-7_25

53. Hofheinz, D., Jager, T., Khurana, D., Sahai, A., Waters, B., Zhandry, M.: How to generate and use universal samplers. In: Cheon, J.H., Takagi, T. (eds.) ASIACRYPT 2016, Part II. LNCS, vol. 10032, pp. 715–744. Springer, Heidelberg (2016). https://doi.org/10.1007/978-3-662-53890-6_24

54. Hohenberger, S., Sahai, A., Waters, B.: Full domain hash from (leveled) multilinear maps and identity-based aggregate signatures. In: Canetti, R., Garay, J.A. (eds.) CRYPTO 2013, Part I. LNCS, vol. 8042, pp. 494–512. Springer, Heidelberg (2013). https://doi.org/10.1007/978-3-642-40041-4_27

55. Jain, A., Lin, H., Matt, C., Sahai, A.: How to leverage hardness of constant-degree expanding polynomials over $\mathbb{R}$ to build $i\mathcal{O}$. In: Ishai, Y., Rijmen, V. (eds.) EUROCRYPT 2019, Part I. LNCS, vol. 11476, pp. 251–281. Springer, Cham (2019). https://doi.org/10.1007/978-3-030-17653-2_9

56. Jain, A., Lin, H., Sahai, A.: Indistinguishability obfuscation from well-founded assumptions. Cryptology ePrint Archive, Report 2020/1003 (2020). https://eprint.iacr.org/2020/1003

57. Joux, A.: A one round protocol for tripartite Diffie–Hellman. In: Bosma, W. (ed.) ANTS 2000. LNCS, vol. 1838, pp. 385–393. Springer, Heidelberg (2000). https://doi.org/10.1007/10722028_23

58. Koppula, V., Lewko, A.B., Waters, B.: Indistinguishability obfuscation for turing machines with unbounded memory. In: STOC (2015)

59. Kothari, P.K., Mori, R., O'Donnell, R., Witmer, D.: Sum of squares lower bounds for refuting any CSP. In: Hatami, H., McKenzie, P., King, V. (eds.) 49th ACM STOC, pp. 132–145. ACM Press, June 2017

60. Lin, H.: Indistinguishability obfuscation from constant-degree graded encoding schemes. In: Fischlin, M., Coron, J.-S. (eds.) EUROCRYPT 2016, Part I. LNCS, vol. 9665, pp. 28–57. Springer, Heidelberg (2016). https://doi.org/10.1007/978-3-662-49890-3_2

61. Lin, H.: Indistinguishability obfuscation from SXDH on 5-linear maps and locality-5 PRGs. In: Katz, J., Shacham, H. (eds.) CRYPTO 2017, Part I. LNCS, vol. 10401, pp. 599–629. Springer, Cham (2017). https://doi.org/10.1007/978-3-319-63688-7_20

62. Lin, H., Matt, C.: Pseudo flawed-smudging generators and their application to indistinguishability obfuscation. IACR Cryptology ePrint Archive 2018:646 (2018)

63. Lin, H., Tessaro, S.: Indistinguishability obfuscation from trilinear maps and blockwise local PRGs. In: Katz, J., Shacham, H. (eds.) CRYPTO 2017, Part I. LNCS, vol. 10401, pp. 630–660. Springer, Cham (2017). https://doi.org/10.1007/978-3-319-63688-7_21

64. Lin, H., Vaikuntanathan, V.: Indistinguishability obfuscation from DDH-like assumptions on constant-degree graded encodings. In: Dinur, I. (ed.) 57th FOCS, pp. 11–20. IEEE Computer Society Press, October 2016

65. Lombardi, A., Vaikuntanathan, V.: Minimizing the complexity of Goldreich's pseudorandom generator. IACR Cryptology ePrint Archive 2017:277 (2017)

66. Micciancio, D., Peikert, C.: Hardness of SIS and LWE with small parameters. In: Canetti, R., Garay, J.A. (eds.) CRYPTO 2013, Part I. LNCS, vol. 8042, pp. 21–39. Springer, Heidelberg (2013). https://doi.org/10.1007/978-3-642-40041-4_2

67. Mossel, E., Shpilka, A., Trevisan, L.: On e-biased generators in NC0. In: 44th FOCS, pp. 136–145. IEEE Computer Society Press, October 2003

68. O'Donnell, R., Witmer, D.: Goldreich's PRG: evidence for near-optimal polynomial stretch. In: IEEE 29th Conference on Computational Complexity, CCC 2014, Vancouver, BC, Canada, 11–13 June 2014, pp. 1–12. IEEE Computer Society (2014)

69. O'Neill, A.: Definitional issues in functional encryption. IACR Cryptology ePrint Archive 2010:556 (2010)

70. Pass, R., Seth, K., Telang, S.: Indistinguishability obfuscation from semantically-secure multilinear encodings. In: Garay, J.A., Gennaro, R. (eds.) CRYPTO 2014, Part I. LNCS, vol. 8616, pp. 500–517. Springer, Heidelberg (2014). https://doi.org/10.1007/978-3-662-44371-2_28

71. Regev, O.: On lattices, learning with errors, random linear codes, and cryptography. In: STOC, pp. 84–93 (2005)

72. Sahai, A., Seyalioglu, H.: Worry-free encryption: functional encryption with public keys. In: Al-Shaer, E., Keromytis, A.D., Shmatikov, V. (eds.) Proceedings of the 17th ACM Conference on Computer and Communications Security, ACM CCS 2010, pp. 463–472. ACM (2010)

73. Sahai, A., Waters, B.: How to use indistinguishability obfuscation: deniable encryption, and more. In: Shmoys, D.B. (ed.) STOC, pp. 475–484. ACM (2014)

74. Sahai, A., Waters, B.: Fuzzy identity-based encryption. In: Cramer, R. (ed.) EUROCRYPT 2005. LNCS, vol. 3494, pp. 457–473. Springer, Heidelberg (2005). https://doi.org/10.1007/11426639_27

# Candidate Obfuscation via Oblivious LWE Sampling

Hoeteck Wee[1] and Daniel Wichs[1,2(✉)]

[1] NTT Research Inc., San Francisco, USA
wichs@ccs.neu.edu
[2] Northeastern University, Boston, USA

**Abstract.** We present a new, simple candidate construction of indistinguishability obfuscation (iO). Our scheme is inspired by lattices and learning-with-errors (LWE) techniques, but we are unable to prove security under a standard assumption. Instead, we formulate a new falsifiable assumption under which the scheme is secure. Furthermore, the scheme plausibly achieves post-quantum security.

Our construction is based on the recent "split FHE" framework of Brakerski, Döttling, Garg, and Malavolta (EUROCRYPT '20), and we provide a new instantiation of this framework. As a first step, we construct an iO scheme that is provably secure assuming that LWE holds *and* that it is possible to obliviously generate LWE samples without knowing the corresponding secrets. We define a precise notion of oblivious LWE sampling that suffices for the construction. It is known how to obliviously sample from any distribution (in a very strong sense) using iO, and our result provides a converse, showing that the ability to obliviously sample from the specific LWE distribution (in a much weaker sense) already also implies iO. As a second step, we give a heuristic contraction of oblivious LWE sampling. On a very high level, we do this by homomorphically generating pseudorandom LWE samples using an encrypted pseudorandom function.

## 1 Introduction

Indistinguishability obfuscation (iO) [BGI+01, GR07] is a probabilistic polynomial-time algorithm $\mathcal{O}$ that takes as input a circuit $C$ and outputs an (obfuscated) circuit $C' = \mathcal{O}(C)$ satisfying two properties: (a) *functionality*: $C$ and $C'$ compute the same function; and (b) *security*: for any two circuits $C_1$ and $C_2$ that compute the same function (and have the same size), $\mathcal{O}(C_1)$ and $\mathcal{O}(C_2)$ are computationally indistinguishable. Since the first candidate for iO was introduced in [GGH+13b], a series of works have shown that iO would have a huge impact on cryptography.

The state-of-the-art iO candidates with concrete instantiations may be broadly classified as follows:

- First, we have fairly simple and direct candidates based on graded "multilinear" encodings [GGH+13b, GGH13a, GGH15, FRS17, CVW18, BGMZ18,

© International Association for Cryptologic Research 2021
A. Canteaut and F.-X. Standaert (Eds.): EUROCRYPT 2021, LNCS 12698, pp. 127–156, 2021.
https://doi.org/10.1007/978-3-030-77883-5_5

CHVW19] and that achieve plausible post-quantum security. These candidates have survived fairly intense scrutiny from cryptanalysts, [CHL+15, MSZ16, CLLT16, ADGM17, CLLT17, CGH17, Pel18, CVW18, CCH+19], and several of them are also provably secure in restricted adversarial models that capture a large class of known attacks. However, none of these candidates have a security reduction to a simple, falsifiable assumption.

- Next, we have a beautiful and remarkable line of works that aims to base iO on a conjunction of simple and well-founded assumptions, starting from [Lin16, LV16, Lin17, LT17], through [AJL+19, Agr19, JLMS19, GJLS20], and culminating in the very recent (and independent) work of Jain, Lin and Sahai [JLS20] basing iO on pairings, LWE, LPN and PRG in NC0. These constructions rely on the prior constructions of iO from functional encryption (FE) [BV15, AJ15], and proceed to build FE via a series of delicate and complex reductions, drawing upon techniques from a large body of works, including pairing-based FE for quadratic functions, lattice-based fully-homomorphic and attribute-based encryption, homomorphic secret-sharing, as well as hardness amplification.

- A number of more recent and incomparable candidates, including a direct candidate based on tensor products [GJK18] and another based on affine determinant programs (with noise) [BIJ+20]; the BDGM candidate based on an intriguing interplay between a LWE-based and a DCR-based cryptosystems [BDGM20a]; the plausibly post-quantum secure candidates in [Agr19, AP20] that replace the use of pairings in the second line of works with direct candidates for FE for inner product plus noise. All of these candidates, as with the first line of work, do not present a security reduction to a simple, falsifiable assumption.[1]

To the best of our knowledge, none of these existing approaches yields a lattice-inspired iO candidate that is plausibly post-quantum secure and enjoys a security reduction under a simple, falsifiable assumption referring solely to lattice-based cryptosystems, which is the focus of this work. We further believe that there is a certain aesthetic and minimalistic appeal to having an iO candidate whose hardness distills to a single source of computational hardness (as opposed to lattice plus pairing/number-theoretic hardness). Such a candidate is also potentially more amenable to crypto-analytic efforts as well as further research to reduce security to more standard lattice problems.

## 1.1 Our Contributions

Our main contribution is a new candidate construction of iO that relies on techniques from lattices and learning-with-errors (LWE). We formulate a new falsifiable assumption on the indistinguishability of two distributions, and show that our construction is secure under this assumption. While we are unable to

---

[1] We defer a comparison with the independent and concurrent works [GP20, BDGM20b] to Sect. 1.3.

prove security under a standard assumption such as LWE, we view our construction as a hopeful step in that direction. To our knowledge, this is the first iO candidate that is simultaneously based on a clearly stated falsifiable assumption and plausibly post-quantum secure. Perhaps more importantly, we open up a new avenue towards iO by showing that, under the LWE assumption, the ability to "obliviously sample from the LWE distribution" (see below) provably implies iO. Unlike prior constructions of iO from simpler primitives (e.g., functional encryption [AJ15,BV15], succinct randomized encodings [LPST16b], XiO [LPST16a], etc.), oblivious LWE sampling does not inherently involve any "computation" and appears to be fundamentally different. Lastly, we believe our construction is conceptually simpler and more self-contained (relying on fewer disjoint components) than many of the prior candidates.

Our main building block is an "oblivious LWE sampler", which takes as input a matrix $\mathbf{A} \in \mathbb{Z}_q^{m \times n}$ and allows us to generate LWE samples $\mathbf{A} \cdot \mathbf{s} + \mathbf{e}$ with some small error $\mathbf{e} \in \mathbb{Z}^m$ without knowing the secrets $\mathbf{s}, \mathbf{e}$. We discuss the notion in more detail below (see the "Our Techniques" section), and provide a formal definition that suffices for our construction. Our notion can be seen as a significant relaxation of "invertible sampling" (in the common reference string model) [IKOS10,DKR15], and the equivalent notion of "pseudorandom encodings" [ACI+20]. The work of [DKR15] showed that, assuming iO, it is possible to invertibly sample from all distributions, and [ACI+20] asked whether it may be possible to do so under simpler assumptions that do not imply iO. As a side result of independent interest, we settle this question by showing that, under LWE, even our relaxed form of invertible sampling for the specific LWE distribution already implies iO.

Overall, our candidate iO construction consists of two steps. The first step is a provably secure construction of iO assuming we have an oblivious LWE sampler and that the LWE assumption holds (both with sub-exponential security). The second step is a candidate heuristic instantiation of an oblivious LWE sampler. On a very high level, our heuristic sampler performs a homomorphic computation that outputs a pseudorandom LWE sample generated using some pseudorandom function (PRF). Security boils down to a clearly stated falsifiable assumption that two distributions, both of which output LWE samples, are indistinguishable even if we give out the corresponding LWE secrets. Our assumption implicitly relies on some form of circular security: we assume that the error term in the pseudorandom LWE sample "drowns out" any error that comes out of the homomorphic computation over the PRF key that was used to generate it. We also discuss how our construction/assumption avoids some simple crypto-analytic attacks.

## 1.2   Technical Overview

Our iO construction is loosely inspired by the "split fully-homomorphic encryption (split FHE)" framework of Brakerski, Döttling, Garg, and Malavolta [BDGM20a] (henceforth BDGM). They defined a new cryptographic primitive called split FHE, which they showed to provably imply iO (under the LWE

| Approach | Falsifiable | Circuit-Independent | Non-Interactive | Post-Quantum |
|---|---|---|---|---|
| mmaps-based iO, cf. [GGH⁺13b] | | | | ✓ |
| NLFE candidates [Agr19, AP20] | | ✓ | | ✓ |
| split-FHE, DCR, LWE [BDGM20a] | | | | |
| LWE, SXDH, LPN, PRG in NC0 [JLS20] | ✓ | ✓ | ✓ | |
| circular-SRL [GP20, BDGM20b] | ✓ | | | ✓ |
| this work (Conjecture 1 HPLS) | ✓ | ✓ | ✓ | ✓ |

**Fig. 1.** Summary of the main approaches and assumptions used for IO. The column "falsifiable" refers to whether there is a reduction to a clearly stated falsifiable assumption (we don't count just assuming the scheme is secure). The term "circuit-independent" means that the assumption does not refer to computation for general circuits (which is closely related to the notion of instance-independent assumptions [GLW14]). We consider assumptions that quantify over worst-case inputs/parameters to be interactive, since the adversary chooses them in the first step.

assumption). They then gave a candidate instantiation of split FHE by heuristically combining decisional composite residue (DCR) and LWE-based techniques, together with the use of a random oracle. We rely on a slight adaptation of their framework by replacing split-FHE with a variant that we call *functional encodings*. Our main contribution is a new instantiation of this framework via "oblivious LWE sampling", relying only on LWE-based techniques (Fig. 1).

We first describe what functional encodings are and how to construct iO from functional encodings. Then we describe our instantiation of functional encodings via oblivious LWE sampling. We defer a detailed comparison to BDGM to Sect. 1.3.

### iO from Functional Encodings

As in BDGM, instead of constructing iO directly, we construct a simpler a primitive called "exponentially efficient iO" XiO, which is known to imply iO under the LWE assumption [LPST16a]. We first describe what XiO is, and then discuss how to construct it from Functional Encodings via the BDGM framework.

**XiO.** An XiO scheme [LPST16a], has the same syntax, correctness and security requirements as iO, but relaxes the efficiency requirement. To obfuscate a circuit $C$ with input length $n$, the obfuscator can run in exponential time $2^{O(n)}$ and the size of the obfuscated circuit can be as large as $2^{n(1-\varepsilon)}$ for some $\varepsilon > 0$. Such a scheme is useful when $n$ is logarithmic in the security parameter, so that $2^n$ is some large polynomial. Note that there is always a trivial obfuscator that outputs the entire truth table of the circuit $C$, which is of size $2^n$. Therefore, XiO is only required to do slightly better than the trivial construction, in that the size of the obfuscated circuit must be non-trivially smaller than the truth table. The work of [LPST16a] showed that XiO together with the LWE assumption (assuming both satisfy sub-exponential security) imply full iO.

**Functional Encodings.** We define a variant of the "split FHE" primitive from BDGM, which we call "functional encodings". A functional encoding can be used to encode a value $x \in \{0,1\}^{\ell}$ to get an encoding $c = \mathsf{Enc}(x; r)$, where $r$ is the randomness of the encoding process. Later, for any function $f : \{0,1\}^{\ell} \to \{0,1\}^m$, we can create an opening $d = \mathsf{Open}(f, x, r)$ for $f$, which can be decoded to recover the function output $\mathsf{Dec}(f, c, d) = f(x)$. We require many-opening simulation based security: the encoding $c = \mathsf{Enc}(x; r)$ together with the many openings $d_1 = \mathsf{Open}(f_1, x, r), \ldots, d_Q = \mathsf{Open}(f_Q, x, r)$ can be simulated given only the functions $f_1, \ldots, f_Q$ and the outputs $f_1(x), \ldots, f_Q(x)$. In other words, nothing about the encoded value $x$ is revealed beyond the function outputs $f_i(x)$ for which openings are given. So far, we can achieve this by simply setting the opening $d$ to be the function output $f(x)$. The notion is made non-trivial, by additionally requiring succinctness: the size of the opening $d$ is bounded by $|d| = O(m^{1-\varepsilon})$ for some $\varepsilon > 0$, and therefore the opening must be non-trivially smaller than the output size of the function. We do not impose any restrictions on the size of the encoding $c$, which may depend polynomially on $m$. Unfortunately, this definition is unachievable in the plain model, as can be shown via a simple incompressibility argument. Therefore, we consider functional encodings in the common reference string (CRS) model and only require many-opening simulation security for some a-priori bound $Q$ on the number of opening (i.e., $Q$-opening security). We allow the CRS size, (but *not* the encoding size or the opening size) to grow polynomially with the bound $Q$.

**XiO from Functional Encodings.** We construct XiO from functional encodings. As a first step, we construct XiO in the CRS model. Let $C : \{0,1\}^n \to \{0,1\}$ be a circuit of size $\ell$ that we want to obfuscate. We can partition the input domain $\{0,1\}^n$ of the circuit into $Q = 2^n/m$ subsets $S_i$, each containing $|S_i| = m$ inputs. We then define $Q$ functions $f_i : \{0,1\}^{\ell} \to \{0,1\}^m$ such that $f_i(C) = (C(x_1), \ldots, C(x_m))$ outputs the evaluations of $C$ on all $m$ inputs $x_j \in S_i$. Finally, we set the obfuscation of the circuit $C$ to be

$$(\mathsf{Enc}(C; r), \mathsf{Open}(f_1, C, r), \ldots, \mathsf{Open}(f_Q, C, r)),$$

which is sufficient to recover the value of the circuit at all $Q \cdot m = 2^n$ possible inputs. By carefully balancing between $m$ and $Q = 2^n/m$, we can ensure that the obfuscated circuit size is $O(2^{n(1-\varepsilon)})$ for some constant $\varepsilon > 0$, and therefore satisfies the non-triviality requirement of XiO. On a high level, we amortize the large size of the encoding across sufficiently many openings to ensure that the total size of the encoding and all the openings together is smaller than the total output size.[2] The above gives us XiO with a strong form of simulation-based security (the obfuscated circuit can be simulated given the truth table) in the CRS model, which also implies the standard indistinguishability-based security in the CRS model.

---

[2] In detail, assume we start with a functional encoding where the encoding size is $O(m^a)$ and the opening size is $O(m^{1-\delta})$ for some constants $a, \delta > 0$, ignoring any other polynomial factors in the security parameter or the input size. The size of the obfuscated circuit above is then bounded by $O(m^a + Qm^{1-\delta})$. By choosing $m = 2^{n/(a+\delta)}$ and recalling $Q = 2^n/m$, the bound becomes $O(2^{n(1-\varepsilon)})$ for $\varepsilon = \delta/(a+\delta)$.

So far, we only got XiO in the CRS model, where the CRS size can be as large as $\mathsf{poly}(Q \cdot m) = 2^{O(n)}$. As the second step, we show that XiO in the CRS model generically implies XiO in the plain model. A naive idea would be to simply make the CRS a part of the obfuscated program, but then we would lose succinctness, since the CRS is large. Instead, we repeat a variant of the previous trick to amortize the cost of the CRS. To obfuscate a circuit $C : \{0,1\}^n \to \{0,1\}$, we partition the domain $\{0,1\}^n$ into $Q = 2^n/m$ subsets containing $m = 2^{n'}$ inputs each, and we define $Q$ sub-circuits $C_i : \{0,1\}^{n'} \to \{0,1\}$, each of which evaluates $C$ on the $m = 2^{n'}$ inputs in the $i$'th subset. We then choose a single CRS for input size $n'$ and obfuscate all $Q$ sub-circuits separately under this CRS; the final obfuscated circuit consists of the CRS and all the $Q$ obfuscated sub-circuits. By carefully balancing between $m = 2^{n'}$ and $Q = 2^n/m$, in the same manner as previously, we can ensure that the total size of the final obfuscated circuit is $O(2^{n(1-\varepsilon)})$ for some constant $\varepsilon > 0$, and therefore the scheme satisfies the non-triviality requirement of XiO.

## Constructing Functional Encodings

We now outline our construction of a functional encoding scheme. We start with a base scheme, which is insecure but serves as the basis of our eventual construction. We show that we can easily make it one-opening simulation secure under the LWE assumption, meaning that security holds in the special case where only a single opening is ever provided (i.e., $Q = 1$). Then we show how to make it many-opening secure via oblivious LWE sampling. Concretely, we obtain a $Q$-opening secure functional encoding candidate for bounded-depth circuits $f : \{0,1\}^\ell \to \{0,1\}^m$ with CRS size $O(Q \cdot m)$, encoding size $O(m^2)$ and opening size $O(1)$, and where $O(\cdot)$ hides factors polynomial in the security parameter, input size $\ell$, and circuit depth.

**Base Scheme.** Our construction of functional encodings is based on a variant of the homomorphic encryption/commitment schemes of [GSW13, GVW15]. Given a commitment to an input $\mathbf{x} = (x_1, \ldots, x_\ell) \in \{0,1\}^\ell$, along with a circuit $f : \{0,1\}^\ell \to \{0,1\}^m$, this scheme allows us to homomorphically compute a commitment to the output $y = f(\mathbf{x})$. Our variant is designed to ensure that the opening for the output commitment is smaller than the output size $m$.

Given a public random matrix $\mathbf{A} \in \mathbb{Z}_q^{m \times n}$ where $m \gg n$, we define a commitment $\mathbf{C}$ to an input $\mathbf{x}$ via

$$\mathbf{C} = (\mathbf{A}\mathbf{R}_1 + x_1\mathbf{G} + \mathbf{E}_1, \ldots, \mathbf{A}\mathbf{R}_\ell + x_\ell\mathbf{G} + \mathbf{E}_\ell)$$

where $\mathbf{R}_i \leftarrow \mathbb{Z}_q^{n \times m \log q}$, $\mathbf{E}_i \leftarrow \chi^{m \times m \log q}$ has its entries chosen from the error distribution $\chi$, and $\mathbf{G} \in \mathbb{Z}_q^{m \times m \log q}$ is the gadget matrix of [MP12]. Although this looks similar to [GSW13, GVW15], we stress that the parameters are different. Namely, in our scheme $\mathbf{A}$ is a tall/thin matrix while in the prior schemes it is a short/fat matrix, we allow $\mathbf{R}_i$ to be uniformly random over the entire space while in the prior schemes it had small entries, and we need to add some error $\mathbf{E}_i$ that was not needed in the prior schemes. The commitment scheme is hiding by the LWE assumption. We can define the functional encoding $\mathsf{Enc}(\mathbf{x}; r) = (\mathbf{A}, \mathbf{C})$

to consist of the matrix $\mathbf{A}$ and the homomorphic commitment $\mathbf{C}$, where $r$ is all the randomness used to sample the above values.

Although we modified several key parameters of [GSW13, GVW15], it turns out that the same homomorphic evaluation procedure there still applies to our modified scheme. In particular, given the commitment $\mathbf{C}$ to an input $\mathbf{x}$ and a boolean circuit $f : \{0,1\}^\ell \to \{0,1\}$, we can homomorphically derive a commitment $\mathbf{C}_f = \mathbf{A}\mathbf{R}_f + f(x)\mathbf{G} + \mathbf{E}_f$ to the output $f(x)$. Furthermore, given a circuit $f : \{0,1\}^\ell \to \{0,1\}^m$ with $m$ bit output, we can apply the above procedure to get commitments to each of the output bits and "pack" them together using the techniques of (e.g.,) [MW16, BTVW17, PS19, GH19, BDGM19] to obtain a vector $\mathbf{c}_f \in \mathbb{Z}_q^m$ such that

$$\mathbf{c}_f = \mathbf{A} \cdot \mathbf{r}_f + f(\mathbf{x}) \cdot \tfrac{q}{2} + \mathbf{e}_f \in \mathbb{Z}_q^m$$

where $f(\mathbf{x}) \in \{0,1\}^m$ is a column vector, $\mathbf{r}_f \in \mathbb{Z}_q^n$, and $\mathbf{e}_f \in \mathbb{Z}^m$ is some small error term.

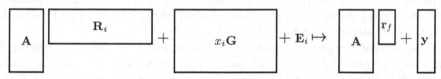

Now, observe that $\mathbf{r}_f$ constitutes a succinct opening to $f(\mathbf{x})$, since $|\mathbf{r}_f| \ll |f(\mathbf{x})|$ and $\mathbf{r}_f$ allows us to easily recover $f(\mathbf{x})$ from $\mathbf{c}_f$ by computing $\mathrm{round}_{q/2}(\mathbf{c}_f - \mathbf{A} \cdot \mathbf{r}_f)$. Furthermore, we can efficiently compute $\mathbf{r}_f$ by applying a homomorphic computation on the opening of the input commitment as in [GVW15], or alternately, we can sample $\mathbf{A}$ with a trapdoor and use the trapdoor to recover $\mathbf{r}_f$. Therefore, we can define the opening procedure of the functional encoding to output the value $\mathbf{r}_f = \mathsf{Open}(f, \mathbf{x}, r)$, and the decoding procedure can recover $f(x) = \mathsf{Dec}(f, (\mathbf{A}, \mathbf{C}), \mathbf{r}_f)$ by homomorphically computing $\mathbf{c}_f$ and using $\mathbf{r}_f$ to recover $f(x)$ as above. This gives us our base scheme (in the plain model), which has the correct syntax and succinctness properties. Unfortunately, the scheme so far does not satisfy even one-opening simulation security, since the opening $\mathbf{r}_f$ (along with the error term $\mathbf{e}_f$ that it implicitly reveals) may leak additional information about $\mathbf{x}$ beyond $f(\mathbf{x})$.

**One-Opening Security from LWE.** We can modify the base scheme to get one-opening simulation security (still in the plain model). In particular, we augment the encoding by additionally including a single random LWE sample $\mathbf{b} = \mathbf{A} \cdot \mathbf{s} + \mathbf{e}$ inside it. We then add this LWE sample to $\mathbf{c}_f$ to "randomize" it, and release $\mathbf{d}_f := \mathbf{r}_f + \mathbf{s}$ as an opening to $f(\mathbf{x})$. Given the encoding $(\mathbf{A}, \mathbf{C}, \mathbf{b})$ and the opening $\mathbf{d}_f$, we can decode $f(\mathbf{x})$ by homomorphically computing $\mathbf{c}_f$ and outputting $y = \mathrm{round}_{q/2}(\mathbf{c}_f + \mathbf{b} - \mathbf{A} \cdot \mathbf{d}_f)$. Correctness follows from the fact that $\mathbf{c}_f + \mathbf{b} \approx \mathbf{A}(\mathbf{r}_f + \mathbf{s}) + f(\mathbf{x}) \cdot q/2$.

With the above modification, we can simulate an encoding/opening pair given only $f(\mathbf{x})$ without knowing $\mathbf{x}$. Firstly, we can simulate the opening without knowing the randomness of the input commitments or the trapdoor for $\mathbf{A}$. In particular, the simulator samples $\mathbf{d}_f$ uniformly at random from $\mathbb{Z}_q^n$, and then "programs" the value $\mathbf{b}$ as $\mathbf{b} := \mathbf{A} \cdot \mathbf{d}_f - \mathbf{c}_f + f(\mathbf{x}) \cdot \tfrac{q}{2} + \mathbf{e}$. The only difference in the distributions is that in the real case the error contained in the LWE sample $\mathbf{b}$ is $\mathbf{e}$, while in the simulated case it is $\mathbf{e} - \mathbf{e}_f$, but we can choose the error $\mathbf{e}$ to be large enough to "smudge out" this difference and ensure that the distributions are statistically close. Once we can simulate the opening without having the randomness of the input commitments or the trapdoor for $\mathbf{A}$, we can rely on LWE to replace the input commitment to $\mathbf{x}$ with a commitment to a dummy value.

**Many-Opening Security via Oblivious LWE Sampling.** We saw that we can upgrade the base scheme to get one-opening simulation security by adding a random LWE sample $\mathbf{b} = \mathbf{A} \cdot \mathbf{s} + \mathbf{e}$ to the encoding. We could easily extend the same idea to achieve $Q$-opening simulation security by adding $Q$ samples $\mathbf{b}_i = \mathbf{A} \cdot \mathbf{s}_i + \mathbf{e}_i$ to the encoding. However, this would require the encoding size to grow with $Q$, which we cannot afford. So far, we have not relied on a CRS, and perhaps the next natural attempt would be to add the $Q$ samples $\mathbf{b}_i$ to the CRS of the scheme. Unfortunately, this also does not work, since the scheme needs to know the corresponding LWE secrets $\mathbf{s}_i$ to generate the openings, and we would not be able to derive them from the CRS.

Imagine that we had an oracle that took as input an arbitrary matrix $\mathbf{A}$ and would output $Q$ random LWE samples $\mathbf{b}_i = \mathbf{A} \cdot \mathbf{s}_i + \mathbf{e}_i$. Such an oracle would allow us to construct $Q$-opening simulation secure functional encodings. The encoding procedure would choose the matrix $\mathbf{A}$ with a trapdoor, call the oracle to get samples $\mathbf{b}_i$ and use the trapdoor to recover the values $\mathbf{s}_i$ that it would use to generate the openings. The decoding procedure would get $\mathbf{A}$ and call the oracle to recover the samples $\mathbf{b}_i$ needed to decode, but would not learn anything else. The simulator would be able to program the oracle and choose the values $\mathbf{b}_i$ itself, which would allow us to prove security analogously to the one-opening setting. We define a cryptographic primitive called an "oblivious LWE sampler", whose goal is to approximate the functionality of the above oracle in the standard model with a CRS. We can have several flavors of this notion, and we start by describing a strong flavor, which we then relax in various ways to get our actual definition.

**Oblivious LWE Sampler (Strong Flavor).** A strong form of oblivious LWE sampling would consist of a deterministic sampling algorithm Sam that takes as input a long CRS along with a matrix $\mathbf{A}$ and outputs $Q$ LWE samples $\mathbf{b}_i = \mathsf{Sam}(\mathsf{CRS}, \mathbf{A}, i)$ for $i \in [Q]$. The size of CRS can grow with $Q$ and the CRS can potentially be chosen from some structured distribution, but it must be independent of $\mathbf{A}$. We want to be able to arbitrarily "program" the outputs of the sampler by programming the CRS. In other words, there is a simulator Sim that gets $\mathbf{A}$ and $Q$ random LWE samples $\{\mathbf{b}_i\}$ as targets; it outputs a programmed string $\mathsf{CRS} \leftarrow \mathsf{Sim}(\mathbf{A}, \{\mathbf{b}_i\})$ that causes the sampler to output the target values $\mathbf{b}_i = \mathsf{Sam}(\mathsf{CRS}, \mathbf{A}, i)$. We want the real and the simulated CRS to be indistinguishable, even for a worst-case choice of $\mathbf{A}$ for which an adversary may know a trapdoor that allows it to recover the LWE secrets. This notion would directly plug in to our construction to get a many-opening secure functional encoding scheme in the CRS model. It turns out that this strong form of oblivious LWE sampling can be seen as a special case of *invertible sampling* (in the CRS model) as proposed by [IKOS10], and can be constructed from iO [DKR15]. Invertible sampling is also equivalent to pseudorandom encodings (with computational security in the CRS model) [ACI+20], and we answer one of the main open problems posed by that work by showing that these notions provably imply iO under the LWE assumption. Unfortunately, we do not know how to heuristically instantiate this strong flavor of oblivious LWE sampling (without already having iO).

**Oblivious LWE Sampler (Relaxed).** We relax the above strong notion in several ways. Firstly, we allow ourselves to "pre-process" the matrix $\mathbf{A}$ using some secret coins to generate a value $\mathsf{pub} \leftarrow \mathsf{Init}(\mathbf{A})$ that is given as an additional input to the sampler $\mathbf{b}_i = \mathsf{Sam}(\mathsf{CRS}, \mathsf{pub}, i)$. We only require that the size of $\mathsf{pub}$ is independent of the number of samples $Q$ that will be generated. The simulator gets to program both $\mathsf{CRS}, \mathsf{pub}$ to produce the desired outcome. Secondly, we relax the requirement that, by programming $\mathsf{CRS}, \mathsf{pub}$, the simulator can cause the sampler output arbitrary target values $\mathbf{b}_i$. Instead, we now give the simulator some target values $\hat{\mathbf{b}}_i$ and the simulator is required to program $(\mathsf{CRS}, \mathsf{pub}) \leftarrow \mathsf{Sim}(\mathbf{A}, \hat{\mathbf{b}}_i)$ to ensure that the sampled values $\mathbf{b}_i = \mathsf{Sam}(\mathsf{CRSpub}, i)$ satisfy $\mathbf{b}_i = \hat{\mathbf{b}}_i + \tilde{\mathbf{b}}_i$ for some LWE sample $\tilde{\mathbf{b}}_i = \mathbf{A} \cdot \tilde{\mathbf{s}}_i + \tilde{\mathbf{e}}_i$ for which the simulator knows the corresponding secrets $\tilde{\mathbf{s}}_i, \tilde{\mathbf{e}}_i$. In other words, the produced samples $\mathbf{b}_i$ need not exactly match the target values $\hat{\mathbf{b}}_i$ given to the simulator, but the difference has to be an LWE sample $\tilde{\mathbf{b}}_i$ for which the simulator can produce the corresponding secrets. Lastly, instead of requiring that the indistinguishability of the real and simulated $(\mathsf{CRS}, \mathsf{pub})$ holds even for a worst-case choice of $\mathbf{A}$ with a known trapdoor, we only require that it holds for a random $\mathbf{A}$, but the adversary is additionally given the LWE secrets $\mathbf{s}_i$ contained in the sampled values $\mathbf{b}_i = \mathbf{A} \cdot \mathbf{s}_i + \mathbf{e}_i$. In other words, we require that real/simulated distributions of $(\mathsf{CRS}, \mathsf{pub}, \{\mathbf{s}_i\})$ are indistinguishable.

We show that this relaxed form of an oblivious LWE sampling suffices in our construction of functional encodings. Namely, we can simply add $\mathsf{pub}$ to the encoding of the functional encoding scheme, since it is short. In the proof, we can replace the real $(\mathsf{CRS}, \mathsf{pub})$ with a simulated one, using some random LWE tuples $\hat{\mathbf{b}}_i$ as target values. Indistinguishability holds even given the LWE secrets $\mathbf{s}_i$ for the produced samples $\mathbf{b}_i = \mathsf{Sam}(\mathsf{CRS}, \mathsf{pub}, i)$, which are used to generate the openings of the functional encoding. The $\hat{\mathbf{b}}_i$ component of the produced samples $\mathbf{b}_i = \hat{\mathbf{b}}_i + \tilde{\mathbf{b}}_i$ is sufficient to re-randomizes the output commitment $\mathbf{c}_f$, and the additional LWE sample $\tilde{\mathbf{b}}_i$ that is added in does not hurt security, since we know the corresponding LWE secret $\tilde{\mathbf{s}}_i$ and can use it to adjust the opening accordingly.

**Constructing an Oblivious LWE Sampler.** We give a heuristic construction of an oblivious LWE sampler, by relying on the same homomorphic commitments that we used to construct our base functional encoding scheme. The high level idea is to give out a commitment to a PRF key $\mathbf{k}$ and let the sampling algorithm homomorphically compute a pseudorandom LWE sample $\mathbf{b}_{\mathsf{prf}} := \mathbf{A} \cdot \mathbf{s}_{\mathsf{prf}} + \mathbf{e}_{\mathsf{prf}}$

where $\mathsf{s}_{\mathsf{prf}}, \mathsf{e}_{\mathsf{prf}}$ are sampled using randomness that comes from the PRF. The overall output of the sampler is a commitment to the above LWE sample, which is itself an LWE sample! While we do not know how to construct a simulator for this basic construction, we conjecture that it may already be sufficient to instantiate functional encodings. To allow the simulator to program the output, we augment the computation to incorporate the CRS. We give a more detailed description below.

The CRS is a uniformly random string, which we interpret as consisting of $Q$ values $\mathsf{CRS}_i \in \mathbb{Z}_q^m$. To generate pub, we sample a random key $\mathbf{k}$ for a pseudorandom function $\mathsf{PRF}(\mathbf{k}, \cdot)$ and set a flag bit $\beta := 0$. We creates a commitment $\mathbf{C}$ to the input $(\mathbf{k}, \beta)$ and we set the public value pub $= (\mathbf{A}, \mathbf{C})$. The algorithm $\mathbf{b}_i = \mathsf{Sample}(\mathsf{CRS}, \mathsf{pub}, i)$ performs a homomorphic computation of the function $g_i$ over the commitment $\mathbf{C}$, where $g_i$ is defined as follows:

$$g_i(\mathbf{k}, \beta): \quad \text{Use } \mathsf{PRF}(\mathbf{k}, i) \text{ to sample } \mathbf{b}_i^{\mathsf{prf}} := \mathbf{A} \cdot \mathbf{s}_i^{\mathsf{prf}} + \mathbf{e}_i^{\mathsf{prf}} \text{ and output}$$
$$\mathbf{b}_i^* := \mathbf{b}_i^{\mathsf{prf}} + \beta \cdot \mathsf{CRS}_i.$$

The output of this computation is a homomorphically evaluated commitment to $\mathbf{b}_i^*$ and has the form $\mathbf{b}_i = \mathbf{A} \cdot \mathbf{s}_i^{\mathsf{eval}} + \mathbf{e}_i^{\mathsf{eval}} + \mathbf{b}_i^*$ where $\mathbf{s}_i^{\mathsf{eval}}, \mathbf{e}_i^{\mathsf{eval}}$ come from the homomorphic evaluation.[3] Overall, the generated samples $\mathbf{b}_i = \mathsf{Sample}(\mathsf{CRS}, \mathsf{pub}, i)$ can be written as

$$\mathbf{b}_i = \mathbf{A} \cdot (\mathbf{s}_i^{\mathsf{eval}} + \mathbf{s}_i^{\mathsf{prf}}) + (\mathbf{e}_i^{\mathsf{eval}} + \mathbf{e}_i^{\mathsf{prf}}) + \beta \cdot \mathsf{CRS}_i$$

where $\mathbf{s}_i^{\mathsf{prf}}, \mathbf{e}_i^{\mathsf{prf}}$ come from the PRF output and $\mathbf{s}_i^{\mathsf{eval}}, \mathbf{e}_i^{\mathsf{eval}}$ come from the homomorphic evaluation.

In the real scheme, the flag $\beta$ is set to 0 and so each output of Sample is an LWE sample $\mathbf{b}_i = \mathbf{A} \cdot (\mathbf{s}_i^{\mathsf{eval}} + \mathbf{s}_i^{\mathsf{prf}}) + (\mathbf{e}_i^{\mathsf{eval}} + \mathbf{e}_i^{\mathsf{prf}})$. In the simulation, the simulator gets some target values $\hat{\mathbf{b}}_i$ and puts them in the CRS as $\mathsf{CRS}_i := \hat{\mathbf{b}}_i$. It sets the flag to $\beta = 1$, which results in the output of Sample being $\mathbf{b}_i = \mathbf{A} \cdot (\mathbf{s}_i^{\mathsf{eval}} + \mathbf{s}_i^{\mathsf{prf}}) + (\mathbf{e}_i^{\mathsf{eval}} + \mathbf{e}_i^{\mathsf{prf}}) + \hat{\mathbf{b}}_i$. Note that the simulator knows the PRF key $\mathbf{k}$ and the randomness of the homomorphic commitment, and therefore knows the values $(\mathbf{s}_i^{\mathsf{eval}} + \mathbf{s}_i^{\mathsf{prf}}), (\mathbf{e}_i^{\mathsf{eval}} + \mathbf{e}_i^{\mathsf{prf}})$. This means that the difference between the target values $\hat{\mathbf{b}}_i$ and the output samples $\mathbf{b}_i$ is an LWE tuple for which the simulator knows the corresponding secrets, as required.

**Security Under a New Conjecture.** We conjecture that the above construction is secure. In particular, we conjecture that the adversary cannot distinguish between $\beta = 0$ and $\beta = 1$ given the values:

$$(\mathsf{CRS} = \{\mathsf{CRS}_i = \mathbf{A}\hat{\mathbf{s}}_i + \hat{\mathbf{e}}_i\}_{i \in [Q]}, \mathsf{pub} = (\mathbf{A}, \mathbf{C} = \mathsf{Commit}(k, \beta)), \{\mathbf{s}_i = \mathbf{s}_i^{\mathsf{eval}} + \mathbf{s}_i^{\mathsf{prf}} + \beta\hat{\mathbf{s}}_i\}_{i \in [Q]})$$

---

[3] Recall that previously we relied on a "packed" homomorphic evaluation, where we could evaluate a function $f : \{0,1\}^\ell \to \{0,1\}^m$ on a commitment to $\mathbf{x}$ to get a commitment $\mathbf{c}_f = \mathbf{A} \cdot \mathbf{s}_f + \mathbf{e}_f + f(\mathbf{x}) \cdot \frac{q}{2}$. The above relies on a slight variant that's even further packed and allows us to homomorphically evaluate a function $g : \{0,1\}^\ell \to \mathbb{Z}_q^m$ over a commitment to $\mathbf{x}$ and derive a commitment $\mathbf{c}_g = \mathbf{A} \cdot \mathbf{s}_g + \mathbf{e}_g + g(\mathbf{x})$.

We refer to this as the *homomorphic pseudorandom LWE samples (HPLS)* conjecture (see Conjecture 1 for a precise statement), and we argue heuristically why we believe it to hold. Since $\mathsf{CRS}, \mathsf{pub}$ completely determine the values $\mathbf{b}_i = \mathbf{A} \cdot \mathbf{s}_i + \mathbf{e}_i$, revealing $\mathbf{s}_i = \mathbf{s}_i^{\mathsf{eval}} + \mathbf{s}_i^{\mathsf{prf}} + \beta \hat{\mathbf{s}}_i$ also implicitly reveals $\mathbf{e}_i = \mathbf{e}_i^{\mathsf{eval}} + \mathbf{e}_i^{\mathsf{prf}} + \beta \hat{\mathbf{e}}_i$. We can think of the HPLS conjecture as consisting of two distinct heuristic components. The first component is to argue that the values $\mathbf{s}_i, \mathbf{e}_i$ look pseudorandom and independent of $\beta$ given only $(\mathsf{CRS}, \mathbf{A})$, but without getting the commitment $\mathbf{C}$. Intuitively, we believe this to hold since $\mathbf{s}_i^{\mathsf{prf}}, \mathbf{e}_i^{\mathsf{prf}}$ are provably pseudorandom (by the security of the PRF). Therefore, as long as we choose the noise $\mathbf{e}_i^{\mathsf{prf}}$ to be large enough to "smudge out" $\hat{\mathbf{e}}_i$, we can provably argue that $\mathbf{s}_i^{\mathsf{prf}} + \beta \hat{\mathbf{s}}_i$ and $\mathbf{e}_i^{\mathsf{prf}} + \beta \hat{\mathbf{e}}_i$ are pseudorandom and independent of $\beta$. Unfortunately, this does not suffice – we still need to rely on a heuristic to ague that there are no computationally discernible correlations between these values and $\mathbf{s}_i^{\mathsf{eval}}, \mathbf{e}_i^{\mathsf{eval}}$ respectively. We believe this should hold with most natural PRFs. Although the first component is already heuristic, there is hope to remove the heuristic nature of this component by explicitly analyzing the distributions $\mathbf{s}_i^{\mathsf{eval}} + \mathbf{s}_i^{\mathsf{prf}}, \mathbf{e}_i^{\mathsf{eval}} + \mathbf{e}_i^{\mathsf{eval}}$ for a specific PRF, and leave this as a fascinating open problem for future work. The second heuristic component is to argue that security holds even in the presence of the commitment $\mathbf{C}$. This part implicitly involves a circular security aspect between the pseudorandom function and the commitment. We'd like to argue that the PRF key $\mathbf{k}$ and the bit $\beta$ are protected by the security of the commitment scheme, but we release $\mathbf{s}_i = \mathbf{s}_i^{\mathsf{eval}} + \mathbf{s}_i^{\mathsf{prf}} + \beta \hat{\mathbf{s}}_i$, where $\mathbf{s}_i^{\mathsf{eval}}$ depends on the commitment randomness; nevertheless we'd like to argue that this does not hurt commitment security since the value $\mathbf{s}_i^{\mathsf{eval}}$ is masked by the PRF output, but this argument is circular since the PRF key is contained in the commitment! This circularity does not easily lend itself to a proof, and we see much less hope in removing the heuristic nature of the second component than the first. Still, this type of circularity also seems difficult to attack: one cannot easily break the security of the commitment without first breaking the security of the PRF and vice versa.

**Simplified Construction.** In the full version, we also give a simplified direct construction of functional encodings in the plain model that we conjecture to satisfy indistinguishability based security. The simplified construction does not go through the intermediate "oblivious LWE sampler" primitive. In contrast to our main construction, which is secure under a non-interactive assumption that two distributions are indistinguishable, the assumption that our simplified construction is secure and interactive.

## 1.3   Discussion and Perspectives

### Comparison to BDGM

We now give a detailed comparison of our results/techniques with those of Brakerski, Döttling, Garg, and Malavolta [BDGM20a] (BDGM). BDGM defined a primitive called split FHE, which they show implies iO under the LWE assumption. They then gave a candidate instantiation of split FHE by heuristically combining decisional composite residue (DCR) and LWE-based techniques, together with the use of a random oracle. While they gave compelling intuition for why they believe this construction of split FHE to be secure, they did not attempt to formulate an assumption under which they could prove security. In our work, we define a variant of split FHE that we call functional encodings. We then provide an entirely new instantiation of functional encodings via oblivious LWE sampling. The main advantages of our approach are:

- We get a provably secure construction of iO under the LWE assumption along with an additional assumption that there is an oblivious LWE sampler, where the latter is a clearly abstracted primitive, which we then instantiate heuristically. In particular, we are able to confine the heuristic portion of our construction to a single well defined component.
- We can prove security of our overall construction under a falsifiable, non-interactive assumption that is independent of the function being obfuscated.
- Our construction of iO relies only on LWE-based techniques rather than the additional use of DCR. In our opinion, this makes the construction conceptually simpler and easier to analyze. Furthermore, the construction is plausibly post-quantum secure.
- We avoid any reliance on random oracles.

On a technical level, we lightly adapt the split FHE framework of BDGM. In particular, our notion of functional encodings can be seen as a relaxed form of split FHE, and our result that functional encodings imply iO closely follows BDGM. The main differences between the two works, lie in the our respective instantiations of split-FHE and functional encodings. We explain the differences in the framework and the instantiation in more detail below.

**Functional Encodings vs Split FHE.** There are two differences between our notion of functional encodings versus the split FHE framework of BDGM. Firstly, our notion of functional encodings has a simplified syntax compared to split FHE (in particular, we do not require any key generation or homomorphic evaluation algorithms and the opening can depend on all of the randomness $r$ used to generate the encoding rather than just a secret key). While we find the simplified syntax conceptually easier, it is not crucial, and our candidate construction of functional encodings can be adapted to also match the syntactic requirements of split FHE. The second difference is that we explicitly allow for a CRS in functional encodings, and show that the CRS can be removed when we go to XiO (in particular, we show that XiO in the CRS model implies XiO in the plain model). In contrast, the work of BDGM considered split FHE in the plain model (with indistinguishability rather than simulation security). Their instantiation relies on a random oracle model and they argued heuristically that the random oracle can be removed. The fact that we explicitly consider the

CRS model allows us to avoid random oracles entirely, and therefore reduce the number of heuristic components in the final construction.[4]

**Heuristic Instantiations.** Both BDGM and our work provide a heuristic instantiation of the main building block: split FHE and functional encodings, respectively. These instantiations are concretely very different, and rely on different techniques. On a conceptual level, they also differ in the role that heuristic arguments play. BDGM constructs a provably secure instantiation of split FHE under the combination of LWE and DCR assumptions, in some idealized oracle world (essentially, the oracle samples Damgard-Jurik encryptions of small values). They then give a heuristic instantiation of their oracle. However, there is no attempt to define any standard-model notion of security that such an instantiation could satisfy to make the overall scheme secure. In contrast, we construct a provably secure instantiation of functional encodings under the LWE assumption and assuming we have an "oblivious LWE sampler", where the latter is a cryptographic primitive in the standard model (with a CRS) with a well-defined security requirement. We then give a heuristic construction of an oblivious LWE sampler using LWE techniques. Although the security notion of oblivious LWE sampling involves a simulator, our heuristic construction comes with a candidate simulator for it. Therefore, the only heuristic component of our construction is a clearly stated falsifiable assumption that two distributions (real and simulated) are indistinguishable.

We conjecture that the split FHE construction of BDGM could similarly be proven secure under the LWE assumption, DCR assumption, and some type of "oblivious sampler" for Damgard-Jurik encryptions of random small values. Moreover, the heuristic instantiation of the oracle in BDGM could likely be seen as a heuristic candidate for such an oblivious sampler. However, BDGM does not appear to have a plausible candidate simulator for this instantiation and hence security does not appear to follow from any simple falsifiable assumption (other than assuming that the full construction of split FHE is secure).

We note that BDGM (Sect. 4.4) also presents an alternate construction of split FHE based only the LWE assumption (without DCR) in some other idealized oracle world. However, they were not able to heuristically instantiate the oracle for this alternate construction, and hence it did not lead to even a heuristic candidate for post-quantum secure iO in their work.[5] Their construction does yield a one-opening secure split-FHE / functional encoding under LWE, and our one-opening secure scheme is in part inspired by it (and can be seen as simplifying it). The main advantage of our scheme is that we can extend it to many-opening security via oblivious LWE sampling, which we then instantiate heuristically to get a candidate iO.

---

[4] We believe that this change could also be applied retroactively to remove the use of a random oracles in BDGM.

[5] As stated in BDGM Sect. 4.4: "We stress that, in contrast with the instantiation based on the Damgard-Jurik encryption scheme (Sect. 4.3), this scheme does not satisfy the syntactical requirements to apply the generic transformations (described in Sect. 4.2) to lift the scheme to the plain model.".

**Comparison with FE**

The line of work on building iO from simple, well-founded assumptions first builds functional encryption (FE). A functional encryption scheme allows us to encrypt a value $x$ and generate secret keys for functions $f$ so that decryption returns $f(x)$ while leaking no additional information about $x$. We also consider $Q$-key security, where an adversary given an encryption of $x$ and $Q$ secret keys for functions $f_1, \ldots, f_Q$ should learn nothing about $x$ beyond $f_1(x), \ldots, f_Q(x)$. A functional encoding scheme can be viewed as a relaxation of a secret-key functional encryption where we allow the key for $f$ to depend on $x$.

The state-of-the-art for functional encryption is analogous to that for functional encoding:

- We have one-key secure public-key FE for bounded-depth circuits $f$ : $\{0,1\}^\ell \to \{0,1\}^m$ from LWE with ciphertext size $O(m)$ and key size $O(1)$ [GKP+13, GVW13, BGG+14].
- A construction of iO from one-key secure public-key FE for bounded-depth circuits $f : \{0,1\}^\ell \to \{0,1\}^m$ with ciphertext size $O(m^{1-\epsilon})$ [BV15, AJ15]. The latter is in turn implied by $Q$-key secure public-key FE for $f : \{0,1\}^\ell \to \{0,1\}$ with ciphertext size $O(Q^{1-\epsilon})$.
- A construction of iO from $Q$-key secure secret-key FE bounded-depth circuits $f : \{0,1\}^\ell \to \{0,1\}^m$ with ciphertext size $Q^{1-\epsilon} \cdot \text{poly}(m)$. Our main candidate is essentially the functional encoding analogue of such a secret-key FE scheme (in the CRS model).

This analogue raises two natural open problems: Do the techniques in this work also yield non-trivial FE schemes (that imply iO) with a polynomial security loss, without passing through iO as an intermediate building block? Can we simplify the constructions or assumptions underlying the FE schemes in [AJL+19, Agr19, JLMS19, GJLS20, JLS20] by relaxing the requirements from FE to functional encodings (which would still suffice for iO)?

**Comparison with Concurrent Works:** [GP20, BDGM20b]

The recent work of [GP20] together with a follow-up to it [BDGM20b] (both of which are concurrent and independent of our work), present new candidate constructions of iO by adapting the BDGM [BDGM20a] framework. Just like our work, they go through the route of constructing XiO in the CRS model, and have instantiations that rely only on LWE-style techniques and are plausibly post-quantum secure. While there are many high-level similarities between these works and our work, the concrete construction and security assumption are different. In terms of construction, the main difference lies in how the works "re-randomize" the opening/hint that allows one to recover the output of the computation. In our case, we do so via an "oblivious LWE sampler", which is instantiated by using an encrypted PRF key to produce an encrypted pseudorandom LWE sample. The two works [GP20, BDGM20b] follow the original construction of [BDGM20a] more closely and rely on homomorphically decrypting random ciphertexts in the CRS using a key cycle.[6] Our overall construction is arguably somewhat simper than the others since it relies on a single homomorphic cryptosystem (a variant of GSW FHE) rather than switching between two different homomorphic cryptosystems with different properties. In terms of assumptions, both of the works [GP20,BDGM20b] prove security under a new assumption that a certain cryptosystem satisfies a strong form of "circular security" in the presence of some oracle. In the full version, we give a more detailed comparison and our take on the circular security assumptions.

## 2 Preliminaries

### 2.1 Notations

We will denote by $\lambda$ the security parameter. The notation $\mathsf{negl}(\lambda)$ denotes any function $f$ such that $f(\lambda) = \lambda^{-\omega(1)}$, and $\mathsf{poly}(\lambda)$ denotes any function $f$ such that $f(\lambda) = \mathcal{O}(\lambda^c)$ for some $c > 0$. For a probabilistic algorithm $\mathsf{alg}(\mathsf{inputs})$, we might explicit the randomness it uses by writing $\mathsf{alg}(\mathsf{inputs}; \mathsf{coins})$. We will denote vectors by bold lower case letters (e.g. $\mathbf{a}$) and matrices by bold upper cases letters (e.g. $\mathbf{A}$). We will denote by $\mathbf{a}^\top$ and $\mathbf{A}^\top$ the transposes of $\mathbf{a}$ and $\mathbf{A}$, respectively. We will denote by $\lfloor x \rceil$ the nearest integer to $x$, rounding towards 0 for half-integers. If $\mathbf{x}$ is a vector, $\lfloor \mathbf{x} \rceil$ will denote the rounded value applied component-wise. For integral vectors and matrices (i.e., those over $\mathbb{Z}$), we use the notation $|\mathbf{r}|, |\mathbf{R}|$ to denote the maximum absolute value over all the entries.

We define the statistical distance between two random variables $X$ and $Y$ over some domain $\Omega$ as: $\mathbf{SD}(X,Y) = \frac{1}{2}\sum_{w \in \Omega}|X(w) - Y(w)|$. We say that two ensembles of random variables $X = \{X_\lambda\}$, $Y = \{Y_\lambda\}$ are *statistically indistinguishable*, denoted $X \overset{\mathrm{s}}{\approx} Y$, if $\mathbf{SD}(X_\lambda, Y_\lambda) \leq \mathsf{negl}(\lambda)$.

We say that two ensembles of random variables $X = \{X_\lambda\}$, and $Y = \{Y_\lambda\}$ are *computationally indistinguishable*, denoted $X \overset{\mathrm{c}}{\approx} Y$, if, for all (non-uniform) PPT distinguishers $\mathsf{Adv}$, we have $|\Pr[\mathsf{Adv}(X_\lambda) = 1] - \Pr[\mathsf{Adv}(Y_\lambda) = 1]| \leq \mathsf{negl}(\lambda)$. We also refer to sub-exponential security, meaning that there exists some $\varepsilon > 0$ such that the distinguishing advantage is at most $2^{-\lambda^\varepsilon}$.

We assume familiarity with the learning-with errors (LWE) assumption [Reg05], noise smudging (e.g., [AJL+12]), the Gadget Matrix $\mathbf{G}$ [MP12] and lattice trapdoors [Ajt96,MP12]. See the full version for details.

## 3 Functional Encodings

### 3.1 Definition of Functional Encodings

A *functional encoding scheme* (in the CRS model) for the family $\mathcal{F}_{\ell,m,t} = \{f : \{0,1\}^\ell \to \{0,1\}^m\}$ of depth-$t$ circuits consists of four PPT algorithms $\mathsf{crsGen}, \mathsf{Enc}, \mathsf{Open}, \mathsf{Dec}$ where $\mathsf{Open}$ and $\mathsf{Dec}$ are deterministic, satisfying the following properties:

---

[6] Interestingly, since decrypting random ciphertexts is a (weak-)PRF, the two approaches may be more similar than may appear.

**Syntax:** The algorithms have the following syntax:

- $\mathsf{CRS} \leftarrow \mathsf{crsGen}(1^\lambda, 1^Q, \mathcal{F}_{\ell,m,t})$ outputs CRS for security parameter $1^\lambda$ and a bound $Q$ on the number of openings;
- $C \leftarrow \mathsf{Enc}(\mathsf{CRS}, x \in \{0,1\}^\ell; r)$ encodes $x$ using randomness $r$;
- $d \leftarrow \mathsf{Open}(\mathsf{CRS}, f : \{0,1\}^\ell \to \{0,1\}^m, i \in [Q], x, r)$ computes the opening corresponding to $i$'th function $f$;
- $y \leftarrow \mathsf{Dec}(\mathsf{CRS}, f, i, C, d)$ computes a value $y$ for the encoding $C$ and opening $d$.

**Correctness:**

$$\mathsf{Dec}(f, \mathsf{Enc}(x, r), \mathsf{Open}(f, x, r)) = f(x)$$

$Q$-**SIM Security:** There exists a PPT simulator $\mathsf{Sim}$ such that the following distributions for all PPT adversaries $\mathcal{A}$ and all $x, f^1, \ldots, f^Q \leftarrow \mathcal{A}(1^\lambda)$, the following distributions of $(\mathsf{CRS}, C, d_1, \ldots, d_Q)$ are computationally indistinguishable (even given $x, f^1, \ldots, f^Q$):

- Real Distribution: $\mathsf{CRS} \leftarrow \mathsf{crsGen}(1^\lambda, 1^Q), C \leftarrow \mathsf{Enc}(\mathsf{CRS}, x; r), d_i \leftarrow \mathsf{Open}(\mathsf{CRS}, f^i, i, x, r), i \in [Q]$.
- Simulated Distribution: $(\mathsf{CRS}, C, d_1, \ldots, d_Q) \leftarrow \mathsf{Sim}(\{f^i, f^i(x)\}_{i \in Q})$.

**Succinctness:** There exists a constant $\epsilon > 0$ such that, for $\mathsf{CRS} \leftarrow \mathsf{crsGen}(1^\lambda, 1^Q, \mathcal{F}_{\ell,m,t}), C \leftarrow \mathsf{Enc}(\mathsf{CRS}, x; r), d \leftarrow \mathsf{Open}(\mathsf{CRS}, f, i, x, r)$ we have:

$$|\mathsf{CRS}| = \mathsf{poly}(Q, \lambda, \ell, m, t), |C| = \mathsf{poly}(\lambda, \ell, m, t), |d| = m^{1-\varepsilon}\mathsf{poly}(\lambda, \ell, t).$$

In our discussion, we also refer to indistinguishability-based security, a relaxation of $Q$-SIM security:

$Q$-**IND Security:** For all PPT adversaries $\mathcal{A}$ and all $\mathbf{x}_0, \mathbf{x}_1, f^1, \ldots, f^Q \leftarrow \mathcal{A}(1^\lambda)$ such that $f^i(\mathbf{x}_0) = f^i(\mathbf{x}_1)$ for all $i \in [Q]$, the following distributions of $(\mathsf{CRS}, C, d_1, \ldots, d_Q)$ are computationally indistinguishable for $\beta = 0$ and $\beta = 1$:

$$\mathsf{CRS} \leftarrow \mathsf{crsGen}(1^\lambda, 1^Q), C \leftarrow \mathsf{Enc}(\mathsf{CRS}, x^\beta; r), d_i \leftarrow \mathsf{Open}(\mathsf{CRS}, f^i, i, x^\beta, r), i \in [Q]$$

*Remark 1 (Comparison with split-FHE).* One can think of functional encodings as essentially a relaxation of split-FHE, where we remove the explicit requirements for decryption (and secret keys) and for homomorphic evaluation. This simplifies both the syntax and the security definition. In the language of BDGM, Open corresponds to a decryption hint for an encryption of $f(x)$, obtained by applying partial decryption to homomorphic evaluation of $f$ on the encryption of $x$. Note that in BDGM, the hint should be computable given the decryption key, whereas we allow the hint to depend on the encryption/commitment randomness. Finally, BDGM circumvents the impossibility of simulation-based security for many-time security in the plain model by turning to indistinguishability-based security, whereas we rely on a CRS.

*Remark 2 (Comparison with functional encryption).* Functional encoding is very similar to (secret-key) functional encryption where given an encryption of $x$ and a secret key for $f$, we learn $f(x)$ and nothing else about $x$. A crucial distinction here is that Open also gets $x$ as input.

# 4  Homomorphic Commitments with Short Openings

In this section, we describe a homomorphic commitment scheme with short openings.

**Lemma 1 (Homomorphic computation on matrices [GSW13, BGG+14]).**
*Fix parameters $m, q, \ell$. Given a matrix $\mathbf{C} \in \mathbb{Z}_q^{m \times \ell m \log q}$ and a circuit $f : \{0, 1\}^\ell \to \{0, 1\}$ of depth $t$, we can efficiently compute a matrix $\mathbf{C}_f$ such that for all $\mathbf{x} \in \{0, 1\}^\ell$, there exists a matrix $\mathbf{H}_{\mathbf{C}, f, \mathbf{x}} \in \mathbb{Z}^{\ell m \log q \times m \log q}$ with $|\mathbf{H}_{\mathbf{C}, f, \mathbf{x}}| = m^{O(t)}$ such that[7]*

$$(\mathbf{C} - \mathbf{x}^\top \otimes \mathbf{G}) \cdot \mathbf{H}_{\mathbf{C}, f, \mathbf{x}} = \mathbf{C}_f - f(\mathbf{x})\mathbf{G} \tag{1}$$

*where $\mathbf{G} \in \mathbb{Z}_q^{m \times m \log q}$ is the gadget matrix. Moreover, $\mathbf{H}_{\mathbf{C}, f, \mathbf{x}}$ is efficiently computable given $\mathbf{C}, f, \mathbf{x}$.*

Using the "packing" techniques in [MW16, BTVW17, PS19], the above relation extends to circuits with $m$-bit output. Concretely, given a circuit $f : \{0, 1\}^\ell \to \{0, 1\}^m$ of depth $t$, we can efficiently compute a vector $\mathbf{c}_f$ such that for all $\mathbf{x} \in \{0, 1\}^\ell$, there exists a vector $\mathbf{h}_{\mathbf{C}, f, \mathbf{x}} \in \mathbb{Z}^{\ell m \log q}$ with $|\mathbf{h}_{\mathbf{C}, f, \mathbf{x}}| = m^{O(t)}$ such that

$$(\mathbf{C} - \mathbf{x}^\top \otimes \mathbf{G}) \cdot \mathbf{h}_{\mathbf{C}, f, \mathbf{x}} = \mathbf{c}_f - f(\mathbf{x}) \cdot \tfrac{q}{2} \tag{2}$$

where $f(\mathbf{x}) \in \{0, 1\}^m$ is a column vector. Concretely, let $f_1, \ldots, f_m : \{0, 1\}^m \to \{0, 1\}$ denote the circuits computing the output bits of $f$. Then, we have:

$$\mathbf{c}_f = \sum_{j=1}^m \mathbf{C}_{f_j} \cdot \mathbf{G}^{-1}(\mathbf{1}_j \cdot \tfrac{q}{2}) \tag{3}$$

$$\mathbf{h}_{\mathbf{C}, f, \mathbf{x}} = \sum_{j=1}^m \mathbf{H}_{\mathbf{C}, f_j, \mathbf{x}} \cdot \mathbf{G}^{-1}(\mathbf{1}_j \cdot \tfrac{q}{2})$$

where $\mathbf{1}_j \in \{0, 1\}^m$ is the indicator column vector whose $j$'th entry is 1 and 0 everywhere else, so that $f(\mathbf{x}) = \sum_j f_i(\mathbf{x}) \cdot \mathbf{1}_j$. Here, $\mathbf{h}_{\mathbf{C}, f, \mathbf{x}}$ is also efficiently computable given $\mathbf{C}, f, \mathbf{x}$.

**Construction 1 (homomorphic commitments pFHC).** *The commitment scheme pFHC ("packed fully homomorphic commitment") is parameterized by $m, \ell$ and $n, q$, and is defined as follows.*

– Gen *chooses a uniformly random matrix $\mathbf{A} \leftarrow \mathbb{Z}_q^{m \times n}$.*

---

[7] Note that if we write $\mathbf{C} = [\mathbf{C}_1 \mid \cdots \mid \mathbf{C}_\ell]$ where $\mathbf{C}_1, \ldots, \mathbf{C}_\ell \in \mathbb{Z}_q^{m \times m \log q}$ and $\mathbf{x} = (x_1, \ldots, x_\ell)$, then

$$\mathbf{C} - \mathbf{x}^\top \otimes \mathbf{G} = [\mathbf{C}_1 - x_1 \mathbf{G} \mid \ldots \mid \mathbf{C}_\ell - x_\ell \mathbf{G}]$$

- $\mathsf{Com}(\mathbf{A} \in \mathbb{Z}_q^{m \times n}, \mathbf{x} \in \{0,1\}^\ell; \mathbf{R} \in \mathbb{Z}_q^{n \times \ell m \log q}, \mathbf{E} \in \mathbb{Z}^{m \times \ell m \log q})$ outputs a commitment
$$\mathbf{C} := \mathbf{AR} + \mathbf{x}^\top \otimes \mathbf{G} + \mathbf{E} \in \mathbb{Z}_q^{m \times \ell m \log q}.$$
Here, $\mathbf{R} \leftarrow \mathbb{Z}_q^{n \times \ell m \log q}, \mathbf{E} \leftarrow \chi^{m \times \ell m \log q}$
- $\mathsf{Eval}(f : \{0,1\}^\ell \to \{0,1\}^m, \mathbf{C} \in \mathbb{Z}_q^{m \times \ell m \log q})$ for a boolean circuit $f : \{0,1\}^\ell \to \{0,1\}^m$, deterministically outputs a (column) vector $\mathbf{c}_f \in \mathbb{Z}_q^m$. Here, $\mathbf{c}_f$ is the same as that given in (2).
- $\mathsf{Eval}_{\mathsf{open}}(f, \mathbf{A} \in \mathbb{Z}_q^{m \times n}, \mathbf{x} \in \{0,1\}^\ell, \mathbf{R} \in \mathbb{Z}_q^{n \times \ell m \log q}, \mathbf{E} \in \mathbb{Z}^{m \times \ell m \log q})$: deterministically outputs (column) vectors $\mathbf{r}_f \in \mathbb{Z}_q^n, \mathbf{e}_f \in \mathbb{Z}_q^m$.

**Lemma 2.** *The above commitment scheme* $\mathsf{pFHC}$ *satisfies the following properties:*

- **Correctness.** *For any boolean circuit* $f : \{0,1\}^\ell \to \{0,1\}^m$ *of depth* $t$, *any* $\mathbf{x} \in \{0,1\}^\ell$, *any* $\mathbf{A} \in \mathbb{Z}_q^{m \times n}, \mathbf{R} \in \mathbb{Z}_q^{n \times \ell m \log q}, \mathbf{E} \in \mathbb{Z}^{m \times \ell m \log q}$, *we have*

$$\mathbf{C} := \mathsf{Com}(\mathbf{A}, \mathbf{x}; \mathbf{R}, \mathbf{E}), \quad \mathbf{c}_f := \mathsf{Eval}(f, \mathbf{C}), \quad (\mathbf{r}_f, \mathbf{e}_f) := \mathsf{Eval}_{\mathsf{open}}(f, \mathcal{A}, \mathbf{x}, \mathbf{R}, \mathbf{E})$$

*satisfies*

$$\mathbf{c}_f = \mathbf{A}\mathbf{r}_f + f(\mathbf{x}) \cdot \tfrac{q}{2} + \mathbf{e}_f \in \mathbb{Z}_q^m$$

*where* $f(\mathbf{x}) \in \{0,1\}^m$ *is a column vector and* $|\mathbf{e}_f| = |\mathbf{E}| \cdot m^{O(t)}$.
- **Privacy.** *Under the LWE assumption, for all* $\mathbf{x} \in \{0,1\}^\ell$, *we have:*

$$\mathbf{A}, \mathsf{Com}(\mathbf{A}, \mathbf{x}) \approx_c \mathbf{A}, \mathsf{Com}(\mathbf{A}, \mathbf{0})$$

*Proof.* Correctness follows from substituting $\mathbf{C} = \mathbf{AR} + \mathbf{x}^\top \otimes \mathbf{G} + \mathbf{E}$ into (2), which yields

$$\mathbf{c}_f = (\mathbf{AR} + \mathbf{E}) \cdot \mathbf{h}_{\mathbf{C},f,\mathbf{x}} + f(x) \cdot \tfrac{q}{2} = \mathbf{A} \cdot \underbrace{\mathbf{R} \cdot \mathbf{h}_{\mathbf{C},f,\mathbf{x}}}_{\mathbf{r}_f} + f(x) \cdot \tfrac{q}{2} + \underbrace{\mathbf{E} \cdot \mathbf{h}_{\mathbf{C},f,\mathbf{x}}}_{\mathbf{e}_f}.$$

The bound on $|\mathbf{e}_f|$ follows from $|\mathbf{h}_{\mathbf{C},f,\mathbf{x}}| = m^{O(t)}$. Privacy follows readily from the pseudorandomness of $(\mathbf{A}, \mathbf{AR} + \mathbf{E})$, as implied by the LWE assumption.

**Handling.** $f : \{0,1\}^\ell \to \mathbb{Z}_q^m$. Next, we observe that we can also augment $\mathsf{pFHC}$ with a pair of algorithms $\mathsf{Eval}^q, \mathsf{Eval}^q_{\mathsf{open}}$ to support bounded-depth circuits $f : \{0,1\}^\ell \to \mathbb{Z}_q^m$ (following [PS19]). That is,

- **Correctness II.** *For any boolean circuit* $f : \{0,1\}^\ell \to \mathbb{Z}_q^m$ *of depth* $t$, *any* $\mathbf{x} \in \{0,1\}^\ell$, *any* $\mathbf{A} \in \mathbb{Z}_q^{m \times n}, \mathbf{R} \in \mathbb{Z}_q^{n \times \ell m \log q}, \mathbf{E} \in \mathbb{Z}^{m \times \ell m \log q}$, *we have*

$$\mathbf{C} := \mathsf{Com}(\mathbf{A}, \mathbf{x}; \mathbf{R}, \mathbf{E}), \quad \mathbf{c}_f := \mathsf{Eval}^q(f, \mathbf{C}), \quad (\mathbf{r}_f, \mathbf{e}_f) := \mathsf{Eval}^q_{\mathsf{open}}(f, \mathcal{A}, \mathbf{x}, \mathbf{R}, \mathbf{E})$$

*satisfies*

$$\mathbf{c}_f = \mathbf{A}\mathbf{r}_f + f(\mathbf{x}) + \mathbf{e}_f \in \mathbb{Z}_q^m$$

*where* $f(\mathbf{x}) \in \mathbb{Z}_q^m$ *is a column vector and* $|\mathbf{e}_f| = |\mathbf{E}| \cdot m^{O(t)}$.

Concretely, let $f_1, \ldots, f_{m \log q} : \{0,1\}^m \to \{0,1\}$ denote the circuits computing the output of $f$ interpreted as bits. Then, we have:

$$\mathbf{c}_f = \sum_{j=1}^{m \log q} \mathbf{C}_{f_j} \cdot \mathbf{G}^{-1}(\mathbf{1}_j \otimes \mathbf{g}^\top) \tag{4}$$

$$\mathbf{h}_{\mathbf{C},f,\mathbf{x}} = \sum_{j=1}^{m \log q} \mathbf{H}_{\mathbf{C},f_j,\mathbf{x}} \cdot \mathbf{G}^{-1}(\mathbf{1}_j \otimes \mathbf{g}^\top)$$

# 5    1-SIM Functional Encoding from LWE

We construct a 1-SIM functional encoding scheme for bounded-depth circuits $\mathcal{F}_{\ell,m,t}$ based on the LWE assumption. The scheme does not require a CRS. Such a result is given in [BDGM20, Sect. 4.4], starting from any FHE scheme with "almost linear" decryption; we provide a more direct construction that avoids key-switching.

## Construction 2

– Enc$(\mathbf{x}; \mathbf{A}, \mathbf{R}, \mathbf{E}, \mathbf{s}, \mathbf{e})$. *Sample*

$$\mathbf{A} \leftarrow \mathbb{Z}_q^{m \times n}, \mathbf{R} \leftarrow \mathbb{Z}_q^{n \times \ell m \log q}, \mathbf{E} \leftarrow \chi^{m \times \ell m \log q}, \mathbf{s} \leftarrow \mathbb{Z}_q^n, \mathbf{e} \leftarrow \hat{\chi}^m$$

*Compute*

$$\mathbf{C} := \mathsf{pFHC.Com}(\mathbf{A}, \mathbf{x}; \mathbf{R}, \mathbf{E}), \quad \mathbf{b} := \mathbf{As} + \mathbf{e}$$

*and output*

$$(\mathbf{A}, \mathbf{C}, \mathbf{b})$$

– Open$(f, \mathbf{x}; \mathbf{A}, \mathbf{R}, \mathbf{E}, \mathbf{s}, \mathbf{e})$: *Compute* $(\mathbf{r}_f, \mathbf{e}_f) := \mathsf{pFHC.Eval}_{\mathsf{open}}(f, \mathbf{A}, \mathbf{x}, \mathbf{R}, \mathbf{E})$
  *and output*

$$\mathbf{d} := \mathbf{r}_f + \mathbf{s} \in \mathbb{Z}_q^n$$

– Dec$(f, (\mathbf{A}, \mathbf{C}, \mathbf{b}), \mathbf{d})$: *Compute* $\mathbf{c}_f := \mathsf{pFHC.Eval}(f, \mathbf{C})$ *and output*

$$\mathsf{round}_{q/2}(\mathbf{c}_f + \mathbf{b} - \mathbf{Ad}) \in \{0,1\}^m$$

*where* $\mathsf{round}_{q/2} : \mathbb{Z}_q^m \to \{0,1\}^m$ *is coordinate-wise rounding to the nearest multiple of* $q/2$.

**Theorem 3.** *Under the* $\mathsf{LWE}_{n,q,\chi}$ *assumption, the construction above is a 1-SIM functional encoding.*

We defer the proof to the full version.

*Remark 3 (An attack given many openings.).* We describe an attack strategy on our 1-SIM scheme in the $Q$-SIM setting, namely, when the adversary gets openings $\mathbf{d}_1, \ldots, \mathbf{d}_Q$ corresponding to many functions $f^1, \ldots, f^Q$. (We stress that this does not contradict our preceding security claim.) Observe that we have

$$\mathbf{d}_i = \mathbf{R} \cdot \mathbf{h}_{\mathbf{C}, f^i, \mathbf{x}} + \mathbf{s}$$

where $\mathbf{h}_{\mathbf{C}, f^i, \mathbf{x}}$ (as defined in (2)) is efficiently computable given $\mathbf{x}, \mathbf{C}, f^i$. In the case of linear functions, $\mathbf{h}_{\mathbf{C}, f^i, \mathbf{x}}$ does not even depend on $\mathbf{x}$. This gives us $Q$ linear equations in the unknowns $\mathbf{R}, \mathbf{s}$, and allows us to recover $\mathbf{R}$ and break many-opening security in both the indistinguishability-based and simulation-based settings as long as we can choose $f^i$'s in such a way that the equations are linearly independent.

# 6   Oblivious Sampling from a Falsifiable Assumption

Oblivious LWE sampling allows us to compute $Q$ seemingly random LWE samples $\mathbf{b}_i = \mathbf{A}\mathbf{s}_i + \mathbf{e}_i$ relative to some LWE matrix $\mathbf{A}$, by applying some deterministic function to a long CRS that is independent of $\mathbf{A}$ along with a short public value pub that can depend on $\mathbf{A}$ but whose length is independent of $Q$. We require that there is a simulator that can indistinguishably program CRS, pub to ensures that the resulting samples $\mathbf{b}_i$ "almost match" some arbitrary LWE samples $\hat{\mathbf{b}}_i$ given to the simulator as inputs. Ideally, the simulator could ensure that $\mathbf{b}_i = \hat{\mathbf{b}}_i$ match exactly. However, we relax this and only require the simulator to ensure that $\mathbf{b}_i = \hat{\mathbf{b}}_i + \tilde{\mathbf{b}}_i$ for some LWE sample $\tilde{\mathbf{b}}_i = \mathbf{A}\tilde{\mathbf{s}}_i + \tilde{\mathbf{e}}_i$ for which the simulator knows the corresponding secret $\tilde{\mathbf{s}}_i$. Note that the simulator does not get the secrets $\hat{\mathbf{s}}_i$ for the target values $\hat{\mathbf{b}}_i = \mathbf{A}\hat{\mathbf{s}}_i + \hat{\mathbf{e}}_i$, but indistinguishability should hold even for a distinguisher that gets the secrets $\mathbf{s}_i$ for the output samples $\mathbf{b}_i = \mathbf{A}\mathbf{s}_i + \mathbf{e}_i$. In the full version, we show that we can construct a strong form of oblivious sampling using the notion of invertible sampling (in the CRS model) from [IKOS10, DKR15, ACI+20], which can be constructed from iO. This highlights that the notion is plausibly achievable. We then give a heuristic constructions of oblivious LWE sampling using LWE-style techniques and heuristically argue that security holds under a new falsifiable assumption.

## 6.1   Definition of Oblivious Sampling

An oblivious LWE sampler consists of four PPT algorithms: CRS $\leftarrow$ crsGen($1^\lambda, 1^Q$), pub $\leftarrow$ Init($\mathbf{A}$), $\mathbf{b}_i =$ Sample(CRS, pub, $i$) and (CRS, pub, $\{\tilde{\mathbf{s}}_i\}_{i \in [Q]}$) $\leftarrow$ Sim($1^\lambda, 1^Q, \mathbf{A}, \{\hat{\mathbf{b}}_i\}_{i \in [Q]}$). The Sample algorithm is required to be deterministic while the others are randomized. Let (TrapGen, LWESolve) be the lattice trapdoor algorithms for generating $\mathbf{A}$ with a trapdoor and solving LWE using the trapdoor respectively.

**Definition 1.** *An* $(n, m, q, \hat{\chi}, B_{\mathsf{OLWE}})$ *oblivious LWE sampler satisfies the following properties:*

**Correctness:** *Let* $Q = Q(\lambda)$ *be some polynomial. Let* $(\mathbf{A}, \mathsf{td}) \leftarrow$ $\mathsf{TrapGen}(1^n, 1^m, q), \mathsf{CRS} \leftarrow \mathsf{crsGen}(1^\lambda, 1^Q), \mathsf{pub} \leftarrow \mathsf{Init}(\mathbf{A}).$ *Then, with over-whelming probability over the above values, for all* $i \in [Q]$ *there exists some* $\mathbf{s}_i \in \mathbb{Z}_q^n$ *and* $\mathbf{e}_i \in \mathbb{Z}_q^m$ *with* $||\mathbf{e}_i||_\infty \leq B_{\mathsf{OLWE}}$ *such that* $\mathbf{b}_i = \mathbf{A}\mathbf{s}_i + \mathbf{e}_i$.

**Security:** *The following distributions of* $(\mathsf{CRS}, \mathbf{A}, \mathsf{pub}, \{\mathbf{s}_i\}_{i \in [Q]})$ *are computationally indistinguishable:*

- *Real Distribution: Sample* $(\mathbf{A}, \mathsf{td}) \leftarrow \mathsf{TrapGen}(1^n, 1^m, q), \mathsf{CRS} \leftarrow$ $\mathsf{crsGen}(1^\lambda, 1^Q), \mathsf{pub} \leftarrow \mathsf{Init}(\mathbf{A}).$ *For* $i \in [Q]$ *set* $\mathbf{b}_i = \mathsf{Sample}(\mathsf{CRS}, \mathsf{pub}, i),$ $\mathbf{s}_i = \mathsf{LWESolve}_{\mathsf{td}}(\mathbf{b}_i).$ *Output* $(\mathsf{CRS}, \mathbf{A}, \mathsf{pub}, \{\mathbf{s}_i\}_{i \in [Q]}).$
- *Simulated Distribution: Sample* $(\mathbf{A}, \mathsf{td}) \leftarrow \mathsf{TrapGen}(1^n, 1^m, q), \hat{\mathbf{s}}_i \leftarrow \mathbb{Z}_q^n, \hat{\mathbf{e}}_i$ $\leftarrow \hat{\chi}^m$ *and let* $\hat{\mathbf{b}}_i = \mathbf{A}\hat{\mathbf{s}}_i + \hat{\mathbf{e}}_i.$ *Sample* $(\mathsf{CRS}, \mathsf{pub}, \{\tilde{\mathbf{s}}_i\}_{i \in [Q]}) \leftarrow \mathsf{Sim}(1^\lambda, 1^Q,$ $\mathbf{A}, \{\hat{\mathbf{b}}_i\}_{i \in [Q]})$ *and let* $\mathbf{s}_i = \hat{\mathbf{s}}_i + \tilde{\mathbf{s}}_i.$ *Output* $(\mathsf{CRS}, \mathbf{A}, \mathsf{pub}, \{\mathbf{s}_i\}_{i \in [Q]}).$

Observe that the algorithm $\mathsf{pub} \leftarrow \mathsf{Init}(\mathbf{A})$ in the above definition does not get $Q$ as an input and therefore the size of $\mathsf{pub}$ is independent of $Q$. On the other hand, the algorithm $\mathsf{CRS} \leftarrow \mathsf{crsGen}(1^\lambda, 1^Q)$ does not get $\mathbf{A}$ as an input and hence $\mathsf{CRS}$ must be independent of $\mathbf{A}$. This is crucial and otherwise there would be a trivial construction where either $\mathsf{CRS}$ or $\mathsf{pub}$ would consist of $Q$ LWE samples with respect to $\mathbf{A}$.

Note that the security property implicitly also guarantees the following correctness property of the simulated distribution. Assume we simulate the values $(\mathsf{CRS}, \mathbf{A}, \mathsf{pub}, \{\tilde{\mathbf{s}}_i\}_{i \in [Q]}) \leftarrow \mathsf{Sim}(1^\lambda, 1^Q, \mathbf{A}, \{\hat{\mathbf{b}}_i\}_{i \in [Q]})$ where the simulator is given LWE samples $\hat{\mathbf{b}}_i = \mathbf{A}\hat{\mathbf{s}}_i + \hat{\mathbf{e}}_i$ as input. Then the resulting $(\mathsf{CRS}, \mathbf{A}, \mathsf{pub})$ will generate samples $\mathbf{b}_i = \mathsf{Sample}(\mathsf{CRS}, \mathsf{pub}, i)$ of the form $\mathbf{b}_i = \hat{\mathbf{b}}_i + \tilde{\mathbf{b}}_i$ where $\tilde{\mathbf{b}}_i = \mathbf{A}\tilde{\mathbf{s}}_i + \tilde{\mathbf{e}}_i$ some small $\tilde{\mathbf{e}}_i$. This is because, in the simulation, we must have $\mathbf{b}_i = \mathbf{A}\mathbf{s}_i + \mathbf{e}_i$ where $||\mathbf{e}_i||_\infty \leq B$ as otherwise it would be trivial to distinguish the simulation from the real case. But $\mathbf{s}_i = \hat{\mathbf{s}}_i + \tilde{\mathbf{s}}_i$ and so $\mathbf{e}_i = \hat{\mathbf{e}}_i + \tilde{\mathbf{e}}_i$. This implies $\tilde{\mathbf{e}}_i = \mathbf{e}_i - \hat{\mathbf{e}}_i$ will be small.

*Remark 4 (Naive construction fails).* Consider the naive construction:

$$\mathsf{pub} := (\mathbf{A}\mathbf{S} + \mathbf{E}), \quad \mathsf{CRS} := (\mathbf{r}_1, \ldots, \mathbf{r}_Q), \quad \mathbf{b}_i := (\mathbf{A}\mathbf{S} + \mathbf{E})\mathbf{r}_i$$

where

$$\mathbf{A} \leftarrow \mathbb{Z}_q^{m \times n}, \quad \mathbf{S} \leftarrow \mathbb{Z}_q^{n \times m \log q}, \quad \mathbf{E} \leftarrow \chi^{m \times m \log q}, \quad \mathbf{r}_i \leftarrow \chi^{m \log q}$$

We stress that the simulator receives a random $\mathbf{A}$ but not the corresponding trapdoor. Indeed, under the LWE assumption, there does not exist an efficient simulator for the naive construction. In more detail, the simulator is required on input $(\mathbf{A}, \{\hat{\mathbf{b}}_i\}_{i \in [Q]})$ to output $(\{\mathbf{r}_i\}_{i \in [Q]}, \mathbf{B}, \{\tilde{\mathbf{s}}_i\}_{i \in [Q]})$ such that

$$(\{\mathbf{r}_i\}_{i \in [Q]}, \mathbf{A}\mathbf{S} + \mathbf{E}, \{\mathbf{S}\mathbf{r}_i\}_{i \in [Q]}) \approx_c (\{\mathbf{r}_i\}_{i \in [Q]}, \mathbf{B}, \{\hat{\mathbf{s}}_i + \tilde{\mathbf{s}}_i\}_{i \in [Q]})$$

We claim that checking whether $\mathbf{B}\mathbf{r}_i \approx \hat{\mathbf{b}}_i + \mathbf{A}\tilde{\mathbf{s}}_i$ yields a distinguisher for whether $(\mathbf{A}, \{\hat{\mathbf{b}}_i\}_{i \in [Q]})$ is drawn from LWE versus uniform distribution. The proof relies on the fact that given $(\{\mathbf{r}_i\}_{i \in [Q]}, \{\mathbf{S}\mathbf{r}_i\}_{i \in [Q]})$ for $Q \gg m$, we can solve for $\mathbf{S}$ via Gaussian elimination, which means that the matrix $\mathbf{B}$ must be of the form

$\mathbf{AS}_0 + \mathbf{E}_0$ and therefore any $\hat{\mathbf{b}}_i$ that passes the check satisfies $\hat{\mathbf{b}}_i \approx \mathbf{A}(\mathbf{S}_0 \mathbf{r}_i - \tilde{\mathbf{s}}_i)$. Note that the LWE distinguisher works even if it does not know $\mathbf{S}_0, \mathbf{E}_0$.

## 6.2 Heuristic Construction

We now give our heuristic construction of an oblivious LWE sampler. Let $n, m, q$ be some parameters and $\chi, \chi_{\mathsf{prf}}, \hat{\chi}$ be distributions over $\mathbb{Z}$ that are $B, B_{\mathsf{prf}}, \hat{B}$ bounded respectively. Let D be an algorithms that samples tuples $(\mathbf{s}, \mathbf{e})$ where $\mathbf{s} \leftarrow \mathbb{Z}_q^n$ and $\mathbf{e} \leftarrow \chi_{\mathsf{prf}}^m$. Assume that D uses $v$ random coins, and for $r \in \{0,1\}^v$ define $(\mathbf{s}, \mathbf{e}) = \mathsf{D}(r)$ to be the output of D with randomness $r$. Let $\mathsf{PRF} : \{0,1\}^\lambda \times \{0,1\}^* \to \{0,1\}^v$ be a pseudorandom function. We rely on the homomorphic commitment algorithms $\mathsf{Com}, \mathsf{Eval}^q, \mathsf{Eval}^q_{\mathsf{open}}$ with parameters $n, m, q, \chi$ from Sect. 4.

**Construction 4.** *We define the oblivious LWE sampler as follows:*

- $\mathsf{CRS} \leftarrow \mathsf{crsGen}(1^\lambda, 1^Q)$: $\mathsf{CRS} := (\mathsf{CRS}_1, \ldots, \mathsf{CRS}_Q)$ *where* $\mathsf{CRS}_i \leftarrow \mathbb{Z}_q^m$.
- $\mathsf{pub} \leftarrow \mathsf{Init}(\mathbf{A})$: *Sample a PRF key* $k \leftarrow \{0,1\}^\lambda$ *and set a flag* $\beta := 0$. *Set* $\mathsf{pub} := (\mathbf{A}, \mathbf{C})$ *where* $\mathbf{C} \leftarrow \mathsf{Com}(\mathbf{A}, (k, \beta))$.
- $\mathbf{b}_i = \mathsf{Sample}(\mathsf{CRS}, \mathsf{pub}, i)$: *Let* $g_{i,\mathsf{CRS}_i, \mathbf{A}} : \{0,1\}^{\lambda+1} \to \mathbb{Z}_q^m$ *be a circuit that contains the values* $(i, \mathbf{A}, \mathsf{CRS}_i)$ *hard-coded and performs the computation:*

$$g_{i,\mathsf{CRS}_i, \mathbf{A}}(k, \beta): \text{ Let } (\mathbf{s}_i^{\mathsf{prf}}, \mathbf{e}_i^{\mathsf{prf}}) = \mathsf{D}(\mathsf{PRF}(k, i)). \text{ Output } \mathbf{A}\mathbf{s}_i^{\mathsf{prf}} + \mathbf{e}_i^{\mathsf{prf}} + \beta \cdot \mathsf{CRS}_i.$$

*Output* $\mathbf{b}_i = \mathsf{Eval}^q(g_{i,\mathsf{CRS}_i, \mathbf{A}}, \mathbf{C})$.
- $(\mathsf{CRS}, \mathsf{pub}, \{\tilde{\mathbf{s}}_i\}_{i \in [Q]}) \leftarrow \mathsf{Sim}(1^\lambda, 1^Q, \mathbf{A}, \{\hat{\mathbf{b}}_i\}_{i \in [Q]})$: *Set* $\mathsf{CRS} := (\hat{\mathbf{b}}_1, \ldots, \hat{\mathbf{b}}_Q)$. *Set the flag* $\beta := 1$ *and* $\mathsf{pub} := (\mathbf{A}, \mathbf{C})$ *for* $\mathbf{C} = \mathsf{Com}((k, \beta); \mathbf{R}, \mathbf{E})$ *where* $\mathbf{R}, \mathbf{E}$ *is the randomness of the commitment. Let* $(\mathbf{r}_i^{\mathsf{eval}}, \mathbf{e}_i^{\mathsf{eval}}) = \mathsf{Eval}^q_{\mathsf{open}}(g_{i,\mathsf{CRS}_i, \mathbf{A}}, \mathbf{A}, (k, \beta), \mathbf{R}, \mathbf{E})$ *and* $(\mathbf{s}_i^{\mathsf{prf}}, \mathbf{e}_i^{\mathsf{prf}}) = \mathsf{D}(\mathsf{PRF}(k, i))$. *Set* $\tilde{\mathbf{s}}_i = \mathbf{r}_i^{\mathsf{eval}} + \mathbf{s}_i^{\mathsf{prf}}$.

**Form of Samples $\mathbf{b}_i$.** Let us examine this construction in more detail and see what the samples $\mathbf{b}_i$ look like.

In the real case, where $\mathsf{pub} \leftarrow \mathsf{Init}(\mathbf{A})$, we have $\mathsf{pub} = (\mathbf{A}, \mathbf{C})$ where $\mathbf{C} = \mathsf{Com}(\mathbf{A}, (k, 0); (\mathbf{R}, \mathbf{E}))$. For $\mathbf{b}_i = \mathsf{Sample}(\mathsf{CRS}, \mathsf{pub}, i)$ we can write

$$\mathbf{b}_i = \mathbf{A}\underbrace{(\mathbf{r}_i^{\mathsf{eval}} + \mathbf{s}_i^{\mathsf{prf}})}_{\mathbf{s}_i} + \underbrace{(\mathbf{e}_i^{\mathsf{eval}} + \mathbf{e}_i^{\mathsf{prf}})}_{\mathbf{e}_i} \tag{5}$$

where $(\mathbf{s}_i^{\mathsf{prf}}, \mathbf{e}_i^{\mathsf{prf}}) = \mathsf{D}(\mathsf{PRF}(k, i))$ are sampled using the PRF and $(\mathbf{r}_i^{\mathsf{eval}}, \mathbf{e}_i^{\mathsf{eval}}) = \mathsf{Eval}^q_{\mathsf{open}}(g_i, \mathbf{A}, (k, 0), \mathbf{R}, \mathbf{E})$ come from the homomorphic evaluation.

In the simulated case, where $\mathsf{CRS}, \mathsf{pub}$ are chosen by the simulator, we have $\mathsf{pub} = (\mathbf{A}, \mathbf{C})$ where $\mathbf{C} = \mathsf{Com}(\mathbf{A}, (k, 1); (\mathbf{R}, \mathbf{E}))$ and $\mathsf{CRS}_i = \hat{\mathbf{b}}_i = \mathbf{A}\hat{\mathbf{s}}_i + \hat{\mathbf{e}}_i$. For $\mathbf{b}_i = \mathsf{Sample}(\mathsf{CRS}, \mathsf{pub}, i)$ we can write

$$\mathbf{b}_i = \mathbf{A} \underbrace{(\overbrace{\mathbf{r}_i^{\mathsf{eval}} + \mathbf{s}_i^{\mathsf{prf}}}^{\tilde{\mathbf{s}}_i} + \hat{\mathbf{s}}_i)}_{\mathbf{s}_i} + \underbrace{(\overbrace{\mathbf{e}_i^{\mathsf{eval}} + \mathbf{e}_i^{\mathsf{prf}}}^{\tilde{\mathbf{e}}_i} + \hat{\mathbf{e}}_i)}_{\mathbf{e}_i} \tag{6}$$

where $(\mathbf{s}_i^{\mathsf{prf}}, \mathbf{e}_i^{\mathsf{prf}}) = \mathsf{D}(\mathsf{PRF}(k, i))$ are sampled using the PRF and $(\mathbf{r}_i^{\mathsf{eval}}, \mathbf{e}_i^{\mathsf{eval}}) = \mathsf{Eval}_{\mathsf{open}}^q(g_{i, \mathsf{CRS}_i, \mathbf{A}}, \mathbf{A}, (k, 0), \mathbf{R}, \mathbf{E})$ come from the homomorphic evaluation.

**Correctness.** Equation 5 implies that the scheme satisfies the correctness of an $n, m, q, \hat{\chi}, B_{\mathsf{OLWE}}$ oblivious LWE sampler, where $B_{\mathsf{OLWE}}$ is a bound $\|\mathbf{e}_i\|_\infty$. In particular, $B \leq B_{\mathsf{prf}} + B \cdot m^{O(t)}$, where $t$ is the depth of the circuit $g_{i, \mathsf{CRS}_i, \mathbf{A}}$ (which is dominated by the depth of the PRF).

## 6.3   Security Under a New Conjecture

The security of our heuristic oblivious sampler boils down to the indistinguishability of the real and simulated distributions, which is captured by the following conjecture:

*Conjecture 1 (HPLS Conjecture).* For $\beta \in \{0, 1\}$, let us define the distribution $\mathsf{DIST}(\beta)$ over

$$(\{\hat{\mathbf{b}}_i = \mathbf{A}\hat{\mathbf{s}}_i + \hat{\mathbf{e}}_i\}_{i \in [Q]}, \mathbf{A}, \mathbf{C}, \{\mathbf{s}_i = \mathbf{r}_i^{\mathsf{eval}} + \mathbf{s}_i^{\mathsf{prf}} + \beta \cdot \hat{\mathbf{s}}_i\}_{i \in [Q]})$$

where

- $\mathbf{A} \leftarrow \mathbb{Z}_q^{m \times n}, \hat{\mathbf{s}}_i \leftarrow \mathbb{Z}_q^n, \hat{\mathbf{e}}_i \leftarrow \chi^m, \hat{\mathbf{b}}_i := \mathbf{A}\hat{\mathbf{s}}_i + \hat{\mathbf{e}}_i$.
- $k \leftarrow \{0, 1\}^\lambda, (\mathbf{C} = \mathbf{A} \cdot \mathbf{R} + \mathbf{E} + (k, \beta) \otimes \mathbf{G}) \leftarrow \mathsf{Com}(\mathbf{A}, (k, \beta); (\mathbf{R}, \mathbf{E}))$
- $(\mathbf{s}_i^{\mathsf{prf}}, \mathbf{e}_i^{\mathsf{prf}}) := \mathsf{D}(\mathsf{PRF}(k, i)), (\mathbf{r}_i^{\mathsf{eval}}, \mathbf{e}_i^{\mathsf{eval}}) := \mathsf{Eval}_{\mathsf{open}}^q(g_{i, \hat{\mathbf{b}}_i, \mathbf{A}}, \mathbf{A}, (k, \beta), \mathbf{R}, \mathbf{E})$
  where

  $g_{i, \hat{\mathbf{b}}_i, \mathbf{A}}(k, \beta):$ Let $(\mathbf{s}_i^{\mathsf{prf}}, \mathbf{e}_i^{\mathsf{prf}}) = \mathsf{D}(\mathsf{PRF}(k, i))$. Output $\mathbf{A}\mathbf{s}_i^{\mathsf{prf}} + \mathbf{e}_i^{\mathsf{prf}} + \beta \cdot \hat{\mathbf{b}}_i$.

- $\mathbf{s}_i := (\mathbf{r}_i^{\mathsf{eval}} + \mathbf{s}_i^{\mathsf{prf}} + \beta \cdot \hat{\mathbf{s}}_i)$.

The (sub-exponential) *homomorphic pseudorandom LWE samples (HPLS)* conjecture with parameters $(n, m, q, \chi, \hat{\chi}, \chi_{\mathsf{prf}})$ and pseudodrandom function PRF says that the distributions $\mathsf{DIST}(0)$ and $\mathsf{DIST}(1)$ are (sub-exponentially) computationally indistinguishable.

When we do not specify parameters, we assume the conjecture holds for some choice of PRF and any choices of $n, q, \chi, \hat{\chi}$ and any polynomial $m$, such that $LWE_{n, q, \chi}$ and $LWE_{n, q, \hat{\chi}}$ assumptions hold and $\chi_{\mathsf{prf}}$ smudges out error of size $\hat{B} + B \cdot m^{O(t)}$, where $t$ is the depth of the circuit $g_{i, \mathsf{CRS}_i, \mathbf{A}}$ (which is dominated by the depth of the PRF).

**Observations.** We begin with two simple observations about the conjecture:

- The distribution $\mathsf{DIST}(\beta)$ satisfies the following consistency check for both $\beta = 0$ and $\beta = 1$, namely

$$\mathsf{Eval}^q(g_{i,\mathbf{A}\hat{\mathbf{s}}_i+\hat{\mathbf{e}}_i,\mathbf{A}}, \mathbf{C}) \approx \mathbf{A}\mathbf{s}_i$$

This means that we cannot rely on homomorphic evaluation to distinguish between the two distributions. In addition, note that the distinguisher can compute

$$\mathbf{e}_i := \mathsf{Eval}^q(g_{i,\mathbf{A}\hat{\mathbf{s}}_i+\hat{\mathbf{e}}_i,\mathbf{A}}, \mathbf{C}) - \mathbf{A}\mathbf{s}_i = \mathbf{e}_i^{\mathsf{eval}} + \mathbf{e}_i^{\mathsf{prf}} + \beta \cdot \hat{\mathbf{e}}_i$$

- If we omit $\mathbf{r}_i^{\mathsf{eval}}$ from $\mathbf{s}_i$, then indistinguishability follows from standard assumptions. Concretely, under the LWE assumption and security of PRF, we have:

$$(\{\mathbf{A}\hat{\mathbf{s}}_i + \hat{\mathbf{e}}_i\}_{i\in[Q]}, \mathbf{A}, \mathbf{C}, \{\mathbf{s}_i^{\mathsf{prf}}, \mathbf{e}_i^{\mathsf{prf}}\}_{i\in[Q]})$$
$$\approx_c (\{\mathbf{A}\hat{\mathbf{s}}_i + \hat{\mathbf{e}}_i\}_{i\in[Q]}, \mathbf{A}, \mathbf{C}, \{\mathbf{s}_i^{\mathsf{prf}} + \hat{\mathbf{s}}_i, \mathbf{e}_i^{\mathsf{prf}} + \hat{\mathbf{e}}\}_{i\in[Q]})$$

By privacy of Com, we can replace $\mathbf{C}$ with a commitment to $\mathbf{0}$, and then security follows from PRF security plus noise smudging. In particular $\mathbf{e}_i^{\mathsf{prf}}$ smudges out $\hat{\mathbf{e}}_i$.

That is, the non-standard/heuristic nature of Conjecture 1 arises from (1) the interaction and potential correlations between $\mathbf{r}_i^{\mathsf{eval}}$ and $\mathbf{s}_i^{\mathsf{prf}}$ (and between $\mathbf{e}_i^{\mathsf{eval}}$ and $\mathbf{e}_i^{\mathsf{prf}}$), and (2) the fact that giving out $\mathbf{C} = \mathsf{Com}(\mathbf{A}, (k, \beta))$ introduces circularity between the PRF key and the commitment randomness – commitment security is needed to ensure PRF security by making sure that the PRF key is hidden by the commitment, while at the same time the PRF security is needed to ensure commitment security by making sure that the values $\mathbf{s}_i^{\mathsf{prf}}, \mathbf{e}_i^{\mathsf{prf}}$ mask any information about the commitment randomness contained in $\mathbf{r}_i^{\mathsf{eval}}, \mathbf{e}_i^{\mathsf{eval}}$. We defer further discussion on the conjecture, its plausibility, and analysis of zeroizing attacks to the full version.

**Oblivious LWE Sampling from the New Conjecture.** We now that the conjecture implies the (sub-exponential security) of our oblivious LWE sampler in Definition 1.

**Lemma 3.** *Under the homomorphic pseudorandom LWE samples (HPLS) conjecture (Conjecture 1) (with sub-exponential security), the oblivious sampler construction is (sub-exponentially) secure.*

We defer the proof to the full version.

# 7    $Q$-SIM Functional Encodings from Oblivious Sampling

We construct a $Q$-SIM functional encoding scheme $(\mathsf{crsGen}, \mathsf{Enc}, \mathsf{Open}, \mathsf{Dec})$ for bounded-depth circuits $\mathcal{F}_{\ell,m,t}$ from LWE and an oblivious LWE sampler $(\mathsf{OLWE.crsGen}, \mathsf{Init}, \mathsf{Sample})$.

## Construction 5

- crsGen($1^\lambda, 1^Q, \mathcal{F}_{\ell,m,t}$). *Output* OLWE.crsGen($1^\lambda, 1^Q$).
- Enc(CRS, $\mathbf{x}$): *Sample*

$$(\mathbf{A}, \mathsf{td}) \leftarrow \mathsf{TrapGen}(1^n, 1^m, q), \mathsf{pub} \leftarrow \mathsf{Init}(\mathsf{CRS}, \mathbf{A}), \mathbf{R} \leftarrow \mathbb{Z}_q^{n \times \ell m \log q}, \mathbf{E} \leftarrow \chi^{m \times \ell m \log q}$$

*Compute* $\mathbf{C} := \mathsf{pFHC.Com}(\mathbf{A}, \mathbf{x}; \mathbf{R}, \mathbf{E})$ *and output* $(\mathsf{pub}, \mathbf{A}, \mathbf{C})$.

- Open($f^i, \mathbf{x}$): *Compute*

$$(\mathbf{r}_{f^i}, \mathbf{e}_{f^i}) := \mathsf{pFHC.Eval}_{\mathsf{open}}(f^i, \mathbf{A}, \mathbf{x}, \mathbf{R}, \mathbf{E}), \quad \mathbf{b}_i := \mathsf{Sample}(\mathsf{CRS}, \mathsf{pub}, i), \quad \mathbf{s}_i := \mathsf{LWESolve}_{\mathsf{td}}(\mathbf{b}_i)$$

*and output* $\mathbf{d}_i := \mathbf{r}_{f^i} + \mathbf{s}_i \in \mathbb{Z}_q^n$.

- Dec($f^i, (\mathsf{pub}, \mathbf{A}, \mathbf{C}), \mathbf{d}_i$): *Compute*

$$\mathbf{c}_{f^i} := \mathsf{pFHC.Eval}(f, \mathbf{C}), \quad \mathbf{b}_i := \mathsf{Sample}(\mathsf{CRS}, \mathsf{pub}, i)$$

*and output* $\mathbf{y}_i := \mathsf{round}_{q/2}(\mathbf{c}_{f^i} + \mathbf{b}_i - \mathbf{A}\mathbf{d}_i) \in \{0,1\}^m$.

**Theorem 6.** *Under the LWE assumption and the existence of a $(n, m, q, \chi, B)$ oblivious LWE sampler, the construction above is a $Q$-SIM functional encoding.*

We defer the proof to the full version.

## 8  IO from Functional Encodings

See the full version for how to construct XiO from functional encodings. We then rely on the work of [LPST16a], which shows that (sub-exponentially secure) XiO + LWE implies iO. Below, we summarize the main results.

**Theorem 7.** *The existence of (sub-exponentially secure) functional encoding implies (sub-exponenitally secure) XiO. In particular, sub-exponentially secure functional encodings and sub-exponential security of LWE imply the existence of iO.*

**Corollary 1.** *Assuming that there exists a sub-exponentially secure oblivious LWE sampler and that the sub-exponentially secure LWE assumption holds, there exists iO.*

**Corollary 2.** *Assuming the sub-exponential security of Conjecture 1 and the sub-exponential security of LWE, there exists iO.*

**Acknowledgments.** We thank Yilei Chen and Vinod Vaikuntanathan for insightful discussions on cryptanalysis and bootstrapping.

# References

[ACI+20] Agrikola, T., Couteau, G., Ishai, Y., Jarecki, S., Sahai, A.: On pseudo-random encodings. In: TCC, Cryptology ePrint Archive, Report 2020/445 (2020). https://eprint.iacr.org/2020/445

[ADGM17] Apon, D., Döttling, N., Garg, S., Mukherjee, P.: Cryptanalysis of indistinguishability obfuscations of circuits over GGH13. In: Chatzigiannakis, I., Indyk, P., Kuhn, F., Muscholl, A. (eds.) ICALP 2017, LIPIcs, Schloss Dagstuhl, vol. 80, pp. 38:1–38:16, July 2017

[Agr19] Agrawal, S.: Indistinguishability obfuscation without multilinear maps: new methods for bootstrapping and instantiation. In: Ishai and Rijmen [IR19], pp. 191–225

[AJ15] Ananth, P., Jain, A.: Indistinguishability obfuscation from compact functional encryption. In: Gennaro, R., Robshaw, M. (eds.) CRYPTO 2015, Part I. LNCS, vol. 9215, pp. 308–326. Springer, Heidelberg (2015). https://doi.org/10.1007/978-3-662-47989-6_15

[AJL+12] Asharov, G., Jain, A., López-Alt, A., Tromer, E., Vaikuntanathan, V., Wichs, D.: Multiparty computation with low communication, computation and interaction via threshold FHE. In: Pointcheval and Johansson [PJ12], pp. 483–501

[AJL+19] Ananth, P., Jain, A., Lin, H., Matt, C., Sahai, A.: Indistinguishability obfuscation without multilinear maps: new paradigms via low degree weak pseudorandomness and security amplification. In: Boldyreva and Micciancio [BM19], pp. 284–332

[Ajt96] Ajtai, M.: Generating hard instances of lattice problems (extended abstract). In: 28th ACM STOC, pp. 99–108. ACM Press, May 1996

[AP20] Agrawal, S., Pellet-Mary, A.: Indistinguishability obfuscation without maps: attacks and fixes for noisy linear FE. In: Canteaut and Ishai [CI20], pp. 110–140

[BDGM19] Brakerski, Z., Döttling, N., Garg, S., Malavolta, G.: Leveraging linear decryption: Rate-1 fully-homomorphic encryption and time-lock puzzles. In: Hofheinz and Rosen [HR19], pp. 407–437

[BDGM20a] Brakerski, Z., Döttling, N., Garg, S., Malavolta, G.: Candidate iO from homomorphic encryption schemes. In: Canteaut and Ishai [CI20], pp. 79–109

[BDGM20b] Brakerski, Z., Döttling, N., Garg, S., Malavolta, G.: Factoring and pairings are not necessary for IO: Circular-secure LWE suffices. Cryptology ePrint Archive, Report 2020/1024 (2020)

[BGG+14] Boneh, D., et al.: Fully key-homomorphic encryption, arithmetic circuit ABE and compact garbled circuits. In: Nguyen, P.Q., Oswald, E. (eds.) EUROCRYPT 2014. LNCS, vol. 8441, pp. 533–556. Springer, Heidelberg (2014). https://doi.org/10.1007/978-3-642-55220-5_30

[BGI+01] Barak, B., et al.: On the (Im)possibility of obfuscating programs. In: Kilian, J. (ed.) CRYPTO 2001. LNCS, vol. 2139, pp. 1–18. Springer, Heidelberg (2001). https://doi.org/10.1007/3-540-44647-8_1

[BGMZ18]  Bartusek, J., Guan, J., Ma, F., Zhandry, M.: Return of GGH15: provable security against zeroing attacks. In: Beimel, A., Dziembowski, S. (eds.) TCC 2018, Part II. LNCS, vol. 11240, pp. 544–574. Springer, Cham (2018). https://doi.org/10.1007/978-3-030-03810-6_20

[BIJ+20]  Bartusek, J., Ishai, Y., Jain, A., Ma, F., Sahai, A., Zhandry, M.: Affine determinant programs: a framework for obfuscation and witness encryption. In: Vidick, T. (ed.) ITCS 2020, LIPIcs, vol. 151, pp. 82:1–82:39, January 2020

[BM19]  Boldyreva, A., Micciancio, D. (eds.): CRYPTO 2019, Part III. LNCS, vol. 11694. Springer, Heidelberg, August 2019

[BRF13]  Boneh, D., Roughgarden, T., Feigenbaum, J. (eds.) 45th ACM STOC. ACM Press, June 2013

[BTVW17]  Brakerski, Z., Tsabary, R., Vaikuntanathan, V., Wee, H.: Private constrained PRFs (and More) from LWE. In: Kalai, Y., Reyzin, L. (eds.) TCC 2017, Part I. LNCS, vol. 10677, pp. 264–302. Springer, Cham (2017). https://doi.org/10.1007/978-3-319-70500-2_10

[BV15]  Bitansky, N., Vaikuntanathan, V.: Indistinguishability obfuscation from functional encryption. In: Guruswami, V. (ed.) 56th FOCS, pp. 171–190. IEEE Computer Society Press, October 2015

[CCH+19]  Cheon, J.H., Cho, W., Hhan, M., Kim, J., Lee, C.: Statistical zeroizing attack: cryptanalysis of candidates of BP obfuscation over GGH15 multilinear map. In: Boldyreva and Micciancio [BM19], pp. 253–283

[CGH17]  Chen, Y., Gentry, C., Halevi, S.: Cryptanalyses of candidate branching program obfuscators. In: Coron, J.-S., Nielsen, J.B. (eds.) EUROCRYPT 2017, Part III. LNCS, vol. 10212, pp. 278–307. Springer, Cham (2017). https://doi.org/10.1007/978-3-319-56617-7_10

[CHL+15]  Cheon, J.H., Han, K., Lee, C., Ryu, H., Stehlé, D.: Cryptanalysis of the multilinear map over the integers. In: Oswald, E., Fischlin, M. (eds.) EUROCRYPT 2015, Part I. LNCS, vol. 9056, pp. 3–12. Springer, Heidelberg (2015). https://doi.org/10.1007/978-3-662-46800-5_1

[CHVW19]  Chen, Y., Hhan, M., Vaikuntanathan, V., Wee, H.: Matrix PRFs: constructions, attacks, and applications to obfuscation. In: Hofheinz, D., Rosen, A. (eds.) TCC 2019, Part I. LNCS, vol. 11891, pp. 55–80. Springer, Cham (2019). https://doi.org/10.1007/978-3-030-36030-6_3

[CI20]  Canteaut, A., Ishai, Y. (eds.): EUROCRYPT 2020, Part I. LNCS, vol. 12105. Springer, Heidelberg, May 2020

[CLLT16]  Coron, J.S., Lee, M.S., Lepoint, T., Tibouchi, M.: Cryptanalysis of GGH15 multilinear maps. In: Robshaw and Katz [RK16], pp. 607–628

[CLLT17]  Coron, J.-S., Lee, M.S., Lepoint, T., Tibouchi, M.: Zeroizing attacks on indistinguishability obfuscation over CLT13. In: Fehr, S. (ed.) PKC 2017, Part I. LNCS, vol. 10174, pp. 41–58. Springer, Heidelberg (2017). https://doi.org/10.1007/978-3-662-54365-8_3

[CVW18]  Chen, Y., Vaikuntanathan, V., Wee, H.: GGH15 beyond permutation branching programs: proofs, attacks, and candidates. In: Shacham, H., Boldyreva, A. (eds.) CRYPTO 2018, Part II. LNCS, vol. 10992, pp. 577–607. Springer, Cham (2018). https://doi.org/10.1007/978-3-319-96881-0_20

[DKR15]  Dachman-Soled, D., Katz, J., Rao, V.: Adaptively secure, universally composable, multiparty computation in constant rounds. In: Dodis and Nielsen [DN15], pp. 586–613

[DN15] Dodis, Y., Nielsen, J.B. (eds.): TCC 2015, Part II. LNCS, vol. 9015. Springer, Heidelberg, March 2015

[FRS17] Fernando, R., Rasmussen, P.M.R., Sahai, A.: Preventing CLT attacks on obfuscation with linear overhead. In: Takagi, T., Peyrin, T. (eds.) ASI-ACRYPT 2017. LNCS, vol. 10626, pp. 242–271. Springer, Cham (2017). https://doi.org/10.1007/978-3-319-70700-6_9

[GGH13a] Garg, S., Gentry, C., Halevi, S.: Candidate multilinear maps from ideal lattices. In: Johansson, T., Nguyen, P.Q. (eds.) EUROCRYPT 2013. LNCS, vol. 7881, pp. 1–17. Springer, Heidelberg (2013). https://doi.org/10.1007/978-3-642-38348-9_1

[GGH+13b] Garg, S., Gentry, C., Halevi, S., Raykova, M., Sahai, A., Waters, B.: Candidate indistinguishability obfuscation and functional encryption for all circuits. In: 54th FOCS, pp. 40–49. IEEE Computer Society Press, October 2013

[GGH15] Gentry, C., Gorbunov, S., Halevi, S.: Graph-induced multilinear maps from lattices. In: Dodis and Nielsen [DN15], pp. 498–527

[GH19] Gentry, C., Halevi, S.: Compressible FHE with applications to PIR. In: Hofheinz and Rosen [HR19], pp. 438–464

[GJK18] Gentry, C., Jutla, C.S., Kane, D.: Obfuscation using tensor products. Cryptology ePrint Archive, Report 2018/756 (2018). https://eprint.iacr.org/2018/756

[GJLS20] Gay, R., Jain, A., Lin, H., Sahai, A.: Indistinguishability obfuscation from simple-to-state hard problems: new assumptions, new techniques, and simplification. Cryptology ePrint Archive, Report 2020/764 (2020). https://eprint.iacr.org/2020/764

[GKP+13] Goldwasser, S., Kalai, Y., Popa, R.A., Vaikuntanathan, V., Zeldovich, N.: Reusable garbled circuits and succinct functional encryption. In: Boneh et al. [BRF13], pp. 555–564

[GLW14] Gentry, C., Lewko, A., Waters, B.: Witness encryption from instance independent assumptions. In: Garay, J.A., Gennaro, R. (eds.) CRYPTO 2014, Part I. LNCS, vol. 8616, pp. 426–443. Springer, Heidelberg (2014). https://doi.org/10.1007/978-3-662-44371-2_24

[GP20] Gay, R., Pass, R.: Indistinguishability obfuscation from circular security. Cryptology ePrint Archive, Report 2020/1010 (2020)

[GR07] Goldwasser, S., Rothblum, G.N.: On best-possible obfuscation. In: Vadhan, S.P. (ed.) TCC 2007. LNCS, vol. 4392, pp. 194–213. Springer, Heidelberg (2007). https://doi.org/10.1007/978-3-540-70936-7_11

[GSW13] Gentry, C., Sahai, A., Waters, B.: Homomorphic encryption from learning with errors: conceptually-simpler, asymptotically-faster, attribute-based. In: Canetti, R., Garay, J.A. (eds.) CRYPTO 2013. LNCS, vol. 8042, pp. 75–92. Springer, Heidelberg (2013). https://doi.org/10.1007/978-3-642-40041-4_5

[GVW13] Gorbunov, S., Vaikuntanathan, V., Wee, H.: Attribute-based encryption for circuits. In: Boneh et al. [BRF13], pp. 545–554

[GVW15] Gorbunov, S., Vaikuntanathan, V., Wichs, D.: Leveled fully homomorphic signatures from standard lattices. In: Servedio, R.A., Rubinfeld, R. (eds.) 47th ACM STOC, pp. 469–477. ACM Press, June 2015

[HR19] Hofheinz, D., Rosen, A. (eds.): TCC 2019, Part II. LNCS, vol. 11892. Springer, Heidelberg, December 2019

[IKOS10] Ishai, Y., Kumarasubramanian, A., Orlandi, C., Sahai, A.: On invertible sampling and adaptive security. In: Abe, M. (ed.) ASIACRYPT 2010. LNCS, vol. 6477, pp. 466–482. Springer, Heidelberg (2010). https://doi.org/10.1007/978-3-642-17373-8_27

[IR19] Ishai, Y., Rijmen, V. (eds.): EUROCRYPT 2019, Part I. LNCS, vol. 11476. Springer, Heidelberg, May 2019

[JLMS19] Jain, A., Lin, H., Matt, C., Sahai, A.: How to leverage hardness of constant-degree expanding polynomials overa $\mathbb{R}$ to build $i\mathcal{O}$. In: Ishai and Rijmen [IR19], pp. 251–281

[JLS20] Jain, A., Lin, H., Sahai, A.: Indistinguishability obfuscation from well-founded assumptions. Cryptology ePrint Archive, Report 2020/1003 (2020)

[KS17] Katz, J., Shacham, H. (eds.): CRYPTO 2017, Part I. LNCS, vol. 10401. Springer, Heidelberg, August 2017

[Lin16] Lin, H.: Indistinguishability obfuscation from constant-degree graded encoding schemes. In: Fischlin, M., Coron, J.-S. (eds.) EUROCRYPT 2016, Part I. LNCS, vol. 9665, pp. 28–57. Springer, Heidelberg (2016). https://doi.org/10.1007/978-3-662-49890-3_2

[Lin17] Lin, H.: Indistinguishability obfuscation from SXDH on 5-linear maps and locality-5 PRGs. In: Katz and Shacham [KS17], pp. 599–629

[LPST16a] Lin, H., Pass, R., Seth, K., Telang, S.: Indistinguishability obfuscation with non-trivial efficiency. In: Cheng, C.-M., Chung, K.-M., Persiano, G., Yang, B.-Y. (eds.) PKC 2016, Part II. LNCS, vol. 9615, pp. 447–462. Springer, Heidelberg (2016). https://doi.org/10.1007/978-3-662-49387-8_17

[LPST16b] Lin, H., Pass, R., Seth, K., Telang, S.: Output-compressing randomized encodings and applications. In: Kushilevitz, E., Malkin, T. (eds.) TCC 2016-A, Part I. LNCS, vol. 9562, pp. 96–124. Springer, Heidelberg (2016). https://doi.org/10.1007/978-3-662-49096-9_5

[LT17] Lin, H., Tessaro, S.: Indistinguishability obfuscation from trilinear maps and block-wise local PRGs. In: Katz and Shacham [KS17], pp. 630–660

[LV16] Lin, H., Vaikuntanathan, V.: Indistinguishability obfuscation from DDH-like assumptions on constant-degree graded encodings. In: Dinur, I. (ed.) 57th FOCS, pp. 11–20. IEEE Computer Society Press, October 2016

[MP12] Micciancio, D., Peikert, C.: Trapdoors for lattices: simpler, tighter, faster, smaller. In: Pointcheval and Johansson [PJ12], pp. 700–718

[MSZ16] Miles, E., Sahai, A., Zhandry, M.: Annihilation attacks for multilinear maps: cryptanalysis of indistinguishability obfuscation over GGH13. In: Robshaw and Katz [RK16], pp. 629–658

[MW16] Mukherjee, P., Wichs, D.: Two round multiparty computation via multi-key FHE. In: Fischlin, M., Coron, J.-S. (eds.) EUROCRYPT 2016, Part II. LNCS, vol. 9666, pp. 735–763. Springer, Heidelberg (2016). https://doi.org/10.1007/978-3-662-49896-5_26

[Pel18] Pellet-Mary, A.: Quantum attacks against indistinguishablility obfuscators proved secure in the weak multilinear map model. In: Shacham, H., Boldyreva, A. (eds.) CRYPTO 2018, Part III. LNCS, vol. 10993, pp. 153–183. Springer, Cham (2018). https://doi.org/10.1007/978-3-319-96878-0_6

[PJ12] Pointcheval, D., Johansson, T. (eds.): EUROCRYPT 2012. LNCS, vol. 7237. Springer, Heidelberg, April 2012

[PS19]   Peikert, C., Shiehian, S.: Noninteractive zero knowledge for NP from (plain) learning with errors. In: Boldyreva, A., Micciancio, D. (eds.) CRYPTO 2019, Part I. LNCS, vol. 11692, pp. 89–114. Springer, Cham (2019). https://doi.org/10.1007/978-3-030-26948-7_4

[Reg05]  Regev, O.: On lattices, learning with errors, random linear codes, and cryptography. In: Gabow, H.N., Fagin, R. (eds.) 37th ACM STOC, pp. 84–93. ACM Press, May 2005

[RK16]   Robshaw, M., Katz, J. (eds.): CRYPTO 2016, Part II. LNCS, vol. 9815. Springer, Heidelberg, August 2016

# Non-Malleable Commitments

# Black-Box Non-interactive Non-malleable Commitments

Rachit Garg[1]([⊠]), Dakshita Khurana[2], George Lu[1], and Brent Waters[1,3]

[1] University of Texas at Austin, Austin, USA
{rachg96,gclu,bwaters}@cs.utexas.edu
[2] University of Illinois Urbana-Champaign, Urbana, USA
dakshita@illinois.edu
[3] NTT Research, Sunnyvale, USA

**Abstract.** There has been recent exciting progress on building non-interactive non-malleable commitments from judicious assumptions. All proposed approaches proceed in two steps. First, obtain simple "base" commitment schemes for very small tag/identity spaces based on a various sub-exponential hardness assumptions. Next, assuming sub-exponential non-interactive witness indistinguishable proofs (NIWIs), and variants of keyless collision resistant hash functions, construct non-interactive compilers that convert tag-based non-malleable commitments for a small tag space into tag-based non-malleable commitments for a larger tag space.

We propose the first black-box construction of non-interactive non-malleable commitments. Our key technical contribution is a novel implementation of the non-interactive proof of consistency required for tag amplification. Prior to our work, the only known approach to tag amplification without setup and with black-box use of the base scheme (Goyal, Lee, Ostrovsky and Visconti, FOCS 2012) added multiple rounds of interaction.

Our construction satisfies the strongest known definition of non-malleability, i.e., CCA (chosen commitment attack) security. In addition to being black-box, our approach dispenses with the need for sub-exponential NIWIs, that was common to all prior work. Instead of NIWIs, we rely on sub-exponential hinting PRGs which can be obtained based on a broad set of assumptions such as sub-exponential CDH or LWE.

## 1  Introduction

Non-malleable commitments have been a well studied primitive in cryptography since their introduction by Dolev, Dwork and Naor [11]. They are an important

This material is based on work supported in part by DARPA under Contract No. HR001120C0024. Any opinions, findings and conclusions or recommendations expressed in this material are those of the author(s) and do not necessarily reflect the views of the United States Government or DARPA.

A. Canteaut and F.-X. Standaert (Eds.): EUROCRYPT 2021, LNCS 12698, pp. 159–185, 2021.
https://doi.org/10.1007/978-3-030-77883-5_6

component of nearly all multi-party protocols including multiparty computation, coin flipping and secure auctions. These commitments ensure security in the presence of "man in the middle" attacks. A man-in-the-middle adversary participates in two or more instantiations of a protocol, trying to use information obtained in one execution to breach security in the other protocol execution. A non-malleable protocol should ensure that an adversary gains no advantage from such behavior.

*Non-Interactive Non-Malleable Commitments.* For several years, provably secure constructions of non-malleable commitments required several rounds of interaction. On the other hand, practical constructions need to be highly efficient and often non-interactive. For these reasons, in practice, we often heuristically assume that a family of (keyless) SHA-like hash functions is non-malleable. Our technique gives the first provably secure black-box construction of non-interactive non-malleable commitments, taking us a step closer to efficient realizations.

We will focus on perfectly binding and computationally hiding non-interactive commitments. For these commitments, the perfect binding requirement asserts that a commitment cannot be opened to two different messages $m \neq m'$. Specifically, even for a maliciously generated commitment string $c$, there do not exist two openings to messages $m$ and $m'$ such that $m \neq m'$. The (computational) hiding property asserts that for any two messages, $m$ and $m'$ (of the same length), the distributions of commitments $\mathsf{com}(m)$ and $\mathsf{com}(m')$ are computationally indistinguishable.

Loosely speaking, a commitment scheme is said to be non-malleable if no adversary, given a commitment $\mathsf{com}(m)$, can efficiently generate a commitment $\mathsf{com}(m')$, such that the message $m'$ is related to the original message $m$. This is equivalent (assuming the existence of one-way functions) to a tag-based notion where the commit algorithm obtains an additional input, a $\mathsf{tag} \in \{0,1\}^{\kappa}$, and where the adversary is restricted to using a tag, or identity, that is different from the tag used to generate its input commitment. We will rely on tag-based definitions throughout this paper. We will also model man-in-the-middle security as a CCA (chosen commitment attack) game between the adversary and a challenger.

Specifically, the hiding game is modified to give the adversary oracle access to an inefficient value function CCA.Val where on input a string $c$, $\mathsf{CCA.Val}(\mathsf{tag}, c)$ returns $m$ if $\mathsf{CCA.Com}(\mathsf{tag}, m; r) \to c$ for some $r$. The adversary must first specify a challenge $\mathsf{tag}^*$ along with messages $m_0^*, m_1^*$. He is then allowed oracle access to $\mathsf{CCA.Val}(\mathsf{tag}, \cdot)$ for every $\mathsf{tag} \neq \mathsf{tag}^*$, and can make an arbitrary (polynomial) number of queries before and after obtaining the challenge commitment.[1] This CCA definition is the strongest known definition of non-malleability. In the non-interactive setting, the often-used definition of (concurrent) non-malleability

---

[1] The assumption that the commitment takes input a $\mathsf{tag}$ is w.l.o.g when the tag space is exponential. As is standard with non-malleable commitments, tags can be generically removed from this construction by setting the tag as the verification key of a signature scheme, and signing the commitment string using the signing key.

w.r.t. commitment is implied by this definition where the adversary is only allowed to make parallel oracle queries once it obtains the challenge commitment.

*Our Results, in a Nutshell.* In this work, we give the first black-box construction of CCA secure commitments, under weaker assumptions than prior work. In terms of assumptions, we substitute NIWIs with hinting PRGs [25] which can be instantiated under several standard assumptions like CDH and LWE. Additionally, while all prior work recursively applied NIWIs to prove cryptographic statements, making heavy non-black-box use of cryptography, our constructions are black-box. Combining this with base schemes due to [21], we obtain CCA secure commitments from black box use of the following assumptions: subexponential hinting PRGs, subexponential keyless collision-resistant hash functions, subexponential one-way functions against quantum adversaries, and subexponential one-way functions in BQP with hardness against classical adversaries. We note that subexponential hinting PRGs can be obtained based on black-box use of any group where CDH is subexponentially hard.

We believe this takes us one step closer to the goal of building provably secure and efficient non-interactive non-malleable commitments.

*Prior Work on Non-Malleable Commitments.* There has been a long line of work constructing non-malleable commitments in the plain model, without trusted setup. This research has been driven by two often competing goals: the first is to reduce the round complexity of commitment, which is important because it directly impacts the round complexity of applications like MPC. The second goal is to achieve non-malleable commitments under the weakest possible assumptions.

This research [1,9,11,14–16,18,26,27,29–32,34,35] culminated in three round stand-alone secure non-malleable commitments based on injective one-way functions [17] and concurrent secure non-malleable commitments based on DDH/LWE [22], or subexponential injective one-way functions [8]. In the two round setting, we now have constructions based on sub-exponential time-lock puzzles [28] and sub-exponential DDH/LWE/QR/NR [23].

Very recently, research in non-malleable commitments moved to a final frontier of achieving non-interactive non-malleable commitments from well-studied assumptions without leveraging setup. In this non-interactive setting, Pandey, Pass and Vaikuntanathan [30] first gave constructions of non-malleable commitments based on a strong non-falsifiable assumption. The primary research challenge has been to improve assumptions while realizing non-malleability without interaction and setup, which does not allow the use of tools like zero knowledge proof systems.

Nevertheless, the recent works of Bitansky and Lin [4] and Kalai and Khurana [21] made progress on improving these assumptions. All of these works [4,21,23,28] proceed in two steps. First, they construct "base" commitment schemes that only support a constant-sized space of tags. Second, they give amplification techniques to convert commitments supporting a small space of tags into commitments that support a much larger tag space. Applying these amplification techniques to the base scheme helps generically increase the space of tags to $\{0,1\}^\kappa$. We summarize known results in the non-interactive setting by splitting up contributions into base constructions and tag amplification results.

*Base Constructions.* Three recent works [4,21,28] build non-interactive base schemes: non-malleable commitments for a tag space of size $c \log \log \kappa$ for a specific constant $c > 0$, based on various hardness assumptions. These are typically only secure in a setting where the adversary is restricted to using the same tag in all its queries to the CCA.Val oracle. This is primarily achieved by using families of assumptions, each of which is harder than the other along some axis of hardness. We list these assumptions below.

1. Lin, Pass and Soni [28] assume a sub-exponential variant of the hardness of time-lock puzzles. Specifically, they define a two-dimensional variant of the Rivest, Shamir and Wagner (RSW) repeated squaring assumption there is a security parameter $n$ and another parameter $t$, and it is required that computing $h = g^{2^{2^t}}$ cannot be done by circuits of overall size $2^{n^\epsilon}$ and depth $2^{t^\delta}$, for constants $\epsilon$ and $\delta$.
2. Bitansky and Lin [4] rely on sub-exponentially hard one-way functions that admit a strong form of hardness amplification. Roughly speaking, they say that a one-way function $f$ is amplifiable, if there is a way to combine (XOR), say $\ell$ hardcore bits corresponding to $\ell$ independent images $f(x_1), \ldots, f(x_\ell)$ that are each hard against $T$-time adversaries, so that the combined bit is $2^{\ell^\epsilon}$-unpredicatable against $T'$-time adversaries; that is, the level of unpredictability increases at least subexponentially as more hardcore bits are combined (their assumption on unpredictability goes beyond the limit $\mathsf{poly}(\frac{T}{T'})$ that is commonly imposed by known provable results on hardness amplification).
3. Kalai and Khurana [21] assume classically sub-exponentially hard but quantum easy one-way functions (which can be based, e.g., on sub-exponential hardness of DDH), and sub-exponentially quantum hard one-way functions (which can be based, e.g., on sub-exponential hardness of LWE).

*Tag Amplification.* Starting with non-malleable commitments for a tag space of size $c \log \log \kappa$ for a specific constant $c > 0$ (or sometimes even smaller), several works develop techniques to achieve non-malleable commitments for a tag space of $\{0,1\}^\kappa$. This is achieved by several applications of a tag-amplification compiler, that increases the tag space exponentially in each application. We also point out that these compilers often obtain as input base schemes that are secure against a restricted adversary; one that uses the same tag in all its queries to the CCA.Val oracle. The end goal, however, is to obtain security against a general adversary, that uses arbitrary tags in its oracle queries – as long as all tags in oracle queries are different from the challenge tag.

Such compilers were developed in [4,21,28] based various assumptions, and we summarize these results below.

- Lin, Pass and Soni [28] assume sub-exponential non-interactive witness indistinguishable (NIWI) proofs and keyless collision resistant hash functions against uniform adversaries. The resulting commitments for larger tags are secure only against uniform adversaries.
- Bitansky and Lin [4] assume sub-exponential non-interactive witness indistinguishable (NIWI) proofs and keyless collision resistant hash functions with limited security against non-uniform adversaries. Such a hash function $H : \{0,1\}^{3\kappa} \to \{0,1\}^{\kappa}$ guarantees that no superpolynomial adversary with non-uniform description of polynomial size $S$ can find more than $K(S)$ collisions in the underlying function. Here, $K$ is a fixed polynomial (e.g., quadratic). The resulting commitments for larger tags are secure against non-uniform adversaries.
- Kalai and Khurana [21] assume sub-exponential non-interactive witness indistinguishable (NIWI) proofs and obtain security against non-uniform adversaries. But their compiler, on input commitments that satisfy a weaker notion of non-malleability w.r.t. replacement generates commitments that are non-malleable w.r.t replacement for a larger tag space.

In [4,28], NIWIs are combined with a hard-to-invert trapdoor statement to enable weak forms of NIZKs without setup. In contrast, [21] use NIWIs without associated trapdoors, but then only achieve weaker forms of non-malleability (that is, w.r.t. replacement).

But a common thread among the amplification techniques is that they all require the use of sub-exponential NIWI proofs. We remind that reader that NIWIs are one round proof systems with statistical soundness, for which no computationally bounded verifier can distinguish which witness in a relation was used to create the proof.

Reliance on NIWIs results in the following less than ideal consequences:

- Subexponential NIWIs are only known based on the hardness of the decisional linear problem over bilinear maps [19], or derandomization assumptions and subexponential trapdoor permutations [2].
- All these compilers use NIWIs to prove complex cryptographic statements, and therefore make non-black box use of the underlying non-malleable commitment for a smaller tag space. On the other hand, from the point of view of efficiency, it is desirable to have constructions that make black-box use of cryptography.

*Our Results.* In this work, we provide a new approach to non-interactive tag amplification for non-malleable commitments. This approach only makes black-box use of cryptography, and achieves provable security under a more diverse set of assumptions. Specifically, this compiler replaces the NIWI assumption with hinting PRGs, that were introduced by Koppula and Waters [25], and can be obtained based on CDH, LWE [25] and also $\phi$-hiding and DBDHI assumptions [13]. (One can also alternatively execute the paradigm from any projective key-dependent secure symmetric key encryption scheme [24] which is realizable from the LPN assumption).

We summarize (a simplification of) our results via the following informal theorems. Recall that base schemes are typically only secure in a setting where the adversary is restricted to using the same tag in all its queries to the oracle. In what follows, we refer to such a commitment scheme that is only secure against this limited class of adversaries as a same-tag CCA secure commitment. We also refer to CCA commitments where the adversary is only allowed to make parallel oracle queries after obtaining the challenge commitment, as non-malleable commitments.

**Theorem 1.** *(Informal) (Removing the Same-Tag Restriction) Assuming the existence of sub-exponentially secure hinting PRGs and keyless hash functions that are collision-resistant against sub-exponential uniform adversaries, there exists a compiler that on input any same-tag CCA (respectively, non-malleable) non-interactive commitment for N tags secure against* non-uniform *adversaries where $N \leq \mathsf{poly}(\kappa)$, outputs a CCA (respectively, non-malleable) non-interactive commitment for N tags secure against* uniform *adversaries.*

**Theorem 2.** *(Informal) (Tag-Amplification for CCA commitments) Assuming the existence of sub-exponentially hinting PRGs and keyless hash functions that are collision-resistant against sub-exponential uniform adversaries, there exists a compiler that on input any CCA (respectively, non-malleable) non-interactive commitment for N tags secure against* non-uniform *adversaries where $N \leq \mathsf{poly}(\kappa)$, outputs a CCA (respectively, non-malleable) non-interactive commitment for $2^{N/2}$ tags secure against* uniform *adversaries.*

Unfortunately, using these informal theorems to amplify tag space from $c \log \log n$ for a small constant $c > 0$ immediately encounters the following issue: the input scheme to the compiler is required to be *non-uniform secure*, whereas the output scheme is only *uniform secure*.

To enable recursion, we strengthen our CCA abstraction. Specifically, we modify the CCA security game to allow an adversary to submit a Turing Machine $P$ to the challenger, and obtain the evaluation of $P$ on an input of the adversary's choice. We say that a scheme is $e$-"computation enabled" if it is secure against all adversaries that submit programs that run in time polynomial in $2^{\kappa^e}$ for constant $e$. As such, we will substitute the *non-uniform security* requirement for the base CCA scheme and instead require it to be $e$-"computation enabled" for an appropriate constant $e$. The output of the compiler will be an $e'$-"computation enabled" commitment for an appropriate constant $e'$. We describe this abstraction, and our techniques, in additional detail in Sect. 1.1.

## 1.1 Our Techniques

We now provide our technical overview. Recall that the core technical goal of our work is to provide a method for amplifying from a commitment scheme for $O(N)$ sized tag space to a $2^N$ sized space. If the computational overhead associated with the amplification step is polynomial in $N$ and the security parameter $\kappa$, then the process can be applied iteratively $c + 1$ times to a base NM commitment scheme that handles tags of size $\lg \lg \cdots \lg(\kappa)$ for a $c$-times iterated log, for arbitrary constant $c$ and results in a scheme that handles tags of size $2^\kappa$. Here, we note that subexponential quantum hardness of LWE and subexponential hardness of DDH [21], or subexponential hardness amplifiable one-way functions [4], or subexponential variants of time-lock puzzles [28] imply base schemes for tags in $(c \lg \lg \kappa)$ for a small constant $c > 0$, which means they imply schemes for tags in $(\lg \lg \lg \kappa)$.

Now the traditional way to amplify such a tag space can be traced back to [11]² They suggested a method of breaking a large tag $T^j$ (say, in $[2^N]$) into $N$ small tags $t_1^j, t_2^j, \ldots t_N^j$, each in $2N$, such that for two different large tags $T^1 \neq T^2$, there exists at least one index $i$ such that $t_i^2 \notin \{t_1^1, t_2^1, \ldots t_N^1\}$. This is achieved by setting $t_i^j = i || T^j[i]$, where $T^j[i]$ denotes the $i^{th}$ bit of $T^j$.

A scheme for tags in $2^N$ will have an algorithm CCA.Com that commits to a message $m$ as $\mathsf{CCA.Com}(1^\kappa, \mathsf{tag}, m; r) \rightarrow \mathsf{com}$. To commit to $m$ under $\mathsf{tag}$ one first creates $N$ tags $t_1, \ldots t_N$ by applying the DDN encoding to $\mathsf{tag}$. Next, these (smaller) tags are used to generate commitments of $m$ in the smaller tag scheme as $c_i = \mathsf{Small.Com}(1^\kappa, (t_i), \mathsf{msg} = m; r_i)$ for $i \in [N]$. Next, the committer attaches a zero knowledge (ZK) proof that all commitments are to the same message $m$ using the random coins as a witness. Since we are interested in non-interactive amplification, the ZK proof will need to be non-interactive. Additionally, we will require it to be ZK against adversaries running in time $T$, where $T$ is the time required to brute-force break the underlying CCA scheme for small tags.

CCA security of the scheme with larger tag space can be argued in two basic steps. Suppose the challenger commits to either $m_0^*$ or $m_1^*$ under tag $T^*$ (we denote the DDN encoding of $T^*$ by $t_1^*, \ldots t_N^*$). The adversary wins if it gets which out of $m_0^*$ and $m_1^*$ was committed. Recall that the adversary can request the CCA oracle to provide openings of commitment string with tags $\mathsf{tag} \neq \mathsf{tag}^* \in \{0,1\}^N$. This oracle generates a response as follows - (1) Verify the ZK proof in the commitment string. Return $\perp$ if verification does not accept. (2) Open the underlying commitment scheme with small tags at position 1 with tag $t_1$.

We will assume, for simplicity, that the adversary makes a single oracle query in the CCA game, with tag $T$, whose DDN encoding is denoted by $t_1, \ldots t_N$. We will focus on the index $i$ in the adversary's oracle query, such that the tag $t_i \notin \{t_1^*, \ldots t_N^*\}$.

As a first step towards proving CCA security, one can modify the oracle to open the commitment string $c$ with small tag $t_i$, in Step 2. Because of the soundness of the ZK proof system, this change cannot be detected by the adversary, except with negligible probability.

At this point, the challenge commitment is modified so that the ZK proof is simulated and does not need the random coins used in the small tag commitments anymore. To argue indistinguishability, we will need to answer the

---

² This was recently further optimized by [23] but in this paper, we use the [11] technique for simplicity.

adversary's oracle queries. This will be done by extracting, via brute-force, the value committed in the adversary's oracle query. As such, we will need to rely on ZK proofs where the ZK property holds even against machines that can (brute-force) break the small tag commitments. Once this is done, we will change each of the small tag commitments in the challenge commitment from committing to the message $m_b^*$ to committing to the all 0's string, one by one. At the same time, the oracle will continue to open the commitment string $c$ with small tag $t_i$, in Step 2. Since $t_i \notin \{t_1^*, \ldots t_N^*\}$, we can rely on CCA security of the underlying small tag scheme and argue that the adversary will not be able to detect these changes. By the end, all information about the bit $b$ will be erased.

Since non-interactive zero-knowledge proofs without setup are impossible, existing non-interactive tag amplification techniques [4,23,28] rely on weaker variants of zero-knowledge proofs, such as ZK with super-polynomial simulation and weak soundness, to perform tag amplification via the afore-mentioned outline. These required variants of non-interactive ZK proofs are obtained by including a trapdoor statement td. To prove that a statement $x$ is in an NP language $L$, one typically provides a NIWI to establish that $(x \in L) \vee$ (td is true). The trapdoor statement helps perform simulation, whereas for soundness it is required that the adversary cannot prove the trapdoor statement. One exception is [21], which only relies on NIWIs and does not make use of on any trapdoor statements, but is limited to the weaker notion of replacement security. However, in addition to relying on NIWIs, the outline above makes non-black-box use of the underlying base commitment scheme.

*Eliminating NIWIs.* Our primary goal in this paper is to perform tag amplification without NIWIs, and while making black-box use of the underlying base commitments. Taking a step back, the reason ZK is required in the tag amplification argument discussed above, is that we can change the oracle to one that opens different underlying tags, without the adversary noticing. In other words, we would like to establish a system where the adversary cannot submit a commitment such that its opening will be different under the original and new oracle functions.

Here, inspired by recent work in chosen ciphertext secure public key encryption [25], our construction will allow the oracle to recover a PRG seed $s$ that gives (a good part of) the randomness used to create the underlying commitments. Specifically, the oracle will use the commitment with a specific small tag to first recover a candidate PRG seed $s'$ and then check for consistency by re-evaluating the underlying commitment pieces, and checking them against the original.

These checks will intuitively serve as a substitution for ZK proofs. Interestingly, our checking algorithm will allow some partially malformed commitments to go through – allowing this is essential to our security argument. This is in contrast to a ZK proof which enforces that all must be commitments to the same message. While creating such partially malformed commitments is actually easy for the adversary, the adversary will still not be able to differentiate between different forms of decryption. (We note that in non-malleable encryption some systems [7,33] allow for somewhat malformed ciphertexts to be let through.)

Importantly, unlike [25] that looked at two possible decryption strategies, we will need to ensure that up to polynomially many such strategies decrypt the same way. Furthermore, we will not be able rely on trusted setup to generate verification keys for a signature scheme. Instead, we will develop a new technique leveraging hinting PRGs, which we outline below.

We now describe our new tag amplification technique that converts CCA commitments with $4N$ tags to CCA commitments with $2^N$ tags. We point out that our technique also applies as is to converting parallel CCA commitments with $4N$ tags to parallel CCA commitments with $2^N$ tags. First, we summarize some of the tools we will use.

- **Hinting PRGs.** A hinting PRG, introduced in [25], satisfies the following property: for a uniformly random short seed $s$, the matrix $M$ obtained by first expanding $PRG(s) = z_0 z_1 z_2 \ldots z_n$, sampling uniformly random $v_1 v_2 \ldots v_n$, and setting for all $i \in [n]$, $M_{s_i, i} = z_i$ and $M_{1-s_i, i} = v_i$, should be indistinguishable from a uniform matrix. Hinting PRGs are known based on CDH, LWE [25] – more generally, any circular secure symmetric key encryption scheme [24].

- **Statistically Equivocal Commitments Without Setup.** We will rely on statistically hiding bit commitments without setup, that satisfy binding against uniform adversaries. Additionally, these commitments will be statistically equivocal, that is, with overwhelming probability, a randomly chosen commitment string can be opened to both a 0 and a 1. These can be obtained from keyless collision resistant hash functions against uniform adversaries, based on the blueprint of [10] and [20], and more recently [3], in the keyless hash setting.

*Outline of Our Tag Amplification Technique.* Let (Small.Com, Small.Val, Small.Recover) be a non malleable commitment for $4N$ tags. We will assume tags take identities of the form $(i, \beta, \gamma) \in [N] \times \{0, 1\} \times \{0, 1\}$ and that the Small.Com algorithm requires randomness of length $\ell(\kappa)$.

Our transformation will produce three algorithms, (CCA.Com, CCA.Val, CCA.Recover). The CCA.Com algorithm on input a tag **tag** from the large tag space, an input message, and uniform randomness, first samples a seed $s$ of size $n$ for a hinting PRG. It uses the first co-ordinate $z_0$ of the output of the hinting PRG on input $s$, as a one-time pad to mask the message $m$, resulting in string $c$. Next, it generates $n$ equivocal commitments $\{\sigma_i\}_{i \in [n]}$, one to each bit of $s$. We will let $y_i$ denote the opening of the $i^{th}$ equivocal commitment (this includes the $i^{th}$ bit $s_i$ of $s$). Finally, it 'signals' each of the bits of $s$ by generating commitments $\{c_{x,i,b}\}_{x \in [N], i \in [n], b \in \{0,1\}}$ using the small tag scheme. For every $i \in [n]$, the commitments $\{c_{x,i,0}\}_{x \in [N]}$ and $\{c_{x,i,1}\}_{x \in [N]}$ are generated as follows:

1. If $s_i = 0$
   (a) $c_{x,i,0} = \mathsf{Small.Com}(1^\kappa, (x, \mathsf{tag}_x, 0), \mathsf{msg} = y_i; r_{x,i})$
   (b) $c_{x,i,1} = \mathsf{Small.Com}(1^\kappa, (x, \mathsf{tag}_x, 1), \mathsf{msg} = y_i; \tilde{r}_{x,i})$

2. If $s_i = 1$
   (a) $c_{x,i,0} = \mathsf{Small.Com}(1^\kappa, (x, \mathsf{tag}_x, 0), \mathsf{msg} = y_i; \tilde{r}_{x,i})$
   (b) $c_{x,i,1} = \mathsf{Small.Com}(1^\kappa, (x, \mathsf{tag}_x, 1), \mathsf{msg} = y_i; r_{x,i})$

where all the $\tilde{r}_{x,i}$ values are uniformly random, whereas $r_{x,i}$ values correspond to the output of the hinting PRG on seed $s$. The output of CCA.Com is $\mathsf{tag}, c, \{\sigma_i\}_{i \in [n]}, \{c_{x,i,b}\}_{x \in [N], i \in [n], b \in \{0,1\}}$.

On an oracle query of the form CCA.Val($\mathsf{tag}, \mathsf{com}$), we must return the message committed in the string com, if one exists. To do this, we parse $\mathsf{com} = \mathsf{tag}, c, \{\sigma_i\}_{i \in [n]}, \{c_{x,i,b}\}_{x \in [N], i \in [n], b \in \{0,1\}}$, and then recover the values committed under small tags $(1, \mathsf{tag}_1, 0)$ and $(1, \mathsf{tag}_1, 1)$, which also helps recover the seed $s$ of the hinting PRG. Next, we check that for every $i \in [n]$, the recovered values correspond to openings of the respective $\sigma_i$. We also compute hinting PRG($s$), and use the resulting randomness to check that for all $x \in [N]$, the commitments that were supposed to use the outcome of the PRG were correctly constructed. If any of these checks fail, we know that the commitment string com cannot be a well-formed commitment to any message. Therefore, if any of the checks fail, the oracle outputs $\bot$. These checks are inspired by [25], and intuitively, ensure that it is computationally infeasible for an adversary to query the oracle on commitment strings that lead to different outcomes differently depending on which small tag was used. If all these checks pass, the CCA.Val algorithm uses $c$ to recover and output $m$.

*Proving Security.* We will prove that the resulting scheme is CCA secure against uniform adversaries. To begin, we note that the set $\{(x, \mathsf{tag}_x)\}_{x \in [N]}$ is nothing but the DDN encoding of the tag $\mathsf{tag}$. Recall that this encoding has the property that for every $\mathsf{tag}, \mathsf{tag}^* \in 2^N$, there exists an index $x \in [N]$ such that $(x, \mathsf{tag}_x) \notin \{(x^*, \mathsf{tag}_{x^*}^*)\}_{x^* \in [N]}$. In the scheme described above, the tag used for each set $\{c_{x,i,b}\}_{i \in [n]}$ is $(x, \mathsf{tag}_x, b)$. This means that for our particular method of generating the commitments $c_{x,i,b}$ described above, for each of the adversary's oracle queries, there will be an index $x' \in [N]$ such that the tags $(x', \mathsf{tag}_{x'}, 0)$ and $(x', \mathsf{tag}_{x'}, 1)$ used to generate $\{c_{x',i,b}\}_{i \in [n], b \in \{0,1\}}$ in that query will differ from *all small tags used to generate the challenge commitment.*

Our first step towards proving security of the resulting commitment with large tags, will be to define an alternative CCA.ValAlt algorithm, that instead of recovering the values committed under tags $(1, \mathsf{tag}_1, 0)$ and $(1, \mathsf{tag}_1, 1)$, recovers values committed under $(x', \mathsf{tag}_{x'}, 0)$ and $(x', \mathsf{tag}_{x'}, 1)$. As already alluded to earlier, this scheme is designed so that it is computationally infeasible for a uniform adversary to query the oracle on commitment strings for which CCA.Val and CCA.ValAlt lead to different outcomes. Formally, we will first switch to a hybrid that uses the CCA.ValAlt algorithm instead of CCA.Val to answer the adversary's oracle queries.

When making this change, because of the checks performed by the valuation algorithms, we can formally argue that any adversary that distinguishes these hybrids must query the oracle with a commitment string that has following property: For some $i \in [n], x \in [N]$, $c_{x,i,0}$ and $c_{x,i,1}$ are small tag commitments to openings of the equivocal commitment to some bit $b$ and $1 - b$

respectively. Assuming that the equivocal commitment satisfies binding against uniform adversaries that run in subexponential time, one can brute-force extract these openings from $c_{x,i,0}$ and $c_{x,i,1}$ to contradict the binding property.

The next hybrid is an exponential time hybrid that samples equivocal commitments $\{\sigma_i\}_{i \in [n]}$, for the challenge commitment, together with randomness $\{y_{0,i}\}_{i \in [n]}$ and $\{y_{1,i}\}_{i \in [n]}$ that can be used to equivocally open these commitments to 0 and 1 respectively.

In the next hybrid, inspired by [25] we modify the components $\{c^*_{x,i,b}\}_{x \in [N], i \in [n], b \in \{0,1\}}$ in the challenge commitment to "drown" out information about $s$ via noise. In particular, while in the real game, the values $c^*_{x,i,1}$ are always commitments to $y_{s_i,i}$, in the challenge commitment these values are modified to become commitments to $y^*_{i,1}$, irrespective of what $s_i$ is. In the next step, the values $c^*_{x,i,0}$ are modified to become commitments to $y^*_{i,0}$, irrespective of what $s_i$ is. We rely on CCA security of the underlying small tag scheme so that we can continue to run the CCA.ValAlt function to recover values committed under $(x', \mathsf{tag}_{x'}, 0)$ and $(x', \mathsf{tag}_{x'}, 1)$ while changing all the components $\{c^*_{x,i,b}\}_{x \in [N], i \in [n], b \in \{0,1\}}$ in the challenge commitment. This step crucially makes use of the fact that the tags $(x', \mathsf{tag}_{x'}, 0)$ and $(x', \mathsf{tag}_{x'}, 1)$ differ from *all small tags used to generate the challenge commitment*. Moreover, in spite of the fact that generating equivocal openings of $\{\sigma_i\}_{i \in [n]}$ takes exponential time, the proof of indistinguishability between this hybrid and the previous one does not need to rely on an exponential time reduction. Instead, we observe that the equivocal commitment strings $\{\sigma_i\}_{i \in [n]}$ together with their openings can be fixed non-uniformly and independently of the strings $c^*_{x,i,b}$, and therefore these hybrids can be proven indistinguishable based on non-malleability of the small tag commitment against non-uniform adversaries. Since we must carefully manipulate the randomness used for $c^*_{x,i,b}$ in both games, this hybrid requires a delicate argument.

At this point, we have eliminated all information about the PRG seed $s$, except from the randomness $r_{x,i}$ and $\tilde{r}_{x,i}$. In the final hybrid, we rely on the security of the hinting PRG to switch to using uniform randomness everywhere. Note that we still need to answer the adversary's oracle queries, but this can be done by ensuring that the time required to run the CCA.ValAlt algorithm is much smaller than that needed to break hinting PRG security. At this point, there is no information about $s$, and therefore about the message being committed to in the challenge commitment.

*Issues with Recursion.* At this point, it may seem like we are done, but the careful reader may have noticed a problem. To prove security, we assumed an input scheme that was secure against *non-uniform* adversaries, but due to the use of equivocal commitments against uniform adversaries, the transformation yields a scheme that is only secure against *uniform* adversaries. This would be no problem if we say were only amplifying once from $\kappa$ to $2^\kappa$ tags. But unfortunately, the recursion will not work if our base scheme starts with $\lg \lg \lg(\kappa)$ size tags (which is the number of tags allowable by most existing base schemes), as we will need to recursively amplify multiple times.

It might seem that we are fundamentally stuck. The first hybrid in our argument requires the equivocal commitment scheme to be more secure than the underlying small tag commitment. Later hybrids require that the small tag commitment to satisfy CCA security even when equivocal commitments with openings to both ones and zeros are generated. If the small tag CCA scheme is only uniformly secure, it seems impossible to satisfy this requirement without violating the previous one.

However, if we peel the recursion back further, there appears to be a glimmer of hope. Suppose we are applying our transformation to an underlying CCA commitment, which is itself the result of applying the transformation one or more times. When our proof arrives at the security of the underlying scheme, the underlying scheme's security will rely both on an equivocal commitment itself, and at the deepest level the non-uniform security of the base scheme. If the equivocal commitments in the underlying scheme use a larger security parameter than the current one, then the lower level scheme may still be secure (and lower level equivocal commitments may still be binding) even when equivocal openings are found at the current level.

*e-Computation Enabled Security.* We capture this intuition by expanding our abstraction to include what we call e-computation enabled CCA commitments. Here, we modify the security game to allow an adversary to submit a Turing Machine $P$ to the challenger. The adversary will receive the evaluation of $P$ on an input of its choice. We say that a scheme is e-computation enabled if it is secure against all adversaries that submit programs that run in time polynomial in $2^{\kappa^e}$ for constant $e$. (The program output size itself is required to be polynomially bounded.)

With this abstraction in place, when proving security, our reduction can pass the task of generating equivocal openings as an appropriate program $P$ to the enhanced CCA security game itself. Implicitly, this allows the equivocal opening requests to be satisfied in different ways depending on what stage the security proof of the lower scheme is at.

While this new property provides a useful tool for recursion, we also need to work a bit harder to prove e-computation enabled CCA security. Specifically, we prove in Sect. 3 that given a hinting PRG and an equivocal commitment scheme that are uniformly secure against $2^{\kappa^\delta}$ time adversaries for $\delta \in (0,1)$, we can transform an e-computation enabled CCA scheme for small tags into one that is $e'$-computation enabled CCA secure for large tags, where $e' = e \cdot \delta$.

In our proof, at the stages where we use a reduction to find equivocal openings, the reduction will run in time $2^{\kappa^{e'}}$ to satisfy the adversary's program request. When contradicting the hinting PRG, the reduction will run in time $2^{\kappa^e}$ to find equivocal openings, and $2^{\kappa^{e'}}$ to satisfy the adversary's program request. To ensure that this gives us a contradiction, we will set the security parameter of the hinting PRG to be large enough. Finally, when the reduction is to the underlying small tag CCA commitment, the program request of the large tag adversary will be passed by the reduction to the interface of the underlying small tag scheme, which is allowed since $e' < e$. In the base case, we note that we start with schemes secure against non-uniform adversaries (for $\lg\lg\lg\kappa$ tags). By definition, any scheme that is secure against non-uniform adversaries is trivially $e$-computation enabled secure for arbitrary $e$.

*Issues due to Same-Tag Restrictions.* The techniques described above capture our main ideas for tag amplification. Unfortunately, the base schemes that we start with may only be same-tag secure. On the other hand, we would like to end up with CCA schemes for $2^\kappa$ tags that do not have this restriction. This is because CCA commitments without such a restriction can be generically transformed, assuming signatures into schemes that do not use tags at all. We remedy the same-tag issue by applying a transformation that takes a scheme supporting a tag space of $N$ tags with same-tag only queries to one that supports $N$ tags without the same-tag restriction, for any $N \leq \mathsf{poly}(\kappa)$.

*Removing the Same-Tag Requirement.* We start with an underlying scheme that has the same-tag requirement, and modify it to remove this requirement as follows. To commit to a message with tag **tag** in the new scheme, commit to it with respect to all $N - 1$ tags *except* **tag** in the underlying same-tag scheme. Similar to the previous construction, we use hinting PRGs and attach a bunch of checks to ensure that recovering the committed value from the adversary's queries using any one tag is computationally indistinguishable from recovering it using a different tag.

The overall mechanics and guarantees are similar to our prior transformation. Suppose an adversary were given a challenge commitment **tag*** in the transformed scheme, and got to make queries to several *different* tags **tag** $\neq$ **tag***. By our construction, the adversary's challenge does not contain an underlying commitment with tag **tag*** whereas all of the adversary's oracle queries will contain an underlying commitment with tag **tag***. We can therefore answer all of these queries by changing the oracle valuation function to one that uses only tag **tag*** in underlying scheme.

We note that since the same-tag transformation incurs a blowup proportional to $N$, it is imperative to apply it early on in the sequence of transformations. If we first amplified the tag space to be of size $2^\kappa$ and then attempted to remove the same-tag restriction, the resulting scheme would have exponential sized commitments. Therefore, we start with a base scheme that is same-tag secure and supports tags of size iterated log, $c$ times, as $\lg\lg\cdots\lg(\kappa)$ for some constant $c$, we will first apply the same-tag to many-tag transformation. Next, we apply the tag amplification transformation $c + 1$ times. We end up with a scheme that is polynomial sized and supports a tag space of size $2^\kappa$ with no same-tag restrictions.

*Non-uniform Security.* Our techniques give a CCA commitment scheme secure against uniform adversaries. One might ask whether we could use similar techniques, perhaps combined with new assumptions such as non-uniformly secure keyless hash functions [3,4] to obtain security against non-uniform adversaries. We address this in two parts.

First, taking a step back, a primary motivation for obtaining non-uniform security is that it is useful for protocol composition. For example, if we were using a cryptographic primitive like public key encryption as an end application say for encrypting email, then obtaining uniform security would arguably be just fine. As the uniform model captures attackers in the real world. However, the extra power of non-uniform security might be helpful if our commitment scheme were a component used in building a larger cryptosystem. Here, we observe that our transformation actually outputs a CCA scheme with properties that are stronger than (plain) uniform security. Specifically, the output scheme satisfies $e$-computation enabled CCA security.

While the initial motivation for this abstraction was that it helps with recursion; we note that it can actually be a useful property for a CCA scheme to have. In particular, it can actually be viewed as a more fine-grained or nuanced view of non-uniform computation. This abstraction gives any adversary non-uniform advice so long as it can be computed in time $2^{\kappa^e}$. If $e$ is set appropriately, then we expect this would suffice in many circumstances, including for protocol composition. Indeed, this was true for the type of protocol composition that we needed to recursively amplify the tag space. Thus our amplification techniques and our abstraction can arguably deliver something that is the "best of both worlds": the outcome is as good as non-uniform security for many applications, but does not make any new non-uniform assumptions about the hash function.

Second, our techniques are also meaningful for constructing black-box two-message non-malleable commitments with (regular) non-uniform security. In our transformation, the primitive that requires uniform security is the keyless hash-based equivocal commitment scheme. In the two-message setting, it seems possible to slightly modify our scheme to have the receiver generate the key for a keyed (non-uniform secure) collision-resistant hash function. All of our other techniques appear to carry over to this setting, and it appears that one would be able to prove that the resulting scheme is a (regular) non-uniform secure non-malleable commitment that only makes black-box use of cryptography.

*Organization.* We define "computation enabled" commitments in Sect. 2, present our tag amplification scheme in Sect. 3, and show how to compile these elements in Sect. 4. Details on preliminaries and proof analyses, as well as recovery-from-randomness and removing the same tag restriction can be found in our full version [12].

## 2   Computation Enabled CCA Commitments

We now define what we describe as "computation enabled" CCA secure commitments. Intuitively, these will be tagged commitments where a commitment to message $m$ under tag $\mathsf{tag}$ and randomness $r$ is created as $\mathsf{CCA.Com}(\mathsf{tag}, m; r) \to \mathsf{com}$. The scheme will be statistically binding if for all $\mathsf{tag}_0, \mathsf{tag}_1, r_0, r_1$ and $m_0 \neq m_1$ we have that $\mathsf{CCA.Com}(\mathsf{tag}_0, m_0; r_0) \neq \mathsf{CCA.Com}(\mathsf{tag}_1, m_1; r_1)$.

Our hiding property follows along the lines of chosen commitment security definitions [6] where an attacker gives a challenge tag $\mathsf{tag}^*$ along with messages

$m_0, m_1$ and receives a challenge commitment com* to either $m_0$ or $m_1$ from the experiment. The attacker's job is to guess the message that was committed to with the aid of oracle access to an (inefficient) value function CCA.Val where CCA.Val(com) will return $m$ if CCA.Com(tag, $m; r$) → com for some $r$. The attacker is allowed oracle access to CCA.Val($\cdot$) for any tag $\neq$ tag*. The traditional notion of non-malleability (as seen in [21], etc.) is simply a restriction of the CCA game where the adversary is only allowed to simultaneously submit a single set of decommitment queries. The proof of this is immediate and can be found in [5].

The primary difference in our definition is that we also allow the attacker to submit a randomized turing machine $P$ at the beginning of the game. The challenger will run $P$ and output its result to the attacker at the beginning of the game. This added property will allow us to successfully apply recursion for tag amplification later in our scheme. In addition, we require a recover from randomness property, which allows one to open the commitment given all the randomness used to generate said commitment.

## 2.1 Definition

A computation enabled CCA secure commitment is parameterized by a tag space of size $N = N(\kappa)$ where tags are in $[1, N]$. It consists of three algorithms:

CCA.Com($1^\kappa$, tag, $m; r$) → com is a randomized PPT algorithm that takes as input the security parameter $\kappa$, a tag tag $\in [N]$, a message $m \in \{0, 1\}^*$ and outputs a commitment com, including the tag com.tag. We denote the random coins explicitly as $r$.

CCA.Val(com) → $m \cup \perp$ is a deterministic inefficient algorithm that takes in a commitment com and outputs either a message $m \in \{0, 1\}^*$ or a reject symbol $\perp$.

CCA.Recover(com, $r$) → $m$ is a deterministic algorithm which takes a commitment com and the randomness $r$ used to generate com and outputs the underlying message $m$.

We now define the correctness, efficiency properties, as well as the security properties of perfectly binding and message hiding.

**Definition 1 (Correctness).** *We say that our computation enabled CCA secure commitment scheme is perfectly correct if the following holds. $\forall m \in \{0, 1\}^*$, tag $\in [N]$ and $r$ we have that*

$$\mathsf{CCA.Val}(\mathsf{CCA.Com}(1^\kappa, \mathsf{tag}, m; r)) = m.$$

**Definition 2 (Efficiency).** *We say that our computation enabled CCA secure commitment scheme is efficient if CCA.Com, CCA.Recover run in time poly($|m|, \kappa$), while CCA.Val runs in time poly($|m|, 2^\kappa$).*

**Definition 3 (Security).** *We say that our computation enabled CCA secure commitment is perfectly binding if* $\forall m_0, m_1 \in \{0,1\}^*$ *s.t.* $m_0 \neq m_1$ *there does not exist* $\mathsf{tag}_0, \mathsf{tag}_1, r_0, r_1$ *such that*

$$\mathsf{CCA.Com}(1^\kappa, \mathsf{tag}_0, m_0; r_0) = \mathsf{CCA.Com}(1^\kappa, \mathsf{tag}_1, m_1; r_1).$$

*Remark 1.* We remark that this is implied by Definition 1, as we know that if $\mathsf{CCA.Com}(1^\kappa, \mathsf{tag}_0, m_0; r_0) = \mathsf{CCA.Com}(1^\kappa, \mathsf{tag}_1, m_1; r_1)$, then

$$m_0 = \mathsf{CCA.Val}(\mathsf{CCA.Com}(1^\kappa, \mathsf{tag}_0, m_0; r_0)) = \mathsf{CCA.Val}(\mathsf{CCA.Com}(1^\kappa, \mathsf{tag}_1, m_1; r_1)) = m_1,$$

but $m_0 \neq m_1$, a contradiction.

We define our message hiding game between a challenger and an attacker. The game is parameterized by a security parameter $\kappa$.

1. The attacker sends a randomized and inputless Turing Machine algorithm $P$. The challenger runs the program on random coins and sends the output to the attacker. If the program takes more than $2^{2^\kappa}$ time to halt, the outputs halts the evaluation and outputs the empty string.[3]
2. The attacker sends a "challenge tag" $\mathsf{tag}^* \in [N]$.
3. The attacker makes repeated commitment queries com. If com.tag $= \mathsf{tag}^*$ the challenger responds with $\perp$. Otherwise it sends

$$\mathsf{CCA.Val(com)}.$$

4. For some $w$, the attacker sends two messages $m_0, m_1 \in \{0,1\}^w$.
5. The challenger flips a coin $b \in \{0,1\}$ and sends $\mathsf{com}^* = \mathsf{CCA.Com}(\mathsf{tag}^*, m_b; r)$ for randomly chosen $r$.
6. The attacker again makes repeated queries of commitment com. If com.tag $= \mathsf{tag}^*$ the challenger sends $\perp$. Otherwise it responds as

$$\mathsf{CCA.Val(com)}.$$

7. The attacker finally outputs a guess $b'$.

We define the attacker's advantage in the game to be $\Pr[b' = b] - \frac{1}{2}$ where the probability is over all the attacker and challenger's coins.

**Definition 4.** *An attack algorithm* $\mathcal{A}$ *is said to be e-conforming for some real value* $e > 0$ *if:*

1. $\mathcal{A}$ *is a (randomized) uniform algorithm.*
2. $\mathcal{A}$ *runs in polynomial time.*
3. *The program* $P$ *output by* $\mathcal{A}$ *in Step 1 of the game will always terminate in time* $p(2^{\kappa^e})$ *time and output at most* $q(\kappa)$ *bits for some polynomial functions* $p, q$ *(For all possible random tapes given to the program* $P$*).*

---

[3] The choice of $2^{2^\kappa}$ is somewhat arbitrary as the condition is in place so that the game is well defined on all $P$.

**Definition 5.** *A computation enabled CCA secure commitment scheme scheme given by algorithms* (CCA.Com, CCA.Val, CCA.Recover) *is said to be e-computation enabled CCA secure if for any e-conforming adversary $\mathcal{A}$ there exists a negligible function* negl($\cdot$) *such that the attacker's advantage in the game is* negl($\kappa$).

We also define another notion of security which we call "same tag" computation enabled secure for a weaker class of adversaries who only submit challenge queries that all have the same tag.

**Definition 6.** *A computation enabled CCA secure commitment scheme scheme given by algorithms* (CCA.Com, CCA.Val, CCA.Recover) *is said to be "same tag" e-computation enabled CCA secure if for any e-conforming adversary $\mathcal{A}$ which generates queries such that all commitment queries submitted by $\mathcal{A}$ are on the same tag, there exists a negligible function* negl($\cdot$) *such that the attacker's advantage in the game is* negl($\kappa$).

*Recovery From Randomness*

**Definition 7.** *We say that our CCA secure commitment scheme can be recovered from randomness if the following holds. For all $m \in \{0,1\}^*$, tag $\in [N]$, and $r$ we have that*

$$\text{CCA.Recover}(\text{CCA.Com}(1^\kappa, \text{tag}, m; r), r) = m.$$

*Claim.* Let (CCA.Com, CCA.Val) be a set of algorithms which satisfy any of Definition 1, Definition 2, Definition 3, Definition 5. Then there exists a set of algorithms (CCA$'$.Com, CCA$'$.Val, CCA$'$.Recover) which satisfy the same properties as well as Definition 7. We defer the construction and proof to our full version [12].

## 2.2 Connecting to Standard Security

We now connect our computation enabled definition to the standard notion of chosen commitment security. In particular, the standard notion of chosen commitment security is simply the computation enabled above, but removing the first step of submitting a program $P$. We prove two straightforward lemmas. The first shows that any computation enabled CCA secure commitment scheme is a standard secure one against uniform attackers. The second is that any non-uniformly secure standard scheme satisfies e-computation enabled security for any constant $e \geq 0$.

**Definition 8.** *A commitment scheme* (CCA.Com, CCA.Val, CCA.Recover) *is said to be CCA secure against uniform/non-uniform attackers if for any poly-time uniform/non-uniform adversary $\mathcal{A}$ there exists a negligible function* negl($\cdot$) *such that $\mathcal{A}$'s advantage in the above game with Step 1 removed is* negl($\kappa$).

**Definition 9.** *A commitment scheme* (CCA.Com, CCA.Val, CCA.Recover) *is said to be "same tag" CCA secure against uniform/non-uniform attackers if for any poly-time uniform/non-uniform adversary* $\mathcal{A}$ *such that all commitment queries submitted by* $\mathcal{A}$ *are on the same tag, there exists a negligible function* negl($\cdot$) *such that* $\mathcal{A}$*'s advantage in the above game with* Step 1 *removed is* negl($\kappa$).

*Claim.* If (CCA.Com, CCA.Val, CCA.Recover) is an $e$-computation enabled CCA secure commitment scheme for some $e$ as per Definition 5, then it is also a scheme that achieves standard CCA security against uniform poly-time attackers as per Definition 8.

*Proof.* This follows from the fact that any uniform attacker $\mathcal{A}$ in the standard security game with advantage $\epsilon(\kappa) = \epsilon$ immediately implies an $e$-conforming attacker $\mathcal{A}'$ with the same advantage where $\mathcal{A}'$ outputs a program $P$ that immediately halts and then runs $\mathcal{A}$.                                             □

*Claim.* If (CCA.Com, CCA.Val, CCA.Recover) achieves standard CCA security against *non-uniform* poly-time attackers as per Definition 8, then it is an $e$-computation enabled CCA secure commitment scheme for any $e$ as per Definition 5.

*Proof.* Suppose $\mathcal{A}$ is an $e$-conforming attacker for some $e$ with some advantage $\epsilon = \epsilon(\kappa)$. Then our non-uniform attacker $\mathcal{A}'$ can fix the random coins of $\mathcal{A}$ and to maximize its probability of success. Since now $\mathcal{A}$ is deterministic save for randomness produced by the challenger in step 5, this deterministically fixes the $P$ $\mathcal{A}$ sends, so $\mathcal{A}'$ can fix the coins of $P$ to maximize success. Thus, $\mathcal{A}'$ can simulate $\mathcal{A}$ given the above aforementioned random coins of $\mathcal{A}$ and the output of $P$, both of which are poly-bounded by the fact that $\mathcal{A}$ is $e$-conforming. Since all non-challenger randomness was non-uniformly fixed to maximize success, $\mathcal{A}'$ has at least advantage $\epsilon$ as well. By our definition of standard security hiding, the advantage of $\mathcal{A}'$ must be negligible, so $\mathcal{A}$'s advantage must be as well.     □

We remark that the above statements are also true for "same tag" conforming adversaries.

## 3  Tag Amplification

In this section we show a process from amplifying a computation enabled CCA commitment scheme for $N' = 4N$ tags to a scheme with $2^N$ tags. The amplification process imposes an overhead that is polynomial in $N$ and the size/time of the original commitment scheme. Thus it is important that $N$ be polynomially bounded in the security parameter.

Let (Small.Com, Small.Val, Small.Recover) be an $e$-computation enabled CCA commitment scheme for $N'(\kappa) = N' = 4N$ tags. We will assume tags take identities of the form $(i, \beta, \Gamma) \in [N] \times \{0,1\} \times \{0,1\}$ and that the Small.Com algorithm take in random coins of length $\ell(\kappa)$. In addition, for some constant $\delta \in (0,1)^4$ we assume a equivocal commitment without setup scheme (Equiv.Com, Equiv.Decom, Equiv.Equivocate) that is $T = 2^{\kappa^\delta}$ binding secure and statistically hiding.

We assume a hinting PRG scheme (Setup, Eval) that is $T = 2^{\kappa^\gamma}$ secure for some constant $\gamma \in (0,1)$ and has seed length $n(\kappa, |m|)$ (represented by $n$ for ease) and block output length of $\max(|m|, \ell \times N)$. For ease of notation we assume that HPRG.Eval(HPRG.pp, $s$, 0) $\in \{0,1\}^{|m|}$ and $\forall i \in [n]$, HPRG.Eval(HPRG.pp, $s$, $i$) $\in \{0,1\}^{\ell \cdot N}$.

Our transformation will produce three algorithms, CCA.Com, CCA.Val, and CCA.Recover which we prove $e'$-computation enabled where we require $e' = e \cdot \delta \geq 1$. We will also present a fourth algorithm CCA.ValAlt, which is only used in the proof. The algorithms will make use of the auxiliary subroutines CCA.Find and CCA.Check described below. CCA.ValAlt(tag*, com) $\rightarrow m \cup \perp$ is a deterministic inefficient algorithm that takes in a tag tag* and a commitment com and outputs either a message $m \in \{0,1\}^*$ or a reject symbol $\perp$. It will be used solely as an instrument in proving the scheme secure and not exported as part of the interface. We describe the transformation and due to space constraints analyze it's properties formally in [12] . We present the security games in the main body to give intuition on how our proof proceeds.

---

**CCA.Find($x'$, com)**

**Inputs:** Index $x' \in [N]$

Commitment com $= \left(\text{tag}, \text{HPRG.pp}, c, (\sigma_i, (c_{x,i,0}, c_{x,i,1})_{x \in [N]})_{i \in [n]})\right)$

**Output:** $\tilde{s} \in \{0,1\}^n$

- For each $i \in [n]$
  1. Let $\tilde{y}_i = \text{Small.Val}(c_{x',i,0})$
  2. Set $\tilde{z}_i = \text{Equiv.Decom}(\sigma_i, \tilde{y}_i)$. If $\tilde{z}_i = \perp$, set $\tilde{s}_i = 1$. Else, set $\tilde{s}_i = \tilde{z}_i$.
- Output $\tilde{s} = \tilde{s}_1, \tilde{s}_2, \ldots, \tilde{s}_n$.

---

**Fig. 1.** Routine CCA.Find

Transformation Amplify(Small $=$ (Small.Com, Small.Val, Small.Recover), HPRG, Equiv, $e'$) $\rightarrow$ NM $=$ (CCA.Com, CCA.Val, CCA.Recover) :

---

[4] The constant $\delta$ must be less than 1 in order to meet the requirement that the Equiv.Equivocate algorithm runs in time polynomial in $2^\kappa$.

CCA.Check($\tilde{s}$, com)

---

**Inputs:** Seed candidate $\tilde{s} = \tilde{s}_1, \tilde{s}_2, \ldots, \tilde{s}_n$

Commitment com $= \Big( \mathsf{tag}, \mathsf{HPRG.pp}, c, (\sigma_i, (c_{x,i,0}, c_{x,i,1})_{x \in [N]})_{i \in [n]}) \Big)$

**Output:** $\{0, 1\}$

- For $i \in [n]$
  1. Compute $(r_{1,i}, r_{2,i}, \ldots, r_{N,i}) = \mathsf{HPRG.Eval}(\mathsf{HPRG.pp}, \tilde{s}, i)$
  2. For $x \in [N]$
     (a) Let $\tilde{y}_i = \mathsf{Small.Recover}(c_{x,i,\tilde{s}_i}, r_{x,i})$. If $\tilde{y}_i = \bot$, output 0.
     (b) If $c_{x,i,\tilde{s}_i} \neq \mathsf{Small.Com}(1^\kappa, (x, \mathsf{tag}_x, \tilde{s}_i), \tilde{y}_i; r_{x,i})$, output 0.
     (c) If $\tilde{s}_i \neq \mathsf{Equiv.Decom}(\sigma_i, \tilde{y}_i)$, output 0.
- If all the above checks have passed, output 1.

**Fig. 2.** Routine CCA.Check

CCA.Com($1^\kappa, \mathsf{tag}, m \in \{0,1\}^*; r$) $\to$ com
  1. Compute $\kappa' = \kappa^{\frac{e'}{\delta}} = \kappa^e$. Compute $\kappa'' = \kappa'^{\frac{1}{\gamma}}$.[5]
  2. Sample $(\mathsf{HPRG.pp}, 1^n) \leftarrow \mathsf{HPRG.Setup}(\kappa'', 1^{\max(|m|, N \cdot \ell)})$.
  3. Sample $s = s_1 \ldots s_n \xleftarrow{R} \{0, 1\}^n$ as the seed of the hinting PRG.
  4. For all $i \in [n]$ run $\mathsf{Equiv.Com}(1^{\kappa'}, s_i) \to (\sigma_i, y_i)$.
  5. Let $r_{x,i}, \tilde{r}_{x,i} \in \{0,1\}^\ell$ be defined as follows:
  6. For $i \in [n]$
     (a) Compute $(r_{1,i}, r_{2,i}, \ldots, r_{N,i}) = \mathsf{HPRG.Eval}(\mathsf{HPRG.pp}, s, i)$
     (b) Sample $(\tilde{r}_{1,i}, \tilde{r}_{2,i}, \ldots, \tilde{r}_{N,i}) \xleftarrow{R} \{0, 1\}^{N \cdot \ell}$
  7. Compute $c = m \oplus \mathsf{HPRG.Eval}(\mathsf{HPRG.pp}, s, 0)$
  8. For $i \in [n], x \in [N]$
     (a) If $s_i = 0$
        i. $c_{x,i,0} = \mathsf{Small.Com}(1^\kappa, (x, \mathsf{tag}_x, 0), \mathsf{msg} = y_i; r_{x,i})$
        ii. $c_{x,i,1} = \mathsf{Small.Com}(1^\kappa, (x, \mathsf{tag}_x, 1), \mathsf{msg} = y_i; \tilde{r}_{x,i})$
     (b) If $s_i = 1$
        i. $c_{x,i,0} = \mathsf{Small.Com}(1^\kappa, (x, \mathsf{tag}_x, 0), \mathsf{msg} = y_i; \tilde{r}_{x,i})$
        ii. $c_{x,i,1} = \mathsf{Small.Com}(1^\kappa, (x, \mathsf{tag}_x, 1), \mathsf{msg} = y_i; r_{x,i})$
  9. Output com $= \Big( \mathsf{tag}, \mathsf{HPRG.pp}, c, (\sigma_i, (c_{x,i,0}, c_{x,i,1})_{x \in [N]})_{i \in [n]}) \Big)$ as the commitment. All of the randomness is used as the decommitment string.
CCA.Val(com) $\to m \cup \bot$
  1. Set $\tilde{s} = \mathsf{CCA.Find}(1, \mathsf{com})$.
  2. If $\mathsf{CCA.Check}(\tilde{s}, \mathsf{com}) = 0$ output $\bot$.
  3. Output $c \oplus \mathsf{HPRG.Eval}(\mathsf{HPRG.pp}, \tilde{s}, 0)$.
CCA.ValAlt($\mathsf{tag}^*, \mathsf{com}$) $\to m \cup \bot$
  1. If $\mathsf{com.tag} = \mathsf{tag}^*$, output $\bot$.
  2. Let $x^*$ be the smallest index where the bits of $\mathsf{tag}^*, \mathsf{tag}$ differ.

---

[5] $\delta$ and $\gamma$ are known from the security guarantees of $\mathsf{Equiv}, \mathsf{HPRG}$ respectively.

3. Set $\tilde{s} = \mathsf{CCA.Find}(x^*, \mathsf{com})$.
4. If $\mathsf{CCA.Check}(\tilde{s}, \mathsf{com}) = 0$ output $\bot$.
5. Output $c \oplus \mathsf{HPRG.Eval}(\mathsf{HPRG.pp}, \tilde{s}, 0)$.

$\mathsf{CCA.Recover}(\mathsf{com}, r) \to m \cup \bot$

1. From $r$, parse the seed $s$ of the Hinting PRG.
2. From $\mathsf{com}$, parse the commitment component $c$ and the public parameter $\mathsf{HPRG.pp}$.
3. Output $c \oplus \mathsf{HPRG.Eval}(\mathsf{HPRG.pp}, s, 0)$

## 3.1 Proof of Security

We now prove security by showing that our transformation leads to an $e' = e \cdot \delta$-computation enabled CCA commitment scheme. We do so in a sequence of security games.

In each proof step we will need to keep in mind that the attacker will be allowed to ask for a program $P$ that runs in time polynomial in $2^{\kappa^{e'}}$ where $e' = e \cdot \delta$. This will be satisfied in one of two ways. In the proof steps that rely on the hinting PRG security or the equivocal commitment without setup scheme we leverage the that that these are subexponentially secure primitives. For relying on security of the equivocal commitment without setup we use security parameter $\kappa' = \kappa^e$, it is secure against attackers that run in time polynomial in $2^{(\kappa')^\delta} = 2^{\kappa^{e\delta}} = 2^{\kappa^{e'}}$ time. Thus our reduction algorithm in these steps can satisfy the requirement by running $P$ itself and still be a legitimate $2^{(\kappa')^\delta}$ time attacker. For relying on security of the hinting PRG scheme, we use security parameter $\kappa'' = \kappa'^{\frac{1}{\gamma}}$, it is secure against attackers that run in time polynomial in $2^{\kappa'}$. Thus our reduction algorithm can run $P$ and the equivocate algorithm.

The second situation is when we rely on the security of the smaller tag space $e$-computation enabled scheme. In this case the reduction will need to be polynomial time so there is no way for it to directly run a program $P$ that takes $2^{\kappa^{e'}}$ time. However, in this case it can satisfy the requirement by creating a program $\tilde{P}$ and passing this onto the security game of the $e$-computation enabled challenger. The program $\tilde{P}$ will run $P$ as well as $n$ invocations of the $\mathsf{Equiv.Equivocate}$ algorithm. We present our sequence of games below, and proofs of indistinguishability between these games can be found in the full version.

*Game 0.* This is the original message hiding game between a challenger and an attacker for $e' = e \cdot \delta$ conforming attackers. The game is parameterized by a security parameter $\kappa$.

1. The attacker sends a randomized and inputless Turing Machine algorithm $P$. The challenger runs the program on random coins and sends the output to the attacker. If the program takes more than $2^{2^\kappa}$ time to halt, the outputs halts the evaluation and outputs the empty string.
2. The attacker sends a "challenge tag" $\mathsf{tag}^* \in \{0, 1\}^N$.

3. **Pre Challenge Phase:** The attacker makes repeated queries commitments

$$\mathsf{com} = \left(\mathsf{tag}, \mathsf{HPRG.pp}, c, (\sigma_i, (c_{x,i,0}, c_{x,i,1})_{x \in [N]})_{i \in [n]}\right).$$

If $\mathsf{tag} = \mathsf{tag}^*$ the challenger responds with $\perp$. Otherwise responds as

$$\mathsf{CCA.Val(com)}.$$

4. **Challenge Phase**
    (a) The attacker sends two messages $m_0^*, m_1^* \in \{0,1\}^w$
    (b) **Part 1:**
        - Compute $\kappa' = \kappa^e$.
        - Compute $\kappa'' = \kappa'^{\frac{1}{\gamma}}$.
        - Sample $(\mathsf{HPRG.pp}^*, 1^n) \leftarrow \mathsf{HPRG.Setup}(\kappa'', 1^{\max(w, N \cdot \ell)})$.
        - Sample $s^* = s_1^* \ldots s_n^* \xleftarrow{R} \{0,1\}^n$ as the seed of the HPRG.
        - Let $r_{x,i}^*, \tilde{r}_{x,i}^* \in \{0,1\}^\ell$ be defined as follows:
        - For $i \in [n]$
            i. Compute $(r_{1,i}^*, r_{2,i}^*, \ldots, r_{N,i}^*) = \mathsf{HPRG.Eval}(\mathsf{HPRG.pp}^*, s^*, i)$
            ii. Sample $(\tilde{r}_{1,i}^*, \tilde{r}_{2,i}^*, \ldots, \tilde{r}_{N,i}^*) \xleftarrow{R} \{0,1\}^{N \cdot \ell}$
        - For all $i \in [n]$ run $\mathsf{Equiv.Com}(1^{\kappa'}, s_i^*) \to (\sigma_i^*, y_i^*)$.
    (c) **Part 2:**
        - It chooses $b \in \{0,1\}$ and sets $c^* = \mathsf{HPRG.Eval}(\mathsf{HPRG.pp}^*, s^*, 0) \oplus m_b^*$.
        - For $i \in [n]$, $x \in [N]$
            i. If $s_i^* = 0$
                A. $c_{x,i,0}^* = \mathsf{Small.Com}(1^\kappa, (x, \mathsf{tag}_x^*, 0), y_i^*; r_{x,i}^*)$
                B. $c_{x,i,1}^* = \mathsf{Small.Com}(1^\kappa, (x, \mathsf{tag}_x^*, 1), y_i^*; \tilde{r}_{x,i}^*)$
            ii. If $s_i^* = 1$
                A. $c_{x,i,0}^* = \mathsf{Small.Com}(1^\kappa, (x, \mathsf{tag}_x^*, 0), y_i^*; \tilde{r}_{x,i}^*)$
                B. $c_{x,i,1}^* = \mathsf{Small.Com}(1^\kappa, (x, \mathsf{tag}_x^*, 1), y_i^*; r_{x,i}^*)$
        - Finally, it sends $\mathsf{com}^* = (\mathsf{tag}^*, \mathsf{HPRG.pp}^*, c^*, (\sigma_i^*, (c_{x,i,0}^*, c_{x,i,1}^*)_{x \in [N]})_{i \in [n]}))$ as the commitment. All of the randomness is used as the decommitment string.
5. **Post Challenge Phase:** The attacker again makes commitment queries com. If $\mathsf{tag} = \mathsf{tag}^*$ the challenger responds with $\perp$. Otherwise it responds as

$$\mathsf{CCA.Val(com)}.$$

6. The attacker finally outputs a guess $b'$.

*Game 1.* This is same as Game 0, except that during the **Pre Challenge Phase** and **Post Challenge Phase**, challenger uses $\mathsf{CCA.ValAlt(tag^*, com)}$ to answer queries.

*Game 2.* In this game in **Part 1** the $(\sigma_i^*, y_i^*)$ are now generated from the Equiv.Equivocate algorithm instead of the Equiv.Com algorithm.

- Compute $\kappa' = \kappa^e$, $\kappa'' = \kappa'^{\frac{1}{\gamma}}$.
- Sample $(\mathsf{HPRG.pp}^*, 1^n) \leftarrow \mathsf{HPRG.Setup}(\kappa'', 1^{\max(w, N \cdot \ell)})$.
- Sample $s^* = s_1^* \ldots s_n^* \xleftarrow{R} \{0,1\}^n$ as the seed of the hinting PRG.
- Let $r_{x,i}^*, \tilde{r}_{x,i}^* \in \{0,1\}^\ell$ be defined as follows, for $i \in [n]$
    1. Compute $(r_{1,i}^*, r_{2,i}^*, \ldots, r_{N,i}^*) = \mathsf{HPRG.Eval}(\mathsf{HPRG.pp}^*, s^*, i)$
    2. Sample $(\tilde{r}_{1,i}^*, \tilde{r}_{2,i}^*, \ldots, \tilde{r}_{N,i}^*) \xleftarrow{R} \{0,1\}^{N \cdot \ell}$
- For all $i \in [n]$ run $\mathsf{Equiv.Equivocate}(1^{\kappa'}) \to (\sigma_i^*, y_{i,0}^*, y_{i,1}^*)$.
- For all $i \in [n]$, set $y_i^* = y_{i,s_i^*}^*$.

*Game 3.* In this game in **Part 2** we move to $c_{x,i,0}^*$ committing to $y_{i,0}^*$ and $c_{x,i,1}^*$ committing to $y_{i,1}^*$ for all $x \in [N], i \in [n]$ independently of $s_i^*$.

- For $i \in [n]$, $x \in [N]$
    1. If $s_i^* = 0$
        1. $c_{x,i,0}^* = \mathsf{Small.Com}(1^\kappa, (x, \mathsf{tag}_x^*, 0), y_{i,0}^*; r_{x,i}^*)$
        2. $c_{x,i,1}^* = \mathsf{Small.Com}(1^\kappa, (x, \mathsf{tag}_x^*, 1), y_{i,1}^*; \tilde{r}_{x,i}^*)$
    2. If $s_i^* = 1$
        (a) $c_{x,i,0}^* = \mathsf{Small.Com}(1^\kappa, (x, \mathsf{tag}_x^*, 0), y_{i,0}^*; \tilde{r}_{x,i}^*)$
        (b) $c_{x,i,1}^* = \mathsf{Small.Com}(1^\kappa, (x, \mathsf{tag}_x^*, 1), y_{i,1}^*; r_{x,i}^*)$

*Game 4.* In all $r_{x,i}^*$ values are chosen uniformly at random (insted of choosing from $\mathsf{HPRG.Eval}(\mathsf{HPRG.pp}^*, s^*, i)$) and $c^*$ is also chosen uniformly at random (instead of choosing $\mathsf{HPRG.Eval}(\mathsf{HPRG.pp}^*, s^*, 0) \oplus m_b^*$).

# 4    Compiling Our Transformations

We conclude by showing how to compile our transformations. Suppose that we begin with a base scheme supporting $32 \cdot \mathsf{ilog}(c, \kappa)^6$ tags for some constant $c$ that is secure against non-uniform attackers that make same tag queries. We will compile this into a scheme supporting $16 \cdot 2^\kappa$ space against uniform attackers with no same tag restriction.

We apply the transformation that removes the same tag restriction [12] to the base scheme which divides the tag space supported by 2 to get a scheme with $16 \cdot \mathsf{ilog}(c, \kappa)$ sized tag space, but removes the same-tag restriction. The we apply the Sect. 3 tag amplification process $c + 1$ times. Recall the transformation takes a $N' = 4N$ scheme to a scheme supporting $2^N$ tags. Since $16/4 = 4$ and $2^4 = 16$ the effect is of each application is to remove one of the lg iterations and keep the factor of 16. Since the transformation imposes a polynomial blowup on

---

[6] For brevity, $\mathsf{ilog}(c, \kappa)$ denotes $\underbrace{\lg \lg \cdots \lg(\kappa)}_{c \text{ times}}$.

the underlying scheme and since it is applied a constant number of times, the size of the resulting scheme is also polynomial.

Below we give a formal construction utilizing the transformations RecoverRandom($\cdot$) presented in [12] , OneToMany($\cdot$) presented in [12] , and Amplify($\cdot$) presented in Section 3. Since we are transforming a scheme that takes $32 \cdot \mathrm{ilog}(c, \kappa)$ tags to $16 \cdot 2^\kappa$ tags, we need to use the amplification transformation $c + 1$ times. OneToMany($\cdot$), Amplify($\cdot$) transformations take in a $e$-computation enabled scheme and output a $e' = e \cdot \delta$-computation enabled scheme where $e' \geq 1$ and $\delta \in (0, 1)$ and the equivocal commitment scheme is $2^{\kappa^\delta}$ hiding secure. We set OneToMany($\cdot$) to take a $e \cdot \delta^{-c-2}$-computation enabled and output a $e \cdot \delta^{-c-1}$-computation enabled scheme. Amplify($\cdot$) takes a $e \cdot \delta^{-c-1}$-computation enabled scheme and outputs a $e$-computation enabled scheme after $c+1$ transformations.

CompiledAmplify(BaseCCA = (BaseCCA.Com, BaseCCA.Val), HPRG, Equiv, $e$)
1. RandomBaseCCA $\leftarrow$ RecoverRandom(BaseCCA)
2. Let $\delta$ be the constant so that Equiv is $2^{\kappa^\delta}$ binding secure and $c$ be the constant such that the base scheme takes $32 \cdot \mathrm{ilog}(c, \kappa)$.
3. AmplifiedCCA$^0$ $\leftarrow$ OneToMany(RandomBaseCCA, HPRG, Equiv, $e \cdot \delta^{-c-1}$).
4. For $i \in [c + 1]$
    (a) AmplifiedCCA$^i$ $\leftarrow$ Amplify(AmplifiedCCA$^{i-1}$, HPRG, Equiv, $e \cdot \delta^{i-c-1}$)
5. Output (AmplifiedCCA$^{c+1}$.Com, AmplifiedCCA$^{c+1}$.Val)

Below we analyze CompiledAmplify by stating theorems on correctness, efficiency and security. Due to space constraints, we defer the proofs of these theorems to the full version of our paper.

**Theorem 3.** *For every $\kappa \in \mathbb{N}$, let BaseCCA = (BaseCCA.Com, BaseCCA.Val) be a perfectly correct CCA commitment scheme by Definition 1. Let Equiv = (Equiv.Com, Equiv.Decom, Equiv.Equivocate) be a perfectly correct equivocal commitment scheme. Then, we have that the scheme CompiledAmplify(BaseCCA, HPRG, Equiv, $e$) is a perfectly correct CCA commitment scheme.*

**Theorem 4.** *For every $\kappa \in \mathbb{N}$, let BaseCCA = (BaseCCA.Com, BaseCCA.Val) be an efficient CCA commitment scheme by Definition 2 with tag space $32 \cdot \mathrm{ilog}(c, \kappa)$. Let Equiv = (Equiv.Com, Equiv.Decom, Equiv.Equivocate) be an efficient equivocal commitment scheme. Then, CompiledAmplify (BaseCCA, HPRG, Equiv, $e$) is an efficient CCA commitment scheme.*

**Theorem 5.** *For every $\kappa \in \mathbb{N}$, let BaseCCA = (BaseCCA.Com, BaseCCA.Val) be a CCA commitment scheme that is hiding against non-uniform "same tag" adversaries according to Definition 9 for tag space $32 \cdot \mathrm{ilog}(c, \kappa)$. HPRG = (HPRG.Setup, HPRG.Eval) be a hinting PRG scheme that is $T = 2^{\kappa^\gamma}$ secure for $\gamma \in (0, 1)$. Equiv be an equivocal commitment without setup scheme that is $T = 2^{\kappa^\delta}$ binding and statistically hiding for some constant $\delta \in (0, 1)$. Then, CompiledAmplify(BaseCCA, HPRG, Equiv, $e$) is a $e$-computation enabled CCA commitment scheme that is hiding against uniform adversaries according to Definition 8 for tag space $16 \cdot 2^\kappa$.*

We import the following theorems about instantiating base schemes, from prior work.

**Theorem 6.** *[21] For every constant $c > 0$, there exist CCA secure commitments satisfying Definition 9 against non-uniform adversaries, with tag space $(c \lg \lg \lg \kappa)$, that make black-box use of subexponential quantum hard one-way functions and subexponential classically hard one-way functions in* BQP.

We point out that while [21] prove that their construction satisfies non-malleability with respect to commitment, their proof technique also directly exhibits same-tag CCA security against non-uniform adversaries.

Combining this theorem with Theorem 5 yields the following corollary.

**Corollary 1.** *There exists a constant $e > 0$ for which there exists a perfectly correct and polynomially efficient e-computation enabled CCA secure commitment satisfying Definition 5 against uniform adversaries, with tag space $2^\kappa$ for security parameter $\kappa$, that makes black-box use of subexponential quantum hard one-way functions, subexponential classically hard one-way functions in* BQP, *subexponential hinting PRGs and subexponential keyless collision-resistant hash functions.*

Alternatively, [28] showed that for every constant $c > 0$, assuming a family of $(c \lg \lg \lg \kappa)$ time-lock puzzles that are simultaneously increasingly depth-robust and decreasingly time-robust, there exist CCA secure commitments satisfying Definition 9 against non-uniform adversaries, with tag space $(c \lg \lg \lg \kappa)$. Our compiler applies to their base scheme as well, yielding $e$-computation enabled CCA secure commitment satisfying Definition 5 against uniform adversaries, with tag space $2^\kappa$, that make black-box use of the LPS base scheme.

Finally, we point out that while all our formal theorems discuss CCA security, our transformations also apply as is to the case of amplifying parallel CCA security (equivalently, concurrent non-malleability w.r.t. commitment). That is, given a base scheme that is only same-tag parallel CCA secure (or non-malleable w.r.t. commitment) for small tags, our transformations yield a scheme for all tags that is parallel CCA secure (or concurrent non-malleable w.r.t. commitment) for tags in $2^\kappa$, without the same tag restriction.

# References

1. Barak, B.: Constant-round coin-tossing with a man in the middle or realizing the shared random string model. In: FOCS (2002)
2. Barak, B., Ong, S.J., Vadhan, S.P.: Derandomization in cryptography. SIAM J. Comput. **37**, 380–400 (2007)
3. Bitansky, N., Kalai, Y.T., Paneth, O.: Multi-collision resistance: a paradigm for keyless hash functions. In: STOC (2018)
4. Bitansky, N., Lin, H.: One-message zero knowledge and non-malleable commitments. In: Beimel, A., Dziembowski, S. (eds.) TCC 2018. LNCS, vol. 11239, pp. 209–234. Springer, Cham (2018). https://doi.org/10.1007/978-3-030-03807-6_8

5. Broadnax, B., Fetzer, V., Müller-Quade, J., Rupp, A.: Non-malleability vs. CCA-security: the case of commitments. In: Abdalla, M., Dahab, R. (eds.) PKC 2018. LNCS, vol. 10770, pp. 312–337. Springer, Cham (2018). https://doi.org/10.1007/978-3-319-76581-5_11
6. Canetti, R., Lin, H., Pass, R.: Adaptive hardness and composable security in the plain model from standard assumptions. In: FOCS (2010)
7. Choi, S.G., Dachman-Soled, D., Malkin, T., Wee, H.: Simple, black-box constructions of adaptively secure protocols. In: Reingold, O. (ed.) TCC 2009. LNCS, vol. 5444, pp. 387–402. Springer, Heidelberg (2009). https://doi.org/10.1007/978-3-642-00457-5_23
8. Ciampi, M., Ostrovsky, R., Siniscalchi, L., Visconti, I.: Concurrent non-malleable commitments (and more) in 3 rounds. In: Robshaw, M., Katz, J. (eds.) CRYPTO 2016. LNCS, vol. 9816, pp. 270–299. Springer, Heidelberg (2016). https://doi.org/10.1007/978-3-662-53015-3_10
9. Ciampi, M., Ostrovsky, R., Siniscalchi, L., Visconti, I.: Four-round concurrent non-malleable commitments from one-way functions. In: Katz, J., Shacham, H. (eds.) CRYPTO 2017. LNCS, vol. 10402, pp. 127–157. Springer, Cham (2017). https://doi.org/10.1007/978-3-319-63715-0_5
10. Damgård, I.B., Pedersen, T.P., Pfitzmann, B.: On the existence of statistically hiding bit commitment schemes and fail-stop signatures. In: Stinson, D.R. (ed.) CRYPTO 1993. LNCS, vol. 773, pp. 250–265. Springer, Heidelberg (1994). https://doi.org/10.1007/3-540-48329-2_22
11. Dolev, D., Dwork, C., Naor, M.: Non-malleable cryptography (extended abstract). In: STOC (1991)
12. Garg, R., Khurana, D., Lu, G., Waters, B.: Black-box non-interactive non-malleable commitments (2020). https://eprint.iacr.org/2020/1197
13. Goyal, R., Vusirikala, S., Waters, B.: New constructions of hinting PRGs, OWFs with encryption, and more. IACR Cryptology ePrint Archive (2019)
14. Goyal, V.: Constant round non-malleable protocols using one-way functions. In: STOC (2011)
15. Goyal, V., Lee, C.K., Ostrovsky, R., Visconti, I.: Constructing non-malleable commitments: a black-box approach. In: FOCS (2012)
16. Goyal, V., Pandey, O., Richelson, S.: Textbook non-malleable commitments. In: STOC (2016)
17. Goyal, V., Richelson, S.: Non-malleable commitments using Goldreich-Levin list decoding. In: FOCS (2019)
18. Goyal, V., Richelson, S., Rosen, A., Vald, M.: An algebraic approach to non-malleability. In: FOCS (2014)
19. Groth, J., Ostrovsky, R., Sahai, A.: New techniques for noninteractive zero-knowledge. J. ACM 59, 1–35 (2012)
20. Halevi, S., Micali, S.: Practical and provably-secure commitment schemes from collision-free hashing. In: Koblitz, N. (ed.) CRYPTO 1996. LNCS, vol. 1109, pp. 201–215. Springer, Heidelberg (1996). https://doi.org/10.1007/3-540-68697-5_16
21. Kalai, Y.T., Khurana, D.: Non-interactive non-malleability from quantum supremacy. In: Boldyreva, A., Micciancio, D. (eds.) CRYPTO 2019. LNCS, vol. 11694, pp. 552–582. Springer, Cham (2019). https://doi.org/10.1007/978-3-030-26954-8_18
22. Khurana, D.: Round optimal concurrent non-malleability from polynomial hardness. In: Kalai, Y., Reyzin, L. (eds.) TCC 2017. LNCS, vol. 10678, pp. 139–171. Springer, Cham (2017). https://doi.org/10.1007/978-3-319-70503-3_5

23. Khurana, D., Sahai, A.: How to achieve non-malleability in one or two rounds. In: FOCS (2017)
24. Kitagawa, F., Matsuda, T., Tanaka, K.: CCA security and trapdoor functions via key-dependent-message security. In: Boldyreva, A., Micciancio, D. (eds.) CRYPTO 2019. LNCS, vol. 11694, pp. 33–64. Springer, Cham (2019). https://doi.org/10.1007/978-3-030-26954-8_2
25. Koppula, V., Waters, B.: Realizing chosen ciphertext security generically in attribute-based encryption and predicate encryption. In: Boldyreva, A., Micciancio, D. (eds.) CRYPTO 2019. LNCS, vol. 11693, pp. 671–700. Springer, Cham (2019). https://doi.org/10.1007/978-3-030-26951-7_23
26. Lin, H., Pass, R.: Non-malleability amplification. In: STOC (2009)
27. Lin, H., Pass, R.: Constant-round non-malleable commitments from any one-way function. In: STOC (2011)
28. Lin, H., Pass, R., Soni, P.: Two-round and non-interactive concurrent non-malleable commitments from time-lock puzzles. In: FOCS (2017)
29. Lin, H., Pass, R., Venkitasubramaniam, M.: Concurrent non-malleable commitments from any one-way function. In: Canetti, R. (ed.) TCC 2008. LNCS, vol. 4948, pp. 571–588. Springer, Heidelberg (2008). https://doi.org/10.1007/978-3-540-78524-8_31
30. Pandey, O., Pass, R., Vaikuntanathan, V.: Adaptive one-way functions and applications. In: Wagner, D. (ed.) CRYPTO 2008. LNCS, vol. 5157, pp. 57–74. Springer, Heidelberg (2008). https://doi.org/10.1007/978-3-540-85174-5_4
31. Pass, R., Rosen, A.: Concurrent non-malleable commitments. In: FOCS (2005)
32. Pass, R., Rosen, A.: New and improved constructions of nonmalleable cryptographic protocols. SIAM J. Comput. 38, 702–752 (2008)
33. Pass, R., shelat, Vaikuntanathan, V.: Construction of a non-malleable encryption scheme from any semantically secure one. In: Dwork, C. (ed.) CRYPTO 2006. LNCS, vol. 4117, pp. 271–289. Springer, Heidelberg (2006). https://doi.org/10.1007/11818175_16
34. Pass, R., Wee, H.: Constant-round non-malleable commitments from sub-exponential one-way functions. In: Gilbert, H. (ed.) EUROCRYPT 2010. LNCS, vol. 6110, pp. 638–655. Springer, Heidelberg (2010). https://doi.org/10.1007/978-3-642-13190-5_32
35. Wee, H.: Black-box, round-efficient secure computation via non-malleability amplification. In: FOCS (2010)

# Non-interactive Distributional Indistinguishability (NIDI) and Non-malleable Commitments

Dakshita Khurana[(✉)]

University of Illinois, Urbana-Champaign, Urbana, USA
dakshita@illinois.edu

**Abstract.** We introduce *non-interactive distributionally indistinguishable arguments* (NIDI) to address a significant weakness of NIWI proofs: namely, the lack of meaningful secrecy when proving statements about NP languages with unique witnesses.

NIDI arguments allow a prover $\mathcal{P}$ to send a single message to verifier $\mathcal{V}$, from which $\mathcal{V}$ obtains a sample $d$ from a (secret) distribution $\mathcal{D}$, together with a proof of membership of $d$ in an NP language $\mathcal{L}$.

The soundness guarantee is that if the sample $d$ obtained by the verifier $\mathcal{V}$ is not in $\mathcal{L}$, then $\mathcal{V}$ outputs $\perp$. The privacy guarantee is that secrets about the distribution remain hidden: for every pair of (sufficiently) hard-to-distinguish distributions $\mathcal{D}_0$ and $\mathcal{D}_1$ with support in NP language $\mathcal{L}$, a NIDI that outputs samples from $\mathcal{D}_0$ with proofs of membership in $\mathcal{L}$ is indistinguishable from one that outputs samples from $\mathcal{D}_1$ with proofs of membership in $\mathcal{L}$.

- We build NIDI arguments for superpolynomially hard-to-distinguish distributions, assuming sub-exponential indistinguishability obfuscation and sub-exponentially secure (variants of) one-way functions.
- We demonstrate preliminary applications of NIDI and of our techniques to obtaining the first (relaxed) non-interactive constructions in the plain model, from well-founded assumptions, of:
  • Commit-and-prove that provably hides the committed message
  • CCA-secure commitments against non-uniform adversaries.

The commit phase of our commitment schemes consists of a single message from the committer to the receiver, followed by a randomized output by the receiver (that need not be returned to the committer).

## 1 Introduction

*Can one non-interactively commit to a plaintext and prove that it satisfies a predicate (e.g., the plaintext is larger than 0) while also ensuring that the plaintext is hidden?*

Work done in part during a visit to the Simons institute, Berkeley. This material is based upon work supported in part by DARPA under Contract No. HR001120C0024. Any opinions, findings and conclusions or recommendations expressed in this material are those of the author(s) and do not necessarily reflect the views of the United States Government or DARPA.

A. Canteaut and F.-X. Standaert (Eds.): EUROCRYPT 2021, LNCS 12698, pp. 186–215, 2021.
https://doi.org/10.1007/978-3-030-77883-5_7

More generally, can a prover send a statement to a verifier and demonstrate that the statement is true without revealing secrets about it? An *interactive* solution to this problem can be obtained via the use of zero-knowledge proofs. These were first introduced in an influential work of Goldwasser, Micali and Rackoff [38], and it was subsequently shown that all languages in NP admit *interactive* ZK proofs [36]. An interactive proof is said to be zero-knowledge if there exist a simulator that can simulate the behavior of any verifier, without having access to the prover, in such a way that its output is indistinguishable from the output of the verifier after having interacted with an honest prover.

Understanding the round complexity of zero knowledge has been an important problem. In particular, zero-knowledge arguments for languages outside BPP, and without any trusted setup, are known to require at least three messages of interaction [37]. This leads to a natural question: *what meaningful relaxations of zero-knowledge are achievable non-interactively and without setup?*

*Existing Relaxations of Zero-Knowledge.* Towards addressing this question, several relaxations of zero-knowledge have been studied over the years.

- **Weak Zero-Knowledge** [28] relaxes zero-knowledge by switching the order of quantifiers. Specficially, weak zero-knowledge requires that for every verifier and every *distinguisher*, there exists a *distinguisher-dependent simulator* that fools this specific pair[1].
  Weak zero-knowledge is known to require at least two messages [37].
- **Witness Hiding** [30] loosely guarantees that a malicious verifier cannot recover a witness from a proof unless the witness can be efficiently computed from the statement alone.
- **Strong Witness Indistinguishability (Strong WI)** [35] requires that for two indistinguishable statement distributions $\mathcal{D}_0, \mathcal{D}_1$, a proof (or argument) for statement $d_0 \leftarrow \mathcal{D}_0$ must be indistinguishable from a proof (or argument) for statement $d_1 \leftarrow \mathcal{D}_1$.
- **Witness indistinguishability (WI)** [30] ensures that proofs of the *same statement* generated using different witnesses are indistinguishable. WI does not hold for statements sampled from different distributions, or statements that have a unique witness associated with them.

Two-message variants of weak zero-knowledge, witness hiding and strong WI have been obtained by [5,12,25,47,57]. But so far, the only relaxation known to be achievable *non-interactively* from well-studied assumptions, is witness indistinguishability. Non-interactive witness indistinguishable proofs (NIWIs) have been obtained by [8,15,44] under various assumptions. While NIWIs are quite natural and are useful as a building blocks in some applications, they are often quite limited. In (common) scenarios like committing to a secret message and proving a predicate about it – where statements being proven often have unique witnesses – the witness indistinguishability guarantee is meaningless.

---

[1] There are several variants of this definition strengthening/weakening different aspects [22,28].

*Commit-and-Prove.* In a "commit-and-prove" protocol, a *prover* commits to (or encrypts) one or more messages, and would like to prove that the secret message(s) satisfy a predicate.

A simplification of the most basic privacy guarantee required in these applications is the following: for every pair of messages $(m_0, m_1)$ that satisfy a (polynomial-time computable) predicate $\phi$ (i.e. $\phi(m_0) = \phi(m_1) = 1$), the following two distributions must be computationally indistinguishable:

$$\left(c_0 = \mathsf{Com}(m_0; r), \Pi_{c_0 \in \mathcal{L}_\phi}\right) \text{ and } \left(c_1 = \mathsf{Com}(m_1; r), \Pi_{c_1 \in \mathcal{L}_\phi}\right)$$

where $\mathsf{Com}$ denotes a perfectly binding commitment (or encryption), and $\Pi_{c \in \mathcal{L}_\phi}$ denotes a proof of the statement $c \in \mathcal{L}_\phi$ where

$$\mathcal{L}_\phi = \{c : \exists (m, r) \text{ such that } (c = \mathsf{Com}(m; r)) \wedge (\phi(m) = 1)\}.$$

In other words, any distributions $c_0 = \mathsf{Com}(m_0; r)$ and $c_1 = \mathsf{Com}(m_1; r)$ that are computationally indistinguishable, must remain indistinguishable even given proofs of membership in $\mathcal{L}_\phi$. Here $\phi$ is any efficiently computable predicate of the message, e.g., $\phi(m) = 1$ if and only if $m > 10$.

*The Insufficiency Of NIWIs.* Because the statements in question clearly have unique witnesses, using NIWIs to generate the proof $\Pi_{c \in \mathcal{L}_\phi}$ does not guarantee that the secret message remains hidden. We note that the notion of *strong witness indistinguishability* would suffice, but whether strong WI can be achieved non-interactively remains an important open problem.

All known constructions [5,12,25,47,57] of *two-message* strong WI arguments follow variants of the common FLS [29] paradigm. Here, the prover provides a WI proof that:

"Either $x \in \mathcal{L}$ or the prover knows some trapdoor".

The trapdoor is designed to be hard for a (cheating) prover to compute, but easy for a simulator. Security is argued by having the simulator extract the secret trapdoor in polynomial or superpolynomial time, and use this trapdoor to generate the proof, instead of relying on a witness for $x$.

In settings where the verifier can send (at least) one message to the prover, the verifier's message can be used to set up a trapdoor, e.g., by sampling $f(z)$ for a one-way permutation $f$ and random trapdoor $z$ [57]. The trapdoor $z$ can be obtained by a simulator non-uniformly or in superpolynomial time (or even in polynomial time via specialized recent techniques [12,25,47]).

*Establishing Trapdoors in the Non-interactive Setting.* In the non-interactive setting, since the verifier does not send any message to the prover, it becomes much more challenging to establish a trapdoor of the form described above, that is easy for a simulator to compute but not for a cheating prover.

Nevertheless, there have been exciting prior attempts. In particular, Barak and Pass [9] obtain variants of one-message zero-knowledge with nonuniform simulation and soundness against uniform provers. They rely on problems that are hard for uniform algorithms (e.g., keyless collision-resistant hash functions) to set up a trapdoor that no *uniform prover* can obtain. Bitansky and Lin [13] propose a clever extension of this to the non-uniform setting by relying on problems that are hard for algorithms with a polynomial amount of non-uniformity. Assuming keyless collision-resistant hash functions with security against non-uniform adversaries, they obtain one-message zero-knowledge with superpolynomial simulation and *weak soundness against non-uniform provers*. They guarantee that the number of false statements a polynomial-time non-uniform prover can convince the verifier to accept is not much larger than its non-uniform advice.

In summary, known constructions of meaningful non-interactive secrecy-preserving arguments either (1) are not adequately sound and rely on non-standard hardness assumptions, or (2) do not provide meaningful secrecy, especially when considering statements with unique witnesses.

*Bottlenecked Applications.* The lack of non-interactive secrecy-preserving proofs for statements with unique witnesses has led to the need for non-standard assumptions in additional applications besides the example commit-and-prove scenario described above.

A prominent example are *non-interactive non-malleable commitments*: for which the only known constructions [13,31,48,54,56] either achieve non-standard forms of security or rely on relatively less standard assumptions like keyless collision resistant hashing with security against non-uniform adversaries. Eliminating non-standard assumptions appears to require appropriate non-interactive secrecy-preserving arguments, which were so far not known under well-founded assumptions. In the following section, we outline our contributions that aim to remedy this situation.

## 1.1  Our Results

We introduce and construct non-interactive distributional indistinguishable (NIDI) arguments without trusted setup from well-founded assumptions. These help overcome some of the drawbacks of existing non-interactive arguments, and enable applications like non-interactive commit-and-prove without trusted setup.

*Non-interactive Distributionally Indistinguishable (NIDI) Arguments.* NIDI arguments enable a prover $\mathcal{P}$ with input a secret *efficiently sampleable* distribution $\mathcal{D}$ to send a single message (a "sampler") to verifier $\mathcal{V}$. Given this sampler, $\mathcal{V}$ can obtain a sample $d$ from the (secret) distribution $\mathcal{D}$ *together with a proof of membership of the sampled instance $d$ in a (public) NP language $\mathcal{L}$*. Specifically, after checking such a proof, the verifier either outputs $\perp$ or a sample $d$. [2]

In more detail, the prover algorithm $\mathcal{P}$ obtains input a security parameter, the description of a (secret) distribution $\mathcal{D}$, and a public NP language $\mathcal{L}$, and

---

[2] Jumping ahead, in our construction, a prover message will take the form of a program, to which the verifier will make a (randomized) query. In response, the program will output a sample $d$ and a proof of membership of $d \in \mathcal{L}$.

generates $\mathcal{P}(1^\kappa, \mathcal{D}, \mathcal{L}) \to \pi$. The verifier $\mathcal{V}$ on input sampler $\pi$ and the language $\mathcal{L}$ computes $\mathcal{V}(1^\kappa, \pi, \mathcal{L}) \to d$ or $\perp$.

- The **soundness** guarantee is that $\mathcal{V}$ does not output $d \notin \mathcal{L}$ (except with negligible probability). In other words, if the sample $d$ obtained by $\mathcal{V}$ is not in $\mathcal{L}$, then the proof allows the verifier to detect this fact, and $\mathcal{V}$ outputs $\perp$ (except with negligible probability over the randomness of $\mathcal{V}$).
- The **secrecy** guarantee is that secrets in the distribution remain hidden from a malicious verifier: i.e., for every pair of (sufficiently) hard-to-distinguish distributions $\mathcal{D}_0 \approx \mathcal{D}_1$ where $\mathsf{Supp}(\mathcal{D}_0) \cup \mathsf{Supp}(\mathcal{D}_1) \in \mathcal{L}$,

$$\mathcal{P}(1^\kappa, \mathcal{D}_0, \mathcal{L}) \approx \mathcal{P}(1^\kappa, \mathcal{D}_1, \mathcal{L})$$

Equivalently, a NIDI that outputs samples from $\mathcal{D}_0$ with proofs of membership in $\mathcal{L}$ is indistinguishable from one that outputs samples from $\mathcal{D}_1$ with proofs of membership in $\mathcal{L}$.

NIDI arguments bear a peripheral resemblance to, and are implied by (non-interactive) strong witness indistinguishable arguments, by simply having the prover on input $\mathcal{D}$ sample $d \leftarrow \mathcal{D}$ and attach a strong WI proof of membership of $d \in \mathcal{L}$. In particular, the secrecy guarantee of NIDI is similar in spirit to that of strong witness indistinguishable arguments. However, we do not know if non-interactive strong WI arguments exist under standard assumptions.

We note that the syntax/completeness properties of NIDI are different from strong WI: in the case of a strong WI proof system, the prover samples $d \leftarrow \mathcal{D}$ and attaches a proof that $d \in \mathcal{L}$. On the other hand, in the case of NIDI, the prover sends a "sampler" to $\mathcal{V}$, and the sample $d$ (together with a proof) are obtained by $\mathcal{V}$ from this sampler. Therefore, while an honest prover knows the distribution $\mathcal{D}$, it may not know the exact value $d$ that was sampled by a (randomized) $\mathcal{V}$.

*Non-interactive Distributionally Indistinguishable (NIDI) Arguments from Subexponential Indistinguishability Obfuscation.* We rely on sub-exponential indistinguishability obfuscation and other standard assumptions to obtain NIDI arguments that satisfy the secrecy guarantee described above as long as the pair of distributions $(\mathcal{D}_0, \mathcal{D}_1)$ are *superpolynomially indistinguishable*.

**Theorem 1.** *(Informal) For every $p(\kappa) = \omega(\log \kappa)$ and every pair of distributions $\mathcal{D}_0, \mathcal{D}_1$ that cannot be distinguished with advantage better than $2^{-p(\kappa)}$ by any polynomial-sized adversary, NIDI arguments exist assuming sub-exponentially secure indistinguishability obfuscation and other standard assumptions.*

*Application 1: Non-interactive Commit-and-Prove.* A commit-and-prove argument is a protocol between a committer $\mathcal{C}$ and receiver $\mathcal{R}$. In the commit phase, the committer sends to the verifier a message that allows it to commit to a value $m \in \{0,1\}^\kappa$. It also proves that the committed value $m$ satisfies a (public) efficiently computable predicate $\phi$. Given the prover's message, the receiver outputs

$\perp$, or a string $c$. Later, $\mathcal{C}$ and $\mathcal{R}$ possibly engage in another decommit phase, at the end of which $\mathcal{R}$ outputs $\perp$ or $m \in \{0,1\}^\kappa$.

The soundness and secrecy guarantees are as expected:

- **Soundness** requires that if the verifier outputs a string $c$ that is not $\perp$, then there does not exist an opening $m'$ of $c$ such that $m'$ does not satisfy $\phi$.
- **Secrecy** guarantees that the message $m$ is hidden, i.e. for all pairs of (equal-sized) messages $(m_0, m_1)$ that satisfy the predicate $\phi$, $\mathcal{C}(1^k, m_0, \phi) \approx \mathcal{C}(1^k, m_1, \phi)$.

**Theorem 2.** *(Informal) Assuming sub-exponentially secure indistinguishability obfuscation and other standard assumptions, there exist commit-and-prove arguments in the plain model that satisfy a relaxed notion of non-interactivity.*

In our construction, the commitment phase consists of a committer sending the receiver a string (representing a program), but the actual commitment transcript is finalized only after the receiver produces an output (based on a randomized query to this program). While the commitment transcript is a deterministic function of the committer's message and the receiver's randomness, the receiver randomness/receiver query *may or may not* have to be known to the committer before or during the decommitment phase. If this randomness needs to be made explicit, then the commitment needs an extra message from the receiver. If it is not necessary to make the receiver randomness explicit, it becomes possible to achieve a truly non-interactive protocol.

For example, in two-party settings where one player establishes a secret trapdoor for use in a larger protocol, the extra message from the receiver may either be unnecessary (since it is not needed for decommitment) or could be clubbed together with other receiver messages. At the same time, there could be multi-party settings where the committer and receiver must agree to an entire commitment transcript before the protocol can proceed. For example, on a blockchain, one may want to commit to the value of a transaction and prove that the committed value is positive. Applying our non-interactive commit-and-prove naively to such a setting, without an explicit receiver message, could allow a malicious committer to trick different verifiers into recording different transactions (although each to a positive value).

*Application 2: Non-interactive Non-malleable (CCA) Commitments.* Very roughly, non-malleability prevents an adversary from modifying a commitment $\text{com}(m)$ to generate a commitment $\text{com}(m')$ to a value $m'$ that is related to the original $m$. This is equivalent (assuming the existence of signatures/one-way functions) to a tag-based notion where the commit algorithm obtains an additional input, a $\text{tag} \in \{0,1\}^\kappa$, and where the adversary is restricted to using a tag, or identity, that is different from the tag used to generate the honest commitment.

We consider a strong form of *non-malleability* for non-interactive commitments: CCA security [21]. Namely, we build commitments that hide the committed value even from an adversary which has access to an oracle that computes decommitments of arbitrary commitment strings that the adversary sends to this oracle, as long as they are different from the challenge string.

**Theorem 3.** *(Informal) CCA commitments for $2^\kappa$ tags satisfying a relaxed notion of non-interactivity exist assuming sub-exponentially secure indistinguishability obfuscation, CCA commitments for $\log\log\log\kappa$ tags and other standard assumptions.*

We note that CCA commitments for $\log\log\log\kappa$ tags can be based on either (1) sub-exponential time-lock puzzles (which can be based on sub-exponential indistinguishability obfuscation and the existence of sub-exponentially hard non-parallelizable languages [11]), or (2) sub-exponential hardness of discrete log and sub-exponential quantum hardness of LWE.

Just like the setting of commit-and-prove, the underlying "committed value" is defined as a function of the (non-interactive) message from the committer, and the receiver's randomness. However, again like the case of commit-and-prove, the receiver can remain *silent* throughout, thereby leading to a truly non-interactive protocol. In this setting, the CCA commitment guarantees that the value underlying a mauled commitment is independent of the honestly committed message, with overwhelming over the randomness of an honest receiver. Therefore this appears to achieve the conceptual objective of completely non-interactive commitments.

In addition, this notion would suffice for classic applications of non-malleable commitments like coin-flipping and auctions, with a non-interactive committer message and without the need for any additional messages from the receiver. An auction would be implemented by having all parties commit to their inputs using the CCA commitment, with just a single (broadcast) message from the committer. In the next round, all committers reveal *all the input and randomness* they used to generate their entire obfuscated program. These openings are accepted only if the honest committer strategy applied to the opened input and randomness results in the same obfuscated program that the committer sent; otherwise the protocol aborts. If the protocol does not abort, then the result of the protocol is computed on these opened values.

Finally, we remark that recent exciting progress [1–3,17,33,34,45] has led to constructions of indistinguishability obfuscation from simpler assumptions, including most recently [18,34,65] that obtain sub-exponentially secure iO from simple-to-state (circular security) assumptions on LWE-based cryptosystems and [46] that obtains iO from the following sub-exponential well-founded assumptions: SXDH, LWE, (a variant of) LPN and boolean PRGs in NC0.

### 1.2  Additional Related Work

*Relaxations of Zero-Knowledge.* Subsequent to the introduction of weak zero-knowledge [28], three-message weak ZK and witness hiding were constructed by [14] from what are now considered implausible assumptions (due to [10, 19]). The work of [22] proved equivalence between different variants of weak zero-knowledge. Next, [47] constructed *distributional* weak-zero-knowledge and witness-hiding protocols for a restricted class of *non-adaptive verifiers* who choose their messages obliviously of the proven statement. They obtain protocols in three messages under standard assumptions, and in two messages under standard, but super-polynomial, assumptions. More recently, [12] obtained two-message weak-zero knowledge (which implies witness hiding and strong WI) in the standard setting via a new simulation technique, and concurrently [25] obtained two-message witness hiding from new assumptions. Even more recently, [51] gave best-possible/universal and non-uniform witness hiding arguments, as well as witness hiding proofs under assumptions on the non-existence of weak forms of witness encryption for certain languages. We note that witness hiding arguments provide a weaker one-wayness guarantee, and are insufficient to achieve, e.g., commit-and-prove with message hiding as discussed in the example in the introduction.

Zero knowledge with simulators that run in super-polynomial time is known in two messages from standard, but super-polynomial, assumptions [5,57]. One-message ZK with super-polynomial simulation can be obtained against uniform provers, assuming uniform collision-resistant keyless hash functions [9], or against non-uniform verifiers, but with *weak soundness*, assuming multi-collision-resistant keyless hash functions [13]. As discussed earlier, these proofs satisfy weak notions of soundness against non-uniform provers (allowing non-uniform provers to cheat on certain instances). This is undesirable in many settings.

*Non-malleable Commitments.* Minimizing the round complexity of non-malleable commitments has been an important research goal in cryptography. Prior work, namely [6,23,24,27,39–41,43,52,53,55,56,58–60,64] culminated in three round non-malleable commitments from standard polynomial-time assumptions [42,49] and two round commitments from sub-exponential assumptions like time-lock puzzles [54] and sub-exponential DDH/LWE/QR/NR [50].

However, achieving non-interactive non-malleable commitments from well-found assumptions has been particularly challenging. In the non-interactive setting, Pandey, Pass and Vaikuntanathan [56] first gave constructions of non-malleable commitments based on a strong non-falsifiable assumption ("adaptive" one-way functions). Recently Bitansky and Lin [13] obtained constructions of non-interactive non-malleable commitments from sub-exponential time-lock puzzles and keyless hash functions with (variants of) collision resistance against non-uniform adversaries. Additionally Kalai and Khurana [48] obtained constructions satisfying a weaker notion of non-malleability w.r.t. 'replacement' (essentially allowing selective-abort attacks) from well-studied assumptions including sub-exponential NIWIs, discrete log and the *quantum* hardness of LWE. Very recently Garg et al. [31] improved upon [13], eliminating the need for NIWIs and making black-box use of cryptography. Despite this substantial progress, prior to this work, there were no known constructions of non-interactive (or relaxed non-interactive) non-malleable commitments from well-founded assumptions.

## 2    Technical Overview

We now walk the reader through our construction and offer additional insight into the notion of a NIDI. Our aim will be to find a meaningful privacy guarantee that *is achievable non-interactively*, and applicable widely. A "commit-and-prove" protocol as described in the introduction will serve as a canonical example of the type of applications that we would like to enable.

### 2.1    Commit-and-Prove Arguments

*Outline: Compressing Interactive Commit-and-Prove via Obfuscation.* Our first stab at constructing non-interactive commit-and-prove with meaningful secrecy is as follows: let us try to *compress* an interactive commit-and-prove protocol to a non-interactive one, as follows.

Let $(\mathsf{ICP}.\mathcal{P}, \mathsf{ICP}.\mathcal{V})$ denote the (honest) prover and verifier circuits for an appropriate *interactive* $n$-round commit-and-prove protocol $\mathsf{ICP}$. The prover in the non-interactive system simply outputs obfuscations of the next-message functions of $\mathsf{ICP}.\mathcal{P}$, one obfuscation for each round. The prover's next-message function $\mathsf{ICP}.\mathcal{P}_j$ for round $j \in [n]$ of $\mathsf{ICP}$ depends on its inputs $m, \phi$ (i.e. the secret message and predicate), and randomness $r$ – all of which are hardwired in the obfuscated circuits. This function on input the transcript through round $(j-1)$, produces as output the next message. The prover must output, for every round $j \in [n]$, the obfuscated circuit

$$\mathcal{C}_j = \mathsf{Obf}\left(\mathsf{ICP}.\mathcal{P}_j(m, \phi, r, \cdot)\right).$$

Given $(\mathcal{C}_1, \ldots, \mathcal{C}_n)$, $\mathcal{V}$ queries these circuits as if it were interacting with $\mathsf{ICP}.\mathcal{P}$, feeding them the current transcript and obtaining the next message. Finally, it accepts if $\mathsf{ICP}.\mathcal{V}$ would have accepted.

But obfuscating the next message function in this manner leads to new vulnerabilities that do not necessarily arise in the interactive setting. Unlike queries to an actual prover, an adversarial verifier can query obfuscated programs $(\mathcal{C}_1, \ldots, \mathcal{C}_n)$ out of order, and may even query them many times, amounting to "resetting" attacks [20]. Thus one would generally need to rely on *resettably zero-knowledge* protocols that satisfy security in the presence of resetting attacks [20].

Second, we note that general-purpose obfuscators satisfying the most natural notion of security (virtual-black-box) cannot exist [7]. We would therefore like to base security of the compressed protocol on the weaker notion of *indistinguishability obfuscation*, for which we know constructions under plausible assumptions (most recently due to [18,34,46,65]).

*Basing Security on Indistinguishability Obfuscation.* Recall that we would like the compressed commit-and-prove argument to hide the committed $m$. This means that for every pair of values $m_0, m_1$ that satisfy a predicate $\phi$, obfuscated next-message circuits that commit to $m_0$ and generate a proof of $m_0$ satisfying $\phi$, should be indistinguishable from obfuscated circuits that generate a similar commit-and-prove argument for $m_1$.

Before going into further detail, we point out that the general paradigm of using obfuscation to compress interactive protocols has been explored in prior work, (e.g., MPC protocols were compressed via obfuscating the next-message function in [4, 26, 32]). However in these works, the set of allowable or meaningful inputs to the program are small in number and are fixed apriori. This makes it possible to hardwire a few meaningful paths in the obfuscated programs and use such paths to argue security.

In our setting, the obfuscated next-message function must remain functional for (nearly) *all* verifier inputs. Because of this, our strategy to prove indistinguishability will iterate over *all possible* verifier inputs. To make this easier, we will begin by fixing a specific two-message interactive protocol, that will then be compressed to a non-interactive protocol via obfuscation.

*Fixing an Interactive Protocol.* To begin with, the interactive protocol that we rely on will be the following two-message protocols due to Pass [57].

- The interactive verifier ICP.$\mathcal{V}$ samples a random $\alpha$ and outputs $f(\alpha)$, where $f$ denotes a one-way function with "efficiently recognizable range": where it is easy to efficiently check given $y$ if there exists $\alpha$ such that $f(\alpha) = y$ (e.g., this is true whenever $f$ is a one-way permutation).
- Next, the prover ICP.$\mathcal{P}$ generates a commitment $c$ to $m$ by means of any perfectly binding non-interactive commitment, and also a non-interactive commitment $c'$ to 0. In addition, it sends a NIWI asserting that:

  "$\big(c$ is a commitment to $m$ such that $\phi(m) = 1\big)$
  OR $\big(c'$ is a commitment to $\alpha$ such that $f(\alpha) = y\big)$."

To argue that this interactive protocol *hides* the value $m$, one can rely on a simulator that extracts $\alpha$ given $y$ in superpolynomial time, and uses the second *trapdoor* statement to generate the NIWI. This makes it possible to rely on the hiding property of the non-interactive commitment and replace $c$ with a commitment to a different message.

*Arguing Security of the Compressed Commit-and-Prove System.* Plugging this two-message argument into the template described above yields the following commit-and-prove protocol:

The non-interactive prover simply obfuscates a circuit that on input an arbitrary string $y$ computes $c, c'$ as commitments to $m$ and 0 respectively, and as described above a NIWI asserting that:

  "$\big(c$ is a commitment to $m$ such that $\phi(m) = 1\big)$
  OR $\big(c'$ is a commitment to $\alpha$ such that $f(\alpha) = y\big)$."

Arguing secrecy of the non-interactive protocol is somewhat more involved as one cannot hope to directly emulate the proof of secrecy of the interactive protocol. In particular, ideally one would like to replace the obfuscated circuit with a different one that has the superpolynomial simulator's code hardwired into it. In the next hybrid step one could hope to switch the commitment string

$c$ to commit to a different value. But this does not immediately work because of the inefficiency introduced by the simulator. In fact, even if we started out with a resettably-secure protocol with a polynomial simulator, it is completely unclear how to replace the next-message circuit with one that generates simulated proofs, unless the simulator is straight-line and black-box. Unfortunately straight-line black-box simulators cannot exist in the plain model without trusted setup, so we explore a different route as described below. In what follows, we will outline a concrete construction by building on the ideas and pitfalls discussed above.

*Towards a Concrete Construction.* The commit-and-prove algorithm $\mathcal{C}(1^k, m, \phi)$ samples a random key $K$ for a *puncturable* PRF, and then outputs an indistinguishability obfuscation $\widetilde{P}$ of the program $P$ described in Fig. 1.

---

**Hardwired:** Puncturable PRF Key $K$, Message $m$, Predicate $\phi$.

**Input:** Query $y \in \{0,1\}^\kappa$.

1. If $y \notin \mathsf{Range}(f)$, output $\bot$. Otherwise, continue.
2. Set $(r_1, r_2, r_3) = \mathsf{PRF}(K, y)$.
3. Set $c = \mathsf{com}(m; r_1)$ and $c' = \mathsf{com}(0^\kappa; r_2)$.
4. Let $e$ be a NIWI, computed with randomness $r_3$, asserting that

   "$\big(c$ is a commitment to $m$ such that $\phi(m) = 1\big)$
   OR $\big(c'$ is a commitment to $\alpha$ such that $f(\alpha) = y\big)$."

5. Output $(c, c', e)$.

---

**Fig. 1.** Program $P$.

The receiver on input the obfuscated program $\widetilde{P}$ samples random $\alpha$, sets $y = f(\alpha)$ and queries the program on $y$ to obtain output some $(c, c', e)$. It parses $e$ as a NIWI and outputs $\bot$ if the NIWI does not verify, otherwise outputs $c$.

*Message Hiding.* Recall that we would like to establish that for all pairs of (equal-sized) messages $(m_0, m_1)$ such that $\phi(m_0) = \phi(m_1) = 1$, $\mathcal{C}(1^\kappa, m_0, \phi) \approx \mathcal{C}(1^\kappa, m_1, \phi)$.

We will prove this by iterating over exponentially many hybrids, corresponding to all possible inputs to the obfuscated program. The $j^{th}$ intermediate hybrid $\mathsf{Hybrid}_j$ for $j \in [0, 2^\kappa]$ will obfuscate a program $P^{(j)}$ that is identical to $P$ except the following. On all inputs $y$ such that $y < j$, $P^{(j)}$ sets $c = \mathsf{com}(m_1)$, and on all inputs $y$ such that $y \geq j$, sets $c = \mathsf{com}(m_0)$. When defined this way, note that $\mathsf{Hybrid}_0 \equiv \mathcal{C}(1^\kappa, m_0, \phi)$ and $\mathsf{Hybrid}_1 \equiv \mathcal{C}(1^\kappa, m_1, \phi)$.

Let us now argue that for all $j \in [1, 2^\kappa]$, $\mathsf{Hybrid}_{j-1} \approx \mathsf{Hybrid}_j$. Note that the only difference between the two hybrids is the difference in behavior of programs

$P^{(j-1)}$ and $P^{(j)}$ on input $y = j$. While $P^{(j-1)}$ on input $y = j$ outputs $\mathsf{com}(m_0)$, $P^{(j-1)}$ on input $y = j$ outputs $\mathsf{com}(m_1)$.

We rely on standard iO techniques to show that $\mathsf{Hybrid}_{j-1}$ and $\mathsf{Hybrid}_j$ are indistinguishable. This is done by first puncturing the key $K$ on input $y = j$, then hardwiring uniform randomness corresponding to input $j$, and then relying on the hiding of the commitments $c$ and $c'$, as well as the witness indistinguishability of NIWI.

Since there are $\sim 2^\kappa$ hybrids, denoting (an upper bound on) the adversary's distinguishing advantage between any consecutive pair $\mathsf{Hybrid}_{j-1}$ and $\mathsf{Hybrid}_j$ by $\mu$, the overall advantage between $\mathcal{C}(1^\kappa, m_0, \phi)$ and $\mathcal{C}(1^\kappa, m_1, \phi)$ can grow to $2^\kappa \cdot \mu$, which is not negligible unless $\mu = \frac{\mathsf{negl}(\kappa)}{2^\kappa}$.

Therefore, we ensure that $\mu$ is small enough by relying on subexponential assumptions. Specifically, we will assume the PRF, non-interactive commitment, and iO allow adversarial advantage to be at most $2^{-k^\epsilon}$ for some arbitrary small $0 < \epsilon < 1$ when executed with security parameter $k$. By setting $k = \kappa^{1/\epsilon}$, we will achieve the desired small $\mu$.

*Proving Soundness: A Subtle Malleability Problem.* Recall also that we would like to ensure soundness, meaning that a malicious prover, by sending an arbitrary obfuscated program $\widetilde{P}$ to a verifier, should not be able to convince such a verifier to output a string $c$ for which the underlying value $m$ does not satisfy predicate $\phi$.

Note that this is only possible if the verifier's query to $\widetilde{P}$ results in output $(c, c')$ and a NIWI $e$ for which verification accepts, and which asserts that:

"($c$ is a commitment to $m$ such that $\phi(m) = 1$)
OR ($c'$ is a commitment to $\alpha$ such that $f(\alpha) = y$)."

By soundness of the NIWI, if the verifier outputs $c$ such that the underlying value $m$ does not satisfy $\phi(m) = 1$, then (w.h.p.) it must be the case that

$c'$ is a commitment to $\alpha$ such that $f(\alpha) = y$.

To rule out this possibility, we would like to argue that it is impossible for a committer to efficiently compute $\mathsf{com}(\alpha)$ given $y = f(\alpha)$. A natural way to achieve this is via complexity leveraging: we could try setting the parameter of the commitment to be relatively small so that it is easy to extract the value $\alpha$ from commitment string $c'$ in time $T$. At the same time, we could require $f$ to be uninvertible in time $T$. This would ensure that any committer that efficiently computes $\mathsf{com}(\alpha)$ given $y = f(\alpha)$, would necessarily be contradicting uninvertibility of $f$ against adversaries running in time $T$.

But this leads to a circularity: recall that we set the size of $y$ to be $\kappa$ bits, and for our hybrid argument to go through, we needed $\mathsf{com}$ to use a security parameter $k = \kappa^{1/\epsilon}$ for the commitment scheme $\mathsf{com}$, such that the commitment scheme can be broken in time $T = 2^k$. But because the size of $y$ is $\kappa$ bits, $f$ cannot be more than $2^\kappa \ll T$-secure. Therefore, our setting of parameters for the proof of secrecy directly contradicts the parameters needed for the proof of soundness described above.

To get around this issue, we replace the commitment scheme used to generate the commitment $c'$ in our construction, with a perfectly correct *public-key encryption scheme.*

Specifically, the commit-and-prove protcol outputs a public key $pk$ in addition to the obfuscated program. And instead of generating $c'$ as a commitment to 0, $c'$ is generated as an encryption of 0, with respect to $pk$. This enables a non-uniform proof of soundness.

Specifically, given $(pk, \widetilde{P})$ if the verifier outputs $c$ such that the underlying value $m$ does not satisfy $\phi(m) = 1$, then (w.h.p.) it must be the case that

$c'$ is an encryption (w.r.t. $pk$) of $\alpha$ such that $f(\alpha) = y$.

Now given $pk$, our reduction/proof of soundness will non-uniformly obtain the corresponding $sk$. Next, given any prover that on input $y$ outputs $c'$ as an encryption of $f^{-1}(y)$, this reduction will be able to use $sk$ to decrypt $c'$ and recover $\alpha$. This will yield a contradiction to the uninvertibility of $f$, and therefore help us obtain a proof of soundness. We note that a similar technique was used in [16] to achieve soundness in the context of post-quantum interactive ZK arguments.

### 2.2   Non-interactive Distributional Indistinguishability

A reader may have already observed that the technique discussed so far is more general: it need not be limited to commit-and-prove, and may be used to prove arbitrary statements about (indistinguishable) distributions.

We distill out a general formulation of this technique into what we call a NIDI argument. The construction of our NIDI argument follows an outline identical to that of our commit-and-prove system. Namely, the prover algorithm $\mathcal{P}(1^\kappa, \mathcal{D}, \mathcal{L})$ is given a secret efficiently sampleable distribution $\mathcal{D}$ and public language $\mathcal{L}$ with corresponding relation $\mathcal{R}_\mathcal{L}$. It outputs a public key $pk$ and an indistinguishability obfuscation of a program $P'$ that is very similar to the program $P$ discussed above. The key difference is that the commitment $c$ to value $m$ in the functionality of the program $P$ is replaced by a general sample $d$ from distribution $\mathcal{D}$. This program is described in Fig. 2. Secrecy and soundness of this program follow identically to the commit-and-prove argument.

### 2.3   Application: CCA Commitments

These techniques also yield (relaxed) non-interactive non-malleable commmitments: in fact, we achieve a strong form of non-malleability, i.e. CCA security.

We model CCA commitments as being associated with identities or tags, where the CCA adversary gets access to a decommitment oracle for all tags/identities different from its own. All non-malleable commitment schemes

---

**Hardwired:** Puncturable PRF Key $K$, Distribution $\mathcal{D}$, Language $\mathcal{L}$, Public key $pk$.

**Input:** Query $y \in \{0,1\}^\kappa$.

1. If $y \notin \mathsf{Range}(f)$, output $\perp$. Otherwise, continue.
2. Set $(r_1, r_2, r_3) = \mathsf{PRF}(K, y)$.
3. Set $d = \mathcal{D}(r_1)$ and $c' = \mathsf{Enc}_{pk}(0^\kappa; r_2)$.
4. Let $e$ be a NIWI, computed with randomness $r_3$, asserting that

$$\text{``}\big(d = \mathcal{D}(r) \text{ for some } \mathcal{D} \text{ and } r \text{ such that } \mathcal{R}_\mathcal{L}(d, \mathcal{D}, r) = 1\big)$$
$$\text{OR } \big(c' \text{ is an encryption w.r.t. } pk, \text{ of } \alpha \text{ such that } f(\alpha) = y\big).\text{''}$$

5. Output $(d, c', e)$.

---

**Fig. 2.** Program $P'$.

assign "tags" (or identities) to parties, and require non-malleability to hold whenever the adversary is trying to generate a commitment $\mathsf{CCACom}_{\widetilde{T}}$ w.r.t. a tag $\widetilde{T}$ that is different from the honest tag $T$. Existing constructions of non-interactive non-malleable commitments (1) develop a scheme for a small (constant) number of tags, and then (2) recursively apply *tag amplification*, discussed below, several times until a scheme supporting $(2^\lambda)$ tags is achieved – which corresponds to supporting every possible $\lambda$-bit identity that a participant can assume.

*Outline of Existing Tag Amplification Techniques.* Non-interactive CCA commitments that support a small space of tags can be bootstrapped into commitments for a larger space of tags by executing (a round optimized variant of) a tag encoding scheme first suggested by [27].

Given a large tag $T$ (in $[2^n]$) where $n \leq \mathsf{poly}(\lambda)$, first encode $T$ into $n$ small tags $t_1, t_2, \ldots t_n$ each in $[2n]$, by setting each $t_i = (i \| T_i)$ where $T_i$ denotes the $i^{th}$ bit of $T$. This encoding ensures that for any different large tags $T \neq \widetilde{T}$, there exists at least one index $i$ such that $\widetilde{t}_i \notin \{t_1, t_2, \ldots t_n\}$, where $(\widetilde{t}_1, \widetilde{t}_2, \ldots \widetilde{t}_n)$ is an encoding of $\widetilde{T}$. Note that when $T \in [2^n]$, each of the small tags $t$ will only be as large as $2n$. Now starting with a CCA commitment 'ComSmall' for tags in $[2n]$, a scheme CCACom for tags in $[2^n]$ can be obtained as follows:

To commit to a message $m$ w.r.t. a tag $T$, set

$$\mathsf{CCACom}_T(m) = \big(\{c_i = \mathsf{ComSmall}_{t_i}(m)\}_{i \in [n]}, \Pi\big), \text{ where}$$

$\Pi$ is (an appropriate variant of a) zero-knowledge argument certifying that:

"All $n$ commitments $c_i$ are to the same message."

*Analysis.* Suppose the adversary used large tag $\widetilde{T} = (\widetilde{t}_1, \ldots, \widetilde{t}_n)$ and the honest party used tag $T = (t_1, \ldots, t_n)$. By the property of the encoding, for any two large tags $T \neq \widetilde{T}$, there exists at least one index $i$ such that $\widetilde{t}_i \notin \{t_1, t_2, \ldots t_n\}$, where $(t_1, t_2, \ldots t_n)$ and $(\widetilde{t}_1, \widetilde{t}_2, \ldots \widetilde{t}_n)$ refer to encodings of $T$ and $\widetilde{T}$ respectively. This means (due to non-malleability of ComSmall) that the message committed by the adversary using tag $\widetilde{t}_i$ must be independent of the honest committer's input. By the soundness of ZK, the message committed by the adversary using each (small) tag $\widetilde{t}_1, \ldots \widetilde{t}_n$ is identical, so independence of the one committed using $\widetilde{t}_i$ implies independence of them all! Loosely, it then suffices to argue that a message corresponding to *any* tag $\widetilde{t}_i$ is generated independently of the honest committer's message.

In some more detail, for the CCA attacker's $j^{th}$ oracle decommitment query, we will focus on the index $i_j$ such that the tag $\widetilde{t}_{i_j} \notin \{t_1^1, t_2^1, \ldots t_n^1\}$. In the real interaction, by soundness of the ZK argument, the value committed by the attacker is identical to the value committed using $\widetilde{t}_{i_j}$. This makes it possible to rely on CCA security of the value committed using $\widetilde{t}_{i_j}$. We note that this method will need rely on a ZK argument that is secure against adversaries running in time $T$, where $T$ is the time required to brute-force break the CCA commitment with $\widetilde{t}_{i,j}$. This is because we will want to argue that the value committed using tag $\widetilde{t}_{i_j}$ remains unchanged even when the challenge commitment is generated by simulating the underlying ZK argument.

Once the ZK argument in the challenge commitment is simulated, it becomes possible to switch all components of the challenge commitment one by one, while arguing CCA security w.r.t. the value committed by the adversary via tag $\widetilde{t}_{i_j}$. This follows because of CCA security of the underlying commitment scheme for small tags.

*The Zero-Knowledge Bottleneck.* Unfortunately, this process makes cricital use of the zero-knowledge argument. Recall that ZK requires more than 2 rounds of interaction, which leads to a clear problem in the non-interactive setting. Existing methods to overcome this problem without interaction rely on special (weak) types of ZK – thus requiring non-standard assumptions [13], or achieving only weak forms of security [31,48,54]. In [13,54], NIWIs are combined with a trapdoor statement to enable weak forms of NIZKs without setup: against uniform provers assuming keyless collision-resistant hash functions in [54], and a weak form of soundness against non-uniform provers under the non-standard assumption of keyless collision-resistant hash against *non-uniform* adversaries in [13]. In addition [48] use NIWIs without trapdoors, but only achieve weaker forms of non-malleability (that is, w.r.t. replacement). Even more recently, [31] replace NIWIs with hinting PRGs and remove the need for non-black-box use of cryptography. However, they also rely on keyless hash functions to set up "trapdoors" for equivocal commitments, thereby achieving only uniform security. In summary, due to the need for (variants of) non-interactive ZK, all known constructions achieving the standard notion of non-malleability w.r.t. commitment (or the stronger notion of CCA security) without trusted setup and against non-uniform adversaries end up having to rely on non-standard assumptions.

In fact by now, CCA commitments – *only* for constant (and slightly super-constant) tags – are *known* based on relatively mild assumptions, whereas tag amplification requires stronger assumptions. We now briefly describe the milder assumptions for schemes with slightly super-constant tags for completeness, before going back to discussing the tag amplification bottleneck.

*Base Schemes.* Three recent works [13,48,54] build non-interactive "base" schemes: i.e. non-malleable commitments for a tag/identity space of size $c \log \log \kappa$ for a specific constant $c > 0$, based on various hardness assumptions. This is achieved by relying on families of assumptions, each of which is harder than the other along some axis of hardness.

Lin, Pass and Soni [54] assume a sub-exponential variant of the hardness of time-lock puzzles. Bitansky and Lin [13] show that base commitments can also rely on sub-exponentially hard one-way functions that admit a strong form of hardness amplification (the assumption is stronger than what is currently known to be provable by known results on hardness amplification). Subsequently, Kalai and Khurana [48] showed that one can assume classically sub-exponentially hard but quantum easy one-way functions (which can be based, e.g., on sub-exponential hardness of DDH), and sub-exponentially quantum hard one-way functions (which can be based, e.g., on sub-exponential quantum hardness of LWE). As discussed above, we would like to enable an alternative tag amplification process.

*Commit-and-Prove.* Going back to the tag amplification process outlined above, one may observe that the type of statement being proved via ZK fits well into the "non-interactive commit-and-prove" paradigm. In particular, one may hope that it would suffice to replace the ZK argument $\Pi$ with (an appropriate) commit-and-prove – which allows a committer to generate $n$ commitments w.r.t. $n$ different small tags, and give a (privacy-preserving) proof that all $n$ strings commit to the same message. As such, by carefully relying on our non-interactive commit-and-prove discussed in Sect. 2.1, it seems like one should be able to achieve generic tag amplification.

In fact, our construction is roughly as expected at this point. The committer $\mathcal{C}$ on input a message $m$ and tag $T$ encoded as $\{t_1, \ldots, t_n\}^3$, outputs a public key $pk$, together with an obfuscation of the program $P_{\mathsf{CCA}}$ described in Fig. 3.

The proof of security of the resulting CCA commitment for large tags relies on a delicate interplay of parameters between the CCA commitment and the zero-knowledge argument. Specifically, recall that the tag amplification method sketched out earlier requires the "strength" of zero-knowledge to be higher than the time needed to brute-force extract the committed value from the underlying CCA commitment for small tags. In our setting, this translates to carefully fine-tuning parameters so that the NIWI, PRF and public key encryption scheme are all secure against $T$-size adversaries, where $T$ is the time needed to break (via brute-force) the underlying CCA commitment for small tags. This requirement for fine-tuned parameters requires us to "open the black-box" and give a

---

[3] In the main technical body, we use a somewhat more optimal encoding scheme due to [50], but we ignore this optimization for the purposes of this overview.

**Hardwired:** Puncturable PRF Key $K$, Message $m$, Tags $t_1, \ldots, t_n$, Public key $pk$.

**Input:** Query $y \in \{0,1\}^{\kappa}$.

1. If $y \notin \mathsf{Range}(f)$, output $\bot$. Otherwise, continue.
2. Set $(r_1, r_2, \ldots, r_{n+2}) = \mathsf{PRF}(K, y)$.
3. Set $c_i = \mathsf{ComSmall}(m; r_i)$ for all $i \in [n]$.
4. Set $c' = \mathsf{enc}_{pk}(0^{\kappa}; r_{n+1})$.
5. Let $e$ be a NIWI, computed with randomness $r_{n+2}$, asserting that

   "(There exist $m$ and $\{r_i\}_{i \in [n]}$ s.t. $\forall i \in [n], c_i = \mathsf{ComSmall}(m; r_i)$)
   OR $\big(c'$ is an encryption w.r.t. $pk$, of $\alpha$ such that $f(\alpha) = y\big)$."

6. Output $(\{c_i\}_{i \in [n]}, c', e)$.

**Fig. 3. Program $P_{\mathsf{CCA}}$.**

monolithic proof of security. By contrast, our (regular) commit-and-prove system makes black-box use of the NIDI abstraction.

*A Final Subtle Issue.* We now point out one additional subtlety that we glossed over the in the overview so far. Existing base schemes [13, 48, 54] (for $O(\log \log \kappa)$ tags) are only secure in a setting where the adversary is restricted to using the same tag in all its queries to the CCA decommitment oracle. Before performing our tag amplification process, we will need to remove this "same-tag" restriction.

We build on a technique proposed by [31] to eliminate this restriction. A CCA commitment scheme without the same-tag restriction, for tags in $[n]$ where $n \leq \mathsf{poly}(\kappa)$, can be obtained from a CCA commitment with the same tag restriction, via the following process: To commit w.r.t. tag $t \in [n]$, send commitments w.r.t. all tags in $[n]$ that are *not equal to* $t$. In more detail,

$$\mathsf{CCACom}_t(m) = (\{\mathsf{CCACom\text{-}same\text{-}tag}_i(m)\}_{i \in [n] \setminus \{t\}}, \Pi),$$

where $\Pi$ is (an appropriate variant of a) ZK argument certifying that

"All $n - 1$ commitments $c_i$ are to the same message."

Let us assume that the adversary's challenge commitment has tag $t^*$. This means that the challenge commitment *does not contain* the underlying commitment $\mathsf{CCACom\text{-}same\text{-}tag}$ w.r.t. tag $t^*$, and on the other hand, all the adversaries oracle decommitment queries *will contain* $\mathsf{CCACom\text{-}same\text{-}tag}$ w.r.t. tag $t^*$. This means that all decommitment queries that the adversary makes contain a commitment w.r.t. tag $t^*$ that does not appear in the challenge commitment. This leads to an identical situation as the setting of tag amplification, and a very similar construction (and proof) helps bootstrap same-tag schemes for $n \leq \mathsf{poly}(\kappa)$ tags to those that do not have such a requirement.

In summary, our final CCA commitment is obtained by first bootstrapping "base" same-tag commitment schemes for small tags to remove the same-tag requirement, and then bootstrapping the resulting small tag commitment via the tag amplification process outlined above.

*Organization.* The rest of this paper is organized as follows. In Sect. 3 we set up notation and define building blocks. In Sect. 4 we define and construct NIDIs, in Sect. 5, we use NIDIs in a black-box way to obtain commit-and-prove, and finally in Sect. 6 we build CCA commitments.

## 3   Preliminaries

We rely on the standard notions of Turing machines and Boolean circuits.

- A polynomial-size circuit family $\mathcal{C}$ is a sequence of circuits $\mathcal{C} = \{C_\kappa\}_{\kappa \in \mathbb{N}}$, such that each circuit $C_\kappa$ is of polynomial size $\kappa^{O(1)}$ and has $\kappa^{O(1)}$ input and output bits. We also consider probabilistic circuits that may toss random coins.
- We follow the standard habit of modeling any efficient adversary as a family of polynomial-size circuits. For an adversary $\mathcal{A}$ corresponding to a family of polynomial-size circuits $\{\mathcal{A}_\kappa\}_{\kappa \in \mathbb{N}}$, we omit the subscript $\kappa$, when it is clear from the context.
- A function $f : \mathbb{N} \to \mathbb{R}$ is $\mathsf{negl}(n)$ if $f(n) = n^{-\omega(1)}$.
- For random variables $X, Y$, and $0 < \mu < 1$, we write $X \approx_{T(\kappa)} Y$ if for all polynomial-sized circuits $\mathcal{A}$, there exists a negligible function $\mu$ such that for all $\kappa$,

$$\big| \Pr[\mathcal{A}(X) = 1] - \Pr[\mathcal{A}(Y) = 1] \big| \leq \mu(T(\kappa)).$$

- We will use $d \leftarrow \mathcal{D}$ to denote a random sample from distribution $\mathcal{D}$. This will sometimes be denoted equivalently as $d = \mathcal{D}(r)$ for $r \leftarrow \{0,1\}^*$. Similarly, we will consider randomized algorithms that obtain inputs, and toss coins. We will use notation $t \leftarrow \mathcal{T}(m)$ to denote the output of randomized algorithm $\mathcal{T}$ on input $m$. Sometimes we will make the randomness of $\mathcal{T}$ explicit, in which case we will use notation $t = \mathcal{T}(m; r)$ for $r \leftarrow \{0,1\}^*$.

## 4   Non-interactive Distributionally Indistinguishable (NIDI) Arguments

In this section, we define and construct NIDI arguments. As discussed earlier, NIDI arguments enable a prover $\mathcal{P}$ with input a secret *efficiently sampleable* distribution $\mathcal{D}$ to send a single message (a "sampler") to verifier $\mathcal{V}$. Given this sampler, $\mathcal{V}$ can obtain a sample $d$ from the (secret) distribution $\mathcal{D}$ *together with a proof of membership of the sampled instance $d$ in a (public) NP language $\mathcal{L}$.* Specifically, after checking such a proof, the verifier either outputs $\perp$ or a sample $d$ from the distribution.

## 4.1   Definitions

In a NIDI, the prover algorithm $\mathcal{P}$ obtains input a security parameter, the description of a (secret) distribution $\mathcal{D}$, and a public NP language $\mathcal{L}$, and generates $\mathcal{P}(1^\kappa, \mathcal{D}, \mathcal{L}) \to \pi$. The verifier $\mathcal{V}$ on input sampler $\pi$ and the language $\mathcal{L}$ computes $\mathcal{V}(1^\kappa, \pi, \mathcal{L}) \to d$ or $\perp$. We formally define this primitive below.

**Definition 1 (Non-interactive        Distributionally-Indistinguishable (NIDI) Arguments).** *A pair of PPT algorithms is $(\mathcal{P}, \mathcal{V})$ is a non-interactive distributionally-indistinguishable (NIDI) argument for* NP *language $\mathcal{L}$ with associated relation $R_\mathcal{L}$ if the non-interactive algorithms $\mathcal{P}(1^\kappa, \mathcal{D}, \mathcal{L})$ and $\mathcal{V}(1^\kappa, \pi, \mathcal{L})$[4] satisfy:*

- **Completeness:** *For every* poly($\lambda$)*-sampleable distribution[5] $\mathcal{D} = (\mathcal{X}, \mathcal{W})$ over instance-witness pairs in $R_\mathcal{L}$ such that* Supp($\mathcal{X}$) $\subseteq \mathcal{L}$,

$$\left( \mathcal{V}(1^\kappa, \pi, \mathcal{L}) : \pi \in \mathsf{Supp}\left(\mathcal{P}(1^\kappa, \mathcal{D}, \mathcal{L})\right) \right) \in \mathsf{Supp}(\mathcal{X}).$$

- **Soundness:** *For every ensemble of polynomial-length strings $\{\pi_\kappa\}_{\kappa \in \mathbb{N}}$ there exists a negligible function $\mu(\cdot)$ such that:*

$$\Pr_{x \leftarrow \mathcal{V}(1^\kappa, \pi, \mathcal{L})} \left[ (x \neq \perp) \wedge (x \notin \mathcal{L}) \right] \leq \mu(\kappa)$$

- **Distributional Indistinguishability:** *For every* poly($\kappa$)*-sampleable pair of distributions $\mathcal{D}_0 = (\mathcal{X}_0, \mathcal{W}_0)$ and $\mathcal{D}_1 = (\mathcal{X}_1, \mathcal{W}_1)$ over instance-witness pairs in $R_\mathcal{L}$ where* Supp($\mathcal{X}_0$) $\cup$ Supp($\mathcal{X}_1$) $\subseteq \mathcal{L}$, *and $\mathcal{X}_0 \approx_\kappa \mathcal{X}_1$,*

$$\mathcal{P}(1^\kappa, \mathcal{D}_0, \mathcal{L}) \approx_\kappa \mathcal{P}(1^\kappa, \mathcal{D}_1, \mathcal{L})$$

**Definition 2 (NIDI Arguments for $T(\kappa)$-Hard Distributions).** *A pair of PPT algorithms is $(\mathcal{P}, \mathcal{V})$ is a non-interactive distributionally-indistinguishable (NIDI) argument for $T(\kappa)$-hard distributions and* NP *language $\mathcal{L}$ with associated relation $\mathcal{R}_\mathcal{L}$ if the non-interactive algorithms $\mathcal{P}(1^\kappa, \mathcal{D}, \mathcal{L})$ and $\mathcal{V}(1^\kappa, \pi, \mathcal{L})$ satisfy the completeness and soundness properties from Definition 1, and additionally satisfy:*

- **Distributional Indistinguishability for $T(\kappa)$-Hard Distributions:** *For every* poly($\kappa$)*-sampleable pair of distributions $\mathcal{D}_0 = (\mathcal{X}_0, \mathcal{W}_0)$ and $\mathcal{D}_1 = (\mathcal{X}_1, \mathcal{W}_1)$ over instance-witness pairs in $R_\mathcal{L}$ where* Supp($\mathcal{X}_0$) $\cup$ Supp($\mathcal{X}_1$) $\subseteq \mathcal{L}$, *and $\mathcal{X}_0 \approx_{T(\kappa)} \mathcal{X}_1$,*

$$\mathcal{P}(1^\kappa, \mathcal{D}_0, \mathcal{L}) \approx_\kappa \mathcal{P}(1^\kappa, \mathcal{D}_1, \mathcal{L})$$

---

[4] Since we define a NIDI for $\mathcal{L}$, it is not necessary to explicitly send $\mathcal{L}$ as input to $\mathcal{P}$ and $\mathcal{V}$ but we nevertheless write it this way for clarity.

[5] Here, we slightly abuse notation and use $\mathcal{D}$ to also denote a circuit that on input uniform randomness, outputs a sample from the distribution $\mathcal{D}$.

## 4.2   Construction and Analysis

We prove the following theorem.

**Theorem 4.** *Assuming the existence of sub-exponentially secure one-way functions with efficiently recognizable range and sub-exponentially secure indistinguishability obfuscation, there exists a constant $c > 1$ s.t. for $T(\kappa) = 2^{(\log \kappa)^c}$ there exist NIDI arguments for $T(\kappa)$-Hard Distributions satisfying Definition 2.*

To prove Theorem 4, we show that there exist NIDI arguments for $T(\kappa)$-hard distributions, where $\log T = (\log \kappa)^c$, and $c > 1$ is some constant. Our construction depends on $T$, and is as follows.

*Construction 4.1.* Let $\epsilon > 0$ be an arbitrarily small constant such that:

- There exists a sub-exponentially secure one-way function $f : \{0,1\}^{\mathsf{poly}(k)} \to \{0,1\}^{\mathsf{poly}(k)}$ with an *efficiently recognizable range*, i.e., given $y$ there is an efficient algorithm to check whether there exists a value $x$ such that $f(x) = y$. Note that permutations have this property, because every $y$ is in the range of the permutation. We require that for security parameter $k'$, this function is invertible with probability at most $\frac{1}{2^{(k')^\epsilon}}$ by machines of size $2^{(k')^\epsilon}$.
- There exists a *perfectly correct, sub-exponentially secure* public-key encryption scheme with key generation, encryption and decryption algorithms $(\mathsf{KeyGen}, \mathsf{Enc}, \mathsf{Dec})$ that for security parameter $1^k$ satisfies $2^{k^\epsilon}$- IND-CPA security against (non-uniform) adversaries[6].
- There exists a *sub-exponentially secure* indistinguishability obfuscation scheme $(\mathsf{iO.Obf}, \mathsf{iO.Eval})$ that for security parameter $1^k$ satisfies $2^{k^\epsilon}$- security against (non-uniform) adversaries.
- There exists a *sub-exponentially secure* puncturable PRF that for security parameter $1^k$ satisfies $2^{k^\epsilon}$- security against (non-uniform) adversaries.
- There exist *sub-exponentially secure* NIWIs that for security parameter $1^k$ satisfy $2^{k^\epsilon}$- security against (non-uniform) adversaries.

Set $c = \frac{1}{\epsilon}$. We construct our non-interactive distributionally-indistinguishable (NIDI) argument below, where letting $\mathcal{R}_{\mathcal{L}}$ denote the relation corresponding to NP language $\mathcal{L}$ we define

$$\mathcal{L}_{\mathsf{NIWI}} = \Big\{ (pk, d_x, c, y) : \exists (d_w, s, sk) \text{ s.t. } ((d_x, d_w) \in \mathcal{R}_{\mathcal{L}}) \bigvee ((pk, sk) \leftarrow \mathsf{KeyGen}(s) \wedge y = f(\mathsf{Dec}_{sk}(c))) \Big\}$$

- The prove algorithm $\mathcal{P}(1^\kappa, \mathcal{D}, \mathcal{L})$ does the following:
  - Set $k = 2^{(\log \kappa)^{c^2}}, k' = 2^{(\log \kappa)^c}$.
  - Sample $s \leftarrow \{0,1\}^k$ and set $(pk, sk) \leftarrow \mathsf{KeyGen}(s)$.
  - Sample $K \leftarrow \{0,1\}^k, R \leftarrow \{0,1\}^k$.
  - Generate program $P_{pk,K,\mathcal{D},\mathcal{L}}$ defined in Fig. 4.
  - Compute $\widetilde{P} = \mathsf{iO.Obf}(P_{pk,K,\mathcal{D},\mathcal{L}}; R)$.
  - Output $(pk, \widetilde{P})$.

---

[6] This can be based on sub-exponential indistinguishability obfuscation and sub-exponential one-way functions following [62].

---

**Hardwired:** Public key $pk$, Puncturable PRF Key $K$, Distribution $\mathcal{D}$, Language $\mathcal{L}$.

**Input:** Query $y \in \{0,1\}^{k'}$.

1. If $y \notin \mathsf{Range}(f)$, output $\perp$. Otherwise, continue.
2. Set $(r_1, r_2, r_3) = \mathsf{PRF}(K, y)$.
3. Set $(d_x, d_w) = \mathcal{D}(r_1)$.
4. Set $c = \mathsf{Enc}_{pk}(0^{k'}; r_2)$.
5. Set $x = (pk, d_x, c, y)$, $w = (d_w, 0^{k'+k})$.
   Then compute $e = \mathsf{NIWI}.\mathcal{P}(1^k, x, w, \mathcal{L}_{\mathsf{NIWI}}; r_3)$.
6. Output $(x, e)$.

---

**Fig. 4. Program** $P_{pk,K,\mathcal{D},\mathcal{L}}$.

– The verify algorithm $\mathcal{V}(1^\kappa, \pi, \mathcal{L})$ on input a proof $\pi = (pk, \widetilde{P})$ does the following:
   • Sample $v \leftarrow \{0,1\}^{k'}$ and set $y = f(v)$.
   • Compute $\mathsf{out} = \mathsf{iO}.\mathsf{Eval}(\widetilde{P}, y)$. Parse $\mathsf{out} = (x, e)$ and parse $x = (pk, d, c, y)$.
   • If $\mathsf{NIWI}.\mathcal{V}(1^k, x, e, \mathcal{L}_{\mathsf{NIWI}})$ rejects, output $\perp$ and stop.
   • Else output $d$.

**Lemma 1.** *Construction 4.1 satisfies completeness according to Definition 1.*

*Proof.* The proof follows by observing that due to perfect correctness of iO, $\mathcal{V}(\pi, \mathcal{L})$ for $\pi = (pk, \widetilde{P})$ obtains $(x, e)$ from $\widetilde{P}$, where $x = (pk, d, c, y)$. By perfect correctness of NIWI, $\mathcal{V}$ will output $d$ with probability 1. Recall that $(d, \cdot) = \mathcal{D}(r_1)$ by construction, and therefore $d \in \mathsf{Supp}(\mathcal{X})$.

**Lemma 2.** *Under the assumptions in Theorem 4, construction 4.1 satisfies soundness according to Definition 1.*

**Lemma 3.** *Under the assumptions in Theorem 4, construction 4.1 satisfies distributional indistinguishability for $T(\kappa)$-hard distributions per Definition 2.*

The proofs of these lemmas appear in the full version but are omitted from this version due to lack of space.

## 5 Commit-and-Prove

A (relaxed) non-interactive commit-and-prove argument is a protocol between a committer $\mathcal{C}$ and receiver $\mathcal{R}$. In the commit phase, $\mathcal{C}$ sends $\mathcal{R}$ a single message to commit to a value $m \in \{0,1\}^\kappa$. The transcript of the commitment is finalized as a function of the receiver's randomness and the committer's message, although the receiver does not need to return this randomness to the committer. It also proves that $m$ satisfies some public predicate $\phi$, in other words it proves that $\phi(m) = 1$. At the end of this phase, $\mathcal{R}$ either outputs $\perp$ (denoting that the commitment phase was rejected) or outputs a commitment string $c$.

Later, the parties $\mathcal{C}$ and $\mathcal{R}$ possibly engage in another decommit phase, at the end of which $\mathcal{R}$ outputs $\perp$ or $m \in \{0,1\}^\kappa$.

**Definition 3 (Non-interactive Commit-and-Prove).** *A pair of PPT algorithms $(\mathcal{C}, \mathcal{R})$ where $\mathcal{R} = (\mathcal{R}_1, \mathcal{R}_2)$ is a non-interactive commit-and-prove argument if it satisfies the following.*

- **Completeness:** *For every $\phi$ and every $m \in \{0,1\}^\kappa$ such that $\phi(m) = 1$,*

$$\Pr\left[\begin{matrix} m \leftarrow \mathcal{R}_2(1^\kappa, c, \mathsf{cert}, \mathsf{st}) & \wedge \\ \phi(m) = 1 \end{matrix}\middle| \begin{matrix} (\pi, \mathsf{st}) \leftarrow \mathcal{C}(1^\kappa, m, \phi) \\ (c, \mathsf{cert}) \leftarrow \mathcal{R}_1(1^\kappa, \pi, \phi) \end{matrix}\right] = 1.$$

- **Soundness:** *For every $\mathsf{poly}(\kappa)$-sized (non-uniform) committer $\mathcal{C}^*$ there exists a negligible function $\mu(\cdot)$ such that for large enough $\kappa \in \mathbb{N}$,*

$$\Pr\left[\begin{matrix} \exists(m^*, \mathsf{st}^*) \text{ s.t. } (m^* \neq \perp) & \wedge \\ m^* \leftarrow \mathcal{R}_2(1^\kappa, c, \mathsf{cert}, \mathsf{st}^*) & \wedge \\ \phi(m^*) \neq 1 \end{matrix}\middle| \begin{matrix} \pi \leftarrow \mathcal{C}^* \\ (c, \mathsf{cert}) \leftarrow \mathcal{R}_1(1^\kappa, \pi, \phi) \end{matrix}\right] \leq \mu(\kappa).$$

- **Computational Hiding:** *For every language $\mathcal{L}$, every pair of messages $(m_0, m_1)$ such that $\phi(m_0) = \phi(m_1) = 1$,*

$$\mathcal{C}(1^\kappa, m_0, \phi) \approx_\kappa \mathcal{C}(1^\kappa, m_1, \phi)$$

*Construction 5.1.* Let $\epsilon > 0$ be a constant such that:

- There exists a non-interactive perfectly binding commitment $\mathsf{Com}$ that satisfies hiding against $2^{\kappa^\epsilon}$-time (non-uniform) adversaries, and
- There exists a NIDI argument for $2^{\kappa^\epsilon}$-hard distributions that satisfies Definition 1.

We define

$$\mathcal{L}_\phi = \left\{ c : \exists(m, r) \text{ s.t. } c = \mathsf{Com}(m; r) \wedge \phi(m) = 1 \right\}$$

- The commit algorithm $\mathcal{C}(1^\kappa, m, \phi)$ does the following:
  - Define distribution $\mathcal{D}_m(r) = \mathsf{Com}(m; r)$.
  - Output $\pi = \mathcal{P}(1^\kappa, \mathcal{D}_m, \mathcal{L}_\phi)$ computed using uniform randomness $r_\mathcal{C}$.
  - Set $\mathsf{st} = (m, r_\mathcal{C})$.
- The receiver algorithm $\mathcal{R}_1(1^\kappa, \pi, \phi)$ does the following.
  - Sample randomness $r_\mathcal{R}$.
  - Obtain $y \leftarrow \mathcal{V}(1^\kappa, \pi, \mathcal{L}_\phi; r_\mathcal{R})$.
  - Output $(y, r_\mathcal{R})$.

– The receiver algorithm $\mathcal{R}_2(1^\kappa, c, \mathsf{cert}, \mathsf{st}^*)$ does the following:
  • Parse $\mathsf{st}^* = (m^*, r_{\mathcal{C}}^*)$ and $\mathsf{cert} = r_{\mathcal{R}}$.
  • Compute $\pi^* = \mathcal{P}(1^\kappa, \mathcal{D}_{m^*}, \mathcal{L}_\phi; r_{\mathcal{C}}^*)$.
  • If $\mathcal{V}(1^\kappa, \pi^*, \mathcal{L}_\phi; r_{\mathcal{R}}) = (c, \cdot)$, output $m^*$.
  • Otherwise, output $\bot$.

**Lemma 4.** *Construction 5.1 satisfies completeness according to Definition 3.*

*Proof.* The proof follows by the perfect correctness of NIDI.

**Lemma 5.** *Construction 5.1 satisfies soundness according to Definition 3.*

*Proof.* We prove that this lemma follows by the soundness of the NIDI according to Definition 2 and the perfect binding property of Com. Towards a contradiction, suppose there exists a $\mathsf{poly}(\kappa)$-sized (non-uniform) committer $\mathcal{C}^*$ for which there exists a polynomial $p(\cdot)$ such that for infinitely many $\kappa \in \mathbb{N}$,

$$\Pr\left[\begin{array}{l} \exists (m^*, \mathsf{st}^*) \text{ s.t. } (m^* \neq \bot) \;\wedge \\ m^* \leftarrow \mathcal{R}_2(1^\kappa, c, \mathsf{cert}, \mathsf{st}^*) \;\wedge \\ \phi(m^*) \neq 1 \end{array} \middle| \begin{array}{l} \pi \leftarrow \mathcal{C}^* \\ (c, \mathsf{cert}) \leftarrow \mathcal{R}_1(1^\kappa, \pi, \phi) \end{array}\right] \geq \frac{1}{p(\kappa)}.$$

Fix any string $\pi$, and let $(c, \mathsf{cert}) \leftarrow \mathcal{R}_1(1^\kappa, \pi, \phi)$.

– By construction, for any $\mathsf{st}^*$ parsed as $(m^*, r_{\mathcal{C}}^*)$, $\mathcal{R}_2(1^\kappa, c, \mathsf{cert}, \mathsf{st}^*)$ outputs $m^* \neq \bot$ if and only if for $\pi^* = \mathcal{P}(1^\kappa, \mathcal{D}_{m^*}, \mathcal{L}_\phi; r_{\mathcal{C}}^*)$, $\mathcal{V}(1^\kappa, \pi^*, \mathcal{L}_\phi; \mathsf{cert}) = (c, \cdot)$. By perfect completeness of NIDI, this implies that $\mathcal{R}_2(1^\kappa, c, \mathsf{cert}, \mathsf{st}^*)$ outputs some $m^* \neq \bot$ if and only if there exists $r_{\mathcal{C}}^*$ such that $c = \mathsf{Com}(m^*; r_{\mathcal{C}}^*)$.
– Next by the perfect binding of Com, for every string $c$, there exists at most one message $m^*$ and randomness $r_{\mathcal{C}}^*$ such that $c = \mathsf{Com}(m^*; r_{\mathcal{C}}^*)$. Then $\phi(m^*) \neq 1 \iff c \notin \mathcal{L}_\phi$.

Taken together, this implies that

$$\Pr\left[(\mathcal{R}(1^\kappa, \pi, \mathcal{L}_\phi) \neq \bot) \wedge (\mathcal{R}(1^\kappa, \pi, \mathcal{L}_\phi) \notin \mathcal{L}) \middle| \pi \leftarrow \mathcal{C}^*\right] \geq \frac{1}{p(\kappa)},$$

which contradicts the soundness of NIDI, as desired.

**Lemma 6.** *Construction 5.1 satisfies computational hiding according to Definition 2.*

*Proof.* This lemma follows almost immediately from the distributional indistinguishability of NIDI.

Specifically, for language $\mathcal{L} = \mathcal{L}_\phi$, for any pair of messages $m_0, m_1$ such that $\phi(m_0) = \phi(m_1) = 1$, define $\mathsf{poly}(\kappa)$-sampleable distributions $(\mathcal{D}_{m_0}, \mathcal{D}_{m_1})$ where $\mathcal{D}_{m_b} = (\mathsf{Com}(m_b; r), (m_b, r))$.

By definition of $\mathcal{L}_\phi$, $\mathsf{Supp}(\mathcal{D}_0) \cup \mathsf{Supp}(\mathcal{D}_0) \subseteq \mathcal{L}_\phi$. Moreover by $2^{\kappa^\epsilon}$-hardness of Com, we have that $\mathsf{Com}(m_0; r) \approx_{2^{\kappa^\epsilon}} \mathsf{Com}(m_1; r)$, Therefore, distributional indistinguishability of NIDI according to Definition 2 implies that: $\mathcal{P}(1^\kappa, \mathcal{D}_{m_0}, \mathcal{L}_\phi) \approx_\kappa \mathcal{P}(1^\kappa, \mathcal{D}_{m_1}, \mathcal{L}_\phi)$ or equivalently, $\mathcal{C}(1^\kappa, m_0, \phi) \approx_\kappa \mathcal{C}(1^\kappa, m_1, \phi)$, as desired.

# 6    CCA Commitments from Indistinguishability Obfuscation

In this section, we prove the following theorem.

**Theorem 5.** *Assume the existence of sub-exponentially secure indistinguishability obfuscation, sub-exponentially secure one-way functions with efficiently recognizable range and sub-exponentially secure CCA commitments for tags in* $[\log \log \log \kappa]$. *Then there exist CCA commitments for tags in* $2^{\kappa}$.

We prove this theorem by building a tag amplification compiler that amplifies CCA commitments for tags in $[t/2]$ for $t \leq \mathsf{poly}(\kappa)$ to tags in $[T]$ where $T = \binom{t}{t/2}$. Applying this compiler 4 times to a CCA commitments for tags in $[\log \log \log \kappa]$ yields the statement of the theorem.

In what follows, let $\epsilon > 0$ be an arbitrarily small constant such that:

- The CCA commitment for small tags and security parameter $\kappa$ is $2^{(\log \kappa)^{1/\epsilon}}$ secure and has a "brute-force" value algorithm CCAVal that recovers the value underlying any commitment, and runs in time at most $\mathsf{poly}(2^{\kappa})$.
- There exists a *subexponentially secure one-way function* $f$ that with security parameter $k$ is $2^{k^{\epsilon}}$ one-way. Furthermore, $f$ has an *efficiently recognizable range*, i.e., given $y$ there is an efficient algorithm to check whether there exists a value $x$ such that $f(x) = y$. Note that permutations have this property, because every $y$ is in the range of a permutation.
- There exists a *perfectly correct, sub-exponentially secure* public-key encryption scheme with key generation, encryption and decryption algorithms (KeyGen, Enc, Dec) that for security parameter $1^k$ satisfies $2^{k^{\epsilon}}$- IND-CPA security against (non-uniform) adversaries.
- There exists a *sub-exponentially secure* indistinguishability obfuscation scheme (iO.Obf, iO.Eval) that for security parameter $1^k$ satisfies $2^{k^{\epsilon}}$- security against (non-uniform) adversaries.
- There exists a *sub-exponentially secure* puncturable PRF that for security parameter $1^k$ satisfies $2^{k^{\epsilon}}$- security against (non-uniform) adversaries.
- There exist *sub-exponentially secure* NIWIs that for security parameter $1^k$ satisfy $2^{k^{\epsilon}}$- security against (non-uniform) adversaries.

Our compiler is described formally below, where letting $\mathcal{R}_{\mathcal{L}}$ denote the relation corresponding to NP language $\mathcal{L}$ we define language

$$\mathcal{L}_{\mathsf{NIWI}} = \Big\{ \{(c_i, s_i)\}_{i \in [t/2]}, (pk, \mathsf{enc}, y) : \exists (M, r_1, \dots, r_{t/2}, s, sk) \text{ s.t.}$$

$$\Big( \forall i \in [t/2], c_i = \mathsf{ComSmall}_{s_i}(M; r_i) \Big)$$

$$\bigvee \Big( (pk, sk) \leftarrow \mathsf{KeyGen}(s) \wedge y = f(\mathsf{Dec}_{sk}(c)) \Big) \Big\}$$

where $s_i$ denotes a tag in $[t/2]$, and ComSmall denotes the commit algorithm for an underlying CCA commitment with tags in $[t/2]$.

*Construction 6.1.* We now describe the CCACom and CCAVal algorithms for the scheme with large tags. We note that just like our commit-and-prove system described in the previous section, the commit phase ends *after* the receiver has queried the committer's program on a random input. The output of the commit phase is the output of such a receiver (and depending on the application, the receiver may or may not need to send its input back to the committer).

On input security parameter $\kappa$, we will set parameters of our building blocks as follows. Our one-way function with efficiently recognizable range and sub-exponential security will have security parameter $k_f$ set to $(\log \kappa)^{1/\epsilon}$. The CCA commitment for small tags will have security parameter set to $\kappa$. Note that this implies (by assumption) that CCAVal runs in time $\text{poly}(2^\kappa)$. Finally, all other primitives including iO, the puncturable PRF and the PKE scheme will have security parameter set to $k = \kappa^{\frac{1}{\epsilon}}$.

**The CCACom Algorithm:** $\text{CCACom}(1^\kappa, m, \text{tag})$ does the following.

- Let $\mathbb{T}$ denote the ordered set of all possible subsets of $[t]$, of size $t/2$. Pick the $i^{th}$ element in set $\mathbb{T}$, for $i = \text{tag}$.[7] Let this element be denoted by $(s_1, \ldots s_{t/2})$.
- The committer $\mathcal{C}(1^\kappa, M, \text{tag})$ does the following:
  - Set $k = \kappa^{\frac{1}{\epsilon}}$, and $k_f = (\log \kappa)^{\frac{1}{\epsilon}}$.
  - Sample $s \leftarrow \{0, 1\}^k$ and set $(pk, sk) \leftarrow \text{KeyGen}(s)$.
  - Sample $K \leftarrow \{0, 1\}^k$ and $R \leftarrow \{0, 1\}^k$.
  - Generate program $P_{pk, K, M, \text{tag}}$ defined in Fig. 5.
  - Compute $\widetilde{P} = \text{iO}(P_{pk, K, M, \text{tag}}; R)$.
  - Output $c = (\text{tag}, pk, \widetilde{P})$.
- The receiver $\mathcal{R}$ on input a commitment $c = (\text{tag}, pk, \widetilde{P})$ does the following.
  - Sample $v \leftarrow \{0, 1\}^\kappa$ and set $y = f(v)$.
  - Compute $\text{out} = \text{iO.Eval}(\widetilde{P}, y)$. Parse $\text{out} = (x, e)$, $x = (d, pk\text{enc}, y)$ and $d = \{c_i\}_{i \in [t/2]}$.
  - Set $x' = \{(c_i, s_i)\}_{i \in [t/2]}, (pk, \text{enc}, y)$. If $\text{NIWI}.\mathcal{V}(1^k, x', e, \mathcal{L}_{\text{NIWI}})$ rejects, output $\perp$ and stop.
  - Else output $v$, and for each $i \in [t/2]$, execute the receiver algorithm $\text{ComSmall}.\mathcal{R}(c_i)$.
    If any of these $(t/2)$ algorithms output $\perp$, then output $\perp$ and stop.
  - At the end of this process, the receiver either outputs $\perp$ or $(\tau_1, \ldots, \tau_{t/2})$ where $\tau_i$ denotes the (non-$\perp$) outcome of $\text{ComSmall}.\mathcal{R}(c_i)$.[8]

**The CCAVal Algorithm:** The CCAVal algorithm obtains as input a commitment string parsed as $\perp$ or $(\tau_1, \ldots, \tau_{t/2})$, generated as the output of the commit phase above, and does the following.

---

[7] Here, we use a different tag encoding scheme due to [50] that offers a slightly more optimized way to the same effect as the DDN encoding [27] discussed in the overview. That is, for every pair of unequal large tags $T$ and $T'$, there is at least one member in the set corresponding to $T$ that is not present in the set corresponding to $T'$, and vice-versa.

[8] Note that for the base scheme, $\mathcal{R}$ simply outputs the string it obtained from the committer.

**Hardwired:** Public key $pk$, Puncturable PRF Key $K$, message $M \in \{0,1\}^p$, small tags $(s_1, \dots s_{t/2})$ corresponding to **tag**.

**Input:** Query $y \in \{0,1\}^{k_f}$.

1. If $y \notin \mathsf{Range}(f)$, output $\perp$. Otherwise, continue.
2. Set $r = (r_1 \| r_2 \| \dots \| r_{t/2} \| r_{t/2+2}) = \mathsf{PRF}(K, y)$.
3. For $i \in [t/2]$, set $c_i = \mathsf{ComSmall}_{s_i}(M; r_i)$. Set $d = \{c_i\}_{i \in [t/2]}$.
4. Set $\mathsf{enc} = \mathsf{Enc}_{pk}(0^\kappa; r_{t/2+1})$.
5. Set $x = d, (pk, \mathsf{enc}, y), w = (M, r_1, \dots, r_{t/2}, 0^{2k})$.
6. Compute $e = \mathsf{NIWI}.\mathcal{P}(1^k, x, w, \mathcal{L}_{\mathsf{NIWI}}; r_{t/2+2})$ and output $(x, e)$.

**Fig. 5. Program** $P_{K,M,\mathsf{tag}}$

- On input a commitment string, if $\perp$, output $\perp$. Otherwise parse the string as $(\tau_1, \dots, \tau_{t/2})$ and execute $\mathsf{ComSmall.CCAVal}(\tau_1)$.

We prove the security of this construction, and discuss how to eliminate the same-tag restriction in the full version of the paper.

**Acknowledgments.** We thank the anonymous Eurocrypt reviewers for their insightful suggestions. We are also grateful to Ran Canetti, Suvradip Chakraborty, Oxana Poburinnaya and Manoj Prabhakaran for useful discussions.

# References

1. Agrawal, S.: Indistinguishability obfuscation without multilinear maps: new methods for bootstrapping and instantiation. In: Ishai, Y., Rijmen, V. (eds.) EUROCRYPT 2019. LNCS, vol. 11476, pp. 191–225. Springer, Cham (2019). https://doi.org/10.1007/978-3-030-17653-2_7
2. Agrawal, S., Pellet-Mary, A.: Indistinguishability obfuscation without maps: attacks and fixes for noisy linear FE. In: Canteaut, A., Ishai, Y. (eds.) EUROCRYPT 2020. LNCS, vol. 12105, pp. 110–140. Springer, Cham (2020). https://doi.org/10.1007/978-3-030-45721-1_5
3. Ananth, P., Jain, A., Lin, H., Matt, C., Sahai, A.: Indistinguishability obfuscation without multilinear maps: new paradigms via low degree weak pseudorandomness and security amplification. In: Boldyreva, A., Micciancio, D. (eds.) CRYPTO 2019. LNCS, vol. 11694, pp. 284–332. Springer, Cham (2019). https://doi.org/10.1007/978-3-030-26954-8_10
4. Ananth, P., Jain, A., Naor, M., Sahai, A., Yogev, E.: Universal constructions and robust combiners for indistinguishability obfuscation and witness encryption. In: Robshaw, M., Katz, J. (eds.) CRYPTO 2016. LNCS, vol. 9815, pp. 491–520. Springer, Heidelberg (2016). https://doi.org/10.1007/978-3-662-53008-5_17. Proceedings, Part II

5. Badrinarayanan, S., Garg, S., Ishai, Y., Sahai, A., Wadia, A.: Two-message witness indistinguishability and secure computation in the plain model from new assumptions. In: Takagi, T., Peyrin, T. (eds.) ASIACRYPT 2017. LNCS, vol. 10626, pp. 275–303. Springer, Cham (2017). https://doi.org/10.1007/978-3-319-70700-6_10. Proceedings, Part III

6. Barak, B.: Constant-round coin-tossing with a man in the middle or realizing the shared random string model. In: FOCS 2002, pp. 345–355 (2002)

7. Barak, B., et al.: On the (im)possibility of obfuscating programs. J. ACM **59**(2), 6:1–6:48 (2012). https://doi.org/10.1145/2160158.2160159

8. Barak, B., Ong, S.J., Vadhan, S.P.: Derandomization in cryptography. SIAM J. Comput. **37**(2), 380–400 (2007). https://doi.org/10.1137/050641958

9. Barak, B., Pass, R.: On the possibility of one-message weak zero-knowledge. In: Naor, M. (ed.) TCC 2004. LNCS, vol. 2951, pp. 121–132. Springer, Heidelberg (2004). https://doi.org/10.1007/978-3-540-24638-1_7. Theory of Cryptography, First Theory of Cryptography Conference

10. Bellare, M., Stepanovs, I., Tessaro, S.: Contention in cryptoland: obfuscation, leakage and UCE. In: Kushilevitz, E., Malkin, T. (eds.) TCC 2016. LNCS, vol. 9563, pp. 542–564. Springer, Heidelberg (2016). https://doi.org/10.1007/978-3-662-49099-0_20

11. Bitansky, N., Goldwasser, S., Jain, A., Paneth, O., Vaikuntanathan, V., Waters, B.: Time-lock puzzles from randomized encodings. In: Sudan, M. (ed.) Proceedings of the 2016 ACM Conference on Innovations in Theoretical Computer Science, Cambridge, MA, USA, 14–16 January 2016, pp. 345–356. ACM (2016). https://doi.org/10.1145/2840728.2840745

12. Bitansky, N., Khurana, D., Paneth, O.: Weak zero-knowledge beyond the black-box barrier. In: Charikar, M., Cohen, E. (eds.) STOC 2019, pp. 1091–1102. ACM (2019). https://doi.org/10.1145/3313276.3316382

13. Bitansky, N., Lin, H.: One-message zero knowledge and non-malleable commitments. In: Beimel, A., Dziembowski, S. (eds.) TCC 2018. LNCS, vol. 11239, pp. 209–234. Springer, Cham (2018). https://doi.org/10.1007/978-3-030-03807-6_8

14. Bitansky, N., Paneth, O.: Point obfuscation and 3-round zero-knowledge. In: Cramer, R. (ed.) TCC 2012. LNCS, vol. 7194, pp. 190–208. Springer, Heidelberg (2012). https://doi.org/10.1007/978-3-642-28914-9_11

15. Bitansky, N., Paneth, O.: ZAPs and non-interactive witness indistinguishability from indistinguishability obfuscation. In: Dodis, Y., Nielsen, J.B. (eds.) TCC 2015. LNCS, vol. 9015, pp. 401–427. Springer, Heidelberg (2015). https://doi.org/10.1007/978-3-662-46497-7_16

16. Bitansky, N., Shmueli, O.: Post-quantum zero knowledge in constant rounds. In: Makarychev, K., Makarychev, Y., Tulsiani, M., Kamath, G., Chuzhoy, J. (eds.) STOC 2020, pp. 269–279. ACM (2020). https://doi.org/10.1145/3357713.3384324

17. Brakerski, Z., Döttling, N., Garg, S., Malavolta, G.: Candidate iO from homomorphic encryption schemes. In: Canteaut, A., Ishai, Y. (eds.) EUROCRYPT 2020. LNCS, vol. 12105, pp. 79–109. Springer, Cham (2020). https://doi.org/10.1007/978-3-030-45721-1_4

18. Brakerski, Z., Döttling, N., Garg, S., Malavolta, G.: Factoring and pairings are not necessary for iO: circular-secure LWE suffices. IACR Cryptol. ePrint Arch. (2020). https://eprint.iacr.org/2020/1024

19. Brzuska, C., Mittelbach, A.: Indistinguishability obfuscation versus multi-bit point obfuscation with auxiliary input. In: Sarkar, P., Iwata, T. (eds.) ASIACRYPT 2014. LNCS, vol. 8874, pp. 142–161. Springer, Heidelberg (2014). https://doi.org/10.1007/978-3-662-45608-8_8

20. Canetti, R., Goldreich, O., Goldwasser, S., Micali, S.: Resettable zero-knowledge (extended abstract). In: Yao, F.F., Luks, E.M. (eds.) Proceedings of the Thirty-Second Annual ACM Symposium on Theory of Computing, 21–23 May 2000, Portland, OR, USA, pp. 235–244. ACM (2000). https://doi.org/10.1145/335305.335334

21. Canetti, R., Lin, H., Pass, R.: Adaptive hardness and composable security in the plain model from standard assumptions. In: Proceedings of the 51th Annual IEEE Symposium on Foundations of Computer Science, FOCS 2010, pp. 541–550 (2010)

22. Chung, K.-M., Lui, E., Pass, R.: From weak to strong zero-knowledge and applications. In: Dodis, Y., Nielsen, J.B. (eds.) TCC 2015. LNCS, vol. 9014, pp. 66–92. Springer, Heidelberg (2015). https://doi.org/10.1007/978-3-662-46494-6_4

23. Ciampi, M., Ostrovsky, R., Siniscalchi, L., Visconti, I.: Concurrent non-malleable commitments (and more) in 3 rounds. In: Robshaw, M., Katz, J. (eds.) CRYPTO 2016. LNCS, vol. 9816, pp. 270–299. Springer, Heidelberg (2016). https://doi.org/10.1007/978-3-662-53015-3_10. Robshaw and Katz [61]

24. Ciampi, M., Ostrovsky, R., Siniscalchi, L., Visconti, I.: Four-round concurrent non-malleable commitments from one-way functions. In: Katz, J., Shacham, H. (eds.) CRYPTO 2017. LNCS, vol. 10402, pp. 127–157. Springer, Cham (2017). https://doi.org/10.1007/978-3-319-63715-0_5

25. Deshpande, A., Kalai, Y.: Proofs of ignorance and applications to 2-message witness hiding. IACR Cryptol. ePrint Arch. 2018, 896 (2018)

26. Dodis, Y., Halevi, S., Rothblum, R.D., Wichs, D.: Spooky encryption and its applications. In: Robshaw, M., Katz, J. (eds.) CRYPTO 2016. LNCS, vol. 9816, pp. 93–122. Springer, Heidelberg (2016). https://doi.org/10.1007/978-3-662-53015-3_4. Robshaw and Katz [61]

27. Dolev, D., Dwork, C., Naor, M.: Non-malleable cryptography (Extended Abstract). In: STOC 1991 (1991)

28. Dwork, C., Naor, M., Reingold, O., Stockmeyer, L.J.: Magic functions. J. ACM 50(6), 852–921 (2003). https://doi.org/10.1145/950620.950623

29. Feige, U., Lapidot, D., Shamir, A.: Multiple noninteractive zero knowledge proofs under general assumptions. SIAM J. Comput. 29(1), 1–28 (1999). https://doi.org/10.1137/S0097539792230010

30. Feige, U., Shamir, A.: Witness indistinguishable and witness hiding protocols. In: Proceedings of the 22nd Annual ACM Symposium on Theory of Computing, 13–17 May 1990, Baltimore, Maryland, USA, pp. 416–426 (1990). https://doi.org/10.1145/100216.100272

31. Garg, R., Khurana, D., Lu, G., Waters, B.: Black-box non-interactive non-malleable commitments. Cryptology ePrint Archive, Report 2020/1197 (2020). https://eprint.iacr.org/2020/1197

32. Garg, S., Gentry, C., Halevi, S., Raykova, M.: Two-round secure MPC from indistinguishability obfuscation. In: Lindell, Y. (ed.) TCC 2014. LNCS, vol. 8349, pp. 74–94. Springer, Heidelberg (2014). https://doi.org/10.1007/978-3-642-54242-8_4

33. Gay, R., Jain, A., Lin, H., Sahai, A.: Indistinguishability obfuscation from simple-to-state hard problems: new assumptions, new techniques, and simplification. IACR Cryptol. ePrint Arch. (2020). https://eprint.iacr.org/2020/764

34. Gay, R., Pass, R.: Indistinguishability obfuscation from circular security. IACR Cryptol. ePrint Arch. (2020). https://eprint.iacr.org/2020/1010

35. Goldreich, O.: The Foundations of Cryptography -Basic Techniques, vol. 1. Cambridge University Press, Cambridge (2001)

36. Goldreich, O., Micali, S., Wigderson, A.: Proofs that yield nothing but their validity for all languages in NP have zero-knowledge proof systems. J. ACM 38(3), 691–729 (1991). https://doi.org/10.1145/116825.116852

37. Goldreich, O., Oren, Y.: Definitions and properties of zero-knowledge proof systems. J. Cryptol. **7**(1), 1–32 (1994). https://doi.org/10.1007/BF00195207
38. Goldwasser, S., Micali, S., Rackoff, C.: The knowledge complexity of interactive proof systems. SIAM J. Comput. **18**(1), 186–208 (1989). https://doi.org/10.1137/0218012
39. Goyal, V.: Constant round non-malleable protocols using one-way functions. In: STOC 2011, pp. 695–704. ACM (2011)
40. Goyal, V., Lee, C.K., Ostrovsky, R., Visconti, I.: Constructing non-malleable commitments: a black-box approach. In: FOCS (2012)
41. Goyal, V., Pandey, O., Richelson, S.: Textbook non-malleable commitments. In: STOC, pp. 1128–1141. ACM, New York (2016). https://doi.org/10.1145/2897518.2897657
42. Goyal, V., Richelson, S.: Non-malleable commitments using goldreich-levin list decoding. In: Zuckerman, D. (ed.) FOCS 2019, pp. 686–699. IEEE Computer Society (2019). https://doi.org/10.1109/FOCS.2019.00047, https://ieeexplore.ieee.org/xpl/conhome/8936052/proceeding
43. Goyal, V., Richelson, S., Rosen, A., Vald, M.: An algebraic approach to non-malleability. In: FOCS 2014, pp. 41–50 (2014). https://doi.org/10.1109/FOCS.2014.13
44. Groth, J., Ostrovsky, R., Sahai, A.: New techniques for noninteractive zero-knowledge. J. ACM **59**(**3**), 11:1–11:35 (2012). https://doi.org/10.1145/2220357.2220358
45. Jain, A., Lin, H., Matt, C., Sahai, A.: How to leverage hardness of constant-degree expanding polynomials over $\mathbb{R}$ to build $i\mathcal{O}$. In: Ishai, Y., Rijmen, V. (eds.) EUROCRYPT 2019. LNCS, vol. 11476, pp. 251–281. Springer, Cham (2019). https://doi.org/10.1007/978-3-030-17653-2_9
46. Jain, A., Lin, H., Sahai, A.: Indistinguishability obfuscation from well-founded assumptions. Cryptology ePrint Archive, Report 2020/1003 (2020). https://eprint.iacr.org/2020/1003
47. Jain, A., Kalai, Y.T., Khurana, D., Rothblum, R.: Distinguisher-dependent simulation in two rounds and its applications. In: Katz, J., Shacham, H. (eds.) CRYPTO 2017. Lecture Notes in Computer Science, vol. 10402, pp. 158–189. Springer (2017). https://doi.org/10.1007/978-3-319-63715-0
48. Kalai, Y.T., Khurana, D.: Non-interactive non-malleability from quantum supremacy. In: Boldyreva, A., Micciancio, D. (eds.) CRYPTO 2019. LNCS, vol. 11694, pp. 552–582. Springer, Cham (2019). https://doi.org/10.1007/978-3-030-26954-8_18
49. Khurana, D.: Round optimal concurrent non-malleability from polynomial hardness. In: Kalai, Y., Reyzin, L. (eds.) TCC 2017. LNCS, vol. 10678, pp. 139–171. Springer, Cham (2017). https://doi.org/10.1007/978-3-319-70503-3_5
50. Khurana, D., Sahai, A.: How to achieve non-malleability in one or two rounds. In: Umans [63], pp. 564–575. https://doi.org/10.1109/FOCS.2017.58
51. Kuykendall, B., Zhandry, M.: Towards non-interactive witness hiding. Cryptology ePrint Archive, Report 2020/1205 (2020). https://eprint.iacr.org/2020/1205
52. Lin, H., Pass, R.: Constant-round non-malleable commitments from any one-way function. In: STOC 2011, pp. 705–714 (2011)
53. Lin, H., Pass, R.: Non-malleability amplification. In: Proceedings of the 41st Annual ACM Symposium on Theory of Computing, STOC 2009, pp. 189–198 (2009)

54. Lin, H., Pass, R., Soni, P.: Two-round and non-interactive concurrent non-malleable commitments from time-lock puzzles. In: Umans [63], pp. 576–587 (2017). https://doi.org/10.1109/FOCS.2017.59
55. Lin, H., Pass, R., Venkitasubramaniam, M.: Concurrent non-malleable commitments from any one-way function. In: TCC 2008, pp. 571–588 (2008)
56. Pandey, O., Pass, R., Vaikuntanathan, V.: Adaptive one-way functions and applications. In: Advances in Cryptology – CRYPTO 2008, pp. 57–74 (2008)
57. Pass, R.: Simulation in quasi-polynomial time, and its application to protocol composition. In: Biham, E. (ed.) EUROCRYPT 2003. LNCS, vol. 2656, pp. 160–176. Springer, Heidelberg (2003). https://doi.org/10.1007/3-540-39200-9_10
58. Pass, R., Rosen, A.: Concurrent non-malleable commitments. In: Proceedings of the 46th Annual IEEE Symposium on Foundations of Computer Science, FOCS 2005, pp. 563–572 (2005)
59. Pass, R., Rosen, A.: New and improved constructions of nonmalleable cryptographic protocols. SIAM J. Comput. **38**(2), 702–752 (2008)
60. Pass, R., Wee, H.: Constant-round non-malleable commitments from sub-exponential one-way functions. In: Gilbert, H. (ed.) EUROCRYPT 2010. LNCS, vol. 6110, pp. 638–655. Springer, Heidelberg (2010). https://doi.org/10.1007/978-3-642-13190-5_32
61. Robshaw, M., Katz, J. (eds.): Advances in Cryptology - CRYPTO 2016–36th Annual International Cryptology Conference, Santa Barbara, CA, USA, August 14–18, 2016, Proceedings, Part III, Lecture Notes in Computer Science, vol. 9816. Springer (2016). https://doi.org/10.1007/978-3-662-53015-3
62. Sahai, A., Waters, B.: How to use indistinguishability obfuscation: deniable encryption, and more. In: Shmoys, D.B. (ed.) STOC 2014, pp. 475–484. ACM (2014). https://doi.org/10.1145/2591796.2591825
63. Umans, C. (ed.): 58th IEEE Annual Symposium on Foundations of Computer Science, FOCS 2017, Berkeley, CA, USA, 15–17 October 2017. IEEE Computer Society (2017). https://ieeexplore.ieee.org/xpl/conhome/8100284/proceeding
64. Wee, H.: Black-box, round-efficient secure computation via non-malleability amplification. In: FOCS 2010, pp. 531–540 (2010). https://doi.org/10.1109/FOCS.2010.87
65. Wee, H., Wichs, D.: Candidate obfuscation via oblivious LWE sampling. IACR Cryptol. ePrint Arch. (2020). https://eprint.iacr.org/2020/1042

# Zero-Knowledge Proofs

# Public-Coin Statistical Zero-Knowledge Batch Verification Against Malicious Verifiers

Inbar Kaslasi[1(✉)], Ron D. Rothblum[1], and Prashant Nalini Vasudevanr[2]

[1] Technion, Haifa, Israel
{inbark,rothblum}@cs.technion.ac.il
[2] UC Berkeley, Berkeley, USA
prashvas@berkeley.edu

**Abstract.** Suppose that a problem $\Pi$ has a statistical zero-knowledge (SZK) proof with communication complexity $m$. The question of batch verification for SZK asks whether one can prove that $k$ instances $x_1, \ldots, x_k$ all belong to $\Pi$ with a statistical zero-knowledge proof whose communication complexity is better than $k \cdot m$ (which is the complexity of the trivial solution of executing the original protocol independently on each input).

In a recent work, Kaslasi *et al.* (TCC, 2020) constructed such a batch verification protocol for any problem having a *non-interactive* SZK (NISZK) proof-system. Two drawbacks of their result are that their protocol is private-coin and is only zero-knowledge with respect to the honest verifier.

In this work, we eliminate these two drawbacks by constructing a public-coin malicious-verifier SZK protocol for batch verification of NISZK. Similarly to the aforementioned prior work, the communication complexity of our protocol is $(k + \mathsf{poly}(m)) \cdot \mathsf{polylog}(k, m)$.

**Keywords:** Statistical zero-knowledge · Batch verification

## 1 Introduction

The concept of zero knowledge proofs, introduced by Goldwasser, Micali and Rackoff [GMR89], is an incredibly deep and fascinating notion that has proven to be a fundamental component in the construction and design of cryptographic protocols (see, e.g., [GMW87]). A zero-knowledge proof allows a prover to convince an efficient verifier that a given statement is true without revealing anything else to the verifier. This is formalized by requiring that for any (possibly malicious) verifier that participates in such a proof, there is an efficient simulation algorithm that simulates its interaction with the prover.

In this work we focus on *statistical zero-knowledge proofs*. In this variant, both the verifier and the prover are guaranteed information-theoretic (rather

The full version is available on the Cryptology ePrint Archive [KRV21].

© International Association for Cryptologic Research 2021
A. Canteaut and F.-X. Standaert (Eds.): EUROCRYPT 2021, LNCS 12698, pp. 219–246, 2021.
https://doi.org/10.1007/978-3-030-77883-5_8

than computational) security. On the one hand, the verifier knows that even an all-powerful prover could not convince it to accept a false statement (other than with negligible probability). On the other hand, the prover knows that any polynomial-time cheating strategy of the verifier can only reveal a negligible amount of information beyond the validity of the statement being proven.

The class of languages having a statistical zero-knowledge protocol is denoted by SZK. This class contains several natural problems like Graph Nonisomorphism, and many of the problems that are central to cryptography such as quadratic residuosity [GMR89], discrete logarithm [GK93, CP92], and various lattice problems [GG00, MV03, PV08, APS18]. It has been found to possess extremely rich structure [For89, AH91, Oka00, SV03, GSV98, GV99, NV06, OV08] and to have fundamental connections to different aspects of cryptography [BL13, KMN+14, LV16, Ost91, OW93, BDRV18, KY18, BBD+20] and complexity theory [For87, AH91, Aar12, GR14, Dru15, AV19, BCH+20].

In a recent work, Kaslasi et al. [KRR+20] raised the question of *batch verification for statistical zero-knowledge proofs*: Suppose $\Pi$ has a statistical zero-knowledge proof (SZK). Can we prove that $x_1, \ldots, x_k \in \Pi$ with communication complexity that beats the naive approach of separately proving that each $x_i \in \Pi$, while still maintaining zero-knowledge? Beyond being of intrinsic interest and teaching us about the structure of SZK, such protocols have potential cryptographic applications such as the batch verification of cryptographic signatures [NMVR94, BGR98, CHP12] or well-formedness of public-keys [GMR98].

The main result of [KRR+20] was such a generic batch verification result for a subclass of languages in SZK – specifically for problems having a *non-interactive* statistical zero-knowledge proof system (NISZK). Kaslasi et al. construct an (interactive) SZK protocol for batching $k$ instances of $\Pi \in$ NISZK, with communication complexity $(k + \text{poly}(n)) \cdot \text{polylog}(k, n)$, where $n$ is the length of each of the $k$ inputs, and poly refers to a fixed polynomial that depends only on the specific problem (and not on $k$). Their result should be contrasted with the naive approach of simply executing the NISZK protocol separately on each input (which has communication complexity $k \cdot \text{poly}(n)$).

Two major drawbacks of the protocol of [KRR+20] are the fact that it is *private-coin* and only *honest-verifier* statistical zero-knowledge (HVSZK). These drawbacks are significant. Recall that private-coin protocols can only be verified by a designated verifier, in contrast to *public-coin* protocols that can be verified by anyone (as long as they can ensure that the coins were truly unpredictable to the prover, e.g., they were generated by some physical phenomenon or a public randomness beacon). Further, public-coin protocols have the added benefit that they can be transformed into *non-interactive* arguments via the Fiat-Shamir transform (either heuristically [FS86], in the random-oracle model [PS96], or, more recently, under concrete cryptographic assumptions (see, e.g., [CCH+19])).

The second drawback is arguably even more significant. Recall that honest-verifier zero-knowledge is a relatively weak privacy guarantee which, in a nutshell, only guarantees that verifiers that follow the protocol to the letter learn nothing in the interaction. Usually this weak privacy guarantee is only used as a stepping stone towards getting full-fledged zero-knowledge (i.e., zero-knowledge that holds even against arbitrary polynomial-time cheating verifiers).

At first glance it may seem straightforward to overcome both drawbacks of the protocol of [KRR+20] by employing the known generic transformations from *private-coin honest-verifier statistical zero-knowledge* to *public-coin malicious-verifier statistical zero-knoweldge* [Oka00, GSV98, HRV18]. Unfortunately, these tranformations incur a large polynomial overhead in communication that we cannot afford in our context (see also Remark 1 below).

## 1.1  Our Results

In this paper we eliminate the two major drawbacks mentioned above by constructing a *public-coin malicious-verifier* SZK batch verification protocol for every problem in NISZK. The communication complexity in our protocol is similar to that of [KRR+20].

**Theorem 1 (Informally Stated, see Theorem 7).** *Let $\Pi \in$ NISZK. There exists a public-coin SZK protocol for verifying that $x_1, \ldots, x_k \in \Pi$, with communication complexity $(k + \mathrm{poly}(n)) \cdot \mathrm{polylog}(n, k)$. The verifier's running time is $k \cdot \mathrm{poly}(n, \log k)$, and the number of rounds is $k \cdot \mathrm{polylog}(n, k)$.*

Our high-level approach for proving Theorem 1 follows a classical approach for constructing malicious-verifier zero-knowledge proofs: first construct a public-coin honest-verifier zero-knowledge batching protocol, and then show how to transform it to be *malicious-verifier* zero-knowledge. The main challenge that we must overcome is in actually implementing these two steps without incurring the exorbitant price of the generic transformations for SZK [Oka00, SV03, GV99, GSV98, HRV18]. Thus, our two main steps are:

1. Construct an efficient *public-coin* HVSZK batch verification protocol.
2. Transform it to be zero-knowledge against malicious verifiers, while preserving its efficiency.

Our first main technical contribution is in implementing Step 1.

**Theorem 2 (Informally Stated, see Theorem 6).** *Let $\Pi \in$ NISZK. There exists a public-coin HVSZK protocol for verifying that $x_1, \ldots, x_k \in \Pi$, with communication complexity $(k + \mathrm{poly}(n)) \cdot \mathrm{polylog}(n, k)$. The verifier's running time is $k \cdot \mathrm{poly}(n, \log k)$, and the number of rounds is $O(k)$.*

Theorem 2 already improves on the main result of [KRR+20], since it gives a *public-coin* batch verification protocol. However, we would like to go further and obtain security even against malicious verifiers. It is tempting at this point to apply the generic transformations of [GSV98, HRV18] from public-coin *honest-verifier* zero-knowledge, to *malicious-verifier*. Unfortunately, the overhead introduced in these transformations is too large and applying them to the protocol of Theorem 1 would yield a trivial result (see Remark 1 for details).

Rather, as our second technical contribution (which may be of independent interest), we show that the communication complexity of the [GSV98] transformation can be significantly improved for protocols satisfying a strong notion of soundness. Specifically, we refer to the notion of *round-by-round soundness*, introduced in a recent work of Canetti *et al.* [CCH+19].

**Theorem 3 (Informally Stated, see Theorem 5).** *Any public-coin* HVSZK *protocol with negligible round-by-round soundness error can be efficiently transformed into a public-coin* SZK *protocol. In particular, a message of length $\ell$ in the original protocol grows to length* poly$(\ell)$ *in the transformed protocol.*

Note that the growth of each message in the transformation above depends only on its own length and not on $n$ or $k$ – this allows us to take advantage of the fact that all but one of the messages in the protocol of Theorem 2 have polylogarithmic length. We show that the protocol of Theorem 2 indeed has round-by-round soundness which, in combination with Theorem 3, yields Theorem 1.

*Remark 1 (On Generic Transformations from the Literature).* We discuss here a few known generic transformations for the class SZK from the literature, and why they are not applicable in our context.

Okamoto [Oka00] showed how to transform any *private-coin* HVSZK protocol into a public-coin one. Unfortunately, we cannot use his transformation to derive Theorem 1 from the private-coin batching protocol of [KRR+20], due to the overhead involved. In more detail, Okamoto's protocol starts by taking a $t$-fold parallel repetition of the private-coin protocol, where $t = \ell^9 \cdot r^9$, where $\ell$ is the round complexity and $r$ is the randomness complexity of the simulator. In our context $\ell = k$ and $r = $ poly$(n)$ and so the overhead from Okamoto's transformation would yield a trivial result (as a matter of fact, we could not even afford an overhead of $t = \ell$, which seems inherent to Okamoto's approach).

Similarly, we cannot derive Theorem 1 from Theorem 2 by applying the generic transformation of [GSV98, HRV18] for transforming honest-verifier public-coin SZK proofs to malicious-verifier ones. In more detail, the transformation of [GSV98] starts by applying an $\ell$-fold parallel repetition of the honest-verifier protocol (where again $\ell$ is the number of rounds). In the context of Theorem 2, $\ell = \Theta(k)$, and so, applying the [GSV98] transformation yields a protocol with communication complexity $k \cdot$ poly$(n)$, which we cannot afford.

The more recent work of Hubáček *et al.* [HRV18] gives an efficiency-preserving transformation from honest-verifier to malicious-verifier. This transformation also incurs a polynomial overhead in the communication complexity. In particular, [HRV18] rely on the instance-dependent commitments of Ong and Vadhan [OV08], which in turn use the SZK completeness of the Entropy Difference (or ED) problem [GV99]. The known reduction from SZK to ED (see [Vad99, Theorem 3.3.13]) generates circuits whose input size is roughly $\ell \cdot r$. This size would correspond to the size of the decommitments in the [HRV18] protocol and again would lead to an overhead that we cannot incur.

Indeed, our work motivates the study of *communication-preserving* transformations for SZK protocols. In particular, obtaining a *generic* communication-preserving transformation from honest-verifier to malicious-verifier SZK is an interesting open question.

## 1.2    Technical Overview

First, in Sect. 1.2, we describe the public-coin honest-verifier statistical zero-knowledge (HVSZK) batching protocol. Then, in Sect. 1.2, we show how to compile honest-verifier protocols *efficiently* to be secure against malicious verifiers.

**Public-Coin HVSZK Batching.** Our starting point is the aforementioned recent work of Kaslasi *et al.* [KRR+20], which gave a *private-coin* HVSZK batching protocol. As their first step, they introduced a new (promise) problem called *approximate injectivety* (AI) and showed that it is NISZK-complete. They then designed a private-coin HVSZK batch verification protocol for AI. We follow a similar route, except that we construct a *public-coin* HVSZK batch verification protocol for AI.

The inputs to the AI problem, which is parameterized by a real number $\delta \in [0,1]$, are circuits $C : \{0,1\}^n \to \{0,1\}^m$. YES instances are circuits $C$ for which all but a $\delta$ fraction of the inputs are mapped injectively to their corresponding outputs (i.e., $\Pr_x\left[|C^{-1}(C(x))| > 1\right] < \delta$). NO instances are circuits for which at most a $\delta$ fraction of the inputs are mapped injectively (i.e., $\Pr_x\left[|C^{-1}(C(x))| > 1\right] > 1 - \delta$).

Since $\mathsf{AI}_\delta$ was shown to be NISZK complete, to prove Theorem 2 it suffices to show a *public-coin* HVSZK batching protocol for $\mathsf{AI}_\delta$. Our main technical result is precisely such a protocol achieving communication roughly $k + \mathsf{poly}(n)$, where $k$ is the number of instances being batched. For simplicity, we first focus on the case that $\delta = 0$ – namely, distinguishing circuits that are injective from those in which no input is mapped injectively to its output. A discussion of the case of $\delta > 0$ is deferred to the end of this overview.

In order to present our approach, following [KRR+20], we will first consider a drastically easier case in which the goal is to distinguish between circuits that are *permutations* (rather than merely being injective) or are far from such.

*Warmup: Batch Verification for Permutations.* We first consider a variant of AI, called PERM. The inputs to PERM are length-preserving circuits $C : \{0,1\}^n \to \{0,1\}^n$. YES instances are circuits that compute permutations over $\{0,1\}^n$, whereas NO instances are circuits that are *far* from being permutations in the sense that no input is mapped injectively (i.e., every image has at least two preimages).

Consider the following batch verification protocol for PERM. Given common input $C_1, \ldots, C_k : \{0,1\}^n \to \{0,1\}^n$ the parties proceed as follows. The verifier V samples $y_k \in \{0,1\}^n$ and sends it to the prover P. Then, P responds with an $x_1$ s.t. $C_k(C_{k-1}(...C_1(x_1))) = y_k$. The verifier checks that indeed $C_k(C_{k-1}(...C_1(x_1))) = y_k$ and accepts or rejects accordingly.

To argue that completeness holds, observe that when all of the $C_i$'s are permutations, there exists a *unique* sequence $x_1, y_1, x_2, y_2, \ldots, x_{k-1}, y_{k-1}, x_k$, where $x_i = y_{i-1}$ for every $i \in [2, k]$, that is consistent with $y_k$. That is, $x_i = C_i^{-1}(y_i)$, for every $i \in [k]$). The prover can thus make the verifier accept (with probability 1) by sending $x_1$ as its message.

For soundness, let $i^* \in [k]$ denote the maximal index $i$ s.t. $C_i$ is a NO instance. Since $C_{i^*}$ is a NO instance, each of its images has at least two preimages and so the size of its image is at most $2^{n-1}$. Since $y_k$ is sampled uniformly and $C_{i^*+1}, \ldots, C_k$ are permutations, we have that $y_{i^*}$ is also random in $\{0, 1\}^n$. In particular this means that with probability at least half it has no preimage under $C_{i^*}$, and the verifier will eventually reject no matter what value of $x_1$ the prover sends. Note that the soundness error, which is $1/2$ here, can be amplified by repetition.

For zero-knowledge, consider the simulator that first samples $x_1 \in \{0, 1\}^n$ and then computes $y_k = C_k(C_{k-1}(\ldots C_1(x_1)))$. Since all circuits are permutations, $y_k$ is distributed uniformly over $\{0, 1\}^n$ as in the real interaction between the honest-verifier and the prover.

The above batch verification protocol for PERM, while simple, will be the basic underlying idea also for our batch verification protocol for $\mathsf{AI}_0$.

*Public-Coin Batch Verification for* $\mathsf{AI}_0$. Let $C_1, \ldots, C_k : \{0, 1\}^n \to \{0, 1\}^m$ be instances of $\mathsf{AI}_0$. Since the output size of each circuit $C_i$ is not compatible with the input size for the following circuit $C_{i+1}$, we cannot directly compose the circuits as we did for PERM.

A natural idea that comes to mind is to use hashing. Namely, choose a hash function[1] $g$ to map $C_i$'s output $y_i \in \{0, 1\}^m$ to the next circuit input $x_{i+1} \in \{0, 1\}^n$, for every $i \in [k]$. Based on this idea it is natural to consider a minor modificition of the batch verification protocol for PERM, where the only difference is that we interleave applications of $g$ as we compose the circuits. Note that we have to hash the last circuit output $y_k$ as well so that we can specify $x_{k+1} = g(y_k)$ to the prover as a genuine unstructured random string.

If we could guarantee that the hash function $g$ maps the image of each circuit *injectively* into the domain of the subsequent circuit, then a similar analysis as in the protocol for PERM could be applied and we would be done. However, finding such a hash function in general seems incredibly difficult. Thus, instead, we choose $g$ to be a random function.[2]

In what follows, for every $i \in [k]$, denote the image of $C_i$ by $S_i \subseteq \{0, 1\}^m$. Note that if $C_i$ is a YES instance (i.e., injective), the size of $S_i$ is exactly $2^n$, and if $C_i$ is a NO instance (entirely non-injective) the size of $S_i$ is at most $2^{n-1}$.

When using a random function $g$ as our hash function, we run into two key challenges that did not exist in the protocol for PERM. The first of these two challenges arises from the fact that for any YES instance circuit $C_i$, with high

---

[1] The specific type of hash function that we use is left vague for now and will be discussed in detail shortly.

[2] Jumping ahead, we note that we cannot afford for $g$ to be entirely random, and will have to settle for some de-randomization. For the moment we ignore this issue.

probability over the choice of $g : \{0,1\}^m \rightarrow \{0,1\}^n$, a constant fraction of the elements in $\{0,1\}^n$ have no preimages (under $g$) in the set $S_i$.[3] If such a situation occurs for *any* of the circuits, a situation which is exceedingly likely, then even the honest prover will not be able to find a suitable preimage $x_1$ and we lose completeness.

The way we solve this difficulty is relatively simple: we add to the hash function $g$ a short random auxiliary input that will be chosen independently for each of the $k$ applications of $g$. We denote the auxiliary input for the $i^{\text{th}}$ application by $z_i$ and its length by $d$ (which we set to $\text{polylog}(n,k)$). Observe that if $g : \{0,1\}^m \times \{0,1\}^d \rightarrow \{0,1\}^n$ is chosen at random, then we expect all $x$'s in the domain of $C_{i+1}$ to have roughly the same number of preimages (under $g$) that lie in the set $S_i \times \{0,1\}^d$.[4]

This brings us to the second challege in using a random hash function $g$, which is slightly more subtle. When considering a YES instance circuit $C_i$, even ignoring the additional auxiliary input, a constant fraction of the domain $\{0,1\}^n$ of $C_{i+1}$ will have *more than one* preimage (under $g$) which falls in $S_i$. Needless to say, this issue is further exacerbated by the addition of the auxiliary input. At first glance this may not seem like much of an issue when we consider a YES circuit. However, on further inspection, we observe that we may very well be in the case that all of the circuits except for the first circuit $C_1$ are YES instances (i.e., injective) and only $C_1$ is a NO instance (i.e., non-injective).

If such is the case, due to the collisions that occur in $g$, it is likely that $y_k$ will have an exponential (in $k$) number of preimages $x_2$ that are consistent with it. If the prover has so much flexibility in its choice of $x_2$ then it is likely that, even though $C_1$ is non-injective, the prover will be able to find a consistent preimage $x_1$ and we lose soundness.

Borrowing an idea from [KRR+20], we solve this challenge using interaction. The high-level approach is for the prover to *commit* to $x_i$ *before* we reveal the auxiliary information for the next circuit. Thus, the protocol proceeds iteratively, where in each iteration first the prover commits to $x_i$, and then the verifier reveals the auxiliary input, which the prover uses to recover $y_{i-1}$, and so on. The commitment has the property that as long as we are processing YES input circuits, with high probability, there is a *unique* $x_i$ that is consistent with the interaction. In particular, when we reach the first NO instance circuit $C_{i^*}$ (recall that $i^*$ denotes the maximal $i$ s.t. $C_i$ is a NO instance) there is a unique $x_{i^*+1}$ that is consistent with the transcript.

*Distinguishing Injective Circuits from Non-Injective Circuits.* Recall that our goal is to distinguish an injective circuit from a highly non-injective circuit. Following our approach thus far, assume that we have processed the circuit

---

[3] This is similar to the fact that when throwing $N$ balls into $N$ bins, in expectation, a constant fraction of the bins remain empty. Here the images of $C_i$ play the role of the balls and the elements in the domain $\{0,1\}^n$ of $C_{i+1}$ play the role of the bins.

[4] Here we rely on the fact that when throwing $N \cdot \text{polylog}(N)$ balls into $N$ bits, with high probability, all bins will contain very close to the expected $\text{polylog}(N)$ balls.

up to the circuit $C_i$ and moreover, that there is a unique $x_{i+1}$ that is consistent with the interaction up to this point.

Recall also that if $C_i$ is injective then $|S_i| = 2^n$, whereas if it is non-injective then $|S_i| \leq 2^{n-1}$. Thus, our approach is to employ a set lower bound protocol (a la [GS89]) as follows. The verifier chooses a "filter" function $h_i \in H_n$, where $H_n$ is a family of pairwise independent hash functions from domain $\{0,1\}^m \times \{0,1\}^d$ to an appropriately chosen range size, as well as a target element $\alpha_i$. If $C_i$ is injective then we expect each $x_{i+1}$ to have very close to $2^d$ preimages $(y_i, z_i) \in S_i \times \{0,1\}^d$ under $g$. On the other hand, if $C_i$ is non-injective, then we expect each $x_{i+1}$ to have roughly $2^{d-1}$ such preimages or less. Thus, by setting the range size to be roughly $2^d$, the probability that one of these preimages hashes correctly via $h_i$ to $\alpha_i$ is larger (by a constant) in the YES case than in the NO case.

*Balancing Completeness, Soundness and Zero-Knowledge.* At this point we observe that even if $g$ and $h_i$ were random functions, the set lower bound approach only yields a small constant gap between completeness and soundness. This is insufficient since the completeness error is accumulating across the $k$ different circuits. Note that we cannot afford a $k$-fold repetition of the set lower bound protocol (since it would be prohibitively expensive in our parameter setting). Moreover, since we cannot generically amplify zero-knowledge, we also need the zero-knowledge error accumulated by the YES instance circuits to be negligible.

We resolve this issue by considering a new variant of the approximate injectivity problem which we denote by $\mathsf{AI}_{L,\delta}$. The YES instances in this variant are identical to the YES instance in $\mathsf{AI}_\delta$ – namely circuits that are injective on all but a $\delta$ fraction of their domain. However, a circuit $C$ is a NO instance if at least $1 - \delta$ fraction of its inputs have at least $L$ "siblings" (i.e., inputs that are mapped to the same output). Thus, the standard $\mathsf{AI}_\delta$ problem corresponds to the case $L = 2$. Using a large enough $L$ increases the gap between the number of preimages in YES and NO instances, letting us set the range size of the $h_i$'s to obtain a larger gap between completeness and soundness.

We show that $\mathsf{AI}_{2,\delta}$ reduces to $\mathsf{AI}_{L,\delta'}$, where $L = 2^{\mathrm{polylog}(n,k)}$ and $\delta'$ is related to $\delta$. The idea for the reduction is to simply concatenate sufficiently many copies of the input circuit.[5] Thus, in the sequel it suffices to consider batch verification for $k$ instances of $\mathsf{AI}_{L,0}$ (and the case that $\delta > 0$ will be discussed later on).

*Over-Simplified Batch Verification Protocol for $\mathsf{AI}_{L,0}$.* With the foregoing insights in mind, consider the following over-simplified batching protocol for $\mathsf{AI}_{L,0}$ (see also the diagram in Fig. 1 which gives a bird's eye view of the flow of the protocol).

1. V samples $g$ and $x_{k+1} \leftarrow \{0,1\}^n$ and sends both to P.
2. For $i = k, ..., 1$:

---

[5] In more detail, we transform an instance $C$ of $\mathsf{AI}_{2,\delta}$ to an instance $C'$ of $\mathsf{AI}_{2^\ell, \delta \cdot \ell}$ by concatenating $\ell$ copies of $C$. It is not hard to see that if $C$ were (almost) injective) then $C'$ is (almost) injective. But, if (almost) every image of $C$ has at least two preimages then (almost) every image of $C'$ has at least $2^\ell$ preimages.

    (a) V samples a filter function $h_i \leftarrow H_n$ and target value $\alpha_i$ (of appropriate length) and sends both to P.

    (b) P selects at random a pair $(x_i, z_i)$ s.t.

        i. $g(C_i(x_i), z_i) = x_{i+1}$

        ii. $h_i(C_i(x_i), z_i) = \alpha_i$

      and sends $(x_i, z_i)$ to V.

3. V sets $x_1' = x_1$ and for $i = 1, \ldots, k$:

    (a) Computes $y_i' = C_i(x_i')$.

    (b) Verifies that $h_i(y_i', z_i) = \alpha_i$.

    (c) Computes $x_{i+1}' = g(y_i', z_i)$.

    (d) Verifies that $x_{i+1}' = x_{i+1}$.

4. If all of V's checks pass then she accepts. Otherwise she rejects.

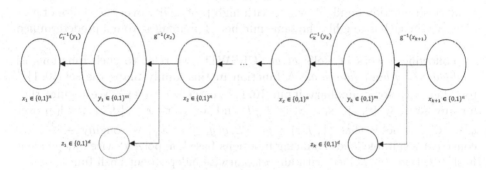

**Fig. 1.** Sampling Process of the Protocol

Note that the communication complexity in this protocol is $\Omega(k \cdot n)$ (since the prover sends $x_1, \ldots, x_k$), which is more than we can afford. This issue will be resolved shortly and so we ignore it for now.

For completeness, if all $C_i$'s are injective, in every iteration $i$, given that there exists a consistent $x_i$ (i.e., $x_i$ for which there exists $z$ where $g(C_i(x_i), z) = x_{i+1}$ and $h_i(C_i(x_i), z) = \alpha_i$), w.h.p. there exists also a consistent $x_{i-1}$. Hence, it is not hard to show, by induction, that with high probability, after the last iteration there exists an $x_1$ that passes the verifier's checks, and so V accepts.

For soundness, consider the iteration $i^*$ which, as defined in the protocol for PERM, denotes the maximal index of a NO instance circuit. Since the number of preimages of $C_{i^*}$ is less than $2^n/L$, by the foregoing discussion it is very likely that there does not exist a pair $(x_{i^*}, z_{i^*})$ that is consistent with the rest of the messages, i.e., s.t. $g(C_{i^*}(x_{i^*}), z_{i^*}) = x_{i^*+1}$ and $h_{i^*}(C_{i^*}(x_{i^*}), z_{i^*}) = \alpha_{i^*}$, and therefore V will eventually reject.

Before arguing why the protocol is zero-knowledge, we first discuss the hash function family that $g$ is sampled from.

*The Hash Function $g$.* One important consideration that arises when derandomizing $g$ is that a cheating prover P\* has some flexibility in the choice of the $x_i$

that she sends for rounds $i > i^*$. Indeed, by design there will be many such $x_i$'s. While the honest prover should choose $x_i$ at random (from this set), a cheating prover may try to cleverly choose $x_i$'s that help her cheat. Since all these choices are made after the function $g$ was revealed, we cannot assume that $x_{i^*+1}, \ldots, x_k$ are uniformly random relative to $g$. Thus, for our analysis it does not suffice that a random $x_{i+1}$ has a suitable number of preimages under $g$.

Instead, we will seek a much stronger, worst-case guarantee, from $g$. Specifically, that for *every* $x_{i+1} \in \{0,1\}^n$, the number of preimages $(y, z) \in g^{-1}(x_{i+1})$, where $y \in S_i$, is close to its expectation, i.e., around $2^d$ for $C_i \in$ YES and around $2^d/L$ for $C_i \in$ NO.

As shown by Alon *et al.* [ADM+99], this type of guarantee is not offered by pairwise independent hash function or even more generally by randomness extractors. On the other hand, what gives us hope is that a totally random function does have such a worst-case guarantee. Thus, we wish to construct a small hash function family $G$ where with high probability over the choice of $g \leftarrow G$, every image has roughly the same number of preimages from a predetermined set.

Following a work of Celis *et al.* [CRSW11], we refer to such functions as *load-balancing hash functions*. A function in this family maps the set $\{0,1\}^m$ together with some auxiliary input $\{0,1\}^d$ to the set $\{0,1\}^n$. We require that for any set $S \subseteq \{0,1\}^n$ s.t. $|S| \geq 2^n/L$ and for every $x \in \{0,1\}^n$, w.h.p over $g \leftarrow G_n$, it holds that $\left|\{(y,z) : y \in S, g(y,z) = x\}\right|$ is roughly $\frac{|S| \cdot 2^d}{2^n}$. We construct a suitable load-balancing functions based on $\mathsf{poly}(n)$-wise independent hash functions (combined with almost pairwise independent hash functions).

*Honest Verifier Statistical Zero-Knowledge.* To argue zero-knowledge, consider a simulator that first samples an initial $x_1$. Then, in each iteration $i$ the simulator samples $z_i$, computes $y_i = C_i(x_i)$ and $x_{i+1} = g(y_i, z_i)$. Then it samples $h_i$ and computes $\alpha_i = h_i(y_i, z_i)$.

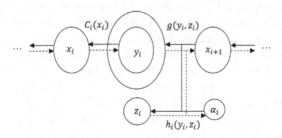

**Fig. 2.** Direction of Protocol Progress vs. Simulator Progress – solid lines represent the protocol, and dashed lines represent the simulator.

Statistical zero-knowledge is not obvious since the protocol and the simulator progress in opposite directions. The simulation progress direction is from circuit

$C_1$ up to circuit $C_k$, while the protocol progress direction is from circuit $C_k$ down to circuit $C_1$, as shown in Fig. 2. However, due to the special property of the the load-balancing function $g$, we manage to achieve statistical zero-knowledge.

We define the hybrid distribution $H_i$ that is sampled as follows:

1. Sample $g \in G_n$ and $x_i \in \{0,1\}^n$.
2. Generate $(x_j, z_j, h_j, \alpha_j)_{j \in \{1,\dots,i-1\}}$ according to the protocol.
3. Generate $(z_j, h_j, \alpha_j, x_{j+1})_{j \in \{i,\dots,k\}}$ according to the simulator.
4. Output $g, x_{k+1}$ and $(x_j, z_j, h_j, \alpha_j)_{j \in \{1,\dots,k\}}$.

Note that the simulator distribution is identical to $H_1$ while the protocol distribution is identical to $H_{k+1}$. We bound the statistical difference between $H_i$ and $H_{i+1}$ and use the hybrid argument.

Note that conditioned on $(g, x_i, z_i, h_i, \alpha_i, x_{i+1})$ the rest of the variables in $H_i, H_{i+1}$ are distributed identically. Therefore it is enough to bound the statistial differences between those variables as sampled in $H_i$ and $H_{i+1}$. Since $g$ is sampled identically in both hybrids, we can fix it and bound the statistical difference of those variables conditioned on some $g$.

For the hybrid $H_{i+1}$, the variables $(x_i, z_i, h_i, \alpha_i, x_{i+1})$ are sampled according to the protocol whereas for the hybrid $H_i$, the variables $(x_i, z_i, h_i, \alpha_i, x_{i+1})$ are sampled according to the simulator. Let $X_S, X_P$ and $X_U$ denotes the distributions of any random variable $X$ according to the simulator, protocol and the uniform distribution respectively.

Consider the distribution of $(x_i, z_i, h_i, \alpha_i, x_{i+1})_P$ which is sampled according to the protocol, i.e., $(h_i, \alpha_i, x_{i+1})$ are sampled uniformly at first, and then $(x_i, z_i)$ are chosen uniformly from the set of $(x, z)$ s.t. $g(C_i(x), z) = x_{i+1}$ and $h_i(C_i(x), z) = \alpha_{i+1}$. Consider also the distribution $(x_i, z_i, h_i, \alpha_i, x_{i+1})_S$ which is sampled according to the simulator, i.e., $(x_i, z_i, h_i)$ are sampled uniformly at first and then it sets $x_{i+1} = g(C_i(x_i), z_i)$ and $\alpha_i = h_i(C_i(x_i), z_i)$. Note that the distributions $(x_i, z_i)_P$ and $(x_i, z_i)_S$ are identical conditioned on specific values of $(h_i, \alpha_i, x_{i+1})$, and therefore, it is enough to bound $\Delta((h_i, \alpha_i, x_{i+1})_P, (h_i, \alpha_i, x_{i+1})_S)$.

We define the function $\varphi_i(x_i, z_i, h_i) = (h_i, \alpha_i, x_{i+1})$, where $x_{i+1} = g(C_i(x_i), z_i)$ and $\alpha_i = h_i(C_i(x_i))$. Note that

$$\Delta\left((h_i, \alpha_i, x_{i+1})_P, (h_i, \alpha_i, x_{i+1})_S\right) = \Delta\left((h_i, \alpha_i, x_{i+1})_U, \varphi_i\left((x_i, z_i, h_i)_U\right)\right).$$

Therefore, what we have left is to show that $\varphi_i$'s output on uniform input is close to uniform.

Consider uniform $(x_i, z_i, h_i)$ and set $x_{i+1} = g(C_i(x_i), z_i)$ and $\alpha_i = h_i(C_i(x_i), z_i)$. $x_{i+1}$ is close to uniform due to the special property of $g$ that every $x_{i+1}$ has roughly the same number of preimages $(y_i, z_i)$, and due to the fact that each image of $C_i$ has exactly one preimage. Now fix $x_{i+1}$. the number of pairs $(x_i, z_i)$ that are mapped to $x_{i+1}$ is roughly $2^d$, i.e., there are $d$ bits of entropy on which $h_i$ is applied. Therefore, since $h_i$ is pairwise independent hash function and as such, also a strong extractor, we get that $(h_i, \alpha_i)$ is also close to uniform.

*Reducing Communication via Hashing.* The foregoing soundness analysis relied on the fact that the prover sent the values $(x_1, \ldots, x_k)$ during the interaction. However, as noted above, this requires $n \cdot k$ communication which we cannot afford. In a nutshell, we resolve this inefficiency by having the prover only send short hashes of the $x_i$'s, details follows.

At the beginning of each round, the verifier $\mathsf{V}$ sends a description of a pairwise independent hash function $f_i$ in addition to the filter function $h_i$ and target value $\alpha_i$. Then, in addition to sending $z_i$, the prover $\mathsf{P}$ in her turn also sends a hash value $\beta_i = f_i(x_i)$ (rather than sending $x_i$ explicitly). In order for the hash value to commit the prover to $x_i$, we would like for the hash function $f_i$ to be injective on the set of consistent $(x, z)$'s (i.e., those for which $g(C_i(x), z) = x_{i+1}$ and $h_i(C_i(x), z) = \alpha_i$). This set is of size roughly $2^d$ where $d = \mathsf{polylog}(n, k)$. Therefore, setting the output size of $f_i$ to be $\mathsf{poly}(d)$ ($= \mathsf{polylog}(n, k)$) bits is sufficient. At the very end of the protocol, the prover $\mathsf{P}$ still needs to explicitly send $x_1'$, so that $\mathsf{V}$ can compute $y_i' = C_i(x_i')$ and $x_{i+1}' = g(y_i', z_i)$, for every $i \in [k]$, and verify that $h_i(y_i', z_i) = \alpha_i$, and lastly that $x_{k+1}' = x_{k+1}$. Note that the verifier can only perform these checks at the end of the interaction (as she did in the simplified protocol) since she must obtain the value of $x_1'$ in order to generate $x_2', \ldots, x_k'$.

Overall, the communication is dominated by the values $x_{k+1}$ and $g$, which are sent by the verifier, and the value $x_1'$ sent by the prover. Each of these messages has length $\mathsf{poly}(n, \log(k))$. All the rest of the messages including the specification of the hash functions $h_i$, $f_i$ as well as the values $\alpha_i$, $\beta_i$ and $z_i$ have length $\mathsf{polylog}(n, k)$. Overall we obtain the desired communication complexity $(k + \mathsf{poly}(n)) \cdot \mathsf{polylog}(n, k)$.

*When $\delta > 0$.* For the case where $\delta > 0$, the arguments we made for completeness and zero-knowledge still hold in a straightforward manner, but we need to be more careful about soundness. More specifically, for some YES instance circuit $C_i$ (where $i > i^*$) and $x_{i+1} \in \{0, 1\}^n$, there potentially can exist a pair $(y_i, z_i) \in g^{-1}(x_{i+1})$ s.t. $h_i(y_i, z_i) = \alpha_i$ and $y_i$ has an exponential number of preimages. Therefore, the set of consistent $(x, z)$ is of exponential size and therefore, in order to fix the chosen $x_i$ by the prover, $\beta_i$ must consist polynomial number of bits, which is of course too expensive for us.

However, since there is only a small number of images $y_i$ that have more then one preimage ($\delta$ fraction of $2^n$), there is also only a small number of pairs $(y_i, z_i) \in g^{-1}(x_{i+1})$ where $y_i$ is such an image. Therefore, w.h.p over $(h_i, \alpha_i)$, none of those problematic pairs satisfy the condition that $h_i(y_i, z_i) = \alpha_i$, and therefore, their preimages are inconsistent which allows the earlier setting of the output size of $f_i$ to work.

*Comparison to the [KRR+20] Protocol.* Our public-coin batching protocol bears some resemblance to the *private-coin* batching protocol of [KRR+20]. We highlight here the similarity and differences between our approaches. We note that readers who are unfamiliar with [KRR+20] can safely skip this discussion and proceed directly to Sect. 1.2.

In the protocol of [KRR+20] the verifier V first samples $x_1$ and auxiliary randomnesses $(z_1, \ldots, z_k)$ as part of her setup. She computes $y_i = C_i(x_i)$ and determines the next circuit input as $x_{i+1} = g(y_i, z_i)$, for every $i \in [k]$, where in contrast to our protocol, the function $g$ is simply a (strong) seeded randomness extractor (where $y_i$ is the min-entropy source and $z_i$ is the extractor's seed).

The actual interaction starts by having the verifier V send $y_k$ to P. The parties then proceed in iterations where in each iteration $i$, given $x_{i+1}$, the prover needs to guess $x_i$ using some additional hints that the verifier supplies. The prover's guesses are communicated by sending a short hash.

While their protocol bears some similarity to ours, we emphasize several fundamental ways in which our approach differs from that of [KRR+20] (beyond the fact that our protocol is public-coin).

- In [KRR+20] the verifier herself samples $(z_1, \ldots, z_k)$ and using it computes $(x_1, \ldots, x_k)$ as part of her setup, and then she reveals these gradually. This means that in the [KRR+20] there is a ground truth that the verifier can compare. In contrast, in our protocol, each $x_i$ is chosen via an interactive process that involves both parties and happens "online". In particular, and as discussed above, this means that a cheating prover can bias the distribution of the $x_i$'s as we process the circuit.
- On a related note, if the prover commits to a wrong $x_i$ in some iteration $i$, then, in [KRR+20], the verifier V can immediately detect this and reject. In contrast, in our protocol we are unable to do so and must wait to detect this at the very end of the interaction.
- In our protocol the $x_i$'s are computed in reverse order starting from $x_k$ down to $x_1$, whereas in the protocol of [KRR+20] the $x_i$'s are computed in order, starting from $x_1$ up to $x_k$. This may seem like a minor difference but turns out to complicate matters significantly when considering zero-knowledge. Indeed, both the [KRR+20] simulator as well as our simulator compute the $x_i$'s in order. This means that in the current work the protocol and the simulator, operate in *different* order. This makes the analysis of the simulation significantly more challenging.
- Lastly, [KRR+20] use extractors in order to map each circuit output $y_i$ to the next circuit input $x_{i+1}$. As discussed in detail in the above technical overview, the average-case guarantee provided by extractors are not good enough for us and we rely on the stronger notion of load-balancing hash functions.

**Efficient Transformation to Public-Coin Malicious Verifier SZK.** Goldreich, Sahai, and Vadhan [GSV98] showed that any public-coin HVSZK protocol can be transformed into a public-coin SZK protocol. Applying their transformation to the public-coin honest-verifier batch verification protocol described above would indeed result in a malicious-verifier SZK batch verification protocol for AI, and thus NISZK. This transformation, however, starts by repeating the HVSZK protocol several times in parallel in order to make the soundness error exponentially small in the number of rounds. This would incur a blowup in communication by a factor of $\Omega(k)$, which we cannot afford.

In order to get around this, we show that the transformation of [GSV98], when used on protocols with a stronger soundness guarantee called *round-by-round soundness* [CCH+19], can be performed without the initial repetition step, and thus achieve a much smaller blowup in communication. Then we show that our honest-verifier batching protocol does indeed provide this guarantee, and thus the transformation can be applied to it with this better blowup, giving us the desired result. We now briefly describe the transformation, the round-by-round soundness property, and how they fit together.

*The GSV Transformation.* Recall that in a public-coin HVSZK protocol, the honest verifier's messages consist of uniformly random strings. What breaks when the verifier is malicious is that it might choose these strings arbitrarily rather than uniformly at random. In the GSV transformation, the prover and verifier essentially run the given HVSZK protocol, but instead of the verifier sending these random strings, they are sampled by the prover and the verifier together using a Random Selection (RS) protocol. This protocol, which is constructed by [GSV98], uses four messages, is public-coin, and produces as output a string $r$ of some desired length $\ell$. It provides, very roughly, the following guarantees when run with security parameter $\lambda$:

1. If the prover is honest, the distribution of $r$ is $2^{-\lambda}$-close to uniform over $\{0,1\}^{\ell}$, and the transcript of the protocol is simulatable given output $r$.
2. If the verifier is honest, for any set $T \subseteq \{0,1\}^{\ell}$, we have $\Pr\left[r \in T\right] \leq 2^{\lambda} \cdot |T|/2^{\ell}$.

The first property above ensures that the resulting protocol is complete and zero-knowledge. The second property ensures that the prover cannot skew the distribution of $r$, and thus soundness is maintained. Following the analysis in [GSV98], however, it turns out that if the original protocol has soundness error $s$ and $r$ rounds, the bound obtained on the soundness error of the new protocol is roughly $2^{r\lambda} \cdot s$. Thus, we would need to start by decreasing the soundness error of the HVSZK protocol to less than $2^{-r\lambda}$. The only way we know to do this generically is by repetition, which results in a multiplicative blowup of at least $\Omega(r)$ in communication – in our case this is $\Omega(k)$, which is too large for us. We get around this by showing that our batch verification protocol has a stronger soundness property that results in a much better bound on the soundness error when this transformation is applied.

*Round-by-Round Soundness.* Typically, the soundness property in an interactive proof places requirements on how likely it is that a verifier accepts on a NO input. Round-by-round soundness, introduced by Canetti et al. [CCH+19], instead places requirements on intermediate stages of the protocol. It involves a mapping State from partial transcripts of the protocol to the set $\{$alive, doomed$\}$. A protocol is $\epsilon$-*round-by-round sound* if there exists a mapping State such that for any input $x$ and partial transcript $\tau$ with $\mathsf{State}(x,\tau) = $ doomed, and any subsequent prover message $\alpha$, the probability over the next verifier message $\beta$

that $\mathsf{State}(x, \tau, \alpha, \beta) = \mathtt{alive}$ is at most $\epsilon$. Further, any complete transcript that is $\mathtt{doomed}$ always results in a rejection by the verifier, and for any NO instance $x$, it is the case that $\mathsf{State}(x, \perp) = \mathtt{doomed}$.

In other words, at a point where a protocol is $\mathtt{doomed}$, irrespective of what the prover does, the set of "bad" verifier messages that make the protocol $\mathtt{alive}$ in the next round has relative size at most $\epsilon$. To see its implications for standard soundness, consider a protocol that has $r$ rounds and is $\epsilon$-round-by-round sound. The probability that the verifier accepts on a NO instance is at most the probability that the complete transcript is $\mathtt{alive}$. Thus, since the protocol has to go from $\mathtt{doomed}$ to $\mathtt{alive}$ in at least one of the $r$ rounds, the probability that the verifier accepts is at most $r\epsilon$.

*Putting it Together.* Now, consider passing an $\epsilon$-round-by-round sound protocol through the GSV transformation described above. Here, each verifier message is replaced by the output of the RS protocol. On a NO instance, in order to successfully cheat, the prover has to make at least one of the $r$ verifier messages fall into the "bad" set for that round. Each of these bad sets, however, has relative size at most $\epsilon$, and thus the RS protocol's output falls in each with probability at most $\epsilon 2^\lambda$. Thus, that total probability that the prover successfully cheats is at most $\epsilon r 2^\lambda$.

So, if the original protocol had round-by-round soundness error somewhat smaller than $(r2^\lambda)^{-1}$, the resulting protocol would still be sound. This is a much more modest requirement than before, and can be achieved with a multiplicative blowup of at most $O(\lambda \log r)$ in communication. Completeness and zero-knowledge follow from the other properties of the RS protocol, and setting $\lambda$ to be $\mathrm{polylog}(n, k)$ gives us the desired SZK protocol.

*Round-by-Round Soundness of our* HVSZK *Batching Protocol.* To show that our protocol described earlier has round-by-round soundness, we define the $\mathsf{State}$ function as follows. Consider the partial transcript $\tau_j$ that corresponds to its $j$'th iteration – this consists of $g$, $x_{k+1}$, $(h_i, \alpha_i, f_i, z_i, \beta_i)_{i \in \{k, \ldots, j+1\}}$, and $(h_j, \alpha_j, f_j)$.

- For $j > i^*$: Output $\mathtt{doomed}$ on the transcript $\tau_j$ if, for any prover message $(z_j, \beta_j)$ that follows, there exists at most one preimage $x_j$ that is consistent with $\tau_j$ and $(z_j, \beta_j)$. Further, if there is no such $x_j$, output $\mathtt{doomed}$ on all future transcripts that extend $\tau_j$.
  - Consider a $\mathtt{doomed}$ transcript $\tau_{j+1}$, a prover message $(z_{j+1}, \beta_{j+1})$, and the unique $x_{j+1}$ that is consistent with them as promised (if it doesn't exist, future transcripts are already $\mathtt{doomed}$). By our earlier discussion, w.h.p., there are very few $x_j$'s which have a $z_i$ such that $g(C_j(x_j), z_j) = x_{j+1}$ and $h_j(C_j(x_j), z_j) = \alpha_j$. Therefore, w.h.p., $f_j$ maps these $x_j$'s injectively. Hence for any prover message $(z_{j+1}, \beta_{j+1})$, we have that w.h.p. $\tau_{j+1}, (z_{j+1}, \beta_{j+1}), (h_j, \alpha_j, f_j)$ is also $\mathtt{doomed}$.
- For $j = i^*$: We define the $\mathsf{State}$ function to output $\mathtt{doomed}$ on the transcript $\tau_{i^*}$ if for any prover message $(z_{i^*}, \beta_{i^*})$, there does not exist $x_{i^*}$ that is consistent with $\tau_{i^*}$ and $(z_{i^*}, \beta_{i^*})$.

- Consider any **doomed** transcripts $\tau_{i^*+1}$, a prover message $(z_{i^*+1}, \beta_{i^*+1})$, and the unique $x_{i^*+1}$ that is consistent with them. As discussed earlier, w.h.p., there does not exist $(x_{i^*}, z_{i^*})$ s.t. $g(C_{i^*}(x_{i^*}), z_{i^*}) = x_{i^*+1}$ and $h_{i^*}(C_{i^*}(x_{i^*}), z_{i^*}) = \alpha_{i^*}$ and therefore for every prover message $(z_{i^*+1}, \beta_{i^*+1})$, it holds w.h.p. that $\tau_{i^*+1}, (z_{i^*+1}, \beta_{i^*+1}), (h_{i^*}, \alpha_{i^*}, f_{i^*})$ is **doomed** too.

– For $j < i^*$: We define the State function to answer according to the partial transcript $\tau_{i^*}$, and therefore round-by-round soundness in this case is immediate.

We set $\mathsf{State}(x, \bot)$ to be **doomed** if $x$ is a NO instance, and anything that is not **doomed** is set to be **alive**. Lastly, consider a complete transcript that is **doomed**; there does not exists $x_{i^*}$ that is consistent with the beginning of the transcript, and therefore V must reject. This function now witnesses the round-by-round soundness of our protocol.

## 1.3 Organization

We start with preliminaries in Sect. 2. In Sect. 3 we formalize our notion of a *load-balancing* hash function and provide a construction based on $k$-wise independent hash functions. In Sect. 4 we introduce our variant of the approximate injectivity (AI) problem and show that it is NISZK-complete. In Sect. 5 we construct our *public-coin honest-verifier* batch verification for AI. In Sect. 6 we show a generic, and efficient, transformation from public-coin HVSZK (having round-by-round soundness) to public-coin full-fledged SZK. Lastly, in Sect. 7 we use the results obtained in the prior sections to obtain our public-coin SZK batch verification protocol for NISZK.

Due to space restrictions, most of the proofs are deferred to the full version [KRV21].

## 2    Preliminaries

For a finite non-empty set $S$, we denote by $x \leftarrow S$ a uniformly distributed element in $S$. We also use $U_\ell$ to denote a random variable uniformly distributed over $\{0, 1\}^\ell$.

For a distribution $X$ over a finite set $U$ and a (non-empty) event $E \subseteq U$, we denote by $X|_E$ the distribution obtained by conditioning $X$ on $E$: namely, $\Pr[X|_E = u] = \Pr[X = u \,|\, E]$, for every $u \in U$. The *support* of $X$ is defined as $\mathsf{supp}(X) = \{u \in U : \Pr[X = u] > 0\}$.

**Definition 1.** *Let* $\Pi = (\mathrm{YES}, \mathrm{NO})$ *be a promise problem, where* $\mathrm{YES} = (\mathrm{YES}_n)_{n \in \mathbb{N}}$ *and* $\mathrm{NO} = (\mathrm{NO}_n)_{n \in \mathbb{N}}$, *and let* $k = k(n) \in \mathbb{N}$. *We define the promise problem* $\Pi^{\otimes k} = (\mathrm{YES}^{\otimes k}, \mathrm{NO}^{\otimes k})$, *where* $\mathrm{YES}^{\otimes k} = (\mathrm{YES}_n^{\otimes k})_{n \in \mathbb{N}}$, $\mathrm{NO}^{\otimes k} = (\mathrm{NO}_n^{\otimes k})_{n \in \mathbb{N}}$ *and*

$$\mathrm{YES}_n^{\otimes k} = (\mathrm{YES}_n)^k$$

*and*

$$\mathrm{NO}_n^{\otimes k} = (\mathrm{YES}_n \cup \mathrm{NO}_n)^k \setminus (\mathrm{NO}_n)^k.$$

The statistical distance between two distributions $P$ and $Q$ over a finite set $U$ is defined as $\Delta(P, Q) = \max_{S \subseteq U} (P(S) - Q(S)) = \frac{1}{2} \sum_{u \in U} |P(u) - Q(u)|$.

## 2.1   Statistical Zero-Knowledge

We use $(\mathsf{P}, \mathsf{V})(x)$ to refer to the *transcript* of an execution of an interactive protocol with prover $\mathsf{P}$ and verifier $\mathsf{V}$ on common input $x$. The transcript includes the input $x$, all messages sent by $\mathsf{P}$ to $\mathsf{V}$ in the protocol and the verifier's random coin tosses. We say that the transcript $\tau = (\mathsf{P}, \mathsf{V})(x)$ is accepting if at the end of the corresponding interaction, the verifier accepts.

**Definition 2 (Interactive proof)**
*Let $c = c(n) \in [0, 1]$ and $s = s(n) \in [0, 1]$. An interactive proof with completeness error $c$ and soundness error $s$ for a promise problem $\Pi = (\Pi_{\mathrm{YES}}, \Pi_{\mathrm{NO}})$, consists of a probabilistic polynomial-time verifier $\mathsf{V}$ and a computationally unbounded prover $\mathsf{P}$ such that following properties hold:*

- **Completeness:** *For any $x \in \Pi_{\mathrm{YES}}$:*

$$\Pr\left[(\mathsf{P}, \mathsf{V})(x) \text{ is accepting}\right] \geq 1 - c(|x|).$$

- **Soundness:** *For any (computationally unbounded) cheating prover $\mathsf{P}^*$ and any $x \in \Pi_{\mathrm{NO}}$:*

$$\Pr\left[(\mathsf{P}^*, \mathsf{V})(x) \text{ is accepting}\right] \leq s(|x|).$$

*We denote this proof system by the pair $(\mathsf{P}, \mathsf{V})$.*

In this paper we focus on *public-coin* interactive proofs. An interactive proof $(\mathsf{P}, \mathsf{V})$ is public-coin if the verifier's messages are selected independently and uniformly at random (and their lengths are fixed independently of the interaction).

We next define *honest-verifier* statistical zero-knowledge proofs, in which zero-knowledge is only guaranteed wrt the *honest* (i.e., prescribed) verifier's behavior.

**Definition 3 (HVSZK).** *Let $z = z(n) \in [0, 1]$. An interactive proof system $(\mathsf{P}, \mathsf{V})$ is an* Honest Verifier SZK Proof-System *(HVSZK), with zero-knowledge error $z$, if there exists a probabilistic polynomial-time algorithm* Sim *(called the simulator) such that for any $x \in \Pi_{\mathrm{YES}}$:*

$$\Delta\left((\mathsf{P}, \mathsf{V})(x), \mathsf{Sim}(x)\right) \leq z(|x|).$$

For the malicious verifier SZK definition, we allow the verifier access to non-uniform advice. Therefore, we also provide the simulator with the same advice. Let $\mathsf{Sim}_{[a]}$ denote the simulator $\mathsf{Sim}$ given access to the some advice string $a \in \{0, 1\}^*$.

**Definition 4 (SZK).** *Let* $z = z(n) \in [0,1]$. *An interactive-proof* $(P, V)$ *is a statistical zero-knowledge proof-system (SZK), with zero-knowledge error* $z$, *if for every probabilistic polynomial-time verifier* $V^*$ *there exists an algorithm* Sim *(called the* simulator*) that runs in (strict) polynomial time such that for any* $x \in \Pi_{YES}$ *and* $a \in \{0,1\}^*$:

$$\Delta\left((P, V^*_{[a]})(x), \mathsf{Sim}_{[a]}(x)\right) \leq z(|x|).$$

If the completeness, soundness and zero-knowledge (resp., honest-verifier zero-knoweldge) errors are all negligible, we simply say that the interactive proof is an SZK (resp., HVSZK) protocol. We also use SZK (resp., HVSZK) to denote the class of promise problems having such an SZK (resp., HVSZK) protocol.

**Non-Interactive Statistical Zero-Knowledge Proofs.** We also define the *non-interactive* variant of SZK as follows.

**Definition 5 (NISZK).** *Let* $c = c(n) \in [0,1]$, $s = s(n) \in [0,1]$ *and* $z = z(n) \in [0,1]$. *An non-interactive statistical zero-knowledge proof (NISZK) with completeness error* $c$, *soundness error* $s$ *and zero-knowledge error* $z$ *for a promise problem* $\Pi = (\Pi_{YES}, \Pi_{NO})$, *consists of a probabilistic polynomial-time verifier* V, *a computationally unbounded prover* P *and a polynomial* $\ell = \ell(n)$ *such that following properties hold:*

- **Completeness:** *For any* $x \in \Pi_{YES}$:

$$\Pr_{r \in \{0,1\}^{\ell(|x|)}} [V(x, r, \pi) \; accepts] \geq 1 - c(|x|),$$

  *where* $\pi = P(x, r)$.
- **Soundness:** *For any* $x \in \Pi_{NO}$:

$$\Pr_{r \in \{0,1\}^{\ell(|x|)}} [\exists \pi^* \; s.t. \; V(x, r, \pi^*) \; accepts] \leq s(|x|).$$

- **Honest Verifier Statistical Zero Knowledge:** *There is a probabilistic polynomial-time algorithm* Sim *(called the* simulator*) such that for any* $x \in \Pi_{YES}$:

$$\Delta\left((U_\ell, P(x, U_\ell)), \mathsf{Sim}(x)\right) \leq z(|x|).$$

(Note that the zero-knowledge property in Definition 5 is referred to as "honest-verifier" simply because the verifier does not send any messages to the prover and so it is meaningless to consider malicious behavior.)

As above, if the errors are negligible, we say that $\Pi$ has a NISZK protocol and use NISZK to denote the class of all such promise problems.

## 2.2   Many-wise Independence

**Definition 6 ($\delta$-almost $\ell$-wise Independent Hash Functions).** *For $\ell = \ell(n) \in \mathbb{N}$, $m = m(n) \in \mathbb{N}$ and $\delta = \delta(n) > 0$, a family of functions $\mathcal{F} = (\mathcal{F}_n)_n$, where $\mathcal{F}_n = \left\{ f : \{0,1\}^m \to \{0,1\}^n \right\}$ is $\delta$-almost $\ell$-wise independent if for every $n \in \mathbb{N}$ and distinct $x_1, x_2, \ldots, x_\ell \in \{0,1\}^m$ the distributions:*

- *$(f(x_1), \ldots, f(x_\ell))$, where $f \leftarrow \mathcal{F}_n$; and*
- *The uniform distribution over $(\{0,1\}^n)^\ell$,*

*are $\delta$-close in statistical distance.*

When $\delta = 0$ we simply say that the hash function family is $\ell$-wise independent. Constructions of (efficiently computable) many-wise hash function families with a very succinct representation are well known. In particular, when $\delta = 0$ we have the following well-known construction:

**Lemma 1 (See, e.g., [Vad12, Section 3.5.5]).** *For every $\ell = \ell(n) \in \mathbb{N}$ and $m = m(n) \in \mathbb{N}$ there exists a family of $\ell$-wise independent hash functions $\mathcal{F}_{n,m}^{(\ell)} = \{f \colon \{0,1\}^m \to \{0,1\}^n\}$ where a random function from $\mathcal{F}_{n,m}^{(\ell)}$ can be selected using $O(\ell \cdot \max(n,m))$ bits, and given a description of $f \in \mathcal{F}_{n,m}^{(\ell)}$ and $x \in \{0,1\}^m$, the value $f(x)$ can be computed in time $\mathsf{poly}(n,m,\ell)$.*

For $\delta > 0$, the seminal work of Naor and Naor [NN93] yields a highly succinct construction.

**Lemma 2 ([NN93, Lemma 4.2]).** *For every $\ell = \ell(n) \in \mathbb{N}$, $m = m(n) \in \mathbb{N}$ and $\delta = \delta(n) > 0$, there exists a family of $\delta$-almost $\ell$-wise independent hash functions $\mathcal{F}_{n,m}^{(\ell)} = \{f \colon \{0,1\}^m \to \{0,1\}^n\}$ where a random function from $\mathcal{F}_{n,m}^{(\ell)}$ can be selected using $O(\ell \cdot n + \log(m) + \log(1/\delta))$ bits, and given a description of $f \in \mathcal{F}_{n,m}^{(\ell)}$ and $x \in \{0,1\}^m$, the value $f(x)$ can be computed in time $\mathsf{poly}(n,m,\ell,\log(1/\delta))$.*

## 2.3   Round-By-Round Soundness

In this section we define the notion of *round-by-round soundness* of interactive proofs, as introduced in the recent work of Canetti *et al.* [CCH+19].

Let $(\mathsf{P}, \mathsf{V})$ be a public-coin interactive proof. We denote by $\mathsf{V}(x, \tau)$ the distribution of the next message (or output) of $\mathsf{V}$ on the input $x$ and partial transcript $\tau$.

**Definition 7.** *Let $(\mathsf{P}, \mathsf{V})$ be a public-coin interactive proof for the promise problem $\Pi = (\Pi_{\mathrm{YES}}, \Pi_{\mathrm{NO}})$.*

*We say that $(\mathsf{P}, \mathsf{V})$ has a round-by-round soundness error $\epsilon = \epsilon(n)$ if there exists some (possibly inefficient) function $\mathsf{State}$ that takes as input the main input $x$ and a partial transcript $\tau$ and outputs either $\mathtt{alive}$ or $\mathtt{doomed}$ and has the following properties:*

1. *If $x \in$ NO, then* $\mathsf{State}(x, \perp) = \boldsymbol{doomed}$ *(where $\perp$ denotes the empty transcript).*
2. *For any transcript prefix $\tau$, if* $\mathsf{State}(x, \tau) = \boldsymbol{doomed}$, *then for any prover message $\alpha$ it holds that*

$$\Pr_{\beta \leftarrow V(x, \tau, \alpha)} \left[ \mathsf{State}(x, \tau, \alpha, \beta) = \boldsymbol{alive} \right] \leq \epsilon(n).$$

3. *For any full transcript $\tau$ (i.e., a transcript in which the verifier halts) such that* $\mathsf{State}(x, \tau) = \boldsymbol{doomed}$, *it holds that $V(x, \tau)$ is rejecting.*

Canetti *et al.* [CCH+19] also show the following simple fact (which follows from the union bound).

**Fact 4.** *Let* $(\mathsf{P}, \mathsf{V})$ *be a $2r$-message interactive proof with round-by-round soundness error $\epsilon$. Then,* $(\mathsf{P}, \mathsf{V})$ *has standard soundness error $r \cdot \epsilon$.*

## 3   Load-Balancing Functions

We now define *load-balancing hash functions*, a central tool in our construction. Loosely speaking, a load balanching hash function is a function mapping a set $\{0,1\}^m$ together with a short auxiliary random string $\{0,1\}^d$ to a range $\{0,1\}^n$. The key property that we seek is that for every subset of $\{0,1\}^m$ of size roughly $2^n$ it holds that every element $x \in \{0,1\}^n$ has roughly the same number of preimages $(y, z) \in S \times \{0,1\}^d$.

**Definition 8 (Load Balancing Hash Function Family).** *Let $m = m(n) \in \mathbb{N}$, $d = d(n) \in \mathbb{N}$ and $\epsilon : \mathbb{N}^4 \to [0,1]$. We say that a family of hash functions $G = (G_n)_n$, where $G_n = \left\{ g : \{0,1\}^m \times \{0,1\}^d \to \{0,1\}^n \right\}$, is $(d, \epsilon)$-load-balancing, if for every $n \in \mathbb{N}$, number of elements $v \in \mathbb{N}$, and set $S \subseteq \{0,1\}^{m(n)}$ of size $|S| \leq 2^n$ it holds that:*

$$\Pr_{g \leftarrow G} \left[ \exists x \in \{0,1\}^n : \left| L_{S,g}(x) - \frac{|S| \cdot 2^d}{2^n} \right| > v \right] \leq \epsilon(n, |S|, v, d),$$

*where $L_{S,g}(x) = \left| \left\{ (y, z) \in S \times \{0,1\}^d \ : \ g(y, z) = x \right\} \right|.$*

**Lemma 3.** *For any values $n, \lambda \in \mathbb{N}$ and $m = m(n), d = d(n)$, there is an explicit family of hash functions $G = (G_n)_n$ that is $(d, \lambda, \epsilon)$-load-balancing, where $G_n = \left\{ g : \{0,1\}^{m(n)} \times \{0,1\}^{d(n)} \to \{0,1\}^n \right\}$ and*

$$\epsilon_\lambda(n, |S|, v, d) = 2^n \cdot \left( 64 \cdot (n + \lambda) \cdot \frac{\mu + (n + \lambda)}{v^2} \right)^{n + \lambda + 4} + 2^{-\lambda - 1},$$

*where $\mu = \frac{|S| \cdot 2^d}{2^n}$, s.t. a random function in the family can be sampled using $O(n^2 + \lambda^2 + d \cdot (n + \lambda))$ uniformly random bits, and each such function can be evaluated in time $\mathsf{poly}(n, m, d, \lambda)$.*

Due to space restrictions, the proof of Lemma 3 is deferred to the full version [KRV21].

**Corollary 1.** *For any* $n, m(n), \lambda, \ell, \epsilon' \in (0, 1]$ *and* $d \geq 3 \log \left( \frac{n+\lambda}{\epsilon'^2} \right) + \ell$, *the family of hash functions from Lemma 3 has the following properties:*

1. *For any set* $S \subseteq \{0, 1\}^m$ *s.t.* $2^{n-\ell} \leq |S| \leq 2^n$ *it holds that*

$$
\Pr_{g \leftarrow G} \left[ \exists x \in \{0, 1\}^n : \left| L_{S,g}(x) - \frac{|S| \cdot 2^d}{2^n} \right| > \frac{|S| \cdot 2^d}{2^n} \cdot \epsilon' \right] \leq 2^{-\lambda}.
$$

2. *For every* $\nu$ *s.t.* $12 \cdot (n + \lambda) \leq \nu$ *and set* $S \subseteq \{0, 1\}^m$ *s.t.* $|S| \leq 2^{n-d}$ *it holds that*

$$
\Pr_{g \leftarrow G} \left[ \exists x \in \{0, 1\}^n : L_{S,g}(x) - \frac{|S| \cdot 2^d}{2^n} > \nu \right] \leq 2^{-\lambda}.
$$

## 4  Approximate Injectivity

In this section we analyze the *approximate injectivity* problem, introduced by Kaslasi *et al.* [KRR+20]. In particular, we consider a variant in which NO cases are (approximately) many-to-one and show that it is NISZK-complete.

We say that $x'$ is a *sibling* of $x$, with respect to the circuit $C$, if $C(x) = C(x')$. We omit $C$ from the notation if it is clear from the context.

**Definition 9.** *The problem* $\mathsf{AI}_{L,\delta}^{n,m}$ *is defined as the promise problem of circuits with* $n$ *input bits and* $m$ *output bits, where*

$$
(\mathsf{AI}_{L,\delta}^{n,m})^Y = \left\{ circuit\ C : \Pr_x \left[ |C^{-1}(C(x))| > 1 \right] < \delta \right\},
$$

*and*

$$
(\mathsf{AI}_{L,\delta}^{n,m})^N = \left\{ circuit\ C : \Pr_x \left[ |C^{-1}(C(x))| < L \right] < \delta \right\}.
$$

*We omit* $m$ *and* $n$ *from the notation when they are clear from the context.*

To show that $\mathsf{AI}_{L,\delta}$ is NISZK-hard, we rely on the fact that it is known to be NISZK-hard in the special case when $L = 2$.

**Lemma 4** ([KRR+20]). *Let* $\delta = \delta(n) \in [0, 1]$ *be a non-increasing function such that* $\delta(n) > 2^{-o(n^{1/4})}$. *Then,* $\mathsf{AI}_{2,\delta}$ *is NISZK-hard.*

Thus, to show that $\mathsf{AI}_{L,\delta}$ is NISZK-hard, it suffices to reduce $\mathsf{AI}_{2,\delta}$ to $\mathsf{AI}_{L,\delta}$.

**Lemma 5.** *For every parameter* $\ell = \mathsf{poly}(n)$, *there exists a polynomial time Karp-reduction from* $\mathsf{AI}_{2,\delta}^{n,m}$ *to* $\mathsf{AI}_{2^\ell, \ell \cdot \delta}^{n \cdot \ell, m \cdot \ell}$.

Before proving Lemma 5, we observe that Lemma 4 together with Lemma 5 immediately implies that $\mathsf{AI}_{L,\delta}$ is NISZK-hard. Since $\mathsf{AI}_{2,\delta}$ is a special case of $\mathsf{AI}_{L,\delta}$, we get also that $\mathsf{AI}_{L,\delta}$ is NISZK-complete.

**Corollary 2.** *Let $\delta = \delta(n) \in [0,1]$ be a non-increasing function and $\ell = \mathsf{poly}(n)$ such that $\delta(n) > \frac{2^{-o(n^{1/4})}}{\ell}$. Then, there exist constants $c, d \in \mathbb{N}$ such that $\mathsf{AI}_{2^\ell,\delta}^{n^c,m^d}$ is NISZK-complete.*

Due to space restrictions, the proof of Lemma 5 is deferred to the full version [KRV21].

## 5   Public-Coin Batch Verification for $\mathsf{AI}_{L,\delta}$

In this section we prove the following lemma by showing a *public-coin* HVSZK protocol for batch verification of $\mathsf{AI}_{L,\delta}$ (as defined in Definition 9).

**Lemma 6.** *Let $\delta = \delta(n) \in [0,1]$ and $k = k(n) \in \mathbb{N}$. Also, let $\lambda = \lambda(n) \in \mathbb{N}$ be a security parameter and let $\ell = \ell(n) \in \mathbb{N}$, with $\ell(n) \geq \lambda(n)$ for all $n$. Set $d = 7 \cdot (\log n + \log k + \lambda) + \ell$ and assume that $\delta \leq 2^{-d}$ and $d < 2\ell - 2\lambda$.*

*Then, $\mathsf{AI}_{2^\ell,\delta}^{\otimes k}$ has an HVSZK public-coin protocol with completeness error $2^{-\lambda+1}$, round-by-round soundness error $2^{-\lambda}$ and statistical zero knowledge error $k \cdot (\delta \cdot 2^{d+2} + 2^{-\lambda+6})$. The communication complexity is $O(n^2) + k \cdot \mathsf{poly}(\log n, \log k, \lambda)$ and the verifier running time is $k \cdot \mathsf{poly}(n, \log k, \lambda)$.*

*Furthermore, the protocol consists of $k$ rounds. The length of the verifier's first message is $O(n^2 + \ell \cdot n \cdot \mathsf{poly}(\log n, \log k, \lambda)$ and the length of all other verifier messages is $\mathsf{poly}(\log n, \log k, \lambda)$.*

The protocol establishing Lemma 6 is presented in Fig. 3. Due to space restrictions, the analysis of the protocol is deferred to the full version [KRV21].

## 6   From Honest to Malicious Verifier

In this section, we show how efficiently to transform an *honest-verifier* SZK protocol with round-by-round soundness, into a *malicious-verifier* SZK protocol. Our transformation builds on the prior work of Goldreich, Sahai and Vadhan [GSV98] who showed a generic transformation from honest to malicious verifiers for SZK, which unfortunately (and as discussed in more detail in the introduction) is not efficient enough for our purposes.

**Theorem 5.** *Suppose a problem $\Pi$ has a public-coin honest-verifier SZK proof system. This protocol can be transformed into a public-coin malicious-verifier SZK proof system for $\Pi$ with the following properties when given security parameter $\lambda$:*

---

**Public-coin HVSZK Batching Protocol for $\mathsf{Al}_{2^\ell,\delta}$.**

PARAMETERS: input length $n$, output length $m$, number of instances $k$, security parameter $\lambda$, arity $\ell$ and seed length $d = 7 \cdot (\log n + \log k + \lambda) + \ell$.

INPUT: Circuits $C_1, \ldots, C_k : \{0,1\}^n \to \{0,1\}^m$, where all circuits[a] have size at most $N$, input length $n$, and output length $m \leq N$.

INGREDIENTS:

- Let $G = (G_n)_n$, where $G_n = \big\{ g : \{0,1\}^m \times \{0,1\}^d \to \{0,1\}^n \big\}$, be the explicit family of load-balancing functions from Lemma 3, with seed length $d$ and accuracy $2^{-\lambda}$ with respect to security parameter $\lambda + \log k + 1$.
- Let $H = (H_n)_n$, where $H_n = \big\{ h : \{0,1\}^m \times \{0,1\}^d \to \{0,1\}^{d/2} \big\}$, be the explicit family of $2^{-3d/2}$-almost pairwise independent hash function from Lemma 2.
- Let $F = (F_n)_n$, where $F_n = \big\{ f : \{0,1\}^n \to \{0,1\}^{2d+\lambda+\log k} \big\}$, be the explicit family of $2^{-(2d+\lambda+\log k)}$-almost pairwise independent hash functions from Lemma 2.

THE PROTOCOL:

1. V samples $g \leftarrow G_n$ and $x_{k+1} \leftarrow \{0,1\}^n$ and sends both to P.
2. For $i = k, \ldots, 1$:
   (a) V samples $\alpha_i \leftarrow \{0,1\}^{d/2}$, $h_i \leftarrow H_n$, and $f_i \leftarrow F_n$, and sends $(\alpha_i, h_i, f_i)$ to P.
   (b) P generates the set

   $$XZ_i = \Big\{ (x,z) \in \{0,1\}^n \times \{0,1\}^d \, : \, g(C_i(x), z) = x_{i+1} \text{ and } h_i(C_i(x), z) = \alpha_i \Big\}.$$

   (c) P samples $(x_i, z_i) \leftarrow XZ_i$, and sends $(z_i, \beta_i)$ to V, where $\beta_i = f_i(x_i)$. In case the set $XZ_i$ is empty, P sends an arbitrary[b] $(z_i, \beta_i) \in \{0,1\}^d \times \{0,1\}^{2d+\lambda+\log k}$.
   We denote the pair received by V by $(z'_i, \beta'_i)$ (allegedly equal to $(z_i, \beta_i)$).
3. P sends $x_1$ to V.
4. V receives $x'_1 \in \{0,1\}^n$ (allegedly equal to $x_1$) and computes:
   (a) For $i = 1, \ldots, k$:
       i. $y'_i = C_i(x'_i)$
       ii. $x'_{i+1} = g(y'_i, z'_i)$
5. V checks that $x_{k+1} = x'_{k+1}$ and that $\forall i \in [k]$, $\beta'_i = f_i(x'_i)$ and $\alpha_i = h_i(y'_i, z'_i)$.
6. If all of V's checks passed then she accepts. Otherwise she rejects.

---

[a] The circuits can be trivially modified to have the same output length $m \leq N$ by padding.

[b] Alternatively, we could simply have the prover abort in this case. However, it will be more convenient for our analysis that P send an arbitrary $(z_i, \beta_i)$ pair rather than sending a special abort symbol.

**Fig. 3.** A Public-coin HVSZK Batching Protocol for $\mathsf{Al}_{2^\ell,\delta}$

1. *Suppose the original protocol has $r$ rounds and the prover and verifier communication in its $i^{th}$ round are $s_i$ and $\ell_i$, respectively. Then the transformed protocol has $2r$ rounds, and its total communication is $\left( \sum_{i \in [r]} s_i + O\left( \sum_{i \in [r]} \ell_i^4 \right) \right)$.*
2. *The completeness and statistical zero-knowledge errors are at most $\mathsf{poly}(r, \ell_{\max}) \cdot 2^{-\Omega(\lambda)}$ more (additively) than the respective errors in the original protocol, where $\ell_{\max} = \max_i \ell_i$.*
3. *If the original protocol has round-by-round soundness error $\epsilon$, then this protocol has soundness error $\left( \epsilon r 2^\lambda + \frac{1}{2^\lambda} \right)$.*
4. *The verifier runs in time polynomial in the input length, $r$, $\ell_{\max}$, and $\lambda$, as does the prover, if given oracle access to the prover from the original protocol.*

The transformation that we use to prove Theorem 5 is almost exactly the same as the one of Goldreich, Sahai and Vadhan [GSV98]. The main difference is that [GSV98] first perform an $O(r)$-fold parallel repetition of the underlying HVSZK protocol, where $r$ is its round complexity. This increases the communication complexity by a factor of $r$, which we cannot afford.

In contrast, in our analysis we avoid the use of parallel repetition and instead rely on the underlying protocol satisfying a stronger notion of soundness - namely, round-by-round soundness (Definition 7).

Due to space restrictions, we defer the proof of Theorem 5 to the full version [KRV21].

# 7 Public-Coin Malicious Verifier SZK Batching for NISZK

In this section we state our main theorems. The proof, which build on results established in the prior sections is deferred to the full version [KRV21]. We first state our public-coin HVSZK batch verification protocol for NISZK.

**Theorem 6.** *Let $\Pi \in$ NISZK and $k = k(n) \in \mathbb{N}$ such that $k(n) \leq 2^{n^{0.01}}$ and let $\lambda = \lambda(n) \in \mathbb{N}$ be a security parameter such that $\lambda(n) \leq n^{0.1}$. Then, $\Pi^{\otimes k}$ has a public-coin HVSZK protocol with completeness, zero-knowledge, and round-by-round soundness errors of $2^{-\lambda}$.*

*The communication complexity is $(k + \mathsf{poly}(n)) \cdot \mathsf{poly}(\log n, \log k, \lambda)$ and the verifier running time is $k \cdot \mathsf{poly}(n, \log k, \lambda)$.*

*Furthermore, the protocol consists of $k$ rounds. The length of the verifier's first message is $\mathsf{poly}(n)$ and the length of each of the verifier's other messages is $\mathsf{polylog}(n, k, \lambda)$.*

Combining Theorem 6 with Theorem 5, we get a *malicious-verifier* SZK batch verification protocol.

**Theorem 7.** *Let $\Pi \in$ NISZK and $k = k(n) \in \mathbb{N}$ such that $k(n) \leq 2^{n^{0.01}}$ and let $\lambda = \lambda(n) \in \mathbb{N}$ be a security parameter such that $\lambda(n) \leq n^{0.09}$. Then, $\Pi^{\otimes k}$ has a public-coin SZK protocol with completeness, soundness, and zero-knowledge errors of $2^{-\Omega(\lambda)}$, and communication complexity of $(k + \mathsf{poly}(n)) \cdot \mathsf{poly}(\log n, \log k, \lambda)$. The verifier running time is $k \cdot \mathsf{poly}(n, \lambda, \log k)$ and the number of rounds is $O(k \cdot \lambda)$.*

**Acknowledgments.** We thank the anonymous Eurocrypt 2021 reviewers for useful comments.

Inbar Kaslasi and Ron Rothblum were supported in part by a Milgrom family grant, by the Israeli Science Foundation (Grants No. 1262/18 and 2137/19), and grants from the Technion Hiroshi Fujiwara cyber security research center and Israel cyber directorate.

Prashant Vasudevan was supported in part by AFOSR Award FA9550-19-1-0200, AFOSR YIP Award, NSF CNS Award 1936826, DARPA and SPAWAR under contract N66001-15-C-4065, a Hellman Award and research grants by the Okawa Foundation, Visa Inc., and Center for Long-Term Cybersecurity (CLTC, UC Berkeley). The views expressed are those of the authors and do not reflect the official policy or position of the funding agencies.

# References

[Aar12] Aaronson, S.: Impossibility of succinct quantum proofs for collision-freeness. Quantum Inf. Comput. **12**(1–2), 21–28 (2012)

[ADM+99] Alon, N., Dietzfelbinger, M., Miltersen, P.B., Petrank, E., Tardos, G.: Linear hash functions. J. ACM **46**(5), 667–683 (1999)

[AH91] Aiello, W., Hastad, J.: Statistical zero-knowledge Languages can be recognized in two rounds. J. Comput. Syst. Sci. **42**(3), 327–345 (1991)

[APS18] Alamati, N., Peikert, C., Stephens-Davidowitz, N.: New (and Old) proof systems for lattice problems. In: Abdalla, M., Dahab, R. (eds.) PKC 2018, Part II. LNCS, vol. 10770, pp. 619–643. Springer, Cham (2018). https://doi.org/10.1007/978-3-319-76581-5_21

[AV19] Applebaum, B., Vasudevan, P.N.: Placing conditional disclosure of secrets in the communication complexity universe. In: Blum, A. (ed.) 10th Innovations in Theoretical Computer Science Conference, ITCS 2019, San Diego, California, USA, 10–12 January 2019. LIPIcs, vol. 124, pp. 4:1–4:14. Schloss Dagstuhl - Leibniz-Zentrum für Informatik (2019)

[BBD+20] Ball, M., et al.: Cryptography from information loss. In: Vidick, T. (ed.) 11th Innovations in Theoretical Computer Science Conference, ITCS 2020, Seattle, Washington, USA, 12–14 January 2020. LIPIcs, vol. 151, pp. 81:1–81:27. Schloss Dagstuhl - Leibniz-Zentrum für Informatikz (2020)

[BCH+20] Bouland, A., Chen, L., Holden, D., Thaler, J., Vasudevan, P.N.: On the power of statistical zero knowledge. SIAM J. Comput. **49**(4) (2020)

[BDRV18] Berman, I., Degwekar, A., Rothblum, R.D., Vasudevan, P.N.: From laconic zero-knowledge to public-key cryptography. In: Shacham, H., Boldyreva, A. (eds.) CRYPTO 2018, Part III. LNCS, vol. 10993, pp. 674–697. Springer, Cham (2018). https://doi.org/10.1007/978-3-319-96878-0_23

[BGR98] Bellare, M., Garay, J.A., Rabin, T.: Fast batch verification for modular exponentiation and digital signatures. In: Nyberg, K. (ed.) EUROCRYPT 1998. LNCS, vol. 1403, pp. 236–250. Springer, Heidelberg (1998). https://doi.org/10.1007/BFb0054130

[BL13] Bogdanov, A., Lee, C.H.: Limits of provable security for homomorphic encryption. In: Canetti, R., Garay, J.A. (eds.) CRYPTO 2013, Part I. LNCS, vol. 8042, pp. 111–128. Springer, Heidelberg (2013). https://doi.org/10.1007/978-3-642-40041-4_7

[CCH+19] Canetti, R., et al.: Fiat-Shamir: from practice to theory. In: Charikar, M., Cohen, E. (eds.) Proceedings of the 51st Annual ACM SIGACT Symposium on Theory of Computing, STOC 2019, Phoenix, AZ, USA, 23–26 June 2019, pp. 1082–1090. ACM (2019)

[CHP12] Camenisch, J., Hohenberger, S., Pedersen, M.Ø.: Batch verification of short signatures. J. Cryptol. 25(4), 723–747 (2011). https://doi.org/10.1007/s00145-011-9108-z

[CP92] Chaum, D., Pedersen, T.P.: Wallet databases with observers. In: Brickell, E.F. (ed.) CRYPTO 1992. LNCS, vol. 740, pp. 89–105. Springer, Heidelberg (1993). https://doi.org/10.1007/3-540-48071-4_7

[CRSW11] Celis, L.E., Reingold, O., Segev, G., Wieder, U.: Smaller hash families and faster evaluation. In: Electronic Colloquium on Computational Complexity (ECCC), vol. 18, p. 68 (2011)

[Dru15] Drucker, A.: New limits to classical and quantum instance compression. SIAM J. Comput. 44(5), 1443–1479 (2015)

[For87] Fortnow, L.: The complexity of perfect zero-knowledge (extended abstract). In: Aho, A.V. (ed.) Proceedings of the 19th Annual ACM Symposium on Theory of Computing, New York, New York, USA, pp. 204–209. ACM (1987)

[For89] Fortnow, L.J.: Complexity-theoretic aspects of interactive proof systems. Ph.D. thesis, Massachusetts Institute of Technology (1989)

[FS86] Fiat, A., Shamir, A.: How to prove yourself: practical solutions to identification and signature problems. In: Odlyzko, A.M. (ed.) CRYPTO 1986. LNCS, vol. 263, pp. 186–194. Springer, Heidelberg (1987). https://doi.org/10.1007/3-540-47721-7_12

[GG00] Goldreich, O., Goldwasser, S.: On the limits of nonapproximability of lattice problems. J. Comput. Syst. Sci. 60(3), 540–563 (2000)

[GK93] Goldreich, O., Kushilevitz, E.: A perfect zero-knowledge proof system for a problem equivalent to the discrete logarithm. J. Cryptol. 6(2), 97–116 (1993). https://doi.org/10.1007/BF02620137

[GMR89] Goldwasser, S., Micali, S., Rackoff, C.: The knowledge complexity of interactive proof systems. SIAM J. Comput. 18(1), 186–208 (1989)

[GMR98] Gennaro, R., Micciancio, D., Rabin, T.: An efficient non-interactive statistical zero-knowledge proof system for quasi-safe prime products. In: Gong, L., Reiter, M.K. (eds.) Proceedings of the 5th ACM Conference on Computer and Communications Security, CCS 1998, San Francisco, CA, USA, 3–5 November 1998, pp. 67–72. ACM (1998)

[GMW87] Goldreich, O., Micali, S., Wigderson, A.: How to play any mental game or A completeness theorem for protocols with honest majority. In: Proceedings of the 19th Annual ACM Symposium on Theory of Computing, New York, New York, USA, pp. 218–229 (1987)

[GR14] Goldwasser, S., Rothblum, G.N.: On best-possible obfuscation. J. Cryptol. 27(3), 480–505 (2014)

[GS89] Goldwasser, S., Sipser, M.: Private coins versus public coins in interactive proof systems. Adv. Comput. Res. 5, 73–90 (1989)

[GSV98] Goldreich, O., Sahai, A., Vadhan, S.: Honest-verifier statistical zero-knowledge equals general statistical zero-knowledge. In: STOC (1998)

[GV99] Goldreich, O., Vadhan, S.P.: Comparing entropies in statistical zero knowledge with applications to the structure of SZK. In: CCC (1999)

[HRV18] Hubáček, P., Rosen, A., Vald, M.: An efficiency-preserving transformation from honest-verifier statistical zero-knowledge to statistical zero-knowledge. In: Nielsen, J.B., Rijmen, V. (eds.) EUROCRYPT 2018, Part III. LNCS, vol. 10822, pp. 66–87. Springer, Cham (2018). https://doi.org/10.1007/978-3-319-78372-7_3

[KMN+14] Komargodski, I., Moran, T., Naor, M., Pass, R., Rosen, A., Yogev, E.: One-way functions and (im)perfect obfuscation. In: 55th IEEE Annual Symposium on Foundations of Computer Science, FOCS 2014, Philadelphia, PA, USA, 18–21 October 2014, pp. 374–383. IEEE Computer Society (2014)

[KRR+20] Kaslasi, I., Rothblum, G.N., Rothblum, R.D., Sealfon, A., Vasudevan, P.N.: Batch verification for statistical zero knowledge proofs. In: Electronic Colloquium on Computational Complexity (ECCC) (2020)

[KRV21] Kaslasi, I., Rothblum, R.D., Vasudevan, P.N.: Public-coin statistical zero-knowledge batch verification against malicious verifiers. Cryptology ePrint Archive, Report 2021/233 (2021). https://eprint.iacr.org/2021/233

[KY18] Komargodski, I., Yogev, E.: On distributional collision resistant hashing. In: Shacham, H., Boldyreva, A. (eds.) CRYPTO 2018, Part II. LNCS, vol. 10992, pp. 303–327. Springer, Cham (2018). https://doi.org/10.1007/978-3-319-96881-0_11

[LV16] Liu, T., Vaikuntanathan, V.: On basing private information retrieval on NP-hardness. In: Kushilevitz, E., Malkin, T. (eds.) TCC 2016, Part I. LNCS, vol. 9562, pp. 372–386. Springer, Heidelberg (2016). https://doi.org/10.1007/978-3-662-49096-9_16

[MV03] Micciancio, D., Vadhan, S.P.: Statistical zero-knowledge proofs with efficient provers: lattice problems and more. In: Boneh, D. (ed.) CRYPTO 2003. LNCS, vol. 2729, pp. 282–298. Springer, Heidelberg (2003). https://doi.org/10.1007/978-3-540-45146-4_17

[NMVR94] Naccache, D., M'Raïhi, D., Vaudenay, S., Raphaeli, D.: Can D.S.A. be improved?—complexity trade-offs with the digital signature standard. In: De Santis, A. (ed.) EUROCRYPT 1994. LNCS, vol. 950, pp. 77–85. Springer, Heidelberg (1995). https://doi.org/10.1007/BFb0053426

[NN93] Naor, J., Naor, M.: Small-bias probability spaces: efficient constructions and applications. SIAM J. Comput. 22(4), 838–856 (1993)

[NV06] Nguyen, M.-H., Vadhan, S.P.: Zero knowledge with efficient provers. In: Proceedings of the 38th Annual ACM Symposium on Theory of Computing, Seattle, WA, USA, 21–23 May 2006, pp. 287–295 (2006)

[Oka00] Okamoto, T.: On relationships between statistical zero-knowledge proofs. J. Comput. Syst. Sci. 60(1), 47–108 (2000)

[Ost91] Ostrovsky, R.: One-way functions, hard on average problems, and statistical zero-knowledge proofs. In: Structure in Complexity Theory Conference, pp. 133–138 (1991)

[OV08] Ong, S.J., Vadhan, S.: An equivalence between zero knowledge and commitments. In: Canetti, R. (ed.) TCC 2008. LNCS, vol. 4948, pp. 482–500. Springer, Heidelberg (2008). https://doi.org/10.1007/978-3-540-78524-8_27

[OW93] Ostrovsky, R., Wigderson, A.: One-way functions are essential for nontrivial zero-knowledge. In: ISTCS, pp. 3–17 (1993)

[PS96] Pointcheval, D., Stern, J.: Security proofs for signature schemes. In: Maurer, U. (ed.) EUROCRYPT 1996. LNCS, vol. 1070, pp. 387–398. Springer, Heidelberg (1996). https://doi.org/10.1007/3-540-68339-9_33

[PV08]  Peikert, C., Vaikuntanathan, V.: Noninteractive statistical zero-knowledge proofs for lattice problems. In: Wagner, D. (ed.) CRYPTO 2008. LNCS, vol. 5157, pp. 536–553. Springer, Heidelberg (2008). https://doi.org/10.1007/978-3-540-85174-5_30

[SV03]  Sahai, A., Vadhan, S.: A complete problem for statistical zero knowledge. J. ACM (JACM) **50**(2), 196–249 (2003)

[Vad99]  Vadhan, S.P.: A study of statistical zero-knowledge proofs. PhD thesis, Massachusetts Institute of Technology (1999)

[Vad12]  Vadhan, S.P.: Pseudorandomness. Found. Trends Theor. Comput. Sci. **7**(1–3), 1–336 (2012)

# Efficient Range Proofs with Transparent Setup from Bounded Integer Commitments

Geoffroy Couteau[1], Michael Klooß[2], Huang Lin[3], and Michael Reichle[4,5]([✉])

[1] CNRS, IRIF, Université de Paris, Paris, France
couteau@irif.fr
[2] Karlsruhe Institute for Technology, Karlsruhe, Germany
michael.klooss@kit.edu
[3] Mercury's Wing and Suterusu Project, Beijing, China
[4] DIENS, École normale supérieure, CNRS, PSL University, 75005 Paris, France
michael.reichle@ens.fr
[5] Inria, Paris, France

**Abstract.** We introduce a new approach for constructing range proofs. Our approach is modular, and leads to highly competitive range proofs under standard assumption, using less communication and (much) less computation than the state of the art methods, and without relying on a trusted setup. Our range proofs can be used as a drop-in replacement in a variety of protocols such as distributed ledgers, anonymous transaction systems, and many more, leading to significant reductions in communication and computation for these applications.

At the heart of our result is a new method to transform any commitment over a finite field into a commitment scheme which allows to commit to and efficiently prove relations about *bounded integers*. Combining these new commitments with a classical approach for range proofs based on square decomposition, we obtain several new instantiations of a paradigm which was previously limited to RSA-based range proofs (with high communication and computation, and trusted setup). More specifically, we get:

- Under the discrete logarithm assumption, we obtain the most compact and efficient range proof among all existing candidates (with or without trusted setup). Our proofs are 12% to 20% shorter than the state of the art Bulletproof (Bootle et al., CRYPTO'18) for standard choices of range size and security parameter, and are more efficient (both for the prover and the verifier) by more than an order of magnitude.
- Under the LWE assumption, we obtain range proofs that improve over the state of the art in a batch setting when at least a few dozen range proofs are required. The amortized communication of our range proofs improves by up to two orders of magnitudes over the state of the art when the number of required range proofs grows.
- Eventually, under standard class group assumptions, we obtain the first concretely efficient standard integer commitment scheme (with-

© International Association for Cryptologic Research 2021
A. Canteaut and F.-X. Standaert (Eds.): EUROCRYPT 2021, LNCS 12698, pp. 247–277, 2021.
https://doi.org/10.1007/978-3-030-77883-5_9

out bounds on the size of the committed integer) which does not assume trusted setup.

**Keywords:** Range proof · Integer commitments

# 1   Introduction

In this work, we develop new techniques to construct range proofs, an important building block in a variety of modern cryptographic protocols such as distributed ledgers, anonymous transactions, e-cash, e-voting, and many more. The range proofs obtained with our methods are highly competitive with the state of the art: they rely on standard assumptions, require less communication and computation, and do not assume any trusted setup. Furthermore, our approach is modular and can be instantiated in the discrete logarithm setting, in the lattice setting (leading to the most efficient post-quantum range proofs in a batch setting), and in the class group setting. Below, we review some background.

**Range Proofs and Anonymous Transactions.** Zero-knowledge proofs, introduced in the seminal work of Goldwasser, Micali, and Rackoff [GMR89], allow a prover to convince a verifier that a statement is true, while concealing all information beyond the truth of the statement. They are a fundamental primitive in cryptography, with inumerable applications. Range proofs, whose genesis can be traced back to [BCDv88], are a particular type of zero-knowledge proof where the prover wishes to convince the verifier that a committed value belongs to a certain range. Range proofs are a core building block in numerous applications such as anonymous credentials [Cha90], e-voting [Gro05], and e-cash [CHL05]. Furthermore, efficient range proofs have recently become central components in distributed ledgers, the prime example being the recent integration of Bulletproof [BBB+18] in the cryptocurrency Monero[1] and later Mimblewimble-based anonymous cryptocurrencies such as Beam[2] and Grin[3]. Range proofs also play an essential role in anonymous payment schemes for smart contract platforms such as Zether [BAZB20].

In most of these anonymous payment schemes, (positive and negative) integers are encoded as finite field elements, and negative spendings constitute a valid transaction in general, if they are not explicitly disallowed. This feature can be exploited to launch a double-spending attack, allowing the adversary to print money out of thin air [MIO18]. In a confidential payment scheme where both inputs and outputs of a transaction are hidden in either a digital commitment (as in Monero) or an encryption (as in Zether), range proofs are necessary to guarantee that the hidden value falls into the correct range and prevent the aforementioned overflow attack.

---

[1]  https://web.getmonero.org/resources/moneropedia/bulletproofs.html.

[2]  https://github.com/BeamMW/beam.

[3]  https://cointelegraph.com/news/cryptocurrency-grin-follows-through-with-anticipated-july-17-mainnet-hardfork.

The maximum throughput of a distributed ledger protocol is mainly determined by the maximum block size and average transaction size [CDE+16]. The smaller the transaction size is, the larger the maximum throughput is. The average transaction size in an anonymous payment scheme is largely determined by the zero-knowledge range proof size. Therefore, the proof size is a crucial parameter for the design of a range proof scheme. The proof generation and verification time are also vital to the performance of the system built on the range proof scheme. In the case of a decentralized anonymous payment scheme, the proof generation time will determine how fast the anonymous payment can be launched and have a direct impact on the user experience and system scalability [CZJ+17]. The proof verification time, on the other hand, has a great impact on the workload of the miners.

## 1.1   Standard Approaches for Building Range Proofs

Due to their wide variety of applications, many constructions of range proofs have been proposed over the past decades. All these constructions can be categorized in two main high level approaches, which we outline below.

*First Method: n-Ary Decomposition.* The first method is the one employed both in the early (folklore) constructions of range proofs, as well as in the latest state-of-the-art constructions (such as Bulletproof). To prove that a committed integer $x$ belong to an interval of the form $[0, n^\ell - 1]$, where $n$ is some small value, this method uses the following high-level template:

1. First, commit to the $n$-ary decomposition of $x$, denoted $(x_0, \cdots, x_{\ell-1})$.
2. Second, prove that the relation $x = \sum_{i=0}^{\ell-1} x_i \cdot n^i$ holds.
3. Third, prove that each component of the committed tuple belongs to $[0, n-1]$. Since $n$ is typically very small, this can be achieved using some brute-force method (for example, when using binary decomposition, it amounts to proving that each component is a bit, which can be done using standard methods).

When the commitment scheme satisfies some homomorphic properties, it is generally simple to lift a proof as above to a proof for a more general interval $[a, b]$. The first instance of this approach is a folklore discrete-logarithm-based construction using the Pedersen commitment scheme to commit to the bit decomposition of $x$. Denoting $\beta = \log(b-a)$ the bitlength of the interval size and $\lambda$ the bitlength of group elements, This leads to a range proof communicating $\mathcal{O}(\lambda \cdot \beta)$ bits. This approach was first improved in [CCs08] to $\mathcal{O}(\lambda \cdot \beta/\log \beta)$ by using decomposition in a larger basis, and later in [Gro11] to $\mathcal{O}(\lambda \cdot \beta^{1/3})$, using pairings.

In a recent breakthrough work, the authors of [BBB+18] introduced Bulletproof, which managed to reduce the communication to $\mathcal{O}(\lambda \cdot \log \beta)$ under the plain DLOG assumption (without pairings) while still remaining computationally efficient. Their approach relies on generalized Pedersen commitment to commit to the entire bit-decomposition of $x$ using few group elements, and on a clever recursive proof strategy to simultaneously prove that all committed values are bits.[4] This comes at the cost of a larger number of rounds $\mathcal{O}(\log \beta)$ (but this is typically not a concern in real-world applications, where the Fiat-Shamir heuristic is used to make the proof non-interactive) and a computational soundness guarantee (leading to a zero-knowledge argument instead of a proof).

A strong advantage of the proofs obtained in this line of work is that they do not require any trusted setup. In real-world applications such as cryptocurrencies, this is an important feature to avoid having to trust any central authority with the secure generation of the parameters (we will discuss this more later). Due to this feature and its good concrete efficiency, Bulletproof is currently considered the state of the art method for range proofs, and has found its way into several real-world protocols.

*Second Method: Square Decomposition.* The second method can be traced back to the work of Boudot [Bou00], and was initially introduced to avoid the large $\mathcal{O}(\lambda \cdot \beta)$ cost of the range proofs obtained (at the time) by the first method. It relies on the following high-level template (or a close variant thereof): first, proving that $x \in [a, b]$ reduces to proving that $x - a$ and $b - x$ (whose commitments can typically be computed homomorphically from a commitment to $x$) are positive. Now, to prove that a committed value $y$ is positive:

1. First, decompose $y$ as $y = \sum_{i=1}^{4} y_i^2$ over the integers. Lagrange's four square theorem guarantees that such a decomposition exists, and efficient algorithms allow to quickly find one.
2. Second, commit to the $y_i$ and prove (using standard methods) that $y = \sum_{i=1}^{4} y_i^2$ *over the integers*.

The advantage of this method is that it requires committing only to a constant number of components (independent of the interval size), instead of $\approx \beta$ components with the first method. This typically leads to proofs with communication $\mathcal{O}(\beta + \lambda)$ bits. However, it is crucial for this method that the relation is proven *over the integers*: standard commitment schemes such as Pedersen only allow committing values over $\mathbb{Z}_p$ for some prime $p$, but finding a 4-square decomposition over $\mathbb{Z}_p$ does not provide any guarantee of positivity. Hence, a core component of this line of work is the notion of *integer commitment schemes*, introduced in [FO97, DF02], which allows to commit and prove relations among values directly over the integers.

The square decomposition method has been refined in [Lip03]. Later, the work of Groth [Gro05] observed that one can instead decompose $4y + 1$ as a sum of three squares (positive integers congruent to 1 modulo 4 can always be decomposed this way) to reduce the proof size, and further efficiency and security improvements were described in [CPP17]. A common issue of all these works is that all known integer commitment schemes require the use of RSA groups or class groups with a hard-to-factor discriminant. This means that the

---

[4] There have been several recent follow up works [HKR19, AC20] to Bulletproof, which expand the set of relations captured by the framework, but do not translate into concrete improvements on the size of the range proofs produced by this framework.

group size is very large (typically 3072 bits), and that these proofs all require a trusted setup to generate a public product of secret prime factors[5]. Assuming a trusted setup is a rather undesirable property in a decentralized anonymous payment scheme: in general, the party responsible for the setup step can exploit the trapdoor information obtained through this process to print an unlimited amount of cryptocurrency without being detected [Sle,Ben]. Although one could potentially mitigate the risk of the above attack by using secure multi-party computation to execute the setup step (as was done e.g. for zcash[6]), it introduces additional engineering complexity and potential vulnerabilities.

Furthermore, even before Bulletproof, these proof systems were competitive with proofs obtained with the first method only for very large intervals. Compared to Bulletproof, they lead to much larger proof sizes for any interval size (and are also computationally less efficient). Due to their higher cost and their need of a trusted setup, this second method is largely considered obsolete and non-competitive with the proofs obtained through the first method.

## 1.2   Our Contribution

In this work, we turn the tables and demonstrate that the square decomposition method can be refined to create highly competitive range proofs, with smaller communication and computation compared to the state of the art Bulletproof, without trusted setup (meaning that our proofs only require a transparent setup), and under standard assumptions. Among other advantages, our method is modular and can also be instantiated in the lattice setting to obtain post-quantum range proofs which are highly competitive with the sate of the art in a batch scenario (where several range proofs must be computed at once), and in the class group setting with prime discriminant. Furthermore, our proofs require only three rounds of interaction, an important feature if one does not want to rely on the Fiat-Shamir heuristic, and can be modified to achieve statistical soundness instead of computational soundness (at a small cost in efficiency). At the heart of our constructions is a new generic method to convert any commitment scheme over $\mathbb{Z}_p$ into a *bounded integer commitment scheme*, i.e., a commitment scheme which allows to commit to bounded-range integers and to prove relations over $\mathbb{Z}$ between committed bounded-range integers.

**Instantiation in the Discrete-Log Setting.** Instantiating our framework with the standard Pedersen commitment scheme, we obtain a bounded integer commitment scheme under the discrete logarithm assumption. When plugging this bounded integer commitment scheme in the range proof of [CPP17], we obtain a range proof which does not require any trusted setup and can benefit simultaneously from the compactness of square-decomposition-based range

---

[5] While it is theoretically possible to use a very large random integer as RSA modulus, without relying on a trusted party to compute a product of safe primes, this approach is completely impractical due to the very large group size and amount of computation, see the discussion on RSA-UFO in [LM19].

[6] https://z.cash/technology/paramgen/.

proofs (i.e., constant number of group elements) and the possibility of instantiating the Pedersen commitment scheme over prime-order elliptic curve, with small group elements[7]. To further optimize the proof size, we describe an optimized variant which relies on the *short-exponents* discrete logarithm assumption (i.e., the assumption that it is hard to compute discrete logarithm even when the exponent is sampled from a large enough bounded range), which is a well-studied variant of the standard discrete log assumption. For example, for an interval size of $2^{32}$ and 128 bits of security, we obtain range proofs of size 501 Bytes, compared to the 608 Bytes of Bulletproof. For the same parameters, the computational cost for both the prover and the verifier are more than an order of magnitude smaller compared to Bulletproof. The high efficiency of prover *and* verifier is crucial for use of (range) proofs on resource constrained devices, such as smartphones. Such devices are of special interest for privacy-enhancing technologies, such as anonymous credentials [Cha90] and payment systems. To achieve practialility, tradeoffs have to made. For example, the work [BBDE19] relies on [CCs08], which requires pairings and relatively large public parameters, whereas the work [HKRR20] relies on *uncompressed*, i.e. linear-size, Bulletproofs, trading communication for computation. Our range proofs are a great fit for these settings.

*Detailed Comparison with Bulletproof.* A more detailed comparison with Bulletproof is given in Table 1. Below, we explain how the numbers in the table have been obtained. Computing the exact costs of our range proof is rather tedious, since it involves careful optimizations with rejection sampling techniques, and optimizations using the short-exponent discrete logarithm assumption. We consider range proofs over an interval $[a, b]$ with $\beta = \log(b - a) \in \{32, 64\}$, a security parameter $\lambda \in \{80, 128\}$, and a group of size $q$ (which might not be the same for Bulletproof and our range proof). The formula below additionally uses parameters $C, S, L'$ corresponding respectively to the challenge size, a bound on the length of short exponents, and a bound for rejection sampling. Our concrete numbers are obtained by setting $C = 2^{\lambda}, S = 2^{2\lambda}, L' = \lceil 256\sqrt{2\lambda} \rceil$. The formulas for computing the range proof size (in the non-interactive setting, when Fiat-Shamir is used), the prover work, and the verifier work, are given below:

- Proof size (in bits): $30(\beta + \log(CL')) + \lceil \log(C)/\lambda \rceil (2\lambda + 4(2\beta + \log(CL') + 2\log(SCL')) + 2)$ (our work) versus $\log q \cdot (2\beta + 9)$ (Bulletproof).
- Prover work (in group multiplications): $2.31 \cdot (4\beta + 8\log S + 6\log C + 7\log L') + 30$ (our work) versus $18 \cdot (\beta \log q)$ (Bulletproof).
- Verifier work (in group multiplications): $4.5\beta + 7\log S + 13\log C + 9\log L' + 10$ versus at least $3\beta \cdot \log q$ (lower bound on the cost for Bulletproof, computed as the cost of a single inner product argument)

---

[7] Since our bounded integer commitment scheme requires the committed values to remain into a bounded range, we actually require slightly larger group size compared to Bulletproof to achieve the same security level; this is accounted for in our concrete comparison and will be covered in details in the technical overview.

- Group size (in bits): $\log q = 32(2^\beta CL')^2 + 1$ (our work) versus $\log q = 2\lambda$ (Bulletproof)

In the above, prover and verifier work are computed as the number of multiplications required for the exponentiations (we do not directly count the exponentiations for fairness of comparison: Bulletproof and our work do not use the same group size, and our optimized construction also uses exponentiations with short exponents), which largely dominate the overall cost. We note that in both our work and Bulletproof, the verifier work can be optimized by relying on multiexponentiations techniques; since these techniques apply identically in both works and do not significantly change the bottom line in terms of comparisons, we ignore them in this overview.

Asymptotically, our proofs have size $O(\lambda + \beta)$, while Bulletproof has size $O(\lambda \log \beta)$. We note that in the range of parameters $\beta = O(\lambda)$, our techniques actually leads to an asymptotic improvement over Bulletproof; for larger ranges, Bulletproof is more efficient, and for very small ranges, the asymptotic costs are the same for both. Previous square-decomposition-based range proofs had asymptotic cost $O(\beta + \lambda^{3-o(1)})$ due to their use of RSA modulus (which allow for subexponential attacks).

We stress that when not using the Fiat-Shamir heuristic, our scheme can be instantiated to have only three rounds (this slightly increases the proof size, because it requires to not use rejection sampling, since the latter causes the protocol to restart with non-negligible probability) while Bulletproof requires $\log \beta$ rounds. Even with rejection sampling and our concrete choice of parameters, the expected number of rounds is less than 5. Thus for sufficiently large $\beta$, our security proof is tighter than the one of Bulletproofs in the random-oracle model.

Furthermore, our scheme can be instantiated to have statistical soundness. On the other hand, Bulletproof allows for extremely efficient batching a large number of range proofs, and would therefore become preferable communication-wise when many range proofs must be performed at once. In any case, and independently of the number of range proofs, our range proofs requires 20 to 40 times less group multiplications for the prover, and 6 to 15 times less for the verifier.

**Instantiation in the Lattice Setting.** For the instantiation of our framework in the lattice setting, we build upon the commitment scheme and proof system from [YAZ+19]. The commitments built this way allow to commit to long vectors over $\mathbb{Z}_q^n$ (think of $n$ as being a few thousands, e.g. $n = 5000$). Our techniques require to use a relatively large modulus $q$ in order to avoid overflows in the computation. As a consequence, our commitments and proofs are quite large.

However, in exchange for using a large modulus, the commitment and proof system obtained by compiling the commitment of [YAZ+19] with our techniques allow to *batch* many range proofs extremely efficiently: we can essentially perform up to $n$ range proofs in parallel for the cost of a single range proof, even if range proofs have different ranges. This improves over the communication achieved by the best LWE-based range proofs [YAZ+19]. Even compared to the more recent

**Table 1.** Comparison between the optimized range proof of Sect. 5.4 and Bulletproof [BBB+18] for various choices of security parameter $\lambda$ and log of interval size $\beta$. Proof size and group size are in Bytes, prover and verifier work are counted as a number of group multiplications, rounded to two decimal places. See the paragraph "detailed comparison with Bulletproof" for the details on our computations.

| $(\beta, \lambda)$ | | Proof size | Prover work | Verifier work | Group size |
|---|---|---|---|---|---|
| $(32, 80)$ | This Work | 339 | 4.6k | 2.4k | 32 |
| | Bulletproof | 380 | 92k | >15k | 20 |
| $(32, 128)$ | This Work | 501 | 7k | 3.7k | 44 |
| | Bulletproof | 608 | 150k | >25k | 32 |
| $(64, 80)$ | This Work | 383 | 4.9k | 2.6k | 40 |
| | Bulletproof | 420 | 180k | >31k | 20 |
| $(64, 128)$ | This Work | 545 | 7.3k | 3.8k | 52 |
| | Bulletproof | 672 | 290k | >49k | 32 |

scheme of [BLLS20], which achieves very compact (single-shot) range proofs under the ring-SIS assumption, our approach starts to become more efficient from about 35 range proofs (and the efficiency gain scales linearly after that). In the limit, when performing a large number of range proofs in parallel, we achieve about two orders of magnitude of communication reduction compared to the state of the art. The comparison is summarized on Table 2.

**Table 2.** Comparison of the range proof size in the lattice setting. Note that the scheme of [YAZ+19] was designed for large ranges. For a fair comparison, we apply similar vector-based batching optimization. The size is given in KB.

| Range | | Batch size | $\lambda = 80$ | $\lambda = 128$ |
|---|---|---|---|---|
| $\beta = 32$ | LWE [YAZ+19] | 31 | 39 | 73 |
| | This Work | 35 | 4.7 | 5.2 |
| | This Work | 5000 | 0.1 | 0.1 |
| $\beta = 64$ | LWE [YAZ+19] | 31 | 77 | 146 |
| | This Work | 35 | 8.4 | 9.7 |
| | This Work | 5000 | 0.16 | 0.16 |

**Instantiation in the Class Group Setting.** Eventually, we also instantiate our method in the class group setting. The proofs obtained this way improve over our DLOG-based proofs only for large ranges, where Bulletproof would be more efficient. On the other hand, instantiating our approach in the class group setting leads to the first concretely efficient construction of *unbounded* integer commitment scheme which does not require a trusted setup (the only known alternative uses RSA-UFO, which is impractical, see the discussion in [LM19]).

**Concurrent Works.** In the DLOG setting, the work of [CHJ+20] recently claimed an improvement in proof size compared to [BBB+18] by slightly reducing the number of group elements required in [BBB+18]. The computational cost of their proof is the same as in [BBB+18]. To our knowledge, their scheme was not peer reviewed yet; we note that our range proofs are still shorter than theirs, and more than an order of magnitude computationally more efficient.

## 2    Technical Overview

As we outlined in the introduction, at the heart of our results is a method to convert standard homomorphic commitment schemes into *bounded integer commitment schemes* – that is, a scheme that allows to commit to integers from a bounded range, but also to *prove in zero-knowledge* relations between commited values *over the integers*, see [FO97,DF02] – with a certain set of additional specific properties. We now provide details on our approach.

### 2.1    A Natural Approach via Σ-Protocols

For simplicity, suppose that we have at our disposal a commitment scheme com with message space and random coin space $\mathbb{Z}_q$, for some large prime $q$, which is homomorphic over the messages and the coins: $\mathsf{com}(m_1; r_1) \cdot \mathsf{com}(m_2; r_2) = \mathsf{com}(m_1 + m_2; r_1 + r_2)$. This is satisfied for example by the Pedersen commitment scheme $\mathsf{com}(m; r) = g^m h^r$ for two group elements $(g, h)$ over a group of order $q$. The transformation works for a more general class of commitments, this choice of structure is for the sake of concreteness. Suppose now that we would like to obtain a bounded integer commitment scheme out of com. The first obvious idea is to proceed as follows:

- map values in $\mathbb{Z}_q$ to integers $[-(q-1)/2, (q-1)/2]$ in the natural way;
- define com' to be exactly like com, but where the committed values are restricted to $[-R, R]$, where $R \ll (q-1)/2$ is some bound.

Intuitively, the bound $R$ is here to ensure that we will have enough "room" to guarantee that if a relation between elements of $[-R, R]$ holds modulo $q$, then it must also hold over the integers. Looking ahead, for building a range proof, we will want to prove relations of the form $x = \sum_i x_i^2$, and we will choose $R$ such that no overflow occurs when computing $\sum_i x_i^2 \bmod q$ with $x_i \in [-R, R]$.

The next step is to equip this commitment com' with a zero-knowledge proof system allowing to prove relations between committed values *over the integers*. However, this turns out to be particularly challenging. To see this, consider the standard Σ-protocol between a prover P and a verifier V for proving knowledge of an opening $(m, r)$ to a commitment $c = \mathsf{com}(m; r)$:

- P: pick $(m', r') \xleftarrow{\$} \mathbb{Z}_q^2$ and send $c' = \mathsf{com}(m'; r')$.
- V: send a challenge $e \xleftarrow{\$} \mathbb{Z}_q$.
- P: send $d_m = em + m'$ and $d_r = er + r'$.
- V: accept if $\mathsf{com}(m; r)^e \cdot \mathsf{com}(m'; r') = \mathsf{com}(d_m; d_r)$.

Using a standard rewinding argument, we can extract a valid opening $(m; r) \in \mathbb{Z}_q^2$ of $c$ from any (potentially malicious) prover $P^*$ which produces accepting proofs with non-negligible probability $\varepsilon$: run $P^*$ to get $c'$, fork it, and run it on two different random challenges $e, e'$, receiving $(d_m, d_r)$ and $(d'_m, d'_r)$. By a standard probability lemma (see the splitting lemma from [PS96, PS00]), $(c', e, d_m, d_r)$ and $(c', e', d'_m, d'_r)$ will both be accepting transcript with non-negligible probability $\Omega(\varepsilon^2)$. From the two accepting equations, one gets

$$c = \mathsf{com}((d_m - d'_m) \cdot (e - e')^{-1}, (d_r - d'_r) \cdot (e - e')^{-1}). \tag{1}$$

To adapt the protocol to $\mathsf{com}'$, we would need to modify the $\Sigma$-protocol such that it additionally guarantees that the extracted value $m$ belongs to $[-R, R]$. This actually seems feasible at first sight if we agree to settle for a relaxed correctness and zero-knowledge guarantee: we only enforce correctness and (honest-verifier) zero-knowledge whenever $m$ belongs to $[-R', R']$, for a bound $R'$ such that $2^{\lambda+\kappa} R' \leq R$, where $\kappa$ is a statistical security parameter for zero-knowledge, and $\lambda$ is a statistical security parameter for soundness (we keep both separate for generality). Then, we can modify the protocol as follows:

- P: pick $(m', r') \xleftarrow{\$} [-2^{\lambda+\kappa} R', 2^{\lambda+\kappa} R'] \times \mathbb{Z}_q$ and send $c' = \mathsf{com}(m'; r')$.
- V: send a challenge $e \xleftarrow{\$} [1, 2^\lambda]$.
- P: send $d_m = em + m'$ and $d_r = er + r'$.
- V: accept if $\mathsf{com}(m; r)^e \cdot \mathsf{com}(m'; r') = \mathsf{com}(d_m; d_r)$ and $d_m \in [-R, R]$.

Intuitively, relaxed correctness and relaxed statistical zero-knowledge follow from the fact that for $m \in [-R', R']$ and $e \in [1, 2^\lambda]$, $d_m = em + m'$ for $m' \xleftarrow{\$} [-2^{\lambda+\kappa} R', 2^{\lambda+\kappa} R']$ will be $2^{-\kappa}$-close to uniform (in statistical distance) over $[-R, R]$. It remains to analyze whether we can extract from an accepting prover a valid witness for $\mathsf{com}'$. However, even though we restricted $e$ and $d_m$ to be small, recall that the extracted value (Eq. 1) is of the form $m = (d_m - d'_m) \cdot (e - e')^{-1} \bmod q$. That is, $m$ is not an element of $[-R, R]$ in general; rather, it is the product of an element in $[-R, R]$ and *the inverse modulo $q$ of an element in* $[1, 2^\lambda]$. Therefore, this approach fails at binding the prover to a value $m \in [-R, R]$.

We note that the failure of this approach – the impossibility of extracting values guaranteed to be short in general – is a well-known problem in the context of lattice-based cryptography. Indeed, standard $\Sigma$-protocol for proving knowledge of a short solution to a system of equation – i.e., a witness for the SIS problem – suffer from exactly the same limitation (see e.g. the discussions in [BCK+14]). The standard solution is to restrict the challenge set to $\{-1, 0, 1\}$ (to guarantee that the inverse of the difference between distinct challenges remains small), and to amplify soudness via parallel repetitions. However, in our context, this would lead to a very inefficient proof system. Unfortunately, finding a different proof system with much better efficiency seems to be a hard problem.

## 2.2   Encoding Integers as Mod-$q$ Rationals

Instead, we follow a different approach by turning the problem around: rather than searching an efficient and sound proof system for the commitment com$'$ above, we seek to find a different construction of bounded integer commitment $\overline{\text{com}}$ such that the above efficient proof system – which is not sound because it only allows extracting fractions of small values modulo $p$ – becomes a sound proof system for $\overline{\text{com}}$ (allowing to extract bounded integers committed with $\overline{\text{com}}$). Abstracting out, we saw above that we can extract from a cheating prover a triple $(y, d, \rho) \in [-R, R] \times [1, 2^\lambda] \times \mathbb{Z}_q$ such that $c = \text{com}(y \cdot d^{-1} \bmod q; \rho)$. Our goal will be to find an appropriate choice of *encoding* Encode satisfying the following properties:

- $\overline{\text{com}}(x; \rho) = \text{com}(\text{Encode}(x); \rho)$, such that a commitment to a value $x'$ with com can be seen as a commitment to some different value $x = \text{Decode}(x')$ with $\overline{\text{com}}$.
- Extracting a tuple $(y, d, \rho) \in [-R, R] \times [1, 2^\lambda] \times \mathbb{Z}_q$ should correspond to extracting a valid opening of $\overline{\text{com}}$ to some *bounded integer* $x$ in an appropriate bounded range.

Looking ahead, we will need a few additional properties to hold for Encode if we want to build an efficient range proofs for $\overline{\text{com}}$.

- First, we want Encode to satisfy some appropriate homomorphic properties. Informally: $\text{Encode}(-x) = -\text{Encode}(x)$, $\text{Encode}(x + a) = \text{Encode}(x) + a$, and $\text{Encode}(a \cdot x) = a \cdot \text{Encode}(x)$, for a sufficiently small integer $a$.
- Second, we want to be able to transfer a square decomposition from encodings modulo $q$ to encoded integers: informally, proving a relation of the form $x' = \sum_i (x'_i)^2 \bmod q$ where $x' = \text{Encode}(x)$ and $x'_i = \text{Encode}(x_i)$ should guarantee that $x = \sum x_i^2$ *over the integers*.

**Our Choice of Encoding.** It turns out that there is a choice of (randomized) encoding that satisfies all of the above constraints simultaneously. In hindsight, this encoding is quite simple and natural: we view any pair $(y, d) \in [-R, R] \times [1, 2^\lambda]$ as an encoding $(y, d) = \text{Encode}(x)$ of the integer

$$ x = \left\lfloor \frac{y}{d} \right\rceil \in [-R, R], $$

where the fraction denotes standard division, and $\lfloor \cdot \rceil$ denotes *rounding to the nearest integer*. Given this choice of encoding, $\overline{\text{com}}$ is defined as follows:

- $\overline{\text{com}}(x)$: pick $\rho \xleftarrow{\$} \mathbb{Z}_q$ and output commitment $c = \text{com}(x; \rho)$ and opening $(x, 1, \rho)$.
- $\overline{\text{com}}.\text{Verify}(c, \boldsymbol{x}, (y, d, \rho))$: check that $c = \text{com}(y \cdot d^{-1}; \rho)$, $x = \lfloor y/d \rceil$, $y \in [-R, R]$, and $d \in [1, 2^\lambda]$.

Some remarks are in order. First, observe that $\overline{\text{com}}(x)$ is defined exactly as $\text{com}(x)$; that is, a honest commitment with $\overline{\text{com}}$ is just a normal commitment with com. This is because we can view any $x \in [-R, R]$ as an encoding $(x, 1)$ of itself (since $x = \lfloor x/1 \rceil$). The only difference is that we relax the verification to accept general openings $(y, d) = \mathsf{Encode}(x)$ of $x$. Second, the fact that extracting a triple $(y, d, \rho)$ in the $\Sigma$-protocol corresponds to extracting a valid opening (w.r.t. $\overline{\mathsf{com}}$) of an integer in $[-R, R]$ becomes trivially true. It remains to check two things:

1. $\overline{\mathsf{com}}$ must remain *binding* and *hiding*;
2. $\overline{\mathsf{com}}$ must satisfy some homomorphic properties that we outlined above.

$\overline{\mathsf{com}}$ **is Binding and Hiding.** That $\overline{\mathsf{com}}$ is hiding follows immediatly from the fact that com is hiding. It remains to consider binding. Suppose that an adversary finds two valid openings $(y, d, \rho)$ and $(y', d', \rho')$ in $[-R, R] \times [1, 2^\lambda] \times \mathbb{Z}_q$ to a commitment $c$; that is, $c = \mathsf{com}(y \cdot d^{-1} \bmod q; \rho) = \mathsf{com}(y' \cdot (d')^{-1} \bmod q; \rho')$. Since com itself is binding, we must have $y \cdot d^{-1} = y' \cdot (d')^{-1} \bmod q$. This last equation implies

$$yd' = y'd \bmod q \implies yd' = y'd \text{ over } \mathbb{Z} \implies \lfloor y/d' \rceil = \lfloor y'/d \rceil,$$

where the first implication holds as long as $q$ is chosen large enough compared to $R$ and $2^\lambda$, i.e., $q/2 > R \cdot 2^\lambda$.

**Properties of $\overline{\mathsf{com}}$.** First, we check some basic homomorphic properties:

– If $(y, d)$ encodes $x = \lfloor y/d \rceil$, then $(-y, d)$ encodes $-x$.
– If $(y, d)$ encodes $x = \lfloor y/d \rceil$ and $a$ is an integer such that $ya \leq R$, then $\overline{\mathsf{com}}(x)^a = \mathsf{com}(ayd^{-1})$ is a valid commitment $\overline{\mathsf{com}}(ax)$.
– If $(y, d)$ encodes $x = \lfloor y/d \rceil$ and $a$ is an integer such that $y + da \leq R$, then $\overline{\mathsf{com}}(x) \cdot \mathsf{com}(a) = \mathsf{com}(yd^{-1} + a) = \mathsf{com}((y + da)d^{-1})$ is a valid commitment $\overline{\mathsf{com}}(x + a)$ since $\lfloor (y + da)/d \rceil = \lfloor y/d + a \rceil = \lfloor y/d \rceil + a$.

Second, in our most optimized range proof constructions, we will reduce the task of proving that $x$ belongs to an interval $[a, b]$ to the task of proving that $x_0 = (x - a)(b - x)$ is positive. To show the latter, we will prove that there exists three integers $(x_1, x_2, x_3)$ such that $4x_0 + 1 = \sum_{i=1}^{3} x_i^3$; such a decomposition exists (and can be found efficiently) if and only if $x_0 \geq 0$ [Gro05]. Now, suppose we extracted encodings $(y, d), ((y_i, d)_{i \leq 3})$ to $4x_0 + 1$ and $(x_1, x_2, x_3)$ respectively, with the following guarantee: $yd^{-1} = \sum_{i=1}^{3}(y_i d^{-1})^2 \bmod q$.

Intuitively, this guarantee will be obtained by using a standard $\Sigma$-protocol to prove knowledge of a 3-square decomposition directly over commitments with com. The extracted encodings will all have a common $d$, because of the structure of the extraction procedure: $d$ corresponds simply to the difference between two distinct challenges for which the prover produced an accepting transcript. The above equation can be rewritten $yd = \sum_{i=1}^{3} y_i^2 \bmod q$, which necessarily holds over the integers (i.e., no overflow occurs) given that $3R^2 < q/2$ and $2^\lambda R < q/2$, since the values $y$ and $y_i$ are bounded by $R$ and $d$ is bounded by $2^\lambda$. From there, dividing both sides by $d^2$ over the rationals, we get that $y/d$ can we written as a sum of three squares over $\mathbb{Q}$. A simple technical lemma shows that this relation over $\mathbb{Q}$ actually suffices to guarantee $x = \lfloor y/d \rceil \in [a, b]$; we omit details in this high level overview.

Note that in related work [FSW03], a similar encoding is used to allow for homomorphic computations with bounded rationals. However in our case, bounded rationals appear as an intermediate result as extracted value $(y - y') \cdot (d - d')^{-1} \bmod q$ of the proof of knowledge. Our encoding is for small integers, hence the rounding. Also, the work [LN17] uses the fact that the extracted value is unique to construct verifiable encryption schemes. Again, the application differs.

## 2.3   Instantiation in the Discrete Log Setting

Equipped with a method to build bounded integer commitment schemes which satisfy some necessary properties, we turn to the problem of instantiating the construction in different settings, and building a range proof from it. In the discrete logarithm setting, we set com to be the standard Pedersen commitment scheme: $\mathsf{com}(m; r) = g^m h^r$ where $(g, h)$ are two random generators over a group where computing discrete logarithms is hard. As for the range proof, we rely on the efficient $\Sigma$-protocol of [CPP17], adapting it to prime order group (since the scheme is described over subgroups of $\mathbb{Z}_n$ for an RSA modulus $n$ in [CPP17]). This is a relatively standard $\Sigma$-protocol where the prover, given an opening $(x, r)$ for a commitment $c = g^x h^r$, commits to three values $(x_1, x_2, x_3)$ such that $4(x - a)(b - x) + 1 = \sum_i x_i^2$, and proves knowledge of openings to $x, x_1, x_2, x_3$ such that this relation is satisfied. We provide a detailed security analysis of the resulting protocol.

The scheme of [CPP17] already includes a standard optimization for $\Sigma$-protocols, which relies on a collision-resistant hash function to compress the first flow while preserving soundness. We introduce two important additional optimizations tailored to our setting.

**First Optimization.** Due to our use of a group with a large order, we can actually reduce the size of the random coins used in the Pedersen commitments, at the cost of relying on the *short-exponent* discrete logarithm assumption (DLSE). This improves the computational efficiency, but also reduces the communication when proving knowledge of an opening. Furthermore, relying on DLSE has an important consequence: while the protocol of [CPP17] has computational soundness (and statistical zero-knowledge), we get an alternative instantiation which satisfies statistical soundness (and computational zero-knowledge).

*On Getting Range Proofs with Statistical Soundness.* This alternative instantiation is obtained by changing the commitment as follows: To commit to $m \in [-R, R]$, sample $r \xleftarrow{\$} [1, K]$ and output $g^m h^r$. Here, $R$ is a bound on the committed messages, and $K$ is chosen such that the short-exponent discrete log assumption, with random exponent chosen from $[1, K]$, is believed to hold. Applying DLSE, $h^r$ is indistinguishable from a uniformly random group element (using a standard search-to-decision reduction for DLSE in prime-order groups [KK04]).

Hence, the scheme remains (computationally) hiding. Furthermore, $g^m h^r$ is perfectly binding: the probability (over the random choice of $s$ such that $g^s = h$) that there exists $(m, r, m', r')$ with $m' \neq m$ such that $m + sr = m' + sr'$ is negligible by the Schwartz-Zippel lemma and a union bound (when $R, K$ are small enough).

Therefore, using our proof system with short randomness in the Pedersen commitments, with appropriate parameter adjustment to guarantee perfect binding, we obtain a range proof with statistical soundness. We note that this is an important feature: the impossibility of getting statistical soundness with Bulletproof is discussed in Sect. 4.6 of the Bulletproof paper [BBB+18]. In anonymous transaction schemes, statistical soundness is more important than statistical zero-knowledge, since the former is crucial for avoiding indetectable creation of coins (which would render the currency useless), while the second is only necessary to guarantee anonymity (without which the currency remains usable). Not getting statistical soundness was generally believed to be inherent to efficient range proofs, since very compact commitments require computational soundness; our method shows that it is actually possible to get competitive range proofs with statistical soundness. Note that there is also a natural instantiation of our approach using ElGamal encryption as the underlying commitment scheme. This also yields a statistically sound range proof but it is less efficient than the variant of this work.

**Second Optimization.** The scheme of [CPP17] relies on standard "flooding" to achieve statistical zero-knowledge: the value $e \cdot m$, where $m \in [-R, R]$ is a secret value and $e \leq 2^\lambda$ is a challenge, is masked with a random $m' \xleftarrow{\$} [1, 2^{\lambda+\kappa} R]$ to ensure that $em + m'$ will be $2^{-\kappa}$-close in statistical distance to the uniform distribution over $[1, 2^{\lambda+\kappa} R]$. However, it turns out that our constraints are closely related to the constraints satisfied by several $\Sigma$-protocols in the *lattice* setting, which also deal with careful bounds on the size of secret values. Building upon this observation, we import a standard optimization of $\Sigma$-protocols in the lattice-setting, namely, the *rejection-sampling* method [Lyu12]. Using rejection sampling allows different tradeoffs between the group size, the number of repetitions of the underlying protocol, and the size of the masks used to hide secret values. We show that an appropriate choice of tradeoff allows to significantly reduce the communication complexity of our protocol.

# 3 Preliminaries

**Notation.** In this work, we generally perform calculations in $\mathbb{Z}/q\mathbb{Z}$ with representatives $\mathbb{Z}_q = [-\frac{q-1}{2}, \frac{q-1}{2}]$ for an odd modulus $q \in \mathbb{N}$, and we identify $\mathbb{Z}_q$ with $\mathbb{Z}/q\mathbb{Z}$, unless stated otherwise. Inside of flooring $\lfloor \frac{a}{b} \rfloor$ or rounding $\lfloor \frac{a}{b} \rceil = \lfloor \frac{a}{b} + \frac{1}{2} \rfloor$ operations, we generally have $a, b$ in $\mathbb{Z}$ with division over $\mathbb{Q}$, i.e. we work with the representatives and not in $\mathbb{Z}/q\mathbb{Z}$.

For some randomized algorithm $\mathscr{A}$ with input $x$, we sometimes write $y \leftarrow \mathscr{A}(x; r)$ for its execution with explicit randomness $r$. If the randomness is not explicit, we write $y \leftarrow \mathscr{A}(x)$ and assume that the randomness was sampled accordingly. We also write $s \xleftarrow{\$} S$ for sampling $s$ uniformly random from a finite set $S$ or $d \xleftarrow{\$} D$ to sample $d$ randomly according to a given probability distribution $D$. Further, we often assume that some public parameters, denoted by pp, and the security parameter, denoted by $\lambda$, are implicitly passed as input to algorithms if it is clear by context.

Throughout, we write integers $a \in \mathbb{Z}$ in lower case letters, vectors as $\boldsymbol{a} \in \mathbb{Z}^n$ with components $a_i$, and matrices $\boldsymbol{A} \in \mathbb{Z}^{m \times n}$ in bold upper case letters. Computations on vectors are performed component-wise, unless stated otherwise. For example, for vectors $\boldsymbol{a} = (a_i)_{i=1..n}, \boldsymbol{b} = (b_i)_{i=1..n} \in \mathbb{Z}^n$ and scalar $x \in \mathbb{Z}$, we write $\boldsymbol{c} = \boldsymbol{a} \cdot \boldsymbol{b} = (a_i \cdot b_i)_{i=1..n}, y^{\boldsymbol{B}} = (y^{b_i})_{i=1..n}$ and $\boldsymbol{B}^y = (b_i^y)_{i=1..n}$. For some constant $c \in \mathbb{Z}$, we let by $\boldsymbol{c} = (c)_{i=1..n}$ the vector with all components equal to $c$.

We denote by $|x|$ the absolute value of $x \in \mathbb{R}$ and by $\|\cdot\|_1, \|\cdot\|_2, \|\cdot\|_\infty$ the norms defined as $\|\boldsymbol{x}\|_1 = \sum_i |x_i|, \|\boldsymbol{x}\|_2 = \sqrt{\sum_i x_i^2}, \|\boldsymbol{x}\|_\infty = \max_i |x_i|$ for $\boldsymbol{x} \in \mathbb{R}^m$.

## 3.1   Commitment Schemes

A commitment scheme com with message space $\mathcal{M}_{\text{com}}$, commitment space $\mathcal{C}_{\text{com}}$ and opening space $\mathcal{R}_{\text{com}}$ is a 3-tuple of PPT algorithms (Setup, Commit, Verify) such that

- com.Setup($1^\lambda$): outputs public parameters pp,
- com.Commit$_{\text{pp}}(x)$: computes a commitment $c \in \mathcal{C}_{\text{com}}$ to $x \in \mathcal{M}_{\text{com}}$ with its opening $d \in \mathcal{R}_{\text{com}}$ and outputs the pair $(c, d)$,
- com.Verify$_{\text{pp}}(c, x, d)$: verifies the commitment $c \in \mathcal{C}_{\text{com}}$ to $x \in \mathcal{M}_{\text{com}}$ with the opening $d \in \mathcal{R}_{\text{com}}$ and outputs a bit $b \in \{0, 1\}$

Further, we require that com is (statistically) correct, and satisfies binding (i.e. it is hard to find two different openings to a commitment) and hiding (i.e. one learns nothing about $x$ from Commit($x$)). We refer to the full version for formal definitions. Often, $d$ consists of the randomness used in the commitment generation, but it can include other auxiliary information.

**(Homomorphic) Integer Commitment Schemes.** In this work, we are interested in integer commitment schemes which allow to commit to an integer $x \in \mathbb{Z}$. An integer commitment scheme has message space $\mathcal{M}_{\text{com}} = \mathbb{Z}$ and allows for proving relations, such as knowledge of an opening, in a zero-knowledge manner (see Sect. 3.2). We also establish bounded integer commitment schemes (Sect. 4.1) where the message space is $\mathcal{M}_{\text{com}} = \{x \in \mathbb{Z} \mid |x| \leq R\}$ for some upper bound $R$. The crucial difference between message space $\mathcal{M}_{\text{com}} = \mathbb{Z}_q$ and $\mathcal{M}_{\text{com}} = \{x \in \mathbb{Z} \mid |x| \leq R\}$ is: The former can have additive homomorphism (over $\mathbb{Z}_q$), but only binds to a representative of $x \in \mathbb{Z}_q$, not to an integer. The latter binds to a (bounded) integer, but has limited homomorphism (over $\mathbb{Z}$).

## 3.2   Zero-Knowledge Proofs

We define zero-knowledge with setup GenCRS, which generates a common reference string (CRS) crs $\leftarrow$ GenCRS(pp). In this work, we only require an unstructured CRS[8]. Let R be a NP-relation over a set $X$ defining a (pp-dependent) NP-language $\mathscr{L} = \{x \in X \mid \exists w : R(pp, x, w) = 1\}$. For simplicity, we suppress the dependency on pp when it is clear. A zero-knowledge proof system for $\mathscr{L}$ is a protocol between a prover P and verifier V. We write $tr \leftarrow \langle P(s), V(t) \rangle$ for the transcript of an interaction where P (resp. V) has input $s$ (resp. $t$) and *implicit inputs* $1^\lambda$, pp, crs. We write $b = \langle P(s), V(t) \rangle$ for the verifier's verdict $b$. A proof system is *public coin* if the verifier's messages are uniformly random and independent of the prover's messages, and the verifier outputs $b = \text{Verify}(x, tr)$ for a PPT algorithm Verify.

Due to rejection sampling, our schemes have non-negligible correctness error.

**Definition 1 (Correctness).** A proof system (GenCRS, P, V) for $\mathscr{L}$ has *correctness error* $\gamma_{\text{err}}$, or is $\gamma_{\text{err}}$-correct, if for every adversary $\mathscr{A}$

$$\Pr\left[\begin{array}{l} pp \leftarrow \text{GenPP}(1^\lambda); crs \leftarrow \text{GenCRS}(pp); \\ (x, w) \leftarrow \mathscr{A}(pp, crs): \langle P(x, w), V(x) \rangle = 1] \end{array}\right] \geq 1 - \gamma_{\text{err}}(\lambda)$$

We call (GenCRS, P, V) *correct* if $\gamma_{\text{err}} = \text{negl}$.

To separate (statistical) simulation and knowledge errors from hardness assumptions as much as possible, we define zero-knowledge and knowledge extraction by means of adversary advantages.

**Definition 2 (HVZK).** A simulator Sim for a public coin proof system (GenCRS, P, V) for $\mathscr{L}$ is a PPT algorithm with input a statement $x$ for which $(pp, x, w) \in R$ and implicit inputs $1^\lambda$, pp, crs, and output a transcript $tr$. Let $\mathscr{A}$ be a stateful algorithm and let

$$\text{Real}_{\mathscr{A}}(\lambda) = \Pr\left[\begin{array}{l} pp \leftarrow \text{GenPP}(1^\lambda); crs \leftarrow \text{GenCRS}(pp); (x, w) \leftarrow \mathscr{A}(pp, crs); \\ tr \leftarrow \langle P(x, w), V(x) \rangle; b \leftarrow \mathscr{A}(tr): b \wedge R(x, w) = 1 \end{array}\right]$$

$$\text{Ideal}_{\mathscr{A}}(\lambda) = \Pr\left[\begin{array}{l} pp \leftarrow \text{GenPP}(1^\lambda); crs \leftarrow \text{GenCRS}(pp); (x, w) \leftarrow \mathscr{A}(pp, crs); \\ tr \leftarrow \text{Sim}(x); b \leftarrow \mathscr{A}(tr): b \wedge R(x, w) = 1 \end{array}\right]$$

Define the advantage of $\mathscr{A}$ by $\text{Adv}^{\text{hvzk}}_{\mathscr{A},P,V}(\lambda) = \text{Real}_{\mathscr{A}}(\lambda) - \text{Ideal}_{\mathscr{A}}(\lambda)$. Then Sim (and by extension (GenCRS, P, V)) is *honest verifier zero-knowledge* with *simulation error* $\sigma_{\text{err}} = \sigma_{\text{err}}(\lambda)$, if for all PPT $\mathscr{A}$ we have $\text{Adv}^{\text{hvzk}}_{\mathscr{A},P,V} \leq \sigma_{\text{err}} + \text{negl}$.

---

[8] Note that the distinction between structured and unstructured random strings is crucial in real-world applications: the former unavoidably requires either a trusted third party, or a secure distributed setup. However, the latter can be instantiated in the real-world using standard heuristic 'nothing-up-my-sleeve' methods.

**Definition 3 (Knowledge error).** Let $(\mathsf{GenCRS}, \mathsf{P}, \mathsf{V})$ be a public coin proof system for $\mathscr{L}$. Let $\mathsf{Ext}$ be an *expected* polynomial time oracle algorithm (with oracle steps counted as one step) with implicit inputs $1^\lambda, \mathsf{pp}, \mathsf{crs}$. Let $\mathscr{A}$ be a (probabilistic) and $\mathsf{P}^*$ be a deterministic algorithm.

$$\mathsf{Real}_{\mathscr{A}}(\lambda) = \Pr \left[ \begin{array}{c} \mathsf{pp} \leftarrow \mathsf{GenPP}(1^\lambda); \mathsf{crs} \leftarrow \mathsf{GenCRS}(\mathsf{pp}); (x, s) \leftarrow \mathscr{A}(\mathsf{pp}, \mathsf{crs}); \\ tr \leftarrow \langle \mathsf{P}^*(x, s), \mathsf{V}(x) \rangle \colon \mathsf{Verify}(x, tr) = 1 \end{array} \right]$$

$$\mathsf{Ideal}_{\mathscr{A}}(\lambda) = \Pr \left[ \begin{array}{c} \mathsf{pp} \leftarrow \mathsf{GenPP}(1^\lambda); \mathsf{crs} \leftarrow \mathsf{GenCRS}(\mathsf{pp}); (x, s) \leftarrow \mathscr{A}(\mathsf{pp}, \mathsf{crs}); \\ (tr, w) \leftarrow \mathsf{Ext}^{\mathsf{P}^*(x,s)} \colon \mathsf{Verify}(x, tr) = 1 \wedge \mathsf{R}(x, w) = 1 \end{array} \right]$$

W.l.o.g. Ext let $w = \bot$ if $\mathsf{Verify}(x, tr) = 1$. The advantage of $(\mathscr{A}, \mathsf{P}^*)$ is $\mathsf{Adv}^{\mathsf{ke}}_{\mathscr{A}, \mathsf{P}^*, \mathsf{V}}(\lambda) = \mathsf{Real}_{\mathscr{A}}(\lambda) - \mathsf{Ideal}_{\mathscr{A}}(\lambda)$. A proof system has knowledge error $\kappa_{\mathsf{err}}$, if for any PPT $\mathscr{A}, \mathsf{P}^*$ we have $\mathsf{Adv}^{\mathsf{ke}}_{\mathscr{A}, \mathsf{P}^*, \mathsf{V}} \leq \kappa_{\mathsf{err}} + \mathsf{negl}$.

Our definition of knowledge error is closely related to witness extended emulation [Lin03, GI08], which also requires that an extractor produces convincing transcripts. This property is trivial to achieve in our setting, but interferes with our definition of knowledge error. All of our proof systems are $\Sigma$-protocols.

**Definition 4.** A $\Sigma$-protocol $\Sigma$ for relation $\mathsf{R}$ is an interactive three-move protocol consisting of four PPT algorithms $(\Sigma.\mathsf{Init}, \Sigma.\mathsf{Chall}, \Sigma.\mathsf{Resp}, \Sigma.\mathsf{Verify})$ between prover $\mathsf{P}$ holding a witness $w$ for the statement $x \in \mathscr{L}$ and verifier $\mathsf{V}$ such that:

- $\Sigma.\mathsf{Init}(1^\lambda, w, x) \to (\alpha, \mathsf{st})$: On input of statement and witness $(x, w)$ with $\mathsf{R}(x, w) = 1$, outputs a first message $\alpha$ and a state $\mathsf{st}$.
- $\Sigma.\mathsf{Chall}(1^\lambda) \to \gamma$: Draw challenge $\gamma$ uniformly from the set of challenges $[0, C]$.
- $\Sigma.\mathsf{Resp}(\mathsf{st}, \gamma) \to \omega$: On input of previous state $\mathsf{st}$ and challenge $\gamma$, outputs a response $\omega$.
- $\Sigma.\mathsf{Verify}(x, \alpha, \gamma, \omega) \to b$: On input statement $x$ and transcript $\alpha, \gamma, \omega$, accepts $(b = 1)$ or rejects $(b = 0)$.

Moreover, $\Sigma$ must satisfy *correctness* and *HVZK*. As usual, the algorithms have implicit inputs $1^\lambda, \mathsf{pp}, \mathsf{crs}$.

The simulators for our $\Sigma$-protocols actually show *special HVZK*, that is, they work given any (adversarial) challenge $\gamma$. Letting $\mathsf{Sim}$ pick $\gamma \overset{\$}{\leftarrow} [0, C]$ yields standard HVZK. To prove knowledge extraction, we rely on $k$-special soundness.

**Definition 5 ($k$-special soundness).** A $k$-special soundness extractor $\mathsf{Ext}$ is a PPT algorithm which takes as input a set of $k$ accepting transcripts $\Gamma = \{(\alpha, \gamma_i, \omega_i) \mid \Sigma.\mathsf{Verify}(x, \alpha, \gamma_i, \omega_i) = 1\}_{i=1..k}$ with fixed $\alpha$ and pair-wise distinct challenges $\gamma_i$, and outputs a valid witness $w \leftarrow \mathsf{Ext}(\Gamma)$, i.e. $\mathsf{R}(w, x) = 1$.

In security proofs, $k$ transcripts will either yield a witness or break an assumption. Formally, we consider the language $\mathscr{L} \vee \mathscr{L}_{\mathsf{hard}}$ instead of $\mathscr{L}$. Finding $k$ transcripts as in Definition 5 is a standard (solved) problem.

*Fiat–Shamir Transformation.* Informally, the Fiat–Shamir transformation applied to a $\Sigma$-protocol replaces the verifier's random challenge by a hash of the initial message $\alpha$, resulting in a non-interactive proof system.

**Range Proofs.** A range proof is essentially a zero-knowledge proof that guarantees that a committed value $x$ resides inside a specified interval $[a, b]$. We can show so by setting $y = (b - x)(x - a)$, computing the commitment to $y$ homomorphically from the commitment to $x$ and the constants $a, b$, and showing that $y \geq 0$ in a zero-knowledge manner. The following lemma yields a strategy to show that committed integers are non-negative.

**Lemma 1 (Decomposition into 3 Squares [RS86, Gro05]).** *Let $y \in \mathbb{Z}$ be an integer. It holds that*

$$y \geq 0 \iff \exists \{x_i\}_{i=1..3} : 4y + 1 = \sum_{i=1..3} x_i^2$$

*Further, the integers $x_i$ can be efficiently computed. In [PS19], the runtime of finding the decomposition was improved to $\mathcal{O}(\log^2(y)/\log\log(y))$ multiplications.*

### 3.3    Tools in the DLOG Setting

**Hardness Assumptions.** First, we establish the hardness assumptions that our scheme in the DLOG setting is based on (see Sect. 5). To avoid trusted setup, we assume a deterministic family $\mathbb{G} = \mathbb{G}_\lambda$ of cyclic groups with generator $g_\lambda$ and known order $q_\lambda$, generated by a group generator $(\mathbb{G}_\lambda, g_\lambda, q_\lambda) = \mathsf{GenGrp}(1^\lambda)$. For notational simplicity, we leave $\mathsf{GenGrp}$ implicit in the rest of the work.

**Definition 6 ($S$-Bounded DLSEand SEIAssumption).** Consider a group $\mathbb{G}$ of order $q$ with generator $g$. Let $S < q$. The $S$-bounded DLSE assumption holds if for all PPT $\mathscr{A}$ there is a negligible negl such that

$$\Pr\left[z \xleftarrow{\$} \{0..S - 1\}, z' \leftarrow \mathscr{A}(g^z): z = z'\right] \leq \mathrm{negl}(\lambda)$$

The $S$-bounded short exponent indistinguishability (SEI) assumption holds if for all PPT $\mathscr{A}$ there is a negligible negl such that

$$\left|\Pr\left[z \xleftarrow{\$} \{0..S - 1\} : \mathscr{A}(g^z) = 1\right] - \Pr\left[z \xleftarrow{\$} \mathbb{Z}_{\mathrm{ord}} : \mathscr{A}(g^z) = 1\right]\right| \leq \mathrm{negl}(\lambda)$$

Throughout this work, we generally set $S = 2^{2\lambda}$. Note that DLOG assumption is equivalent to the $q$-bounded DLSE assumption.

**Tools.** Now, we introduce some lemmas and a commitment scheme that we later on utilize for constructing the bounded integer commitment and range proof.

**Lemma 2 ([KK04]).** *Let $\mathbb{G}$ be a group of prime order $q$ with generator $g \in \mathbb{G}$. For $S < q/2$, the $S$-bounded DLSE and SEI assumptions are equivalent.*

We consider a Pedersen commitment scheme [Ped92] with smaller openings in exchange for a computational (instead of statistical) hiding property.

**Definition 7 (Pedersen Commitments with Short Openings).** Let $\mathbb{G}$ be a group of prime order $q$ and consists of a 3-tuple of PPT algorithms (Ped.Setup, Ped.Commit, Ped.Verify) such that

- Ped.Setup($1^\lambda$): samples $g, h \xleftarrow{\$} \mathbb{G}$ and outputs public parameters pp $= (g, h)$,
- Ped.Commit$_{pp}(x)$: samples $d \xleftarrow{\$} [0, 2^{2\lambda}]$ for $x \in \mathbb{Z}_q$, sets $c = g^x h^d$ and outputs the pair $(c, d)$,
- Ped.Verify$_{pp}(c, x, d)$: outputs 1 iff $c = g^x h^d$.

Using $d \xleftarrow{\$} [0, 2^{2\lambda}]$ instead of $d \xleftarrow{\$} [0, q - 1]$ (as in [Ped92]) still achieves computational hiding: Under SEI (or equivalently DLSE), we can replace the short random exponent $d$ in $h^d$ with a full random $d \xleftarrow{\$} [0..q - 1]$ in a hybrid game. Now $g^x h^d$ is uniformly distributed, independent of $x$.

### 3.4  Tools for Zero-Knowledge

As a technical tool for achieving zero knowledge, our protocols use additive masking of the witness. We recall the tools for masking here.

**Lemma 3 (Masking with the Security Parameter).** *For any $C, B, L \in \mathbb{N}$ and fixed $x \in [-B, B], \gamma \in [-C, C]$, the distributions $U = \mathcal{U}[0, BCL]$ and $V = \{m + \gamma \cdot x \mid m \xleftarrow{\$} [0, BCL]\}$ have statistical distance at most $1/L$.*

Rejection sampling and Gaussian noise allow to use smaller masks.

**Definition 8 (Discrete Gaussian Distributions, [YAZ+19]).** *The continuous Gaussian distribution over $\mathbb{R}^m$ centered around $v \in \mathbb{R}^m$ with standard deviation $\sigma$ is defined by the density function $\rho^m_{v,\sigma}(x) = (\frac{1}{\sqrt{2\pi\sigma^2}})^m e^{\frac{-\|x-v\|^2_2}{2\sigma^2}}$. The discrete Gaussian distribution over $\mathbb{Z}^m$ centered around $v \in \mathbb{Z}^m$ with standard deviation $\sigma$ is defined as $D^m_{v,\sigma}(x) = \rho^m_{v,\sigma}(x)/\rho^m_\sigma(\mathbb{Z}^m)$, where $\rho^m_\sigma(\mathbb{Z}^m) = \sum_{x \in \mathbb{Z}^m} \rho^m_\sigma(x)$. We write $D^m_\sigma(x) = D^m_{0,\sigma}(x)$ for short.*

**Lemma 4 (Relationship between norms).** *For $v \in \mathbb{R}^m$, the inequalities of norms, $\|v\|_\infty \leq \|v\|_1 \leq \sqrt{N}\|v\|_2 \leq N\|v\|_\infty$, are well known.*

**Lemma 5 (Lemma 4.4, [Lyu12]).**

- *For any $k > 0$ it holds that $\Pr[|z| > k\sigma \mid z \xleftarrow{\$} D_\sigma] \leq 2e^{\frac{-k^2}{2}}$.*
- *For any $k > 1$ it holds that $\Pr[\|z\|_2 > k\sigma\sqrt{m} \mid z \xleftarrow{\$} D^m_\sigma] < k^m e^{\frac{m}{2}(1-k^2)}$.*

**Lemma 6 (Theorem 4.6, [Lyu12]).** *Let $V$ be a subset of $\mathbb{Z}^m$ in which all elements have $\|\cdot\|_2$ norms less than $T$, $\sigma \in \mathbb{R}$ such that $\sigma = \omega(T\sqrt{\log m})$ and $h : V \mapsto \mathbb{R}$ a probability distribution. Define algorithms $\mathscr{T}$ (resp. $\mathscr{S}$) as follows:*

1. $v \xleftarrow{\$} h$
2. $t \xleftarrow{\$} D_{v,\sigma}^m$ (resp. $t \xleftarrow{\$} D_{\sigma}^m$)
3. output $(t, v)$ with probability $\min \left( \frac{D_{\sigma}^m(t)}{M \cdot D_{v,\sigma}^m(t)}, 1 \right)$ (resp. with probability $1/M$)

Then there exists a constant $M = O(1)$ such that the output distributions of $\mathscr{T}$ and $\mathscr{S}$ are within statistical distance $\frac{2^{-\omega(\log m)}}{M}$. Moreover, the probability that $\mathscr{T}$ outputs something is at least $\frac{1-2^{-\omega(\log m)}}{M}$.

Note that if $\sigma = \alpha T$ for some $\alpha > 0$, then $M = e^{13.3/\alpha + 1/(2\alpha^2)}$, the output of algorithm $\mathscr{T}$ is within statistical distance $2^{-128}/M$ of the output of $\mathscr{S}$ and the probability that $\mathscr{T}$ outputs something is at least $\frac{1-2^{-128}}{M}$ [YAZ+19,HPWZ17].

## 4    Integer Commitments from Rounding Fractions

In this section, we introduce bounded integer commitments and motivate the construction of range proofs based on these commitments.

### 4.1    Bounded Integer Commitment Scheme

We introduce a commitment scheme transformation that allows to commit to bounded integers. The core feature of this transformation is its proof-friendliness: standard $\Sigma$-protocols for proving knowledge of a square decomposition (or, more generally, any low-degree polynomial relation) with the original commitment (over a field $\mathbb{Z}_q$) can be re-interpreted (with minor adaptations) as $\Sigma$-protocols for proving knowledge of a square decomposition (resp. low-degree relation) over $\mathbb{Z}$ with respect to the transformed commitment scheme. In addition, the transformation preserves some homomorphic properties of the underlying scheme, which turns out to be crucial in the application to range proofs.

**Definition 9 (The Transformation).** Let com be a commitment scheme with message space $\text{com}.\mathcal{M}_{\text{com}} = \mathbb{Z}_q^n$ and random space $\text{com}.\mathcal{R}_{\text{com}}$. We define the commitment scheme $\overline{\text{com}}$ over parameters $U, C \in \mathbb{N}$ such that $U < \frac{q-1}{2}$ with

- $\overline{\text{com}}.\mathcal{M}_{\text{com}} = \{ \boldsymbol{x} \in \mathbb{Z}^n \mid \|\boldsymbol{x}\|_\infty \leq U/C \}$
- $\overline{\text{com}}.\mathcal{R}_{\text{com}} = \{ (d, \gamma, \boldsymbol{y}) \in \mathcal{R}_{\text{com}} \times \mathbb{Z} \times \mathbb{Z}^n \mid \gamma \leq C, \|\boldsymbol{y}\|_\infty \leq U/C \}$

as follows:

- $\overline{\text{com}}.\text{Setup}(1^\lambda)$: outputs $\text{pp} \leftarrow \text{com}.\text{Setup}(1^\lambda)$.
- $\overline{\text{com}}.\text{Commit}_{\text{pp}}(\boldsymbol{x})$: computes $(c, r) \leftarrow \text{com}.\text{Commit}_{\text{pp}}(\boldsymbol{x})$ and outputs $(c, (r, 1, \boldsymbol{x}))$.
- $\overline{\text{com}}.\text{Verify}_{\text{pp}}(c, \boldsymbol{x}, (r, \gamma, \boldsymbol{y}))$: sets $\boldsymbol{z} = \boldsymbol{y} \cdot \gamma^{-1} \mod q$ and checks $\boldsymbol{x} = \lfloor \frac{\boldsymbol{y}}{\gamma} \rceil, |\gamma| \leq C, \gamma \neq 0, \|\boldsymbol{y}\|_\infty \leq U/C, \text{com}.\text{Verify}_{\text{pp}}(c, \boldsymbol{z}, r) = 1$ as well as $\boldsymbol{x} = \lfloor \frac{\boldsymbol{y}}{\gamma} \rceil$, where division is performed in $\mathbb{Q}^n$.

**Lemma 7.** The commitment scheme $\overline{\text{com}}$ is correct, binding and hiding.

The correctness and hiding properties follow directly from the security of com. The binding property can be argued similarly.

Let $\mathscr{A}$ be a PPT adversary breaking the binding property of $\overline{\mathsf{com}}$. We design a PPT adversary $\mathscr{B}$ that breaks the binding property of com with challenger $\mathcal{C}$.

On receiving pp from the challenger $\mathcal{C}$, $\mathscr{B}$ forwards pp to $\mathscr{A}$ and receives $(c, (d_0, \gamma_0, \boldsymbol{y}_0), ((d_1, \gamma_1, \boldsymbol{y}_1), \boldsymbol{x}_0, \boldsymbol{x}_1)$. $\mathscr{B}$ sets $\boldsymbol{z}_i = \boldsymbol{y}_i \cdot \gamma_i^{-1} \mod q$ and just forwards $(c, d_0, d_1, \boldsymbol{z}_0, \boldsymbol{z}_i)$ to $\mathcal{C}$. If $\mathscr{A}$ is successful, both commitments verify correctly with respect to $\overline{\mathsf{com}}$ and $\boldsymbol{x}_0 \neq \boldsymbol{x}_1$. Thus by definition of $\overline{\mathsf{com}}$.Verify, the verification check for the sent openings are valid with respect to the scheme com. Note that $\|\boldsymbol{y}_i\|_\infty \leq U/C, |\gamma_i| \leq C$ for $i \in [0,1]$. So $\|\boldsymbol{y}_i \cdot \gamma_i\|_\infty \leq U \leq \frac{q-1}{2}$. Assume for the sake of contradiction that $\boldsymbol{z}_0 = \boldsymbol{z}_1$:

$$\boldsymbol{z}_0 = \boldsymbol{z}_1 \implies \boldsymbol{y}_0 \cdot \gamma_1 = \boldsymbol{y}_1 \cdot \gamma_0 \mod q \implies \boldsymbol{y}_0 \cdot \gamma_1 = \boldsymbol{y}_1 \cdot \gamma_0 \text{ in } \mathbb{Q}$$

$$\implies \frac{\boldsymbol{y}_0}{\gamma_0} = \frac{\boldsymbol{y}_1}{\gamma_1} \text{ in } \mathbb{Q} \implies \left\lfloor \frac{\boldsymbol{y}_0}{\gamma_0} \right\rfloor = \left\lfloor \frac{\boldsymbol{y}_1}{\gamma_1} \right\rfloor \text{ in } \mathbb{Q}$$

This contradicts $\boldsymbol{x}_0 \neq \boldsymbol{x}_1$ and thus the advantage of $\mathscr{B}$ is the same as $\mathscr{A}$.

**Arguing over the Integers.** Now, we motivate how to perform proofs over the integers on the example Ped. Let $\overline{\mathsf{Ped}}$ be the scheme obtained by the above transformation applied to Ped. Let $C = 2^\lambda$ determine the challenge space, $S = 2^{2\lambda}$ determine the size of the randomness and $L = 2^\lambda$ be the masking overhead. Let $2^\lambda = C < U \in \mathbb{N}$ and let $q$ be prime with $2U < q$. Let $\mathbb{G}$ be a group of order $q$. For clarity, we restate the scheme:

- $\overline{\mathsf{Ped}}.\mathsf{Setup}(1^\lambda)$: outputs $\mathsf{pp} = (g,h) \xleftarrow{\$} \mathbb{G}^2$.
- $\overline{\mathsf{Ped}}.\mathsf{Commit}(\mathsf{pp}, x)$: samples $r \xleftarrow{\$} [0, S]$ and outputs $(c = g^x h^r, (r, 1, x))$.
- $\overline{\mathsf{Ped}}.\mathsf{Verify}(\mathsf{pp}, c, x, (r, \gamma, y))$: checks $g^{y \cdot \gamma^{-1}} h^r = c$ as well as $x = \lfloor \frac{y}{\gamma} \rceil$, where the division is performed in $\mathbb{Q}$, $|\gamma| \leq C, \gamma \neq 0$ and $|y| \leq U/C$.

The most essential protocol is the proof of knowledge of an opening. We now establish an unoptimized version in order to gain a basic understanding of the underlying arguments. The relation we prove is

$$\mathsf{R} = \{(c, (x, (r, \gamma, y))) \mid \overline{\mathsf{Ped}}.\mathsf{Verify}(c, x, (r, \gamma, y)) = 1\}.$$

For the correctness property, we are only interested in honest openings, so $\gamma = 1, y = x$. The proof scheme follows the conventional strategy of blinding the witnesses $(x, r)$ with a mask. We add a size check for the masked witness to ensure the shortness of the opening. Note that the message space of $\overline{\mathsf{Ped}}$ is $\{x \in \mathbb{Z} \mid x \leq U/C\}$ but we can only perform proofs for smaller $x$ values because the commitments need to stay binding after the masking process. In more detail, we let $B \in \mathbb{N}$ such that $2BCL \leq U/C$ and we allow for messages $|x_i| \leq B$. The following protocol proves knowledge of an opening.

- $\mathsf{Init}(c, (x \in [-B, B], r \in [0, S]))$: $m \xleftarrow{\$} [0, BCL], s \xleftarrow{\$} [0, SCL]$; outputs $d = g^m h^s$.

- Chall(): outputs $\gamma \xleftarrow{\$} [0, C]$
- Resp($\gamma$): sets $z = m + \gamma \cdot x, t = s + \gamma \cdot r$. Outputs $(z, t)$
- Verify($d, \gamma, z, t$): checks $|z| \le BCL$ and $g^z h^t = d \cdot c^\gamma$.

The first verification check succeeds with overwhelming probability since the probability that the random $m$ is too close to $BCL$ is small. The second check succeeds due to

$$g^z h^t = g^{m + \gamma \cdot x} h^{s + \gamma \cdot r} = g^m h^s \cdot (g^x h^r)^\gamma = d \cdot c^\gamma.$$

Further, Lemma 3 also implies that $z, t$ hide the witnesses $x, r$ statistically and using $d = g^z h^t \cdot c^{-\gamma}$, a valid transcript can be computed for a given challenge $\gamma$. Thus, the scheme honest-verifier is zero-knowledge. The following soundness argument shows how to extract correct openings.

First, let $(d, \gamma, z, t), (d, \gamma', z', t')$ be two accepting transcripts with $\gamma \ne \gamma'$. Without loss of generality, we assume that $\gamma' > \gamma$. We denote $\bar{z} = z' - z, \bar{t} = t' - t$ and $\bar{\gamma} = \gamma' - \gamma$. We know that $g^{z' - z} h^{t' - t} = c^{\gamma' - \gamma}$ which directly implies $g^{\bar{z}/\bar{\gamma}} h^{\bar{t}/\bar{\gamma}} = c$. Thus, $\gamma^* = \bar{\gamma}, r^* = \bar{t}/\bar{\gamma}, y^* = \bar{z}$ and $x^* = \lfloor \frac{y^*}{\gamma^*} \rceil$ is a valid opening for $c$. Note that the size checks are satisfied:

$$|\gamma^*| \le C, \qquad\qquad |y^*| \le 2BCL \le U/C.$$

Note that we know that $x^*$ is short because $\gamma^*$ and $y^*$ are short, so the above protocol can already be seen as range proof that guarantees that the committed value lies in $[-2BCL, 2BCL]$. Nonetheless, this is not very satisfying yet because the slackness of $2CL = 2^{2\lambda + 1}$ is very large. But the shortness of the extracted values can be used to argue in $\mathbb{Z}$ instead of $\mathbb{Z}_q$ which opens the door for more sophisticated arguments.

**On Retaining Homomorphism.** If the original scheme is homomorphic, the transformation retains (restricted) homomorphic properties. Firstly, if the commitments are generated honestly, the homomorphic property is retained as long as the homomorphic calculation is performed inside the bound $U/C$ of the scheme. In case of dishonest commitments, the scheme still retains a more limited form of homomorphic properties.

If the scheme com allows for addition of constants to the committed value, the homomorphic property is retained up to overflow over the bound $U/C$. To illustrate, let $\boldsymbol{t} \in \mathbb{Z}_q^n$ be some constant and $c$ a commitment to message $\boldsymbol{m} = \lfloor \boldsymbol{y}/\gamma \rceil$ with opening $(r, \gamma, \boldsymbol{y})$. Note that $c$ commits to $\boldsymbol{y}/\gamma$ modulo $q$ with respect to com and we can use the homomorphic operations. We have

$$(\boldsymbol{y}/\gamma) + \boldsymbol{t} = \boldsymbol{y}/\gamma + (\boldsymbol{t} \cdot \gamma)/\gamma = (\boldsymbol{y} + \boldsymbol{t} \cdot \gamma)/\gamma \quad \mod q$$

and $\lfloor \frac{\boldsymbol{y} + \boldsymbol{t} \cdot \gamma}{\gamma} \rceil = \lfloor \boldsymbol{y}/\gamma \rceil + \boldsymbol{t} = \boldsymbol{m} + \boldsymbol{t}$. So the result of the homomorphic operation is actually exact because the additional operand does not introduce an additional error term. Note that for the opening to be correct, the norm $\|\boldsymbol{y} + \boldsymbol{t} \cdot \gamma\|_\infty$ needs to be smaller than $U/C$. So, enough space needs to be guaranteed to perform homomorphic operations. The analysis for retaining multiplicative homomorphic properties for small constants is similar.

In the case of additive and multiplicative homomorphisms between dishonest commitments, there are some small error terms and thus, the properties do not translate as directly. We refer to the full version for more details.

For range proofs, the homomorphism with small constants can be used to prove the 3-square decomposition of the integer and the complications from multiplicative and the additive homomorphic error terms can be balanced out such that we can still prove the relation with the homomorphic property of the underlying schemes.

**Ensuring Membership of an Interval.** We use the 3 square decomposition in order to show membership of $[0, B]$. This can be extended to a range proof for interval $[a, b]$ by setting $B = b - a$. Since $\overline{\text{com}}$ allows for addition of constants, the prover can show $x - a \in [0, B] \implies x \in [a, b]$. Note that the values still need to lie inside the given bounds.

We are using the 3 square decomposition to show that $x \in [0, B]$. Since the extracted $x$ is a rounded fraction, we still need to ensure that the decomposition shows the desired range membership.

**Lemma 8 (Three Square for Rounded Fractions).** *Let $n, d \in \mathbb{Z}$ and $x = \lfloor \frac{n}{d} \rceil, \{x_i\}_{i=1..3} \in \mathbb{Q}$ and $B \geq 2$. Then:*

$$1 + 4\frac{n}{d}\left(B - \frac{n}{d}\right) = \sum_{i=1}^{3} x_i^2 \implies x \in [0, B].$$

*Proof.* A simple calculation shows that $\frac{n}{d} \in [\frac{1}{2}(B - \sqrt{B^2 + 1}), \frac{1}{2}(B + \sqrt{B^2 + 1})]$. This interval can further be bound as follows:

$$\frac{1}{2}(B + \sqrt{B^2 + 1}) = \frac{1}{2}B(1 + \sqrt{1 + \tfrac{1}{B^2}}) \leq \frac{1}{2}B(1 + 1 + \tfrac{1}{B^2}) = B + \tfrac{1}{2B}$$

A similar computation for the left bound shows that the 3-squares decomposition implies $\frac{n}{d} \in [-\frac{1}{2B}, B + \frac{1}{2B}]$. Since $B \geq 2$, we find $\frac{n}{d} \in [-\frac{1}{4}, B + \frac{1}{4}]$. Rounding leads to the desired result. (In fact, this holds even for $B = 1$.)

**Further Properties.** Our adapted commitment scheme and range proofs have additional useful properties.

*Remark 1 (RP for com).* For denominator $\gamma = 1$, $\overline{\text{com}}$ coincides with com. Under this precondition, our range proofs establish $x \in [0, B]$ for also com-commitments.

*Remark 2 (Positivity).* Our proofs show $x \in [0, B]$. However, in many applications, proofs of positivity ($x \geq 0$) suffice. That is, $B$ could be made into a zero-knowledge threshold (used for masking only), so that for $x > B$ no zero-knowledge guarantees hold.[9] This change is achieved by proving $1 + 4x = \sum_{i=1}^{3} x_i^2$. Now, soundness guarantees $x \in [0, \frac{q-1}{2}]$.

---

[9] In fact, masking and hence zero-knowledge degrades gracefully in the size of $x$.

*Remark 3 (Denominators).* A closer look at soundness shows, that a denominator $\gamma > 1$ leads to a rejection with probability $1 - \frac{1}{\gamma}$. Thus, the larger $\gamma$, the less likely will a (malicious) verifier succeed.

# 5 Range Proof in a DLOG Setting

## 5.1 Overview

In this section, we present the range proof in the setting of a group $\mathbb{G}$ with prime order $q$ under the DLOG (or DLSE) assumption.[10] As basis, we use Pedersen commitments Ped, which we transform in a bounded rational commitment schemes $\overline{\text{Ped}}$ as in Sect. 4.1. Recall that the difference of Ped and $\overline{\text{Ped}}$ is mostly in the interpretation of the committed values.

Our protocol reuses the structure of existing range proofs based on Pedersen commitments in the RSA setting (see [Lip03, Gro05, CPP17]). For a given commitment $c = g^x h^r$, the prover computes the square decomposition $1 + 4(b-x)x = \sum_{i=1..3} x_i^2$ and lets $x_0 = b - x$. Thus, we prove $1 + 4x_0 x = \sum_{i=1..3} x_i^2$. Note that all $x_i$ are in the range $[0, B]$. The prover commits to $c_i = g^{x_i} h^{r_i}$ for some randomly sampled $r_i$ for $i \in [1, 3]$, and sets $c_0 = g^b c^{-1}$. For a proof of knowledge of $x_i$, he computes mask commitments $d_i = g^{m_i} h^{s_i}$ (and an additional "garbage" term $d$), and sends them to the verifier. After receiving the challenge $\gamma$, the prover reveals $z_i = m_i + \gamma x_i$ and $t_i = s_i + \gamma r_i$ and the verifier can check whether the equation $g^{z_i} h^{t_i} = c_i^\gamma d_i$ holds (and an equation for the square decomposition).[11] The verifier checks the proof of knowledge and accepts only if $z_i$ and $t_i$ are small. As usual, if the prover can answer two different challenges $\gamma, \tilde{\gamma}$, openings can be extracted. These openings are $x_i = \frac{z_i - \tilde{z}_i}{\gamma - \tilde{\gamma}}$ with short nominator and denominator, and they satisfy the square decomposition (or DLOG is broken). This shows soundness (for $\overline{\text{Ped}}$ openings), Furthermore, as we sketched in the introduction, when small exponents are used for the masking term $h^y$, and by adjusting the parameters, soundness can actually be proven *statistically*. In our parameter choice, however, we will optimize for efficiency and focus on computational soundness.

For zero-knowledge, the witness is blinded by the masks $m_i$. Since the $m_i$'s must be small (hence are not uniform in $\mathbb{Z}_q$), we do not get perfect zero-knowledge. However, $x_i + m_i$ still statistically hides $x_i$. This is enough to establish (statistical) zero-knowledge by the usual "simulation by execution in reverse". The construction and proof is somewhat complicated by using *small* exponents for the masking term $h^y$, which consequently must be masked itself.

---

[10] The optimization of the Pedersen commitment scheme with short exponents relies on the SEI, which for relevant ranges is equivalent to DLSE.

[11] In the scheme, we use a hash function to avoid having to send the mask commitments to the verifier to save space.

## 5.2   Parameters

Let $\mathsf{pp} = (g, h, q)$ be the public parameters of the commitment scheme $\mathsf{Ped}$ in group $\mathbb{G}$ with order $q$, let $\mathsf{H} : \{0,1\}^* \mapsto \{0,1\}^{2\lambda}$ be a collision resistant hash function, and let $[0, B]$ be the range with $B \geq 2$. Let $[0, C]$ be the challenge set. Let $S$ be the size of small exponents in the $\mathsf{SEI}$ assumption, and let $L$ be the growth factor of masked intervals due to additive noise, that is, masking $[0, B]$ results in $[0, BL]$. We define $U = 32B^2C^2L^2$ and note that it serves as an upper bound for the integers appearing in the security proof. In particular, we require $U < \frac{q-1}{2}$. The prover shows that he knows $x, r$ committed in $c = g^x h^r = \overline{\mathsf{Ped}}.\mathsf{Commit}(x; r)$ and that $x \in [0, B]$. (Other commitments are interpreted as $\mathsf{Ped}$).

## 5.3   Scheme

The scheme $\mathsf{RP}_{\mathsf{Log}}$ follows the structure of the line of work [Lip03, Gro05, CPP17]. We adapt the scheme to the $\mathsf{DLOG}$ setting and apply our encoding technique.

- $\mathsf{RP}_{\mathsf{Log}}.\mathsf{Init}(c = g^x h^r, x \in [0, B], r \in [0, S])$:
    1. compute $x_i$ s.t. $4x(B - x) + 1 = \sum_{i=1}^{3} x_i^2$
    2. Set $r_0 = -r, x_0 = B - x$
    3. Set $c_0 = c^{-1} g^B$
    4. Set $\forall i \in [1, 3] : r_i \xleftarrow{\$} [0, S], c_i = g^{x_i} h^{r_i}$
    5. Set $\forall i \in [0, 3] : m_i \xleftarrow{\$} [0, BCL], s_i \xleftarrow{\$} [0, SCL], d_i = g^{m_i} h^{s_i}$
    6. Set $\sigma \xleftarrow{\$} [0, 4SBCL], d = h^\sigma c^{4m_0} \prod_{i=1..3} c_i^{-m_i}$
    7. Set $\Delta = H(\{d_i\}_{i=0..3}, d)$
    8. Outputs $\{c_i\}_{i=1..3}, \Delta$
- $\mathsf{RP}_{\mathsf{Log}}.\mathsf{Chall}()$: outputs $\gamma \xleftarrow{\$} [0, C]$
- $\mathsf{RP}_{\mathsf{Log}}.\mathsf{Resp}(\gamma)$:
    1. Sets $\forall i \in [0, 3] : z_i = m_i + \gamma \cdot x_i, t_i = s_i + \gamma \cdot r_i$
    2. Sets $\tau = \sigma + \gamma(\sum_{i=1..3} x_i r_i + 4x_0 r_0)$
    3. Outputs $\{z_i, t_i\}_{i=0..3}, \tau$
- $\mathsf{RP}_{\mathsf{Log}}.\mathsf{Verify}(\{c_i\}_{i=1..3}, \Delta, \gamma, \{z_i, t_i\}_{i=0..3}, \tau)$:
    1. Compute $c_0 = c^{-1} g^B$
    2. Compute $\forall i \in [0, 3] : f_i = g^{z_i} h^{t_i} c_i^{-\gamma}$
    3. Compute $f = h^\tau \cdot g^\gamma \cdot c^{4z_0} \cdot \prod_{i=1..3} c_i^{-z_i}$
    4. Check $\Delta = H(\{f_i\}_{i=0..3}, f)$
    5. Check $z_i \in [0, BC(L + 1)]$

The scheme is perfectly correct. Note that any interval $[0, T]$, where term $T$ contains $S$, may be replaced by $[0, \max(q - 1, T)]$, as these masks only serve zero-knowledge and do not affect soundness, hence wraparound is not a problem. In particular, the scheme is correct, sound and HVZK if $S = q - 1$.

**Theorem 1.** *Suppose $L \geq 32$. The range proof $\mathsf{RP}_{\mathsf{Log}}$ for $[0, B]$ is 2-special sound with knowledge error $\frac{1}{(C+1)}$ under $\mathsf{DLOG}$ and $\mathsf{CRHF}$ assumptions. More precisely, for every adversary $\mathscr{A}$ with strict running time $T$ there are adversaries $\mathscr{B}_1, \mathscr{B}_2$ with expected running time roughly $2T$ and $\mathsf{Adv}_{\mathscr{A}}^{\mathsf{ke}} \leq \frac{1}{(C+1)} + \mathsf{Adv}_{\mathscr{B}_1}^{\mathsf{dlog}} + \mathsf{Adv}_{\mathscr{B}_2}^{\mathsf{crhf}}$.*

*Proof.* Assume we have two accepting transcripts for distinct challenges $\gamma \neq \tilde{\gamma}$ with witnesses $z_i, t_i, \tau$ and $\tilde{z}_i, \tilde{t}_i, \tilde{\tau}$ respectively. Without loss of generality, say $\gamma > \tilde{\gamma}$. We show that either we obtain a valid witness, or we break DLOG or collision resistance.

By collision resistance of H, we have $d = f = \tilde{f}$ and $\forall i \in [0,3] : d_i = f_i = \tilde{f}_i$. Denote by $\overline{a}$ the difference of $a - \tilde{a}$ for $a \in \{z_i, t_i, \tau\}$. From $f_i = \tilde{f}_i$ we find

$$g^{z_i} h^{t_i} c_i^{-\gamma} = g^{\tilde{z}_i} h^{\tilde{t}_i} c_i^{-\tilde{\gamma}} \iff g^{\overline{z_i}} h^{\overline{t_i}} = c_i^{\overline{\gamma}} \iff g^{\overline{z_i}/\overline{\gamma}} h^{\overline{t_i}/\overline{\gamma}} = c_i.$$

Thus for all $i \in [1,3]$, we have valid openings $x_i = \overline{z_i}/\overline{\gamma}$ and $r_i = \overline{t_i}/\overline{\gamma}$ for commitment $c_i$. For $c_0$, we obtain $c = g^{(\overline{\gamma} \cdot B - \overline{z_0})/\overline{\gamma}} h^{-\overline{t_0}/\overline{\gamma}}$ and therefore $x_0 = \overline{z_0}/\overline{\gamma}$ and $r_0 = \overline{t_0}/\overline{\gamma}$ is an opening to $c^{-1} g^B$. Moreover $x = B - \overline{z_0}/\overline{\gamma} = B - x_0$ is the committed value in $c$.

Now we turn to the square decomposition. We have

$$f = \tilde{f} \implies h^{\overline{\tau}} \cdot g^{\overline{\gamma}} \cdot c^{4\overline{z_0}} = \prod_{i=1..3} c_i^{\overline{z_i}}$$

$$\implies h^{\overline{\tau}} \cdot g^{\overline{\gamma}} \cdot g^{4(B - \overline{z_0}/\overline{\gamma})\overline{z_0}} \cdot h^{4r \cdot \overline{z_0}} = \prod_{i=1..3} g^{x_i \cdot \overline{z_i}} h^{r_i \cdot \overline{z_i}}$$

$$\implies g^{\overline{\gamma}} \cdot g^{4(B - \overline{z_0}/\overline{\gamma})\overline{z_0}} \cdot \prod_{i=1..3} g^{-x_i \cdot \overline{z_i}} = h^{-4r \cdot \overline{z_0}} \cdot h^{-\overline{\tau}} \cdot \prod_{i=1..3} h^{r_i \cdot \overline{z_i}}$$

$$\implies g^{\overline{\gamma} + 4(B - \overline{z_0}/\overline{\gamma})\overline{z_0} - \sum_{i=1..3} x_i \cdot \overline{z_i}} = h^{-4r \cdot \overline{z_0} - \overline{\tau} + \sum_{i=1..3} r_i \cdot \overline{z_i}}.$$

Under the DLOG assumption (or statistically, when the exponent of $h$ remains small enough), this forces

$$\overline{\gamma} + 4(B - \overline{z_0}/\overline{\gamma})\overline{z_0} - \sum_{i=1..3} x_i \cdot \overline{z_i} = 0 \quad \mathrm{mod}\ q$$

$$\implies \overline{\gamma} + 4(B - \overline{z_0}/\overline{\gamma})\overline{z_0} = \sum_{i=1..3} \overline{z_i}^2/\overline{\gamma} \quad \mathrm{mod}\ q$$

$$\implies \overline{\gamma}^2 + 4(\overline{\gamma} \cdot B - \overline{z_0})\overline{z_0} = \sum_{i=1..3} \overline{z_i}^2 \quad \mathrm{mod}\ q$$

The final equality holds over the integers, because all values are small enough so that there is no wrap-around. More precisely: Let $K = BC(L+1)$ be the maximal (accepting) value of $|z_i|$. For the right hand side, $|\overline{z_i}| \leq |z_i| + |\tilde{z}_i| \leq 2K$ and hence $\sum_{i=1..3} \overline{z_i}^2 \leq 16K^2 \leq U < \frac{q-1}{2}$. Rewrite the left hand side as $\overline{\gamma}^2 + 4\overline{\gamma}B\overline{z_0} - \overline{z_0}^2$. Shortness follows from $|\gamma|B \leq K$ and thus $K^2 + 8K^2 + 16K^2 \leq 25K^2 \leq U < \frac{q-1}{2}$. Here we use that $25K^2 = 25(BC(L+1))^2 \leq 32(BCL)^2 = U$ since $L \geq 32$.

Since the equality holds over the integers, after dividing by $\overline{\gamma}^2$ it holds over $\mathbb{Q}$. Using $\overline{z_0} = \overline{\gamma}(B - x)$, we see that $\overline{\gamma}^2 + 4\overline{\gamma}x(\overline{\gamma}B - \overline{\gamma}x) = \sum_{i=1}^3 \overline{\gamma}^2 x_i^2$ and hence $1 + 4x(B - x) = \sum_{i=1}^3 x_i^2$ for $x = B - \frac{\overline{z_0}}{\overline{\gamma}}$. Now, Lemma 8 finishes the proof. (Note that we extracted a valid opening for $c$.)

**Theorem 2.** *The proof system* $\mathsf{RP_{Log}}$ *is HVZK with simulation error* $9/L$. *If* $S = q - 1$, *this holds against unbounded adversaries.*
*More precisely, for every HVZK adversary* $\mathscr{A}$, *there is a* $\mathsf{SEI}$ *adversary* $\mathscr{B}$ *with roughly the same running time as* $\mathscr{A}$, *such that* $\mathsf{Adv}_{\mathscr{A}}^{\mathrm{hvzk}} \leq 9/L + 4\mathsf{Adv}_{\mathscr{B}}^{\mathrm{sei}}$.

The proof works by simulation via "execution in reverse". That is, the simulator Sim picks random messages $z_i, t_i$ first and lets $x_i = 0$. Then it uses the challenge to compute the messages from the first round. Due to masking, this distribution is $L^{-1}$-close to the real one. And due to SEI, replacing commitments to $x_i$ by commitments to 0 is also indistinguishable. The full proof is in the full version.

## 5.4   Optimizations

We discuss some optimizations to either reduce the proof size or the group size.

*Rejection Sampling for Smaller Group Size.* In $\mathsf{RP_{Log}}$, we hide the values $\gamma \cdot x_i \in [0, BC]$ by an additive uniformly random mask $z \in [0, BCL]$. So the masking has an overhead of $\log(L)$ bits. By using rejection sampling for masking, as used in the lattice setting, this overhead can be traded for a (small) correctness error. For this, we apply Lemma 6 instead of Lemma 3. That is, we choose the mask from a discrete Gaussian distribution with large enough standard deviation $\sigma_x$, and the prover aborts in Resp with (small) probability.

More concretely: Let the parameters for rejection sampling be standard deviation $\sigma_x = \alpha \cdot BC$ and $M = e^{13.3/\alpha + 1/(2\alpha^2)}$ for some $\alpha$. Let $k = \sqrt{2\lambda}$ and let $L' = \lceil k\alpha \rceil$. Then the probability that the mask $m \leftarrow D_{\sigma_x}$ is too large (and causes verification to abort) is $O(2e^{-k^2/2}) = \mathrm{negl}(\lambda)$ by Lemma 5. The protocol is adapted as follows[12]:

- In Init, sample $m_i \leftarrow D_{\sigma_x}$ for $i \in [0, 3]$ (instead of $m_i \leftarrow [0, BCL']$).
- In Resp, abort with probability $1 - \min\left(\frac{D_{\sigma_x}(z_i)}{M \cdot D_{\gamma \cdot x_i, \sigma_x}(z_i)}, 1\right)$ for $i \in [0, 3]$,
- In Verify, check $|z_i| \leq BC(L' + 1)$ for $i \in [0, 3]$ instead of $z_i \in [0, BC(L' + 1)]$.

Since $|m_i| \leq BCL'$ (and thus $|z_i| \leq BC(L' + 1)$) with overwhelming probability, the completeness is mostly affected by aborting in Resp. For the concrete value $\alpha = 256$ which implies $M \approx 1.05$, the abort probability is very small (roughly 0.05). The statistical distance between honest masking and "simulated" masked values is at most $\delta = 2^{-120}$, by Lemma 6. Using this property the HVZK simulator is easily adapted and achieves simulation error $4\delta + 5L^{-1}$. (Note that $s_i$ and $\sigma$ are sampled as before.) The soundness proof uses $L'$ but is otherwise unchanged.

---

[12] For more details on the technique and the proof of security, we refer to the range proof in the lattice setting of the full version. It uses rejection sampling for masking the randomness of the commitment scheme.

To achieve non-negligible completeness, the protocol needs to be repeated, increasing computation and communication. For the Fiat–Shamir transformation, only computation increases.

Lastly, note that $2U = 32(BCL')^2$ is a lower bound on the group size $q$. With rejection sampling, we can choose smaller $L'$, and hence smaller $q$. One can use rejection sampling for the masks $\sigma$ and $s_i$ as well, but these do not affect the group size, only the communication (and the simulation error). More concretely, let $\sigma_r = \alpha \cdot SCL$ and further modify the protocol as follows:

- In Init choose $s_i \leftarrow D_{\sigma_r}$ for $i \in [0, 3]$.
- In Resp abort with probability $1 - \min\left(\frac{D_{\sigma_r(t_i)}}{M \cdot D_{\gamma \cdot r_i, \sigma_r}(t_i)}, 1\right)$ for $i \in [0, 3]$.

This results in a size of $|t_i| \leq SCL'$. Also applying this to $\sigma$ yields $|\tau| \leq 4SBCL'$. In the full version, we detail the concrete impact of these changes on the efficiency.

*Soundness Amplification for Smaller Group Size.* The soundness error of the scheme is $1/(C+1)$, and since $C$ affects $U$ and hence the group size, decreasing it allows smaller groups. However, to achieve negligible soundness error, multiple iterations are required, namely $\lambda/\log(C)$ iterations for a soundness error of $2^{-\lambda}$. Note that the commitments $c_i$ only need to be sent in the first repetition and can be reused in the following ones.

*Efficiency.* Efficiency estimations are given in the introduction. Details on our calculations and the Python scripts used to compute the costs are given in the full version.

# References

[AC20] Attema, T., Cramer, R.: Compressed $\Sigma$-protocol theory and practical application to plug & play secure algorithmics. In: Micciancio, D., Ristenpart, T. (eds.) CRYPTO 2020, Part III. LNCS, vol. 12172, pp. 513–543. Springer, Cham (2020). https://doi.org/10.1007/978-3-030-56877-1_18

[BAZB20] Bünz, B., Agrawal, S., Zamani, M., Boneh, D.: Zether: towards privacy in a smart contract world. In: Bonneau, J., Heninger, N. (eds.) FC 2020. LNCS, vol. 12059, pp. 423–443. Springer, Cham (2020). https://doi.org/10.1007/978-3-030-51280-4_23

[BBB+18] Bünz, B., Bootle, J., Boneh, D., Poelstra, A., Wuille, P., Maxwell, G.: Bulletproofs: short proofs for confidential transactions and more. In: 2018 IEEE Symposium on Security and Privacy, pp. 315–334. IEEE Computer Society Press, May 2018

[BBDE19] Blömer, J., Bobolz, J., Diemert, D., Eidens, F.: Updatable anonymous credentials and applications to incentive systems. In: ACM CCS 2019, pp. 1671–1685. ACM Press, November 2019

[BCDv88] Brickell, E.F., Chaum, D., Damgård, I., van de Graaf, J.: Gradual and verifiable release of a secret (extended abstract). In: Pomerance, C. (ed.) CRYPTO 1987. LNCS, vol. 293, pp. 156–166. Springer, Heidelberg (1988). https://doi.org/10.1007/3-540-48184-2_11

[BCK+14]  Benhamouda, F., Camenisch, J., Krenn, S., Lyubashevsky, V., Neven, G.:
          Better zero-knowledge proofs for lattice encryption and their application to
          group signatures. In: Sarkar, P., Iwata, T. (eds.) ASIACRYPT 2014, Part
          I. LNCS, vol. 8873, pp. 551–572. Springer, Heidelberg (2014). https://doi.
          org/10.1007/978-3-662-45611-8_29

[Ben]     Benarroch, D.: Diving into the zk-SNARKs setup phase. https://medium.
          com/qed-it/diving-into-the-snarks-setup-phase-b7660242a0d7

[BLLS20]  Bootle, J., Lehmann, A., Lyubashevsky, V., Seiler, G.: Compact privacy
          protocols from post-quantum and timed classical assumptions. In: Ding,
          J., Tillich, J.-P. (eds.) PQCrypto 2020. LNCS, vol. 12100, pp. 226–246.
          Springer, Cham (2020). https://doi.org/10.1007/978-3-030-44223-1_13

[Bou00]   Boudot, F.: Efficient proofs that a committed number lies in an interval.
          In: Preneel, B. (ed.) EUROCRYPT 2000. LNCS, vol. 1807, pp. 431–444.
          Springer, Heidelberg (2000). https://doi.org/10.1007/3-540-45539-6_31

[CCs08]   Camenisch, J., Chaabouni, R., Shelat, A.: Efficient protocols for set mem-
          bership and range proofs. In: Pieprzyk, J. (ed.) ASIACRYPT 2008. LNCS,
          vol. 5350, pp. 234–252. Springer, Heidelberg (2008). https://doi.org/10.
          1007/978-3-540-89255-7_15

[CDE+16]  Croman, K., et al.: On scaling decentralized blockchains. In: Clark, J., Meik-
          lejohn, S., Ryan, P.Y.A., Wallach, D., Brenner, M., Rohloff, K. (eds.) FC
          2016. LNCS, vol. 9604, pp. 106–125. Springer, Heidelberg (2016). https://
          doi.org/10.1007/978-3-662-53357-4_8

[Cha90]   Chaum, D.: Showing credentials without identification transferring sig-
          natures between unconditionally unlinkable pseudonyms. In: Seberry, J.,
          Pieprzyk, J. (eds.) AUSCRYPT 1990. LNCS, vol. 453, pp. 245–264.
          Springer, Heidelberg (1990). https://doi.org/10.1007/BFb0030366

[CHJ+20]  Chung, H., Han, K., Ju, C., Kim, M., Seo, J.H.: Bulletproofs+: shorter
          proofs for privacy-enhanced distributed ledger. Cryptology ePrint Archive,
          Report 2020/735 (2020). https://eprint.iacr.org/2020/735

[CHL05]   Camenisch, J., Hohenberger, S., Lysyanskaya, A.: Compact E-cash. In:
          Cramer, R. (ed.) EUROCRYPT 2005. LNCS, vol. 3494, pp. 302–321.
          Springer, Heidelberg (2005). https://doi.org/10.1007/11426639_18

[CPP17]   Couteau, G., Peters, T., Pointcheval, D.: Removing the strong RSA assump-
          tion from arguments over the integers. In: Coron, J.-S., Nielsen, J.B. (eds.)
          EUROCRYPT 2017. LNCS, vol. 10211, pp. 321–350. Springer, Cham
          (2017). https://doi.org/10.1007/978-3-319-56614-6_11

[CZJ+17]  Cecchetti, E., Zhang, F., Ji, Y., Kosba, A., Juels, A., Shi, E.: Solidus:
          confidential distributed ledger transactions via pvorm. In: Proceedings of
          the 2017 ACM SIGSAC Conference on Computer and Communications
          Security, pp. 701–717 (2017)

[DF02]    Damgård, I., Fujisaki, E.: A statistically-hiding integer commitment scheme
          based on groups with hidden order. In: Zheng, Y. (ed.) ASIACRYPT 2002.
          LNCS, vol. 2501, pp. 125–142. Springer, Heidelberg (2002). https://doi.
          org/10.1007/3-540-36178-2_8

[FO97]    Fujisaki, E., Okamoto, T.: Statistical zero knowledge protocols to prove
          modular polynomial relations. In: Kaliski, B.S. (ed.) CRYPTO 1997. LNCS,
          vol. 1294, pp. 16–30. Springer, Heidelberg (1997). https://doi.org/10.1007/
          BFb0052225

[FSW03]   Fouque, P.-A., Stern, J., Wackers, G.-J.: Cryptocomputing with rationals.
          In: Blaze, M. (ed.) FC 2002. LNCS, vol. 2357, pp. 136–146. Springer, Hei-
          delberg (2003). https://doi.org/10.1007/3-540-36504-4_10

[GI08]    Groth, J., Ishai, Y.: Sub-linear zero-knowledge argument for correctness of a shuffle. In: Smart, N. (ed.) EUROCRYPT 2008. LNCS, vol. 4965, pp. 379–396. Springer, Heidelberg (2008). https://doi.org/10.1007/978-3-540-78967-3_22

[GMR89]    Goldwasser, S., Micali, S., Rackoff, C.: The knowledge complexity of interactive proof systems. SIAM J. Comput. 18(1), 186–208 (1989)

[Gro05]    Groth, J.: Non-interactive zero-knowledge arguments for voting. In: Ioannidis, J., Keromytis, A., Yung, M. (eds.) ACNS 2005. LNCS, vol. 3531, pp. 467–482. Springer, Heidelberg (2005). https://doi.org/10.1007/11496137_32

[Gro11]    Groth, J.: Efficient zero-knowledge arguments from two-tiered homomorphic commitments. In: Lee, D.H., Wang, X. (eds.) ASIACRYPT 2011. LNCS, vol. 7073, pp. 431–448. Springer, Heidelberg (2011). https://doi.org/10.1007/978-3-642-25385-0_23

[HKR19]    Hoffmann, M., Klooß, M., Rupp, A.: Efficient zero-knowledge arguments in the discrete log setting, revisited. In: ACM CCS 2019, pp. 2093–2110. ACM Press, November 2019

[HKRR20]    Hoffmann, M., Klooß, M., Raiber, M., Rupp, A.: Black-box wallets: fast anonymous two-way payments for constrained devices. PoPETs 2020(1), 165–194 (2020)

[HPWZ17]    Hoffstein, J., Pipher, J., Whyte, W., Zhang, Z.: A signature scheme from learning with truncation. Cryptology ePrint Archive, Report 2017/995 (2017). http://eprint.iacr.org/2017/995

[KK04]    Koshiba, T., Kurosawa, K.: Short exponent Diffie-Hellman problems. In: Bao, F., Deng, R., Zhou, J. (eds.) PKC 2004. LNCS, vol. 2947, pp. 173–186. Springer, Heidelberg (2004). https://doi.org/10.1007/978-3-540-24632-9_13

[Lin03]    Lindell, Y.: Parallel coin-tossing and constant-round secure two-party computation. J. Cryptol. 16(3), 143–184 (2003)

[Lip03]    Lipmaa, H.: On diophantine complexity and statistical zero-knowledge arguments. In: Laih, C.-S. (ed.) ASIACRYPT 2003. LNCS, vol. 2894, pp. 398–415. Springer, Heidelberg (2003). https://doi.org/10.1007/978-3-540-40061-5_26

[LM19]    Lai, R.W.F., Malavolta, G.: Subvector commitments with application to succinct arguments. In: Boldyreva, A., Micciancio, D. (eds.) CRYPTO 2019, Part I. LNCS, vol. 11692, pp. 530–560. Springer, Cham (2019). https://doi.org/10.1007/978-3-030-26948-7_19

[LN17]    Lyubashevsky, V., Neven, G.: One-shot verifiable encryption from lattices. In: Coron, J.-S., Nielsen, J.B. (eds.) EUROCRYPT 2017, Part I. LNCS, vol. 10210, pp. 293–323. Springer, Cham (2017). https://doi.org/10.1007/978-3-319-56620-7_11

[Lyu12]    Lyubashevsky, V.: Lattice signatures without trapdoors. In: Pointcheval, D., Johansson, T. (eds.) EUROCRYPT 2012. LNCS, vol. 7237, pp. 738–755. Springer, Heidelberg (2012). https://doi.org/10.1007/978-3-642-29011-4_43

[MIO18]    Miola, A.: Addressing privacy and fungibility issues in bitcoin: confidential transactions (2018)

[Ped92]    Pedersen, T.P.: Non-interactive and information-theoretic secure verifiable secret sharing. In: Feigenbaum, J. (ed.) CRYPTO 1991. LNCS, vol. 576, pp. 129–140. Springer, Heidelberg (1992). https://doi.org/10.1007/3-540-46766-1_9

[PS96]  Pointcheval, D., Stern, J.: Security proofs for signature schemes. In: Maurer, U. (ed.) EUROCRYPT 1996. LNCS, vol. 1070, pp. 387–398. Springer, Heidelberg (1996). https://doi.org/10.1007/3-540-68339-9_33

[PS00]  Pointcheval, D., Stern, J.: Security arguments for digital signatures and blind signatures. J. Cryptol. **13**(3), 361–396 (2000)

[PS19]  Pollack, P., Schorn, P.: Dirichlet's proof of the three-square theorem: an algorithmic perspective. Math. Comput. **88**(316), 1007–1019 (2019)

[RS86]  Rabin, M.O., Shallit, J.O.: Randomized algorithms in number theory, pp. S239–S256 (1986)

[Sle]   Slepak, G.: How to compromise zcash and take over the world. https://blog.okturtles.org/2016/09/how-to-compromise-zcash-and-take-over-the-world/

[YAZ+19] Yang, R., Au, M.H., Zhang, Z., Xu, Q., Yu, Z., Whyte, W.: Efficient lattice-based zero-knowledge arguments with standard soundness: construction and applications. In: Boldyreva, A., Micciancio, D. (eds.) CRYPTO 2019, Part I. LNCS, vol. 11692, pp. 147–175. Springer, Cham (2019). https://doi.org/10.1007/978-3-030-26948-7_6

# Towards Accountability in CRS Generation

Prabhanjan Ananth[1]([✉]), Gilad Asharov[2], Hila Dahari[3], and Vipul Goyal[4]

[1] University of California, Santa Barbara, Santa Barbara, USA
prabhanjan@cs.ucsb.edu
[2] Bar-Ilan University, Ramat Gan, Israel
gilad.asharov@biu.ac.il
[3] Weizmann Institute, Rehovot, Israel
hila.dahari@weizmann.ac.il
[4] NTT Research and Carnegie Mellon University, Pittsburgh, USA
vipul@cmu.edu

**Abstract.** It is well known that several cryptographic primitives cannot be achieved without a common reference string (CRS). Those include, for instance, non-interactive zero-knowledge for NP, or maliciously secure computation in fewer than four rounds. The security of those primitives heavily relies upon on the assumption that the trusted authority, who generates the CRS, does not misuse the randomness used in the CRS generation. However, we argue that there is no such thing as an unconditionally trusted authority and every authority must be held accountable for any trust to be well-founded. Indeed, a malicious authority can, for instance, recover private inputs of honest parties given transcripts of the protocols executed with respect to the CRS it has generated.

While eliminating trust in the trusted authority may not be entirely feasible, can we at least move towards achieving some notion of accountability? We propose a new notion in which, if the CRS authority releases the private inputs of protocol executions to others, we can then provide a publicly-verifiable proof that certifies that the authority misbehaved. We study the feasibility of this notion in the context of non-interactive zero knowledge and two-round secure two-party computation.

## 1  Introduction

Very broadly, cryptography can be seen as having two parallel lines of research: one where the parties don't trust anyone but themselves, and another where security relies on some kind of trust assumption. Most notably, many works have relied on the common reference string (CRS) model where a trusted party chooses and publishes a public string. The advantage of relying on a CRS depends upon the setting. For example, for ZK it is known that while in the CRS model, a non-interaction solution can be achieved [9,17] one needs at least 3 rounds in the plain model [22]. For MPC, two rounds are sufficient in the CRS model [8,21,29] while the best known constructions in the plain model require at least

© International Association for Cryptologic Research 2021
A. Canteaut and F.-X. Standaert (Eds.): EUROCRYPT 2021, LNCS 12698, pp. 278–308, 2021.
https://doi.org/10.1007/978-3-030-77883-5_10

4-rounds [1,4,10,15,27,28]. Furthermore, UC security is known to be impossible to achieve in the plain model [11,12] while this impossibility can be bypassed in the CRS model [11,13]. Thus, while one might prefer to obtain constructions in the plain model, it seems unlikely that the CRS model will be abandoned anytime soon.

**Do There Really Exist Trusted Parties?** We argue that in real life, there is no such thing as an unconditional trusted party. We argue that the only reason we trust a party is because the cost of cheating (if caught) for that party would be much higher than the potential gains obtained by cheating successfully. Indeed this applies everywhere in our society. We are more comfortable trusting a large bank with our personal information compared to a small individual lender only because a large bank will pay a much higher cost (loss of reputation and potential future business) if it behaves maliciously. However if the cost to the large bank was zero, the reasons for placing this trust would be unfounded. There are multiple examples where even large entities systematically participated in an activity which would be generally unacceptable only because they thought the activity would not become public knowledge (e.g., Facebook selling data to Cambridge Analytica, or Wells Fargo opening accounts without customer knowledge).

Compared to real life, in cryptography, life is largely black and white: dishonest parties can be arbitrarily bad and trusted parties are unconditionally trusted. For example, the party generating a CRS (referred to as the CRS authority from hereon) in a NIZK system can potentially even recover your witness entirely and sell it for profit. Similarly, in MPC, the CRS authority may recover your input and pass it on to another party. Even if you detect that the authority is doing that, it's not clear how to prove it in a court of law and seek damages. You can publicly blame the authority for doing that. But this is then indistinguishable from a malicious party blaming an honest authority.

These concerns have motivated the study of weaker notions such as ZAPs [16] and super-polynomial simulation security [30]. Groth and Ostrovsky studied the so called multi-string model [25] where multiple authorities publish common reference strings such that a majority of them are guaranteed to be honest. Goyal and Katz [24], and later Garg et al. [20] studied UC security with an unreliable CRS if the CRS turns out to be malicious, some other setup or an honest majority can come to the rescue. Bellare et al. [7] studied NIZKs with an untrusted CRS where even if the CRS is malicious, some weaker security properties still hold.

In this work, we focus on a single CRS while providing some notion of accountability towards the CRS generation authority. Our direction is orthogonal to many of the works mentioned and, to our knowledge, largely unexplored.

**Towards Accountability in CRS Generation:** While eliminating trust in the CRS authority entirely may not be feasible, can we at least move towards achieving some notion of accountability? As an example, suppose you find out that the CRS authority decrypted your input used in an execution of MPC protocol and sold to another party for profit. Can you obtain a cryptographic proof of this fact? Can you convince others that such an incident has happened? Indeed there are limits on what can and cannot be achieved. For example, if the authority sells your input and you never find out, it's unclear if something can be done. But if the decrypted input indeed falls into your hand (e.g., the person buying the input from the authority was your own agent), you know for sure that the authority is dishonest (although you may not be able to prove it to others).

In this work, we study if there is *any* meaningful notion of accountability that can be achieved with respect to a CRS authority. We focus specifically on the case of NIZK, and two-round MPC which are both known to be impossible in the plain model and yet achievable with a CRS. Our work runs into several novel technical challenges as we discuss later. We note that our study is far from complete and leaves open various intriguing questions.

## 1.1   Our Results

In this work, we propose novel notions of accountability in the context of two party secure computation protocols and NIZKs. We also accompany these definitions with constructions realizing these notions.

**Secure Two-Party Computation (2PC).** Our definition of malicious authority security first requires the same security guarantees as in regular secure computation, that is, if the CRS was honestly generated, then the protocol achieves simulation security in the presence of a malicious adversary. To capture the setting when the CRS authority is malicious, we require the following two security properties:

– **Accountability.** Suppose the authority generated a CRS maliciously. At a later point in time, it offers a service to recover the honest parties' inputs from the transcripts of protocol executions between these parties, using the trapdoors it embedded in the CRS. The accountability property guarantees that we can hold such a CRS authority accountable by producing a piece of publicly verifiable evidence that incriminates this authority for its malpractice. This evidence can then be presented in a court of law to penalize this authority. We formalize this by defining an efficient extractor that can interact[1] with this malicious authority and outputs a piece of evidence (a string). We associate with the scheme an algorithm Judge, which then determines whether this evidence is valid or not.

  The authority should not distinguish whether it interacts with the extractor (who is trying to incriminate the authority) or with a real party (who is trying to learn the inputs of the honest parties). Note that if the authority has some auxiliary information about the honest party's input, it can possibly

---

[1] We stress that this extractor interacts with the malicious authority online *without being able to rewind the authority*. This is because, if we want to implicate the authority in the real world then we would not have the ability to rewind such an authority.

produce the input without using the CRS trapdoor at all. In that case, it seems impossible to obtain incriminating evidence from the response of the authority. To avoid this issue, we specify a distribution $\mathcal{D}$ such that the inputs of the honest parties are sampled from this distribution in the security experiment. We stress that this requirement is only for the accountability security experiment. Our construction satisfies the usual definition of 2PC (without requiring any distribution on the inputs) in case the CRS is honest.

– **Defamation-free.** Of course, accountability cannot stand by itself. This notion opens up the possibility of falsely accusing even an honest CRS authority (who never partakes in running the input recovery service mentioned above) of malpractice. We complement the definition of accountability by defining another property called *defamation-free*. Roughly speaking, this definition states that just given an honestly generated CRS, it should be computationally infeasible to come up with an evidence that would incriminate an honest authority.

We study two variants of accountability. First, we study the scenario mentioned above in which two parties engage in a secure protocol. Then, one of them comes to the authority *after the fact* and asks to open the honest party's input. That party has to provide to the authority its view, which includes its own input and randomness. In the second (stronger) definition, we imagine the authority will be more cautious and refuse to answer such queries. Instead, the authority will insist on being involved from the beginning. In this model, the authority completely controls one of the parties, actively participates in the protocol execution on behalf of this party, and finally recovers and provides to this party the honest party's input. We refer to these notions as weak and strong accountability.

**Impossibility Result.** The first question is whether this new notion can be realized at all. Unfortunately, we show that even the weak definition cannot be realized for all functions. We show the following.

**Theorem 1.1** (Informal). *There exists a two-party functionality $\mathcal{F}$ such that there does not exist any secure two-party computation protocol for $\mathcal{F}$ in the CRS model satisfying both (weak) accountability and defamation-free properties.*

Specifically, the class of functionalities for which the above impossibility result hold are functionalities where given the output, we can efficiently recover the inputs. Indeed, an impossibility result is easy to see in this case since the authority can recover the input without even using any trapdoor related to the CRS (and in fact, anyone can recover the input of any party). Since this class of functionalities is somewhat trivial, and such functions are usually considered as functions where secure computation is not necessary (a trivial protocol where a party just gives its input suffices), this gives us hope that we can come up with positive results for large class of interesting functionalities. We focus on the setting of maliciously secure *two-round* two-party since that is known to be impossible to achieve in the plain model.

**Construction.** We then study the following class of (asymmetric) two-party functionalities $\mathcal{F}$: the two-party functionality takes as input $(x, y)$ and outputs $g(\{x_i\}_{y_i=1})$ to the second party (with input $y$) for some function $g$. That is, it outputs $g$ on only those bits of $x$ that are indexed by the bits of $y$ set to 1. This class of functions includes for instance, oblivious transfer, private information retrieval, subset sum, and more. We show the following:

**Theorem 1.2** (Informal). *Assuming SXDH (Symmetric External Diffie-Hellman) on bilinear maps, there exists a two-round maliciously secure two-party computation protocol for $\mathcal{F}$ satisfying both weak accountability (with respect to the uniform distribution over the inputs) and defamation-free.*

Indeed, obtaining such a construction turns out to be surprisingly non-trivial and requires one to overcome novel technical challenges. We refer the reader to Sect. 2 (Technical Overview) for a summary of techniques.

**Strong Accountability for Oblivious Transfer.** As mentioned, we study weak and strong accountability, depending on whether the malicious authority actively participates in the protocol execution or not. We focus on the oblivious transfer functionality and demonstrate that strong accountability is possible to achieve, based on a (seemingly) stronger assumption.

**Theorem 1.3** (Informal). *Assuming indistinguishability obfuscation for P/poly [5,19] and SXDH in bilinear groups, there exists a two-round maliciously secure oblivious transfer protocol in the CRS model satisfying both strong accountability and defamation-free properties, with respect to the uniform distribution over the inputs.*

The techniques developed in the above construction can potentially be extended also for the class of functions in $\mathcal{F}$ for which Theorem 1.2 holds, although we focused on oblivious transfer for simplicity.

**Non-Interactive Zero-Knowledge (NIZK).** Another basic cryptographic primitive which relies on a CRS is NIZK. Indeed, CRS shows up in several cryptographic constructions primarily because they use NIZK as a building block. Similar to the 2PC case, we require the same guarantees as a regular NIZK when the CRS is honestly generated, namely, completeness, soundness and zero-knowledge. We associate with the proof system a Judge algorithm and require accountability and defamation free properties:

- **Accountability.** For any CRS* that might be maliciously produced by the CRS authority, if there exists an adversary that upon receiving pairs $(x, \pi)$ can recover the witness $w$, (where $x$ is an instance, $\pi$ is a proof that $x$ is in the associated language, and $w$ is the secret witness), then there exists an extractor that can create a piece of evidence $\tau$ that is accepted by Judge.
  As before, our accountability property is parameterized by a distribution $\mathcal{D}$ defined on the instance-witness pairs. Indeed this is necessary since if the authority can guess the witness without using the CRS trapdoor, the security guarantees we have in mind are impossible to achieve.

- **Defamation-free.** This states that no non-uniform probabilistic polynomial-time adversary $\mathcal{A}$ upon receiving a CRS that was honestly generated can come up with a piece of evidence $\tau$ that makes Judge accept.

We consider a NP language $L$ consisting of instances of the form $(C, c_1, \ldots, c_m, b)$ such that $C : \{0,1\}^m \to \{0,1\}$ is a boolean circuit, each $c_i$ is a commitment of $x_i$ and moreover, $C(x_1, \ldots, x_n) = b$. We note that we can reduce any NP-complete language to this language based on the existence of rerandomizable commitments. We show the following.

**Theorem 1.4** (Informal). *Assuming SXDH on bilinear maps, there exists a NIZK for $L$ in the CRS model satisfying both the accountability and the defamation-free properties.*

We can handle a class of distributions $\mathcal{D}$ with the only requirement being that a distribution in this class computes the commitments using uniform randomness while the circuit $C$ and inputs $(x_1, \ldots, x_n)$ can be arbitrarily chosen.

**Open Problems.** We believe that a systematic study of the notions of accountability in the CRS model is an exciting line of research. Our work leaves open several natural questions. Can we broaden and characterize the class of functionalities for which accountable 2PC can be achieved? Can we extend our construction to more than two parties? While we focus on two rounds, obtaining even three round constructions would be valuable since the best known constructions in the plain model require at least four rounds.

One could also consider stronger notions where the authority only supplies some information about the input (e.g. the first bit of the input) rather than the entire input. In this setting, it seems the extractor would need to obtain multiple responses from the authority and somehow combine them into a single proof. Furthermore, while we focus on privacy (of the input in case of secure computation, or the witness in case of NIZK) in this work, what if the authority instead attacks correctness or soundness?

Another interesting direction is to consider other settings where CRS is used such as obtaining UC security.

**Related Works.** Our notion is inspired, in part, by broadcast encryption with traitor tracing [14] where, given a decryption box, there is a trace algorithm (similar to our Judge algorithm) which identifies the cheating party. However there are crucial differences. Our Judge algorithm does not have direct access to the CRS authority and only gets to see a string produced by the extractor. Furthermore, our extractor only gets to interact with the CRS authority *online* and, in particular, *does not get to rewind the CRS authority*. In another related line of research, Goyal [23] introduced what is known as accountable authority (AA) identity-based encryption (IBE) where if the authority generating the IBE public parameters is dishonest and releases a "decryption box", the authority can be implicated in a court. Our definition is also inspired by public verifiability in covert security, introduced by Asharov and Orlandi [3]. This definition shows how one can extract, given a transcript of the protocol, a piece of evidence showing that there was a misbehavior in the execution. The definition also requires defamation free, so that innocents cannot be implicated.

Another related notion of our work is subversion security, suggested by Bellare, Fuchsbauer, and Scafuro [7] (see also [18]). The work studies the security of NIZKs in the presence of a maliciously chosen common reference string. It shows that several security properties can still be preserved when the CRS is maliciously generated. Nevertheless, it is shown that zero-knowledge cannot be preserved simultaneously with soundness when the common reference string is maliciously generated. Our work takes a different approach and seeks accountability when such misbehavior is detected. It will be intriguing to see how these two notions can intertwine.

## 2    Technical Overview

We start by explaining the main idea that underpins the constructions of NIZK, oblivious transfer and secure two-party computation with malicious authority security. Realizing this insight will lead us to different challenges in the context of designing each of the different primitives; we discuss the challenges for each of these primitives separately.

**Main Idea.** Our main idea is to force the CRS authority to include a transcript of execution of the protocol as part of the CRS, where the transcript has a secret $x$ embedded inside. In the context of NIZKs, we force the authority to include a NIZK proof in the CRS where the witness contains the secret $x$. In the case of oblivious transfer and secure two-party computation, the sender and the receiver's input in the transcript are generated as a function of $x$.

In the honest execution, the transcript in the CRS is ignored. However, to argue accountability, the extractor will cleverly maul this transcript in the CRS to generate another transcript in such a way that the mauled transcript now has the embedded secret $x \oplus y$, where $y$ is sampled by the extractor. The extractor then sends this mauled transcript to the malicious CRS authority. Since this authority offers a service to recover the inputs of the honest parties (or witness in the context of NIZKs), it recovers $x \oplus y$ and outputs this. Note that the authority was tricked into recovering an input that was in reality related to the secret that it hardwired inside the CRS. Now, the extractor has $x \oplus y$, and it can easily recover $x$. It recovers $x$ and presents it as evidence to implicate the authority. The extractor could never recover $x$ by itself without the "help" of the malicious authority, which also implies defamation free.

While this initial idea sounds promising, its realization involves technical challenges. We highlight some of them below.

- The first and foremost challenge is malleability. We hinged on the fact that the extractor can maul the transcript in the CRS. It turns out that malleability is a challenging problem. Malleability of transcripts has not been studied in the context of interactive protocols before and moreover, even in the setting of NIZKs, this has only been studied in the context of restricted relations.

– Another challenge is to ensure that the malicious authority cannot distinguish whether it is interacting with an extractor, who is trying to incriminate it, or is it interacting with a malicious party who only intends to learn the inputs of the honest parties. In other words, we need an extractor who can produce transcripts that are computationally indistinguishable from the transcripts produced by real protocol executions (not the ones obtained by mauling the CRS).

– We mentioned above that we force the authority to include a transcript in the CRS. How do we ensure that the authority did indeed include a valid transcript in the CRS? The standard solution to employ a NIZK proof cannot work because the authority can violate soundness since it is the one who generates the CRS.

– Finally, to prove the defamation-free property, we need to argue that any probabilistic polynomial time adversary, (no matter how hard it tries) cannot come up with an evidence to implicate an honest authority. In other words, given the transcript in the CRS, it should be computationally infeasible to recover the secret $x$.

We now show how to implement our main idea, to construct NIZKs, oblivious transfer and secure 2PC with malicious authority security, and in the process we also discuss how to address the above challenges.

## 2.1   Malicious Authority Security for NIZK

We start by describing the NP relation associated with the proof system.

**NP Relation.** Every instance in this relation is of the form $(C, c_1, \ldots, c_m, b)$, consisting of three components: (1) A boolean circuit $C : \{0,1\}^m \to \{0,1\}$; (2) Committed input $\mathbf{c} = (c_1, \ldots, c_m)$ hiding some bits $(x_1, \ldots, x_m)$ using decommitments $(r_1, \ldots, r_m)$; (3) A bit $b$ satisfying $b = C(x_1, \ldots, x_m)$. The witness is therefore the bits $(x_1, \ldots, x_m)$ and their associated decommitments $(r_1, \ldots, r_m)$. In particular, embedding the commitments in the language guarantees average case hardness, as opposed to regular circuit satisfiability that might have only worst case hardness.

**Base Proof System.** We start with a NIZK proof system and then modify this system to satisfy the desired properties. The proof system is obtained by employing the standard FLS trick [17].

To prove an instance $(C, c_1, \ldots, c_m, b)$ using a witness $\mathbf{x} = (x_1, \ldots, x_m)$ and de-commitments $\mathbf{r} = (r_1, \ldots, r_m)$, we simply use a NIWI proof system in which the prover can show that either it knows the witness $(\mathbf{x}, \mathbf{r})$, or that it knows a seed $\mathsf{s_{in}}$ for some string $y$ that appears in the CRS, i.e., $y = \mathsf{PRG}(\mathsf{s_{in}})$. When the CRS is honestly generated, with overwhelming probability, such a pre-image does not exist, and thus the proof system is sound. Moreover, the simulator can generate an indistinguishable CRS in which $y = \mathsf{PRG}(\mathsf{s_{in}})$ for some trapdoor $\mathsf{s_{in}}$, enabling it to provide proofs without knowing the witnesses.

**Accountability.** To achieve accountability, we need to provide more information in the CRS. As a warmup, we will include the commitments $\mathbf{c}^0 = \mathsf{Com}(0; \mathbf{r}^0)$ and $\mathbf{c}^1 = \mathsf{Com}(1; \mathbf{r}^1)$ for random $\mathbf{r}^0, \mathbf{r}^1$. To prove accountability, we define an extractor who first samples a circuit $C$ and a string $\mathbf{x} = (x_1 \cdots x_n)$ according to the distribution of the honest prover, chooses a subset of the commitments $(\mathbf{c}^{x_1}, \ldots, \mathbf{c}^{x_n})$, where $\mathbf{c}^{x_i}$ is a commitment of the bit $x_i$ and is taken from the extra information in the CRS. Then, the extractor computes a proof $\pi$ on the instance $(C, (\mathbf{c}^{x_1}, \ldots, \mathbf{c}^{x_n}), C(\mathbf{x}))$. The authority, given the instance and the proof, will output the witness $(\mathbf{x}, \mathbf{r}^{x_1}, \ldots, \mathbf{r}^{x_n})$. This witness itself serves as an evidence that can be used to incriminate the authority; this is because it can be publicly verified that $(x_i, \mathbf{r}^{x_i})$ is a valid opening for $\mathbf{c}^{x_i}$. Moreover, just given the CRS, it is computationally infeasible to produce an opening; thus, defamation-free is guaranteed as well.

There are four major issues with this approach. The *first* issue is the following: the authority upon recovering the witness $(\mathbf{x}, \mathbf{r}^{x_1}, \ldots, \mathbf{r}^{x_n})$, or even by just viewing the instance $(C, (\mathbf{c}^{x_1}, \ldots, \mathbf{c}^{x_n}), C(\mathbf{x}))$ to be opened, will realize that it corresponds to the randomness associated with the commitments in the CRS. So, it will be able to figure out that it is the extractor who submitted the proof. The *second* issue is that it is unclear how the extractor will be able to produce a valid proof on the instance $(\mathbf{c}^{x_1}, \ldots, \mathbf{c}^{x_n})$. Indeed, the binding property of the commitment scheme and the soundness of the NIWI proof tell us that this should not be possible. The *third* issue is that the authority is the one who generates the public parameters of the commitment scheme, and might generate them as computationally binding instead of perfectly binding. This means that even if the authority opens the input, it might open $\mathbf{c}^{x_i}$ to $1 - x_i$. In this case, it is unclear how to implicate the authority. Finally, the *fourth* issue is that we need to verify that the malicious authority included commitments of 0 and 1 only.

- To get around the first issue, we use a rerandomizable commitment scheme. Given commitment to a message $m$, we can rerandomize this commitment in such a way that randomness of the new commitment information-theoretically hides the randomness used in the old commitment. To see why this is useful, note that the extractor can rerandomize the commitments $(\mathbf{c}^{x_1}, \ldots, \mathbf{c}^{x_n})$. Now, the randomness recovered by the authority is identically distributed to fresh commitments of $(x_1, ..., x_n)$.
- To get around the second issue, we add to the language of our NIWI a third branch: given a statement $(C, \mathbf{c}_1, \ldots, \mathbf{c}_m, b)$, the commitments $(\mathbf{c}_1, \ldots, \mathbf{c}_m)$ were obtained as re-randomizations of the two commitments $\mathbf{c}^0$ and $\mathbf{c}^1$ in the CRS, and the extractor has to provide the re-randomization information. Thus, to generate an implicating transcript, the extractor chooses any circuit $C$ and input $(x_1, \ldots, x_m)$ according to the distribution of the honest prover. Moreover, it evaluates $C(x_1, \ldots, x_m) = b$, re-randomizes the commitments $\mathbf{c}^{x_1}, \ldots, \mathbf{c}^{x_m}$ to obtain $(\mathbf{c}_1, \ldots, \mathbf{c}_m)$. The extractor then gets an instance $(C, \mathbf{c}_1, \ldots, \mathbf{c}_m, b)$ with a proof $\pi_{\mathsf{NIWI}}$.
- For the third issue, we show that it does not matter whether the commitment $\mathbf{c}^{x_i}$ is opened to $x_i$ or $1 - x_i$. In particular we show that, using the reran-

domizability property of the commitment scheme, having either of the two openings is sufficient to implicate the authority.

- Finally, to overcome the forth issue, the authority will provide four commitments as part of the CRS, $((c_0^0, c_1^0), (c_0^1, c_1^1))$, and prove using a NIWI proof (which does not require CRS) that one of the branches $(c_0^0, c_1^0)$ or $(c_0^1, c_1^1)$ consists of commitments to 0 and 1. Before participating in proving any statement with respect to this CRS, one has to check using the proof provided in the CRS that the CRS is correctly computed, i.e., that there is a method to implicate the authority if corrupted.

To argue accountability with the modified CRS, the extractor needs to pick the correct branch to rerandomize. However, it does not know which is the right branch. Instead it samples one of the branches uniformly at random and proceeds. If we had the guarantee that the authority recovered the witness with non-negligible probability then we have the guarantee that the extractor still succeeds in coming up with an incriminating evidence with non-negligible probability.

We can argue defamation-free using the witness-indistinguishability property of the proof in the CRS in conjunction with the hiding property of the commitment scheme.

## 2.2 Malicious Authority Security for Oblivious Transfer

We now focus our attention on secure two party computation protocols. To gain better intuition and to understand the difficulties we cope with, we start with studying a specific functionality—oblivious transfer. The solutions and techniques developed in addressing this functionality will also be useful in understanding the general case.

As opposed to NIZK which consists of one message and only the prover has some private input (the witness), in oblivious transfer both parties have private inputs. We consider a parallel repetition of 1-out-of-2 bit oblivious transfer, in which the receiver holds a string $\sigma = (\sigma_1, \ldots, \sigma_n) \in \{0, 1\}^n$, and the sender holds two messages $\mathbf{m}_0 = (m_1^0, \ldots, m_n^0)$, $\mathbf{m}_1 = (m_1^1, \ldots, m_n^1) \in \{0, 1\}^n$. Only the receiver receives the output which is $m_1^{\sigma_1}, \ldots, m_n^{\sigma_n}$. A two-round protocol of oblivious transfer in the CRS model consists CRS generation algorithm GenCRS (run by the authority) that outputs $\mathsf{CRS}_{\mathsf{OT}}$, and two algorithms $\mathsf{OT}_1, \mathsf{OT}_2$ for generating the transcript. The receiver runs $\mathsf{msg}_R = \mathsf{OT}_1(\mathsf{CRS}_{\mathsf{OT}}, \sigma)$ to obtain the message $\mathsf{msg}_R$ from the receiver to the sender, followed by a message $\mathsf{msg}_S = \mathsf{OT}_2(\mathsf{CRS}_{\mathsf{OT}}, \mathbf{m}_0, \mathbf{m}_1, \mathsf{msg}_R)$ from the sender to the receiver. The receiver then makes some local computation to output $m_1^{\sigma_1}, \ldots, m_n^{\sigma_n}$.

As the functionality hides information for both the receiver $(m_1^{1-\sigma_1}, \ldots, m_n^{1-\sigma_n})$ and the sender $(\sigma)$, both parties might come to the malicious authority and ask to open the same transcript, while extracting different information from it. We, therefore, have to discuss two different scenarios and show that in either case, if the authority offers help to either of the two parties, it can be implicated. In the first scenario, which we call *malicious sender*, the sender submits

its view to the authority and tries to learn the input of the receiver. We define *malicious receiver* analogously. We follow the same oblivious transfer protocol that is secure against malicious adversaries. As mentioned earlier in our discussion, to achieve the protocol's security, we cannot hope to prevent the malicious authority from making any trapdoors in $\mathsf{CRS}_{\mathsf{OT}}$. Those trapdoors are essential ingredients when proving the simulation security of the protocol. All we can do is to prevent it from using that trapdoor, and specifically from divulging secrets to others.

**Dealing with a Malicious Sender.** Following our general template, the authority generates $\mathsf{CRS}_{\mathsf{OT}}$. Moreover, it randomly samples a challenge $\boldsymbol{\sigma} = (\sigma_1, \ldots, \sigma_m)$, for some sufficiently long $m$, and appends $f(\boldsymbol{\sigma})$ to the CRS, where $f$ is a one-way function. Then, we want to embed $\boldsymbol{\sigma}$ in transcript of OT, i.e., add $\mathsf{msg}_R^\sigma = \mathsf{OT}_1(\boldsymbol{\sigma})$. Without knowing the receiver's randomness, no one can learn $\boldsymbol{\sigma}$ just from seeing the message $\mathsf{OT}_1(\boldsymbol{\sigma})$, as guaranteed from the receiver's security in the protocol against the malicious sender. This guarantees defamation free. Yet, our goal is give the extractor the ability to maul those transcripts such that if ever opened, we will have a piece of evidence to implicate the authority.

A natural idea is to just complete the transcript with any $\mathbf{m}_0, \mathbf{m}_1$ to obtain $\mathsf{msg}_S = \mathsf{OT}_2(\mathsf{CRS}_{\mathsf{OT}}, \mathbf{m}_0, \mathbf{m}_1, \mathsf{msg}_R^\sigma)$. Then, to come up with the pair ($\mathsf{msg}_S$, $\mathsf{msg}_R$) to the authority. But, the authority will refuse to open such a transcript – it can clearly identify that the receiver's secret input is $\boldsymbol{\sigma}$, i.e., the secret challenge it generated! Moreover, it can identify that the message $\mathsf{msg}_R$ in the transcript is identical to the message it published in the CRS. We need a stronger method that enables us to complete transcripts to any input of the sender and to maul the receiver's input and re-randomizes it.

To achieve that, we again successfully avoid the issue of malleability using rerandomization and by adding more information in the CRS. Recall that the protocol is a parallel repetition of bit OT, i.e., $\mathsf{OT}_1(\boldsymbol{\sigma}) = \mathsf{OT}_1^{bit}(\sigma_1), \ldots,$ $\mathsf{OT}_1^{bit}(\sigma_m)$, where $(\mathsf{OT}_1^{bit}, \mathsf{OT}_2^{bit})$ is the underlying bit OT protocol. The authority will have to generate for every bit two transcripts, $\alpha_{i,0} = \mathsf{OT}_1^{bit}(\sigma_i \oplus 0)$ and $\alpha_{i,1} = \mathsf{OT}_1^{bit}(\sigma_i \oplus 1)$. This enables the extractor to obtain a transcript for $\boldsymbol{\sigma} \oplus \Delta$ for the receiver for every $\Delta = (\Delta_1, \ldots, \Delta_n)$ of its choice, and any input $(\mathbf{m}_0, \mathbf{m}_1)$ of the sender of its choice. That is, to generate $\mathsf{OT}_1(\boldsymbol{\sigma} \oplus \Delta)$, do the following:

$$\mathsf{OT}_1(\boldsymbol{\sigma} \oplus \Delta) = (\alpha_{1,\Delta_1}, \ldots, \alpha_{n,\Delta_n}) = \left(\mathsf{OT}_1^{bit}(\sigma_1 \oplus \Delta_1), \ldots, \mathsf{OT}_1^{bit}(\sigma_n \oplus \Delta_n)\right).$$

It re-randomizes each one of these messages, and completes it to full transcript with any messages $\mathbf{m}_0, \mathbf{m}_1$ of its choice. The authority receiving such a transcript has no way to tell that this transcript was generated using the transcripts it published in the CRS. By extracting the input of the receiver it discloses itself.

**Dealing with a Malicious Receiver.** Following a similar approach, recall that on input $(\mathbf{m}_0, \mathbf{m}_1)$ for the sender and $\boldsymbol{\sigma}$ for the receiver, the oblivious transfer functionality hides only $(m_1^{1-\sigma_1}, \ldots, m_n^{1-\sigma_n})$ but reveals $(m_1^{\sigma_1}, \ldots, m_n^{\sigma_n})$ to the receiver. Therefore, it seems natural to embed the challenge in the hidden part of the message. The authority chooses a new challenge $\mathbf{x} = (x_1, \ldots, x_n)$ and publishes $f(\mathbf{x})$ in the CRS. Moreover, it creates transcripts that correspond to $\mathbf{x}$ and enables the extractor to produce transcript for every input $\mathbf{r} = (r_1, \ldots, r_n)$ of the receiver and "shift" $\Delta = (\Delta_1, \ldots, \Delta_n)$, while embedding $x_i$ in position $1 - r_i$ (which is not revealed), to obtain $((x_1 \oplus \Delta_1)^{1-r_1}, \ldots, (x_n \oplus \Delta_n)^{1-r_n})$. If the malicious authority ever opens the transcript, that is, it recovers $((x_1 \oplus \Delta_1)^{1-r_1}, \ldots, (x_n \oplus \Delta_n)^{1-r_n})$, it can then extract $\mathbf{x}$ from this (since it knows the "shift") and implicate the authority. To do that, first observe that there are 8 possible transcripts for each bit OT: the input of the receiver is $r_i \in \{0,1\}$ and the input of the sender is $(m_0, m_1) \in \{0,1\}^2$. To enable the extractor to generate any transcript it wishes, for every bit-OT $i \in \{1, \ldots, n\}$, the CRS authority is expected to produce (as part of the CRS generation) four values as follows: For every $\mu, \Delta_i \in \{0,1\}$:

$$\beta^i_{0,\mu,\Delta_i} = \mathsf{OT}(0, (\mu, x_i \oplus \Delta_i)) \quad \text{and} \quad \beta^i_{1,\mu,\Delta_i} = \mathsf{OT}(1, (x_i \oplus \Delta_i, \mu)),$$

while $\mathsf{OT}(\sigma, (m_0, m_1))$ denotes a full transcript of a bit OT where the input of the receiver is $\sigma$ and the sender is $(m_0, m_1)$, and we omit $\mathsf{CRS}_{\mathsf{OT}}$ for brevity. Observe that for each $i \in \{1, \ldots, n\}$ of the bit-OTs provided in the CRS, the bit $x_i$ is not revealed in the transcript, as it corresponds to the input of the sender that is not revealed. On the other hand, the randomness and the input of the receiver is given in the clear.

The extractor can now choose any message $\mathbf{m} = (m_1, \ldots, m_n)$ of its choice and any $\Delta = (\Delta_1, \ldots, \Delta_n)$, and for every input $\mathbf{r} = (r_1, \ldots, r_n)$ of the receiver, it can generate a transcript $(\beta^1_{r_1, m_1, \Delta_1}, \ldots, \beta^n_{r_n, m_n, \Delta_n})$, which embeds a masking of $\mathbf{x}$. The extractor rerandomizes this transcript and, if opened by the authority, the extractor can easily recover $\mathbf{x}$.

Finally, as the authority has to produce many transcripts that are correlated with the challenge, it has to prove that it generated all of them as specified. Just as in malicious authority security for NIZK, we double all the new information in the CRS and ask it to prove using a NIWI that one of the branches was generated as specified.

**Re-randomizable Oblivious Transfer.** As mentioned above, to allow this to work, we must ensure that the oblivious transfer transcript is *rerandomizable*. Informally, we say that an OT transcript is rerandomizable if given a transcript of execution of OT, we should be able to transform into another transcript on the same inputs. The rerandomization guarantee is that even given the secret randomness and the input of both parties in the original transcript, a distinguisher receiving a view of one of the parties should not be able to figure out whether the view comes from a new transcript (with the same inputs), or the view was rerandomized. We show that the oblivious transfer protocol of Peikert, Vaikuntanathan, and Waters [31] is a perfect fit for our needs: it is a two-round oblivious transfer in the CRS model, and we augment the protocol with rerandomization procedures.

**Strong Accountability.** The protocol described above works when the malicious authority does not participate actively in the protocol execution. To understand why, we first remark that for a malicious receiver, the authority provides transcripts where the input and randomness of the receiver are in the clear (i.e., provides the complete view of the receiver).

However, in strong accountability, the extractor now talks directly to the adversary. It receives the first message in the protocol from the adversary, and it cannot know the randomness and the private input of the adversary. Matching the correct transcript from the CRS to the one just received by the adversary is impossible, due to the receiver's privacy. Specifically, to embed $x_i$ in position $1 - r_i$, we have to know $r_i$.

On the other hand, this problem does not occur for the malicious sender's case, as it sends the second message in the protocol. In fact, the above-described method already achieves strong accountability against malicious sender.

**Achieving Strong Accountability via Indistinguishability Obfuscation.** We first start with the following idea. As now the transcripts are given "on the fly" to the extractor, we do not even try to embed the secret challenge into the transcript. Instead, we generate an honestly generated transcript using random messages $\mathbf{m}_0, \mathbf{m}_1$ that the extractor itself *does not even know*, and give it also $\mathbf{m}_0 \oplus \mathbf{m}_1 \oplus \mathbf{x}$. Now the bits $(m_1^{1-r_1}, \ldots, m_n^{1-r_n})$ are not known to the sender and the receiver, and thus $\mathbf{x}$ is protected using one-time pad.

To implement this idea, we use indistinguishability obfuscation[2]. The authority obfuscates a circuit $C$ that on input $\mathsf{msg}_R$ generates $\mathsf{msg}_S$ on random inputs $\mathbf{m}_0, \mathbf{m}_1$ and gives also $\mathbf{m}_0 \oplus \mathbf{m}_1 \oplus \mathbf{x}$. Crucially, the evaluator of the circuit (the extractor) does not know $\mathbf{m}_0, \mathbf{m}_1$. The messages $\mathbf{m}_0, \mathbf{m}_1$ are generated using a pseudorandom key chosen by the CRS authority and was hardwired in the circuit. Moreover, the defamation free proof is now rather involved as it requires showing that the hardwired value $\mathbf{x}$ is not revealed even though it is also hardwired in the circuit.

This description is too simplified and is not sound. If the extraction just sends the message $\mathsf{msg}_R$ as received from the obfuscated circuit, the authority can clearly identify it as it had generated the obfuscated circuit. The extractor therefore has to rerandomize the message it receives as output from the circuit. But this still does not suffice, as the authority can also identify that two messages $\mathbf{m}_0, \mathbf{m}_1$ were generated by the circuit, as those are pseudorandom and it knows the key used to generate them. Therefore, we modify the circuit such that given a message $\mathsf{msg}_R$ it generates four different transcripts, i.e.,

$$\beta_{\tau_0, \tau_1} = \mathsf{OT}_2(\mathbf{m}_0 \oplus \tau_0^n, \mathbf{m}_1 \oplus \tau_1^n, \mathsf{msg}_R)$$

---

[2] An indistinguishability obfuscator [5,19] is a compiler that on input circuit $C$ outputs a functionally equivalent circuit $\widehat{C}$. Moreover, it gurantees that the obfuscations of two functionally equivalent circuits (of the same size) are computationally indistinguishable.

for every $\tau_0, \tau_1 \in \{0, 1\}$. This enables the extractor to pick any masking it wishes to $\mathbf{m}_0, \mathbf{m}_1$, similarly to the case of weak accountability. Whenever the authority opens such a message, the extractor recovers $\mathbf{m}_0, \mathbf{m}_1$ and thus also $\mathbf{x}$.

## 2.3    Malicious Authority Security for Two Party Computation

We now focus our attention on general purpose secure two party computation protocols. We first start with an overview that shows that it is not possible to achieve general purpose secure computation protocols for all functions. We then complement our negative result by identifying a class of functionalities (which subsumes oblivious transfer functionalities) for which we can achieve a positive result.

**Impossibility Result.** When it comes to tackling the problem of designing secure computation for general functionalities, we realize that we cannot simultaneously achieve accountability and defamation-free properties. Since the authority recovers the inputs of the honest parties, it has to be the case that the output of the functionality does not trivially leak the inputs, i.e., each party really needs the help of the authority to recover the inputs of the honest parties. When considering functions that do not provide such secrecy, we show that there does not exists a protocol that can address malicious authority security. Luckily, those functions, at least intuitively, are the functions for which secure computation is not necessary to begin with. We formalize this intuition and show that it is impossible to achieve secure two party computation for any functionality, as there exists functions for which achieving malicious authority security is impossible.

Observe also that so far, both in the NIZK example and in oblivious transfer, the functionality hides sufficient information (in NIZK this is the witness $w$; in oblivious transfer these are the choice bits of the receiver and for the sender, those are the bits in the input that were not selected by the receiver). This is very intuitive: If the function is not hiding, then there is no need for help from the authority to recover the private inputs.

**Positive Result.** We therefore restrict our attention to a specific class of functions $\mathcal{F}$ that is guaranteed to have some form of secrecy. We also focus on the asymmetric case where only one of the parties (designated as the receiver) gets an output. Specifically we look at functions in which the inputs of both parties is sufficiently long, and for every input of the receiver, there exists at least $\lambda$ bits in the inputs of the sender that are not meaningful and do not affect the output, where $\lambda$ denotes the security parameter. Interesting functions that are captured in this class are oblivious transfer, private information retrieval, subset sum, and more.

We describe a two-round secure computation protocol for computing all the functions in the family in the CRS model, and then show how to enhance its security to achieve malicious authority security.

The base protocol is a standard two-round two-party secure computation protocol that combines two-round oblivious transfer with garbled circuits. Denoting the sender's input as $\mathbf{x} = (x_1, \ldots, x_\ell)$ and the receiver's input as $\mathbf{y} = (y_1, \ldots, y_\ell)$, the receiver's first message is simply $\mathsf{msg}_R = \mathsf{OT}_1(\mathbf{y})$. The second message of the sender is a bit more involved, and this complication comes to accommodate malicious authority security at a later stage. Given a circuit $C$ for computing the function $F \in \mathcal{F}$, the sender generates a garbled circuit $\mathsf{GC}$ together with the labels $K_{i,0}^{(x)}, K_{i,1}^{(x)}$ for each input of the sender, and labels $K_{i,0}^{(y)}, K_{i,1}^{(y)}$ for each input of the receiver. To receive the output on $\mathbf{x}, \mathbf{y}$, the receiver has to obtain the labels $K_{i,x_i}^{(x)}, K_{i,y_i}^{(y)}$ and output $\mathsf{Eval}(\mathsf{GC}, K_{i,x_i}^{(x)}, K_{i,y_i}^{(y)})$. To do that, the "classic" approach is to instruct the sender to send the following message:

$$\{K_{i,x_i}^{(x)}\}_{i \in [\ell]}, \quad \mathsf{OT}_2\left((K_{i,0}^{(y)})_{i \in [\ell]}, (K_{i,1}^{(y)})_{i \in \ell}, \mathsf{msg}_R\right), \tag{1}$$

i.e., sending the labels that correspond to the sender's input, and the labels correspond to the receiver's input are obtained using the oblivious transfer. For the generation of the transcript by the extractor, it would be easier to send the labels of the sender also in an OT message. We instead send the following message:

$$\mathsf{OT}_2\left((K_{i,0}^{(x)} \parallel K_{i,0}^{(y)})_{i \in [\ell]}, \quad (K_{i,x_i}^{(x)} \parallel K_{i,1}^{(y)})_{i \in \ell}, \mathsf{msg}_R\right). \tag{2}$$

That is, the receiver always receives labels that corresponds to its input, as before. As for the labels that correspond to the input of the sender, in case $y_i = 1$, then the receiver obtains $K_{i,x_i}^{(x)}$, i.e., the "correct" label. On the other hand, in case $y_i = 0$ then the receiver obtains $K_{i,0}^{(x)}$, regardless of what the input of the sender is, i.e., it receives a label that corresponds to $x_i = 0$. This still guarantees correctness as in the case where $y_i = 0$, the input $x_i$ does not affect the output, and the evaluation of the circuit when $x_i = 0$ and $x_i = 1$ gives the same result. Here we rely on the structure of functions that we compute. Together with this $\mathsf{OT}_2$ message, the sender also sends a NIWI proof that it either generated the message correctly as instructed, or it knows some trapdoor in the CRS.

**Enhancing to Malicious Authority Security.** Since the first message in the protocol of the receiver is just $\mathsf{OT}_1(\mathbf{y})$, this case reduces to the case of obtaining malicious authority security in the case of a malicious receiver in oblivious transfer.

For the case of malicious sender, we again follow our general template and the CRS authority chooses a random challenge $\mathbf{r} = (r_1, \ldots, r_\lambda) \in \{0, 1\}^\lambda$, and gives out $f(\mathbf{r})$. The goal now is to find what transcripts to provide such that the extractor will be able to embed $\mathbf{r}$ to the input of the sender. If we would have sent the keys as described in Eq. (1), then to let the extractor choose inputs of the sender as a function of $\mathbf{r}$, the authority would have to give both keys $K_{i,r_i}^{(x)}, K_{i,1-r_i}^{(x)}$. This implies that the extractor will be able to evaluate the function on both values of $r_i$, breaking defamation free. Embedding the changes inside the $\mathsf{OT}_2$ message enables us to maul that message without giving away any information about **r**. Specifically, we always maul the part that the receiver did not ask for, similarly to the way it is done for oblivious transfer.

**Organization.** The remaining of the paper is organized as follows. We provide the necessary preliminaries in Sect. 3. In Sect. 4 we formally define our new notion. In Sect. 5 we provide the construction of NIZK. Due to lack of space, the construction of oblivious transfer and the two-party computation are deferred to the full version of this paper.

# 3  Preliminaries

**Notation and Conventions.** We let $\lambda$ denote the security parameter. We let $[n]$ denote the set $\{1, \ldots, n\}$. We use PPT as shorthand for probabilistic polynomial time. A function $\mu$ is **negligible** if for every positive polynomial $p(\cdot)$ and all sufficiently large $\lambda$'s, it holds that $\mu(\lambda) < 1/p(\lambda)$.

A probability ensemble $X = \{X(a, \lambda)\}_{a \in \{0,1\}^*; \lambda \in \mathbb{N}}$ is an infinite sequence of random variables indexed by $a \in \{0, 1\}^*$ and $\lambda$. In the context of zero knowledge, the value $a$ will represent the parties' inputs and $\lambda$ will represent the security parameter. All parties are assumed to run in time that is polynomial in the security parameter. Two probability ensembles $X = \{X(a, \lambda)\}_{a \in \{0,1\}^*; \lambda \in \mathbb{N}}$, $Y = \{Y(a, \lambda)\}_{a \in \{0,1\}^*; \lambda \in \mathbb{N}}$ are are said to be **computationally indistinguishable**, denoted by $X \approx_c Y$, if for every non-uniform polynomial-time algorithm $D$ there exists a negligible function $\mu$ such that for every $a \in \{0, 1\}^*$ and every $\lambda \in \mathbb{N}$,

$$|\Pr[D(X(a, \lambda)) = 1] - \Pr[D(Y(a, \lambda)) = 1]| \leq \mu(\lambda)$$

We denote by $x \leftarrow D$ a sampling of an instance $x$ according to the distribution $D$.

We denote vectors using a **bold** font, e.g., $\boldsymbol{\alpha} \in \{0, 1\}^n$, when it is usually clear from context what the vector size is. We let $\boldsymbol{\alpha}[i]$ denote the $i$th coordinate of the vector.

## 3.1  Rerandomizable Commitment Scheme

Commitment scheme is a basic tool in cryptographic protocols. Informally, we require the commitment scheme to satisfy two properties, the first is called **perfect binding**, which means that the sets of all commitments to different values are disjoint; for all $x \neq x'$ it holds that $\mathsf{Com}(x) \cap \mathsf{Com}(x') = \emptyset$ where $\mathsf{Com}(x) = \{c \mid \exists r \text{ such that } \mathsf{c} = \mathsf{Com}(x; r)\}$ and $\mathsf{Com}(x') = \{c \mid \exists r \text{ such that } \mathsf{c} = \mathsf{Com}(x'; r)\}$. The second property is **computational hiding**; which means that the commitments to different strings are computationally indistinguishable.

In addition to the perfect binding and computational hiding properties, we also require the commitment scheme to be rerandomizable. The commitment scheme $\mathsf{C} = (\mathsf{Setup}, \mathsf{Com}, \mathsf{Rerand}, f_{\mathsf{com}})$ has the following syntax and properties:

- $\mathsf{p} \leftarrow \mathsf{Setup}(1^\lambda)$: outputs some public parameters $\mathsf{p}$. Let the message space be $\mathcal{M}$ and the commitment space be $\mathcal{C}$.

- $\mathbf{c} \leftarrow \mathsf{Com}(\mathsf{p}, \mathbf{m}; \mathbf{r})$: The algorithm gets $m \in \mathcal{M}$ and outputs a commitment $c \in \mathcal{C}$. The opening of the commitment is simply $r$.
- $\mathbf{c}' \leftarrow \mathsf{Rerand}(\mathsf{p}, \mathbf{c}; \mathbf{s})$: On input parameters $\mathsf{p}$, commitment $\mathbf{c}$ and randomness $s$, Rerand outputs a randomized commitment $\mathbf{c}'$ to the same value. Moreover, we require the existence of an efficient function $f_{\mathsf{com}}$ such that for any randomness $m, r, s$ the following holds:
  - $\mathsf{Rerand}(\mathsf{p}, \mathsf{Com}(\mathsf{p}, m; r); s) = \mathsf{Com}(\mathsf{p}, m, s')$ where $s' = f_{\mathsf{com}}(r, s)$.
    Moreover, it is required that for every fixed $s$, the function $f_{\mathsf{com}}(\cdot, s)$ is bijection, and for every $r$, the function $f_{\mathsf{com}}(r, \cdot)$ is a bijection as well. In particular, this means that given $s', s$ one can find $r$ for which $s' = f_{\mathsf{com}}(r, s)$.

Such a scheme can be constructed from the DLIN assumption, as showed in [26]. It's rerandomization properties were discussed in [2].

## 3.2  Non-Interactive Zero Knowledge (NIZK)

Let $L$ be an $NP$ language and let $R_L$ be its associated relation. For $(x, w) \in R_L$ we sometimes denote $x$ the statement and $w$ its associated witness.

**Definition 3.1.** *Let $L \in$ NP and let $R_L$ be the corresponding NP relation. A triple of algorithms $\Pi = (\mathsf{GenCRS}, \mathsf{Prove}, \mathsf{Verify})$ is called* non interactive zero knowledge *(NIZK) argument for $L$ if it satisfies:*

- **Perfect completeness:** *For all security parameters $\lambda \in \mathbb{N}$ and for all $(x, w) \in R_L$,*

$$\Pr\left[\mathsf{CRS} \leftarrow \mathsf{GenCRS}(1^\lambda);\ \pi \leftarrow \mathsf{Prove}(\mathsf{CRS}, x, w) : \mathsf{Verify}(\mathsf{CRS}, x, \pi) = 1\right] = 1$$

- **Adaptive Soundness:** *For all prover $P^*$, there exists a negligible function $\mu$ such that for all $\lambda$:*

$$\Pr\left[\mathsf{CRS} \leftarrow \mathsf{GenCRS}(1^\lambda); (x, \pi) \leftarrow P^*(\mathsf{CRS}) : \mathsf{Verify}(\mathsf{CRS}, x, \pi) \wedge x \notin L\right] \leq \mu(\lambda)$$

  *When this probability is 0, we say that $\Pi$ is perfectly sound.*
- **Adaptive Zero Knowledge:** *There exists a PPT simulator $\mathcal{S} = (\mathcal{S}_1, \mathcal{S}_2)$ where $\mathcal{S}_1(1^\lambda)$ outputs $(\mathsf{CRS}_\mathcal{S}, \tau)$ and $\mathcal{S}_2(\mathsf{CRS}_\mathcal{S}, \tau, x)$ outputs $\pi_\mathcal{S}$ such that for all non-uniform PPT adversaries $\mathcal{A}$,*

$$\left\{\mathsf{CRS} \leftarrow \mathsf{GenCRS}(1^\lambda) \ : \ \mathcal{A}^{\mathcal{O}_1(\mathsf{CRS}, \cdot, \cdot)}(\mathsf{CRS})\right\}$$

$$\approx_c \left\{(\mathsf{CRS}_\mathcal{S}, \tau) \leftarrow \mathcal{S}_1(1^\lambda) \ : \ \mathcal{A}^{\mathcal{O}_2(\mathsf{CRS}, \tau, \cdot, \cdot)}(\mathsf{CRS}_\mathcal{S})\right\}$$

  *where $\mathcal{O}_1, \mathcal{O}_2$ on input $(x, w)$ first check that $(x, w) \in R_L$, else output $\bot$. Otherwise, $\mathcal{O}_1$ outputs $\mathsf{Prove}(\mathsf{CRS}, x, w)$ and $\mathcal{O}_2$ outputs $\mathcal{S}_2(\mathsf{CRS}_\mathcal{S}, \tau, x)$.*

## 3.3 Non-Interactive Witness Indistinguishability (NIWI)

One building block that we often use in our construction is non-interactive witness indistinguishability. It is useful for our purposes as it does not require a common-reference string. NIWI in the plain model can be constructed based on the DLIN assumption [26] and can be constructed assuming either trapdoor permutations and derandomization assumptions [6].

**Definition 3.2.** *A pair of PPT algorithms* (Prove, Verify) *is a NIWI for an* NP *relation $R_L$ if it satisfies:*

1. **Completeness:** *For every $(x, w) \in R_L$,*

$$\Pr\left[\text{Verify}(x, w) = 1 \ : \ \pi \leftarrow \text{Prove}(x, w)\right] = 1.$$

2. **Soundness:** *There exists a negligible function $\mu$ such that for every $x \notin L$ and $\pi \in \{0, 1\}^*$:*
$$\Pr\left[\text{Verify}(x, \pi) = 1\right] \leq \mu(|x|).$$

3. **Witness indistinguishability:** *For any sequence $\{(x, w_1, w_2) \ : \ w_1, w_2 \in R_L(x)\} \in \mathcal{I}$:*

$$\{\pi_1 : \pi_1 \leftarrow \text{Prove}(x, w_1)\}_{(x, w_1, w_2) \in \mathcal{I}} \approx_c \{\pi_2 : \pi_2 \leftarrow \text{Prove}(x, w_2)\}_{(x, w_1, w_2) \in \mathcal{I}}.$$

# 4 Defining Malicious Authority Security

In this section, we define the notion of malicious authority security for cryptographic protocols defined in the CRS model. There are two aspects to our definition, depending on whether CRS is honestly generated or if its generated by a malicious authority. In the first case, if the CRS is honestly generated, we require that the protocol satisfies the same traditional security requirements described in the literature. In the second case, suppose that the CRS is generated by a malicious authority and specifically, if the malicious authority runs a service that let the adversarial entities, participating in the protocol, to recover the inputs of the honest parties. In this setting, we should be able to implicate the malicious authority of its wrongdoing. Formally speaking, we define an extractor that interacts with the malicious authority and comes up with an evidence $\tau$ that can presented to a Judge, defined by a Judge algorithm, who verifies whether the presented evidence is valid. At the same time, we require the property that no efficiency adversary can present an evidence that can falsely accuse the honest authority of running a service.

We first discuss the definition of malicious authority security for NIZK (Sect. 4.1), and then extend the ideas to general secure two party computation (Sect. 4.2).

## 4.1  Malicious Authority Security for NIZK

We start by defining malicious authority security in the context of non-interactive zero-knowledge systems.

A NIZK system consists of a triplet of algorithms $\Pi$ = (GenCRS, Prove, Verify). In addition, we define a PPT algorithm Judge, which will be necessary for malicious authority security.

- $b \leftarrow$ Judge(CRS, $\tau$) where $b \in \{\text{honest}, \text{corrupted}\}$: The algorithm receives as input the (possibly corrupted) CRS and some transcript $\tau$, and outputs a $b$, indicating whether the $\tau$ proves that the CRS CRS is corrupted or not.

**Definition 4.1.** *Let $L \in$ NP and let $R_L$ be the corresponding NP relation. We say that a NIZK system $\Pi$ = (GenCRS, Prove, Verify, Judge) has malicious authority security with respect to distribution $\mathcal{D}$ if:*

1. *The system $\Pi'$ = (GenCRS, Prove, Verify) is a NIZK proof system for L.*
2. **(Accountability:)** *We say that the NIZK scheme $\Pi$ achieves* accountability *with respect to distribution $\mathcal{D}$ if for all sufficiently large security parameter $\lambda \in \mathbb{N}$, any adversary $\mathcal{A}$, if there exists a non-negligible function $\epsilon_1(\cdot)$ such that*

$$\Pr[\text{Acc.Real}_{\Pi,\mathcal{A},q}(\lambda) = 1] \geq \epsilon_1(\lambda)$$

*then there exists a probabilistic polynomial time oracle-aided algorithm Ext making at most $q$ queries, and a non-negligible function $\epsilon_2(\cdot)$ such that:*

$$\Pr[\text{Acc.Ext}_{\pi,\mathcal{A},\mathcal{E},q}(\lambda) = 1] \geq \epsilon_2(\lambda)$$

*where the random variables $\text{Acc.Real}_{\pi,\mathcal{A},\mathcal{E},q}(\lambda)$ and $\text{Acc.Ext}_{\pi,\mathcal{A},\mathcal{E},q}(\lambda)$ are defined below.*

<u>Acc.Real$_{\Pi,\mathcal{A},q}(\lambda)$:</u>
*The adversary $\mathcal{A}(1^\lambda)$ outputs some* CRS$^*$*, and we repeat the following for $q$ iterations:*
- *$(x_i, w_i) \leftarrow \mathcal{D}$ and then $\pi_i \leftarrow$ Prove(CRS$^*$, $(x_i, w_i)$).*
- *If Verify(CRS$^*$, $x_i, \pi_i$) $\neq 1$ then abort and the output of the experiment is 0.*
- *$\mathcal{A}$ is given $(x_i, \pi_i)$.*
*$\mathcal{A}$ outputs some $(i, x_i', w_i')$ for $i \in [q]$. The output of the experiment is 1 if $x_i = x_i'$ and $R_L(x_i, w_i') = 1$.*

<u>Acc.Ext$_{\pi,\mathcal{A},\mathcal{E},q}(\lambda)$:</u>
*The adversary $\mathcal{A}(1^\lambda)$ outputs some* CRS$^*$*, and we invoke the extractor $\mathcal{E}$ on input (CRS$^*$). We run $q$ iterations in which in each iteration $\mathcal{E}$ outputs some $(x_i, \pi_i)$ that is forwarded to $\mathcal{A}$. After all iterations, $\mathcal{A}$ outputs some $(i, x_i', w_i')$ for some $i \in [q]$. The extractor $\mathcal{E}$ then outputs $\tau$, and the output of the experiment is 1 if Judge(CRS$^*$, $\tau$) = corrupted.*

3. **(Defamation-free:)** *For every* PPT *adversary* $\mathcal{A}$, *there exists a negligible function* $\mu(\cdot)$, *such that for all* $\lambda$:

$$\Pr\left[\mathsf{Judge}(\mathsf{CRS}, \mathcal{A}(\mathsf{CRS})) = \mathsf{corrupted}\right] \leq \mu(\lambda) \ ,$$

*where* $\mathsf{CRS} \leftarrow \mathsf{GenCRS}(1^\lambda)$.

**Discussion.** We would like to highlight the following aspects of the above definition:

- **Maliciously generated** $\mathsf{CRS}^*$: In the above definition, the adversary is the one who is choosing the $\mathsf{CRS}^*$ which might be maliciously generated. Naturally, our aim is to capture the case where the maliciously generated $\mathsf{CRS}^*$ is indistinguishable from an honestly generated one, but the malicious authority has some trapdoors that enable it to extract sensitive information. However, the definition also has to capture the case where $\mathsf{CRS}^*$ might be far from an honestly generated $\mathsf{CRS}$, to the extent where the scheme does not even provide correctness with respect to that $\mathsf{CRS}^*$. In that case, the output of the real experiment is 0, and it is easy to implicate the adversary.
- **Oracle access to the adversary:** We remark that the extractor only has an oracle access to the authority and does not get the code of the authority. Giving the code of the authority to the extractor is unrealistic - in real life, the authority is an actual entity, and so the extractor will not have access to its code. Moreover, we want to explicitly prevent the extractor from "rewinding" the authority, as this is not realistic in the real world.
- **The distribution of the queries of the extractor:** The malicious authority $\mathcal{A}$ is the same in both experiments, and as such its view, as generated by the extractor, should be indistinguishable from the view in the real execution. In particular, this means that the malicious authority should receive from $\mathcal{E}$ in each iteration a pair $(x_i, \pi_i)$ where the marginal distribution on $x_i$ is computationally indistinguishable from the marginal distribution on $x_i$ sampled according to the distribution $(x_i, w_i) \leftarrow \mathcal{D}$ and then setting $\pi_i = \mathsf{Prove}(\mathsf{CRS}^*, x_i, w_i)$.

### 4.2  Malicious Authority for Secure Two-Party Computation

We now extend the above definition to general two-party computation in the CRS model. We again assume that the reader is familiar with the standard (standalone) definition of secure computation, and refer to the full version for a formal definition. We require that the protocol $\Pi$ simulates some functionality $\mathcal{F}$ in the CRS model. Then, we add the malicious authority capability. We first provide the definition and then discuss its changes from the NIZK definition. We define a judgement algorithm similarly to the NIZK case:

- $b \leftarrow \mathsf{Judge}(\mathsf{CRS}, \tau)$: It takes as input a common reference string $\mathsf{CRS}$, a certificate $\tau$ and outputs a bit $b$, indicating whether the common reference string $\mathsf{CRS}$ is corrupted or not.

**Definition 4.2.** *We say that a protocol* $\Pi = (\pi, \mathsf{Judge})$ *has malicious authority security for the functionality* $\mathcal{F}$ *with respect to the distribution* $\mathcal{D}$ *if the following conditions hold:*

1. **Simulation security:** $\pi$ *satisfies simulation security for the functionality* $\mathcal{F}$.
2. **Accountability:** *We say that* $\pi$ *satisfies* security against malicious authority *with respect to the distribution* $\mathcal{D}$ *if the same conditions as in Definition 4.1 hold, where now the random variables* $\mathsf{Acc.Real}_{\pi,\mathcal{A},q}(\lambda)$ *and* $\mathsf{Acc.Ext}_{\pi,\mathcal{A},\mathcal{E},q}(\lambda)$ *are defined as follows.*

$\underline{\mathsf{Acc.Real}_{\pi,\mathcal{A},q}(\lambda):}$

(a) $\mathcal{A}(1^\lambda)$ *is invoked and outputs a common reference string* $\mathsf{CRS}^*$.
(b) *The protocol* $\pi$ *is executed* $q$ *number of times, where in the* $k$th *execution:*
   - *The adversary* $\mathcal{A}$ *chooses some input* $x_i^{(k)}$ *and randomness* $r_i^{(k)}$ *for* $P_i$.
   - *The input* $x_j^{(k)}$ *of the honest party is sampled according to* $\mathcal{D}$.
   - *The protocol is run on these inputs; let* $\mathsf{trans}_k$ *be the resulting transcript.*
   - *The adversary* $\mathcal{A}$ *receives* $\mathsf{trans}_k$.
(c) *The adversary outputs* $(k, x_j^{(k)})$ *for some* $k \in [q]$.
(d) *The output of the experiment is 1 if the input of* $P_j$ *in the* $k$th *execution was* $x_j^{(k)}$.

$\underline{\mathsf{Acc.Ext}_{\pi,\mathcal{A},\mathcal{E},q}(\lambda):}$

(a) $\mathcal{A}(1^\lambda)$ *is invoked and output common reference string* $\mathsf{CRS}^*$.
(b) *The following is run for* $q$ *number of times:*
   - *The adversary outputs some input* $x_i^{(k)}$ *and randomness* $r_i^{(k)}$ *for* $P_i$.
   - *The extractor replies with* $\mathsf{trans}_k$.
(c) *The* $\mathcal{A}$ *receives the* $q$ *queries, it outputs* $\left(k, x_j^{(k)}\right)$ *for some* $k \in [q]$. *The extractor* $\mathcal{E}$ *then outputs* $\tau$.
(d) *The experiment outputs 1 if* $\mathsf{Judge}(\mathsf{CRS}^*, \tau) = \mathsf{corrupted}$.

3. **Defamation free:** *Same as in Definition 4.1.*

**Comparison to the Malicious Authority Security of NIZK.** Malicious authority security of NIZK is a special case of the above definition for two-party computation. In NIZK, the functionality involves a prover and a verifier, where the prover sends the functionality some $(x, w)$. If $(x, w) \in R_L$ then the functionality sends $(x, \mathsf{yes})$ to the verifier and otherwise it sends $(x, \mathsf{no})$. The protocol in the CRS model consists of a single message from the Prover to the Verifier. As we are interested in the privacy of the witness, we focus on the case where the verifier is corrupted. As a result, the input of the honest party (the prover) is chosen according to the distribution $\mathcal{D}$ and the input of the corrupted party (the verifier) is chosen by the adversary, which is empty in the case of NIZK. The adversary receives the transcript and at some point has to come up with the input of the honest party, i.e., extract from $(x_i, \pi_i)$ some $(x_i, w_i)$.

## 4.3    Strong Accountability

So far, we considered adversaries that are passive - while they contribute the input and randomness of the corrupted party in the protocol, the malicious authority expects to get back a full transcript of the protocol, i.e., the adversary is semi-malicious. Here, we model the case where the malicious authority is part of the protocol and colludes with one of the parties. Recall that simulation security is guaranteed only if the CRS authority honestly generated the CRS. If it does not, then we just have accountability as defined next. Defamation free is defined similarly to the previous definitions.

**Definition 4.3.** *We say that $\pi$ satisfies* strong security *against malicious authority with respect to the distribution $\mathcal{D}$ if the conditions as in Definition 4.1 hold, where now the random variables* $\mathsf{StrongAcc.Real}_{\pi,\mathcal{A},q}(\lambda)$ *and* $\mathsf{StrongAcc.Ext}_{\pi,\mathcal{A},\mathcal{E},q}(\lambda)$ *are defined as follows.*

$\mathsf{StrongAcc.Real}_{\pi,\mathcal{A},q}(\lambda)$:

1. $\mathcal{A}(1^\lambda)$ *is invoked and outputs a common reference string* CRS*.
2. *The protocol $\pi$ is executed $q$ number of times where in the $k$th execution:*
   - *The adversary $\mathcal{A}$ participates in the protocol and corrupts party $P_i$.*
   - *The input $x_j^{(k)}$ of the honest party is sampled according to $\mathcal{D}$.*
3. *The adversary outputs $(k, x_j^{(k)})$ for some $k \in [q]$ and $j \neq i$.*
4. *The output of the experiment is 1 if the input of $P_j$ in the $k$th execution was $x_j^{(k)}$.*

$\mathsf{StrongAcc.Ext}_{\pi,\mathcal{A},\mathcal{E},q}(\lambda)$:

1. $\mathcal{A}(1^\lambda)$ *is invoked and outputs a common reference string* CRS*.
2. $\mathcal{A}$ *and $\mathcal{E}$ engage in $q$ executions of a secure computation protocol, where the party $P_i$ is controlled by $\mathcal{A}$.*
3. *After the $q$ executions, $\mathcal{A}$ outputs $(k, x_j^{(k)})$ for some $k \in [q]$ and $j \neq i$. The extractor $\mathcal{E}$ then outputs $\tau$.*
4. *The experiment outputs 1 if* $\mathsf{Judge}(\mathsf{CRS}^*, \tau) = \mathsf{corrupted}$.

## 5    Malicious Authority Security for NIZK

In this section we construct a NIZK satisfying malicious authority security for the language of circuit satisfiability on committed inputs. The instance is a circuit $C : \{0,1\}^m \to \{0,1\}$, some committed values $\mathbf{c} = (c_1, \ldots, c_m)$ and the output $b$. The claim is that $\mathbf{c}$ are commitments of bits $\mathbf{x} = (x_1, \ldots, x_m)$, and that $C(x_1, \ldots, x_m) = b$. Formally:

$$R_{\mathsf{p}}(L) = \Big\{ (C, c_1, \ldots, c_m, b) \mid \exists (x_1, \ldots, x_m) \in \{0,1\}^m,$$

$$(r_1, \ldots, r_m) \in \{0,1\}^{\mathsf{poly}(\lambda)} \text{ s.t. } C(x_1, \ldots, x_m) = b$$

$$\land \ \forall i \in [m] \ c_i = \mathsf{Com}(\mathsf{p}, x_i; r_i) \Big\}$$

The public parameters p associated with the commitment scheme are part of the CRS. We let $\mathcal{C}$ be the set of all circuits that map $m$-bit input to 1 bit output.

**Tools.** The construction is based on the following components:

- A pseudorandom generator $\mathsf{PRG} : \{0,1\}^\lambda \to \{0,1\}^{\mathsf{poly}(\lambda)}$.
- A rerandomizable bit commitment scheme which is perfectly binding and computationally hiding, denoted as $\mathsf{C} = (\mathsf{Setup}, \mathsf{Com}, \mathsf{Rerand})$, where $\mathsf{Setup}(1^\lambda)$ outputs some public parameters p, $\mathbf{c} \leftarrow \mathsf{Com}(\mathsf{p}, m; r)$ where $m$ is a bit and $r$ is the de-commitment. $\mathbf{c}' \leftarrow \mathsf{Rerand}(\mathsf{p}, \mathbf{c}; s)$ takes a commitment $\mathbf{c}$ and randomness $s$ and outputs some commitment $\mathbf{c}'$.
  It holds that $\mathsf{Rerand}(\mathsf{p}, \mathsf{Com}(\mathsf{p}, m; r); s) = \mathsf{Com}(\mathsf{p}, m, s')$ for some $s' = f_{\mathsf{com}}(r, s)$, and for every fixed $s, r$, the two functions $f_{\mathsf{com}}(\cdot, s)$ and $f_{\mathsf{com}}(r, \cdot)$ are bijections.
- Two non-interactive witness-indistinguishable proof systems $(\mathsf{Prove}, \mathsf{Verify})$, denoted as $\Pi_{\mathsf{NIWI}}^{(1)}, \Pi_{\mathsf{NIWI}}^{(2)}$, associated with the languages $L_1$ and $L_2$, respectively, which are defined as follows:
  - **The language $L_1$:**
$$\text{Statement} : \left(\mathsf{p}, (c_0^0, c_1^0), (c_0^1, c_1^1)\right)$$
$$\text{Witness} : \left((r, \mathbf{r}_0^0, \mathbf{r}_1^0), (r, \mathbf{r}_0^1, \mathbf{r}_1^1)\right),$$

  such that *one* of the following conditions hold:
    1. $\mathsf{p} = \mathsf{Setup}(1^\lambda; r)$ and $(c_0^0, c_1^0) = (\mathsf{Com}(\mathsf{p}, 0, \mathbf{r}_0^0), \mathsf{Com}(\mathsf{p}, 1, \mathbf{r}_1^0))$, or
    2. $\mathsf{p} = \mathsf{Setup}(1^\lambda; r)$ and $(c_0^1, c_1^1) = (\mathsf{Com}(\mathsf{p}, 0, \mathbf{r}_0^1), \mathsf{Com}(\mathsf{p}, 1, \mathbf{r}_1^1))$.
  - **The language $L_2$:**
$$\text{Statement} : \left(\mathsf{CRS}, C, \{c_i\}_{i \in [m]}, b\right)$$
$$\text{Witness} : \left(\mathsf{s_{in}}, \{x_i\}_{i \in [m]}, \{r_i\}_{i \in [m]}, \sigma, \{s_i\}_{i \in [m]}\right)$$

  such that *one* of the following conditions hold:
    1. $\mathsf{PRG}(\mathsf{s_{in}}) = \mathsf{s_{out}}$, or,
    2. $C(x_1, \ldots, x_m) = b$, and $\forall i \in [m]$ it holds that $c_i = \mathsf{Com}(\mathsf{p}, x_i; r_i)$.
    3. $C(x_1, \ldots, x_m) = b$, and $\forall i \in [m]$ it holds that $c_i = \mathsf{Rerand}(\mathsf{p}, c_{x_i}^\sigma; s_i)$.
  where $\mathsf{s_{out}}$ and $(c_0^0, c_1^0), (c_1^0, c_1^1)$ are taken from the CRS as given in Step 5 of GenCRS in Construction 5.1.

---

**Construction 5.1 [NIZK with Malicious Authority Security]**

**GenCRS $\left(1^{1^\lambda}\right)$:**

1. Compute $\mathsf{p} \leftarrow \mathsf{Setup}(1^{1^\lambda}; r)$ for a random $r$.
2. Sample $\mathsf{s_{out}} \leftarrow \{0,1\}^{\mathsf{poly}(\lambda)}$
3. For $\sigma = 0$ and $\sigma = 1$, do the following:
   - Compute $(c_0^\sigma, c_1^\sigma) = (\mathsf{Com}(\mathsf{p}, 0, \mathbf{r}_0^\sigma), \mathsf{Com}(\mathsf{p}, 1, \mathbf{r}_1^\sigma))$, for $\mathbf{r}_0^\sigma, \mathbf{r}_1^\sigma \leftarrow \{0,1\}^{\mathsf{poly}(\lambda)}$.

4. Compute $\pi^{(1)} \leftarrow \Pi_{\mathsf{NIWI}}^{(1)}.\mathsf{Prove}\left(\left((c_0^0, c_1^0), (c_0^1, c_1^1)\right), (r, \mathbf{r}_0^0, \mathbf{r}_1^0, \bot, \bot, \bot\right)$.

5. Output $\mathsf{CRS} = \left(\mathsf{p}, \mathsf{s}_{\mathsf{out}}, \ (c_0^0, c_1^0), (c_0^1, c_1^1), \ \pi^{(1)}\right)$.

**Prove$(\mathsf{CRS}, (C, c_1, \ldots, c_m, b), \mathbf{w})$:** On input CRS, circuit $C : \{0, 1\}^m \to \{0, 1\}$, commitments $(c_1, \ldots, c_m)$, output bit $b \in \{0, 1\}$, and witness $\mathbf{w}$ do the following:

1. Parse $\mathbf{w} = ((x_1, \ldots, x_m), (r_1, \ldots, r_m))$ where $x_i \in \{0, 1\}, r_i \in \{0, 1\}^{\mathsf{poly}(\lambda)}$ for all $i \in [m]$, and compute

$$\pi^{(2)} \leftarrow \Pi_{\mathsf{NIWI}}^{(2)}.\mathsf{Prove}\left((\mathsf{CRS}, C, \{c_i\}_{i \in [m]}, b), \ (\bot, \{x_i\}_{i \in [m]}, \{r_i\}_{i \in [m]}, \bot, \bot)\right) \ .$$

Output $\pi = \pi^{(2)}$.

**Verify$(\mathsf{CRS}, (C, \mathbf{c}, b), \pi)$:** On input CRS, instance $(C, \mathbf{c}, b)$, proof $\pi$,

1. Output the decision of $\Pi_{\mathsf{NIWI}}^{(2)}.\mathsf{Verify}((\mathsf{CRS}, C, \mathbf{c}, b), \pi)$.

**Judge$(\mathsf{CRS}^*, \tau)$ :** On input (possibly maliciously generated) $\mathsf{CRS}^*$ and a transcript $\tau$, do the following:

1. Check that the $\mathsf{CRS}^*$ is well formed. That is:
   (a) Parse $\mathsf{CRS}^* = \left(\mathsf{p}, \mathsf{s}_{\mathsf{out}}, \ (c_0^0, c_1^0), (c_0^1, c_1^1), \ \pi^{(1)}\right)$.
   (b) Verify that $\Pi_{\mathsf{NIWI}}^{(1)}.\mathsf{Verify}\left((\mathsf{p}, (c_0^0, c_1^0), (c_0^1, c_1^1)), \pi^{(1)}\right) = 1$.
   If the verification fails then abort and output corrupted.
2. If $\tau = (\mathsf{open}, \sigma, \rho, \mathbf{r})$, where $\sigma, \rho \in \{0, 1\}$ and $\mathbf{r} \in \{0, 1\}^{\mathsf{poly}(\lambda)}$ then: If $c_\rho^\sigma = \mathsf{Com}(\mathsf{p}, \rho; \mathbf{r})$ then output corrupted.
3. If $\tau = (\mathsf{rerandomize}, \sigma, \rho, \mathbf{r}, c, \mathbf{s})$ where $\sigma, \rho \in \{0, 1\}$ and $\mathbf{r}, \mathbf{s} \in \{0, 1\}^{\mathsf{poly}(\lambda)}$, and $c$ is a commitment, then: If $c = \mathsf{Rerand}(\mathsf{p}, c_\rho^\sigma; \mathbf{s})$ and $c = \mathsf{Com}(\mathsf{p}, 1 - \rho; \mathbf{r})$ then output corrupted.
4. Otherwise, output honest.

---

**The Distribution $\mathcal{D}(\mathcal{D}_{\mathcal{C}}, \mathcal{D}_{\mathbf{x}})$.** We define now the family of distributions $\mathcal{D}$ associated with the accountability property. We only place a restriction on the generation of commitments; that is, the commitments need to be honestly generated, i.e., the randomness $r_i$ is uniformly distributed in $\{0, 1\}^{\mathsf{poly}(\lambda)}$.

Formally, for any distribution over $\mathcal{C}$ (recall that $\mathcal{C}$ denotes the set of all circuits with $m$-bit input and 1-bit output) and for any distribution $\mathcal{D}_{\mathbf{x}}$ over $\{0, 1\}^m$, the distribution $\mathcal{D}(\mathcal{D}_{\mathcal{C}}, \mathcal{D}_{\mathbf{x}})$ samples the input and witness as follows:

1. Sample a circuit $C$ according to $\mathcal{D}_{\mathcal{C}}$.
2. Sample the bits $(x_1, \ldots, x_m)$ according to $\mathcal{D}_{\mathbf{x}}$ and evaluate $b = C(x_1, \ldots, x_m)$.
3. For every $i \in [m] \cup \{M\}$ compute $c_i = \mathsf{C.Com}(\mathsf{p}, x_i; r_i)$ for a uniform $r_i$.
4. Output $(C, c_1, \ldots, c_m, b)$ as the instance and $(x_1, \ldots, x_m), (r_1, \ldots, r_m)$ as the witness.

**Theorem 5.2.** *For every $\mathcal{D_C}, \mathcal{D_x}$, Construction 5.1 is a NIZK proof system with malicious authority security with respect to the distribution $\mathcal{D}(\mathcal{D_C}, \mathcal{D_x})$, assuming the security of* PRG, $\Pi_{\mathsf{Comm}}$, $\Pi_{\mathsf{NIWI}}^{(1)}$ *and* $\Pi_{\mathsf{NIWI}}^{(2)}$.

*Proof.* We show completeness, soundness, zero-knowledge, accountability and defamation-free properties.

**Completeness.** The completeness property follows from the completeness property of $\Pi_{\mathsf{NIWI}}^{(2)}$.

**Soundness.** Let CRS $\leftarrow$ GenCRS($1^\lambda$), and fix any PPT adversary (corrupted prover) $\mathcal{A}$ and any $(C, \mathbf{c}, b) \notin R_\mathsf{p}(L)$. We show that the probability that the adversary outputs a proof $\pi$ such that Verify(CRS, $(C, \mathbf{c}, b), \pi) = 1$ is negligible.

We claim that $(\mathsf{s_{out}}, C, \mathbf{c}, b) \notin L_2$. Once we prove this, it then follows from the perfect soundness of $\Pi_{\mathsf{NIWI}}^{(2)}$ that the probability that the adversary outputs a valid proof is negligible.

To show this, it suffices to argue that there does not exist any witness $(\mathsf{s_{in}}, (x_1, \ldots, x_m), (r_1, \ldots, r_m), \sigma, \{s_i\}_{i \in [m]})$ for the instance $(\mathsf{s_{out}}, C, \mathbf{c}, b)$.

1. Firstly, with overwhelming probability it holds that $\mathsf{PRG}(\mathsf{s_{in}}) \neq \mathsf{s_{out}}$ since $\mathsf{s_{out}}$ is sampled uniformly at random.
2. Since $(C, \mathbf{c}, b) \notin R_\mathsf{p}(L)$, it holds that either $C(x_1, \ldots, x_m) \neq b$, or there exists some $i \in [m]$ such that $c_i \neq \mathsf{Com}(\mathsf{p}, x_i; r_i)$.
3. Finally, we argue that there exists some $i \in [m]$ such that $\mathsf{Rerand}(\mathsf{p}, c_{x_i}^\sigma; s_i) \neq c_i$. Observe that if $c_i$ was obtained as a rerandomization of some $c_{x_i}^\sigma$, then still there exists a unique opening to $x_i$ (or no opening at all). This would then violate $(C, \mathbf{c}, b) \notin R_\mathsf{p}(L)$.

**Zero-Knowledge.** We describe a PPT simulator Sim. The simulator Sim runs GenCRS, but compute $\mathsf{s_{out}}$ as an output of PRG where the seed $\mathsf{s_{in}}$ is sampled uniformly at random from $\{0, 1\}^\lambda$ and stores the trapdoor $\mathsf{s_{in}}$. Then, whenever it is given an instance (CRS, $C, \mathbf{c}, b$) it uses $(\mathsf{s_{in}}, \perp, \perp, \perp, \perp)$ as a witness to compute the proof $\pi_{\mathsf{NIWI}}^{(2)}$.

The computational indistinguishability of the real world and the ideal world follows from the witness-indistinguishability of $\Pi_{\mathsf{NIWI}}^{(2)}$, and the pesudorandomness of PRG.

**Accountability.** We first describe the extractor $\mathcal{E}$. On input (possibly maliciously generated) CRS\* generated by the malicious authority, it does the following:

1. It checks that CRS\* is well formed, as described in Step 1 in Judge algorithm. If CRS\* is not well formed, then it halts and outputs $\tau = \perp$.
2. It chooses a branch $\sigma \in \{0, 1\}$ uniformly at random and runs the following for $q$ iterations. For every $j \in [q]$:
   (a) It samples a circuit $C^{(j)} = C$ according to the distribution $\mathcal{D_C}$.
   (b) It samples an input $\mathbf{x}^{(j)} = \mathbf{x} = (x_1, \ldots, x_m)$ according to the distribution $\mathcal{D_x}$.

(c) It evaluates $b^{(j)} = b = C(x_1, \ldots, x_m)$.

(d) For every $i \in [m]$, it generates the commitment $\hat{c}_{x_i} = \mathsf{C.Rerand}(\mathsf{p}, c_{x_i}^{\sigma}, s_i)$ for a uniformly random $s_i^{(j)} = s_i \in \{0,1\}^{\mathsf{poly}(\lambda)}$.

Let $\hat{\mathbf{c}}^{(j)} = \hat{\mathbf{c}} = (\hat{c}_{x_1}, \ldots, \hat{c}_{x_m})$ be the sequence of all commitments.

(e) It generates $\pi = \pi^{(2)} \leftarrow \Pi_{\mathsf{NIWI}}^{(2)}.\mathsf{Prove}\left((\mathsf{CRS}, C, \hat{\mathbf{c}}, b), (\perp, \perp, \perp, \sigma, \{s_i\}_{i \in [m]})\right)$.

(f) It sends $((C, \hat{\mathbf{c}}, b), \pi)$ to the malicious authority.

3. After $q$ iterations, the malicious authority might reply with some input $(j, (C, \hat{\mathbf{c}}, b))$ with witness $\{x_i\}_{i \in [m]}$ and $\{r_i\}_{i \in [m]}$ for which $\hat{c}_i = \mathsf{Com}(\mathsf{p}, x_i; r_i)$ for all $i \in [m]$ and $C(x_1, \ldots, x_m) = b$.

(a) If $(x_1, r_1)$ satisfies $c_{x_1}^{\sigma} = \mathsf{Com}(\mathsf{p}, x_1; r_1)$ where $c_{x_1}^{\sigma}$ is taken from the CRS, then output $\tau = (\mathsf{open}, \sigma, x_1, r_1)$.

(b) Otherwise, if it holds that $c' := \mathsf{Rerand}(\mathsf{p}, c_{1-x_1}^{\sigma}, s_1^{(j)}) = \mathsf{Com}(\mathsf{p}, x_1, r_1)$, output $\tau = (\mathsf{rerandomize}, \sigma, x_1, \mathbf{r}, c', s_1^{(j)})$.

We claim that if the extractor chooses $\sigma$ to be the "correct branch", i.e., the one for which $\pi^{(1)}$ from the CRS is correct, then the view of the malicious authority is indistinguishable between Acc.Real and Acc.Ext. We then claim that the extractor always outputs a transcript that is accepted by Judge if the malicious authority outputs a valid witness $(j, (C, \hat{\mathbf{c}}, b))$ for the $j \in [q]$ iteration. To show this, we need to argue that the view of the authority when interacting with the real parties is computationally indistinguishable from the view of the authority when interacting with the extractor.

**Indistinguishability of Views.** Consider the following hybrids:

- $\mathbf{H}_1$: We change the way CRS is generated, such that $\mathsf{s}_{\mathsf{out}}$ is an output of PRG where the seed $\mathsf{s}_{\mathsf{in}}$ is sampled uniformly at random from $\{0,1\}^{\lambda}$. The output of the hybrid is 1 if the adversary succeeds to output $\pi$ for which $\mathsf{Verify}(\mathsf{CRS}, (C, \mathbf{c}, b), \pi) = 1$.

- $\mathbf{H}_2$: This is the experiment $\mathsf{Acc.Real}_{\Pi, \mathcal{A}, q}(\lambda)$.

- $\mathbf{H}_3$: This hybrid is inefficient. The prover in the real experiment works as follows: It samples $C \leftarrow \mathcal{D}_C$ and $\mathbf{x} \leftarrow \mathcal{D}_{\mathbf{x}}$. Then, instead of directly committing to the $\mathbf{x} = (x_1, \ldots, x_m)$ it takes $c_{x_1}^{\sigma}, \ldots, c_{x_m}^{\sigma}$. It then rerandomizes all the commitments to obtain rerandomized commitments $\hat{c}_{x_1}^{\sigma}, \ldots, \hat{c}_{x_m}^{\sigma}$. It then runs in exponential time and determines the randomness $\{r_i\}_{i \in [m]}$ such that $\hat{c}_{x_i}^{\sigma} = \mathsf{Com}(\mathsf{p}, x_i; r_i)$. It uses $(\perp, x, \{r_i\}_{i \in [m]}, \perp, \perp)$ to compute the proof $\pi_{\mathsf{NIWI}}^{(2)}$ for the instance $(C, \tilde{\mathbf{c}}, b)$, where $b = C(x)$. The rest of the hybrid is the same as before.

- $\mathbf{H}_4$: This is $\mathsf{Acc.Ext}_{\Pi, \mathcal{A}, q}(\lambda)$ with branch $\sigma$.

From the security of PRG, it follows that the view of the adversary in $\mathbf{H}_1$ is computational indistinguishale from the real view. The view of the adversary in $\mathbf{H}_2$ and $\mathbf{H}_3$ is identical, which follows from the fact that the rerandomization procedure of the commitment scheme generates commitments that are identically distributed to fresh commitments.

The two hybrids $\mathbf{H}_3$ and $\mathbf{H}_4$ are computationally indistinguishable, follows from the witness-indistinguishability of $\Pi_{\mathsf{NIWI}}^{(2)}$. We consider a non-uniform reduction which gets as input the CRS and the decommitments of the commitments in the CRS as non-uniform advice. Using this, the (efficient) reduction computes and sends the instance $(C, \hat{c}, b)$, where $b = C(x)$, along with two witnesses to the challenger of the WI game. The challenger then sends the proof $\pi_{\mathsf{NIWI}}^{(2)}$ to the reduction, who forwards it to the adversary. If the adversary can distinguish the hybrids $\mathbf{H}_3$ and $\mathbf{H}_4$ with non-negligible probability then the reduction can break the witness-indistinguishability property with non-negligible probability, a contradiction.

Once the authority gives a witness $\{x_i\}_{i \in [m]}$ and $\{r_i\}_{i \in [m]}$ for the $j$th execution, from inspection it is easy to see that the extractor outputs a transcript that implicates the authority. Thus, if the authority succeeds in Acc.Real with some non-negligible probability $\epsilon_1(\lambda)$ then the extractor succeeds with probability negligibly close to $\epsilon_1(\lambda)/2$, where the loss occurs from guessing $\sigma$ and the indistinguishability of the proof $\pi$.

**Defamation-Free.** For every PPT adversary $\mathcal{A}$ there exists a negligible function $\mu(\cdot)$ such that: $\Pr[\mathsf{Judge}(\mathsf{CRS}, \mathcal{A}(\mathsf{CRS})) = \mathsf{corrupted}] \le \mu(\lambda)$, where CRS $\leftarrow$ GenCRS$(1^\lambda)$. First, since CRS is honestly generated, it always passes the verification of Step 1 in the Judge algorithm. We now show that for every $\sigma \in \{0, 1\}$, no PPT adversary can output $\tau = (\mathsf{open}, \sigma, \cdot)$ or $\tau = \mathsf{rerandomize}, \sigma, \cdot, \cdot, \cdot)$ with non-negligible probability. For that, fix $\sigma \in \{0, 1\}$, and consider the following sequence of hybrid experiments:

1. $\mathbf{H}_1$: In this hybrid, the adversary receives CRS $\leftarrow$ GenCRS$(1^\lambda)$ and the output of the hybrid is 1 if it outputs $\tau = (\mathsf{open}, \sigma, \cdot\cdot)$ or $\tau = (\mathsf{rerandomize}, \sigma, \cdot, \cdot, \cdot, \cdot)$ that is accepted by Judge.
2. $\mathbf{H}_2$: We modify the way CRS is generated, such that for proving the instance $((c_0^0, c_1^0), (c_0^1, c_1^1))$ using $\Pi_{\mathsf{NIWI}}^{(1)}$, we use the witness of $1 - \sigma$. That is,
   (a) If $\sigma = 0$ we prove $\pi^{(1)}$ using the witness $(\bot, \bot, \bot, r, \mathbf{r}_0^1, \mathbf{r}_1^1)$.
   (b) If $\sigma = 1$ we prove $\pi^{(1)}$ using the witness $(r, \mathbf{r}_0^0, \mathbf{r}_1^0, \bot, \bot)$.

Clearly, the views of the adversary in both the experiments are computationally indistinguishable from the witness-indistinguishability property of $\Pi_{\mathsf{NIWI}}^{(1)}$. Next, we claim that the probability that the adversary outputs an accepted transcript in $\mathbf{H}_2$ is negligible. At this point, the proof $\pi^{(1)}$ is independent of the randomness used to create the commitments $c_0^\sigma, c_1^\sigma$. Outputting $\tau = (\mathsf{open}, \sigma, \rho, \mathbf{r})$ is equivalent to violating the hiding property of the commitment scheme. Outputting $\tau = (\mathsf{rerandomize}, \sigma, \cdot, \cdot, \cdot, \cdot)$ is impossible in case p is perfectly binding. In case p just satisfies computational hiding, coming up with the rerandomization is equivalent to violating the (computationally infeasible) "rerandomize and open" property, as we formalize in the full version.

# 6  Malicious Authority Security for Oblivious Transfer

## 6.1  Oblivious Transfer with Weak Accountability

Due to lack of space, we just state our results and refer the reader to the full version for further details. Our construction is based on a rerandomizable oblivious transfer, which intuitively mean that a transcript of a given execution of two-round oblivious transfer can be re-randomized, i.e., look like a fresh execution on the same inputs. We show that [31] achieves this notion. We denote by $n \times$ OT the functionality of $n$ parallel instance of 1-out-of-2 bit OT.

**Theorem 6.1.** *Assuming one-way functions, non-interactive witness indistinguishability proof system, and two-round rerandomizable oblivious transfer for bit OT, there exists a construction of two-round $n \times$ OT with (weak) malicious authority with respect to the uniform distribution over the inputs for any $n \in \Omega(\lambda)$, where $\lambda$ is the security parameter.*

## 6.2  Oblivious Transfer with Strong Accountability

Moreover, we show that strong accountability is possible but we need stronger assumptions:

**Theorem 6.2.** *Assuming the security of one-way function, indistinguishability obfuscator, non-interactive witness-indistinguishability proof system, and the existence of a rerandomizable oblivious transfer, there exists a construction that achieves **strong** malicious authority security for the functionality $n \times$ OT with respect to the uniform distribution over the inputs for any $n \in \Omega(\lambda)$, where $\lambda$ is the security parameter.*

# 7  Malicious Authority Secure for Secure 2PC

In this section, we investigate malicious authority security for secure two party computation. Due to lack of space, we just give the statements of the results and refer the reader to the full version for more details.

**Lemma 7.1.** *There exists a two-party functionality $F$ such that for any secure computation protocol for $F$ between parties $P_1$ and $P_2$, the following events cannot simultaneously hold:*

- *$P_i$, for some $i \in \{1, 2\}$ receives the output of the protocol and,*
- *The following properties are satisfied: (i) defamation-free property and, (ii) accountability holds when the malicious authority corrupts the party $P_i$.*

**Positive Result - the Class of Functions.** For $\ell > \lambda$, we let $\mathcal{F}$ be a family of all functions over $F : \{0,1\}^\ell \times \mathcal{Y} \to \{0,1\}^\ell$ such that

$$F\left((x_1, \ldots, x_\ell), (y_1, \ldots, y_\ell)\right) = g\left(\{x_i\}_{y_i=1}\right),$$

for some function $g$. Namely, whenever $y_i = 0$, then the $x_i$ does not affect the output. The set $\mathcal{Y} \subset \{0,1\}^\ell$ contains all elements with hamming weight at most $\ell - \lambda$.

**Theorem 7.2.** *For every function $F \in \mathcal{F}$, there exists a construction that achieves (weak) malicious authority security with respect to the uniform distribution over the inputs, assuming the existence of maliciously secure rerandomizable oblivious transfer in the CRS model, non-interactive witness-indistinguishability proofs, and pseudorandom generator.*

**Acknowledgements.** The authors thank the anonymous reviewers of EUROCRYPT 2021 for many helpful comments.

Gilad Asharov is sponsored by the Israel Science Foundation (grant No. 2439/20), and by the BIU Center for Research in Applied Cryptography and Cyber Security in conjunction with the Israel National Cyber Bureau in the Prime Minister's Office. This project has received funding from the European Union's Horizon 2020 research and innovation programme under the Marie Skłodowska-Curie grant agreement No. 891234. Hila Dahari is a fellow of the Ariane de Rothschild Women Doctoral Program and supported in part by grants from the Israel Science Foundation (No. 950/15 and 2686/20) and by the Simons Foundation Collaboration on the Theory of Algorithmic Fairness. Vipul Goyal is supported in part by the NSF award 1916939, DARPA SIEVE program, a gift from Ripple, a DoE NETL award, a JP Morgan Faculty Fellowship, a PNC center for financial services innovation award, and a Cylab seed funding award.

# References

1. Ananth, P., Choudhuri, A.R., Jain, A.: A new approach to round-optimal secure multiparty computation. In: Katz, J., Shacham, H. (eds.) CRYPTO 2017. LNCS, vol. 10401, pp. 468–499. Springer, Cham (2017). https://doi.org/10.1007/978-3-319-63688-7_16
2. Ananth, P., Deshpande, A., Kalai, Y.T., Lysyanskaya, A.: Fully homomorphic NIZK and NIWI proofs. In: Hofheinz, D., Rosen, A. (eds.) TCC 2019. LNCS, vol. 11892, pp. 356–385. Springer, Cham (2019). https://doi.org/10.1007/978-3-030-36033-7_14
3. Asharov, G., Orlandi, C.: Calling out cheaters: covert security with public verifiability. In: Wang, X., Sako, K. (eds.) ASIACRYPT 2012. LNCS, vol. 7658, pp. 681–698. Springer, Heidelberg (2012). https://doi.org/10.1007/978-3-642-34961-4_41
4. Badrinarayanan, S., Goyal, V., Jain, A., Kalai, Y.T., Khurana, D., Sahai, A.: Promise zero knowledge and its applications to round optimal MPC. In: Shacham, H., Boldyreva, A. (eds.) CRYPTO 2018. LNCS, vol. 10992, pp. 459–487. Springer, Cham (2018). https://doi.org/10.1007/978-3-319-96881-0_16
5. Barak, B., et al.: On the (im)possibility of obfuscating programs. In: Kilian, J. (ed.) CRYPTO 2001. LNCS, vol. 2139, pp. 1–18. Springer, Heidelberg (2001). https://doi.org/10.1007/3-540-44647-8_1
6. Barak, B., Ong, S.J., Vadhan, S.: Derandomization in cryptography. In: Boneh, D. (ed.) CRYPTO 2003. LNCS, vol. 2729, pp. 299–315. Springer, Heidelberg (2003). https://doi.org/10.1007/978-3-540-45146-4_18
7. Bellare, M., Fuchsbauer, G., Scafuro, A.: NIZKs with an untrusted CRS: security in the face of parameter subversion. In: Cheon, J.H., Takagi, T. (eds.) ASIACRYPT 2016. LNCS, vol. 10032, pp. 777–804. Springer, Heidelberg (2016). https://doi.org/10.1007/978-3-662-53890-6_26

8. Benhamouda, F., Lin, H.: k-round multiparty computation from k-round oblivious transfer via garbled interactive circuits. In: Nielsen, J.B., Rijmen, V. (eds.) EURO-CRYPT 2018. LNCS, vol. 10821, pp. 500–532. Springer, Cham (2018). https://doi.org/10.1007/978-3-319-78375-8_17

9. Blum, M., Feldman, P., Micali, S.: Non-interactive zero-knowledge and its applications (extended abstract). In: Symposium on Theory of Computing (STOC), pp. 103–112. ACM (1988)

10. Brakerski, Z., Halevi, S., Polychroniadou, A.: Four round secure computation without setup. In: Kalai, Y., Reyzin, L. (eds.) TCC 2017. LNCS, vol. 10677, pp. 645–677. Springer, Cham (2017). https://doi.org/10.1007/978-3-319-70500-2_22

11. Canetti, R., Fischlin, M.: Universally composable commitments. In: Kilian, J. (ed.) CRYPTO 2001. LNCS, vol. 2139, pp. 19–40. Springer, Heidelberg (2001). https://doi.org/10.1007/3-540-44647-8_2

12. Canetti, R., Kushilevitz, E., Lindell, Y.: On the limitations of universally composable two-party computation without set-up assumptions. In: Biham, E. (ed.) EUROCRYPT 2003. LNCS, vol. 2656, pp. 68–86. Springer, Heidelberg (2003). https://doi.org/10.1007/3-540-39200-9_5

13. Canetti, R., Lindell, Y., Ostrovsky, R., Sahai, A.: Universally composable two-party and multi-party secure computation. In: ACM Symposium on Theory of Computing (STOC), pp. 494–503 (2002)

14. Chor, B., Fiat, A., Naor, M.: Tracing traitors. In: Desmedt, Y.G. (ed.) CRYPTO 1994. LNCS, vol. 839, pp. 257–270. Springer, Heidelberg (1994). https://doi.org/10.1007/3-540-48658-5_25

15. Choudhuri, A.R., Ciampi, M., Goyal, V., Jain, A., Ostrovsky, R.: Round optimal secure multiparty computation from minimal assumptions. In: Theory of Cryptography - TCC 2020 (2020, to appear)

16. Dwork, C., Naor, M.: Zaps and their applications. In: Foundations of Computer Science, FOCS 2000, pp. 283–293 (2000)

17. Feige, U., Lapidot, D., Shamir, A.: Multiple noninteractive zero knowledge proofs under general assumptions. SIAM J. Comput. 29, 1–28 (1999)

18. Fuchsbauer, G.: Subversion-zero-knowledge SNARKs. In: Abdalla, M., Dahab, R. (eds.) PKC 2018. LNCS, vol. 10769, pp. 315–347. Springer, Cham (2018). https://doi.org/10.1007/978-3-319-76578-5_11

19. Garg, S., Gentry, C., Halevi, S., Raykova, M., Sahai, A., Waters, B.: Candidate indistinguishability obfuscation and functional encryption for all circuits. SIAM J. Comput. 45(3), 882–929 (2016)

20. Garg, S., Goyal, V., Jain, A., Sahai, A.: Bringing people of different beliefs together to Do UC. In: Ishai, Y. (ed.) TCC 2011. LNCS, vol. 6597, pp. 311–328. Springer, Heidelberg (2011). https://doi.org/10.1007/978-3-642-19571-6_19

21. Garg, S., Srinivasan, A.: Two-round multiparty secure computation from minimal assumptions. In: Nielsen, J.B., Rijmen, V. (eds.) EUROCRYPT 2018. LNCS, vol. 10821, pp. 468–499. Springer, Cham (2018). https://doi.org/10.1007/978-3-319-78375-8_16

22. Goldreich, O., Oren, Y.: Definitions and properties of zero-knowledge proof systems. J. Cryptol. 7, 1–32 (1994)

23. Goyal, V.: Reducing trust in the PKG in identity based cryptosystems. In: Menezes, A. (ed.) CRYPTO 2007. LNCS, vol. 4622, pp. 430–447. Springer, Heidelberg (2007). https://doi.org/10.1007/978-3-540-74143-5_24

24. Goyal, V., Katz, J.: Universally composable multi-party computation with an unreliable common reference string. In: Canetti, R. (ed.) TCC 2008. LNCS, vol. 4948, pp. 142–154. Springer, Heidelberg (2008). https://doi.org/10.1007/978-3-540-78524-8_9

25. Groth, J., Ostrovsky, R.: Cryptography in the multi-string model. In: Menezes, A. (ed.) CRYPTO 2007. LNCS, vol. 4622, pp. 323–341. Springer, Heidelberg (2007). https://doi.org/10.1007/978-3-540-74143-5_18

26. Groth, J., Ostrovsky, R., Sahai, A.: Non-interactive zaps and new techniques for NIZK. In: Dwork, C. (ed.) CRYPTO 2006. LNCS, vol. 4117, pp. 97–111. Springer, Heidelberg (2006). https://doi.org/10.1007/11818175_6

27. Halevi, S., Hazay, C., Polychroniadou, A., Venkitasubramaniam, M.: Round-optimal secure multi-party computation. In: Shacham, H., Boldyreva, A. (eds.) CRYPTO 2018. LNCS, vol. 10992, pp. 488–520. Springer, Cham (2018). https://doi.org/10.1007/978-3-319-96881-0_17

28. Katz, J., Ostrovsky, R.: Round-optimal secure two-party computation. In: Franklin, M. (ed.) CRYPTO 2004. LNCS, vol. 3152, pp. 335–354. Springer, Heidelberg (2004). https://doi.org/10.1007/978-3-540-28628-8_21

29. Mukherjee, P., Wichs, D.: Two round multiparty computation via multi-key FHE. In: Fischlin, M., Coron, J.-S. (eds.) EUROCRYPT 2016. LNCS, vol. 9666, pp. 735–763. Springer, Heidelberg (2016). https://doi.org/10.1007/978-3-662-49896-5_26

30. Pass, R.: Simulation in quasi-polynomial time, and its application to protocol composition. In: Biham, E. (ed.) EUROCRYPT 2003. LNCS, vol. 2656, pp. 160–176. Springer, Heidelberg (2003). https://doi.org/10.1007/3-540-39200-9_10

31. Peikert, C., Vaikuntanathan, V., Waters, B.: A framework for efficient and composable oblivious transfer. In: Wagner, D. (ed.) CRYPTO 2008. LNCS, vol. 5157, pp. 554–571. Springer, Heidelberg (2008). https://doi.org/10.1007/978-3-540-85174-5_31

# Property-Preserving Hash Functions and ORAM

# Robust Property-Preserving Hash Functions for Hamming Distance and More

Nils Fleischhacker[1]([envelope]) and Mark Simkin[2]

[1] Ruhr University Bochum, Bochum, Germany
`mail@nilsfleischhacker.de`
[2] Aarhus University, Aarhus, Denmark

**Abstract.** Robust property-preserving hash (PPH) functions, recently introduced by Boyle, Lavigne, and Vaikuntanathan [ITCS 2019], compress large inputs $x$ and $y$ into short digests $h(x)$ and $h(y)$ in a manner that allows for computing a predicate $P$ on $x$ and $y$ while only having access to the corresponding hash values. In contrast to locality-sensitive hash functions, a robust PPH function guarantees to correctly evaluate a predicate on $h(x)$ and $h(y)$ even if $x$ and $y$ are chosen adversarially *after* seeing $h$.

Our main result is a robust PPH function for the exact hamming distance predicate

$$\mathsf{HAM}^t(x,y) = \begin{cases} 1 & \text{if } d(x,y) \geq t \\ 0 & \text{Otherwise} \end{cases}$$

where $d(x,y)$ is the hamming-distance between $x$ and $y$. Our PPH function compresses $n$-bit strings into $\mathcal{O}(t\lambda)$-bit digests, where $\lambda$ is the security parameter. The construction is based on the q-strong bilinear discrete logarithm assumption.

Along the way, we construct a robust PPH function for the set intersection predicate

$$\mathsf{INT}^t(X,Y) = \begin{cases} 1 & \text{if } |X \cap Y| > n - t \\ 0 & \text{Otherwise} \end{cases}$$

which compresses sets $X$ and $Y$ of size $n$ with elements from some arbitrary universe $U$ into $\mathcal{O}(t\lambda)$-bit long digests. This PPH function may be of independent interest. We present an almost matching lower bound of $\Omega(t \log t)$ on the digest size of any PPH function for the intersection predicate, which indicates that our compression rate is close to optimal. Finally, we also show how to extend our PPH function for the intersection predicate to more than two inputs.

N. Fleischhacker—Funded by the Deutsche Forschungsgemeinschaft (DFG, German Research Foundation) under Germany's Excellence Strategy - EXC 2092 CASA - 390781972.

M. Simkin—Supported by a DFF Sapere Aude Grant 9064-00068B.

A. Canteaut and F.-X. Standaert (Eds.): EUROCRYPT 2021, LNCS 12698, pp. 311–337, 2021.
https://doi.org/10.1007/978-3-030-77883-5_11

# 1   Introduction

Compressing data while maintaining some of its properties is one of the most fundamental tasks in computer science. Approximate set membership data structures, such as Bloom Filters [2] or Cuckoo Hashing [16], allow for compressing large data sets into small digests that can afterwards be used to test whether some element $x$ was a member of the original data set or not. Locality-sensitive hash functions [11] allow for compressing data points $x$ and $y$ independently into short digests $h(x)$ and $h(y)$ such that the hash values can be used to check whether the original points were close or far apart according to some metric like the euclidean or angular distance. Streaming algorithms [14] enable an observer of a data stream to estimate certain statistics about the stream while using only a small amount of local storage. All of these algorithms have two things in common. They are all randomized and thus may fail on certain inputs with some, usually small, probability and they all assume that the inputs are chosen *independently* of the random coins used by the data structure.

Over the past years, a series of works [1,4,5,10,13,15] have investigated such data structures in the presence of adversarial inputs that are chosen *after* seeing the random coins of the data structure. Naor and Yogev [15], for instance, study the robustness of Bloom filters in the presence of an adversary that aims to find an input set $X$ and a value $z \notin X$ such that the approximate membership test on a digest of $X$ and the value $z$ incorrectly reports that $z \in X$. Clayton, Patton, and Shrimpton [5] extend the work of Naor and Yogev to other data structures such as counting Bloom filters and count-min sketches. Boyle, LaVigne and Vaikuntanathan [4], referenced as BLV hereafter, initiated the study of *robust property-preserving hash (PPH) functions*, which, in a nutshell, combine the security guarantees of collision-resistant and the functionality of locality-sensitive hash functions.

A bit more formally, a PPH function $h : X \to Y$ with evaluation algorithm Eval $: Y \times Y \to \{0,1\}$ for some predicate $P : X \times X \to \{0,1\}$ is said to be robust, if no PPT adversary $\mathcal{A}$, who is given $(h, \mathsf{Eval})$, can produce an output $(x,y)$ such that $P(x,y) \neq \mathsf{Eval}(h(x), h(y))$. The authors construct such a hash function, which compresses $n$-bit inputs by some small constant factor, for the gap-hamming predicate

$$\mathsf{GAP\text{-}HAM}_\epsilon^t(x,y) = \begin{cases} 1 & \text{if } d(x,y) \geq t(1+\epsilon) \\ 0 & \text{if } d(x,y) \leq t(1-\epsilon) \\ \star & \text{Otherwise} \end{cases}$$

for $t = \mathcal{O}(n/\log n)$ and an arbitrary small, but constant, non-zero value $\epsilon$, where $d$ is the hamming distance. This means that the Eval function can only guarantee that the Hamming distance is *at most* $t(1+\epsilon)$ for output 0 or *at least* $t(1-\epsilon)$ for output 1. In the gap between the two values either output is possible and we get no correctness or security guarantees. It would therefore be desirable to close this gap, i.e., to obtain a construction for $\epsilon = 0$, which was left open by the work of BLV. In addition to their positive results, BLV also proved that a compressing PPH function for $\epsilon = 0$ and $t = n/2$ cannot exist.

## 1.1   Our Contribution

In this work, we construct a robust PPH function for the exact hamming distance predicate, which essentially corresponds to $\mathsf{GAP\text{-}HAM}_\epsilon^t(x, y)$ with $\epsilon = 0$, for $t \leq n/c\lambda$ for some small constant $c > 1$. We also show how to generalize our result to strings over large alphabets, e.g. alphanumeric sequences, and the corresponding generalized hamming distance, which counts the number of positions in which the strings differ.[1] Our construction is based on the q-strong bilinear discrete logarithm assumption in pairing-friendly groups and compresses $n$-bit inputs into $\mathcal{O}(t\lambda)$-bit hash values. Our results are not covered by the impossibility results of BLV, since we restrict $t$ to be sufficiently small in comparison to the input bit-length $n$.

Along the way, we consider the symmetric set difference predicate, which takes two sets $X$ and $Y$ of size $n$ from some universe $U$ as input and checks whether $|(X \setminus Y) \cup (Y \setminus X)| < t$. We construct a PPH function for this predicate from the same assumptions and with the same $\mathcal{O}(t\lambda)$-bit long hash values as above. Here it is insightful to note that for two-input predicates, the symmetric set difference and an intersection predicate with a threshold on the minimum intersection size are equivalent.

For the symmetric set difference and the intersection predicate, we show that any PPH function has to have $\Omega(t \log t)$-bit long hash values, which indicates that our hash functions are close to optimal in terms of compression factor.

Finally, we show how to construct PPH functions for the intersection predicate with more than two inputs.

## 1.2   Technical Overview

We will start our overview by constructing a robust PPH function for the two-input symmetric set difference predicate. Obtaining our PPH function for the exact hamming distance predicate will only require one additional step of encoding the input bit strings into appropriate sets.

The starting point of our work is a simple, yet beautiful, observation about polynomials and rational function interpolation made by Minsky et al. [12][2]. Consider sets $A = \{a_1, \ldots, a_n\}$ and $B = \{b_1, \ldots, b_n\}$ which are encoded into the roots of some polynomials $u(x) = \prod_{i=0}^n (x - a_i)$ and $v(x) = \prod_{i=0}^n (x - b_i)$ over

---

[1] Note that encoding strings from a large alphabet into bit strings and then using our construction for binary inputs does not work, since the hamming distance of the encoded strings has no meaningful interpretation.

[2] The work of Minsky et al. has recently found other applications in the context of cryptography in the domain of communication efficient private set intersection protocols [7].

some finite field $\mathbb{F}$, and consider the rational function[3]

$$w(x) := \frac{u(x)}{v(x)} = \frac{\prod_{a_i \in A \setminus B}(x - a_i)}{\prod_{b_j \in B \setminus A}(x - b_j)}.$$

The main observation behind the work of Minsky et al. was the following: the larger the intersection of $A$ and $B$, the smaller their symmetric set difference, the more roots of the polynomials $u(x)$ and $v(x)$ "cancel out". Furthermore, the smaller the degrees of the remaining polynomials in the numerator and denominator, the fewer evaluation points are needed for correctly interpolating $w(x)$. More precisely, the degree each polynomial, once they have been reduced to lowest terms, is exactly $|A \setminus B| = |B \setminus A|$, thus if the symmetric set difference is at most $2t$ large, then $w(x)$ can be correctly interpolated from $\ell$ evaluation points of $w(x)$, where $\ell \in \mathcal{O}(t)$. Importantly for us, $\ell$ can be chosen such that $\ell - 1$ points are not sufficient for correctly interpolating the rational function if $|(A \setminus B) \cup (B \setminus A)| > 2t$.

As a first attempt towards compressing sets $A$ and $B$ of size $n$ into appropriate hash values, one might want to compute $(u(\alpha_1), \ldots, u(\alpha_\ell))$ and $(v(\alpha_1), \ldots, v(\alpha_\ell))$, where $\alpha_1, \ldots, \alpha_\ell$ are some distinct publicly known fixed evaluation points. Given these two hash values, the evaluation algorithm Eval could now compute $w(\alpha_i) := u(\alpha_i)/v(\alpha_i)$ for $i \in [n]$ and attempt to interpolate a rational function $\hat{w}(x)$ using these points. Recall that $w(x) = \hat{w}(x)$ if $|(A \setminus B) \cup (B \setminus A)| \leq 2t$ and $w(x) \neq \hat{w}(x)$ otherwise.

At this point we are left with the task of checking whether the interpolated function is the correct one. Ideally, we would like to simply evaluate the polynomials $u(x)$ and $v(x)$ on some random point $r$ and check whether $u(r)/v(r) = \hat{w}(r)$. Over a large enough field and using a uniformly and independently sampled random value $r$ this allows us to efficiently test the equality of two (rational) functions with only negligible error. Unfortunately, since we are designing a hash function, rather than an interactive protocol, $u(r)$ and $v(r)$ would need to be part of the corresponding hash value. This means, $r$ would need to be fixed at the time of hashing and needs to be the same for all inputs to the hash function. Thus, it has to already be fixed as part of the sampling of the hash function from its corresponding family and an adversary can choose sets $A$ and $B$ *conditioned* on $r$. Since $r$ is now no longer distributed independently of $A, B$ the adversary could potentially find two such input sets with $|(A \setminus B) \cup (B \setminus A)| > 2t$, which result in an interpolation of a function $\hat{w}(x) \neq w(x)$ that still passes the check, because the sets are chosen such that $\hat{w}(r) = w(r)$.

To get around this problem, we need to hide $r$ from the adversary. Towards this goal, we fix a uniformly random *hidden* value $r$ in a way that allows for performing the check described above *obliviously*. Assume the PPH function description includes values $\vec{\Gamma} = (g, g^r, g^{r^2}, \ldots, g^{r^n})$ for some uniformly random

---

[3] Note, that the equality does not strictly hold, since the function on the right is defined for $x \in A \cup B$, whereas the one on the left is not. However, the two functions are equivalent for all $x$ except for the removable singularities of $u(x)/v(x)$ which is exactly what we need.

value $r$. Now given the coefficients of polynomials $u(x)$, $v(x)$, and $\vec{\Gamma}$, we can evaluate our polynomials in the exponent to obtain $g^{u(r)}$ and $g^{v(r)}$. Under an appropriate $q$-type discrete logarithm assumption we can argue that the actual value $r$ remains hidden and the attack outlined above is no longer possible.

To see how to perform the rational function equality check in the exponent, assume that the interpolation of $\hat{w}(x)$ gives us the coefficients of the polynomials $\hat{v}(x)$ and $\hat{u}(x)$ with $\hat{w}(x) = \hat{u}(x)/\hat{v}(x)$. The equation

$$w(x) = \frac{u(x)}{v(x)} = \frac{\hat{u}(x)}{\hat{v}(x)} = \hat{w}(x)$$

holds if and only if

$$u(x)\hat{v}(x) = \hat{u}(x)v(x)$$

holds. Finally, given $g^{u(r)}, g^{v(r)}$, which are computed independently during hashing, the vector $\vec{\Gamma}$, which is part of the hash function description, and the coefficients of $\hat{u}(x)$ and $\hat{v}(x)$, which we obtain from the interpolation, we can use a bilinear pairing, which allows us to perform a multiplication in the exponent, to check the desired equation.

To obtain our construction for the hamming distance predicate, we need to encode the input bit strings into sets in a way that allows us to translate a threshold on the hamming distance to a threshold on the size of the symmetric set difference of the corresponding sets. Towards this goal, we simply encode a bit string $x = x_1 x_2 \ldots x_n$ into a set $S_x := \{2i - x_i \mid i \in [n]\}$. For two strings $x$ and $y$ and each bit position $i$ with $x_i = y_i$ the corresponding sets $S_x$ and $S_y$ will have one element $2i - x_i = 2i - y_i$ in common. For each position $i$ with $x_i \neq y_i$, the sets will contain distinct elements $2i$ and $2i - 1$. With this in mind, it is straightforward to see that

$$d(x, y) = \frac{|(S_x \setminus S_y) \cup (S_y \setminus S_x)|}{2},$$

which means that we can reduce the problem of computing the hamming distance between bit strings to computing the size of the symmetric set difference of the corresponding set encodings.

## 2   Preliminaries

This section introduces notation, some basic definitions and lemmas that we will use throughout this work. We denote by $\lambda \in \mathbb{N}$ the security parameter and by $\mathsf{poly}(\lambda)$ any function that is bounded by a polynomial in $\lambda$. A function $f$ is negligible if for every $c \in \mathbb{N}$, there exists some $N \in \mathbb{N}$ such that for all $\lambda > N$ it holds that $f(\lambda) < 1/\lambda^c$. We denote by $\mathsf{negl}(\lambda)$ any negligible function. An algorithm is PPT if it is modeled by a probabilistic Turing machine with a running time bounded by $\mathsf{poly}(\lambda)$.

Let $n \in \mathbb{N}$, we denote by $[n]$ the set $\{1, \ldots, n\}$. Let $X, Y$ be sets, we denote by $|X|$ the size of $X$ and by $X \triangle Y$ the symmetric set difference of $X$ and $Y$, i.e., $X \triangle Y = (X \cup Y) \setminus (X \cap Y) = (X \setminus Y) \cup (Y \setminus X)$. Further, we denote by $\mathcal{P}_n(X) = \{S \subseteq X \mid |S| = n\}$ the set of all subsets of size $n$ of $X$ and by $x \leftarrow X$ the process of sampling an element of $X$ uniformly at random. Let $x, y \in \{0,1\}^n$, we write $w(x)$ to denote the Hamming weight of $x$ and we write $d(x,y)$ to denote the Hamming distance between $x$ and $y$, i.e., $d(x,y) = w(x \oplus y)$. For a polynomial $p = \sum_{i=0}^{n} c_i x^i$, we write $\mathsf{coef}(p,i) = c_i$ to denote the $i$-th coefficient of $p$.

**Rational Functions.** A rational function is the fraction of two polynomials. The total degree of a rational function is the sum of the degrees of the numerator and the denominator after they have been reduced to lowest terms. More precisely, it is defined as follows.

**Definition 1 (Total Degree).** *Let $f$ and $g$ be arbitrary non-zero polynomials. Let $r, f', g'$ be polynomials, such that $f = rf'$, $g = rg'$ and $f'$ and $g'$ are coprime. Note that $r, f', g'$ always exist and are unique. The total degree of the rational function $f/g$ is then defined as $\mathsf{tdeg}(f/g) = \deg(f') + \deg(g')$.*

**Encoding Bit Strings as Sets.** A given bit string $x \in \{0,1\}^n$ can be efficiently encoded into a set as $S_x := \{2i - x_i \mid i \in [n]\}$. We have that $S_x \in \mathcal{P}_n([2n])$, i.e. the size of $S_x$ is $n$ and its description length in bits is $n\lceil \log 2n \rceil$. We call $S_x$ the *set encoding* of $x$.

**Lemma 1.** *Let $n \in \mathbb{N}$. For any $x, y \in \{0,1\}^n$, it holds that*

$$2d(x,y) = |S_x \triangle S_y|.$$

*Proof.* We denote by $I := \{i \in [n] \mid x_i = y_i\}$ the set of indices $i$ where $x_i = y_i$. Similarly, we denote by $J := \{j \in [n] \mid x_j \neq y_j\}$ the set of indices $j$ where $x_j \neq y_j$. By definition of the Hamming distance, we have $|J| = d(x,y)$ and $|I| = n - |J|$.

We can now write $S_x, S_y$ in terms of $I$ and $J$ as

$$S_x = \{2i - x_i \mid i \in I\} \cup \{2j - x_j \mid j \in J\}$$
$$S_y = \{2i - y_i \mid i \in I\} \cup \{2j - y_j \mid j \in J\}.$$

By definition of $I$, we have that $\{2i - x_i \mid i \in I\} = \{2i - y_i \mid i \in I\}$ and therefore that

$$S_x \cup S_y = \{2i - x_i \mid i \in [n]\} \cup \{2j - y_j \mid j \in J\} = S_x \cup \{2j - y_j \mid j \in J\}$$

Since, by definition of $J$ it must also hold that $S_x \cap \{2j - y_j \mid j \in J\} = \emptyset$ we thus have

$$|S_x \cup S_y| = |S_x| + |J| = n + d(x,y). \tag{1}$$

Similarly, by the above observations, it holds that $S_x \cap S_y = \{2i - x_i \mid i \in I\}$ and thereby

$$|S_x \cap S_y| = |I| = n - |J| = n - d(x,y) \tag{2}$$

Finally, combining the definition of symmetric set difference and Eqs. 1 and 2 we thus have

$$|S_x \triangle S_y| = |(S_x \cup S_y) \setminus (S_x \cap S_y)| = |S_x \cup S_y| - |S_x \cap S_y|$$
$$= n + d(x,y) - (n - d(x,y)) = 2d(x,y)$$

as claimed. □

**Encoding Sets as Polynomials.** We define the *polynomial encoding* of a set $S = \{s_1, \ldots, s_n\} \subseteq [N]$ as the polynomial $p_S(z) = \prod_{i=1}^{n}(z - s_i)$ over some field $\mathbb{Z}_q$ of prime order $q > N$. For a bit string $x \in \{0,1\}^n$, we will abuse notation and write $p_x$ to denote the polynomial encoding of the set encoding of $x$. Observe that the roots of $p_x$ are all in $[2n]$.

**Lemma 2.** *Let $n, N \in \mathbb{N}$ such that $n < N$. For any pair of sets $X, Y \in \mathcal{P}_n([N])$, it holds that*

$$|X \triangle Y| = \mathrm{tdeg}\left(\frac{p_X}{p_Y}\right).$$

*Proof.* Let $X' := X \setminus Y$, $Y' := Y \setminus X$ and $W := X \cap Y$. We have by definition of the polynomial encoding that

$$p_X(z) = \prod_{x \in X}(z - x) = \left(\prod_{w \in W}(z - w)\right) \cdot \left(\prod_{x \in X'}(z - x)\right)$$

and

$$p_Y(z) = \prod_{y \in Y}(z - y) = \left(\prod_{w \in W}(z - w)\right) \cdot \left(\prod_{y \in Y'}(z - y)\right).$$

Since $X' \cap Y' = \emptyset$, the two polynomials $\prod_{x \in X'}(z - x)$ and $\prod_{y \in Y'}(z - y)$ are coprime, while $\prod_{w \in W}(z - w)$ is a common factor in $p_X$ and $p_Y$. By Definition 1, it thus holds that

$$\mathrm{tdeg}\left(\frac{p_X(z)}{p_Y(z)}\right) = \deg\left(\prod_{x \in X'}(z - x)\right) + \deg\left(\prod_{y \in Y'}(z - y)\right)$$
$$= |X'| + |Y'| = |X' \cup Y'| = |(X \setminus Y) \cup (Y \setminus X)|$$
$$= |X \triangle Y|$$

as claimed. □

**Proposition 3** ([12]). *For polynomials $f \in \mathbb{F}_{\leq n}[X]$ and $g \in \mathbb{F}_{\leq m}[X]$, the rational function $h(z) = f(z)/g(z)$ can be uniquely interpolated (up to equivalences) from distinct evaluation points $z_1, \ldots, z_d$ and $f(z_1), g(z_1), \ldots, f(z_d), g(z_d)$, where $d = n + m + 1$, as well as upper bounds on $n$ and $m$.*

*Remark 1.* We denote by RatInt the algorithm that takes as input a list of $d$ points $(x_1, y_1), \ldots, (x_d, y_d) \in \mathbb{F}_q$ and tries to find a rational function $p/q$ with degrees of $p$ and $q$ at most $\lfloor (d-1)/2 \rfloor$, such that $p(x_i)/q(x_i) = y_i$ for $1 \leq i \leq d$. Upon success it outputs $(p, q)$. Otherwise it outputs the constant 0 function.

**Two-Input Predicates.** We define the following two-input predicates, which will be the main focus of this work.

**Definition 2 (Hamming Predicate).** *For $x, y \in \{0, 1\}^n$ and $t > 0$, the two-input predicate is defined as*

$$\mathsf{HAM}^t(x, y) = \begin{cases} 1 & \text{if } d(x, y) \geq t \\ 0 & \text{Otherwise} \end{cases}$$

**Definition 3 (Symmetric Set Difference Predicate).** *For a universe $U$, natural number $n$, $X, Y \in \mathcal{P}_n(U)$, and $t > 0$, the two-input symmetric set difference predicate is defined as*

$$\mathsf{SSD}^t(X, Y) = \begin{cases} 1 & \text{if } |X \triangle Y| \geq t \\ 0 & \text{Otherwise} \end{cases}$$

**Bilinear Groups and Pairings.** A bilinear group is described by a tuple $(\mathbb{G}_1, \mathbb{G}_2, \mathbb{G}_T, q, e)$, where $\mathbb{G}_1, \mathbb{G}_2, \mathbb{G}_T$ are groups of order $q$ and $e : \mathbb{G}_1 \times \mathbb{G}_2 \to \mathbb{G}_T$ is a (non-degenerate) bilinear asymmetric map, called pairing, such that for all $a, b \in \mathbb{Z}_q$ and $g_1 \in \mathbb{G}_1$ and $g_2 \in \mathbb{G}_2$ it holds that

$$e(g_1^a, g_2^b) = e(g_1, g_2)^{ab}.$$

If $\mathbb{G}_1$ and $\mathbb{G}_2$ are cyclic and $g_1$ and $g_2$ are generators of those groups respectively, then $e(g_1, g_2)$ is a generator of $\mathbb{G}_T$.

Let GGen be a PPT algorithm that takes the security parameter $1^\lambda$ as input and outputs bilinear map parameters $(\mathbb{G}_1, \mathbb{G}_2, \mathbb{G}_T, q, e, g_1, g_2)$, where $\mathbb{G}_1, \mathbb{G}_2, \mathbb{G}_T$ are the groups of prime order $q = q(\lambda)$. $e : \mathbb{G}_1 \times \mathbb{G}_2 \to \mathbb{G}_T$ is a (non-degenerate) bilinear map and $g_1$ and $g_2$ are generators of $\mathbb{G}_1$ and $\mathbb{G}_2$ respectively. Our constructions will rely on the following $q$-type extension of the discrete logarithm assumption over bilinear groups.

**Definition 4 (The $n$-Strong Bilinear Discrete Logarithm ($n$-SBDL) Assumption).** *The $n$-SBDL assumption holds relative to GGen if for all PPT algorithms $\mathcal{A}$ it holds that*

$$\Pr\left[ r = \mathcal{A}\left( \mathbb{G}_1, \mathbb{G}_2, \mathbb{G}_T, q, e, \begin{pmatrix} g_1 \ g_1^r \ \cdots \ g_1^{r^n} \\ g_2 \ g_2^r \ \cdots \ g_2^{r^n} \end{pmatrix} \right) \right] \leq \mathsf{negl}(\lambda),$$

*where the probability is taken over $(\mathbb{G}_1, \mathbb{G}_2, \mathbb{G}_T, q, e, g_1, g_2) \leftarrow \mathsf{GGen}(1^\lambda)$ and $r \leftarrow \mathbb{Z}_q$.*

To the best of our knowledge, and unlike the regular $n$-strong discrete logarithm ($n$-SDL) assumption [9], this exact assumption has not been used before. However, it is in fact implied by, and thus weaker than, other related $q$-type assumptions such as the $n$-BDHI [3] assumption.

**Hash Functions.** We first recall the standard definition of collision-resistant hash functions.

**Definition 5 (Collision Resistant Hash Function Family).** *For a $\lambda \in \mathbb{N}$ a hash function family $\mathcal{F} = \{f : \{0,1\}^* \to \{0,1\}^\lambda\}$ consists of a pair of efficiently computable algorithms:*

Sample$(1^\lambda) \to f$ *is an efficient randomized algorithm that samples an efficiently computable random hash function from $\mathcal{F}$ with security parameter $\lambda$.*
Hash$(f, x) \to y$ *is an efficient deterministic algorithm that evaluates the hash function $h$ on $x$.*

*The family $\mathcal{F}$ is collision resistant if, for any PPT adversary $\mathcal{A}$ it holds that,*

$$\Pr[f \leftarrow \mathsf{Sample}(1^\lambda); (x_1, x_2) \leftarrow \mathcal{A}(f) : f(x_1) = f(x_2)] \leq \mathsf{negl}(\lambda),$$

*where the probability is taken over the internal random coins of* Sample *and* $\mathcal{A}$.

The following definition of property-preserving hash functions is taken almost verbatim from [4]. In this work, we consider the strongest of several different security notions that were proposed by BLV.

**Definition 6 (Property-Preserving Hash).** *For a $\lambda \in \mathbb{N}$ an $\eta$-compressing property preserving hash function family $\mathcal{H}_\lambda = \{h : X \to Y\}$ for a two-input predicate requires the following three efficiently computable algorithms:*

Sample$(1^\lambda) \to h$ *is an efficient randomized algorithm that samples an efficiently computable random hash function from $\mathcal{H}$ with security parameter $\lambda$.*
Hash$(h, x) \to y$ *is an efficient deterministic algorithm that evaluates the hash function $h$ on $x$.*
Eval$(h, y_1, y_2) \to \{0, 1\}$: *is an efficient deterministic algorithm that on input $h$, and $y_1, y_2 \in Y$ outputs a single bit.*

*We require that $\mathcal{H}$ must be compressing, meaning that $\log |Y| \leq \eta \log |X|$ for $0 < \eta < 1$.*

For notational convenience we write $h(x)$ for Hash$(h, x)$.

**Definition 7 (Direct-Access Robustness).** *A family of PPH functions $\mathcal{H} = \{h : X \to Y\}$ for a two-input predicate $P : X \times X \to \{0, 1\}$ is a family of direct-access robust PPH functions if, for any PPT adversary $\mathcal{A}$ it holds that,*

$$\Pr\left[\begin{array}{l} h \leftarrow \mathsf{Sample}(1^\lambda); \\ (x_1, x_2) \leftarrow \mathcal{A}(h) \end{array} : \mathsf{Eval}(h, h(x_1), h(x_2)) \neq P(x_1, x_2)\right] \leq \mathsf{negl}(\lambda),$$

*where the probability is taken over the internal random coins of* Sample *and* $\mathcal{A}$.

$$
\begin{array}{ll}
\hline
\mathsf{Sample}(1^\lambda) & \mathsf{Hash}(h, X) \\
\hline
(\mathbb{G}_1, \mathbb{G}_2, \mathbb{G}_T, q, e, g_1, g_2) \leftarrow \mathsf{GGen}(1^\lambda) & \textbf{parse } h \textbf{ as } (\mathbb{G}_1, \mathbb{G}_2, \mathbb{G}_T, q, e, \boldsymbol{\Gamma}) \\
r \leftarrow \mathbb{Z}_q \setminus [N] & \boldsymbol{a} := \big(p_X(N+1), \ldots, p_X(N+t)\big) \\
\boldsymbol{\Gamma} := \begin{pmatrix} g_1 \ g_1^r \cdots g_1^{r^n} \\ g_2 \ g_2^r \cdots g_2^{r^n} \end{pmatrix} & b := \prod_{i=0}^{n} \Gamma_{1,i+1}^{\mathrm{coef}(p_X, i)} = g_1^{p_X(r)} \\
\textbf{return } h := (\mathbb{G}_1, \mathbb{G}_2, \mathbb{G}_T, q, e, \boldsymbol{\Gamma}) & \textbf{return } (\boldsymbol{a}, b) \\
\hline
\end{array}
$$

$$
\begin{array}{l}
\hline
\mathsf{Eval}(h, (\boldsymbol{a}, b), (\tilde{\boldsymbol{a}}, \tilde{b})) \\
\hline
\textbf{parse } h \textbf{ as } (\mathbb{G}_1, \mathbb{G}_2, \mathbb{G}_T, q, e, \boldsymbol{\Gamma}) \\
\textbf{for } 1 \le i \le t \\
\quad s_i := \left( N+i, \dfrac{a_i}{\tilde{a}_i} \right) \\
\quad (u, v) := \mathsf{RatInt}(s_1, \ldots, s_t) \\
\textbf{return } e\left( b, \prod_{i=0}^{n} \Gamma_{2,i+1}^{\mathrm{coef}(v,i)} \right) \overset{?}{\ne} e\left( \tilde{b}, \prod_{i=0}^{n} \Gamma_{2,i}^{\mathrm{coef}(u,i)} \right) \\
\hline
\end{array}
$$

**Fig. 1.** A family of direct-access robust PPH for the predicate $\mathsf{SSD}^t$ over the domain $\mathcal{P}_n([N])$ for any $N \in \mathbb{N}$ with $N \le 2^{\lambda-1}$.

## 3    PPH for Symmetric Set Difference

In this section we construct property preserving hash functions for symmetric set difference. We start by presenting a construction for sets with elements from a universe of bounded size in Sect. 3.1 and show how to extend the construction to sets with elements from an arbitrarily large universe in Sect. 3.2.

### 3.1    PPH for Symmetric Set Difference of $\mathcal{P}_n([N])$

**Theorem 4.** *Let* $\mathsf{GGen}$ *be a bilinear group generation algorithm that generates groups of prime order* $q = q(\lambda)$ *with* $q > 2^\lambda$. *Then, for any* $n = \mathsf{poly}(\lambda)$, $N \in \mathbb{N}$ *with* $n \le N \le 2^{\lambda-1}$ *and any* $t < \frac{n(\log N - \log n)}{\log q(\lambda)} - 1$, *the construction in Fig. 1 is a* $\frac{(t+1)\log q(\lambda)}{\log\binom{N}{n}} \le \frac{(t+1)\log q(\lambda)}{n(\log N - \log n)}$-*compressing direct-access robust property preserving hash function family for the two-input predicate* $\mathsf{SSD}^t$ *and domain* $\mathcal{P}_n([N])$, *if the* $n$-$SBDL$ *assumption holds relative to* $\mathsf{GGen}$.

*Proof.* Let $\mathcal{A}$ be an arbitrary PPT adversary against the direct access robustness of $\mathcal{H}$. We have

$$\Pr[\mathsf{Eval}(h, h(X_1), h(X_2)) \neq \mathsf{SSD}^t(X_1, X_2)]$$
$$= \Pr[\mathsf{Eval}(h, h(X_1), h(X_2)) = 1 \mid \mathsf{SSD}^t(X_1, X_2) = 0] \cdot \Pr[\mathsf{SSD}^t(X_1, X_2) = 0]$$
$$+ \Pr[\mathsf{Eval}(h, h(X_1), h(X_2)) = 0 \mid \mathsf{SSD}^t(X_1, X_2) = 1] \cdot \Pr[\mathsf{SSD}^t(X_1, X_2) = 1],$$

where the probabilities are taken over $h \leftarrow \mathsf{Sample}(1^\lambda)$ and $(X_1, X_2) \leftarrow \mathcal{A}(h)$. We consider the two cases separately.

**Claim 5.** $\Pr[\mathsf{Eval}(h, h(X_1), h(X_2)) = 1 \mid \mathsf{SSD}^t(X_1, X_2) = 0] = 0$

*Proof (claim 5).* Since $\mathsf{SSD}^t(X_1, X_2) = 0$, we know that $|X_1 \triangle X_2| < t$. By Lemma 2 this means that

$$\mathsf{tdeg}\left(\frac{p_{X_1}}{p_{X_2}}\right) < t.$$

From Proposition 3 it follows that the rational function $p_{X_1}/p_{X_2}$ can (up to equivalences) be uniquely interpolated from $t$ points. We observe that for $1 \leq i \leq t$ it holds that $p_{X_2}(N + i) \neq 0$, since roots of $p_{X_2}$ are in the interval $[N]$ by construction. Therefore, $s_i = p_{X_1}(N + i)/p_{X_2}(N + i)$ is well-defined and thus

$$\frac{p_{X_1}}{p_{X_2}} = \frac{u}{v}$$

where $u/v$ is the rational function computed by $\mathsf{RatInt}$ in $\mathsf{Eval}(h, h(X_1), h(X_2))$. Finally, we observe that

$$e\left(g_1^{p_{X_1}(r)}, \prod_{i=0}^n \Gamma_{2,i+1}^{\mathsf{coef}(v,i)}\right) = e\left(g_1^{p_{X_2}(r)}, \prod_{i=0}^n \Gamma_{2,i}^{\mathsf{coef}(u,i)}\right)$$
$$\iff e(g_1, g_2)^{p_{X_1}(r) \sum_{i=0}^n (\mathsf{coef}(v,i) \cdot r^i)} = e(g_1, g_2)^{p_{X_2}(r) \sum_{i=0}^n (\mathsf{coef}(u,i) \cdot r^i)}$$
$$\iff e(g_1, g_2)^{p_{X_1}(r) v(r)} = e(g_1, g_2)^{p_{X_2}(r) u(r)},$$

which is true whenever

$$p_{X_1}(r) \cdot v(r) = p_{X_2}(r) \cdot u(r)$$
$$\iff \frac{p_{X_1}(r)}{p_{X_2}(r)} = \frac{u(r)}{v(r)},$$

which is true for all $r$ and thus the last inequality in $\mathsf{Eval}(h, h(X_1), h(X_2))$ is never satisfied. $\square$

**Claim 6.** *If the $n$-SBDL assumption holds relative to* $\mathsf{GGen}$, *then*

$$\Pr[\mathsf{Eval}(h, h(X_1), h(X_2)) = 0 \mid \mathsf{SSD}^t(X_1, X_2) = 1] \cdot \Pr[\mathsf{SSD}^t(X_1, X_2) = 1]$$
$$\leq \mathsf{negl}(\lambda).$$

*Proof (claim 6).* Since $\mathsf{SSD}^t(X_1, X_2) = 1$, it must hold that $t \leq |X_1 \triangle X_2| \leq 2n$. By Lemma 2 this means that

$$t \leq \mathsf{tdeg}\left(\frac{p_{x_1}}{p_{x_2}}\right) \leq 2n.$$

On the other hand, by construction $u/v$ is the rational function of total degree at most $t - 1$ uniquely determined by $s_1, \ldots, s_t$. It must therefore hold that

$$\frac{u}{v} \neq \frac{p_{x_1}}{p_{x_2}}.$$

For the last inequality in $\mathsf{Eval}(h, h(X_1), h(X_2))$ to hold, $p_{X_1}/p_{X_2}$ and $u/v$ must therefore be two *different* rational functions that agree on point $r$. This means that $r$ must be one of the at most $n + (t-1)/2$ roots of the rational function

$$\frac{p_{X_1}}{p_{X_2}} - \frac{u}{v} = \frac{p_{X_1} \cdot v - p_{X_2} \cdot u}{p_{X_2} \cdot v}.$$

Whenever $\mathcal{A}$ would be successful, we could therefore find $r$ by testing the roots of the polynomial $p_{X_1} \cdot v - p_{X_2} \cdot u$. We give a formal reduction as follows:

$\mathcal{R}$ takes as input

$$\mathbb{G}_1, \mathbb{G}_2, \mathbb{G}_T, q, e, \vec{\Gamma} := \begin{pmatrix} g_1 \; g_1^r \; \cdots \; g_1^{r^n} \\ g_2 \; g_2^r \; \cdots \; g_2^{r^n} \end{pmatrix}$$

and invokes $\mathcal{A}$ on $h := (\mathbb{G}_1, \mathbb{G}_2, \mathbb{G}_T, q, e, \vec{\Gamma})$ and receives $X_1, X_2$.

If $\mathsf{SSD}^t(X_1, X_2) = 0$, $\mathcal{R}$ aborts. Otherwise it computes $(u, v)$ as in $\mathsf{Eval}$ and determines the set $X$ of roots of the polynomial $p_{X_1} \cdot v - p_{X_2} \cdot u$. For each $r' \in X$, $\mathcal{R}$ checks whether $g_1^{r'} \stackrel{?}{=} \Gamma_{1,2}$ and returns $r'$ if it holds. If the equality holds for no $r' \in X$, $\mathcal{R}$ aborts.

Since $\mathcal{A}$ is PPT and finding the roots of a polynomial is possible in polynomial time, it follows that $\mathcal{R}$ is PPT and must, by assumption, have a negligible success probability against the $n$-SBDL problem.

Note that $r$ from the input of the reduction is distributed uniformly in $\mathbb{Z}_q$, while $\mathcal{A}$ expects $r$ to be uniformly distributed in $\mathbb{Z}_q \setminus [N]$. However, since $N \leq 2^{\lambda-1}$ and $q > 2^\lambda$, it holds that $r \in \mathbb{Z}_q \setminus [N]$ with probability at least $1/2$. Furthermore, once we condition on $r \notin [N]$, the distribution of $h$ is identical to the one expected by $\mathcal{A}$.

Now, observe that the reduction $\mathcal{R}$ is successful, if $\mathcal{A}$ outputs $X_1, X_2$, such that $\mathsf{SSD}^t(X_1, X_2) = 1$ and $r$ is one of the roots of $p_{X_1} \cdot v - p_{X_2} \cdot u$. As argued above, the latter must be true, if $\mathsf{Eval}(h, h(x_1), h(x_2)) = 0$. Therefore, it holds that

$$\mathsf{negl}(\lambda)$$

$$\geq \Pr\left[r = \mathcal{R}\left(\mathbb{G}_1, \mathbb{G}_2, \mathbb{G}_T, q, e, \begin{pmatrix} g_1 \; g_1^r \; \cdots \; g_1^{r^n} \\ g_2 \; g_2^r \; \cdots \; g_2^{r^n} \end{pmatrix}\right)\right]$$

$$\geq \Pr\left[r \notin [N]\right] \cdot \Pr\left[r = \mathcal{R}\left(\mathbb{G}_1, \mathbb{G}_2, \mathbb{G}_T, q, e, \begin{pmatrix} g_1 \ g_1^r \ \cdots \ g_1^{r^n} \\ g_2 \ g_2^r \ \cdots \ g_2^{r^n} \end{pmatrix}\right)\right) \Big| r \notin [N]\right]$$

$$\geq \frac{1}{2} \cdot \Pr[\mathsf{Eval}(h, h(X_1), h(X_2)) = 0 \mid \mathsf{SSD}^t(X_1, X_2) = 1] \cdot \Pr[\mathsf{SSD}^t(X_1, X_2) = 1]$$

and, thus, the claim follows. □

Using Claims 5 and 6 we can thus conclude that

$$\Pr[\mathsf{Eval}(h, h(X_1), h(X_2)) \neq \mathsf{SSD}^t(X_1, X_2)] \leq 0 + \mathsf{negl}(\lambda) = \mathsf{negl}(\lambda).$$

Therefore, $\mathcal{H}$ is direct access robust as claimed. It remains to show that it is also compressing. The domain of the hash function is $\mathcal{P}_n([N])$, the codomain is $\mathbb{Z}_{q(\lambda)}^t \times \mathbb{G}_1$. It follows that the compression factor is

$$\eta = \frac{\log |\mathbb{Z}_{q(\lambda)}^t \times \mathbb{G}_1|}{\log |\mathcal{P}_n([N])|} = \frac{\log q(\lambda)^{t+1}}{\log \binom{N}{n}} \leq \frac{\log q(\lambda)^{t+1}}{\log\left(\frac{N}{n}\right)^n} = \frac{(t+1)\log q(\lambda)}{n(\log N - \log n)}$$

as claimed. The construction is thus compressing, if

$$\frac{(t+1)\log q(\lambda)}{n(\log N - \log n)} < 1 \iff t < \frac{n(\log N - \log n)}{\log q} - 1.$$

□

## 3.2 PPH for Symmetric Set Difference of Arbitrary Sets

To obtain our construction for sets with elements from an arbitrarily large universe, we make use of a collision-resistant hash function. We simply first hash the elements of the input sets into a smaller universe and then apply our construction from the previous section.

| Sample($1^\lambda$) | Hash($(h, f), X$) | Eval($(h, f), y, \tilde{y}$) |
|---|---|---|
| $h \leftarrow \mathcal{H}.\mathsf{Sample}(1^\lambda)$ | $X' := \{f(x) \mid x \in X\}$ | $b := \mathcal{H}.\mathsf{Eval}(h, y, \tilde{y})$ |
| $f \leftarrow \mathcal{F}.\mathsf{Sample}(1^\lambda)$ | $y := h(X')$ | **return** $b$ |
| **return** $h' := (h, f)$ | **return** $y$ | |

**Fig. 2.** A family of direct-access robust PPH for $\mathsf{SSD}^t$ on $\mathcal{P}_n(\{0,1\}^\ell)$.

**Theorem 7.** *Let* $\mathcal{H}_\lambda = \{h : \mathcal{P}_n(\{0,1\}^\lambda) \to Y\}$ *be an* $\eta$-*compressing direct-access robust property preserving hash function family for* $\mathsf{SSD}^t$. *Let* $\mathcal{F} = \{f : \{0,1\}^\ell \to \{0,1\}^\lambda\}$ *be a collision resistant hash function family. Then the construction in Fig. 2 is a* $\eta \cdot \frac{\log \binom{2^\lambda}{n}}{\log \binom{2^\ell}{n}} \leq \eta \cdot \frac{\log e + \lambda - \log n}{\ell - \log n}$-*compressing direct-access robust PPH for* $\mathsf{SSD}^t$ *and domain* $\mathcal{P}_n(\{0,1\}^\ell)$.

*Proof.* Let $\mathcal{A}$ be an arbitrary PPT adversary against the direct-access robustness of $\mathcal{H}'$. We have that

$$\Pr[\mathsf{Eval}(h', h'(X_1), h'(X_2)) \neq \mathsf{SSD}^t(X_1, X_2)]$$
$$= \Pr[\mathcal{H}.\mathsf{Eval}(h, h(X_1'), h(X_2')) \neq \mathsf{SSD}^t(X_1, X_2)]$$
$$= \Pr\Big[\mathcal{H}.\mathsf{Eval}(h, h(X_1'), h(X_2')) \neq \mathsf{SSD}^t(X_1, X_2) \;\Big|\; |X_1' \triangle X_2'| = |X_1 \triangle X_2|\Big]$$
$$\cdot \Pr\Big[|X_1' \triangle X_2'| = |X_1 \triangle X_2|\Big] \tag{3}$$
$$+ \Pr\Big[\mathcal{H}.\mathsf{Eval}(h, h(X_1'), h(X_2')) \neq \mathsf{SSD}^t(X_1, X_2) \;\Big|\; |X_1' \triangle X_2'| \neq |X_1 \triangle X_2|\Big]$$
$$\cdot \Pr\Big[|X_1' \triangle X_2'| \neq |X_1 \triangle X_2|\Big]$$

where the probability is taken over the sampling of $h' = (h, f) \leftarrow \mathsf{Sample}'(1^\lambda)$ and $(X_1, X_2) \leftarrow \mathcal{A}(h')$. Equation 3 follows by applying the definition of $\mathcal{H}'$ and then splitting the probability. We will now upper bound the two parts of the sum in Claims 8 and 9.

**Claim 8.** *If $\mathcal{H}$ is direct-access robust, it holds that*

$$\Pr\Big[\mathcal{H}.\mathsf{Eval}(h, h(X_1'), h(X_2')) \neq \mathsf{SSD}^t(X_1, X_2) \;\Big|\; |X_1' \triangle X_2'| = |X_1 \triangle X_2|\Big]$$
$$\cdot \Pr\Big[|X_1' \triangle X_2'| = |X_1 \triangle X_2|\Big] \leq \mathsf{negl}(\lambda).$$

*Proof (claim 8).* By the direct access robustness of $\mathcal{H}$, we have

$$\mathsf{negl}(\lambda)$$
$$\geq \Pr\Big[\mathcal{H}.\mathsf{Eval}(h, h(X_1'), h(X_2')) \neq \mathsf{SSD}^t(X_1', X_2')\Big]$$
$$\geq \Pr\Big[\mathcal{H}.\mathsf{Eval}(h, h(X_1'), h(X_2')) \neq \mathsf{SSD}^t(X_1', X_2') \;\Big|\; |X_1' \triangle X_2'| = |X_1 \triangle X_2|\Big]$$
$$\cdot \Pr\Big[|X_1' \triangle X_2'| = |X_1 \triangle X_2|\Big]$$
$$= \Pr\Big[\mathcal{H}.\mathsf{Eval}(h, h(X_1'), h(X_2')) \neq \mathsf{SSD}^t(X_1, X_2) \;\Big|\; |X_1' \triangle X_2'| = |X_1 \triangle X_2|\Big]$$
$$\cdot \Pr\Big[|X_1' \triangle X_2'| = |X_1 \triangle X_2|\Big]$$

where the last equality follows from the fact that $|X_1' \triangle X_2'| = |X_1 \triangle X_2|$ implies that $\mathsf{SSD}^t(X_1', X_2') = \mathsf{SSD}^t(X_1, X_2)$. Thus the claim follows. $\square$

**Claim 9.** *If $\mathcal{F}$ is collision resistant, it holds that*

$$\Pr\Big[|X_1' \triangle X_2'| \neq |X_1 \triangle X_2|\Big] \leq \mathsf{negl}(\lambda).$$

*Proof (claim 9).* Note that, since $f$ is a function, it must hold that $|X_1' \cup X_2'| \leq |X_1 \cup X_2|$. Further, if $|X_1' \cup X_2'| = |X_1 \cup X_2|$ then it must hold that $|X_1' \cap X_2'| \geq |X_1 \cap X_2|$. By definition of symmetric set difference it therefore holds that

$$\Pr\Big[|X_1' \triangle X_2'| \neq |X_1 \triangle X_2|\Big]$$

$$\leq \Pr\big[|X_1' \cup X_2'| < |X_1 \cup X_2| \vee |X_1' \cap X_2'| > |X_1 \cap X_2|\big]$$
$$= \Pr\big[\exists\, x_1, x_2 \in X_1 \cup X_2 \colon x_1 \neq x_2 \wedge f(x_1) = f(x_2)\big].$$

Since $\mathcal{F}$ is a family of collision resistant hash functions, the probability that $\mathcal{A}$ finds a collision is negligible and thus the claim follows. □

Combining Eq. 3 with Claims 8 and 9, it thus follows that

$$\Pr[\mathsf{Eval}(h', h'(X_1), h'(X_2)) \neq \mathsf{SSD}^t(X_1, X_2)] \leq \mathsf{negl}(\lambda)$$

and the theorem follows. □

We obtain the following Corollary by combining Theorems 7 and 4.

**Corollary 10.** *Let* GGen *be a bilinear group generation algorithm that generates bilinear groups of prime order* $q = q(\lambda)$ *with* $q > 2^\lambda$ *relative to which the* $n$-SBDL *assumption holds. Let* $\mathcal{F} = \{f : \{0,1\}^\ell \to \{0,1\}^\lambda\}$ *be a collision resistant hash function family. Then for any* $n = \mathsf{poly}(\lambda)$, *and any* $t < \frac{n(\ell - \log n)}{\log q(\lambda)} - 1$ *there exists a* $\frac{(t+1)\log q(\lambda)}{\log \binom{2^\ell}{n}} \leq \frac{(t+1)\log q(\lambda)}{n(\ell - \log n)}$-*compressing direct-access robust PPH for the two-input predicate* $\mathsf{SSD}^t$ *and domain* $\mathcal{P}_n(\{0,1\}^\ell)$.

# 4  PPH for Hamming Distance

In this section, we construct a PPH function for the hamming distance predicate. To hash a string $x \in \{0,1\}^n$, we apply our PPH function for the symmetric set difference predicate to the set encoding $S_x$ of $x$.

**Theorem 11.** *Let* $\mathcal{H}_\lambda = \{h : \mathcal{P}_n([2n]) \to Y\}$ *be an* $\eta$-*compressing direct-access robust property preserving hash function family for* $\mathsf{SSD}^{2t}$. *Then the following construction* $\mathcal{H}'$ *is a* $\eta \cdot \frac{\log \binom{2n}{n}}{n} \leq \eta \cdot (1 + \log e)$-*compressing direct-access robust PPH for* $\mathsf{HAM}^t$ *and domain* $\{0,1\}^n$. $\mathcal{H}'$ *is defined by* (Sample', Hash', Eval') *with* Sample' = Sample, Hash'$(x) := $ Hash$(S_x)$, *and* Eval' = Eval.

*Proof.* Let $\mathcal{A}$ be an arbitrary PPT adversary against the direct-access robustness of $\mathcal{H}'$. We have that

$$\Pr[\mathsf{Eval}'(h', h'(x_1), h'(x_2)) \neq \mathsf{HAM}^t(x_1, x_2)]$$
$$= \Pr[\mathsf{Eval}(h, h(S_{x_1}), h(S_{x_2})) \neq \mathsf{HAM}^t(x_1, x_2)] \tag{4}$$
$$= \Pr[\mathsf{Eval}(h, h(S_{x_1}), h(S_{x_2})) \neq \mathsf{SSD}^{2t}(S_{x_1}, S_{x_2})] \tag{5}$$
$$\leq \mathsf{negl}(\lambda) \tag{6}$$

where Eq. 4 follows from the definition of $\mathcal{H}'$, Eq. 5 follows from the fact that by Lemma 1 for any $x, y \in \{0,1\}^n$ it holds that $d(x_1, x_2) > t \iff |S_{x_1} \triangle S_{x_2}| > 2t$. Finally Eq. 6 follows from the direct-access robustness of the underlying property preserving hash function family $\mathcal{H}$.

The inputs to the hash functions are of length $n$ and are first mapped to elements of $\mathcal{P}_n([2n])$ before being hashed with an $\eta$-compressing function. The total compression is thus

$$\eta \cdot \frac{\log\binom{2n}{n}}{n} \leq \eta \cdot \frac{\log\left(\frac{e \cdot 2n}{n}\right)^n}{n} = \eta \cdot \log 2e = \eta \cdot (1 + \log e)$$

as claimed.                                                                                      □

Combining Theorems 11 and 4, we immediately get the following Corollary.

**Corollary 12.** *Let* GGen *be a bilinear group generation algorithm that generates bilinear groups of prime order* $q = q(\lambda)$ *with* $q > 2^\lambda$ *relative to which the* $n$-SBDL *assumption holds. Then for any* $n = \mathsf{poly}(\lambda)$, *and any* $t < \frac{n}{2\log q(\lambda)} - \frac{1}{2}$ *there exists a* $\frac{(2t+1)\log q(\lambda)}{n}$-*compressing direct-access robust PPH for the two-input predicate* $\mathsf{HAM}^t$ *and domain* $\{0,1\}^n$.

### 4.1  Generalization to Different Alphabets

Previously, we have defined Hamming distance specifically for binary strings. This notion, however, as well as the corresponding predicate, can easily be generalized to strings over an arbitrary alphabet $\Sigma$. Let $\Sigma$ be an alphabet and let $x, y \in \Sigma^n$ be strings. The Hamming distance between the two strings is the number of indices $i \in [n]$, such that $x_i \neq y_i$, formally $d(x,y) = |\{i \in [n] \mid x_i \neq y_i\}|$.

Using this generalized definition of Hamming distance, it is straightforward to generalize the Hamming predicate defined in Definition 2 to a predicate $\mathsf{HAM}^{\Sigma,t}$ for strings over an arbitrary alphabet $\Sigma$.

To generalize the construction from Theorem 11 to this predicate, we merely need to define a set-encoding for strings over $\Sigma$. Let $\Sigma = \{a_1, \ldots, a_\ell\}$ be an alphabet of size $\ell$ and let $x = x_i \ldots x_n = a_{i_1} \ldots a_{i_n} \in \Sigma^n$ be an arbitrary string over $\Sigma$. We define the set encoding of $x$ as $S_x = \{\ell \cdot j - i_j \mid j \in [n]\}$. Using this set encoding in the construction from Theorem 11 immediately gives us a PPH function for $\mathsf{HAM}^{\Sigma,t}$ as stated in the following.

**Proposition 13.** *Let* $\mathcal{H} = \{h : \mathcal{P}_n([\ell n]) \to Y\}$ *be an* $\eta$-compressing direct-access robust property preserving hash function family for $\mathsf{SSD}^{2t}$. Then the following construction* $\mathcal{H}'$ *is a* $\eta \cdot \frac{\log\binom{\ell n}{n}}{\log \ell^n} \leq \eta \cdot (1 + \frac{\log e}{\log \ell})$-*compressing direct-access robust PPH for* $\mathsf{HAM}^{\Sigma,t}$ *and domain* $\Sigma^n$. $\mathcal{H}'$ *is defined by* (Sample', Hash', Eval') *with* Sample' = Sample, Hash'$(x) := $ Hash$(S_x)$, *and* Eval' = Eval.

The proof easily follows from the proof of Theorem 11, by extending Lemma 1 to strings over arbitrary alphabets. Note, that the proof of Lemma 1 already proves this stronger statement.

## 5   PPH for Multi-input Predicates

In this section, we show how to extend our constructions to the multi-input
intersection predicate, which we introduce below. The basic idea underlying our
construction is reminiscent to an idea used by Ghosh and Simkin [7][4] for constructing interactive protocols that are secure against semi-honest adversaries
for the so-called multiparty threshold private set intersection problem. Since we
consider an active adversary and would like to construct a non-interactive primitive, our setting is quite a bit more challenging and requires a more intricate
security analysis.

**Definition 8 (Intersection Predicate).** *For sets $X_1, \ldots, X_\ell \in \mathcal{P}_n(U)$ of size
$n$ with elements from the universe $U$ and threshold $t > 0$, the multi-input set
intersection predicate is defined as*

$$\mathsf{INT}_\ell^t(X_1, \ldots, X_\ell) = \begin{cases} 1 & \text{if } |X_1 \cap \cdots \cap X_\ell| > n - t \\ 0 & \text{Otherwise} \end{cases}$$

Before presenting our construction in this section, we observe that the symmetric set difference and the intersection predicate are equivalent for the two-
input setting.

**Proposition 14.** *For all $n \in \mathbb{N}$, for all sets $X, Y \in \mathcal{P}_n(U)$ of size $n$ with
elements from the universe $U$ and for all $t \in \mathbb{N}$, it holds that $\mathsf{INT}_2^t(X, Y) = 1 - \mathsf{SSD}^{2t}(X, Y)$.*

*Proof.* Let $X$ and $Y$ be two sets of size $n$ with elements from an arbitrary
universe $U$. We observe that

$$\begin{aligned}
|X \triangle Y| &= |(X \setminus Y) \cup (Y \setminus X)| \\
&= |(X \setminus (X \cap Y)) \cup (Y \setminus (X \cap Y))| \\
&= n - |X \cap Y| + n - |X \cap Y| \\
&= 2n - 2|X \cap Y|
\end{aligned}$$

and therefore

$$\begin{aligned}
\mathsf{SSD}^{2t}(X, Y) = 1 &\iff |X \triangle Y| \geq 2t \\
&\iff 2n - 2|X \cap Y| \geq 2t \\
&\iff n - t \geq |X \cap Y| \iff \mathsf{INT}_2^t(X, Y) = 0
\end{aligned}$$

and equivalently $\mathsf{SSD}^{2t}(X, Y) = 0 \iff \mathsf{INT}_2^t(X, Y) = 1$.     □

---

[4] Their multiparty protocols can be found in the extended abstract [8] on ePrint.

## 5.1   PPH for the Intersection Predicate $\mathsf{INT}_\ell^t$

The intuition for our PPH function for $\mathsf{INT}_\ell^t$ is as follows. Let $X_1, \ldots, X_\ell$ be sets encoded into polynomials $p_{X_1}(z), \ldots, p_{X_\ell}(z)$ over a field $\mathbb{Z}_q$ of prime order. Let $W = X_1 \cap \cdots \cap X_\ell$ be the intersection of those sets and let $c_1, \ldots, c_\ell$ be field elements, then

$$\frac{c_1 \cdot p_{X_1}(z) + \cdots + c_{\ell-1} \cdot p_{X_{\ell-1}}(z)}{c_1 \cdot p_{X_\ell}(z)}$$

$$= \frac{p_W(z)\left(c_1 \cdot p_{X_1 \setminus W}(z) + \cdots + c_{\ell-1} \cdot p_{X_{\ell-1} \setminus W}(z)\right)}{p_W(z) \cdot c_\ell \cdot p_{X_\ell \setminus W}(z)}$$

$$= \frac{c_1 \cdot p_{X_1 \setminus W}(z) + \cdots + c_{\ell-1} \cdot p_{X_{\ell-1} \setminus W}(z)}{c_\ell \cdot p_{X_\ell \setminus W}(z)}$$

If $|W| > n - t$, then for each $i \in [\ell]$ the degree of $p_{X_i \setminus W}(z)$ is upper bounded by $t$. This implies that the degree of the two polynomials in the numerator and denominator are upper bounded by $t$ respectively, resulting in an upper bound of $2t$ for the total degree of the rational function. This is stated formally in the following lemma.

**Lemma 15.** *Let $n, N \in \mathbb{N}$ such that $n < N$ and let $\mathbb{Z}_q$ be a field of prime order $q > N$. For all $X_1, \ldots, X_\ell \in \mathcal{P}_n([N])$ and all $c_1, \ldots, c_\ell \in \mathbb{Z}_q^*$ it holds that*

$$2\left(n - \left|\bigcap_{i \in [\ell]} X_i\right|\right) \geq \mathsf{tdeg}\left(\frac{\sum_{i \in [\ell-1]} c_i \cdot p_{X_i}}{c_\ell \cdot p_{X_\ell}}\right)$$

*Proof.* Let $W = X_1 \cap \cdots \cap X_\ell$ be the intersection of the sets. We have

$$p_{X_\ell}(z) = \prod_{x \in X_\ell}(z - x) = \left(\prod_{x \in X_\ell \setminus W}(z - x)\right) \cdot \left(\prod_{x \in W}(z - x)\right) = p_{X_\ell \setminus W}(z) \cdot p_W(z)$$

and thus the degree of the denominator is at most $n - |W|$. Similarly, for any $1 \leq i \leq \ell - 1$, we have

$$c_i \cdot p_{X_i}(z) = c_i \cdot p_{X_i \setminus W}(z) \cdot p_W(z)$$

and thus the degree of each individual polynomial in the numerator is at most $n - |W|$. Since the sum of polynomials of degrees $d_1, \ldots, d_{\ell-1}$ is a new polynomial of degree $\max(d_1, \ldots, d_\ell)$, the lemma follows.  $\square$

To obtain something equivalent to Lemma 2, i.e. that the degree of the rational function corresponds *exactly* to $n - t$, we would like to argue that if $|W| \leq n - t$, then the degree of numerator and denominator are also *at least* $t$. However, this is not necessarily the case. Even though, after factoring out $p_W(z)$ the remaining polynomials $p_{X_i \setminus W}(x)$ no longer share any common roots, the *sum of polynomials* in the numerator *could* share an additional root with the numerator. However, by choosing the $c_i$ with a random oracle and choosing our parameters appropriately, we can ensure that no efficient algorithm will be able to *find* such a combination with non-negligible probability. We formally state the following lemma.

**Lemma 16.** *Let $n, N \in \mathbb{N}$ with $n < N$ and let $\delta \geq \lambda + \ell \log^2 \lambda + \log N + 1$. Let $\mathbb{Z}_q$ be a field of prime order $q > 2^\delta$ and let $R : \mathcal{P}_n([N]) \to \mathbb{Z}_q^*$ be a random oracle. Then for any PPT algorithm $\mathcal{A}$ it holds that*

$$
\Pr\left[ 2\left(n - \left|\bigcap_{i \in [\ell]} X_i\right|\right) > \mathrm{tdeg}\left( \frac{\sum_{i \in [\ell-1]} R(X_i) \cdot p_{X_i}}{R(X_\ell) \cdot p_{X_\ell}} \right) \right] \leq \mathsf{negl}(\lambda),
$$

*where the randomness is taken over $(X_1, \ldots, X_\ell) \leftarrow \mathcal{A}^{R(\cdot)}(1^\lambda)$ and the choice of the random oracle.*

*Proof.* Denote by $(X_1, \ldots, X_\ell)$ the output of $\mathcal{A}$ and by $W = \{w \mid p_{X_1}(w) = \cdots = p_{X_{\ell-1}}(w) = 0\}$ the set of common roots of the polynomials *in the numerator*. We first note, that the degree of the rational function can only be smaller than $(n - |\bigcap_{i \in [\ell]} X_i|)$, if an additional root of $p_{X_1}$ cancels out. For this to be the case, the sum in the numerator must have a root $z \in [N] \setminus W$. To prove the lemma, it thus suffices to show that

$$
\Pr\left[ \sum_{i \in [\ell-1]} R(X_i) \cdot p_{X_i}(z) = 0 \wedge \exists i \in [\ell-1]. \ p_{X_i}(z) \neq 0 \right] \leq \mathsf{negl}(\lambda).
$$

Denote by $Q$ the set of queries made to the random oracle $R$ before $\mathcal{A}$ produces its output. For any fixed $z \in [N] \setminus W$, and any index $i$ it holds that

$$
\Pr\left[ \sum_{j \in [\ell-1]} R(X_j) \cdot p_{X_j}(z) = 0 \ \middle|\ \exists X_i \notin Q. \ p_{X_i}(z) \neq 0 \right]
$$
$$
= \Pr\left[ R(X_i) = -p_{X_i}^{-1}(z) \cdot \sum_{j \in [\ell-1] \setminus \{i\}} R(X_j) \cdot p_{X_j}(z) \ \middle|\ \exists X_i \notin Q. \ p_{X_i}(z) \neq 0 \right] \leq 2^{-\delta},
$$

since the left-hand side is an independently and uniformly distributed element of $\mathbb{Z}_q^*$. By a union bound this gives us the following probability that there exists any such $z \in [N] \setminus W$ and $X_i \notin Q$:

$$
\Pr\left[ \exists z \in [N] \setminus W. \ \sum_{j \in [\ell-1]} R(X_j) \cdot p_{X_j}(z) = 0 \wedge \exists X_i \notin Q. \ p_{X_i}(z) \neq 0 \right]
$$
$$
\leq \sum_{z \in [N] \setminus W} \Pr\left[ \sum_{j \in [\ell-1]} R(X_j) \cdot p_{X_j}(z) = 0 \wedge \exists X_i \notin Q. \ p_{X_i}(z) \neq 0 \right]
$$
$$
\leq \sum_{z \in [N] \setminus W} \Pr\left[ \sum_{j \in [\ell-1]} R(X_j) \cdot p_{X_j}(z) = 0 \ \middle|\ \exists X_i \notin Q. \ p_{X_i}(z) \neq 0 \right]
$$
$$
= \sum_{z \in [N] \setminus W} 2^{-\delta} \leq N \cdot 2^{-\delta}.
$$

Thus we can conclude that for any $z$ and any $(X_1, \ldots, X_\ell)$ the adversary has to query $R$ on all polynomials that are not vanishing at $z$ to have any hope of succeeding at that evaluation point. At this point, the adversary's task is effectively reduced to finding a sequence $(X_1, \ldots, X_k) \in Q^k$ of length $k \in [\ell - 1]$ such that $p_X(z) \neq 0$ for all $X_i$, but

$$\sum_{i \in [k]} R(X_i) \cdot p_{X_i}(z) = 0.$$

Given such a sequence, the adversary can win by simply "filling up" the sequence to length $\ell - 1$ using sets corresponding to polynomials that vanish at $z$.

Since $\mathcal{A}$ runs in polynomial time, there exists a $\mu = \mathsf{poly}(\lambda)$ such that $|Q| = \mu$. Let $Y_i$ denote the $i$th query made by $\mathcal{A}$ and let $Q_i = \{Y_1, \ldots, Y_i\} \subseteq Q$ denote the set of the first $i$ queries.

Fix an arbitrary $z \in [N]$ and consider the set $Z_i = \{R(Y) \cdot p_Y(z) \mid Y \in Q_i \wedge p_Y(z) \neq 0\}$ with $|Z_i| \leq |Q_i| = i$, which is a set of independent uniformly random elements of $\mathbb{Z}_q^*$ because $R$ is a random oracle and none of the involved polynomials is 0 at point $z$. The number of sequences[5] of elements from $Z_i$ of length at most $\ell - 1$ can be bounded as

$$\left| \bigcup_{k \in [\ell-1]} Z_i^k \right| \leq \sum_{k \in [\ell-1]} i^k \leq 2i^{\ell-1},$$

Assume that a sequence that sums up to zero does *not* exist in $Z_{i-1}$. Then for each of those sequences of $Z_i$ elements, there is *at most* one value of $R(Y_i) \cdot p_{Y_i}(z)$ that would make the sequence sum up to zero. Let ZERO be the event that at least one sequence summing up to zero occurs in $Z_\mu$ and let $\mathsf{ZERO}_i$ be the event that the first such sequence occurs after the $i$th query. Then by the above observation, we have

$$\Pr[\mathsf{ZERO}] = \sum_{i=1}^{\mu} \Pr[\mathsf{ZERO}_i] \leq \sum_{i=1}^{\mu} \Pr\left[ \bigwedge_{j \in [i-1]} \neg \mathsf{ZERO}_j \right] \cdot \frac{2i^{\ell-1}}{2^\delta}$$

$$\leq 2^{1-\delta} \cdot \sum_{i=1}^{\mu} i^{\ell-1}$$

$$\leq 2^{1-\delta} \mu^\ell$$

$$\leq 2^{1-\delta} \lambda^{\ell \log \lambda} = 2^{1+\ell \log^2 \lambda - \delta}$$

where the last inequality follows from the fact that $\mu \leq \lambda^{\log \lambda}$ for large enough $\lambda$. By a union bound over $z \in [N]$, we get that

$$\Pr\left[ \exists z \in [N]. \ \exists (X_1, \ldots, X_k) \in \bigcup_{j \in [\ell-1]} Q^j. \ \sum_{i \in [k]} p_{X_i}(z) = 0 \right] = 2^{\log N + 1 + \ell \log^2 \lambda - \delta}.$$

---

[5] Taking into account the commutativity of addition in $\mathbb{F}$, many of these sequences are actually equivalent. It would be sufficient to count the number of possible *multi-sets* instead. However, counting sequences is an upper bound on this actual number and gives a simpler, though slightly worse, bound for $\delta$.

$$\text{Sample}(1^\lambda)$$

$$(\mathbb{G}_1, \mathbb{G}_2, \mathbb{G}_T, q, e, g_1, g_2) \leftarrow \text{GGen}(1^\lambda)$$

$$r \leftarrow \mathbb{Z}_q \setminus [N]$$

$$\boldsymbol{\Gamma} := \begin{pmatrix} g_1 \ g_1^r \ \cdots \ g_1^{r^n} \\ g_2 \ g_2^r \ \cdots \ g_2^{r^n} \end{pmatrix}$$

$$\textbf{return } h := (\mathbb{G}_1, \mathbb{G}_2, \mathbb{G}_T, q, e, \boldsymbol{\Gamma})$$

$$\text{Hash}^R(h, X)$$

$$\textbf{parse } h \textbf{ as } (\mathbb{G}_1, \mathbb{G}_2, \mathbb{G}_T, q, e, \boldsymbol{\Gamma})$$

$$c := R(X)$$

$$\boldsymbol{a} := \begin{pmatrix} c \cdot p_X(N+1) \\ \vdots \\ c \cdot p_X(N+2t) \end{pmatrix}$$

$$b := \prod_{i=0}^{n} \Gamma_{1,i+1}^{\text{coef}(c \cdot p_X, i)} = g_1^{c \cdot p_X(r)}$$

$$\textbf{return } (\boldsymbol{a}, b)$$

$$\text{Eval}^R\big(h, \big(\boldsymbol{a}^{(1)}, b^{(1)}\big), \ldots, \big(\boldsymbol{a}^{(\ell)}, b^{(\ell)}\big)\big)$$

$$\textbf{parse } h \textbf{ as } (\mathbb{G}_1, \mathbb{G}_2, \mathbb{G}_T, q, e, \boldsymbol{\Gamma})$$

$$\textbf{for } 1 \le i \le 2t$$

$$s_i := \left( N+i, \frac{\sum_{j \in [\ell-1]} a_i^{(j)}}{a_i^{(\ell)}} \right)$$

$$(u, v) := \text{RatInt}(s_1, \ldots, s_t)$$

$$\textbf{return } e\Big(\prod_{j \in [\ell-1]} b^{(j)}, \prod_{i=0}^{n} \Gamma_{2,i+1}^{\text{coef}(v,i)}\Big) \stackrel{?}{=} e\Big(b^{(\ell)}, \prod_{i=0}^{n} \Gamma_{2,i}^{\text{coef}(u,i)}\Big)$$

**Fig. 3.** A family of direct-access robust PPHs for $\text{INT}_\ell^t$.

Note that this event is exactly the event that the adversary can find the desired sequence described above. Since by the lemma statement, $\delta \ge \lambda + (\ell+1) \log^2 \lambda + \log N + 1$ the lemma follows.                                                    □

Equipped with these observations, our construction will now be a natural extension of our previous constructions for the two-input case. The proof of Theorem 17 will therefore mirror the proof of Theorem 4 closely.

**Theorem 17.** *Let* $n = \text{poly}(\lambda)$, $N \in \mathbb{N}$ *with* $n \le N \le 2^\lambda$. *Let* $\text{GGen}$ *be a bilinear group generation algorithm that generates bilinear groups of prime order* $q(\lambda) > 2^\delta$, *where* $\delta \ge \lambda + \ell \log^2 \lambda + \log N + 1$ *and let* $R : \mathcal{P}_n([N]) \to \mathbb{Z}_q^*$ *be a random oracle. Then for any* $t < \frac{n(\log N - \log n)}{2 \log q(\lambda)} - \frac{1}{2}$ *the construction in Fig. 3 is a* $\frac{(2t+1) \log q(\lambda)}{n(\log N - \log n)}$ *-compressing direct-access robust PPH for the multi-input predicate* $\text{INT}_\ell^t$ *and domain* $\mathcal{P}_n([N])$ *if the* $n$-SBDL *assumption holds relative to* $\text{GGen}$.

*Proof.* Let $\mathcal{A}$ be an arbitrary PPT adversary against the direct access robustness of $\mathcal{H}$. We have

$$\Pr[\text{Eval}(h, h(X_1), \ldots, h(X_\ell)) \ne \text{INT}_\ell^t(X_1, \ldots, X_\ell)]$$

$$= \quad \Pr[\mathsf{Eval}(h, h(X_1), \ldots, h(X_\ell)) = 0 \mid \mathsf{INT}_\ell^t(X_1, \ldots, X_\ell) = 1]$$
$$\cdot \Pr[\mathsf{INT}_\ell^t(X_1, \ldots, X_\ell) = 1]$$
$$+ \Pr[\mathsf{Eval}(h, h(X_1), \ldots, h(X_\ell)) = 1 \mid \mathsf{INT}_\ell^t(X_1, \ldots, X_\ell) = 0]$$
$$\cdot \Pr[\mathsf{INT}_\ell^t(X_1, \ldots, X_\ell) = 0],$$

where the probabilities are taken over $h \leftarrow \mathsf{Sample}(1^\lambda)$ and $(X_1, \ldots, X_\ell) \leftarrow \mathcal{A}(h)$. We consider the two cases separately.

**Claim 18.** $\Pr[\mathsf{Eval}(h, h(X_1), \ldots, h(X_\ell)) = 0 \mid \mathsf{INT}_\ell^t(X_1, \ldots, X_\ell) = 1] = 0$

*Proof (claim 18).* Let $c_i = R(X_i)$. Since $\mathsf{INT}_\ell^t(X_1, \ldots, X_\ell) = 1$, it holds that $|X_1 \cap \cdots \cap X_\ell| > n - t$ and by Lemma 15 that

$$\mathsf{tdeg}\left(\frac{\sum_{i \in [\ell-1]} c_i \cdot p_{X_i}}{c_\ell \cdot p_{X_\ell}}\right) < 2t.$$

By Proposition 3, it follows that the rational function can thus be uniquely (up to equivalences) interpolated from $2t$ points. We observe that for $1 \leq i \leq 2t$ it holds that $c_\ell \cdot p_{X_\ell}(N + i) \neq 0$, since the roots of $p_{X_\ell}$ are in the interval $[N]$ by construction and $c_1 \in \mathbb{Z}_q^*$. Therefore,

$$s_i = \frac{\sum_{j \in [\ell-1]} c_j \cdot p_{X_j}(N + i)}{c_\ell \cdot p_{X_\ell}(N + i)}$$

are well-defined and thus

$$\frac{\sum_{j \in [j-1]} c_j \cdot p_{X_j}}{c_\ell \cdot p_{X_\ell}} = \frac{u}{v} \tag{7}$$

where $u/v$ is the rational function computed by $\mathsf{RatInt}$ in $\mathsf{Eval}(h, h(X_1), \ldots, h(X_\ell))$. Finally we observe that

$$e\left(\prod_{j \in [\ell-1]} b^{(j)}, \prod_{i=0}^{n} \Gamma_{2,i+1}^{\mathsf{coef}(v,i)}\right) = e\left(b^{(\ell)}, \prod_{i=0}^{n} \Gamma_{2,i}^{\mathsf{coef}(u,i)}\right)$$

$$\iff e\left(g_1^{\sum_{j \in [\ell-1]} c_j \cdot p_{X_j}(r)}, g_2^{v(r)}\right) = e\left(g_1^{c_\ell \cdot p_{X_\ell}(r)}, g_2^{u(r)}\right)$$

$$\iff e(g_1, g_2)^{\left(\sum_{j \in [\ell-1]} c_j \cdot p_{X_j}(r)\right) \cdot v(r)} = e(g_1, g_2)^{c_\ell \cdot p_{X_\ell}(r) \cdot u(r)}$$

$$\iff \left(\sum_{j \in [\ell-1]} c_j \cdot p_{X_j}(r)\right) \cdot v(r) = c_\ell \cdot p_{X_\ell}(r) \cdot u(r)$$

$$\iff \frac{\sum_{j \in [\ell-1]} c_j \cdot p_{X_j}(r)}{c_\ell \cdot p_{X_\ell}(r)} = \frac{u(r)}{v(r)},$$

which due to Eq. 7 is always true and thus $\mathsf{Eval}$ always returns 1 in this case. $\square$

**Claim 19.** *If the $n$-SBDL assumption holds relative to* GGen, *then*

$$\mathsf{negl}(\lambda) \geq \Pr[\mathsf{Eval}(h, h(X_1), \ldots, h(X_\ell)) = 1 \mid \mathsf{INT}_\ell^t(X_1, \ldots, X_\ell) = 0]$$
$$\cdot \Pr[\mathsf{INT}_\ell^t(X_1, \ldots, X_\ell) = 0].$$

*Proof (claim 19).* Since $\mathsf{INT}_\ell^t(X_1, \ldots, X_\ell) = 0$, it must hold that $0 \leq |X_1 \cap \cdots \cap X_\ell| \leq n - t$. By Lemma 16, since $\mathcal{A}$ is a PPT algorithm, this means that except with negligible probability

$$2t \leq \mathsf{tdeg}\left(\frac{\sum_{i \in [\ell-1]} c_i \cdot p_{X_i}}{c_\ell \cdot p_{X_\ell}}\right) \leq 2n.$$

On the other hand, by construction $u/v$ is the rational function of total degree at most $2t - 1$ uniquely determined by $s_1, \ldots, s_{2t}$. It must therefore hold that

$$\frac{u}{v} \neq \frac{\sum_{i \in [\ell-1]} c_i \cdot p_{X_\ell}}{c_\ell \cdot p_{X_\ell}}.$$

For the last inequality in $\mathsf{Eval}(h, h(X_1), \ldots, h(X_\ell))$ to hold, $(\sum_{i \in [\ell-1]} c_i \cdot p_{X_\ell})/(c_1 \cdot p_{X_\ell})$ and $u/v$ must therefore be two *different* rational functions that agree on point $r$. This means that $r$ must be one of the at most $n + (t-1)/2$ roots of the rational function

$$\frac{\sum_{i \in [\ell-1]} c_i \cdot p_{X_\ell}}{c_\ell \cdot p_{X_\ell}} - \frac{u}{v} = \frac{v \cdot \sum_{i \in [\ell-1]} c_i \cdot p_{X_\ell} - c_\ell \cdot p_{X_\ell} \cdot u}{c_\ell \cdot p_{X_\ell} \cdot v}.$$

Whenever $\mathcal{A}$ would be successful, we could therefore find $r$ by testing the roots of the polynomial $v \cdot \sum_{i \in [\ell-1]} c_i \cdot p_{X_\ell} - c_\ell \cdot p_{X_\ell} \cdot u$. We give a formal reduction as follows:

$\mathcal{R}$ takes as input

$$\mathbb{G}_1, \mathbb{G}_2, \mathbb{G}_T, q, e, \vec{\Gamma} := \begin{pmatrix} g_1 \ g_1^r \ \cdots \ g_1^{r^n} \\ g_2 \ g_2^r \ \cdots \ g_2^{r^n} \end{pmatrix}$$

and invokes $\mathcal{A}$ on $h := (\mathbb{G}_1, \mathbb{G}_2, \mathbb{G}_T, q, e, \vec{\Gamma})$ and receives $X_1, \ldots, X_\ell$.

The reduction then checks whether $\mathsf{INT}_\ell^t(X_1, \ldots, X_\ell) = 0$ and aborts otherwise. We denote this event as $\mathsf{INT}_0$. Next $\mathcal{R}$ checks whether

$$\mathsf{tdeg}\left(\frac{\sum_{i \in [\ell-1]} c_i \cdot p_{X_i}}{c_\ell \cdot p_{X_\ell}}\right) \geq 2t$$

and again aborts otherwise. We denote this event as $\mathsf{TDEG}_{\geq 2t}$. Note, that as argued above, by Lemma 16

$$\Pr[\mathsf{TDEG}_\geq \mid \mathsf{INT}_0] \geq 1 - \mathsf{negl}(\lambda).$$

If it has not aborted, $\mathcal{R}$ then computes $(u, v)$ as in Eval and determines the set $X$ of roots of the polynomial $v \cdot \sum_{i \in [\ell-1]} c_i \cdot p_{X_\ell} - c_\ell \cdot p_{X_\ell} \cdot u$. For each $r' \in X$, $\mathcal{R}$ checks whether $g_1^{r'} \overset{?}{=} \Gamma_{1,2}$ and returns $r'$ if it holds. If the equality holds for no $r' \in X$, $\mathcal{R}$ aborts.

The reduction $\mathcal{R}$ essentially performs three steps, executing $\mathcal{A}$, checking the total degree of a rational function, and finding the roots of a polynomial. Each of those steps can be performed in polynomial time. It follows that $\mathcal{R}$ is PPT and must, by assumption, have a negligible success probability against the $n$-SBDL problem.

Note that $r$ from the input of the reduction is distributed uniformly in $\mathbb{Z}_q$, while $\mathcal{A}$ expects $r$ to be uniformly distributed in $\mathbb{Z}_q \setminus [N]$. However, since and $q > 2^\delta \geq 2^{\lambda + \ell \log^2 \lambda + \log N + 1} \geq N \cdot 2^{\lambda + \ell \log^2 \lambda + 1}$, it holds that $r \in \mathbb{Z}_q \setminus [N]$ with probability at least $1 - 2^{-\lambda - \ell \log^2 \lambda - 1}$. Furthermore, once we condition on $r \notin [N]$, the distribution of $h$ is identical to the one expected by $\mathcal{A}$.

Now, observe that the reduction $\mathcal{R}$ is successful, if $\mathcal{A}$ outputs $X_1, \ldots, X_\ell$, such that $\mathsf{INT}_0$ and $\mathsf{TDEG}_{\geq 2t}$ both occur and $r$ is one of the roots of $v \cdot \sum_{i \in [\ell-1]} c_i \cdot p_{X_\ell} - c_\ell \cdot p_{X_\ell} \cdot u$. As argued above, conditioned on the first two, the latter must be true, if $\mathsf{Eval}(h, h(X_1), \ldots, h(X_\ell)) = 1$. Therefore, it holds that

$$\mathsf{negl}(\lambda)$$

$$\geq \Pr\left[ r = \mathcal{R}\left( \mathbb{G}_1, \mathbb{G}_2, \mathbb{G}_T, q, e, \begin{pmatrix} g_1 \ g_1^r \ \cdots \ g_1^{r^n} \\ g_2 \ g_2^r \ \cdots \ g_2^{r^n} \end{pmatrix} \right) \right]$$

$$\geq \Pr[r \notin [N]] \cdot \Pr\left[ r = \mathcal{R}\left( \mathbb{G}_1, \mathbb{G}_2, \mathbb{G}_T, q, e, \begin{pmatrix} g_1 \ g_1^r \ \cdots \ g_1^{r^n} \\ g_2 \ g_2^r \ \cdots \ g_2^{r^n} \end{pmatrix} \right) \ \middle| \ r \notin [N] \right]$$

$$\geq (1 - \mathsf{negl}(\lambda)) \cdot \Pr[\mathsf{Eval}(h, h(X_1), \ldots, h(X_\ell)) = 1 \mid \mathsf{INT}_0, \mathsf{TDEG}_{\geq 2t}]$$
$$\cdot \Pr[\mathsf{TDEG}_{\geq 2t} \mid \mathsf{INT}_0] \cdot \Pr[\mathsf{INT}_0]$$

$$\geq \Pr[\mathsf{Eval}(h, h(X_1), \ldots, h(X_\ell)) = 1 \mid \mathsf{INT}_0, \mathsf{TDEG}_{\geq 2t}]$$
$$\cdot \Pr[\mathsf{TDEG}_{\geq 2t} \mid \mathsf{INT}_0] \cdot \Pr[\mathsf{INT}_0] - \mathsf{negl}(\lambda)$$

$$\geq \Pr[\mathsf{Eval}(h, h(X_1), \ldots, h(X_\ell)) = 1 \mid \mathsf{INT}_0] \cdot \Pr[\mathsf{INT}_0]$$
$$- \Pr[\neg \mathsf{TDEG}_{\geq 2t} \mid \mathsf{INT}_0] - \mathsf{negl}(\lambda)$$

$$\geq \Pr[\mathsf{Eval}(h, h(X_1), \ldots, h(X_\ell)) = 1 \mid \mathsf{INT}_0] \cdot \Pr[\mathsf{INT}_0] - \mathsf{negl}(\lambda)$$

and the claim follows.    □

Using Claims 18 and 19 we can thus conclude that

$$\Pr[\mathsf{Eval}(h, h(X_1), \ldots, h(X_\ell)) \neq \mathsf{INT}_\ell^t(X_1, \ldots, X_\ell)] \leq 0 + \mathsf{negl}(\lambda) = \mathsf{negl}(\lambda).$$

Therefore, $\mathcal{H}$ is direct access robust as claimed. It remains to show that it is also compressing. The domain of the hash function is $\mathcal{P}_n([N])$, the codomain is $\mathbb{Z}_{q(\lambda)}^t \times \mathbb{G}_1$. It follows that the compression factor is

$$\eta \leq \frac{\log |\mathbb{Z}_{q(\lambda)}^{2t} \times \mathbb{G}_1|}{\log |\mathcal{P}_n([N])|} = \frac{\log q(\lambda)^{2t+1}}{\log \binom{N}{n}} \leq \frac{\log q(\lambda)^{2t+1}}{\log(\frac{N}{n})^n} = \frac{(2t+1) \log q(\lambda)}{n(\log N - \log n)}$$

as claimed. The construction is thus compressing, if

$$\frac{(2t+1)\log q(\lambda)}{n(\log N - \log n)} < 1 \iff t < \frac{n(\log N - \log n)}{2 \log q} - \frac{1}{2}.$$

$\square$

# 6   Lower Bounds

In this section, we show that the compression rate of our constructions for the $\mathsf{SSD}^t$ and $\mathsf{INT}_2^t$ predicates are close to optimal. We prove our lower bound on the size of a hash value by drawing connections to one-round communication complexity lower bounds. Such a connection was already observed in the work of BLV[6], but we state our lower bound and full proof here for the sake of completeness.

**Theorem 20** ([6]). *For a universe $U$, let $X, Y \subseteq \mathcal{P}_n(U)$. Let the set disjointness predicate be defined as follows:*

$$\mathsf{DISJ}(X,Y) = \begin{cases} 1 & \text{if } X \cap Y = \emptyset \\ 0 & \text{Otherwise} \end{cases}$$

*For $n < \sqrt{|U|}$ the one-way randomized communication complexity of $\mathsf{DISJ}(X,Y)$ in the common random string model is $\Omega(n \log n)$.*

In contrast to BLV, who prove the non-existence of PPH functions for certain parameters, we prove a lower bound on the size of the hash value for parameters where PPH functions are feasible.

**Theorem 21.** *Let $\mathcal{H} = \{h : \mathcal{P}_n(U) \to Y\}$ be a family of direct-access robust PPH functions for the symmetric set difference predicate $\mathsf{SSD}^t$ for some universe $U$ with $|U| > t^2/4 + n - t/2$. Then,*

$$\log |Y| \in \Omega(t \log t).$$

*Proof.* We assume without loss of generality, that $t$ is even.[7] Fix an arbitrary set $S \in \mathcal{P}_{n-t/2}(U)$. We prove the stated theorem by using $\mathcal{H}$ to construct a communication efficient one-round protocol for the set disjointness problem for input sets of size $t/2$ from the universe $U' = U \setminus S$. Let $R$ be the common random string that the parties can access in the set disjointness problem. Let $A, B \in \mathcal{P}_{n'}(U')$ be the input sets of the two parties. The protocol proceeds as follows:

The parties define $A' = A \cup S$ and $B' = B \cup S$. We note that $|A'| = |B'| = n$ and that $\mathsf{SSD}^t(A', B') = 1$ if and only if $A \cap B = \emptyset$. I.e.,

---

[6] See Theorem 36 in [4].

[7] Note that for sets of equal size, the symmetric set difference is always even and therefore $\mathsf{SSD}^{2i-1} = \mathsf{SSD}^{2i}$ for all $i \in \mathbb{N}_+$.

$\mathsf{SSD}^t(A', B') = \mathsf{DISJ}(A, B)$. Both parties then sample a hash function $h \in \mathcal{H}$ using randomness $R$ and security parameter $n$. We let party $P_A$ holding $A$ send $z = h(A')$ to party $P_B$ holding $B$. Party $P_B$ computes $b = \mathsf{Eval}(h, z, h(B'))$ and outputs $b$. Note, that $A', B'$ are fixed before and independently of $h$. It follows from the direct access robustness of $\mathcal{H}$ that for any such a priori fixed $A', B'$ it holds that

$$\Pr[\mathsf{Eval}(h, h(A'), h(B') = \mathsf{SSD}^t(A', B')] \geq 1 - \mathsf{negl}(n)$$

where the probability is taken over the random choice of $h \in \mathcal{H}$. It therefore holds that $\Pr[b = \mathsf{DISJ}^t(A, B)] \geq 1 - \mathsf{negl}(n)$.

Observe that by definition of $U'$ and $S$, it holds that $|U'| = |U| - |S| = |U| - (n - t/2)$. By the condition on $|U|$ from the theorem statement, it thus follows that

$$|U'| > \frac{t^2}{4} + n - t/2 - (n - t/2) = \frac{t^2}{4},$$

and thereby $\sqrt{|U'|} > t/2$. Since the protocol described above works for sets of size $t/2$, Theorem 20 therefore applies. The total communication of our protocol consists of $z \in Y$, thus by Theorem 20 we have that $\log|Y| \in \Omega(t \log t)$.     $\square$

Via the equivalence of the $\mathsf{SSD}^t$ and $\mathsf{INT}^t$ predicate proven in Proposition 14, we immediately also get the following lower bound on size of a hash value of a PPH function for $\mathsf{INT}_2^t$.

**Corollary 22.** *Let $\mathcal{H} = \{h : \mathcal{P}_n(U) \to Y\}$ be a family of direct-access robust PPH functions for the two-input intersection predicate $\mathsf{INT}_2^t$ for some universe $U$ with $|U| > t^2 + n - t$. Then,*

$$\log|Y| \in \Omega(t \log t).$$

# References

1. Ben-Eliezer, O., Jayaram, R., Woodruff, D.P., Yogev, E.: A framework for adversarially robust streaming algorithms. In: Proceedings of the 39th ACM SIGMOD-SIGACT-SIGAI Symposium on Principles of Database Systems, pp. 63–80 (2020). https://doi.org/10.1145/3375395.3387658
2. Bloom, B.H.: Space/time trade-offs in hash coding with allowable errors. Commun. ACM **13**(7), 422–426 (1970). https://doi.org/10.1145/362686.362692
3. Boneh, D., Boyen, X.: Efficient selective-ID secure identity-based encryption without random oracles. In: Cachin, C., Camenisch, J.L. (eds.) EUROCRYPT 2004. LNCS, vol. 3027, pp. 223–238. Springer, Heidelberg (2004). https://doi.org/10.1007/978-3-540-24676-3_14
4. Boyle, E., LaVigne, R., Vaikuntanathan, V.: Adversarially robust property-preserving hash functions. In: Blum, A. (ed.) ITCS 2019: 10th Innovations in Theoretical Computer Science Conference, vol. 124, pp. 16:1–16:20. LIPIcs, San Diego, 10–12 January 2019. https://doi.org/10.4230/LIPIcs.ITCS.2019.16

5. Clayton, D., Patton, C., Shrimpton, T.: Probabilistic data structures in adversarial environments. In: Cavallaro, L., Kinder, J., Wang, X., Katz, J. (eds.) ACM CCS 2019: 26th Conference on Computer and Communications Security, pp. 1317–1334. ACM Press, 11–15 November 2019. https://doi.org/10.1145/3319535.3354235
6. Dasgupta, A., Kumar, R., Sivakumar, D.: Sparse and lopsided set disjointness via information theory. In: Gupta, A., Jansen, K., Rolim, J., Servedio, R. (eds.) APPROX/RANDOM -2012. LNCS, vol. 7408, pp. 517–528. Springer, Heidelberg (2012). https://doi.org/10.1007/978-3-642-32512-0_44
7. Ghosh, S., Simkin, M.: The communication complexity of threshold private set intersection. In: Boldyreva, A., Micciancio, D. (eds.) CRYPTO 2019. LNCS, vol. 11693, pp. 3–29. Springer, Cham (2019). https://doi.org/10.1007/978-3-030-26951-7_1
8. Ghosh, S., Simkin, M.: The communication complexity of threshold private set intersection. Cryptology ePrint Archive, Report 2019/175 (2019). https://eprint.iacr.org/2019/175
9. Goyal, V., O'Neill, A., Rao, V.: Correlated-input secure hash functions. In: Ishai, Y. (ed.) TCC 2011. LNCS, vol. 6597, pp. 182–200. Springer, Heidelberg (2011). https://doi.org/10.1007/978-3-642-19571-6_12
10. Hardt, M., Woodruff, D.P.: How robust are linear sketches to adaptive inputs? In: Boneh, D., Roughgarden, T., Feigenbaum, J. (eds.) 45th Annual ACM Symposium on Theory of Computing, pp. 121–130. ACM Press, Palo Alto, 1–4 June 2013. https://doi.org/10.1145/2488608.2488624
11. Indyk, P., Motwani, R.: Approximate nearest neighbors: towards removing the curse of dimensionality. In: 30th Annual ACM Symposium on Theory of Computing, pp. 604–613. ACM Press, Dallas, 23–26 May 1998. https://doi.org/10.1145/276698.276876
12. Minsky, Y., Trachtenberg, A., Zippel, R.: Set reconciliation with nearly optimal communication complexity. IEEE Trans. Inf. Theory 49(9), 2213–2218 (2003). https://doi.org/10.1109/TIT.2003.815784
13. Mironov, I., Naor, M., Segev, G.: Sketching in adversarial environments. In: Ladner, R.E., Dwork, C. (eds.) 40th Annual ACM Symposium on Theory of Computing, pp. 651–660. ACM Press, Victoria, 17–20 May 2008. https://doi.org/10.1145/1374376.1374471
14. Muthukrishnan, S.: Data streams: algorithms and applications. In: 14th Annual ACM-SIAM Symposium on Discrete Algorithms, pp. 413–413. ACM-SIAM, Baltimore, 12–14 January 2003
15. Naor, M., Yogev, E.: Bloom filters in adversarial environments. In: Gennaro, R., Robshaw, M. (eds.) CRYPTO 2015. LNCS, vol. 9216, pp. 565–584. Springer, Heidelberg (2015). https://doi.org/10.1007/978-3-662-48000-7_28
16. Pagh, R., Rodler, F.F.: Cuckoo hashing. J. Algorithms 51(2), 122–144 (2004). https://doi.org/10.1016/j.jalgor.2003.12.002

# Alibi: A Flaw in Cuckoo-Hashing Based Hierarchical ORAM Schemes and a Solution

Brett Hemenway Falk[1]([✉]), Daniel Noble[1], and Rafail Ostrovsky[2]

[1] University of Pennsylvania, Philadelphia, USA
{fbrett,dgnoble}@cis.upenn.edu
[2] UCLA, Los Angeles, USA
rafail@cs.ucla.edu

**Abstract.** *There once was a table of hashes*
*That held extra items in stashes*
*It all seemed like bliss*
*But things went amiss*
*When the stashes were stored in the caches*
The first Oblivious RAM protocols introduced the "hierarchical solution," (STOC '90) where the server stores a series of hash tables of geometrically increasing capacities. Each ORAM query would read a small number of locations from each level of the hierarchy, and each level of the hierarchy would be reshuffled and rebuilt at geometrically increasing intervals to ensure that no single query was ever repeated twice at the same level. This yielded an ORAM protocol with polylogarithmic overhead.

Future works extended and improved the hierarchical solution, replacing traditional hashing with cuckoo hashing (ICALP '11) and cuckoo hashing with a combined stash (Goodrich et al. SODA '12). In this work, we identify a subtle flaw in the protocol of Goodrich et al. (SODA '12) that uses cuckoo hashing with a stash in the hierarchical ORAM solution.

We give a concrete distinguishing attack against this type of hierarchical ORAM that uses cuckoo hashing with a *combined* stash. This security flaw has propagated to at least 5 subsequent hierarchical ORAM protocols, including the recent optimal ORAM scheme, OptORAMa (Eurocrypt '20).

In addition to our attack, we identify a simple fix that does not increase the asymptotic complexity.

We note, however, that our attack only affects more recent *hierarchical ORAMs*, but does not affect the early protocols that predate the use of cuckoo hashing, or other types of ORAM solutions (e.g. Path ORAM or Circuit ORAM).

## 1 Introduction

In this work, we describe an attack on a wide variety of *hierarchical Oblivious RAM (ORAM)* protocols in the literature. Oblivious RAM is a cryptographic primitive designed to allow a client to securely execute RAM programs using an

© International Association for Cryptologic Research 2021
A. Canteaut and F.-X. Standaert (Eds.): EUROCRYPT 2021, LNCS 12698, pp. 338–369, 2021.
https://doi.org/10.1007/978-3-030-77883-5_12

*untrusted* memory. ORAM provides a method for simulating a virtual memory array, such that for any two equal-length sequences of reads and writes into the virtual array, the sequences of accesses to the underlying *physical memory* are indistinguishable.

Typically, encryption protects the data *content*, however, even when the underlying data are encrypted simply observing the *data access pattern* can leak significant information.

ORAM is applicable in several different types of scenarios, including:

1. **Outsourced storage:** If a client makes use of an outsourced (cloud) storage provider, even if the content is encrypted, the storage provider can observe the client's access pattern. This may leak sensitive information. ORAM allows all sequences of accesses (of equal length) to be indistinguishable to the server. (Note that if the *amount* of data that the user accesses is sensitive, then ORAM cannot hide this.)
2. **Secure hardware:** If a small, trusted hardware component makes use of a (cheaper) untrusted memory, observing the memory access pattern can compromise the security of the processes running within the trusted component. This was the original proposed application [Ost90] and is a concern where memory side-channel attacks exist. A secure enclave, such as Intel SGX, is a recent real-world computing environment in which computation is performed on secure hardware, but the application needs the memory resources of an untrusted operating system. A series of works have shown that revealing memory access patterns is indeed a problem for SGX [BMD+17, GESM17, MIE17, JHOvD17], and this leakage can be mitigated using ORAM and other oblivious data structures to allow enclaves to use untrusted memory without leaking access patterns [SGF17].
3. **Secure multiparty computation (MPC):** ORAM is also useful in secure multiparty computation (MPC), where a group of parties engage in a distributed protocol to compute a joint function of their private data. Most MPC protocols use cryptographic secret sharing to protect the *content* of the data, and execute computations in the *circuit model* to ensure that the computation's control flow remains independent of the private data. Efficient ORAM protocols have the potential for allowing efficient, secure multiparty computation in the *RAM model* [OS97, LHS+14, Ds17, WHC+14].

The first ORAM construction [Ost90], introduced the *hierarchical solution*, and many subsequent works have expanded and built on this paradigm [Ost92, GO96, GMOT12, KLO12, LO13, PPRY18, AKL+20]. We review the hierarchical solution in Sect. 2.5.

The original Hierarchical ORAM builds a hierarchy of $\mathcal{O}(\log(n))$ levels, each containing a hash table with buckets of size $\mathcal{O}(\log(n))$, leading to lookups (ignoring the costs of rebuilds[1]) having a cost of $\mathcal{O}(\log^2(n))$.

---

[1] Rebuilds require constructing oblivious hash tables, which is relatively costly, so the amortized cost of lookups is usually dominated by the rebuild cost. Much of the progress in the literature has been towards reducing this cost, but to simplify the narrative, we focus here only on the costs of lookups without rebuilds.

To reduce the cost of each lookup, the traditional hash tables at each level can be replaced with cuckoo hashing, which reduces the cost of accessing each hash table to $\mathcal{O}(1)$ per virtual access. The initial solution [PR10] allowed cuckoo hashing to fail with some non-negligible probability, and in the case that it did, the hash table would be reconstructed. The failure (and rebuilding) of a cuckoo hash led to security problems, however, since the ORAM protocol would rebuild the hash table until there were no collisions, an adversary who observed a collision in the *physical access pattern*, would learn that the client had made queries for elements not stored in that level [GM11].

This problem was resolved by reducing the cuckoo hash failure probability by including a stash [PR04]. If each Cuckoo Hash Table in the hierarchy includes a $\mathcal{O}(\log(n))$-sized stash, the probability of a build failure becomes negligible, and no rehashing is needed [GM11].[2] At query time, every element of the stash at each level needed to be accessed, so although this eliminated the security problem created by cuckoo hashing failures, it did not improve the asymptotic overhead, which remained $\mathcal{O}\left(\log^2(n)\right)$.

Scanning separate cuckoo stashes at every level of the hierarchy significantly adds to the query complexity, and Goodrich et al. [GMOT12] then observed that even though the size of the stash for *each* level needs to be $\mathcal{O}(\log(n))$ in order to ensure a negligible probability of failure, the same failure probability could be maintained by combining the stashes at all levels into a single $\mathcal{O}(\log(n))$-sized stash. Similarly, Kushilevitz et al. [KLO12] proposed that elements that would otherwise be placed in a cuckoo stash could instead be re-inserted directly into the ORAM data structure. Both these techniques improved the asymptotic complexity of accesses in the hierarchical solution to $\mathcal{O}(\log(n))$ physical accesses per virtual access.

In this work, we show that the techniques of combining cuckoo stashes across different levels of the hierarchy (introduced by Goodrich et al. and Kushilevitz et al.) creates a subtle security flaw which gives an adversary non-negligible advantage in distinguishing access patterns. The problem is similar to the problem in [PR10], where rehashing in the event of a build failure leaked information about the elements being stored at that level. Removing the elements from the stash on each level, like performing a rehashing, causes the elements that would have been in the stash to no longer be in that level. Therefore, if these elements are searched for they will be found before this level is reached, so instead of accessing the locations for the stashed elements at that level, random locations will be accessed instead. This means that, if all elements that were placed in a given level are searched for (including the items that were stashed), the access pattern of that level is less likely to contain any collisions in the *physical access pattern*. In contrast, if no elements from that level are accessed, all accessed locations

---

[2] Even though a logarithmic-sized stash provides a negligible failure probability, for the smaller levels, a failure probability that is negligible in the size of the *level* may be non-negligible in the overall size of the ORAM. To avoid this problem, [GM11] suggested using traditional hash tables (rather than cuckoo hashing) for the smaller levels of the hierarchy, *i.e.*, until the level size reached $\mathcal{O}\left(\log^7(n)\right)$.

will be random. The expected number of collisions will therefore be higher in the second case, and we will show that this difference is non-negligible.

This flaw affects a large number of papers [GMOT12, KLO12, LO13, PPRY18, KM19, AKL+20] which combine stashes in order to eliminate super-constant sized stashes at each level. This does not affect earlier hierarchical solutions that did not combine the stash e.g. [Ost90, Ost92, GO96] or non-hierarchical ORAMs such as PathORAM [SvDS+13] or Circuit ORAM [WCS15]. In addition to finding this flaw, we present a simple solution. Our solution applies to all schemes which suffer from the flaw without affecting their asymptotic complexity.

In Sect. 2.3, we review cuckoo hashing, and in Sect. 2.5 we review the basic hierarchical ORAM construction. In Sect. 3, we present our concrete attack that allows an adversary to distinguish two different access patterns with non-negligible probability in hierarchical ORAM solutions that use Cuckoo Hashing with a *combined stash*. This attack has a nice intuitive interpretation. However, this attack does not apply directly to PanORAMa and OptORAMa, so in Sect. 4 we present a generic version of our attack which does apply to these protocols. The generic attack is also shorter and simpler. In Sect. 5 we present our solution and prove that it is correct. Finally, we present the protocols that have been affected by this flaw in Sect. 6.

## 2 Preliminaries

### 2.1 Notation and Model

For any positive integer $x$, $[x] \stackrel{\text{def}}{=} \{1, \dots, x\}$. For a set $Z$, $z \stackrel{\$}{\leftarrow} Z$ denotes that $z$ is chosen uniformly at random from $Z$ and $2^Z$ denotes the powerset of $Z$.

We denote a sequence using parenthesis as follows: $v = (v_1, \dots, v_t)$. Sequences can alternatively be thought of as vectors or tuples, and we use the standard subscript $v_i$ to denote the element at location $i$ of sequence $v$. Set notation (e.g. $\in, \cup$) is often applied to sequences, in which case the sequence is implicitly first mapped to the set of elements it contains.

We think of an ORAM as an oblivious implementation of a RAM. Therefore, the index space, which we denote $\mathcal{V}$, is simply $[N]$, where $N$ is the size of the ORAM.[3] We assume that the payloads are chosen from a space $\mathcal{W}$. For all $w \in \mathcal{W}$ we assume that $|w|$, the length of the bit-representation of $w$, is the same, so that items cannot be distinguished by volumetric attacks.

As is standard practice, we model the hash functions as truly random functions (see [Mit09] for a discussion of this assumption). Assuming that the hash functions are truly random implies that the adversary (who only learns outputs of the hash function) cannot gain any additional information about the hash function. Our protocols are secure against computationally *unbounded* adversaries in this model.[4] We consider protocols secure (information-theoretically

---

[3] With some additional work, an ORAM scheme can be made to be an oblivious implementation of a *dictionary*, *i.e.*, that have keys chosen from a space different than $[N]$, but we avoid this version for simplicity.

[4] In practice, implementations must use hash functions that are not truly random, but seem sufficiently random to a computationally bounded adversary.

secure in the random hash function model) if the distributions of adversary views do not change much based on sensitive data. Formally, let $D(x)$, $D(x')$ be two distributions of views of the adversary on differing sensitive data $x$ and $x'$. Let $\Delta(D(x), D(x'))$ denote the statistical distance between two distributions. Protocols are secure if $\Delta(D(x), D(x'))$ is negligible (in $N$) for all pairs $x$, $x'$.

## 2.2   Oblivious Hash Tables

The hierarchical ORAM scheme builds on Oblivious Hash Tables which we formalize and abstract in Definition 1. We view a hash table as a method for storing $(v, w)$ pairs, where $v \in \mathcal{V} = [N]$ is a (virtual) index, and $w \in \mathcal{W}$ is a payload. Let $\mathcal{X} = \mathcal{V} \times \mathcal{W}$.

**Definition 1 (Oblivious Hash Tables).** *An Oblivious Hash Table*

$$T = (\mathsf{Gen}, \mathsf{Build}, \mathsf{Lookup}, \mathsf{Delete}, \mathsf{Extract})$$

*is a tuple of polynomial-time algorithms*

- **Setup:** $\mathsf{k} \leftarrow \mathsf{Gen}(N, m)$ *generates a key for a hash table of capacity $m$, storing (virtual) indices from $[N]$. In most cases, the key is simply the description of the hash functions.*
- **Building:** *The function $T \leftarrow \mathsf{Build}(\mathsf{k}, X)$ takes a set, $X \subset \mathcal{X}$, $|X| \leq m$ and builds a table, $T$, containing the elements in $X$. For any $X$, the probability that $\mathsf{Build}(\mathsf{k}, X)$ fails is negligible in $N$, i.e., is bounded by $N^{-\omega(1)}$.*
- **Lookup:** *The deterministic function $Q \leftarrow \mathsf{Lookup}(\mathsf{k}, v)$ takes a (virtual) index $v \in \mathcal{V}$, and returns a set of query locations $Q \subset [|T|]$.*
- **Delete:** *The deterministic function $\mathsf{Delete}(\mathsf{k}, v, T)$ removes items $(v, w)$ if they exist in any location $T[i]$ where $i \in Q \leftarrow \mathsf{Lookup}(\mathsf{k}, v)$. Delete accesses exactly the indexes of $T$ in $Q$ and does not access any other memory.*
- **Extract:** *The function $\bar{X} \leftarrow \mathsf{Extract}(\mathsf{k}, T)$, takes a key $\mathsf{k}$ and a table $T$ and returns a set of elements $\bar{X}$.*

*These algorithms satisfy the following correctness properties. Suppose $\mathsf{k} \leftarrow \mathsf{Gen}(N, m)$ and $X \subset \mathcal{X}$ with $|X| \leq m$.*

- **Building:** *If $T \leftarrow \mathsf{Build}(\mathsf{k}, X)$, then $T \in \mathcal{X}^{|T|}$. For every $(v, w) \in X$, we say that the payload $w$ was stored in virtual location $v$ and that $(v, w)$ is stored in $T$.*
- **Lookup:** *If $T \leftarrow \mathsf{Build}(\mathsf{k}, X)$, then for any $(v, w) \in X$, if $v$ has not been deleted from $T$, the lookup $Q \leftarrow \mathsf{Lookup}(\mathsf{k}, v)$ produces a set of indices, $Q \subset [|T|]$ such that $(v, w) \in T[i]$ for some $i \in Q$ with probability at least $1 - N^{-\omega(1)}$.*
- **Extraction:** *If $\mathsf{k}, T$ are constructed as above, and $D$ is the set of items deleted from table $T$, and $\bar{X} \leftarrow \mathsf{Extract}(\mathsf{k}, T)$ then $x = (v, w) \in \bar{X}$ iff $(v, w) \in X$, $v \notin D$,*

*Additionally, these algorithms will need to allow the above functions to be executed obliviously. We define two notions of obliviousness: access-obliviousness and full obliviousness. Full obliviousness includes access-obliviousness. In our attack, we show that "combined-stash" cuckoo hashing schemes are not access-oblivious, and hence cannot be fully oblivious. Since the techniques used to obliviously perform builds and extractions are complex and varied, focusing on access-obliviousness will simplify exposition.*

*In brief, a protocol is access-oblivious if equal-length non-repeating sequences of indexes have indistinguishable outputs from* Lookup. *This is the best that can be achieved. Since* Lookup *is deterministic, repeated indexes in the input to* Lookup *will result in repeated outputs, so if one sequence contains repeats and another doesn't the outputs of* Lookup *will be easily distinguishable. ORAM can be viewed as a way of modifying an Oblivious Hash Table to allow repeated queries of the same index.*

**Definition 2.** *A sequence $v = (v_1, \ldots, v_t)$ is said to be* non-repeating *if for all $1 \leq i < j \leq t$, $v_i \neq v_j$.*

– *Obliviousness:*

 • *Access-obliviousness: For any two sets $X, X' \subset \mathcal{X}$ with $|X|, |X'| \leq m$ and any* non-repeating *sequences of virtual indices $v, v' \in \mathcal{V}^t$ the sequence of outputs of* Lookup(k, ·) *on $v$ and $v'$ have negligible statistical distance (in $N$). In other words*

$$\Delta \left( (Q_1, \ldots, Q_t), (Q'_1, \ldots, Q'_t) \right) < N^{\omega(1)}$$

*where the sequence of queries $(Q_1, \ldots, Q_t)$ and $(Q'_1, \ldots, Q'_t)$ are generated according to the following experiments:*

$$\left\{ (Q_1, \ldots, Q_t) \; \middle| \; \begin{array}{l} T \leftarrow \mathsf{Build}(\mathsf{k}, X) \\ Q_1 \leftarrow \mathsf{Lookup}(\mathsf{k}, v_1) \\ \vdots \\ Q_t \leftarrow \mathsf{Lookup}(\mathsf{k}, v_t) \end{array} \right\}$$

*and*

$$\left\{ (Q'_1, \ldots, Q'_t) \; \middle| \; \begin{array}{l} T' \leftarrow \mathsf{Build}(\mathsf{k}', X') \\ Q'_1 \leftarrow \mathsf{Lookup}(\mathsf{k}', v'_1) \\ \vdots \\ Q'_t \leftarrow \mathsf{Lookup}(\mathsf{k}', v'_t) \end{array} \right\}.$$

 • *Full obliviousness: The complete sequence of accesses from building, lookups, deletions and extractions are oblivious, provided that the lookup and deletion sequences are the same, and the sequences are non-repeating. Note that deletions access the same locations as the results of lookups, so the access pattern of deletions do not provide additional information and can be ignored. Concretely, for any two sets* $X, X' \subset \mathcal{X}$ *with* $|X|, |X'| \leq m$ *and any non-repeating sequences* $v, v' \in \mathcal{V}^t$ *and*

$$A \stackrel{def}{=} \left\{ \mathsf{Acc} \left( \begin{array}{l} T \leftarrow \mathsf{Build}(\mathsf{k}, X) \\ \bar{X} \leftarrow \mathsf{Extract}(\mathsf{k}, T) \end{array} \right) \ \middle| \ \mathsf{k} \leftarrow \mathsf{Gen}(N, m) \right\}$$

*and*

$$A' \stackrel{def}{=} \left\{ \mathsf{Acc} \left( \begin{array}{l} T' \leftarrow \mathsf{Build}(\mathsf{k}', X') \\ \bar{X}' \leftarrow \mathsf{Extract}(\mathsf{k}', T') \end{array} \right) \ \middle| \ \mathsf{k}' \leftarrow \mathsf{Gen}(N, m) \right\}$$

*where* $\mathsf{Acc}(f(\cdot))$ *are the set of physical memory accesses when executing function* $f$ *and* $Q_i$, $Q'_i$ *are defined as above using the same* $v, v', X, X', \mathsf{k}, \mathsf{k}'$, *then*

$$\Delta \left( (A, Q_1, \ldots, Q_t), (A', Q'_1, \ldots, Q'_t) \right) < N^{\omega(1)}$$

*Remark 1 (Full Obliviousness).* In a single-party ORAM setting, the hash-table must provide full obliviousness. It is possible in a multi-party setting to have the construction, accessing and extraction of the hash table be performed by different parties (*e.g.,* [LO13]). In this case, the set of functions executed by each individual party must be oblivious, but the combined set of all functions need not be.

*Remark 2 (Insertions).* Although most hash tables support *insertion*, the hierarchical ORAM construction does not require this feature – instead, elements are inserted into the ORAM only during rebuilds. Thus we do not include insertion as a necessary functionality in our formal definition of a hash table.

*Remark 3 (Deletions and Extraction).* Some ORAM schemes do not delete items as they are accessed, but rather extract data from all levels and then perform deduplication. However, the definition presented here simplifies proofs.

## 2.3   Cuckoo Hashing

Cuckoo hashing was introduced in [PR04] as a method of multiple-choice hashing with expected constant-time lookups. Since its introduction, many variants of cuckoo hashing have been proposed and analyzed (see [Mit09] for a review). In this section, we review a basic common form of cuckoo hashing, but we emphasize that our attack works for almost all types of hashing with a stash.

We view a Cuckoo Hash Table as an array, $T$, with $cn + s$ locations, each having capacity one. Each element, $x$, can be placed in one of $d$ locations given by $h_i(x)$ for $i = 1, \ldots, d$ where $h_i(x) \in [cn]$. If an element cannot be placed in one of its $d$ locations, it is placed in a logarithmic-sized "stash," *i.e.,* a location in $cn + 1, \ldots, cn + s$.

With appropriate choices of constants $c$ and $d$, and a stash of size $s = \log(n)$, cuckoo hashing will succeed except with probability negligible in $n$ (Theorem 2 of [ADW14]).

- **Key generation:** Generate $d \geq 2$ hash functions $h_i : \mathcal{V} \rightarrow [cn]$ for $i \in [d]$.
- **Building:** The build algorithm must place each element $(v, w) \in X$ in either $T[h_i(v)]$ for some $1 \leq i \leq d$ or in $T[cn + j]$ for some $1 \leq j \leq s$. If there is no allocation of elements that satisfies this condition, the build fails. Building can be accomplished by repeated insertions, or an "offline" algorithm. We do not specify how the build is accomplished obliviously as this varies significantly between protocols.
- **Lookups:** Return $Q = (h_1(v), \ldots, h_d(v), cn + 1, \ldots, cn + s)$. To read an element from a virtual index, $v$, read $T[h_i(v)]$ for $i = 1, \ldots, d$, and check if any of the elements retrieved are of the form $(v, x)$ for some $x$.
- **Deletions:** Find $Q \leftarrow \mathsf{Lookup}(k, v)$ and for any $i \in Q$ if $T[i] = (v, x)$ set $T[i] = (\perp, \perp)$.
- **Extractions:** Again, the method for performing extractions obliviously varies significantly between protocols, so we do not outline it here.

**Fig. 1.** Cuckoo Hash Table (1-table version) [PR04]

**Lemma 1.** *Cuckoo Hash Tables, as presented in Fig. 1 are* access oblivious.

*Proof.* Since each hash function is truly random, the first time an item is queried to a hash function, the result is chosen uniformly at random and independent of all previous choices. Therefore, within the scope of the access obliviousness experiment, the values $Q_i$ and $Q_i'$ will all be chosen uniformly at random and independently, since each access sequence is distinct, and the keys are different in the two experiments. Therefore, $(Q_1, \ldots, Q_t)$ and $(Q_1', \ldots Q_t')$ will actually be chosen from the same random distribution, and the statistical distance between them is 0.

*Remark 4 (Set Membership in Table).* The *access pattern* of a Cuckoo Hash Table does not reveal whether the queried elements were present in the table or not. This follows because non-stash locations accessed are always chosen uniformly at random from $[cm]^d$ (and the stash locations are always accesssed).

Unlike some other constructions, Cuckoo Hash Tables hide set membership *without* the insertion of dummy elements, *i.e.*, pre-inserted elements that should be searched for in the case the item is not in the table.

If Cuckoo hashing is combined with an appropriate Build and Extract construction, it can be fully oblivious. Note that this not only requires that the Build and Extract functions are oblivious in themselves, but that when Build, Lookup and Extract are all performed by a single entity, that the *combined* sequence of accesses is still oblivious.

*Remark 5 (1-table vs d-table cuckoo hashing).* We describe a single-table cuckoo hashing scheme, where all $d$ hash functions hash into the same table. Alternatively, some cuckoo hashing constructions use $d$ tables, and hash function $i$ hashes into table $i$. Setting $d$ to 2 is a common choice, resulting in 2-table cuckoo hashing. Using 1- vs $d$-table cuckoo hashing does not change the asymptotic performance of the hashing scheme, although it does change some details in the analysis.

A single-table Cuckoo Hash Table corresponds naturally to bipartite multigraph with $n$ left-hand nodes (corresponding to $[n]$) and $cn$ right-hand nodes corresponding to the hash buckets (*i.e.*, the first $cn$ locations in the array $T$). Then a left hand node, $v$, is connected to $d$ right hand neighbors given by $\{h_i(v)\}_{i=1}^{d}$. It is straightforward to see that the build procedure can succeed if there is a bipartite matching that includes $|X| - s$ left-hand vertices. The matched elements can be placed in their right-hand neighbors (given by the matching) and the remaining $s$ elements can be placed in the stash.

This also shows that the build procedure can be implemented by building this bipartite multigraph and calculating a maximum matching. We assume that whatever build procedure is used does find such a maximum matching. In practice, analyses of build processes generally assume that a maximum matching is found, even if they use an algorithm which is not known to provide a maximum matching. For instance, in [KMW09] builds use a bounded-time insertion which is not guaranteed to find an optimal allocation, but is heuristically found to be nearly optimal.

To be an Oblivious Hash Table, the functions Build and Lookup need to fail with probability $N^{-\omega(1)}$. If a Cuckoo Hash Table is successfully built, the locations returned by Lookup will always include the location of the queried item if it is stored in the table, so the probability of failure is 0. Build, however, can fail. If the stash is chosen by finding a maximum matching, the probability of failure is $\mathcal{O}(n^{-s})$ for any constant $s$ [KMW09]. A similar result holds for $s = \mathcal{O}(\log n)$, for which the probability of failure is $\mathcal{O}(n^{-\frac{s}{2}})$ [ADW14]. Therefore, if $s = \Theta(\log(n))$ the failure probability is $\mathcal{O}(n^{-\Theta(\log n)})$, which is negligible in $n$. Note that for ORAMs, the failure probability needs to be negligible not in the capacity of the Cuckoo Hash Table, $n$, but in the capacity of the ORAM, $N$. If $N$ is polynomial in $n$ this will hold. Goodrich and Mitzenmacher show that if the stash size is $\Theta(\log(N))$ and $n = \Omega(\log^7(N))$ the failure probability is still negligible in $N$ and propose using another type of oblivious hash table for $n = o(\log^7(N))$ [GM11]. We similarly assume that for $n = o(\log^7(N))$ some alternative Oblivious Hash Table is used so that the failure probability of each hash table is indeed negligible in $N$, rather than $n$.

We have shown here that the Cuckoo Hash Table presented here, with appropriate Build and Extract functions, is an example of an oblivious hash table (with failure negligible in $n$). We next show how oblivious hash tables can be used to construct a hierarchical ORAM. This is secure, but we will later show that if the stashes are combined this breaks obliviousness.

## 2.4   ORAM

An Oblivious RAM (ORAM) provides access to a virtual memory such that all equal-length sequences of virtual memory accesses have indistinguishable physical access sequences. We define an ORAM formally below.

**Definition 3 (ORAM).** *An ORAM* $O = (\mathsf{Init}, \mathsf{Query})$ *is a tuple of polynomial-time algorithms:*

- **Init:** $O \leftarrow \mathsf{Init}(A, N)$, *where* $N$ *is an integer, and* $A$ *is an array of length* $N$ *of elements from some space* $\mathcal{W}$. *This initializes the value of index* $i \in \mathcal{V} = [N]$ *to* $A[i] \in \mathcal{W}$.
- **Query:** $w' \leftarrow \mathsf{Query}(O, v, w)$ *where* $O$ *is an ORAM object,* $v \in \mathcal{V}$ *is an index and* $w \in \mathcal{W} \cup \{\bot\}$. *If* $w = \bot$ *this is a read query and it returns the value at index* $v$. *If* $w \neq \bot$ *this is a write query and it returns* $\bot$ *and sets the value at index* $v$ *to* $w$.

*The ORAM must satisfy the following correctness guarantee.*

- **Consistency:** *When a read is performed on index* $v$, *the result equals the value that was last written to index* $v$, *or if a write has never been performed on index* $v$, *it returns the initial value of index* $v$, $A[v]$.

*The ORAM must additionally satisfy the following security property.*

- **Obliviousness:**
  *Regardless of the data, or the sequence of queries, the access pattern to the physical memory is indistinguishable. Formally, for any initial arrays* $A$, $A'$ *of length* $N$ *and any sequence of queries* $(v_1, w_1), \ldots, (v_t, w_t)$, $(v'_1, w'_1), \ldots, (v'_t, w'_t)$, *where* $v_i, v'_i \in \mathcal{V}$, $w_i, w'_i \in \mathcal{W} \cup \{\bot\}$, *given*

$$
C \stackrel{def}{=} \left\{ \mathsf{Acc} \begin{pmatrix} O \leftarrow \mathsf{Init}(A, N) \\ \mathsf{Query}(O, v_1, w_1) \\ \cdots \\ \mathsf{Query}(O, v_t, w_t) \end{pmatrix} \right\}
$$

  *and*

$$
C' \stackrel{def}{=} \left\{ \mathsf{Acc} \begin{pmatrix} O' \leftarrow \mathsf{Init}(A', N) \\ \mathsf{Query}(O', v'_1, w'_1) \\ \cdots \\ \mathsf{Query}(O', v'_t, w'_t) \end{pmatrix} \right\}
$$

  *then*

$$
\Delta(C, C') < N^{\omega(1)}
$$

Note that the basic ORAM security definition only gives the adversary the ability to see the *access pattern*, but not the underlying data itself. To hide the data, each record can be encrypted under the client's key using a symmetric-key cryptosystem, or, in multi-server ORAMs, each record can be secret-shared among the servers (e.g. [KM19]).

## 2.5    Hierarchical ORAM

The hierarchical ORAM construction was originally put forward in [Ost90, Ost92, GO96] and has since been used as a basis for many future ORAM protocols including [GMOT12, LO13, PPRY18, AKL+20]. In this section, we lay out a generic version of hierarchical ORAM and show it to be secure. In Sect. 3, we show how modifications to this basic scheme caused a subtle security problem that caused future schemes (using this modification) to be insecure.

A hierarchical ORAM consists of $\ell + 1$ levels. Of these, there are $\ell$ levels each consisting of an Oblivious Hash Table of increasing capacities. Additionally, there is one level $L_0$, also called the cache, which is an oblivious object similar to an Oblivious Hash Table but that additionally supports insertions and repeated queries in the access sequence. The cache only ever contains at most $\mathfrak{c}$ elements (where typically $\mathfrak{c} = \Theta(\log(N))$). We choose $\ell$ such that $\mathfrak{c}2^\ell \geq N$. Since $\mathfrak{c}$ is small, the cache can be implemented easily by performing a linear scan of its contents on each access.

We present the Hierarchical ORAM formally in Fig. 2. We will now show why such ORAMs are secure, provided that the hash tables are fully oblivious. First, we need the following lemma.

**Lemma 2.** *The ORAM of Fig. 2 satisfies an invariant that all possible indexes $v \in \mathcal{V}$ are stored in exactly one level in the ORAM. This invariant holds after initialization, after each cache insertion and after each rebuild, though need not hold between these points.*

*Proof.* By induction. The ORAM is initialized to store all indexes $v \in \mathcal{V}$ in level $L_\ell$. Each query is to some $v \in \mathcal{V}$. When a lookup to some index $v$ is made, by induction this index will exist at some level. Since each level is searched, this index will be found and deleted from this level. It will then be placed in the cache. Therefore, once the item has been inserted into the cache, each index $v \in \mathcal{V}$ will be stored in exactly one location. If a rebuild occurs, certain levels will be emptied and merged into a larger level. However, this merge preserves the set of indexes in the ORAM, since all indexes from levels $i = 0, \ldots, i^*$ are extracted and placed in level $i^*$.

**Lemma 3.** *An index is queried at most once at each (non-cache) level between rebuilds of that level, or equivalently, an index is queried at most once to any Oblivious Hash Table.*

*Proof.* If an index, $v \in \mathcal{V}$ is queried at a level $L_i$, it will be found at some level, (since by Lemma 2 it must exist at *some* level). It will then be placed in the cache. Until $L_i$ is rebuilt, it will not exist in $L_i$, since the tables only support deletions, not insertions. Since the sizes of the tables are exponentially increasing, if $L_j$ is rebuilt for some $j > i$, $L_i$ will also be rebuilt (possibly to an empty table) so conversely, if $L_i$ has *not* been rebuilt, $L_j$ will also have not been rebuild for all $j > i$. Therefore, the index will not be stored at $L_j$ for any $j > i$. Therefore, since the index must be stored somewhere, it is stored at some level

---

- **Input:** A virtual memory size $N$. An array of initial values $A$.
- **Init:** Set $t = 0$
  Set $X = (v, A[v])$ for all $1 \leq v \leq N$.
  For $i = 0, \ldots, \ell - 1$, set $\mathsf{k}_i \leftarrow \mathsf{Gen}(N, \mathsf{c}2^i)$, $T_i \leftarrow \mathsf{Build}(\mathsf{k}_i, \emptyset)$.
  Set $\mathsf{k}_\ell \leftarrow \mathsf{Gen}(N, \mathsf{c}2^\ell)$, $T_\ell \leftarrow \mathsf{Build}(\mathsf{k}_\ell, X)$.

---

Hierarchical ORAM Initialization

---

- **Input:** A virtual memory address, $v$. A payload, $x$. (For read queries $x = \bot$.)
- **State:** A counter, $t$. Hash tables $\{T_i\}_{i \in [\ell]}$. Hash keys $\{\mathsf{k}_i\}_{i \in [\ell]}$. Local memory, $m$.
- **Scan the cache:** Initialize found = false. Read every element in the cache $L_0$. If a pair $(v, w)$ is found, set $m = w$, found = true, and delete the old item from the cache.
- **Search each level:** For $i$ in $1, \ldots, \ell$
  - If found = false set $Q_i \leftarrow \mathsf{Lookup}(\mathsf{k}_i, v)$, otherwise set $Q_i \leftarrow \mathsf{Lookup}(\mathsf{k}_i, \mathsf{dummy} \circ t)$ where $\circ$ denotes concatenation, ensuring $\mathsf{dummy} \circ t \notin \mathcal{V}$.
  - Access $T_i[j]$ for all $j \in Q_i$. If there is a $j \in Q_i$, and a $w$ such that $T_i[j] = (v, w)$, then set $m = w$ and found = true.
  - $\mathsf{Delete}(\mathsf{k}_i, v, T_i)$
- **Insert into the cache:** If $x \neq \bot$ (*i.e.*, it was a write query), insert $(v, x)$ into the cache, otherwise insert $(v, m)$ into the cache.
- **Rebuilding:** Increment $t$. Let $\tau = 2\mathsf{c}$ be the rebuild period. If $t$ is a multiple of $\tau$ initiate a rebuild (as described below).
- **Output:** Output $m$. If it was a read query, $m$ will contain the read value.

---

Hierarchical ORAM queries.

---

- **State:** A counter, $t$. Hash tables $\{T_i\}_{i \in [\ell]}$. Hash keys $\{\mathsf{k}_i\}_{i \in [\ell]}$.
- **Identify level:** Let $\bar{i}$ be the largest value such that $\frac{t}{\tau} = 0 \bmod 2^{\bar{i}}$. Let $i^* = \min(\bar{i} + 1, \ell)$. We will merge levels $0, \ldots, i^*$ into level $i^*$.
- **Merge levels:** Initialize $X = \emptyset$. For $i = 0, \ldots, i^*$, and obliviously evaluate $X = X \cup \mathsf{Extract}(\mathsf{k}_i, T_i)$. Set $\mathsf{k}_{i^*} \leftarrow \mathsf{Gen}(N, \mathsf{c}2^{i^*})$, and $T_{i^*} = \mathsf{Build}(\mathsf{k}_{i^*}, X)$.
- **Clear lower levels:** For $i = 0, \ldots, i^* - 1$, set $\mathsf{k}_i \leftarrow \mathsf{Gen}(N, \mathsf{c}2^i)$, $T_i \leftarrow \mathsf{Build}(\mathsf{k}_i, \emptyset)$.

---

Hierarchical ORAM rebuilds.

**Fig. 2.** Hierarchical ORAM

$L_k$, where $k < i$. Since the Hierarchical ORAM searches levels sequentially, it will find the item before $L_i$ is reached, will set $found = true$ and will therefore search for $dummy \circ t$. Therefore each $v \in \mathcal{V}$ will only be searched for once in $L_i$ between rebuilds of $L_i$. The values of $t$ increment with each ORAM query, so each query of form $dummy \circ t$ will also be queried at most once at any level.

We now show that the oblivious property of the ORAM follows easily from this lemma and the properties of Oblivious Hash Tables:

**Theorem 1.** *The Hierarchical ORAM protocol in Fig. 2, when using an Oblivious Hash Table at each level, is oblivious as per Definition 3.*

*Proof.* The security of the ORAM protocol rests on two key facts: (1) *No repeated accesses:* An index is queried once in each level between rebuilds, or equivalently, the sequence of queries to each hash table is non-repeating. This was demonstrated in Lemma 3. (2) *Oblivious accesses:* Our definition of an Oblivious Hash Table (Definition 1) produces indistinguishable physical access patterns provided that the two sequences of virtual indices are *non-repeating*. This is satisfied as per fact (1), so the combined access patterns of builds, lookups, deletions and extractions at each level have distributions separated by negligible statistical distances. Accesses to the cache are always the same, so these do not increase the statistical distance between access distributions. Furthermore the access patterns of builds, lookups, deletions and extractions of each Oblivious Hash Table are independent of each other Oblivious Hash Table, since different keys are used each time. Therefore the combined access pattern of the entire data structure also has distributions separated by negligible statistical distances so is secure by Definition 3.

*Remark 6 (Efficiency).* While rebuilding the hash tables is expensive,[5] these rebuilds occur at a frequency proportional to the capacity of the table, thus the *amortized* cost can remain low. The exact communication cost depends on how the hash tables are implemented, and how the oblivious functions Build and Extract are implemented. We do not focus on these details here, as they do not bear directly on our attack.

## 3    The Attack

In this section, we describe a novel attack on hierarchical ORAM protocols that use cuckoo hashing with a combined stash. This attack applies directly to [GMOT12,KLO12,LO13] and Instantiation 2 of [KM19]. The recent works of PanORAMa [PPRY18] and OptORAMa [AKL+20] use a modified hierarchical solution with multiple cuckoo tables at each level. Since the attack presented here assumes that the adversary can know which indexes are stored in the

---

[5] In the client-server setting expense is measured by communication between the client and the server. In the MPC setting, expense is measured as the communication between the parties in the computation.

Cuckoo Hash Table, it does not apply directly to PanORAMa and OptORAMa. In Sect. 4 we present a more general attack that also applies to PanORAMa and OptORAMa. The general attack is also simpler, but this attack has the advantage of having an intuitive interpretation.

## 3.1  Simplified Attack

First, we describe this attack in a simplified setting, which we later show is equivalent to the ORAM setting.

Imagine the following construction of a hash table. A Cuckoo Hash Table, as defined in Fig. 1, is modified in the following way. When querying some item $v \in \mathcal{V}$, the stash will be searched first. If the item is found in the stash, then some new unique index $v' \notin \mathcal{V}$ will be searched for in the remainder of the table, i.e., $h_i(v')$ will be accessed for $1 \leq i \leq d$. This construction is presented in Fig. 3. We will show that this object is no longer an Oblivious Hash Table.

---

Build, Delete and Extract are the same as in Cuckoo Hash Tables (Figure 1)

- **Lookups:** Lookup takes the key k, an index $v$ and the table object $T$, and returns a set of indexes, $Q$. If $v$ is not in the stash, (i.e., $T[j] \neq (v, w)$ for any $cm + 1 \leq j \leq cm + s$) return $Q = (cm + 1, \ldots, cm + s, h_1(v), \ldots, h_d(v))$. However, if $v$ is in the stash pick a new $v' \notin \mathcal{V}$, using an internal counter to ensure that the same $v'$ is never selected twice, and return $Q = (cm + 1, \ldots, cm + s, h_1(v'), \ldots, h_d(v'))$.

---

**Fig. 3.** Stash-resampling cuckoo hash table

Observe that previously, Lookup only took k and $v$ as parameters, whereas in this definition, its behavior depends on an additional parameter $T$. Specifically, Lookup now depends on which items were placed in $T$'s stash. The fact that the access pattern changes depending on how the table is constructed breaks the abstraction of an Oblivious Hash Table. We will next show that this break leads to a concrete vulnerability.

*Remark 7.* We describe our attack in terms of cuckoo hashing, but essentially the same argument goes through with other hashing schemes that use a stash.

Let $T$ be a Stash-Resampling Cuckoo Hash Table containing indices $v = (v_1, \ldots, v_t)$ and using hash functions $h = (h_1, \ldots, h_d)$. Imagine computing Lookup$(k, v_i, T)$ for $1 \leq i \leq t$. Let $v'$ be the sequence of inputs to the hash functions. If $v_i$ was not stashed, $v'_i = v_i$, but if $v_i$ was stashed, $v'_i$ will be some other unique value.

Now imagine that a Cuckoo Hash Table is constructed using hash functions $h$, but with indices $v'$. All items that were already stored in the table can continue to be stored in the table. However, it is likely that if $v_i$ was stashed, $v_i'$ will not need to be stashed, since it is hashed to new locations, one of which is probably empty. Therefore the stash size of this Cuckoo Hash Table is smaller than usual. Now, an adversary does not know $h$ or $v'$, but it *does* learn $h_j(v_i')$ since these are returned by Lookups. Therefore, it can learn what the stash size *would have been* in a table that used hash functions $h$ and indexes $v'$.

In contrast, let $v''$ be a sequence of $t$ accesses, none of which are in $T$. Since none are in the stash, $v''$ are also the inputs to the hash functions and the adversary can learn from the access pattern the size the stash would have been if the table stored $v''$. The values of $h_j(v_i'')$ will be chosen uniformly at random, so this stash would be chosen from the usual stash size distribution. Hence, if the adversary calculates what the stash size *would have been* if a table was constructed from the hash function inputs, the distribution of stash sizes will be *smaller* if $v$ is queried than if $v''$ is queried.

We now prove formally that a Stash-Resampling Cuckoo Hash Table is not access-oblivious. We formalize the intuition above by representing the accesses as a bipartite graph, with $m$ left-vertices corresponding to the $m$ inputs to the hash functions, with $cm$ right-vertices corresponding to the non-stash locations in the table and edges from a left-vertex to a right-vertex if one of the hash functions maps the left-vertex to the right-vertex. A maximum matching in the graph therefore corresponds to a possible assignment of elements to locations in the hypothetical hash table constructed by the adversary. The number of unmatched elements then will correspond to the stash size. Below, we formalize the correspondance from access sequences to graphs and show that the distribution of the number of unmatched elements in the graphs indeed differs non-negligibly.

**Definition 4 (Graph Representation of an Access-Pattern).** *The Graph Representation of an Access Pattern, $B(m, c, Q)$ is a function that takes as inputs integers $m$ and $c$ and a sequence of access sets, $Q = Q_1, \ldots, Q_m$, and returns a bipartite multigraph with left vertices $a_1, \ldots, a_m$, right vertices $b_1, \ldots, b_{cm}$ and edges $(a_i, b_j)$ for $j \in Q_i \cap [cm]$.*

**Definition 5 (Left-regular bipartite multigraph).** *We define a left-regular bipartite multigraph to be a graph $G = (L \cup R, E)$ with the following properties.*

- *It is bipartite, with vertex sets $L$ and $R$, and each edge being directed from $L$ to $R$, i.e., $\forall (u, v) \in E, u \in L, v \in R$.*
- *Every vertex in $L$ has a constant number of edges, denoted $d$.*
- *$E$ is a multiset, i.e., the edge $(u, v)$ may occur multiple times.*

**Definition 6 (Random left-regular bipartite multigraph).** *We define $H_0(m, c, d)$ to be a function that produces a random left-regular bipartite multigraph, where $|L| = m$, $|R| = c \cdot m$, $d \geq 1$ is the degree of each vertex in $L$ and where each outgoing edge from a vertex $u \in L$ has an end-point, $v \in R$, that is chosen uniformly at random from $R$ (and independent of all other choices).*

If $Q = (Q_1, \ldots, Q_m)$ is the result of outputs of Lookup to a sequence of queries to a (Stash-Resampling) Cuckoo Hash Table with capacity $m$ and degree

$d$, then $G \leftarrow B(m, c, Q)$ will be a left-regular bipartite multigraph, since every $Q_i$ will contain $d$ vertices in $[cm]$. We will soon show that for a Stash-Resampling Cuckoo Hash Table, if none of the queried elements are in the table, $G$ will be sampled as a *random* left-regular bipartite multigraph, but if the table contents are queried, the left-regular bipartite multigraph will be sampled from a *different* distribution of graphs which will have fewer unmatched elements.

**Definition 7 (Matching of a bipartite multigraph).** *For a bipartite multigraph $G = (L \cup R, E)$, a matching is a set of edges $E' \subseteq E$ such that*

$$(u, v), (u', v') \in E' \Rightarrow u \neq u', v \neq v'.$$

*A maximum matching is a matching of maximum size. There may be multiple such matchings, but they will all be the same size; we use $M(G)$ to denote some such matching and $|M(G)|$ to be this size, which is independent of which matching is chosen. $S(G) \overset{def}{=} m - |M(G)|$ is the number of unmatched elements on the left-hand side.*

Note that for any $G$, $1 \leq |M(G)| \leq m$, so $0 \leq S(G) \leq m - 1$.

**Lemma 4 (Lower bound on unmatched elements).** *For all $0 \leq s \leq m-1$ and $G \leftarrow H_0(m, c, d)$, where $d$, $c$ are constants,*

$$\Pr[S(G) \geq s] \geq \left(\frac{1}{cm}\right)^{ds+d-1}$$

*which is non-negligible in $m$.*

*Proof.* Pick $s+1$ elements of $L$. The probability that *all* $d \cdot (s+1)$ edges of these elements will have the same endpoint $v \in R$ is $\left(\frac{1}{cm}\right)^{d(s+1)-1} = \left(\frac{1}{cm}\right)^{ds+d-1}$. If this occurs, any matching can contain at most 1 of these elements, which means that at least $s$ of these elements will be unmatched. Thus $S(G) \geq s$. Note that for any constant $d$ and $s$, this probability is non-negligible.

Next, we describe two distributions on the integers $[m-1]$.

**Definition 8.** *Fix constants $d, m \in \mathbb{N}$, and $c > 1$. Let $M(\cdot)$ be an algorithm that takes a bipartite multigraph $G$, and returns a maximum matching $M(G)$.*

- **Distribution 0:** *Let $s_0$ be the random variable denoting the number of unmatched elements in a random bipartite multigraph. $s_0 \overset{def}{=} S(H_0(m, c, d))$.*
- **Distribution 1:** *Define a distribution of graphs according to the following process. First construct a graph $G' \leftarrow H_0(m, c, d)$. Let $G' = (L \cup R, E')$. Let $M(G')$ be a maximum matching in $G'$. Initialize $E = E'$. For every $u \in L$ s.t. $\nexists (u, v) \in M(G')$, remove every edge $(u, v) \in E'$, and replace it with a new edge $(u, v')$ where $v'$ is chosen uniformly at random from $R$. Let $G = (L_1 \cup R_1, E)$ be the modified graph. Let $H_1(m, c, d, M(\cdot))$ denote the function that samples a graph from this distribution. Define $s_1$ to be the number of unmatched elements in this experiment, i.e., $s_1 \overset{def}{=} S(H_1(m, c, d, M(\cdot)))$.*

*Although the distributions $s_0$ and $s_1$ depend on parameters, we generally suppress these dependencies for notational convenience.*

Intuitively, the expected value of $s_1$ should be smaller than the expected value of $s_0$, since the vertices which were not matched get another chance to be matched when new end-points are chosen for them. In Lemma 5 we show that this is indeed the case, and that the distributions of $s_0$ and $s_1$ are statistically different (*i.e.*, non-negligibly different).

**Lemma 5.** *If $s_0$ and $s_1$ are the random variables described above, then the statistical distance between $s_0$ and $s_1$ is at least $\frac{1}{m}\left(1-\left(\frac{1}{c}\right)^d\right)\left(\frac{1}{cm}\right)^{2d-1}$ which is non-negligible in $m$.*

*Proof.* Consider the graph $G' = (L \cup R, E') \leftarrow H_0(m,c,d)$ generated as the first step in generating distribution $s_1$, where $|R| = c \cdot m$. Let $M = M(G')$. Let $S \subset L$ be the unmatched vertices in $L$. We know $|S|$ is distributed by $s_0$. When $G$ is constructed (as the second step of distribution $s_1$), each $u \in S$ will receive $d$ new random neigbors. For $v \in L/S$ we can use the existing matching $M$ for $G$ and for $u \in S$ we can match it to a neighbor directly if this neighbor is not already matched.[6] Since at most $m$ elements of $R$ will ever be matched, the probability that a new random neighbor is already matched is at most $\frac{1}{c}$. There is then at most a $\left(\frac{1}{c}\right)^d$ probability that *all* $d$ right-hand neighbors of $u$ are already matched. Let $e'_i$ be the event that $v_i$ is unmatched in $G'$, and $e_i$ the event that $v_i$ is unmatched in $G$. This shows:

$$Pr[e_i] \leq \left(\frac{1}{c}\right)^d Pr[e'_i]$$

Thus by linearity of expectation

$$E[s_1] = \sum_{1 \leq i \leq m} Pr[e_i] \leq \sum_{1 \leq i \leq m} \left(\frac{1}{c}\right)^d Pr[e'_i] = \left(\frac{1}{c}\right)^d E[s_0].$$

By Lemma 4, $Pr(s_0 \geq s) \geq \left(\frac{1}{cm}\right)^{ds+d-1}$. Since $s_0$ is a non-negative distribution, $E[s_0] \geq Pr(s_0 \geq 1) \geq \left(\frac{1}{cm}\right)^{2d-1}$ so

$$|E[s_0] - E[s_1]| \geq \left(1-\left(\frac{1}{c}\right)^d\right)\left(\frac{1}{cm}\right)^{2d-1}.$$

In particular, this means that the expected values, $E[s_0]$ and $E[s_1]$ are non-negligibly different. Finally, notice that $0 \leq s_0, s_1 \leq m$, so

$$\Delta(s_0, s_1) \geq \frac{1}{m}|E[s_0] - E[s_1]| \geq \frac{1}{m}\left(1-\left(\frac{1}{c}\right)^d\right)\left(\frac{1}{cm}\right)^{2d-1}$$

which means that $\Delta(s_0, s_1)$ is also non-negligible.

---

[6] This greedy matching assignment not give an optimal matching for $G$, but it will provide an upper bound for $s_1$ in terms of $s_0$.

Now we show that the Stash-Resampling Cuckoo Hash Table is not access oblivious.

**Theorem 2.** *The Stash-Resampling Cuckoo table presented in Fig. 3 is not access-oblivious.*

*Proof.* Let $X = X' = \{1, \ldots, m\}$ for some $m \leq \frac{N}{2}$. Let $v_i = i + m$ and let $v'_i = i$ for $1 \leq i \leq m$. The adversary will generate a table with the input data, lookup the sequence of virtual indices and construct a bipartite graph based on these lookup results.

Let there be two experiments:

$$\left\{ \begin{array}{l} k \leftarrow \mathsf{Gen}(N, m) \\ T \leftarrow \mathsf{Build}(k, X) \\ \{Q_i \leftarrow \mathsf{Lookup}(k, v_i, T)\}_{i \in [m]} \\ G \leftarrow B(m, c, Q) \\ s = S(G) \end{array} \right\} \text{ and } \left\{ \begin{array}{l} k' \leftarrow \mathsf{Gen}(N, m) \\ T' \leftarrow \mathsf{Build}(k, X') \\ \{Q'_i \leftarrow \mathsf{Lookup}(k', v'_i, T')\}_{i \in [m]} \\ G' \leftarrow B(m, c, Q') \\ s' = S(G') \end{array} \right\}$$

In the first experiment, none of the queries are in $X$, therefore none will be in the stash. Therefore $Q_i = (cm + 1, \ldots, cm + s, h_1(v_i), \ldots, h_d(v_i))$. Since the $v_i$ are distinct from each other and the elements stored in the table, $h_j(v_i)$ will be chosen uniformly at random from $[cm]$ and independently of all previous variables. Therefore, each left-vertex in $G$ will have $d$ neighbors, chosen uniformly at random from $b_j$. Therefore $G$ is chosen exactly according to $H_0$.

In the second experiment, all of the queries are in $X'$. If we were to search according to the oblivious Cuckoo Hash Table of Fig. 1 then the corresponding graph would be distributed according to $H_0(m, c, d)$. However, for any element that was not in the maximum matching, (*i.e.*, the elements in the stash) the Stash-Resampling Cuckoo Hash Table will instead pick new indices to query, $\bar{v}'_j$ and return locations $h_i(\bar{v}'_j)$ which will not have been queried before so will be new random locations. Therefore, for these elements that were not in the maximum matching, the corresponding edges will be re-chosen uniformly at random. The graph from the second experiment will therefore be constructed according to distribution $H_1(m, c, d, M(\cdot))$, assuming the stash was chosen by some maximum matching algorithm $M(\cdot)$.

We have already shown that distributions $H_0(m, c, d)$ and $H_1(m, c, d, M(\cdot))$ are distinguishable. Therefore an adversary can distinguish the two experiments, so Stash-Resampling Cuckoo Hash Tables are not access-oblivious.

*Remark 8.* Note that the attack described above is immediately applicable in cases where the stash is accessed *before* the associated Cuckoo Hash Table, and if the target is found in the stash, the protocol searches for dummy elements in the table. For instance, our attack would apply to a hierarchical ORAM that stored a stash at the same level, but accessed the stash *first*, and searches for a dummy in the rest of the table if the element is found in the stash.

## 3.2   Hierarchical ORAM with a Combined Stash

We now present how hierarchical ORAMs were constructed using a combined stash. We will show that this breaks the abstraction of an Oblivious Hash Table, and results in access patterns identical to those of the Stash-Resampling Cuckoo Hash Table, which breaks obliviousness.

Beginning with the protocol of Goodrich et al. [GMOT12], a number of hierarchical ORAM schemes stored stashed items from a table construction in a shared stash or re-inserted them into the cache. Since most schemes re-insert stash items into the cache, we will present this version. Figure 4 presents the changes between the stash-reinserting hierarchical ORAM and the original hierarchical ORAM protocol from Sect. 2.5. All other parts of the protocol remain the same.

---

A Stash-Reinserting ORAM is an ORAM equivalent to that of Figure 2 with the following modifications:

- **Rebuild:** Rather than table $T_{i*}$ storing all elements in $X$, at most $c$ of these elements can be stored in a stash. The stash is not stored at this level, but is is padded to size $c$ and inserted into the cache.
- **Rebuild frequency:** Since the cache is of size $c$ after a rebuild, the rebuild period is now $\tau = c$.

---

**Fig. 4.** Stash-reinserting hierachical ORAM

**Theorem 3.** *The Stash-Reinserting ORAM of Fig. 4 is insecure; i.e., it does not satisfy the oblivious property in Definition 3.*

*Proof.* Let $A = A' = 0^N$. Let the hierarchical ORAM be such that there will be some level $L_i$ of capacity $m \leq \frac{N}{2}$ that is implemented using a Cuckoo Hash Table.[7]

Let $U = ((1,0),\ldots,(2m,0))$ and $U' = ((1,0),\ldots,(m,0),(1,0),\ldots,(m,0))$ be two sequences of ORAM queries.

---

[7] Some schemes use a mixture of hash table types at different levels. We do not require that all levels use a Cuckoo Hash Table, only that there is at least one such level of size $\leq \frac{N}{2}$ that has its stash re-inserted into the ORAM data structure.

After $m$ queries, $L_i$ will be constructed.[8] In both experiments $L_i$ will be constructed using the elements $(1, 0), \ldots, (m, 0)$. A Cuckoo Hash Table will be constructed in both cases, with these contents.[9]

The stash will be re-inserted in both cases. We have from Lemma 2 that each of these stashed elements will exist at a single location at the start of each access. Since levels $L_j$ for all $j \geq i$ will only be rebuilt when $L_i$ is also rebuilt, we know that these elements must remain in some level $L_k$ with $k < i$ until $L_i$ is rebuilt. This means that, until this point in time, they will always be found *before* $L_i$ is accessed. Thus, by the ORAM query algorithm, a dummy query will be performed in $L_i$.

Therefore, the access pattern in the Cuckoo Hash Table at $L_i$ will be the same as that of the Stash-Resampling Cuckoo Hash Table in Fig. 3, where elements were searched in the stash first, and if found in the stash a dummy was searched in the remainder of the table. The only difference is that in the Stash-Resampling Cuckoo Hash Table, the algorithm also accessed a pre-assigned stash, but this is not an issue since the attack to the stash-resampling algorithm does not use the access pattern to the stash (as this access pattern is always the same). Observe that, exactly like in the attack of Theorem 2, one sequence of accesses ($U$) will only access elements that were *not* in the data table, and the other sequence ($U'$) will only access elements that *were* in the data table (including the stash). Therefore, by the same argument as Theorem 2 the statistical distance between ORAM access pattern distributions is non-negligible. Therefore, the ORAM protocol is insecure.

## 4   The Generic Attack

The attack in Sect. 3 assumes that an adversary knows all $m$ elements that were placed in the Cuckoo Hash Table. However, in PanORAMa [PPRY18] and OptORAMa [AKL+20] each level contains multiple Cuckoo Hash Tables and only some of the elements are placed in any given table. We therefore now construct a more general attack that assumes only that the adversary knows a *superset* of the elements that were placed in the table. More formally, we can weaken the definition of Access-Obliviousness in Definition 1 such that the

---

[8] This is not quite true. We would like to construct $L_i$ such that it contains indices $1, \ldots, m$ (although some may of these may be stashed). However, due to reinsersions of the stash this will actually need to occur in a level with capacity roughly $2m$. If additional accesses are needed to trigger the rebuild, then the same element, *e.g.,* $(1, 0)$ can be looked up multiple times. The exact details of what sequence of accesses is needed in order to cause elements $1, \ldots, m$ to be inserted into a particular level also varies depending on how exactly the ORAM is constructed. More generally, the sequence $(1, 0), \ldots, (m, 0)$ at the beginning of both $U$ and $U'$ should be replaced with whatever sequence in the given ORAM is needed in order to instantiate a level to contain exactly the indices $1, \ldots, m$.

[9] It is possible that when the ORAM is initialized, elements from $L_\ell$ are stashed and stored in the cache. These elements would inadvertently also be stored in $L_i$. The effect of this on the Cuckoo Hash Table is small.

contents of the data in the two experiments are the same, and the access patterns cannot depend directly on the table contents, but are functions of any superset of the contents.

**Definition 9.** *A hash-table is* access-oblivious in the knowledge of a content superset *if for all datasets $X \subset \mathcal{X}$ with indices $V \subset \mathcal{V}$, and all PPT algorithms $f, f' : 2^{\mathcal{V}} \to \mathcal{V}^t$, there exists $Y$, with $V \subset Y \subset \mathcal{V}$, $|Y| \leq |\mathcal{V}| - 3$ such that the distribution of outputs of $\mathsf{Lookup}(k, f(Y), T)$ has negligible (in $|Y|$) statistical distance from the distribution of outputs of $\mathsf{Lookup}(k', f'(Y), T')$ where $T \leftarrow \mathsf{Build}(k, X)$, $T' \leftarrow \mathsf{Build}(k', T')$.*

We show that a Stash-Resampling Cuckoo Hash Table (Fig. 3) does not satisfy this weaker security guarantee. We will then show that an adversary can then use this to differentiate sequences in PanORAMa and OptORAMa with non-negligible probability. For simplicity, our proof assumes $d = 2$ hash functions, which is the choice used by PanORAMa and OptORAMa, but can easily be extended to any constant number of hash functions.

### 4.1   Generic Stash-Resampling Cuckoo Hash Table Attack

**Theorem 4.** *Stash-Resampling Cuckoo Hash Tables with $d = 2$ are not access-oblivious in the knowledge of a content superset.*

*Proof.* Let $|X| = |V| = n' \geq 3$ and $|Y| = m$. The adversary algorithms are as follows: $f$ chooses distinct $v_1, v_2, v_3 \overset{\$}{\leftarrow} Y$ and outputs $A = (v_1, v_2, v_3)$. $f'$ chooses distinct $v'_1, v'_2, v'_3 \overset{\$}{\leftarrow} \mathcal{V}/Y$ and outputs $A' = (v'_1, v'_2, v'_3)$.

Let the set $S \subset V$ denote the indexes stored in the stash constructed by the table $T$, that is built in the first experiment, and let $|S| = s$. Define $B = V/S$ to be the indexes that were successfully stored in their hashed locations in $T$ and define $C = S \cup Y/V = Y/B$ to denote indexes in $Y$ that are not (either because they weren't in $V$ to begin with, or because they were stashed). As previously assumed, there are 2 hash functions. By the definition of a Stash Resampling Cuckoo Hash Table, if $v_1, v_2, v_3 \in B$ are distinct elements, it is impossible for $(h_1(v_i), h_2(v_i))$ to be equal for all $i \in \{1, 2, 3\}$. Let $r$ be the size of the set of outputs of $(h_1(v), h_2(v))$. For the Cuckoo Hash Table of Fig. 1 $r = (cn')^2$. Let $Q_i = \mathsf{Lookup}(k, T, v_i)$ and $Q'_i = \mathsf{Lookup}(k', T', v'_i)$ be the results of Lookups in the first and second experiments respectively, but ignoring the stash locations (since these are chosen deterministically). We now show that $\Delta((Q_1, Q_2, Q_3), (Q'_1, Q'_2, Q'_3)) \geq m^{-\Theta(1)}$, i.e., that the accesses to $A$ and $A'$ are statistically different.

Let us first look at the distribution of $(Q_1, Q_2)$ and $(Q'_1, Q'_2)$. Since $v'_1, v'_2 \notin Y \supset V$, $Q'_1$ and $Q'_2$ contain random locations in the table. Therefore, the probability that $Q'_1 = Q'_2$ is exactly $\frac{1}{r}$.

Now let us look at the distribution of $(Q_1, Q_2)$. If both $v_1, v_2 \in C$, $Q_1$ and $Q_2$ will both be chosen uniformly at random, and the probability that $Q_1 = Q_2$ would be $\frac{1}{r}$. Even if only one of $v_1$ or $v_2$ is in $C$, the locations returned by Lookup for this element will be chosen uniformly at random and independent from all previous choices, so the probability that $Q_1 = Q_2$ would be $\frac{1}{r}$ in this case also.

Now let us examine the probability that $Q_1 = Q_2$ for a randomly selected $v_1, v_2 \in B$. Let this probability be denoted by $p$ for a given Cuckoo Hash Table implementation. For a random $v_1, v_2 \in V$, the probability that $(h_1(v_1), h_2(v_1)) = (h_1(v_2), h_2(v_2))$ is $\frac{1}{r}$. However, the build algorithm has some choice in which items it places in the stash. It is possible that elements that cause collisions are either more, or less, likely to be placed in $S$. Therefore $p$ could be different from $\frac{1}{r}$, but we show it cannot be much different without making the output distributions non-negligibly statistically distant.

$$Pr(Q_1 = Q_2) = \frac{\binom{|B|}{2}}{\binom{|Y|}{2}} p + \left(1 - \frac{\binom{|B|}{2}}{\binom{|Y|}{2}} \frac{1}{r}\right)$$

$$Pr(Q_1 = Q_2) - Pr(Q_1' = Q_2') = \frac{\binom{|B|}{2}}{\binom{|Y|}{2}} \left(p - \frac{1}{r}\right)$$

There are two cases. In the first case $|p - \frac{1}{r}| \geq m^{\Theta(1)}$ then $|Pr(Q_1 = Q_2) - Pr(Q_1' = Q_2')|$ is non-negligible in $m$, $(Q_1, Q_2)$ and $(Q_1', Q_2')$ will be statistically different, and the proof is done. In the second case $|p - \frac{1}{r}| = m^{\omega(1)}$ and we will proceed to show that then $(Q_1, Q_2, Q_3)$ and $(Q_1', Q_2', Q_3')$ are statistically different.

Let us examine the probability that $Q_1 = Q_2 = Q_3$. If $v_1, v_2, v_3 \in C$, then this probability is $\frac{1}{r^2}$, since we can imagine one $v_i$ being pre-set, and each other $v_j$ is chosen uniformly at random and independently from a space of size $\frac{1}{r}$. If at least two of $v_1, v_2, v_3$ are in $C$, then the one that is not can be pre-set, and by the same argument as above the probability that $Q_1 = Q_2 = Q_3$ is $\frac{1}{r^2}$.

Now if $v_i, v_j \in B$, $v_k \in C$ for some distinct $i, j, k \in \{1, 2, 3\}$, the probability that $Q_i = Q_j$ is exactly $p$, by our definition of $p$. $Q_k$ is chosen uniformly at random and independently from a space of size $\frac{1}{r}$, so the probability that $Q_i = Q_j = Q_k$ is $p\frac{1}{r}$.

Finally, let us examine the case where $v_1, v_2, v_3 \in B$. Since these items were successfully stored in the table, they cannot all have been hashed to the same 2 locations. Therefore in this case $Pr(Q_1 = Q_2 = Q_3) = 0$.

We therefore have:

$$Pr(Q_1 = Q_2 = Q_3) - Pr(Q_1' = Q_2' = Q_3') = \frac{\binom{|C|}{1}\binom{|B|}{2}}{\binom{|Y|}{3}} \left(p - \frac{1}{r}\right) - \frac{\binom{|B|}{3}}{\binom{|Y|}{3}} \frac{1}{r}$$

But we are looking at the case that $p - \frac{1}{r}$ is negligible. On the other hand $\frac{\binom{|B|}{3}}{\binom{|Y|}{3}} \frac{1}{r} = \frac{n'(n'-1)(n'-2)}{m(m-1)(m-2)r}$ which, since $r = \mathcal{O}(m^2)$, is non-negligible in $m$.

Therefore $|Pr(Q_1 = Q_1 = Q_3) - Pr(Q_1' = Q_2' = Q_3')|$ and subsequently $\Delta((Q_1, Q_2, Q_3), (Q_1', Q_2', Q_3'))$ are also non-negligible in $m$.

## 4.2   Attack Against PanORAMa and OptORAMa

In PanORAMa and OptORAMa, rather than each ORAM level containing a single Cuckoo Hash Table, each level has a number of equal-size bins, an Overflow Table and a (level-specific) Combined Stash. The bins, the Overflow Table and the Combined Stash are all implemented as Cuckoo Hash Tables. The Combined Stash Table contains the combined stashes of all bins on that level. The Overflow Table and the Combined Stash additionally have their own stashes. These stashes are removed from the level and reinserted into the ORAM.

Provided that items found in the Combined Stash are still searched for at each bin, the fact that the stashes of all bins in a given level are combined is not an issue.[10] However, the fact that the stashes of the Overflow Table and of the (level-specific) Combined Stash are removed from the level and re-inserted into the ORAM makes the protocols vulnerable to the attack described in this paper.

Like in the regular ORAM attack, let $u_1, \ldots, u_m$ be a sequence of distinct accesses of length $m \leq N - 3$ such that following this sequence of accesses, a level $L_i$ is built with the set $Y = \{u_1, \ldots, u_m\}$ as input.

Let $T$ be the Overflow Hash Table,[11] and $X$ be the set of items input the Build function. $X$ is unknown to the adversary, but it is guaranteed that $X \subseteq Y$. Let $S$ be the set of stashed elements in the Overflow Hash Table.

Observe that if an index $x \in S$ is queried, PanORAMa and OptORAMa will find $x$ before reaching $L_i$ and will query a nonce in $T$ instead. Therefore, the access sequence to the Overflow Hash Table in the ORAM is the same as that of a Stash-Resampling Cuckoo Hash Table.

Since the Overflow Hash Table is not access-oblivious, to an adversary that knows $Y \supseteq X$, by Theorem 4, the ORAM protocols are not access-oblivious either. In particular, let the adversary choose distinct $v_1, v_2, v_3$ uniformly at random from $Y$. Let $A = (u_1, \ldots, u_m, v_1, v_2, v_3)$. Let $v_1', v_2', v_3' \notin Y$ be distinct elements and $A' = (u_1, \ldots, u_m, v_1', v_2', v_3')$. The access sequences of the ORAM on $A$ and $A'$ will have non-negligible statistical distance in $m$ (and $N$).

## 5   Alibi: Secure Hierarchical ORAM with Reinserted Stashes

The basic problem arises when a stashed element is found *before* the appropriate level of the ORAM hierarchy is searched. As a successful criminal needs not only

---

[10] OptORAMa seaches in the Combined Stash *after* searching in the bins, so the access pattern in the bins will be the same for items that are later found in the Combined Stash. However, in PanORAMa, the Combined Stash is accessed *before* the bins are accessed and a random bin is chosen in the case that the data is found in the Combined Stash. Therefore, the access patterns in the individual bins are also vulnerable to a distinguishing attack based on the fact that stashed elements will not be searched for. This can simply be solved by searching the bins before searching the Combined Stash.

[11] The proof would work out the same if $T$ was the Combined Stash Hash Table.

to be hidden in the location where they committed a crime, but also needs an alibi who claims to have seen them enacting their everyday life, likewise the stashed elements need not only hide their presence in the levels to which they are reinserted, but also need to hide their absence from the levels from which they came. To fix this problem, we need to ensure that even when an element cannot be *stored* at a certain level of the ORAM hierarchy (*i.e.,* because it falls in the cuckoo stash), it must still be *searched for* at this level. This way, the set of physical accesses at a level will always be chosen uniformly at random and be fully independent. Each element therefore needs to store a record of the locations where it would have been, and needs to be searched for in these locations if accessed.

There are some small subtleties here. First, an element needs to store the fact that it was ejected from a level not only when it is in the cache, but at least until this level is rebuilt or the item is searched for, since if it is looked up at *any* point before this level is rebuilt it needs to be searched for in this level. Second, it is entirely possible that the same element that had been stashed at some level $L_i$ could be stashed again at some level $L_k$ with $k < i$, *before $L_i$ is rebuilt* or the element queried. Therefore each element needs to store the location of all levels from which it was ejected due to having fallen in the stash. Since there are $\ell \leq \log N$ levels in the hierarchical ORAM, it is possible to store which levels the item was ejected from using $\log N$ bits.

The flaw can be fixed using the following simple modification. For each element $(v, x)$ the algorithm will additionally store a bit array $\mathfrak{e}$ of length $\ell$, which records at which levels the item was "stashed."

Our solution modifies the generic hierarchical ORAM protocol of Fig. 2; these modifications[12] are presented in Fig. 5.

**Lemma 6.** *In the Alibi protocol presented in Fig. 5 there is an invariant that given a tuple $(v, w, \mathfrak{e})$ stored at some level, $\mathfrak{e}[i] = 1$ if and only if $v$ was stashed at level $L_i$ during the last rebuild and $v$ has not been queried by the ORAM since this rebuild. This invariant holds initially, after each query and after each rebuild.*

*Proof.* By induction. This is initially true, as no items have been stashed and $\mathfrak{e}[i] = 0$ for all items.

If a level $L_i$ is rebuilt, all levels $L_j$ for $j < i$ will be rebuilt as empty levels. Therefore following the rebuild $\mathfrak{e}[j] = 0$ for all such levels, satisfying the invariant for these levels. For level $L_i$, some elements may be stashed after the rebuild, $\mathfrak{e}[i] = 1$ for exactly these elements, so the invariant is satisfied for level $i$. For any level $L_j$ with $j > i$, the level has not been rebuilt and $\mathfrak{e}[j]$ is not modified, so the invariant will hold if it held before.

After a query $\mathfrak{e}[j]$ is set to 0 for all $j$, so $\mathfrak{e}[i]$ will only be 1 if there has not been a query since the last rebuild.

---

[12] This protocol uses a slightly definition of Oblivious Hash Tables. Rather than returning a single array, Build returns a tuple $(T_i, S_i)$, where $T_i$ is the main table and $S_i$ is the stash. Lookup only contains the non-stash locations.

- **Initializing records:** When initializing the ORAM, for each input tuple $(v, x)$ store the tuple $(v, x, 0^\ell)$ in the ORAM.
- **On rebuilds:** When a hash table, $T_i$, is constructed at level $i$, suppose $(T_i, S_i) \leftarrow \mathsf{Build}(\mathsf{k}_i, X)$.
  - **Stashed records:** For each record $(v, x, \mathfrak{e}) \in S_i$, set $\mathfrak{e}[i] = 1$, and $\mathfrak{e}[j] = 0$ for $j = 1, \ldots, i - 1$. Finally, insert $(v, x, \mathfrak{e})$ into the cache (or combined stash) as usual.
  - **Regular records:** For each record $(v, x, \mathfrak{e}) \in T_i$, set $\mathfrak{e}[i] = 0$, and $\mathfrak{e}[j] = 0$ for $j = 1, \ldots, i - 1$.
- **On queries:** On input $(v, x)$, initialize $\mathsf{found} = \mathsf{false}$, $\mathfrak{f} = 0^\ell$.
  - **Scan the cache:** If a record $(v, w, \mathfrak{e})$ is found in the cache, set $m = w$, $\mathsf{found} = \mathsf{true}$ and $\mathfrak{f} = \mathfrak{e}$ and delete the item from the cache.
  - **Search each level:** For $i$ in $1, \ldots, \ell$
    * If $\mathsf{found} = \mathsf{true}$ and $\mathfrak{f}[i] = 0$ then set $Q_i \leftarrow \mathsf{Lookup}(\mathsf{k}_i, \mathsf{dummy} \circ t)$. Otherwise set $Q_i \leftarrow \mathsf{Lookup}(\mathsf{k}_i, v)$,
    * Probe locations $T_i[j]$ for $j \in Q_i$.
    * If there is a $j \in Q_i$, such that $T_i[j] = (v, w, \mathfrak{e})$, then set $m = w$, $\mathsf{found} = \mathsf{true}$ and $\mathfrak{f} = \mathfrak{e}$.
    * Execute $\mathsf{Delete}(\mathsf{k}_i, v, T_i)$
  - **Rewrite the cache:** If $x \neq \perp$ (*i.e.*, it was a write query), insert $(v, x, 0^\ell)$ into the cache. Otherwise insert $(v, m, 0^\ell)$ into the cache.

**Fig. 5.** Alibi Hierarchical ORAM protocol (delta to standard protocol of Fig. 2)

Therefore, by induction, this invariant always holds.

**Theorem 5.** *Let $(v_1, \cdots, v_m)$ be the sequence of indices that are looked up at level $L_i$ with $i > 0$, between two subsequent rebuilds of that level. Then the Alibi protocol satisfies the following property. If $v_k = v'_{k'}$ for some $k' < k$, then $Q_k = \mathsf{Lookup}(\mathsf{k}_i, \mathsf{dummy} \circ t)$ else $Q_k = \mathsf{Lookup}(\mathsf{k}_i, v_k)$.*

*Proof.* Immediately after $L_i$ is rebuilt, all levels $L_j$ for $0 < j < i$ are empty. Furthermore, the cache $L_0$ contains only elements from $S_i$, the stash of level $i$. Therefore, by Lemma 6 every element $(v, w, \mathfrak{e})$ either exists in level $L_j$ for some $j \geq i$ or has $\mathfrak{e}[i] = 1$. This will remain true until $L_i$ is rebuilt or $v$ is queried. If $v_k = v$ is queried and $v$ is stored at some level $j \geq i$, then it will be looked up at level $i$, *i.e.*, $Q_k = \mathsf{Lookup}(\mathsf{k}_i, v_k)$. Similarly, if $v_k = v$ is queried, and $\mathfrak{e}[i] = 1$ then when $v$ is found $\mathfrak{f}[i]$ will be set to $\mathfrak{e}[i]$ so $v$ will still be looked up at level $L_i$, *i.e.*, $Q_k = \mathsf{Lookup}(\mathsf{k}_i, v_k)$. In both cases $\mathfrak{e}[i]$ will be set to 0 (if it wasn't already) and it will be moved to a level $j < i$ (if it wasn't already). Only a rebuild on level $L_i$ could change either of these facts. Therefore, until $L_i$ is rebuilt, for any subsequent queries $v'_k = v$, a dummy item will be looked for in $L_i$, *i.e.*, $Q'_k = \mathsf{Lookup}(\mathsf{k}_i, \mathsf{dummy} \circ t)$.

**Theorem 6.** *The Alibi Stash-Reinserting ORAM protocol, when instantiated with an Oblivious Hash Table with a stash, is secure, i.e., it satisfies the security property of Definition 3.*

*Proof.* This follows similarly to the proof of Theorem 1. The ORAM satisfies two properties: (1) *No repeated accesses:* Each query is queried at most once to each level between rebuilds. This follows directly from Theorem 5. Any query in the form $v \in \mathcal{V}$ is queried at most once, since the theorem implies that any future accesses will be to dummy items. Any query in the form dummy $\circ\, t$ is queried at most once, because $t$ is incremented after each query. Therefore the lookups to the Oblivious Hash Table are *non-repeating*. (2) *Oblivious accesses:* The Oblivious Hash Table satisfies a property that the results of Lookup have distributions with negligible distances for all non-repeating access patterns. We know from (1) that in an ORAM the accesses to each Oblivious Hash Table are indeed non-repeating. The ORAM only accesses the non-stash part of the Oblivious Hash Table, and since it is only accessing a subset, the distribution of access patterns of the ORAM on each level still differ negligibly. Furthermore, for an Oblivious Hash Table satisfying Full Obliviousness, the distribution of all memory accesses by an ORAM on each level differ negligibly.

Since each Oblivious Hash Table is built independently, the distance between distributions of their combined accesses will be at most the sum of the distances between distributions of accesses at each Oblivious Hash Table. Also, the distribution of accesses to the cache is the same each time, since the entire cache is scanned initially and a single item is written at the end, so this does not increase the distance between the access patterns of the ORAM. The distance between distributions of the entire sequences of $t_{max}$ queries to an ORAM system with $\ell$ levels, will therefore be at most $\ell t_{max}$ times that of any individual Oblivious Hash Table. Since the latter is negligible in $N$, and $\ell t_{max}$ is polynomial in $N$, then the the total distance between distributions of ORAM access will also be negligible in $N$. Therefore the ORAM is oblivious.

*Remark 9.* It may initially seem that the proof of security above would apply to the flawed schemes as well. However, because the schemes *resample* the queries based on whether they were stored in the stash, the access pattern of the remaining table changes, and changes specifically in a way that depends on the structure of the table. We showed that in the case of Cuckoo Hashing this change causes a change in the combined set of accesses that is distinguishable.

**Complexity:** Since each element only needs to store one bit for each level, and there are at most $\log N$ levels, then the additional size of each element is increased by $\log N$ bits. Since the index is at least $\log N$ bits and the payload is $\Omega(\log n)$ the items still have the same asymptotic sizes so this does not change the asymptotic communication complexity. All of the modifications above only involve modifying or reading $\mathfrak{e}$ when $v$ and/or $x$ would also be read or modified. We have that $|\mathfrak{e}| = \mathcal{O}(|v|)$, $|\mathfrak{e}| = \mathcal{O}(|x|)$. Therefore the modification only increases communication costs by up to constant factors.

**Correctness:** The modifications do not change the output of the program, only the access patterns. The only operation that does not involve only modifications of $\epsilon$ is that during an access, if the item has already been found, the real item may be searched for in subsequent levels rather than a random item. This does not change the output of the program, since the value that was already found is the one that will be used.

Note that this fix also applies to PanORAMa and OptORAMa. Even though these protocols contain multiple Cuckoo Hash Tables at each level, it is possible to view the entire level as a single Oblivious Hash Table with a stash. (The stash of the level would be the union of the stashes of the Overflow Table and the level-specific Combined Stash Table).

# 6    Summary of Affected Papers

Goodrich et al. [GMOT12] introduced the idea of using Cuckoo tables with combined stashes for Hierarchical ORAM. This introduced the flaw described in this paper. Kushilevitz et al. [KLO12] introduced the alternative approach of reinserting elements from the stash into the ORAM ("cache the stash"). While there are differences between these approaches, in either case an element that was stashed will be found prior to the level from which it was ejected and random locations accessed at this level instead. Therefore both approaches are vulnerable to our attack.

Lu and Ostrovsky [LO13] then used the stash-reinsertion of [KLO12] in their 2-server ORAM protocol, inheriting this vulnerability. Similarly Kushilevitz and Mour [KM19] created a 3-server ORAM that also uses cuckoo hashing (Instantiation 2) based on [KLO12], but using a shared stash [GMOT12] rather than reinserting the stash. This ORAM protocol is therefore vulnerable to the attack from this paper. Kushilevitz and Mour also present other multi-party ORAM protocols based on other techniques which are not subject to this attack.

Two alternative Hierarchical ORAM protocols were also published that avoided the flaw described in this paper. The Hierarchical ORAM protocol [MZ14] of Mitchell and Zimmerman uses a different model where the client can keep track of which level each item should be stored at. Knowing before-hand that an element does not exist at a certain level allows the algorithm to search for *pre-inserted dummy elements* at these levels. The data-structure therefore no longer needs to hide where data is stored, but only whether an element is real or a dummy, so any standard hash tables can be used instead of Cuckoo hashing. The two-tiered Hierarchical ORAM protocol of Chan et al. [CGLS17] then presented an alternative to cuckoo hashing with a stash. Instead, two hash tables existed, each with bins of size $\log^\epsilon(\lambda)$ for some constant $\epsilon \in (0.5, 1)$ and security parameter $\lambda$. They presented an oblivious construction in which elements would be placed in the first hash table if possible and in the second if not. They showed that the probability that an element could not be placed was negligible. Since this protocol used two-tier hashing rather than Cuckoo hashing with a combined stash it is immune to the attack we have presented.[13]

However, the flaw resurfaced again in the recent asymptotic breakthroughs of PanORAMa [PPRY18] and OptORAMa [AKL+20].[14] These achieved efficiency by storing most of the data in small bins, which are small enough to be sorted without increasing the asymptotic performance, while remaining items are placed in an overflow pile. Each of these bins is implemented as a cuckoo table and stashes are shared, but the combined stash for the bins is kept at the same level as the bins. Therefore it is possible to search the bins for the stashed elements and then to access the single-level combined stash, so the bin tables are not vulnerable to this attack. However, in both papers, the overflow and single-level combined stash cuckoo tables both have stashes that are re-inserted into the ORAM data structure. They are therefore vulnerable to the variant of our attack in Sect. 4.

Our attack *does not* affect the tree-based ORAM protocols, such as Binary Tree ORAM [SCSL11], Path ORAM [SvDS+13] and Circuit ORAM [WCS15], as these do not use cuckoo hashing.

In summary, this flaw existed in the ORAM literature for almost a decade and has affected six significant protocols, including the most recent asymptotic breakthroughs. The fact that such a flaw could exist unnoticed for so long motivates the development of simpler protocols for oblivious data structures.

**Acknowledgements.** This research was sponsored in part by ONR grant (N00014-15-1-2750) "SynCrypt: Automated Synthesis of Cryptographic Constructions". This research was supported in part by DARPA under Cooperative Agreement No: HR0011-20-2-0025, NSF-BSF Grant1619348, US-Israel BSF grant 2012366, Google Faculty Award, JP Morgan Faculty Award, IBM Faculty Research Award, Xerox Faculty Research Award, OKAWA Foundation Research Award, B. John Garrick Foundation Award, Teradata Research Award, and Lockheed-Martin Corporation Research Award. The views and conclusions contained herein are those of the authors and should not be interpreted as necessarily representing the official policies, either expressed or implied, of DARPA, the Department of Defense, or the U.S. Government. The U.S. Government is authorized to reproduce and distribute reprints for governmental purposes not withstanding any copyright annotation therein.

---

[13] Chan et al. also presented a concrete instantiation of Goodrich and Mitzenmacher's ORAM protocol in an appendix of the full version of their paper. The protocol they present uses a Cuckoo Hash Table at each level and a shared stash, so is vulnerable to the attack described in this paper. However, they recommend, somewhat clairvoyantly, that since Cuckoo hashing is complex and hard to prove correct, that their two-tier hash-table protocol should be used rather than the Cuckoo-hashing protocol.

[14] In response to our preprint, Asharov et al. have updated the OptORAMa paper to include a fix.

## Supplementary Material

## A    Distinguishing Distributions

In this section, we review a basic fact that if two distributions are statistically different, and supported on polynomial-sized sets, then they are polynomial-time distinguishable.

**Lemma 7.** *Let $\{X_n\}$, $\{Y_n\}$ denote two sequences of distributions supported on polynomial-sized sets, i.e., there is a constant c, such that $\max(|X_n|, |Y_n|) < n^c$. In addition, assume that $X_n$ and $Y_n$ are efficiently samplable.*

*Then if $\Delta(X_n, Y_n)$ is non-negligible, the distributions $\{X_n\}$ and $\{Y_n\}$ are polynomial-time distinguishable.*

*Proof.* Consider the following maximum likelihood distinguisher, $D$. Let $W = \mathrm{supp}(X_n) \cup \mathrm{supp}(Y_n)$, and $m = |W|$. Define

$$p_z \stackrel{\mathrm{def}}{=} \Pr\left[X_n = z\right]$$

$$q_z \stackrel{\mathrm{def}}{=} \Pr\left[Y_n = z\right]$$

Fix $t = \mathrm{poly}(n)$.

Recall that if $W = X_n \cup Y_n$,

$$\sum_{w \in W} \max(p_w, q_w) = \frac{1}{2} \sum_{w \in W} \left[\left[\max(p_w, q_w) + \min(p_w, q_w)\right] + \left[\max(p_w, q_w) - \min(p_w, q_w)\right]\right]$$

$$= \frac{1}{2}\left[2 + \sum_{w \in W} \left[\max(p_w, q_w) - \min(p_w, q_w)\right]\right]$$

$$= \frac{1}{2}\left[2 + 2\Delta(X_n, Y_n)\right]$$

$$= 1 + \Delta(X_n, Y_n)$$

First, $D$ will estimate the frequency of elements in both $X_n$ and $Y_n$ by sampling. First $D$ will draw $tm$ samples from $X_n$, let $X_{\mathrm{sampled}}$ denote the multiset corresponding to these samples. Similarly $D$ will draw $tm$ samples from $Y_n$. Let $Y_{\mathrm{sampled}}$ be the multiset corresponding to these samples.

Then $D$ defines

$$\tilde{p}_w \stackrel{\mathrm{def}}{=} \frac{\text{number of times } w \text{ occurred in } X_{\mathrm{sampled}}}{tm}$$

$$\tilde{q}_w \stackrel{\mathrm{def}}{=} \frac{\text{number of times } w \text{ occurred in } Y_{\mathrm{sampled}}}{tm}$$

Finally, given a sample $z$ from a distribution $Z \in \{X_n, Y_n\}$, the adversary will guess

$$A(z) = \begin{cases} X \text{ if } \tilde{p}_z \geq \tilde{q}_z \\ Y \text{ if } \tilde{p}_z < \tilde{q}_z. \end{cases}$$

A Hoeffding bound shows that

$$\Pr\left[|\tilde{p}_z - p_z| > \delta\right] < 2e^{-2mt\delta^2}$$

and similarly

$$\Pr\left[|\tilde{q}_z - q_z| > \delta\right] < 2e^{-2mt\delta^2}$$

Fix $\delta > 0$, and define

$$G \stackrel{\text{def}}{=} \{z \in W \mid |p_z - q_z| > 2\delta\}$$

$$B \stackrel{\text{def}}{=} \{z \in W \mid |p_z - q_z| \le 2\delta\}$$

Now, notice that

$$\max(p_z, q_z) - 2\delta < \min(p_z, q_z) \qquad \text{for all } z \in B \ . \tag{1}$$

The Hoeffding bounds give

$$\Pr\left[\max(p_z, q_z) = \max\left(\tilde{p}_z, \tilde{q}_z\right)\right] > 1 - 2e^{-2mt\delta^2} \qquad \text{for } z \in G \tag{2}$$

Let $\epsilon = \max_z \left(|\Pr(X_n = z) - \Pr(Y_n = z)|\right)$. Thus $\epsilon \ge \frac{\Delta(X_n, Y_n)}{m}$, which is non-negligible.

$\Pr\left[\ A \text{ is correct }\right]$

$$= \frac{1}{2}\left[\sum_{z \in Z} \Pr\left[\max\left(\tilde{p}_z, \tilde{q}_z\right) = \max\left(p_z, q_z\right)\right] \max\left(p_z, q_z\right) + \sum_{z \in Z} \Pr\left[\max\left(\tilde{p}_z, \tilde{q}_z\right) \ne \max\left(p_z, q_z\right)\right] \min\left(p_z, q_z\right)\right]$$

$$= \frac{1}{2}\left[\sum_{z \in Z} \Pr\left[\max\left(\tilde{p}_z, \tilde{q}_z\right) = \max\left(p_z, q_z\right)\right] \max\left(p_z, q_z\right) + \sum_{z \in B} \Pr\left[\max\left(\tilde{p}_z, \tilde{q}_z\right) \ne \max\left(p_z, q_z\right)\right] \min\left(p_z, q_z\right)\right]$$

$$\ge \frac{1}{2}\left[\sum_{z \in G} \Pr\left[\max\left(\tilde{p}_z, \tilde{q}_z\right) = \max\left(p_z, q_z\right)\right] \max\left(p_z, q_z\right) + \sum_{z \in B} \left[\max\left(p_z, q_z\right) - 2\delta\right]\right]$$

$$\ge \frac{1}{2}\left[\left(1 - 2e^{-2mt\delta^2}\right) \sum_{z \in Z} \max\left(p_z, q_z\right) - 2m\delta\right]$$

$$= \frac{1}{2}\left[\left(1 - 2e^{-2mt\delta^2}\right) [1 + \Delta(X_n, Y_n)] - 2m\delta\right]$$

$$= \left(1 - 2e^{-2mt\delta^2}\right)\left[\frac{1}{2} + \frac{1}{2}\Delta(X_n, Y_n)\right] - m\delta$$

Which is a non-negligible advantage for sufficiently large $t$ and sufficiently small $\delta$.

# References

[ADW14] Aumüller, M., Dietzfelbinger, M., Woelfel, P.: Explicit and efficient hash families suffice for cuckoo hashing with a stash. Algorithmica **70**(3), 428–456 (2014)

[AKL+20] Asharov, G., Komargodski, I., Lin, W.-K., Nayak, K., Peserico, E., Shi, E.: OptORAMa: optimal oblivious RAM. In: Canteaut, A., Ishai, Y. (eds.) EUROCRYPT 2020. LNCS, vol. 12106, pp. 403–432. Springer, Cham (2020). https://doi.org/10.1007/978-3-030-45724-2_14

[BMD+17] Brasser, F., Müller, U., Dmitrienko, A., Kostiainen, K., Capkun, S., Sadeghi, A.-R.: SGX cache attacks are practical. In: WOOT, Software Grand Exposure (2017)

[CGLS17] Chan, T.-H.H., Guo, Y., Lin, W.-K., Shi, E.: Oblivious hashing revisited, and applications to asymptotically efficient ORAM and OPRAM. In: Takagi, T., Peyrin, T. (eds.) ASIACRYPT 2017. LNCS, vol. 10624, pp. 660–690. Springer, Cham (2017). https://doi.org/10.1007/978-3-319-70694-8_23

[Ds17] Doerner, J., Shelat, A.: Scaling ORAM for secure computation. In: CCS, pp. 523–535 (2017)

[GESM17] Götzfried, J., Eckert, M., Schinzel, S., Müller, T.: Cache attacks on Intel SGX. In: Proceedings of the 10th European Workshop on Systems Security, pp. 1–6 (2017)

[GM11] Goodrich, M.T., Mitzenmacher, M.: Privacy-preserving access of outsourced data via oblivious RAM simulation. In: Aceto, L., Henzinger, M., Sgall, J. (eds.) ICALP 2011. LNCS, vol. 6756, pp. 576–587. Springer, Heidelberg (2011). https://doi.org/10.1007/978-3-642-22012-8_46

[GMOT12] Goodrich, M.T., Mitzenmacher, M., Ohrimenko, O., Tamassia, R.: Privacy-preserving group data access via stateless oblivious RAM simulation. In: SODA, pp. 157–167. SIAM (2012)

[GO96] Goldreich, O., Ostrovsky, R.: Software protection and simulation on oblivious RAMs. JACM **43**(3), 431–473 (1996)

[JHOvD17] John, T.M., Haider, S.K., Omar, H., van Dijk, M.: Connecting the dots: privacy leakage via write-access patterns to the main memory. IEEE Trans. Dependable Secure Comput. (2017)

[KLO12] Kushilevitz, E., Lu, S., Ostrovsky, R.: On the (in) security of hash-based oblivious RAM and a new balancing scheme. In: SODA, pp. 143–156. SIAM (2012)

[KM19] Kushilevitz, E., Mour, T.: Sub-logarithmic distributed oblivious RAM with small block size. In: Lin, D., Sako, K. (eds.) PKC 2019. LNCS, vol. 11442, pp. 3–33. Springer, Cham (2019). https://doi.org/10.1007/978-3-030-17253-4_1

[KMW09] Kirsch, A., Mitzenmacher, M., Wieder, U.: More robust hashing: Cuckoo hashing with a stash. SIAM J. Comput. **39**(4), 1543–1561 (2009)

[LHS+14] Liu, C., Huang, Y., Shi, E., Katz, J., Hicks, M.: Automating efficient RAM-model secure computation. In: S&P, pp. 623–638. IEEE (2014)

[LO13] Lu, S., Ostrovsky, R.: Distributed oblivious RAM for secure two-party computation. In: Sahai, A. (ed.) TCC, pp. 377–396. Springer, Heidelberg (2013). https://doi.org/10.1007/978-3-642-36594-2_22

[MIE17] Moghimi, A., Irazoqui, G., Eisenbarth, T.: CacheZoom: how SGX amplifies the power of cache attacks. In: Fischer, W., Homma, N. (eds.) CHES 2017. LNCS, vol. 10529, pp. 69–90. Springer, Cham (2017). https://doi.org/10.1007/978-3-319-66787-4_4

[Mit09] Mitzenmacher, M.: Some open questions related to cuckoo hashing. In: ESA, pp. 1–10 (2009)

[MZ14] Mitchell, J.C., Zimmerman, J.: Data-oblivious data structures. In: STACS. Schloss Dagstuhl-Leibniz-Zentrum fuer Informatik (2014)

[OS97] Ostrovsky, R., Shoup, V.: Private information storage. In: STOC, vol. 97, pp. 294–303. Citeseer (1997)

[Ost90] Ostrovsky, R.: Efficient computation on oblivious RAMs. In: STOC, pp. 514–523 (1990)

[Ost92] Ostrovsky, R.: Software protection and simulation on oblivious RAMs. Ph.D. thesis, Massachusetts Institute of Technology (1992)

[PPRY18] Patel, S., Persiano, G., Raykova, M., Yeo, K.: PanORAMa: oblivious RAM with logarithmic overhead. In: FOCS, pp. 871–882. IEEE (2018)

[PR04] Pagh, R., Rodler, F.F.: Cuckoo hashing. J. Algorithms **51**, 122–144 (2004)

[PR10] Pinkas, B., Reinman, T.: Oblivious RAM revisited. In: Rabin, T. (ed.) CRYPTO 2010. LNCS, vol. 6223, pp. 502–519. Springer, Heidelberg (2010). https://doi.org/10.1007/978-3-642-14623-7_27

[SCSL11] Shi, E., Chan, T.-H.H., Stefanov, E., Li, M.: Oblivious RAM with $O((\log N)^3)$ worst-case cost. In: Lee, D.H., Wang, X. (eds.) ASIACRYPT 2011. LNCS, vol. 7073, pp. 197–214. Springer, Heidelberg (2011). https://doi.org/10.1007/978-3-642-25385-0_11

[SGF17] Sasy, S., Gorbunov, S., Fletcher, C.W.: Zerotrace: oblivious memory primitives from Intel SGX. IACR Cryptol. ePrint Arch., 2017:549 (2017)

[SvDS+13] Stefanov, E.: Path ORAM: an extremely simple oblivious RAM protocol. In: CCS, pp. 299–310 (2013)

[WCS15] Wang, X., Chan, H., Shi, E.: Circuit ORAM: on tightness of the Goldreich-Ostrovsky lower bound. In: CCS, pp. 850–861 (2015)

[WHC+14] Wang, X.S., Huang, Y., Chan, T.-H.H., Shelat, A., Shi, E.: SCORAM: oblivious RAM for secure computation. In: CCS, pp. 191–202. ACM (2014)

# Structured Encryption and Dynamic Leakage Suppression

Marilyn George[1][(⊠)], Seny Kamara[1], and Tarik Moataz[2]

[1] Brown University, Providence, USA
marilyn_george@brown.edu
[2] Aroki Systems, Providence, USA

**Abstract.** Structured encryption (STE) schemes encrypt data structures in such a way that they can be privately queried. Special cases of STE include searchable symmetric encryption (SSE) and graph encryption. Like all sub-linear encrypted search solutions, STE leaks information about queries against persistent adversaries. To address this, a line of work on *leakage suppression* was recently initiated that focuses on techniques to mitigate the leakage of STE schemes.

A notable example is the query equality suppression framework (Kamara et al. *CRYPTO'18*) which transforms dynamic STE schemes that leak the query equality into new schemes that do not. Unfortunately, this framework can only produce static schemes and it was left as an open problem to design a solution that could yield dynamic constructions.

In this work, we propose a dynamic query equality suppression framework that transforms volume-hiding semi-dynamic or mutable STE schemes that leak the query equality into new *fully-dynamic* constructions that do not. We then use our framework to design three new fully-dynamic STE schemes that are "almost" and fully zero-leakage which, under natural assumptions on the data and query distributions, are asymptotically more efficient than using black-box ORAM simulation. These are the first constructions of their kind.

## 1   Introduction

The problem of encrypted search has received a lot of attention over the years from both the research community and industry. The ability to efficiently search and query encrypted data has the potential to change how we store and process data and help increase the wide-scale deployment of end-to-end encryption. A key requirement for any practical encrypted search solution is handling search queries in sub-linear time. Sub-linear encrypted search can be achieved based on several cryptographic primitives, including property-preserving encryption (PPE), structured encryption (STE) and oblivious RAM (ORAM). Each of these primitives have been heavily investigated and are known to achieve different tradeoffs between efficiency, expressiveness and security/leakage.

**Leakage.** All sub-linear encrypted search primitives leak information which has motivated the study of leakage attacks to investigate the real-world security

A. Canteaut and F.-X. Standaert (Eds.): EUROCRYPT 2021, LNCS 12698, pp. 370–396, 2021.
https://doi.org/10.1007/978-3-030-77883-5_13

of these primitives. In 2015, Naveed, Kamara and Wright [34] described data-recovery attacks in the snapshot setting against schemes that leak data equality and order. In 2012, Islam, Kuzu and Kantarcioglu [23] described a query-recovery attack against schemes that leak query co-occurrences (i.e., whether two keywords appear in the same document). The IKK attack was subsequently shown not to work in the standard adversarial model [10] but followup work described attacks in stronger adversarial models where the adversary is assumed to either know or choose a fraction of the client's data [6,10]. The known-data attacks of [10] exploit co-occurrence leakage and require a large fraction of known data whereas the attacks of [6] require a smaller fraction of known-data and exploit response length leakage; making them applicable to ORAM-based solutions as well. The chosen-data attacks of [46] exploit the response identity (i.e., identifiers of the files that contain the keyword) whereas the recent attacks of [6] only exploit response lengths; again, making them applicable to ORAM-based solutions. Several works have also described leakage attacks on the profiles of known oblivious and encrypted range schemes [21,22,30,32]. In [2], it is shown that highly-efficient STE schemes with zero-leakage queries can be achieved in the snapshot model.

**Leakage suppression.** Recently, Kamara, Moataz and Ohrimenko initiated the study of leakage suppression [27], which are methods to diminish and eradicate the leakage of STE schemes. There are two kinds of leakage suppression techniques: compilers and data transformations. Compilers take an STE scheme and transform it into a new scheme with similar efficiency but with an improved leakage profile. An example is the cache-based compiler (CBC) of [27] which is a generalization of the seminal Square Root ORAM construction of Goldreich and Ostrovsky [19]. The CBC takes any rebuildable STE scheme that leaks the query equality and possibly some other pattern patt, and transforms it into a new scheme that leaks only the non-repeating sub-pattern of patt. The non-repeating sub-pattern of a leakage pattern is the leakage it produces when queried only on non-repeating query sequences.

Data transformations change plaintext data structures in such a way that leakage is less harmful. The simplest example of a data transformation is padding, which mitigates response length leakage, but more sophisticated approaches include the clustering-based techniques of Bost and Fouque [8] and the transformation that underlies the PBS construction [27], both of which mitigate volume leakage. Recently, Kamara and Moataz also introduced computationally-secure transformations (as opposed to the previously mentioned approaches which are information-theoretic) to mitigate volume leakage [26].

**Dynamic leakage suppression.** The main advantage of suppression compilers over transformations is that they can be applied to large classes of schemes. For example, the CBC can be applied to any rebuildable STE scheme and, furthermore, [27] shows that any semi-dynamic STE scheme can be made rebuildable. An STE scheme is semi-dynamic if it supports additions but not deletions, and it is fully-dynamic if it supports both. The main limitation of the techniques from [27] is that they only produce *static* schemes even if the base construction is dynamic. While static STE schemes have several applications, dynamic schemes allow the encrypted data structure to adapt to changing data, which is more useful from a practical standpoint.

## 1.1 Our Contributions

In this work, we address the main problem left open by [27] which is to design a dynamic leakage suppression framework for the query equality. As we will see, solving this open problem results in three new low- and zero-leakage dynamic constructions that, under natural conditions on the data and queries, are asymptotically more efficient than black-box ORAM simulation.

**Dynamic compilers.** The suppression framework of [27], which includes the CBC and the rebuild compiler (RBC), can be used to compile any semi-dynamic STE scheme that leaks the query equality into a new scheme that does not. But, as discussed, this framework can only produce static schemes; i.e., it does not preserve the (semi-)dynamism of the base scheme. In this work, we propose dynamic variants of the CBC and RBC that suppress the query equality while preserving the dynamism of the base scheme.

Designing such compilers is challenging for several reasons. For example, consider that if the base scheme leaks the response length as well as the operation identity pattern (i.e., whether an operation is a query or an update), the adversary can learn the query equality as follows. Suppose that the largest response length observed is $n$ and that it occurs at some time $t$. Furthermore, suppose that at time $t + 1$ an update operation occurs and that at some time $t' > t + 1$ another query occurs with response larger than $n$. For some datasets and query distributions, it would be reasonable for the adversary to infer that the two queries are for the same value which, effectively, is the query equality. Unfortunately, all currently-known fully-dynamic STE schemes leak both the response length and the operation identity patterns.

Our approach, therefore, is to start with schemes that do not leak the response length like PBS [27] and AVLH [26]. The challenge in using these schemes, however, is that they are not dynamic but only semi-dynamic or mutable (i.e., they only support edit operations). To address this, our compiler is designed to work with these limited forms of dynamism but this requires overcoming a set of additional technical challenges like "upgrading" the base scheme's dynamism from semi-dynamic or mutable to fully-dynamic without leaking any additional information.

**New constructions.** We apply our compilers to three base multi-map encryption schemes to construct dynamic zero- and almost zero-leakage multi-map encryption schemes. Our first construction results from applying our compilers to the PBS construction of [27]. This results in a dynamic variant of the AZL scheme [27] which, given a sequence of operations $(\mathsf{op}_1, \ldots, \mathsf{op}_t)$, reveals nothing on operations $(\mathsf{op}_1, \ldots, \mathsf{op}_{t-1})$ and then reveals the sum of the operations' response lengths on operation $\mathsf{op}_t$. Similarly, our second construction results from applying our compilers to a variant of PBS and is a dynamic variant of the FZL scheme of [27]. This scheme has zero-leakage queries but only achieves probabilistic correctness. Our third construction, which results from applying our compilers to the AVLH construction of [26], also has ZL queries but achieves perfect correctness. We show that all three schemes are asymptotically more efficient than state-of-the-art black-box ORAM simulation under natural assumptions.

## 2    Related Work

**Structured encryption.** Structured encryption was introduced by Chase and Kamara in [14] as a generalization of searchable symmetric encryption (SSE) [15,41]. Several aspects of STE and SSE have been studied including dynamism [11,28,29,35], expressiveness [12,17,24,25,37], locality and I/O-efficiency [3,4, 11,13,16], security [2,7,9,18,42] and cryptanalysis [6,10,23,30,32,46].

**Leakage suppression.** Leakage suppression was first proposed by Kamara, Moataz and Ohrimenko [27] who generalized and adapted the techniques from Goldreich and Ostrovsky's seminal Square-Root ORAM to STE. Recently, Kamara and Moataz showed, for the first time, how to design volume-hiding STE schemes [26] without making use of padding. In follow up work, Patel, Persiano, Yeo and Yung [39] proposed new volume-hiding constructions that achieve better query and storage efficiency.

**Oblivious RAM.** Oblivious RAM was first proposed by Goldreich and Ostrovsky [19]. Several aspects of ORAM have been studied and improved in the last twenty years including its communication complexity, the number of rounds and client and server storage [18,20,31,36,38,40,43,45]. Another line of work initiated by Wang et al. [44] considers the design of oblivious data structures, without making use of general-purpose ORAM techniques. These constructions are typically more efficient than using general-purpose ORAM but are usually static or require setting an upper bound the structure at setup time.

## 3    Preliminaries and Notation

**Notation.** We denote the security parameter as $k$, and all algorithms run in time polynomial in $k$. The set of all binary strings of length $n$ is denoted as $\{0,1\}^n$, and the set of all finite binary strings as $\{0,1\}^*$. $[n]$ is the set of integers $\{1,\ldots,n\}$, and $2^{[n]}$ is the corresponding power set. We write $x \leftarrow \chi$ to represent an element $x$ being sampled from a distribution $\chi$, and $x \xleftarrow{\$} X$ to represent an element $x$ being sampled uniformly at random from a set $X$. The output $x$ of an algorithm $\mathcal{A}$ is denoted by $x \leftarrow \mathcal{A}$. Given a sequence $\mathbf{v}$ of $n$ elements, we refer to its $i^{th}$ element as $v_i$ or $\mathbf{v}[i]$. If $S$ is a set then $\#S$ refers to its cardinality. If $s$ is a string then $|s|_2$ refers to its bit length.

**Sorting networks.** A sorting network is a circuit of comparison-and-swap gates. A sorting network for $n$ elements takes as input a collection of $n$ elements

$(a_1, \ldots, a_n)$ and outputs them in increasing order. Each gate $g$ in an $n$-element network $\mathrm{SN}_n$ specifies two input locations $i, j \in [n]$ and, given $a_i$ and $a_j$, returns the pair $(a_i, a_j)$ if $i < j$ and $(a_j, a_i)$ otherwise. Sorting networks can be instantiated with the asymptotically-optimal Ajtai-Komlos-Szemeredi network [1] which has size $O(n \log n)$ or Batcher's more practical network [5] with size $O(n \log^2 n)$ but with small constants.

**The word RAM.** Our model of computation is the word RAM. In this model, we assume memory holds an infinite number of $w$-bit words and that arithmetic, logic, read and write operations can all be done in $O(1)$ time. We denote by $|x|_w$ the word-length of an item $x$; that is, $|x|_w = |x|_2/w$. Here, we assume that $w = \Omega(\log k)$.

**Abstract data types.** An *abstract data type* specifies the functionality of a data structure. It is a collection of data objects together with a set of operations defined on those objects. Examples include sets, dictionaries (also known as key-value stores or associative arrays) and graphs. The operations associated with an abstract data type fall into one of two categories: query operations, which return information about the objects; and update operations, which modify the objects. If the abstract data type supports only query operations it is *static*, otherwise it is *dynamic*. We model a dynamic data type $\mathbf{T}$ as a collection of four spaces: the object space $\mathbb{D} = \{\mathbb{D}_k\}_{k \in \mathbb{N}}$, the query space $\mathbb{Q} = \{\mathbb{Q}_k\}_{k \in \mathbb{N}}$, the response space $\mathbb{R} = \{\mathbb{R}_k\}_{k \in \mathbb{N}}$ and the update space $\mathbb{U} = \{\mathbb{U}_k\}_{k \in \mathbb{N}}$. We also define the query map $\mathsf{qu} : \mathbb{D} \times \mathbb{Q} \rightarrow \mathbb{R}$ and the update map $\mathsf{up} : \mathbb{D} \times \mathbb{U} \rightarrow \mathbb{D}$ to represent operations associated with the dynamic data type. We refer to the query and update spaces of a data type as the operation space $\mathbb{O} = \mathbb{Q} \cup \mathbb{U}$. When specifying a data type $\mathbf{T}$ we will often just describe its maps $(\mathsf{qu}, \mathsf{up})$ from which the object, query, response and update spaces can be deduced. The spaces are ensembles of finite sets of finite strings indexed by the security parameter. We assume that $\mathbb{R}$ includes a special element $\perp$ and that $\mathbb{D}$ includes an empty object $d_0$ such that for all $q \in \mathbb{Q}$, $\mathsf{qu}(d_0, q) = \perp$.

**Data structures.** A type-$\mathbf{T}$ data *structure* is a representation of data objects in $\mathbb{D}$ in some computational model (as mentioned, here it is the word RAM). Typically, the representation is optimized to support $\mathsf{qu}$ as efficiently as possible; that is, such that there exists an efficient algorithm $\mathsf{Query}$ that computes the function $\mathsf{qu}$. For data types that support multiple queries, the representation is often optimized to efficiently support as many queries as possible. As a concrete example, the dictionary type can be represented using various data structures depending on which queries one wants to support efficiently. Hash tables support $\mathsf{Get}$ and $\mathsf{Put}$ in expected $O(1)$ time whereas balanced binary search trees support both operations in worst-case $O(\log n)$ time.

**Definition 1 (Structuring scheme).** *Let* $\mathbf{T} = (\mathsf{qu} : \mathbb{D} \times \mathbb{Q} \rightarrow \mathbb{R}, \mathsf{up} : \mathbb{D} \times \mathbb{U} \rightarrow \mathbb{D})$ *be a dynamic type. A type-$\mathbf{T}$ structuring scheme* $\mathsf{SS} = (\mathsf{Setup}, \mathsf{Query}, \mathsf{Update})$ *is composed of three polynomial-time algorithms that work as follows:*

- $\mathsf{DS} \leftarrow \mathsf{Setup}(d)$: *is a possibly probabilistic algorithm that takes as input a data object* $d \in \mathbb{D}$ *and outputs a data structure* $\mathsf{DS}$. *Note that $d$ can be represented* *in any arbitrary manner as long as its bit length is polynomial in $k$. Unlike* DS, *its representation does not need to be optimized for any particular query.*

- $r \leftarrow$ Query(DS, $q$): *is an algorithm that takes as input a data structure* DS *and a query* $q \in \mathbb{Q}$ *and outputs a response* $r \in \mathbb{R}$.
- DS $\leftarrow$ Update(DS, $u$): *is a possibly probabilistic algorithm that takes as input a data structure* DS *and an update* $u \in \mathbb{U}$ *and outputs a new data structure* DS.

Here, we allow Setup and Update to be probabilistic but not Query. This captures most data structures but the definition can be extended to include structuring schemes with probabilistic query algorithms. We say that a data structure DS *instantiates* a data object $d \in \mathbb{D}$ if for all $q \in \mathbb{Q}$, Query(DS, $q$) = qu($d, q$). We denote this by DS $\equiv d$. We denote the set of queries supported by a structure DS as $\mathbb{Q}_{\text{DS}}$; that is,

$$\mathbb{Q}_{\text{DS}} \stackrel{def}{=} \left\{ q \in \mathbb{Q} : \text{Query(DS}, q) \neq \perp \right\}.$$

Similarly, the set of responses supported by a structure DS is denoted $\mathbb{R}_{\text{DS}}$.

**Definition 2 (Correctness).** *Let* $\mathbf{T} = (\text{qu} : \mathbb{D} \times \mathbb{Q} \to \mathbb{R}, \text{up} : \mathbb{D} \times \mathbb{U} \to \mathbb{D})$ *be a dynamic type. A type-$\mathbf{T}$ structuring scheme* SS = (Setup, Query, Update) *is perfectly correct if it satisfies the following properties:*

1. *(static correctness) for all* $d \in \mathbb{D}$,

$$\Pr\left[\, \text{DS} \equiv d : \text{DS} \leftarrow \text{Setup}(d) \,\right] = 1,$$

   *where the probability is over the coins of* Setup.
2. *(dynamic correctness) for all* $d \in \mathbb{D}$ *and* $u \in \mathbb{U}$, *for all* DS $\equiv d$,

$$\Pr\left[\, \text{Update(DS}, u) \equiv \text{up}(d, u) \,\right] = 1,$$

   *where the probability is over the coins of* Update.

Note that the second condition guarantees the correctness of an updated structure whether the original structure was generated by a setup operation or a previous update operation. Weaker notions of correctness (e.g., for data structures like Bloom filters) can be derived from Definition 2.

**Basic data structures.** We use structures for several basic data types including arrays, dictionaries and multi-maps which we recall here. An array RAM of capacity $n$ stores $n$ items at locations 1 through $n$ and supports read and write operations. We write $v := \text{RAM}[i]$ to denote reading the item at location $i$ and $\text{RAM}[i] := v$ the operation of storing an item at location $i$. A dictionary structure DX of capacity $n$ holds a collection of $n$ label/value pairs $\{(\ell_i, v_i)\}_{i \leq n}$ and supports get and put operations. We write $v_i := \text{DX}[\ell_i]$ to denote getting the value associated with label $\ell_i$ and $\text{DX}[\ell_i] := v_i$ to denote the operation of associating the value $v_i$ in DX with label $\ell_i$. A multi-map structure MM with capacity $n$ is a collection of $n$ label/tuple pairs $\{(\ell_i, \mathbf{v}_i)_i\}_{i \leq n}$ that supports get and put operations. Similarly to dictionaries, we write $\mathbf{v}_i := \mathsf{MM}[\ell_i]$ to denote getting the tuple associated with label $\ell_i$ and $\mathsf{MM}[\ell_i] := \mathbf{v}_i$ to denote operation of associating the tuple $\mathbf{v}_i$ to label $\ell_i$. Multi-maps are the abstract data type instantiated by an inverted index. In the encrypted search literature multi-maps are sometimes referred to as indexes, databases or tuple-sets (T-sets).

**Data structure logs.** Given a structure DS that instantiates an object $d$, we will be interested in the sequence of update operations needed to create a new structure $\mathsf{DS}'$ that also instantiates $d$. We refer to this as the *query log* of DS and assume the existence of an efficient algorithm Log that takes as input DS and outputs a tuple $(u_1, \ldots, u_n)$ such that adding $u_1, \ldots, u_n$ to an empty structure results in some $\mathsf{DS}' \equiv d$.

**Extensions.** An important property we will need from a data structure is that it be *extendable* [27] in the sense that, given a structure DS one can create another structure $\overline{\mathsf{DS}} \neq \mathsf{DS}$ that is functionally equivalent to DS but that also supports a number of *dummy* queries. We say that a structure is efficiently extendable if there exist a query set $\overline{\mathbb{Q}} \supset \mathbb{Q}$ and a PPT algorithm $\mathsf{Ext_T}$ that takes as input a structure DS of type $\mathbf{T}$ and a *capacity* $\lambda \geq 1$ and returns a new structure $\overline{\mathsf{DS}}$ also of type $\mathbf{T}^1$ such that: (1) $\overline{\mathsf{DS}} \equiv d$; and (2) for all $q \in \overline{\mathbb{Q}} \setminus \mathbb{Q}$, $\mathsf{Query}(\overline{\mathsf{DS}}, q) = \perp$. We say that $\overline{\mathsf{DS}}$ is an extension of DS and that DS is a sub-structure of $\overline{\mathsf{DS}}$.

**Cryptographic protocols.** We denote by $(\mathsf{out}_A, \mathsf{out}_B) \leftarrow \Pi_{A,B}(X, Y)$ the execution of a two-party protocol $\Pi$ between parties $A$ and $B$, where $X$ and $Y$ are the inputs provided by $A$ and $B$, respectively; and $\mathsf{out}_A$ and $\mathsf{out}_B$ are the outputs returned to $A$ and $B$, respectively.

### 3.1   Structured Encryption

We recall the syntax definition of STE.

**Definition 3 (Structured encryption [14]).** *An interactive structured encryption scheme $\Sigma = (\mathsf{Setup}, \mathsf{Operate})$ consists of an algorithm and a two-party protocol that work as follows:*

- $(K, st, \mathsf{EDS}) \leftarrow \mathsf{Setup}(1^k, \lambda, \mathsf{DS})$: *is a probabilistic polynomial-time algorithm that takes as input a security parameter $1^k$, a query capacity $\lambda \geq 1$ and a type-$\mathbf{T}$ structure DS. It outputs a secret key $K$, a state $st$ and an encrypted structure EDS. If $\mathsf{DS} \equiv d_0$, it outputs an empty EDS.*
- $((st', r), \mathsf{EDS}') \leftarrow \mathsf{Operate}_{\mathsf{C,S}}((K, st, \mathsf{op}), \mathsf{EDS})$: *is a two-party protocol executed between a client and a server where the client inputs a secret key $K$, a state $st$ and an operation op and the server inputs an encrypted structure EDS. The client receives as output a (possibly) updated state $st'$ and a response $r \in \mathbb{R} \cup \perp$ while the server receives a (possibly updated) encrypted structure EDS'.*

---

[1] We consider that the inclusion of dummy queries in a query space does not impact the type of a structure.

*If $\Sigma$ also has a* Rebuild *protocol as defined below, we say that it is rebuildable,*

- $((st', K'), \mathsf{EDS}') \leftarrow \mathsf{Rebuild}_{\mathsf{C},\mathsf{S}}((K, st), \mathsf{EDS})$: *is a two-party protocol executed between the client and server where the client inputs a secret key $K$ and a state $st$. The server inputs an encrypted data structure* EDS. *The client receives an updated state $st'$ and a new key $K'$ as output while the server receives a new structure* EDS'.

**Operations.** Note that an STE schemes usually supports more than a single operation and the syntax above can be used (or extended) to capture this in one of two ways. The first is to notice that the Operate protocol can take as input an operation op that describes one of a set of operations and its operands. For example, if $\Sigma_{\mathsf{DS}} = (\mathsf{Setup}, \mathsf{Operate})$ supports both query and add operations, then op can have the form $\mathsf{op} = (\mathsf{qry}, q)$ to denote a query operation for $q$ or $\mathsf{op} = (\mathsf{add}, a)$ to denote an add operation for $a$. The Operate protocol can then operate on EDS accordingly and output $((st, r), \mathsf{EDS}')$, where $r \neq \bot$ and $\mathsf{EDS}' = \mathsf{EDS}$ in the case of a query, and where $r = \bot$ and $\mathsf{EDS}' \neq \mathsf{EDS}$ in the case of an add. For notational convenience we will usually omit the flags qry or add and just write $\mathsf{op} = q$ or $\mathsf{op} = a$ to denote that it is a query or and add. This formulation is particularly convenient when working with schemes that hide which operation is being executed, as will be the case with our main constructions. Another approach is to include the different operations explicitly in $\Sigma_{\mathsf{DS}}$'s syntax. For example, if it supports queries and adds, then we would write $\Sigma_{\mathsf{DS}} = (\mathsf{Setup}, \mathsf{Query}, \mathsf{Add})$, where Query is a special case of Operate that (usually) outputs a response $r \neq \bot$ and an $\mathsf{EDS}' = \mathsf{EDS}$ and Add is a special case that (usually) outputs $r = \bot$ and $\mathsf{EDS}' \neq \mathsf{EDS}$. This formulation is particularly convenient when working with schemes that reveal which operation is being executed, as will be the case with the constructions we use as building blocks.

**Dynamism.** We consider several kinds of dynamic STE schemes. The first are *fully-dynamic* schemes which support add and delete operations. We usually refer to such schemes simply as *dynamic*. Add operations insert a query/response pair $(q, r)$ into the data structure whereas delete operations remove query/response pairs $(q, r)$ associated with a given query $q$. If a scheme only handles add operations we say it is *semi-dynamic*. Finally, we consider *mutable* schemes which are schemes that support an edit operation which takes as input a query/response pair $(q, r')$ and changes a pre-existing pair $(q, r)$ to $(q, r')$. If a scheme is either semi-dynamic or mutable we say that it is *weakly dynamic*.

**Security.** We recall the notion of adaptive semantic security for STE.

**Definition 4 (Security [14, 15]).** *Let $\Sigma = (\mathsf{Setup}, \mathsf{Operate}_{\mathsf{C},\mathsf{S}}, \mathsf{Rebuild}_{\mathsf{C},\mathsf{S}})$ be a structured encryption scheme and consider the following probabilistic experiments where $\mathcal{C}$ is a stateful challenger, $\mathcal{A}$ is a stateful adversary, $\mathcal{S}$ is a stateful simulator, $\Lambda = (\mathsf{patt}_{\mathsf{S}}, \mathsf{patt}_{\mathsf{O}}, \mathsf{patt}_{\mathsf{R}})$ is a leakage profile, $\lambda \geq 1$ and $z \in \{0, 1\}^*$:*

$\mathbf{Real}_{\Sigma, \mathcal{C}, \mathcal{A}}(k)$: *given $z$ and $\lambda$ the adversary $\mathcal{A}$ outputs a structure* DS *and receives* EDS *from the challenger, where $(K, st, \mathsf{EDS}) \leftarrow \mathsf{Setup}(1^k, \lambda, \mathsf{DS})$. $\mathcal{A}$ then*

*adaptively chooses a polynomial-size sequence of operations* $(\mathsf{op}_1, \ldots \mathsf{op}_m)$.
*For all* $1 \leq i \leq m$ *the challenger and adversary do the following:*

1. *if* $\mathsf{op}_i$ *is a query or an update, they execute* $\mathsf{Operate}_{\mathcal{C},\mathcal{A}}\big((K, st, \mathsf{op}_i), \mathsf{EDS}\big)$;
2. *if* $\mathsf{op}_i$ *is a rebuild, they execute* $\mathsf{Rebuild}_{\mathcal{C},\mathcal{A}}\big((K, st), \mathsf{EDS}\big)$.

*Finally,* $\mathcal{A}$ *outputs a bit b that is output by the experiment.*

$\mathbf{Ideal}_{\Sigma,\mathcal{A},\mathcal{S}}(k)$: *given z and* $\lambda$ *the adversary* $\mathcal{A}$ *outputs a structure* $\mathsf{DS}$ *of type*
$\mathbf{T}$. *Given* $\mathsf{patt}_\mathsf{S}(\mathsf{DS})$, *the simulator returns an encrypted structure* $\mathsf{EDS}$
*to* $\mathcal{A}$. $\mathcal{A}$ *then adaptively chooses a polynomial-size sequence of operations*
$(\mathsf{op}_1, \ldots, \mathsf{op}_m)$. *For all* $1 \leq i \leq m$, *the challenger, simulator and adversary*
*do the following:*

1. *if* $\mathsf{op}_i$ *is either a query or an update,* $\mathcal{S}$ *is given* $\mathsf{patt}_\mathsf{O}(\mathsf{DS}, \mathsf{op}_1, \ldots, \mathsf{op}_i)$
   *and it executes* $\mathsf{Operate}_{\mathcal{S},\mathcal{A}}$ *with* $\mathcal{A}$;
2. *if* $\mathsf{op}_i$ *is a rebuild,* $\mathcal{S}$ *is given* $\mathsf{patt}_\mathsf{R}(\mathsf{DS})$ *and it executes* $\mathsf{Rebuild}_{\mathcal{S},\mathcal{A}}$ *with*
   $\mathcal{A}$;

*Finally,* $\mathcal{A}$ *outputs a bit b that is output by the experiment.*

We say that $\Sigma$ is $\Lambda$-secure if there exists a PPT simulator $\mathcal{S}$ such that for all
PPT adversaries $\mathcal{A}$, for all $\lambda \geq 1$ and all $z \in \{0,1\}^*$,

$$\left|\Pr\left[\mathbf{Real}_{\Sigma,\mathcal{A}}(k) = 1\right] - \Pr\left[\mathbf{Ideal}_{\Sigma,\mathcal{A},\mathcal{S}}(k) = 1\right]\right| \leq \mathsf{negl}(k).$$

Note that security of non-rebuildable schemes can be recovered by not allowing
rebuild operations.

**Leakage.** We extend the leakage patterns defined in [27] to the dynamic setting.
In particular [27] defined leakage patterns as functions of queries on a static data
type. We will have to extend the definitions to account for general operations
(queries or updates) on a dynamic data type. Let $\mathbf{T} = (\mathsf{qu} : \mathbb{D} \times \mathbb{Q} \to \mathbb{R}, \mathsf{up} :$
$\mathbb{D} \times \mathbb{U} \to \mathbb{D})$ be a dynamic data type. We assume that updates can be written as
query/response pairs, i.e., $\mathbb{U} = \mathbb{Q} \times \mathbb{R}$. Given a data structure $d$ and a sequence
of $t$ operations $\mathsf{op}_1, \ldots, \mathsf{op}_t$, we denote by $d_t$ the structure that results from
applying the given sequence of operations to $d$. Consider the following leakage
patterns,

- the *operation identity pattern* is the function family $\mathsf{oid} = \{\mathsf{oid}_{k,t}\}_{k,t \in \mathbb{N}}$ with
  $\mathsf{oid}_{k,t} : \mathbb{D}_k \times \mathbb{O}_k^t \to \{0,1\}^t$ such that $\mathsf{oid}_{k,t}(d, \mathsf{op}_1, \ldots, \mathsf{op}_t) = \mathbf{m}$, where $\mathbf{m}$ is
  a binary $t$-dimensional vector such that $\mathbf{m}[i] = 0$ if $\mathsf{op}_i \in \mathbb{Q}$ and $\mathbf{m}[i] = 1$ if
  $\mathsf{op}_i \in \mathbb{U}$;
- the *update query equality pattern* is the function family $\mathsf{uqeq} = \{\mathsf{uqeq}_{k,t}\}_{k,t \in \mathbb{N}}$
  with $\mathsf{uqeq}_{k,t} : \mathbb{D}_k \times \mathbb{U}_k^t \to \{0,1\}^{t \times t}$ such that $\mathsf{uqeq}_{k,t}(d, u_1, \ldots, u_t) = M$,
  where $M$ is a binary $t \times t$ matrix such that for updates $u_i = (q_i, r_i)$ and
  $u_j = (q_j, r_j)$, $M[i,j] = 1$ if $q_i = q_j$ and $M[i,j] = 0$ otherwise;
- the *operation total response length pattern* is the function family $\mathsf{otrlen} =$
  $\{\mathsf{otrlen}_k\}_{k \in \mathbb{N}}$ with $\mathsf{otrlen}_k : \mathbb{D}_k \times \mathbb{O}_k^t \to \mathbb{N}$ such that $\mathsf{otrlen}_k(d, \mathsf{op}_1, \ldots, \mathsf{op}_t) =$
  $\sum_{q \in \mathbb{Q}_k} |\mathsf{qu}(d_t, q)|_w$ and $d_t$ is $d$ after $t$ operations.;
- the *operation data size pattern* is the function family $\mathsf{odsize} = \{\mathsf{odsize}_k\}_{k \in \mathbb{N}}$
  with $\mathsf{odsize}_k : \mathbb{D}_k \times \mathbb{O}_k^t \to \mathbb{N}$ such that $\mathsf{odsize}_k(d, \mathsf{op}_1, \ldots, \mathsf{op}_t) = |d_t|_w$;

- the *operation log size pattern* is the function family olsize $= \{\text{olsize}_k\}_{k\in\mathbb{N}}$ with olsize$_k : \mathbb{D}_k \times \mathbb{O}_k^t \rightarrow \mathbb{N}$ such that olsize$_k(d, \text{op}_1, \ldots, \text{op}_t) = \#\text{Log}(\text{DS})$ where DS is an instantiation of $d_t$ such that DS $\equiv d_t$;
- the *operation max log length pattern* is the function family omllen $= \{\text{omllen}_k\}_{k\in\mathbb{N}}$ with omllen$_k : \mathbb{D}_k \times \mathbb{O}_k^t \rightarrow \mathbb{N}$ such that omllen$_k(d, \text{op}_1, \ldots, \text{op}_t) = \max_{\text{op}\in\text{Log}(d_t)} |\text{op}|_w$.

Note that in the static setting, i.e., when $\mathbb{O} = \mathbb{Q}$, the leakage patterns otrlen, odsize, olsize, omllen are equivalent to the patterns trlen, dsize, lsize, mllen originally defined in [27].

**Leakage sub-patterns.** We recall the notion of leakage sub-patterns introduced in [27]. Given a leakage pattern patt, it can be decomposed into sub-patterns capturing its behavior on restricted classes of query sequences. In particular, we can decompose a leakage pattern into repeating and non-repeating sub-patterns. The non-repeating sub-pattern is pattern that results from evaluating patt on non-repeating query sequences (i.e., where all queries are unique).

**Definition 5 (Non-repeating sub-patterns).** *Let* $\mathbf{T} = (\text{qu} : \mathbb{D} \times \mathbb{Q} \rightarrow \mathbb{R}, \text{up} : \mathbb{D} \times \mathbb{U} \rightarrow \mathbb{D})$ *be a dynamic data type and* patt $: \mathbb{D} \times \mathbb{Q}^t \rightarrow \mathbb{X}$ *be a query leakage pattern. The non-repeating sub-pattern of* patt *is the function* uniq *such that*

$$\text{patt}(\text{DS}, q_1, \ldots, q_t) = \begin{cases} \text{uniq}(\text{DS}, q_1, \ldots, q_t) & \text{if } q_i \neq q_j \text{ for all } i, j \in [t], \\ \text{other}(\text{DS}, q_1, \ldots, q_t) & \text{otherwise.} \end{cases}$$

**Safe extensions.** We recall and extend the notion of safe extension from [27] to support updates.

**Definition 6 (Safe extensions).** *Let* $\Lambda = (\text{patt}_\text{S}, \text{patt}_\text{Q}, \text{patt}_\text{U}, \text{patt}_\text{R})$ *be a leakage profile. We say that an extension* Ext *is* $\Lambda$-*safe if for all* $k \in \mathbb{N}$, *for all* $d \in \mathbb{D}_k$, *for all* DS $\equiv d$, *for all* $\lambda \geq 1$, *for all* $\overline{\text{DS}}$ *output by* Ext$(\text{DS}, \lambda)$, *for all* $t \in \mathbb{N}$, *for all* $\mathbf{op} = (\text{op}_1, \ldots, \text{op}_t) \in \mathbb{O}_k^t$,

- patt$_\text{S}(\overline{\text{DS}}) \leq$ patt$_\text{S}(\text{DS})$;
- patt$_\text{Q}(\overline{\text{DS}}, q_1, \ldots, q_p) \leq$ patt$_\text{Q}(\text{DS}, q_1, \ldots, q_p)$, *where* $(q_1, \ldots, q_p)$ *is the sub-sequence of queries in* $\mathbf{op}$;
- patt$_\text{U}(\overline{\text{DS}}, u_1, \ldots, u_w) \leq$ patt$_\text{U}(\text{DS}, u_1, \ldots, u_w)$, *where* $(u_1, \ldots, u_w)$ *is the sub-sequence of updates in* $\mathbf{op}$;
- patt$_\text{R}(\overline{\text{DS}}) \leq$ patt$_\text{R}(\text{DS})$,

*where* patt$_1 \leq$ patt$_2$ *means that* patt$_1$ *can be simulated from* patt$_2$.

## 4   Our Dynamic Suppression Framework

In this section, we present a dynamic variant of the query equality suppression framework proposed by [27]. Our framework transforms non-rebuildable weakly-dynamic STE schemes that leak the query equality into fully-dynamic STE schemes that do not. Recall that the static framework relies on two compilers: (1) a rebuild compiler (RBC) which transforms a semi-dynamic and non-rebuildable scheme into a static and rebuildable one; and (2) the cache-based compiler (CBC) which transforms a static and rebuildable scheme that leaks the query equality into a static scheme that does not.

**Challenges.** One of the challenges in designing a dynamic variant of the CBC is handling subtle correlations between various leakage patterns. For example, suppose the base STE scheme leaks the response length and the operation identity patterns and consider a sequence of operations $(\mathsf{op}_1, \ldots, \mathsf{op}_4)$ such that $\mathsf{op}_1 = q_1$, $\mathsf{op}_2 = q_2$, $\mathsf{op}_3 = u_3$ and $\mathsf{op}_4 = q_4$. Now, given the operation identities and the response lengths, suppose the adversary observes that: $q_1$ has the largest response length $\ell_1$; that $q_3$ is an update operation; and that $q_4$ has response length $\ell_1 + 1$. From this, it can reasonably infer that $q_1$ might be equal to $q_4$ which is a "probabilistic" variant of the query equality. It is therefore not enough to suppress the exact query equality but also the patterns that can reveal partial information about it.

To address this, our compiler will have to suppress the response length and the operation identity in addition to the query equality. One can trivially suppress the former by padding responses to the maximum length but this induces a large storage cost; especially when the response lengths are skewed. A better approach would be to start with base schemes that are volume-hiding in the sense that they hide the response lengths (without naive padding). Unfortunately, all volume-hiding constructions we are aware of [26,39] are only weakly dynamic. Our goal, therefore, will be to design a compiler that suppresses the query equality, the operation identity and the response length while upgrading the base scheme from being weakly-dynamic to fully-dynamic.

Another important challenge we must overcome is making the base scheme rebuildable. [27] already showed how to make semi-dynamic schemes rebuildable but, in our setting, we also need to handle mutable constructions which do not support add operations but only edits. To summarize, our compiler has to handle the following challenges:

- *(weak dynamism)* it must transform a weakly-dynamic (i.e., either semi-dynamic or mutable) scheme to a fully-dynamic one;
- *(operation identity)* it must suppress the operation identity; that is, queries and updates should look identical.
- *(rebuild)* it must make the base scheme rebuildable even if it is only weakly dynamic.

**Overview of the dynamic CBC.** The dynamic CBC is similar to the static CBC of [27] with the exception of a few steps to handle adds and edits. Let $\Sigma_{\mathsf{DS}} =$ (Setup, Query, Add) be a semi-dynamic STE scheme and let $\Sigma_{\mathsf{DX}} =$ (Setup, Get, Put) be a semi-dynamic and zero-leakage dictionary encryption scheme. The compiler produces a new scheme $\Sigma_{\mathsf{DDS}} =$ (Setup, Operate) that works as follows.

Given a structure DS and a capacity $\lambda \geq 1$, its setup algorithm outputs a structure EDDS $= (\overline{\text{EDS}}, \text{EDX})$, where $\overline{\text{EDS}}$ is the encryption of a $\lambda$-extension of DS and EDX is an encryption of a dictionary with capacity $\lambda$. Operations on EDDS are handled as follows:

- *(queries)* to make a query $q$, the client first executes a get on EDX for $q$. If this returns $\bot$ (i.e., $q$ has never been issued before) the client queries $\overline{\text{EDS}}$ for $q$ and receives a response $r$. The client then does a put on EDX to add the query/response pair $(q, r)$. If, on the other hand, the get on the cache returned a response $r \neq \bot$, the client queries $\overline{\text{EDS}}$ for an unused dummy value and puts the query/response pair $(q, r)$ in EDX;
- *(adds)* to add a query/response pair $(q, r)$, the client executes a get on EDX for an arbitrary query and ignores the response. It then queries $\overline{\text{EDS}}$ for an unused dummy and puts $(q, r)$ in EDX;
- *(edits)* to edit the response of an existing query $q$ (e.g., by either adding to it, deleting from it or changing it), the client first executes a get on EDX for $q$. If this returns $\bot$, the client queries $\overline{\text{EDS}}$ for $q$ and receives a response $r$. It then edits $r$, which results in a new response $r'$, and puts $(q, r')$ in EDX. If, on the other hand, the get on the cache returned a response $r \neq \bot$, the client queries $\overline{\text{EDS}}$ for an unused dummy, edits $r$ and puts the edited query/response pair $(q, r')$ in EDX.

Note that for every operation, the dynamic CBC executes a get on EDX, then a query on $\overline{\text{EDS}}$ and, finally, a put on EDX. Furthermore, $\overline{\text{EDS}}$ is never queried for a query $q$ more than once. Intuitively, the first property will guarantee that the scheme suppresses the operation identity while the second will guarantee that it suppresses the query equality.

Every operation executed on EDDS consumes a (unique) dummy item from $\overline{\text{EDS}}$. And since it holds $\lambda$ dummies, it needs to be rebuilt after $\lambda$ operations so that it can continue to be used. We now describe how this rebuild is achieved.

**Overview of the dynamic RBC.** We have two main goals when rebuilding EDDS $= (\overline{\text{EDS}}, \text{EDX})$. The first is to build a new $\overline{\text{EDS}}$ structure $\overline{\text{EDS}'}$ that holds the $\lambda$ dummies. The second is to make sure that $\overline{\text{EDS}'}$ holds the most up-to-date responses for all the queries. Note that the second goal is non-trivial because of the way adds and edits are handled. In particular, the most up-to-date response for a query $q$ can be either in $\overline{\text{EDS}}$ or in EDX depending on whether it has been added, edited or never modified. More precisely, we have hat after $\lambda$ operations, if a query/response pair $(q, r)$ is in the cache then $r$ is the most up-to-date response for $q$. On the other hand, if a pair $(q, r)$ is not in the cache then the main structure $\overline{\text{EDS}}$ holds the most up-to-date response for $q$. In the following, we refer to a query/response pair $(q, r)$ as *valid* if $r$ is the most up-to-date response for $q$ and as *invalid* if it is not. Our rebuild protocol must then extract the valid query/response pairs from EDX and $\overline{\text{EDS}}$ and add them to $\overline{\text{EDS}'}$ with a minimal amount of leakage.[2]

---

[2] Note that invalid query/response pairs in $\overline{\text{EDS}}$ result from the pair existing in $\overline{\text{EDS}}$ from setup (i.e., not being added) but being edited during the last $\lambda$ operations.

The protocol consists of five phases: (1) *initialization*, where an array RAM is initialized at the server; (2) *extract-and-tag*, where all the query/response pairs are retrieved from $\overline{\text{EDS}}$ and EDX, tagged according to their validity and stored in an encrypted array at the server; (3) *sort-and-shuffle*, where the encrypted array is (obliviously) sorted to partition the invalid and valid query/response pairs so that the former can be deleted and the latter are randomly shuffled; (4) *update*, where the valid query/response pairs in the array are added to a new $\overline{\text{EDS}'}$ structure; and (5) *cache setup*, where a new cache structure EDX' is created. More precisely, it works as follows:

1. *(initialization):* the server initializes an array RAM.
2. *(extract-and-tag)* the client sequentially retrieves all the query/response pairs $(q, r)$ in $\overline{\text{EDS}}$ and EDX. For all $(q, r)$ in EDX, it adds an encryption of $(q, r, f)$ to RAM, where $f$ is a random non-zero $k$-bit value we refer to as a validity tag. If there are less than $\lambda$ entries in EDX, it queries it on arbitrary values until it reaches $\lambda$ queries and for each of these arbitrary queries it adds an encryption of $(\bot, \bot, 0)$ to RAM. For all query/response pairs $(q, r)$ in $\overline{\text{EDS}}$, it adds an encryption of $(q, r, f)$ to RAM, where $f$ is set to 0 if $q$ was present in EDX and $f$ is set to a random non-zero $k$-bit value otherwise. For each dummy in $\overline{\text{EDS}}$, the client adds an encryption of $(\bot, \bot, f)$ to RAM, where $f$ is a random non-zero $k$-bit value. Throughout this phase, the client also keeps count of the number of entries with 0 tags. Notice that the valid query/response pairs and the dummies are all tagged with random non-zero validity tags whereas the invalid pairs and the entries that result from the "arbitrary" queries on EDX are tagged with 0.
3. *(sort-and-shuffle)* the client obliviously sorts RAM according to the validity tags. Since the valid pairs and the dummies have random non-zero tags and the rest have 0 tags, this step will randomly shuffle the valid pairs and dummies and store the rest at the start of the array. The client then asks the server to delete the first $t$ entries, where $t$ is the number of entries with 0 tags. At this point, the array only holds valid query/response pairs.
4. *(update)* the client creates a new structure $\overline{\text{EDS}'}$ by retrieving the query/response pairs in RAM and adding them to $\overline{\text{EDS}'}$. How exactly this is done depends on the kind of dynamism $\Sigma_{\text{DS}}$ supports:
   - *(semi-dynamic)* if it is semi-dynamic, the client initializes an empty structure $\text{DS}_0$ and encrypts it with $\Sigma_{\text{DS}}$ before storing it at the server. This new encrypted structure is $\overline{\text{EDS}'}$. The client sequentially retrieves the query/response pairs $(q, r)$ from RAM and adds them to $\overline{\text{EDS}'}$.
   - *(mutable)* if $\Sigma_{\text{DS}}$ is mutable we can only use edit operations. The client then sets up "placeholder" structure $\widetilde{\text{DS}}$ that it will encrypt and edit until it holds the necessary data. Note that for this to work, the placeholder must be large enough to hold the latest version of DS (i.e., the structure DS after the $\lambda$ operations) and it must be "safe" in the sense that encrypting and editing the placeholder must not leak more than operating on the original structure.

5. *(cache setup)* the client generates an empty dictionary with capacity $\lambda$ and encrypts it with $\Sigma_{DX}$ and sets it to be $\mathsf{EDX}'$.

Finally, the protocol outputs a rebuilt structure $\mathsf{EDDS}' = (\overline{\mathsf{EDS}'}, \mathsf{EDX}')$.

## 4.1 Security

We now analyze the security of our dynamic suppression framework. We present two theorems whose proofs are in the full version of this work. Theorem 1 analyzes the case when $\Sigma_{DS}$ is semi-dynamic and Theorem 2 analyzes the case where $\Sigma_{DS}$ is mutable. For Theorem 1, we assume $\Sigma_{DS}$ has leakage profile

$$\Lambda_{DS} = (\mathcal{L}_S, \mathcal{L}_Q, \mathcal{L}_A) = \left(\mathsf{patt}_S^{ds}, (\mathsf{qeq}^{ds}, \mathsf{patt}_Q^{ds}), \mathsf{patt}_A^{ds}\right),$$

and $\Sigma_{DX}$ has profile

$$\Lambda_{DX} = (\mathcal{L}_S, \mathcal{L}_G, \mathcal{L}_P) = \left(\mathsf{patt}_S^{dx}, \bot, \bot\right).$$

**Theorem 1 (Semi-dynamic).** *If $\Sigma_{DS}$ is $\Lambda_{DS}$-secure, if Ext is $(\mathsf{patt}_S^{ds}, \mathsf{uniq}, \mathsf{patt}_A^{ds})$-safe, and if $\Sigma_{DX}$ is $\Lambda_{DX}$-secure, then $\Sigma_{DDS}$ is $\Lambda_{DDS}$-secure, where*

$$\Lambda_{DDS} = (\mathcal{L}_S, \mathcal{L}_O, \mathcal{L}_R) = \left(\left(\mathsf{patt}_S^{ds}, \mathsf{patt}_S^{dx}\right), \mathsf{uniq}, \left(\mathsf{patt}_S^{dx}, \mathsf{patt}_1, \mathsf{patt}_2, \mathsf{patt}_3\right)\right)$$

*and $\mathsf{patt}_1$, $\mathsf{patt}_2$ and $\mathsf{patt}_3$ are defined as,*

- $\mathsf{patt}_1(\mathsf{DS}) = \left(\mathsf{patt}_S^{ds}(\mathsf{DS}_0), \mathsf{lsize}, \mathsf{olsize}, \mathsf{omllen}\right)$
- $\mathsf{patt}_2(\mathsf{DS}) = \left(\mathsf{patt}_Q^{ds}(\mathsf{DS}, q)\right)_{q \in \mathbb{Q}_{DS}}$
- $\mathsf{patt}_3(\mathsf{DS}) = \left(\mathsf{patt}_A^{ds}(\mathsf{DS}_0, a)\right)_{a \in \mathsf{Log}(\mathsf{DS}_\lambda)},$

*where $\mathsf{uniq}$ is the non-repeating sub-pattern of $\mathsf{patt}_Q^{ds}$, $\mathsf{DS}_0 \equiv d_0$ and $\mathsf{DS}_\lambda$ is the updated $\mathsf{DS}$ after $\lambda \geq 1$ operations.*

Before we state our Theorem for mutable schemes, recall that the rebuild protocol needs to setup a placeholder structure that can be edited to realize the new data object. This placeholder must be setup and edited with minimal leakage. We do this with the notion of a safe placeholder which we define below.

**Definition 7 (Safe placeholder).** *A placeholder structure $\widetilde{\mathsf{DS}}$ is $(\mathsf{patt}_S, \mathsf{patt}_Q, \mathsf{patt}_E)$-safe for a structure $\mathsf{DS}$ if, for all queries $q_1, \ldots, q_t$, for all edits $e_1, \ldots, e_t$,*

- $\mathsf{patt}_S(\widetilde{\mathsf{DS}}) \leq \mathsf{patt}_S(\mathsf{DS})$,
- $\mathsf{patt}_Q(\widetilde{\mathsf{DS}}, q_1, \ldots, q_t) \leq \mathsf{patt}_Q(\mathsf{DS}, q_1, \ldots, q_t)$,
- $\mathsf{patt}_E(\widetilde{\mathsf{DS}}, e_1, \ldots, e_t) \leq \mathsf{patt}_A(\mathsf{DS}, e_1, \ldots, e_t)$.

We assume that there exists an efficient algorithm $\mathsf{GenPlaceholder}$ that takes as input some state information and generates a safe placeholder. We now state Theorem 2 whose proof is deferred to the full version of this work. Here, we assume $\Sigma_{DS}$ has leakage profile

$$\Lambda_{DS} = (\mathcal{L}_S, \mathcal{L}_Q, \mathcal{L}_E) = \left(\mathsf{patt}_S^{ds}, (\mathsf{qeq}^{ds}, \mathsf{patt}_Q^{ds}), \mathsf{patt}_E^{ds}\right),$$

and $\Sigma_{DX}$ has the same profile as above.

**Theorem 2 (Mutable).** *If $\Sigma_{\mathsf{DS}}$ is $\Lambda_{\mathsf{DS}}$-secure, if $\mathsf{Ext}$ is $(\mathsf{patt}_{\mathsf{S}}^{\mathsf{ds}}, \mathsf{uniq}, \mathsf{patt}_{\mathsf{E}}^{\mathsf{ds}})$-safe, if $\widetilde{\mathsf{DS}}$ is an $(\mathsf{patt}_{\mathsf{S}}^{\mathsf{ds}}, \mathsf{patt}_{\mathsf{Q}}^{\mathsf{ds}}, \mathsf{patt}_{\mathsf{E}}^{\mathsf{ds}})$-safe placeholder for $\mathsf{DS}_\lambda$, and if $\Sigma_{\mathsf{DX}}$ is $\Lambda_{\mathsf{DX}}$-secure, then $\Sigma_{\mathsf{DDS}}$ is $\Lambda_{\mathsf{DDS}}$-secure, where*

$$\Lambda_{\mathsf{DDS}} = (\mathcal{L}_{\mathsf{S}}, \mathcal{L}_{\mathsf{O}}, \mathcal{L}_{\mathsf{R}}) = \left( \left(\mathsf{patt}_{\mathsf{S}}^{\mathsf{ds}}, \mathsf{patt}_{\mathsf{S}}^{\mathsf{dx}}\right), \mathsf{uniq}, \left(\mathsf{patt}_{\mathsf{S}}^{\mathsf{dx}}, \mathsf{patt}_1, \mathsf{patt}_2, \mathsf{patt}_3\right) \right)$$

*and $\mathsf{patt}_1$, $\mathsf{patt}_2$ and $\mathsf{patt}_3$ are defined as,*

- $\mathsf{patt}_1(\mathsf{DS}) = \left(\mathsf{patt}_{\mathsf{S}}^{\mathsf{ds}}(\mathsf{DS}_\lambda), \mathsf{lsize}, \mathsf{olsize}, \mathsf{omllen}\right)$
- $\mathsf{patt}_2(\mathsf{DS}) = \left(\mathsf{patt}_{\mathsf{Q}}^{\mathsf{ds}}(\mathsf{DS}, q)\right)_{q \in \mathbb{Q}_{\mathsf{DS}}}$
- $\mathsf{patt}_3(\mathsf{DS}_\lambda) = \left(\mathsf{patt}_{\mathsf{E}}(\mathsf{DS}_\lambda, e)\right)_{e \in \mathsf{Log}(\mathsf{DS}_\lambda)},$

*where $\mathsf{uniq}$ is the non-repeating sub-pattern of $\mathsf{patt}_{\mathsf{Q}}^{\mathsf{ds}}$, and $\mathsf{DS}_\lambda$ is the updated DS after $\lambda \geq 1$ operations.*

## 4.2   Efficiency of the Dynamic Cache-Based Compiler

We now analyze the efficiency of the schemes produced by our suppression framework and compare it to using black-box ORAM simulation.

**Operation complexity.** The efficiency of $\Sigma_{\mathsf{DDS}}$ clearly depends on the efficiency of its building blocks $\Sigma_{\mathsf{DS}}$ and $\Sigma_{\mathsf{DX}}$. Recall that for every operation op on EDDS, the client executes: one get operation on EDX, one query operation on $\overline{\mathsf{EDS}}$ and one put operation on EDX. This leads to an operation complexity of

$$\mathsf{time}_{\mathsf{O}}^{\mathsf{dds}} = \mathsf{time}_{\mathsf{Q}}^{\mathsf{ds}} + \mathsf{time}_{\mathsf{G}}^{\mathsf{dx}} + \mathsf{time}_{\mathsf{P}}^{\mathsf{dx}},$$

where $\mathsf{time}_{\mathsf{Q}}^{\mathsf{ds}}$ is the query complexity of $\Sigma_{\mathsf{DS}}$, and $\mathsf{time}_{\mathsf{G}}^{\mathsf{dx}}$ and $\mathsf{time}_{\mathsf{P}}^{\mathsf{dx}}$ are the get and put complexities of $\Sigma_{\mathsf{DX}}$.

**Rebuild complexity.** Recall that the Rebuild protocol of $\Sigma_{\mathsf{DDS}}$ executes: (1) $\lambda$ gets on EDX; (2) $\#\mathbb{Q}_{\mathsf{DS}}$ queries on EDS; (3) an oblivious sort on an array of size $\#\mathbb{Q}_{\mathsf{DS}} + 2 \cdot \lambda$; and (4) $\#\mathbb{Q}_{\mathsf{DS}_\lambda}$ adds or edits on EDS. The complexity of steps (1) and (2) is

$$\lambda \cdot \mathsf{time}_{\mathsf{G}}^{\mathsf{dx}} + \#\mathbb{Q}_{\mathsf{DS}} \cdot \mathsf{time}_{\mathsf{Q}}^{\mathsf{ds}}.$$

The complexity of steps (3) and (4) depend on the sorting network used and the storage at the client. Using Batcher's bitonic sort [5] with $O(1)$ client storage [27], steps (3) and (4) have complexity

$$O\left( \#\mathbb{Q}_{\mathsf{DS}_\lambda} \cdot \max_{r \in \mathbb{R}_{\mathsf{DS}_\lambda}} |r|_w \cdot \log^2 \#\mathbb{Q}_{\mathsf{DS}_\lambda} + \#\mathbb{Q}_{\mathsf{DS}_\lambda} \cdot \max_{u \in U} \mathsf{time}_{\mathsf{U}}^{\mathsf{ds}}(|u|) \right), \quad (1)$$

where $\mathsf{time}_{\mathsf{U}}^{\mathsf{ds}}(|u|)$ is either the add or the edit complexity of $\Sigma_{\mathsf{DS}}$, $\mathbb{Q}_{\mathsf{DS}_\lambda}$ is the query space of $\mathsf{DS}_\lambda$, and $\mathbb{R}_{\mathsf{DS}_\lambda}$ is the corresponding response space for the queries $q \in \mathbb{Q}_{\mathsf{DS}_\lambda}$. Note that if $\max_{u \in U} \mathsf{time}_{\mathsf{U}}^{\mathsf{ds}}(|u|) = O\left(\log^2 \#\mathbb{Q}_{\mathsf{DS}_\lambda}\right)$, then Eq. (1) above is

$$O\left( \#\mathbb{Q}_{\mathsf{DS}_\lambda} \cdot \max_{r \in \mathbb{R}_{\mathsf{DS}_\lambda}} |r|_w \cdot \log^2 \#\mathbb{Q}_{\mathsf{DS}_\lambda} \right).$$

Adding steps (1) through (4) we have

$$\text{time}_R^{\text{dds}} = \lambda \cdot \text{time}_G^{\text{dx}} + \#\mathbb{Q}_{\text{DS}} \cdot \text{time}_Q^{\text{ds}} + O\left(\#\mathbb{Q}_{\text{DS}_\lambda} \cdot \max_{r \in \mathbb{R}_{\text{DS}_\lambda}} |r|_w \cdot \log^2 \#\mathbb{Q}_{\text{DS}_\lambda}\right). \quad (2)$$

**Operations & rebuild.** It follows from the above that the time $\text{time}_{\lambda O + R}^{\text{ds}}$ to execute $\lambda$ operations and to rebuild the structure is

$$\begin{aligned}
\text{time}_{\lambda O + R}^{\text{dds}} &= \lambda \cdot \text{time}_O^{\text{dds}} + \text{time}_R^{\text{dds}} \\
&= \lambda \cdot \left(\text{time}_Q^{\text{ds}} + 2 \cdot \text{time}_G^{\text{dx}} + \text{time}_P^{\text{dx}}\right) + \#\mathbb{Q}_{\text{DS}} \cdot \text{time}_Q^{\text{ds}} \\
&\quad + O\left(\#\mathbb{Q}_{\text{DS}_\lambda} \cdot \max_{r \in \mathbb{R}_{\text{DS}_\lambda}} |r|_w \cdot \log^2 \#\mathbb{Q}_{\text{DS}_\lambda}\right). \quad (3)
\end{aligned}$$

The complexity above depends in part on the efficiency of the scheme $\Sigma_{\text{DX}}$ used for the underlying cache. Several constructions can be used including the "standard" cache, square-root ORAM or the more efficient tree-based ORAM [43]. In the following, we analyze the complexity of $\Sigma_{\text{DDS}}$ based on different instantiations of $\Sigma_{\text{DX}}$.

**Using the standard cache.** The standard (zero-leakage) cache is an array of size $\lambda$ that stores encryptions of label/value pairs $(\ell, v)$ where the labels all have the same size and where the values are padded to the maximum value length. To execute a get for a label $\ell$, the client retrieves the entire encrypted array, decrypts it and keeps the value associated with $\ell$. To insert or edit a label/value pair, the client retrieves the entire encrypted array, decrypts it, inserts the new pair or modifies an existing pair, re-encrypts the array and sends it back to he server. It follows that the get and put complexities of the standard cache are

$$\text{time}_G^{\text{dx}} = \text{time}_P^{\text{dx}} = O\left(\lambda \cdot \max_{r \in \mathbb{R}_{\text{DS}_\lambda}} |r|_w\right),$$

Combining this with Eq. (3), we have

$$\begin{aligned}
\text{time}_{\lambda O + R}^{\text{dds}} &= (\lambda + \#\mathbb{Q}_{\text{DS}}) \cdot \text{time}_Q^{\text{ds}} + O\left(\lambda^2 \cdot \max_{r \in \mathbb{R}_{\text{DS}_\lambda}} |r|_w\right) \\
&\quad + O\left(\#\mathbb{Q}_{\text{DS}_\lambda} \cdot \max_{r \in \mathbb{R}_{\text{DS}_\lambda}} |r|_w \cdot \log^2 \#\mathbb{Q}_{\text{DS}_\lambda}\right).
\end{aligned}$$

**Using a tree-based cache.** The scheme $\Sigma_{\text{DX}}$ can also be instantiated with a tree-based ORAM like Path ORAM [43] which has get and put complexity

$$\text{time}_G^{\text{dx}} = \text{time}_P^{\text{dx}} = O\left(\max_{r \in \mathbb{R}_{\text{DS}_\lambda}} |r|_w \cdot \log^2 \lambda\right),$$

where $\lambda$ is the number of entries stored in the ORAM. Combining this with Eq. 3, we have

$$\mathsf{time}^{\mathsf{dds}}_{\lambda\mathsf{O}+\mathsf{R}} = (\lambda + \#\mathbb{Q}_{\mathsf{DS}}) \cdot \mathsf{time}^{\mathsf{ds}}_{\mathsf{Q}} + O\left(\lambda \cdot \max_{r \in \mathbb{R}_{\mathsf{DS}_\lambda}} |r|_w \cdot \log^2 \lambda\right)$$

$$+ O\left(\#\mathbb{Q}_{\mathsf{DS}_\lambda} \cdot \max_{r \in \mathbb{R}_{\mathsf{DS}_\lambda}} |r|_w \cdot \log^2 \#\mathbb{Q}_{\mathsf{DS}_\lambda}\right). \tag{4}$$

**Comparison to black-box ORAM simulation.** With the exception of the construction of [33], ORAM does not traditionally support re-sizing. So to compare our constructions with black-box ORAM simulation based on state-of-the-art ORAMs (e.g., Path ORAM [43])[3] we have to assume that the ORAM is initialized with some upper-bound on the size. We use an "upper-bound" data structure which we denote $\mathsf{DS}^*$. More precisely, to setup the ORAM simulation for a structure $\mathsf{DS}$, the ORAM is initialized to hold $\mathsf{DS}^*$ so that $\mathsf{DS}$ can expand to fill the allocated space. The ORAM simulation of one operation on $\mathsf{DS}$ using a tree-based ORAM then has complexity,

$$\mathsf{time}^{\mathsf{tree}}_{\mathsf{O}} = \mathsf{B}^{\mathsf{ds}}_{\mathsf{Q}} \cdot O\left(\log^2 \frac{|\mathsf{DS}^*|_2}{B}\right) \cdot \frac{B}{w},$$

where $\mathsf{B}^{\mathsf{ds}}_{\mathsf{Q}}$ is the number of blocks that need to be read to answer a query, $B$ is the block size of the ORAM and $w$ is the word length (in bits). Since the ORAM does not have to be rebuilt, $\mathsf{time}^{\mathsf{tree}}_{\lambda\mathsf{O}+\mathsf{R}}$ is the same as the time complexity of $\lambda$ operations. Setting $B = \max_{r \in \mathbb{R}_{\mathsf{DS}^*}} |r|_2$ as an upper limit on possible response length, we have,

$$\mathsf{time}^{\mathsf{tree}}_{\lambda\mathsf{O}} = \lambda \cdot \mathsf{B}^{\mathsf{ds}}_{\mathsf{Q}} \cdot O\left(\log^2 \frac{|\mathsf{DS}^*|_2}{\max_{r \in \mathbb{R}_{\mathsf{DS}^*}} |r|_2}\right) \cdot \max_{r \in \mathbb{R}_{\mathsf{DS}^*}} |r|_w. \tag{5}$$

To compare the efficiency of our schemes with black-box ORAM simulation, we examine Eq. (4). Assuming that $\lambda = O(\#\mathbb{Q}_{\mathsf{DS}})$,[4] and $\mathsf{time}^{\mathsf{ds}}_{\mathsf{Q}} = O(\log \#\mathbb{Q}_{\mathsf{DS}})$ we have that $\#\mathbb{Q}_{\mathsf{DS}_\lambda} \leq \#\mathbb{Q}_{\mathsf{DS}} + \lambda = O(\#\mathbb{Q}_{\mathsf{DS}})$. Combining the first two terms in Eq. (4) we get,

$$\mathsf{time}^{\mathsf{dds}}_{\lambda\mathsf{O}+\mathsf{R}} = O(\#\mathbb{Q}_{\mathsf{DS}} \cdot \log \#\mathbb{Q}_{\mathsf{DS}}) + O\left(\lambda \cdot \max_{r \in \mathbb{R}_{\mathsf{DS}_\lambda}} |r|_w \cdot \log^2 \lambda\right)$$

$$+ O\left(\#\mathbb{Q}_{\mathsf{DS}} \cdot \max_{r \in \mathbb{R}_{\mathsf{DS}_\lambda}} |r|_w \cdot \log^2 \#\mathbb{Q}_{\mathsf{DS}}\right). \tag{6}$$

---

[3] Note that some ORAM constructions can achieve better asymptotic query complexity [38] but we use Path ORAM for its simplicity and real-world practicality.

[4] This is a conservative assumption on $\lambda$. In practice, the selection of $\lambda$ is crucial to the efficiency of the scheme. The question of selecting the optimal $\lambda$ for efficiency is interesting and can be further explored.

From Eq. (6), we observe that $\text{time}^{\text{dds}}_{\lambda\text{O+R}}$ is asymptotically dominated by

$$O\left(\#\mathbb{Q}_{\text{DS}} \cdot \max_{r\in\mathbb{R}_{\text{DS}_\lambda}} |r|_w \cdot \log^2 \#\mathbb{Q}_{\text{DS}}\right).$$

Comparing Eqs. (5) and (6), we have the following proposition.

**Proposition 1.** *If* $\lambda = O(\#\mathbb{Q}_{\text{DS}})$, $\#\mathbb{Q}_{\text{DS}} = O(\#\mathbb{Q}_{\text{DS}^*})$ *and* $B^{\text{ds}}_{\text{Q}} = \omega(1)$, *then*

$$\text{time}^{\text{dds}}_{\lambda\text{O+R}} = o\left(\text{time}^{\text{tree}}_{\lambda\text{O}}\right).$$

For structures with constant-time queries, $B^{\text{ds}}_{\text{Q}} = 1$ so our approach improves asymptotically over ORAM simulation whenever

$$\max_{r\in\mathbb{R}_{\text{DS}_\lambda}} |r|_w = o\left(\max_{r\in\mathbb{R}_{\text{DS}^*}} |r|_w\right).$$

For a concrete efficiency comparison we refer the reader to Sect. 5.3.

## 5  Concrete Instantiations

In this section we show how to apply our framework to two concrete schemes: the piggyback scheme PBS from [27] which is a semi-dynamic construction and the advanced volume-hiding scheme AVLH$^d$ from [26] which is mutable. The leakage profiles of the resulting schemes is minimal and only reveal information pertaining to the total size of the structure.

### 5.1  Our PBS-Based Constructions

PBS is a non-rebuildable semi-dynamic STE scheme. It is parameterized with a batch size $\alpha$ and supports query and add operations. PBS queries and adds in batches in the sense that when executing a query $q_1$ it only retrieves a fixed number of batches from $q_1$'s response and retrieves the next set of batches only when a new query $q_2$ occurs. In the meantime, $q_2$ is inserted into a queue until enough queries are made for the client to retrieve $q_1$'s entire response. Adds are handled similarly. When a sequence of queries or adds is complete, all the remaining batches in the queue are retrieved or pushed.

PBS has two variants. The first is a perfectly correct variant which incurs some small amount of query leakage; namely, for sequences of non-repeating queries, it leaks the number of batches required to process the sequence; and for sequences with repeating queries, it reveals the query equality and the response lengths. The second variant achieves only probabilistic correctness but the non-repeating sub-pattern of its query leakage is $\bot$. The application of our framework to the first variant results in a dynamic variant of the AZL construction from

[27] whereas applying it to the second variant results in a dynamic variant of the FZL construction from [27].

**Leakage profile of** PBS. The leakage profile of the perfectly correct variant of PBS is

$$\Lambda_{\mathsf{PBS}} = (\mathcal{L}_{\mathsf{S}}, \mathcal{L}_{\mathsf{Q}}, \mathcal{L}_{\mathsf{A}}) = (\mathsf{tbrlen}, \mathsf{rqeq}, \mathsf{alen}),$$

where tbrlen, rqeq and alen are defined as follows. The *total batched response length*

$$\mathsf{tbrlen}_{k,\alpha}(\mathsf{DS}) = \mathsf{trlen}(\mathsf{DS}) + \sum_{q \in \mathbb{Q}_{\mathsf{DS}}} \alpha - \big(|\mathsf{qu}(\mathsf{DS}, q)|_w \mod \alpha\big)$$

reveals the number of batches needed to store the responses in the structure. The *repeated query equality* pattern

$$\mathsf{rqeq}_{k,m}(\mathsf{DS}, q_1, \ldots, q_t) = \begin{cases} \bot & \text{if } m < t \text{ and } q_i \neq q_j \text{ for all } i, j \in [t], \\ \gamma_m & \text{if } m = t \text{ and } q_i \neq q_j \text{ for all } i, j \in [t], \\ \mathsf{qeq} \times \mathsf{rlen}(\mathsf{DS}, q_1, \ldots, q_t) & \text{otherwise,} \end{cases}$$

where

$$\gamma_m \stackrel{def}{=} \left( \sum_{i \in [m]} |\mathsf{qu}(\mathsf{DS}, q_i)|_w + \alpha - \big(|\mathsf{qu}(\mathsf{DS}, q_i)|_w \mod \alpha\big) \right) \cdot \alpha^{-1} - (m - 1).$$

Note that the non-repeating sub-pattern of rqeq is uniq where

$$\mathsf{uniq}_{k,m}(\mathsf{DS}, q_1, \ldots, q_t) = \begin{cases} \bot & \text{if } m < t \text{ and } q_i \neq q_j \text{ for all } i, j \in [t], \\ \gamma_m & \text{if } m = t \text{ and } q_i \neq q_j \text{ for all } i, j \in [t]. \end{cases}$$

The *add length* pattern

$$\mathsf{alen}_{k,m}(\mathsf{DS}, u_1, \ldots, u_t) = \begin{cases} \bot & \text{if } m < t, \\ \gamma_m & \text{if } m = t, \end{cases}$$

reveals nothing until the last add of the sequence, and then reveals the number of batches required to finish the add sequence.

When PBS is modified to support only probabilistic correctness for queries, the non-repeating sub-pattern of its query leakage is $\bot$. The leakage profile of the probabilistic variant of PBS is therefore $(\mathcal{L}_{\mathsf{S}}^{\mathsf{pbs}}, \mathcal{L}_{\mathsf{Q}}^{\mathsf{pbs}}, \mathcal{L}_{\mathsf{U}}^{\mathsf{pbs}}) = (\mathsf{tbrlen}, \mathsf{patt}_{\mathsf{Q}}, \mathsf{alen})$ where

$$\mathsf{patt}_{\mathsf{Q}}(\mathsf{DS}, q_1, \ldots, q_t) = \begin{cases} \bot & \text{if } q_i \neq q_j \text{ for all } i, j \in [t], \\ \mathsf{qeq} \times \mathsf{rlen}(\mathsf{DS}, q_1, \ldots, q_t) & \text{otherwise.} \end{cases}$$

**Safe extension for** PBS. Let $(\widetilde{q}_1, \cdots, \widetilde{q}_\lambda)$ be dummy queries. For all $1 \leq i \leq \lambda$, compute $\overline{\mathsf{DS}} \leftarrow \mathsf{Add}(\overline{\mathsf{DS}}, (\widetilde{q}_i, \mathbf{0}))$, where $|\mathbf{0}|_w = \max_{r \in \mathbb{R}_{\mathsf{DS}}} |r|_w$.

**Theorem 3.** *If $\lambda$ and $\alpha$ are publicly-known parameters and if all queries in $\mathbb{Q}_{DS}$ have the same bit length, the extension scheme described above is* $(\mathsf{tbrlen}, \mathsf{uniq}, \mathsf{alen})$-*safe.*

**Dynamic AZL.** Let dynamic AZL be the perfectly-correct fully-dynamic rebuildable scheme that results from applying our framework to the perfectly-correct variant of PBS. Its security is stated in the following Theorem whose proof is in the full version.

**Theorem 4.** *If $\Sigma_{DX}$ is $\Lambda_{DX}$-secure where $\Lambda_{DX} = (\mathcal{L}_S, \mathcal{L}_G, \mathcal{L}_P) = (\mathsf{mllen}, \perp, \perp)$, then dynamic AZL is $\Lambda_{AZL}$-secure where*

$$\Lambda_{AZL} = (\mathcal{L}_S, \mathcal{L}_O, \mathcal{L}_R)$$
$$= \big((\mathsf{tbrlen}, \mathsf{mllen}), \mathsf{uniq}', (\mathsf{lsize}, \mathsf{tbrlen}, \mathsf{olsize}, \mathsf{omllen}, \mathsf{otbrlen})\big)$$

*where* $\mathsf{otbrlen}(DS, op_1, \ldots, op_\lambda) = \mathsf{tbrlen}_{k,\alpha}(DS_\lambda)$ *and*

$$\mathsf{uniq}'_{k,m}(DS, op_1, \ldots, op_t) = \mathsf{uniq}_{k,m}(DS, q_1, \ldots, q_t),$$

*where* $op_i$ *is either a query* $q_i$ *or an update* $u_i = (q_i, r_i)$.

**Efficiency of dynamic AZL.** It follows from Eq. (4) that the complexity of dynamic AZL when $\Sigma_{DX}$ is initialized with a tree-based ORAM is

$$\mathsf{time}^{\mathsf{azl}}_{\lambda O + R} = (\lambda + \#\mathbb{Q}_{DS}) \cdot \mathsf{time}^{\mathsf{pbs}}_Q + O\left(\lambda \cdot \max_{r \in \mathbb{R}_{DS_\lambda}} |r|_w \cdot \log^2 \lambda\right)$$
$$+ O\left(\#\mathbb{Q}_{DS} \cdot \max_{r \in \mathbb{R}_{DS_\lambda} |r|_w} \cdot \log^2 \#\mathbb{Q}_{DS_\lambda}\right),$$

where $\mathsf{time}^{\mathsf{pbs}}_Q$ is the query complexity of PBS which is equal to the query complexity of is underlying multi-map encryption scheme. The storage complexity of dynamic AZL is the sum of the storage required for the cache and the storage required for the PBS structure. This results in storage complexity

$$O\left(\lambda \cdot (\alpha + \max_{a \in \mathsf{Log}(DS_\lambda)} |a|_w) + \#\mathbb{Q}_{DS} \cdot (\alpha + \max_{r \in \mathbb{R}_{DS}} |r|_w)\right).$$

**Dynamic FZL.** Dynamic FZL is the probabilistically-correct fully-dynamic scheme that results from applying our framework to the probabilistically-correct variant of PBS. Its security is analyzed in the following Theorem whose proof is in the full version of this work.

**Theorem 5.** *If $\Sigma_{DX}$ is $\Lambda_{DX}$ where $\Lambda_{DX} = (\mathcal{L}_S, \mathcal{L}_G, \mathcal{L}_P) = (\mathsf{mllen}, \perp, \perp)$, then dynamic FZL is $\Lambda_{FZL}$-secure where*

$$\Lambda_{FZL} = (\mathcal{L}_S, \mathcal{L}_O, \mathcal{L}_R) = \big((\mathsf{tbrlen}, \mathsf{mllen}), \perp, (\mathsf{lsize}, \mathsf{olsize}, \mathsf{omllen}, \mathsf{otbrlen})\big).$$

**Efficiency of dynamic FZL.** The efficiency of dynamic FZL is the same as that of dynamic AZL.

## 5.2   Our AVLH-Based Construction

We now apply our framework to the mutable variant of the advanced volume-hiding multi-map encryption scheme $\mathsf{AVLH}^d$ from [26]. Note that here we do not consider the variant that exploits concentrated components for storage improvements.

**Overview of** $\mathsf{AVLH}$. At a high level, the scheme uses $n$ bins to store a multi-map of size $N$, where $N$ is the sum over all labels of the labels' tuple lengths. The scheme uses a random bipartite graph to map labels to bins. More precisely, each label $\ell$ is mapped at random to $t$ out of $n$ bins, where $t$ is the maximum tuple length. The elements of the tuple corresponding to a label $\ell$ are placed in each bin mapped to $\ell$. If there are more bins mapped than the length of the tuple, some bins are left empty. The bins are then padded to the size of the maximum bin, encrypted and stored on the server. To query for a label $\ell$, the client retrieves all the bins mapped to $\ell$. The scheme hides the tuple lengths, i.e., the response length rlen. It also supports restricted edits in the sense that one can edit/change the values in a tuple but not add values to it. The leakage profile of $\mathsf{AVLH}^d$ is

$$\Lambda_{\mathsf{AVLH}} = (\mathcal{L}_S, \mathcal{L}_Q, \mathcal{L}_E) = (\mathsf{trlen}, \mathsf{qeq}, (\mathsf{oid}, \mathsf{uqeq})).$$

**Extension.** Let $(\widetilde{q}_1, \cdots, \widetilde{q}_\lambda)$ be dummy queries and $(\widetilde{r}_1, \cdots, \widetilde{r}_\lambda)$ be the corresponding dummy responses such that $|\widetilde{r}_i| = 1$. For all $i \in [\lambda]$, compute $\overline{\mathsf{MM}} \leftarrow \mathsf{Add}(\overline{\mathsf{MM}}, (\widetilde{q}_i, \widetilde{r}_i))$. We state the security of this extension in the Theorem below whose proof is deferred to the full version.

**Theorem 6.** *If $\lambda$ is a publicly-known parameter and that all queries in the query space $\mathbb{Q}_{\mathsf{DS}}$ have the same bit length, the above extension scheme is* $(\mathsf{trlen}, \perp, (\mathsf{oid}, \mathsf{uqeq}))$-*safe.*

**Safe placeholder.** Since $\mathsf{AVLH}^d$ is mutable we define a safe placeholder multi-map $\overline{\mathsf{MM}}$. Note that the placeholder must have the following properties:

1. $\overline{\mathsf{MM}}$ must have enough space to hold the tuples of all the labels $\ell \in \mathbb{L}_{\mathsf{MM}_\lambda}$[5];
2. the setup, query and edit leakages on $\overline{\mathsf{MM}}$ must be at most the setup, query and edit leakages on $\mathsf{MM}$.

The placeholder structure is created as follows during rebuilds. During the extract-and-tag phase, the client learns which labels are valid and their tuple lengths. During the update phase it creates, for every valid label $\ell$ a dummy tuple $\mathbf{t}$ of the same length and inserts $(\ell, \mathbf{t})$ in $\overline{\mathsf{MM}}$. We state the security of the placeholder in the Theorem below, whose proof is deferred to the full version.

**Theorem 7.** *The placeholder above is* $(\mathsf{trlen}, \mathsf{qeq}, (\mathsf{oid}, \mathsf{uqeq}))$-*safe.*

---

[5] For any multi-map data structure MM, the query space $\mathbb{Q}_{\mathsf{DS}}$ is the label space $\mathbb{L}_{\mathsf{MM}}$.

**Zero-leakage advanced volume-hiding.** Let ZAVLH be the dynamic rebuild-able multi-map encryption scheme that results from applying our framework to $\mathsf{AVLH}^d$ with the above placeholder structure and a dictionary encryption scheme $\Sigma_{\mathsf{DX}}$ with leakage profile $\Lambda_{\mathsf{DX}} = (\mathcal{L}_{\mathsf{S}}^{\mathsf{dx}}, \mathcal{L}_{\mathsf{G}}^{\mathsf{dx}}, \mathcal{L}_{\mathsf{P}}^{\mathsf{dx}}) = (\mathsf{mllen}, \bot, \bot)$. Theorem 8 below, whose proof is in the full version of this work, states the security of ZAVLH.

**Theorem 8.** *If $\Sigma_{\mathsf{DX}}$ is $\Lambda_{\mathsf{DX}}$-secure, then* ZAVLH *is $\Lambda_{\mathsf{ZAVLH}}$-secure where*

$$\Lambda_{\mathsf{ZAVLH}} = (\mathcal{L}_{\mathsf{S}}, \mathcal{L}_{\mathsf{O}}, \mathcal{L}_{\mathsf{R}}) = ((\mathsf{trlen}, \mathsf{mllen}), \bot, (\mathsf{lsize}, \mathsf{olsize}, \mathsf{omllen}, \mathsf{otrlen})).$$

**Efficiency of ZAVLH.** We now analyze the efficiency of our dynamic cache-based compiler with a tree-based cache and the $\mathsf{AVLH}^d$ scheme. The query complexity for ZAVLH is

$$\mathsf{time}_{\mathsf{Q}}^{\mathsf{zavlh}} = O(t \cdot N/n)$$

If $t = O(1)$ and $n = O(N/\log N)$ where $t$ is the maximum tuple length and $n$ is the number of bins, the query complexity is $O(\log N)$ for zero-leakage operations. From Eq. (4) we have,

$$\mathsf{time}_{\lambda\mathsf{O+R}}^{\mathsf{zavlh}} = O\left(\#\mathbb{L}_{\mathsf{MM}} \cdot \log N\right) + O\left(\lambda \cdot \max_{r \in \mathbb{R}_{\mathsf{MM}_\lambda}} |r|_w \cdot \log^2 \lambda\right) \tag{7}$$

$$+ O\left(\#\mathbb{L}_{\mathsf{MM}} \cdot \max_{r \in \mathbb{R}_{\mathsf{MM}_\lambda}} |r|_w \cdot \log^2 \#\mathbb{L}_{\mathsf{MM}_\lambda}\right) \tag{8}$$

### 5.3   Concrete Comparisons

In Sect. 4.2, we showed that our framework can asymptotically outperform black-box ORAM simulation under natural assumptions on the data and queries. In this section, we are interested in gaining a better understanding of the practical gains in different settings. Specifically, we compare the concrete efficiency of our ZAVLH scheme to an oblivious multi-map constructed via black-box ORAM simulation and to a standard dynamic encrypted multi-map called $\Pi_{\mathsf{bas}}^{\mathsf{dyn}}$ [11]. Since the latter has optimal storage and query complexities, this comparison highlights the cost of leakage suppression.

**Parameters and notation.** For our comparison, we consider a multi-map MM with $t$ labels and $N = \sum_{\ell \in \mathbb{L}_{\mathsf{MM}}} \#\mathsf{MM}[\ell]$ total values and maximum tuple length $l$. After $\lambda$ Add operations on MM, the resulting multi-map is denoted $\mathsf{MM}_\lambda$. We denote the number of labels in $\mathsf{MM}_\lambda$ as $t_\lambda$ and the total values in $\mathsf{MM}_\lambda$ as $N_\lambda$. The maximum tuple size in $\mathsf{MM}_\lambda$ is denoted by $l_\lambda$. All PRF keys and outputs are of length $k = 256$ bits, all values in the multi-maps are 64 bits and $N$ is set to $2^{16}$.

**Parameters for ZAVLH.** The number of bins in AVLH are chosen such that each bin contains $(\log N)/2$ values on average. The tree-based cache used in the dynamic CBC is instantiated with Path ORAM with $\lambda$ leaf nodes; one for

**Table 1.** Parameters for the efficiency comparison of dynamic CBC, black-box ORAM simulation, and $\Pi_{\mathsf{bas}}^{\mathsf{dyn}}$, given a multi-map MM and a sequence of $\lambda$ add operations.

| Parameters | Setting 1 | Setting 2 | Setting 3 | Setting 4 |
|---|---|---|---|---|
| General: | | | | |
| length of PRF output (bits) | 256 | 256 | 256 | 256 |
| length of MM value (bits) | 64 | 64 | 64 | 64 |
| cache size ($\lambda$) | 64 | 64 | 64 | 64 |
| MM: | | | | |
| max. tuple length ($l$) | 512 | 512 | 512 | 512 |
| total # of labels ($t$) | 256 | 256 | 256 | 256 |
| total # of values ($N$) | $2^{16}$ | $2^{16}$ | $2^{16}$ | $2^{16}$ |
| total # of AVLH bins ($n$) | 8192 | 8192 | 8192 | 8192 |
| Updated MM$_\lambda$: | | | | |
| max. tuple length ($l_\lambda$) | 512 | 512 | 512 | 512 |
| total # of labels ($t_\lambda$) | 256 | 256 | 256 | 256 |
| total # of values ($N_\lambda$) | 65600 | 65600 | 65600 | 65600 |
| total # of AVLH bins ($n_\lambda$) | 8199 | 8199 | 8199 | 8199 |
| Upper-bound MM$_*$: | | | | |
| factor of growth | 25 | 50 | 150 | 1000 |
| max. tuple length ($l_*$) | $1.28 \times 10^4$ | $2.56 \times 10^4$ | $7.68 \times 10^4$ | $51.2 \times 10^4$ |
| total # of labels ($t_*$) | $0.64 \times 10^4$ | $1.28 \times 10^4$ | $3.84 \times 10^4$ | $25.6 \times 10^4$ |
| total # of values ($N_*$) | $163.84 \times 10^4$ | $327.68 \times 10^4$ | $983.04 \times 10^4$ | $6553.6 \times 10^4$ |

**Table 2.** Concrete efficiency comparison. The efficiency numbers shown for ORAM correspond to each of the 4 settings for the ORAM upper-bound data structure.

| Efficiency Measure | ZAVLH (OPS) | ZAVLH (E&T) | ZAVLH (S&S) | ZAVLH (UP) | ZAVLH (Total) | Path ORAM EMM$^{(*)}$ | Std EMM ($\Pi_{\mathsf{bas}}^{\mathsf{dyn}}$) |
|---|---|---|---|---|---|---|---|
| Client State (Mbits) | 0.401 | 0.084 | – | 0.401 | 0.486 | 4.78 10.058 32.539 244.137 | 0.066 |
| Server Storage (Mbits) | 29.704 | 14.352 | – | 29.71 | 44.062 | 52424.704 209707.008 1887412.224 83885916.16 | 20.992 |
| Communication (Mbits) | 166.739 | 211.042 | 1181.008 | 268.294 | 1827.084 | 1995.534 4306.721 14421.059 113419.012 | 10.485 |
| Leakage | $l, N$ | $t$ | $t_\lambda$ | $l_\lambda, N_\lambda$ | $l, N, t$ $l_\lambda, N_\lambda, t_\lambda$ | $l_*, t_*$ | vol, qeq |

each tuple in the cache. Each block is initialized to hold one tuple and therefore $(l + \lambda)$ values at most. Each node/bucket in the binary tree holds $Z = 5$ blocks. The position map maps every label to a leaf node in the ORAM and has size $\lambda(k + \log \lambda)$. The stash stores at most $\log \lambda$ blocks and therefore $\log \lambda(l + \lambda)$ values. A query to the cache reads and writes a path of $\log \lambda$ buckets in the tree. The multi-map MM stores $t + \lambda$ labels and $N + \lambda$ total values. We summarize the cost of ZAVLH in Table 2 breaking it down into the cost to execute $\lambda$ operations (OPS) and the costs of the different rebuild phases: extract-and-tag (E&T), sort-and-shuffle (S&S) and update (UP).

**Black-box ORAM simulation.** To manage the dynamic multi-map MM with Path ORAM, we initialize an *upper-bound* structure $\mathsf{MM}_*$ with $t_*$ labels and $N_*$ values.[6] Specifically, we use upper-bound structures that are $25, 50, 150$, and $1000$ times larger than the multi-map's original size (Table 1). The maximum length of a tuple in $\mathsf{MM}_*$ is $l_*$. The Path ORAM that manages $\mathsf{MM}_*$ has $t_*$ leaf nodes, one for each label in $\mathsf{MM}_*$. Each block is initialized to hold $l_*$ values and each node/bucket in the binary tree holds $Z = 5$ blocks. This ORAM has a position map of size $t_*(q + \log t_*)$ and a stash that holds at most $\log t_*$ blocks at any given time.

**Comparison.** Table 2 shows the costs in Mbits for each of the 4 settings for ZAVLH, black-box ORAM simulation, and $\Pi_{\mathsf{bas}}^{\mathsf{dyn}}$. We can see that ZAVLH outperforms black-box ORAM simulation in both space and communication for our chosen parameters. In particular, the storage cost of ZAVLH is 3 to 7 orders of magnitude smaller than black-box ORAM simulation and only a factor of 2 larger than $\Pi_{\mathsf{bas}}^{\mathsf{dyn}}$. We also observe that the communication cost of ZAVLH is up to 60 times smaller than black-box ORAM simulation, but 180 times larger than $\Pi_{\mathsf{bas}}^{\mathsf{dyn}}$ which is optimal but incurs more leakage.

# References

1. Ajtai, M., Komlós, J., Szemerédi, E.: An o(n log n) sorting network. In: ACM Symposium on Theory of Computing (STOC 1983), pp. 1–9 (1983)
2. Amjad, G., Kamara, S., Moataz, T.: Breach-resistant structured encryption. In: Proceedings on Privacy Enhancing Technologies (Po/PETS 2019) (2019)
3. Asharov, G., Naor, M., Segev, G., Shahaf, I.: Searchable symmetric encryption: optimal locality in linear space via two-dimensional balanced allocations. In: Wichs, D., Mansour, Y. (eds.) Proceedings of the 48th Annual ACM SIGACT Symposium on Theory of Computing, STOC 2016, Cambridge, MA, USA, 18–21 June 2016, pp. 1101–1114. ACM (2016)
4. Asharov, G., Segev, G., Shahaf, I.: Tight tradeoffs in searchable symmetric encryption. In: Shacham, H., Boldyreva, A. (eds.) CRYPTO 2018. LNCS, vol. 10991, pp. 407–436. Springer, Cham (2018). https://doi.org/10.1007/978-3-319-96884-1_14
5. Batcher, K.: Sorting networks and their applications. In: Proceedings of the Joint Computer Conference, pp. 307–314 (1968)

---

[6] This is due to Path ORAM's inability to resize.

6. Blackstone, L., Kamara, S., Moataz, T.: Revisiting leakage abuse attacks. In: Network and Distributed System Security Symposium (NDSS 2020) (2020)
7. Bost, R.: Sophos - forward secure searchable encryption. In: ACM Conference on Computer and Communications Security (CCS 2016) (2016)
8. Bost, R., Fouque, P.-A.: Thwarting leakage abuse attacks against searchable encryption - a formal approach and applications to database padding. Technical Report 2017/1060, IACR Cryptology ePrint Archive (2017)
9. Bost, R., Minaud, B., Ohrimenko, O.: Forward and backward private searchable encryption from constrained cryptographic primitives. In: ACM Conference on Computer and Communications Security (CCS 2017) (2017)
10. Cash, D., Grubbs, P., Perry, J., Ristenpart, T.: Leakage-abuse attacks against searchable encryption. In: ACM Conference on Communications and Computer Security (CCS 2015), pp. 668–679. ACM (2015)
11. Cash, D., Jaeger, J., Jarecki, S., Jutla, C., Krawczyk, H., Rosu, M., Steiner, M.: Dynamic searchable encryption in very-large databases: data structures and implementation. In: Network and Distributed System Security Symposium (NDSS 2014) (2014)
12. Cash, D., Jarecki, S., Jutla, C., Krawczyk, H., Roşu, M.-C., Steiner, M.: Highly-scalable searchable symmetric encryption with support for Boolean queries. In: Canetti, R., Garay, J.A. (eds.) CRYPTO 2013. LNCS, vol. 8042, pp. 353–373. Springer, Heidelberg (2013). https://doi.org/10.1007/978-3-642-40041-4_20
13. Cash, D., Tessaro, S.: The locality of searchable symmetric encryption. In: Nguyen, P.Q., Oswald, E. (eds.) EUROCRYPT 2014. LNCS, vol. 8441, pp. 351–368. Springer, Heidelberg (2014). https://doi.org/10.1007/978-3-642-55220-5_20
14. Chase, M., Kamara, S.: Structured encryption and controlled disclosure. In: Abe, M. (ed.) ASIACRYPT 2010. LNCS, vol. 6477, pp. 577–594. Springer, Heidelberg (2010). https://doi.org/10.1007/978-3-642-17373-8_33
15. Curtmola, R., Garay, J., Kamara, S., Ostrovsky, R.: Searchable symmetric encryption: improved definitions and efficient constructions. In: ACM Conference on Computer and Communications Security (CCS 2006), pp. 79–88. ACM (2006)
16. Demertzis, I., Papadopoulos, D., Papamanthou, C.: Searchable encryption with optimal locality: achieving sublogarithmic read efficiency. In: Shacham, H., Boldyreva, A. (eds.) CRYPTO 2018. LNCS, vol. 10991, pp. 371–406. Springer, Cham (2018). https://doi.org/10.1007/978-3-319-96884-1_13
17. Faber, S., Jarecki, S., Krawczyk, H., Nguyen, Q., Rosu, M., Steiner, M.: Rich queries on encrypted data: beyond exact matches. In: Pernul, G., Ryan, P.Y.A., Weippl, E. (eds.) ESORICS 2015. LNCS, vol. 9327, pp. 123–145. Springer, Cham (2015). https://doi.org/10.1007/978-3-319-24177-7_7
18. Garg, S., Mohassel, P., Papamanthou, C.: TWORAM: efficient oblivious RAM in two rounds with applications to searchable encryption. In: Robshaw, M., Katz, J. (eds.) CRYPTO 2016. LNCS, vol. 9816, pp. 563–592. Springer, Heidelberg (2016). https://doi.org/10.1007/978-3-662-53015-3_20
19. Goldreich, O., Ostrovsky, R.: Software protection and simulation on oblivious RAMs. J. ACM **43**(3), 431–473 (1996)
20. Goodrich, M., Mitzenmacher, M., Ohrimenko, O., Tamassia, R.: Oblivious RAM simulation with efficient worst-case access overhead. In: ACM Workshop on Cloud Computing Security Workshop (CCSW 2011), pp. 95–100 (2011)

21. Grubbs, P., Lacharité, M., Minaud, B., Paterson, K.G.: Pump up the volume: practical database reconstruction from volume leakage on range queries. In: Lie, D., Mannan, M., Backes, M., Wang, X. (eds.) Proceedings of the 2018 ACM SIGSAC Conference on Computer and Communications Security, CCS 2018, Toronto, ON, Canada, 15–19 October 2018, pp. 315–331. ACM (2018)
22. Grubbs, P., Lacharité, M.S., Minaud, B., Paterson, K.G.: Learning to reconstruct: learning theory and encrypted database attacks. In: 2019 IEEE Symposium on Security and Privacy, SP 2019, San Francisco, CA, USA, 19–23 May 2019, pp. 1067–1083. IEEE (2019)
23. Islam, M.S., Kuzu, M., Kantarcioglu, M.: Access pattern disclosure on searchable encryption: ramification, attack and mitigation. In: Network and Distributed System Security Symposium (NDSS 2012) (2012)
24. Kamara, S., Moataz, T.: Boolean searchable symmetric encryption with worst-case sub-linear complexity. In: Coron, J.-S., Nielsen, J.B. (eds.) EUROCRYPT 2017. LNCS, vol. 10212, pp. 94–124. Springer, Cham (2017). https://doi.org/10.1007/978-3-319-56617-7_4
25. Kamara, S., Moataz, T.: SQL on structurally-encrypted databases. In: Peyrin, T., Galbraith, S. (eds.) ASIACRYPT 2018. LNCS, vol. 11272, pp. 149–180. Springer, Cham (2018). https://doi.org/10.1007/978-3-030-03326-2_6
26. Kamara, S., Moataz, T.: Computationally volume-hiding structured encryption. In: Ishai, Y., Rijmen, V. (eds.) EUROCRYPT 2019. LNCS, vol. 11477, pp. 183–213. Springer, Cham (2019). https://doi.org/10.1007/978-3-030-17656-3_7
27. Kamara, S., Moataz, T., Ohrimenko, O.: Structured encryption and leakage suppression. In: Shacham, H., Boldyreva, A. (eds.) CRYPTO 2018. LNCS, vol. 10991, pp. 339–370. Springer, Cham (2018). https://doi.org/10.1007/978-3-319-96884-1_12
28. Kamara, S., Papamanthou, C.: Parallel and dynamic searchable symmetric encryption. In: Financial Cryptography and Data Security (FC 2013) (2013)
29. Kamara, S., Papamanthou, C., Roeder, T.: Dynamic searchable symmetric encryption. In: ACM Conference on Computer and Communications Security (CCS 2012). ACM Press (2012)
30. Kellaris, G., Kollios, G., Nissim, K., Neill, A.O.: Generic attacks on secure outsourced databases. In: ACM Conference on Computer and Communications Security (CCS 2016) (2016)
31. Kushilevitz, E., Lu, S., Ostrovsky, R.: On the (in) security of hash-based oblivious RAM and a new balancing scheme. In: ACM-SIAM Symposium on Discrete Algorithms (SODA 2012), pp. 143–156 (2012)
32. Lacharité, M., Minaud, B., Paterson, K.G.: Improved reconstruction attacks on encrypted data using range query leakage. In: 2018 IEEE Symposium on Security and Privacy, SP 2018, Proceedings, San Francisco, California, USA, 21–23 May 2018, pp. 297–314. IEEE Computer Society (2018)
33. Moataz, T., Mayberry, T., Blass, E.-O., Chan, A.H.: Resizable tree-based oblivious RAM. In: Böhme, R., Okamoto, T. (eds.) FC 2015. LNCS, vol. 8975, pp. 147–167. Springer, Heidelberg (2015). https://doi.org/10.1007/978-3-662-47854-7_9
34. Naveed, M., Kamara, S., Wright, C.V.: Inference attacks on property-preserving encrypted databases. In: ACM Conference on Computer and Communications Security (CCS), CCS 2015, pp. 644–655. ACM (2015)
35. Naveed, M., Prabhakaran, M., Gunter, C.: Dynamic searchable encryption via blind storage. In: IEEE Symposium on Security and Privacy (S&P 2014) (2014)
36. Ostrovsky, R., Shoup, V.: Private information storage. In: ACM Symposium on Theory of Computing (STOC 1997), pp. 294–303 (1997)

37. Pappas, V., et al.: Blind seer: a scalable private DBMS. In: 2014 IEEE Symposium on Security and Privacy (SP), pp. 359–374. IEEE (2014)
38. Patel, S., Persiano, G., Raykova, M., Yeo, K.: Panorama: oblivious RAM with logarithmic overhead. In: 2018 IEEE 59th Annual Symposium on Foundations of Computer Science (FOCS), pp. 871–882. IEEE (2018)
39. Patel, S., Persiano, G., Yeo, K.,Yung, M.: Mitigating leakage in secure cloud-hosted data structures: volume-hiding for multi-maps via hashing. In: Conference on Computer and Communications Security (CCS 2019), pp. 79–93 (2019)
40. Shi, E., Chan, T.-H.H., Stefanov, E., Li, M.: Oblivious RAM with $O((\log N)^3)$ worst-case cost. In: Lee, D.H., Wang, X. (eds.) ASIACRYPT 2011. LNCS, vol. 7073, pp. 197–214. Springer, Heidelberg (2011). https://doi.org/10.1007/978-3-642-25385-0_11
41. Song, D., Wagner, D., Perrig, A.: Practical techniques for searching on encrypted data. In: IEEE Symposium on Research in Security and Privacy, pp. 44–55. IEEE Computer Society (2000)
42. Stefanov, E., Papamanthou, C., Shi, E.: Practical dynamic searchable encryption with small leakage. In: Network and Distributed System Security Symposium (NDSS 2014) (2014)
43. Stefanov, E., et al.: Path ORAM: an extremely simple oblivious RAM protocol. In: ACM Conference on Computer and Communications Security (CCS 2013) (2013)
44. Wang, X.S., et al.: Oblivious data structures. In: Proceedings of the 2014 ACM SIGSAC Conference on Computer and Communications Security, pp. 215–226 (2014)
45. Williams, P., Sion, R., Carbunar, B.: Building castles out of mud: practical access pattern privacy and correctness on untrusted storage. In: ACM Conference on Computer and Communications Security (CCS 2008), pp. 139–148 (2008)
46. Zhang, Y., Katz, J., Papamanthou, C.: All your queries are belong to us: the power of file-injection attacks on searchable encryption. In: USENIX Security Symposium (2016)

# Blockchain

# Dynamic Ad Hoc Clock Synchronization

Christian Badertscher[1](✉)(iD), Peter Gaži[1], Aggelos Kiayias[1,2],
Alexander Russell[1,3](iD), and Vassilis Zikas[4]

[1] IOHK, Hong Kong, China
{christian.badertscher,peter.gazi}@iohk.io
[2] University of Edinburgh, Edinburgh, UK
aggelos.kiayias@ed.ac.uk
[3] University of Connecticut, Mansfield, USA
acr@cse.uconn.edu
[4] Purdue University, West Lafayette, USA
vzikas@cs.purdue.edu

**Abstract.** Clock synchronization allows parties to establish a common
notion of global time by leveraging a weaker synchrony assumption, i.e.,
local clocks with approximately the same speed. Despite intensive investigation of the problem in the fault-tolerant distributed computing literature, existing solutions do not apply to settings where participation is
unknown, e.g., the ad hoc model of Beimel *et al.* [EUROCRYPT 17], or
is dynamically shifting over time, e.g., the fluctuating/sleepy/dynamic-
availability models of Garay *et al.* [CRYPTO 17], Pass and Shi [ASI-
ACRYPT 17] and Badertscher *et al.* [CCS 18].

We show how to apply and extend ideas from the blockchain literature to devise synchronizers that work in such dynamic ad hoc settings
and tolerate corrupted minorities under the standard assumption that
local clocks advance at approximately the same speed. We discuss both
the setting of honest-majority hashing power and that of a PKI with
honest majority. Our main result is a synchronizer that is directly integrated with a new proof-of-stake (PoS) blockchain protocol, Ouroboros
Chronos, which we construct and prove secure; to our knowledge, this is
the first PoS blockchain protocol to rely only on *local* clocks, while tolerating worst-case corruption and dynamically fluctuating participation.
We believe that this result might be of independent interest.

## 1 Introduction

Global clock synchronization [13, 19, 24] allows a set of mutually distrustful parties to approximate a global notion of "time," in such a manner that if some

---

C. Badertscher—Work done while the author was at the University of Edinburgh,
Scotland.

A. Kiayias—Research partly supported by EU Project No. 780477, PRIVILEDGE.

A. Russell—This material is based upon work supported by the National Science Foundation under Grant No. 1717432.

V. Zikas—Work done in part while the author was at the University of Edinburgh and
while visiting the Simons Institute for the Theory of Computing, UC Berkeley. Work
supported in part by IOHK.

A. Canteaut and F.-X. Standaert (Eds.): EUROCRYPT 2021, LNCS 12698, pp. 399–428, 2021.
https://doi.org/10.1007/978-3-030-77883-5_14

party believes that the global time is $t$ then every party believes it to be $t \pm \epsilon$ for some small $\epsilon > 0$. This allows for an (approximately) synchronous (or partially synchronous) execution of distributed protocols which has placed the study of such *synchronizers* at a prominent position in theoretical computer science research. A number of works investigated feasibility across the spectrum of security/adversary models—from perfect to computational security and for different types of network synchronization assumptions [2,13–15,19,24,25,28,32,33]. We defer a full description of the current landscape of feasibility to the full version of this work [4] due to space constraints. The common assumption of such synchronizers is that the (honest) parties have local (initially desynchronized) clocks which advance at (roughly) the same speed.

Notwithstanding, existing synchronization techniques rely on accurate knowledge of the total number of parties present in the system and smart counting of received messages (or message chains). Consequently these techniques are inapplicable in the *ad hoc secure multi-party computation* setting of Beimel *et al.* [6], where the universe of parties is known but not all parties participate in the protocol and the identities of those that do participate are not known to the other parties. As discussed in [6], what makes this model challenging is the fact that it aims for non-interactive secure computation in the private simultaneous message (PSM) model [16,20]. Indeed, if one allows multiple rounds of interaction, then the parties assumed to be online can try to figure out the active identities, taking the problem's difficulty away.

In this work we study a synchronization challenge which arises in the *dynamic* variant of the ad hoc model, where not only the parties do not know who is actually playing the protocol, but the set of active participants might change in every round (this change is further allowed to be under adversarial control). This is not only a natural extension of [6] but is also motivated by real-world considerations in the blockchain setting. Indeed, the *sleepy model* of consensus proposed by Pass and Shi [31]—and later generalized in the UC setting [8,9] by Badertscher *et al.* [3] under the term *dynamic availability*—puts forth such a *dynamic ad hoc* model for capturing participation fluctuation in distributed ledger protocols. In a nutshell, these works allow for parties to (re)join the protocol at any time and to temporarily *sleep*—i.e., drop out of (certain processes of) the protocol—according to an arbitrary (or even adversarial) sleep pattern.

This dynamic ad hoc setting limits the power of existing synchronization techniques, since the lack of agreement of participation patterns makes counting ineffective for taking consistent decisions. The lack of such synchronization makes any distributed cryptography primitive [1] in this dynamic ad hoc setting reliant on a (possible imperfect) global notion of time. In fact, even the formal cryptographic analyses of proof-of-work (PoW) and proof-of-stake (PoS) blockchains have typically assumed a (partially) synchronous model with a notion of global time. For instance, standard references for the proven security of Bitcoin [17,18,29] implicitly use the fact that they can refer to a global round index in order to prove the desired properties of the protocol. Indeed, the common-prefix property is defined to require that if an honest party holds a chain at round $\rho$, then the prefix of this chain—obtained by removing the $k$ most recent blocks—will eventually become prefix of the chain of any honest party (at some round $\rho' \geq \rho$). The assumption was made explicit in [5] by assuming a global clock in the global UC setting [9]: this permits every party to query a common clock on demand and from that deduce the current round. A similar approach, assuming access to a global clock, was also adopted in the constructions of PoS blockchains, such as Sleepy Consensus [31], Snow White [11], and Ouroboros [3, 12, 23].

The natural question that we address in this work is the following: *Is global clock synchronization from standard assumptions possible in the dynamic ad hoc setting?* By "standard assumptions" in the above question we mean the common assumptions underlying traditional synchronizers—that is, local (initially desynchronized) clocks which advance at (roughly) the same speed and an honest majority of parties.[1] —along with standard cryptographic assumptions such as a public-key infrastructure (PKI) and existentially unforgeable digital signatures.

As discussed above, counting arguments of the sort used in classical synchronizers does not seem to help. Therefore, to answer this question we turn to techniques from the cryptographic literature on blockchain ledgers, which has already come a long way in addressing other security challenges that the dynamic ad hoc model creates. In fact, it is not hard to verify that in a resource-restricted scenario, such as the one created by assuming honest majority of hashing power, the above question can be answered by relying on a simplified version of the Bitcoin backbone protocol [17]. In particular, one can observe that the description of the Bitcoin blockchain (without difficulty recalibration) can rely on a purely *execution-driven* notion of time and explicit knowledge of current global time is not required. In the static difficulty setting, proving security in this way follows immediately from [17, 29]. As a result, a synchronizer can be trivially inferred by defining the clock to be the current blockchain length in each party's local state.

The above observation is a good indication that blockchain techniques can help answering our question, but it unfortunately does not provide a satisfying answer, as it relies on a non-standard—from the perspective of synchronizers and/or general multi-party computation (MPC) literature—assumption, i.e., that the honest parties control the majority of the computing power per unit of time. To avoid such non-standard assumptions we turn to proof of stake (PoS). Here, an execution-driven notion of time similar to the aforementioned notion achieved by Bitcoin without difficulty recalibration can actually be achieved by certain PoS-based iterated-Byzantine Fault Tolerant (iBFT) ledger protocols such as Algorand [10]. Indeed, given access to the genesis block (which can be seen as an initial PKI) a party can use the index (sequence number) of the current block as global time. This suggests the following as a solution to our synchronization problem: The assumed PKI—which in the ad hoc model would

---

[1] In the static ad hoc setting [6], this assumption becomes honest majority of active parties; and in the dynamic, it would be honest majority among the parties that are actively participating in any given round.

include the keys of all parties, active or not—is interpreted as a genesis block where every key is associated with a unit of stake. Then a simplified version of the Algorand ledger protocol is executed, i.e., without any stake shift and where the contents of the blocks are independent messages, in particular they are not interpreted as transactions of any kind. Whenever a party becomes active in the computation, he uses the length of the blockchain as his global time. If a $(2/3 + \epsilon)$-majority of active parties is honest (for some constant $\epsilon > 0$), it follows that in the above execution of simplified-Algorand, a $(2/3 + \epsilon)$-majority of the (implicit) stake must be in honest hands and therefore security follows by the security proof of Algorand. It is not hard to verify that the protocol yields a good synchronizer, where, not surprisingly, the network delay lower-bounds the maximum skew of synchronized parties' clocks. However, the above solution works only under a concession which severely limits the nature of the dynamic ad hoc model. We need to demand explicit participation thresholds that are part of the protocol logic. Stated differently, each protocol participant at any given time must be aware of a sufficiently accurate estimate of how many parties are active at that time. To our knowledge, such a property, which in [10] is referred to as *lazy honesty*, is necessary for the security analysis of [10]. We note in passing that such a rigid participation restriction is not necessary for the Bitcoin blockchain or its PoS variants in the sleepy/dynamic-availability setting.

Although it does not solve our question, the above idea still points to the right direction: Concretely, if we could use the above idea but with a PoS protocol which does not rely on explicit participation bounds, e.g., [3,11,12,23,31], then we would have answered our question to the affirmative. And even better, our synchronizer would work assuming an honest majority ($1/2 + \epsilon$ of parties for some suitably chosen $\epsilon$), since the above protocols are secure w.r.t. such an assumption on the stake distribution. Unfortunately, unlike Algorand, these protocols use a notion of (approximate) global time hardwired in the protocol logic, and the protocol is unspecified without such global knowledge of time/round. In fact, as explained below, there does not seem to be a simple way to removing this dependence of global time, and replace it by local clocks —even, perfectly-coordinated ones that advance at exactly the same speed—while preserving the security guarantees.[2] The reason is that in these PoS blockchains a party's right to create a block is always associated with a concrete round (also called "slot"), and in order to verify that a block is created by an eligible party, that party must include a proof explicitly referring to the slot number. This means that a new party that joins the blockchain—or one that has been sleeping for long—cannot prune-off chains with adversarial timestamps so that it eventually adopts the right chain. Thus if a new party with an incorrect local time joins the protocol and sees a chain that includes blocks which appear to be far in the future (according to her local time), she cannot decide whether the chain is adversarial—in

---

[2] Of course, one could include such a notion of (approximate) global time in a trusted *checkpointing assumption* [11], but this defeats the purpose of decoupling the protocol from an explicitly assumed trusted source of global time when a party (re)joins, which is the main challenge of our work.

which case she needs to ignore or truncate it—or her local time is far behind absolute time. It is worth adding that these are not merely theoretical considerations: in a real world deployment the dependency on a global clock is typically met by using a global time synchronization service such as NTP [27] and hence the security of all these protocols becomes compromised if such service fails to deliver a truly reliable clock, a possibility that cannot be excluded [26].

Note that all previous PoS protocols which can operate in a participation-unrestricted setting [3,11,12,23,31] require an upper bound on the network delay $\Delta$ which is a necessary assumption, see [30], due to the participation uncertainty. However, knowledge of an upper bound on $\Delta$ does not help the parties in any direct way to assess the actual time (e.g., by locally counting time intervals of length $\Delta$), as participation gaps can invalidate their local timer with respect to the implicit global execution-driven time.

It seems we have hit a deadlock: if the protocol itself crucially relies on global time, then how can it be used to remove global time and replace it with loosely synchronized clocks? Unfortunately, there seems to be no way to use these blockchain protocols (or their properties) in a black-box manner to realize a global clock from standard assumptions. Nonetheless, as we prove here, we can draw inspiration from these works to design new a new PoS blockchain protocol *from scratch*, so that it *does not rely on a global clock* and can be used as a synchronizer to obtain an approximate global clock from standard synchronizer assumptions. Our approach to building the new blockchain extends in a highly non-trivial manner ideas from the recent PoS literature.

Our blockchain protocol works not only for static stake, but can even accommodate stake transfers and new keys being generated (and potentially allocated stake) as in existing PoS blockchains. Thus, we actually not only solve the synchronizer problem in the dynamic ad hoc setting, but we provide the first full fledged PoS blockchain in the dynamic availability setting which relies *not* on global time but on the weaker and more realistic assumption of local (initially desynchronized) clocks which advance at (roughly) the same speed. We believe that this result might be both of independent interest for the distributed ledgers literature as well as of practical importance. We note in passing that given our new synchronizer, a potential alternative construction of a blockchain would be to use it in a black-box way to first realize a global clock, and then use this within an existing PoS blockchain. However, this would yield a highly suboptimal use of resources as it would effectively mean running two blockchains. This works shows that one does not need this redundancy and use our construction both as a PoS blockchain and as means to simulate a global clock (and potentially export it to other calling protocols) at the same time.

## 2   Overview of Our Techniques

At the core of our global synchronization procedure is a new PoS blockchain ledger protocol which (1) does not rely on global clocks but merely on local clocks with (approximately) the same speed, (2) accommodates dynamic ad hoc participation, and (3) assigns timestamps to each block so that they can be used by any external observer to deduce an (approximate) notion of global time/round (see Theorem 1). We refer to this new blockchain protocol as *Ouroboros Chronos*, or simply *Chronos*, and discuss it below. As discussed above, it would be sufficient for our synchronizer's needs to just design a blockchain that works in the static stake setting. Nonetheless, for full generality, we design Chronos to accommodate (and tolerate) stake-shift, which makes it the first fully-functional PoS blockchain, yielding the same guarantees as existing ones [3,10,11], but without reliance on a global clock or restricting dynamic participation.

First, observe that if all the parties running the blockchain protocol would be guaranteed to be around from its beginning and throughout its lifetime (i.e., in the static ad hoc model of [6]) then one could use an existing PoS blockchain for honest majority, e.g., [3,11] with the convention described above to assign one unit of stake per public key. A synchronizer could be derived from the length of the blockchain while the security assumptions and parties never joining or leaving the system would guarantee that parties stay synchronized. What makes the problem challenging and excludes the above solution is, thus, the combination of lack of a global clock with dynamic (ad hoc) participation. In the following we focus on how to redesign the mechanism of the above PoS protocols to allow (re)joining parties to get in sync with parties that have been around sufficiently long and are, therefore, already in-sync with each other—we refer to these latter parties as *alert*.

The central idea of our mechanism is the continuous recording of individually submitted clock readings and the clock adjustment of the alert parties' local clocks based on these readings at regular recalibration points. This mechanism is based on a VRF-based probabilistic sampling of the local clocks of all active parties using the blockchain to consistently record this operation over the protocol execution. As we demonstrate, this opens the opportunity for a safe (re)joining procedure; newly joining parties will be able to "hook" themselves into the next recalibration point and become fully alert.

In more details, here is how our new (re)joining procedure works: (Re)joining parties, start with listening on the network for some time, collecting broadcasted chains and following a "densest chain" chain-selection rule similar to [3]. Informally, this rule mandates that if two chains $\mathcal{C}$ and $\mathcal{C}'$ start diverging at some time $t$—according to the reported time-stamps in $\mathcal{C}$ and $\mathcal{C}'$—then choose the chain which is denser in a sufficiently long interval after that time. Our first key observation is that this rule offers a useful (albeit in itself insufficient) guarantee in our setting: the joining party will end up with some blockchain that, although *arbitrarily long*, is at worst forking from a chain held by an honest and already synchronized party by a bounded number of blocks (equal to a security parameter) with overwhelming probability. This observation is the key to start building our synchronization mechanism. More concretely, we prove that the above process guarantees to eventually prune-off all chains with bad prefixes, i.e., prefixes that do not largely coincide with the prefixes of the other already synchronized honest parties' chains. In fact, as we show, the parties can compute an upper bound on the time (according to their local clocks) they need to remain in the above self-synchronization state before they build confidence in the above guarantee, i.e., before they know that their locally held chain is consistent with a long and stable prefix that already-synchronized honest parties adopt.

The second key observation is that once a joining party has converged to such a *fresh*—i.e., produced after the joining party was activated— prefix of an honest chain, it may use the difference between its current local time and the (local) time recorded when this chain (and other control information) was received to adjust its local clock so that its local time is consistent with the times reported on the prefix. The hope would be that a clever adjustment will bring this local time sufficiently close to that of an honest and already synchronized party.

Designing and analyzing such an updating process is challenging. Indeed, consider the following straw man attempt: The party resets its local clock so that the time reported in, say, the last block of the prefix is the time this block was received. Before discussing the limitations of this proposal, let us first discuss an inherent property when dealing with clock synchronization in the setting with $\Delta$-bounded (but adversarially controlled) delay networks. A message received by a party might have been sent up to $\Delta$ rounds before, hence the time that the party will set its clock to might be up to $\Delta$ rounds away from the clock of the sender (at the point of update). This delay-induced imprecision is unavoidable, so when we assess a given proposal we accept that clocks only need to be "loosely" synchronized; specifically, clocks of honest parties might differ by a bounded amount, where the bound is known and depends only on $\Delta$. In fact, this relaxation is common and believed to be necessary even in the permissioned model [19, 24].[3]

However, the above simple solution is problematic even when there are no delays: Although the chain that the newly joining party recovered is guaranteed to have a prefix consistent with the already synchronized honest parties, individual blocks might be originating from the adversary and therefore contain a time stamp very different from the true sending time of that block. To make matters worse, the rate of honestly generated blocks in a chain of an honest party can be quite low as implied by the known bounds of chain quality [12, 18], and thus the time inaccuracy of any individual block can be significant.

A second attempt would be to have in every round (or at regular intervals) every party use the credentials of all the coins it owns to broadcast a signed timestamp, i.e., every party acts as a verifiable *synchronization (or timestamping) beacon* on behalf of all the coins it owns. The joining party receives all these broadcasted timestamps, and uses their majority to compute the value of its clock. Still, this solution has drawbacks: The first is scalability; this is not severe, as existing ideas can be employed such as using the protocol history as input to a verifiable random function (VRF) to identify eligible parties (or, as in the case of Algorand, by using Bracha-style committees [7]) to send time-

---

[3] The model from [24] with honest clocks that report values differing by up to $\Delta$ is equivalent to a situation in which clocks report the right value, but parties might receive it with a difference of up to $\Delta$ rounds.

stamping beacons in every synchronization round. The second, harder problem is that in order to use the majority, the local clocks of the parties that report time need to be perfectly synchronized so that their majority agrees. If their clocks have any small drift, this fails. Furthermore, even with identical speed clocks, dynamic participation allows parties to drop off and rejoin, which means that, due to the network delay the honest parties will end up with only loosely synchronized local clocks. Using the average instead of the majority function does not help out here either since a single adversarial timestamp can throw off the average arbitrarily far. Hence, taking the median of the received timestamps promises to be more stable against extreme values. Observe that as long as synchronized honest parties' local clocks are not far apart, the times they report will be concentrated to a sufficiently small time interval, and the median will fall in this interval.

The above insight brings us closer, but is still insufficient: If the adversary can serve to, say, two different joining parties different and possibly disjoint sets of timestamps (on behalf of eligible corrupted synchronization-beacon parties) then he could force an opposing clock adjustment between the two that will increase their clock drift well beyond the drift of any pair of already synchronized parties. To resolve this issue, we need to ensure that the parties agree on the set of eligible timestamps (whether honest or corrupted) that they use for adjusting their local time. This is a classical consensus problem. Luckily, our synchronizer runs in tandem with a PoS-based blockchain which solves consensus with dynamic availability, and which can assist in reaching agreement on the synchronization-beacon values for recalibration. And thanks to the property discussed at the beginning of the section—namely that even joining parties (without accurate time) will eventually be able to bootstrap a sufficiently long prefix of the blockchain—the joining parties will agree on the set of beacons for recalibration.

Our solution follows the spirit of the above conclusion. In a nutshell, we will use the VRF to assign timestamping-beacon parties to slots according to their state. Parties who are synchronized and active when their assigned slot is encountered will broadcast a timestamp and a VRF-proof of their eligibility for the current timeslot (together, we call this a *synchronization beacon*). And to agree on the set of eligible parties that will be used (including the dishonest ones) these beacons will also be included in the blockchain by the already synchronized parties, similarly to transactions. Any party who joins and tries to get synchronized will gather chains and record any broadcasted beacons (and keep track of the local time these were received). Once the party is confident it has a sufficiently long prefix of the honest chain, it will retrospectively use this gathered information to extract the agreed-upon set of beacons, compute a good approximation of the clocks parties had when they broadcasted these beacons and apply a median rule to set its local clock to at most a small distance from other honest and synchronized parties. In order to ensure that already synchronized parties adjust in tandem with joining parties we will have them also periodically execute the synchronization algorithm—but of course using their local blockchain, which they know is guaranteed to have a large common prefix with any other honest and synchronized party. Evidently, to turn this high-level idea of our solution into a provably secure protocol requires appropriate design choices that we present in Sect. 4. Nonetheless, by a careful analysis (cf. Sect. 5) we can show that not only the above construction yields a PoS blockchain that does not rely on global time, but, also, the reported timestamps are (approximately) consistent among long-term (alert) participants and can, with a suitable encoding mechanism, be used to devise a synchronizer satisfied the guarantees of the following theorem.

**Theorem 1.** *There is a synchronizer protocol in the dynamic ad hoc setting, so that the following properties hold:*

1. *(Completeness) Any alert party in the protocol reports some time $t \in \mathbb{N}$.*
2. *(Approximate synchrony) For any two alert parties $p_1$ and $p_2$ reporting times $t_1$ and $t_2$, respectively, it holds $|t_1 - t_2| \leq 2\Delta$, where $\Delta$ is an upper bound on the network delay.*
3. *(Monotonicity) If an alert party reports times $t_1$ and then $t_2$ at two consecutive steps[4] in its execution, then $t_1 \leq t_2 \leq t_1 + 2\Delta$.*
4. *(Liveness) For any alert party, if time $t_2$ is reported $2\Delta$ local rounds after time $t_1$, then $t_1 < t_2$.*

Note that the above theorem provides a clock that might make "jumps" (i.e., skip some rounds for certain parties). However, these jumps are bounded by $2\Delta$. Hence, it is straightforward to turn this clock into a clock that does not make jumps (albeit slower) and where synchronized parties are within a round from each other: Every party reports time $\lfloor \frac{t}{2\Delta} \rfloor$, where $t$ is the value it sees from the above "jumpy" clock.

## 3    Our Model

**Basic Notation.** For $n \in \mathbb{N}$ we use the notation $[n]$ to refer to the set $\{1, \ldots, n\}$. For brevity, we often write $\{x_i\}_{i=1}^n$ and $(x_i)_{i=1}^n$ to denote the set $\{x_1, \ldots, x_n\}$ and the tuple $(x_1, \ldots, x_n)$, respectively. For a tuple $(x_i)_{i=1}^n$, we denote by $\mathsf{med}((x_i)_{i=1}^n)$ the (lower) median of the tuple, i.e., $\mathsf{med}((x_i)_{i=1}^n) \triangleq x'_{\lceil n/2 \rceil}$, where $(x'_i)_{i=1}^n$ is a (non-decreasing) sorted permutation of $(x_i)_{i=1}^n$. For a blockchain (or chain) $\mathcal{C}$, which is a sequence of blocks, we denote by $\mathcal{C}^{\lceil k}$ the chain that is obtained by removing the last $k$ blocks; and by $\mathsf{head}(\mathcal{C})$ the last block of $\mathcal{C}$. We write $\mathcal{C}_1 \preceq \mathcal{C}_2$ if $\mathcal{C}_1$ is a prefix of $\mathcal{C}_2$.

We discuss the model and the hybrid functionalities assumed in the protocol below. The formal descriptions are given in the full version of this work [4].

**Relaxed Synchrony.** The synchrony assumption that parties advance at exactly the same pace can be captured by the global-setup variant of the clock

---

[4] In this context, a step in the execution corresponds to the action(s) a party takes during a single local round (i.e., between two "ticks" of its local clock.).

functionality from [22]. This is a weaker version of the global clock used in previous analyses of blockchains [3,5] in that it does not keep a counter representing the global system time, but rather maintains for each party (resp. ideal functionality) an indicator bit $d_\mathsf{P}$ (resp. $d_{(\mathcal{F},\mathrm{sid})}$) of whether or not a new round has started. Each party's indicator is accessible by a standard CLOCK-GET command. All indicators are set to 0 at the beginning of each round; once any party or functionality finishes its round it issues a CLOCK-UPDATE command that updates his indicator to 1. Once every party and functionality has updated its indicator, the clock resets all of them to 0; this switch allows the parties to detect that the previous round has ended and move on to the next round.

Arguably the above clock offers very strong synchronization guarantees, since once a round switches, every party is informed about it in the next activation. In [22] a relaxed version of this clock was introduced which allowed the adversary to delay notifying the parties about a round switch by bounded amount of fetch-attempts. This behavior relaxes the perfect nature of the clock, but it still ensures that no party advances to a next round before all parties have completed their current round.

In this work we consider parties that advance at roughly the same speed, which means that a party might advance its round even before another party has finished with its current round, and even multiple times, as long as its is ensured that no honest party is left too far behind. For this purpose we introduce an even more relaxed version of the (global-setup variant) of the clock from [22] which, intuitively, allows a party to advance to its next round multiple times *before* some honest parties have completed their current round, as long as the relative pace of advancement for any two honest parties stays below a drift parameter $\Delta_\mathrm{clock}$. We note in passing that a similar guarantee was formulated in the timing model [21]; however, the solution there notified the underlying model of computation which creates complications with the (G)UC composition theorem which would need to be reproved. To avoid such complications, in this work we capture the above relaxed synchrony assumption as a global functionality.[5] and call it $\mathcal{G}^{\Delta_\mathrm{clock}}_{\mathrm{IMPERFLCLOCK}}$.

Similar to the perfect clock above, the imperfect clock stores an indicator bit $d_\mathsf{P}$ which is used to keep track of when everyone has completed a round (not necessarily the same round)—one can think of this indicator as corresponding to a baseline round-switch, which is however hidden from the parties and might only be observed by ideal functionalities. Additionally, for every party the imperfect clock keeps an imperfect version of the indicator bit $d_\mathsf{P}^{Imp}$ (corresponding to switches P's *local*, e.g., hardware, clock switches) which is what is exported when the party attempts to check his clock.

This local indicator is used similarly to how synchronous protocols would use the perfect indicator in [22]; but we allow the adversary to control when this

---

[5] In [22] a functionality corresponding to the timing-model assumptions [21] was proposed along with a reduction to the (local) clock functionality. However, both the fact that their clock functionality is local and that their reduction uses a complete network of (known) bounded-delay authenticated channels—which we do not assume here—makes that result incompatible with our model and goals.

local indicator is updated under the restrictions that (a) $d_P^{Imp}$ cannot advance in the middle of P's round, (b) it cannot fall behind the baseline induced by the indicator $d_P$, and (c) it cannot advance ahead of the baseline by more than $\Delta_{clock}$. This is achieved by the imperfect clock keeping track of the relative difference/distance $\texttt{drift}_P$ between the number of local advances of each registered P from the baseline updates; this distance is increased whenever $d_P^{Imp}$ is reset (by the adversary) to 0 and decreased whenever the baseline indicator $d_P \in \{0,1\}$ is reset to 0; if the distance of some party from the baseline falls below 0 (i.e., the adversary attempts to stall a party when the baseline advances[6]) then the local indicator is reset to $d_P^{Imp} = 0$ (which allows P to advance his round) and the corresponding distance is also reset to 0.

**Modeling Peer-to-Peer Communication.** We assume a diffusion network, denoted by and we denote it by $\mathcal{F}_{\text{N-MC}}^{\Delta_{\text{net}}}$, in which all messages sent by honest parties are guaranteed to be fetched by protocol participants after a specific delay $\Delta_{\text{net}}$. Additionally, the network guarantees that once a message has been fetched by an honest party, this message is fetched by any other honest party within a delay of at most $\Delta_{\text{net}}$, even if the sender of the message is corrupted. We note that this network model is not substantially stronger than in previous works [3,5], which use a network functionality providing bounded-delay message delivery. Our model is equivalent via an unconditional reduction: echoing received messages. In practice, this reduction of course needs to be applied prudently to avoid saturating the network. This is exactly done by the relevant networking protocols: e.g. in Bitcoin, when a new block is received its hash is advertised and then propagated and validated by the network as needed. Chronos can use the same mechanism.

**Genesis Block Distribution and Weak Start Agreement.** Our model allows parties' local time-stamps to drift apart over the course of an execution; additionally the model makes no assumption that the initialization of the initial stakeholders is completed in the same round, i.e., honest parties might start staking at different rounds of the execution. To this aim, we weaken the functionality $\mathcal{F}_{\text{INIT}}$ adopted by [3] to allow for bounded delays when initial stakeholders receive the genesis blocks. Namely, our $\mathcal{F}_{\text{INIT}}^{\Delta_{\text{net}}}$ functionality merely guarantees genesis block delivery to initial stakeholder not more than $\Delta_{\text{net}}$ rounds apart from each other; the offsets are under adversarial control.

**Further Hybrids.** The protocol makes use of a VRF (verifiable random function) functionality $\mathcal{F}_{\text{VRF}}$, a KES (key-evolving signature) functionality $\mathcal{F}_{\text{KES}}$, and a (global) random oracle functionality $\mathcal{G}_{\text{RO}}$ (to model ideal hash functions).

### 3.1   Dynamic (Ad Hoc) Participation

To support a fine-grained dynamic participation model, we follow the approach of [3] and categorize the parties into *party types*. Recall that the dynamic partic-

---

[6] Note that by definition the baseline advances when all parties have completed their current round.

ipation model allows to capture the security of the protocol in a realistic fashion, by considering that some parties might be stalling their computation, some might accidentally lose network access and hence disappear unannounced, and others might lose track of the passage of time due to some failure. In our model, we formally let the environment be in charge of connecting and disconnecting to its resources. (This is done by equipping the functionalities, global setups, and the protocol with explicit registration/de-registration commands, thereby keeping track of when parties are joining and adjusting their guarantees depending based on this information.) The various basic and derived types of parties are summarized in Fig. 1.

| Resource (Res.) | Basic types of *honest* parties | |
| --- | --- | --- |
| | Res. unavailable | Res. available |
| random oracle $\mathcal{G}_{RO}$ | *stalled* | *operational* |
| network $\mathcal{F}_{N\text{-}MC}$ | *offline* | *online* |
| clock $\mathcal{G}_{PERFLCLOCK}$ | *time-unaware* | *time-aware* |
| synchronized state, local time | *desynchronized* | *synchronized* |
| KES capable of signing (w.r.t. local time) | *sign-capable* | *sign-uncapable* |

**Derived types:**

*alert* :⇔ *operational* ∧ *online* ∧ *time-aware* ∧ *synchronized* ∧ *sign-capable*

*active* :⇔ *alert* ∨ *adversarial* ∨ *time-unaware*

Note: *alert* parties are honest, *active* parties also contain all adversarial parties.

**Fig. 1.** Party types.

For a given point in execution, a party is considered *offline* if it is not registered with the network, otherwise it is considered *online*. A party is *time-aware* if it is registered with the clock, otherwise we call it *time-unaware*. We say that a party is *operational* if it is registered with the random oracle, otherwise we call it *stalled*. Finally, we say that a party is *sign-capable* if the counter in $\mathcal{F}_{KES}$ is less or equal to its local time-stamp.

Additionally, an honest party is called *synchronized* if it has been continuously connected to all its resources for a sufficiently long interval to make sure that, roughly speaking, (i) it holds a chain that shares a common prefix with other synchronized parties (synchronized state) and (ii) its local time does not differ by much from other synchronized parties (synchronized time). Our protocol's resynchronization procedure JoinProc will guarantee the party that after executing it for the prescribed number of rounds, it will achieve both properties (i) and (ii) above. In addition, such a party will eventually become sign-capable in future rounds (in case the KES is "evolved" too far into the future due to a desynchronized time-stamp before joining). We note that an honest party always knows whether it is synchronized or sign-capable and (in contrast to the treatment in [3]), it maintains its synchronization state in a local variable isSync and makes its actions depend on it.

Based on these four basic attributes, we define *alert* and *active* parties similarly to [3]. Alert parties are considered the core set of honest parties that have access to all necessary resources, are synchronized and sign-capable. On the other hand, *potentially active* parties (or *active* for short) are those (honest or corrupted) parties that can potentially act (propose a block, send a synchronization beacon) in its current status; in other words, we cannot guarantee their inactivity. Formally, it includes alert parties, corrupted (i.e., adversarial) parties, and moreover any party that is time-unaware (independently of the other attributes; this is because those parties are in particular not capable of evolving their signing keys reliably and hence it cannot be excluded that if they later get corrupted, they might retroactively perform protocol operations in a malicious way).

The definition of a party type is extended now, namely from single points in an execution to the natural numbers, which we refer to as *logical slots* in this context. As we see in Sect. 4, to each logical slot, a leader election process is associated, which every honest party will run when its local clock localTime equals sl for the first time. The definition of party types w.r.t. logical slots is as follows: a party P is counted as alert (resp. operational, online, time-aware, synchronized, sign-capable) for a slot sl if the first time its local clock passes through the (logical) slot sl, it maintains this state *throughout the whole slot*, otherwise it is considered not alert (resp. stalled, offline, time-unaware, desynchronized, sign-uncapable) for sl. It is considered corrupted (i.e., adversarial) for sl if it was corrupted by the adversary $\mathcal{A}$ when its local clock satisfied localTime $\leq$ sl. Finally, it is active for sl if it is either corrupted for that slot, or it is alert or time-unaware *at any point* during the interval when its local clock for the first time passes through slot sl.

# 4   The Blockchain Protocol

At a high level, the protocol we present is a Nakamoto-style proof-of-stake based protocol for the so-called semi-synchronous setting; this is the same model used for standard analyses of Bitcoin. In this model, parties have a somewhat accurate common notion of elapsed time (rather than absolute time information) and the network has an upper bound on the delay which is not known to the parties. At a very high-level the protocol attempts to imitate a process which resembles a situation in which state (including time) is continuously passed on to currently alert stakeholders. The honest majority of active stake assumption that is explicit in [3,12] will then ensure that the adversary cannot destroy this state by using his ability to tune participation.

To ease into the main protocol ideas it is useful to imagine a situation in which there is a core of parties with sufficient stake that has been around from the onset of the blockchain. (These parties have a common, albeit somewhat imperfect, understanding of how much time has passed since the protocol started and can contribute this information to the synchronization procedure.) We stress that the continuous or indefinite presence of such parties is not needed in our final protocol which will ensure that the information that these parties would safeguard is passed on to new parties if/when such inaugural parties go to sleep or deregister.

Here is how such an inaugural participant (i.e., a participant who is assigned stake at the outset of the computation by $\mathcal{F}_{\mathsf{INIT}}$) executes the protocol. With access to the provided genesis block, which reveals an initial record $S_1 = ((P_1, v_1^{\mathrm{vrf}}, v_1^{\mathrm{kes}}, s_1), \ldots, (P_n, v_n^{\mathrm{vrf}}, v_n^{\mathrm{kes}}, s_n))$ that associates each participant $P_i$[7] to its chosen public keys used for verification purposes of the staking process and its initial stake $s_i$, each party begins the so-called first epoch of the staking procedure and sets its local clock localTime to the value 1. The party has to execute a certain set of tasks per round. Note that two inaugural parties have only a somewhat accurate notion of elapsed time and receiving the genesis block might be delayed, it might very well be that a party $P_1$ has executed three rounds, while $P_2$ has only executed one so far, or has not even received the genesis block. The bounds on the clock drifts and the network delay however ensure that the difference of the number of completed protocol rounds does not drift too far apart.

A participant's main task (per round) is to evaluate whether it is elected to produce a block for the current local time, which we refer to as a *slot*. For this, it evaluates a verifiable random function (VRF) on input $x := \eta_1 \,\|\, \mathtt{localTime} \,\|\, \mathtt{TEST}$, where $\eta_1$ is a truly random seed provided by $\mathcal{F}_{\mathsf{INIT}}$. If the returned value $y$ is smaller than a threshold value $T_P^{\mathrm{ep}}$, which is derived from the stake associated with $P$, then the participant is called a slot leader. The threshold is computed to yield a higher probability of slot leadership the higher the stake of the party. The main task of the slot leader is to create a valid block for this slot that contains, as control information (alongside the transactions), the VRF proof of slot leadership, an additional random nonce, and the hash to the head of the chain it connects to. Each block is signed using a key-evolving signature scheme.[8] As typical in these systems, the block is made to extend (essentially) the longest valid chain known to the party. Due to the slightly shifted local clocks, some care has to be taken to not disregard entirely chains that contain blocks in the logical future of a party. However, the chain a party adopts (and computes the ledger state from) at slot localTime shall never contain a block with a higher time-stamp.[9]

In addition to the above actions, or if a party is not slot leader, it must play the lottery once more on input $x' := \eta_1 \,\|\, \mathtt{localTime} \,\|\, \mathtt{SYNC}$. If the party is lucky this time and receives a return value smaller than the threshold (defined shortly), it must emit a so-called synchronization beacon containing the VRF proof and

---

[7] More precisely, $P_i$ denotes just a bitstring in the model that formally identifies a machine and is used to identify which keys (and hence stake) are controlled by corrupted machines. Note that we write participant or party instead of machine.

[8] The KES ensures that if a participants gets corrupted, no blocks can be created in retrospect.

[9] Some further care has to be taken in proof of stake to detect chains that try to perform a long-range attack. We describe this in the next section in more detail when we recall the Genesis chain-selection rule.

the current time `localTime`. Synchronization beacons are treated similarly to transactions and are contained into blocks if valid. If a party has done all its tasks, it increments `localTime` and waits until the round is over. Except for the generation of synchronization beacons, which is only done in a first fraction of an epoch, the above round procedure iterates over the entire first epoch, where the length of an epoch is $R$, a parameter of the protocol. Our security proof shows that this first epoch does result in a blockchain satisfying common prefix, chain growth, and chain quality properties for specific parameters, as long as the leader-election per slot is to the advantage of honest protocol participants.[10]

At the epoch boundary to the second epoch, two important things happen. First the stake-distribution and the epoch randomness change: they are derived from specific blocks contained in the guaranteed common prefix established by the first epoch. In particular, we must ensure that at the time the stake distribution is fixed, the epoch randomness cannot be predicted to ensure the freshness of the slot leader election lottery for the second epoch. The second critical update at the epoch boundary is the local time: each party performs a local-clock adjustment, outlined in Sect. 4.1, which ensures that after the adjustment parties are still close together, where "close" means within $\Delta = \Delta_{net} + \Delta_{clock}$ (two sources of bounded variance contribute to this: delay and drift) and that performed shifts of the local clock remain small (which is crucial for security). The desired property follows from the common-prefix guarantee (enabling an agreement on beacons), the honest majority assumption (enabling small clock shifts), and the network properties and clock properties (which ensure correlated arrival times). With some additional considerations detailed in Sect. 4.1, the protocol proceeds executing the above round tasks for the entire second epoch until the next boundary is met. This iterated process, where one epoch bootstraps the next, is backed by an inductive security argument, following previous works [3,12,23], that shows how the overall security is a consequence of the first epoch achieving the desired blockchain properties to serve as a good basis for the second, etc.

The reason to perform a local-clock adjustment is to enable the main goal of our construction: to enable new parties to safely join the system and to determine, just by observing the network and without any further help, an accurate and up-to-date local-clock value and ledger state with respect to the existing honest parties in the system, i.e., being within a $\Delta$ interval of their clock values and obtaining the same common-prefix, chain-quality and chain-growth guarantees. After this, newly joining parties can start contributing to the security of the system.

The bootstrapping procedure for newcomers is quite involved due to a combination of obstacles: First, the joining party needs to obtain a blockchain that shares some common prefix with the common prefix established by the existing parties. This is achieved by having the joining party listen to the network for some rounds, and picking the "best" chain $C$ it sees in the following sense: when compared with any other seen valid chain $C'$, $C$ contains more blocks in an

---

[10] We note that the leader election is per logical slot and honest parties will all pass through the same logical not at the same time, but at related times.

interval of slots of size $s$ starting from the forking point of $\mathcal{C}$ and $\mathcal{C}'$. We prove that based on the honest-majority assumption, such a densest chain must share a large common prefix with the chains honest parties currently hold. However, $\mathcal{C}$ could still be adversarially crafted and for example be much longer than what honest parties agreed on by extending into the future, hence a reliable ledger state cannot yet be computed. However, it will become possible once the joining party succeeds in bootstrapping also an accurate time-stamp in the $\Delta$ interval of honest participants' timestamps, which is the second obstacle to overcome. After the party is guaranteed to be hooked to a large prefix of the honest parties' common-prefix, it begins recording all synchronization beacons it receives on the network for a long enough period of time, a parameter of the system. The length of the waiting time is set in order to ensure that, after the newly joining party started listening to the network, the parties at least once seeded the slot-leadership lottery with a fresh nonce that was unpredictable at the time of joining the system. After an additional waiting time, the agreed-upon set of beacons (with proofs referring to the fresh lottery) will be part of the common prefix and eventually be part of what is known to the joining party. We prove that based on this agreement on beacons found in the blockchain, the clock-adjustments procedure by the current participants in the system can be retraced and will yield a clock adjustment to the newly joining party's local clock that will directly push it into the interval of existing honest participants' local clock. At this point, the party runs the normal chain-selection mechanism, essentially cutting off blocks in its logical future and obtains a reliable ledger state as well.

### 4.1   The Protocol with Static Ad Hoc Participation

Towards a modular description of our protocol, let us first focus on how the protocol would work in the static ad hoc setting, where all parties are alert. In particular, we discuss what such alert parties need to do in order to accommodate synchronization of joining and rejoining parties. The description of what joining and rejoining parties do—i.e., how they use the help of alert parties to get in-sync—is the included in Sect. 4.2. Every alert party runs the following round instructions. For the pseudo-code of all involved tasks (and more detailed explanations), we refer to the full version of this work [4].

1. Fetch information from the network over which transactions, beacons, and blocks are sent and further update the current time-stamp and epoch number. A party locally advances its time-stamp whenever it realizes that a new (local) round has started by a call to $\mathcal{G}_{\mathrm{IMPERFLCLOCK}}$.
2. Record the arrival times of the synchronization beacons produced by all protocol participants. This is discussed in more detail below.
3. Process the received chains: as some chains might have been created by parties whose time-stamps are ahead of local time, the future chains are stored in a specific buffer for later usage (and importantly, not discarded). Among the

remaining chains, the protocol will decide whether any chain is more prefer-able than the local chain using a chain-selection rule inspired by Ouroboros Genesis [3] which we thus refer to as the Genesis rule. An important property of the Genesis rule is that chain selection is secure without requiring a mov-ing checkpoint: roughly speaking, a chain $\mathcal{C}_1$ is preferred over $\mathcal{C}_2$ if they have a large common history, except possibly the last $k$ blocks (where $k$ is some parameter) and $\mathcal{C}_1$ is longer. If however, they fork even before, chain $\mathcal{C}_1$ is preferred if it is block density is higher compared to $\mathcal{C}_2$ in a carefully selected interval of size $s$ slots after the forking point.

4. Run the main staking procedure to evaluate slot leadership, and potentially create and emit a new block or synchronization beacon. Before the main staking procedure is executed, the local state is updated including the current stake distribution. We provide more details on some of these aspects below.

5. If the end of the round coincides with the end of an epoch, the *synchronization procedure* (denoted SyncProc) is executed.

While the above only gives a broad overview of different tasks per round, we cover some of those in more detail below.

**Stake Distribution and Leader Election.** A party P is an eligible slot-leader for a particular slot sl in an epoch ep if its VRF-output (for an input dependent on sl) is smaller than a threshold value $T_P^{ep}$. The threshold is derived from the (local) stake distribution $\mathbb{S}_{ep}$ assigned to an ep which in turn is defined by the (local) blockchain $\mathcal{C}_{loc}$, that is we assume an abstract mapping that assigns to a party (identified by an encoding of its public keys) its stake derived as a function of the transactions in $\mathcal{C}_{loc}$, the genesis block, and the epoch the party is currently in. As described above, the stake distribution is only updated once a party enters a new epoch, i.e., once localTime mod $R = 1$. Say a party enters in epoch ep + 1, then the distribution is defined by the state contained in the block sequence up to and including the last block in epoch ep − 1 (or the genesis block for the first two epochs). Furthermore, the epoch randomness for epoch ep + 1 (to refresh the lottery) is extracted from the previous randomness and the seeds defined by the first two-thirds of the blocks in epoch ep (for the first epoch, the randomness is defined by the genesis block). Both of these updates thus derived based on the (supposedly) established common prefix among participants.

The relative stake of P in the stake distribution $\mathbb{S}_{ep}$ is denoted as $\alpha_p^{ep} \in [0, 1]$. The mapping $\phi_f(\cdot)$ is defined as

$$\phi_f(\alpha) \triangleq 1 - (1 - f)^\alpha \qquad (1)$$

and is parametrized by a quantity $f \in (0, 1]$ called the *active slots coefficient* [12].

Finally, the threshold $T_p^{ep}$ is determined as

$$T_p^{ep} = 2^{\ell_{VRF}} \phi_f(\alpha_p^{ep}), \qquad (2)$$

where $\ell_{VRF}$ denotes the output length of the VRF (in bits).

Note that by (2), a party with relative stake $\alpha \in (0,1]$ becomes a slot leader in a particular slot with probability $\phi_f(\alpha)$, independently of all other parties. We clearly have $\phi_f(1) = f$, hence $f$ is the probability that a hypothetical party controlling all 100% of the stake would be elected leader for a particular slot. Furthermore, the function $\phi$ has an important property called "independent aggregation" [12]:

$$1 - \phi \left( \sum_i \alpha_i \right) = \prod_i (1 - \phi(\alpha_i)). \tag{3}$$

In particular, when leadership is determined according to $\phi_f$, the probability of a stakeholder becoming a slot leader in a particular slot is independent of whether this stakeholder acts as a single party in the protocol, or splits its stake among several "virtual" parties.

The technical code of the staking procedure is not given here due to space constraints. Briefly, it starts by two calls evaluating the VRF in two different points, using constants NONCE and TEST to provide domain separation, and receiving $(y_\rho, \pi_\rho)$ and $(y, \pi)$, respectively. The value $y$ is used to evaluate slot leadership: if $y < T_p^{\mathrm{ep}}$ then the party is a slot leader and continues by processing its current transaction buffer to form a new block $B$. Aside of this application data, each block contains control information. The information includes the proof of leadership $(y, \pi)$, additional VRF-output $(y_\rho, \pi_\rho)$ that influences the epoch-randomness for the next epoch, and the block signature $\sigma$ produced using $\mathcal{F}_{\mathrm{KES}}$. Finally, an updated blockchain $\mathcal{C}_{\mathrm{loc}}$ containing the new block $B$ is multicast over the network (note that in practice, the protocol would only diffuse the new block $B$). A slot leader embeds a sequence of valid transactions into a block. As in [3], we abstract block formation and transaction validity into predicates $\mathsf{blockify}_{\mathrm{OC}}$ and $\mathsf{ValidTx}_{\mathrm{OC}}$. The function $\mathsf{blockify}_{\mathrm{OC}}$ takes as input a plain sequence of transactions and outputs a block, whereas $\mathsf{ValidTx}_{\mathrm{OC}}$ takes as input a single transaction and the ledger state. A transaction is said to be valid with respect to the ledger state if and only if it fulfills the predicate. The transaction validity predicate $\mathsf{ValidTx}_{\mathrm{OC}}$ induces a natural transaction validity on blockchain-states that we succinctly denote by the predicate $\mathsf{isvalidstate}(\mathsf{st})$ that decides that a state is valid if it can be constructed sequentially by adding one transaction at a time and viewing the already added transactions as part of the state.

**Eligibility to Emit Synchronization Beacons.** An alert party emits so-called *synchronization beacons* in the first $R/6$ slots of an epoch ep. To be admissible to emit a beacon, the party evaluates the VRF again as for slot-leadership. To obtain an independent evaluation, we use a new constant called SYNC to obtain domain separation. If the returned value $y \leq T_{\mathsf{P}}^{\mathrm{ep,bc}}$, where in this case we can simply use a linear scaling of the domain, i.e., we define the threshold

$$T_p^{\mathrm{ep,bc}} := 2^{\ell_{\mathrm{VRF}}} \cdot \alpha_p^{\mathrm{ep}}, \tag{4}$$

then the party will create a block header and send it on the broadcast network.

**Embedding Synchronization Beacons in Blocks.** Part of the staking procedure is to embed synchronization beacons in the first $2R/3$ slots of an epoch ep.

A synchronization beacon is embedded if the creator of the beacon was elected to emit a beacon (according to the current stake distribution in epoch ep) in the first $R/6$ slots of this epoch, and if no other beacon in the chain already specifies the same slot and party identifiers. Like this, an alert party is assured to produce a valid chain. Validity is decided according to a predicate whose description appears as part of the protocol's code in the full version [4].

**Details of the Synchronization Process.** At the end of an epoch, parties run the synchronization procedure based on the beacons recorded in this epoch. The entire synchronization can be logically partitioned into seven logical building blocks. The first five items are definitions and necessary preparatory tasks in order to have the synchronization procedure perform its tasks at the end of an epoch.

1.) *Synchronization* slots: Once a party's local time-stamp reaches a defined synchronization slot for the first time, it will adjust its local time-stamp before moving to the next slot. The protocol will specify the necessary actions for the cases where the local time-stamp is shifted forward or backward. We define the synchronization slots to be the slots with numbers $i \cdot R$ for $i \geq 1$ and hence they coincide with the end of an epoch. In a real-word execution (which is a random experiment with discrete steps), we say that a party P *has passed its synchronization slot* $i \cdot R$ (e.g., at step $x$ of the experiment) if it has already concluded its operations in a round where P.localTime $= i \cdot R$ holds for the first time.

2.) *Synchronization Beacons:* In addition to the other messages, the parties in Chronos generate synchronization messages or "beacons" as follows: an alert party P evaluates the VRF functionality by sending the input (EvalProve, sid, $\eta_j \parallel$ P.localTime $\parallel$ SYNC) to $\mathcal{F}_{\mathsf{VRF}}$ in order to receive the response (Evaluated, sid, $y, \pi$). The beacon message is then defined as

$$\mathsf{SB} \triangleq (\mathsf{P.localTime}, \mathsf{P}, y, \pi),$$

where P.localTime is the current slot number party P reports and the triple $(\mathsf{P}, y_\rho, \pi)$ is the usual attestation of slot leadership by party (or stakeholder) P. In the following, let slotnum($\cdot$) be the function that returns the first element (the reported slot number) of a beacon.

3.) *Arrival times bookkeeping:* Every party P maintains an array P. Timestamp$_{SB}(\cdot)$ that assigns to each synchronization beacon SB a pair $(n, \mathsf{flag}) \in \mathbb{N} \times \{\mathsf{final}, \mathsf{temp}\}$. Assume a beacon SB with slotnum(SB) $\in [j \cdot R + 1, \ldots, j \cdot R + R/6]$, $j \in \mathbb{N}$ and party P' is fetched by party P (for the first time). If the pair (slotnum(SB), P') is new, the recorded arrival time is defined as follows:

  - If P has already passed synchronization slot $j \cdot R$ but not yet passed synchronization slot $(j+1) \cdot R$, Timestamp$_{SB}$(SB) is defined as the current slot number and the value is considered final, i.e., Timestamp$_{SB}$(SB) $\triangleq$ (P.localTime, final).

- If party P has not yet passed synchronization slot $j \cdot R$ (and thus the beacon belongs logically to this party's next epoch), $\mathsf{Timestamp}_{SB}(\mathsf{SB})$ is defined as the current slot number $\mathsf{P.localTime}$ and the decision is marked as temporary, i.e., $\mathsf{Timestamp}_{SB}(\mathsf{SB}) \triangleq (\mathsf{P.localTime}, \mathsf{temp})$. This value will be adjusted once this party adjusts its local time-stamp for the next epoch (when arriving at the next synchronization slot $j \cdot R$). If a party has already received a beacon for the same slot and creator, it will set the arrival time equal to the first one received among those.

4.) *The synchronization interval*: the interval based on which the adjustment of the local time-stamp is computed. For a synchronization slot $i \cdot R$ ($i \geq 1$), its associated synchronization interval is the interval $I_{\mathrm{sync}}(i) \triangleq [(i-1) \cdot R + 1, \ldots (i-1) \cdot R + R/6]$ and hence encompasses the first sixth of the epoch that is now ending.

5.) *Emitting Beacons and inclusion into the chain*: An alert party sends out a synchronization beacon during a synchronization interval (i.e., if the current local time reports a slot number that falls into a synchronization interval) if and only if the VRF evaluation $(\mathsf{EvalProve}, \mathsf{sid}, \eta_j \parallel \mathsf{P.localTime} \parallel \mathsf{SYNC})$ to $\mathcal{F}_{\mathsf{VRF}}$ returned $(\mathsf{Evaluated}, \mathsf{sid}, y, \pi)$ with $y < T_{\mathsf{P}}^{\mathrm{ep}}$ where $T_{\mathsf{P}}^{\mathrm{ep,bc}}$ is the beacon threshold in the current epoch as defined in Eq. 4. An alert slot leader $\mathsf{P}'$ on the other hand will include any valid synchronization beacon in its new block as long as $\mathsf{P}'.\mathsf{localTime}$ reports a slot number within the first two-thirds of an epoch (and if the beacon has not been included yet). This process is part of the main staking procedure and was describe in the previous paragraph.

The remaining three steps are implemented as part of the core synchronization procedure SyncProc.

6.) *Computing the adjustment evidence:* The adjustment will be computed based on evidence from the set $\mathcal{S}_i^{\mathsf{P}}$ that is defined with respect to the current view of P in the execution: Let $\mathcal{S}_i^{\mathsf{P}}$ contain all beacons SB that report a slot number $\mathsf{slotnum}(\mathsf{SB}) \in [(i-1) \cdot R + 1, \ldots, (i-1) \cdot R + R/6]$ (of the synchronization interval) and which are included in a block $B$ of $\mathsf{P}.\mathcal{C}_{\mathsf{loc}}$ that reports a slot number $\mathsf{slotnum}(B) \leq (i-1) \cdot R + 2R/3$. Based on these beacons and their recorded arrival times, the shift will be computed. More precisely, if a beacon SB is recorded in $\mathsf{P}.\mathcal{C}_{\mathsf{loc}}$, then the arrival time used in the computation will be based on a the valid[11] beacon $\mathsf{SB}'$ that reports the same slot number and party identity as SB and which has arrived first— either as part of some blockchain block or as a standalone message. By our choice of parameters, parties will have assigned an arrival value to any such beacon with overwhelming probability.

7.) *Adjusting the local clock:* The shift $\mathsf{shift}_i^{\mathsf{P}}$ a party P computes to adjust its clock in synchronization slot $i \cdot R$ is defined by

$$\mathsf{shift}_i^{\mathsf{P}} \triangleq \mathsf{med}\left\{\mathsf{slotnum}(\mathsf{SB}) - \mathsf{Timestamp}(\mathsf{SB}) \mid \mathsf{SB} \in \mathcal{S}_i^{\mathsf{P}}\right\}.$$

---

[11] Evaluated using this epoch's stake distribution.

Recall that Timestamp(SB) is shorthand for the first element of the pair Timestamp$_{SB}$(SB). As we will show, this adjustment ensures that the local time stamps of alert parties report values in a sufficiently narrow interval (depending on the network delay) to provide all protocol properties we need. Furthermore, for each beacon SB with P.Timestamp$_{SB}$(SB) $= (a, \text{temp})$ and slot number slotnum(SB) $> i \cdot R$ the arrival time is adjusted by P.Timestamp$_{SB}$(SB) $\triangleq (a + \text{shift}_i^P, \text{final})$. This ensures that eventually the arrival times of all beacons that logically belong to epoch $i + 1$ will be expressed in terms of the newly adjusted local time-stamp computed at synchronization slot $i \cdot R$. At this point, the party is further capable of excluding invalid beacons.

8.) At the beginning of the next round the party will report a local time equal to $i \cdot R + \text{shift} + 1$. If shift $\geq 0$, the party proceeds by emulating its actions for shift rounds. If shift $< 0$, the party remains a silent observer (recording arrival times for example) until its local time has advanced to slot $i \cdot R + 1$ and resumes normally at that round. Note that in this time, an alert party will not revert any previously reported ledger state with overwhelming probability. The reason is that the party will stick to $\mathcal{C}_{\text{loc}}$ during this waiting time and only replace it by longer chains that do not fork by more than $k$ blocks from $\mathcal{C}_{\text{loc}}$ which is a direct consequence of the security guarantees implied by the Genesis chain-selection rule. (An alert party reverting a previously reported state implies a common-prefix violation.)

## 4.2    (Re)Joining Procedures

**De-Registration and Re-Joining.** If a party is alert, it can lose in several ways its status of being alert. If a party loses access to the random oracle only, then it will still be able to observe the protocol execution and record message arrivals. The main issue is that such a party—when it is fully operational again—will have to retrace what it missed. This is slightly complicated due to the adjustments to the local clock in the course of the execution. However, the party has all reliable information to actually retrace the actions as if it was present as a passive observer all the time. This special procedure SimulateClockAdjustments is given in the full version of this work [4] and it is invoked as part of the main round tasks before performing the actions as an alert party (again).

On the other hand, if any alert party loses access to $\mathcal{G}_{\text{IMPERFLCLOCK}}$ or $\mathcal{F}_{\text{N-MC}}$ by the respective de-registration queries, or if it joins anew only late in the execution, then it considers itself as de-synchronized. Parties are aware of their synchronization status, and any party that is de-synchronized will have to run through the main joining procedure that we call JoinProc in order to become alert. Due to lack of space, we cannot provide the code of this procedure and refer to [4]. Below we give an overview of this procedure.

**Description of JoinProc.** Introducing synchronization slots into the protocol serves the main purpose of enabling a novel joining procedure that newly joining (or resynchronizing) parties can execute to bootstrap an actual reliable time-stamp and ledger state, where a reliable time-stamp is one that lies in the interval of time stamps reported by alert parties. The joining procedure is divided into several phases where the party gathers reliable information, identifies a good synchronization interval and finally applies the shift(s) that will allow it to report a local time-stamp that is sufficiently close to the alert parties in the system. The procedure refers to a couple of parameters. Their concrete values is not necessary to understand its dynamics.

**Phase A:** A joining party with all resources available invokes the main round procedure triggering the join procedure that first resets the local variables.

**Phase B:** In the second activation upon a MAINTAIN-*ledger* command, the party will jump to phase B and continue to do so until and including round $t_{off}$. During this interval, the party applies the Genesis chain selection rule maxvalid-bg to filter its incoming chains. It will apply the chain selection rule to all valid chains it receives. Since the party does not have reliable time, it will consider also future chains as valid, as long as they satisfy all remaining validity predicates. As we prove in the security analysis, at the end of this phase, the party adopts chain $\mathcal{C}$ that stands in a particularly useful relation to any chain $\mathcal{C}'$ an alert party adopts. Roughly, the relation says that the point at which the two chains fork is about $k$ blocks behind the tip of $\mathcal{C}'$. This follows from the Genesis chain selection rule and the fact that $\mathcal{C}'$ is more dense than $\mathcal{C}$ shortly after the fork. However, this also means that P could still hold an extremely long chain served by the adversary (namely, an adversarial extension of an alert party's chain at some point less than $k$ blocks behind the tip into the future). On the positive side, the stake distribution used for general validation of blocks and beacons logically associated to the time before the fork are reliable.

**Phase C:** If a party arrives at local time $t_{off} + 1$, it starts with phase C, the gathering phase. The party still filters chains as before, but now processes the arrival times of beacons from the network (or indirectly via the received chains). This phase is parameterized by two quantities: the sum of $t_{minSync}$ and $t_{stable}$ define the total duration of this round, where intuitively, $t_{minSync}$ guarantees that enough arrival times are recorded to compute a reliable estimate of the time-shift, and $t_{stable}$ ensures that the blockchain reaches agreement on which (valid) synchronization beacons to use. After this phase, a party can reliably judge valid arrival times.

**Phase D:** The party collects the valid evidence and computes the adjustment based on the first synchronization interval $I = [(i-1)R, \ldots, (i-1)R + R/6]$ identified on the blockchain that reports beacons that arrived sufficiently later than the start of phase C (parameter $t_{pre}$). Party P computes the adjustment value that alert parties would do at synchronization slot $i \cdot R$ based on the recorded beacon arrival times associated with interval $I$. The party P is done if its adjusted time does not indicate that it should have passed another synchronization slot (and otherwise, the above is repeated with adjusted arrival times of already recorded beacons).

# 5  Security Analysis

We begin by setting down notation and defining the conventions we adopt for measuring stake ratios. The following definition is adapted from [3]; the crucial difference is that it refers to the types of parties with respect to a *logical slot* as defined in Sect. 3.1.

**Definition 1 (Classes of parties and their relative stake).** *Let $\mathcal{P}[\mathtt{sl}]$ denote the set of all parties in a logical slot $\mathtt{sl}$ and let $\mathcal{P}_{type}[\mathtt{sl}]$, for any type of party described in Fig. 1 (e.g. alert, active), denote the set of all parties of the respective type in the slot $\mathtt{sl}$. For a set of parties $\mathcal{P}_{type}[\mathtt{sl}]$, let $\mathcal{S}^{-}(\mathcal{P}_{type}[\mathtt{sl}]) \in [0,1]$ (resp. $\mathcal{S}^{+}(\mathcal{P}_{type}[\mathtt{sl}]) \in [0,1]$) denote the minimum (resp., maximum), taken over the views of all alert parties, of the total relative stake of all the parties in $\mathcal{P}_{type}[\mathtt{sl}]$ in the stake distribution used for sampling the slot leaders for slot $\mathtt{sl}$.*

Looking ahead, we remark that even though we give the general definition above, our protocol will have the desirable property that for all party types and all time slots, $\mathcal{S}^{-}(\mathcal{P}_{\mathsf{type}}[\mathtt{sl}]) = \mathcal{S}^{+}(\mathcal{P}_{\mathsf{type}}[\mathtt{sl}])$ with overwhelming probability, as all the alert parties will agree on the distribution used for sampling slot leaders with overwhelming probability.

**Definition 2 (Alert ratio, participating ratio).** *For any logical slot $\mathtt{sl}$ during the execution, we let: (i.) the* alert stake ratio *be the fraction of stake $\mathcal{S}^{-}(\mathcal{P}_{alert}[\mathtt{sl}])/\mathcal{S}^{+}(\mathcal{P}_{active}[\mathtt{sl}])$; and (ii.) the (potentially)* participating stake *ratio be $\mathcal{S}^{-}(\mathcal{P}_{active}[\mathtt{sl}])$.*

It is instructive to see that the potentially participating stake ratio allows us to infer the ratio of stake belonging to parties that cannot participate in slot $\mathtt{sl}$. Intuitively speaking, we will prove the security of our protocol under the assumption that both stake ratios from Definition 2 are sufficiently lower-bounded (the former one by $1/2 + \varepsilon$, the latter one by a constant). We remark that it is easy to verify that in particular, such an assumption also implies the existence of alert parties at any point in the execution.

## 5.1  Blockchain Security Properties

We now define the standard security properties of blockchain protocols: *common prefix*, *chain growth* and *chain quality*. These will later be useful as an intermediate step in establishing the UC-security guarantees.

Similarly to [3], we only grant these guarantees to *alert* parties. More importantly for this work, the definitions from [3] need to be adjusted to take into account the fact that the local clocks of the parties are not synchronized. To this end, we choose now to define the properties below with respect to the *logical* timestamps (i.e., slot numbers) contained in blocks, and the local clocks of the parties. Namely, we refer to logical slots below, and a party is considered to *be on the onset* of slot $\mathtt{sl}$ (or *enter* slot $\mathtt{sl}$) if her local clock just switched to $\mathtt{sl}$.

**Common Prefix (CP); with parameters** $k \in \mathbb{N}$. The chains $\mathcal{C}_1, \mathcal{C}_2$ possessed by two alert parties at the onset of the slots $\mathtt{sl}_1 < \mathtt{sl}_2$ are such that $\mathcal{C}_1^{\lceil k} \preceq \mathcal{C}_2$, where $\mathcal{C}_1^{\lceil k}$ denotes the chain obtained by removing the last $k$ blocks from $\mathcal{C}_1$, and $\preceq$ denotes the prefix relation.

**Chain Growth (CG); with parameters** $\tau \in (0,1], s \in \mathbb{N}$. Consider a chain $\mathcal{C}$ possessed by an alert party at the onset of a slot $\mathtt{sl}$. Let $\mathtt{sl}_1$ and $\mathtt{sl}_2$ be two previous slots for which $\mathtt{sl}_1 + s \le \mathtt{sl}_2 \le \mathtt{sl}$, so $\mathtt{sl}_2$ is at least $s$ slots ahead of $\mathtt{sl}_1$. Then $|\mathcal{C}[\mathtt{sl}_1 : \mathtt{sl}_2]| \ge \tau \cdot s$. We call $\tau$ the *speed coefficient*.

**Chain Quality (CQ); with parameters** $\mu \in (0,1]$ **and** $k \in \mathbb{N}$. Consider any portion of length at least $k$ of the chain possessed by an alert party at the onset of a slot; the ratio of blocks originating from alert parties is at least $\mu$. We call $\mu$ the chain quality coefficient.

**Existential Chain Quality ($\exists$CQ); with parameter** $s \in \mathbb{N}$. Consider a chain $\mathcal{C}$ possessed by an alert party at the onset of a slot $\mathtt{sl}$. Let $\mathtt{sl}_1$ and $\mathtt{sl}_2$ be two previous slots for which $\mathtt{sl}_1 + s \le \mathtt{sl}_2 \le \mathtt{sl}$. Then $\mathcal{C}[\mathtt{sl}_1 : \mathtt{sl}_2]$ contains at least one alertly generated block (i.e., block generated by an alert party).

The first 3 properties are standard, the last one is a slight variant of chain quality fitting better our analysis. For brevity we sometimes write $\mathsf{CP}(k)$ (resp., $\mathsf{CG}(\tau, s)$, $\mathsf{CQ}(\mu, k)$, $\exists\mathsf{CQ}(s)$) to refer to these properties.

While these definitions based on the logical time allow us to talk about the logical structure of the forks created by the parties and reuse parts of the technical machinery given in [3,12,23] to analyze it, providing only guarantees based on the logical time would be unsatisfactory, as the parties running Chronos desire persistence and liveness with respect to a more "real-time" notion (that we define in a moment). We will address this translation from logical-time to real-time guarantees later in Sect. 5.2.

For many of the security arguments it will be convenient to define a notion of *nominal time*; even though inaccessible to alert parties, we will use it in the proofs to express time-relevant properties of an execution.

**Definition 3 (Nominal Time).** *Given an execution of Chronos, any prefix of the execution can be mapped deterministically to an integer $t$, which we call nominal time, as follows: parsing the prefix from genesis and keeping track of the honest party set registered with the imperfect clock functionality (bootstrapped with the set of inaugural alert parties), $t$ is the number of times the functionality internally switches all flags $d_\mathsf{P}, \mathsf{P} \in \mathcal{P}$ from 1 to 0 until the final step of the execution prefix. (In case no honest party exists in the execution $t$ is undefined).*

Nominal time is a technical definition useful for the analysis. It naturally coincides with the idea of defining a baseline that runs at a certain speed, but where parties have some varying (but bounded) lead ahead of the baseline. For example, if a set of alert parties execute Chronos from the beginning, then nominal time lower bounds the *number* of rounds completed by any of them. Furthermore, by the bounded (absolute) drift enforced by $\mathcal{G}_{\mathrm{IMPERFLCLOCK}}^{\Delta_{\mathrm{clock}}}$, the number of locally completed rounds by these alert parties can each be decomposed to be $t + \delta$ (nominal) rounds, where $t$ is the baseline, and $\delta$ is bounded by $\Delta_{\mathrm{clock}}$.

We next state a definition that will help us quantify how much parties' (local) timestamps deviate from the nominal time and from each other.

**Definition 4. (Clock skew and $Skew_\Delta$).** *Given an honest party* P, *we define its skew in slot* sl *(denoted $Skew^P[sl]$) as the difference between* sl *and the nominal time t when* P *enters slot* sl. *For any $\Delta \geq 0$ and a slot* sl, *we denote by $Skew_\Delta[sl]$ the predicate that for all parties that are synchronized in slot* sl, *their skew in this slot differs by at most $\Delta$; formally*

$$Skew_\Delta[sl] :\Leftrightarrow \left( \forall P_1, P_2 \in \mathcal{P}_{alert}[sl] : \left| Skew^{P_1}[sl] - Skew^{P_2}[sl] \right| \leq \Delta \right).$$

Note that in the static-registration setting (where parties do not join or leave), all honest parties are synchronized (and hence are considered for $Skew_\Delta[sl]$).

**Definition 5 (Joining party).** *We say that an honest party* P *is joining the protocol execution at time $t_{join} > 0$ if $t_{join}$ is the nominal time at the point of the execution where* P *becomes operational, time-aware and online for the first time.*

### 5.2  Proving the Blockchain Properties

We phrase here the asymptotic version of our main result, its concrete-security variant is proven in the full version [4].

**Theorem 2.** *Consider an execution of the protocol* Chronos *in the dynamic-availability setting and let $\kappa$ denote a security parameter. Let $f$ be the active-slot coefficient and $R$ the epoch length, let $\Delta$ be the upper bound on the sum of the maximum network delay and maximum local clock drifts, and let $\widetilde{\Delta} \triangleq 2\Delta$. Let $\alpha, \beta \in [0,1]$ denote a lower bound on the alert and participating stake ratios throughout the whole execution, respectively. Assume that for some $\epsilon \in (0,1)$ we have*

$$\alpha \cdot (1 - f)^{\widetilde{\Delta}+1} \geq (1 + \epsilon)/2,$$

*and that the* maxvalid-bg *parameters, $k$ and $s$, satisfy*

$$k > 192\widetilde{\Delta}/(\epsilon\beta) \quad \text{and} \quad R/6 \geq s = k/(4f) \geq 48\widetilde{\Delta}/(\epsilon\beta f).$$

*Then, all blockchain properties $CP(k')$, $CG(\tau, s')$, $CQ(\mu, k')$, $\exists CQ(s')$ (for concrete coefficients $\tau$ and $\mu$ defined in the proof) hold except with negligible probability in $\kappa$ whenever $s'$ and $k'$ as well as the chain-selection parameters $k$ and $s$ of* maxvalid-bg *are functions in $\omega(\log \kappa)$.*

Note that the bound on $s$ implies that the epoch length $R$ has a lower bound in $\omega(\log \kappa)$ in such an asymptotic treatment.

**Outline of the Proof.** We only give a brief overview of the proof and refer to the full version of this work [4]. To handle the proof complexity, the proof is divided into a sequence of logical steps:

1. A proof that the blockchain properties CP, CG, CQ, and ∃CQ hold in a static registration setting (where parties do not join or leave) and for a single epoch. In view of an inductive proof, this serves as the security base case.
2. Once we can rely on the blockchain properties, we can as a second step analyze the synchronization procedure and prove that no matter what the adversary does, the parties will always stay close together when transitioning from one epoch, say $i$ where the security properties hold, to the next and that the clock-adjustments are very small. Two properties are important:

   SyncProc **maintains** Skew$_\Delta$. If (some parametrizations of) CG and CP are not violated up to the end of epoch $i$, then Skew$_\Delta$ is satisfied in the first slot of epoch $i + 1$.

   **Bounded** shift. If the lower bound on $\alpha$, some parametrization of ∃CQ, and Skew$_\Delta$ are not violated up to epoch $i$, then the value shift by which an alert party updates its local clock in SyncProc right before epoch $i + 1$ satisfies $|\text{shift}| \leq 2\Delta$.

   Here we only briefly comment on the proof of the first property, which relies on two intermediate claims: The first is that all alert parties use the same set of synchronization beacons in their execution of the procedure SyncProc between epochs ep and ep + 1; the second is that for any fixed beacon SB $\in \mathcal{S}_j^{P_1} = \mathcal{S}_j^{P_2}$ (in the $j$th synchronization slot), the quantity $\mu(P_i, \text{SB}) \triangleq \text{Skew}^{P_i}[\text{sl}] + \text{slotnum}(\text{SB}) - P_i.\text{Timestamp}(\text{SB})$ will differ by at most $\Delta$ between any two alert parties $P_1$ and $P_2$.
3. By an inductive argument, if we start with a bounded-skew initial epoch (which is guaranteed by the weak start agreement), the above two steps allow us to conclude the security of the (multi-epoch) blockchain protocol, but without parties joining.
4. A party joining the network acts like an observer of the network (i.e., it does not interfere with the protocol) and becomes synchronized after extracting enough information from the network, at which point it can start to be an active protocol participant. This step of the security proof can hence be conducted based on the previous analysis. Our analysis shows two properties of the joining process of $P_{\text{join}}$ that hold as long as the established properties CP, CG, ∃CQ remain satisfied throughout the joining process:
   (a) After Phase B, $P_{\text{join}}$ will be holding a chain $\mathcal{C}_{\text{join}}$ that satisfies $\mathcal{C}_{\text{alert}}^{\lceil k} \preceq \mathcal{C}_{\text{join}}$ with respect to any $\mathcal{C}_{\text{alert}}$ held by an alert party at least $\Delta$ time steps ago.
   (b) In Phase D, $P_{\text{join}}$ correctly identifies an epoch $i^*$ for which it has collected all the beacons that alert parties had used in their execution of SyncProc after epoch $i^*$, and based on these beacons mimics the synchronization procedure so that starting with epoch $i^* + 1$, $P_{\text{join}}$ does not violate Skew$_\Delta$ as it becomes alert.
5. At this point, we are ready to derive the CP, CG, CQ, and ∃CQ guarantees for the entire protocol in a fully dynamic world, where parties join any time, might be temporarily stalled, and disappear unannounced. This can be argued based on a case distinction on different party types (cf. Sect. 3.1) and quantify their impact on the security guarantees established above. This concludes the proof.

**From Logical-Time to Real-Time Guarantees for Chain Growth.** Recall that eventually, we are interested in a ledger that provides consistency and liveness and they typically follow black-box from the blockchain properties above. However, since in our protocol, parties emulate a global time themselves, we must make related logical time advancement with the nominal time, which is especially important for liveness. Since parties adjust their timestamps at the boundary of every epoch, an external observer that takes nominal time as the baseline, would conclude that parties are slightly off. To quantify the general relationship, we introduce a concrete discount factor $\tau_{\text{TG}}$. We state the informal lemma here, which is proven with a concrete expression for $\tau_{\text{TG}}$ in the full version [4].

**Lemma 1 (Nominal vs. logical time, informal).** *Consider an execution of the full protocol Chronos in the dynamic-availability setting, let P be a party that is synchronized between (and including) slots $\mathsf{sl}$ and $\mathsf{sl}'$, let $t$ and $t'$ be the nominal times when P enters slot $\mathsf{sl}$ and $\mathsf{sl}'$ for the first time, respectively. Denote by $\delta\mathsf{sl}$ and $\delta t$ the respective differences $|\mathsf{sl}' - \mathsf{sl}|$ and $|t' - t|$. Then, under the same assumptions as before, we have $\delta\mathsf{sl} \geq \tau_{\text{TG}} \cdot \delta t$ for large enough $\delta t$.*

It is important to point out that the $\tau_{\text{TG}}$ is close to 1 for typical parameter choices and that the lower bound on $\delta t$ does depend on $\Delta$ and not on the security parameter. We are ready to state chain-growth with respect to nominal time. Again, the formal statement with concrete bounds is given in the full version [4].

**Corollary 1 (Nominal time CG, informal).** *Consider the event that the execution of Chronos under the assumptions as above does not violate property CG with parameters $\tau \in (0,1], s \in \mathbb{N}$. Let $\tau_{\text{CG,glob}} \triangleq \tau \cdot \tau_{\text{TG}}$. Consider a chain $\mathcal{C}$ possessed by an alert party at a point in the execution where the party is at an onset of a (local) round and where the nominal time is $t$. Let further $t_1, t_2$, and $\delta t$ be such that $t_1 + \delta t \leq t_2 \leq t$. Let $\mathsf{sl}_1$ and $\mathsf{sl}_2$ be the last slot numbers that P reported in the execution when nominal time was $t_1$ (resp. $t_2$) Then it must hold that $|\mathcal{C}[\mathsf{sl}_1 : \mathsf{sl}_2]| \geq \tau_{\text{CG,glob}} \cdot \delta t$ whenever $\delta t$ is sufficiently large.*

## 6   The Synchronizer

We now explore the properties of the time-stamps that are recorded by our blockchain protocol and how to export a clock based on them. Recall that in the view of each party P, blocks feature *extended* local timestamps $\mathsf{time_P}$, equal to the pair $\mathsf{time_P} = (e, t)$, where $t$ is the time-value, and $e$ is the number of non-monotone adjustments to $t$, i.e., the number of epoch switches that P has observed (and hence the synchronization procedure was executed). The following lemma (proven in the full version [4]) captures the properties of these timestamps.

**Lemma 2 (Quality of Exported Time-Stamps).** *Consider an execution of the full protocol Chronos in the dynamic-availability setting, let P be a party* and let the sequence $(e_1, t_1), \ldots, (e_n, t_n)$ denote the updates that P makes to its exported time-stamp between two arbitrary instances in the execution where in between P is synchronized throughout. Then the timestamps satisfy the following properties:

1. No reported time stamp $t_i$ is further than $2\Delta$ slots apart from any other alert party's time value and no other alert party reports an e-value that differs by more than 1. If another alert party reports the same e-value, then the exported times are at most $\Delta$ apart.
2. Any subsequence of the same epoch $(e, t_j), \ldots, (e, t_k)$, $k > j$ has monotone increasing time-stamps with increments of 1 happening whenever P locally completes a round in the execution.
3. The only non-monotone behavior of the exported time can occur at most once per epoch, namely at the epoch boundary $(e, t) \rightarrow (e+1, t')$ with $t \mod R = 0$, and it holds $t' \leq t + \Delta$ and $t' \geq t - 2\Delta$.

Having established this final piece, we can couple it with the statements above, notably with Theorem 2—which guarantees that we have achieved a blockchain protocol in the dynamic availability setting with all required properties—which overall assures that we have a protocol that outputs reliable, accurate two-dimensional time-stamps in the dynamic availability setting: any party and any observer is able to compute a reliable time-stamp, no matter when he or she joined or started observing the system.

**Proof of Theorem 1 [The synchronizer].** Theorem 1 follows as a simple corollary of the above. In fact, we just need to map the above 2D time-stamps to the natural numbers: an alert party, obtaining sequences of (2-dimensional) time-stamps from the underlying protocol over the course of an execution, say $E = (e_1, t_1), \ldots, (e_n, t_n)$, simply maps this to an integer by the map $\tau_i \leftarrow \max_{j \in [i]}\{t_j\}$. This integer time-stamp satisfies the abstract properties 1. to 4. demanded by Theorem 1. Clearly, the outputs are natural numbers, then by property 1. of Lemma 2 we obtain the bound between time-stamps of $2\Delta$, and by combining properties 2. and 3. of Lemma 2, the third and fourth properties of Theorem 1 follow, i.e., the final sequence of time values are non-decreasing and guaranteed to increase after a constant number of local rounds have elapsed (since the underlying 2D timestamps never roll back more than $2\Delta$ in the second coordinate).

In the full version of this paper [4], we additionally give a UC proof of the protocol that follows in a straightforward way from the above properties. The protocol UC-realizes a functionality that combines a ledger with a clock. We analyze in a modular way further settings, including optimistic network models with known expectation and variance of delay to show that it is possible to approximate real-time progression extremely accurately.

# References

1. Andrychowicz, M., Dziembowski, S.: PoW-based distributed cryptography with no trusted setup. In: Gennaro, R., Robshaw, M. (eds.) CRYPTO 2015. LNCS,

vol. 9216, pp. 379–399. Springer, Heidelberg (2015). https://doi.org/10.1007/978-3-662-48000-7_19

2. Attiya, H., Herzberg, A., Rajsbaum, S.: Optimal clock synchronization under different delay assumptions (preliminary version). In: Anderson, J., Toueg, S. (eds.) 12th ACM PODC, pp. 109–120. ACM, August 1993

3. Badertscher, C., Gaži, P., Kiayias, A., Russell, A., Zikas, V.: Ouroboros genesis: composable proof-of-stake blockchains with dynamic availability. In: Lie, D., Mannan, M., Backes, M., Wang, X. (eds.) ACM CCS 2018, pp. 913–930. ACM Press, October 2018

4. Badertscher, C., Gaži, P., Kiayias, A., Russell, A., Zikas, V.: Ouroboros chronos: permissionless clock synchronization via proof-of-stake. Cryptology ePrint Archive, Report 2019/838 (2019). https://eprint.iacr.org/2019/838

5. Badertscher, C., Maurer, U., Tschudi, D., Zikas, V.: Bitcoin as a transaction ledger: a composable treatment. In: Katz, J., Shacham, H. (eds.) CRYPTO 2017. LNCS, vol. 10401, pp. 324–356. Springer, Cham (2017). https://doi.org/10.1007/978-3-319-63688-7_11

6. Beimel, A., Ishai, Y., Kushilevitz, E.: Ad hoc PSM protocols: secure computation without coordination. In: Coron, J.-S., Nielsen, J.B. (eds.) EUROCRYPT 2017. LNCS, vol. 10212, pp. 580–608. Springer, Cham (2017). https://doi.org/10.1007/978-3-319-56617-7_20

7. Bracha, G.: An asynchronous $[(n-1)/3]$-resilient consensus protocol. In: Probert, R.L., Lynch, N.A., Santoro, N. (eds.) 3rd ACM PODC, pp. 154–162. ACM, August 1984

8. Canetti, R.: Universally composable security: a new paradigm for cryptographic protocols. In: 42nd FOCS, pp. 136–145. IEEE Computer Society Press, October 2001

9. Canetti, R., Dodis, Y., Pass, R., Walfish, S.: Universally composable security with global setup. In: Vadhan, S.P. (ed.) TCC 2007. LNCS, vol. 4392, pp. 61–85. Springer, Heidelberg (2007). https://doi.org/10.1007/978-3-540-70936-7_4

10. Chen, J., Micali, S.: Algorand: a secure and efficient distributed ledger. Theor. Comput. Sci. **777**, 155–183 (2019)

11. Daian, P., Pass, R., Shi, E.: Snow White: robustly reconfigurable consensus and applications to provably secure proof of stake. In: Goldberg, I., Moore, T. (eds.) FC 2019. LNCS, vol. 11598, pp. 23–41. Springer, Cham (2019). https://doi.org/10.1007/978-3-030-32101-7_2

12. David, B., Gaži, P., Kiayias, A., Russell, A.: Ouroboros praos: an adaptively-secure, semi-synchronous proof-of-stake blockchain. In: Nielsen, J.B., Rijmen, V. (eds.) EUROCRYPT 2018. LNCS, vol. 10821, pp. 66–98. Springer, Cham (2018). https://doi.org/10.1007/978-3-319-78375-8_3

13. Dolev, D., Halpern, J.Y., Strong, H.R.: On the possibility and impossibility of achieving clock synchronization. In: 16th ACM STOC, pp. 504–511. ACM Press (1984)

14. Dolev, S., Welch, J.L.: Wait-free clock synchronization (extended abstract). In: Anderson, J., Toueg, S. (eds.) 12th ACM PODC, pp. 97–108. ACM, August 1993

15. Dolev, S., Welch, J.L.: Self-stabilizing clock synchronization in the presence of byzantine faults (abstract). In: Anderson, J.H. (ed.) 14th ACM PODC, p. 256. ACM, August 1995

16. Feige, U., Kilian, J., Naor, M.: A minimal model for secure computation (extended abstract). In: 26th ACM STOC, pp. 554–563. ACM Press, May 1994

17. Garay, J., Kiayias, A., Leonardos, N.: The bitcoin backbone protocol: analysis and applications. In: Oswald, E., Fischlin, M. (eds.) EUROCRYPT 2015. LNCS, vol. 9057, pp. 281–310. Springer, Heidelberg (2015). https://doi.org/10.1007/978-3-662-46803-6_10

18. Garay, J.A., Kiayias, A., Leonardos, N.: The bitcoin backbone protocol with chains of variable difficulty. Cryptology ePrint Archive, Report 2016/1048 (2016). http://eprint.iacr.org/2016/1048

19. Halpern, J.Y., Simons, B.H., Strong, R., Dolev, D.: Fault-tolerant clock synchronization. In: Probert, R.L., Lynch, N.A., Santoro, N. (eds.) 3rd ACM PODC, pp. 89–102. ACM, August 1984

20. Ishai, Y., Kushilevitz, E.: Private simultaneous messages protocols with applications. In: ISTCS 1997, pp. 174–184. IEEE Computer Society (1997)

21. Kalai, Y.T., Lindell, Y., Prabhakaran, M.: Concurrent composition of secure protocols in the timing model. J. Cryptol. **20**(4), 431–492 (2007)

22. Katz, J., Maurer, U., Tackmann, B., Zikas, V.: Universally composable synchronous computation. In: Sahai, A. (ed.) TCC 2013. LNCS, vol. 7785, pp. 477–498. Springer, Heidelberg (2013). https://doi.org/10.1007/978-3-642-36594-2_27

23. Kiayias, A., Russell, A., David, B., Oliynykov, R.: Ouroboros: a provably secure proof-of-stake blockchain protocol. In: Katz, J., Shacham, H. (eds.) CRYPTO 2017. LNCS, vol. 10401, pp. 357–388. Springer, Cham (2017). https://doi.org/10.1007/978-3-319-63688-7_12

24. Lamport, L., Melliar-Smith, P.M.: Byzantine clock synchronization. In: Probert, R.L., Lynch, N.A., Santoro, N. (eds.) 3rd ACM PODC, pp. 68–74. ACM, August 1984

25. Lenzen, C., Locher, T., Wattenhofer, R.: Clock synchronization with bounded global and local skew. In: 49th FOCS, pp. 509–518. IEEE Computer Society Press, October 2008

26. Malhotra, A., Van Gundy, M., Varia, M., Kennedy, H., Gardner, J., Goldberg, S.: The security of NTP's datagram protocol. In: Kiayias, A. (ed.) FC 2017. LNCS, vol. 10322, pp. 405–423. Springer, Cham (2017). https://doi.org/10.1007/978-3-319-70972-7_23

27. Mills, D.L.: Computer Network Time Synchronization: The Network Time Protocol on Earth and in Space, 2nd edn. CRC Press, Boca Raton (2010)

28. Ostrovsky, R., Patt-Shamir, B.: Optimal and efficient clock synchronization under drifting clocks. In: Coan, B.A., Welch, J.L. (eds.) 18th ACM PODC, pp. 3–12. ACM, May 1999

29. Pass, R., Seeman, L., Shelat, A.: Analysis of the blockchain protocol in asynchronous networks. In: Coron, J.-S., Nielsen, J.B. (eds.) EUROCRYPT 2017. LNCS, vol. 10211, pp. 643–673. Springer, Cham (2017). https://doi.org/10.1007/978-3-319-56614-6_22

30. Pass, R., Shi, E.: Rethinking large-scale consensus. In: 30th IEEE Computer Security Foundations Symposium, CSF 2017, Santa Barbara, CA, USA, 21–25 August 2017, pp. 115–129. IEEE Computer Society (2017)

31. Pass, R., Shi, E.: The sleepy model of consensus. In: Takagi, T., Peyrin, T. (eds.) ASIACRYPT 2017. LNCS, vol. 10625, pp. 380–409. Springer, Cham (2017). https://doi.org/10.1007/978-3-319-70697-9_14

32. Simons, B.: An overview of clock synchronization. In: Simons, B., Spector, A. (eds.) Fault-Tolerant Distributed Computing. LNCS, vol. 448, pp. 84–96. Springer, New York (1990). https://doi.org/10.1007/BFb0042327

33. Srikanth, T.K., Toueg, S.: Optimal clock synchronization. In: Malcolm, M.A., Strong, H.R. (eds.) 4th ACM PODC, pp. 71–86. ACM, August 1985

# TARDIS: A Foundation of Time-Lock Puzzles in UC

Carsten Baum[1](✉), Bernardo David[2], Rafael Dowsley[3], Jesper Buus Nielsen[1],
and Sabine Oechsner[1]

[1] Aarhus University, Aarhus, Denmark
cbaum@cs.au.dk
[2] IT University of Copenhagen, Copenhagen, Denmark
[3] Monash University, Melbourne, Australia

**Abstract.** Time-based primitives like time-lock puzzles (TLP) are finding widespread use in practical protocols, partially due to the surge of
interest in the blockchain space where TLPs and related primitives are
perceived to solve many problems. Unfortunately, the security claims
are often shaky or plainly wrong since these primitives are used under
composition. One reason is that TLPs are inherently not UC secure and
time is tricky to model and use in the UC model. On the other hand, just
specifying standalone notions of the intended task, left alone correctly
using standalone notions like non-malleable TLPs only, might be hard
or impossible for the given task. And even when possible a standalone
secure primitive is harder to apply securely in practice afterwards as its
behavior under composition is unclear. The ideal solution would be a
model of TLPs in the UC framework to allow simple modular proofs. In
this paper we provide a foundation for proving composable security of
practical protocols using time-lock puzzles and related timed primitives
in the UC model. We construct UC-secure TLPs based on random oracles and show that using random oracles is *necessary*. In order to prove
security, we provide a simple and abstract way to reason about time in
UC protocols. Finally, we demonstrate the usefulness of this foundation
by constructing applications that are interesting in their own right, such
as UC-secure two-party computation with output-independent abort.

C. Baum—This work was funded by the European Research Council (ERC) under
the European Unions' Horizon 2020 research and innovation programme under grant
agreement No. 669255 (MPCPRO).

B. David—This work was supported by the Concordium Foundation, by Protocol Labs
grant S²LEDGE and by the Independent Research Fund Denmark with grants number
9040-00399B (TrA²C) and number 9131-00075B (PUMA).

R. Dowsley—This work was partially done while Rafael Dowsley was with Bar-Ilan
University and was supported by the BIU Center for Research in Applied Cryptography
and Cyber Security in conjunction with the Israel National Cyber Bureau in the Prime
Minister's Office.

J. B. Nielsen—Partially funded by The Concordium Foundation; The Danish Independent Research Council under Grant-ID DFF-8021-00366B (BETHE); The Carlsberg
Foundation under the Semper Ardens Research Project CF18-112 (BCM).

S. Oechsner—Supported by the Danish Independent Research Council under Grant-ID
DFF-8021-00366B (BETHE).

A. Canteaut and F.-X. Standaert (Eds.): EUROCRYPT 2021, LNCS 12698, pp. 429–459, 2021.
https://doi.org/10.1007/978-3-030-77883-5_15

# 1 Introduction

The Universal Composability (UC) framework [18] is widely used for formally analyzing cryptographic protocols as it provides strong security guarantees that allow UC-secure protocols to be arbitrarily composed. This is a very useful property and enables the modular design of cryptographic protocols. However, the original UC framework is inherently asynchronous and does not support the notion of time. Katz et al. [35] introduced a clock functionality in order to define universally composable synchronous computation. Their clock functionality captures the essence of synchronized wall clocks that are available to all parties. This notion is particularly useful in reasoning about synchronous protocols in the UC framework, since the honest parties can use the clock to achieve synchronization.

However, many cryptographic protocols do not depend on concrete time provided by a wall clock, but just on the relative order of events, such as the arrival of messages or the completion of some computation. In particular, protocols in a semi-synchronous communication model (*e.g.* [5,24]) rely on the fact that there exists a finite (but unknown) upper bound for the delay in communication channels, without requiring that events (*e.g.* the arrival of a message) occur at a specific wall clock time (or even within a concrete delay) as long as they occur in a certain order. In this case, using a clock can make the design and security analysis of such protocols unnecessarily complicated.

Another important challenge lies in modeling sequential computation and computational delays in the UC framework. Since the environment may operate in many parallel sessions and activate parties arbitrarily, it obtains an unfair computational advantage in relation to the parties. For example, even if its computational power is constrained within a session, the environment can use multiple sessions to solve faster than a regular party a computational problem assumed to require at least a certain amount of computational steps (and thus time). This precludes the UC modeling and construction of primitives based on sequential computation and computational delays, such as time-lock puzzles [44].

## 1.1 Our Contributions

In this work, we introduce a new abstract notion of time in the UC framework that allows us to reason about communication channels with delays as well as delays induced by sequential computation. We demonstrate the power of our approach by introducing the first definition and construction of composable time-lock puzzles (TLPs) without resorting to clocks, which we use to obtain the first two-party computation protocol with output-independent abort. Finally, we establish that a programmable random oracle is necessary for obtaining UC-secure TLPs. Our contributions are summarized below:

- **Abstract Time in UC:** we put forth a novel abstract notion of time for the UC framework capturing relative event ordering without a clock.
- **Impossibility of UC-Secure TLPs without Programmable Random Oracles:** we prove that programmable random oracles are necessary

for constructing UC-secure TLPs, yielding a new separation between programmable and non-programmable random oracles.

- **First Composable Treatment of Time-Lock Puzzles (TLPs):** we introduce the first composable definition and construction of time-lock puzzles. Our construction uses a RO, as it must. However, it has a flavor of "graceful degradation": if the hash function is not modeled as a random oracle, our TLPs are still non-malleable, which is in some sense optimal without a RO.
- **First Two-Party Computation Protocol with Output Independent Abort:** we use TLPs to construct a UC-secure two-party computation protocol where the adversary cannot see the output before deciding to abort.

The incompatibility of time-lock puzzles and UC security is easy to explain. All that is needed is to recall that UC has straight-line simulation. Let $P = \mathsf{TLP}(x, T, t)$ be a timed commitment to $x$ which can be opened in time $T$ and is hiding for time $t < T$. Consider simultaneous message exchange. In the UC functionality Alice inputs $a$, Bob inputs $b$ and only then are both given $(a, b)$. Here is a toy protocol which does not work for many reasons. Alice and Bob each publish $P_A = \mathsf{TLP}(a, T, t)$ and $P_B = \mathsf{TLP}(b, T, t)$ and then open the puzzles or brute force them. Assume that Alice is supposed to send her puzzle first, and Bob is corrupted. In the security proof, the UC simulator needs to extract Bob's input $b$ in order to query the ideal functionality and learn $a$. However, the simulator needs to learn $P_B$ for that. $P_B$ though is only sent by Bob *after* seeing $P_A$. As a result, the simulator has to produce $P_A$ without knowing $a$. Rewinding is not allowed, so the simulator cannot go back and replace the puzzle $P_A$. The simulator had to put some $a'$ inside $P_A$ and is now committed to it. If $a$ is random then with noticeable probability $a' \neq a$. In UC these problems are typically handled by having trapdoors which allow to do equivocation. Had $P_A$ been a UC commitment we could have changed $a'$ to $a$ before opening. But $P_A$ is a TLP, so there is no way to cheat. The UC environment can simply take $P_A$ and brute-force it open. So the $a'$ is irrevocably committed to by $P_A$. A shorter way to explain the problem is as follows. In a UC simulation the simulator must for all puzzles it sends agree on what is inside at the point in time where they were sent. And the UC experiment will keep running as long as the environment wants, so it can allow itself time enough to open all puzzles eventually. Hence puzzles will not afford us the power of a UC commitment which can be equivocated. Unfortunately, equivocation is exactly the power needed for simulating time-lock puzzles in the UC framework for most interesting applications.

Although the above argument only shows that one particular protocol does not work, we show that the problem cannot be circumvented by any protocol even allowing setup like a CRS. Assuming a random oracle, however, one can cheat and use the random oracle to get equivocation. Note the if we model $H$ as a random oracle and send $\mathsf{TLP}(r), H(r) \oplus m$ in a simulation, we can reprogram $H$ at $r$ as long as $\mathsf{TLP}(r)$ is hiding $r$ such that $H$ was not queried at $r$. This is of course an unsatisfactory solution, but some comfort can be gained from the fact that we provably cannot do without such a cheat if we want UC security.

There is a clear need for a UC model of time-lock puzzles and other time-based primitives, since those are finding widespread use in complex scenarios like the widely distributed and concurrent blockchain setting, where there is no way around having composable security for the protocol building blocks. Many of the proposed uses are often relatively simple *a la* the above simultaneous message exchange example. However, the security statements are often provably wrong, as TLPs for instance cannot yield composable simultaneous message exchange. Reverting to non-composable game-based definitions of the intended tasks and using non-malleable TLPs for the standard model is in principle a solution, but the proofs are typically complicated and the protocols inefficient. We therefore introduce a foundation for practical TLP-based protocols using a UC model of TLPs that allows simple analysis of practical protocols. This model is motivated in the same vein as the random oracle model, which was also proposed as a basis for analysing efficient, practical protocols.

Clearly, when using TLPs we also need a notion of time. If a TLP that can be broken in an hour is received through a network, it should not be trusted to be hiding an hour later. That requires a notion of time (*e.g.* a clock). Often the reliance on time in practical protocols using TLPs if fairly light. In line with the motivation above, we therefore provide also a simple abstract notion of time.

The advantage of our new abstract notion of time for the UC framework is twofold: 1. it captures delays without explicitly referring to wall clock time and 2. it allows for modeling delays induced by sequential computation. This notion makes it possible to state protocols and security proofs in terms of the relative delays between events (*e.g.* the arrival of a message or completion of a computation) and the existence of large enough delays that ensure that these events occur in a certain order.

Building on this model, we introduce the first definition and construction of UC-secure time-lock puzzles. Our construction is based on the classical time-lock assumption of Rivest *et al.* [44] and uses a restricted programmable and observable global random oracle, which we prove to be *necessary*. As an application of our composable TLPs, we introduce the notion of two-party computation (2PC) with output independent abort (OIA) along with the first OIA-2PC protocol. This new security notion for secure computation guarantees that an adversary who aborts the execution cannot learn any information about the output *before* deciding to abort, only obtaining the output after this decision is made. Our new definition improves on the standard security notion with abort (realized by all known 2PC protocols), which allows for the adversary to decide whether to force the honest parties to abort without obtaining the output *after* learning the output itself. We argue that this new security notion is optimal, since fairness (*i.e.* ensuring all parties obtain the output if the adversary does so) for 2PC protocols is impossible [21].

## 1.2  Related Work

*Composition Frameworks with Time and Fairness.* Composition frameworks for cryptographic protocols (e.g. UC [18], constructive cryptography [39], the reactive simulatability (RSIM) framework [42]) provide strong security guarantees for protocols under concurrent composition. In all mentioned frameworks, communication is through inherently *asynchronous* channels. Several works have therefore studied general composition guarantees with *synchronous* communication by introducing a shared source of time or restricting adversarial scheduling. Modeling network timing assumptions such as bounded message delay and clock drift and the resulting concurrent composition guarantees for specific tasks was studied for zero-knowledge [25,29] and MPC [33]. In the context of composition frameworks, Backes et al. [4] model traffic-related timing attacks in GNUC [31] by allowing the adversary to measure the local time at which a message arrives. In this setting, each party has a local execution time, and the EXEC function of GNUC maps the local times into a global time. Backes et al. [3] studied fairness in the RSIM framework and achieve a composable notion of fairness by restricting the adversary model to fair schedulers who deliver any message after at most a polynomial number of steps.

The work that is most closely related to ours is that of Kiayias *et al.* [36], which points out limitations of the local clock functionality of Katz *et al.* [35] and adapts it to the Global UC (GUC) framework [19] to provide all parties with access to a global clock functionality for the purpose of synchronization. Their model requires all parties executing a (semi-)synchronous protocol to keep track of current global clock time and to actively query the global clock functionality in order to advance of time. In particular, even if their model is used to define semi-synchronous communication, it implies that all parties are kept synchronized and may learn how much time has elapsed since their last activation (*i.e.* by obtaining the current time from the global clock), which is a rather strong synchrony assumption. However, many protocols cast in this model do not crucially rely on obtaining concrete time stamps or determining concrete delays between party activations, as long as messages are guaranteed to be delivered within certain delays and in a certain order (*e.g.* as in [5]). This is exactly the kind of guarantees that our model captures without explicitly exposing time keeping to parties or requiring them to keep track of concrete time sources. By doing that, our model allows us to analyse many protocols cast in their model while significantly relaxing synchrony assumptions. Moreover, our model can be used to capture delays induced by sequential computation, which is not captured by the global clock model of Kiayias *et al.*.

Another work technically related to ours is the notion of resource-fairness for protocols in UC introduced by Garay *et al.* [28]. Resource fairness ensures that honest parties who invest a certain amount of resources (*e.g.* computational time) can always recover from an abort and obtain the protocol output in case the adversary causes an abort in such a way that it learns the output. In order to realize this notion, Garay *et al.* show a generic compiler based on a "time-line" construction and a secure computation functionality. Essentially, this time-line encodes a number of computational states into a programmable common reference, which parties use in order to commit to messages that can be recovered by another party who invests enough computational steps. This idea differs from our work in that it limits TLP delay a priori, since the maximum number of computational states used to ensure delay is fixed by the CRS. This crucial difference also forces the resource-fairness framework to modify the UC framework in such a way that environments, adversaries and simulators must have an a priori bounded running time. On the other hand, our modelling of computational time and TLPs does not make modifications or restrictions to the UC environment, as well as allowing us to define TLPs in a more natural way where there's no a priori bound to the TLP delay. In particular, this means that TLPs can be parameterized with any arbitrary delay and that honest parties are always able to solve a TLP, which also allows us to realize our notion of output independent abort in such a way that honest parties can always either retrieve the output of the computation or determine that the adversary has aborted (by solving the adversary's TLPs).

Another relation to [28] is that both papers circumvent the problem that TLPs are not UC simulatable. We do it using the simple hack of using a random oracle, to get a simple model to work with. In [28] it is done by letting the simulator depend on the running time of the environment.

As an example of how to exploit this consider a party that wants to commit to $s$. It secret shares it into $(s_1, \ldots, s_k)$ and makes public $P_1 = \mathsf{TLP}(s_1), \ldots, P_k = \mathsf{TLP}(s_k)$. The hardness of $P_i$ is set to $2^i$ and $k$ is the security parameter. So $P_k$ cannot be brute-forced open. For each $s_i$ it also gives a UC commitment to $s_i$ and a ZK proof that the commitment is to the value in the TLP. To do fair message exchange both Alice and Bob do the above with $s = a$ and $s = b$. Then the parties open the commitments (not the TLPs) to the shares in the order $s_k, s_{k-1}, \ldots$, taking turns to reveal a share. If a party stops opening commitments, then use the TLPs to learn the remaining shares, if the hardness of the remaining TLPs is feasible. Now in the simulation, if the running time of the environment is upper bounded to some polynomial $t$, then there exists $i_0 < k$ such that $2^{i_0} > t$. Now the simulator can put dummy shares $s_i'$ in $P_j$ for $j \geq i$. When it learns the message $a$ of Alice it can then adjust the UC commitments to be a secret sharing of $a$. It does not have to adjust the TLPs as the environment will not have time to open them. The fact that there is an "end of time" in the simulation allows to simulate some TLPs. On the other hand, the fact that there is an "end of time" in the simulation makes composition cumbersome. Indeed [28] gets a complicated notion of security where a protocol to be called secure must be secure in two ways. It must be secure in a so-called resource game, and it must also be so-called full simulation secure. This requires [28] to develop a new variant of the UC framework. This variant does not imply security in the normal UC model which does not have an "end of time".

It also seems hard to prove security of most practical protocols in [28]. The reason is that it seems hard to exploit the simulator's knowledge of the running time of the environment (which can be any polynomial) without using TLPs of super-polynomial running time, as in the above examples with TLPs of doubling hardness. This seems to make it hard to prove security of many simple and intuitively secure scheme like the first protocol above with two TLPs for simultaneous message exchange. Either these two TLPs have a hardness set such that real-world parties can brute-force them (and then so can the environment) or it is set so hard that the environment cannot brute-force them, then neither can the parties. In the first case the protocols falls prey to our impossibility result. In the later case the TLPs seems useless.

We find the techniques and models in our paper and [28] complementary. Our model is built on the normal (G)UC model without modifying it and is simple to specify and use. But needs a random oracle. The paper [28] shows that even without random oracles not everything is lost. It is possible to get models and some constructions with UC like security.

*Time-Lock Puzzles and Computational Delay.* The original construction of time-lock puzzles was proposed by Rivest, Shamir and Wagner [44]. Boneh and Naor [15] introduced the notion of timed commitments. An alternative construction of time-lock puzzles was presented by Bitansky et al. [13]. Recently, the related notion of verifiable delay functions has been investigated [14,43,48]. These constructions are closely related in that they rely on sequential computational tasks that force parties to spend a certain amount of time before they are able to obtain an output. However, none of these works have considered composability issues for such time-based primitives. In particular, the issues of malleability for these time-based primitives and the relationship between computational and communication delay are notably ignored in previous works. The lack of composabillity guarantees for time-lock puzzles is a significant shortcoming, since these primitives are mostly used as building blocks for more complex protocols and current constructions do not ensure that their security guarantees are retained when composed with other primitives to obtain such protocols. Our composable treatment of time-lock puzzles addresses theses issues by introducing constructions that can be arbitrarily composed along with a framework for analysing complex protocols whose security relies on the relative delays in computation and communication.

Concurrently to us, Katz et al. [34] as well as Ephraim et al. [26] have constructed Non-Malleable Timed Commitments. Among others, [23] have shown that UC (non-timed) Commitments imply Non-Malleable Commitments. A similar argument can be made for timed commitments as well. In that sense, our construction of UC-secure TLPs implies [26,34]. At the same time, our work crucially relies on a programmable Random Oracle (and indeed shows that it is necessary to achieve UC security). Neither [34] nor [26] require such strong assumptions and can be seen as realising the strongest notion of non-malleability achievable without using a (programmable) random oracle or similar assumption: the beautiful construction of [34] does not require any Random Oracle-type assumption and builds upon RSW-TLPs in the Algebraic Group Model, while [26] use an observable Random Oracle but their construction can be realized from a generic TLP. At the same time, [26] also constructs publicly verifiable TLPs departing from generic strong trapdoor VDFs. We'd like to stress that our construction of a UC-secure TLP is publicly verifiable, although this is only shown in recent follow-up work [7]. We further note that the work of [26] shows a bound on the composability of non-malleable TLPs, but their bound does not apply to our setting as they assume a distinguisher with an arbitrary runtime, while the UC environment is computationally restricted in our setting.

*Aborts and Fairness in Secure Computation.* An MPC protocol is said to be fair if a party can obtain the output if and only if all other parties also obtain the output. It is a well-known fact that fair MPC in the standard communication model is impossible with a dishonest majority [21]. Given the impossibility to achieve fairness, techniques for identifying misbehaving parties responsible for causing an abort have been investigated [9,10,32]. In the last few years a line of work developed which imposes financial penalties on parties who are identified as misbehaving by using cryptocurrencies and smart contracts, thus giving financial incentives for rational parties to behave in a fair way. Protocols have been designed to punish misbehavior at any point of the protocol execution (Fair Computation with Penalties) [2,36,38] or to only punish participants that learn the output but prevent others from doing the same (Fair Output Delivery with Penalties) [1,6,12,37]. However, these protocols allow the adversary to make a decision on whether to abort or not *after* seeing the output that will be obtained by the honest parties in case the execution proceeds.

The recent work of Couteau et al. [22] studies the problem of obtaining partially-fair exchange from time-lock puzzles, but in much weaker security and adversarial models. In particular, their work does not consider composability issues and is limited to the specific problem of fair exchange rather than the general problem of secure computation considered in our results.

*Random Oracle Separation Results.* Our impossibility result provides yet another separation between the programmable and non-programmable random oracle models, complementing the few previously known separations [11,27,40,47].

### 1.3  Our Techniques

In the remainder of this section, we briefly outline the new techniques behind our results and their implications.

*Abstract Time:* Our goal is to express different timing assumptions (possibly related) within the GUC framework in such a way that protocols are oblivious to them. We do so by providing the adversary with a way of advancing time in the form of *ticks*. A tick represents a discrete unit of time. Time can only be advanced, and moreover only one unit at a time. In contrast to Katz et al. [35,36], however, these ticks and thus the passing of time are not supposed to be directly visible to the protocol. Thus instead of a (global) clock that parties can ask for the current time, we add a ticking interface to ideal functionalities. This way, timing-related observable behavior becomes an assumption of the underlying functionalities, e.g. of a computational problem or a channel. Parties may now observe events triggered by elapsed time, but not the time itself. Ticked functionalities are free to interpret ticks in any way they like; this way we can synchronize and relate ticks representing elapsed time in different "units" like passed time or computation steps. The technical challenge is to ensure in a composable way that all honest parties have a chance at observing all relevant timing-related events. Katz et al. solved this issue inside the clock by keeping track of which parties have been activated in the current time period (and thus asked for the time) and refusing to advance time if necessary. We enforce the requirement that all honest parties must be activated between ticks by defining a global ticker functionality that makes sure this constraint is obeyed. In contrast to the global clock, our global ticker does not provide any information about the time elapsed between queries by functionalities, only informing functionalities that a new tick has occurred. From the point of view of honest parties, our global ticker is even more restricted, since it does not inform parties whether a tick has occurred or not. To further control the observable side effects of ticks, we restrict protocols and ideal functionalities to interact in the "pull model" known from Constructive Cryptography, precluding functionalities from implicitly providing communication channels between parties and instead requiring parties to actively query functionalities in order to obtain new messages. Apart from presenting a clear abstraction of time, this notion explicitly exposes issues that must be taken in consideration when implementing protocols that realize our functionalities, *i.e.* the concrete delays in real world communication channels and computation. In particular, while the theoretical protocol description and security analysis can be carried in terms of such abstract delays, our techniques clarify the relationship between concrete time-based parameters (*e.g.* timeouts vs. network delays) that must be respected in protocol implementations. We will go into this in more detail in Sect. 2.

*Composable Treatment of Time-Lock Puzzles:* To illustrate the potential uses of our framework, we present the first definition and construction of UC-secure Time-Lock Puzzles (TLP). We depart from the classical construction by Rivest et al. [44] and provide the first UC abstraction of the Time-Lock Assumption, which is modeled in a "generic group model" style, hiding the group description from the environment and limiting its access to group operations. A party acting as the "owner" of an instance of the TLP functionality can generate a puzzle containing a certain message that should be revealed after a certain number of computational steps. The functionality allows the parties to make progress on the solution of the puzzle every time that it is ticked. Once a party solves a puzzle, it can check that a certain message was contained in that puzzle. The ticks given to this functionality come externally from the adversary and we require in the framework that the parties get activated often enough. We show that our UC abstraction of the Time-Lock Assumption allows us to implement UC-secure TLPs in the restricted programmable and observable global random oracle model of Camenisch et al. [16] (which turns out to be necessary for UC-realizing TLPs). We introduce our notion of TLP in the UC model with a global ticker in Sect. 4 and our construction of a protocol realizing this notion in Sect. 5.

*Two-Party Computation with Output Independent Abort:* To further showcase our framework we construct the first protocol for secure two-party computation (2PC) with output-independent abort, i.e., the adversary must decide whether to abort or not before seeing the output. In order to do so, we build on techniques from [6]: there, the authors combine an MPC protocol with linearly secret-shared outputs and an additively homomorphic commitment by having each party commit to its share of the output and then reconstruct the output inside the commitments. In [6], the output of the secure computation is obtained by opening the final commitments resulting from the reconstruction procedure, which allows the adversary to learn the output before the honest parties do. He can then refuse to open its commitment, causing the protocol to abort, based on this information. Similarly to [6], we combine a 2PC protocol with secret-shared outputs and an additively homomorphic commitment, but we define and construct commitments with a new delayed opening interface. When a delayed opening happens, the receiver is notified after a communication delay but only receives the revealed message after an *opening delay*. Hence, we can obtain output independent abort by delayed opening the final commitments obtained after reconstructing the output and considering that a party aborts if it does not execute a delayed opening of their commitments before the other parties delayed openings reveal their messages. Finally, we show how to obtain UC-secure additively homomorphic commitments with delayed opening by modifying the scheme of Cascudo et al. [20] with the help of the delayed secure message transmission and TLP functionalities. We present these results in Sect. 6.

*Impossibility Result.* Finally, we prove that a non-programmable random oracle is not sufficient for obtaining UC-secure fair-coin flip, secure 2PC with output-independent abort or TLP. Therefore a programmable random oracle is necessary to implement these primitives, yielding a separation between the programmable and non-programmable random oracle models. This also shows that our TLP construction which requires this strong assumption is in that sense "optimal". We present this impossibility result in Sect. 7.

## 2   UC with Relative Time

This section describes our notion of abstract time. In order to obtain universal composability, we model our ideas on top of the GUC framework [19]. The goal is to capture time in such a way that parties are oblivious to it and can only observe the progression of time indirectly through events like the arrival of messages or the completion of a computation. At the same time, the passing of abstract time is completely under adversarial control. And most importantly, the notion is meant to be composable.

**Timing Assumptions.** Our first observation is that timing assumptions are assumptions about physical systems and should thus be captured at the level of ideal functionalities. Such a timed functionality has a notion of passing time and can adapt its behavior as time progresses. This will allow us to reduce properties of a protocol that require concrete timing assumptions. Note that the time is only a proof construct, it is not visible to the actual protocol, much like physical time. Most importantly, having a notion of passing time should not imply synchrony like in the UC clock models of [35,36].

---

**Functionality $\mathcal{G}_{\text{ticker}}$**

Initialize a set of registered parties $\mathcal{P} = \emptyset$, a set of registered functionalities $F = \emptyset$, a set of activated parties $L_P = \emptyset$, and a set of functionalities $L_F = \emptyset$ that have been informed about the current tick. $\mathcal{G}_{\text{ticker}}$ communicates with an adversary $\mathcal{S}$.

**Party registration:** Upon receiving (register, pid) from honest party $\mathcal{P}_i$ with pid pid, add pid to $\mathcal{P}$ and send (registered) to $\mathcal{P}_i$.

**Functionality registration:** Upon receiving (register) from $\mathcal{F}$, add $\mathcal{F}$ to $F$ and send (registered) to $\mathcal{F}$.

**Tick:** Upon receiving (tick) from the environment, do the following:
1. If $\mathcal{P} = L_P$, reset $L_P = \emptyset$ and $L_F = \emptyset$, and send (ticked) to $\mathcal{S}$.
2. Else, send (notticked) to the environment.

**Ticked request:** Upon receiving (ticked?) from $\mathcal{F} \in F$, do the following:
- If $\mathcal{F} \notin L_F$, add $\mathcal{F}$ to $L_F$ and send (ticked) to $\mathcal{F}$.
- If $\mathcal{F} \in L_F$, send (notticked) to $\mathcal{F}$.

**Record party activation:** Upon receiving (activated) from party $\mathcal{P}_i$ with pid pid $\in \mathcal{P}$, add pid to $L_P$ and send (recorded) to $\mathcal{P}_i$.

---

**Fig. 1.** Global ticker functionality $\mathcal{G}_{\text{ticker}}$.

**Global Ticker Functionality $\mathcal{G}_{\text{ticker}}$ (Fig. 1).** This idea leads to natural questions. Where does this "time" come from? And if there are multiple timed functionalities, how is it coordinated between them to support the kind of reductions we want? The first question can be answered by the well-known concept of adversarial "ticks" that model discrete units of passing time. To answer the second question, we propose a global ticker functionality $\mathcal{G}_{\text{ticker}}$ that receives ticks from the environment and makes them available for ticked functionalities upon request. Parties themselves have no access to the ticker.

Note that $\mathcal{G}_{\text{ticker}}$ captures an assumption on the physical world and can therefore not be instantiated. It is only a tool for proofs. Similar to the synchronous setting with a global clock where the next logical round can only start after all parties have been activated, the global ticker implicitly enforces that all honest parties can finish their computations for the current tick before advancing to the next tick. This ensures all honest parties are activated and given a chance to perform computation without the need to modify the (G)UC framework. Notice that, while the assumption of a global time is a poor model of reality, we do not envision our model being used for protocols running in relativistic conditions.

While $\mathcal{G}_{\text{ticker}}$ allows the ideal adversary to take actions as soon as every tick happens, it gives no information about passing time to the honest parties. The only interaction that honest parties have with $\mathcal{G}_{\text{ticker}}$ is in confirming that they have been activated. A new tick only happens once all honest parties confirm they have been activated after the last tick. This mechanism ensures that the environment or the adversary do not get an unfair advantage in accessing timed functionalities while preventing the honest parties from also doing so (since in this case the honest parties will not confirm they have been activated and time will not progress).

Only other functionalities (and the ideal adversary) can detect elapsed time by querying $\mathcal{G}_{\text{ticker}}$ and receiving a notification in case a new tick happened. In our model, functionalities take actions such as delivering a message or the output of a computation once a new tick happens. Hence, honest parties only perceive time through messages received by other functionalities that have their behavior conditioned on the progression of time. In particular, if one wants to instantiate synchronized clocks from $\mathcal{G}_{\text{ticker}}$, it would be possible to instantiate a version of the UC clocks of [35,36] where the clock only progresses when a new tick is issued by $\mathcal{G}_{\text{ticker}}$. With such a construction, parties can access the number of ticks issued up to a certain point of the execution by querying the clock functionality (but not $\mathcal{G}_{\text{ticker}}$). Note that in this setting, honest parties need to query the clock functionality regularly to ensure that the clock can in turn query $\mathcal{G}_{\text{ticker}}$ for ticks.

**Conventions.** For the sake of readability, we will omit the calls of ideal functionalities to $\mathcal{G}_{\text{ticker}}$ which would in the worst case have to occur at every activation. Functionalities are instead assumed to query $\mathcal{G}_{\text{ticker}}$ with (tick?) whenever they are activated, and the behavior upon a positive answer is described as **Tick** in the ideal functionality description.

## 3   Communication Delay

In the context of communication, we interpret abstract time ticks in order to model message transmission delays. That is, we model the fact that message transmission is never instantaneous and thus takes time. Moreover, we model the different synchrony assumptions for communication channels in current literature. As a concrete example, we will study the secure message transmission functionality $\mathcal{F}_{\text{smt}}^{\ell}$. Any implementation of an interactive functionality must strictly speaking be in a $\mathcal{F}_{\text{smt}}^{\ell}$ (or similar) hybrid model and hence our modeling can be adapted to any interactive functionality. Notice that by interactive functionalities we mean any functionality that transmits information between parties, a task that is often done implicitly by UC ideal functionalities such as those for secure computation.

### 3.1   Secure Message Transmission with Delays

Secure message transmission (SMT) is the problem of securely sending a single message $m$ from a sender $\mathcal{P}_S$ to a receiver $\mathcal{P}_R$. Secure means that the power of an eavesdropper intercepting the channel is restricted to learning some leakage $\ell(m)$ on the message and delaying the message delivery. The standard formulation of $\mathcal{F}_{\text{smt}}^{\ell}$ [17, 2019 version] assumes that message delivery can be delayed infinitely by an adversary. Here, we want to add an upper bound on the message delay. The exact constraints on this upper bound will determine whether a protocol operates over synchronous, semi-synchronous or asynchronous channels, as discussed further in Sect. 3.2.

In order to capture elapsed time according to our model, we add a **Tick** procedure to obtain a ticked ideal functionality. As mentioned in the previous

---

**Functionality $\mathcal{F}^{\Delta}_{\text{smt,delay}}$**

$\mathcal{F}^{\Delta}_{\text{smt,delay}}$ proceeds as follows, when parameterized by maximal delay $\Delta > 0$, sender $\mathcal{P}_S$, receiver $\mathcal{P}_R$ and adversary $\mathcal{S}$. Internal variable $t$ is initally set to 0, and flags msg, released, done to $\perp$.

**Send:** Upon receiving an input (Send, sid, $\mathcal{P}_R$, $m$) from party $\mathcal{P}_S$, do:
- If msg $= \perp$, record $m$, set msg $= \top$, and send (Sent, sid, $\mathcal{P}_R$, $\ell(m)$) to $\mathcal{S}$.
- If msg $= \top$, send (None, sid) to $\mathcal{P}_S$.

**Receive:** Upon receiving (Rec, sid, $R$) from $\mathcal{P}_R$, do:
- If released $= \perp$ and done $= \perp$, then send (None, sid) to $\mathcal{P}_R$.
- If released $= \top$ and done $= \perp$, then msg $= \top$ as well and there exists a recorded message $m$. Set done $= \top$ and send (Sent, sid, $\mathcal{P}_S$, $\mathcal{P}_R$, $m$) to $\mathcal{P}_R$.
- If done $= \top$, then send (done, sid) to $\mathcal{P}_R$.

**Release message:** Upon receiving an input (ok, sid, $\mathcal{P}_S$, $\mathcal{P}_R$) from $\mathcal{S}$, do:
- If msg $= \perp$, then send (None, sid, $\mathcal{P}_S$, $\mathcal{P}_R$) to $\mathcal{S}$.
- If msg $= \top$ and released $= \perp$, then set released $= \top$.
- If released $= \top$, then send (None, sid, $\mathcal{P}_S$, $\mathcal{P}_R$) to $\mathcal{S}$.

**Tick:**
- If msg $= \perp$, then send (None, sid, $\mathcal{P}_S$, $\mathcal{P}_R$) to $\mathcal{S}$.
- If msg $= \top$ and released $= \perp$, then set $t = t + 1$. If now $t = \Delta$, set released $= \top$. Then send (Ticked, sid) to $\mathcal{S}$.
- If released $= \top$, then send (None, sid, $\mathcal{P}_S$, $\mathcal{P}_R$) to $\mathcal{S}$.

**Corrupt:** Upon receiving (Corrupt, sid, $\mathcal{P}$) from $\mathcal{S}$ where $\mathcal{P} \in \{\mathcal{P}_S, \mathcal{P}_R\}$, do:
- If $\mathcal{P} = \mathcal{P}_S$ and msg $= \perp$, send (None, sid, $\mathcal{P}_S$, $\mathcal{P}_R$) to $\mathcal{S}$.
- If $\mathcal{P} = \mathcal{P}_S$ and msg $= \top$, then there exists a recorded message $m$. Send (Sent, sid, $m$, $\mathcal{P}_S$, $\mathcal{P}_R$) to $\mathcal{S}$.
- If $\mathcal{P} = \mathcal{P}_R$ and done $= \perp$, send (None, sid, $\mathcal{P}_S$, $\mathcal{P}_R$) to $\mathcal{S}$.
- If $\mathcal{P} = \mathcal{P}_R$ and done $= \top$, then there exists a recorded message $m$. Send (Sent, sid, $m$, $\mathcal{P}_S$, $\mathcal{P}_R$) to $\mathcal{S}$.

---

**Fig. 2.** Ticked ideal functionality $\mathcal{F}^{\Delta}_{\text{smt,delay}}$ for secure message transmission with maximal message delay $\Delta$.

section, **Tick** is run upon each activation if $\mathcal{G}_{\text{ticker}}$ indicates that a new tick happened. The functionality is parameterized by a maximal delay $\Delta > 0$. Requiring $\Delta > 0$ models the fact that communication always takes time. After a message is input to the functionality by the sender, each tick will increase a counter. The message is released to the receiver after at most $\Delta$ ticks are counted or whenever the ideal adversary instructs the functionality to release it.[1] However, a tick cannot directly trigger the activation of parties other than the adversary. Otherwise, we would be exposing the elapsed time towards the parties and implicitly synchronizing them. As a consequence, the functionality cannot send the message to the receiver as in [17]. We solve this issue by requiring the receiver to actively

---

[1] The delay model could generalized even further by introducing two delay parameters $\Delta_{min}$ and $\Delta_{max}$ to model that communication *must* take time. In that case, messages are only forwarded after $\Delta_{min}$ ticks were received.

query the functionality for newly released messages. Finally, the adversary can adaptively request to corrupt a party $\mathcal{P} \in \{\mathcal{P}_S, \mathcal{P}_R\}$, in which case they will learn the message if the corresponding party knows it already. Note that this corruption behavior differs crucially from Canetti's formulation: Since message transmission is explicitly taking time, adaptive corruptions at runtime are actually meaningful now. In particular, it is no longer possible to first observe leakage on a sent message to then corrupt the sender and change the message that was sent. The resulting ideal functionality $\mathcal{F}_{\mathsf{smt,delay}}^{\Delta}$ is shown in Fig. 2.

In principle, one can transform a UC-functionality also by adding a wrapper that buffers messages and handles ticks. Due to the differences in handling adaptive corruption, we chose a standalone solution for this concrete example.

## 3.2  Modeling (Semi)-Synchronous Channels

Besides establishing that all messages must be delivered with a maximal delay $\Delta$, our formulation of $\mathcal{F}_{\mathsf{smt,delay}}^{\Delta}$ does not specify if it operates as a synchronous, semi-synchronous or asynchronous channel. This modeling choice is made so that this single model can capture all of these assumptions on communication synchrony by imposing constraints of the maximal delay $\Delta$. We obtain a channel satisfying each communication synchrony assumption by constraining $\Delta$ as follows:

- **Synchronous Channel, finite and publicly known $\Delta$:** a synchronous channel is modeled by setting a finite $\Delta > 0$ and allowing all parties to learn $\Delta$, which makes it possible for parties to determine if a given message was sent or not (since a message must be delivered within the known delay $\Delta$).
- **Semi-Synchronous Channel, finite but unknown $\Delta$:** a semi-synchronous channel is modeled by setting a finite $\Delta > 0$ that is only known to the adversary, which ensures parties that all messages will be eventually delivered but does not allow them to explicitly distinguish a delayed message from a dropped message (since they do not know the maximal delay $\Delta$ after which messages are guaranteed to be delivered).
- **Asynchronous Channel, infinite $\Delta$:** an asynchronous channel is modeled by setting $\Delta = \infty$, which allows the adversary to never release messages sent through $\mathcal{F}_{\mathsf{smt,delay}}^{\Delta}$ (*i.e.* essentially dropping these messages).

In the synchronous and asynchronous cases, the constraints on $\Delta$ simply model the usual notions of synchronous and asynchronous channels. In the semi-synchronous case, the constraints limit the way a protocol can use $\Delta$, since no information about it is given to honest parties, precluding them from setting other parameters of the protocol relatively to a previously known $\Delta$. We remark that $\Delta$ can potentially be chosen by the adversary itself or preset before execution starts, as long as the right constraints for the communication synchrony assumption considered in the proof are obeyed (*i.e.* in the synchronous case the adversarially chosen $\Delta$ must be made public to the honest parties and in the semi-synchronous case $\Delta$ is not revealed to the honest parties). Notice that the exact value of $\Delta$ does not affect the behavior of honest parties in our model because the honest parties cannot perceive the advance of abstract time (*i.e.* the honest parties cannot tell when a tick happened).

# 4    Modeling Time-Lock Puzzles and Computational Delay

We will now introduce a concept for modeling sequential computation inside the UC framework that does not suffer from degradation through composition or adversarially chosen activation of parties. As an example, we will realize the notion of a "time-lock puzzle" [44] in a composable fashion. In a time-lock puzzle (TLP), the owner generates a computational puzzle that outputs a message to the receiver when solved. The main property of the construction is that none of the solvers can obtain the message from the puzzle substantially faster than any other solvers, thus introducing problems that cannot be parallelized.

To the best of our knowledge, this has not been formalized in the UC framework before and there are multiple pitfalls that one has to avoid when formalizing TLPs. First, UC allows the environment to activate parties at its will throughout the session and it might be that an honest party does not even get activated before the puzzle was solved by the adversary. Even worse, such a modeling might permit that the environment can solve the puzzle in another session, so even by enforcing regular activation inside a session (as in the previous section) or equal computational powers between the iTM modeling the parties as well as the adversary one cannot achieve the aforementioned notion.

Ticked ideal functionalities help us to overcome both issues, and the resulting ticked time lock puzzle ideal functionality $\mathcal{F}_{\text{tlp}}$ is shown in Fig. 3. It can easily be seen that the functionality fulfills our definitions as outlined before. First, any new instance of a puzzle can be tied to a specific party, namely the owner $\mathcal{P}_o$, who can initialize the puzzle by providing a number of computation steps $\Gamma$ and a message $m$. The functionality outputs a puzzle $\text{puz} = (\text{st}_0, \Gamma, \text{tag})$ consisting of an initial state $\text{st}_0$, the number of steps $\Gamma$ needed for reaching a final state and tag $\text{tag}$ used to encode the message. After every tick, each party can use a puzzle state $\text{st}_i$ to call the **Solve** interface, which will append the next state $\text{st}_{i+1}$ to a list of messages delivered to the party after the next tick. By buffering messages containing the next states, we essentially limit all parties' (and the environment's and adversary's) ability to attempt performing more than one solving step per tick and puzzle. Notice that any party who tries to call **Solve** more than once per tick for a puzzle would have to guess the next state $\text{st}_{i+1}$ in order to perform the second call, which can only be done with negligible probability. Once the final state $\text{st}_\Gamma$ is reached, parties can call the **Get Message** interface in order to retrieve the message associated with the puzzle by presenting the puzzle $\text{puz}$ and the final state $\text{st}_\Gamma$ obtained through successive calls to **Solve**. Finally, $\mathcal{F}_{\text{tlp}}$ will at the beginning of any activation query $\mathcal{G}_{\text{ticker}}$ if a clock-tick happened and execute the Tick procedure if it indeed did. This will allow each party to obtain a new value, which may get it closer to the solution of the puzzle.

Observe that this model does neither restrict the actual computational power of the environment nor any other iTM. The environment can activate any party arbitrarily often, as long as the honest parties also occasionally can have the ability to access the restricted resource. Care must also be taken to allow limited ideal adversarial control over the functionality's answers to queries to **Solve**

---

Functionality $\mathcal{F}_{\text{tlp}}$

$\mathcal{F}_{\text{tlp}}$ is parameterized by a set of parties $\mathcal{P}$, an owner $\mathcal{P}_o \in \mathcal{P}$, a computational security parameter $\tau$, a state space $\mathcal{ST}$ and a tag space $\mathcal{TAG}$. In addition to $\mathcal{P}$ the functionality interacts with an adversary $\mathcal{S}$. $\mathcal{F}_{\text{tlp}}$ contains initially empty lists **steps** (honest puzzle states), **omsg** (output messages), **in** (inbox) and **out** (outbox).

**Create puzzle:** Upon receiving the first message $(\text{CreatePuzzle}, \text{sid}, \Gamma, m)$ from $\mathcal{P}_o$ where $\Gamma \in \mathbb{N}^+$ and $m \in \{0,1\}^\tau$, proceed as follows:

1. If $\mathcal{P}_o$ is honest, sample $\text{tag} \xleftarrow{\$} \mathcal{TAG}$ and $\Gamma + 1$ random distinct states $\text{st}_j \xleftarrow{\$} \{0,1\}^\tau$ for $j \in \{0, \dots, \Gamma\}$. If $\mathcal{P}_o$ is corrupted, let $\mathcal{S}$ provide values $\text{tag} \in \mathcal{TAG}$ and $\Gamma + 1$ distinct values $\text{st}_j \in \mathcal{ST}$.
2. Append $(\text{st}_0, \text{tag}, \text{st}_\Gamma, m)$ to **omsg**, append $(\text{st}_j, \text{st}_{j+1})$ to **steps** for $j \in \{0, \dots, \Gamma - 1\}$, and output $(\text{CreatedPuzzle}, \text{sid}, \text{puz} = (\text{st}_0, \Gamma, \text{tag}))$ to $\mathcal{P}_o$ and $\mathcal{S}$. $\mathcal{F}_{\text{tlp}}$ stops accepting messages of this form.

**Solve:** Upon receiving $(\text{Solve}, \text{sid}, \text{st})$ from party $\mathcal{P}_i \in \mathcal{P}$ with $\text{st} \in \mathcal{ST}$, if there exists $(\text{st}, \text{st}') \in \text{steps}$, append $(P_i, \text{st}, \text{st}')$ to **in** and ignore the next steps. If there is no $(\text{st}, \text{st}') \in \text{steps}$, proceed as follows:

- If $\mathcal{P}_o$ is honest, sample $\text{st}' \xleftarrow{\$} \mathcal{ST}$.
- If $\mathcal{P}_o$ is corrupted, send $(\text{Solve}, \text{sid}, \text{st})$ to $\mathcal{S}$ and wait for answer $(\text{Solve}, \text{sid}, \text{st}, \text{st}')$.

Append $(\text{st}, \text{st}')$ to **steps** and append $(P_i, \text{st}, \text{st}')$ to **in**.

**Get Message:** Upon receiving $(\text{GetMsg}, \text{sid}, \text{puz}, \text{st})$ from party $\mathcal{P}_i \in \mathcal{P}$ with $\text{st} \in \mathcal{ST}$, parse $\text{puz} = (\text{st}_0, \Gamma, \text{tag})$ and proceed as follows:

- If $\mathcal{P}_o$ is honest and there is no $(\text{st}_0, \text{tag}, \text{st}, m) \in \text{omsg}$, append $(\text{st}_0, \text{tag}, \text{st}, \bot)$ to **omsg**.
- If $\mathcal{P}_o$ is corrupted and there exists no $(\text{st}_0, \text{tag}, \text{st}, m) \in \text{omsg}$, send $(\text{GetMsg}, \text{sid}, \text{puz}, \text{st})$ to $\mathcal{S}$, wait for $\mathcal{S}$ to answer with $(\text{GetMsg}, \text{sid}, \text{puz}, \text{st}, m)$ and append $(\text{st}_0, \text{tag}, \text{st}, m)$ to **omsg**.

Get $(\text{st}_0, \text{tag}, \text{st}, m)$ from **omsg** and output $(\text{GetMsg}, \text{sid}, \text{st}_0, \text{tag}, \text{st}, m)$ to $\mathcal{P}_i$.

**Output:** Upon receiving $(\text{Output}, \text{sid})$ by $\mathcal{P}_i \in \mathcal{P}$, retrieve the set $L_i$ of all entries $(\mathcal{P}_i, \cdot, \cdot)$ in **out**, remove $L_i$ from **out** and output $(\text{Complete}, \text{sid}, L_i)$ to $\mathcal{P}_i$.

**Tick:** Set $\text{out} \leftarrow \text{in}$ and set $\text{in} = \emptyset$.

---

**Fig. 3.** Functionality $\mathcal{F}_{\text{tlp}}$ for time-lock puzzles.

containing undefined states and queries to **Get Message** containing undefined $(\text{puz}, \text{st})$ tuples. While the adversary is allowed to provide an arbitrary sequence of states $\text{st}_0, \dots, \text{st}_\Gamma$ and an arbitrary tag $\text{tag}$, the functionality enforces the fact that, once defined, the same sequence of steps will be deterministically obtained by all honest parties invoking **Solve**. However, queries to $\mathcal{F}_{\text{tlp}}$ involving undefined states and puzzles are answered with messages provided by the ideal adversary. This is necessary for capturing adversaries that construct different versions of a puzzle departing from different initial states of the original sequence $\text{st}_0, \dots, \text{st}_\Gamma$ or from an arbitrary state that eventually leads to this sequence.

# 5   Constructing Time-Lock Puzzles in UC

The functionality given in Fig. 3 from Sect. 4 describes how we ideally model a TLP in our framework. We will now instantiate $\mathcal{F}_{\mathsf{tlp}}$ departing from the well-known construction by Rivest et al. [44]. In order to obtain a UC-secure protocol, we will first model the assumption that underpins Rivest *et al.*'s construction under our notion of sequential computation with ticks. Moreover, we will resort to a global random oracle, which turns out to be *necessary* for UC-realizing $\mathcal{F}_{\mathsf{tlp}}$ as discussed later in this section.

The TLP construction of Rivest *et al.* [44] is based on the assumption that it is hard to compute successive squarings of an element of $(\mathbb{Z}/N\mathbb{Z})^{\times}$ (*i.e.* the group of primitive residues modulo $N$) with a large $N$ in less time than it takes to compute each of the squarings sequentially, unless the factorization of $N$ is known. In other words, for a random element $g \xleftarrow{\$} (\mathbb{Z}/N\mathbb{Z})^{\times}$ and a large $N$ whose factorization is unknown, this assumptions says that it is hard to compute $g^{2^{\Gamma}}$ in less time than it takes to compute $\Gamma$ sequential squarings $g^2, g^{2^2}, g^{2^3}, \ldots, g^{2^{\Gamma}}$. On the other hand, if $N = pq$ is generated following the key generation algorithm of the RSA cryptosystem, one obtains a trapdoor (*i.e.* the order of $(\mathbb{Z}/N\mathbb{Z})^{\times}$) $\phi(N) = (p-1)(q-1)$ that allows for fast computation of $g^{2^{\Gamma}}$ requiring two exponentiations: first compute $t = 2^{\Gamma} \mod \phi(N)$ and then $g^t$. Hence, a TLP encoding a message $m \in (\mathbb{Z}/N\mathbb{Z})^{\times}$ with a number of steps $\Gamma$ can be generated by a party who knows $N = pq, p, q$ by sampling a random $g \xleftarrow{\$} (\mathbb{Z}/N\mathbb{Z})^{\times}$, computing $t = 2^{\Gamma} \mod \phi(N)$, $g^{2^{\Gamma}} = g^t$ and $mg^{2^{\Gamma}}$, arriving at a puzzle $\mathsf{puz} = (g, \Gamma, mg^{2^{\Gamma}})$. From the assumption of Rivest *et al.*, it follows that any party must compute $\Gamma$ sequential squarings departing from $g$ in order to obtain $g^{2^{\Gamma}}$ and compute $m = mg^{2^{\Gamma}}g^{-2^{\Gamma}}$.

In employing Rivest *et al.*'s time-lock assumption to UC-realize $\mathcal{F}_{\mathsf{tlp}}$ we face an important challenge: even if the environment is computationally constrained in a session, it can use the representation of $(\mathbb{Z}/N\mathbb{Z})^{\times}$ (*i.e.* $N$) to compute all $\Gamma$ squarings needed to obtain $g^{2^{\Gamma}}$ from $g$ across multiple sessions. Hence, it would be impossible to construct a simulator for a protocol realizing $\mathcal{F}_{\mathsf{tlp}}$, since the environment would be able to immediately extract the message encoded in the puzzle. Notice that an environment that can immediately solve a TLP makes it impossible for the simulator to provide a TLP containing a random message and later equivocate the opening of this TLP so that it yields an arbitrary message obtained from $\mathcal{F}_{\mathsf{tlp}}$. In order to address this issue, we need to model this time-lock assumption using our notion of sequential computation with ticks, which will limit the environment's power for computing squarings of elements of $(\mathbb{Z}/N\mathbb{Z})^{\times}$.

## 5.1   Modeling Rivest *et al.*'s Time-Lock Assumption [44]

We describe in Fig. 4 an ideal functionality $\mathcal{F}_{\mathsf{rsw}}$ that captures the hardness assumption used by Rivest et al. [44] to build a time-lock puzzle protocol. This functionality essentially treats group $(\mathbb{Z}/N\mathbb{Z})^{\times}$ as in the generic group model [46]

---

### Functionality $\mathcal{F}_{\mathsf{rsw}}$

$\mathcal{F}_{\mathsf{rsw}}$ is parameterized by a set of parties $\mathcal{P}$, an owner $\mathcal{P}_o \in \mathcal{P}$, an adversary $\mathcal{S}$ and a computational security parameter $\tau$ and a parameter $N \in \mathbb{N}^+$. $\mathcal{F}_{\mathsf{rsw}}$ contains a map group which maps strings $\mathsf{el} \in \{0,1\}^\tau$ to $\mathbb{N}$ as well as maps in and out associating parties in $\mathcal{P}$ to a list of entries from $(\{0,1\}^\tau)^2$ or $(\{0,1\}^\tau)^3$. The functionality maintains the group of primitive residues modulo $N$ with order $\phi(N)$ denoted as $(\mathbb{Z}/N\mathbb{Z})^\times$.

**Create Group:** Upon receiving the first message $(\mathsf{Create}, \mathsf{sid})$ from $\mathcal{P}_o$:
1. If $\mathcal{P}_o$ is corrupted then wait for message $(\mathsf{Group}, \mathsf{sid}, N, \phi(N))$ from $\mathcal{S}$ with $N \in \mathbb{N}^+$, $N < 2^\tau$ and store $N, \phi(N)$.
2. If $\mathcal{P}_o$ is honest then sample two random distinct prime numbers $p, q$ of length approximately $\tau/2$ bits according to the RSA key generation procedure. Set $N = pq$ and $\phi(N) = (p-1)(q-1)$.
3. Set $\mathsf{td} = \phi(N)$ and output $(\mathsf{Created}, \mathsf{sid}, \mathsf{td})$ to $\mathcal{P}_o$.

**Random:** Upon receiving $(\mathsf{Rand}, \mathsf{sid}, \mathsf{td}')$ from $\mathcal{P}_i \in \mathcal{P}$, if $\mathsf{td}' \neq \mathsf{td}$, send $(\mathsf{Rand}, \mathsf{sid}, \mathsf{Invalid})$ to $\mathcal{P}_i$. Otherwise, sample $\mathsf{el} \xleftarrow{\$} \{0,1\}^\tau$ and $g \xleftarrow{\$} (\mathbb{Z}/N\mathbb{Z})^\times$, add $(\mathsf{el}, g)$ to group and output $(\mathsf{Rand}, \mathsf{sid}, \mathsf{el})$ to $\mathcal{P}_i$.

**GetElement:** Upon receiving $(\mathsf{GetElement}, \mathsf{sid}, \mathsf{td}', g)$ from $\mathcal{P}_i \in \mathcal{P}$, if $g \notin (\mathbb{Z}/N\mathbb{Z})^\times$ or $\mathsf{td}' \neq \mathsf{td}$, send $(\mathsf{GetElement}, \mathsf{sid}, \mathsf{td}', q, \mathsf{Invalid})$ to $\mathcal{P}_i$. Otherwise, if there exists an entry $(\mathsf{el}, g)$ in group then retrieve $\mathsf{el}$, else sample a random string $\mathsf{el}$ and add $(\mathsf{el}, g)$ to group. Output $(\mathsf{GetElement}, \mathsf{sid}, \mathsf{td}', g, \mathsf{el})$ to $\mathcal{P}_i$.

**Power:** Upon receiving $(\mathsf{Pow}, \mathsf{sid}, \mathsf{td}', \mathsf{el}, x)$ from $\mathcal{P}_i \in \mathcal{P}$ with $x \in \mathbb{Z}$, if $\mathsf{td}' \neq \mathsf{td}$ or there is no $a$ such that $(\mathsf{el}, a) \in$ group, output $(\mathsf{Pow}, \mathsf{sid}, \mathsf{td}', \mathsf{el}, x, \mathsf{Invalid})$ to $\mathcal{P}_i$. Otherwise, proceed:
1. Convert $x \in \mathbb{Q}$ into a representation $\bar{x} \in \mathbb{Z}_{\varphi(N)}$. If no such $\bar{x}$ exists in $\mathbb{Z}_{\varphi(N)}$ then output $(\mathsf{Pow}, \mathsf{sid}, \mathsf{td}', \mathsf{el}, x, \mathsf{Invalid})$ to $\mathcal{P}_i$.
2. Compute $y \leftarrow a^{\bar{x}} \bmod N$. If there is no $(\mathsf{el}', y) \in$ group then sample $\mathsf{el}' \xleftarrow{\$} \{0,1\}^\tau$ randomly but different from all group entries and add $(\mathsf{el}', y)$ to group.
3. Output $(\mathsf{Pow}, \mathsf{sid}, \mathsf{td}, \mathsf{el}, x, \mathsf{el}')$ to $\mathcal{P}_i$.

**Multiply:** Upon receiving $(\mathsf{Mult}, \mathsf{sid}, \mathsf{el}_1, \mathsf{el}_2)$ from $\mathcal{P}_i \in \mathcal{P}$:
1. If there are no $a, b$ s.t. $(\mathsf{el}_1, a), (\mathsf{el}_2, b) \in$ group, then output $(\mathsf{Invalid}, \mathsf{sid})$ to $\mathcal{P}_i$.
2. Compute $c \leftarrow ab \bmod N$. If there is no $(\mathsf{el}_3, c) \in$ group then sample $\mathsf{el}_3 \xleftarrow{\$} \{0,1\}^\tau$ randomly but different from all group entries and add $(\mathsf{el}_3, c)$ to group.
3. Add $(\mathcal{P}_i, (\mathsf{el}_1, \mathsf{el}_2, \mathsf{el}_3))$ to in and return $(\mathsf{Mult}, \mathsf{sid}, \mathsf{el}_1, \mathsf{el}_2)$ to $\mathcal{P}_i$.

**Invert:** Upon receiving $(\mathsf{Inv}, \mathsf{sid}, \mathsf{el})$ from some party $\mathcal{P}_i \in \mathcal{P}$:
1. If there is no $a$ such that $(\mathsf{el}, a) \in$ group then output $(\mathsf{Invalid}, \mathsf{sid})$ to $\mathcal{P}_i$.
2. Compute $y \leftarrow a^{-1} \bmod N$. If there is no $\mathsf{el}'$ s.t. $(\mathsf{el}', y) \in$ group, sample $\mathsf{el}' \xleftarrow{\$} \{0,1\}^\tau$ randomly but different from all group entries and add $(\mathsf{el}', y)$ to group.
3. Add $(\mathcal{P}_i, (\mathsf{el}, \mathsf{el}'))$ to in and return $(\mathsf{Inv}, \mathsf{sid}, \mathsf{el})$ to $\mathcal{P}_i$.

**Output:** Upon receiving $(\mathsf{Output}, \mathsf{sid})$ by $\mathcal{P}_i \in \mathcal{P}$, retrieve the set $L_i$ of all entries $(\mathcal{P}_i, \cdot)$ in out, remove $L_i$ from out and output $(\mathsf{Complete}, \mathsf{sid}, L_i)$ to $\mathcal{P}_i$.

**Tick:** Set out $\leftarrow$ in and in $= \emptyset$.

---

**Fig. 4.** Functionality $\mathcal{F}_{\mathsf{rsw}}$ capturing the time lock assumption of [44].

and only gives handles to the group elements to all parties. In order to perform operations, the parties then need to interact with the functionality. They can ask for any number of operations to be performed between two computational ticks. However, the outcome of the operation (*i.e.* the handle of the resulting group element) will only be released after the next computational tick occurs. However, a special owner party $\mathcal{P}_o$ who initializes $\mathcal{F}_{rsw}$ receives a trapdoor td that allows it to perform arbitrary operations on group elements. Upon learning td any party gains the power to perform arbitrary operations in $\mathcal{F}_{rsw}$ but parties who do not know td are restricted to sequential operations and have no information about the group representation. In particular, in case of an honestly generated group the order will remain completely hidden from the adversary. Finally, this functionality is treated as a global functionality in order to make sure that a simulator does not obtain an unreal advantage in computing the solution of a TLP without waiting for enough ticks.

We remark that our modeling of this time-lock assumption is corroborated by a recent result [45] showing that delay functions (such as TLPs) based on cyclic groups that do not exploit any particular property of the underlying group cannot be constructed if the order is known. It is clear that we cannot reveal any information about the group structure to the environment, since it could use this information across multiple sessions to solve TLPs quicker than the parties. Hence, in order to make it possible to UC-realize $\mathcal{F}_{tlp}$ based on cyclic groups (and in particular the time-lock assumption of Rivest et al. [44]), we must model the underlying group in such a way that both its structure and its order are hidden from the environment and the parties.

## 5.2  Realizing $\mathcal{F}_{tlp}$ in the $\mathcal{F}_{rsw}, \mathcal{G}_{rpoRO}$-Hybrid Model

Using Rivest *et al.*'s time-lock assumptions modeled in $\mathcal{F}_{rsw}$ following our sequential computation with ticks framework, we can instantiate Rivest *et al.*'s original time-lock puzzle without running into the issues described before. However, we now face different issues: 1. because all parties are forced by $\mathcal{F}_{rsw}$ to do sequential computation, a simulator for Rivest *et al.*'s construction would not be able to extract $m$ from $mg^{2^\Gamma}$; 2. because $\mathcal{F}_{rsw}$ deterministically assigns handles to each group element, a simulator would not be able to equivocate $mg^{2^\Gamma}$ in such a way that it yields an arbitrary message $m'$. In order to address these issues, we must resort to a random oracle. More specifically, we work in the restricted programmable and observable global random oracle model $\mathcal{G}_{rpoRO}$ of [16] (see the full version for the description). It turns out that a programmable random oracle is indeed necessary for UC-realizing $\mathcal{F}_{tlp}$, as it implies coin flipping with output independent abort as shown in Sect. 6, which is impossible without a programmable random oracle as shown in Sect. 7.

We present Protocol $\pi_{tlp}$ in Fig. 5. The main idea behind this protocol is to follow Rivest *et al.*'s construction to compute $\text{puz} = (\text{el}_0, \Gamma, \text{tag})$ while encoding the initial random group element $\text{el}_0$, the message $m$, the final group element $\text{el}_\Gamma$ and the trapdoor td for $\mathcal{F}_{rsw}$ in a tag generated with the help of the random

---

Protocol $\pi_{\mathsf{tlp}}$

Protocol $\pi_{\mathsf{tlp}}$ is parameterized by a security parameter $\tau$, a state space $\mathcal{ST} = \{0,1\}^{\tau}$ and a tag space $\mathcal{TAG} = \{0,1\}^{\tau} \times \{0,1\}^{\tau}$. $\pi_{\mathsf{tlp}}$ is executed by an owner $\mathcal{P}_o$ and a set of parties $\mathcal{P}$ interacting among themselves and with functionalities $\mathcal{F}_{\mathsf{rsw}}$, $\mathcal{G}_{\mathsf{rpoRO1}}$ (an instance of $\mathcal{G}_{\mathsf{rpoRO}}$ with domain $\{0,1\}^{2\tau}$ and output size $\{0,1\}^{2\tau}$) and $\mathcal{G}_{\mathsf{rpoRO2}}$ (an instance of $\mathcal{G}_{\mathsf{rpoRO}}$ with domain $\{0,1\}^{4\tau}$ and output size $\{0,1\}^{\tau}$).

**Create Puzzle:** Upon receiving input $(\mathsf{CreatePuzzle}, \mathsf{sid}, \varGamma, m)$ for $m \in \{0,1\}^{\tau}$, $\mathcal{P}_o$ proceeds as follows:
1. Send $(\mathsf{Create}, \mathsf{sid})$ to $\mathcal{F}_{\mathsf{rsw}}$ obtaining $(\mathsf{Created}, \mathsf{sid}, \mathsf{td})$.
2. Send $(\mathsf{Rand}, \mathsf{sid}, \mathsf{td})$ to $\mathcal{F}_{\mathsf{rsw}}$, obtaining $(\mathsf{Rand}, \mathsf{sid}, \mathsf{el}_0)$.
3. Send $(\mathsf{Pow}, \mathsf{sid}, \mathsf{td}, \mathsf{el}_0, 2^{\varGamma})$ to $\mathcal{F}_{\mathsf{rsw}}$, obtaining $(\mathsf{Pow}, \mathsf{sid}, \mathsf{td}, \mathsf{el}_0, 2^{\varGamma}, \mathsf{el}_{\varGamma})$.
4. Send $(\textsc{Hash-Query}, (\mathsf{el}_0|\mathsf{el}_{\varGamma}))$ to $\mathcal{G}_{\mathsf{rpoRO1}}$, obtaining $(\textsc{Hash-Confirm}, h_1)$.
5. Send $(\textsc{Hash-Query}, (h_1|m|\mathsf{td}))$ to $\mathcal{G}_{\mathsf{rpoRO2}}$, obtaining $(\textsc{Hash-Confirm}, h_2)$.
6. Compute $\mathsf{tag}_1 = h_1 \oplus (m|\mathsf{td})$ and $\mathsf{tag}_2 = h_2$, set $\mathsf{tag} = (\mathsf{tag}_1, \mathsf{tag}_2)$ and output $(\mathsf{CreatedPuzzle}, \mathsf{sid}, \mathsf{puz} = (\mathsf{el}_0, \varGamma, \mathsf{tag}))$ to $\mathcal{P}_o$. Send $(\mathsf{activated})$ to $\mathcal{G}_{\mathsf{ticker}}$.

**Solve:** Upon receiving input $(\mathsf{Solve}, \mathsf{sid}, \mathsf{el})$, a party $\mathcal{P}_i \in \mathcal{P}$, send $(\mathsf{Mult}, \mathsf{sid}, \mathsf{el}, \mathsf{el})$ to $\mathcal{F}_{\mathsf{rsw}}$. If $\mathcal{P}_i$ obtains $(\mathsf{Invalid}, \mathsf{sid})$, it aborts. Send $(\mathsf{activated})$ to $\mathcal{G}_{\mathsf{ticker}}$.

**Get Message:** Upon receiving $(\mathsf{GetMsg}, \mathsf{puz}, \mathsf{el})$ as input, a party $\mathcal{P}_i \in \mathcal{P}$ parses $\mathsf{puz} = (\mathsf{el}_0, \varGamma, \mathsf{tag})$, parses $\mathsf{tag} = (\mathsf{tag}_1, \mathsf{tag}_2)$ and proceeds as follows:
1. Send $(\textsc{Hash-Query}, (\mathsf{el}_0|\mathsf{el}))$ to $\mathcal{G}_{\mathsf{rpoRO1}}$, obtaining $(\textsc{Hash-Confirm}, h_1)$.
2. Compute $(m|\mathsf{td}) = \mathsf{tag}_1 \oplus h_1$ and send $(\textsc{Hash-Query}, (h_1|m|\mathsf{td}))$ to $\mathcal{G}_{\mathsf{rpoRO2}}$, obtaining $(\textsc{Hash-Confirm}, h_2)$.
3. Send $(\mathsf{Pow}, \mathsf{sid}, \mathsf{td}, \mathsf{el}_0, 2^{\varGamma})$ to $\mathcal{F}_{\mathsf{rsw}}$, obtaining $(\mathsf{Pow}, \mathsf{sid}, \mathsf{td}, \mathsf{el}_0, 2^{\varGamma}, \mathsf{el}_{\varGamma})$.
4. Send $(\textsc{IsProgrammed}, (\mathsf{el}_0|\mathsf{el}))$ and $(\textsc{IsProgrammed}, (h_1|m|\mathsf{td}))$ to $\mathcal{G}_{\mathsf{rpoRO1}}$ and $\mathcal{G}_{\mathsf{rpoRO2}}$, obtaining $(\textsc{IsProgrammed}, b_1)$ and $(\textsc{IsProgrammed}, b_2)$, respectively. Abort if $b_1 = 0$ or $b_2 = 0$,.
5. If $\mathsf{tag}_2 = h_2$ and $\mathsf{el} = \mathsf{el}_{\varGamma}$, output $(\mathsf{GetMsg}, \mathsf{sid}, \mathsf{el}_0, \mathsf{tag}, \mathsf{el}, m)$. Otherwise, output $(\mathsf{GetMsg}, \mathsf{sid}, \mathsf{el}_0, \mathsf{tag}, \mathsf{el}, \bot)$. Send $(\mathsf{activated})$ to $\mathcal{G}_{\mathsf{ticker}}$.

**Output:** Upon receiving $(\mathsf{Output}, \mathsf{sid})$ as input, a party $\mathcal{P}_i \in \mathcal{P}$ sends $(\mathsf{Output}, \mathsf{sid})$ to $\mathcal{F}_{\mathsf{rsw}}$, receiving $(\mathsf{Complete}, \mathsf{sid}, L_i)$ and outputting it. Send $(\mathsf{activated})$ to $\mathcal{G}_{\mathsf{ticker}}$.

**Fig. 5.** Protocol $\pi_{\mathsf{tlp}}$ realizing time-lock puzzle functionality $\mathcal{F}_{\mathsf{tlp}}$ in the $\mathcal{F}_{\mathsf{rsw}}, \mathcal{G}_{\mathsf{rpoRO}}$-hybrid model.

oracle. This tag is generated in such a way that a party who solves the puzzle can retrieve $\mathsf{td}, m$ and test whether the tag is consistent with these values and with initial and final group elements $\mathsf{el}_0, \mathsf{el}_{\varGamma}$. More specifically, the tag $\mathsf{tag} = (\mathsf{tag}_2, \mathsf{tag}_2)$ is generated by computing $h_1 = H_1(\mathsf{el}_0|\mathsf{el}_{\varGamma})$, $\mathsf{tag}_1 = h_1 \oplus (m|\mathsf{td})$ and $\mathsf{tag}_2 = H_2(h_1|m|\mathsf{td})$, where $H_1(\cdot), H_2(\cdot)$ are random oracles. A party who solves this puzzle obtaining $\mathsf{el}_{\varGamma}$ by performing $\varGamma$ sequential squarings of $\mathsf{el}_0$ can retrieve $h_1$, obtain $(m|\mathsf{td})$ and check that these values are consistent with $h_2$. Notice that this also allows a simulator who observes queries to random oracles $H_1(\cdot), H_2(\cdot)$ to extract all parameters of a puzzle (including the message) and check whether it is a valid puzzle. A simulator who also has the additional (and provably necessary) power of programming the output of these random oracles can deliver an arbitrary message $m'$ to a party who solves the puzzle. We formally state the security of $\pi_{\mathsf{tlp}}$ in Theorem 1. Due to space limitations, the proof is contained in the full version.

**Theorem 1.** *Protocol $\pi_{\mathsf{tlp}}$ UC-realizes $\mathcal{F}_{\mathsf{tlp}}$ in the $\mathcal{G}_{\mathsf{rpoRO}}, \mathcal{F}_{\mathsf{rsw}}$-hybrid model with computational security against a static adversary. Formally, for every static adversary $\mathcal{A}$ there exists a simulator $\mathcal{S}$ such that for any environment $\mathcal{Z}$, the environment cannot distinguish $\pi_{\mathsf{tlp}}$ composed with $\mathcal{G}_{\mathsf{rpoRO}}, \mathcal{F}_{\mathsf{rsw}}$ and $\mathcal{A}$ from $\mathcal{S}$ composed with $\mathcal{F}_{\mathsf{tlp}}$.*

# 6  Secure Two-Party Computation with Output-Independent Abort

We show how to obtain 2PC with output independent abort from any 2PC with secret-shared outputs using homomorphic commitments with delayed opening.

**Functionalities.** We will use the following functionalities, for which we present new definitions which take time into consideration:

- The functionality $\mathcal{F}_{\mathsf{2pcoia}}^{\Delta,\delta}$ (Fig. 6) for 2PC with Output-Independent Abort.
- The functionality $\mathcal{F}_{\mathsf{2pcsso}}^{\Delta}$ (Fig. 7 and Fig. 8) for secure 2PC with secret-shared output which naturally arises from existing protocols.
- The functionality $\mathcal{F}_{\mathsf{ahcom}}^{\Delta,\delta}$ (see full version) for homomorphic commitments with delayed non-interactive openings that naturally arises from homomorphic commitments that are combined with $\mathcal{F}_{\mathsf{tlp}}$.

An additional functionality $\mathcal{F}_{\mathsf{ct}}$ for coin-flipping with abort in the timed message model appears in the full version [8]. All of the functionalities assume that one of the parties is honest while the other is corrupted, but this is only for simplicity of exposition of the functionalities. We write functionalities where the parties have to send messages to trigger "regular behavior" instead of giving full one-sided control to $\mathcal{S}$ as this appears more natural. Messages to dishonest parties, on the other hand, go directly to $\mathcal{S}$ that can act upon them.

**2PC with Output-Independent Abort.** The functionality $\mathcal{F}_{\mathsf{2pcoia}}^{\Delta,\delta}$ as outlined in Fig. 6 shows how Output-Independent Abort for 2PC can be modeled. Similar to other 2PC functionalities, it allows parties to fix the circuit $C$ to be computed, provide inputs, compute with these inputs and then obtain the result of the computation. In comparison to regular UC functionalities, there are two differences how this is handled:

- Parties using $\mathcal{F}_{\mathsf{2pcoia}}^{\Delta,\delta}$ do not receive messages from $\mathcal{F}_{\mathsf{2pcoia}}^{\Delta,\delta}$ in a push-model where they get activated upon each new message, but instead they have to pull messages from the functionality (which was also already the case for $\mathcal{F}_{\mathsf{smt,delay}}^{\Delta}$). The reasoning behind this is that the functionality is ticked and it might happen that multiple messages arrive to multiple receivers in the same

---

**Functionality $\mathcal{F}_{\text{2pcoia}}^{\Delta,\delta}$**

The functionality runs with parties $\mathcal{P}_1, \mathcal{P}_2$ and an adversary $\mathcal{S}$ who may corrupt either of the parties. It is parameterized by parameters $\Delta, \delta \in \mathbb{N}^+$. The computed circuit is defined over $\mathbb{F}_2$. The functionality internally has three lists $\mathcal{M}, \mathcal{Q}, \mathcal{O}$ and flags $\text{output}, \text{noabort} \leftarrow \perp$.

**Init:** On input $(\text{Init}, \text{sid}, C)$ by $\mathcal{P}_i \in \{\mathcal{P}_1, \mathcal{P}_2\}$:
1. Add $(\Delta, \text{mid}, \text{sid}, \mathcal{P}_{3-i}, (\text{Init}, C))$ to $\mathcal{Q}$ for an unused mid.
2. If both parties sent $(\text{Init}, \text{sid}, C)$ then store $C$ locally.
3. Send $(\text{Init}, \text{sid}, \mathcal{P}_i, C, \text{mid})$ to $\mathcal{S}$.

**Input:** On first input $(\text{Input}, \text{sid}, i, x_i)$ by $\mathcal{P}_i$ for $i \in \{1, 2\}$:
1. Add $(\Delta, \text{mid}, \text{sid}, \mathcal{P}_{3-i}, (\text{Input}, \mathcal{P}_i))$ to $\mathcal{Q}$ for an unused mid.
2. Accept $x_i$ as input for $\mathcal{P}_i$.
3. Send $(\text{Input}, \text{sid}, \mathcal{P}_i, x_i, \text{mid})$ to $\mathcal{S}$ if $\mathcal{P}_i$ is corrupted and $(\text{Input}, \text{sid}, \mathcal{P}_i, \text{mid})$ otherwise.

**Computation:** On first input $(\text{Compute}, \text{sid})$ by $\mathcal{P}_i \in \{\mathcal{P}_1, \mathcal{P}_2\}$ and if both $x_1, x_2$ were accepted:
1. Add $(\Delta, \text{mid}, \text{sid}, \mathcal{P}_{3-i}, (\text{Compute}))$ to $\mathcal{Q}$ for an unused mid.
2. If both parties sent $(\text{Compute}, \text{sid})$ compute $y = C(x_1, x_2)$ and store $y$.
3. Send $(\text{Compute}, \text{sid}, \mathcal{P}_i, \text{mid})$ to $\mathcal{S}$.

**Output:** On first input $(\text{Output}, \text{sid})$ by both parties and if $y$ has been stored then add $(\delta, \text{sid}, \mathcal{S}, (\text{Output}, y))$ to $\mathcal{O}$.

**Fetch Message:** Upon receiving $(\text{FetchMsg}, \text{sid})$ by $\mathcal{P} \in \{\mathcal{P}_1, \mathcal{P}_2\}$ retrieve the set $L$ of all entries $(\mathcal{P}, \text{sid}, \cdot)$ in $\mathcal{M}$, remove $L$ from $\mathcal{M}$ and return $(\text{FetchMsg}, \text{sid}, L)$ to $\mathcal{P}$.

**Scheduling:** On input from $\mathcal{S}$:
- If $\mathcal{S}$ sent $(\text{Deliver}, \text{sid}, \text{mid})$ and then remove each $(c, \text{mid}, \text{sid}, \mathcal{P}, m)$ from $\mathcal{Q}$ and add $(\mathcal{P}, \text{sid}, m)$ to $\mathcal{M}$.
- If $\mathcal{S}$ sent $(\text{Abort}, \text{sid})$ and $\text{noabort} = \perp$ then add $(\mathcal{P}_1, \text{sid}, \text{Abort}), (\mathcal{P}_2, \text{sid}, \text{Abort})$ to $\mathcal{M}$ and ignore all further calls to the functionality except to **Fetch Message**.

**Tick:**
1. For each query $(0, \text{mid}, \text{sid}, \mathcal{P}, m) \in \mathcal{Q}$:
   (a) Remove $(0, \text{mid}, \text{sid}, \mathcal{P}, m)$ from $\mathcal{Q}$.
   (b) Add $(\mathcal{P}, \text{sid}, m)$ to $\mathcal{M}$.
2. Replace each $(c, \text{mid}, \text{sid}, \mathcal{P}, m)$ in $\mathcal{Q}$ with $(c - 1, \text{mid}, \text{sid}, \mathcal{P}, m)$.
3. For each entry $(c, \text{sid}, \mathcal{S}, y) \in \mathcal{O}$, proceed as follows:
   - If $c = 0$, send $(\text{OutputOrAbort}, \text{sid})$ to $\mathcal{S}$. Sample a fresh mid and set $\text{noabort} \leftarrow \top$. If $\mathcal{S}$ responds with $(\text{Abort}, \text{sid})$ then add $(\Delta, \text{mid}, \text{sid}, \mathcal{P}_j, (\text{Abort}))$ to $\mathcal{Q}$ for the honest party $\mathcal{P}_j$, otherwise add $(\Delta, \text{mid}, \text{sid}, \mathcal{P}_j, (\text{Output}, y))$. Finally send $(\text{Output}, \text{sid}, \text{mid}, y)$ to $\mathcal{S}$.
   - If $c > 0$, replace $(c, \text{sid}, \mathcal{S}, y)$ with $(c - 1, \text{sid}, \mathcal{S}, y)$ in $\mathcal{O}$.

---

**Fig. 6.** The $\mathcal{F}_{\text{2pcoia}}^{\Delta,\delta}$ functionality for 2PC with output-independent abort.

"tick" round. But upon receiving a message from $\mathcal{F}_{\text{2pcoia}}^{\Delta,\delta}$, a party may not return activation to it. This means that another "tick" may happen before another message gets delivered, which would break the guaranteed delivery requirement. A pull-model is a solution as each party is guaranteed to get activated between any two "ticks" in our model, allowing it to receive messages if it wants to. We will also use this modeling for the other functionalities in this section.

- The functionality does not directly deliver messages to receivers, but instead internally queries them first. This is because it is necessary to use communication using $\mathcal{F}^{\Delta}_{\mathsf{smt,delay}}$, which means that the adversary may arbitrarily control how messages get delivered, and he may reorder delivery at his will within the maximal delay that $\mathcal{F}^{\Delta}_{\mathsf{smt,delay}}$ permits. We also allow the adversary to influence delivery "adaptively", meaning depending on other events outside of $\mathcal{F}^{\Delta,\delta}_{\mathsf{2pcoia}}$'s scope.

Towards achieving this pull-model and adversarial reordering of messages, $\mathcal{F}^{\Delta,\delta}_{\mathsf{2pcoia}}$ has three internal lists $\mathcal{Q}$, $\mathcal{M}$ and $\mathcal{O}$. $\mathcal{Q}$ contains all the buffered messages which can be delivered in the future, while messages in $\mathcal{M}$ can be retrieved right now by the respective receivers. Whenever $\mathcal{F}^{\Delta,\delta}_{\mathsf{2pcoia}}$ notices that a tick happened it will run **Tick**, which will then move all messages from $\mathcal{Q}$ to $\mathcal{M}$ which get available in the next round, and which can be retrieved via the interface **Fetch Message**.

$\mathcal{S}$ may use **Scheduling** to prematurely move messages to $\mathcal{M}$ by sending a special message that contains the message id mid—that means that $\mathcal{S}$ gets notified about every new mid whenever a message is added to $\mathcal{Q}$ which $\mathcal{S}$ can influence. $\mathcal{S}$ may also cancel the delivery of messages, though this will lead to a break-down of the functionality as $\mathcal{F}^{\Delta}_{\mathsf{smt,delay}}$ does not allow to drop messages altogether.

We let **Tick** be responsible to realize the output-independent abort property of $\mathcal{F}^{\Delta,\delta}_{\mathsf{2pcoia}}$. To see why this is the case, observe that once both parties activate the output phase the functionality stores a message to $\mathcal{S}$ that represents the output in $\mathcal{O}$. In comparison to $\mathcal{Q}$, $\mathcal{S}$ cannot make $\mathcal{F}^{\Delta,\delta}_{\mathsf{2pcoia}}$ output values in $\mathcal{O}$ any faster. Once this message will be delivered to $\mathcal{S}$, the functionality will then ask $\mathcal{S}$ if the honest party should obtain the output or not. It will also give $\mathcal{S}$ control over when the output message should be delivered to the honest party. Observe that once $\mathcal{S}$ obtained the output then the Abort command cannot be used anymore.

**Two-Party Computation with Secret-Shared Output.** In Fig. 7 and Fig. 8 we describe a 2PC functionality $\mathcal{F}^{\Delta}_{\mathsf{2pcsso}}$ which will be the foundation for our compiler that will realise $\mathcal{F}^{\Delta,\delta}_{\mathsf{2pcoia}}$. $\mathcal{F}^{\Delta}_{\mathsf{2pcsso}}$ has the same initialization, input and computation interfaces as other 2PC functionalities. The two main differences between a standard 2PC functionality and $\mathcal{F}^{\Delta}_{\mathsf{2pcsso}}$ are: first, $\mathcal{F}^{\Delta}_{\mathsf{2pcsso}}$ is again a "ticked" functionality, meaning that it similarly to $\mathcal{F}^{\Delta,\delta}_{\mathsf{2pcoia}}$ considers a 2PC protocol that implements communication via $\mathcal{F}^{\Delta}_{\mathsf{smt,delay}}$. Second, $\mathcal{F}^{\Delta}_{\mathsf{2pcsso}}$ does not directly output the outcome of the computation. Instead, it reveals a secret-sharing of it to both parties. The parties can then manipulate shares using the functionality, generate additional random shares or reconstruct them.

We will not show in this work how to realize $\mathcal{F}^{\Delta}_{\mathsf{2pcsso}}$. This is because it's output-sharing property is rather standard (albeit not always modeled as explicitly as here) and it follows directly from any 2PC protocol that is

---

**Functionality** $\mathcal{F}_{2pcsso}^{\Delta}$ **(Computation, Message Handling)**

The functionality interacts with two parties $\mathcal{P}_1, \mathcal{P}_2$ and an adversary $\mathcal{S}$ which may corrupt either of the parties. The functionality will internally have two lists $\mathcal{M}, \mathcal{Q}$.

**Init:** On input $(\mathsf{Init}, \mathsf{sid}, C)$ by $\mathcal{P}_i \in \{\mathcal{P}_1, \mathcal{P}_2\}$:
1. Add $(\Delta, \mathsf{mid}, \mathsf{sid}, \mathcal{P}_{3-i}, (\mathsf{Init}, C))$ to $\mathcal{Q}$ for an unused $\mathsf{mid}$.
2. If both parties sent $(\mathsf{Init}, \mathsf{sid}, C)$ then store $C$ locally and let $m$ be the length of the output of $C$. Then send $(\mathsf{Init}, \mathsf{sid}, \mathcal{P}_i, C, \mathsf{mid})$ to $\mathcal{S}$.

**Input:** On first input $(\mathsf{Input}, \mathsf{sid}, i, x_i)$ by $\mathcal{P}_i$ for $i \in \{1, 2\}$:
1. Add $(\Delta, \mathsf{mid}, \mathsf{sid}, \mathcal{P}_{3-i}, (\mathsf{Input}, \mathcal{P}_i))$ to $\mathcal{Q}$ for an unused $\mathsf{mid}$.
2. Accept $x_i$ as input for $\mathcal{P}_i$. Then send $(\mathsf{Input}, \mathsf{sid}, \mathcal{P}_i, x_i, \mathsf{mid})$ to $\mathcal{S}$ if $\mathcal{P}_i$ is corrupted and $(\mathsf{Input}, \mathsf{sid}, \mathcal{P}_i, \mathsf{mid})$ otherwise.

**Computation:** On first input $(\mathsf{Compute}, \mathsf{sid})$ by $\mathcal{P}_i \in \{\mathcal{P}_1, \mathcal{P}_2\}$ and if both $x_1, x_2$ were accepted:
1. Add $(\Delta, \mathsf{mid}, \mathsf{sid}, \mathcal{P}_{3-i}, (\mathsf{Compute}))$ to $\mathcal{Q}$ for an unused $\mathsf{mid}$.
2. If both parties sent $(\mathsf{Compute}, \mathsf{sid})$ compute $\boldsymbol{y} = (y_1, \ldots, y_m) \leftarrow C(x_1, x_2)$ and store $\boldsymbol{y}$. Then send $(\mathsf{Compute}, \mathsf{sid}, \mathcal{P}_i, \mathsf{mid})$ to $\mathcal{S}$.

**Fetch Message:** Upon receiving $(\mathsf{FetchMsg}, \mathsf{sid})$ by $\mathcal{P} \in \{\mathcal{P}_1, \mathcal{P}_2\}$ retrieve the set $L$ of all entries $(\mathcal{P}, \mathsf{sid}, \cdot)$ in $\mathcal{M}$, remove $L$ from $\mathcal{M}$ and return $(\mathsf{Output}, \mathsf{sid}, L)$ to $\mathcal{P}$.

**Scheduling:** On input of $\mathcal{S}$:
- If $\mathcal{S}$ sent $(\mathsf{Deliver}, \mathsf{sid}, \mathsf{mid})$ then remove each $(\mathsf{c}, \mathsf{mid}, \mathsf{sid}, \mathcal{P}, m)$ from $\mathcal{Q}$ and add $(\mathcal{P}, \mathsf{sid}, m)$ to $\mathcal{M}$.
- If $\mathcal{S}$ sent $(\mathsf{Abort})$ add $(\mathcal{P}_S, \mathsf{sid}, \mathsf{Abort}), (\mathcal{P}_R, \mathsf{sid}, \mathsf{Abort})$ to $\mathcal{M}$ and ignore all further calls to the functionality except to **Fetch Message**.

**Tick:**
1. For each query $(0, \mathsf{mid}, \mathsf{sid}, \mathcal{P}, m) \in \mathcal{Q}$:
   (a) Remove $(0, \mathsf{mid}, \mathsf{sid}, \mathcal{P}, m)$ from $\mathcal{Q}$.
   (b) Add $(\mathcal{P}, \mathsf{sid}, m)$ to $\mathcal{M}$.
2. Replace each $(\mathsf{c}, \mathsf{mid}, \mathsf{sid}, \mathcal{P}, m)$ in $\mathcal{Q}$ with $(\mathsf{c} - 1, \mathsf{mid}, \mathsf{sid}, \mathcal{P}, m)$.

---

**Fig. 7.** 2PC with secret-shared output and linear share operations.

entirely based on secret-sharing [41] or BMR protocols that secret-share the output [6,30].

**Additively Homomorphic Commitments with Delayed Openings.** In order to implement $\mathcal{F}_{2pcoia}^{\Delta,\delta}$ we also need a special commitment scheme that allows for delayed openings. The functionality is naturally ticked, as its implementation will use both $\mathcal{F}_{smt,delay}^{\Delta}$ and $\mathcal{F}_{tlp}$. Due to space limitations, the functionality as well as its implementation is delayed to the full version [8]. In addition to regular commit and opening procedures, the functionality has a special **Delayed Open** command which releases the message in a commitment after a delay $\delta$. The adversary $\mathcal{A}$ may introduce a (communication) delay of maximum $\Delta$ ticks before the honest party receives the delayed opening notification (or it may decide to abort the opening process altogether). However, $\mathcal{A}$ cannot choose to abort the delayed opening anymore once the honest party has received the notification.

---

**Functionality $\mathcal{F}_{2\mathsf{pcsso}}^{\Delta}$ (Computation on Outputs)**

**Share Output:** Upon input $(\mathsf{ShareOut}, \mathsf{sid}, \mathcal{I})$ by $\mathcal{P}_i \in \{\mathcal{P}_1, \mathcal{P}_2\}$ for fresh identifiers $\mathcal{I} = \{\mathsf{cid}_1, \ldots, \mathsf{cid}_m\}$ and if **Computation** was finished:

1. Add $(\Delta, \mathsf{mid}, \mathsf{sid}, \mathcal{P}_{3-i}, (\mathsf{ShareOut}))$ to $\mathcal{Q}$ for an unused $\mathsf{mid}$. Then send $(\mathsf{ShareOut}, \mathsf{sid}, \mathcal{P}_i, \mathsf{mid})$ to $\mathcal{S}$.

2. If both parties sent **ShareOut** (and letting $\mathcal{P}_j$ be the corrupted party):
   (a) Send $(\mathsf{ReqShares}, \mathsf{sid}, \mathcal{I})$ to $\mathcal{S}$, which replies with $(\mathsf{OutShares}, \mathsf{sid}, \{(\mathsf{cid}, s_{j,\mathsf{cid}})\}_{\mathsf{cid} \in \mathcal{I}})$ for the corrupted party $\mathcal{P}_j$. Then set $s_{3-j,\mathsf{cid}_h} = y_h \oplus s_{j,\mathsf{cid}_h}$.
   (b) For $\mathsf{cid} \in \mathcal{I}$ store $(\mathsf{cid}, s_{1,\mathsf{cid}}, s_{2,\mathsf{cid}})$. Then add $(\Delta, \mathsf{mid}_1, \mathsf{sid}, \mathcal{P}_{3-j}, (\mathsf{OutShares}, \{(\mathsf{cid}, s_{3-j,\mathsf{cid}})\}_{\mathsf{cid} \in \mathcal{I}}))$ for a fresh $\mathsf{mid}_1$ to $\mathcal{Q}$ and send $(\mathsf{OutShares}, \mathsf{sid}, \mathcal{P}_{3-j}, \mathsf{mid}_1)$ to $\mathcal{S}$.

**Share Random Value:** Upon input $(\mathsf{ShareRand}, \mathsf{sid}, \mathcal{I})$ by both parties, for fresh identifiers $\mathcal{I}$ and letting $\mathcal{P}_j$ be the corrupted party:

1. Send $(\mathsf{ReqShares}, \mathsf{sid}, \mathcal{I})$ to $\mathcal{S}$, which replies with $(\mathsf{RandShares}, \mathsf{sid}, \{(\mathsf{cid}, s_{j,\mathsf{cid}})\}_{\mathsf{cid} \in \mathcal{I}})$ for the corrupted party $\mathcal{P}_j$. Then sample $s_{3-j,\mathsf{cid}} \overset{\$}{\leftarrow} \mathbb{F}$ for each $\mathsf{cid} \in \mathcal{I}$.

2. For each $\mathsf{cid} \in \mathcal{I}$ store $(\mathsf{cid}, s_{1,\mathsf{cid}}, s_{2,\mathsf{cid}})$. Then add $(\Delta, \mathsf{mid}_1, \mathsf{sid}, \mathcal{P}_{3-j}, (\mathsf{RandShares}, \{(\mathsf{cid}, s_{3-j,\mathsf{cid}})\}_{\mathsf{cid} \in \mathcal{I}}))$ for a fresh $\mathsf{mid}_1$ to $\mathcal{Q}$ and send $(\mathsf{RandShares}, \mathsf{sid}, \mathcal{P}_{3-j}, \mathsf{mid}_1)$ to $\mathcal{S}$.

**Linear Combination:** Upon input $(\mathsf{Linear}, \mathsf{sid}, \{(\mathsf{cid}, \alpha_{\mathsf{cid}})\}_{\mathsf{cid} \in \mathcal{I}}, \mathsf{cid}')$ from both parties: If all $\alpha_{\mathsf{cid}} \in \mathbb{F}$, all $\mathsf{cid} \in \mathcal{I}$ have stored values and $\mathsf{cid}'$ is unused, set $s_{i,\mathsf{cid}'} \leftarrow \sum_{\mathsf{cid} \in \mathcal{I}} \alpha_{\mathsf{cid}} \cdot s_{i,\mathsf{cid}}$ for $i \in \{1, 2\}$ and record $(\mathsf{cid}', s_{1,\mathsf{cid}'}, s_{2,\mathsf{cid}'})$.

**Reveal:** Upon input $(\mathsf{Reveal}, \mathsf{sid}, \mathsf{cid})$ by $\mathcal{P}_i \in \{\mathcal{P}_1, \mathcal{P}_2\}$, if $(\mathsf{cid}, s_1, s_2)$ is stored and $\mathcal{P}_j$ is corrupted:

1. Add $(\Delta, \mathsf{mid}, \mathsf{sid}, \mathcal{P}_i, (\mathsf{Reveal}))$ to $\mathcal{Q}$ for an unused $\mathsf{mid}$. Then send $(\mathsf{Reveal}, \mathsf{sid}, \mathcal{P}_i, \mathsf{mid})$ to $\mathcal{S}$.

2. If both parties sent $(\mathsf{Reveal}, \mathsf{sid}, \mathsf{cid})$ then send $(\mathsf{Reveal}, \mathsf{sid}, \mathsf{cid}, s_1 \oplus s_2)$ to $\mathcal{S}$.

3. If $\mathcal{S}$ sends $(\mathsf{DeliverReveal}, \mathsf{sid}, \mathsf{cid})$ then add $(\Delta, \mathsf{mid}, \mathsf{sid}, \mathcal{P}_{3-j}, (\mathsf{Reveal}, \mathsf{cid}, s_1 \oplus s_2))$ for a fresh $\mathsf{mid}$ to $\mathcal{Q}$.

4. Send $(\mathsf{DeliverReveal}, \mathsf{sid}, \mathsf{cid}, \mathcal{P}_{3-j}, \mathsf{mid})$ to $\mathcal{S}$.

---

**Fig. 8.** 2PC with secret-shared output and linear share operations, part 2.

$\mathcal{A}$ will learn the opening $\delta$ ticks after $\mathcal{P}_R$ initiated the delayed opening (as he receives messages immediately), while an honest receiver $\mathcal{P}_R$ might have to wait $\delta + \Delta$ ticks in total as the ticking for the delayed opening of a commitment can only happen once the opening notification arrives on the receiver's side.

**Coin Tossing.** In our protocol we additionally need to use a functionality for coin tossing, as mentioned before. It could actually already be implemented, albeit inefficiently, using $\mathcal{F}_{\mathsf{ahcom}}^{\Delta,\delta}$. For completeness, we instead use the functionality $\mathcal{F}_{\mathsf{ct}}$ which can be found in the full version.

---

**Protocol** $\pi_{\text{2pcoia}}$

This protocol is for two parties $\mathcal{P}_1, \mathcal{P}_2$ and uses the functionalities $\mathcal{F}_{\text{ahcom}}^{\Delta,\delta}$, $\mathcal{F}_{\text{2pcsso}}^{\Delta}$ and $\mathcal{F}_{\text{ct}}$. The parties compute the circuit $C$ over $\mathbb{F}$ with output length $m$. We assume that the commitment functionality $\mathcal{F}_{\text{ahcom}}^{\Delta,\delta}$ commits to vectors of length $m$. Throughout the protocol, we say "$\mathcal{P}_i$ ticks" when we mean that it sends (activated) to $\mathcal{G}_{\text{ticker}}$. We say that "$\mathcal{P}_i$ waits" when we mean that it, upon each activation, first checks if the event happened and if not, sends (activated) to $\mathcal{G}_{\text{ticker}}$.

**Init:** Each $\mathcal{P}_i$ sends (Init, sid, $C$) to $\mathcal{F}_{\text{2pcsso}}^{\Delta}$ and ticks. Then it waits and queries $\mathcal{F}_{\text{2pcsso}}^{\Delta}$ for an output (Init, sid, $C$).

**Input:** Each $\mathcal{P}_i$ sends (Input, sid, $i$, $x_i$) to $\mathcal{F}_{\text{2pcsso}}^{\Delta}$ and ticks. Then it waits and queries $\mathcal{F}_{\text{2pcsso}}^{\Delta}$ for an output (Input, sid, $\mathcal{P}_{3-i}$).

**Computation:** Each $\mathcal{P}_i$ sends (Compute, sid) to $\mathcal{F}_{\text{2pcsso}}^{\Delta}$ and ticks. Then it waits and queries $\mathcal{F}_{\text{2pcsso}}^{\Delta}$ for an output (Compute, sid).

**Output:**

1. Each party $\mathcal{P}_i$ sends (ShareOutput, sid, $\text{cid}_1, \ldots, \text{cid}_m$) for fixed $\text{cid}_h$ to $\mathcal{F}_{\text{2pcsso}}^{\Delta}$ and ticks. Then it waits and queries $\mathcal{F}_{\text{2pcsso}}^{\Delta}$ to receive its shares $s_{1,i}, \ldots, s_{m,i}$.

2. Each party $\mathcal{P}_i$ sends (RandomOutput, sid, $\widehat{\text{cid}}_1, \ldots, \widehat{\text{cid}}_{m \cdot \kappa}$) for fixed $\widehat{\text{cid}}_t$ to $\mathcal{F}_{\text{2pcsso}}^{\Delta}$ and ticks. Then it waits and queries $\mathcal{F}_{\text{2pcsso}}^{\Delta}$ until it receives its shares $r_{1,i}, \ldots, r_{m \cdot \kappa, i}$.

3. Each party uses $\mathcal{F}_{\text{ahcom}}^{\Delta,\delta}$ to commit to $\boldsymbol{s}_i = (s_{1,i}, \ldots, s_{m,i})$ as well as $\boldsymbol{r}_{k,i} = (r_{(k-1) \cdot m + 1, i}, \ldots, r_{k \cdot m, i})$ for $k \in [\kappa]$ using the cid's $\text{cid}_i^s, \text{cid}_{1,i}^r, \ldots, \text{cid}_{\kappa,i}^r$ and ticks. Then it waits and queries $\mathcal{F}_{\text{ahcom}}^{\Delta,\delta}$ to see if the other party committed.

4. Each $\mathcal{P}_i$ sends (Toss, sid, $\kappa$) to $\mathcal{F}_{\text{ct}}$ and ticks. Then it waits and queries $\mathcal{F}_{\text{ct}}$ until obtains $\alpha_1, \ldots, \alpha_\kappa$.

5. For $i \in [2]$, $k \in [\kappa]$ the parties use **Linear Combination** on $\mathcal{F}_{\text{ahcom}}^{\Delta,\delta}$ to compute commitments for the $\kappa$ values $d_{k,i} = \alpha_k \cdot \boldsymbol{s}_i \oplus \boldsymbol{r}_{k,i}$. These have cid's $\text{cid}_{1,i}^d, \ldots, \text{cid}_{\kappa,i}^d$.

6. For $k \in [\kappa]$, $h \in [m]$ the parties use **Linear Combination** on $\mathcal{F}_{\text{2pcsso}}^{\Delta}$ to compute the linear relations $d_{k,h} = \alpha_k \cdot s_h \oplus r_{(k-1) \cdot m + h}$.

7. The parties use **Reveal** on $\mathcal{F}_{\text{2pcsso}}^{\Delta}$ to open $d_{k,h}$ for all $k \in [\kappa], h \in [m]$.

8. Each $\mathcal{P}_i$ sends (DOpen, sid, $\text{cid}_i^s, \text{cid}_{1,i}^d, \ldots, \text{cid}_{\kappa,i}^d, \delta$) to its instance of $\mathcal{F}_{\text{ahcom}}^{\Delta,\delta}$.

9. Each party $\mathcal{P}_i$ now waits and:
   (a) Queries the instance of $\mathcal{F}_{\text{ahcom}}^{\Delta,\delta}$ where $\mathcal{P}_i$ was a receiver to see if it obtained a message (DOpen, $\text{cid}_{3-i}^s, \text{cid}_{1,3-i}^d, \ldots, \text{cid}_{\kappa,3-i}^d$). If so, then exit the loop.
   (b) Queries the instance of $\mathcal{F}_{\text{ahcom}}^{\Delta,\delta}$ where $\mathcal{P}_i$ was a sender to see if it obtained a message (DOpened, $\text{cid}_i^s, \text{cid}_{1,i}^d, \ldots, \text{cid}_{\kappa,i}^d$). If so, then exit the loop.

10. After having obtained either of the above messages, $\mathcal{P}_i$ does the following:
    - If DOpened arrived before DOpen then output $\perp$.
    - If DOpen arrived before DOpened then wait until $\tilde{\boldsymbol{s}}_{3-1}, \tilde{\boldsymbol{d}}_{1,3-i}, \ldots, \tilde{\boldsymbol{d}}_{\kappa,3-i}$ is obtained from $\mathcal{F}_{\text{ahcom}}^{\Delta,\delta}$. Then output $\boldsymbol{y} = \boldsymbol{s}_i \oplus \tilde{\boldsymbol{s}}_{3-i}$ if $\tilde{\boldsymbol{d}}_{k,3-i}[h] = d_{k,h} \oplus \boldsymbol{d}_{k,i}[h]$ for all $k \in [\kappa], h \in [m]$ and $\perp$ otherwise.

---

**Fig. 9.** Protocol $\pi_{\text{2pcoia}}$ For 2PC with output-independent abort.

## 6.1  Achieving Output-Independent Abort for 2PC in UC

Intuitively, the protocol realizing $\mathcal{F}_{2\text{pcoia}}^{\Delta,\delta}$ works as follows: first, both parties use $\mathcal{F}_{2\text{pcsso}}^{\Delta}$ to perform the secure computation. They then don't directly obtain an output, but instead each get a vector of shares $s_i$. Afterwards, the parties will commit to $s_i$ using $\mathcal{F}_{\text{ahcom}}^{\Delta,\delta}$ and use the homomorphic property of $\mathcal{F}_{\text{ahcom}}^{\Delta,\delta}$ to show consistency between the values in $\mathcal{F}_{2\text{pcoia}}^{\Delta,\delta}, \mathcal{F}_{\text{ahcom}}^{\Delta,\delta}$. For this, they sample a random matrix using $\mathcal{F}_{\text{ct}}$ and perform an identical linear operation on both functionalities.

At this stage the protocol might still fail and an adversary might still abort, but no information will leak as the consistency check does only reveal a uniformly random value. Finally, both parties use the **Delayed Open** to reveal their share $s_i$ which allows each party to reconstruct the output. At this stage, $\mathcal{A}$ might decide not to activate **Delayed Open**, but we can set the parameters of $\mathcal{F}_{\text{ahcom}}^{\Delta,\delta}$ such that it will have to do so before the commitment of the honest party opens. If it does not activate its delayed opening before that point, then the honest party will decide that an abort happened and just ignore any future messages of $\mathcal{A}$. The full protocol $\pi_{2\text{pcoia}}$ can be found in Fig. 9. In the full version [8], we show the following theorem:

**Theorem 2.** *Let $\delta > \Delta$ and $\kappa \in \mathbb{N}^+$ be a statistical security parameter. Then the protocol $\pi_{2\text{pcoia}}$ UC-implements $\mathcal{F}_{2\text{pcoia}}^{\Delta,\delta}$ in the $\mathcal{F}_{2\text{pcsso}}^{\Delta}, \mathcal{F}_{\text{ahcom}}^{\Delta,\delta}, \mathcal{F}_{\text{ct}}$-hybrid model against any static active adversary corrupting at most one of the two parties.*

## 7  The Impossibility Result

We show that in the UC model one cannot implement fair coin-flip without using a random oracle, or similar programmable setup assumption. This holds even if one is allowed to use time-lock puzzles, and non-programmable random oracles and 2PC with abort. We first show the impossibility result for the *simple case* where we assume there is no setup, no random oracles and that the protocol has a fixed round complexity. This allows us to focus on the central new idea. After that we show the result for the full case.

The ideal functionality $\mathcal{F}_{\text{cf}}$ for fair coin-flip (without abort) proceeds as follows. When activated by any party in round 0 it will sample a uniformly random bit $c$ and output it to both parties in some round $\rho$ specified by the adversary. The adversary cannot refuse the output to be given. The ideal functionality is rushing: the adversary gets $c$ in round 0. The honest parties do not get the coin until round $\rho$.

**Implications.** Below we show that in several settings, called the excluded settings, one cannot UC securely realize $\mathcal{F}_{\text{cf}}$. By the UC composition theorem this impossibility result has wide implications. In particular, it holds for all ideal functionalities $\mathcal{G}$ that if one can UC securely realize $\mathcal{F}_{\text{cf}}$ in the $\mathcal{G}$-hybrid model, then one cannot UC realize $\mathcal{G}$ in the excluded settings either.

**Impossibility of Two-Party Coinflip with Output-Independent Abort.** It follows that two-party coin-flip with output-independent abort is impossible in the excluded settings. Namely, given a protocol $\pi_{\mathsf{cfoia}}$ for two-party coin-flip with output-independent abort one can get a two-party coin-flip protocol $\pi_{\mathsf{cf}}$ without abort as follows. We describe the protocol in the $\mathcal{F}_{\mathsf{cfoia}}$-hybrid model and get the result by composition. Run $\mathcal{F}_{\mathsf{cfoia}}$. If neither of the parties aborts, take the output of $\mathcal{F}_{\mathsf{cfoia}}$ to be the output. If one of the parties aborts, let the other party sample and announce a uniformly random $c$ and take $c$ as the output. To simulate the protocol, get from $\mathcal{F}_{\mathsf{cf}}$ the coin $c$ to hit in the simulation. Simulate a copy of $\mathcal{F}_{\mathsf{cfoia}}$ to the adversary. If the adversary does not abort, let the output of $\mathcal{F}_{\mathsf{cfoia}}$ be $c$. Otherwise, let the output of $\mathcal{F}_{\mathsf{cfoia}}$ be a uniformly random $c'$, and then simulate that the honest party samples and announces $c$.

Notice that it was crucial for this simulation that we could change the output of $\mathcal{F}_{\mathsf{cfoia}}$ from $c$ to an independent $c'$ when there was an abort. Namely, when there is an abort we still need to hit the $c$ output by $\mathcal{F}_{\mathsf{cf}}$ in the simulation, so we are forced to simulate that the honest party samples and announces $c$ in the simulation. But if we were then also forced to let $\mathcal{F}_{\mathsf{cfoia}}$ output $c$, then in the simulation the bits output by $\mathcal{F}_{\mathsf{cfoia}}$ and the honest party when there is an abort will always be the same. In the protocol they are independent. This would make it easy to distinguish. A generalisation of this observation will later be the basis for our impossibility result.

**Impossibility of UC 2PC with Output-Independent Abort.** It also follows that 2PC with output-independent abort is impossible in the excluded settings. Namely, given a functionality $\mathcal{F}_{\mathsf{2pcoia}}$ for 2PC with output-independent abort (as described in the previous section) one can UC securely realize $\mathcal{F}_{\mathsf{cfoia}}$. Namely, use $\mathcal{F}_{\mathsf{2pcoia}}$ to compute the function which takes one bit as input from each party and outputs the exclusive or. Let each party input a uniformly random bit. If any party aborts on $\mathcal{F}_{\mathsf{2pcoia}}$, abort in $\pi_{\mathsf{cfoia}}$. It is straight forward to simulate $\pi_{\mathsf{cfoia}}$ given $\mathcal{F}_{\mathsf{2pcoia}}$.

**Impossibility of UC Time-Lock Puzzles.** It also follows that UC time-lock puzzles are impossible in the excluded settings. Namely, we have shown that given UC time-lock puzzles one can UC securely realize $\mathcal{F}_{\mathsf{2pcoia}}$, which was excluded above. Due to space constraints, proofs are left to the full version [8].

# References

1. Andrychowicz, M., Dziembowski, S., Malinowski, D., Mazurek, Ł.: Fair two-party computations via bitcoin deposits. In: Böhme, R., Brenner, M., Moore, T., Smith, M. (eds.) FC 2014. LNCS, vol. 8438, pp. 105–121. Springer, Heidelberg (2014). https://doi.org/10.1007/978-3-662-44774-1_8
2. Andrychowicz, M., Dziembowski, S., Malinowski, D., Mazurek, L.: Secure multiparty computations on bitcoin. In: 2014 IEEE Symposium on Security and Privacy. IEEE Computer Society Press, May 2014

3. Backes, M., Hofheinz, D., Müller-Quade, J., Unruh, D.: On fairness in simulatability-based cryptographic systems. In: FMSE 2005, pp. 13–22. ACM (2005)
4. Backes, M., Manoharan, P., Mohammadi, E.: TUC: time-sensitive and modular analysis of anonymous communication. In: Computer Security Foundations Symposium, CSF 2014. IEEE Computer Society Press (2014)
5. Badertscher, C., Gazi, P., Kiayias, A., Russell, A., Zikas, V.: Ouroboros genesis: composable proof-of-stake blockchains with dynamic availability. In: ACM CCS 2018. ACM Press, October 2018
6. Baum, C., David, B., Dowsley, R.: Insured MPC: efficient secure computation with financial penalties. In: Bonneau, J., Heninger, N. (eds.) FC 2020. LNCS, vol. 12059, pp. 404–420. Springer, Cham (2020). https://doi.org/10.1007/978-3-030-51280-4_22
7. Baum, C., David, B., Dowsley, R., Nielsen, J.B., Oechsner, S.: Craft: composable randomness and almost fairness from time. Cryptology ePrint Archive, Report 2020/784 (2020). https://eprint.iacr.org/2020/784
8. Baum, C., David, B., Dowsley, R., Nielsen, J.B., Oechsner, S.: TARDIS: time and relative delays in simulation. Cryptology ePrint Archive, Report 2020/537 (2020). https://eprint.iacr.org/2020/537
9. Baum, C., Orsini, E., Scholl, P.: Efficient secure multiparty computation with identifiable abort. In: Hirt, M., Smith, A. (eds.) TCC 2016, Part I. LNCS, vol. 9985, pp. 461–490. Springer, Heidelberg (2016). https://doi.org/10.1007/978-3-662-53641-4_18
10. Baum, C., Orsini, E., Scholl, P., Soria-Vazquez, E.: Efficient constant-round MPC with identifiable abort and public verifiability. In: Micciancio, D., Ristenpart, T. (eds.) CRYPTO 2020, Part II. LNCS, vol. 12171, pp. 562–592. Springer, Cham (2020). https://doi.org/10.1007/978-3-030-56880-1_20
11. Bellare, M., Dowsley, R., Waters, B., Yilek, S.: Standard security does not imply security against selective-opening. In: Pointcheval, D., Johansson, T. (eds.) EUROCRYPT 2012. LNCS, vol. 7237, pp. 645–662. Springer, Heidelberg (2012). https://doi.org/10.1007/978-3-642-29011-4_38
12. Bentov, I., Kumaresan, R.: How to use bitcoin to design fair protocols. In: Garay, J.A., Gennaro, R. (eds.) CRYPTO 2014, Part II. LNCS, vol. 8617, pp. 421–439. Springer, Heidelberg (2014). https://doi.org/10.1007/978-3-662-44381-1_24
13. Bitansky, N., Goldwasser, S., Jain, A., Paneth, O., Vaikuntanathan, V., Waters, B.: Time-lock puzzles from randomized encodings. In: ITCS 2016. ACM, January 2016
14. Boneh, D., Bonneau, J., Bünz, B., Fisch, B.: Verifiable delay functions. In: Shacham, H., Boldyreva, A. (eds.) CRYPTO 2018, Part I. LNCS, vol. 10991, pp. 757–788. Springer, Cham (2018). https://doi.org/10.1007/978-3-319-96884-1_25
15. Boneh, D., Naor, M.: Timed commitments. In: Bellare, M. (ed.) CRYPTO 2000. LNCS, vol. 1880, pp. 236–254. Springer, Heidelberg (2000). https://doi.org/10.1007/3-540-44598-6_15
16. Camenisch, J., Drijvers, M., Gagliardoni, T., Lehmann, A., Neven, G.: The wonderful world of global random oracles. In: Nielsen, J.B., Rijmen, V. (eds.) EUROCRYPT 2018, Part I. LNCS, vol. 10820, pp. 280–312. Springer, Cham (2018). https://doi.org/10.1007/978-3-319-78381-9_11
17. Canetti, R.: Universally composable security: a new paradigm for cryptographic protocols. Cryptology ePrint Archive, Report 2000/067 (2000). http://eprint.iacr.org/2000/067

18. Canetti, R.: Universally composable security: a new paradigm for cryptographic protocols. In: 42nd FOCS. IEEE Computer Society Press, October 2001
19. Canetti, R., Dodis, Y., Pass, R., Walfish, S.: Universally composable security with global setup. In: Vadhan, S.P. (ed.) TCC 2007. LNCS, vol. 4392, pp. 61–85. Springer, Heidelberg (2007). https://doi.org/10.1007/978-3-540-70936-7_4
20. Cascudo, I., Damgård, I., David, B., Döttling, N., Dowsley, R., Giacomelli, I.: Efficient UC commitment extension with homomorphism for free (and applications). In: Galbraith, S.D., Moriai, S. (eds.) ASIACRYPT 2019, Part II. LNCS, vol. 11922, pp. 606–635. Springer, Cham (2019). https://doi.org/10.1007/978-3-030-34621-8_22
21. Cleve, R.: Limits on the security of coin flips when half the processors are faulty (extended abstract). In: 18th ACM STOC. ACM Press, May 1986
22. Couteau, G., Roscoe, B., Ryan, P.: Partially-fair computation from timed-release encryption and oblivious transfer. Cryptology ePrint Archive, Report 2019/1281 (2019). https://eprint.iacr.org/2019/1281
23. Damgård, I., Groth, J.: Non-interactive and reusable non-malleable commitment schemes. In: 35th ACM STOC. ACM Press, June 2003
24. David, B., Gaži, P., Kiayias, A., Russell, A.: Ouroboros Praos: an adaptively-secure, semi-synchronous proof-of-stake blockchain. In: Nielsen, J.B., Rijmen, V. (eds.) EUROCRYPT 2018, Part II. LNCS, vol. 10821, pp. 66–98. Springer, Cham (2018). https://doi.org/10.1007/978-3-319-78375-8_3
25. Dwork, C., Naor, M., Sahai, A.: Concurrent zero-knowledge. In: 30th ACM STOC. ACM Press, May 1998
26. Ephraim, N., Freitag, C., Komargodski, I., Pass, R.: Non-malleable time-lock puzzles and applications. Cryptology ePrint Archive, Report 2020/779 (2020). https://eprint.iacr.org/2020/779
27. Fischlin, M., Lehmann, A., Ristenpart, T., Shrimpton, T., Stam, M., Tessaro, S.: Random oracles with(out) programmability. In: Abe, M. (ed.) ASIACRYPT 2010. LNCS, vol. 6477, pp. 303–320. Springer, Heidelberg (2010). https://doi.org/10.1007/978-3-642-17373-8_18
28. Garay, J., MacKenzie, P., Prabhakaran, M., Yang, K.: Resource fairness and composability of cryptographic protocols. In: Halevi, S., Rabin, T. (eds.) TCC 2006. LNCS, vol. 3876, pp. 404–428. Springer, Heidelberg (2006). https://doi.org/10.1007/11681878_21
29. Goldreich, O.: Concurrent zero-knowledge with timing, revisited. In: 34th ACM STOC. ACM Press, May 2002
30. Hazay, C., Scholl, P., Soria-Vazquez, E.: Low cost constant round MPC combining BMR and oblivious transfer. In: Takagi, T., Peyrin, T. (eds.) ASIACRYPT 2017, Part I. LNCS, vol. 10624, pp. 598–628. Springer, Cham (2017). https://doi.org/10.1007/978-3-319-70694-8_21
31. Hofheinz, D., Shoup, V.: GNUC: a new universal composability framework. J. Cryptol. **28**(3), 423–508 (2015)
32. Ishai, Y., Ostrovsky, R., Zikas, V.: Secure multi-party computation with identifiable abort. In: Garay, J.A., Gennaro, R. (eds.) CRYPTO 2014, Part II. LNCS, vol. 8617, pp. 369–386. Springer, Heidelberg (2014). https://doi.org/10.1007/978-3-662-44381-1_21
33. Kalai, Y.T., Lindell, Y., Prabhakaran, M.: Concurrent general composition of secure protocols in the timing model. In: 37th ACM STOC. ACM Press, May 2005

34. Katz, J., Loss, J., Xu, J.: On the security of time-lock puzzles and timed commitments. In: Pass, R., Pietrzak, K. (eds.) TCC 2020, Part III. LNCS, vol. 12552, pp. 390–413. Springer, Cham (2020). https://doi.org/10.1007/978-3-030-64381-2_14

35. Katz, J., Maurer, U., Tackmann, B., Zikas, V.: Universally composable synchronous computation. In: Sahai, A. (ed.) TCC 2013. LNCS, vol. 7785, pp. 477–498. Springer, Heidelberg (2013). https://doi.org/10.1007/978-3-642-36594-2_27

36. Kiayias, A., Zhou, H.-S., Zikas, V.: Fair and robust multi-party computation using a global transaction ledger. In: Fischlin, M., Coron, J.-S. (eds.) EUROCRYPT 2016, Part II. LNCS, vol. 9666, pp. 705–734. Springer, Heidelberg (2016). https://doi.org/10.1007/978-3-662-49896-5_25

37. Kumaresan, R., Bentov, I.: How to use bitcoin to incentivize correct computations. In: ACM CCS 2014. ACM Press, November 2014

38. Kumaresan, R., Moran, T., Bentov, I.: How to use bitcoin to play decentralized poker. In: ACM CCS 2015. ACM Press, October 2015

39. Maurer, U.: Constructive cryptography – a new paradigm for security definitions and proofs. In: Mödersheim, S., Palamidessi, C. (eds.) TOSCA 2011. LNCS, vol. 6993, pp. 33–56. Springer, Heidelberg (2012). https://doi.org/10.1007/978-3-642-27375-9_3

40. Nielsen, J.B.: Separating random oracle proofs from complexity theoretic proofs: the non-committing encryption case. In: Yung, M. (ed.) CRYPTO 2002. LNCS, vol. 2442, pp. 111–126. Springer, Heidelberg (2002). https://doi.org/10.1007/3-540-45708-9_8

41. Nielsen, J.B., Nordholt, P.S., Orlandi, C., Burra, S.S.: A new approach to practical active-secure two-party computation. In: Safavi-Naini, R., Canetti, R. (eds.) CRYPTO 2012. LNCS, vol. 7417, pp. 681–700. Springer, Heidelberg (2012). https://doi.org/10.1007/978-3-642-32009-5_40

42. Pfitzmann, B., Waidner, M.: A model for asynchronous reactive systems and its application to secure message transmission. In: 2001 IEEE Symposium on Security and Privacy. IEEE Computer Society Press, May 2001

43. Pietrzak, K.: Simple verifiable delay functions. In: ITCS 2019. LIPIcs, January 2019

44. Rivest, R.L., Shamir, A., Wagner, D.A.: Time-lock puzzles and timed-release crypto (1996)

45. Rotem, L., Segev, G., Shahaf, I.: Generic-group delay functions require hidden-order groups. In: Canteaut, A., Ishai, Y. (eds.) EUROCRYPT 2020, Part III. LNCS, vol. 12107, pp. 155–180. Springer, Cham (2020). https://doi.org/10.1007/978-3-030-45727-3_6

46. Shoup, V.: Lower bounds for discrete logarithms and related problems. In: Fumy, W. (ed.) EUROCRYPT 1997. LNCS, vol. 1233, pp. 256–266. Springer, Heidelberg (1997). https://doi.org/10.1007/3-540-69053-0_18

47. Wee, H.: Zero knowledge in the random oracle model, revisited. In: Matsui, M. (ed.) ASIACRYPT 2009. LNCS, vol. 5912, pp. 417–434. Springer, Heidelberg (2009). https://doi.org/10.1007/978-3-642-10366-7_25

48. Wesolowski, B.: Efficient verifiable delay functions. In: Ishai, Y., Rijmen, V. (eds.) EUROCRYPT 2019, Part III. LNCS, vol. 11478, pp. 379–407. Springer, Cham (2019). https://doi.org/10.1007/978-3-030-17659-4_13

# Privacy and Law Enforcement

# On the Power of Multiple Anonymous Messages: Frequency Estimation and Selection in the Shuffle Model of Differential Privacy

Badih Ghazi[1]($\boxtimes$), Noah Golowich[2], Ravi Kumar[1], Rasmus Pagh[3], and Ameya Velingker[1]

[1] Google Research, Mountain View, USA
[2] MIT EECS, Cambridge, USA
nzg@mit.edu
[3] BARC and University of Copenhagen, Copenhagen, Denmark
pagh@di.ku.dk

**Abstract.** It is well-known that general secure multi-party computation can in principle be applied to implement differentially private mechanisms over distributed data with utility matching the curator (a.k.a. central) model. In this paper we study the power of protocols running on top of a much weaker primitive: A non-interactive anonymous channel, known as the *shuffle* model in the differential privacy literature. Such protocols are implementable in a scalable way using known cryptographic methods and are known to enable non-interactive, differentially private protocols with error much smaller than what is possible in the local model. We study fundamental counting problems in the shuffle model and obtain tight, up to polylogarithmic factors, bounds on the error and communication in several settings.

For the classic problem of *frequency estimation* for $n$ users and a domain of size $B$, we obtain:
- A nearly tight lower bound of $\tilde{\Omega}(\min(\sqrt[4]{n}, \sqrt{B}))$ on the $\ell_\infty$ error in the *single-message* shuffle model. This implies that the protocols obtained from the amplification via shuffling work of Erlingsson et al. (SODA 2019) and Balle et al. (Crypto 2019) are nearly optimal for single-message protocols.
- Protocols in the *multi-message* shuffle model with poly$(\log B, \log n)$ bits of communication per user and $\ell_\infty$ error at most poly

---

N. Golowich—This work was done while interning at Google Research. Supported at MIT by a Fannie & John Hertz Foundation Fellowship and an NSF Graduate Fellowship.

R. Pagh—This work was initiated while visiting Google Research. Supported by VILLUM Foundation grant 16582.

---

**Electronic supplementary material** The online version of this chapter (https://doi.org/10.1007/978-3-030-77883-5_16) contains supplementary material, which is available to authorized users.

A. Canteaut and F.-X. Standaert (Eds.): EUROCRYPT 2021, LNCS 12698, pp. 463–488, 2021.
https://doi.org/10.1007/978-3-030-77883-5_16

$(\log B, \log n)$, which provide an exponential improvement on the error compared to what is possible with single-message algorithms. This implies protocols with similar error and communication guarantees for several well-studied problems such as heavy hitters, $d$-dimensional range counting, M-estimation of the median and quantiles, and more generally sparse non-adaptive statistical query algorithms.

For the *selection* problem on a domain of size $B$, we prove:

- A nearly tight lower bound of $\Omega(B)$ on the number of users in the single-message shuffle model. This significantly improves on the $\Omega(B^{1/17})$ lower bound obtained by Cheu et al. (Eurocrypt 2019).

A key ingredient in our lower bound proofs is a lower bound on the error of *locally*-private frequency estimation in the low-privacy (a.k.a. high $\varepsilon$) regime. For this we develop new tools to improve the results of Duchi et al. (FOCS 2013; JASA 2018) and Bassily & Smith (STOC 2015), whose techniques only gave tight bounds in the high-privacy setting.

# 1   Introduction

With increased public awareness and the introduction of stricter regulation of how personally identifiable data may be stored and used, user privacy has become an issue of paramount importance in a wide range of practical applications. While many formal notions of privacy have been proposed (see, e.g., [76]), *differential privacy (DP)* [44,46] has emerged as the gold standard due to its broad applicability and nice features such as composition and post-processing (see, e.g., [51,93] for a comprehensive overview). A primary goal of DP is to enable processing of users' data in a way that (i) does not reveal substantial information about the data of any single user, and (ii) allows the accurate computation of functions of the users' inputs. The theory of DP studies what trade-offs between privacy and accuracy are feasible for desired families of functions.

Most work on DP has been in the *central* (a.k.a. *curator*) setup, where numerous private algorithms with small error have been devised (see, e.g., [18,49,50]). The premise of the central model is that a curator can access the raw user data before releasing a differentially private output. In distributed applications, this requires users to transfer their raw data to the curator—a strong limitation in cases where users would expect the entity running the curator (e.g., a government agency or a technology company) to gain little information about their data.

To overcome this limitation, recent work has studied the *local* model of DP [71] (also [97]), where each individual message sent by a user is required to be private. Indeed, several large-scale deployments of DP in practice, at companies such as Apple [5,62], Google [55,87], and Microsoft [40], have used local DP. While estimates in the local model require weaker trust assumptions than in the central model, they inevitably suffer from significant error. For many types of queries, the estimation error is provably larger than the error incurred in the central model by a factor growing with the square root of the number of users.

*Shuffle Privacy Model.* The aforementioned trade-offs have motivated the study of the *shuffle* model of privacy as a middle ground between the central and local models. While a similar setup was first studied in cryptography in the work of Ishai et al. [68] on cryptography from anonymity, the shuffle model was first proposed for privacy-preserving protocols by Bittau et al. [16] in their Encode-Shuffle-Analyze architecture. In the shuffle setting, each user sends one or more messages to the analyzer using an *anonymous* channel that does not reveal where each message comes from. Such anonymization is a common procedure in data collection and is easy to explain to regulatory agencies and users. The anonymous channel is equivalent to all user messages being randomly shuffled (i.e., permuted) before being operated on by the analyzer, leading to the model illustrated in Fig. 1; see Sect. 2 for a formal description of the shuffle model. In this work, we treat the shuffler as a black box, but note that various efficient cryptographic implementations of the shuffler have been considered, including onion routing, mixnets, third-party servers, and secure hardware (see, e.g., [16, 68]). A comprehensive overview of recent work on anonymous communication can be found on Free Haven's Selected Papers in Anonymity website [57].

The DP properties of the shuffle model were first analytically studied, independently, in the works of Erlingsson et al. [54] and Cheu et al. [29]. Protocols within the shuffle model are non-interactive and fall into two categories: *single-message* protocols, in which each user sends one message (as in the local model), and *multi-message* protocols, in which a user can send more than one message. In both variants, the messages sent by all users are shuffled before being passed to the analyzer. The goal is to design private protocols in the shuffle model with as small error and total communication as possible. An example of the power of the shuffle model was established by Erlingsson et al. [54] and extended by Balle et al. [9], who showed that every locally differentially private algorithm directly yields a single-message protocol in the shuffle model with significantly better privacy. In this paper we study the optimal error achievable for fundamental tasks such as frequency estimation (i.e., histograms) and selection in the shuffle model of differential privacy. We show that in many settings, multi-message protocols can achieve significantly smaller error than single-message protocols, and we introduce such low-error multi-message protocols that have the additional property of having low communication.

The study of differential privacy in the shuffle model can be seen as part of a movement towards an integrated study of differential privacy and cryptographic protocols, i.e., "DP-cryptography" [94].

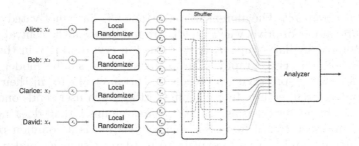

**Fig. 1.** Computation in the shuffle model consists of local randomization of inputs in the first stage, followed by a shuffle of all outputs of the local randomizers, after which the shuffled output is passed on to an analyzer.

**Overview.** The remainder of the paper is organized as follows. In Sect. 2 we review some preliminaries for differential privacy and the shuffle model. In Sect. 3 we give an overview of our main theorems for the frequency estimation and selection problems, and in Sect. 4 we overview the proofs of our main results. In Sect. 5 we discuss applications of our results to problems such as range queries and median estimation. In Sect. 6 we discuss related work in detail, and we conclude in Sect. 7. Full proofs of our results as well as the precise statements of some theorems are relegated to the supplementary material; see Section A.

## 2   Preliminaries

Before stating our main results, we formally introduce the basics of differential privacy and the shuffle model.

*Notation.* For a positive real number $a$, we use $\log(a)$ to denote the logarithm base 2 of $a$, and $\ln(a)$ to denote the natural logarithm of $a$. For any positive integer $B$, let $[B] = \{1, 2, \ldots, B\}$. For any set $\mathcal{Y}$, we denote by $\mathcal{Y}^*$ the set consisting of sequences of elements of $\mathcal{Y}$, i.e., $\mathcal{Y}^* = \bigcup_{n \geq 0} \mathcal{Y}^n$. For positive integers $n, B$, we write $\text{polylog}(n, B)$ to denote the class of functions $f(n, B)$ for which there is a constant $C$ so that for all $n, B \in \mathbb{N}$, $f(n, B) \leq C(\log(nB))^C$.

*Datasets.* Fix a finite set $\mathcal{X}$, the space of reports of users. A *dataset* is an element of $\mathcal{X}^*$, namely a tuple consisting of elements of $\mathcal{X}$. Let $\text{hist}(X) \in \mathbb{N}^{|\mathcal{X}|}$ be the histogram of $X$: for any $x \in \mathcal{X}$, the $x$th component of $\text{hist}(X)$ is the number of occurrences of $x$ in the dataset $X$. We will consider datasets $X, X'$ to be *equivalent* if they have the same histogram (i.e., the ordering of the elements $x_1, \ldots, x_n$ does not matter). For a multiset $\mathcal{S}$ whose elements are in $\mathcal{X}$, we will also write $\text{hist}(\mathcal{S})$ to denote the histogram of $\mathcal{S}$ (so that the $x$th component is the number of copies of $x$ in $\mathcal{S}$).

*Differential Privacy.* Two datasets $X, X'$ are said to be *neighboring* if they differ in a single element, meaning that we can write (up to equivalence) $X = (x_1, \ldots, x_{n-1}, x_n)$ and $X' = (x_1, \ldots, x_{n-1}, x'_n)$, for $x_1, \ldots, x_n, x'_n \in \mathcal{X}$. In this case, we write $X \sim X'$. Let $\mathcal{Z}$ be a set; we now define the differential privacy of a randomized function $P : \mathcal{X}^n \to \mathcal{Z}$:

**Definition 21 (Differential privacy [44,46]).** *A randomized algorithm $P :$ $\mathcal{X}^n \to \mathcal{Z}$ is $(\varepsilon, \delta)$-differentially private (DP) if for every pair of neighboring datasets $X \sim X'$ and for every set $\mathcal{S} \subset \mathcal{Z}$, we have*

$$\mathbb{P}[P(X) \in \mathcal{S}] \leqslant e^\varepsilon \cdot \mathbb{P}[P(X') \in \mathcal{S}] + \delta,$$

*where the probabilities are taken over the randomness in $P$. Here, $\varepsilon \geqslant 0, \delta \in [0,1]$.*

We will use the following compositional property of differential privacy.

**Lemma 1 (Post-processing, e.g., [50]).** *If $P$ is $(\varepsilon, \delta)$-differentially private, then for every randomized function $A$, the composed function $A \circ P$ is $(\varepsilon, \delta)$-differentially private.*

*Shuffle Model.* We review the *shuffle model* of differential privacy [16,29,54]. The input to the model is a dataset $(x_1, \ldots, x_n) \in \mathcal{X}^n$, where item $x_i \in \mathcal{X}$ is held by user $i$. A protocol in the shuffle model is the composition of three algorithms:

- The *local randomizer* $R : \mathcal{X} \to \mathcal{Y}^*$ takes as input the data of one user, $x_i \in \mathcal{X}$, and outputs a sequence $(y_{i,1}, \ldots, y_{i,m_i})$ of *messages*; here $m_i$ is a positive integer. In the *single-message* shuffle model, we require $m_i = 1$ for each $i$; in the *multi-message* shuffle model, $m_i$ may be any positive integer.
- The *shuffler* $S : \mathcal{Y}^* \to \mathcal{Y}^*$ takes as input a sequence of elements of $\mathcal{Y}$, say $(y_1, \ldots, y_m)$, and outputs a random permutation, i.e., the sequence $(y_{\pi(1)}, \ldots, y_{\pi(m)})$, where $\pi \in S_m$ is a uniformly random permutation on $[m]$. The input to the shuffler will be the concatenation of the outputs of the local randomizers.
- The *analyzer* $A : \mathcal{Y}^* \to \mathcal{Z}$ takes as input a sequence of elements of $\mathcal{Y}$ (which will be taken to be the output of the shuffler) and outputs an answer in $\mathcal{Z}$ which is taken to be the output of the protocol $P$.

We will write $P = (R, S, A)$ to denote the protocol whose components are given by $R$, $S$, and $A$. The main distinction between the shuffle and local model is the introduction of the (trusted) shuffler $S$ between the local randomizer and the analyzer. Similar to the local model, in the shuffle model the analyzer is untrusted; hence privacy must be guaranteed with respect to the input to the analyzer, i.e., the output of the shuffler. Formally, we have:

**Definition 22 (Differential privacy in the shuffle model, [29,54]).** *A protocol $P = (R, S, A)$ is $(\varepsilon, \delta)$-differentially private if, for any dataset $X = (x_1, \ldots, x_n)$, the algorithm*

$$(x_1, \ldots, x_n) \mapsto S(R(x_1), \ldots, R(x_n))$$

*is $(\varepsilon, \delta)$-differentially private.*

Notice that the output of $S(R(x_1), \ldots, R(x_n))$ can be simulated by an algorithm that takes as input the *multiset* consisting of the union of the elements of $R(x_1), \ldots, R(x_n)$ (which we denote as $\bigcup_i R(x_i)$, with a slight abuse of notation) and outputs a uniformly random permutation of them. Thus, by Lemma 1, it can be assumed without loss of generality for privacy analyses that the shuffler simply outputs the multiset $\bigcup_i R(x_i)$. For the purpose of analyzing accuracy of the protocol $P = (R, S, A)$, we define its *output* on the dataset $X = (x_1, \ldots, x_n)$ to be $P(X) := A(S(R(x_1), \ldots, R(x_n)))$. We also remark that the case of *local differential privacy*, formalized in Definition 23, is a variant of the shuffle model where the shuffler $S$ is replaced by the identity function.

**Definition 23 (Local differential privacy [71]).** *A protocol $P = (R, A)$ is $(\varepsilon, \delta)$-differentially private in the local model (or $(\varepsilon, \delta)$-locally differentially private) if the function $x \mapsto R(x)$ is $(\varepsilon, \delta)$-differentially private in the sense of Definition 21. We say that the output of the protocol $P$ on an input dataset $X = (x_1, \ldots, x_n)$ is $P(X) := A(R(x_1), \ldots, R(x_n))$.*

## 3   Overview of Results

In this work, we study several basic problems related to *counting* in the shuffle model of DP. In these problems, each of $n$ users holds an element from a domain of size $B$. We consider the problems of frequency estimation, variable selection, heavy hitters, median estimation, and range counting and study whether it is possible to obtain $(\varepsilon, \delta)$-DP in the shuffle model with accuracy close to what is possible in the central model, while keeping communication low. This section contains an overview of our main results.

The *frequency estimation* problem (also known as computing *histograms*) is at the core of many of the problems we study. In the simplest version, for some positive integer $B$, each of $n$ users gets an element of the domain $\mathcal{X} := [B]$, and the goal is to estimate the number of users in a dataset $X$ holding element $j$, namely $\mathrm{hist}(X)_j$, for each query element $j \in [B]$. We study frequency estimation with the $\ell_\infty$ error, meaning that we define the error of a frequency estimation protocol to be the maximum additive error for the frequency estimate of any coordinate $j$. In particular, if $\hat{f} \in \mathbb{R}^B$ is a vector of frequency estimates for a dataset $X$, then the $\ell_\infty$ error is $\|\mathrm{hist}(X) - \hat{f}\|_\infty = \max_{j \in [B]} |\mathrm{hist}(X)_j - \hat{f}_j|$. Frequency estimation is a fundamental primitive that is used in various data structural, sketching, and streaming applications (see Sect. 5 for its use in the shuffled protocols for range counting and median estimation as well as Sect. 6 for a sample of related work on the problem). Frequency estimation has been extensively studied in DP where in the central model, the smallest possible error is $\Theta(\min(\log(1/\delta)/\varepsilon, \log(B)/\varepsilon, n))$ (see, e.g., [93, Section 7.1]). By contrast, in the local model of DP, the smallest possible error is known to be $\Theta(\min(\sqrt{n \log(B)}/\varepsilon, n))$ under the assumption that $\delta < o(1/n)$ [12] (this regime for $\delta$ covers all values for $\delta$ of interest in the setting of differential privacy).[1]

---

[1] Most of the large-scale deployments of local DP in practice (e.g., [5,55]) have been variants of frequency estimation protocols.

In the high-level exposition of our results given below, we let $n$ and $B$ be any positive integers. We typically take $\varepsilon > 0$ to be any constant, and $\delta > 0$ to be inverse polynomial in $n$. This assumption on $\varepsilon$ and $\delta$ covers a regime of parameters that is relevant in practice. We will make use of tilde notation (e.g., $\tilde{O}, \tilde{\Theta}$) to indicate the suppression of multiplicative factors that are polynomial in $\log B$ and $\log n$. Theorem statements which do not make such assumptions and contain full dependence on all parameters may be found in the supplementary material.

*Single-Message Bounds for Frequency Estimation.* For the frequency estimation problem, we show the following result in the shuffle model where each user sends a single message.

**Theorem 1 (Informal version of Theorems 5 & 7).** *Any $(O(1), o(1/n))$-differentially private frequency estimation protocol in the single-message shuffle model has expected $\ell_\infty$ error $\tilde{\Omega}(\min(\sqrt[4]{n}, \sqrt{B}))$. Moreover, there is a single-message $(O(1), o(1/n))$-differentially private protocol with error $\tilde{O}(\min(\sqrt[4]{n}, \sqrt{B}))$.*

The main contribution of Theorem 1 is the lower bound. To prove this result, we obtain improved bounds on the error needed for frequency estimation in local DP in the weak privacy regime where $\varepsilon$ is around $\ln n$. The upper bound in Theorem 1 follows by combining the recent result of Balle et al. [9] (building on the earlier result of Erlingsson et al. [54]) with RAPPOR [55] and $B$-ary randomized response [97] (see Sect. 4.1 and Section C for more details).

The precise version of Theorem 1 with polylogarithmic factors (i.e., Theorem 5) implies that in order for a single-message differentially private protocol to get error $o(n)$ one needs to have $n = \omega\left(\frac{\log B}{\log \log B}\right)$ users; see Corollary 2. This improves on a result of Cheu et al. [29, Corollary 32], which gives a lower bound of $n = \omega(\log^{1/17} B)$ for this task.

*Multi-message Protocols for Frequency Estimation.* Theorem 1 implies that in the single-message shuffle model, the error has to grow polynomially with $\min(n, B)$, even with unbounded communication (i.e., message length). We next present (non-interactive) *multi-message* protocols in the shuffle model of DP for frequency estimation with only *polylogarithmic* error and communication. One of the protocols is a *public-coin* protocol, meaning that it makes use of a source of public randomness (known to all parties, including the adversary); the other protocol is a *private-coin* protocol, meaning that no such assumption is made. In addition to error and communication, a parameter of interest is the *query time*, which is the time to estimate the frequency of any element $j \in [B]$ from the data structure constructed by the analyzer.[2]

---

[2] The analyzers for both protocols in Theorem 2 have pre-processing time $\tilde{O}(n)$ on the output of the shuffler. In the regime $B \gg n$ (which is often of interest), this running time precludes them from computing all frequencies up-front.

**Table 1.** Upper and lower bounds on expected maximum error (over all $B$ queries, where the sum of all frequencies is $n$) for frequency estimation in different models of DP. The bounds are stated for fixed, positive privacy parameters $\varepsilon$ and $\delta$, and $\tilde{\Theta}/\tilde{O}/\tilde{\Omega}$ asymptotic notation suppresses factors that are polylogarithmic in $B$ and $n$. The communication per user is in terms of the total number of bits sent. In all upper bounds, the protocol is symmetric with respect to the users, and no public randomness is needed. References are to the first results we are aware of that imply the stated bounds.

| | Local | | Local + shuffle | Shuffle, single-message | Shuffle, multi-message | Central |
|---|---|---|---|---|---|---|
| Expected max. error | $\tilde{O}(\sqrt{n})$ | $\tilde{\Omega}(\sqrt{n})$ | $\tilde{O}(\min(\sqrt[4]{n}, \sqrt{B}))$ | $\tilde{\Omega}(\min(\sqrt[4]{n}, \sqrt{B}))$ | $\mathrm{polylog}(n, B)$ | $\mathrm{polylog}(n, B)$ |
| Comm. per user | $\Theta(1)$ | Any | $O(B)$ (err $\sqrt[4]{n}$) $\log B$ (err $\sqrt{B}$) | Any | $\mathrm{polylog}(n, B)$ | n.a. |
| References | [11] | [12] | [9,55,97] | Thms. 7 & 5 | Thm. 15 | [78,90] |

**Theorem 2 (Informal version of Theorems 15 & 16).** *There are private-coin and public-coin multi-message $(O(1), 1/n^{O(1)})$-DP protocols in the shuffle model for frequency estimation satisfying the following:*

- *The private-coin protocol has $\ell_\infty$ error $O(\max\{\log B, \log n\})$, total communication of $O(\log B \log^2 n)$ bits per user, and query time $\tilde{O}(n)$.*
- *The public-coin protocol has $\ell_\infty$ error $O(\log^{3/2}(B)\sqrt{\log(n \log(B))})$, total communication of $O(\log^4(B) \log^2(n))$ bits per user, and query time $O(\log B)$.*

Combining Theorems 1 and 2 yields the first separation between single-message and multi-message protocols for frequency estimation. Moreover, Theorem 2 can be used to obtain multi-message protocols with small error and small communication for several other widely studied problems (e.g., heavy hitters, range counting, and median and quantile estimation), discussed in Sect. 5. Finally, Theorem 2 implies the following consequence for statistical query (SQ) algorithms with respect to a distribution $\mathcal{D}$ on $\mathcal{X}$ (see Section G for the basic definitions). We say that a non-adaptive SQ algorithm $\mathcal{A}$ making at most $B$ queries $q : \mathcal{X} \to \{0, 1\}$ is $k$-*sparse* if for each $x \in \mathcal{X}$, the Hamming weight of the output of the queries is at most $k$. Then, under the assumption that users' data is drawn i.i.d. from $\mathcal{D}$, the algorithm $\mathcal{A}$ can be efficiently simulated in the shuffle model as follows (Table 1):

**Corollary 1 (Informal version of Corollary 4).** *For any non-adaptive $k$-sparse SQ algorithm $\mathcal{A}$ with $B$ queries of tolerance $\tau > 0$ and any $\beta \in (0, 1)$, there is a (private-coin) shuffle model protocol satisfying $(\varepsilon, \delta)$-DP whose output has total variation distance at most $\beta$ from that of $\mathcal{A}$, such that the number of users is $n \leqslant \tilde{O}\left(\frac{k}{\varepsilon\tau} + \frac{1}{\tau^2}\right)$, and the per-user communication is $\tilde{O}\left(\frac{k^2}{\varepsilon^2}\right)$, where $\tilde{O}(\cdot)$ hides logarithmic factors in $B, n, 1/\delta, 1/\varepsilon$, and $1/\beta$.*

Corollary 1 improves upon the simulation of non-adaptive SQ algorithms in the *local model* [71], for which the number of users must grow as $\frac{k}{\varepsilon^2\tau^2}$ as opposed to

$\frac{1}{\tau^2} + \frac{k}{\varepsilon\tau}$ in the shuffle model. We emphasize that the main novelty of Corollary 1 is in the regime that $k^2/\varepsilon^2 \ll B$; in particular, though prior work on low-communication private summation in the shuffle model [10,29,59] implies an algorithm for simulating $\mathcal{A}$ with roughly the same bound on the number of users $n$ as in Corollary 1 and communication $\Omega(B)$, it was unknown whether the communication could be reduced to have logarithmic dependence on $B$, as in Corollary 1.

*Single-Message Bounds for Selection.* The techniques that we develop to prove the lower bound in Theorem 1 can be used to get a nearly tight $\Omega(B)$ lower bound on the number of users necessary to solve the *selection* problem. In the selection problem[3], each user $i \in [n]$ is given an arbitrary subset of $[B]$, represented by the indicator vector $x_i \in \{0,1\}^B$, and the goal is for the analyzer to output an index $j^* \in [B]$ such that

$$\sum_{i\in[n]} x_{i,j^*} \geqslant \max_{j\in[B]} \sum_{i\in[n]} x_{i,j} - \frac{n}{10}. \tag{1}$$

In other words, the analyzer's output should be the index of a domain element that is held by an approximately maximal number of users. The choice of the constant 10 in (1) is arbitrary; any constant larger than 1 may be used.

The selection problem has been studied in several previous works on differential privacy, and it has many applications to machine learning, hypothesis testing and approximation algorithms (see [41,90,92] and the references therein). Our work improves an $\Omega(B^{1/17})$ lower bound on $n$ in the single-message shuffle model due to Cheu et al. [29]. For $\varepsilon = 1$, the exponential mechanism [78] implies an $(\varepsilon, 0)$-DP algorithm for selection with $n = O(\log B)$ users in the central model, whereas in the local model, it is known that any $(\varepsilon, 0)$-DP algorithm for selection requires $n = \Omega(B \log B)$ users [92].

**Theorem 3 (Informal version of Theorem 11).** *For any single-message* $(O(1), o(1/(nB)))$-*DP protocol in the shuffle model that solves the selection problem given in Eq. (1), the number $n$ of users should be $\Omega(B)$.*

The lower bound in Theorem 3 nearly matches the $O(B \log B)$ upper bound on the required number of users that holds even in the local model (and hence in the single-message shuffle model) and that uses the $B$-randomized response [92,97]. Cheu et al. [29] have previously obtained a multi-message protocol for selection with $O(\sqrt{B})$ users, and combined with this result Theorem 3 yields the first separation between single-message and multi-message protocols for selection.

In subsequent work Chen et al. [28] have extended Theorem 3 to the setting when each user only sends *few* messages; in particular, they show that if each user sends at most $m$ messages in the shuffle model, then the number of users should be $\Omega(B/m)$. Their proof uses generally similar techniques to ours.

---

[3] Sometimes also referred to as *variable selection*.

# 4  Proof Outlines

## 4.1  Overview of Single-Message Lower Bounds

We start by giving an overview of the lower bound of $\tilde{\Omega}(\min\{n^{1/4}, \sqrt{B}\})$ in Theorem 1 on the error of any single-message frequency estimation protocol. We first focus on the case where $n \leqslant B^2$ and thus $\min\{n^{1/4}, \sqrt{B}\} = n^{1/4}$. The main component of the proof in this case is a lower bound of $\tilde{\Omega}(n^{1/4})$ for frequency estimation for $(\varepsilon_L, \delta_L)$-*local* DP protocols[4] when $\varepsilon_L = \ln(n) + O(1)$. In fact, we prove lower bounds for $(\varepsilon_L, \delta_L)$-locally differentially protocols for a broader range of parameters $\varepsilon_L, \delta_L$ in Theorem 6; a special case of this result which includes the setting $\varepsilon_L = \ln(n) + O(1)$ relevant for the shuffle model is stated below:

**Theorem 4 (Local DP lower bound; informal version of Theorem 6).**
*Suppose that $\varepsilon_L, \delta_L > 0$ satisfy*

$$\frac{2}{3} \cdot \ln n \leqslant \varepsilon_L + \ln(1 + \varepsilon_L) \leqslant \min\{2\ln(B) - O(1), 2\ln(n) - 2\ln\ln(B)\},$$

*and $\delta_L < o\left(\min\left\{\frac{1}{n \ln n}, \exp(-\varepsilon_L)\right\}\right)$. Then any $(\varepsilon_L, \delta_L)$-locally differentially private protocol for frequency estimation on $[B]$ must have $\ell_\infty$ error at least $\tilde{\Omega}\left(\frac{\sqrt{n}}{e^{\varepsilon_L/4}}\right)$, where the tilde hides factors polynomial in $\log B, \log n$.*

While lower bounds for local DP frequency estimation were previously obtained in the seminal works of Bassily and Smith [12] and Duchi, Jordan and Wainwright [42], two critical reasons make them less useful for our purposes: (i) for $\varepsilon_L = \omega(1)$ (i.e., in the low-privacy regime) they only apply to the case where $\delta_L = 0$ (i.e., pure privacy)[5], and (ii) even for $\delta_L = 0$, their dependence on $\varepsilon_L$ is sub-optimal when $\varepsilon_L = \omega(1)$: the results of [42], for instance, imply a lower bound of $\Omega\left(\frac{\sqrt{n \log B}}{e^{\varepsilon_L}}\right)$ on the $\ell_\infty$ error.[6] By contrast, Theorem 4 covers the *low and approximate privacy* regime; we next discuss its proof.

Let $R$ be an $(\varepsilon_L, \delta_L)$-locally differentially private randomizer. The general approach in the proof of Theorem 4, which was also taken in [12,42], is to show that if $V$ is a random variable drawn uniformly at random from $[B]$ and

---

[4] Note that we use the subscripts in $\varepsilon_L$ and $\delta_L$ to distinguish the privacy parameters of the *local* model from the $\varepsilon$ and $\delta$ parameters (without a subscript) of the shuffle model.

[5] As we discuss in Remark 1, generic reductions [20,29] showing that one can efficiently simulate an approximately differentially private protocol (i.e., with $\delta_L > 0$) with a pure differentially private protocol (i.e., with $\delta_L = 0$) are insufficient to obtain tight lower bounds.

[6] If we were to ignore the assumption of $\delta_L = 0$ and try to use this bound for $\varepsilon_L = \ln(n) + O(1)$ to attempt to derive a lower bound in the single-message shuffle model in the context of Theorem 1, we would get a lower bound of $\Omega(\sqrt{\log(B)/n})$ on the $\ell_\infty$ error, which for $n \gg \log B$ is (much) worse than even the lower bound of $\Omega(\min\{\log B, \log n\})$ from the *central* model.

if $X$ is a random variable that is equal to $V$ with some appropriate choice of $\alpha \in (0,1)$, and is drawn uniformly at random from $[B]$ otherwise, then the mutual information between $V$ and the local randomizer output $R(X)$ satisfies

$$I(V; R(X)) \leqslant \frac{\log B}{4n}. \tag{2}$$

Once (2) is established, the chain rule of mutual information implies that $I(V; R(X_1), \ldots, R(X_n)) \leqslant \frac{\log B}{4}$, where $X_1, \ldots, X_n$ are independent and identically distributed given $V$. Fano's inequality [38] then implies that the probability that any analyzer receiving $R(X_1), \ldots, R(X_n)$ correctly guesses $V$ is at most $1/4$; on the other hand, an $\Omega(\alpha n)$-accurate analyzer must be able to determine $V$ with high probability since its frequency in the dataset $X_1, \ldots, X_n$ is roughly $\alpha n$, greater than the frequency of all other $v \in [B]$. This approach thus yields a lower bound of $\Omega(\alpha n)$ on frequency estimation.

To prove the lower bound of Theorem 4 using this approach, we choose $\alpha n = \tilde{\Theta}(\sqrt{n}/e^{\varepsilon_L/4})$, and show that

$$I(V; R(X)) \leqslant \tilde{O}(\alpha^4 n e^{\varepsilon_L}) \leqslant \frac{\log B}{4n}. \tag{3}$$

For the application to the single-message shuffle model, we will have $\varepsilon_L = \ln(n) + O(1)$ and so $\alpha = \tilde{\Theta}(n^{-3/4})$; as we will discuss later, (3) is essentially tight in this regime.

*Limitations of Previous Approaches.* We first state the existing upper bounds on $I(V; R(X))$, which only use the privacy of the local randomizer. Bassily and Smith [12, Claim 5.4] showed an upper bound of $I(V; R(X)) \leqslant O(\varepsilon_L^2 \alpha^2)$ with $\varepsilon_L = O(1)$ and $\delta_L = o(1/(n \log n))$, which thus satisfies (2) with $\alpha = \Theta\left(\sqrt{\frac{\log B}{\varepsilon_L^2 n}}\right)$. For $\delta_L = 0$, Duchi et al. [42] generalized this result to the case $\varepsilon_L \geqslant 1$, proving that[7] $I(V; R(X)) \leqslant O(\alpha^2 e^{2\varepsilon_L})$. Even ignoring the constraint $\delta_L = 0$, this bound of [42] is weaker than (3) for the above setting of $\alpha$ and $\varepsilon_L$.

However, proving the mutual information bound in (3) turns out to be impossible if we only use the privacy of the local randomizers! In particular, the bound can be shown to be *false* if all we assume about $R$ is that it is $(\varepsilon_L, \delta_L)$-locally differentially private for some $\varepsilon_L \approx \ln n$ and $\delta_L \leqslant n^{-O(1)}$. For instance, it is violated if one takes $R$ to be $R_{\mathrm{RR}}$, the local randomizer of the $B$-randomized response [97]. Consider for example the regime where $B \leqslant n \leqslant B^2$, and the setting where $R_{\mathrm{RR}}(v)$ is equal to $v$ with probability $1 - B/n$, and is uniformly random over $[B]$ with the remaining probability of $B/n$. In this case, the local randomizer $R_{\mathrm{RR}}(\cdot)$ is $(\ln(n) + O(1), 0)$-differentially private. A simple calculation shows that $I(V; R_{\mathrm{RR}}(X)) = \tilde{\Theta}(\alpha)$. Whenever $\alpha \ll 1/n^{2/3}$, which is the regime we have to consider in order to prove Theorem 1[8], it holds that $\alpha \gg \alpha^4 n \exp(\ln(n))$, thus

---

[7] This bound is not stated explicitly in [42], though [42, Lemma 7] proves a similar result whose proof can readily be modified appropriately.

[8] i.e., we will take $\alpha n = \tilde{\Theta}(n^{1/4})$, so $\alpha = \tilde{\Theta}(n^{-3/4})$.

contradicting (3). (See also Remark 4 for an explanation of how a slightly different strategy also fails.) The insight derived from this counterexample is crucial,
as we describe in our new technique next.

*Mutual Information Bound from Privacy and Accuracy.* Departing from previous work, we manage to prove the stronger bound (3) as follows. Inspecting
the counterexample based on the $B$-randomized response outlined above, we
first observe that any analyzer must have error at least $\Omega(\sqrt{B})$ when combined with $R_{\mathrm{RR}}(\cdot)$, which is larger than $\alpha n$, the error that would be ruled out
by the subsequent application of Fano's inequality. This leads us to appeal to
accuracy, in addition to privacy, when proving the mutual information upper
bound. We thus leverage the additional available property that the local randomizer $R$ can be combined with an analyzer $A$ in such a way that the mapping
$(x_1, \ldots, x_n) \mapsto A(R(x_1), \ldots, R(x_n))$ computes the frequencies of elements of
every dataset $(x_1, \ldots, x_n)$ accurately, i.e., to within an error of $O(\alpha n)$. At a high
level, our approach for proving the bound in (3) then proceeds by:

(i) Proving a structural property satisfied by the randomizer corresponding to
    any accurate frequency estimation protocol. Namely, we show in Lemma 10
    that if there is an accurate analyzer, the total variation distance between
    the output of the local randomizer on any given input, and its output on a
    uniform input, is close to 1.

(ii) Using the $(\varepsilon_L, \delta_L)$-DP property of the randomizer along with the structural
     property in (i) in order to upper-bound the mutual information $I(V; R(X))$.

We believe that the application of the structural property in (i) to proving
bounds of the form (3) is of independent interest. As we further discuss below,
this property is, in particular, used (together with privacy of $R$) to argue that
for most inputs $v \in [B]$, the local randomizer output $R(v)$ is unlikely to equal
a message that is much less likely to occur when the input is uniformly random
than when it is $v$. Note that it is somewhat counter-intuitive that accuracy is
used in the proof of this fact, as one way to achieve very accurate protocols is to
ensure that $R(v)$ is equal to a message which is unlikely when the input is any
$u \neq v$. We now outline the proofs of (i) and (ii) in more detail.

The gist of the proof of (i) is an anti-concentration statement. Let $v$ be a
fixed element of $[B]$ and let $U$ be a random variable uniformly distributed on $[B]$.
Assume that the total variation distance $\Delta(R(v), R(U))$ is not close to 1, and that
a small fraction of the users have input $v$ while the rest have uniformly random
inputs. Let $\mathcal{Z}$ denote the range of the local randomizer $R$. First, we consider the
special case where $\mathcal{Z}$ is $\{0, 1\}$. Then the distribution of the histogram of outputs
of the users with $v$ as their input is in bijection with a binomial random variable
with parameter $p := \mathbb{P}[R(v) = 1]$, and the same is true for the distribution of
the shuffled outputs of the users with uniform random inputs $U$ (with parameter
$q := \mathbb{P}[R(U) = 1]$). Then, we use the anti-concentration properties of binomial
random variables in order to argue that if $|p - q| = \Delta(R(v), R(U))$ is too small,
then with nontrivial probability the shuffled outputs of the users with input $v$
will be indistinguishable from the shuffled outputs of the users with uniform

random inputs. This is then used to contradict the supposed accuracy of the analyzer. To deal with the general case where the range $\mathcal{Z}$ is any finite set, we repeatedly apply the data processing inequality for total variation distance in order to reduce to the binary case (Lemma 13). The full proof appears in Lemma 10.

Equipped with the property in (i), we now outline the proof of the mutual information bound in (ii). Denote by

- $\mathcal{T}_v$ the set of messages *much more likely* to occur when the input is $v$ than when it is uniform,
- $\mathcal{Y}_v$ the set of messages *less likely* to occur when the input is $v$ than when it is uniform.

Note that the union $\mathcal{T}_v \cup \mathcal{Y}_v$ is *not* the entire range $\mathcal{Z}$ of messages; in particular, it does not include messages that are *a bit more likely* to occur when the input is $v$ than when it is uniform.[9] On a high level, it turns out that the mutual information $I(V; R(X))$ will be large, i.e., $R(X)$ will reveal a significant amount of information about $V$, if either of the following events occurs:

(a) There are not enough inputs $v \in [B]$ such that the mass $\mathbb{P}[R(X) \in \mathcal{Y}_v]$ is large. Intuitively, for $v$ so that $\mathbb{P}[R(X) \in \mathcal{Y}_v]$ is large, the local randomizer "effectively hides" the fact that the uniform input $X$ is $v$ given that $X$ indeed equals $v$ and $R(v) \in \mathcal{Y}_v$.
(b) There are too many inputs $v \in [B]$ such that the mass $\mathbb{P}[R(v) \in \mathcal{T}_v]$ is large. Such inputs make it too likely that $X = v$ given that $R(X) \in \mathcal{T}_v$, which makes it more likely in turn that $V = v$.

We first note that the total variation distance $\Delta(R(v), R(X))$ is upper-bounded by $\mathbb{P}[R(X) \in \mathcal{Y}_v]$. On the other hand, the accuracy of the protocol along with property (i) imply that $\Delta(R(v), R(X))$ is close to 1 for all $v$. By putting these together, we can conclude that event (a) does not occur (see Lemma 10 for more details).

To prove that event (b) does not occur, we use the $(\varepsilon_L, \delta_L)$-DP guarantee of the local randomizer $R$. Namely, we will use the inequality $\mathbb{P}[R(v) \in \mathcal{S}] \leqslant e^{\varepsilon_L} \cdot \mathbb{P}[R(X) \in \mathcal{S}] + \delta$ for various subsets $\mathcal{S}$ of $\mathcal{Z}$. Unfortunately, setting $\mathcal{S} = \mathcal{T}_v$ does not lead to a good enough upper bound on $\mathbb{P}[R(v) \in \mathcal{T}_v]$; indeed, for the local randomizer $R = R_{\mathrm{RR}}$ corresponding to the $B$-ary randomized response, we will have $\mathcal{T}_v = \{v\}$ for $n \gg B$, and so $\mathbb{P}[R(v) \in \mathcal{T}_v] = 1 - B/n \approx 1$ for any $v$. Thus, to establish (b), we need to additionally use the accuracy of the analyzer $A$ (i.e., property (i) above), together with a careful double-counting argument to enumerate the probabilities that $R(v)$ belongs to subsets of $\mathcal{T}_v$ of different granularity (with respect to the likelihood of occurrence under input $v$ versus a uniform input). For the details, we refer the reader to Section B.3 and Lemma 9.

Having established Theorem 4 giving a lower bound for locally differentially private estimation in the low-privacy regime, Theorem 1 follows in a straightforward manner: the only step is to apply a lemma of Cheu et al. [29] (restated as

---

[9] For clarity of exposition in this overview, we refrain from quantifying the likelihoods in each of these cases; for more details on this, we refer the reader to Section B.3.

Lemma 2 below), stating that any lower bound for $(\varepsilon + \ln(n), \delta)$-locally differentially private protocols implies a lower bound for $(\varepsilon, \delta)$-differentially private protocols in the single-message shuffle model (i.e., we take $\varepsilon_L = \varepsilon + \ln(n)$). Indeed, for $\varepsilon_L = \ln(n) + O(1)$, the error lower bound from Theorem 4 is $\tilde{\Omega}(\sqrt{n}/e^{\varepsilon_L/4}) = \tilde{\Omega}(n^{1/4})$. Finally, we point out that while the above outline assumed that $n \leq B^2$, it turns out that this is essentially without loss of generality as the other case where $n > B^2$ can be reduced to the former (see Lemma 6).

*Tightness of Lower Bounds.* The lower bounds sketched above are nearly tight. The upper bound of Theorem 1 follows from combining existing results showing that the single-message shuffle model provides privacy amplification of locally differentially private protocols [9,54], with known locally differentially private protocols for frequency estimation [9,42,55,97]. In particular, as recently shown by Balle et al. [9], a pure $(\varepsilon_L, 0)$-differentially private local randomizer yields a protocol in the shuffle model that is $\left( O\left( e^{\varepsilon_L} \sqrt{\frac{\log(1/\delta)}{n}} \right), \delta \right)$-differentially private and that has same level of accuracy.[10] Then:

- When combined with RAPPOR [42,55], we get an upper bound of $\tilde{O}(n^{1/4})$ on the error.
- When combined with the $B$-randomized response [3,97], we get an error upper bound of $\tilde{O}(\sqrt{B})$.

The full details appear in Section C. Put together, these imply that the minimum in our lower bound in Theorem 1 is tight (up to logarithmic factors). It also follows that the mutual information bound in Eq. (3) is tight (up to logarithmic factors) for $\varepsilon_L = \ln(n) + O(1)$ and $\alpha = n^{-3/4}$ (which is the parameter settings corresponding to the single-message shuffle model); indeed, a stronger bound in Eq. (3) would lead to larger lower bounds in the single-message shuffle model thereby contradicting the upper bounds discussed in this paragraph.

*Lower Bound for Selection: Sharp Bound on Level-1 Weight of Probability Ratio Functions.* We now outline the proof of the nearly tight lower bound on the number of users required to solve the *selection* problem in the single-message shuffle model (Theorem 3). The main component of the proof in this case is a lower bound of $\Omega(B)$ users for selection for $(\varepsilon_L, \delta_L)$-*local* DP protocols when $\varepsilon_L = \ln(n) + O(1)$.

In the case of local $(\varepsilon_L, 0)$-DP (i.e., pure) protocols, Ullman [92] proved a lower bound $n = \Omega\left( \frac{B \log B}{(\exp(\varepsilon_L)-1)^2} \right)$. There are two different reasons why this lower bound is not sufficient for our purposes:

1. It does not rule out DP protocols with $\delta_L > 0$ (i.e., approximate protocols), which are necessary to consider for our application to the shuffle model.

---

[10] Note that we cannot use the earlier amplification by shuffling result of [54], since it is only stated for $\varepsilon_L = O(1)$ whereas we need to amplify a much less private local protocol, having an $\varepsilon_L$ close to $\ln n$.

2. For the low privacy setting of $\varepsilon_L = \ln(n) + O(1)$, the bound simplifies to $n = \tilde{\Omega}(B/n^2)$, i.e., $n = \tilde{\Omega}(B^{1/3})$, weaker than what we desire.

To prove our near-optimal lower bound, we remedy both of the aforementioned limitations by allowing positive values of $\delta_L$ and achieving a better dependence on $\varepsilon_L$. As in the proof of frequency estimation, we reduce proving Theorem 3 to the task of showing the following mutual information upper bound:

$$I((L,J); R(X_{L,J})) \leqslant \tilde{O}\left(\frac{1}{B}\right) + O(\delta_L(B+n)), \tag{4}$$

where $L$ is a uniform random bit, $J$ is a uniform random coordinate in $[B]$, and $X_{L,J}$ is uniform over the subcube $\{x \in \{0,1\}^B : x_J = L\}$. Indeed, once (4) holds and $\delta_L < o(1/(Bn))$, the chain rule implies that the mutual information between all users' messages and the pair $(L, J)$ is at most $O\left(\frac{n \ln(B)}{B}\right)$. It follows by Fano's inequality that if $n = o(B)$, no analyzer can determine the pair $(L, J)$ with high probability (which any protocol for selection must be able to do).

For any message $z$ in the range of $R$, define the Boolean function $f_z(x) := \frac{\mathbb{P}[R(x)=z]}{\mathbb{P}[R(X_{L,J})=z]}$ where $x \in \{0,1\}^B$. Let $\mathbf{W}^1[f]$ denote the level-1 Fourier weight of a Boolean function $f$. To prove inequalities of the form (4), the prior work of Ullman [92] shows that $I((L,J); R(X_{L,J}))$ is determined by $\mathbf{W}^1[f_z]$, up to normalization constants. In the case where $\delta_L = 0$ and $\varepsilon_L = \ln(n) + O(1)$, $f_z \in [0, e^{\varepsilon_L}]$, and by Parseval's identity $\mathbf{W}^1[f_z] \leqslant O(e^{2\varepsilon_L})$ for any message $z$, leading to

$$I((L,J); R(X_{L,J})) \leqslant O\left(\frac{e^{2\varepsilon_L}}{B}\right). \tag{5}$$

Unfortunately, for our choice of $\varepsilon_L = \ln(n) + O(1)$, (5) is weaker than (4).

To show (4), we depart from the previous approach in the following ways:

(a) We show that the functions $f_z$ take values in $[0, O(e^{\varepsilon_L})]$ for *most* inputs $x$; this uses the $(\varepsilon_L, \delta_L)$-local DP of the local randomizer $R$ (we cannot show this for all $x$ as in general $\delta_L > 0$).

(b) Using the *Level-1 inequality* from the analysis of Boolean functions [84] (see Theorem 13 below), we upper bound $\mathbf{W}^1[g_z]$ by $O(\varepsilon_L)$, where $g_z$ is the truncation of $f_z$ defined by $g_z(x) = f_z(x)$ if $f_z(x) \leqslant O(n)$ and $g_z(x) = 0$ otherwise.

(c) We bound $I((L,J); R(X_{L,J}))$ by $\mathbf{W}^1[g_z]$, using the fact $f_z$ is sufficiently close to its truncation $g_z$.

The above line of reasoning, formalized in Section B.5, allows us to show

$$I((L,J); R(X_{L,J})) \leqslant O\left(\frac{\varepsilon_L}{B} + \delta \cdot (B + e^{\varepsilon_L})\right),$$

which is sufficient to establish that (4) holds.

Having proved a lower bound on the error of any $(\varepsilon+\ln n, \delta)$-local DP protocol for selection with $\varepsilon = O(1)$, the final step in the proof is to apply a lemma of [29] to deduce the desired lower bound in the single-message shuffle model.

## 4.2   Overview of Multi-message Protocols

An important consequence of our lower bound in Theorem 1 is that one cannot achieve an error of polylog($n, B$) using *single-message* protocols. This in particular rules out any approach that uses the following natural two-step recipe for getting a private protocol in the shuffle model with accuracy better than in the local model:

1. Run any known locally differentially private protocol with a setting of parameters that enables high-accuracy estimation at the analyzer, but exhibits low privacy locally.
2. Randomly shuffle the messages obtained when each user runs step 1 on their input, and use the privacy amplification by shuffling bounds [9,54] to improve the privacy guarantees.

Thus, shuffled versions of the $B$-randomized response [3,97], RAPPOR [3,42, 55], the Bassily–Smith protocol [12], TreeHist and Bitstogram [11], and the Hadamard response protocol [2,3], will still incur an error of $\Omega(\min(\sqrt[4]{n}, \sqrt{B}))$.

Moreover, although the single-message protocol of Cheu et al. [29] for binary aggregation (as well as the multi-message protocols given in [7,8,59,60] for the more general task of real-valued aggregation) can be applied to the one-hot encodings of each user's input to obtain a multi-message protocol for frequency estimation with error polylog($n, B$), the communication per user would be $\Omega(B)$ bits, which is clearly undesirable.

Recall that the main idea behind (shuffled) randomized response is for each user to send their input with some probability, and random noise with the remaining probability. Similarly, the main idea behind (shuffled) Hadamard response is for each user to send a uniformly random index from the support of the Hadamard codeword corresponding to their input with some probability, and a random index from the entire universe with the remaining probability. In both protocols, the user is sending a message that either depends on their input or is noise; this restriction turns out to be a significant limitation. Our main insight is that multiple messages allows users to simultaneously send both types of messages, leading to a sweet spot with exponentially smaller error and communication.

*Our Protocols.* We design a multi-message version of the private-coin Hadamard response of Acharya et al. [2,3] where each user sends a small *subset* of indices sampled uniformly at random from the support of the Hadamard codeword corresponding to their input, and in addition sends a small subset of indices sampled uniformly at random from the entire universe [$B$]. To get accurate results it is crucial that a subset of indices is sampled, as opposed to just a single index (as in the local model protocol of [2,3]). We show that in the regime where the number of indices sampled from inside the support of the Hadamard codeword and the number of noise indices sent by each user are both logarithmic, the resulting multi-message algorithm is private in the shuffle model, and it has polylogarithmic error and communication per user (see Theorem 15, Lemmas 17, 18, and 19 for more details).

A limitation of our private-coin algorithm outlined above is that the time for the analyzer to answer a single query is $\tilde{O}(n)$. This might be a drawback in applications where the analyzer is CPU-limited or where it is supposed to produce real-time answers. In the presence of public randomness, we design an algorithm that remedies this limitation, having error, communication per user, and query time all bounded above by $\text{polylog}(n, B)$. This algorithm is based on a multi-message version of randomized response combined in a delicate manner with the Count Min data structure [34] (for more details, see Section D.2). Previous work [11,12] on DP has used Count Sketch [24], which is a close variant of Count Min, to reduce heavy hitter computation to frequency estimation. In contrast, our use of Count Min has the purpose of reducing the amount of communication per user.

## 5 Applications

*Heavy Hitters.* Another algorithmic task that is closely related to frequency estimation is computing the *heavy hitters* in a dataset distributed across $n$ users, where the goal of the analyzer is to (approximately) retrieve the identities and counts of all elements that appear at least $\tau$ times, for a given threshold $\tau$. It is well-known that in the central DP model, it is possible to compute $\tau$-heavy hitters for $\tau = \text{polylog}(n, B)$ whereas in the local DP model, it is possible to compute $\tau$-heavy hitters if and only if $\tau = \tilde{\Theta}(\sqrt{n})$. By combining with known reductions (e.g., from Bassily et al. [11]), our multi-message protocols for frequency estimation yield multi-message protocols for computing the $\tau$-heavy hitters with $\tau = \text{polylog}(n, B)$ and total communication of $\text{polylog}(n, B)$ bits per user (for more details, see Section H).

*Range Counting.* In range counting, each of the $n$ users is associated with a point in $[B]^d$ and the goal of the analyzer is to answer arbitrary queries of the form: given a rectangular box in $[B]^d$, how many of the points lie in it?[11] This is a basic algorithmic primitive that captures an important family of database queries and is useful in geographic applications. This problem has been well-studied in the central model of DP, where Chan et al. [22] obtained an upper bound of $(\log B)^{O(d)}$ on the error (see Sect. 6 for more related work). It has also been studied in the local DP model [33]; in this case, the error has to be at least $\Omega(\sqrt{n})$ even for $d = 1$.

We obtain private protocols for range counting in the multi-message shuffle model with exponentially smaller error than what is possible in the local model (for a wide range of parameters). Specifically, we give a private-coin multi-message protocol with $(\log B)^{O(d)}$ messages per user each of length $O(\log n)$ bits, error $(\log B)^{O(d)}$, and query time $\tilde{O}(n \log^d B)$. Moreover, we obtain a public-coin protocol with similar communication and error but with a much smaller query time of $\tilde{O}(\log^d B)$ (see Section F for more details).

---

[11] We formally define range queries as a special case of counting queries in Section F.

We now briefly outline the main ideas behind our multi-message protocols for range counting. We first argue that even for $d = 2$, the total number of queries is $\Theta(B^2)$ and the number of possible queries to which a user positively contributes is also $\Theta(B^2)$. Thus, direct applications of DP algorithms for aggregation or for frequency estimation would result in polynomial error and polynomial communication per user. Instead, we combine our multi-message protocol for frequency estimation (Theorem 2) with a communication-efficient implementation, in the multi-message shuffle model, of the space-partitioning data structure used in the central model protocol of Chan et al. [22]. The idea is to use a collection $\mathcal{B}$ of $O(B \log^d B)$ $d$-dimensional rectangles in $[B]^d$ (so-called *dyadic intervals*) with the property that an arbitrary rectangle can be formed as the disjoint union of $O(\log^d B)$ rectangles from $\mathcal{B}$. Furthermore, each point in $[B]^d$ is contained in $O(\log^d B)$ rectangles from $\mathcal{B}$. This means that it suffices to release a private count of the number of points inside each rectangle in $\mathcal{B}$—a frequency estimation task where each user input contributes to $O(\log^d B)$ buckets. To turn this into a protocol with small maximum communication in the shuffle model, we develop an approach analogous to the matrix mechanism [74,75]. We argue that the transformation of the aforementioned central model algorithm for range counting into a private protocol in the multi-message shuffle model with small communication and error is non-trivial and relies on the specific protocol structure. In fact, the state-of-the-art range counting algorithm of Dwork et al. [48] in the central model does not seem to transfer to the shuffle model.

*M-Estimation of Median.* A very basic statistic of any dataset of real numbers is its *median*. For simplicity, suppose our dataset consists of real numbers lying in $[0, 1]$. It is well-known that there is no DP algorithm for estimating the *value* of the median of such a dataset with error $o(1)$ (i.e., outputting a real number whose absolute distance to the true median is $o(1)$) [93, Section 3]. This is because the median of a dataset can be highly sensitive to a single data point when there are not many individual data points near the median. Thus in the context of DP, one has to settle for weaker notions of median estimation. One such notion is *M-estimation*, which amounts to finding a value $\tilde{x}$ that approximately minimizes $\sum_i |x_i - \tilde{x}|$ (recall that the median is the minimizer of this objective). This notion has been studied in previous work on DP including by [42,73] (for more on related work, see Sect. 6 below). Our private range counting protocol described above yields a multi-message protocol with communication polylog($n$) per user and that $M$-estimates the median up to error polylog($n$), i.e., outputs a value $y \in [0, 1]$ such that $\sum_i |x_i - y| \leq \min_{\tilde{x}} \sum_i |x_i - \tilde{x}| + \text{polylog}(n)$ (see Theorem 23 in Section I). Beyond $M$-estimation of the median, our work implies private multi-message protocols for estimating *quantiles* with polylog($n$) error and polylog($n$) bits of communication per user (see Section I for more details).

# 6  Related Work

*Shuffle Privacy Model.* Following the proposal of the Encode-Shuffle-Analyze architecture by Bittau et al. [16], several recent works have sought to formalize the trade-offs in the shuffle model with respect to standard local and central

DP [9,54] as well as devise private schemes in this model for tasks such as secure aggregation [7–9,29,59,60]. In particular, for the task of *real* aggregation, Balle et al. [9] showed that in the single-message shuffle model, the optimal error is $\Theta(n^{1/6})$ (which is better than the error in the local model which is known to be $\Theta(n^{1/2})$).[12] By contrast, recent follow-up work gave multi-message protocols for the same task with error and communication of polylog($n$) [7,8,59,60][13]. Our work is largely motivated by the aforementioned body of works demonstrating the power of the shuffle model, namely, its ability to enable private protocols with lower error than in the local model while placing less trust in a central server or curator.

Wang et al. [96] recently designed an extension of the shuffle model and analyzed its trust properties and privacy-utility tradeoffs. They studied the basic task of frequency estimation, and benchmarked several algorithms, including one based on single-message shuffling. However, they did not consider improvements through multi-message protocols, such as the ones we propose in this work. Very recently, Erlingsson et al. [53] studied multi-message ("report fragmenting") protocols for frequency estimation in a practical shuffle model setup. Though they make use of a sketching technique, like we do, their methods cannot be parameterized to have communication and error polylogarithmic in $n$ and $B$ (which our Theorem 2 achieves). This is a result of using an estimator (based on computing a mean) that does not yield high-probability guarantees.

*(Private) Frequency Estimation, Heavy Hitters, and Median.* Frequency estimation (and its extensions considered below) is a fundamental problem that has been extensively studied in numerous computational models including data structures, sketching, streaming, and communication complexity, (in particular, [24,31,34,35,56,61,63,70,77,79,80,101]). Heavy hitters and frequency estimation have also been studied extensively in the standard models of DP, e.g., [2,11,12,20,67,95,97]. The other problems we consider in the shuffle model, namely, range counting, M-estimation of the median, and quantiles, have been well-studied in the literature on data structures and sketching [37] as well as in the context of DP in the central and local models. Dwork and Lei [45] initiated work on establishing a connection between DP and robust statistics, and gave private estimators for several problems including the median, using the paradigm of propose-test-release. Subsequently, Lei [73] provided an approach in the central DP model for privately releasing a wide class of M-estimators (including the median) that are statistically consistent. While such M-estimators can also be obtained indirectly from non-interactive release of the density function [98], the aforementioned approach exhibits an improved rate of convergence. Furthermore, motivated by risk bounds under privacy constraints, Duchi et al. [42]

---

[12] Although the single-message real summation protocol of Balle et al. [9] uses the $B$-ary randomized response, when combined with their lower bound on single-message protocols, it does not imply any lower bound on single-message frequency estimation protocols. The reason is that their upper bound doe not use the $\ell_\infty$ error bound for the $B$-ary randomized response as a black box.

[13] A basic primitive in these protocols is a "split-and-mix" procedure that goes back to the work of Ishai et al. [68].

provided private versions of information-theoretic bounds for minimax risk of M-estimation of the median.

Frequency estimation can be viewed as the problem of distribution estimation in the $\ell_\infty$ norm where the distribution to be estimated is the empirical distribution of a dataset $(x_1, \ldots, x_n)$. Some works [69,100] have established tight lower bounds for locally differentially private distribution estimation in the weak privacy setting with loss instead given by either $\ell_1$ or $\ell_2^2$. However, their techniques proceed by using Assouad's method [42] and are quite different from the approach we use for the $\ell_\infty$ norm in the proof of Theorem 1 (specifically, in the proof of Theorem 6).

We also note that an anti-concentration lemma qualitatively similar to our Lemma 10 was used by Chan et al. [23, Lemma 3] to prove lower bounds on private aggregation, but they operated in a multi-party setting with communication limited by a sparse communication graph. After the initial release of this paper, Ghazi et al. [58] proved a similar anti-concentration lemma to establish a lower bound on private summation for protocols with short messages. The lemmas in both of these papers do not apply to the more general case of frequency estimation with an arbitrary number $B$ of buckets, as is the case throughout this paper.

*Range Counting.* Range counting queries have also been an important subject of study in several areas including database systems and algorithms (see [30] and the references therein). Early works on differentially private frequency estimation , e.g., [43,64], apply naturally to range counting, though the approach of summing up frequencies yields large errors for queries with large ranges.

For $d = 1$, Dwork et al. [47] obtained an upper bound of $O\left(\frac{\log^2 B}{\varepsilon}\right)$ and a lower bound of $\Omega(\log B)$ for obtaining $(\varepsilon, 0)$-DP. Chan et al. [22] extended the analysis to $d$-dimensional range counting queries in the central model, for which they obtained an upper bound of roughly $(\log B)^{O(d)}$. Meanwhile, a lower bound of Muthukrishnan and Nikolov [81] showed that for $n \approx B$, the error is lower bounded by $\Omega\left((\log n)^{d-O(1)}\right)$. Since then, the best-known upper bound on the error for general $d$-dimensional range counting has been $(\log B + \log(n)^{O(d)})/\varepsilon$ [48], obtained using ideas from [22,47] along with a k-d tree-like data structure. We note that for the special case of $d = 1$, it is known how to get a much better dependence on $B$ in the central model, namely, exponential in $\log^* B$ [14,21].

Xiao et al. [99] showed how to obtain private range count queries by using Haar wavelets, while Hay et al. [66] formalized the method of maintaining a hierarchical representation of data; the aforementioned two works were compared and refined by Qardaji et al. [85]. Cormode et al. [33] showed how to translate many of the previous ideas to the local model of DP. We also note that the matrix mechanism of Li et al. [74,75] also applies to the problem of range counting queries. An alternate line of work for tackling multi-dimensional range counting that relied on developing private versions of k-d trees and quadtrees was presented by Cormode et al. [36].

*Secure Multi-party Computation.* If we allow user interaction in the computation of the queries, then there is a rich theory, within cryptography, of *secure multi-party computation* (SMPC) that allows $f(x_1, \ldots, x_n)$ to be computed without revealing anything about $x_i$ except what can be inferred from $f(x_1, \ldots, x_n)$ itself (see, e.g., the book of Cramer et al. [39]). Kilian et al. [72] studied SMPC protocols for heavy hitters, obtaining near-linear communication complexity with a multi-round protocol. In contrast, all results in this paper are about *non-interactive* (single-round) protocols in the shuffle model (in the multi-message setting, all messages are generated at once). Though generic SMPC protocols can be turned into differentially private protocols (see, e.g., Sect. 10.2 in [93] and the references therein), they almost always use multiple rounds, and often have large overheads compared to the cost of computing $f(x_1, \ldots, x_n)$ in a non-private setting.

# 7 Conclusions and Open Problems

The shuffle model is a promising new privacy framework motivated by the significant interest in anonymous communication. In this paper, we studied the fundamental task of frequency estimation in this setup. In the single-message shuffle model, we established nearly tight bounds on the error for frequency estimation: while in the local model the error is well-known to be $\tilde{\Theta}(\sqrt{n})$, we proved that the right bound in the single-message model is the minimum of $\tilde{\Theta}(n^{1/4})$ and $\tilde{\Theta}(\sqrt{B})$, which interestingly are achieved by shuffling the widely used RAPPOR and the $B$-randomized response protocols, respectively. Moreover, we proved a nearly tight lower bound on the number of users required to solve the selection problem in the single-message shuffle model. We also obtained communication-efficient multi-message private-coin protocols with exponentially smaller error for frequency estimation, heavy hitters, range counting, and M-estimation of the median and quantiles (and more generally sparse non-adaptive SQ algorithms). We also gave public-coin protocols with, in addition, small query times. Our work raises several interesting open questions and points to fertile future research directions.

Our $\tilde{\Omega}(B)$ lower bound for selection (Theorem 3) holds for single-message protocols even with unbounded communication. We conjecture that a lower bound on the error of $B^{\Omega(1)}$ should hold even for multi-message protocols (with unbounded communication) in the shuffle model, and we leave this as a very interesting open question. Such a lower bound would imply a first separation between the central and (unbounded communication) multi-message shuffle model.

Another interesting question is to obtain a private-coin protocol for frequency estimation with polylogarithmic error, communication per user, and query time; reducing the query time of our current protocol below $\tilde{O}(n)$ seems challenging. In general, it would also be interesting to reduce the polylogarithmic factors in our guarantees for range counting as that would make them practically useful.

Another interesting direction for future work is to determine whether our efficient protocols for frequency estimation with much less error than what is possible in the local model could lead to more accurate and efficient shuffle model protocols for fundamental primitives such as clustering [91] and distribution testing [1], for which current locally differentially private protocols use frequency estimation as a black box.

Finally, a promising future direction is to extend our protocols for sparse non-adaptive SQ algorithms to the case of sparse aggregation. Note that the queries made by sparse non-adaptive SQ algorithms correspond to the special case of sparse aggregation where all non-zero queries are equal to 1. Extending our protocols to the case where the non-zero coordinates can be arbitrary numbers would, e.g., capture sparse stochastic gradient descent (SGD) updates, an important primitive in machine learning. More generally, it would be interesting to study the complexity of various other statistical and learning tasks [13, 25–27, 88, 98] in the shuffle privacy model.

# References

1. Acharya, J., Canonne, C., Freitag, C., Tyagi, H.: Test without trust: optimal locally private distribution testing. In: AISTATS, pp. 2067–2076 (2019)
2. Acharya, J., Sun, Z.: Communication complexity in locally private distribution estimation and heavy hitters. ICML **97**, 51–60 (2019)
3. Acharya, J., Sun, Z., Zhang, H.: Hadamard response: estimating distributions privately, efficiently, and with little communication. In: AISTATS, pp. 1120–1129 (2019)
4. Agarwal, N., Suresh, A.T., Yu, F.X.X., Kumar, S., McMahan, B.: cpSGD: communication-efficient and differentially-private distributed SGD. In: Advances in Neural Information Processing Systems, pp. 7564–7575 (2018)
5. Apple Differential Privacy Team: Learning with privacy at scale. Apple Mach. Learn. J. (2017). https://machinelearning.apple.com/docs/learning-with-privacy-at-scale/appledifferentialprivacysystem.pdf
6. Balcer, V., Cheu, A.: Separating local & shuffled differential privacy via histograms. In: ITC, pp. 1:1–1:14 (2020)
7. Balle, B., Bell, J., Gascón, A., Nissim, K.: Differentially private summation with multi-message shuffling. CoRR arXiv:1906.09116 (2019)
8. Balle, B., Bell, J., Gascón, A., Nissim, K.: Improved summation from shuffling. arXiv:1909.11225 (2019)
9. Balle, B., Bell, J., Gascón, A., Nissim, K.: The privacy blanket of the shuffle model. In: Boldyreva, A., Micciancio, D. (eds.) CRYPTO 2019. LNCS, vol. 11693, pp. 638–667. Springer, Cham (2019). https://doi.org/10.1007/978-3-030-26951-7_22
10. Balle, B., Bell, J., Gascón, A., Nissim, K.: Private summation in the multi-message shuffle model. arXiv:2002.00817 (2020)
11. Bassily, R., Nissim, K., Stemmer, U., Thakurta, A.G.: Practical locally private heavy hitters. In: NIPS, pp. 2288–2296 (2017)
12. Bassily, R., Smith, A.: Local, private, efficient protocols for succinct histograms. In: STOC, pp. 127–135 (2015)
13. Bassily, R., Smith, A.D., Thakurta, A.: Private empirical risk minimization: efficient algorithms and tight error bounds. In: FOCS, pp. 464–473 (2014)

14. Beimel, A., Nissim, K., Stemmer, U.: Private learning and sanitization: pure vs. approximate differential privacy. In: Raghavendra, P., Raskhodnikova, S., Jansen, K., Rolim, J.D.P. (eds.) APPROX/RANDOM -2013. LNCS, vol. 8096, pp. 363–378. Springer, Heidelberg (2013). https://doi.org/10.1007/978-3-642-40328-6_26
15. Bentley, J.L.: Decomposable searching problems. IPL **8**(5), 244–251 (1979)
16. Bittau, A., et al.: Prochlo: strong privacy for analytics in the crowd. In: SOSP, pp. 441–459 (2017)
17. Blum, A., Dwork, C., Nissim, K., McSherry, F.: Practical privacy: the SuLQ framework. In: PODS, pp. 128–138 (2005)
18. Blum, A., Ligett, K., Roth, A.: A learning theory approach to non-interactive database privacy. In: STOC, pp. 609–618 (2008)
19. Boucheron, S., Lugosi, G., Massart, P.: Concentration Inequalities: A Nonasmpytotic Theory of Independence. Clarendon Press, Oxford (2012)
20. Bun, M., Nelson, J., Stemmer, U.: Heavy hitters and the structure of local privacy. In: PODS, pp. 435–447 (2018)
21. Bun, M., Nissim, K., Stemmer, U., Vadhan, S.: Differentially private release and learning of threshold functions. In: FOCS, pp. 634–649 (2015)
22. Chan, T.H., Shi, E., Song, D.: Private and continual release of statistics. ACM Trans. Inf. Syst. Secur. **14**(3), 26:1–26:24 (2011)
23. Chan, T.H.H., Shi, E., Song, D.: Optimal lower bound for differentially private multi-part aggregation. In: European Symposium on Algorithms (2012)
24. Charikar, M., Chen, K., Farach-Colton, M.: Finding frequent items in data streams. In: Widmayer, P., Eidenbenz, S., Triguero, F., Morales, R., Conejo, R., Hennessy, M. (eds.) ICALP 2002. LNCS, vol. 2380, pp. 693–703. Springer, Heidelberg (2002). https://doi.org/10.1007/3-540-45465-9_59
25. Chaudhuri, K., Monteleoni, C.: Privacy-preserving logistic regression. In: NIPS, pp. 289–296 (2008)
26. Chaudhuri, K., Monteleoni, C., Sarwate, A.D.: Differentially private empirical risk minimization. JMLR **12**, 1069–1109 (2011)
27. Chaudhuri, K., Sarwate, A.D., Sinha, K.: A near-optimal algorithm for differentially-private principal components. JMLR **14**(1), 2905–2943 (2013)
28. Chen, L., Ghazi, B., Kumar, R., Manurangsi, P.: On distributed differential privacy and counting distinct elements. arXiv:2009.09604 (2020)
29. Cheu, A., Smith, A.D., Ullman, J., Zeber, D., Zhilyaev, M.: Distributed differential privacy via mixnets. In: EUROCRYPT, pp. 375–403 (2019)
30. Cormode, G.: Sketch techniques for approximate query processing. In: Foundations and Trends in Databases. Now Publishers (2011)
31. Cormode, G., Hadjieleftheriou, M.: Finding frequent items in data streams. VLDB **1**(2), 1530–1541 (2008)
32. Cormode, G., Kulkarni, T., Srivastava, D.: Marginal release under local differential privacy. In: SIGMOD, pp. 131–146 (2018)
33. Cormode, G., Kulkarni, T., Srivastava, D.: Answering range queries under local differential privacy. In: Proceedings of International Conference on Management of Data (SIGMOD), pp. 1832–1834 (2019)
34. Cormode, G., Muthukrishnan, S.: An improved data stream summary: the Count-Min sketch and its applications. J. Algorithms **55**(1), 58–75 (2005)
35. Cormode, G., Muthukrishnan, S.: What's hot and what's not: tracking most frequent items dynamically. TODS **30**(1), 249–278 (2005)
36. Cormode, G., Procopiuc, C., Srivastava, D., Shen, E., Yu, T.: Differentially private spatial decompositions. In: ICDE, pp. 20–31 (2012). https://doi.org/10.1109/ICDE.2012.16

37. Cormode, G., Yi, K.: Small Summaries for Big Data. Cambridge University Press, Cambridge (2020). http://cormode.org/ssbd
38. Cover, T.A., Thomas, J.M.: Elements of Information Theory. Wiley, New York (1991)
39. Cramer, R., Damgård, I.B., Nielsen, J.B.: Secure Multiparty Computation. Cambridge University Press, Cambridge (2015)
40. Ding, B., Kulkarni, J., Yekhanin, S.: Collecting telemetry data privately. In: NIPS, pp. 3571–3580 (2017)
41. Duchi, J.C., Jordan, M.I., Wainwright, M.J.: Local privacy and statistical minimax rates. In: FOCS, pp. 429–438 (2013)
42. Duchi, J.C., Jordan, M.I., Wainwright, M.J.: Minimax optimal procedures for locally private estimation. JASA **113**(521), 182–201 (2018)
43. Dwork, C.: Differential privacy. In: Bugliesi, M., Preneel, B., Sassone, V., Wegener, I. (eds.) ICALP 2006. LNCS, vol. 4052, pp. 1–12. Springer, Heidelberg (2006). https://doi.org/10.1007/11787006_1
44. Dwork, C., Kenthapadi, K., McSherry, F., Mironov, I., Naor, M.: Our data, ourselves: privacy via distributed noise generation. In: Vaudenay, S. (ed.) EUROCRYPT 2006. LNCS, vol. 4004, pp. 486–503. Springer, Heidelberg (2006). https://doi.org/10.1007/11761679_29
45. Dwork, C., Lei, J.: Differential privacy and robust statistics. In: STOC, pp. 371–380 (2009)
46. Dwork, C., McSherry, F., Nissim, K., Smith, A.: Calibrating noise to sensitivity in private data analysis. In: Halevi, S., Rabin, T. (eds.) TCC 2006. LNCS, vol. 3876, pp. 265–284. Springer, Heidelberg (2006). https://doi.org/10.1007/11681878_14
47. Dwork, C., Naor, M., Pitassi, T., Rothblum, G.N.: Differential privacy under continual observation. In: STOC, pp. 715–724 (2010)
48. Dwork, C., Naor, M., Reingold, O., Rothblum, G.N.: Pure differential privacy for rectangle queries via private partitions. In: Iwata, T., Cheon, J.H. (eds.) ASIACRYPT 2015. LNCS, vol. 9453, pp. 735–751. Springer, Heidelberg (2015). https://doi.org/10.1007/978-3-662-48800-3_30
49. Dwork, C., Naor, M., Reingold, O., Rothblum, G.N., Vadhan, S.: On the complexity of differentially private data release: efficient algorithms and hardness results. In: STOC, pp. 381–390 (2009)
50. Dwork, C., Roth, A.: The Algorithmic Foundations of Differential Privacy. Now Publishers Inc., Delft (2014)
51. Dwork, C., Roth, A., et al.: The algorithmic foundations of differential privacy. Found. Trends Theoret. Comput. Sci. **9**(3–4), 211–407 (2014)
52. Edmonds, A., Nikolov, A., Ullman, J.: The power of factorization methods in local and central differential privacy. In: Symposium on the Theory of Computing (2020)
53. Erlingsson, Ú., et al.: Encode, shuffle, analyze privacy revisited: formalizations and empirical evaluation. arXiv preprint arXiv:2001.03618 (2020)
54. Erlingsson, Ú., Feldman, V., Mironov, I., Raghunathan, A., Talwar, K., Thakurta, A.: Amplification by shuffling: from local to central differential privacy via anonymity. In: SODA, pp. 2468–2479 (2019)
55. Erlingsson, Ú., Pihur, V., Korolova, A.: RAPPOR: randomized aggregatable privacy-preserving ordinal response. In: CCS, pp. 1054–1067 (2014)
56. Estan, C., Varghese, G.: New directions in traffic measurement and accounting: focusing on the elephants, ignoring the mice. TOCS **21**(3), 270–313 (2003)
57. Free Haven: Selected papers in anonymity. https://www.freehaven.net/anonbib/

58. Ghazi, B., Golowich, N., Kumar, R., Manurangsi, P., Pagh, R., Velingker, A.: Pure differentially private summation from anonymous messages. In: Information Theoretic Cryptography (ITC) (2020)
59. Ghazi, B., Manurangsi, P., Pagh, R., Velingker, A.: Private aggregation from fewer anonymous messages. arXiv:1909.11073 (2019)
60. Ghazi, B., Pagh, R., Velingker, A.: Scalable and differentially private distributed aggregation in the shuffled model. arXiv:1906.08320 (2019)
61. Gilbert, A.C., Guha, S., Indyk, P., Kotidis, Y., Muthukrishnan, S., Strauss, M.J.: Fast, small-space algorithms for approximate histogram maintenance. In: STOC, pp. 389–398 (2002)
62. Greenberg, A.: Apple's "differential privacy" is about collecting your data - but not your data. Wired, 13 June 2016
63. Greenwald, M., Khanna, S., et al.: Space-efficient online computation of quantile summaries. ACM SIGMOD Rec. 30(2), 58–66 (2001)
64. Hardt, M., Ligett, K., McSherry, F.: A simple and practical algorithm for differentially private data release. In: NIPS, pp. 2339–2347 (2012). http://dl.acm.org/citation.cfm?id=2999325.2999396
65. Hardt, M., Rothblum, G.N.: A multiplicative weights mechanism for privacy-preserving data analysis. In: FOCS, pp. 61–70 (2010)
66. Hay, M., Rastogi, V., Miklau, G., Suciu, D.: Boosting the accuracy of differentially private histograms through consistency. VLDB 3(1–2), 1021–1032 (2010). https://doi.org/10.14778/1920841.1920970
67. Hsu, J., Khanna, S., Roth, A.: Distributed private heavy hitters. In: Czumaj, A., Mehlhorn, K., Pitts, A., Wattenhofer, R. (eds.) ICALP 2012. LNCS, vol. 7391, pp. 461–472. Springer, Heidelberg (2012). https://doi.org/10.1007/978-3-642-31594-7_39
68. Ishai, Y., Kushilevitz, E., Ostrovsky, R., Sahai, A.: Cryptography from anonymity. In: FOCS, pp. 239–248 (2006)
69. Kairouz, P., Bonawitz, K., Ramage, D.: Discrete distribution estimation under local privacy. In: ICML, pp. 2436–2444 (2016)
70. Karnin, Z., Lang, K., Liberty, E.: Optimal quantile approximation in streams. In: FOCS, pp. 71–78 (2016)
71. Kasiviswanathan, S.P., Lee, H.K., Nissim, K., Rashkodnikova, S., Smith, A.: What can we learn privately? In: FOCS, pp. 531–540 (2008)
72. Kilian, J., Madeira, A., Strauss, M.J., Zheng, X.: Fast private norm estimation and heavy hitters. In: Canetti, R. (ed.) TCC 2008. LNCS, vol. 4948, pp. 176–193. Springer, Heidelberg (2008). https://doi.org/10.1007/978-3-540-78524-8_11
73. Lei, J.: Differentially private m-estimators. In: NIPS, pp. 361–369 (2011)
74. Li, C., Hay, M., Rastogi, V., Milau, G., McGregor, A.: Optimizing linear counting queries under differential privacy. In: PODS, pp. 123–134 (2010)
75. Li, C., Miklau, G.: An adaptive mechanism for accurate query answering under differential privacy. VLDB 5(6), 514–525 (2012)
76. Li, N., Li, T., Venkatasubramanian, S.: t-closeness: privacy beyond k-anonymity and l-diversity. In: ICDE, pp. 106–115 (2007)
77. Manku, G.S., Rajagopalan, S., Lindsay, B.G.: Approximate medians and other quantiles in one pass and with limited memory. ACM SIGMOD Rec. 27(2), 426–435 (1998)
78. McSherry, F., Talwar, K.: Mechanism design via differential privacy. In: FOCS, pp. 94–103 (2007)
79. Misra, J., Gries, D.: Finding repeated elements. Sci. Comput. Program. 2(2), 143–152 (1982)

80. Munro, J.I., Paterson, M.S.: Selection and sorting with limited storage. TCS **12**(3), 315–323 (1980)
81. Muthukrishnan, S., Nikolov, A.: Optimal private halfspace counting via discrepancy. In: STOC, pp. 1285–1292 (2012)
82. Nguyen, T., Xiao, X., Yang, Y., Hui, S.C., Shin, H., Shin, J.: Collecting and analyzing data from smart device users with local differential privacy. arXiv:1606.05053 (2016)
83. Nikolov, A., Talwar, K., Zhang, L.: On the geometry of differential privacy: the sparse and approximate cases. In: STOC, pp. 351–360 (2013)
84. O'Donnell, R.: Analysis of Boolean Functions. Cambridge University Press, Cambridge (2014)
85. Qardaji, W., Yang, W., Li, N.: Understanding hierarchical methods for differentially private histograms. VLDB **6**(14), 1954–1965 (2013). https://doi.org/10.14778/2556549.2556576
86. Roos, B.: Binomial approximation to the Poisson binomial distribution: the Krawtchouk expansion. Theory Prob. Appl. **45**(2), 258–272 (2006)
87. Shankland, S.: How Google tricks itself to protect Chrome user privacy. CNET, October 2014
88. Smith, A.D.: Privacy-preserving statistical estimation with optimal convergence rates. In: STOC, pp. 813–822 (2011)
89. Steinke, T., Ullman, J.: Between pure and approximate differential privacy. J. Priv. Confid. **7**(2), 3–22 (2016)
90. Steinke, T., Ullman, J.: Tight lower bounds for differentially private selection. In: FOCS, pp. 552–563 (2017)
91. Stemmer, U.: Locally private k-means clustering. In: Proceedings of the 2020 Symposium on Discrete Algorithms (2020)
92. Ullman, J.: Tight lower bounds for locally differentially private selection. arXiv:1802.02638 (2018)
93. Vadhan, S.: The complexity of differential privacy. In: Lindell, Y. (ed.) Tutorials on the Foundations of Cryptography. ISC, pp. 347–450. Springer, Cham (2017). https://doi.org/10.1007/978-3-319-57048-8_7
94. Wagh, S., He, X., Machanavajjhala, A., Mittal, P.: DP-cryptography: marrying differential privacy and cryptography in emerging applications. CoRR abs/2004.08887 (2020). https://arxiv.org/abs/2004.08887, to appear in Communications of the ACM
95. Wang, T., Blocki, J., Li, N., Jha, S.: Locally differentially private protocols for frequency estimation. In: USENIX Security, pp. 729–745 (2017)
96. Wang, T., Xu, M., Ding, B., Zhou, J., Li, N., Jha, S.: Practical and robust privacy amplification with multi-party differential privacy. arXiv:1908.11515 (2019)
97. Warner, S.L.: Randomized response: a survey technique for eliminating evasive answer bias. JASA **60**(309), 63–69 (1965)
98. Wasserman, L., Zhou, S.: A statistical framework for differential privacy. JASA **105**(489), 375–389 (2010)
99. Xiao, X., Wang, G., Gehrke, J.: Differential privacy via wavelet transforms. TKDE **23**(8), 1200–1214 (2010)
100. Ye, M., Barg, A.: Optimal schemes for discrete distribution estimation under local differential privacy. In: ISIT, pp. 759–763 (2017)
101. Yi, K., Zhang, Q.: Optimal tracking of distributed heavy hitters and quantiles. Algorithmica **65**(1), 206–223 (2013)

# Non-Interactive Anonymous Router

Elaine Shi$^{(\boxtimes)}$ and Ke Wu

Carnegie Mellon University, Pittsburgh, USA

**Abstract.** Anonymous routing is one of the most fundamental online privacy problems and has been studied extensively for decades. Almost all known approaches for anonymous routing (e.g., mix-nets, DC-nets, and others) rely on multiple servers or routers to engage in some *interactive* protocol; and anonymity is guaranteed in the *threshold* model, i.e., if one or more of the servers/routers behave honestly.

Departing from all prior approaches, we propose a novel *non-interactive* abstraction called a Non-Interactive Anonymous Router (NIAR), which works even with a *single untrusted router*. In a NIAR scheme, suppose that $n$ senders each want to talk to a distinct receiver. A one-time trusted setup is performed such that each sender obtains a sending key, each receiver obtains a receiving key, and the router receives a *token* that "encrypts" the permutation mapping the senders to receivers. In every time step, each sender can encrypt its message using its sender key, and the router can use its token to convert the $n$ ciphertexts received from the senders to $n$ *transformed ciphertexts*. Each transformed ciphertext is delivered to the corresponding receiver, and the receiver can decrypt the message using its receiver key. Imprecisely speaking, security requires that the untrusted router, even when colluding with a subset of corrupt senders and/or receivers, should not be able to compromise the privacy of honest parties, including who is talking to who, and the message contents.

We show how to construct a communication-efficient NIAR scheme with provable security guarantees based on the standard Decision Linear assumption in suitable bilinear groups. We show that a compelling application of NIAR is to realize a Non-Interactive Anonymous Shuffler (NIAS), where an untrusted server or data analyst can only decrypt a permuted version of the messages coming from $n$ senders where the permutation is hidden. NIAS can be adopted to construct privacy-preserving surveys, differentially private protocols in the shuffle model, and pseudonymous bulletin boards.

Besides this main result, we also describe a variant that achieves fault tolerance when a subset of the senders may crash. Finally, we further explore a paranoid notion of security called full insider protection, and show that if we additionally assume sub-exponentially secure Indistinguishability Obfuscation and as sub-exponentially secure one-way functions, one can construct a NIAR scheme with paranoid security.

---

A full version of the paper can be found online [68].

© International Association for Cryptologic Research 2021
A. Canteaut and F.-X. Standaert (Eds.): EUROCRYPT 2021, LNCS 12698, pp. 489–520, 2021.
https://doi.org/10.1007/978-3-030-77883-5_17

# 1    Introduction

The Internet has become a platform that billions of users rely on in their daily lives, and protecting users' online privacy is a significant challenge we face. Anonymous communication systems provide a way for users to communicate without leaking their identities or message contents. There has been several decades of work dedicated to the design, implementation, and deployment of anonymous communication systems [8,18,34,35,38,39,42,50,64,70,71,74], and numerous abstractions and techniques have been explored, including mix-nets [8,18,34], the Dining Cryptographers' nets [9,35,39], onion routing [29, 41,42,50], multi-party-computation-based approaches [13], multi-server PIR-write [38,48,60], as well as variants/improvements of the above [70,71,74]. We refer the readers to several excellent surveys on this rich line of work [40,44,69].

To the best of our knowledge, almost all known anonymous routing schemes rely on *multiple* routers or servers to engage in an *interactive protocol*, and moreover, security is guaranteed in the *threshold* model, i.e., assuming that one or more of the routers remain honest. For example, the mix-net family of schemes typically require each router along the way to shuffle the input ciphertexts and remove a layer of encryption; the DC-net family of schemes require multiple parties to engage in a cryptographic protocol, and so on.

Departing from all prior approaches which are interactive and rely on some form of threshold cryptography, we ask the following natural question:

Can we achieve anonymous routing *non-interactively* on a *single untrusted* router?

## 1.1    Defining Non-Interactive Anonymous Router (NIAR)

Our first contribution is a conceptual one: we formulate a new abstraction called a non-interactive anonymous router (NIAR). The abstraction is in fact quite natural, and in hindsight, it may even be a little surprising why it has not been considered before.

**Non-Interactive Anonymous Router.** Imagine that there are $n$ senders and $n$ receivers, and each sender wishes to speak with a distinct receiver. Henceforth let $\pi$ denote the permutation that maps each sender to its intended receiver, i.e., each sender $i \in [n]$ wants to speak to receiver $\pi(i)$. A NIAR scheme has the following syntax:

- $(\{\mathsf{ek}_i, \mathsf{rk}_i\}_{i \in [n]}, \mathsf{tk}) \leftarrow \mathbf{Setup}(1^\kappa, n, \pi)$: First, we run a one-time trusted setup procedure that takes the security parameter $1^\kappa$, the number of senders/receivers $n$, and the routing permutation $\pi$, and produces a *sender key* $\mathsf{ek}_i$ for each sender $i \in [n]$, and a *receiver key* $\mathsf{rk}_i$ for each receiver $i \in [n]$. Moreover, the setup procedure also produces a *token* $\mathsf{tk}$ for the router which encodes the secret permutation $\pi$. Note that the trusted setup can be decentralized using standard multi-party computation techniques.

- $\mathsf{ct}_{i,t} \leftarrow \mathbf{Enc}(\mathsf{ek}_i, x_{i,t}, t)$: With this one-time setup, we can allow the $n$ senders to anonymously send $T$ number of packets to their intended receivers. In every time step $t \in [T]$, each sender $i \in [n]$ encrypts its message $x_{i,t}$ using its secret key $\mathsf{ek}_i$ by calling $\mathbf{Enc}(\mathsf{ek}_i, x_{i,t}, t)$, and sends the resulting ciphertext $\mathsf{ct}_{i,t}$ to the router.
- $\{\mathsf{ct}'_{i,t}\}_{i \in [n]} \leftarrow \mathbf{Rte}(\mathsf{tk}, \{\mathsf{ct}_{i,t}\}_{i \in [n]})$: The untrusted router uses its token to convert the $n$ ciphertexts collected from the senders into $n$ *transformed ciphertexts*. This is accomplished by calling $\mathbf{Rte}(\mathsf{tk}, \{\mathsf{ct}_{i,t}\}_{i \in [n]})$. The router then forwards each transformed ciphertext $\mathsf{ct}'_{i,t}$ to the corresponding recipient $i$.
- $x_i \leftarrow \mathbf{Dec}(\mathsf{rk}_i, \mathsf{ct}'_{i,t})$: Finally, the recipients use their respective secret keys to decrypt the plaintexts by calling $\mathbf{Dec}(\mathsf{rk}_i, \mathsf{ct}'_{i,t})$.

At a very high level, we want that the untrusted router learns no information about the routing permutation $\pi$ as well as the messages exchanged. Moreover, the scheme should offer robustness even when a (potentially majority) subset of the senders and/or receivers collude with the untrusted router. It turns out that defining robustness under collusion is non-trivial and the security requirements can vary from application to application—we will discuss the security definitions in more detail later.

**Communication Efficiency.** The first naïve idea is to let each sender-receiver pair share a freshly and randomly chosen secret key during the setup. During each time step, each sender encrypts its messages using its secret key, and sends the ciphertext to the router. The router then forwards all $n$ ciphertexts to each of the $n$ receivers; and each receiver's secret key allows it to decrypt exactly one among the $n$ ciphertexts received. This scheme protects the plaintext messages as well as the routing permutation $\pi$ from the untrusted router; unfortunately, it incurs *quadratic* communication overhead in each time step[1].

Throughout the rest of the paper, we will require that the NIAR scheme preserve *communication efficiency*, that is, the communication blowup relative to sending the messages in the clear must be upper bounded by $\mathsf{poly}(\kappa)$ where $\kappa$ is the security parameter. In other words, suppose, without loss of generality, that in each time step, each sender has one bit to send, then the total communication (among all senders and receivers) per time step must be upper bounded by $O(n) \cdot \mathsf{poly}(\kappa)$.

**Non-Interactive Anonymous Shuffler.** One important application and special case of NIAR is to realize a non-interactive anonymous shuffler (NIAS). To understand what is a non-interactive anonymous shuffler, it helps to think of the following application. Suppose that during a pandemic, University X wants to implement a privacy-preserving daily check mechanism, where students and faculty each send a short message to report their health conditions every day, and whether they could have been exposed to the virus. To protect each individual's

---

[1] Furthermore, while this naïve scheme works for a private-messaging scenario, and does not work for the non-interactive anonymous shuffler application to be described later, due to the fact that a receiver colluding with the router can learn which sender it is paired with. We will elaborate on this point when we define security.

privacy, we want to shuffle the messages according to some randomly chosen permutation $\pi$, such that the history of an individual's reports is pseudonymous. In this scenario, we can employ a NIAR scheme, and give the data analyst the token tk as well as *all n* receiver keys. This ensures that the data analyst can decrypt only a shuffled list of the plaintexts, and moreover the permutation is hidden from the data analyst.

In other words, a Non-Interactive Anonymous Shuffler (NIAS) is a special case of NIAR where the router and all the receivers are a single party. In Sect. 1.4, we will present numerous applications of NIAR and NIAS. We point out that the NIAS special case in fact imposes some extra security requirements on top of our basic security notion for NIAR, in the sense that even a receiver cannot know which sender it is paired up with—we will discuss how to define security next.

## 1.2    Defining Security Requirements

If all receivers were fully trusted, then another naïve idea would be to have every sender encrypt its message along with its respective destination using a Fully Homomorphic Encryption (FHE) scheme. In this way, the untrusted router can accomplish the routing through homomorphic evaluation. However, all receivers must be given the FHE's secret key to decrypt the messages. Therefore, if even a single receiver colludes with the untrusted router, then all other honest players' anonymity would be broken. This is clearly unacceptable since in most applications of anonymous routing, anyone can become a sender or a receiver, including the owner of the router. Approaches that construct special-purpose homomorphic encryption schemes optimized for shuffling suffer from the same drawback [11].

We therefore require a security notion that provides robustness even when a subset of the senders and receivers can be corrupt, and potentially colluding with the untrusted router. It turns out that how to define robustness against collusion requires some careful thinking, since the security requirements can vary from application to application.

**Basic Notion.** Our basic security notion is motivated by a private-messaging scenario, e.g., members of a secret society wish to send private emails without revealing their identities and their correspondence to the public. In this case, each player (i.e., either sender or receiver) knows who it is talking to. Therefore, if the adversary who controls the router additionally corrupts a subset of the senders and receivers, the adversary can learn who the corrupt senders and receivers are paired up with, as well as the messages received by corrupt receivers (from honest senders) in every time step. Our basic security notion requires that besides this natural leakage, the adversary should not learn any additional information. Observe that our communication-inefficient naïve solution that forwards all ciphertexts to every receiver would satisfy this basic notion.

**Receiver-Insider Protection.** The basic security notion, however, turns out to be insufficient for the NIAS application. In the NIAS application, a single entity acts as the router and all $n$ receivers—for example, in our earlier "anonymous daily check-in" application, the data analyst has all receiver keys $\{\mathsf{rk}_i\}_{i \in [n]}$ as well as the token tk. To protect the users' pseudonymity, it is important that the data analyst does not learn which decrypted report corresponds to which user. In Sect. 1.4, we present more applications for NIAS, and all of them have the same security requirement.

We therefore propose a strengthened security notion, called receiver-insider protection, that is suitable and sufficient for NIAS-type applications. Here, we require that even a receiver does not learn which sender it is speaking with; however, a sender may learn which receiver it is speaking with. Now, if the adversary who controls the router additionally corrupts a subset of the senders and receivers, the adversary can learn the *corrupt-to-*$*$ part[2] of the permutation $\pi$ as well as the messages received by corrupt receivers in every time step. Besides this natural leakage, the adversary should not learn anything else.

**Full Insider Protection.** While receiver-insider protection seems sufficient for most applications including NIAS, we additionally explore a *paranoid* notion of security. Here, we want that every player has no idea who it is speaking with, including both senders and receivers. Nonetheless, the *corrupt-to-corrupt* part of the permutation is *inherently* leaked to the adversary and this leakage cannot be avoided: since a corrupt sender can always try encrypting some message and check whether any corrupt receiver received the corresponding message. Therefore, our most paranoid notion, which we call *full insider protection*, requires that an adversary controlling the router and a subset of corrupt senders and receivers learns only the corrupt-to-corrupt part of the permutation $\pi$, as well as the messages received by corrupt receivers in every time step, but nothing else.

In Sect. 1.4, we describe more applications of NIAR and NIAS, and at that point, the reader can see how different applications require different notions. Of course, one can always go for the most paranoid notion; but the weaker notions suffice for a wide range of natural applications. Therefore, differentiating between these notions can lead to more efficient constructions.

**Equivalence Between Simulation- and Indistinguishability-Based Notions.** Later in the paper, we shall formalize the above security notions using two definitional approaches: *simulation-based* notions and *indistinguishability-based* notions. We then prove that in fact, *each simulation-based notion* (without insider protection, with receiver-insider protection, or with full insider protection) *is equivalent to the corresponding indistinguishability-based notion*. While the simulation-based notion more naturally captures the security requirements we want to express, the indistinguishability-based notions are often easier to work with in proofs.

*Remark 1 (NIAR/NIAS requires no network-layer anonymity protection).* We point out that whenever a NIAR or NIAS scheme is deployed, one advantage

---

[2] Here, $*$ denotes a wildcard; thus the corrupt-to-$*$ part of the permutation includes who every corrupt sender is speaking with.

is that *we would no longer need any network-layer anonymity protection* (e.g., Tor [42] or DC nets [35]). This is in contrast to a vast line of works that leverage cryptographic techniques such as zero-knowledge proofs for anonymity protection, e.g., E-Cash [32,33], e-voting [10,62], anonymous credentials [14,20], ZCash [21], and others [53,54]—in these cases, an Internet Service Provider controlling the network routers can completely break anonymity despite the cryptographic techniques employed.

### 1.3   Our Results

**Main Construction: NIAR with Receiver-Insider Protection and NIAS.** To situate our results in context, it helps to first think of the following naïve construction based on a virtual-blackbox (VBB) obfuscator. During setup, we publish the public key pk of a public-key encryption (PKE) scheme, and moreover, we give each sender-receiver pair a symmetric encryption key. During each routing step, each sender uses its symmetric key to encrypt its respective message, resulting what we henceforth call an *inner ciphertext*. The sender then encrypts the inner ciphertext with the public key encryption scheme, resulting in an *outer ciphertext*. During the setup, we give the router a VBB obfuscation of the following program: use the PKE's secret key to decrypt each sender's outer ciphertext, obtain a list of $n$ inner ciphertexts, and then apply the permutation $\pi$ to the $n$ inner ciphertexts and output the result. Now, during each routing step, the router can simply apply its VBB obfuscated program to the list of $n$ outer ciphertexts collected from the senders, and the result would be $n$ permuted inner ciphertexts. The $i$-th inner ciphertext is then forwarded to the $i$-th receiver where $i \in [n]$. Note that in this VBB-based solution, the program obfuscation hides the secret key of the PKE scheme as well as the secret permutation $\pi$. One can verify that indeed, this VBB-based construction satisfies security with *receiver-insider protection*; but it does *not* provide full insider protection. Specifically, a corrupt sender $i^* \in [n]$ colluding with the router can simply plant a random inner ciphertext $c$, and see which of the receivers receives $c$ at the end—this must be the receiver $i^*$ is speaking with[3].

The drawback with this naïve solution is obvious: it is well-known that VBB obfuscation is impossible to attain for general functions if one-way functions exist [17]. We therefore ask,

*Can we construct a NIAR scheme from standard cryptographic assumptions?*

We construct a NIAR scheme that achieves security with receiver-insider protection, relying on the Decisional Linear assumption in suitable bilinear groups. Our scheme satisfies communication efficiency: in each time step, each player sends or receives only $\mathsf{poly}(\kappa)$ bits of data (assuming, without loss of generality, that each sender wants to send one bit during each time step). Furthermore, the

---

[3] In general, achieving full insider security appears much more challenging than our basic notion or receiver-only insider protection. Indeed, we will discuss this in further detail later on.

public and secret key sizes are $\mathsf{poly}(n, \kappa)$; and yet the scheme can support an *unbounded* number of time steps.

At a high level, in our construction, each sender creates an inner encryption of its message using a symmetric key shared with its receiver, and then encrypts the inner ciphertext again using a special outer encryption scheme. With an appropriately constructed token, the router can output a permuted list of inner ciphertexts. We state the aforementioned result in the following theorem:

**Theorem 1 (NIAR with receiver-insider protection).** *Assume that the Decisional Linear assumption holds in certain bilinear groups. Then, there exists a NIAR scheme with receiver-insider protection, where the public key and secret key sizes are at most $\mathsf{poly}(n, \kappa)$ bits, and the per-player communication cost in each routing step is only $\mathsf{poly}(\kappa)$ assuming that each sender has one bit to send per time step. Further, the scheme supports an unbounded number of time steps.*

The above theorem also implies a NIAS scheme with the same performance bounds. Although our work should primarily be viewed as an initial exploration of NIAR, the constructions that led to Theorem 1 is potentially implementable.

**NIAR with Full Insider Protection.** The receiver-insider protection achieved by Theorem 1 is sufficient for most application scenarios including NIAS. Nonetheless, it is interesting to ask whether one can achieve full insider protection. As mentioned, full insider protection is the strongest security notion one can hope for in the context of NIAR, since here we leak only the inevitable. Achieving full insider security, however, appears much more challenging. The reason is that we do not even want a corrupt sender to learn which honest receiver it is talking to. However, in our schemes so far (even the aforementioned VBB-based construction), a corrupt sender $i^* \in [n]$ colluding with the router can choose a random inner ciphertext $c$ and just check which receiver receives $c$. In this way, the adversary can learn the corrupt-to-$*$ part of the permutation $\pi$.

Again, it is instructive to first consider how to achieve full insider protection using VBB obfuscation. To achieve such paranoid security, one way is to modify the previous VBB-based scheme such that inside the VBB, we decrypt the $n$ input ciphertexts, permute them, and then *reencrypt* them under the receivers' keys, respectively. To defeat the aforementioned attack, it is important that the reencryption step produces *random* transformed ciphertexts. In fact, one useful insight we can draw here is that for any scheme that provides full insider protection, if the adversary controlling a corrupt sender $\widetilde{i} \in [n]$ switches $\widetilde{i}$'s input ciphertext, the transformed ciphertexts corresponding to *all* receivers output by the **Rte** procedure must all change.

We show how to achieve full insider protection by additionally relying on sub-exponentially secure indistinguishability obfuscation and sub-exponentially secure one-way functions.

**Theorem 2 (NIAR with full insider protection).** *Assume the existence of sub-exponentially secure indistinguishability obfuscator, sub-exponentially secure* *one-way functions, and that the Decisional Linear assumption (with standard polynomial security) holds in certain bilinear groups. Then, there exists a NIAR scheme with full insider protection, and whose key sizes and communication cost match those of Theorem 1.*

Notably, a flurry of very recent works [27,47,56,73] show that sub-exponentially secure indistinguishability obfuscator can be constructed under a variety of assumptions some of which are considered well-founded.

**Extension: Fault-Tolerant NIAR.** Similar to the line of work on Multi-Client Functional Encryption (MCFE) [2,37,37,51,66], a drawback with the present formulation is that a single crashed sender can hamper liveness. Basically, the router must collect ciphertexts from all senders in each time step to successfully evaluate the **Rte** procedure. To the best of our knowledge, fault tolerance has been little investigated in this line of work.

We therefore formulate a variation of our basic NIAR abstraction, called *fault-tolerant NIAR*. In a fault-tolerant NIAR, if a subset of the senders have crashed, the remaining set of senders can encrypt their messages in a way that is aware of the set of senders who are known to be still online (henceforth denoted $\mathcal{O}$). Similarly, the router will perform the **Rte** procedure in a way that is aware of $\mathcal{O}$, too. In this way, the router can continue to perform the routing, without being stalled by the crashed senders. Similar to our basic notion, we define receiver-insider protection and full-insider protection for our fault-tolerant NIAR abstraction, and show that the most natural simulation-based and indistinguishability-based notions are equivalent.

We show that our previous NIAR constructions of Theorem 1 and Theorem 2 can be extended to the fault-tolerant setting, and the result is stated in the following theorem.

**Theorem 3 (Informal: fault-tolerant NIAR).** *Suppose that the Decisional Linear assumption holds in suitable bilinear groups. Then, there exists a fault-tolerant NIAR scheme that leaks only the (corrupt+crashed)-to-\* part of the permutation as well as messages received by corrupt receivers, but nothing else (see the online full version [68] for formal security definitions).*

*Suppose that the Decisional Linear assumption (with standard polynomial security) holds in suitable bilinear groups, and assume the existence of sub-exponentially secure indistinguishability obfuscation and one-way functions. Then, there exists a fault-tolerant NIAR scheme that leaks only the inherent leakage, that is, the (corrupt+crashed)-to-corrupt part of the permutation as well as messages received by corrupt receivers, but nothing else (see the online full version [68] for formal security definitions).*

*Furthermore, both schemes achieve the same key sizes and communication efficiency as in Theorem 1.*

## 1.4   Applications of NIAR and NIAS

NIAR adds to the existing suite of primitives [8,18,34,35,38,39,42,50,70,71,74] that enable anonymous routing. In comparison with prior works, NIAR adopts a different trust model since it does not rely on threshold cryptography. Arguably it also has a somewhat simpler abstraction than most existing primitives, partly due to the non-interactive nature.

We discuss two flavors of applications for NIAR, including 1) using NIAR in private messaging, which is the more classical type of application; and 2) using NIAR as a non-interactive anonymous shuffler (NIAS). We will use these applications to motivate the need for the different security notions, without insider protection, with receiver-insider protection, or with full insider protection. We shall begin with NIAS-type applications since some of these applications are of emerging interest.

**Using NIAR as a Non-Interactive Anonymous Shuffler.** NIAR can serve as *a non-interactive anonymous shuffler* (NIAS), which shuffles $n$ senders' messages in a non-interactive manner, such that the messages become unlinkable to their senders. This allows the senders to publish messages under a pseudonym, and the pseudonymity does not have to rely on the network layer being anonymous. In a non-interactive shuffler type of application, typically a single entity acts as the router and all $n$ receiver—therefore, typically these applications require *receiver-insider* protection. To understand what is a non-interactive anonymous shuffler, it is most instructive to look at some example applications.

*Anonymous Bulletin Board or Forum.* Imagine that a group of users want to post messages *pseudonymously* to a website every day, e.g., to discuss some sensitive issues. The users act as the NIAR senders and encrypt their messages every day. The server, which acts as both the router and all the receivers in NIAR, decrypts a permuted list of the messages and posts them on the website. In this way, the untrusted server can mix the $n$ senders' messages, and the pseudonymity guarantee need not rely on additional network-layer anonymity protection. In other words, even a powerful attacker controlling all routers in the world as well as the server cannot break the pseudonymity guarantees.

Since the server takes the role of the router and all $n$ receivers, we would need a NIAR scheme that provides *receiver-insider protection*. This way, even when all the receivers are in the control of the adversary, the adversary cannot deanonymize honest senders.

*Distributed Differential Privacy in the Shuffle Model.* There has been a growing appetite for large-scale, privacy-preserving federated learning, especially due to interest and investment from big players such as Google and Facebook. Unlike the classical "central model" where we have a trusted database curator [43], in a federated learning scenario, the data collector is not trusted, and yet it wants to learn interesting statistics and patterns over data collected by multiple users' mobile phones, web browsers, and so on. This model is often referred to the "local model". It is understood that without any additional assumptions and without cryptographic hardness, mechanisms in the local model incur a utility loss [19,31,67] that is significantly worse than the central model (given a fixed privacy budget).

Recently, an elegant line of work [15,16,23,36,45,49] emerged, and showed that if there exists a shuffler that randomly shuffles the users' input data, then we can design (information-theoretic) distributed differential privacy mechanisms that are often competitive to the central model. This is commonly referred to as the "shuffle model".

NIAR can be potentially employed to implement a shuffler for the shuffle model. In particular, it is suited for a setting like Google's RAPPOR project [46], where data was repeatedly collected from the users' Chrome browsers on a daily basis. In this scenario, the data collector acts as the NIAR router and all the receivers too; therefore, we also need the NIAR scheme to satisfy receiver-insider protection. Again, we do not need network-level anonymity protection.

*Privacy-Preserving "Daily Check" During a Pandemic.* This application was described earlier in this section. We additionally point out an interesting variation of the same application: we can *create the inner layer of encryption using not symmetric-key encryption, but rather, a predicate encryption scheme* [7,25,26,52,61,65]. In this way, a data analyst can be granted special tokens that would permit her to decrypt the data, only if some predicate is satisfied over the user's encrypted daily report (e.g., the user has come in contact with an infected person and needs to be quarantined).

*Pseudonymous Survey Systems.* Another application is to build a pseudonymous survey system. For example, we can allow students to pseudonymously and regularly post course feedback to an instructor throughout the semester, or ask questions that they would otherwise feel embarrassed to ask. We can also create periodic surveys and allow members of an underrepresented minority group to pseudonymously report if they have been the victims of discrimination or harassment. Similar applications have been considered and implemented in the past [10,54]. However, in such existing mechanisms [10,54], the cryptographic protection alone is insufficient, and one must additionally rely on the network layer to be anonymous too. By contrast, with NIAR, we no longer need the network layer to provide anonymity protection.

*Other Applications.* Besides these aforementioned applications, it is also known that a shuffler can lend to the design of light-weight multi-party computation (MPC) protocols [55].

**Private Messaging.** NIAR can also be used to enable private messaging, which is the more traditional application of anonymous routing. We give a few scenarios to motivate the different security requirements.

In the first scenario, we may imagine that members of a secret society wish to send private messages or emails to one another without identified. To do so, pairs of members that wish to communicate regularly can join a NIAR group. In this scenario, each pair of communicating parties know each other's identities, and therefore we only need the basic security notion, i.e., without insider protection.

Another application is to build an anonymous mentor-mentee system, or an anonymous buddy or mutual-support system. For example, some scientists have relied on Slack to provide such functionalities [1], where members can anonymously post questions, and others can anonymously provide advice. Currently, the anonymity guarantee is provided solely by the Slack server. However, one can easily imagine scenarios where trusting a centralized party for anonymity is undesirable. In these cases, we can rely on NIAR to build an anonymous buddy system. Each pair of buddies can regularly engage in conversations to provide mutual support, and the untrusted router (e.g., Slack) cannot learn the communication pattern or the messages being exchanged. Like the earlier mentor-mentee scenario, the buddies themselves may not wish to reveal their identities to each other. Therefore, in this scenario, we would need the NIAR scheme to provide *full insider protection*.

## 1.5   Open Questions

Partly, our work makes a conceptual contribution since we are the first to define the NIAR and NIAS abstractions. Our work should be viewed as an initial exploration of these natural abstractions, inspired by a fundamental and long-standing online privacy problem. Many open questions arise given our new abstractions, and our work lays the groundwork for further exploring exciting future directions. We present a list of open questions in the online full version [68].

## 1.6   Technical Highlight

**Why Existing Approaches Fail.** A first strawman attempt is to rely on a Multi-Client Functional Encryption (MCFE) scheme for inner products, also known as Multi-Client Inner-Product Encryption (MCIPE) [2,4,37,51]. In a Multi-Client Inner-Product Encryption scheme, each of the $n$ clients obtains a secret encryption key during a setup phase. During every time step $t$, each client $i$ uses its secret encryption key to encrypt a message $x_{i,t}$—henceforth the $i$-th ciphertext is denoted $\mathsf{ct}_{i,t}$ for $i \in [n]$, and moreover, let $\mathbf{x}_t := (x_{1,t}, \ldots, x_{n,t})$. An authority with a master secret key can generate a functional key $\mathsf{sk}_\mathbf{y}$ for a vector $\mathbf{y}$ whose length is also $n$. Given the collection of ciphertexts $\{\mathsf{ct}_{i,t}\}_{i\in[n]}$ and the functional key $\mathsf{sk}_\mathbf{y}$, one can evaluate the function $\langle \mathbf{x}_t, \mathbf{y} \rangle$ of the encrypted plaintexts but nothing else is revealed.

Our idea is to express the permutation $\pi$ as $n$ selection vectors, and each is used to select what one receiver would receive from the vector of input messages. The router receives one functional key for each selection vector. A selection vector $\mathbf{y}$ has exactly one coordinate that is set to 1, whereas all other coordinates are set to 0. In this way, the inner product of $\mathbf{x}_t$ and $\mathbf{y}$ selects exactly one coordinate of $\mathbf{x}_t$. In our NIAR construction, the input messages $\mathbf{x}_t$ to the MCFE-for-selection scheme will be inner ciphertexts encrypted under keys shared between each pair of sender and receiver, such that the router cannot see to the plaintext message.

At first sight, an MCFE scheme for inner products may seem like a good match for our problem, but upon more careful examination, all known MCFE schemes, including those based on program obfuscation, fail in our context. To the best of our knowledge, *all existing MCFE schemes* (for evaluating any function, not just inner products) *are NOT function-hiding*. In our context, this means that the functional key $\mathsf{sk_y}$ is allowed to reveal the selection vector $\mathbf{y}$. This unfortunately means that the token could leak the routing permutation $\pi$ and thus violate anonymity. Not only so, in fact, it appears that *no prior work has attempted to define or construct function-hiding MCFE* [2,4,37,57,66], likely because we currently lack techniques to get function privacy for MCFE schemes, even allowing RO and program obfuscation [51]. The known techniques for upgrading Functional Encryption and Multi-Input Functional Encryption to have function privacy [5,22,58,59,63] do not apply to MCFE, because they are fundamentally *incompatible with the scenario where some clients can be corrupt*.

Finally, we point out that a related line of work called *Multi-Input* Inner-Product Encryption [5,6,28,51] also fails to solve our problem, because its security definition is too permissive: specifically, mix-and-matching ciphertexts from multiple time steps is allowed during evaluation, and this could be exploited by an adversary to break anonymity in our context.

**Key Insights and Roadmap.** We are the first to define function-hiding MCFE, and demonstrate a construction for a meaningful functionality, i.e., *selection*. Selection is a special case of inner product computation, and is structurally simpler than inner product. Leveraging this structural simplicity, we develop new construction and proof techniques that allow us to prove function-hiding security even when some of the clients can be corrupted. We use the resulting "function-hiding MCFE for selection" as a core building block to realize NIAR.

At a very high level, the structural simplicity of selection helps us in the following way. First, in a more general MCIPE scheme, even without function privacy, one must prevent mix-and-match attacks—in other words, the adversary should not be able to take clients' ciphertext from different time steps and combine them in the same inner-product evaluation. When it comes to the special case of selection, however, we can *defer* the handling of such mix-and-match attacks. Specifically, if we were not concerned about function privacy, then mix-and-match attacks turned out to be a non-issue in an MCFE-for-selection scheme. With this observation, we first construct a conceptually simple MCFE-for-selection scheme *without* function privacy. Essentially, the construction runs $n$ independent instances of semantically secure public-key encryption (PKE), one for each client. The functional key for selecting one client's plaintext is simply the corresponding PKE's secret key.

Next, we perform a function-privacy upgrade—during this function-privacy upgrade, we do need to take care and prevent the aforementioned *mix-and-match* attacks. The function-privacy upgrade is technically much more involved, and we will give an informal overview in Sect. 3. What lends to the function-privacy upgrade is the fact that the underlying MCFE scheme (without function privacy) is essentially "decomposable" into $n$ independent components. This is an important reason why we can accomplish the function privacy upgrade *even when some of the clients can be corrupted.* In comparison, prior MCFE schemes for general inner-products [2,4,37] need more structurally complicated techniques to prevent mix-and-match, even without function privacy. For this reason, our techniques in the current form are not capable of getting a *function-private* MCFE scheme for general inner-products—this remains a challenging open question.

Once we construct a function-hiding MCFE-for-selection scheme, we then use it to construct two NIAR schemes: one with receiver-insider protection, and one with full insider protection. The scheme with receiver-insider protection can be constructed without introducing additional assumptions—and this notion of security suffices for most applications including NIAS. As explained in Sect. 1.3, full insider protection seems much more challenging and a natural class of approaches fail. To get a paranoid construction with full insider protection, we additionally rely on sub-exponentially secure indistinguishability obfuscation and sub-exponentially one-way functions.

# 2 New Definitions: Non-Interactive Anonymous Router

We now define the syntax and security requirements of NIAR. Since our approach relies on a single untrusted router and is non-interactive, both the syntax and security definitions are incomparable to the formal definitions of anonymous routing in prior works, all of which involve multiple routers and interactive protocols [13,29,41].

## 2.1 Syntax

Suppose that there are $n$ senders and $n$ receivers, and each sender wants to talk to a distinct receiver. They would like to route their messages anonymously to hide who is talking to who. The routing is performed by a single router non-interactively.

Let $\mathsf{Perm}([n])$ denote the set of all permutations on the set $[n]$. Let $\pi \in \mathsf{Perm}([n])$ be a permutation that represents the mapping between the sender and the receivers. For example, $\pi(1) = 3$ means that sender 1 wants to talk to receiver 3.

A Non-Interactive Anonymous Router (NIAR) is a cryptographic scheme consisting of the following, possibly randomized algorithms:

- $(\{\mathsf{ek}_i\}_{i \in [n]}, \{\mathsf{rk}_i\}_{i \in [n]}, \mathsf{tk}) \leftarrow \mathbf{Setup}(1^\kappa, n, \pi)$: the trusted $\mathbf{Setup}$ algorithm takes the security parameter $1^\kappa$, the number of senders/receivers $n$, and a permutation $\pi \in \mathsf{Perm}([n])$ that represents the mapping between the senders and the receivers. The $\mathbf{Setup}$ algorithm outputs a sender key for each sender denoted $\{\mathsf{ek}_i\}_{i \in [n]}$, a receiver key for each receiver denoted $\{\mathsf{rk}_i\}_{i \in [n]}$, and a token for the router denoted $\mathsf{tk}$.

- $\mathsf{ct}_{i,t} \leftarrow \mathbf{Enc}(\mathsf{ek}_i, x_{i,t}, t)$: sender $i$ uses its sender key $\mathsf{ek}_i$ to encrypt the message $x_{i,t}$ where $t \in \mathbb{N}$ denotes the current time step. The **Enc** algorithm produces a ciphertext $\mathsf{ct}_{i,t}$.
- $(\mathsf{ct}'_{1,t}, \mathsf{ct}'_{2,t}, \dots, \mathsf{ct}'_{n,t}) \leftarrow \mathbf{Rte}(\mathsf{tk}, \mathsf{ct}_{1,t}, \mathsf{ct}_{2,t}, \dots, \mathsf{ct}_{n,t})$: the routing algorithm **Rte** takes its token $\mathsf{tk}$ (which encodes some permutation $\pi$), and $n$ ciphertexts received from the $n$ senders denoted $\mathsf{ct}_{1,t}, \mathsf{ct}_{2,t}, \dots, \mathsf{ct}_{n,t}$, and produces *transformed ciphertexts* $\mathsf{ct}'_{1,t}, \mathsf{ct}'_{2,t}, \dots, \mathsf{ct}'_{n,t}$ where $\mathsf{ct}'_{i,t}$ is destined for the receiver $i \in [n]$.
- $x \leftarrow \mathbf{Dec}(\mathsf{rk}_i, \mathsf{ct}'_{i,t})$: the decryption algorithm **Dec** takes a receiver key $\mathsf{rk}_i$, a transformed ciphertext $\mathsf{ct}'_{i,t}$, and outputs a decrypted message $x$.

In our formulation above, the permutation $\pi$ is known a-priori at **Setup** time. Once **Setup** has been run, the senders can communicate with the receivers over multiple time steps $t$.

**Correctness.** Without loss of generality, we may assume that each plaintext message is a single bit—if the plaintext contains multiple bits, we can always split it bit by bit and encrypt it over multiple time steps. Correctness requires that with probability 1, the following holds for any $\kappa \in \mathbb{N}$, any $(x_1, x_2, \dots, x_n) \in \{0,1\}^n$ and any $t \in \mathbb{N}$: let $(\{\mathsf{ek}_i\}_{i \in [n]}, \{\mathsf{rk}_i\}_{i \in [n]}, \mathsf{tk}) \leftarrow \mathbf{Setup}(1^\kappa, n, \pi)$, let $\mathsf{ct}_{i,t} \leftarrow \mathbf{Enc}(\mathsf{ek}_i, x_i, t)$ for $i \in [n]$, let $(\mathsf{ct}'_{1,t}, \mathsf{ct}'_{2,t}, \dots, \mathsf{ct}'_{n,t}) \leftarrow \mathbf{Rte}(\mathsf{tk}, \mathsf{ct}_{1,t}, \mathsf{ct}_{2,t}, \dots, \mathsf{ct}_{n,t})$, and let $x'_i \leftarrow \mathbf{Dec}(\mathsf{rk}_i, \mathsf{ct}'_{i,t})$ for $i \in [n]$; it must be that

$$x'_{\pi(i)} = x_i \text{ for every } i \in [n].$$

**Communication Compactness.** We require our NIAR scheme to have *compact communication*, that is, the total communication cost per time step should be upper bounded by $\mathsf{poly}(\kappa) \cdot O(n)$. Furthermore, we would like that the token $\mathsf{tk}$, and every sender and receiver's secret key $\mathsf{ek}_i$ and $\mathsf{rk}_i$ respectively, are all upper bounded by a fixed polynomial in $n$.

### 2.2 Simulation-Based Security

We consider static corruption where the set of corrupt players are chosen prior to the **Setup** algorithm.

**Real-World Experiment** $\mathsf{Real}^{\mathcal{A}}(1^\kappa)$. The real-world experiment is described below where $\mathcal{K}_S \subseteq [n]$ denotes the set of corrupt senders, and $\mathcal{K}_R \subseteq [n]$ denotes the set of corrupt receivers. Let $\mathcal{H}_S = [n] \setminus \mathcal{K}_S$ be the set of honest senders and $\mathcal{H}_R = [n] \setminus \mathcal{K}_R$ be the set of honest receivers. Let $\mathcal{A}$ be a *stateful* adversary:

- $n, \pi, \mathcal{K}_S, \mathcal{K}_R \leftarrow \mathcal{A}(1^\kappa)$
- $(\{\mathsf{ek}_i\}_{i \in [n]}, \{\mathsf{rk}_i\}_{i \in [n]}, \mathsf{tk}) \leftarrow \mathbf{Setup}(1^\kappa, n, \pi)$
- For $t = 1, 2, \dots$:
  - if $t = 1$ then $\{x_{i,t}\}_{i \in \mathcal{H}_S} \leftarrow \mathcal{A}(\mathsf{tk}, \{\mathsf{ek}_i\}_{i \in \mathcal{K}_S}, \{\mathsf{rk}_i\}_{i \in \mathcal{K}_R})$; else $\{x_{i,t}\}_{i \in \mathcal{H}_S} \leftarrow \mathcal{A}(\{\mathsf{ct}_{i,t-1}\}_{i \in \mathcal{H}_S})$;
  - for $i \in \mathcal{H}_S$, $\mathsf{ct}_{i,t} \leftarrow \mathbf{Enc}(\mathsf{ek}_i, x_{i,t}, t)$

**Ideal-World Experiment** $\mathsf{Ideal}^{\mathcal{A},\mathsf{Sim}}(1^\kappa)$. The ideal-world experiment involves not just $\mathcal{A}$, but also a p.p.t. (stateful) simulator denoted $\mathsf{Sim}$, who is in charge of simulating $\mathcal{A}$'s view knowing essentially only what corrupt senders and receivers know. Further, the $\mathsf{Ideal}^{\mathcal{A},\mathsf{Sim}}(1^\kappa)$ experiment is parametrized by a leakage function denoted $\mathsf{Leak}$ to be defined later. Henceforth for $\mathcal{C} \subseteq [n]$, we use $\pi(\mathcal{C})$ to denote the set $\{\pi(i) : i \in \mathcal{C}\}$.

- $n, \pi, \mathcal{K}_S, \mathcal{K}_R \leftarrow \mathcal{A}(1^\kappa)$
- $(\{\mathsf{ek}_i\}_{i\in[n]}, \{\mathsf{rk}_i\}_{i\in[n]}, \mathsf{tk}) \leftarrow \mathsf{Sim}(1^\kappa, n, \mathcal{K}_S, \mathcal{K}_R, \mathsf{Leak}(\pi, \mathcal{K}_S, \mathcal{K}_R))$
- For $t = 1, 2, \ldots$:
  - if $t = 1$ then $\{x_{i,t}\}_{i\in\mathcal{H}_S} \leftarrow \mathcal{A}(\mathsf{tk}, \{\mathsf{ek}_i\}_{i\in\mathcal{K}_S}, \{\mathsf{rk}_i\}_{i\in\mathcal{K}_R})$; else $\{x_{i,t}\}_{i\in\mathcal{H}_S} \leftarrow \mathcal{A}(\{\mathsf{ct}_{i,t-1}\}_{i\in\mathcal{H}_S})$;
  - $\{\mathsf{ct}_{i,t}\}_{i\in\mathcal{H}_S} \leftarrow \mathsf{Sim}\left(\{\forall i \in \mathcal{K}_R \cap \pi(\mathcal{H}_S) : (i, x_{j,t}) \text{ for } j = \pi^{-1}(i)\}\right)$. In other words, the simulator $\mathsf{Sim}$ is allowed to see for each corrupt receiver talking to an honest sender, what message it receives.

**Defining the Insider Information** $\mathsf{Leak}(\pi, \mathcal{K}_S, \mathcal{K}_R)$ **Known to Corrupt Players.** We require that *when no sender or receiver is corrupt, the adversary should not learn anything about the routing permutation $\pi$*. When some senders and receivers are corrupt, the adversary *may learn the insider information about $\pi$ known to the corrupt players, but nothing else*. We use the function $\mathsf{Leak}(\pi, \mathcal{K}_S, \mathcal{K}_R)$ to describe the insider information known to corrupt senders and receivers about the routing permutation $\pi$. We define three natural notions of insider information:

1. *Every player knows who it is talking to.* The first natural notion is to assume that each sender or receiver knows whom the player itself is talking to, but it is not aware who others are talking to. By corrupting some senders and receivers, the adversary should not learn more about the routing permutation $\pi$ beyond what the corrupt senders and receivers know. In other words, the part of the permutation $\pi$ containing "corrupt $\rightarrow$ *" and "* $\rightarrow$ corrupt" is leaked. More formally, we can define leakage as below:

$$\mathsf{Leak}^{\mathrm{SR}}(\pi, \mathcal{K}_S, \mathcal{K}_R) := \{\forall i \in \mathcal{K}_S : (i, \pi(i))\} \cup \{\forall i \in \mathcal{K}_R : (\pi^{-1}(i), i)\}$$

2. *Every sender knows who it is talking to.* Another natural notion is when a sender knows which receiver it is talking to, but a receiver may not know who it is receiving from. By corrupting a subset of the senders and receivers, the adversary should not learn more than what those corrupt players know. In other words, the "corrupt $\rightarrow$ *" part of the permutation $\pi$ is leaked. More formally, we can formally define leakage as below:

$$\mathsf{Leak}^{\mathrm{S}}(\pi, \mathcal{K}_S, \mathcal{K}_R) := \{\forall i \in \mathcal{K}_S : (i, \pi(i))\}$$

3. *Inherent leakage.* The least possible leakage is when only the "corrupt $\rightarrow$ corrupt" part of the permutation $\pi$ is leaked. Note that this leakage is inherent because a corrupt sender can always encrypt multiple random messages in

the same time slot, and observe whether any corrupt receiver received this message. In the minimum, inherent leakage scenario, we require that only this is leaked about the permutation $\pi$ and nothing else. More formally, we can formally define leakage as below:

$$\mathsf{Leak}^{\min}(\pi, \mathcal{K}_S, \mathcal{K}_R) := \{\forall i \in \mathcal{K}_S \cap \pi^{-1}(\mathcal{K}_R) : (i, \pi(i))\}$$

*Remark 2.* Note that even in the minimum, inherent leakage scenario, knowing the leaked information $\mathsf{Leak}^{\min}(\pi, \mathcal{K}_S, \mathcal{K}_R) := \{\forall i \in \mathcal{K}_S \cap \pi^{-1}(\mathcal{K}_R) : (i, \pi(i))\}$ as well as $\mathcal{K}_R$, one can efficiently compute the set $\mathcal{K}_R \cap \pi(\mathcal{H}_S)$. Therefore, during the encryption phase, by learning $\{\forall i \in \mathcal{K}_R \cap \pi(\mathcal{H}_S) : (i, x_j) \text{ for } j = \pi^{-1}(i)\}$, i.e., the set of leaked messages received by corrupt receivers from honest senders, the simulator Sim does not learn anything extra about the routing permutation $\pi$ beyond what it already learned earlier in the experiment, that is, $\mathsf{Leak}^{\min}(\pi, \mathcal{K}_S, \mathcal{K}_R)$.

**Definition 1 (NIAR simulation security).** *We define simulation security of a NIAR scheme as below depending on which leakage function is used in the* $\mathsf{Ideal}^{\mathcal{A},\mathsf{Sim}}$ *experiment:*

1. *We say that a Non-Interactive Anonymous Routing (NIAR) scheme is SIM-secure iff the following holds when using* $\mathsf{Leak} := \mathsf{Leak}^{\mathsf{SR}}$ *in the* $\mathsf{Ideal}^{\mathcal{A},\mathsf{Sim}}$ *experiment: there exists a p.p.t. simulator Sim such that for any non-uniform p.p.t. adversary* $\mathcal{A}$, $\mathcal{A}$*'s view in* $\mathsf{Real}^{\mathcal{A}}(1^\kappa)$ *and* $\mathsf{Ideal}^{\mathcal{A},\mathsf{Sim}}(1^\kappa)$ *are computationally indistinguishable.*
2. *We say that a NIAR scheme is SIM-secure with receiver-insider protection, iff the above holds when using* $\mathsf{Leak} := \mathsf{Leak}^{\mathsf{S}}$ *in the* $\mathsf{Ideal}^{\mathcal{A},\mathsf{Sim}}$ *experiment.*
3. *We say that a NIAR scheme is SIM-secure with full insider protection, iff the above holds when using* $\mathsf{Leak} := \mathsf{Leak}^{\min}$ *in the* $\mathsf{Ideal}^{\mathcal{A},\mathsf{Sim}}$ *experiment.*

### 2.3 Equivalence to Indistinguishability-Based Security

In our online full version [68], we define an alternative, indistinguishability-based security notion, and prove that it is equivalent to the simulation-based notion.

## 3 Informal Overview of Our Construction

We now give an informal overview of our constructions.

### 3.1 Notations and Building Block

We will concretely instantiate a scheme using a cyclic group $\mathbb{G}$ of prime order $q$. Therefore, we introduce some notations for group elements and group operations.

*Group Notation and Implicit Notation for Group Exponentiation.* Throughout the paper, we use the notation $[\![x]\!]$ to denote a group element $g^x \in \mathbb{G}$ where $g \in \mathbb{G}$ is the generator of an appropriate cyclic group of prime order $q$ where $x \in \mathbb{Z}_q$. Similarly, $[\![\mathbf{x}]\!]$ denotes a vector of group elements where $\mathbf{x} \in \mathbb{Z}_q^{|\mathbf{x}|}$ is the exponent vector. If we know $[\![x]\!] \in \mathbb{G}$ and $y \in \mathbb{Z}_p$, we can compute $[\![xy]\!] \in \mathbb{G}$. Therefore, whenever an algorithm needs to compute $[\![xy]\!]$, it only needs to know one of the exponents $x$ or $y$. The same implicit notation is used for vectors too.

*Correlated Pseudorandom Functions.* We will need a building block which we call a correlated pseudorandom function, denoted CPRF. A CPRF scheme has the following possibly randomized algorithms:

- $(K_1, K_2, \ldots, K_n) \leftarrow \mathbf{Gen}(1^\kappa, n, q)$: takes a security parameter $1^\kappa$ and the number of users $n$, some prime $q$, and outputs the user secret key $K_i$ for each $i \in [n]$.
- $v \leftarrow \mathbf{Eval}(K_i, x)$: given a user secret key $K_i$ and an input $x \in \{0,1\}^\kappa$, output an evaluation result $v \in \mathbb{Z}_q$.

For correctness, we require that the following always holds if $\{K_i\}_{i \in [n]}$ is in the support of $\mathbf{Gen}(1^\kappa, n, q)$:

$$\sum_{i \in [n]} \mathsf{CPRF}.\mathbf{Eval}(K_i, x) = 0 \mod q \tag{1}$$

For security, we require that even when a subset of the keys $\mathcal{K} \subset [n]$ can be corrupted by the adversary, it must be that for every fresh $x$, all honest evaluations $\{\mathsf{CPRF}.\mathbf{Eval}(K_i, x)_{i \notin \mathcal{K}}\}$ are computationally indistinguishable from random terms subject to the constraint $\sum_{i \notin \mathcal{K}} \mathsf{CPRF}.\mathbf{Eval}(K_i, x) = -\sum_{i \in \mathcal{K}} \mathsf{CPRF}.\mathbf{Eval}(K_i, x) \mod q$—note that the adversary can compute the right-hand-side of the equation.

Intuitively, such a correlated PRF guarantees that even when some players' keys can be corrupt, honest players' evaluations for any fresh input $x$ must appear random, except that they are subject to the constraint in Eq. 1. A couple earlier works [2,24] showed how to construct such a CPRF from ordinary PRFs. We will present more formal definitions and construction in the online full version [68].

### 3.2   A Simple, Function-Revealing MCFE Scheme for Selection

Multi-client functional encryption for summation was first suggested by Shi et al. [66] (coined "private stream aggregation" in their paper). Later, Goldwasser et al. [51] defined multi-client functional encryption for general functions, and constructed a scheme assuming indistinguishable obfuscation, random oracles, and other assumptions. Subsequently, a line of work focused on constructing MCFE schemes for inner-products.

We consider MCFE for "selection", which can be viewed as a special case of inner-product computation. An MCFE-for-selection scheme has four possibly randomized algorithms (**Setup, KGen, Enc, Dec**)—in our definition below, we allow each client to encrypt a vector $\mathbf{x}_{i,t} \in \{0,1\}^m$ of length $m$, and the selection vector $\mathbf{y} \in \{0,1\}^{mn}$ selects exactly one coordinate from one client's plaintext vector[4]:

- The **Setup**$(1^\kappa, m, n)$ algorithm[5] outputs a secret key for each of the $n$ clients where the $i$-th client's key is denoted $\mathsf{ek}_i$, and a master public- and secret-key pair $(\mathsf{mpk}, \mathsf{msk})$.
- The **KGen**$(\mathsf{mpk}, \mathsf{msk}, \mathbf{y})$ algorithm takes the master public-key $\mathsf{mpk}$ and the master secret-key $\mathsf{msk}$, and outputs a functional key $\mathsf{sk}_\mathbf{y}$ for the selection vector $\mathbf{y} \in \{0,1\}^{mn}$. It is promised that the input $\mathbf{y}$ has only one coordinate set to 1, and the rest are set to 0.
- The **Enc**$(\mathsf{mpk}, \mathsf{ek}_i, \mathbf{x}_{i,t}, t)$ algorithm lets client $i \in [n]$ use its secret key $\mathsf{ek}_i$ to encrypt a plaintext $\mathbf{x}_{i,t} \in \{0,1\}^m$ for the time step $t$.
- Finally, given the $n$ ciphertexts $\mathsf{ct}_1, \ldots, \mathsf{ct}_n$ collected from all clients pertaining to the same time step, as well as the functional key $\mathsf{sk}_\mathbf{y}$, one can call **Dec**$(\mathsf{mpk}, \mathsf{sk}_\mathbf{y}, \{\mathsf{ct}_i\}_{i \in [n]})$ to evaluate the selection outcome $\langle \mathbf{x}, \mathbf{y} \rangle$ where $\mathbf{x}$ denotes the concatenation of the plaintexts encrypted under $\mathsf{ct}_1, \ldots, \mathsf{ct}_n$.

If we did not care about function privacy, it turns out that we can construct a very simple MCFE-for-selection scheme as follows. Basically, for each of the $n$ clients, there is a separate symmetric-key encryption instance. During **Setup**, client $i$ obtains the secret keys $\mathsf{sk}_{i,1}, \ldots, \mathsf{sk}_{i,m}$ corresponding to $m$ independent encryption instances. For client $i$ to encrypt a message of $m$ bits during some time step $t$, it simply encrypts each bit $j \in [m]$ using $\mathsf{sk}_{i,j}$, and output the union of the ciphertexts. To generate a functional key for selection vector $\mathbf{y}$ that selects the $j$-th coordinate of the client $i$'s message, simply output $(\mathbf{y}, \mathsf{sk}_{i,j})$, and decryption can be completed, i.e., using $\mathsf{sk}_{i,j}$ to decrypt the coordinate in the ciphertext that is being selected.

### 3.3 Preparing the MCFE Scheme for Function Privacy Upgrade

The next challenge is how to upgrade the above MCFE-for-selection scheme to have function privacy. Function privacy in inner-product functional encryption (FE) was first studied by Shen, Shi, and Waters [63], who considered single-input FE and a weaker notion of function privacy than what we will need. Subsequent works have generalized and improved the techniques of Shen, Shi, and Waters [63] to achieve stronger notions of function privacy [58], and have extended the techniques to a multi-input FE context [5].

Our function privacy upgrade techniques are inspired by these earlier works [5,58,63], but we need non-trivial new techniques to make it work in our

---

[4] Our scheme can support the case where each coordinate of the plaintext vector $\mathbf{x}_{i,t}$ comes from a polynomially sized space, but we simply assume each coordinate is a bit for simplicity.

[5] In our subsequent formal sections, for notational reasons needed to make our presentation formal, we shall separate the **Setup** algorithm into a parameter generation algorithm **Gen** and a **Setup** algorithm, respectively.

context. Specifically, previous function privacy techniques assume the encryptor to be trusted, and thus they are not directly applicable to the MCFE setting in which some of the clients may be corrupted, and their secret keys become known to the adversary.

To enable the function-private upgrade, let us first understand where the above MCFE-for-selection scheme in Sect. 3.2 leaks information about the selection vector $\mathbf{y}$. First, the scheme blantantly embeds the selection vector $\mathbf{y}$ in cleartext in the functional key $\mathsf{sk_y}$. Second, the decryption process itself also reveals $\mathbf{y}$ because decryption works on only the coordinate being selected. To fix the above problems, we would like to first modify the idea in Sect. 3.2 to satisfy the following two requirements:

1. We change the decryption process such that decryption involves all coordinates, and not just the coordinate being selected.
2. Further, we want to randomize the partial decryption outcome corresponding to every client such that from the partial decryptions alone, one cannot tell which coordinate is being selected.

We can instantiate an MCFE-for-selection scheme satisfying the above requirements in a cyclic group $\mathbb{G}$ of prime order $q$. The resulting scheme is still *function-revealing*—at this point, we have merely "prepared" the scheme for the function privacy upgrade described later in Sect. 3.4. We describe this scheme below where we use $\mathsf{CPRF}(K_i, t)$ as an abbreviation for $\mathsf{CPRF}.\mathbf{Eval}(K_i, t)$:

---

**MCFE: function-revealing MCFE for selection, w/ randomized partial decryptions**

$\mathsf{mpk} = [\![w]\!]$,   $\mathsf{msk} = \{\mathbf{S}_i, a_i\}_{i \in [n]}$,   $\mathsf{ek}_i = (K_i, a_i)$ where each $\mathbf{S}_i \in \mathbb{Z}_q^{m \times 2}$

Ciphertext for $t$ where each $\mathbf{x}_{i,t} \in \{0,1\}^m$

$$\forall i \in [n]: \quad \left( [\![\mathbf{x}_{i,t} + \mathbf{S}_i \mathbf{r}_i]\!], \; [\![\mathbf{r}_i]\!], \; [\![\mathsf{CPRF}(K_i, t) + a_i w \mu_i]\!], \; [\![w \mu_i]\!] \right)$$

where $\mathbf{r}_i$ and $\mu_i$ are chosen at random

Functional key for $\mathbf{y} := (\mathbf{y}_1, \ldots, \mathbf{y}_n)$ where each $\mathbf{y}_i \in \{0,1\}^m$

$$\forall i \in [n]: \quad \left( \mathbf{y}_i, \quad -\mathbf{S}_i^\top \mathbf{y}_i, \quad \rho, \quad -\rho a_i \right)$$

where $\rho$ is chosen at random

---

Henceforth, we will name $[\![\mathbf{c}_{i,1}]\!] := [\![\mathbf{x}_{i,t} + \mathbf{S}_i \mathbf{r}_i]\!]$, $[\![\mathbf{c}_{i,2}]\!] := [\![\mathbf{r}_i]\!]$, and $[\![\widetilde{\mathbf{c}}]\!] := [\![\mathsf{CPRF}(K_i, t) + a_i w \mu_i, w \mu_i]\!]$. Additionally, let $\mathbf{k}_{i,1} := \mathbf{y}_i$, $\mathbf{k}_{i,2} := \mathbf{S}_i^\top \mathbf{y}_i$, and $\widetilde{\mathbf{k}}_i := (\rho, -\rho a_i)$.

For the above scheme to be a correct function-revealing MCFE-for-selection, we only need the first two terms of the ciphertext and functional keys, i.e.,

($[\![\mathbf{c}_{i,1}]\!]$, $[\![\mathbf{c}_{i,2}]\!]$) and ($\mathbf{k}_{i,1}$, $\mathbf{k}_{i,2}$). Essentially, these terms can be viewed as a concrete instantiation of the ideas mentioned in Sect. 3.2: the $j$-th row of $\mathbf{S}_i$ is used to encrypt the $j$-th coordinate of $x_{i,t}$; further, to compute a functional key for $\mathbf{y}$ which is selecting the $j$-th coordinate of the $i$-th client's message, simply output $\mathbf{y}$ and the $j$-th row of $\mathbf{S}_i$ (which is equal to $\mathbf{S}_i^\top \mathbf{y}_i$). Security of the encryption follows from the Decisional Linear assumption. The extra terms in the ciphertexts and functional keys, denoted $\widetilde{\mathbf{c}}_i$ and $\widetilde{\mathbf{k}}_i$ are randomizing terms added to satisfy the aforementioned randomized partial decryption requirement as we explain below.

We now explain how decryption works. Given a ciphertext vector for $n$ all clients $[\![\mathbf{c}]\!] := (([\![\mathbf{c}_{1,1}]\!], [\![\mathbf{c}_{1,2}]\!], [\![\widetilde{\mathbf{c}}_1]\!]), \ldots, ([\![\mathbf{c}_{n,1}]\!], [\![\mathbf{c}_{n,2}]\!], [\![\widetilde{\mathbf{c}}_n]\!]))$, and a key vector $\mathbf{k} := ((\mathbf{k}_{1,1}, \mathbf{k}_{1,2}, \widetilde{\mathbf{k}}_1), \ldots, (\mathbf{k}_{n,1}, \mathbf{k}_{n,2}, \widetilde{\mathbf{k}}_n))$, decryption computes the "inner-product-in-the-exponent" of the ciphertext vector and the token vector, i.e.,

$$[\![\langle \mathbf{c}, \mathbf{k} \rangle]\!] = \prod_{i \in [n]} \left( [\![\langle \mathbf{c}_{i,1}, \mathbf{k}_{i,1} \rangle]\!] \cdot [\![\langle \mathbf{c}_{i,2}, \mathbf{k}_{i,2} \rangle]\!] \cdot [\![\langle \widetilde{\mathbf{c}}_i, \widetilde{\mathbf{k}}_i \rangle]\!] \right).$$

Finally, we output the discrete logarithm of the above expression as the decrypted message[6].

The decryption can alternatively be viewed as computing the partial decryption of each client and then multiplying the partial decryptions together. Henceforth, let $\mathsf{MCFE.Dec}^i$ denote the function that computes the partial decryption corresponding to client $i$, and let $p_{i,t}$ denote the $i$-th partial decryption:

$$p_{i,t} := \mathsf{MCFE.Dec}^i(\mathsf{sk}_i, \mathsf{ct}_{i,t}) = \left( [\![\langle \mathbf{c}_{i,1}, \mathbf{k}_{i,1} \rangle]\!] \cdot [\![\langle \mathbf{c}_{i,2}, \mathbf{c}_{i,2} \rangle]\!] \cdot [\![\langle \widetilde{\mathbf{c}}_i, \widetilde{\mathbf{k}}_i \rangle]\!] \right),$$

and then multiplying all the randomized partially decrypted results. Note that the partial decryption function $\mathsf{MCFE.Dec}^i(\mathsf{sk}_i, \mathsf{ct}_{i,t})$ also evaluates an inner-product in the exponent. One can verify the following: let $\mathbf{x}_{i,t} := (x_{i,1,t}, \ldots, x_{i,m,t})$ be the plaintext message encrypted under $\mathsf{ct}_{i,t}$, we have that

$$p_{i,t} = \begin{cases} [\![\mathsf{CPRF}(K_i, t) \cdot \rho]\!] & \text{if client } i\text{'s vector is not being selected} \\ [\![x_{i,j,t} + \mathsf{CPRF}(K_i, t) \cdot \rho]\!] & \text{if the } j\text{-th coordinate of the } i\text{-th client is being selected} \end{cases}$$

Thus, the above decryption indeed involves all coordinates, and moreover, the partial decryption results $\{p_{i,t}\}_{i \in [n]}$ are randomized due to the use of the CPRF.

*Remark 3 (Technical condition needed for the function privacy upgrade).* Informally speaking, we want the following (necessary but not sufficient) condition to hold for our function privacy upgrade to work. Let $\mathcal{H} \subseteq [n]$ be the set of honest clients. Assume that the Decisional Linear assumption holds. We want that even after having seen the public key, honest ciphertexts in all time steps other than $t$, honest ciphertexts in time step $t$, i.e., $\{\mathsf{ct}_{i,t}\}_{i \in \mathcal{H}}$, as well as $[\![\rho]\!]$ for a fresh random $\rho \in \mathbb{Z}_q$, the terms $\{[\![\mathsf{CPRF}(K_i, t) \cdot \rho]\!]\}_{i \in \mathcal{H}}$ must be computationally indistinguishable from random, except that their product is equal to

---

[6] Note that because decryption involves computing a discrete logarithm, we require the plaintext space to be small.

some fixed term known to the adversary. This condition is needed in the proof of a key lemma in the function privacy upgrade proof (see our the online full version [68]).

## 3.4 Function Privacy Upgrade

Since we do not want the functional key to leak the selection vector $\mathbf{y}$, we want to encrypt the functional key $\mathsf{sk_y}$; but how can we use the encrypted $\mathsf{sk_y}$ for correct decryption? Inspired by earlier works [5,58], our idea is to adopt $n$ instances (single-input) functional encryption henceforth denoted $\mathsf{FE}$, such that the $i$-th client obtains the master secret key of the $i$-th instance, henceforth denoted $\mathsf{msk}_i$. During **KGen**, we encrypt the $i$-th coordinate of $\mathsf{sk_y}$ using the $i$-th $\mathsf{FE}$, and let the result be $\overline{\mathsf{sk}}_i$. To encrypt its message $\mathbf{x}_{i,t}$, the $i$-th client first encrypts $\mathbf{x}_{i,t}$ using the MCFE-for-selection scheme and obtains the ciphertext $\mathsf{ct}_{i,t}$; then it calls $\overline{\mathsf{ct}}_{i,t} := \mathsf{FE.KGen}(\mathsf{msk}_i, f^{\mathsf{ct}_{i,t}})$ to transform $\mathsf{ct}_{i,t}$ into an $\mathsf{FE}$ token for the function $f^{\mathsf{ct}_{i,t}}(\star) := \mathsf{MCFE.Dec}^i(\star, \mathsf{ct}_{i,t})$. Recall that $\mathsf{MCFE.Dec}^i$ computes the MCFE's partial decryption for the $i$-th coordinate. In this way, an evaluator can invoke $\mathsf{FE.Dec}$ on the pair $\overline{\mathsf{ct}}_{i,t}$ and $\overline{\mathsf{sk}}_i$ to obtain the $i$-th partial decryption.

To make this idea work, in fact, we do not even need $\mathsf{FE}$ for general circuits. Recall that in our MCFE-for-selection scheme above, each partial decryption function $\mathsf{MCFE.Dec}^i$ computes an inner-product in the exponent. We therefore only need an $\mathsf{FE}$ scheme capable of computing an inner-product in the exponent. Several earlier works [3,12,72] showed how to construct inner-product function encryption based on the DDH assumption. By slightly modifying these constructions, one can construct an $\mathsf{FE}$ scheme for evaluating "inner-product-in-the-exponent" as long as the Decisional Linear assumption holds in certain bilinear groups. For completeness, we shall present this special $\mathsf{FE}$ scheme for computing "inner-product-in-the-exponent" in the online full version [68].

**From Weak to Full Function Privacy.** Although intuitively, the above idea seems like it should work, it turns out for technical reasons, we can only prove that it satisfies a weak form of function privacy henceforth called *weak function hiding*. We defer its detailed technical definition to the online full version [68]. Fortunately, we can borrow a two-slot trick from various prior works on Functional Encryption [5,22,63] and Indistinguishability Obfuscation [58,59], and upgrade a weakly function-hiding MCFE-for-selection scheme to a fully function-hiding one. At a very high level, to achieve this, instead of having each client $i \in [n]$ encrypt its plaintext $\mathbf{x}_i \in \{0,1\}^m$, we have each client $i$ encrypt the expanded vector $(\mathbf{x}_i, \mathbf{0})$ instead where $\mathbf{0}$ is also of length $m$. Similarly, the selection vector's length will need to be doubled accordingly too, i.e., to compute a functional key for $\mathbf{y} = (\mathbf{y}_1, \ldots, \mathbf{y}_n)$ where each $\mathbf{y}_i \in \{0,1\}^m$, we instead compute a functional key for the expanded vector $((\mathbf{y}_1, \mathbf{0}), \ldots, (\mathbf{y}_n, \mathbf{0}))$.

By expanding the plaintext and selection vectors, we gain some spare slots which can serve as "wiggle room" during our security proofs. This way, in our security proofs, we can make incremental modifications in every step of the hybrid sequence and make progress with the proof.

Our exposition above is geared towards understandability and is sometimes informal. The actual details and proofs are somewhat more involved and we refer the reader to the online full version [68] for a formal exposition.

Summarizing the above, we can construct an MCFE-for-selection scheme with (full) function privacy, henceforth denoted MCFE$^{\text{ffh}}$, presented more formally below. In the description below, MCFE is the aforementioned function-revealing MCFE for selection, augmented to have randomized partial decryptions; FE is a single-input functional encryption scheme for computing inner-products in exponents, formally defined in the online full version [68].

---

### MCFE$^{\text{ffh}}$: function-hiding MCFE for selection

- **Gen**($1^\kappa$): Sample a suitable prime $q$, and generate a suitable bilinear group of order $q$, with the pairing function $e : \mathbb{G}_1 \times \mathbb{G}_2 \to \mathbb{G}_T$. Let $H : \{0,1\}^* \to \mathbb{G}_1$ be a random oracle. The public parameter pp contains the prime $q$, and the description of the bilinear group; the parameters pp$'$ contains a description of $\mathbb{G}_1$, its order $q$, and a description of $H$.
- **Setup**(pp, $m$, $n$): Call $(\text{mpk}', \text{msk}', \{\text{ek}'_i\}_{i\in[n]}) \leftarrow$ MCFE.Setup (pp$'$, $2m$, $n$). For $i \in [n]$, call $(\text{mpk}_i, \text{msk}_i) \leftarrow$ FE.Setup(pp, $2m + 2$). Output:

$$\text{mpk} := (\text{pp}, \text{mpk}', \{\text{mpk}_i\}_{i\in[n]}), \quad \text{msk} := (\text{msk}', \{\text{msk}_i, \text{ek}_i\}_{i\in[n]}),$$
$$\forall i \in [n] : \text{ek}_i := (\text{msk}_i, \text{ek}'_i)$$

- **Enc**(mpk, ek$_i$, **x**, $t$):
  1. Let ct $:=$ MCFE.**Enc**(mpk$'$, ek$'_i$, (**x**, **0**), $t$) $\in \mathbb{G}_1^{2m+2}$.
  2. Let $\overline{\text{ct}} :=$ FE.**KGen**(msk$_i$, ct).
  3. Output CT $:=$ (ct, $\overline{\text{ct}}$).
- **KGen**(mpk, msk, **y**):
  1. Parse **y** $:= (\mathbf{y}_1, \ldots, \mathbf{y}_n)$ where each $\mathbf{y}_i \in \{0,1\}^m$.
  2. Let $\widetilde{\mathbf{y}} = ((\mathbf{y}_1, \mathbf{0}), \ldots, (\mathbf{y}_n, \mathbf{0})) \in \{0,1\}^{2mn}$.
  3. Call $(\mathbf{k}_1, \ldots, \mathbf{k}_n) :=$ MCFE.**KGen**(mpk$'$, msk$'$, $\widetilde{\mathbf{y}}$) where each $\mathbf{k}_i \in \mathbb{Z}_q^{2m+2}$ for $i \in [n]$.
  4. For $i \in [n]$, call $\overline{\mathbf{k}}_i :=$ FE.**Enc**(mpk$_i$, $\mathbf{k}_i$).
  5. Output sk$_{\mathbf{y}} := (\overline{\mathbf{k}}_1, \ldots, \overline{\mathbf{k}}_n)$.
- **Dec**(mpk, sk$_{\mathbf{y}}$, $\{\text{CT}_i\}_{i\in[n]}$): Parse each CT$_i := (\text{ct}_i, \overline{\text{ct}}_i)$. Parse sk$_{\mathbf{y}} := (\overline{\mathbf{k}}_1, \ldots, \overline{\mathbf{k}}_n)$. For $i \in [n]$, call $v_i :=$ FE.**Dec**($\overline{\text{ct}}_i$, ct$_i$, $\overline{\mathbf{k}}_i$). Output $\log(\prod_{i=1}^n v_i)$.

---

Our MCFE$^{\text{ffh}}$ scheme will be at the core of both our NIAR schemes, the one with receiver-insider protection, and the one with full insider protection.

**Proof Roadmap for MCFE$^{\text{ffh}}$.** To prove our MCFE$^{\text{ffh}}$ scheme secure, a critical stepping stone is to prove that it satisfies a weak notion of function privacy—afterwards we can rely on known techniques [5,22,58,59] to prove full function privacy. Roughly speaking, we say that an MCFE scheme for selection satisfies weak function privacy iff no p.p.t.*admissible* adversary $\mathcal{A}$ can distinguish two worlds indexed by $b \in \{0, 1\}$. In world $b$:

- the adversary $\mathcal{A}$ first specifies a set of corrupt clients, and obtains the public parameters as well as secret keys for corrupt clients;
- the adversary $\mathcal{A}$ now submits multiple **KGen** queries, each time specifying $\mathbf{y}^{(0)}$ and $\mathbf{y}^{(1)}$; and the challenger computes and returns tokens for $\mathbf{y}^{(b)}$;
- then $\mathcal{A}$ makes **Enc** queries for each time step $t$ by specifying $\{\mathbf{x}_{i,t}^{(0)}\}_{i \in \mathcal{H}}$ and $\{\mathbf{x}_{i,t}^{(1)}\}_{i \in \mathcal{H}}$ where $\mathcal{H} \subseteq [n]$ denotes the set of honest clients; and the challenger computes and returns encryptions for $\{\mathbf{x}_{i,t}^{(b)}\}_{i \in \mathcal{H}}$.

Moreover, an *admissible* adversary $\mathcal{A}$ must respect the following constraints:

1. for $i \in [n] \backslash \mathcal{H}$, $\mathbf{y}_i^{(0)} = \mathbf{y}_i^{(1)}$.
2. for any $\{\mathbf{x}_{i,t}^{(0)}, \mathbf{x}_{i,t}^{(1)}\}_{i \in \mathcal{H}}$ submitted in an **Enc** query,

$$\left\langle (\mathbf{x}_{i,t}^{(0)})_{i \in \mathcal{H}}, (\mathbf{y}_i^{(0)})_{i \in \mathcal{H}} \right\rangle = \left\langle (\mathbf{x}_{i,t}^{(1)})_{i \in \mathcal{H}}, (\mathbf{y}_i^{(0)})_{i \in \mathcal{H}} \right\rangle = \left\langle (\mathbf{x}_{i,t}^{(1)})_{i \in \mathcal{H}}, (\mathbf{y}_i^{(1)})_{i \in \mathcal{H}} \right\rangle$$

In our proof, we start from world 0, and through a sequence of hybrids, we switch to world 1; and every adjacent pair of hybrids are computationally indistinguishable. First, we use the function-revealing privacy of the underlying MCFE scheme to switch the encrypted vectors from $\{\mathbf{x}_{i,t}^{(0)}\}_{i \in \mathcal{H}}$ to $\{\mathbf{x}_{i,t}^{(1)}\}_{i \in \mathcal{H}}$—this step is possible due to the aforementioned admissibility rule $\mathcal{A}$ must respect. Next, we want to switch to using $\mathbf{y}^{(1)}$ in each **KGen** query. To accomplish this, we rely on a hybrid sequence over the multiple **KGen** queries one by one. Essentially, in the $\ell$-th hybrid, the first $\ell$ **KGen** queries are answered with $\mathbf{y}^{(1)}$, and the rest of the **KGen** queries are answered using $\mathbf{y}^{(0)}$. It suffices to argue that the $(\ell - 1)$-th hybrid and the $\ell$-th hybrid are computationally indistinguishable, and this turns out to be the most subtle step in our proof. To achieve this, let us consider the following modification of the $(\ell - 1)$-th hybrid. Henceforth the $\ell$-th **KGen** query is also called the *challenge* **KGen** query, and the two vectors submitted during this query are denoted $\mathbf{y}_*^{(0)}$ and $\mathbf{y}_*^{(1)}$ respectively:

1. During the $\ell$-th **KGen** quer, for computing components of the key corresponding to honest players, the challenger switches the FE.**Enc** inside the challenge **KGen** query to a simulated encryption which does not use the underlying MCFE's functional key as input. Corrupt players' key components are still computed honestly.

   Correspondingly, in every time step, the challenger answers **Enc** queries by calling the a simulated FE.**KGen** for every honest client $i$'s ciphertext component: the $i$-th simulated FE.**KGen** embeds the $i$-th partial decryption when paired with the challenge key for $\mathbf{y}_*^{(0)}$ of the underlying MCFE scheme. This step relies on the 1-SEL-SIM security of the single-input FE scheme (defined in the online full version [68]).

2. At this moment, due to the randomizing terms, and the aforementioned admissibility rule, we argue that during each **Enc** query, instead of encoding in the simulated FE.**KGen** the partial decryptions when paired with the challenge key for $\mathbf{y}_*^{(0)}$ of the underlying MCFE scheme, we could use $\mathbf{y}_*^{(1)}$ instead. This step is more involved and requires the technical condition in Remark 3.

From this point onwards, we can use a symmetric argument to switch all the way to the aforementioned $\ell$-th hybrid, in which the first $\ell$ **KGen** queries are answered with $\mathbf{y}^{(1)}$, and the remaining answered with $\mathbf{y}^{(0)}$. We defer the detailed proof to the subsequent formal sections.

### 3.5   Constructing NIAR with Receiver-Insider Protection

**Construction.** With a function-hiding MCFE-for-selection scheme henceforth denoted $\mathsf{MCFE}^{\mathsf{ffh}}$, we can construct a NIAR scheme in a natural fashion informally described below:

- **Setup:** The idea is to use the $\mathsf{MCFE}^{\mathsf{ffh}}$ scheme to generate functional keys for $n$ selection vectors, denoted $\mathsf{tk}_1, \ldots, \mathsf{tk}_n$, where $\mathsf{tk}_i$ is for selecting the message received by receiver $i \in [n]$. The collection $\{\mathsf{tk}_i\}_{i \in [n]}$ is given to the router as the token. The $\mathsf{MCFE}^{\mathsf{ffh}}$ also generates $n$ secret encryption keys denoted $\{\mathsf{ek}_i\}_{i \in [n]}$, one for each sender. Finally, the setup procedure generates $n$ symmetric encryption keys, one for each sender-receiver pair.
- **Enc:** During each time step $t$, to encrypt a message $x_{i,t}$, the $i$-th sender first encrypts $x_{i,t}$ with its symmetric key shared with its receiver—let $c_{i,t}$ denote the resulting ciphertext. Now, call $\mathsf{ct}_{i,t} := \mathsf{MCFE}^{\mathsf{ffh}}.\mathbf{Enc}(\mathsf{mpk}, \mathsf{ek}_i, c_{i,t})$ to further encrypt $c_{i,t}$ and obtain a final ciphertext $\mathsf{ct}_{i,t}$. Here, we abuse notation slightly and use $\mathsf{MCFE}^{\mathsf{ffh}}.\mathbf{Enc}(\mathsf{mpk}, \mathsf{ek}_i, c_{i,t})$ to mean encrypting $c_{i,t}$ bit by bit with the $\mathsf{MCFE}^{\mathsf{ffh}}$ scheme.
- **Rte:** Using the $n$ functional keys $\{\mathsf{tk}_i\}_{i \in [n]}$, a router can call $\mathsf{MCFE}^{\mathsf{ffh}}.\mathbf{Dec}$ to obtain the $n$ inner ciphertexts encrypted under the symmetric keys, and send the corresponding inner ciphertext to each receiver.
- **Dec:** Finally, each receiver uses its symmetric key to decrypt the final outcome.

**Proof Roadmap.** In the online full version [68], we shall prove that as long as $\mathsf{MCFE}^{\mathsf{ffh}}$ satisfies function-hiding security and the symmetric-key encryption scheme employed is secure, then, the above NIAR construction satisfies *receiver-insider protection*. To prove this, we use the indistinguishability security notion for NIAR, which is shown to be equivalent to the simulation-based notion. Rouhgly speaking, the indistinguishability game for NIAR, denoted $\mathsf{NIAR\text{-}Expt}^b$ is indexed by a bit $b \in \{0, 1\}$: imagine the adversary $\mathcal{A}$ chooses two permutations $\pi^{(0)}$ and $\pi^{(1)}$, and specifies two sets of messages $\{x_{i,t}^{(0)}\}_{i \in \mathcal{H}_S}$ and $\{x_{i,t}^{(1)}\}_{i \in \mathcal{H}_S}$ to query in each time step $t$. The challenger gives $\mathcal{A}$ a token for $\pi^{(b)}$, and ciphertexts for $\{x_{i,t}^{(b)}\}_{i \in \mathcal{H}_S}$ in each time step $t$. An *admissible* adversary must choose the permutations and messages such that the leakage in the two worlds are the same, where the leakage contains the corrupt-to-* part of the permutation and the messages received by corrupt receivers in every time step. We want to prove that any efficient, admissible $\mathcal{A}$ cannot distinguish whether it is playing NIAR-Expt$^0$ or NIAR-Expt$^1$.

To prove this, we first modify NIAR-Expt$^b$ slightly to obtain a hybrid Hyb$^b$ for $b \in \{0,1\}$: in Hyb$^b$, we replace the inner symmetric-key encryption from honest senders to honest receivers with simulated ciphertexts. We can easily show that Hyb$^b$ is computationally indistinguishable from NIAR-Expt$^b$ by reducing to the security of the symmetric encryption scheme.

To complete the proof, the more challenging step is to show that Hyb$^0$ is computationally indistinguishable from Hyb$^1$ for any efficient, admissible adversary $\mathcal{A}$. Here, we want to leverage $\mathcal{A}$ to create an efficient reduction $\mathcal{B}$ that breaks the function-hiding security of the underlying MCFE$^{\mathrm{ffh}}$ scheme. The subtlety is to make sure that $\mathcal{B}$ indeed respects the MCFE$^{\mathrm{ffh}}$'s admissibility rules. In our formal proofs, we fix the randomness $\psi$ consumed by the SE instances corresponding to each receiver in the set $\pi^{(0)}(\mathcal{H}_S) = \pi^{(1)}(\mathcal{H}_S)$, and prove that the two experiments are indistinguishability for every choice of fixed $\psi$. We then define the reduction $\mathcal{B}$ in a natural manner, and make a careful argument that if $\mathcal{A}$ satisfies the NIAR game's admissibility rule (for the receiver-insider protection notion), then $\mathcal{B}$ will indeed respect the admissibility rules of the underlying MCFE$^{\mathrm{ffh}}$.

We defer the formal description and proofs to the online full version [68].

### 3.6  Achieving Full Insider Protection

To upgrade our NIAR scheme to have full insider protection turns out to be more involved. As explained earlier in Sect. 1.3, for such a scheme to work, *all* the transformed ciphertexts output by **Rte** must change when a single sender's input ciphertext changes.

**Construction (Sketch).** To accomplish this, we leverage a indistinguishability obfuscator for probabilistic circuits (piO) whose existence is implied by sub-exponentially secure indistinguishability obfuscation and sub-exponentially secure one-way functions [30].

- **Setup**: during the trusted setup, each receiver $i$ receives the secret key of a PKE scheme (with special properties mentioned later); and each sender receives the encryption key generated by an MCFE$^{\mathrm{ffh}}$ scheme.
  The router's token tk is a piO which encodes the MCFE$^{\mathrm{ffh}}$ scheme's functional keys for all $n$ selection vectors. Inside the piO, the following probabilistic program is evaluated:
  1. first, use the MCFE$^{\mathrm{ffh}}$ functional keys to decrypt the messages that each receiver should receive;
  2. next, encrypt the messages under each receiver's respective public keys, and output the encrypted ciphertexts—note that the encryption scheme is randomized.

- **Enc:** in every time step, senders encrypt their messages using $\mathsf{MCFE}^{\mathsf{ffh}}$.
- **Rte:** in each time step, the router applies its token $\mathsf{tk}$, which is an obfuscated program, to the $n$ ciphertexts collected from senders. The outcome will be $n$ transformed ciphertexts.
- **Dec:** When a receiver receives a transformed ciphertext, it simply uses its secret key to decrypt it.

Observe that in this construction, indeed, if a single sender's input ciphertext changes, *all* transformed ciphertexts output by the **Rte** procedure will change.

**Proof Roadmap and Subtleties.** We encounter some more subtleties when we attempt to prove the above construction secure. First, it turns out that for technical reasons, to prove the above scheme secure, we need the public-key encryption (PKE) scheme used by the piO to reencrypt output messages to satisfy a special property: the PKE must be a special trapdoor mode in which encryptions of 0 and 1 are identically distributed. Obviously, the trapdoor mode loses information and cannot support correct decryption. In fact, in the real world, we will never use the trapdoor mode—it is used only inside our security proofs. We henceforth call a PKE scheme with this special property a perfectly hiding trapdoor encryption (tPKE). Such a tPKE scheme can be constructed assuming DDH [30].

Informally, our proof strategy is the following: First, we modify the real-world experiment (in which $\pi^{(0)}$ and $x_{i,t}^{(0)}$ are used), and switch the tPKE instances corresponding to honest receivers' to use a trapdoor setup. This step can be reduced to the tPKE's security, since the adversary does not have the tPKE instances' secret keys corresponding to honest receivers. Next, we modify the obfuscated program to *no longer use the functional keys corresponding to the honest receivers*; instead, the obfuscated program will simply output encryptions of 0 under the trapdoor public keys for honest receivers. For corrupt receivers, the obfuscated program still behaves like the real world: use the $\mathsf{MCFE}^{\mathsf{ffh}}$ scheme's **Dec** procedure to decrypt the messages they ought to receive, and output encryptions of these messages under each corrupt receiver's public keys, respectively. This step relies on the security of the piO and the fact that the modified program is "distributionally equivalent" to the original program. At this moment, the obfuscated program *no longer uses the functional keys for honest receivers*, and only at this point can we rely on the $\mathsf{MCFE}^{\mathsf{ffh}}$'s security and switch from using $\pi^{(0)}$ in the setup and encrypting $x_{i,t}^{(0)}$ to using $\pi^{(1)}$ in the setup and encrypting $x_{i,t}^{(1)}$. The remaining hybrids are symmetric to the above, such that eventually we arrive at an experiment that is the same as the real-world experiment in which $\pi^{(1)}$ and $x_{i,t}^{(1)}$ are used by the challenger.

Notice that in our construction, we use the piO to obfuscate the $\mathsf{MCFE}^{\mathsf{ffh}}$ scheme's **Dec** procedure using all $n$ functional keys. One natural question is why we did not directly use the piO to obfuscate a program that calls the **Rte** procedure of our earlier NIAR scheme (with receiver-insider protection) and then encrypts the $n$ outcomes using $n$ instances of tPKE. It turns out that our proof strategy would not have worked for the latter, exactly because in our proofs, we needed an intermediate hybrid to completely stop using functional keys for honest receivers—intuitively, this is how we can prove the privacy of messages received by honest receivers. This explains why in our construction and proofs, we need to open up the NIAR scheme and directly manipulate the functional keys of the underlying MCFE$^{\text{ffh}}$.

## 3.7    Achieving Fault Tolerance

So far in our constructions, unless all senders send their encryption during a certain time step, the router would fail to perform the **Rte** operation. Such a scheme relies all senders to be online all the time, and thus is not fault-tolerant.

We modify our earlier NIAR abstraction to one that is fault-tolerant. The idea is to let **Enc** and **Rte** take an extra parameter $\mathcal{O} \subseteq [n]$ which denotes the set of senders that remain online. Additionally, **Rte** now takes in only ciphertexts from those in $\mathcal{O}$. In fact, our fault-tolerant NIAR abstraction can be viewed as a generalization of the non-fault-tolerant version.

To achieve fault tolerance, we observe that the underlying CPRF construction we use has a nice fault-tolerance property. In fact, we can modify the CPRF's evaluation function to take in $\mathcal{O}$, such that the following is satisfied:

$$\forall t \in \mathbb{N} : \quad \sum_{i \in \mathcal{O}} \text{CPRF.Eval}(K_i, t, \mathcal{O}) = 0$$

This way, for every receiver whose corresponding sender is in the online set $\mathcal{O}$, the router can correctly perform the MCFE$^{\text{ffh}}$'s decryption procedure using only ciphertexts from those in $\mathcal{O}$. Note that the recent elegant work of Bonawitz et al. [24] also made a similar observation of the fault-tolerance of the CPRF, and leveraged it to enable fault-tolerant, privacy-preserving federated learning—this is not explicitly stated in their paper but implicit in their constructions.

If a receiver $i$'s corresponding sender is no longer online, however, then the MCFE$^{\text{ffh}}$'s decryption procedure will output an inner ciphertext of **0** for receiver $i$. Since receiver $i$ cannot decrypt the **0** ciphertext using its symmetric key, it will simply output $\perp$—this is inevitable since the corresponding sender is no longer around. However, the router can also observe that receiver $i$ received an inner-ciphertext **0**. In this way, if the adversary is able to drop the senders one by one and check which receiver starts to receive an inner ciphertext of **0**, it can learn the receivers paired up with crashed senders. In our subsequent formal sections, we shall prove that in this fault-tolerant NIAR scheme, indeed the adversary can learn only the (corrupt+crashed)-to-* part of the permutation $\pi$, as well as the messages received by corrupt receivers every time step, and nothing else.

Finally, using techniques similar to those sketched in Sect. 3.6, we can upgrade the security of the above fault-tolerant scheme to full insider protection, i.e., only the (corrupt + crashed)-to-corrupt part of the permutation is leaked as well as the messages received by corrupt receivers, but nothing else. As mentioned earlier, this leakage is inherent and unavoidable for any fault-tolerant NIAR scheme, since the adversary can always make the senders crash one by one and check which corrupt receiver now starts to receive $\perp$.

Of course, the above description is a gross simplification omitting various subtleties both in definitions and constructions. We refer the reader to the online full version [68] for the detailed definitions, constructions, and proofs.

**Deferred Contents.** Due to lack of space, the formal definitions, constructions and proofs can be found in our online full version [68].

**Acknowledgments.** This work is in part supported by a Packard Fellowship, a DARPA SIEVE grant under a sub-contract from SRI, and NSF grants under award numbers 2001026 and 1601879.

# References

1. Computer science research and practice on slack
2. Abdalla, M., Benhamouda, F., Gay, R.: From single-input to multi-client inner-product functional encryption. In: Galbraith, S.D., Moriai, S. (eds.) ASIACRYPT 2019. LNCS, vol. 11923, pp. 552–582. Springer, Cham (2019). https://doi.org/10.1007/978-3-030-34618-8_19
3. Abdalla, M., Bourse, F., De Caro, A., Pointcheval, D.: Better security for functional encryption for inner product evaluations. Cryptology ePrint 2016/011 (2016)
4. Abdalla, M., Bourse, F., Marival, H., Pointcheval, D., Soleimanian, A., Waldner, H.: Multi-client inner-product functional encryption in the random-oracle model. Cryptology ePrint Archive, Report 2020/788 (2020)
5. Abdalla, M., Catalano, D., Fiore, D., Gay, R., Ursu, B.: Multi-input functional encryption for inner products: function-hiding realizations and constructions without pairings. In: Shacham, H., Boldyreva, A. (eds.) CRYPTO 2018. LNCS, vol. 10991, pp. 597–627. Springer, Cham (2018). https://doi.org/10.1007/978-3-319-96884-1_20
6. Abdalla, M., Gay, R., Raykova, M., Wee, H.: Multi-input inner-product functional encryption from pairings. In: Coron, J.-S., Nielsen, J.B. (eds.) EUROCRYPT 2017. LNCS, vol. 10210, pp. 601–626. Springer, Cham (2017). https://doi.org/10.1007/978-3-319-56620-7_21
7. Abdalla, M., Gong, J., Wee, H.: Functional encryption for attribute-weighted sums from $k$-Lin. In: Micciancio, D., Ristenpart, T. (eds.) CRYPTO 2020. LNCS, vol. 12170, pp. 685–716. Springer, Cham (2020). https://doi.org/10.1007/978-3-030-56784-2_23
8. Abe, M.: Mix-networks on permutation networks. In: Lam, K.-Y., Okamoto, E., Xing, C. (eds.) ASIACRYPT 1999. LNCS, vol. 1716, pp. 258–273. Springer, Heidelberg (1999). https://doi.org/10.1007/978-3-540-48000-6_21
9. Abraham, I., Pinkas, B., Yanai, A.: Blinder: MPC based scalable and robust anonymous committed broadcast. In: ACM CCS (2020)
10. Adida, B.: Helios: web-based open-audit voting. In: USENIX Security (2008)
11. Adida, B., Wikström, D.: How to shuffle in public. In: Vadhan, S.P. (ed.) TCC 2007. LNCS, vol. 4392, pp. 555–574. Springer, Heidelberg (2007). https://doi.org/10.1007/978-3-540-70936-7_30
12. Agrawal, S., Libert, B., Stehlé, D.: Fully secure functional encryption for inner products, from standard assumptions. In: Robshaw, M., Katz, J. (eds.) CRYPTO 2016. LNCS, vol. 9816, pp. 333–362. Springer, Heidelberg (2016). https://doi.org/10.1007/978-3-662-53015-3_12

13. Alexopoulos, N., Kiayias, A., Talviste, R., Zacharias, T.: MCMix: anonymous messaging via secure multiparty computation. In: USENIX Security (2017)
14. Baldimtsi, F., Lysyanskaya, A.: Anonymous credentials light. In: CCS (2013)
15. Balle, B., Bell, J., Gascón, A., Nissim, K.: Differentially private summation with multi-message shuffling. CoRR, abs/1906.09116 (2019)
16. Balle, B., Bell, J., Gascón, A., Nissim, K.: The privacy blanket of the shuffle model. In: Boldyreva, A., Micciancio, D. (eds.) CRYPTO 2019. LNCS, vol. 11693, pp. 638–667. Springer, Cham (2019). https://doi.org/10.1007/978-3-030-26951-7_22
17. Barak, B., et al.: On the (im)possibility of obfuscating programs. In: Kilian, J. (ed.) CRYPTO 2001. LNCS, vol. 2139, pp. 1–18. Springer, Heidelberg (2001). https://doi.org/10.1007/3-540-44647-8_1
18. Bayer, S., Groth, J.: Efficient zero-knowledge argument for correctness of a shuffle. In: Pointcheval, D., Johansson, T. (eds.) EUROCRYPT 2012. LNCS, vol. 7237, pp. 263–280. Springer, Heidelberg (2012). https://doi.org/10.1007/978-3-642-29011-4_17
19. Beimel, A., Nissim, K., Omri, E.: Distributed private data analysis: simultaneously solving how and what. In: Wagner, D. (ed.) CRYPTO 2008. LNCS, vol. 5157, pp. 451–468. Springer, Heidelberg (2008). https://doi.org/10.1007/978-3-540-85174-5_25
20. Belenkiy, M., Chase, M., Kohlweiss, M., Lysyanskaya, A.: P-signatures and non-interactive anonymous credentials. In: Canetti, R. (ed.) TCC 2008. LNCS, vol. 4948, pp. 356–374. Springer, Heidelberg (2008). https://doi.org/10.1007/978-3-540-78524-8_20
21. Ben-Sasson, E., et al.: Zerocash: decentralized anonymous payments from bitcoin. In: IEEE S & P (2014)
22. Bishop, A., Jain, A., Kowalczyk, L.: Function-hiding inner product encryption. In: Iwata, T., Cheon, J.H. (eds.) ASIACRYPT 2015. LNCS, vol. 9452, pp. 470–491. Springer, Heidelberg (2015). https://doi.org/10.1007/978-3-662-48797-6_20
23. Bittau, A., et al.: Prochlo: strong privacy for analytics in the crowd. In: SOSP (2017)
24. Bonawitz, K., et al.: Practical secure aggregation for privacy-preserving machine learning. In: CCS (2017)
25. Boneh, D., Sahai, A., Waters, B.: Functional encryption: definitions and challenges. In: Ishai, Y. (ed.) TCC 2011. LNCS, vol. 6597, pp. 253–273. Springer, Heidelberg (2011). https://doi.org/10.1007/978-3-642-19571-6_16
26. Boneh, D., Waters, B.: Conjunctive, subset, and range queries on encrypted data. In: Vadhan, S.P. (ed.) TCC 2007. LNCS, vol. 4392, pp. 535–554. Springer, Heidelberg (2007). https://doi.org/10.1007/978-3-540-70936-7_29
27. Brakerski, Z., Dottling, N., Garg, S., Malavolta, G.: Factoring and pairings are not necessary for iO: circular-secure LWE suffices. Cryptology ePrint 2020/1024 (2020)
28. Brakerski, Z., Komargodski, I., Segev, G.: Multi-input functional encryption in the private-key setting: stronger security from weaker assumptions. J. Cryptol. 31(2), 434–520 (2018). https://doi.org/10.1007/s00145-017-9261-0
29. Camenisch, J., Lysyanskaya, A.: A formal treatment of onion routing. In: Shoup, V. (ed.) CRYPTO 2005. LNCS, vol. 3621, pp. 169–187. Springer, Heidelberg (2005). https://doi.org/10.1007/11535218_11
30. Canetti, R., Lin, H., Tessaro, S., Vaikuntanathan, V.: Obfuscation of probabilistic circuits and applications. In: Dodis, Y., Nielsen, J.B. (eds.) TCC 2015. LNCS, vol. 9015, pp. 468–497. Springer, Heidelberg (2015). https://doi.org/10.1007/978-3-662-46497-7_19

31. Chan, T.-H.H., Shi, E., Song, D.: Optimal lower bound for differentially private multi-party aggregation. In: Epstein, L., Ferragina, P. (eds.) ESA 2012. LNCS, vol. 7501, pp. 277–288. Springer, Heidelberg (2012). https://doi.org/10.1007/978-3-642-33090-2_25

32. Chaum, D.: Blind signatures for untraceable payments. In: Chaum, D., Rivest, R.L., Sherman, A.T. (eds.) Advances in Cryptology, pp. 199–203. Springer, Boston, MA (1983). https://doi.org/10.1007/978-1-4757-0602-4_18

33. Chaum, D., Fiat, A., Naor, M.: Untraceable electronic cash. In: Goldwasser, S. (ed.) CRYPTO 1988. LNCS, vol. 403, pp. 319–327. Springer, New York (1990). https://doi.org/10.1007/0-387-34799-2_25

34. Chaum, D.L.: Untraceable electronic mail, return addresses, and digital pseudonyms. Commun. ACM **24**(2), 84–90 (1981)

35. Chaum, D.L.: The dining cryptographers problem: unconditional sender and recipient untraceability. J. Cryptol. **1**(1), 65–75 (1988). https://doi.org/10.1007/BF00206326

36. Cheu, A., Smith, A., Ullman, J., Zeber, D., Zhilyaev, M.: Distributed differential privacy via shuffling. In: Ishai, Y., Rijmen, V. (eds.) EUROCRYPT 2019. LNCS, vol. 11476, pp. 375–403. Springer, Cham (2019). https://doi.org/10.1007/978-3-030-17653-2_13

37. Chotard, J., Dufour Sans, E., Gay, R., Phan, D.H., Pointcheval, D.: Decentralized multi-client functional encryption for inner product. In: Peyrin, T., Galbraith, S. (eds.) ASIACRYPT 2018. LNCS, vol. 11273, pp. 703–732. Springer, Cham (2018). https://doi.org/10.1007/978-3-030-03329-3_24

38. Corrigan-Gibbs, H., Boneh, D., Mazières, D.: Riposte: an anonymous messaging system handling millions of users. In: S & P (2015)

39. Corrigan-Gibbs, H., Ford, B.: Dissent: accountable anonymous group messaging. In: CCS, ppp. 340–350 (2010)

40. Danezis, G., Diaz, C.: A survey of anonymous communication channels. Technical Report MSR-TR-2008-35. Microsoft Research (2008)

41. Degabriele, J.P., Stam, M.: Untagging tor: a formal treatment of onion encryption. In: Nielsen, J.B., Rijmen, V. (eds.) EUROCRYPT 2018. LNCS, vol. 10822, pp. 259–293. Springer, Cham (2018). https://doi.org/10.1007/978-3-319-78372-7_9

42. Dingledine, R., Mathewson, N., Syverson, P.: Tor: the second-generation onion router. In: USENIX Security Symposium (2004)

43. Dwork, C., McSherry, F., Nissim, K., Smith, A.: Calibrating noise to sensitivity in private data analysis. In: Halevi, S., Rabin, T. (eds.) TCC 2006. LNCS, vol. 3876, pp. 265–284. Springer, Heidelberg (2006). https://doi.org/10.1007/11681878_14

44. Edman, M., Yener, B.: On anonymity in an electronic society: a survey of anonymous communication systems. ACM Comput. Surv. **42**(1), 1–35 (2009)

45. Erlingsson, Ú., Feldman, V., Mironov, I., Raghunathan, A., Talwar, K., Thakurta, A.: Amplification by shuffling: from local to central differential privacy via anonymity. In: SODA (2019)

46. Erlingsson, U., Pihur, V., Korolova, A.: RAPPOR: randomized aggregatable privacy-preserving ordinal response. In: CCS (2014)

47. Gay, R., Pass, R.: Indistinguishability obfuscation from circular security. Cryptology ePrint Archive, Report 2020/1010 (2020)

48. Gertner, Y., Ishai, Y., Kushilevitz, E., Malkin, T.: Protecting data privacy in private information retrieval schemes. J. Comput. Syst. Sci. **60**(3), 592–629 (2000)

49. Ghazi, B., Pagh, R., Velingker, A.: Scalable and differentially private distributed aggregation in the shuffled model. CoRR, abs/1906.08320 (2019)

50. Goldschlag, D., Reed, M., Syverson, P.: Onion routing for anonymous and private internet connections. Commun. ACM **42**, 39–41 (1999)
51. Goldwasser, S.: Multi-input functional encryption. In: Nguyen, P.Q., Oswald, E. (eds.) EUROCRYPT 2014. LNCS, vol. 8441, pp. 578–602. Springer, Heidelberg (2014). https://doi.org/10.1007/978-3-642-55220-5_32
52. Gorbunov, S., Vaikuntanathan, V., Wee, H.: Predicate encryption for circuits from LWE. In: Gennaro, R., Robshaw, M. (eds.) CRYPTO 2015. LNCS, vol. 9216, pp. 503–523. Springer, Heidelberg (2015). https://doi.org/10.1007/978-3-662-48000-7_25
53. Heilman, E., Alshenibr, L., Baldimtsi, F., Scafuro, A., Goldberg, S.: TumbleBit: an untrusted bitcoin-compatible anonymous payment hub. In: NDSS (2017)
54. Hohenberger, S., Myers, S., Pass, R.: ANONIZE: a large-scale anonymous survey system. In: IEEE S & P (2014)
55. Ishai, Y., Kushilevitz, E., Ostrovsky, R., Sahai, A.: Cryptography from anonymity. In: FOCS (2006)
56. Jain, A., Lin, H., Sahai, A.: Indistinguishability obfuscation from well-founded assumptions. Cryptology ePrint Archive, Report 2020/1003 (2020)
57. Libert, B., Ţiţiu, R.: Multi-client functional encryption for linear functions in the standard model from LWE. In: Galbraith, S.D., Moriai, S. (eds.) ASIACRYPT 2019. LNCS, vol. 11923, pp. 520–551. Springer, Cham (2019). https://doi.org/10.1007/978-3-030-34618-8_18
58. Lin, H.: Indistinguishability obfuscation from SXDH on 5-linear maps and locality-5 PRGs. In: Katz, J., Shacham, H. (eds.) CRYPTO 2017. LNCS, vol. 10401, pp. 599–629. Springer, Cham (2017). https://doi.org/10.1007/978-3-319-63688-7_20
59. Lin, H., Vaikuntanathan, V.: Indistinguishability obfuscation from DDH-like assumptions on constant-degree graded encodings. In: FOCS, pp. 11–20 (2016)
60. Ostrovsky, R., Shoup, V.: Private information storage (extended abstract). In: STOC, pp. 294–303 (1997)
61. Sahai, A., Waters, B.: Fuzzy identity-based encryption. In: Cramer, R. (ed.) EUROCRYPT 2005. LNCS, vol. 3494, pp. 457–473. Springer, Heidelberg (2005). https://doi.org/10.1007/11426639_27
62. Sako, K., Kilian, J.: Receipt-free mix-type voting scheme: a practical solution to the implementation of a voting booth. In: Guillou, L.C., Quisquater, J.-J. (eds.) EUROCRYPT 1995. LNCS, vol. 921, pp. 393–403. Springer, Heidelberg (1995). https://doi.org/10.1007/3-540-49264-X_32
63. Shen, E., Shi, E., Waters, B.: Predicate privacy in encryption systems. In: Reingold, O. (ed.) TCC 2009. LNCS, vol. 5444, pp. 457–473. Springer, Heidelberg (2009). https://doi.org/10.1007/978-3-642-00457-5_27
64. Sherwood, R., Bhattacharjee, B., Srinivasan, A.: P5: a protocol for scalable anonymous communication. In: IEEE S & P (2002)
65. Shi, E., Bethencourt, J., Chan, T.H., Song, D., Perrig, A.: Multi-dimensional range query over encrypted data. In: S & P (2007)
66. Shi, E., Chan, T.H., Rieffel, E., Chow, R., Song, D.: Privacy-preserving aggregation of time-series data. In: NDSS (2011)
67. Shi, E., Chan, T.-H.H., Rieffel, E., Song, D.: Distributed private data analysis: lower bounds and practical constructions. ACM Trans. Algorithms **13**(4), 1–38 (2017)
68. Shi, E., Wu, K.: Non-interactive anonymous router (2021)
69. Shirazi, F., Simeonovski, M., Asghar, M.R., Backes, M., Diaz, C.: A survey on routing in anonymous communication protocols (2018)

70. Tyagi, N., Gilad, Y., Leung, D., Zaharia, M., Zeldovich, N.: Stadium: a distributed metadata-private messaging system. In: SOSP (2017)
71. Van Den Hooff, J., Lazar, D., Zaharia, M., Zeldovich, N.: Vuvuzela: scalable private messaging resistant to traffic analysis. In: SOSP (2015)
72. Wee, H.: New techniques for attribute-hiding in prime-order bilinear groups. Manuscript (2016)
73. Wee, H., Wichs, D.: Candidate obfuscation via oblivious LWE sampling. Cryptology ePrint Archive, Report 2020/1042 (2020)
74. Zhuang, L., Zhou, F., Zhao, B.Y., Rowstron, A.: Cashmere: resilient anonymous routing. In: NSDI (2005)

# Bifurcated Signatures: Folding the Accountability vs. Anonymity Dilemma into a Single Private Signing Scheme

Benoît Libert[1,2]([✉]), Khoa Nguyen[3], Thomas Peters[4], and Moti Yung[5]

[1] CNRS, Laboratoire LIP, Lyon, France
[2] ENS de Lyon, Laboratoire LIP (U. Lyon, CNRS, ENSL, Inria, UCBL), Lyon, France
[3] Nanyang Technological University, SPMS, Singapore, Singapore
[4] FNRS and UCLouvain (ICTEAM), Louvain-la-Neuve, Belgium
[5] Google and Columbia University, New York City, USA

**Abstract.** Over the development of modern cryptography, often, alternative cryptographic schemes are developed to achieve goals that in some important respect are orthogonal. Thus, we have to choose either a scheme which achieves the first goal and not the second, or vice versa. This results in two types of schemes that compete with each other. In the basic area of user privacy, specifically in anonymous (multi-use credentials) signing, such an orthogonality exists between anonymity and accountability.

The conceptual contribution of this work is to reverse the above orthogonality by design, which essentially typifies the last 25 years or so, and to suggest an alternative methodology where the opposed properties are carefully folded into a single scheme. The schemes will support both opposing properties simultaneously in a bifurcated fashion, where:

- First, based on rich semantics expressed over the message's context and content, the user, etc., the relevant property is applied pointwise per message operation depending on a predicate; and
- Secondly, at the same time, the schemes provide what we call "branch-hiding;" namely, the resulting calculated value hides from outsiders which property has actually been locally applied.

Specifically, we precisely define and give the first construction and security proof of a "Bifurcated Anonymous Signature" (BiAS): A scheme which supports either absolute anonymity or anonymity with accountability, based on a specific contextual predicate, while being branch-hiding. This novel signing scheme has numerous applications not easily implementable or not considered before, especially because: (i) the conditional traceability does *not* rely on a trusted authority as it is (non-interactively) encapsulated into signatures; and (ii) signers *know* the predicate value and can make a conscious choice at each signing time.

© International Association for Cryptologic Research 2021
A. Canteaut and F.-X. Standaert (Eds.): EUROCRYPT 2021, LNCS 12698, pp. 521–552, 2021.
https://doi.org/10.1007/978-3-030-77883-5_18

Technically, we realize BiAS from homomorphic commitments for a general family of predicates that can be represented by bounded-depth circuits. Our construction is generic and can be instantiated in the standard model from lattices and, more efficiently, from bilinear maps. In particular, the signature length is independent of the circuit size when we use commitments with suitable efficiency properties.

**Keywords:** New primitive · Privacy · Anonymity · Accountability · Group signatures · Conditional traceability · Predicate-based privacy

# 1 Introduction

Properties provided by cryptographic primitives (such as confidentiality and anonymity) generate a natural tension between the requirements of individual users (such as privacy and other rights), and those of society (such as safety and individual accountability). This fact has created a very rigid positioning of cryptosystems: Designs that serve individual needs, and those which serve societal concerns. A classical example of the above rigidity is the scenario of anonymous signing. On the one hand, there are group signatures [18], central privacy tools allowing users to anonymously sign messages in the name of a population of users they belong to. In order to keep users accountable for their actions, group signatures involve a trusted opening authority (OA) which is called upon when needed only, and is endowed with some privileged information allowing it to trace any signature back to its author. This accountability mechanism, therefore, in these cases, revokes the anonymity of that user. On the other hand, ring signatures [45] and related primitives [11,19,30,39] allow users to sign whatever they like in the name of a population while retaining unconditional anonymity.

In light of this over quarter-of-a-century old situation, we claim that for many applications, in fact, group and ring signatures fall short of providing an appropriate tradeoff between anonymity and accountability that would be sufficiently fair for, both, signers and authorities. Privacy-aware signers naturally want to protect their privacy as much as possible. At the same time, authorities aim to ensure that signers of all problematic signatures can be caught. What we argue in this work is that in many real-life situations, the ability to trace a signature or not should actually depend on the content and context of the message, and should be provided programmatically by the primitive rather than being supported by a one sided mechanism which is part of the primitive specification.

Consider the scenario where each signature authenticates an anonymous financial transaction associated with a hidden amount of money and between users in different countries that should only be known to the payer and the payee (this can be done by employing additional cryptographic mechanisms, e.g., the amount and countries are encrypted or committed to, as in the privacy-preserving cryptocurrency system Monero [41]). For money-laundering detection purposes, the authorities would like to make sure that transactions with amounts above a certain threshold between two specific countries can be traced. On the other hand, to satisfy privacy-aware users, the system should also provide absolute anonymity for transactions amounts below the traceability threshold or within the same country, say, or for any other messages of harmless content. Importantly, for privacy reasons as well (e.g., keeping statistics of the financial transactions hidden), the public should not be able to determine whether a given signed transaction, corresponds to a traceable or to an untraceable type.

As another example, imagine that visitors of a digital library are required to register and sign before reviewing specific e-books. The ability/ inability to identify signers should naturally depend on whether the books in question are totally benign (e.g., comics, essays containing controversial but inoffensive political opinions, etc.) or potentially harmful (like chemistry books explaining how to produce bombs, any form of advocacy of hatred, etc.).

As yet another example, note that service providers often ask users to attest to personal attributes, for example, to guarantee the veracity of answers to questions like "Have you been to one of these countries in the last 6 months?", "Are you above 18?", etc. In this case we argue that while suspicious online activities and alert-raising messages should be traceable by some warranted authority, regular well-behaved typical users should not have to reveal their history and information to service providers that verify their signatures.

The above examples motivate the design of a new anonymous signature primitive where the ability to trace a signature back to its source is determined by a predicate that depends on the signed message and the user's credential, and where the traceability property of a signature is hidden from the general public. Such schemes are highly desirable, so that they can support the above scenarios, since they provide a fair privacy-preserving non-rigid setting which users and authorities both have strong incentives to deploy. However, to our knowledge, a non-rigid conditional setting, and such signatures have never been considered so far. We call this type of schemes that allow this on the fly flexibility "Bifurcated Cryptosystems."

## 1.1 Our Contributions

We introduce the study of cryptographic primitives that provide tradeoffs between competing requirements like end-to-end privacy and accountability, by suggesting *bifurcated anonymous signatures* (BiAS). In short, BiAS schemes are anonymous signature schemes allowing to bifurcate into absolute anonymity and identity escrow at the signing time, where computing signatures is associated with a predicate $P$. They enable unconditional anonymity when the predicate $P(M, \mathsf{id}, w)$ evaluates to 1 on input of the message $M$, the user's identity $\mathsf{id}$ and some secret context-dependent piece of information $w$ which we call a witness. At the same time, signatures should be traceable by an authority whenever $P(M, \mathsf{id}, w) = 0$.

As a first major requirement, BiAS must be *branch-hiding*: verifiers as well as the issuing credential authority should be unable to figure out whether a signature is traceable or not.

In our BiAS primitive, whether a signature is traceable or not depends on the content which is being signed and the user's identity. Since users know the predicate and its value before signing, they know beforehand when they will be subject to tracing and they can make an educated decision as to whether they can afford to sign a specific message or not. At the same time, *only* the tracing authority will be able to learn whether the signatures are traceable or not. The users are assured that if their signature is not traceable, no one, even if the authority's keys are available, will be able to trace them. In fact, let us emphasize that this is an unconditional anonymity property, which is of high importance in some applications, such as the case of journalists signing an article unfavorable to the local regime, in a place where their life is in danger upon eventual identification.

As a natural second requirement, we pair the notion of branch-hiding with the notion of *branch-soundness*. Branch-soundness prevents users from generating untraceable signatures when the signer should have been identified or vice versa. Said otherwise, no signers can fool the system even with the help of the authorities and be able to produce a signature of which the traceability does not respect the predicate.

We first give precise syntax and security definitions for the BiAS primitive. The guarantee offered by this notion allows us to extend the notions of traceability, non-frameability, and anonymity, borrowed from ordinary group signatures to our more general predicate-based primitive.

Secondly, we provide a generic BiAS realization where predicates may consist of polynomial-size circuits of a priori bounded depth. As building blocks, our construction relies on the homomorphic equivocal commitment (HEC) primitive defined by Katsumata *et al.* [27], dual-mode non-interactive zero-knowledge (NIZK) arguments [24,26,42], and a variant of the $\mathcal{R}$-lossy encryption primitive of Boyle *et al.* [14]. Our constructions are instantiable in the standard model for arbitrary polynomial-size Boolean circuits under the Learning-With-Errors (LWE) assumption [44]. For Boolean formulas (equivalently, $NC^1$ circuits), more efficient instantiations are possible under falsifiable assumptions in groups endowed with a bilinear map. In both cases, our schemes enjoy the property that the signature size only depends on the maximal circuit depth, and not on its size. The signature size is dominated by $O((\log N + |w|) \cdot \lambda^c)$ bits (where $N$ is the group size and $c$ is a constant) committing to the witness $w$ and the user's identity together with NIZK arguments showing that the ciphertexts were properly generated.

### 1.2   Technical Overview

DEFINING SECURITY. Our security model puts forth the notions of branch-hiding and branch-soundness for our bifurcated anonymous signature (BiAS) primitive. We advocate, more generally, that it is the first instance of a new fundamental notion of bifurcated cryptosystems (balancing based on a predicate in one scheme, both, user concerns and public safety issues). Further, to capture anonymity we extend the CCA-like notion of unlinkability of signatures which can be now produced from different predicate values. We call the resulting notion anonymity "in the traceable case" which implies the branch-hiding property of BiAS. We augment this anonymity notion with the anonymity "in the non-traceable case" where all the signatures are generated from a predicate value equals to 1, i.e., from the branch leading to unconditional anonymity. A BiAS is, then, called fully anonymous if it fulfills both anonymity notions. Branch-hiding and full anonymity, primarily, take care of privacy of BiAS.

To prevent misuse of the BiAS functionality, we build on two security notions from the Kiayias-Yung model [29] of group signatures. First, the security against *mis-identification attacks* (a.k.a. traceability) which requires that, even if the adversary can introduce users under its control in the group of signers, it cannot produce a signature that traces outside the dishonest coalition. Second, the notion of security against *framing attacks* which implies that honest users can never be falsely accused of having signed messages, even if the whole system conspires against them. However, extending these security notions is not straightforward or immediate in our model, since we have to detect whether a given signature contradicts one of these properties even, if that signature is untraceable. Indeed, to build a reduction in a security proof, for instance, we have to figure out if a given untraceable signature has been generated honestly by a legitimate signer or if it is a forgery. However, being able to do so, in fact, seems to contradict statistical (unconditional) anonymity.

To circumvent the apparent incompatibility between privacy and security, we rely on our branch-soundness notion. It is a two-stage definition which first defines an extractable mode of the scheme only useful for the sake of proving security: it generates parameters of the scheme allowing to extract the identity and the witness behind *any* valid signatures. Such an extraction allows evaluating the predicate a posteriori given any signature. As a second stage, we require that the (real) tracing algorithm can be indistinguishably emulated from the (ideal) extractable mode, even when the authorities' keys are exposed. A BiAS satisfying branch-soundness thus ensures the hardness of "cheating" with the predicate, even for corrupt authorities. The reason is that it implies the infeasibility of producing signatures that: (i) can be traced while the context allows retaining statistical anonymity, i.e., $P(M, \mathsf{id}, w) = 1$, and conversely (ii) cannot be traced while the context allows retaining identity escrow, i.e., $P(M, \mathsf{id}, w) = 0$. We stress that the indistinguishability in branch-soundness cannot be statistical since, otherwise, untraceable signatures would no longer be statistically anonymous. Based on the branch-soundness notion, we can now extend the security notion of [29] from the (ideal) extractable mode of the BiAS.

UNDERLYING PRIMITIVES. Our construction for bounded-depth circuits is based on combining a number of primitives. First, it is built on the homomorphic equivocal commitments (HEC) of Katsumata *et al.* [27]. An HEC is a commitment scheme that allows committing to a message $\vec{x}$ using random coins $R$ in such a way that anyone can publicly evaluate a circuit $C$ over the commitment com to obtain an evaluated commitment $\mathsf{com}_{ev} = \mathsf{Eval}(C, \mathsf{com}_{ev})$ to $C(\vec{x})$. Using the pair $(\vec{x}, R)$, the committer can internally run a private evaluation algorithm over

$(\vec{x}, R)$ in order to compute a proof $\pi$ which will convince a verifier that $\mathsf{com}_{ev}$ is a commitment to $C(\vec{x})$. The primitive is instantiatable for all circuits via the fully homomorphic commitments of Gorbunov, Vaikuntanathan and Wichs [23], which in turn, is built on the FHE scheme of Gentry, Sahai and Waters (GSW) [22]. Katsumata *et al.* [27] also gave a construction for log-depth circuits under pairing-related assumptions [27]. In order to combine statistical anonymity in non-tracing mode and extractability in the security proofs, we employ a dual-mode NIZK argument, which either provides statistical zero-knowledge and computational soundness or vice versa, depending on the distribution of the common reference string. In the public verifiability setting, dual-mode NIZK is known to exist under standard assumptions in pairing-friendly groups, as shown by Groth, Ostrovsky and Sahai [24]. Peikert and Shiehian [42] (inspired by the earlier work of Canetti *et al.* [17]) recently gave constructions under the Learning-With-Errors (LWE) assumption. In order to smoothly interact with HEC schemes, the dual-mode NIZK system makes use of dual-mode commitments [24], where the commitment key can be tuned to give either statistically hiding or extractable commitments.

CONSTRUCTION. At a high level, our construction proceeds as follows. When a user joins the group, he generates a fresh public key for a digital signature $\mathsf{pk}_{\mathsf{id}}$ and obtains from the group manager (GM) a membership certificate $\mathsf{cert}_{\mathsf{id}}$ consisting of the GM's signature on the pair $(\mathsf{id}, \mathsf{pk}_{\mathsf{id}})$, where $\mathsf{id}$ is the user's identity. In order to sign a message w.r.t. the predicate $P$, a group member computes an HEC commitment $\mathsf{com}_{(\mathsf{id},w)}$ to the witness $w$ and his identity $\mathsf{id}$. At the same time, the signer computes a dual-mode commitment to $(\mathsf{id}, w)$, which is configured to be statistically hiding in the real scheme. The signer then considers the message-dependent circuit $C_M(.,.)$ which evaluates $C_M(\mathsf{id}, w) = P(M, \mathsf{id}, w)$ on input of $(\mathsf{id}, w)$. He runs the private HEC evaluation algorithm to compute a proof $\pi_{C,M}$ that $\mathsf{com}_{ev} = \mathsf{Eval}(C_M, \mathsf{com}_{ev})$ is really a commitment to $C_M(\mathsf{id}, w)$. It finally computes a public key encryption $\mathsf{ct}_{\mathsf{id}} \leftarrow \mathsf{Encrypt}(\mathsf{pk}, (1 - C_M(\mathsf{id}, w)) \cdot \mathsf{id})$ of the product $(1 - C_M(\mathsf{id}, w)) \cdot \mathsf{id}$, so that $\mathsf{ct}_{\mathsf{id}}$ encrypts 0 when unconditional anonymity is enabled (i.e., when $C_M(\mathsf{id}, w) = 1$) and $\mathsf{id}$ otherwise. A dual-mode NIZK argument then allows arguing that all steps were properly carried out.

When the tracing capability is enabled (namely, when $C_M(\mathsf{id}, w) = 0$), we need to rely on a special kind of dual-mode commitment to prove computational anonymity in the CCA sense (i.e., when the adversary has access to a signature opening oracle). Specifically, we need to program the commitment key to make commitments extractable in all signature opening queries and statistically hiding in the challenge phase. This is achieved using tag-based commitments, where each commitment is computed under a tag-dependent commitment key that either provides statistically hiding or extractable commitments, depending on the tag. In order to instantiate these dual-mode tag-based commitments, we use a recent variant [34] of the $\mathcal{R}$-lossy encryption of Boyle *et al.* [14], for which we give a DDH-based realization (as well as an LWE-based realization adapted from [34]). Using this $\mathcal{R}$-lossy encryption to instantiate the dual-mode commitment component, we can make it statistically hiding in the challenge phase (for a specific tag corresponding to a one-time verification key $\mathsf{VK}^\star$) and statistically extractable for all other tags $\mathsf{VK} \neq \mathsf{VK}^\star$. This allows us to proceed with a sequence of hybrid games where, instead of answering opening queries by decrypting the ciphertext $\mathsf{ct}_{\mathsf{id}}$, we can extract the committed $(\mathsf{id}, w)$. This can be seen as applying the two-key paradigm of Naor and Yung [40] for CCA2-secure encryption.

The above construction crucially relies on HEC to avoid the signature length from depending on the circuit size. If we were to give up the circuit-size independent property, constructions would be possible from any non-interactive statistically hiding commitment.

OPEN QUESTIONS. Naturally, our work, being in a new area (with some new technical and definitional challenges as described above), leaves many open problems which we believe to be interesting. Conceptually, one can ask how bifurcated cryptography applies elsewhere. Technically, the first problem that comes to mind is finding practically efficient instantiations from lattice assumptions (even in the random oracle model) as our LWE-based construction is only meant to be a first feasibility result. In particular, it would be interesting to provide more efficient lattice-based solutions using, e.g., the Fiat-Shamir-with-abort method [10,37] or the techniques recently suggested in [49]. The second open problem is to determine the extent to which more specific predicate families can be realized more efficiently (with or without random oracles) and under different assumptions. While the work of Katsumata et al. [27] implies a pairing-based construction for Boolean formulas, it is only known to achieve circuit-size independence under a $q$-type (although falsifiable) assumption. A sufficient condition to avoid relying on variable-size assumptions in the pairing setting would be to build an HEC scheme based on simple assumptions, where the size of partial openings does not depend on the circuit size. Finally, while the rest of the paper will concentrate on BiAS, exploring further primitives providing point-wise predicate-based built-in privacy or confidentiality bifurcated tradeoffs seems like a new area for broader investigations.

### 1.3    Related Work

The rigid anonymity vs. accountability situation indeed generated much discomfort in the community. Group signatures traditionally allow opening authorities to identify the author of any signature. As advocated by Sakai et al. [46], it may be desirable to prevent the OA from seeing the entire signature history of all group members. Restricting the power of the opening authorities is a challenging research direction, where a few steps have been taken. For example, traceable signatures [28], group signatures with message-dependent opening [46], and accountable tracing signatures [33] can all be viewed as group signatures with restricted opening authorities. However, the OA can still freely break the anonymity of some subset of signatures without the user's agreement. These primitives offer more privacy to users than ordinary group signatures, but not at a level that privacy-sensitive users would hope for.

Ring signatures [6,45] confer everlasting anonymity to group members. They depart from group signatures in that signers are not required to register in the system and signers have complete freedom on the list of their ring-mates at each signature. Compared to group signatures, they stand at the opposite extreme of the spectrum as they do not provide any accountability at all. Linkable ring signature [36], traceable ring signatures [20], as well as $k$-time anonymous authentication systems [47] only introduce a weak form of accountability in ring signatures as users only lose anonymity to some extent: for example, if they issue two or more signatures for some message, their signatures become linkable but they can still create one controversial signature and disappear from the system without being caught.

Accountable tracing signatures (ATS) [32,33] take a different approach to balance accountability and anonymity, by allowing the two extreme settings of ring signatures and group signatures to co-exist. In ATS schemes, a given user is either always unconditionally anonymous or always traceable, based on a decision made by the authority when the user joins the system. In addition, users are never notified about their traceability status. In our setting and use-cases, the ability to trace or not should depend point-wise on the message and not only on group members' identities. Moreover, we deliberately aim at leaving users some control on when and under which circumstances they want to accept traceability.

Accountable ring signatures (ARS) [9,48] provide another kind of tradeoff where anonymity and traceability can live together. Xu and Yung [48] consider a threshold opening mechanism where no single opener is given the entire power. The ARS model of Bootle $et\ al.$ [9] also provides some flexibility in the choice of tracing authorities as signers are allowed to choose which opener they trust without necessarily leaving the full tracing capability to a pre-determined authority. On the other hand, neither of these models [9,48] provides full expressiveness as to which messages can be signed with unconditional anonymity and which ones should always be traceable.

Bangerter $et\ al.$ [2] considered an informal framework allowing to monitor the release of certified data. Their (interactive) model fully trusts the opening authority to only disclose users' data when specific conditions are met. In contrast, BiAS does not trust the opener when de-anonymization conditions are not fulfilled and even requires unconditional anonymity in this case.

Boyen and Delerablée [12] introduced a variant of group signatures allowing group members to flexibly and expressively choose a subgroup wherein they hide their identity. Our goals are orthogonal to theirs since their model always allows tracing authorities to identify signers whereas we accurately control the conditions under which the signer's identity can be uncovered.

Garms and Lehmann [21] put forth the concept of convertably linkable signatures (CLS) which are group signatures where a "converter" can blindly relate a bunch of signatures to some randomized pseudonyms. To convert the given signatures into linkable ones, another authority first blinds the signatures in order to mitigate the power of the converter. However, the converter is actually an opening authority that can always trace a given signature as long as it was not blinded. At any time, CLS thus "only" provide computational anonymity.

Attribute-based signatures (ABS) [38] allow a signer to sign a message while simultaneously showing possession of credentials satisfying a public predicate.

Policy-based signatures (PBS) [3] are signature schemes where users obtain a policy-based signing key (associated with some predicate $P$) from some authority, which allows them to sign exactly those messages $M$ for which $P(M) = 1$. ABS and PBS address different problems than our BiAS primitive in that they provide fine-grained control over "who can sign" and "which messages can be signed at all", respectively. As such, they do not give users control over which signatures can be traced (with user knowledge of it). Our BiAS functionality departs from PBS [3] in that predicates are not associated with keys but with signed messages and may vary across signatures. In terms of generic implications, PBS were shown [3] to imply digital signatures, NIZK [7] and CCA-secure encryption [43]. However, they are not known to imply homomorphic equivocal commitments with circuit-size independent verification, and the relationship between PBS and BiAS thus remains unclear. In particular, we do not see any obvious way to obtain BiAS realizations by generically using a PBS.

Functional signatures [13] differ from conditionally traceable signatures in that, in the same spirit as PBS, they accurately control which messages can be signed. In contrast, BiAS controls which signatures can be traced.

In the context of anonymous compact e-cash [15], Camenisch $et\ al.$ [16] were bothered by the anonymity vs. accountability issue in a specific scenario. They considered a conditional anonymity setting which restricts transactions to be untraceable only when they do not exceed a specific amount. In their model, the threshold amount is fixed for each merchant over multiple transactions. If a user performs a number of transactions with total values exceeding a threshold, he can be traced based on public records. On the other hand, if the total amount remains under the threshold, the traceable authority is unable to extract the user's identity. However, the anonymity remains computational even in that case. In contrast, our BiAS primitive is a generic add-on mechanism, and ensures the statistical anonymity of signers as long as the predicate equals 1, e.g., the amount does not reach a fixed threshold.

In summary, there was a lot of discomfort with the existing dichotomy between anonymity and accountability. This has produced a large number of interesting and useful cases and solutions. However, a bifurcated solution with choice at the user's hand folded into a single scheme, where the choice is driven by a local predicate which further remains undetected by others, has not been considered. This new BiAS system, which gives the user the best possible (i.e., unconditional) anonymity when permitted, in fact, constitutes the most private and the most versatile solution for the problem of balancing user's vs. society's needs within anonymous signing scenarios.

## 2    Preliminaries

### 2.1    $\mathcal{R}$-Lossy Public-Key Encryption

Boyle $et\ al.$ [14] formalized the notion of $\mathcal{R}$-lossy encryption. The primitive is a tag-based encryption scheme [31] where the tag space $\mathcal{T}$ is partitioned into $injective$ tags and $lossy$ tags. When ciphertexts are generated under an injective tag, the decryption algorithm recovers the underlying plaintext. On lossy tags, the ciphertext statistically hides the underlying plaintext. In $\mathcal{R}$-lossy PKE schemes, the tag space is partitioned according to a binary relation $\mathcal{R} \subseteq \mathcal{K} \times \mathcal{T}$. The key generation algorithm inputs an initialization value $K \in \mathcal{K}$ and partitions $\mathcal{T}$ in such a way that injective tags $t \in \mathcal{T}$ are exactly those for which $(K, t) \in \mathcal{R}$ (i.e., all tags $t$ for which $(K, t) \notin \mathcal{R}$ are lossy).

Libert et al. [34] considered a flavor of $\mathcal{R}$-lossy PKE schemes with two distinct key generation algorithms and equivocal lossy ciphertexts. For our purposes, we do not need to equivocate lossy ciphertexts but we still need two distinct key generation algorithms. Looking ahead, our proof of anonymity (in Lemma 4), requires to switch from a setting where all tags are lossy to a setting where only one tag is lossy. Also, proving other security notions requires to move from the "all lossy" setting to the "all injective" setting in the proof of Theorem 1.

**Definition 1.** *Let $\mathcal{R} \subseteq \mathcal{K}_\lambda \times \mathcal{T}_\lambda$ be an efficiently computable binary relation. An $\mathcal{R}$-lossy PKE scheme with efficient opening is a 5-uple of PPT algorithms* (Par-Gen, Keygen, LKeygen, Encrypt, Decrypt) *such that:*

**Parameter generation:** *On input of a security parameter $\lambda$, a desired length of initialization values $L \in \mathsf{poly}(\lambda)$ and a lower bound $B \in \mathsf{poly}(\lambda)$ on the message length,* Par-Gen$(1^\lambda, 1^L, 1^B)$ *outputs public parameters $\Gamma$ that specify a tag space $\mathcal{T}$, a space of initialization values $\mathcal{K}$, a public key space $\mathcal{PK}$ and a secret key space $\mathcal{SK}$.*

**Key generation:** *For an initialization value $K \in \mathcal{K}$ and public parameters $\Gamma$, algorithm* Keygen$(\Gamma, K)$ *outputs an injective public key $\mathsf{pk} \in \mathcal{PK}$ and a decryption key $\mathsf{sk} \in \mathcal{SK}$. The public key specifies a ciphertext space* CtSp *and a randomness space $R^{\mathsf{RLE}}$.*

**Lossy Key generation:** *Given an initialization value $K \in \mathcal{K}$ and public parameters $\Gamma$, the lossy key generation algorithm* LKeygen$(\Gamma, K)$ *outputs a lossy public key $\mathsf{pk} \in \mathcal{PK}$ and a lossy secret key $\mathsf{sk} \in \mathcal{SK}$.*

**Decryption under injective tags:** *For any $\Gamma \leftarrow$ Par-Gen$(1^\lambda, 1^L, 1^B)$, any $K \in \mathcal{K}$, any $t \in \mathcal{T}$ such that $(K, t) \in \mathcal{R}$, and any* Msg $\in$ MsgSp, *we have*

$$\Pr\left[\exists r \in R^{\mathsf{RLE}} : \mathsf{Decrypt}(\mathsf{sk}, t, \mathsf{Encrypt}(\mathsf{pk}, t, \mathsf{Msg}; r)) \neq \mathsf{Msg}\right] < \nu(\lambda) ,$$

*for some negligible function $\nu(\lambda)$, where* $(\mathsf{pk}, \mathsf{sk}) \leftarrow$ Keygen$(\Gamma, K)$ *and the probability is taken over the randomness of* Keygen.

**Indistinguishability:** *For any $\Gamma \leftarrow$ Par-Gen$(1^\lambda, 1^L, 1^B)$, the key generation algorithms* LKeygen *and* Keygen *satisfy the following:*

(i) *For any $K \in \mathcal{K}$, the distributions $D_{\mathsf{inj}} = \{\mathsf{pk} \mid (\mathsf{pk}, \mathsf{sk}) \leftarrow$ Keygen$(\Gamma, K)\}$ and $D_{\mathsf{loss}} = \{\mathsf{pk} \mid (\mathsf{pk}, \mathsf{sk}) \leftarrow$ LKeygen$(\Gamma, K)\}$ are computationally indistinguishable.*

(ii) *For any initialization values $K, K' \in \mathcal{K}$, the two distributions $\{\mathsf{pk} \mid (\mathsf{pk}, \mathsf{sk}) \leftarrow$ LKeygen$(\Gamma, K)\}$ and $\{\mathsf{pk} \mid (\mathsf{pk}, \mathsf{sk}) \leftarrow$ LKeygen$(\Gamma, K')\}$ are statistically indistinguishable.*

**Lossiness:** *For any* $\Gamma \leftarrow \mathsf{Par\text{-}Gen}(1^\lambda, 1^L, 1^B)$, *any initialization value* $K \in \mathcal{K}$ *and tag* $t \in \mathcal{T}$ *such that* $(K, t) \notin \mathcal{R}$, *any* $(\mathsf{pk}, \mathsf{sk}) \leftarrow \mathsf{Keygen}(\Gamma, K)$, *and any* $\mathsf{Msg}_0, \mathsf{Msg}_1 \in \mathsf{MsgSp}$, *the following distributions are statistically close:*

$$\{C \mid C \leftarrow \mathsf{Encrypt}(\mathsf{pk}, t, \mathsf{Msg}_0)\} \quad \approx_s \quad \{C \mid C \leftarrow \mathsf{Encrypt}(\mathsf{pk}, t, \mathsf{Msg}_1)\}.$$

*For any* $(\mathsf{pk}, \mathsf{sk}) \leftarrow \mathsf{LKeygen}(\Gamma, K)$, *the above holds for any tag* $t$.

We will use an $\mathcal{R}$-lossy encryption scheme for the inequality relation.

**Definition 2.** *Let* $\mathcal{K} = \{0, 1\}^L$ *and* $\mathcal{T} = \{0, 1\}^L \setminus \{0^L\}$, *for some* $L \in \mathsf{poly}(\lambda)$. *The* **inequality relation** $\mathcal{R}_{\mathsf{NEQ}} : \mathcal{K} \times \mathcal{T} \to \{0, 1\}$ *is the relation for which we have* $\mathcal{R}_{\mathsf{NEQ}}(K, t) = 1$ *if and only if* $K \neq t$.

We note that, since we exclude the all-zeroes string $0^L$ from $\mathcal{T}$, running Keygen on input of the initialization value $K = 0^L$ produces a key pk that is injective for *all* tags. In contrast LKeygen produces keys that are lossy for any tag and any initialization value.

We now give an $\mathcal{R}_{\mathsf{NEQ}}$-Lossy PKE realization under the Decision Diffie-Hellman (DDH) assumption (MDDH generalization is obvious).

In the full version, we also provide a construction from the LWE assumption.

**An $\mathcal{R}_{\mathsf{NEQ}}$-Lossy PKE Scheme from DDH.** The construction below is inspired from [35], which is itself inspired from Groth-Sahai commitments [25] to scalars. We first recall the definition of the DDH problem.

**Definition 3.** *In a cyclic group* $\mathbb{G}$ *of prime order* $p$, *the* **Decision Diffie-Hellman Problem** (DDH) *in* $\mathbb{G}$, *is to distinguish the distributions* $(g, g^a, g^b, g^{ab})$ *and* $(g^a, g^b, g^c)$, *with* $a, b, c \leftarrow \mathbb{Z}_p$. *The* **Decision Diffie-Hellman** *assumption is the intractability of* DDH *for any PPT algorithm* $\mathcal{D}$.

**Par-Gen**$(1^\lambda, 1^L, 1^B)$: Define $\mathcal{K} = \{0, 1\}^L$, and $\mathcal{T} = \{0, 1\}^L \setminus \{0^L\}$. Define public parameters as $\Gamma = (1^\lambda, 1^L, 1^B)$.

**Keygen**$(\Gamma, K)$: On input of $\Gamma$ and $K \in \mathcal{K}$, generate a key pair as follows.

1. Choose a cyclic group $\mathbb{G}$ or prime order $p > 2^\lambda$ with a generator $g \leftarrow U(\mathbb{G})$. Choose $\alpha \leftarrow U(\mathbb{Z}_p)$ and compute $h = g^\alpha$. Define $\vec{g}_0 = (g, h) \in \mathbb{G}^2$ and $\vec{g} = \vec{g}_0^\beta \cdot (1, g) \in \mathbb{G}^2$, where $\beta \leftarrow U(\mathbb{Z}_p)$.
2. Pick $\gamma \leftarrow U(\mathbb{Z}_p)$ and compute $\vec{u} = \vec{g}_0^\gamma \cdot \vec{g}^{-K} \in \mathbb{G}^2$, where $K \in \{0, 1\}^L$ is interpreted as an element of $\mathbb{Z}_p$.

Define $R^{\mathsf{RLE}} = \mathbb{Z}_p^B$ and output $\mathsf{sk} = (\alpha, K)$ as well as $\mathsf{pk} := \left( \mathbb{G}, \vec{g}_0, \vec{g}, \vec{u} \right)$.

**LKeygen**$(\Gamma, K)$: This algorithm is identical to Keygen with the difference that, at step 1, it computes $\vec{g}$ as $\vec{g} = \vec{g}_0^\beta \in \mathbb{G}^2$, where $\beta \leftarrow U(\mathbb{Z}_p)$. It defines $R^{\mathsf{RLE}} = \mathbb{Z}_p^B$ and outputs $\mathsf{sk} = (\alpha, K)$ as well as $\mathsf{pk} := \left( \mathbb{G}, \vec{g}_0, \vec{g}, \vec{u} \right)$.

**Encrypt**$(\mathsf{pk}, t, \mathsf{Msg})$: To encrypt $\mathsf{Msg} \in \{0, 1\}^B$, interpret the tag $t \in \mathcal{T}$ as an element of $\mathbb{Z}_p$. For each index $i \in [B]$, pick $r_i \leftarrow U(\mathbb{Z}_p^*)$ and compute $\mathsf{ct}_i = \left( \vec{u} \cdot \vec{g}^t \right)^{\mathsf{Msg}[i]} \cdot \vec{g}_0^{r_i} \in \mathbb{G}^2$. Then, output $\mathsf{ct} = (\mathsf{ct}_1, \ldots, \mathsf{ct}_B) \in \mathbb{G}^{2B}$.

**Decrypt**(sk, $t$, ct): Given sk $= (\alpha, K)$ and $t \in \{0,1\}^L$, interpret $t$ as an element of $\mathbb{Z}_p$. If $t = K$, return $\perp$. Otherwise, for each $i \in [B]$, do the following:

1. Parse $\mathsf{ct}_i$ as $(\mathsf{ct}_{i,1}, \mathsf{ct}_{i,2}) \in \mathbb{G}^2$
2. Set $\mathsf{Msg}[i] = 0$ if $\mathsf{ct}_{i,2} = \mathsf{ct}_{i,1}^\alpha$ and $\mathsf{Msg}[i] = 1$ otherwise.

Output $\mathsf{Msg} \in \{0,1\}^B$.

The proof of Lemma 1 is straightforward. The first indistinguishability property follows immediately from the semantic security of ElGamal and the observation that Keygen and LKeygen only differ in the distribution of $\vec{g}$. The second indistinguishability property follows from the fact that, for any $K \in \mathcal{K}$ and any public key pk generated by LKeygen, $\vec{u} \in \mathbb{G}^2$ is uniformly distributed in the subspace spanned by $\vec{g}_0$. The same holds for any ciphertext encrypted under an injective key for the lossy tag $t = K$ or a lossy key for any tag. The construction readily extends to rely on the $k$-linear assumption [8] for $k > 1$.

**Lemma 1.** *The above construction is an $\mathcal{R}_{\mathsf{NEQ}}$-lossy public-key encryption scheme under the* DDH *assumption.*

### 2.2 Homomorphic Equivocal Commitments

We now recall the definition of homomorphic equivocal commitment, as formalized by Katsumata *et al.* [27].

**Definition 4.** *A HEC scheme with message space $\mathcal{X}$, randomness space $R^{\mathsf{HEC}}$ and randomness distribution $\mathcal{D}^{\mathsf{HEC}}$ over $R^{\mathsf{HEC}}$ for a circuit class $\mathcal{C} = \{C : \mathcal{X} \to \{0,1\}\}$ is a tuple of PPT algorithms $\mathsf{HEC} = (\mathsf{Setup}, \mathsf{Commit}, \mathsf{Open}, \mathsf{Eval}^{in}, \mathsf{Eval}^{out}, \mathsf{Verify})$ with the following specifications:*

**Setup**$(1^\lambda)$: *Inputs a security parameter $1^\lambda$ and outputs public parameters* pp, *an evaluation key* ek *and a master secret key* msk.
**Commit**(pp, $\vec{x}$, $r$): *Takes as input public parameters* pp, *a message $\vec{x} \in \mathcal{X}$ and randomness $r \in R^{\mathsf{HEC}}$. It outputs a commitment* com. *When $r$ is omitted from the notation* Commit(pp, $\vec{x}$), *we man that $r$ is sampled from $\mathcal{D}^{\mathsf{HEC}}$.*
**Open**(msk, $\vec{x}$, $r$, $\vec{x}'$): *Takes as input a master secret key* msk, *messages $\vec{x}, \vec{x}' \in \mathcal{X}$, and randomness $r \in R^{\mathsf{HEC}}$. It outputs fake randomness $r' \in R^{\mathsf{HEC}}$.*
**Eval**$^{in}$(ek, $C$, $\vec{x}$, $r$): *The inner evaluation algorithm inputs a key* ek, *a circuit $C \in \mathcal{C}$, a message $\vec{x}$ and randomness $r \in R^{\mathsf{HEC}}$. It outputs a proof $\pi$.*
**Eval**$^{out}$(ek, $C$, com): *The outer evaluation algorithm is a deterministic algorithm that inputs an evaluation key* ek, *a circuit $C \in \mathcal{C}$ and a commitment* com. *It outputs an evaluated commitment* $\mathsf{com}_{ev}$.
**Verify**(pp, $\mathsf{com}_{ev}$, $z$, $\pi$): *The verification algorithm takes as input public parameters* pp, *an evaluated commitment $\mathsf{com}_{ev}$, a message $z \in \{0,1\}$, and a proof $\pi$. It outputs 0 or 1.*

In addition, it should satisfy the following properties:

**Evaluation correctness:** For all $\lambda \in \mathbb{N}$, all $(\mathsf{pp}, \mathsf{ek}, \mathsf{msk}) \leftarrow \mathsf{HEC.Setup}(1^\lambda)$, any input $\vec{x} \in \mathcal{X}$, any randomness $r \in R^{\mathsf{HEC}}$, and any circuit $C \in \mathcal{C}$, if $\mathsf{com} = \mathsf{HEC.Commit}(\mathsf{pp}, \vec{x}; r)$, $\pi \leftarrow \mathsf{HEC.Eval}^{in}(\mathsf{msk}, C, \vec{x}, r)$, and

$$\mathsf{com}_{ev} = \mathsf{HEC.Eval}^{out}(\mathsf{ek}, C, \mathsf{com}),$$

then $\Pr[\mathsf{HEC.Verify}(\mathsf{pp}, \mathsf{com}_{ev}, C(\vec{x}), \pi) = 1] \geq 1 - \nu(\lambda)$, for some function $\nu(\lambda) \in \mathsf{negl}(\lambda)$.

**Distributional equivalence of Open:** For all $\lambda \in \mathbb{N}$, any $(\mathsf{pp}, \mathsf{ek}, \mathsf{msk}) \leftarrow \mathsf{HEC.Setup}(1^\lambda)$, any $\vec{x}, \bar{\vec{x}} \in \mathcal{X}$, randomness $r, r' \hookleftarrow \mathcal{D}^{\mathsf{HEC}}$, the distributions $\{(\mathsf{pp}, \mathsf{ek}, \mathsf{msk}, \vec{x}, r, \mathsf{com}) \mid r \hookleftarrow \mathcal{D}^{\mathsf{HEC}},\ \mathsf{com} = \mathsf{HEC.Commit}(\mathsf{pp}, \vec{x}; r)\}$ and

$$\{(\mathsf{pp}, \mathsf{ek}, \mathsf{msk}, \vec{x}, r' = \mathsf{HEC.Open}(\mathsf{msk}, \bar{\vec{x}}, \bar{r}, \vec{x}), \mathsf{com}') \mid$$
$$\bar{r} \hookleftarrow \mathcal{D}^{\mathsf{HEC}},\ \mathsf{com}' = \mathsf{HEC.Commit}(\mathsf{pp}, \bar{\vec{x}}; \bar{r})\}$$

are statistically close.

**Computational binding on evaluated commitments:** For any PPT adversary $\mathcal{A}$, we have

$$\Pr\left[\mathsf{HEC.Verify}(\mathsf{pp}, \mathsf{com}_{ev}, z^*, \pi^*) = 1\ \wedge\ z^* \neq C(\vec{x})\right|$$
$$(\mathsf{pp}, \mathsf{ek}, \mathsf{msk}) \leftarrow \mathsf{HEC.Setup}(1^\lambda),$$
$$(\vec{x}, r, C, z^*, \pi^*) \leftarrow \mathcal{A}(\mathsf{pp}, \mathsf{ek}),$$
$$\mathsf{com} = \mathsf{HEC.Commit}(\mathsf{pp}, \vec{x}; r),$$
$$\mathsf{com}_{ev} = \mathsf{HEC.Eval}^{out}(\mathsf{ek}, C, \mathsf{com})\right] \in \mathsf{negl}(\lambda)$$

**Efficient committing:** There exists a polynomial $\mathsf{poly}(\lambda)$ such that, for all $(\mathsf{pp}, \mathsf{ek}, \mathsf{msk}) \leftarrow \mathsf{HEC.Setup}(1^\lambda)$, $\vec{x} \in \mathcal{X}$ and $r \in R^{\mathsf{HEC}}$, the running time of $\mathsf{com} = \mathsf{HEC.Commit}(\mathsf{pp}, \vec{x}; r)$ is bounded by $|\vec{x}| \cdot \mathsf{poly}(\lambda)$.

**Efficient verification:** There exists a polynomial $\mathsf{poly}(\lambda)$ such that, for all $(\mathsf{pp}, \mathsf{ek}, \mathsf{msk}) \leftarrow \mathsf{HEC.Setup}(1^\lambda)$ and any $\vec{x} \in \mathcal{X}$, $r \in R^{\mathsf{HEC}}$, $C \in \mathcal{C}$ and $z \in \{0, 1\}$, if $\mathsf{com} = \mathsf{HEC.Commit}(\mathsf{pp}, \vec{x}; r)$, $\pi \leftarrow \mathsf{HEC.Eval}^{in}(\mathsf{msk}, C, \vec{x}, r)$ and $\mathsf{com}_{ev} = \mathsf{HEC.Eval}^{out}(\mathsf{ek}, C, \mathsf{com})$, then $|\pi|, |\mathsf{com}_{ev}| \leq \mathsf{poly}(\lambda)$ and the running time of $\mathsf{HEC.Verify}(\mathsf{pp}, \mathsf{com}_{ev}, z, \pi)$ is at most $\mathsf{poly}(\lambda)$ (which does not depend on $|C|$).

**Context hiding:** There exists a PPT simulator $\mathsf{HEC.ProofSim}$ such that, for all $\lambda \in \mathbb{N}$, $(\mathsf{pp}, \mathsf{ek}, \mathsf{msk}) \leftarrow \mathsf{HEC.Setup}(1^\lambda)$, $\vec{x} \in \mathcal{X}$, $C \in \mathcal{C}$, $r \in R^{\mathsf{HEC}}$ and $\mathsf{com} = \mathsf{HEC.Commit}(\mathsf{pp}, \vec{x}; r)$, the distribution $\{\pi \leftarrow \mathsf{HEC.Eval}^{in}(\mathsf{msk}, C, \vec{x}, R)\}$ is statistically indistinguishable from $\{\pi' \leftarrow \mathsf{HEC.ProofSim}(\mathsf{msk}, \mathsf{com}, C, C(\vec{x}))\}$.

We note that the distributional equivalence of Open implies that the commitment is statistically hiding. Here, we only need the statistically hiding property and we do not rely on equivocation. We do not explicitly rely on the context hiding property either since partial openings $\pi$ produced by Open will be part of witnesses in a NIZK argument. On the other hand, we will exploit the efficient verification property to achieve circuit-size independence in terms of signature size.[1]

## 3   Bifurcated Anonymous Signatures

This section formalizes the primitive of bifurcated anonymous signature (BiAS). BiAS is the first general signature primitive reconciling statistical anonymity and accountability in front of dishonest authorities in a single scheme. Nevertheless, our model and syntax are inspired by those in the context of dynamic group signatures given by Kiayias and Yung [29] —who extended the work of Bellare, Micciancio and Warinschi [4] on static group signatures.

### 3.1   Syntax

Like in [29], we consider dynamically growing groups. The syntax includes an interactive protocol which allows users to be enrolled as new members of the group at any time. Analogously to the similar model of Bellare, Shi and Zhang [5], the Kiayias-Yung (KY) model assumes an interactive *join* protocol whereby a prospective user becomes a group member by interacting with the group manager responsible to issuing credentials. This protocol provides the user with a membership certificate, $\mathsf{cert}_i$, and a membership secret, $\mathsf{sec}_i$.

In the syntax below, we define a space $\mathcal{ID}$ of user identifiers as well as a space of witnesses $\mathcal{W}$. For any message-identity-witness triple $(M, \mathsf{id}, w) \in \mathcal{M} \times \mathcal{ID} \times \mathcal{W}$, we adopt the convention that $P(M, \mathsf{id}, w) = 0$ whenever the user of identity id was only allowed to sign $M$ using the witness $w$ while being subject to tracing, by the opening authority. In contrast, having $P(M, \mathsf{id}, w) = 1$ allows the user to use the witness $w$ to generate a signature on $M$ while retaining unconditional anonymity. For generality and more applicability, a BiAS defines a family $\mathcal{P}$ of authorized *public* predicates $P$ which are needed to verify signatures.

**Definition 5 (Bifurcated Anonymous Signature).** *A bifurcated anonymous signature (BiAS) scheme for a predicate family $\mathcal{P}$ consists of the following algorithms or protocols.*

**Setup**$(1^\lambda, 1^N)$: *given a security parameter $\lambda$ and a maximal number of group members $N \in \mathsf{poly}(\lambda) \cap \mathbb{N}$, this algorithm is run by a trusted party to generate a group public key $\mathcal{Y}$ associated to the predicate family $\mathcal{P}_\lambda$, which specifies a message space $\mathcal{M}$, a space of user identifiers $\mathcal{ID}$, and a witness space $\mathcal{W}$. It also outputs the group manager's private key $\mathcal{S}_{\mathsf{GM}}$ and the opening authority's private key $\mathcal{S}_{\mathsf{OA}}$. Each key is given to the appropriate authority while $\mathcal{Y}$ is made public. The algorithm also initializes a public state St comprising a set data structure $St_{\mathsf{users}} = \emptyset$ and a string data structure $St_{\mathsf{trans}} = \epsilon$. From now on we assume $\lambda$ is implicit.*

---

[1] As pointed out in [27, Remark 3.3], it is straightforward to build an HEC without the context-hiding and efficient verification properties, using any statistically hiding commitment.

**Join:** *is an interactive protocol between the group manager GM and a user $\mathcal{U}$ who gets a unique identifier id $\in \mathcal{ID}$ (both are responsible for enforcing the uniqueness of the identifier). The protocol involves two interactive Turing machines $J_{user}$ and $J_{GM}$ that both take $\mathcal{Y}$ as input. The execution, denoted as $[J_{user}(\mathcal{Y}), J_{GM}(\mathcal{Y}, \mathcal{S}_{GM}, St)]$, ends with user $\mathcal{U}_{id} := \mathcal{U}$ obtaining a membership secret $sec_{id}$, that no one else knows, and a membership certificate $cert_{id}$. If the protocol is successful, the group manager updates the public state $St$ by setting $St_{users} := St_{users} \cup \{id\}$ as well as $St_{trans} := St_{trans}||\langle id, transcript_{id}\rangle$.*

**Sign(id, $cert_{id}$, $sec_{id}$, $M, w, P$):** *given an identifier id $\in \mathcal{ID}$, a membership certificate $cert_{id}$, a membership secret $sec_{id}$, a message $M \in \mathcal{M}$, a witness $w \in \mathcal{W}$, and a predicate $P \in \mathcal{P}$, this probabilistic algorithm outputs a signature $\sigma$.*

**Verify($\mathcal{Y}, M, \sigma, P$):** *given a message $M \in \mathcal{M}$, a signature $\sigma$, a predicate $P \in \mathcal{P}$ and a group public key $\mathcal{Y}$, this deterministic algorithm returns either 0 or 1.*

**Open($\mathcal{Y}, \mathcal{S}_{OA}, M, \sigma, P, St$):** *takes as input the opening authority's private key $\mathcal{S}_{OA}$, a message $M \in \mathcal{M}$, a signature $\sigma$ w.r.t. $\mathcal{Y}$ and a predicate $P \in \mathcal{P}$ as well as the public state $St$. It outputs id $\in St_{users} \cup \{\bot\}$, which is the identity of a group member or a symbol indicating anonymity.*

Correctness basically requires that, if all parties *honestly* run the protocols, all algorithms are correct with respect to their specification described as above.

*Correctness of Bifurcated Anonymous Signatures.* Following the Kiayias-Yung terminology [29], we say that a public state $St$ is *valid* if it can be reached from $St = (\emptyset, \epsilon)$ by a Turing machine having oracle access to $J_{GM}$. Also, a state $St'$ is said to *extend* another state $St$ if it is within reach from $St$. Moreover, we write $cert_{id} \leftrightharpoons_\mathcal{Y} sec_{id}$ to mean that there exists coin tosses $\varpi$ for $J_{GM}$ and $J_{user}$ such that, for some valid public state $St'$, the execution of the interactive protocol $[J_{user}(\mathcal{Y}), J_{GM}(\mathcal{Y}, \mathcal{S}_{GM}, St')](\varpi)$ provides $J_{user}$ with $\langle id, sec_{id}, cert_{id}\rangle$.

**Definition 6 (Correctness).** *A BiAS scheme is correct if the following conditions are all satisfied for any $(St, \mathcal{Y}, \mathcal{S}_{GM}, \mathcal{S}_{OA}) \leftarrow \mathsf{Setup}(1^\lambda, 1^N)$:*

*(1) In a valid state $St$, $|St_{users}| = |St_{trans}|$ always holds and two distinct entries of $St_{trans}$ always contain certificates with distinct id.*

*(2) If $[J_{user}(\mathcal{Y}), J_{GM}(\mathcal{Y}, \mathcal{S}_{GM}, St)]$ is run by two honest parties following the protocol and $\langle id, cert_{id}, sec_{id}\rangle$ is obtained by $J_{user}$, then we have $cert_{id} \leftrightharpoons_\mathcal{Y} sec_{id}$.*

*(3) For each $\langle id, cert_{id}, sec_{id}\rangle$ such that $cert_{id} \leftrightharpoons_\mathcal{Y} sec_{id}$, any message $M \in \mathcal{M}$, any witness $w \in \mathcal{W}$ and any predicate $P \in \mathcal{P}$, we have*

$$\mathsf{Verify}\big(\mathcal{Y}, M, \mathsf{Sign}(id, cert_{id}, sec_{id}, M, w, P), P\big) = 1.$$

*(4) For any $M \notin \mathcal{M}$ or any $P \notin \mathcal{P}$, and any $\sigma$, we have $\mathsf{Verify}(\mathcal{Y}, M, \sigma, P) = 0$.*

*(5) $\mathsf{Open}(\mathcal{Y}, \mathcal{S}_{OA}, M, \sigma, P, St) \in \mathcal{ID} \cup \{\bot\}$ as long as $\mathsf{Verify}(\mathcal{Y}, M, \sigma, P) = 1$.*

*(6) For any outcome $\langle id, cert_{id}, sec_{id}\rangle$ of $[J_{user}(.,.), J_{GM}(., St, ., .)]$, for some valid $St$, any predicate $P \in \mathcal{P}$, any message $M \in \mathcal{M}$, any witness $w \in \mathcal{W}$ and $\sigma \leftarrow \mathsf{Sign}(id, cert_{id}, sec_{id}, M, w, P)$, with overwhelming probability:*

    *(a) if $P(M, id, w) = 0$, then $\mathsf{Open}(\mathcal{Y}, \mathcal{S}_{OA}, M, \sigma, P, St) = id$;*

(b) if $P(M, \text{id}, w) = 1$, then $\mathsf{Open}(\mathcal{Y}, \mathcal{S}_{\mathsf{OA}}, M, \sigma, P, St) = \bot$.

We formalize security properties via experiments where the adversary interacts with a stateful interface $\mathcal{I}$ that maintains the following variables:

- $\mathsf{state}_{\mathcal{I}}$: is a data structure representing the state of the interface as the adversary invokes the various oracles available in the attack games. It is initialized as $\mathsf{state}_{\mathcal{I}} = (St, \mathcal{Y}, \mathcal{S}_{\mathsf{GM}}, \mathcal{S}_{\mathsf{OA}}) \leftarrow \mathsf{Setup}(1^{\lambda}, 1^{N})$. It includes the (initially empty) set $St_{\mathsf{users}}$ of group members and a dynamically growing database $St_{\mathsf{trans}}$ storing the transcripts of previously executed join protocols.
- $n = |St_{\mathsf{users}}| \leq N$ denotes the current cardinality of the group.
- $\mathsf{Sigs}$: is a database of honestly generated signatures created by the signing oracle. Each entry consists of a tuple $(\text{id}, M, w, \sigma, P)$ indicating that message $M$ was signed by user id with respect to the witness $w$ and the predicate $P$.
- $U^{a}$: is an initially empty set of users that are introduced by the adversary in the system in an execution of the join protocol.
- $U^{b}$: is an initially empty set of honest users introduced in the system by the adversary acting as a dishonest group manager. For these users, the adversary obtains the transcript of $[\mathsf{J}_{\mathsf{user}}, \mathsf{J}_{\mathsf{GM}}]$ but not the user's membership secret.

In attack games, adversaries are granted access to the following oracles:

- $Q_{\mathsf{pub}}$, $Q_{\mathsf{keyGM}}$ and $Q_{\mathsf{keyOA}}$: when these oracles are invoked, the interface looks up $\mathsf{state}_{\mathcal{I}}$ and returns the group public key $\mathcal{Y}$, the GM's private key $\mathcal{S}_{\mathsf{GM}}$ and the opening authority's private key $\mathcal{S}_{\mathsf{OA}}$ respectively. Once the oracle $Q_{\mathsf{keyGM}}$ (resp. $Q_{\mathsf{keyOA}}$) is invoked, it updates the initially empty key state $St_{\mathsf{GM}} \leftarrow \{\mathcal{S}_{\mathsf{GM}}\}$ (resp. $St_{\mathsf{OA}} \leftarrow \{\mathcal{S}_{\mathsf{OA}}\}$).
- $Q_{\mathsf{a\text{-}join}}$: allows the adversary to introduce users under its control in the group. On behalf of the GM, the interface runs $\mathsf{J}_{\mathsf{GM}}$ in interaction with the $\mathsf{J}_{\mathsf{user}}$-executing adversary who plays the role of the prospective user in the join protocol. At the beginning of $\mathsf{J}_{\mathsf{user}}$, the user chooses an identifier id and the interface aborts if id was previously assigned to a different user in $U^{a}$. If this protocol successfully ends, the interface updates $St$ by inserting the new user id in both sets $St_{\mathsf{users}}$ and $U^{a}$. It also sets $St_{\mathsf{trans}} := St_{\mathsf{trans}} || \langle \text{id}, \mathsf{transcript}_{\mathsf{id}} \rangle$.
- $Q_{\mathsf{b\text{-}join}}$: allows the adversary, acting as a corrupted group manager, to introduce new honest group members of its choice. The interface triggers an execution of $[\mathsf{J}_{\mathsf{user}}, \mathsf{J}_{\mathsf{GM}}]$ and runs $\mathsf{J}_{\mathsf{user}}$ in interaction with the adversary who runs $\mathsf{J}_{\mathsf{GM}}$. If the protocol successfully completes, the interface adds user id to $St_{\mathsf{users}}$ and $U^{b}$ and sets $St_{\mathsf{trans}} := St_{\mathsf{trans}} || \langle \text{id}, \mathsf{transcript}_{\mathsf{id}} \rangle$. It stores the membership certificate $\mathsf{cert}_{\mathsf{id}}$ and the membership secret $\mathsf{sec}_{\mathsf{id}}$ in a *private* part of $\mathsf{state}_{\mathcal{I}}$.
- $Q_{\mathsf{sig}}$: given a tule $(M, w, P)$ and an identifier id, the interface returns $\bot$ if id $\notin U^{b}$. Otherwise, the private area of $\mathsf{state}_{\mathcal{I}}$ must contain a certificate $\mathsf{cert}_{\mathsf{id}}$ and a membership secret $\mathsf{sec}_{\mathsf{id}}$. The interface outputs a signature $\sigma$ on behalf of user id and also updates $\mathsf{Sigs} \leftarrow \mathsf{Sigs} || (\text{id}, M, w, \sigma, P)$.
- $Q_{\mathsf{open}}$: when this oracle is invoked on input of a valid triple $(M, \sigma, P)$, the interface runs algorithm $\mathsf{Open}$ using the current state $St$. When $S$ is a set of tuples of the form $(M, \sigma, P)$, $Q_{\mathsf{open}}^{\neg S}$ denotes a restricted oracle that only applies the opening algorithm to tuples $(M, \sigma, P)$ which are not in $S$.

– $Q_{\text{read}}$ and $Q_{\text{write}}$: are used by the adversary to read and write the content of $St$. At each invocation, $Q_{\text{read}}$ outputs the state $St$ of the interface. By using $Q_{\text{write}}$, the adversary can modify $St$ at will as long as it does not invalidate $St$: for example, the adversary is allowed to create dummy users as long as it does not re-use already existing certificates.

In the random oracle model we implicitly assume that all the BiAS algorithms and protocols have access to the random oracle.

## 3.2   Branch-Hiding and Privacy

*Branch-Hiding.* The notion of branch-hiding captures the infeasibility, even for a corrupt group manager, to decide whether a user signs a message $M$ for a given predicate $P$ while enabling traceability or not. In particular, $P(M, \text{id}, w)$ remains computationally hidden. Said otherwise, signatures do not betray any potential intent of a user to remain untraceable or accept traceability. The formal description is given in the full version as we require a stronger privacy notion.

*Full Anonymity.* The notion of anonymity is formalized via two games parametrized by a bit $d$ and involving a two-stage adversary. The first stage is called play stage and allows the adversary $\mathcal{A}$ to modify $\text{state}_\mathcal{I}$ via $Q_{\text{write}}$-queries and open arbitrary signatures by probing $Q_{\text{open}}$. When the play stage ends, $\mathcal{A}$ chooses a message-predicate pair $(M^\star, P^\star)$ as well as two 4-ules $(\text{id}_0^\star, w_0^\star, \text{sec}_0^\star, \text{cert}_0^\star)$ and $(\text{id}_1^\star, w_1^\star, \text{sec}_1^\star, \text{cert}_1^\star)$, both containing a valid membership certificate and a corresponding membership secret. Then, depending on $d \in \{0, 1\}$, the adversary is given a challenge signature $\sigma^\star$ computed using $(\text{id}_d^\star, w_d^\star, \text{sec}_d^\star, \text{cert}_d^\star)$ with the task of eventually guessing the bit $d \in \{0, 1\}$. Before doing so, it is allowed further oracle queries throughout the second stage, called guess stage, but is restricted not to query $Q_{\text{open}}$ for $(M^\star, \sigma^\star, P^\star)$. We note that the adversary is allowed to choose $(\text{id}_0^\star, \text{sec}_0^\star, \text{cert}_0^\star)$ and $(\text{id}_1^\star, \text{sec}_1^\star, \text{cert}_1^\star)$ such that $P^\star(M^\star, \text{id}_0^\star, w_0^\star) \neq P^\star(M^\star, \text{id}_1^\star, w_1^\star)$. Our definition of anonymity thus reflects the inability of a verifier to distinguish signatures that are traceable from those that are not. To strengthen the model, the definition even allows the adversary to corrupt the opening authority as long as $P^\star(M^\star, \text{id}_0^\star, w_0^\star) = 1 = P^\star(M^\star, \text{id}_1^\star, w_1^\star)$. In such a non-traceable case, we require that the indistinguishability is statistically independent of the bit $d$. We elaborate more on this adversarial complexity just after.

**Definition 7.** *A BiAS is fully anonymous if it satisfies the next conditions:*

**Traceable case.** *For any* PPT *adversary $\mathcal{A}$ the following advantage is negligible.*

$$\mathbf{Adv}_{\mathcal{A},N}^{\text{anon}}(\lambda) := \left| \Pr\left[ \mathbf{Exp}_{\mathcal{A},N}^{\text{anon-1}}(\lambda) = 1 \right] - \Pr\left[ \mathbf{Exp}_{\mathcal{A},N}^{\text{anon-0}}(\lambda) = 1 \right] \right|$$

**Non-traceable case.** *For any (unbounded) adversary involved in $\mathbf{Exp}_{\mathcal{A},N}^{\text{anon-}d}$ and $\mathbf{Exp}_{\mathcal{A},N}^{\text{anon-ntr-}d}$ (defined in Fig. 1), the following advantage is negligible.*

$$\mathbf{Adv}_{\mathcal{A},N}^{\text{anon-ntr}}(\lambda) := \left| \Pr\left[ \mathbf{Exp}_{\mathcal{A},N}^{\text{anon-ntr-1}}(\lambda) = 1 \right] - \Pr\left[ \mathbf{Exp}_{\mathcal{A},N}^{\text{anon-ntr-0}}(\lambda) = 1 \right] \right|$$

$\texttt{1}$ $\mathrm{state}_{\mathcal{I}} := (St, \mathcal{Y}, \mathcal{S}_{\mathsf{GM}}, \mathcal{S}_{\mathsf{OA}}) \leftarrow \mathsf{Setup}(1^\lambda, 1^N);$

$\texttt{2}$ $\bigl(aux, M^\star, w_0^\star, w_1^\star, (\mathsf{id}_0^\star, \mathsf{sec}_0^\star, \mathsf{cert}_0^\star), (\mathsf{id}_1^\star, \mathsf{sec}_1^\star, \mathsf{cert}_1^\star), P^\star\bigr)$
$\qquad \leftarrow \mathcal{A}(\mathsf{play}; Q_{\mathsf{pub}}, Q_{\mathsf{keyGM}}, Q_{\mathsf{open}}, Q_{\mathsf{read}}, Q_{\mathsf{write}}, Q_{\mathsf{keyOA}});$

$\texttt{3}$ if $\neg(\mathsf{cert}_{\mathsf{id}_0^\star} \leftrightharpoons_{\mathcal{Y}} \mathsf{sec}_{\mathsf{id}_0^\star}) \vee \neg(\mathsf{cert}_{\mathsf{id}_1^\star} \leftrightharpoons_{\mathcal{Y}} \mathsf{sec}_{\mathsf{id}_1^\star})$ then return $0;$

$\texttt{4}$ if $(M^\star \notin \mathcal{M}) \vee (w_0^\star, w_1^\star \notin \mathcal{W}) \vee (P^\star \notin \mathcal{P})$ then return $0;$

$\texttt{5}$ $\sigma_d \leftarrow \mathsf{Sign}(\mathcal{Y}, \mathsf{id}_d^\star, \mathsf{cert}_d^\star, \mathsf{sec}_d^\star, M^\star, w_d^\star, P^\star)\ ;$

$\texttt{6}$ $d' \leftarrow \mathcal{A}(\mathsf{guess}; \sigma_d, aux, Q_{\mathsf{pub}}, Q_{\mathsf{keyGM}}, Q_{\mathsf{open}}^{\neg\{(M^\star, \sigma_d, P^\star)\}}, Q_{\mathsf{read}}, Q_{\mathsf{write}}, Q_{\mathsf{keyOA}});$

$\texttt{7}$ if $\boxed{\left(P^\star(M^\star, \mathsf{id}_0^\star, w_0^\star) = 1\right) \wedge \left(P^\star(M^\star, \mathsf{id}_1^\star, w_1^\star) = 1\right)}$ then return $\boxed{d'}\ ;$

$\texttt{8}$ if $\boxed{(St_{\mathsf{OA}} = \emptyset)}$ then return $\boxed{d'}\ ;$

$\texttt{9}$ return $0;$

**Fig. 1.** Experiment $\mathbf{Exp}_{\mathcal{A},N}^{\mathrm{anon}\text{-}d}(\lambda)$ (*resp.* $\mathbf{Exp}_{\mathcal{A},N}^{\mathrm{anon}-\mathrm{ntr}\text{-}d}(\lambda)$) excluding the dotted (*resp.* solid) box.

The anonymity definition has two parts: a first one that captures the (CCA) unlinkability against all entities but the OA regardless of the predicate value; and a second one which captures the unlinkability even against the OA when the predicate evaluates to 1. Clearly, the first case can never be statistical if the predicate is not constantly equal to 1. However, while the requirement of the second case could only have been computational, we stress that having two cases has nothing to do with the running time of the adversary.

The reason we are requiring statistical anonymity is because we advocate the need to enhance the privacy branch in the context of anonymous signatures. When the predicate equals 1, the signer should have full confidence in his anonymity. Allowing computational anonymity leaves room for a potential backdoor in the system, which could be exploitable in an unexpected way in some applications.

In the full version of this paper, we suggest an even stronger notion of anonymity, called unsubversive anonymity, in the non-traceable case. This notion allows for adversarially-generated authorities' keys. Since it only seems achievable in the random oracle model, we do not include it in the general BiAS model and leave the design of a BiAS achieving it for future research.

### 3.3   Branch-Soundness and Security

Defining strong unforgeability-related notions requires being able to check whether an adversary fools the underlying predicate value embedded into signatures. However, checking such a relation needs extracting meaningful information even from (statistically) non-traceable signatures. To circumvent this apparent conflicting requirements we first define the branch-soundness notion which sets an indistinguishable extractable mode even if all the keys are exposed. It also captures the inability of any efficient adversary to produce valid signatures in the extractable mode that contradict the openability of signatures in the real mode. Equipped with a setting where identities and witnesses are extractable "all the time" we can turn to other security notions.

*Branch-Soundness.* To be able to extract $(\text{id}, w)$ from *any* valid signatures, we introduce an indistinguishable setting allowing such extractions for the purpose of testing the underlying predicate value $P(M, \text{id}, w)$. As long as signatures are traceable, we require id to be consistent with the outcome of Open.

**Definition 8.** *A BiAS scheme satisfies the* branch-soundness *property if there is a pair of efficient algorithms with the following specifications:*

**SimSetup**$(1^\lambda, 1^N)$: *given a security parameter $\lambda$ and a maximal number of users $N \in \text{poly}(\lambda) \cap \mathbb{N}$, this algorithm generates a group public key $\mathcal{Y}$, the group manager's secret key $\mathcal{S}_{\text{GM}}$, the opening authority's secret key $\mathcal{S}_{\text{OA}}$ as well as an extraction trapdoor $\tau_{\text{ext}}$. The algorithm also initializes a public state $St = (St_{\text{users}}, St_{\text{trans}}) := (\emptyset, \epsilon)$ as in* Setup;

**Extract**$(\mathcal{Y}, \tau_{\text{ext}}, M, \sigma, P, St)$: *inputs a valid message-signature pair $(M, \sigma)$ w.r.t. $\mathcal{Y}$ and a predicate $P \in \mathcal{P}$, the extraction trapdoor $\tau_{\text{ext}}$ as well as the public state $St$. It outputs an identity $\text{id} \in \mathcal{ID}$ and a witness $w \in \mathcal{W}$.*

*In addition, these algorithms must satisfy the following notions.*

***Extractable correctness:*** *for any $(St, \mathcal{Y}, \mathcal{S}_{\text{GM}}, \mathcal{S}_{\text{OA}}, \tau_{\text{ext}}) \leftarrow \text{SimSetup}(1^\lambda, 1^N)$, for any outcome $\langle \text{id}, \text{cert}_{\text{id}}, \text{sec}_{\text{id}} \rangle$ such that $\text{cert}_{\text{id}} \rightleftharpoons_{\mathcal{Y}} \text{sec}_{\text{id}}$, any message $M$, any witness $w$, and any predicate $P \in \mathcal{P}$: if $\sigma \leftarrow \text{Sign}(\text{id}, \text{cert}_{\text{id}}, \text{sec}_{\text{id}}, M, w, P)$ and $(\text{id}', w') \leftarrow \text{Extract}(\mathcal{Y}, \tau_{\text{ext}}, M, \sigma, P, St)$, then $(\text{id}, w) = (\text{id}', w')$ with overwhelming probability.*

***Extractable soundness:*** *For any* PPT *adversary $\mathcal{A}$ involved in the experiments defined in Fig. 2, the following advantage function must be negligible:*

$$\mathbf{Adv}_{\mathcal{A}}^{\text{ext-s}}(\lambda) = \left| \Pr\left[ \mathbf{Exp}_{\mathcal{A}}^{\text{real}}(\lambda) = 1 \right] - \Pr\left[ \mathbf{Exp}_{\mathcal{A}}^{\text{ext}}(\lambda) = 1 \right] \right|.$$

---

1   $(St, \mathcal{Y}, \mathcal{S}_{\text{GM}}, \mathcal{S}_{\text{OA}}) \leftarrow \text{Setup}(1^\lambda, 1^N)$   $(St, \mathcal{Y}, \mathcal{S}_{\text{GM}}, \mathcal{S}_{\text{OA}}, \tau_{\text{ext}}) \leftarrow \text{SimSetup}(1^\lambda, 1^N)$;

2   $(M, \sigma, P, st) \leftarrow \mathcal{A}(St, \mathcal{Y}, \mathcal{S}_{\text{GM}}, \mathcal{S}_{\text{OA}})$;

3   **if** $\text{Verify}(\mathcal{Y}, M, \sigma, P) = 0$   **then return** 0;

4   $\text{id}^* \leftarrow \text{Open}(\mathcal{S}_{\text{OA}}, \mathcal{Y}, M, \sigma, P, St)$   $(\text{id}, w) \leftarrow \text{Extract}(\tau_{\text{ext}}, \mathcal{Y}, M, \sigma, P, St)$;

5   **if** $P(\text{id}, M, w) = 1$ **then** $\text{id}^* \leftarrow \bot$ **else** $\text{id}^* \leftarrow \text{id}$;

6   **return** $\mathcal{A}(st, \text{id}^*)$;

**Fig. 2.** Experiment $\mathbf{Exp}_{\mathcal{A}}^{\text{real}}(\lambda)$ (resp. $\mathbf{Exp}_{\mathcal{A}}^{\text{ext}}(\lambda)$) excluding the dotted (resp. solid) boxes.

In the random oracle model, Item 2 of Fig. 2 is modified as follows:

2'  $(M, \sigma, P, st) \leftarrow \mathcal{A}^{H_0}(St, \mathcal{Y}, \mathcal{S}_{\mathsf{GM}}, \mathcal{S}_{\mathsf{OA}})$ | $(M, \sigma, P, st) \leftarrow \mathcal{A}^{H_1}(St, \mathcal{Y}, \mathcal{S}_{\mathsf{GM}}, \mathcal{S}_{\mathsf{OA}})$;

Here, $H_0$ and $H_1$ are random oracles which privately evaluate and return the digests of given inputs. In the real setup, the BiAS algorithms have access to $H_0$ whereas, in the extractable setup, they have access to $H_1$.

We stress that all secret keys but the extraction trapdoor are given to the distinguisher/adversary. This is necessary because we need the extractable properties even in presence of dishonest authorities. In the extractable setting, we require Extract to output a potential identifier id $\in \mathcal{ID}$ and a witness $w \in \mathcal{W}$ with overwhelming probability, even on adversarially-chosen verifying signatures and when both authorities are corrupted. This extractable mode makes it possible to compute the predicate in a meaningful way. Further, the extractable soundness property implies the hardness of computing a valid signature that traces to some user id for some predicate $P$ although this predicate would have allowed user id to sign the message with statistical anonymity. While Extract is consistent with Open, we still do not have the complementary property of the hardness of computing a valid signature that cannot be traced although the tracing operation should have been possible. Indeed, if Open identifies a signature as non-traceable, we still have no clue about the meaning of the identity-witness pair produced by Extract on adversarially generated valid signatures that are not honestly generated (as otherwise, extractable-correctness implies the match with the actual pair).

*Security Against Misidentification Attacks (a.k.a. traceability).* In a misidentification attack, the adversary can corrupt the opening authority using the $Q_{\mathsf{keyOA}}$ oracle and introduce malicious users in $U^a$ via $Q_{\mathsf{a\text{-}join}}$-queries. It aims at producing a valid signature $\sigma^*$ that does not open to any adversarially-controlled user.

**Definition 9.** *A BiAS scheme is secure against* misidentification attacks *if it is branch-sound and, for any* PPT *adversary $\mathcal{A}$ involved in experiment* $\mathbf{Exp}_{\mathcal{A},N}^{\mathrm{mis\text{-}id}}$ *(as defined in Fig. 3), we have:* $\mathbf{Adv}_{\mathcal{A},N}^{\mathrm{mis\text{-}id}}(\lambda) = \Pr\left[\mathbf{Exp}_{\mathcal{A},N}^{\mathrm{mis\text{-}id}}(\lambda) = 1\right] \in$ negl $(\lambda)$.

---

1  $\mathrm{state}_{\mathcal{I}} := (St, \mathcal{Y}, \mathcal{S}_{\mathsf{GM}}, \mathcal{S}_{\mathsf{OA}});$ $(St, \mathcal{Y}, \mathcal{S}_{\mathsf{GM}}, \mathcal{S}_{\mathsf{OA}}, \tau_{\mathsf{ext}}) \leftarrow \mathsf{SimSetup}(1^\lambda, 1^N)$ ;

2  $(M, \sigma, P) \leftarrow \mathcal{A}(Q_{\mathsf{pub}}, Q_{\mathsf{a\text{-}join}}, Q_{\mathsf{read}}, Q_{\mathsf{write}}, Q_{\mathsf{keyOA}});$

3  if $\mathsf{Verify}(\mathcal{Y}, M, \sigma, P) = 0$ then return 0;

4  $(\mathsf{id}, w) \leftarrow \mathsf{Extract}(\tau_{\mathsf{ext}}, \mathcal{Y}, M, \sigma, P, St);$

5  if id $\in \mathcal{ID} \setminus U^a$ then return 1;

6  return 0;

**Fig. 3.** Experiment $\mathbf{Exp}_{\mathcal{A},N}^{\mathrm{mis\text{-}id}}(\lambda)$.

The winning condition is also checkable without the extractor if we rather define id$^\star$ ← Open($\mathcal{S}_{\mathsf{OA}}, \mathcal{Y}, M, \sigma, P, St$) in the experiment, as long as id$^\star \neq \perp$ in the winning condition of line 5. In that case, the analogue security with the real setup is implied by the extractable soundness property. Nevertheless, in the extractable mode the definition also captures the unforgeability of anonymous signatures, i.e. those which would have made Open to return id$^\star = \perp$ at line 5, if the extracted id does not correspond to a corrupt user when the group manager remains honest.

*Non-Frameability.* Framing attacks consider the case where the entire system is colluding against some honest user. The adversary can corrupt the group manager as well as the opening authority (via oracles $Q_{\mathsf{keyGM}}$ and $Q_{\mathsf{keyOA}}$, respectively). It can also introduce honest group members (via $Q_{\mathsf{b\text{-}join}}$-queries), observe the system while these users sign messages and create dummy users using $Q_{\mathsf{write}}$. The adversary aims at framing an honest group member. Moreover, the adversary is also deemed successful if it is able to create a non-traceable valid signature which could have been created by an honest user but who never computed it: even a corrupted group manager is unable to compute a non-traceable signature using the identity of an honest user. For example, if the predicate of a BiAS only allows some users to compute perfectly anonymous signatures, it is infeasible to compute such signatures without corrupting at least one of these users. The definition follows the indistinguishable approach of security against misidentification attacks.

**Definition 10.** *A BiAS scheme is secure against* framing attacks *if it satisfies branch-soundness and, for any* PPT *adversary* $\mathcal{A}$ *involved in experiment* $\mathbf{Exp}^{\mathrm{fra}}_{\mathcal{A},N}$ *(as defined in Fig. 4), we have:* $\mathbf{Adv}^{\mathrm{fra}}_{\mathcal{A},N}(\lambda) = \Pr\left[\mathbf{Exp}^{\mathrm{fra}}_{\mathcal{A},N}(\lambda) = 1\right] \in \mathsf{negl}(\lambda).$

---

1  state$_\mathcal{I} := (St, \mathcal{Y}, \mathcal{S}_{\mathsf{GM}}, \mathcal{S}_{\mathsf{OA}})$; $(St, \mathcal{Y}, \mathcal{S}_{\mathsf{GM}}, \mathcal{S}_{\mathsf{OA}}, \tau_{\mathsf{ext}}) \leftarrow \mathsf{SimSetup}(1^\lambda, 1^N)$ ;

2  $(M^\star, \sigma^\star, P^\star) \leftarrow \mathcal{A}(Q_{\mathsf{pub}}, Q_{\mathsf{keyGM}}, Q_{\mathsf{keyOA}}, Q_{\mathsf{b\text{-}join}}, Q_{\mathsf{sig}}, Q_{\mathsf{read}}, Q_{\mathsf{write}})$;

3  **if** $\mathsf{Verify}(\mathcal{Y}, M^\star, \sigma^\star, P^\star) = 0$ **then return** 0;

4  $(\mathsf{id}, w) \leftarrow \mathsf{Extract}(\tau_{\mathsf{ext}}, \mathcal{Y}, M^\star, \sigma^\star, P^\star, St)$;

5  **if** $(\mathsf{id} \in U^b) \wedge (\mathsf{id}, M^\star, w, \sigma^\star, P^\star) \notin \mathsf{Sigs}$ **then return** 1;

6  **return** 0;

---

**Fig. 4.** Experiment $\mathbf{Exp}^{\mathrm{fra}}_{\mathcal{A},N}(\lambda)$

Let id$^\star$ = Open($\mathcal{S}_{\mathsf{OA}}, \mathcal{Y}, M^\star, \sigma^\star, P^\star, St$) in the framing experiment. Then, we can derive two winning conditions depending on whether id$^\star \in \mathcal{ID}$ or id$^\star = \perp$. In the former case, the branch-soundness tells us that id$^\star$ = id. This traceable case is thus the analogue of the usual framing attack of KY in group signature transposed to our BiAS primitive. In the latter case, the signature $\sigma^\star$ of a successful adversary is deemed non-traceable, but it would have been created on behalf of an honest signer with identifier id who never produced it. This further justifies the need of all these security notions as we now have the complementary property discussed after Definition 8: a branch-sound BiAS scheme whose extracting algorithm returns independent identity-witness pairs given non-honest valid signatures cannot be secure against framing attacks.

Finally, we note that a signature does not only authenticate the message $M$, but it also binds the predicate value as well as the hidden (id, $w$) to $M$. The framing resistance also guarantees that the signature itself is not malleable as the winning condition is akin to the "strong"-unforgeability notion of standard signatures. This requirement is actually necessary since, in order to achieve anonymity in the "CCA sense", we need to prevent signatures from being malleable.

*Discussion on the witness.* Our model does not assume any property of the witness. At first glance, it may seem strange to apparently let the users choose their witnesses arbitrarily at the signature generation time. This syntactic choice makes BiAS more flexible to be combined with other building blocks. For instance, the witness $w$ may already be committed in an external commitment, i.e. outside our syntax, and bound by the application. Additional zero-knowledge proofs between $w$, the context, and the BiAS scheme are of course possible, which might prevent the user from choosing $w$ freely.

In a money-laundering prevention application, a signer has no incentive in authenticating a transaction for a big amount of money $w$ if he does not want to pay such an amount. Therefore, even if $P(M, \text{id}, w)$ may vary when $w$ varies at each transaction, the context prevents the user with identity id from fixing $w$ in an arbitrary way. We thus leave it to the applications to define their own rules on the $w$'s and the desire and the way to keep their level of secrecy.

## 4   Generic Construction

We provide a generic construction of BiAS for an arbitrary predicate family $\mathcal{P} : \{0,1\}^* \rightarrow \{0,1\}$. Our construction relies on the following building blocks:

- An $\mathcal{R}_{\mathsf{NEQ}}$-lossy PKE scheme $\Pi^{\mathsf{RLE}} = (\mathsf{Par\text{-}Gen}, \mathsf{Keygen}, \mathsf{Encrypt}, \mathsf{Decrypt})$;
- An ordinary lossy PKE scheme $\Pi^{\mathsf{lpke}} = (\mathsf{Keygen}, \mathsf{LKeygen}, \mathsf{Encrypt}, \mathsf{Decrypt})$ where the message space has size at least $N$ and forms an additive group;
- A digital signature scheme $\Pi^{\mathsf{sig}} = (\mathsf{Kg}, \mathsf{Sign}, \mathsf{Verify})$ with signature space $\mathcal{S}$ and public key space $\mathcal{VK}$;
- A one-time signature $\Pi^{\mathsf{ots}} = (\mathsf{Kg}, \mathsf{Sign}, \mathsf{Verify})$;
- A homomorphic equivocal commitment scheme $\mathsf{HEC} = (\mathsf{Setup}, \mathsf{Commit}, \mathsf{Open}, \mathsf{Eval}^{in}, \mathsf{Eval}^{out}, \mathsf{Verify})$, where $\mathsf{Commit}$ samples its random coins from a distribution $\mathcal{D}^{\mathsf{HEC}}$ over a randomness space $R^{\mathsf{HEC}}$;
- A dual-mode statistical NIZK argument system $\mathsf{NIZK} = (\mathsf{Setup}, \mathsf{ExtSetup}, \mathsf{Prove}, \mathsf{Verify}, \mathsf{Sim}, \mathsf{Extract})$, as defined in the full version.

Since an $\mathcal{R}_{\mathsf{NEQ}}$-lossy PKE scheme implies a standard lossy PKE scheme, the only ingredients we need are an $\mathcal{R}_{\mathsf{NEQ}}$-lossy PKE system, a digital signature, a homomorphic equivocal commitment and a dual-mode NIZK argument.

For our purposes, it is sufficient to use an HEC scheme without the context-hiding property since we combine it with NIZK arguments where its partial openings serve as witnesses.[2] By using an HEC with the efficient verification property, we can make the signature length independent of the circuit size. Katsumata *et al.* [27] gave such a pairing-based HEC construction under a $q$-type assumption for $NC^1$ circuits. In the lattice setting, the fully homomorphic commitments of Gorbunov *et al.* [23] provide efficient verification (for bounded-depth circuits) under the Short Integer Solution [1] assumption, as recalled in the full version. At the expense of a signature length depending on the circuit size, the construction can be simplified to use any statistically hiding commitment instead of an efficiently verifiable HEC. However, we aim at avoiding the circuit-size dependency.

Intuitively, the construction encrypts the group member's identity id and the witness $w$ using an HEC *and* simultaneously encrypts them into $\mathsf{ct}_{(\mathsf{id},w)}$ using the $\mathcal{R}_{\mathsf{NEQ}}$-lossy PKE scheme, which realizes either a statistically hiding or an extractable commitment to $(\mathsf{id}, w)$. Our proofs of anonymity require statistically-hiding commitments (as in the real scheme). In our proofs of security against mis-identification attacks and framing attacks, we will switch $\mathsf{ct}_{(\mathsf{id},w)}$ to its extractable mode because we need to be able to extract the underlying $w$ and id.

In the signing algorithm, the group member next computes an evaluated HEC commitment $\mathsf{com}_{ev}$ of the predicate evaluation $C_M(\mathsf{id}, w)$ by homomorphically computing over $\mathsf{com}_{(\mathsf{id},w)}$ (note that $\mathsf{com}_{ev}$ need not be included in the signature since the verifier can recompute if from $\mathsf{com}_{(\mathsf{id},w)}$). Then, the signer computes a ciphertext $\mathsf{ct}_{\mathsf{id}}$ that verifiably encrypts a product $(1 - C_M(\mathsf{id}, w)) \cdot \mathsf{id}$ of his identity id and the logical NOT of $C_M(\mathsf{id}, w)$. When the predicate evaluates to $C_M(\mathsf{id}, w) = 0$, $\mathsf{ct}_{\mathsf{id}}$ is distributed as a lossy encryption[3] of id. When $C_M(\mathsf{id}, w) = 1$, $\mathsf{ct}_{\mathsf{id}}$ is completely independent of the signer's identity as it encrypts $0^{|\mathsf{id}|}$.

**Setup**$(1^\lambda, 1^N, \mathcal{P}_d)$**:** Given a security parameter $\lambda$, a predicate family $\mathcal{P}_d$ modeled by circuits of depth $d = d(\lambda)$ and the maximal number of group members $N = 2^\ell \in \mathsf{poly}(\lambda)$, do the following.

1. Generate a key pair $(\mathsf{pk}_{sig}, \mathsf{sk}_{sig}) \leftarrow \Pi^{\mathsf{sig}}.\mathsf{Kg}(1^\lambda)$ for the signature scheme. We assume that each public key has bitlength $\ell_{sig} \in \mathsf{poly}(\lambda)$.
2. Run $(\mathsf{pp}, \mathsf{ek}, \mathsf{msk}) \leftarrow \mathsf{HEC.Setup}(1^\lambda)$ to generate parameters for the homomorphic equivocal commitment, together with an evaluation key $\mathsf{ek}$ and a master key $\mathsf{msk}$.

---

[2] A context-hiding construction can still improve the efficiency by outputting partial openings in the clear in each signature.

[3] It is possible to compute $\mathsf{ct}_{\mathsf{id}}$ using an ordinary (i.e., non-lossy) PKE scheme but it requires to rely on the simulation-soundness of NIZK in the proof of Lemma 4.

3. Choose a one-time signature scheme $\Pi^{\mathsf{ots}} = (\mathsf{Kg}, \mathsf{Sign}, \mathsf{Verify})$ with verification key space $\{0,1\}^L$, for some $L \in \mathsf{poly}(\lambda)$.
4. Choose public parameters $\Gamma \leftarrow \Pi^{\mathsf{RLE}}.\mathsf{Par\text{-}Gen}(1^\lambda, 1^L, 1^B)$ for an $\mathcal{R}_{\mathsf{NEQ}}$-lossy PKE scheme with tag space $\mathcal{K} = \mathcal{T} = \{0,1\}^L$ and message length $B = \ell + \ell_w$, where $\ell_w \in \mathsf{poly}(\lambda)$ is the bitlength of witnesses from the witness space $\mathcal{W} = \{0,1\}^{\ell_w}$. Then, generate lossy keys $(\mathsf{pk}_{\mathsf{RLE}}, \mathsf{sk}_{\mathsf{RLE}}) \leftarrow \Pi^{\mathsf{RLE}}.\mathsf{LKeygen}(\Gamma, \mathbf{0}^L)$ for the initialization value $K = \mathbf{0}^L$.
5. Generate an injective key pair $(\mathsf{pk}_e, \mathsf{sk}_e) \leftarrow \Pi^{\mathsf{lpke}}.\mathsf{Keygen}(1^\lambda)$ for the standard lossy PKE scheme.
6. Generate a common reference string $\rho$ from $(\rho, \varsigma) \leftarrow \mathsf{NIZK}.\mathsf{Setup}(1^\lambda)$ for a dual-mode NIZK argument in its statistical ZK mode.

The algorithm outputs $(\mathcal{Y}, \mathcal{S}_{\mathsf{GM}}, \mathcal{S}_{\mathsf{OA}})$, where the group public key is as

$$\mathcal{Y} := \big(\rho, \mathsf{pk}_{sig}, (\mathsf{pp}, \mathsf{ek}), (\Gamma, \mathsf{pk}_{\mathsf{RLE}}), \mathsf{pk}_e\big),$$

the opening authority's private key is $\mathcal{S}_{\mathsf{OA}} := \mathsf{sk}_e$ and the private key of the group manager consists of $\mathcal{S}_{\mathsf{GM}} := \mathsf{sk}_{sig}$. $\mathcal{Y}$ implicitly initializes $St$.

**Join**$^{(\mathsf{GM}, \mathcal{U}_{\mathsf{id}})}$: the group manager and the prospective user $\mathcal{U}_{\mathsf{id}}$ run the following interactive protocol $[\mathsf{J}_{\mathsf{user}}(\lambda, \mathcal{Y}), \mathsf{J}_{\mathsf{GM}}(\lambda, St, \mathcal{Y}, \mathcal{S}_{\mathsf{GM}})]$:

1. User $\mathcal{U}_{\mathsf{id}}$ generates a key pair $(\mathsf{sk}_{\mathsf{id}}, \mathsf{pk}_{\mathsf{id}}) \leftarrow \Pi^{\mathsf{sig}}.\mathsf{Kg}(1^\lambda)$ and sends the public key $\mathsf{pk}_{\mathsf{id}}$ together with his identity id $\in \{0,1\}^\ell \backslash \{\mathbf{0}^\ell\}$ and an ordinary signature $sig_{\mathsf{id}} \leftarrow \Pi^{\mathsf{sig}}.\mathsf{Sign}(\mathsf{usk}[\mathsf{id}], (\mathsf{id}, \mathsf{pk}_{\mathsf{id}}))$ to GM.
2. $\mathsf{J}_{\mathsf{GM}}$ verifies that: id $\neq \mathbf{0}^\ell$; id was not previously used by a registered user; $sig_{\mathsf{id}}$ is a valid signature on (id, $\mathsf{pk}_{\mathsf{id}}$) w.r.t. $\mathsf{upk}[\mathsf{id}]$. It aborts if this is not the case. Otherwise, it computes $\mathsf{cert}_{\mathsf{id}} \leftarrow \Pi^{\mathsf{sig}}.\mathsf{Sign}(\mathsf{sk}_{sig}, (\mathsf{id}, \mathsf{pk}_{\mathsf{id}}))$ as a signature on the message (id, $\mathsf{pk}_{\mathsf{id}}$). The membership certificate $\mathsf{cert}_{\mathsf{id}}$ is sent to $\mathcal{U}_{\mathsf{id}}$. Then, $\mathsf{J}_{\mathsf{user}}$ verifies that $\Pi^{\mathsf{sig}}.\mathsf{Verify}(\mathsf{pk}_{sig}, (\mathsf{id}, \mathsf{pk}_{\mathsf{id}}), \mathsf{cert}_{\mathsf{id}}) = 1$. If this condition is not satisfied, $\mathsf{J}_{\mathsf{user}}$ aborts. Otherwise, $\mathsf{J}_{\mathsf{user}}$ defines the membership certificate as $\mathsf{cert}_{\mathsf{id}}$. The membership secret $\mathsf{sec}_{\mathsf{id}}$ is defined to be $\mathsf{sec}_{\mathsf{id}} = \mathsf{sk}_{\mathsf{id}}$. $\mathsf{J}_{\mathsf{GM}}$ stores $\mathsf{transcript}_{\mathsf{id}} = (\mathsf{id}, \mathsf{pk}_{\mathsf{id}}, \mathsf{cert}_{\mathsf{id}}, \mathsf{upk}[\mathsf{id}], sig_{\mathsf{id}})$ in the database $St_{\mathsf{trans}}$ of joining transcripts.

**Sign**(id, $\mathsf{cert}_{\mathsf{id}}, \mathsf{sec}_{\mathsf{id}}, M, w, P$): To sign a message $M \in \{0,1\}^{\ell_m}$ using the witness $w = w[1] \ldots w[\ell_w] \in \{0,1\}^{\ell_w}$ w.r.t. the predicate $P \in \mathcal{P}_d$, let $C_M : \{0,1\}^{\ell_w} \times \{0,1\}^\ell \rightarrow \{0,1\}$ be the message-dependent Boolean circuit of depth $\leq d$ that evaluates $P(M, \mathsf{id}, w)$ on input of $(w[1], \ldots, w[\ell_w], \mathsf{id}[1], \ldots, \mathsf{id}[\ell])$.

1. Generate a one-time signature key pair $(\mathsf{VK}, \mathsf{SK}) \leftarrow \Pi^{\mathsf{ots}}.\mathsf{Kg}(1^\lambda)$.
2. Choose $r_{\mathsf{id},w} \hookleftarrow R^{\mathsf{RLE}}$ in the randomness space of $\Pi^{\mathsf{RLE}}$ and encrypt the identity-witness pair (id, $w$) $\in \{0,1\}^{\ell+\ell_w}$ as an $\mathcal{R}_{\mathsf{NEQ}}$-lossy encryption

$$\mathsf{ct}_{(\mathsf{id},w)} = \Pi^{\mathsf{RLE}}.\mathsf{Encrypt}(\mathsf{pk}_{\mathsf{RLE}}, \mathsf{VK}, (\mathsf{id}, w); r_w) \tag{1}$$

under the tag $\mathsf{VK} \in \{0,1\}^L$.

3. Sample random coins $r^{\mathsf{hec}} \hookleftarrow \mathcal{D}^{\mathsf{HEC}}$ and compute a commitment

$$\mathsf{com}_{(\mathsf{id},w)} = \mathsf{HEC.Commit}(\mathsf{pp}, \mathsf{ek}, (\mathsf{id}, w); r^{\mathsf{hec}}). \qquad (2)$$

4. Using the homomorphic evaluation algorithm of HEC, compute

$$\pi_{C,M} \leftarrow \mathsf{HEC.Eval}^{in}(\mathsf{ek}, C_M, (\mathsf{id}, w), r^{\mathsf{hec}})$$
$$\mathsf{com}_{ev} = \mathsf{HEC.Eval}^{out}(\mathsf{ek}, C_M, \mathsf{com}_{(\mathsf{id},w)}).$$

5. Choose $r^{\mathsf{lpke}} \hookleftarrow R^{\mathsf{lpke}}$ and compute

$$\mathsf{ct}_{\mathsf{id}} = \Pi^{\mathsf{lpke}}.\mathsf{Encrypt}(\mathsf{pk}_e, (1 - c_{ev}) \cdot \mathsf{id}; r^{\mathsf{lpke}}), \qquad (3)$$

where $c_{ev} = C_M(w_1, \ldots, w_{\ell_w}, \mathsf{id}_1, \ldots, \mathsf{id}_\ell) \in \{0, 1\}$.
6. Generate $\sigma \leftarrow \Pi^{\mathsf{sig}}.\mathsf{Sign}(\mathsf{sk}_{\mathsf{id}}, (M, P, \mathsf{ct}_{(\mathsf{id},w)}))$ as a signature on the message $(M, P, \mathsf{ct}_{(\mathsf{id},w)})$.
7. Generate a NIZK argument $\vec{\pi} \leftarrow \mathsf{NIZK.Prove}(\rho, \vec{x}, \vec{w})$ for the statement $\vec{x}$ that there exists a witnesses $\vec{w}$ comprised of $(\mathsf{id}, w) \in \{0, 1\}^{\ell + \ell_w}$, $(\mathsf{pk}_{\mathsf{id}}, \mathsf{cert}_{\mathsf{id}}, \sigma) \in \mathcal{VK} \times \mathcal{S} \times \mathcal{S}$, $r_{\mathsf{id},w} \in R^{\mathsf{RLE}}$, $r^{\mathsf{hec}} \in R^{\mathsf{HEC}}$, $r^{\mathsf{lpke}} \in R^{\mathsf{lpke}}$, $c_{ev} \in \{0, 1\}$ and $\pi_{C,M}$, which satisfy the relations (1)–(3) as well as

$$\Pi^{\mathsf{sig}}.\mathsf{Verify}(\mathsf{pk}_{sig}, (\mathsf{id}, \mathsf{pk}_{\mathsf{id}}), \mathsf{cert}_{\mathsf{id}}) = 1$$
$$\Pi^{\mathsf{sig}}.\mathsf{Verify}(\mathsf{pk}_{\mathsf{id}}, (M, P, \mathsf{ct}_{(\mathsf{id},w)}), \sigma) = 1 \qquad (4)$$
$$\mathsf{HEC.Verify}(\mathsf{pp}, \mathsf{com}_{ev}, c_{ev}, \pi_{C,M}) = 1.$$

8. Compute $sig \leftarrow \Pi^{\mathsf{ots}}.\mathsf{Sign}(\mathsf{SK}, (\mathsf{ct}_{(\mathsf{id},w)}, \mathsf{com}_{(\mathsf{id},w)}, \mathsf{ct}_{\mathsf{id}}, \vec{\pi}))$.

Return the signature

$$\Sigma = (\mathsf{VK}, (\mathsf{ct}_{(\mathsf{id},w)}, \mathsf{com}_{(\mathsf{id},w)}, \mathsf{ct}_{\mathsf{id}}, \vec{\pi}), sig) \qquad (5)$$

**Verify**$(\mathcal{Y}, M, \Sigma, P)$: Parse $\Sigma$ as above. Return 1 if and only if: (i) $sig$ is a valid one-time signature on $(\mathsf{ct}_{(\mathsf{id},w)}, \mathsf{com}_{(\mathsf{id},w)}, C_{\mathsf{id}}, \vec{\pi})$ for the verification key $\mathsf{VK}$; (ii) The NIZK argument $\vec{\pi}$ properly verifies for the commitment $\mathsf{com}_{ev}$ publicly obtained as $\mathsf{com}_{ev} = \mathsf{HEC.Eval}^{out}(\mathsf{ek}, C_M, \mathsf{com}_{(\mathsf{id},w)})$.

**Open**$(\mathcal{Y}, \mathcal{S}_{\mathsf{OA}}, M, \Sigma, P, St)$: Given the opener's secret key $\mathcal{S}_{\mathsf{OA}} := \mathsf{sk}_e$, parse the signature $\Sigma$ as in (5). Compute $t_{\mathsf{id}} = \Pi^{\mathsf{lpke}}.\mathsf{Decrypt}(\mathsf{sk}_e, \mathsf{ct}_{\mathsf{id}})$. If $t_{\mathsf{id}} = \mathbf{0}^\ell$, return $\bot$. Otherwise, check if the string $t_{\mathsf{id}} \in \{0, 1\}^\ell$ appears in a record $(t_{\mathsf{id}}, \mathsf{transcript}_{\mathsf{id}} = (t_{\mathsf{id}}, \mathsf{pk}_{\mathsf{id}}, \mathsf{cert}_{\mathsf{id}}, \mathsf{upk}[\mathsf{id}], sig_{\mathsf{id}}))$ of $St_{\mathsf{trans}}$. If it does, output $\mathsf{id} = t_{\mathsf{id}} \in \{0, 1\}^\ell$ (and, optionally, $\mathsf{upk}[\mathsf{id}]$). Otherwise, output $\bot$.

In the full version, we provide details on instantiations from lattices and bilinear maps. The lattice-based construction is only a feasibility result based on generic NIZK for NP statements [42]. In the case of NC$^1$ circuits, the scheme can be instantiated with Groth-Sahai proofs [25] to provide much shorter signatures than using the Groth-Ostrovsky-Sahai techniques [24].

### 4.1  Branch-Soundness and Security

To prove security under our definitions, we first consider the following SimSetup and Extract algorithms associated to our BiAS construction.

**SimSetup**$(1^\lambda, 1^N, \mathcal{P}_d)$: This algorithm is exactly as Setup$(1^\lambda, 1^N, \mathcal{P}_d)$ except that steps 4 and 6 are modified in the following way:

4. Choose public parameters $\Gamma \leftarrow \Pi^{\mathsf{RLE}}.\mathsf{Par\text{-}Gen}(1^\lambda, 1^L, 1^B)$ for an $\mathcal{R}_{\mathsf{NEQ}}$-lossy PKE scheme with tag space $\mathcal{K} = \mathcal{T} = \{0,1\}^L$ and message length $B = \ell + \ell_w$, where $\ell_w \in \mathsf{poly}(\lambda)$ is the bitlength of witnesses from the witness space $\mathcal{W} = \{0,1\}^{\ell_w}$. Then, generate *injective* keys $(\mathsf{pk_{RLE}}, \mathsf{sk_{RLE}}) \leftarrow \Pi^{\mathsf{RLE}}.\mathsf{Keygen}(\Gamma, \mathbf{0}^L)$ for the initialization value $K = \mathbf{0}^L$.

6. Generate a common reference string $\rho$ from $(\rho, \xi) \leftarrow \mathsf{NIZK.ExtSetup}(1^\lambda)$ for an extractable (and thus statistically sound) NIZK proof system.

The algorithm returns the same output as Setup, together with an extraction trapdoor $\tau_{\mathsf{ext}} = (\mathsf{sk_{RLE}}, \xi)$, where $\xi$ is the extraction trapdoor of NIZK.

**Extract**$(\mathcal{Y}, \tau_{\mathsf{ext}}, M, \Sigma, P, St)$: Write $\Sigma$ as $\big(\mathsf{VK}, (\mathsf{ct}_{(\mathsf{id},w)}, \mathsf{com}_{(\mathsf{id},w)}, \mathsf{ct_{id}}, \vec{\pi}), sig\big)$ and return $\perp$ if its components do not parse properly. Otherwise, use $\mathsf{sk_{RLE}}$ to decrypt the $\mathcal{R}_{\mathsf{NEQ}}$-lossy PKE ciphertexts $\mathsf{ct}_{(\mathsf{id},w)}$ (recall that the NEQ relations makes all tags injective on a public key produced by Keygen for the initialization value $K = \mathbf{0}^\ell$). If any decryption fails, return $\perp$. Otherwise, output $w \in \{0,1\}^{\ell_w}$ and $\mathsf{id} \in \{0,1\}^\ell$.

The security properties of the NIZK argument system ensure that the common reference strings $\rho$ produced by NIZK.Setup and NIZK.ExtSetup are computationally indistinguishable. Moreover, in the $\mathcal{R}_{\mathsf{NEQ}}$-lossy PKE scheme, the public keys produced by LKeygen and Keygen are computationally indistinguishable as well.

Next, we will show that this extractable BiAS satisfies the extractable soundness notion unless the adversary can break the (statistical) soundness of the proof $\vec{\pi}$ included in a valid signature $\Sigma$.

**Theorem 1.** *The scheme satisfies branch-soundness if: (i) $\Pi^{\mathsf{RLE}}$ is a secure $\mathcal{R}_{\mathsf{NEQ}}$-lossy PKE scheme; (ii) NIZK is a dual-mode NIZK argument system (i.e., its statistically sound and statistically ZK modes are computationally indistinguishable); (iii) HEC is computationally binding for evaluated commitments.*

*Proof.* To prove the result, we consider a sequence of games. In each game, we call $W_i$ the event that the challenger outputs 1.

**Game 0:** This is the real experiment $\mathbf{Exp}_{\mathcal{A}}^{\mathsf{real}}(\lambda)$, where the adversary $\mathcal{A}$ is given $(\mathcal{Y}, \mathcal{S}_{\mathsf{GM}}, \mathcal{S}_{\mathsf{OA}})$, where $(St, \mathcal{Y}, \mathcal{S}_{\mathsf{GM}}, \mathcal{S}_{\mathsf{OA}}) \leftarrow \mathsf{Setup}(1^\lambda, 1^N)$. The adversary outputs a tuple $(M, \Sigma, P, st)$, where $\Sigma = \big(\mathsf{VK}, (\mathsf{ct}_{(\mathsf{id},w)}, \mathsf{com}_{(\mathsf{id},w)}, \mathsf{ct_{id}}, \vec{\pi}), sig\big)$. If $\Sigma$ does not verify, the challenger outputs 0. Otherwise, it runs Open to obtain $\mathsf{id}^\star \in \{0,1\}^\ell$ and feeds $\mathcal{A}$ with $\mathsf{id}^\star$. Then, the challenger outputs whatever $\mathcal{A}$ outputs. By definition, $\Pr[W_0] = \Pr[\mathbf{Exp}_{\mathcal{A}}^{\mathsf{real}}(\lambda) = 1]$.

**Game 1:** This game is identical to Game 0 except that, at step 4 of the Setup algorithm, the challenger computes $(\mathsf{pk}_{\mathsf{RLE}}, \mathsf{sk}_{\mathsf{RLE}}) \leftarrow \Pi^{\mathsf{RLE}}.\mathsf{Keygen}(\Gamma, \mathbf{0}^L)$ instead of $(\mathsf{pk}_{\mathsf{RLE}}, \mathsf{sk}_{\mathsf{RLE}}) \leftarrow \Pi^{\mathsf{RLE}}.\mathsf{LKeygen}(\Gamma, \mathbf{0}^L)$. By the first indistinguishability property of $\Pi^{\mathsf{RLE}}$, we have $|\Pr[W_1] - \Pr[W_0]| \in \mathsf{negl}(\lambda)$.

**Game 2:** This game is like Game 1 except that, at step 6 of the Setup algorithm, the challenger generates $(\rho, \xi) \leftarrow \mathsf{NIZK}.\mathsf{ExtSetup}(1^\lambda)$ instead of $(\rho, \zeta) \leftarrow \mathsf{NIZK}.\mathsf{Setup}(1^\lambda)$ and keeps the extraction trapdoor $\tau_{\mathsf{ext}} = (\mathsf{sk}_{\mathsf{RLE}}, \xi)$ to itself. By the dual-mode property of NIZK, the CRSes produced by NIZK.Setup and NIZK.ExtSetup have computationally indistinguishable distributions, thus ensuring that $|\Pr[W_2] - \Pr[W_1]| \in \mathsf{negl}(\lambda)$ for any PPT adversary $\mathcal{A}$.

**Game 3:** In this game, the challenger makes use of the trapdoor $\tau_{\mathsf{ext}} = (\mathsf{sk}_{\mathsf{RLE}}, \xi)$. When $\mathcal{A}$ outputs a tuple $(M, \Sigma, P, st)$, the challenger parses the signature $\Sigma$ as $\left(\mathsf{VK}, (\mathsf{ct}_{(\mathsf{id}, w)}, \mathsf{com}_{(\mathsf{id}, w)}, \mathsf{ct}_{\mathsf{id}}, \vec{\pi}), sig\right)$ and uses $\mathsf{sk}_{\mathsf{RLE}}$ to extract $(\mathsf{id}^\dagger, w^\dagger)$. From the NIZK proof $\vec{\pi}$, it uses $\xi$ to extract the witnesses $(\mathsf{id}, w) \in \{0, 1\}^{\ell_w + \ell}$, $(\mathsf{pk}_{\mathsf{id}}, \mathsf{cert}_{\mathsf{id}}, \sigma) \in \mathcal{VK} \times \mathcal{S} \times \mathcal{S}$, $r_{\mathsf{id}, w} \in R^{\mathsf{RLE}}$, $r^{\mathsf{hec}} \in R^{\mathsf{HEC}}$, $r^{\mathsf{lpke}} \in R^{\mathsf{lpke}}$, $c_{ev} \in \{0, 1\}$ and $\pi_{C,M}$. Then, the challenger halts and outputs a random bit if $c_{ev} \neq C_M(w_1, \dots, w_{\ell_w}, \mathsf{id}[1], \dots, \mathsf{id}[\ell])$.

We claim that $|\Pr[W_3] - \Pr[W_2]| \in \mathsf{negl}(\lambda)$ as the two games only differ when $\mathcal{A}$ breaks the computational binding property of HEC for evaluated commitments. Indeed, by the statistical soundness of NIZK on a CRS $\rho$ produced by NIZK.ExtSetup, we have $(\mathsf{id}, w) = (\mathsf{id}^\dagger, w^\dagger)$ and extracted witnesses satisfy the relations (1)–(3). In particular, we have $\mathsf{com}_{(\mathsf{id}, w)} = \mathsf{HEC}.\mathsf{Commit}(\mathsf{pp}, \mathsf{ek}, (\mathsf{id}, w); r^{\mathsf{hec}})$ and the extracted $c_{ev} \in \{0, 1\}$, $\pi_{C,M}$ satisfy $\mathsf{HEC}.\mathsf{Verify}(\mathsf{pp}, \mathsf{com}_{ev}, c_{ev}, \pi_{C,M}) = 1$, where $\mathsf{com}_{ev} = \mathsf{HEC}.\mathsf{Eval}^{out}(\mathsf{ek}, C_M, \mathsf{com}_{(\mathsf{id}, w)})$. It is easy to see that $\mathsf{Game}_3$ only differs from $\mathsf{Game}_2$ when the extracted $\pi_{C,M}$ differs from

$$\bar{\pi}_{C,M} \leftarrow \mathsf{HEC}.\mathsf{Eval}^{in}(\mathsf{ek}, C_M, (\mathsf{id}, w), r^{\mathsf{hec}}),$$

which is the value that would satisfy $\mathsf{HEC}.\mathsf{Verify}(\mathsf{pp}, \mathsf{com}_{ev}, C_M(w, \mathsf{id}), \bar{\pi}_{C,M}) = 1$. Hence, if $|\Pr[W_3] - \Pr[W_2]|$ is noticeable, the challenger can break the binding property of HEC by outputting $\left((\mathsf{id}, w), r^{\mathsf{hec}}, C_M, c_{ev}, \pi_{C,M}\right)$.

**Game 4:** This game is identical to Game 3 with the difference that, after having extracted $(\mathsf{id}, w)$, the challenger computes $C_M(w, \mathsf{id}) \in \{0, 1\}$, which is identical to the extracted $c_{ev} \in \{0, 1\}$ unless the failure event of Game 3 occurs. If $C_M(w, \mathsf{id}) = 0$, it overwrites $\mathsf{id}^\star \leftarrow \mathsf{Open}(\mathcal{S}_{\mathsf{OA}}, \mathcal{Y}, M, \sigma, P, St)$ with $\mathsf{id}^\star = \mathsf{id}$, which was extracted from $\mathsf{ct}_{(\mathsf{id}, w)}$. If $C_M(w, \mathsf{id}) = 1$, it sets $\mathsf{id}^\star = \perp$. In both cases, it feeds $\mathcal{A}$ with $\mathsf{id}^\star$ and returns whatever $\mathcal{A}$ outputs in reaction. This change does not modify the output distribution of $\mathcal{A}$ because, as long as $c_{ev} = C_M(w, \mathsf{id})$, the statistical soundness of $\vec{\pi}$ ensures that $\mathsf{ct}_{\mathsf{id}} = \Pi^{\mathsf{lpke}}.\mathsf{Encrypt}(\mathsf{pk}_e, (1 - C_M(w, \mathsf{id})) \cdot \mathsf{id}; r^{\mathsf{lpke}})$, where $r^{\mathsf{lpke}}$ and $\mathsf{id}$ are extracted from $\vec{\pi}$. Hence, unless $\mathcal{A}$ breaks the statistical soundness of $\vec{\pi}$, Game 4 eventually returns $\mathsf{id} = \perp$ or $\mathsf{id} = \mathsf{id}^\star$ to $\mathcal{A}$ whenever Game 3 does.

**Game 5:** This game is like Game 4 but we remove the restriction introduced in Game 3. Namely, the challenger does no longer replace $\mathcal{A}$'s output by a random bit when the witnesses $c_{ev} \in \{0,1\}$, $(\mathsf{id}, w) \in \{0,1\}^{\ell_w + \ell}$ extracted from $\vec{\pi}$ are such that $c_{ev} \neq C_M(w_1, \ldots, w_{\ell_w}, \mathsf{id}[1], \ldots, \mathsf{id}[\ell])$. The same arguments as those in the transition between the first two games show that $|\Pr[W_5] - \Pr[W_4]| \in \mathsf{negl}(\lambda)$ so long as HEC is computationally binding.

We conclude the proof by noting that Game 5 is identical to $\mathbf{Exp}_{\mathcal{A}}^{\mathrm{ext}}(\lambda)$, so that we have $|\Pr[\mathbf{Exp}_{\mathcal{A}}^{\mathrm{real}}(\lambda) = 1] - \Pr[\mathbf{Exp}_{\mathcal{A}}^{\mathrm{ext}}(\lambda) = 1]| = [\Pr[W_0] - \Pr[W_5]|$.     □

*Security Against Mis-Identification and Framing Attacks.*

**Lemma 2.** *The scheme is secure against misidentification attacks if: (i) $\Pi^{\mathrm{sig}}$ is existentially unforgeable under chosen-message attacks; (ii) The NIZK argument is computationally sound.* (The proof is given in the full version.)

**Lemma 3.** *The scheme is secure against framing attacks provided: (i) $\Pi^{\mathrm{sig}}$ is strongly unforgeable under chosen-message attacks; (ii) The NIZK argument is computationally sound.* (The proof is given in the full version.)

### 4.2   Branch-Hiding and Privacy

The branch-hiding property follows from the full anonymity of our scheme.

**Theorem 2.** *The scheme provides full anonymity if: $\Pi^{\mathrm{RLE}}$ and $\Pi^{\mathrm{lpke}}$ are secure $\mathcal{R}_{\mathrm{NEQ}}$-lossy PKE and standard lossy PKE schemes, respectively; (ii) NIZK is a computationally sound NIZK argument; (iii) $\Pi^{\mathrm{ots}}$ is strongly unforgeable.*

To prove Theorem 2, we separately consider the tracing and non-tracing modes. Lemma 4 first considers the former case where the adversary does not corrupt the opening authority. Lemma 5 shows that even an unbounded adversary is unable to distinguish group members' signatures in non-tracing mode.

**Lemma 4.** *The scheme provides anonymity in tracing mode assuming that: (i) $\Pi^{\mathrm{RLE}}$ is a secure $\mathcal{R}_{\mathrm{NEQ}}$-lossy PKE scheme; (ii) $\Pi^{\mathrm{lpke}}$ is a standard lossy PKE scheme; (ii) The NIZK argument system provides soundness; (iii) $\Pi^{\mathrm{ots}}$ is strongly unforgeable.* (The proof is given in the full version.)

**Lemma 5.** *The scheme provides statistical anonymity in non-tracing mode.*

*Proof.* Recall that experiment $\mathbf{Exp}_{\mathcal{A}}^{\mathrm{anon\text{-}ntr}\text{-}d}(\lambda)$ allows the adversary to obtain a challenge for the non-tracing mode. Namely, it is allowed to corrupt the opening authority and obtain $\mathcal{S}_{\mathsf{OA}}$ as long as, in the challenge phase, it chooses a pair $(M^\star, P^\star)$ and two tuples $(\mathsf{id}_0^\star, w_0^\star, \mathsf{sec}_0^\star, \mathsf{cert}_0^\star)$ and $(\mathsf{id}_1^\star, w_1^\star, \mathsf{sec}_1^\star, \mathsf{cert}_1^\star)$, such that $P^\star(M^\star, \mathsf{id}_0^\star, w_0^\star) = P^\star(M^\star, \mathsf{id}_1^\star, w_1^\star) = 1$. In this scenario, we will prove that, even after having obtained $\mathcal{S}_{\mathsf{OA}}$, an unbounded adversary $\mathcal{A}$ remains unable to infer anything about the bit $d \in \{0,1\}$ used by the challenger to compute the signature $\Sigma^\star = \left(\mathsf{VK}^\star, (\mathsf{ct}_{(\mathsf{id}, w)}^\star, \mathsf{com}_{(\mathsf{id}, w)}^\star, \mathsf{ct}_{\mathsf{id}}^\star, \vec{\pi}^\star), sig^\star\right)$ using $(\mathsf{id}_d^\star, w_d^\star, \mathsf{sec}_d^\star, \mathsf{cert}_d^\star)$.

To this end, we consider two statistically indistinguishable games. The first one is the real game whereas the second one appeals to the statistical honest-verifier zero-knowledge simulator of the argument system.

**Game**$^{(d)}$ 0: This is the real game, which is as in the proof of Lemma 4.

**Game**$^{(d)}$ 1: This game is like **Game**$^{(d)}$ 0 except that, in the challenge signature $\Sigma^\star$, we use the simulation trapdoor $\zeta$ generated from NIZK.Setup and the statistical NIZK simulator NIZK.Sim to generate $\vec{\pi}^\star$. Owing to the statistical ZK property of NIZK, the simulated $\vec{\pi}^\star$ is statistically close to a real $\vec{\pi}^\star$ that would be generated using the witnesses. Moreover, it is statistically independent of the witnesses used to compute $\mathsf{ct}^\star_{(\mathsf{id},w)}$, $\mathsf{com}^\star_{(\mathsf{id},w)}$ and $\mathsf{ct}^\star_{\mathsf{id}}$.

In **Game**$^{(d)}$ 1, we note that, when $C_{M^\star}(w_1^\star, \ldots, w_{\ell_w}^\star, \mathsf{id}_1^\star, \ldots, \mathsf{id}_\ell^\star) = 1$, the ciphertext $\mathsf{ct}^\star_{\mathsf{id}}$ is of the form $\mathsf{ct}^\star_{\mathsf{id}} = \Pi^{\mathsf{lpke}}.\mathsf{Encrypt}(\mathsf{pk}_e, \mathbf{0}^\ell; r^{\mathsf{lpke}\star})$, where $r^{\mathsf{lpke}\star} \hookleftarrow R^{\mathsf{lpke}}$, so that $\mathsf{ct}^\star_{\mathsf{id}}$ is independent of $d \in \{0,1\}$ although $\mathsf{pk}_e$ is an injective public key. Moreover, $\mathsf{ct}^\star_{(\mathsf{id},w)}$, $\mathsf{com}^\star_{(\mathsf{id},w)}$ statistically hide the underlying pair $(\mathsf{id}, w)$ since, by definition, the homomorphic equivocal commitment $\mathsf{com}^\star_{(\mathsf{id},w)}$ is statistically hiding and the $\mathcal{R}_{\mathsf{NEQ}}$-lossy encryption $\mathsf{ct}^\star_{(\mathsf{id},w)}$ is computed under a lossy key produced by LKeygen. □

**Acknowledgements.** Part of this research was funded by the French ANR ALAMBIC project (ANR-16-CE39-0006). This work was also supported in part by the European Union PROMETHEUS project (Horizon 2020 Research and Innovation Program, grant 780701). Khoa Nguyen was supported in part by the Gopalakrishnan - NTU PPF 2018, by A*STAR, Singapore under research grant SERC A19E3b0099, and by Vietnam National University HoChiMinh City (VNU-HCM) under grant number NCM2019-18-01. Thomas Peters is a research associate of the Belgian Fund for Scientific Research (F.R.S.-FNRS).

# References

1. Ajtai, M.: Generating hard instances of lattice problems. In: STOC (1996)
2. Bangerter, E., Camenisch, J., Lysyanskaya, A.: A cryptographic framework for the controlled release of certified data. In: Christianson, B., Crispo, B., Malcolm, J.A., Roe, M. (eds.) Security Protocols 2004. LNCS, vol. 3957, pp. 20–42. Springer, Heidelberg (2006). https://doi.org/10.1007/11861386_4
3. Bellare, M., Fuchsbauer, G.: Policy-based signatures. In: Krawczyk, H. (ed.) PKC 2014. LNCS, vol. 8383, pp. 520–537. Springer, Heidelberg (2014). https://doi.org/10.1007/978-3-642-54631-0_30
4. Bellare, M., Micciancio, D., Warinschi, B.: Foundations of group signatures: formal definitions, simplified requirements, and a construction based on general assumptions. In: Biham, E. (ed.) EUROCRYPT 2003. LNCS, vol. 2656, pp. 614–629. Springer, Heidelberg (2003). https://doi.org/10.1007/3-540-39200-9_38
5. Bellare, M., Shi, H., Zhang, C.: Foundations of group signatures: the case of dynamic groups. In: Menezes, A. (ed.) CT-RSA 2005. LNCS, vol. 3376, pp. 136–153. Springer, Heidelberg (2005). https://doi.org/10.1007/978-3-540-30574-3_11
6. Bender, A., Katz, J., Morselli, R.: Ring signatures: stronger definitions, and constructions without random oracles. J. Cryptol. **22**(1), 114–138 (2009)
7. Blum, M., Feldman, M., Micali, S.: Non-interactive zero-knowledge and its applications. In: STOC (1988)

8. Boneh, D., Boyen, X., Shacham, H.: Short group signatures. In: Franklin, M. (ed.) CRYPTO 2004. LNCS, vol. 3152, pp. 41–55. Springer, Heidelberg (2004). https://doi.org/10.1007/978-3-540-28628-8_3

9. Bootle, J., Cerulli, A., Chaidos, P., Ghadafi, E., Groth, J., Petit, C.: Short accountable ring signatures based on DDH. In: Pernul, G., Ryan, P.Y.A., Weippl, E. (eds.) ESORICS 2015. LNCS, vol. 9326, pp. 243–265. Springer, Cham (2015). https://doi.org/10.1007/978-3-319-24174-6_13

10. Bootle, J., Lyubashevsky, V., Seiler, G.: Algebraic techniques for short(er) exact lattice-based zero-knowledge proofs. In: Boldyreva, A., Micciancio, D. (eds.) CRYPTO 2019. LNCS, vol. 11692, pp. 176–202. Springer, Cham (2019). https://doi.org/10.1007/978-3-030-26948-7_7

11. Boyen, X.: Mesh signatures. In: Naor, M. (ed.) EUROCRYPT 2007. LNCS, vol. 4515, pp. 210–227. Springer, Heidelberg (2007). https://doi.org/10.1007/978-3-540-72540-4_12

12. Boyen, X., Delerablée, C.: Expressive subgroup signatures. In: Ostrovsky, R., De Prisco, R., Visconti, I. (eds.) SCN 2008. LNCS, vol. 5229, pp. 185–200. Springer, Heidelberg (2008). https://doi.org/10.1007/978-3-540-85855-3_13

13. Boyle, E., Goldwasser, S., Ivan, I.: Functional signatures and pseudorandom functions. In: Krawczyk, H. (ed.) PKC 2014. LNCS, vol. 8383, pp. 501–519. Springer, Heidelberg (2014). https://doi.org/10.1007/978-3-642-54631-0_29

14. Boyle, E., Segev, G., Wichs, D.: Fully leakage-resilient signatures. In: Paterson, K.G. (ed.) EUROCRYPT 2011. LNCS, vol. 6632, pp. 89–108. Springer, Heidelberg (2011). https://doi.org/10.1007/978-3-642-20465-4_7

15. Camenisch, J., Hohenberger, S., Lysyanskaya, A.: Compact e-cash. In: Cramer, R. (ed.) EUROCRYPT 2005. LNCS, vol. 3494, pp. 302–321. Springer, Heidelberg (2005). https://doi.org/10.1007/11426639_18

16. Camenisch, J., Hohenberger, S., Lysyanskaya, A.: Balancing accountability and privacy using e-cash (extended abstract). In: De Prisco, R., Yung, M. (eds.) SCN 2006. LNCS, vol. 4116, pp. 141–155. Springer, Heidelberg (2006). https://doi.org/10.1007/11832072_10

17. Canetti, R., et al.: Fiat-Shamir: from practice to theory. In: STOC (2019)

18. Chaum, D., van Heyst, E.: Group signatures. In: Davies, D.W. (ed.) EUROCRYPT 1991. LNCS, vol. 547, pp. 257–265. Springer, Heidelberg (1991). https://doi.org/10.1007/3-540-46416-6_22

19. Dodis, Y., Kiayias, A., Nicolosi, A., Shoup, V.: Anonymous identification in ad-hoc groups. In: Cachin, C., Camenisch, J.L. (eds.) EUROCRYPT 2004. LNCS, vol. 3027, pp. 609–626. Springer, Heidelberg (2004). https://doi.org/10.1007/978-3-540-24676-3_36

20. Fujisaki, E., Suzuki, K.: Traceable ring signature. In: Okamoto, T., Wang, X. (eds.) PKC 2007. LNCS, vol. 4450, pp. 181–200. Springer, Heidelberg (2007). https://doi.org/10.1007/978-3-540-71677-8_13

21. Garms, L., Lehmann, A.: Group signatures with selective linkability. In: Lin, D., Sako, K. (eds.) PKC 2019. LNCS, vol. 11442, pp. 190–220. Springer, Cham (2019). https://doi.org/10.1007/978-3-030-17253-4_7

22. Gentry, C., Sahai, A., Waters, B.: Homomorphic encryption from learning with errors: conceptually-simpler, asymptotically-faster, attribute-based. In: Canetti, R., Garay, J.A. (eds.) CRYPTO 2013. LNCS, vol. 8042, pp. 75–92. Springer, Heidelberg (2013). https://doi.org/10.1007/978-3-642-40041-4_5

23. Gorbunov, S., Vaikuntanathan, V., Wichs, D.: Leveled fully homomorphic signatures from standard lattices. In: STOC (2015)

24. Groth, J., Ostrovsky, R., Sahai, A.: Perfect non-interactive zero knowledge for NP. In: Vaudenay, S. (ed.) EUROCRYPT 2006. LNCS, vol. 4004, pp. 339–358. Springer, Heidelberg (2006). https://doi.org/10.1007/11761679_21
25. Groth, J., Sahai, A.: Efficient non-interactive proof systems for bilinear groups. In: Smart, N. (ed.) EUROCRYPT 2008. LNCS, vol. 4965, pp. 415–432. Springer, Heidelberg (2008). https://doi.org/10.1007/978-3-540-78967-3_24
26. Hofheinz, D., Ursu, B.: Dual-mode NIZKs from obfuscation. In: Galbraith, S.D., Moriai, S. (eds.) ASIACRYPT 2019. LNCS, vol. 11921, pp. 311–341. Springer, Cham (2019). https://doi.org/10.1007/978-3-030-34578-5_12
27. Katsumata, S., Nishimaki, R., Yamada, S., Yamakawa, T.: Exploring constructions of compact NIZKs from various assumptions. In: Boldyreva, A., Micciancio, D. (eds.) CRYPTO 2019. LNCS, vol. 11694, pp. 639–669. Springer, Cham (2019). https://doi.org/10.1007/978-3-030-26954-8_21
28. Kiayias, A., Tsiounis, Y., Yung, M.: Traceable signatures. In: Cachin, C., Camenisch, J.L. (eds.) EUROCRYPT 2004. LNCS, vol. 3027, pp. 571–589. Springer, Heidelberg (2004). https://doi.org/10.1007/978-3-540-24676-3_34
29. Kiayias, A., Yung, M.: Secure scalable group signature with dynamic joins and separable authorities. Int. J. Secur. Netw. 1(1), 24–45 (2006)
30. Kilian, J., Petrank, E.: Identity escrow. In: Krawczyk, H. (ed.) CRYPTO 1998. LNCS, vol. 1462, pp. 169–185. Springer, Heidelberg (1998). https://doi.org/10.1007/BFb0055727
31. Kiltz, E.: Chosen-ciphertext security from tag-based encryption. In: Halevi, S., Rabin, T. (eds.) TCC 2006. LNCS, vol. 3876, pp. 581–600. Springer, Heidelberg (2006). https://doi.org/10.1007/11681878_30
32. Kohlweiss, M., Miers, I.: Accountable tracing signatures. IACR Cryptology ePrint Archive, 2014:824 (2014)
33. Kohlweiss, M., Miers, I.: Accountable metadata-hiding escrow: a group signature case study. In: PoPETs (2015)
34. Libert, B., Nguyen, K., Passelègue, A., Titiu, R.: Simulation-sound arguments for LWE and applications to KDM-CCA2 security. In: Moriai, S., Wang, H. (eds.) ASIACRYPT 2020. LNCS, vol. 12491, pp. 128–158. Springer, Cham (2020). https://doi.org/10.1007/978-3-030-64837-4_5
35. Libert, B., Yung, M.: Non-interactive CCA-secure threshold cryptosystems with adaptive security: new framework and constructions. In: Cramer, R. (ed.) TCC 2012. LNCS, vol. 7194, pp. 75–93. Springer, Heidelberg (2012). https://doi.org/10.1007/978-3-642-28914-9_5
36. Liu, J., Wei, V., Wong, D.: Linkable spontaneous anonymous group signature for ad hoc groups. In: Wang, H., Pieprzyk, J., Varadharajan, V. (eds.) ACISP 2004. LNCS, vol. 3108, pp. 325–335. Springer, Heidelberg (2004). https://doi.org/10.1007/978-3-540-27800-9_28
37. Lyubashevsky, V.: Fiat-shamir with aborts: applications to lattice and factoring-based signatures. In: Matsui, M. (ed.) ASIACRYPT 2009. LNCS, vol. 5912, pp. 598–616. Springer, Heidelberg (2009). https://doi.org/10.1007/978-3-642-10366-7_35
38. Maji, H., Prabhakaran, M., Rosulek, M.: Attribute-based signatures. In: Kiayias, A. (ed.) CT-RSA 2011. LNCS, vol. 6558, pp. 376–392. Springer, Heidelberg (2011). https://doi.org/10.1007/978-3-642-19074-2_24
39. Naor, M.: Deniable ring authentication. In: Yung, M. (ed.) CRYPTO 2002. LNCS, vol. 2442, pp. 481–498. Springer, Heidelberg (2002). https://doi.org/10.1007/3-540-45708-9_31

40. Naor, M., Yung, M.: Public-key cryptosystems provably secure against chosen ciphertext attacks. In: STOC (1990)
41. Noether, S., Mackenzie, A.: Ring confidential transactions. Ledger **1**, 1–18 (2016)
42. Peikert, C., Shiehian, S.: Non-interactive zero knowledge for NP from (plain) learning with errors. In: Boldyreva, A., Micciancio, D. (eds.) CRYPTO 2019. LNCS, vol. 11692, pp. 89–114. Springer, Cham (2019). https://doi.org/10.1007/978-3-030-26948-7_4
43. Rackoff, C., Simon, D.: Non-interactive zero-knowledge proof of knowledge and chosen ciphertext attack. In: Feigenbaum, J. (ed.) CRYPTO 1991. LNCS, vol. 576, pp. 433–444. Springer, Heidelberg (1992). https://doi.org/10.1007/3-540-46766-1_35
44. Regev, O.: On lattices, learning with errors, random linear codes, and cryptography. In: STOC (2005)
45. Rivest, R., Shamir, A., Tauman, Y.: How to leak a secret. In: Boyd, C. (ed.) ASIACRYPT 2001. LNCS, vol. 2248, pp. 552–565. Springer, Heidelberg (2001). https://doi.org/10.1007/3-540-45682-1_32
46. Sakai, Y., Emura, K., Hanaoka, G., Kawai, Y., Matsuda, T., Omote, K.: Group signatures with message-dependent opening. In: Abdalla, M., Lange, T. (eds.) Pairing 2012. LNCS, vol. 7708, pp. 270–294. Springer, Heidelberg (2013). https://doi.org/10.1007/978-3-642-36334-4_18
47. Teranishi, I., Furukawa, J., Sako, K.: k-times anonymous authentication (extended abstract). In: Lee, P.J. (ed.) ASIACRYPT 2004. LNCS, vol. 3329, pp. 308–322. Springer, Heidelberg (2004). https://doi.org/10.1007/978-3-540-30539-2_22
48. Xu, S., Yung, M.: Accountable ring signatures: a smart card approach. In: Quisquater, J.-J., Paradinas, P., Deswarte, Y., El Kalam, A.A. (eds.) CARDIS 2004. IIFIP, vol. 153, pp. 271–286. Springer, Boston, MA (2004). https://doi.org/10.1007/1-4020-8147-2_18
49. Yang, R., Au, M.-H., Zhang, Z., Xu, Q., Yu, Z., Whyte, W.: Efficient lattice-based zero-knowledge arguments with standard soundness: construction and applications. In: Boldyreva, A., Micciancio, D. (eds.) CRYPTO 2019. LNCS, vol. 11692, pp. 147–175. Springer, Cham (2019). https://doi.org/10.1007/978-3-030-26948-7_6

# Abuse Resistant Law Enforcement Access Systems

Matthew Green[1]([⊠]), Gabriel Kaptchuk[2], and Gijs Van Laer[1]

[1] Johns Hopkins University, Baltimore, USA
mgreen@cs.jhu.edu, gijs.vanlaer@jhu.edu
[2] Boston University, Boston, USA
kaptchuk@bu.edu

**Abstract.** The increasing deployment of end-to-end encrypted communications services has ignited a debate between technology firms and law enforcement agencies over the need for lawful access to encrypted communications. Unfortunately, existing solutions to this problem suffer from serious technical risks, such as the possibility of operator abuse and theft of escrow key material. In this work we investigate the problem of constructing law enforcement access systems that mitigate the possibility of unauthorized surveillance. We first define a set of desirable properties for an abuse-resistant law enforcement access system (ARLEAS), and motivate each of these properties. We then formalize these definitions in the Universal Composability (UC) framework, and present two main constructions that realize this definition. The first construction enables *prospective* access, allowing surveillance only if encryption occurs after a warrant has been issued and activated. The second, more powerful construction, allows *retrospective* access to communications that occurred prior to a warrant's issuance. To illustrate the technical challenge of constructing the latter type of protocol, we conclude by investigating the minimal assumptions required to realize these systems.

## 1 Introduction

Communication systems are increasingly deploying end-to-end (E2E) encryption as a means to secure physical device storage and communications traffic. E2E encryption systems differ from traditional link encryption mechanisms in that keys are not available to service providers, but are instead held by endpoints: typically end-user devices such as phones or computers. This approach ensures that plaintext data cannot be accessed by providers and manufacturers, or by attackers who may compromise their systems. Widely-deployed examples include messaging protocols [6,73,78], telephony [4], and device encryption [5,43], with some systems deployed to billions of users.

The adoption of E2E encryption in commercial services has provoked a backlash from the law enforcement and national security communities around the world, based on concerns that encryption will hamper agencies' investigative

© International Association for Cryptologic Research 2021
A. Canteaut and F.-X. Standaert (Eds.): EUROCRYPT 2021, LNCS 12698, pp. 553–583, 2021.
https://doi.org/10.1007/978-3-030-77883-5_19

and surveillance capabilities [10,36,77]. The U.S. Federal Bureau of Investigation has mounted a high-profile policy campaign called "Going Dark" around these issues [34], and similar public outreach has been conducted by agencies in other countries [55]. These campaigns have resulted in legislative proposals in the United States [46,66,71] that seek to discourage the deployment of "warrant-proof" end-to-end encryption, as well as adopted legislation in Australia that requires providers to guarantee access to plaintext in commercial communication systems [76].

The various legislative proposals surrounding encryption have ignited a debate between technologists and policymakers. Technical experts have expressed concerns that these proposals, if implemented, will undermine the security offered by encryption systems [1,61,74], either by requiring unsafe changes or prohibiting the use of E2E encryption altogether. Law enforcement officials have, in turn, exhorted researchers to develop new solutions that resolve these challenges [10]. However, even the basic technical requirements of such a system remain unspecified, complicating both the technical and policy debates.

**Existing Proposals for Law Enforcement Access.** A number of recent and historical technical proposals have been advanced to resolve the technical questions raised by the encryption policy debate [13,14,30,55,68,75,79]. With some exceptions, the bulk of these proposals are variations on the classical *key escrow* [31] paradigm. In key escrow systems, one or more trusted authorities retain key material that can be used to decrypt targeted communications or devices.

Technologists and policymakers have criticized key escrow systems [1,33,62], citing concerns that, without additional protection measures, these systems could be abused to covertly conduct mass surveillance of citizens. Such abuses could result from a misbehaving operator or a compromised escrow keystore. Two recent policy working group reports [33,62] provide evidence that, at least for the case of communications services, these concerns are shared by members of the policy and national security communities.[1] Reflecting this consensus, recent high-profile technical proposals have limited their consideration only to the special case of *device encryption*, where physical countermeasures (*e.g.,* physical possession of a device, tamper-resistant hardware) can mitigate the risk of mass surveillance [14,68]. Unfortunately, expanding the same countermeasures to messaging or telephony software seems challenging.

**Abuse of Surveillance Mechanisms.** Escrow-based access proposals suffer from three primary security limitations. First, key escrow systems require the storage of valuable key material that can decrypt most communications in the system. This material must be accessible to satisfy law enforcement request, but must simultaneously be defended against sophisticated, nation-state supported

---

[1] The Carnegie Institution report [33] concludes that "In the case of data in motion, for example, our group could identify no approach to increasing law enforcement access that seemed reasonably promising to adequately balance all of the various concerns".

attackers. Second, in the event that key material is surreptitiously exfiltrated from a keystore, it may be difficult or impossible to detect its subsequent misuse. This is because escrow systems designed to allow lawful access to encrypted data typically store *decryption keys*, which can be misused without producing any detectable artifact.[2] Finally, these access systems require a human operator to interface between the digital escrow technology and the non-digital legal system, which raises the possibility of misbehavior by operators. These limitations must be addressed before any law enforcement access system can be realistically considered, as they are not merely theoretical: wiretapping and surveillance systems have proven to be targets for both nation-state attacks and operator abuse [19,44,60].

Overcoming these challenges is further complicated by law enforcement's desire to access data that was encrypted before an investigation is initiated. For example, several recent investigations requested the unlocking of suspects' phones or message traffic in the wake of a crime or terrorist attack [56]. Satisfying these requests would require *retrospectively* changing the nature of the encryption scheme used: ciphertext must be strongly protected before an investigation begins, but they must become accessible to law enforcement after an investigation begins. Satisfying these contradictory requirements is extraordinarily challenging without storing key material that can access all past ciphertexts, since a ciphertext may be created *before* it is known if there will be a relevant investigation in the future.

Law enforcement access systems that do not fail open in the face of lost key material or malicious operators have been considered in the past, *e.g.*, [13,16,79]. Bellare and Rivest [13] proposed a mechanism to build *probabilistic* law enforcement access, in order to mitigate the risk of mass surveillance. Wright and Varia [79] proposed cryptographic puzzles as a means to increase the financial cost of abuse. While these might be theoretically elegant solutions, such techniques have practical limitations that may hinder their adoption: law enforcement is unlikely to tolerate arbitrary barriers or prohibitive costs that might impede legitimate investigations. Moreover, these proposals do little to enable detection of key theft or to prevent more subtle forms of misuse.

**Towards Abuse Resistant Law Enforcement Access.** In this work, we explore if it is technically possible to limit abuse while giving law enforcement the capabilities they are truly seeking: quickly decrypting relevant ciphertexts during legally compliant investigations. To do this, we provide a new cryptographic definition for an *abuse resistant law enforcement access system*. This definition focuses on abuse resistance by weaving *accountability* features throughout the access process. More concretely, our goal is to construct systems that realize the following three main features:

---

[2] This contrasts with the theft of *e.g.*, digital certificates or signing keys, where abuse may produce artifacts such as fraudulent certificates [64] or malware artifacts that can be detected through Internet-wide surveillance.

- **Global Surveillance Policies.** To prohibit abuse by authorized parties, access systems must enforce specific and *fine-grained* global policies that restrict the types of surveillance that may take place. These policies could, for example, encompass limitations on the number of messages decrypted, the total number of targets, and the types of data accessed. They can be agreed upon in advance and made publicly available. This approach ensures that global limits can be developed that meet law enforcement needs, while also protecting the population against unlimited surveillance.
- **Detection of Abuse.** We require that any unauthorized use of escrow key material can be detected, either by the public or by authorized auditing parties. Achieving this goal ensures that even fully-adversarial use of escrow key material (*e.g.,* following an undetected key exfiltration) can be detected, and the system's security can be renewed through rekeying.
- **Operability.** At the same time, escrow systems must remain *operable*, in the sense that honest law enforcement parties should be able to access messages sent through a compliant system. We aim to guarantee this feature by ensuring that it is easy to verify that a message has been correctly prepared.

We stress that the notion of abuse-resistance is different from *impossible to abuse*. Under our definitions abuse may still happen, but the features described above will allow the abuse to be quickly identified and system security renewed. The most critical aspect of our work is that we seek to enforce these features *through the use of cryptography*, rather than relying on correct implementation of key escrow hardware or software, or proper behavior by authorities.

*Prospective vs. Retrospective Surveillance.* We will divide the access systems we discuss into two separate categories: *prospective* and *retrospective*. When using a *prospective* system, law enforcement may only access information encrypted sent or received from suspects *after* those suspects have been explicitly selected as targets for surveillance: this is analogous to "placing an alligator clip on a wire" in an analog wiretap. A *retrospective* access system, as described above, allows investigators to decrypt past communications, even those from suspects who were not the target of surveillance when encryption took place. Retrospective access clearly offers legitimate investigators more capabilities, but may also present a greater risk of abuse. Indeed, achieving accountable access in the challenging setting of retrospective key escrow, where encryption may take place *prior* to any use of escrow decryption keys, is one of the most technically challenging aspects of this work.

**Our Contributions.** More concretely, in this work we make the following contributions.

- **Formalizing security notions for abuse resistant law enforcement access systems.** We first provide a high-level discussion of the properties required to prevent abuse in a key escrow system, with a primary focus on the general data-in-motion setting: *i.e.,* we do not assume that targets possess trusted hardware. Based on this discussion, we formalize the roles and protocol interface of an Abuse-Resistant Law Enforcement Access System (ARLEAS): a message transmission framework that possesses law enforcement access capability with strong accountability guarantees. Finally, we provide an ideal functionality $\mathcal{F}_{ARLEAS}$ in Canetti's Universal Composability framework [21].

- **A prospective ARLEAS construction from non-interactive secure computation.** We show how to realize ARLEAS that is restricted to the case of *prospective* access: this restricts the use of ARLEAS such that law enforcement must commit to surveillance parameters before a target communication occurs. Each message contains a message for a non-interactive secure computation protocol [49] that will release plaintext only if law enforcement has activated a relevant warrant before encryption. We note that more simple and efficient constructions are possible if restrictions are put on warrants, *e.g.* warrants must list specific receivers; due to space constraints, we discuss these approaches in the full version of the paper.

- **A retrospective ARLEAS construction from proof-of-publication ledgers and extractable witness encryption.** We show how to realize ARLEAS that admits *retrospective* access, while still maintaining the auditability and detectability requirements of the system. The novel idea behind our construction is to use secure *proof-of-publication ledgers* to condition cryptographic escrow operations. The cryptographic applications of proof-of-publication ledgers have recently been explored (under slightly different names) in several works [25,45,51,69]. Such ledgers may be realized using recent advances in consensus networking, a subject that is part of a significant amount of research.

- **Evaluating the difficulty of retrospective systems.** Finally, we investigate the *minimal* assumptions for realizing retrospective access in an accountable law enforcement access system. As a concrete result, we present a lower-bound proof that any protocol realizing retrospective ARLEAS implies the existence of an extractable witness encryption scheme for some language $L$ which is related to the ledger functionality and policy functions of the system. While this proof does not imply that all retrospective ARLEAS realizations require extractable witness encryption for general languages (*i.e.*, it may be possible to construct languages that have trivial EWE realizations), it serves as a guidepost to illustrate the barriers that researchers may face in seeking to build accountable law enforcement access systems.

## 1.1   Towards Abuse Resistance

In this work we consider the problem of constructing secure message transmission protocols with abuse resistant law enforcement access, which can be seen as an extension of secure message transmission as formalized in the UC framework by Canetti [21,22]. Before discussing our technical contributions, we present the parties that interact with such a system and discuss several of the security properties we require.

**The ARLEAS Setting.** An ARLEAS system is comprised of three types of parties:

1. **Users:** Users employ a secure message transmission protocol to exchange messages with other users. From the perspective of these users, this system acts like a normal messaging service, with the additional ability to view public audit log information about the use of warrants on information sent through the system.
2. **Law Enforcement:** Law enforcement parties are responsible for initiating surveillance and accessing encrypted messages. This involves determining the scope of a surveillance request, obtaining a digital warrant, publishing transparency information, and then accessing the resulting data.
3. **Judiciary:** The final class of parties act as a check on law enforcement, determining whether a surveillance request meets the necessary legal requirements. In our system, any surveillance request must be approved by a judge before it is activated on the system. In our model we assume a single judge per system, though in practice this functionality can be distributed.

At setup time an ARLEAS system is parameterized by three functions, which we refer to as the global policy function, $p(\cdot)$, the warrant transparency function, $t(\cdot)$, and the warrant scope check function, $\theta(\cdot)$.[3] The purpose of these functions will become clear as we discuss operation and desired properties below. Finally, our proposals assume the existence of a verifiable, public broadcast channel, such as an append-only ledger. While this ledger may be operated by a centralized party, in practice we expect that such systems would be highly-distributed, *e.g.* using blockchain or consensus network techniques.

*ARLEAS Operation.* To initiate a surveillance request, law enforcement must first identify a specific class of messages (*e.g.* by metadata or sender/receiver); it then requests a surveillance warrant $w$ from a judge. The judge reviews the request and authorizes or rejects the request. If the judge produces an authorized warrant, law enforcement must take a final step to *activate* the warrant in order to initiate surveillance. This activation process is a novel element of an abuse resistant access scheme, and it is what allows for the detection of misbehavior. To enforce this, we require that activation of a warrant $w$ results in the publication of some information that is viewable by all parties in the system. This information consists of two parts: (1) a proof that the warrant is *permissible* in accordance with the global policy function, *i.e.* $p(w) = 1$, and (2) some transparency data associated with the warrant. The amount and nature of the transparency data to be published is determined by the warrant transparency function $t(w)$. Once the warrant has been activated, and the relevant information has been made public, law enforcement will be able to access any message that is within the scope of the warrant, as defined by the warrant scope check function $\theta(w)$.

---

[3] We later introduce a fourth parameterizing function, but omit it here for the clarity of exposition.

## 1.2   Technical Overview

We now present an overview of the key technical contributions of this work. We will consider this in the context of secure message transmission systems, which can be generalized to the setting of encrypted storage. Our overview will begin with intuition for building prospective ARLEAS, and then we will proceed to retrospective ARLEAS.

**Accountability From Ledgers.** For an ARLEAS the most difficult properties to satisfy are accountability and detectability. Existing solutions attempt to achieve this property by combining auditors and key escrow custodians; in order to retrieve key material that facilitates decryption, law enforcement must engage with an auditor. This solution, however, does not account for dishonest authorities, and is therefore vulnerable to covert key exfiltration and collusion. In our construction, we turn to public ledgers—a primitive that can be realized using highly-decentralized and auditable systems—as a way to reduce these trust assumptions.

Ledgers have the property that any party can access their content. Importantly, they also have the property that any parties can be convinced that other parties have access to these contents. Thus, if auditing information is posted on a ledger, all parties are convinced that that information is truly public. We note that using ledgers in this way is fundamentally different from prior work addressing encrypted communications; our ledger is a public functionality that does not need to have any escrow secrets. As such, if it is corrupted, there is no private state that can be exploited by an attacker.

**Warm up: Prospective ARLEAS.** To build to our main construction, we first consider the simpler problem of constructing a *prospective* access system, one that is capable of accessing messages that are sent subsequent to a warrant being activated.

A key aspect of this construction is that we consider a relatively flexible setting where parties have network access, and can receive periodic communications from escrow system operators prior to transmitting messages. We employ a public ledger for transmission of these messages, which provides an immutable record as well as a consistent view of these communications. The goal in our approach is to ensure that escrow updates embed information about the specifics of surveillance warrants that are active, while ensuring that even corrupted escrow parties cannot abuse the system.

**Prospective ARLEAS for Arbitrary Predicates.** The core intuition of our approach is to construct a "dual-trapdoor" public-key encryption system that senders can use to encrypt messages to specific parties. This scheme is designed with two ciphertexts $c_1$ and $c_2$, such that $c_1$ can be decrypted by the intended recipient using a normal secret key, while $c_2$ can be decrypted by law enforcement only if the recipient is under active surveillance, *i.e.* law enforcement has a warrant $w$ that applies to the message and has posted any necessary transparency information. A feature of this scheme is that for all recipients not the target of surveillance, $c_2$ should leak no information about the plaintext to law enforcement. In this work, we use non-interactive secure computation (NISC) [49], a reusable, non-interactive version of two-party computation to "encrypt" the ciphertext $c_2$. NISC for an arbitrary function $f$ allows a receiver to post an encryption of some secret $x_1$ such that all players can reveal $f(x_1, x_2)$ to the receiver with only one message, without revealing anything about $x_2$ beyond the output of the function.

In prospective surveillance, law enforcement must activate their warrant before it can be used to decrypt traffic. When activating a warrant, law enforcement computes the transparency information for their warrant info $\leftarrow t(w)$ along with the first message of the NISC scheme, embedding the warrant, and posts these onto the ledger. Whenever a sender sends a message $m$, they retrieve law enforcement's latest post, generate $c_1$ as using a normal public key encryption scheme and then generate $c_2$ which, using the NISC scheme, allows law enforcement to compute $f(w, (m, \mathsf{meta})) = m \wedge \theta(\mathsf{meta}, w)$, where $\theta(\cdot, \cdot)$ evaluates if the warrant applies to this particular message (we will discuss $\theta(\cdot, \cdot)$ in more detail in Sect. 3). Notice that if $\theta(\mathsf{meta}, w) = 0$, then the output of the NISC evaluation is uncorrelated with the message. However, if $\theta(\mathsf{meta}, w) = 1$, meaning law enforcement has been issued a valid warrant, then the message is recovered. We note that it is possible to construct a more concretely efficient scheme that uses lossy encryption instead of NISC, as long as warrants specify the *identity* of users; we discuss this construction in the full version of the paper.

**From Prospective to Retrospective.** The major limitation of the ARLEAS construction above is that it is fundamentally restricted to the case of *prospective* access. Abuse resistance derives from the fact that "activation" of a warrant results in a distribution of fresh encryption parameters to users, and each of these updates renders only a subset of communications accessible to law enforcement. A second drawback of the prospective protocol is that it requires routine communication between escrow authorities and the users of the system, which may not be possible in all settings.

Updating these ideas to provide *retrospective* access provides a stark illustration of the challenges that occur in this setting. In the retrospective setting, the space of targeted communications is unrestricted at the time that encryption takes place. By the time this information is known, both sender and recipient may have completed their interaction and gone offline. Using some traditional, key based solution to this problem implies the existence of powerful master decryption keys that can access *every* ciphertext sent by users of the system. Unfortunately, granting such power to any party (or set of parties) in our system is untenable; if this key material is compromised, any message can be decrypted without leaving a detectable artifact. The technical challenge in the retrospective setting is to find an alternative means to enable decryption, such that decryption is only possible on the conditions that (1) a relevant warrant has been issued that is compliant with the global policy function, (2) a detectable artifact has been made public. This mechanism must remain secure even when encryption occurs significantly before the warrant is contemplated.

*Ledgers as a Cryptographic Primitive.* A number of recent works [24,25,45,51, 69] have proposed to use public ledgers as a means to *condition* cryptographic operations on published events. This paradigm was initially used by Choudhuri *et al.* [25] to achieve fairness in MPC computations, while independently a variant was proposed by Goyal and Goyal [45] to construct one-time programs without the need for trusted hardware. Conceptually, these functionalities all allow decryption or program execution to occur only *after* certain information has been made public. This model assumes the existence of a secure global ledger $\mathcal{L}$ that is capable of producing a publicly-verifiable proof $\pi$ that a value has been made public on the ledger. In principle, this ledger represents an alternative form of "trusted party" that participates in the system. However, unlike the trusted parties proposed in past escrow proposals [30], ledgers do not store any decryption secrets. Moreover, recent advances in consensus protocols, and particularly the deployment of proof-of-work and proof-of-stake cryptocurrency systems. *e.g.,* [17,28,40,52], provide evidence that these ledgers can be operated safely at large scale.

Following the approach outlined by Choudhuri *et al.* [25], we make use of the ledger to *conditionally encrypt* messages such that decryption is only possible following the verifiable publication of the transparency function evaluated over a warrant on the global ledger. For some forms of general purpose ledgers that we seek to use in our system, this can be accomplished using extractable witness encryption (EWE) [18].[4] EWE schemes allow a sender to encrypt under a statement such that decryption is possible only if the decryptor knows of a witness $\omega$ that proves that the statement is in some language $L$, where $L$ parameterizes the scheme. While candidate schemes for witness encryption are known for specific languages (*e.g.* hash proof systems [26,39]), EWE for general languages is unlikely to exist [38].

*Building Retrospective ARLEAS from EWE.* Our retrospective ARLEAS construction assumes the existence of a global ledger that produces verification proofs $\pi$ that a warrant has been published to a ledger. As mentioned before, we aim to condition law enforcement access on the issuance of a valid warrant and the publication of a detectable artifact. In a sense, we want to use this published detectable artifact as a key to decrypt relevant ciphertexts. Thus, in this construction, a sender encrypts each message under a statement with a witness that shows evidence that these conditions have been met. This language reasons over (1) the warrant transparency function, (2) a function determining the relevance of the warrant to ciphertext, (3) the global policy function, (4) the judge's warrant approval mechanism, and (5) the ledger's proof of publication function.

**On the Requirement of EWE.** We justify the use of EWE in our construction by showing that the existence of a secure protocol realizing retrospective ARLEAS implies the existence of a secure EWE scheme for a related language that is deeply linked to the ARLEAS protocol. Intuitively, the witness for this

---

[4] Using the weaker witness encryption primitive may be possible if the ledger produces *unique* proofs of publication.

language should serve as proof that the protocol has been correctly executed; law enforcement should be able to learn information about a message if and only if the accountability and detectability mechanisms have been run. For the concrete instantiation of retrospective ARLEAS, we give in Sect. 6, this would include getting a valid proof of publication from the ledger. If the protocol is realized with a different accountability mechanism, the witness encryption language will reason over that functionality. No matter the details of the accountability mechanism, we note that it should be difficult for law enforcement to locally simulate the mechanism. If it were computationally feasible, then law enforcement would be able to circumvent the accountability mechanism with ease.

### 1.3   Contextualizing ARLEAS In The Encryption Debate

This work is motivated by the active global debate on whether to mandate law enforcement access to encrypted communication systems via key escrow. Reduced to its essentials, this debate incorporates two broad sub-questions. First: can mandatory key escrow be deployed safely? Secondly, if the answer to the first question is positive: *should it be deployed?*

We do not seek to address the second question in this work. Many scholars in the policy and technical communities have made significant efforts in tackling this issue [1,11,33,62] and we do not believe that the current work can make a substantial additional contribution. We stress, therefore, that our goal in this work is not to propose techniques for real-world deployment. Numerous practical questions and technical optimizations would need to be considered before ARLEAS could be deployed in practice.

Instead, the purpose of this work is to provide data to help policymakers address the first question. We have observed a growing consensus among stakeholders that key escrow systems should provide strong guarantees of information security as a precondition for deployment. Some stakeholders in the law-enforcement and national security communities grant that key escrow systems *should not be deployed* unless they can mitigate the risk of mass-surveillance via system abuse or compromise.[5] Unfortunately, there is no agreement on the definition of safety, and the technical community remains divided on whether traditional key escrow security measures (such as the use of secure hardware, threshold cryptography and policy safeguards) will be sufficient. We believe that the research community can help to provide answer these questions, and a failure to do so will increase the risk of unsound policy.

Our contribution in this paper is therefore to take a first step towards this goal. We attempt to formalize a notion of abuse-resilient key escrow, and to

---

[5] For evidence of this consensus, see *e.g.,* the 2018 National Academies of Sciences Report [62], which provides a framework for discussing such questions. See also a recent report by the Carnegie Endowment [33] which chooses to focus only on the problem of escrow for physical devices rather than data in motion, providing the following explanation: "it is much harder to identify a potential solution to the problems identified regarding data in motion in a way that achieves a good balance" (p. 10).

determine whether it can be realized using modern cryptographic techniques. Our work is focused on *feasibility*. With this perspective in mind, we believe that our work makes at least three necessary contributions to the current policy debate:

*Surface the notion of cryptographic abuse-resistance.* We raise the question of whether key escrow can be made *abuse resistant* using modern cryptographic technologies, and investigate what such a notion would imply. A key aspect of this discussion is the question of detectability: by making abuse and key exfiltration publicly detectable, we can test law enforcement's belief that back-door secrets can remain secure, and renew security by efficiently re-keying the system.

*Separate the problems of prospective and retrospective surveillance.* By emphasizing the technical distinctions between prospective and retrospective surveillance, we are able to highlight the design space in which it is realistic to discuss law enforcement access mechanisms. In particular, our technical results in this work illustrate the cryptographic implausibility of retrospective ARLEAS: this may indicate that retrospective surveillance systems are innately susceptible to abuse.

*Shift focus to public policy.* In defining and providing constructions for prospective and retrospective ARLEAS, we formalize the notion of a global policy function and a transparency function (see Sect. 3). By making these functions explicit, we hope to highlight the difficult policy issues that must be solved before deploying any access mechanism. As noted by Feigenbaum and Weitzner [35], there are limits what cryptography can contribute to this debate; legal and policy experts must do a better job reducing the gray area between rules and principles so that technical requirements can be better specified.

Finally, we note that the existence of a cryptographic construction for ARLEAS may not be sufficient to satisfy lawn enforcement needs. The mathematics for cryptographically strong encryption systems is already public and widespread, and determined criminals may simply implement their own secure messaging systems [32]. Alternatively, they may use steganography or pre-encrypt their messages with strong encryption to prevent "real" plaintext from being recovered by law enforcement while still allowing contacts to read messages [47]. These practical problems will likely limit the power of any ARLEAS and must be considered carefully by policy makers before pushing for deployment.

## 2    Related Work

The past decade has seen the start of academic work investigating the notion of accountability for government searches. Bates *et al.* [12] focus specifically on CALEA wiretaps and ensuring that auditors can ensure law enforcement compliance with court orders. In the direct aftermath of the Snowden leaks, Segal *et al.* [70] explored how governments could accountably execute searches without resorting to dragnet surveillance. Liu *et al.* [57] focus on making the number of searches more transparent, to allow democratic processes to balance social welfare and individual privacy. Kroll *et al.* [53,54] investigate different accountability mechanisms for key escrow systems, but stop short of addressing end-to-end encryption systems and the collusion problems we address in this work. Kamara [50] investigates cryptographic means of restructuring the NSA's metadata program. Backes considered anonymous accountable access control [7], while Goldwasser and Park [42] investigate similar notions with the limitation that policies themselves may be secret, due to national security concerns. Frankle *et al.* [37] make use of ledgers to get accountability for search procedures, but their solution cannot be extended to the end-to-end encryption setting. Wright and Varia [79] give a construction that uses cryptographic puzzles to impose a high cost for law enforcement to decrypt messages. Servan-Schreiber and Wheeler [72] give a construction for accountability that randomly selects custodians that law enforcement must access to decrypt a message. Panwar *et al.* [65] attempt to integrate the accountability systems closely with ledgers, but do not use the ledgers to address access to encryption systems. Finally, Scafuro [69] proposes a closely related concept of "break-glass encryption" and give a construction that relies on trusted hardware.

## 3   Definitions

*Notation.* Let $\lambda$ be an adjustable security parameter and $\mathsf{negl}(\lambda)$ be a negligible function in $\lambda$. We use $\|$ to denote concatenation, $\overset{c}{\approx}$ to denote computational indistinguishability, and $\overset{s}{\approx}$ to denote statistical indistinguishability. We will write $x \leftarrow \mathsf{Algo}(\cdot)$ to say that $x$ is a specific output of running the algorithm $\mathsf{Algo}$ on specific inputs and will write $x \in \mathsf{Algo}(\cdot)$ to indicate that $x$ is an element in the output distribution of $\mathsf{Algo}$, when run with honest random coins. We write $\mathsf{Algo}^{\mathsf{Par}}$ to say that the algorithm $\mathsf{Algo}$ is parameterized by the algorithm $\mathsf{Par}$.

*Defining ARLEAS.* We now formally define the notion of an Abuse-Resistant Law Enforcement Access System (ARLEAS). An ARLEAS is a form of message transmission scheme that supports accountable access by law enforcement officials. To emphasize the core functionality, we base our security definitions on the UC Secure Message Transmission ($\mathcal{F}_{\mathsf{SMT}}$) notion originally introduced by Canetti [21]. Indeed, our systems can be viewed as an extension of a multi-message SMT functionality [22], with added escrow capability.

*Parties and System Parameters.* An ARLEAS is an interactive message transmission protocol run between several parties and network components:

– User $P_i$: Users are the primary consumer of the end-to-end encrypted service or application. These parties, which may be numerous, interact with the system by sending messages to other users.

- Judge $P_J$: The judge is responsible for determining the validity of a search and issuing search warrants to law enforcement. The judge interacts with the system by receiving warrant requests and choosing to deny or approve the request.
- LawEnforcement $P_{LE}$: Law enforcement is responsible for conducting searches pursuant to valid warrants authorized by a judge. Law enforcement interacts with the system by requesting warrants from the judge and collecting the plaintext messages relevant to their investigations.

A concrete ARLEAS system also assumes the existence of a communication network that parties can use to transmit encrypted messages to other users. To support law enforcement access, it must be possible for law enforcement to "tap" this network and receive encrypted communications between targeted users. For the purposes of this exposition, we will assume that law enforcement agents have access to any communications transmitted over the network (*i.e.*, the network operates as a transparent channel.) In practice, a service provider would handle the transmissions of ciphertexts. This service provider would also be responsible for storing ciphertext and metadata, and providing this information to law enforcement. Our simplified model captures the worst case network security assumption, where the service provider cooperates with all law enforcement requests. Service providers would also be responsible for checking that messages sent by users are compliant with the law enforcement access protocol. We move this responsibility to the receiver for simplicity. We discuss the role of service providers in more detail in the full version.

An ARLEAS system is additionally parameterized by four functions, which are selected during a trusted setup phase:

- $t(w)$: the deterministic *transparency function* takes as input a warrant $w$ and outputs specific information about the warrant that can be published to the general public.
- $p(w)$: the deterministic *global policy* function takes as input a warrant $w$ and outputs 1 if this warrant is allowed by the system.
- $\theta(w, \mathsf{meta})$: the deterministic *warrant scope check* takes as input a warrant $w$ and per-message metadata $\mathsf{meta}$. It outputs 1 if $\mathsf{meta}$ is in scope of $w$ for surveillance.
- $v(\mathsf{meta}, aux)$: The deterministic *metadata verification functionality* takes as input metadata associated with some message $\mathsf{meta}$ and some auxiliary information $aux$ and determines if the metadata is correct. This auxiliary information could contain the ciphertext, global timing information, or some authenticated side channel information.

We discuss concrete instantiations of these functions in the full version of the paper.

*ARLEAS Scheme.* An ARLEAS scheme comprises a set of six possibly interactive protocols. We provide a complete API specification for these protocols in later sections:

- Setup. On input a security parameter, this trusted setup routine generates all necessary parameters and keys needed to run the full system.
- SendMessage. On input a message $m$, metadata meta, and a recipient identity, this protocol sends an encrypted message from one party to another.
- RequestWarrant. On input a description of the warrant request, this procedure allows law enforcement to produce a valid warrant.
- ActivateWarrant. Given a warrant $w$, this protocol allows law enforcement and a judge to confirm and activate a warrant.
- VerifyWarrantStatus. Given a warrant $w$, this protocol is used to verify that a warrant is valid and active.
- AccessMessage. In the retrospective case, this protocol is used by law enforcement to open a message.

*UC Ideal Functionality.* To define the properties of an ARLEAS system, we present a formal UC ideal functionality $\mathcal{F}_{\text{ARLEAS}}$ in Fig. 1. Recalling that ARLEAS can be instantiated in one of two modes, supporting only prospective or retrospective surveillance, we present a single definition that supports a parameter, mode $\in \{\text{pro}, \text{ret}\}$.

*Ideal World.* For any ideal-world adversary $\mathcal{S}$ with auxiliary input $z \in \{0,1\}^*$, input vector $x$, and security parameter $\lambda$, we denote the output of the ideal world experiment by $\mathbf{Ideal}_{\mathcal{S}, \mathcal{F}_{\text{ARLEAS}}^{v,t,p,\theta,\text{mode}}}(1^\lambda, x, z)$.

*Real World.* The real world protocol starts with the adversary $\mathcal{A}$ selecting a subset of the parties to compromise $\mathcal{P}^{\mathcal{A}} \subset \mathcal{P}$, where $\mathcal{P}^{\mathcal{A}} \subset \{\{P_i\}, \{P_{\text{LE}}\}, \{P_{\text{LE}}, P_J\}\}$, where we denote sender with $P_i$ and receiver with $P_j$. We limit the subsets of parties that can be compromised to these cases, because any other combination is trivial to simulate or can be deducted from the other cases. For example, if both $P_i$ and $P_j$ would be corrupted, there is nothing stopping them from not using the system. Moreover, we also don't consider the case where $P_J$ is the only corrupted party, this case is a more specific then when both $P_{\text{LE}}$ and $P_J$ are corrupted and $P_J$ on its own doesn't have any additional information to achieve anything different. All parties engage in a real protocol execution $\Pi$, the adversary $\mathcal{A}$ sends all messages on behalf of the corrupted parties and can choose any polynomial time strategy.

In a real world protocol we assume that communication between a sender $P_i$ and receiver $P_j$ happens over a transparent channel, meaning all other parties are able to receive all communication. We make this choice to simplify the protocol and security proofs. In the real world, this can be modeled with a service provider relaying messages between $P_i$ and $P_j$ that always complies with law enforcement requests and hands over encrypted messages when presented with a valid warrant. Note that this makes our modeling the worst case scenario, and therefore captures more selective service providers. Additionally, in practice, this service provider would validate if messages are well-formed to make sure $P_i$ and $P_j$ follow the real protocol.

For any adversary $\mathcal{A}$ with auxiliary input $z \in \{0,1\}^*$, input vector $x$, and security parameter $\lambda$, we denote the output of $\Pi$ by $\mathbf{Real}_{\mathcal{A},\Pi}(1^\lambda, x, z)$.

---

Functionality $\mathcal{F}_{\text{ARLEAS}}^{v,t,p,\theta,\text{mode}}$

---

The ideal functionality is parameterized by $\text{mode} \in \{\text{pro}, \text{ret}\}$, a metadata verification function $v : \{0,1\}^* \times \{0,1\}^* \to \{0,1\}$, the transparency function $t(\cdot)$, the global policy function $p(\cdot)$, and the warrant scope check functionality $\theta(\cdot, \cdot)$. The three latter functions are as defined above. We denote the session identifier as sid to separate different runs of the same protocol. We have several parties:

- $P_1, \ldots, P_n$: participants in the system
- $P_J$: the generator of a warrant
- $P_{\text{LE}}$: Law enforcement that can read the message given a valid warrant

**Send Message:** Upon receiving a message $(\text{SendMessage}, \text{sid}, P_j, m, \text{meta}, \text{valid})$ where $\text{valid} \in \{0, 1\}$ from party $P_i$, it sends $(\text{Sent}, \text{sid}, \text{meta})$ to the adversary. If $(\text{sid}, c)$ is received from the adversary,

- If $\text{valid} = 0$ or $v(\text{meta}, aux) = 0$, send $(\text{Sent}, \text{sid}, \text{meta}, c, m)$ to $P_i$ and send $(\text{Sent}, \text{sid}, \text{meta}, c, 0)$ to $P_{\text{LE}}$.
- If $\text{valid} = 1$, $v(\text{meta}, aux) = 1$, and there is no entry $w$ in the active warrant table $W_{\text{active}}$ send $(\text{Sent}, \text{sid}, \text{meta}, c, m)$ to $P_i$ and $P_j$, and send $(\text{Sent}, \text{sid}, \text{meta}, c)$ to $P_{\text{LE}}$.
- If $\text{valid} = 1$, $v(\text{meta}, aux) = 1$, and there is an entry $w$ in the active warrant table $W_{\text{active}}$ send $(\text{Sent}, \text{sid}, \text{meta}, c, m)$ to $P_i$, $P_j$, and $P_{\text{LE}}$.

Finally, store $(\text{Sent}, \text{sid}, \text{meta}, c, m)$ in the message table $M$.

**Request Warrant:** Upon receiving a message $(\text{RequestWarrant}, \text{sid}, w)$ from $P_{\text{LE}}$, the ideal functionality first checks if $p(w) = 1$, responding with $\perp$ and aborting if not. Otherwise, the ideal functionality sends $(\text{ApproveWarrant}, w)$ to $P_J$. If $P_J$ responds with $(\text{Disapprove})$, the trusted functionality sends $\perp$ to $P_{\text{LE}}$. If $P_J$ responds with $(\text{Approve})$, the trusted functionality sends $(\text{Approve})$ to $P_{\text{LE}}$, and stores the entry $w$ in the issued warrant table $W_{\text{issued}}$.

**Activate Warrant:** Upon receiving a message $(\text{ActivateWarrant}, \text{sid}, w)$ from $P_{\text{LE}}$, the ideal functionality checks to see if $w \in W_{\text{issued}}$, responding with $\perp$ and aborting if not. If $w \in W_{\text{issued}}$, the trusted functionality adds the entry $w$ to the active warrant table $W_{\text{active}}$, computes $t(w)$, and sends $(\text{NotifyWarrant}, t(w))$ to all parties and the adversary.

**Verify Warrant Status:** Upon receiving message $(\text{VerifyWarrantStatus}, \text{sid}, c, \text{meta}, w)$ from $P_{\text{LE}}$, if $\text{mode} = \text{pro}$, the ideal functionality responds with $\perp$ and aborts. Otherwise, if $(\text{Sent}, \text{sid}, \text{meta}, c, m) \in M$ and $w \in W_{\text{active}}$ such that $\theta(w, \text{meta}) = 1$, the ideal functionality returns 1. Finally, if $\theta(w, \text{meta}) = 0$ or $w \notin W_{\text{active}}$, it returns 0.

**Access message:** Upon receiving message $(\text{AccessData}, \text{sid}, c, \text{meta}, w)$ from $P_{\text{LE}}$, if $\text{mode} = \text{pro}$, the ideal functionality responds with $\perp$ and aborts. Otherwise, if $(\text{Sent}, \text{sid}, \text{meta}, c, m) \in M$ and $w \in W_{\text{active}}$ such that $\theta(w, \text{meta}) = 1$, the ideal functionality returns $m$. Finally, if $\theta(w, \text{meta}) = 0$, it returns 0.

**Fig. 1.** Ideal functionality for an Abuse Resistant Law Enforcement Access System.

---

### Protocol $\mathbf{Real}_{\mathcal{A},\Pi}(1^{\lambda}, x, z)$

$\mathbf{Real}_{\mathcal{A},\Pi}(1^{\lambda}, x, z)$ is parameterized by the protocol $\Pi$ = (Setup, SendMessage, RequestWarrant, ActivateWarrant, VerifyWarrantStatus, AccessMessage) and a variable mode $\in$ {pro, ret}.

1. When $\mathbf{Real}_{\mathcal{A},\Pi}(1^{\lambda}, x, z)$ is initialized, then all parties engage in the interactive protocol $\Pi$.Setup
2. When $P_i$ is activated with (SendMessage, sid, $P_j$, $m$, 1), parties $P_i$, $P_j$, and $P_{\mathrm{LE}}$ engage in the interactive protocol $\Pi$.SendMessage. $P_{\mathrm{LE}}$ learns some metadata meta about the message.
3. When $P_i$ is activated with (SendMessage, sid, $P_j$, $m$, 0), parties $P_i$, and $P_{\mathrm{LE}}$ engage in the interactive protocol $\Pi$.SendMessage (with $P_j$ not getting output). $P_{\mathrm{LE}}$ learns some metadata meta about the message.
4. When $P_{\mathrm{LE}}$ is activated with (RequestWarrant, sid, $\hat{w}$), parties $P_{\mathrm{LE}}$ and $P_J$ engage in the interactive protocol $\Pi$.RequestWarrant.
5. When $P_{\mathrm{LE}}$ is activated with (ActivateWarrant, sid, $w$), all parties engage in the interactive protocol $\Pi$.ActivateWarrant.
6. When $P_{\mathrm{LE}}$ is activated with (VerifyWarrantStatus, sid, $c$, meta, $w$), if mode = pro, $P_{\mathrm{LE}}$ returns $\bot$. Otherwise, $P_{\mathrm{LE}}$ calls the non-interactive functionality $\Pi$.VerifyWarrantStatus($c$, meta, $w$)
7. When $P_{\mathrm{LE}}$ is activated with (AccessData, sid, $c$, meta, $w$), if mode = pro, $P_{\mathrm{LE}}$ returns $\bot$. Otherwise, $P_{\mathrm{LE}}$ calls the non-interactive functionality $\Pi$.AccessMessage($c$, meta, $w$)

---

**Fig. 2.** The real world experiment for a protocol implementing $\mathcal{F}_{\mathrm{ARLEAS}}^{v,t,p,\theta,\mathrm{mode}}$

---

**Functionality** $\mathcal{L}^{\mathsf{Verify}}$

**GetCounter**: Upon receiving (GetCounter) from any party, return $\ell$.

**Post**: Upon receiving (Post, $x$), the trusted party increments $\ell$ by 1, computes the proof of publication $\pi_{\mathsf{publish}}$ on $(\ell\|x)$ such that $\mathsf{Verify}((\ell\|x), \pi_{\mathsf{publish}}) = 1$. Add the entry $(\ell, x, \pi_{\mathsf{publish}})$ to the entry table $T$. Respond with $(\ell, x, \pi_{\mathsf{publish}})$

**GetVal**: Upon receiving (GetVal, $\ell$), check if there is an entry $(\ell, x, \pi_{\mathsf{publish}})$ in the entry table $T$. If not, return $\bot$. Otherwise, return $(\ell, x, \pi_{\mathsf{publish}})$.

---

**Fig. 3.** Ideal functionality for a proof-of-publication ledger, from [25].

**Definition 1.** *A protocol $\Pi$ is said to be a secure ARLEAS protocol computing $\mathcal{F}_{ARLEAS}^{v,t,p,\theta,mode}$ if for every PPT real-world adversary $\mathcal{A}$, there exists an ideal-world PPT adversary $\mathcal{S}$ corrupting the same parties such that for every input $x$ and auxiliary input $z$ it holds that*

$$\mathbf{Ideal}_{\mathcal{S}, \mathcal{F}_{ARLEAS}^{v,t,p,\theta,mode}}(1^{\lambda}, x, z) \stackrel{c}{\approx} \mathbf{Real}_{\mathcal{A},\Pi}(1^{\lambda}, x, z)$$

$\pi_{PRO}^{v,t,p,\theta}$.Setup:

- All users send (CRS) to $\mathcal{F}_{CRS}^{\Pi_{NIZK}}$.ZKSetup to retrieve the common reference string for the NIZK scheme and all users send (CRS) to $\mathcal{F}_{CRS}^{\Pi_{NISC}}$.GenCRS to retrieve the common reference string for the NISC scheme $CRS_{NISC}$.
- Each user $P_j$ computes $(pk_j, sk_j) \leftarrow \Pi_{Enc}$.KeyGen($1^\lambda$) and sends $pk_j$ to $P_{LE}$ and to each $P_i$ via $\mathcal{F}_{AUTH}$.
- The judge $P_J$ computes $(pk_{sign}, sk_{sign}) \leftarrow \Pi_{Sign}$.KeyGen($1^\lambda$) and send $pk_{sign}$ to all other users via $\mathcal{F}_{AUTH}$.
- Law enforcement $P_{LE}$ runs $\pi_{PRO}^{v,t,p,\theta}$.ActivateWarrant with an empty set $\emptyset$ as the valid warrants.

$\pi_{PRO}^{v,t,p,\theta}$.SendMessage :

- The sender $P_i$ computes the ciphertext $(c_1, c_2, \pi, \text{meta})$ as follows, and sends it to $P_j$ and $P_{LE}$ via $\mathcal{F}_{AUTH}$:
  - Send (GetCounter) to $\mathcal{L}^{Verify}$ and receive the current counter $\ell$. Then query $\mathcal{L}^{Verify}$ on (GetVal, $\ell$) to receive the latest posting $(\ell, x, \pi_{publish})$. Parse $x$ as $(nisc_1^{public}, \pi, info)$. If $\Pi_{NIZK}$.ZKVerify($nisc_1^{public}, info, \pi$) = 0 or $\mathcal{L}^{Verify}$.Verify($\ell \| (nisc_1^{public}, \pi, info), \pi_{publish}$) = 0 return $\perp$ and halt.
  - $c_1 \leftarrow \Pi_{Enc}$.Enc($pk_j, m; r_1$), where $r_1 \xleftarrow{\$} \{0,1\}^\lambda$
  - Create meta
  - $nisc_2 \leftarrow \Pi_{NISC}$.NISC$_2$($CRS_{NISC}, I_{|info|}, (m, \text{meta}), nisc_1^{public}; r_2$), where $r_2 \xleftarrow{\$} \{0,1\}^\lambda$
  - $c_2 \leftarrow nisc_2$
  - Use $\Pi_{NIZK}$.ZKProve to compute $\pi$ such that

$$\pi \leftarrow NIZK \left\{ (m, r_1, r_2) : \begin{array}{l} c_1 = \Pi_{Enc}.\text{Enc}(pk_j, m; r_1) \wedge \\ c_2 = \Pi_{NISC}.\text{NISC}_2(CRS_{NISC}, I_{|info|}, (m, \text{meta}), nisc_1^{public}; r_2) \end{array} \right\}$$

- Upon receiving $c$ from $P_i$, $P_j$ calls $\pi_{PRO}^{v,t,p,\theta}$.VerifyMessage on $c$. If the output is 1, then recover the message as $m \leftarrow \Pi_{Enc}$.Dec($sk_j, c_2$)
- Upon receiving $c$ from $P_i$, $P_{LE}$ calls $\pi_{PRO}^{v,t,p,\theta}$.VerifyMessage on $c$. If the output is 1, then recover the message as $m \leftarrow \Pi_{NISC}$.Evaluate($CRS_{NISC}, nisc_2, nisc_1^{private}$)

$\pi_{PRO}^{v,t,p,\theta}$.VerifyMessage :

- Any party parses $(c_1, c_2, \pi, \text{meta}) \leftarrow c$ and verifies that $\pi$ is correct and computes $v(\text{meta}, aux)$, aborting if the output is 0. Otherwise, output 1.

$\pi_{PRO}^{v,t,p,\theta}$.RequestWarrant:

- $P_{LE}$ sends (RequestWarrant, $\hat{w}$) to $P_J$ via $\mathcal{F}_{AUTH}$. $P_J$ then either decides to send (Disapprove) to $P_{LE}$ and halt or executes the following:
  - Verify that $p(\hat{w}) = 1$. If not send (Disapprove) to $P_{LE}$ and abort.
  - $\sigma \leftarrow \Pi_{Sign}$.Sign($sk_{sign}, \hat{w}$)
  - Send the signed warrant $w = (\hat{w}, \sigma)$ to $P_{LE}$ via $\mathcal{F}_{AUTH}$.

$\pi_{PRO}^{v,t,p,\theta}$.ActivateWarrant:

- $P_{LE}$ adds the new warrant $w$ to the set of valid warrants $\mathcal{W}$. Let $w^* = w_1 \| \ldots \| w_{|\mathcal{W}|}$ for $w_i = (\hat{w}_i, \sigma_i) \in \mathcal{W}$.
- $(nisc_1^{public}, nisc_1^{private}) \leftarrow \Pi_{NISC}$.NISC$_1$($CRS_{NISC}, w^*; r$) and record $nisc_1^{private}$
- Compute info $\leftarrow \{t(w) | w \in \mathcal{W}\}$
- Use $\Pi_{NIZK}$.ZKProve to compute $\pi$ such that

$$\pi \leftarrow NIZK \left\{ (\mathcal{W}, nisc_1^{private}, r) : \begin{array}{l} info = \{t(w) | w \in \mathcal{W}\} \wedge \\ (nisc_1^{public}, nisc_1^{private}) \leftarrow \Pi_{NISC}.\text{NISC}_1(CRS_{NISC}, w^*; r) \wedge \\ \forall (\hat{w}, \sigma) \in \mathcal{W}, \Pi_{Sign}.\text{Verify}(pk_{sign}, \hat{w}, \sigma) = p(\hat{w}) = 1 \end{array} \right\}$$

- Send (Post, $(nisc_1^{public}, \pi, info)$) to $\mathcal{L}^{Verify}$ and receive $(\ell, x, \pi_{publish})$.

**Fig. 4.** Our construction of a protocol $\pi_{PRO}^{v,t,p,\theta}$ that UC-realizes $\mathcal{F}_{ARLEAS}^{v,t,p,\theta,pro}$

# 4   Building Blocks

***Proof-of-Publication Ledgers.*** Our work makes use of a public append-only ledger that can produce a publicly-verifiable *proof of publication*. This concept was formalized by Goyal *et al.* [45], Choudhuri *et al.* [25], and Kaptchuk *et al.* [51], but related ideas have also been previously used by Liu *et al.* to realize time-lock encryption [58]. Plausible candidates for such ledgers have been the subject of great interest, due to the deployment of blockchains and other consensus networks [59]. Significant work has been done to formalize the notion of a public, append-only ledger [8,9,24,45] and study its applications to cryptographic protocols [3,15,25]. This work uses a simplified ledger interface formalized in [25] that abstracts away details such as timing information and temporary inconsistent views that are modeled in [9]. However, this simplified view captures the *eventual* functionality of the complex models, and is therefore equivalent for our purposes (Fig. 2).

The ledger ideal functionality is provided in Fig. 3. This functionality allows users to post arbitrary information to the ledger; this data is associated with a particular index on the ledger, with which any user can retrieve the original data as well as a proof of publication. For security, our functionality encodes a notion we refer to as *ledger unforgeability*, which requires that there exists an algorithm to verify a proof that a message has been posted to the ledger, and that adversaries cannot forge this proof.

***Authenticated Communication.*** We use a variant of Canetti's ideal functionality for authenticated communication, $\mathcal{F}_{AUTH}$, to abstract the notion of message authentication [21]. Due to space constraints, we omit the ideal functionality in this shortened version. Since we restrict our analysis to static corruption, we simplify this functionality to remove the adaptive corruption interface.[6]

***Simulation Extractable Non-interactive Zero Knowledge.*** In our protocols we require non-interactive zero knowledge proofs of knowledge that are simulation extractable. To preserve space, we refer the reader to the definitions of Sahai [67] and De Santis *et al.* [29]. Rather than rely on UC functionalities, we employ a NIZK directly in our protocols.

***Multi-sender Non-interactive Secure Computation.*** When instantiating our prospective protocol for arbitrary predicates in Sect. 5, we will require the use of Non-interactive Secure Computation (NISC) [2,49]. In NISC, a receiver can post an encryption embedding a secret $x_1$ such that senders with secret $x_2$ can reveal $f(x_1, x_2)$ to the receiver by sending only a single message. Realizing such a scheme (see [49]) is feasible in the CRS model [21,23] from two-round, UC-secure malicious oblivious transfer [27,63], Yao's garbled circuits [48], and generic non-interactive zero knowledge (see Sect. 4). The resulting protocols,

---

[6] Note that this ideal functionality only handles a single message transfer, but to achieve multiple messages, we rely on universal composition and use multiple instances of the functionality.

however, are very inefficient and require non-blackbox use of the underlying cryptographic primitives. While this is sufficient for our purposes, we note that depending on specific functionality required in an instantiation of ARLEAS, it may be possible to use more efficient constructions (*i.e.* depending on the size of the predicate circuit, etc.) Because the notation for NISC protocols varies, we fix it for this work below. We omit the ideal functionality of multi-sender NISC from [2], due to space constraints. Because we require non-blackbox use of the primitive, we will use it directly rather than as a hybrid.

**Definition 2 (Multi-sender Non-interactive Secure Computation).** *A garbling scheme for a functionality* $f : \{0,1\}^{\mathsf{input}_1} \times \{0,1\}^{\mathsf{input}_2} \to \{0,1\}^{\mathsf{output}}$ *is a tuple of PPT algorithms* $\Pi_{NISC} := (\mathsf{GenCRS}, \mathsf{NISC}_1, \mathsf{NISC}_2, \mathsf{Evaluate})$ *such that*

- $\mathsf{GenCRS}(1^\lambda, \mathsf{input}; r) \to (\mathsf{CRS}_{\mathsf{NISC}}, \tau_{\mathsf{NISC}})$: *GenCRS takes the security parameter* $1^n$ *and outputs a CRS, along with a simulation backdoor* $\tau_{\mathsf{NISC}}$. *When we explicitly need to specify the randomness, we will include it as $r$ as here.*
- $\mathsf{NISC}_1(\mathsf{CRS}_{\mathsf{NISC}}, x_1; r) \to (\mathsf{nisc}_1^{public}, \mathsf{nisc}_1^{private})$: *NISC$_1$ takes in the CRS and an input* $x \in \{0,1\}^{\mathsf{input}_1}$ *and outputs the first message NISC$_1$. When we explicitly need to specify the randomness, we will include it as $r$ as here.*
- $\mathsf{NISC}_2(\mathsf{CRS}_{\mathsf{NISC}}, f, x_2, \mathsf{nisc}_1^{public}; r) \to \mathsf{nisc}_2$: *NISC$_2$ takes in the CRS, a circuit* $C$, *an input* $x_2 \in \{0,1\}^{\mathsf{input}_2}$ *and the first garbled circuit message* $\mathsf{nisc}_1^{public}$. *It outputs the second message* $\mathsf{nisc}_2$. *When we explicitly need to specify the randomness, we will include it as $r$ as here.*
- $\mathsf{Evaluate}(\mathsf{CRS}_{\mathsf{NISC}}, \mathsf{nisc}_2, \mathsf{nisc}_1^{private})$: *Evaluate takes as input the second GC message* $\mathsf{nisc}_2$ *along with the private information* $\mathsf{nisc}_1^{private}$ *and outputs* $y \in \{0,1\}^{\mathsf{output}}$ *or the error symbol* $\perp$

*We omit the ideal world security definition for multi-sender NISC, due to space constraints. It can be found in [2].*

***Witness Encryption and Extractable Witness Encryption.*** Our *retrospective* constructions require extractable witness encryption (EWE) [18], a variant of witness encryption in which the existence of a distinguisher can be used to construct an extractor for the necessary witness [41]. While EWE is a strong assumption, in later sections of this work we show that it is a minimal requirement for the existence of retrospective ARLEAS.

To preserve space we give the formal definition in the full version of our paper and we describe it informally here. An extractable witness encryption scheme is parameterized by an NP-language $L$ and has two algorithms $\Pi_{\mathrm{EWE}} = (\mathsf{Enc}, \mathsf{Dec})$. Encryption uses a statement $x$ to encrypt a plaintext message $m$, while decryption uses a witness $\omega$ such that $(x, \omega) \in \mathcal{R}_L$ to recover the plaintext.

This scheme has two properties: correctness and extractable security. Correctness implies decryption recovers the plaintext if the witness is valid. Extractable security says that if an adversary can distinguish between two encrypted messages, there exists an extractor that can extract the witness of the statement.

$\pi_{RET}^{v,t,p,\theta}$.Setup:

- All users send (CRS) to $\mathcal{F}_{CRS}^{\Pi_{NIZK}}$.ZKSetup to retrieve the common reference string for the NIZK scheme.
- $P_J$ computes $(\mathsf{pk_{sign}}, \mathsf{sk_{sign}}) \leftarrow \Pi_{Sign}$.KeyGen$(1^\lambda)$ and sends $\mathsf{pk_{sign}}$ to all other users via $\mathcal{F}_{AUTH}$.

$\pi_{RET}^{v,t,p,\theta}$.SendMessage:

- The sender $P_i$ computes the ciphertext $(c_1, c_2, c_3, \pi, \mathsf{meta})$ as follows, and sends it to $P_j$ and $P_{LE}$ via $\mathcal{F}_{AUTH}$:
  - Sample $r \leftarrow \{0,1\}^\lambda$
  - Query the random oracle to obtain the hashes:
    $(\mathsf{HashConfirm}, r_1) \leftarrow \mathcal{G}_{pRO}(\mathsf{HashQuery}, (\text{"ENC"} \| r \| m))$,
    $(\mathsf{HashConfirm}, r_2) \leftarrow \mathcal{G}_{pRO}(\mathsf{HashQuery}, (\text{"WE"} \| r \| m))$, and
    $(\mathsf{HashConfirm}, r_3) \leftarrow \mathcal{G}_{pRO}(\mathsf{HashQuery}, (\text{"RP"} \| r))$
  - $c_1 \leftarrow \Pi_{Enc}$.Enc$(pk, r; r_1)$, $c_2 \leftarrow \Pi_{EWE}$.Enc$(\mathsf{meta}, r; r_2)$, and $c_3 \leftarrow m \oplus r_3$
  - Use $\Pi_{NIZK}$.ZKProve to compute $\pi \leftarrow NIZK\{(r, r_1, r_2) : c_1 = \Pi_{Enc}.\mathsf{Enc}(pk_j, r; r_1) \wedge c_2 = \Pi_{EWE}.\mathsf{Enc}(\mathsf{meta}, r; r_2)\}$
- Upon receiving (send, $c$), $P_j$ performs the following steps:
  - Call $\pi_{RET}^{v,t,p,\theta}$.VerifyMessage on $c$, aborting if the output is 0;
  - Compute $r' \leftarrow \Pi_{Enc}$.Dec$(sk_j, c_1)$
  - $(\mathsf{HashConfirm}, r_3) \leftarrow \mathcal{G}_{pRO}(\mathsf{HashQuery}, (\text{"RP"} \| r'))$
  - Compute $m' \leftarrow c_3 \oplus r_3$
  - $(\mathsf{HashConfirm}, r_1) \leftarrow \mathcal{G}_{pRO}(\mathsf{HashQuery}, (\text{"ENC"} \| r' \| m'))$
  - $(\mathsf{HashConfirm}, r_2) \leftarrow \mathcal{G}_{pRO}(\mathsf{HashQuery}, (\text{"WE"} \| r' \| m'))$
  - Then to verify that the message has not been mauled, $P_j$ recomputes $c_1' \leftarrow \Pi_{Enc}$.Enc$(pk_j, r'; r_1)$ and $c_2' \leftarrow \Pi_{EWE}$.Enc$(\mathsf{meta}, r'; r_2)$. If $c_1 \neq c_1'$ or $c_2 \neq c_2'$, return $\perp$. Otherwise, return $m'$.
- Upon receiving (send, $c$), $P_{LE}$ calls $\pi_{RET}^{v,t,p,\theta}$.VerifyMessage on $c$, aborting if the output is 0, and then calls $\pi_{RET}^{v,t,p,\theta}$.AccessMessage on $c$.

$\pi_{RET}^{v,t,p,\theta}$.VerifyMessage :

- Any party parses $(c_1, c_2, c_3, \pi, \mathsf{meta}) \leftarrow c$ and verifies that $\pi$ is correct and computes $v(\mathsf{meta}, aux)$, aborting if the output is 0. Otherwise, output 1.

$\pi_{RET}^{v,t,p,\theta}$.RequestWarrant:

- $P_{LE}$ sends (RequestWarrant, $\hat{w}$) to $P_J$ via $\mathcal{F}_{AUTH}$. $P_J$ then either decides to send (Disapprove) to $P_{LE}$ and halt or executes the following:
  - Verify that $p(\hat{w}) = 1$. If not send (Disapprove) to $P_{LE}$ and abort.
  - $\sigma \leftarrow \Pi_{Sign}$.Sign$(wsk, \hat{w})$
  - Send the signed warrant $w = (\hat{w}, \sigma)$ to $P_{LE}$ via $\mathcal{F}_{AUTH}$.

$\pi_{RET}^{v,t,p,\theta}$.ActivateWarrant:

- $P_{LE}$ computes info $\leftarrow t(w)$; uses $\Pi_{NIZK}$.ZKProve to compute $\pi \leftarrow NIZK\{(w) : w = (\hat{w}, \sigma), \Pi_{Sign}.\mathsf{Verify}(pk_{sign}, \hat{w}, \sigma) = 1 \wedge \mathsf{info} \leftarrow t(w)\}$; and sends (Post, (info, $\pi$)) to $\mathcal{L}^{Verify}$. It receives and returns $(\ell, \mathsf{info}, \pi_{publish})$.

$\pi_{RET}^{v,t,p,\theta}$.VerifyWarrantStatus:

- $P_{LE}$ calls $\Pi_{EWE}$.Dec$(c_2, \mathsf{meta}, (\hat{w}, \sigma), (\ell, \mathsf{info}, \pi_{publish}))$. If the output is $\perp$, return 0. Otherwise, return 1.

$\pi_{RET}^{v,t,p,\theta}$.AccessMessage:

- $P_{LE}$ computes $r' \leftarrow \Pi_{EWE}$.Dec$(c_2, \mathsf{meta}, (\hat{w}, \sigma), (\ell, \mathsf{info}, \pi_{publish}))$.
- $(\mathsf{HashConfirm}, r_3) \leftarrow \mathcal{G}_{pRO}(\mathsf{HashQuery}, (\text{"RP"} \| r'))$
- Recovers $m' \leftarrow c_3 \oplus r_3$.
- $(\mathsf{HashConfirm}, r_1) \leftarrow \mathcal{G}_{pRO}(\mathsf{HashQuery}, (\text{"ENC"} \| r' \| m'))$
- $(\mathsf{HashConfirm}, r_2) \leftarrow \mathcal{G}_{pRO}(\mathsf{HashQuery}, (\text{"WE"} \| r' \| m'))$
- Recomputes $c_1' \leftarrow \Pi_{Enc}$.Enc$(pk_j, r'; r_1)$ and $c_2' \leftarrow \Pi_{EWE}$.Enc$(\mathsf{meta}, r'; r_2)$. If $c_1' = c_1$ and $c_2' = c_2$, $P_{LE}$ returns $m'$ and $\perp$ otherwise.

**Fig. 5.** Our construction of a protocol $\pi_{RET}^{v,t,p,\theta}$ that UC-realizes $\mathcal{F}_{ARLEAS}^{v,t,p,\theta,\mathsf{ret}}$

***Programmable Global Random Oracle Model.*** The security proof for our retrospective construction makes use of the programmable global random oracle model, introduced in [20]. We omit the ideal functionality $\mathcal{G}_{pRO}$ from [20] due to space constraints.

# 5    Prospective Solution

In this section we describe a prospective ARLEAS scheme, which supports arbitrary predicates. Recall that the key feature of the prospective case is that warrants must be activated *before* targets perform encryption. A key implication of this setting is that new cryptographic material can be generated and distributed to users each time law enforcement updates the set of active warrants. The technical challenge, therefore, is to ensure that this material is distributed in such a way that the surveillance it permits is *accountable*, without revealing to targets any confidential information about which messages are being accessed.

For generality, our main construction supports targeting by allowing warrants to specify an arbitrary predicate over the *metadata* of a transmitted messages. In practice, we realize this functionality through the use of public ledgers and non-interactive secure computation techniques.

## 5.1    UC-Realizing $\mathcal{F}_{ARLEAS}^{v,t,p,\theta,pro}$ for Arbitrary Predicates

To realize prospective ARLEAS, each user must encrypt each message in two separate forms. The first ciphertext uses standard PKE ciphertext to encrypt the message directly to the recipient, as is standard in many end-to-end encrypted messaging systems. The second ciphertext represents a "law enforcement access field" that is designed to permit authorized surveillance. To construct the second ciphertext, we require a mechanism that enables law enforcement access if and only if the warrant is active and valid for the specific message metadata being transmitted. To ensure that the transmission is consistent (*i.e.*, the plaintexts contained in each ciphertext is the same), the two ciphertexts are bound together by using non-interactive zero knowledge proof of knowledge that can be verified by all parties in the system.

Our construction relies on non-interactive secure computation (NISC) [49]. Recall that a NISC scheme for some function $f$ allows a receiver to post an encryption of some secret $x_1$ such that all players can reveal $f(x_1, x_2)$ to the receiver with only one message, without revealing anything about $x_2$ beyond the output of the function. For the following construction, we require a NISC scheme for the function $I_k$, defined as $I_k((w_1, w_2, \ldots, w_k), (m, \text{meta})) = m \wedge (\theta(\text{meta}, w_1) \vee \ldots \vee \theta(\text{meta}, w_k))$.

This function evaluates the warrant scope check functionality on the metadata over $k$ different warrants. If any of them evaluate to true, the message is output. Otherwise, $I_k$ outputs 0. Note that the number of warrants is an explicit parameter of the function and its circuit representation.

Law enforcement begins by posting the first message of the NISC scheme, embedding as input their $k$ warrants, along with the transparency information and proof of correctness. Senders generate and send the ciphertext $(c_1, c_2, \pi)$, generated as follows. $c_1$ remains a normal public key ciphertext for the recipient. $c_2$ is the second message of the NISC scheme, for the function $I_k$ and embedding the inputs $m$, meta. Most known realizations of NISC rely on garbled circuits, with the second message containing the garbling of the intended function and hardcoding the sender's inputs. $\pi$ is a zero-knowledge proof demonstrating that the two ciphertexts contain the same message and that they were each generated correctly with respect to the first message of the NISC.

Upon receiving the resulting ciphertext, law enforcement can attempt to decrypt by evaluating the NISC ciphertext. By the security of the NISC scheme, law enforcement will only learn information about the plaintext if they have a relevant warrant and posted the required transparency information, accomplishing our goal.

We give a description of the prospective ARLEAS protocol $\pi_{\text{PRO}}^{v,t,p,\theta}$ in Fig. 4.

**Theorem 1.** *Assuming a CCA secure public key encryption scheme $\Pi_{Enc}$, a SUF-CMA secure signature scheme $\Pi_{Sign}$, a NIZK scheme $\Pi_{NIZK}$, and an NISC scheme $\Pi_{NISC}$, $\pi_{PRO}^{v,t,p,\theta}$ (presented in Fig. 4) UC-realizes $\mathcal{F}_{ARLEAS}^{v,t,p,\theta,pro}$ initialized in prospective mode in the $\mathcal{L}^{\text{Verify}}$, $\mathcal{F}_{CRS}^{\Pi_{NIZK}.\text{ZKSetup}}$, $\mathcal{F}_{CRS}^{\Pi_{NISC}.\text{GenCRS}}$, $\mathcal{F}_{AUTH}-hybrid$ model.*

**Security Proof.** We give the security proof in the full version of the paper. The simulator is straight forward, taking advantage of the NIZKs and the NISC to facilitate extraction. The proof first simulates just a user, then law enforcement, and then both the judge and law enforcement.

# 6    Retrospective Solution

In the previous section we proposed a protocol to realize ARLEAS under the restriction that access would be prospective only. That protocol requires that law enforcement must activate a warrant and post the resulting parameters on the ledger before any targeted communication occurs. In this section we address the retrospective case. The key difference in this protocol is that law enforcement may activate a warrant at any stage of the protocol, even after a target communication has occurred.

In this setting we assume law enforcement has a way of getting messages that were sent in the past. As described before, we take the simplifying assumption that messages automatically get send to law enforcement. In practice, either a service provider can forward them, after checking the warrant. One can try to avoid surveillance by using expiring messages, but service providers can be forced to keep encrypted messages for a certain period of time. Or law enforcement can actively record messages in transit.

Our construction makes use of an extractable witness encryption scheme $\Pi_{\mathrm{EWE}}$ to encrypt the law enforcement ciphertext $c_2$. This scheme is parameterized by a language $L_{\mathrm{EWE}}$ that is defined with respect to the transparency function $t(\cdot)$, the policy function $p(\cdot)$, the targeting function $\theta(\cdot,\cdot)$, the warrant signing key $\mathsf{pk}_{\mathsf{sign}}$, and the ledger verification function $\mathcal{L}.\mathsf{Verify}$, as follows:

$$
L_{\mathrm{EWE}} = \left\{ \mathsf{meta} \;\middle|\; \exists w, (t, \mathsf{info}, \pi_{\mathsf{publish}}) \text{ s.t. } \begin{array}{l} w = (\hat{w}, \sigma), \mathcal{L}.\mathsf{Verify}((\ell\|\mathsf{info}), \pi_{\mathsf{publish}}) = 1, \\ \mathsf{info} = t(w), \Pi_{\mathsf{Sign}}.\mathsf{Verify}(\mathsf{pk}_{\mathsf{sign}}, \hat{w}, \sigma) = 1, \\ p(\hat{w}) = 1, \theta(\hat{w}, \mathsf{meta}) = 1 \end{array} \right\}
$$

Intuitively, these ciphertexts can only be decrypted by law enforcement once they have performed all the accountability tasks required by the ARLEAS.

We will describe our protocol in a hybrid model that makes use of several functionalities. These include $\mathcal{L}$, $\mathcal{F}_{CRS}^{D}$, $\mathcal{G}_{\mathsf{pRO}}$ and $\mathcal{F}_{AUTH}$.

## 6.1 UC-Realizing $\mathcal{F}_{\mathrm{ARLEAS}}^{v,t,p,\theta,\mathsf{ret}}$

We give a description of the retrospective ARLEAS protocol $\pi_{\mathrm{RET}}^{v,t,p,\theta}$ in Fig. 5.

**Theorem 2.** *Assuming a CCA-secure public key encryption scheme $\Pi_{Enc}$, an extractable witness encryption scheme for $L_{EWE}$, a SUF-CMA secure signature scheme $\Pi_{Sign}$, and a simulation-extractable NIZK scheme $\Pi_{NIZK}$, $\pi_{RET}^{v,t,p,\theta}$ (presented in Fig. 5) UC-realizes $\mathcal{F}_{ARLEAS}^{v,t,p,\theta,\mathsf{ret}}$ in the $\mathcal{L}^{\mathsf{Verify}}, \mathcal{F}_{CRS}^{\Pi_{NIZK}.\mathsf{ZKSetup}}, \mathcal{G}_{\mathsf{pRO}}-hybrid$ model.*

**Security Proof.** We show the full security proof in the full version of the paper. The proof proceed similarly to the prospective case, with the exception that the simulator needs to equivocate on the context of ciphertexts once law enforcement is able to decrypt them. This equivocation is facilitated by the random oracle.

# 7  On the Need for Extractable Witness Encryption

The retrospective solution we present in Sect. 6 relies on extractable witness encryption. Intuitively, this strong assumption is required in our construction because a user must encrypt in a way that decryption is only possible under certain circumstances. Because the description of these circumstances can be phrased as an NP relation, witness encryption represents a "natural" primitive for realizing it. However, thus far we have not shown that the use of extractable witness encryption is *strictly* necessary. Given the strength (and implausibility [38]) of the primitive, it is important to justify its use. We do this by showing that any protocol $\Pi_A$ that UC-realizes $\mathcal{F}_{ARLEAS}^{v,t,p,\theta,\mathsf{ret}}$ implies the existence of extractable witness encryption for a related language. Notice that this does not mean the existence of a particular ARLEAS instantiation implies the existence of generic extractable witness encryption scheme, but rather a specific, non-trivial scheme.

Before proceeding to formally define this related language, we give some intuition about its form. We wish to argue that a protocol $\Pi_A$ *acts like* an extractable witness encryption scheme in the specific case where an adversary has corrupted the escrow authorities $P_{LE}$ and $P_J$ (along with an arbitrary number of unrelated users). Recall that in order to learn any information about a message sent in $\Pi_A$, the following conditions must be met: specifically, law enforcement must correctly run the protocol for $\Pi_A$.RequestWarrant and $\Pi_A$.ActivateWarrant such that if $\Pi_A$.VerifyWarrantStatus were to be called, it would output 1.[7] For the protocol we presented in Sect. 6, this corresponds to obtaining a correct proof of publication from the ledger. Importantly, it must be impossible for law enforcement and judges to generate this information independently; if it were possible, it would be easy for these parties to circumvent the accountability mechanism.

We give a formal definition of this language $L$ below. We denote the view of a user $P_i$ as $\mathcal{V}_{P_i}$, where this view is a collection of the views of running all algorithms that appear. We abuse notation slightly and denote the protocol transcript resulting from a sender $P_S$ sending a message $m$ to $P_R$ as $\Pi_A$.SendMessage$(\cdot, P_S, P_R, m)$

$$
L = \left\{ (\text{meta}, \text{sid}) \,\middle|\, \exists \left( w, c, \left\{ \begin{array}{c} \mathcal{V}_{P_{LE}}, \mathcal{V}_{P_J}, \\ \{\mathcal{V}_{P_i}\}_{P_i \in \{P_1, \ldots, P_n\}/\{P_S, P_R\}} \end{array} \right\} \right) \right\} \text{ s.t.}
$$
$$
\left. \begin{array}{r} c, \text{meta} \leftarrow \Pi_A.\text{SendMessage}(\text{sid}, P_S, P_R, m), \\ (\text{Approve}) \leftarrow \Pi_A.\text{RequestWarrant}(\text{sid}, w), \\ (\text{NotifyWarrant}, t(w)) \leftarrow \Pi_A.\text{ActivateWarrant}(\text{sid}, w), \\ 1 \leftarrow \Pi_A.\text{VerifyWarrantStatus}(\text{sid}, w, \text{meta}, c) \end{array} \right\}
$$

In this language, the statement comprises some specified metadata and a valid instance of the protocol $\Pi_A$ from the perspectives of the parties $P_{LE}, P_J$, and the users $P_i$ without the sender and receiver. This setup specifies all the relevant components of the protocol (including the ledger functionality, in the case of the protocol presented in Sect. 6). The witness is a valid transcript starting with that setup, that includes the sending party sending a message with the appropriate metadata and concludes with a call to $\Pi_A$.VerifyWarrantStatus that returns 1. Note that if VerifyWarrantStatus returns 1, then in the real protocol, AccessMessage would return the relevant plaintext. Unlike other common witness encryption languages, we note that all correctly sampled statements are trivially in the language and have multiple witnesses. Therefore, we need the strong notion of extractable witness encryption. As we will discuss, finding a witness for the statement remains a difficult task.

Consider the implications if it were computationally feasible for an adversary to generate a witness for an honestly sampled statement for $L$. This would imply that an adversary corrupting $P_{LE}$ and $P_J$ interacting with the real protocol has a correct witness, which includes a call to ActivateWarrant, this implies

---

[7] As specified in the ideal functionality, during verification it will be checked that a warrant was properly requested and activated.

our accountability property. Such a protocol could never succeed in meeting our original goals; law enforcement would always be able to simulate the steps required for proper accountability. An accountability mechanism that can be locally simulated cannot guarantee that all parties can monitor the mechanism, undermining the purpose of the protocol.

To formalize this intuition, we begin by describing an extractable witness encryption scheme $\Pi_{\text{EWE}}$ for language $L$ given access to an ARLEAS protocol $\Pi_A$.

- $\text{Enc}(x, m)$ parses $(\text{meta}, \text{sid})$ from $x$ and calls $\Pi_A.\text{SendMessage}(\text{sid}, m, P_S, P_R)$ such that it outputs $\text{meta}, c$. It then returns the views $\{\mathcal{V}_{P_{\text{LE}}}, \mathcal{V}_{P_J}, \mathcal{V}_{P_0}, \ldots, \mathcal{V}_{P_n}\}$ resulting from that run, excluding the private information associated with sending the message.
- $\text{Dec}(c, \omega)$ first parses $c, w, \text{meta}, \text{sid}$ from the inputs $c$ and $\omega$, then calls $m \leftarrow \Pi_A.\text{AccessMessage}(\text{sid}, w, \text{meta}, c)$ and returns the result.

It is easy to see that this construction satisfies the correctness property of extractable witness encryption. Notice that a valid witness needs to contain inputs to $\text{VerifyWarrantStatus}$ such that it outputs 1. Because $\text{VerifyWarrantStatus}$ is defined to return 1 exactly when $\text{AccessMessage}$ will return a message, the above decryption algorithm will return a message only with a valid witness.

We introduce the metadata in the statement in order to fix a witness to a particular statement. Note that our protocol generates an encryption as running part of the protocol, actually generating part of the witness. If metadata is not included in the statement, then *any* witness for a particular setup can be used to decrypt *any* ciphertext generated by the encryption oracle under the same statement. While this is not inherently problematic for extractable witness encryption, it no longer corresponds neatly to ARLEAS. Recall that warrants in ARLEAS specify the metadata for which they are relevant through the warrant scope check functionality $\theta(\cdot, \cdot)$ and this property must be enforced in the language. We now proceed to show that the above scheme $\Pi_{\text{EWE}}$ satisfies extractable security if $\Pi_A$ UC-realizes $\mathcal{F}_{\text{ARLEAS}}^{v,t,p,\theta,\text{ret}}$.

**Theorem 3.** *Given a protocol $\Pi_A$ that UC-realizes $\mathcal{F}_{\text{ARLEAS}}^{v,t,p,\theta,\text{ret}}$, $\Pi_{EWE}$ is a secure extractable witness encryption scheme for the language $L$.*

*Proof.* Given an adversary $\mathcal{A}$ with non-negligible advantage in the extractable witness encryption game for language $L$, either

1. We construct an extractor $\text{Ext}_{\mathcal{A}}(1^\lambda, x, aux)$ by verifying if the adversary $\mathcal{A}$ ran $\Pi_A.\text{RequestWarrant}(\text{sid}, w)$ and $\Pi_A.\text{ActivateWarrant}(\text{sid}, w)$ such that $\Pi_A.\text{VerifyWarrantStatus}(\text{sid}, w, \text{meta}, c) = 1$. If this was the case, the extractor would have all information to form a witness that it can output;
2. else, if such extractor does not exist, we construct a distinguisher $\mathcal{Z}$ that distinguishes between $\Pi_A$ and ARLEAS ideal functionality. $\mathcal{Z}$ proceeds as follows

(a) When $\mathcal{A}$ asks to sample a statement, $\mathcal{Z}$ instantiates $\Pi_A$ with parties $\{P_{LE}, P_J, P_0, \ldots P_n, P_S, P_R\}$ on honest random coins. $\mathcal{Z}$ then generates some arbitrary metadata meta associated with a message that $P_S$ could send in the future. and returns meta, sid to $\mathcal{A}$.

(b) When $\mathcal{A}$ sends the challenge plaintexts $m_0, m_1$ (such that $|m_0| = |m_1|$) on statement $x$, $\mathcal{Z}$ then flips a coin $b \xleftarrow{\$} \{0,1\}$, $\mathcal{Z}$ has $P_S$ call

$$\Pi_A.\mathsf{SendMessage}(\mathsf{sid}, m_b, P_S, P_R)$$

such that it outputs $c$, meta. $\mathcal{Z}$ then returns the updated views of $P_{LE}, P_J$ and the $N$ other users to $\mathcal{A}$.

(c) When $\mathcal{A}$ outputs the guess $b'$ and halts, $\mathcal{Z}$ outputs $b' == b$, where 1 indicates the real world and 0 indicates the ideal world.

Note that in the ideal functionality, the joint views of law enforcement and the judge contain no information about the plaintext, because the ciphertext is chosen by the ideal world adversary without access to the plaintext. As such, if the adversary is able to distinguish between messages with non-negligible probability, $\mathcal{Z}$ must be interacting with the real world protocol.

**Implications For Practical Retrospective ARLEAS.** The relationship between retrospective ARLEAS and extractable witness encryption is an indication of the difficulty of realizing retrospective ARLEAS in practice. In very specific cases, it may be possible to phrase certain existing encryption schemes as witness encryption schemes, for example some IBE schemes. General purpose extractable witness encryption, on the other hand, is considered implausible [38]. The extractable witness encryption language we have described above must reason over the ledger authentication language and the various functionalities that parameterize an retrospective ARLEAS system. As such, the difficulty of realizing a practical retrospective ARLEAS will hinge on the complexity of the ledger and the parameterizing functionalities. If they are centralized and simple, it may be possible to instantiate an retrospective ARLEAS using the protocol we provided in Sect. 6 and known encryption techniques. However, the security provided by a centralized ledger is not significant, as a compromised central authority could circumvent the accountability properties of the system. Thus, we believe that this result indicates that instantiating an retrospective ARLEAS with meaningful security is impractical with known techniques.

**Acknowledgments.** The first author funded in part from the National Science Foundation under awards CNS-1653110 and CNS-1801479, a Google Security & Privacy Award. The second author is supported by the National Science Foundation under Grant #2030859 to the Computing Research Association for the CIFellows Project. Additionally, this material is based upon work supported by DARPA under Agreements No. HR00112020021 and Agreements No. HR001120C0084. Any opinions, findings and conclusions or recommendations expressed in this material are those of the author(s) and do not necessarily reflect the views of the United States Government or DARPA.

# References

1. Abelson, H., et al.: Keys under doormats: mandating insecurity by requiring government access to all data and communications. J. Cybersecur. **1**(1), 69–79 (2015)
2. Afshar, A., Mohassel, P., Pinkas, B., Riva, B.: Non-interactive secure computation based on cut-and-choose. In: Nguyen, P.Q., Oswald, E. (eds.) EUROCRYPT 2014. LNCS, vol. 8441, pp. 387–404. Springer, Heidelberg (2014). https://doi.org/10.1007/978-3-642-55220-5_22
3. Andrychowicz, M., Dziembowski, S., Malinowski, D., Mazurek, L.: Secure multiparty computations on bitcoin. In: 2014 IEEE Symposium on Security and Privacy, pp. 443–458. IEEE Computer Society Press, May 2014
4. Apple. Facetime. https://apps.apple.com/us/app/facetime/id1110145091
5. Apple. icloud security overview. https://support.apple.com/en-us/HT202303
6. Apple. imessage. https://support.apple.com/explore/messages
7. Backes, M., Camenisch, J., Sommer, D.: Anonymous yet accountable access control. In: Proceedings of the 2005 ACM Workshop on Privacy in the Electronic Society, WPES 2005, pp. 40–46. Association for Computing Machinery, New York (2005)
8. Badertscher, C., Gazi, P., Kiayias, A., Russell, A., Zikas, V.: Ouroboros genesis: composable proof-of-stake blockchains with dynamic availability. In: Lie, D., Mannan, M., Backes, M., Wang, X. (eds.) ACM CCS 2018, pp. 913–930. ACM Press (2018)
9. Badertscher, C., Maurer, U., Tschudi, D., Zikas, V.: Bitcoin as a transaction ledger: a composable treatment. In: Katz, J., Shacham, H. (eds.) CRYPTO, Part I. LNCS, vol. 10401, pp. 324–356. Springer, Cham (2017). https://doi.org/10.1007/978-3-319-63688-7_11
10. Barr, W.: Attorney general William P. Barr delivers keynote address at the international conference on cyber security, July 2019
11. Barr, W.: Attorney general William P. Barr delivers keynote address at the international conference on cyber security, July 2019. https://www.justice.gov/opa/speech/attorney-general-william-p-barr-delivers-keynote-address-international-conference-cyber
12. Bates, A.M., Butler, K.R.B., Sherr, M., Shields, C., Traynor, P., Wallach, D.S.: Accountable wiretapping -or- I know they can hear you now. In: NDSS 2012. The Internet Society, February 2012
13. Bellare, M., Rivest, R.L.: Translucent cryptography - an alternative to key escrow, and its implementation via fractional oblivious transfer. J. Cryptol. **12**(2), 117–139 (1999)
14. Bellovin, S.M., Blaze, M., Boneh, D., Landau, S., Rivest, R.R.: Analysis of the CLEAR protocol per the National Academies' framework. Technical report CUCS-003-18, Columbia University, May 2018
15. Bentov, I., Kumaresan, R.: How to use bitcoin to design fair protocols. In: Garay, J.A., Gennaro, R. (eds.) CRYPTO 2014, Part II. LNCS, vol. 8617, pp. 421–439. Springer, Heidelberg (2014). https://doi.org/10.1007/978-3-662-44381-1_24
16. Blaze, M.: Oblivious key escrow. In: Anderson, R. (ed.) IH 1996. LNCS, vol. 1174, pp. 335–343. Springer, Heidelberg (1996). https://doi.org/10.1007/3-540-61996-8_50
17. Boneh, D., Bonneau, J., Bünz, B., Fisch, B.: Verifiable delay functions. In: Shacham, H., Boldyreva, A. (eds.) CRYPTO 2018, Part I. LNCS, vol. 10991, pp. 757–788. Springer, Cham (2018). https://doi.org/10.1007/978-3-319-96884-1_25

18. Boyle, E., Chung, K.-M., Pass, R.: On extractability obfuscation. In: Lindell, Y. (ed.) TCC 2014. LNCS, vol. 8349, pp. 52–73. Springer, Heidelberg (2014). https://doi.org/10.1007/978-3-642-54242-8_3

19. Bryan-Low, C.: Vodafone, Ericsson get hung up in Greece's phone-tap scandal. Wall Street J. (2006)

20. Camenisch, J., Drijvers, M., Gagliardoni, T., Lehmann, A., Neven, G.: The wonderful world of global random oracles. In: Nielsen, J.B., Rijmen, V. (eds.) EUROCRYPT 2018, Part I. LNCS, vol. 10820, pp. 280–312. Springer, Cham (2018). https://doi.org/10.1007/978-3-319-78381-9_11

21. Canetti, R.: Universally composable security: a new paradigm for cryptographic protocols. In: 42nd FOCS, pp. 136–145. IEEE Computer Society Press, October 2001

22. Canetti, R., Krawczyk, H., Nielsen, J.B.: Relaxing chosen-ciphertext security. In: Boneh, D. (ed.) CRYPTO 2003. LNCS, vol. 2729, pp. 565–582. Springer, Heidelberg (2003). https://doi.org/10.1007/978-3-540-45146-4_33

23. Canetti, R., Lindell, Y., Ostrovsky, R., Sahai, A.: Universally composable two-party and multi-party secure computation. In: 34th ACM STOC, pp. 494–503. ACM Press, May 2002

24. Choudhuri, A.R., Goyal, V., Jain, A.: Founding secure computation on blockchains. In: Ishai, Y., Rijmen, V. (eds.) EUROCRYPT 2019, Part II. LNCS, vol. 11477, pp. 351–380. Springer, Cham (2019). https://doi.org/10.1007/978-3-030-17656-3_13

25. Choudhuri, A.R., Green, M., Jain, A., Kaptchuk, G., Miers, I.: Fairness in an unfair world: fair multiparty computation from public bulletin boards. In: Thuraisingham, B.M., Evans, D., Malkin, T., Xu, D. (eds.) ACM CCS 2017, pp. 719–728. ACM Press, October/November 2017

26. Cramer, R., Shoup, V.: Universal hash proofs and a paradigm for adaptive chosen ciphertext secure public-key encryption. In: Knudsen, L.R. (ed.) EUROCRYPT 2002. LNCS, vol. 2332, pp. 45–64. Springer, Heidelberg (2002). https://doi.org/10.1007/3-540-46035-7_4

27. Damgård, I., Nielsen, J.B., Orlandi, C.: Essentially optimal universally composable oblivious transfer. In: Lee, P.J., Cheon, J.H. (eds.) ICISC 2008. LNCS, vol. 5461, pp. 318–335. Springer, Heidelberg (2009). https://doi.org/10.1007/978-3-642-00730-9_20

28. David, B., Gaži, P., Kiayias, A., Russell, A.: Ouroboros praos: an adaptively-secure, semi-synchronous proof-of-stake blockchain. In: Nielsen, J.B., Rijmen, V. (eds.) EUROCRYPT 2018, Part II. LNCS, vol. 10821, pp. 66–98. Springer, Cham (2018). https://doi.org/10.1007/978-3-319-78375-8_3

29. De Santis, A., Di Crescenzo, G., Ostrovsky, R., Persiano, G., Sahai, A.: Robust non-interactive zero knowledge. In: Kilian, J. (ed.) CRYPTO 2001. LNCS, vol. 2139, pp. 566–598. Springer, Heidelberg (2001). https://doi.org/10.1007/3-540-44647-8_33

30. Denning, D.E.: The US key escrow encryption technology. Comput. Commun. **17**(7), 453–457 (1994)

31. Denning, D.E., Branstad, D.K.: A taxonomy for key escrow encryption systems. Commun. ACM **39**(3), 34–40 (1996)

32. EncroChat. Encrochat network. http://encrochat.network/

33. Encryption Working Group: Moving the Encryption Policy Conversation Forward. Technical report, Carnegie Endowment for International Peace (2019)

34. Federal Bureau of Investigation. Going Dark. https://www.fbi.gov/services/operational-technology/going-dark

35. Feigenbaum, J., Weitzner, D.J.: On the incommensurability of laws and technical mechanisms: or, what cryptography can't do. In: Matyáš, V., Švenda, P., Stajano, F., Christianson, B., Anderson, J. (eds.) Security Protocols 2018. LNCS, vol. 11286, pp. 266–279. Springer, Cham (2018). https://doi.org/10.1007/978-3-030-03251-7_31

36. Franceschi-Bicchierai, L.: FBI director: encryption will lead to a 'very dark place'. Mashable, October 2014

37. Frankle, J., Park, S., Shaar, D., Goldwasser, S., Weitzner, D.J.: Practical accountability of secret processes. In: Enck, W., Felt, A.P. (eds.) USENIX Security 2018, pp. 657–674. USENIX Association, August 2018

38. Garg, S., Gentry, C., Halevi, S., Wichs, D.: On the implausibility of differing-inputs obfuscation and extractable witness encryption with auxiliary input. In: Garay, J.A., Gennaro, R. (eds.) CRYPTO 2014, Part I. LNCS, vol. 8616, pp. 518–535. Springer, Heidelberg (2014). https://doi.org/10.1007/978-3-662-44371-2_29

39. Garg, S., Ostrovsky, R., Visconti, I., Wadia, A.: Resettable statistical zero knowledge. In: Cramer, R. (ed.) TCC 2012. LNCS, vol. 7194, pp. 494–511. Springer, Heidelberg (2012). https://doi.org/10.1007/978-3-642-28914-9_28

40. Gazi, P., Kiayias, A., Zindros, D.: Proof-of-stake sidechains. In: 2019 IEEE Symposium on Security and Privacy, pp. 139–156. IEEE Computer Society Press, May 2019

41. Gentry, C., Lewko, A., Waters, B.: Witness encryption from instance independent assumptions. In: Garay, J.A., Gennaro, R. (eds.) CRYPTO 2014, Part I. LNCS, vol. 8616, pp. 426–443. Springer, Heidelberg (2014). https://doi.org/10.1007/978-3-662-44371-2_24

42. Goldwasser, S., Park, S.: Public accountability vs. secret laws: can they coexist? A cryptographic proposal. In: Proceedings of the 2017 on Workshop on Privacy in the Electronic Society, WPES 2017, pp. 99–110. Association for Computing Machinery, New York (2017)

43. Google. Encrypt your data - pixel phone help. https://support.google.com/pixelphone/answer/2844831?hl=en

44. Gorman, S.: NSA officers spy on love interests. Wall Street J. (2013)

45. Goyal, R., Goyal, V.: Overcoming cryptographic impossibility results using blockchains. In: Kalai, Y., Reyzin, L. (eds.) TCC 2017, Part I. LNCS, vol. 10677, pp. 529–561. Springer, Cham (2017). https://doi.org/10.1007/978-3-319-70500-2_18

46. Graham, S.L.: Eliminating abusive and rampant neglect of interactive technologies act of 2020, March 2020

47. Horel, T., Park, S., Richelson, S., Vaikuntanathan, V.: How to subvert backdoored encryption: security against adversaries that decrypt all ciphertexts. In: Blum, A. (ed.) ITCS 2019, vol. 124, pp. 42:1–42:20. LIPIcs (2019)

48. Horvitz, O., Katz, J.: Universally-composable two-party computation in two rounds. In: Menezes, A. (ed.) CRYPTO 2007. LNCS, vol. 4622, pp. 111–129. Springer, Heidelberg (2007). https://doi.org/10.1007/978-3-540-74143-5_7

49. Ishai, Y., Kushilevitz, E., Ostrovsky, R., Prabhakaran, M., Sahai, A.: Efficient non-interactive secure computation. In: Paterson, K.G. (ed.) EUROCRYPT 2011. LNCS, vol. 6632, pp. 406–425. Springer, Heidelberg (2011). https://doi.org/10.1007/978-3-642-20465-4_23

50. Kamara, S.: Restructuring the NSA metadata program. In: Böhme, R., Brenner, M., Moore, T., Smith, M. (eds.) FC 2014. LNCS, vol. 8438, pp. 235–247. Springer, Heidelberg (2014). https://doi.org/10.1007/978-3-662-44774-1_19

51. Kaptchuk, G., Green, M., Miers, I.: Giving state to the stateless: augmenting trust-worthy computation with ledgers. In: NDSS 2019. The Internet Society, February 2019

52. Kiayias, A., Russell, A., David, B., Oliynykov, R.: Ouroboros: a provably secure proof-of-stake blockchain protocol. In: Katz, J., Shacham, H. (eds.) CRYPTO 2017, Part I. LNCS, vol. 10401, pp. 357–388. Springer, Cham (2017). https://doi.org/10.1007/978-3-319-63688-7_12

53. Kroll, J., Felten, E., Boneh, D.: Secure protocols for accountable warrant execution (2014)

54. Kroll, J.A., Zimmerman, J., Wu, D.J., Nikolaenko, V., Felten, E.W., Boneh, D.: Accountable cryptographic access control (2018)

55. Levy, I., Robinson, C.: Principles for a more informed exceptional access debate. Lawfare (2018)

56. Lichtblau, E., Goldstein, J.: Apple faces U.S. demand to unlock 9 more iPhones. The New York Times, February 2016

57. Liu, J., Ryan, M.D., Chen, L.: Balancing societal security and individual privacy: accountable escrow system. In: 2014 IEEE 27th Computer Security Foundations Symposium, pp. 427–440, July 2014

58. Liu, J., Jager, T., Kakvi, S.A., Warinschi, B.: How to build time-lock encryption. Des. Codes Crypt. **86**(11), 2549–2586 (2018)

59. Nakamoto, S.: Bitcoin: a peer-to-peer electronic cash system (2008)

60. Nakashima, E.: Chinese hackers who hacked Google gained access to sensitive data, U.S. officials say. The Washington Post, May 2013

61. National Academies of Sciences, Engineering, and Medicine. Exploring Encryption and Potential Mechanisms for Authorized Government Access to Plaintext, The National Academies Press (2016)

62. National Academies of Sciences, Engineering, and Medicine. Decrypting the Encryption Debate: A Framework for Decision Makers: The National Academies Press, Washington, DC (2018)

63. Nielsen, J.B., Orlandi, C.: LEGO for two-party secure computation. In: Reingold, O. (ed.) TCC 2009. LNCS, vol. 5444, pp. 368–386. Springer, Heidelberg (2009). https://doi.org/10.1007/978-3-642-00457-5_22

64. Nightingale, J.: Fraudulent *.google.com Certificate, August 2011

65. Panwar, G., Vishwanathan, R., Misra, S., Bos, A.: SAMPL: scalable auditability of monitoring processes using public ledgers. In: Cavallaro, L., Kinder, J., Wang, X., Katz, J. (eds.) ACM CCS 2019, pp. 2249–2266. ACM Press, November 2019

66. Poplin, C.M.: Burr-feinstein encryption legislation officially released. Lawfare, April 2016

67. Sahai, A.: Non-malleable non-interactive zero knowledge and adaptive chosen-ciphertext security. In: 40th FOCS, pp. 543–553. IEEE Computer Society Press, October 1999

68. Savage, S.: Lawful device access without mass surveillance risk: a technical design discussion. In: Proceedings of the 2018 ACM SIGSAC Conference on Computer and Communications Security, CCS 2018, pp. 1761–1774. Association for Computing Machinery, New York (2018)

69. Scafuro, A.: Break-glass encryption. In: Lin, D., Sako, K. (eds.) PKC 2019, Part II. LNCS, vol. 11443, pp. 34–62. Springer, Cham (2019). https://doi.org/10.1007/978-3-030-17259-6_2

70. Segal, A., Ford, B., Feigenbaum, J.: Catching bandits and only bandits: Privacy-preserving intersection warrants for lawful surveillance. In: 4th USENIX Workshop on Free and Open Communications on the Internet (FOCI 14). USENIX Association, San Diego, CA, August 2014
71. Blackburn, Sen.M., Graham, Sen.L., Cotton, Sen.T.: Lawful access to 5 encrypted data act, June 2020
72. Servan-Schreiber, S., Wheeler, A.: Judge, jury & encryptioner: exceptional access with a fixed social cost (2019)
73. Signal. Signal secure messaging system
74. Sing, M.: Over two dozen encryption experts call on India to rethink changes to its intermediary liability rules. TechCrunch, February 2020
75. Tait, M.: An approach to James Comey's technical challenge. Lawfare, April 2016
76. Tarabay, J.: Australian government passes contentious encryption law. The New York Times, December 2018
77. Watt, N., Mason, R., Traynor, I.: David Cameron pledges anti-terror law for internet after Paris attacks. The Guardian, January 2015
78. WhatsApp. WhatsApp Encryption Overview, December 2017
79. Wright, C., Varia, M.: Crypto crumple zones: enabling limited access without mass surveillance. In: 2018 IEEE European Symposium on Security and Privacy (EuroS P), pp. 288–306, April 2018

# Author Index

Agarwal, Amit I-435
Aggarwal, Divesh I-467
Albrecht, Martin R. I-528
Alwen, Joël I-87
Amon, Ohad II-127
Ananth, Prabhanjan II-501, II-754, III-278
Andreeva, Elena II-92
Asharov, Gilad III-278

Badertscher, Christian III-399
Bao, Zhenzhen I-771
Bartusek, James I-435
Baum, Carsten III-429
Beck, Gabrielle II-663
Beierle, Christof II-155
Belaïd, Sonia II-313
Benamira, Adrien I-805
Ben-Efraim, Aner III-33
Benhamouda, Fabrice I-33, II-724
Beullens, Ward I-348
Bhattacharyya, Rishiraj II-92
Biryukov, Alex II-219
Blanchet, Bruno I-87
Bordes, Nicolas II-283
Bossuat, Jean-Philippe I-587
Bossuet, Lilian II-438
Boyle, Elette II-871
Brian, Gianluca II-408
Burdges, Jeffrey I-302

Cayrel, Pierre-Louis II-438
Chandran, Nishanth II-871
Cheng, Qi I-559
Chung, Kai-Min II-598
Ciampi, Michele III-64
Colombier, Brice II-438
Cong, Kelong III-33
Costello, Craig I-272
Couteau, Geoffroy II-842, III-247
Coutinho, Murilo I-711

Dahari, Hila III-278
Datta, Pratish I-177
David, Bernardo III-429

De Feo, Luca I-302
Deaton, Joshua I-329
Delpech de Saint Guilhem, Cyprien I-213
Derbez, Patrick II-155
Ding, Jintai I-329
Dinur, Itai I-374
Dobraunig, Christoph II-3, II-377
Dong, Xiaoyang I-771
Dowsley, Rafael III-429
Drăgoi, Vlad-Florin II-438
Ducas, Léo II-249
Dunkelman, Orr II-127

Faonio, Antonio II-408
Farshim, Pooya II-64
Faust, Sebastian II-782
Fehr, Serge II-598
Fleischhacker, Nils III-311

Galbraith, Steven D. I-213
Garg, Rachit III-159
Gay, Romain III-97
Gaži, Peter III-399
George, Marilyn III-370
Gerault, David I-805
Ghazi, Badih III-463
Gilboa, Niv II-871
Goel, Aarushi II-663
Golowich, Noah III-463
Gordon, S. Dov II-694
Goyal, Vipul I-435, II-468, III-64, III-278
Grassi, Lorenzo II-3
Green, Matthew III-553
Grilo, Alex B. II-531
Guinet, Anna II-3
Guo, Jian I-771
Gupta, Divya II-871
Gurkan, Kobi I-147

Hauck, Eduard I-87
Hazay, Carmit II-782
Heath, David III-3
Hemenway Falk, Brett III-338
Heninger, Nadia I-528

Huang, Yu-Hsuan  II-598
Hubaux, Jean-Pierre  I-587

Ishai, Yuval  II-871

Jager, Tibor  I-117
Jain, Aayush  II-724, III-97
Jain, Abhishek  I-3, II-663, II-754
Jin, Zhengzhong  I-3, II-754
Jovanovic, Philipp  I-147

Kamara, Seny  III-370
Kaptchuk, Gabriel  II-663, III-553
Karpman, Pierre  II-283
Kaslasi, Inbar  III-219
Katsumata, Shuichi  I-404
Keller, Nathan  II-35, II-127
Khurana, Dakshita  I-435, III-159, III-186
Kiayias, Aggelos  III-399
Kiltz, Eike  I-87, I-117
Kim, Young-Sik  I-618
Klooß, Michael  III-247
Kolesnikov, Vladimir  III-3
Komargodski, Ilan  I-177, II-724
Kretzler, David  II-782
Kuijsters, Daniël  II-3
Kumar, Nishant  II-871
Kumar, Ravi  III-463
Kutas, Péter  I-242

La Placa, Rolando L.  II-501
Lai, Qiqi  I-498
Lai, Yi-Fu  I-213
Leander, Gregor  II-155
Lee, Eunsang  I-618
Lee, Joon-Woo  I-618
Lee, Yongwoo  I-618
Lepoint, Tancrède  I-33
Leurent, Gaëtan  I-54, II-155
Li, Baiyu  I-648
Li, Chao  I-741
Li, Zeyong  I-467
Li, Zheng  I-771
Liao, Tai-Ning  II-598
Libert, Benoît  III-521
Lin, Huang  III-247
Lin, Huijia  II-531, II-724, III-97
Lipp, Benjamin  I-87
Liu, Feng-Hao  I-498
Liu, Yunwen  I-741

Loss, Julian  I-33
Lu, George  III-159

Maji, Hemanta K.  II-344
Malavolta, Giulio  I-435, II-754
Maller, Mary  I-147
Meiklejohn, Sarah  I-147
Mennink, Bart  II-377
Menu, Alexandre  II-438
Merz, Simon-Philipp  I-242
Meyer, Michael  I-272
Meyer, Pierre  II-842
Micciancio, Daniele  I-648
Moataz, Tarik  III-370
Mouchet, Christian  I-587

Naehrig, Michael  I-272
Nguyen, Hai H.  II-344
Nguyen, Khoa  III-521
Nielsen, Jesper Buus  III-429
Nishimaki, Ryo  I-404
No, Jong-Seon  I-618
Noble, Daniel  III-338

Obremski, Maciej  II-408
Oechsner, Sabine  III-429
Omri, Eran  III-33
Orlandi, Claudio  I-678
Orrù, Michele  I-33
Orsini, Emmanuela  III-33
Ostrovsky, Rafail  III-64, III-338

Pagh, Rasmus  III-463
Pan, Yanbin  I-559
Paskin-Cherniavsky, Anat  II-344
Pernot, Clara  I-54
Peters, Thomas  III-521
Petit, Christophe  I-242
Peyrin, Thomas  I-805
Polychroniadou, Antigoni  II-812

Raddum, Håvard  II-155
Rathee, Mayank  II-871
Raykova, Mariana  I-33
Reichle, Michael  III-247
Ribeiro, João  II-408
Riepel, Doreen  I-87, I-117
Rindal, Peter  II-901
Rivain, Matthieu  II-313
Roberts, Bhaskar  II-562

Ronen, Eyal    II-127
Rosemarin, Asaf    II-35
Rotella, Yann    II-155
Rothblum, Ron D.    III-219
Roy, Arnab    II-92
Rupprecht, David    II-155
Russell, Alexander    III-399

Sahai, Amit    III-97
Schäge, Sven    I-117
Schlosser, Benjamin    II-782
Scholl, Peter    I-678
Schoppmann, Phillipp    II-901
Shamir, Adi    II-127
Shi, Danping    I-771
Shi, Elaine    III-489
Simkin, Mark    II-408, III-311
Skórski, Maciej    II-408
Smart, Nigel P.    III-33
Song, Fang    II-531
Song, Yifan    II-812
Soria-Vazquez, Eduardo    III-33
Souza Neto, Tertuliano C.    I-711
Srinivasan, Akshayaram    II-468
Starin, Daniel    II-694
Stennes, Lukas    II-155
Stephens-Davidowitz, Noah    I-467
Stern, Gilad    I-147
Stevens, Marc    II-249
Suad, Tom    II-344
Sun, Siwei    I-741, I-771

Taleb, Abdul Rahman    II-313
Tan, Quan Quan    I-805
Tessaro, Stefano    II-64
Tomescu, Alin    I-147
Troncoso-Pastoriza, Juan    I-587

Udovenko, Aleksei    II-219

Vaikuntanathan, Vinod    II-531
Van Laer, Gijs    III-553
van Woerden, Wessel    II-249
Vasudevanr, Prashant Nalini    III-219
Velingker, Ameya    III-463
Venturi, Daniele    II-408
Vidick, Thomas    II-630
Vishakha    I-329

Wadleigh, Nick    I-559
Wang, Mingyuan    II-344
Wang, Xiaoyun    I-771
Wang, Zhedong    I-498
Waters, Brent    I-177, III-159
Wee, Hoeteck    III-127
Weitkämper, Charlotte    I-242
Wichs, Daniel    III-127
Wu, Ke    III-489

Xu, Guangwu    II-187
Xu, Jun    I-559

Yakoubov, Sophia    I-678
Yamada, Shota    I-404
Yamakawa, Takashi    I-404, II-568
Yang, Bo-Yin    I-329
Yerukhimovich, Arkady    II-694
Yu, Wei    II-187
Yung, Moti    III-521

Zhandry, Mark    II-568
Zhang, Tina    II-630
Zhu, Chenzhi    II-468
Zikas, Vassilis    III-399

Printed in the United States
by Baker & Taylor Publisher Services